PERSPECTIVES
ON THE
WORLD
CHRISTIAN
MOVEMENT

A Reader

REVISED EDITION

Contributing Editors:

David J. Hesselgrave
Director, School of World Mission and Evangelism
Trinity Evangelical Divinity School

J. Herbert Kane
Professor Emeritus, School of World Mission and Evangelism
Trinity Evangelical Divinity School

Lloyd E. Kwast
Chairman, Department of Missions
Talbot Theological Seminary

Donald A. McGavran
Dean Emeritus, School of World Mission and Institute of Church Growth
Fuller Theological Seminary

PERSPECTIVES
ON THE WORLD CHRISTIAN MOVEMENT

A Reader
REVISED EDITION

RALPH D. WINTER
Founder
U.S. Center for World Mission

STEVEN C. HAWTHORNE
Director of Curriculum Development
Institute of International Studies

Associate Editors:

Darrell R. Dorr

D. Bruce Graham

William Carey Library
Pasadena, California

European Distributor
THE PATERNOSTER PRESS LTD.
Carlisle, United Kingdom

Published by
William Carey Library
P.O. Box 40129
Pasadena, California 91114
Phone (818) 798-0819
ISBN 0-87808-228-X

European distributor (this title only):
The Paternoster Press Ltd.
P.O. Box 300
Kingstown Broadway
Carlisle, UK CA3 0QS
Phone 0228 512512
ISBN 0-85364-539-6

Cover design: Gene Keller

Printed in the United States of America

Library of Congress Cataloging in Publication Date

Main entry under title;

Perspectives on the world Christian movement

Includes index
1. Missions—Addresses, essays, lectures. 2. Evangelistic work—Addresses, essays, lectures. I. Winter, Ralph D. II. Hawthorne, Steven C. 1953—

BV2070.P46 266   81-69924
ISBN 0-87808-228-X (US)   AACR2
ISBN 0-85364-539-6 (UK)

25   24   23   22   21   20   19

00   99   98   97   96   95

Contents

88482

B.   THE HISTORICAL PERSPECTIVE

The Expansion of the Christian Movement

Pioneers of the Christian Movement

Cross-Cultural Communication

Gospel and Culture

D. THE STRATEGIC PERSPECTIVE

Strategies for World Evangelization

Strategies for Church Planting

Strategies for Development

World Christian Teamwork

Foreword

God is raising up a new army of Kingdom volunteers in our day.

Across every continent are emerging "World Christians"—young women and men with world horizons, committed to "Exodus" lifestyles, possessed by the goal of discipling the nations to Jesus Christ the Lord.

At the close of a recent conference in Korea, a hundred thousand Korean youth pledged to spend a year overseas spreading the good seed of the gospel!

In Europe the periodic Lausanne Mission Conferences are now drawing over 10,000 young people.

And in North America the Urbana Conventions of Inter-Varsity, as well as, the training programs of Campus Crusade, the Navigators, Inter-Varsity, Youth With A Mission, and many groups and denominations, are part of this stirring.

Like a great eagle, God is hovering over his people's nest, stirring the young birds to spread their wings and carry the eternal gospel to every nation.

At the dedication of the Billy Graham Center at Wheaton College, the Student Body President gave a most moving call for us to be World Christians— dedicated to reaching the lost and feeding the hungry peoples of the world.

At some secular campuses, the Christian student groups are seemingly outstripping some of their Christian-college counterparts with their zeal for evangelism, discipleship and missions!

At the secular university which my son and daughter have attended, the Christian movement has grown from seven to seven hundred in less than a decade! Many of them are eager for their lives to count for more than merely secular success.

We may be on the verge of a movement comparable to the great waves of student volunteers at the beginning of the century.

If so, *Perspectives on the World Christian Movement can be a key tool. The editors have given to us an impressive (if not exhaustive) collection of readings. I know of nothing quite like it. (Incidentally, the editorial partnership of Dr. Ralph Winter with Steven Hawthorne and friends is in itself a splendid example of the possibilities of partnership between senior missionary experience and younger missionary vision).*

I commend this volume because it sets world evangelization in its proper priority. What beats centrally in the heart of our missionary God, as revealed in the Scriptures, must always be central in the agenda of his missionary people.

Then also, world evangelization appears here as a *possibility*. No sub-Christian pessimism arising from false guilt rules here. Nor is the "vision glorious" intimidated by false Messiahs. Jesus said, "This Gospel of the Kingdom will be preached in all the world as a testimony, then will the end come (Matt. 24:14)." Without apology, arrogance, or timidity, the viewpoint represented in this volume believes that what He has said will be done *will* be done, and wants to be part of it.

Then, as the title says, this volume gives to world evangelization *perspectives*. Today's aspiring missionaries need to understand first the biblical mandate, but also history and culture and strategy. Understanding of the history of missions and the challenge of cross-cultural communication may help to save us from fear on the one hand, and unnecessary mistakes on the other. When Billy Graham was a college president in the late forties his school adopted the slogan, "Knowledge on Fire." This book is based on a belief that missionaries have a calling to *think* as well as to *love* and *give* and *speak*! As John Wesley once said to a critic who was downplaying his education, "God may not need my education, but he doesn't need your ignorance either."

In addition, *Perspectives on the World Christian Movement* can help eager-hearted disciples to see world evangelization also in terms of *passion, power*, and *participation*. Before evangelism is a program it *is* a passion. Always, the key to missionary enterprise can be summed up: "Jesus, priceless treasure." Only a new wave of missionaries in love with Jesus, and captured by His boundless promise of the Spirit will truly be His witnesses "to the uttermost parts."

God had one Son and he made him a missionary. My prayer is that the Father would use this book to help equip and send a great host of sons and daughters from every nation to every nation until His name is known and praised by every people.

> Leighton Ford, Chairman
> Lausanne Committee for World Evangelization
> North Carolina
> October, 1981

Preface

The phrase in our title, "The World Christian Movement," speaks simply of a movement that is now worldwide. But beyond that simple meaning of the phrase, we should clarify what we do not mean. The movement of which we speak is not a single organization, although in many ways it is strikingly coherent and unified, especially by comparison to the next largest world religion, Islam. In using this phrase, we do not speak of the spread of something with the secular muscle of the Communist movement. Yet we do believe that the blessings God gave to Abraham on the basis of his "obedience of faith" will indeed be extended to all people groups on the face of the earth. These blessings are both physical and spiritual, and indeed are conditioned upon that most important relationship—the obedience of faith. But we do not contemplate any physical or human organizational centralization of that obedience.

We understand, with Jesus, that the Kingdom of God relentlessly pressing back the darkness of the world today is, nevertheless, '~not of this world." We seek not the subjugation of all nations (not "countries") to ourselves nor to our own nation. Thus, while God is calling to Himself a new creation, a new people, we do not believe He is doing away with the nations. All nations must become equidistant to the grace and the blessings of our living Lord.

Due to a paralyzing combination of factors, it is virtually impossible today to get any very detailed or comprehensive grasp of the World Christian movement. Is this because those actively engaged in the cause are too few in number? Hardly. There are more than 100,000 people working full-time in Christian mission efforts far from their home and kindred. Is it because the cause is too small or has failed? Hardly. You cannot account for a single nation of Africa or Asia represented in the United Nations that is not there for reasons significantly related to the Christian mission. Indeed, the formation of the United Nations itself has some amazing relationships to key people produced by the missionary movement. Is it because missions are in the decline and are virtually out of date? America's overseas mission force is larger today in personnel and in money than ever in history, and you will soon see that this cause is *not* out of date. The *least* likely reason is that the cause of missions is too new to get into the curriculum. On the contrary, it is in fact the largest and longest standing concerted effort in the annals of human history, and certainly the most influential.

xiv

Why, then, can you search the libraries of the nation, scan college and university catalogs, or peruse the curricula of public schools or even private Christian schools and fail to find a single, substantive course on the nature, the purpose, the achievements, the present deployment, and the unfinished task of the Christian world mission?

We offer this volume as part of an attempt to fill this vacuum and provide such a critical course. We have sought to help the inquirer know the heart and purpose of the reigning, redeeming God of mission, revealed in the *Biblical* drama of the coming of His kingdom and the *historical* record of His people's checkered obedience to that purpose. We have also sought, while presenting this unfolding drama, to encourage an appreciation of the marvelous *cultural* diversity of mankind, thereby introducing the student to the complexity and yet the possibility of cross-cultural communication. Building upon such an understanding, we then focus on the *strategic* possibilities which challenge us all to complete the task of world evangelization.

It is natural and proper, then, that we have chosen to subsume these readings under Biblical, Historical, Cultural, and Strategic divisions. Undoubtedly the drama could be presented otherwise. Its complexity, in fact, gives tribute to the interdisciplinary nature of this book and the course of which it is part. Biblical Theology, History of the Christian Movement, Cultural Anthropology, Community Development, Cross-Cultural Communication, Social Movements, and Sociology of Cultural Change, among others, vie as titles and disciplines that would claim this volume as their own.

The editors make no claim that this book constitutes a comprehensive introduction to the growing field of missiology. We acknowledge two guiding factors in the selection and treatment of these readings. First, *Perspectives on the World Christian Movement* is designed as the core textbook for the Institute of International Studies and the elective courses it promotes. Students in these courses are typically undergraduate students in or from state colleges and universities. We have chosen and edited these readings primarily for them, intending that they use an accompanying study guide. Secondly, our emphasis throughout is on reaching all the earth's unreached peoples, those human societies in which there is still no culturally relevant, evangelizing church. Having said this, we anticipate and welcome other uses of this volume as a resource for introductory courses in missions or even for graduate programs in missiology.

The special Study Guide which has been developed for this book will quite likely be of assistance in many instances. It transforms this volume from an assortment of readings into a well-defined course of study entitled *Understanding the World Christian Movement*. The conceptual structure and educational objectives of the Study Guide in fact underlie the choice of documents in this book. This Study Guide, available as well from William Carey Library, covers the following exciting topics, for each one offering study outlines, learning exercises, bibliographies, quotes and quizzes.

We must acknowledge that the painstaking task of selecting and editing was done with a great deal of help from our colleagues who served as contributing editors: J. Herbert Kane, Lloyd Kwast, David Hesselgrave, and Donald McGavran. Space does not permit the listing of the dozens of other missions professors and leaders who have generously offered their critique and encouragement. All of these have given valued counsel, but none can be held accountable for the shortcomings and errors of the editors.

Special thanks goes to the Haggai Community and the United States Center for World Mission, two organizations which took considerable risk and gave much time to facilitate this project. The dozens of dedicated and skilled volunteers who gave themselves tirelessly in the production of the text are too numerous to mention, but their help is too enormous to forget. Many thanks to them.

The entire IIS staff has labored long and well in every phase of the preparation of this book. Their dedication and zeal epitomize the best of the World Christian movement. Two of them deserve special mention: Barbara Hawthorne accomplished a myriad of editorial tasks with tireless, cheerful grace. Linda Dorr capably supervised the production of the text.

The editors have leaned heavily on the magnificent assistance of Darrell Dorr and Bruce Graham. Their combined wisdom and editorial skill have immeasurably strengthened this book.

The senior editor gladly acknowledges the fact that the younger editor is the chief architect of this collection. The basic outline of the course, the fundamental direction of its purpose, and the alertness and assistance of many other staff members of the Institute of International Studies across the years have, of course, entered in. But under the circumstances, it is only fair to say that the role of the senior editor has been more of an honor than actuality, and certainly it has been a great joy to have been involved with Steve and a number of other dedicated younger leaders who will likely go far in a new era into which our Lord has called us.

It is our aim that these readings will not only inform and stimulate a new wave of pioneer missionaries, but will also encourage a rising *tide* of highly informed, supporting mission activists. Only thus shall we move ever closer to that day when "the earth will be full of the knowledge of the Lord as the waters cover the sea" (Isaiah 11:9).

October 28, 1981

PREFACE TO THE SECOND EDITION, 1992

In the process of developing a second volume to this Perspectives *Reader*, working with Dr. Steven Hoke this time as co-editor, we have not only approached over 100 additional authors, professors and leaders, we have churned through this volume also and made many revisions as well. In the latter, Steven Hawthorne has continued to be active, although as a senior editor. I have, this time, a bit more of the blame for any shortcomings than in the original volume.

At the same time the vast majority of the readings are the same as before. The main "changes" have been updatings and/or revisions of the existing chapters—in some cases original authors have requested that we replace their chapter with something similar but mainly new. There are a few select additions of new chapters from new authors. The additional volume on which we continue to work will have a strikingly different cast. It will highlight leaders and their roles in the global Cause, rather than subjects as such, as does this volume.

The accompanying *Study Guide* is being revised to draw upon the new resources of this volume as well as the preliminary material for the additional reader, those materials simply being added to the Study Guide itself for the meantime.

I am delighted to mention all the new personalities who have labored so eagerly and effectively in this undertaking. Linda Woodward, an engineer turned mission mobilizer, has headed the project, along with the help of Lee Purgason, who continues to direct our Perspectives office. But Steve Hoke, although mainly at work on the additional volume, has been very helpful here as well, since the two volumes will work together. Then, add in Liza West and Deb Conklin for computer formatting; special thanks to Anne Bolcom, Brad Cronbaugh, Lynette Matthews, and Craig Soderberg, the core Perspectives team who assisted in various ways, as well as others: Kara Anderson, Phil Bogosian, Robby Butler, Keith Carey, Dick Cotton, Mary Cotton, Ada Eng, Bob Hall, Gina Markow, Jane Mees, Enid Miller, Danette Olson, Greg and Kathleen Parsons, Ron Shaw, Joanna Shive, Charlie and Barb Sturges, Mike and Ginny Thorne, and Gary Velis, all faithful contributors to this project and the World Christian Movement itself!

Ralph D. Winter

Pasadena, California,   June 1992

Acknowledgements

The following mission leaders were among those who offered significant suggestions and critique. Much of the strength of the Reader is the direct fruit of this help. Any weakness or inadequacy should only be attributed to the editors.

Mr. Dan Bacon, Overseas Missionary Fellowship; Mr. John Bennett, The Association of Church Missions Committees; Dr. Ron Blue, Dallas Theological Seminary; Dr. E. Thomas and Elizabeth S. Brewster, Fuller School of World Mission; Mr. Dave Bryant, Inter-Varsity Missions; Mr. Wade Coggins, EFMA; Dr. Harvie Conn, Westminster Theological Seminary; Dr. Ralph Covell; Denver Conservative Baptist Theological Seminary; Dr. Edward R. Dayton, Missions Advanced Research and Communication Center; Dr. Richard DeRidder, Calvin Theological Seminary; Mr. Bob Douglas, Mission Training and Resource Center; Mr. Phil Elkins, Mission Training and Resource Center; Dr. Arthur F. Glasser, Fuller School of World Mission; Dr. Martin Goldsmith, All Nations Christian College; Dr. John A. Gration, Wheaton College; David Howard, Evangelism Explosion International; Dr. Terry Hulbert, Columbia Bible College; Dr. Arthur P. Johnston, Trinity Evangelical Divinity School; Dr. Water Kaiser, Jr., Trinity Evangelical Divinity School; Dr. Dale Keitzman, Christian Resource Management; Dr. Charles Kraft, Fuller School of World Mission; Dr. John Kyle, Inter-Varsity Missions; Dr. Donald N. Larson, Toronto Institute of Linguistics; Greg Livingston, North Africa Mission; Lois McKinney, Committee to Assist Ministry Education Overseas; Dr. J. R. McQuilkin, Columbia Bible College; Dr. Charles Mellis, Missionary Internship; Dr. Ken Mulholland, Columbia Bible College; Mr. Michael Pocock, The Evangelical Alliance Mission; Dr. Roger Randall, Campus Crusade for Christ; Mr. Don Richardson, Institute of Tribal Studies; Mr. Waldron Scott, American Leprosy Mission; Dr. Charles R. Tabor, Milligan College; Dr. C. Peter Wagner, Fuller School of World Mission; Dr. Ted Ward, Michigan State University; Dr. Warren Webster, Conservative Baptist Foreign Mission Society; Dr. Sam Wilson, Missions Advanced Research and Communication Center.

Those enjoying the relatively low cost of this collection of readings are in a sense indebted to the dozens of workers who volunteered their time and talent to produce this book. We list the principal workers trusting that none have been omitted.

Susie Adams, Gordon Aeschliman, Sherrie Aeschliman, Patty Aker, Ralph

Alpha, Kevin Berasley, Gertrude Bergman, Tim Brenda, Robby Butler, Randy Chan, Karen Clewis, John Cochran, Brad Cronbaugh, Dave Delozier, Lisa Delozier, Linda Dorr, Jan Elder, Jim Fox, Jane Foxwell, Jay Gary, Olgy Gary, Brad Gill, Beth Gill, Christy Graham, Kathy Gunderson, Gene Keller, Lyn Haugh, Barbara Hawthorne, Nancy Hawthorne, Carol Hill, Jerry Hogshead, Marilyn Hogshead, Kitty Holloway, Steve Holloway, Mark Jeffery, Jan Jensen, Jan Josephson, Noelle Lamborn, Shirley Lawson, Helen Lingerfelt, Annette Matsuda, Koleen Matsuda, Jane Mees, Barb Overgaard, Grace Patton, Jack Price, Mary Fran Redding, Cheryl Rose, Joe Ryan, Debbie Sanders, Bob Sjogren, Claudia Smith, Suzanne Smith, Kris Storey, Jodie Van Loon, Tina Warath, Ginny Williamson, Roberta Winter, H. L. Wyatt, Carol Yuke.

Graphics by: Carol Hill, Gene Keller, and Kris Storey.

Photography Credits

The photos on pages B—196 and B—202, are courtesy of World Vision International, Monrovia, California.

The photos on pages B—198, C—135 and D—150 are courtesy of Paul Felitis and the Zwemer Institute, Pasadena, California.

The photos on pages B—206, B—211, C—14 (Dick Loving), C—103 (Ralph McIntosh), C—118, C—128, C—157, and D—118 (Paul Smith) are courtesy of Wycliffe Bible Translators, Huntington Beach, California.

The photo on page B—209 is courtesy of Steven C. Hawthorne, Austin, Texas.

The photos on pages C—33 and D—99 are courtesy of John Shindeldecker,

The photo on page C—69 is courtesy of Don Richardson, Woodland Hills, California.

The photo on page D—226 is courtesy of Phil Elkins, Altadena, California.

The photos on pages D—127, D—131 and D—139 are courtesy of Bruce Graham, Bremerton, Washington

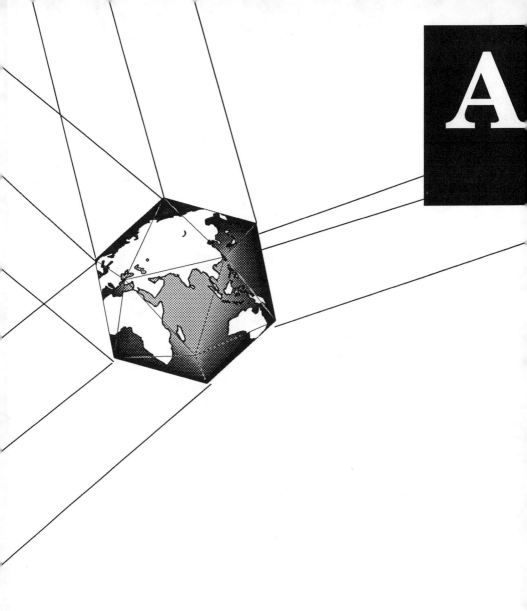

THE BIBLICAL PERSPECTIVE

1

The Bible in World Evangelization

John R. W. Stott

Without the Bible world evangelization would be not only impossible but actually inconceivable. It is the Bible that lays upon us the responsibility to evangelize the world, gives us a gospel to proclaim, tells us to how to proclaim it, and promises us that it is God's power for salvation to every believer.

It is, moreover, an observable fact of history, both past and contemporary, that the degree of the church's commitment to world evangelization is commensurate with the degree of its conviction about the authority of the Bible. Whenever Christians lose their confidence in the Bible, they also lose their zeal for evangelism. Conversely, whenever they are convinced about the Bible, then they are determined about evangelism.

Let me develop four reasons why the Bible is indispensable to world evangelization.

Mandate for World Evangelization

First, the Bible gives us the *mandate* for world evangelization. We certainly need one. Two phenomena are everywhere on the increase. One is religious fanaticism, and the other, religious pluralism. The fanatic displays the kind of irrational zeal which (if it could) would use force to compel belief and eradicate disbelief. Religious pluralism encourages the opposite tendency.

Whenever the spirit of religious fanaticism or of its opposite, religious indifferentism, prevails, world evangelization is bitterly resented. Fanatics refuse to countenance the rival evangelism represents, and pluralists its exclusive claims. The Christian evangelist is regarded as making an unwarrantable intrusion into other people's private affairs.

John R. W. Stott is Rector Emeritus of All Souls Church in London, President of Christian Impact, and an Extra Chaplain to Queen Elizabeth II. For 25 years (1952-77) he led university missions on five continents. He still travels widely, especially in the Two-Thirds World, as a lecturer and speaker. Formerly he addressed five Urbana Student Missions Conventions. His many books include *Basic Christianity, Christian Mission in the Modern World, The Cross of Christ* and *The Spirit, the Church and the World*. Adapted from an address delivered in a plenary session of the Consultation on World Evangelization at Pattaya, Thailand, in June 1980. Used by permission.

In the face of this opposition we need to be clear about the mandate the Bible gives us. It is not just the Great Commission (important as that is) but the entire biblical revelation. Let me rehearse it briefly.

There is but one living and true God, the Creator of the universe, the Lord of the nations and the God of the spirits of all flesh. Some 4,000 years ago he called Abraham and made a covenant with him, promising not only to bless him but also through his posterity to bless all the families of the earth (Gen. 12:1-4). This biblical text is one of the foundation stones of the Christian mission. For Abraham's descendants (through whom all nations are being blessed) are Christ and the people of Christ. If by faith we belong to Christ, we are Abraham's spiritual children and have a responsibility to all mankind. So, too, the Old Testament prophets foretold how God would make his Christ the heir and the light of the nations (Ps. 2:8; Isa. 42:6, 49:6).

When Jesus came, he endorsed these promises. True, during his own earthly ministry he was restricted "to the lost sheep of the house of Israel" (Matt. 10:6, 15:24), but he prophesied that many would "come from east and west, and from north and south," and would "sit at table with Abraham, Isaac, and Jacob in the kingdom of heaven" (Matt. 8:11, Luke 13:29). Further, after his resurrection and in anticipation of his ascension he made the tremendous claim that "all authority in heaven and on earth" had been given to him (Matt. 28:18). It was in consequence of his universal authority that he commanded his followers to make all nations his disciples, baptizing them into his new community and teaching them all his teaching (Matt. 28:19).

And this, when the Holy Spirit of truth and power had come upon them, the early Christians proceeded to do. They became the witnesses of Jesus, even to the ends of the earth (Acts 1:8). Moreover, they did it "for the sake of his name" (Rom. 1:5; III John 7). They knew that God had superexalted Jesus, enthroning him at his right hand and bestowing upon him the highest rank, in order that every tongue should confess his lordship. They longed that Jesus should receive the honor due to his name. Besides, one day he would return in glory, to save, to judge, and to reign. So what was to fill the gap between his two comings? The worldwide mission of the church! Not till the gospel had reached the ends of the world, he said, would the end of history come (cf. Matt. 24:14, 28:20; Acts 1:8). The two ends would coincide.

Our mandate for world evangelization, therefore, is the whole Bible. It is to be found in the creation of God (because of which all human beings are responsible to him), in the character of God (as outgoing, loving, compassionate, not willing that any should perish, desiring that all should come to repentance), in the promises of God (that all nations will be blessed through Abraham's seed and will become the Messiah's inheritance), in the Christ of God (now exalted with universal authority, to receive universal acclaim), in the Spirit of God (who convicts of sin, witnesses to Christ, and impels the church to evangelize) and in the Church of God (which is a multinational, missionary community, under orders to evangelize until Christ returns).

This global dimension of the Christian mission is irresistible. Individual Christians and local churches not committed to world evangelization are contradicting (either through blindness or through disobedience) an essential part of their God-given identity. The biblical mandate for world evangelization cannot be escaped.

Message for World Evangelization

Secondly, the Bible gives us the *message* for world evangelization. The Lausanne Covenant defined evangelism in terms of the evangel. Paragraph four begins: "to evangelize is to spread the good news that Jesus Christ died for our sins and was raised from the dead according to the Scriptures, and that as the reigning Lord he now offers the forgiveness of sins and the liberating gift of the Spirit to all who repent and believe."

Our message comes out of the Bible. As we turn to the Bible for our message, however, we are immediately confronted with a dilemma. On the one hand the message is given to us. We are not left to invent it; it has been entrusted to us as a precious "deposit," which we, like faithful stewards, are both to guard and to dispense to God's household (I Tim. 6:20; II Tim. 1:12-14; II Cor. 4:1-2). On the other hand, it has not been given to us as a single, neat, mathematical formula, but rather in a rich diversity of formulations, in which different images or metaphors are used.

So there is only one gospel, on which all the apostles agreed (I Cor. 15:11), and Paul could call down the curse of God upon anybody—including himself—who preached a "different" gospel from the original apostolic gospel of God's grace (Gal. 1:6-8). Yet the apostles expressed this one gospel in various ways—now sacrificial (the shedding and sprinkling of Christ's blood), now messianic (the breaking in of God's promised rule), now legal (the Judge pronouncing the unrighteous righteous), now personal (the Father reconciling his wayward children), now salvific (the heavenly Liberator coming to rescue the helpless), now cosmic (the universal Lord claiming universal dominion); and this is only a selection.

The gospel is thus seen to be one, yet diverse. It is "given," yet culturally adapted to its audience. Once we grasp this, we shall be saved from making two opposite mistakes. The first I will call "total fluidity." I recently heard an English church leader declare that there is no such thing as the gospel until we enter the situation in which we are to witness. We take nothing with us into the situation, he said; we discover the gospel only when we have arrived there. Now I am in full agreement with the need to be sensitive to each situation, but if this was the point which the leader in question was wanting to make, he grossly overstated it. There is such a thing as a revealed or given gospel, which we have no liberty to falsify.

The opposite mistake I will call "total rigidity." In this case the evangelist behaves as if God had given a series of precise formulas that we have to repeat more or less word for word, and certain images that we must invariably employ. This leads to bondage to either words or images or both. Some evangelists lapse into the use of stale jargon, while others feel obliged on every occasion to mention "the blood of Christ" or "justification by faith" or "the kingdom of God" or some other image.

Between these two extremes there is a third and better way. It combines commitment to the fact of revelation with commitment to the task of contextualization. It accepts that only the biblical formulations of the gospel are permanently normative, and that every attempt to proclaim the gospel in modern idiom must justify itself as an authentic expression of the biblical gospel.

But if it refuses to jettison the biblical formulations, it also refuses to recite them in a wooden and unimaginative way. On the contrary, we have to engage in the continuous struggle (by prayer, study, and discussion) to relate the given gospel to the given situation. Since it comes from God we must guard it; since it is intended for modern men and women we must interpret it. We have to combine fidelity (constantly studying the biblical text) with sensitivity (constantly studying the contemporary scene). Only then can we hope with faithfulness and relevance to relate the Word to the world, the gospel to the context, Scripture to culture.

Model for World Evangelization

Thirdly, the Bible gives us the *model* for world evangelization. In addition to a message (what we are to say) we need a model (how we are to say it). The Bible supplies this too: for the Bible does not just *contain* the gospel; it *is* the gospel. Through the Bible God is himself actually evangelizing, that is, communicating the good news to the world. You will recall Paul's statement about Genesis 12:3 that "the scripture...preached the gospel beforehand to Abraham" (Gal. 3:8; RSV). All Scripture preaches the gospel; God evangelizes through it.

If, then, Scripture is itself divine evangelization, it stands to reason that we can learn how to preach the gospel by considering how God has done it. He has given us in the process of biblical inspiration a beautiful evangelistic model.

What strikes us immediately is the greatness of God's condescension. He had sublime truth to reveal about himself and his Christ, his mercy and his justice, and his full salvation. And he chose to make this disclosure through the vocabulary and grammar of human language, through human beings, human images, and human cultures.

Yet through this lowly medium of human words and images, God was speaking of his own Word. Our evangelical doctrine of the inspiration of Scripture emphasizes its double authorship. Men spoke and God spoke. Men spoke from God (II Pet. 1:21) and God spoke through men (Heb. 1:1). The words spoken and written were equally his and theirs. He decided what he wanted to say, yet did not smother their human personalities. They used their faculties freely, yet did not distort the divine message. Christians want to assert something similar about the Incarnation, the climax of the self-communicating God. "The Word became flesh" (John 1:14). That is, God's eternal Word, who from eternity was with God and was God, the agent through whom the universe was created, became a human being, with all the particularity of a first-century Palestinian Jew. He became little, weak, poor, and vulnerable. He experienced pain and hunger, and exposed himself to temptation. All this was included in the "flesh," the human being he became. Yet when he became one of us, he did not cease to be himself. He remained forever the eternal Word or Son of God.

Essentially the same principle is illustrated in both the inspiration of the Scripture and the incarnation of the Son. The Word became flesh. The divine was communicated through the human. He identified with us, though without surrendering his own identity. And this principle of "identification without loss of identity" is the model for all evangelism, especially cross-cultural evangelism.

Some of us refuse to identify with the people we claim to be serving. We remain ourselves, and do not become like them. We stay aloof. We hold on desperately to our own cultural inheritance in the mistaken notion that it is an indispensable part of our identity. We are unwilling to let it go. Not only do we maintain our own cultural practices with fierce tenacity, but we treat the cultural inheritance of the land of our adoption without the respect it deserves. We thus practice a double kind of cultural imperialism, imposing our own culture on others and despising theirs. But this was not the way of Christ, who emptied himself of his glory and humbled himself to serve.

Other cross-cultural messengers of the gospel make the opposite mistake. So determined are they to identify with the people to whom they go that they surrender even their Christian standards and values. But again this was not Christ's way, since in becoming human he remained truly divine. The Lausanne Covenant expressed the principle in these words: "Christ's evangelists must humbly seek to empty themselves of all but their personal authenticity, in order to become the servants of others" (paragraph 10).

We have to wrestle with the reasons why people reject the gospel, and in particular give due weight to the cultural factors. Some people reject the gospel not because they perceive it to be false, but because they perceive it to be alien.

Dr. René Padilla was criticized at Lausanne [*the 1974 Congress on World Evangelization—ed.*] for saying that the gospel some European and North American missionaries have exported was a "culture-Christianity," a Christian message that is distorted by the materialistic, consumer culture of the West. It was hurtful to us to hear him say this, but of course he was quite right. All of us need to subject our gospel to more critical scrutiny, and in a cross-cultural situation, visiting evangelists need humbly to seek the help of local Christians in order to discern the cultural distortions of their message.

Others reject the gospel because they perceive it to be a threat to their own culture. Of course Christ challenges every culture. Whenever we present the gospel to Hindus or Buddhists, Jews or Muslims, secularists or Marxists, Jesus Christ confronts them with his demand to dislodge whatever has thus far secured their allegiance and replace it with himself. He is Lord of every person and every culture. That threat, that confrontation, cannot be avoided. But does the gospel we proclaim present people with other threats that are unnecessary, because it calls for the abolition of harmless customs or appears destructive of national art, architecture, music, and festivals, or because we who share it are culture-proud and culture-blind?

To sum up, when God spoke to us in Scripture he used human language, and when he spoke to us in Christ he assumed human flesh. In order to reveal himself, he both emptied and humbled himself. That is the model of evangelism which the Bible supplies. There is self-emptying and self-humbling in all authentic evangelism; without it we contradict the gospel and misrepresent the Christ we proclaim.

Power for World Evangelization

Fourthly, the Bible gives us the *power* for world evangelization. It is hardly necessary for me to emphasize our need for power, for we know how feeble our human resources are in comparison with the magnitude of the task. We also know how armor-plated are the defenses of the human heart. Worse still, we know the personal reality, malevolence and might of the Devil, and of the demonic forces at his command.

Sophisticated people may ridicule our belief, and caricature it, too, in order to make their ridicule more plausible. But we evangelical Christians are naive enough to believe what Jesus and his apostles taught. To us it is a fact of great solemnity that, in John's expression, "the whole world is in the power of the evil one" (I John 5:19). For until they are liberated by Jesus Christ and transferred into his kingdom, all men and women are the slaves of Satan. Moreover, we see his power in the contemporary world—in the darkness of idolatry and of the fear of spirits, in superstition and fatalism, in devotion to gods which are no gods, in the selfish materialism of the West, in the spread of atheistic communism, in the proliferation of irrational cults, in violence and aggression, and in the widespread declension from absolute standards of goodness and truth. These things are the work of him who is called in Scripture a liar, a deceiver, a slanderer, and a murderer.

So Christian conversion and regeneration remain miracles of God's grace. They are the culmination of a power struggle between Christ and Satan or (in vivid apocalyptic imagery) between the Lamb and the Dragon. The plundering of the strong man's palace is possible only because he has been bound by the One who is stronger still, and who by his death and resurrection disarmed and discarded the principalities and powers of evil (Matt. 12:27-29; Luke 11:20-22; Col. 2:15).

How then shall we enter into Christ's victory and overthrow the Devil's power? Let Luther answer our question: *ein wörtlein will ihn fällen* ("one little word will knock him down"). There is power in the Word of God and in the preaching of the gospel. Perhaps the most dramatic expression of this in the New Testament is to be found in II Corinthians 4. Paul portrays "the god of this world" as having "blinded the minds of the unbelievers, to keep them from seeing the light of the gospel of the glory of Christ..." (v. 4).

If human minds are blinded, how then can they ever see? Only by the creative Word of God. For it is the God who said "let light shine out of darkness" who has shone in our hearts to "give the light of the knowledge of the glory of God in the face of Christ" (v. 6). The apostle thus likens the unregenerate heart to the dark primeval chaos and attributes regeneration to the divine fiat, "Let there be light."

If then Satan blinds people's minds, and God shines into people's hearts, what can we hope to contribute to this encounter? Would it not be more modest for us to retire from the field of conflict and leave them to fight it out? No, this is not the conclusion Paul reaches.

On the contrary, in between verses 4 and 6, which describe the activities of God and Satan, verse 5 describes the work of the evangelist: "We preach....Jesus Christ as Lord." Since the light which the Devil wants to prevent people seeing and which God shines into them is the gospel, we had better preach it! Preaching the gospel, far from being unnecessary, is indispensable. It is the God-appointed means by which the prince of darkness is defeated and the light comes streaming into people's hearts. There is power in God's gospel—his power for salvation (Rom. 1:16).

We may be very weak. I sometimes wish we were weaker. Faced with the forces of evil, we are often tempted to put on a show of Christian strength and engage in a little evangelical saber rattling. But it is in our weakness that Christ's strength is made perfect and it is words of human weakness that the Spirit endorses with his power. So it is when we are weak that we are strong (I Cor. 2:1-5; II Cor. 12:9-10).

Let It Loose in the World!

Let us not consume all our energies arguing about the Word of God; let's start using it. It will prove its divine origin by its divine power. Let's let it loose in the world! If only every Christian missionary and evangelist proclaimed the biblical gospel with faithfulness and sensitivity, and every Christian preacher were a faithful expositor of God's Word! Then God would display his saving power.

Without the Bible world evangelization is impossible. For without the Bible we have no gospel to take to the nations, no warrant to take it to them, no idea of how to set about the task, and no hope of any success. It is the Bible that gives us the mandate, the message, the model, and the power we need for world evangelization. So let's seek to repossess it by diligent study and meditation. Let's heed its summons, grasp its message, follow its directions, and trust its power. Let's lift up our voices and make it known.

Study Questions

1. What is the foundational conviction of this article? Explain the difference this conviction might make in a potential missionary candidate's life.

2. A field missionary, after facing many criticisms about his work, began to grope for an explanation as to why he had come in the first place. "Why was he doing this work?" What would you say to him, referring to the content of this article?

2

The Living God is a Missionary God

John R. W. Stott

Millions of people in today's world are extremely hostile to the Christian missionary enterprise. They regard it as politically disruptive (because it loosens the cement which binds the national culture) and religiously narrowminded (because it makes exclusive claims for Jesus), while those who are involved in it are thought to suffer from an arrogant imperialism. And the attempt to convert people to Christ is rejected as an unpardonable interference in their private lives. "My religion is my own affair," they say. "Mind your own business, and leave me alone to mind mine."

It is essential, therefore, for Christians to understand the grounds on which the Christian mission rests. Only then shall we be able to persevere in the missionary task, with courage and humility, in spite of the world's misunderstanding and opposition. More precisely, biblical Christians need biblical incentives. For we believe the Bible to be the revelation of God and of his will. So we ask: Has he revealed in Scripture that "mission" is his will for his people? Only then shall we be satisfied. For then it becomes a matter of obeying God, whatever others may think or say. Here we shall focus on the Old Testament, though the entire Bible is rich in evidence for the missionary purpose of God.

The Call of Abraham

Our story begins about four thousand years ago with a man called Abraham, or more accurately, Abram as he was called at that time. Here is the account of God's call to Abraham.

> Now the LORD said to Abram, "Go from your country and kindred and your father's house to the land that I will show you. And

John R. W. Stott is Rector Emeritus of All Souls Church in London, President of Christian Impact, and an Extra Chaplain to Queen Elizabeth II. For 25 years (1952-77) he led university missions on five continents. He still travels widely, especially in the Two-Thirds world, as a lecturer and speaker. Formerly he addressed five Urbana Student Missions Conventions. His many books include *Basic Christianity, Christian Mission in the Modern World, The Cross of Christ* and *The Spirit, the Church and the World* . Taken from *You Can Tell the World*, edited by James E. Berney. Copyright 1979 by Inter-Varsity Christian Fellowship of the USA and used by permission of Inter-Varsity Press.

I will make of you a great nation, and I will bless you, and make your name great, so that you will be a blessing. I will bless those who bless you, and him who curses you I will curse; and by you all the families of the earth shall bless themselves." So Abram went, as the LORD had told him; and Lot went with him. Abram was seventy-five years old when he departed from Haran. (Gen. 12:1-4).

God made a promise (a composite promise, as we shall see) to Abraham. And an understanding of that promise is indispensable to an understanding of the Bible and of the Christian mission. These are perhaps the most unifying verses in the Bible; the whole of God's purpose is encapsulated here.

By way of introduction we shall need to consider the setting of God's promise, the context in which it came to be given. Then we shall divide the rest of our study into two. First, *the promise* (exactly what it was that God said he would do) and second—at greater length—*its fulfillment* (how God has kept and will keep his promise). We start, however, with the setting.

Genesis 12 begins: "Now the LORD said to Abram." It sounds abrupt for an opening of a new chapter. We are prompted to ask: "Who is this 'Lord' who spoke to Abraham?" and "Who is this 'Abraham' to whom he spoke?" They are not introduced into the text out of the blue. A great deal lies behind these words. They are a key which opens up the whole of Scripture. The previous eleven chapters lead up to them; the rest of the Bible follows and fulfills them.

What, then, is the background to this text? It is this. "The Lord" who chose and called Abraham is the same Lord who in the beginning created the heavens and the earth, and who climaxed his creative work by making man and woman unique creatures in his own likeness. In other words, we should never allow ourselves to forget that the Bible begins with the universe, not with the planet earth; then with the earth, not with Palestine, then with Adam the father of the human race, not with Abraham the father of the chosen race. Since, then, God is the Creator of the universe, the earth and all mankind, we must never demote him to the status of a tribal deity or petty godling like Chemosh the god of the Moabites, or Milcom (or Molech) the god of the Ammonites, or Baal the male deity, or Ashtoreth the female deity, of the Canaanites. Nor must we suppose that God chose Abraham and his descendants because he had lost interest in other peoples or given them up. Election is not a synonym for elitism. On the contrary, as we shall soon see, God chose one man and his family in order, through them, to bless *all* the families of the earth.

We are bound, therefore, to be deeply offended when Christianity is relegated to one chapter in a book on the world's religions as if it were one option among many, or when people speak of "the Christian God" as if there were others! No, there is only one living and true God, who has revealed himself fully and finally in his only Son Jesus Christ. Monotheism lies at the basis of mission. As Paul wrote to Timothy, "There is one God, and there is one mediator between God and men, the man Christ Jesus" (I Tim. 2:5).

The Genesis record moves on from the creation of all things by the one God and of human beings in his likeness, to our rebellion against our own Creator and to God's judgment upon his rebel creatures—a judgment which is relieved, however, by his first gospel promise that one day the woman's seed would "bruise," indeed "crush," the serpent's head (3:15).

The following eight chapters (Genesis 4-11) describe the devastating results of the Fall in terms of the progressive alienation of human beings from God and from our fellow human beings. This was the setting in which God's call and promise came to Abraham. All around was moral deterioration, darkness and dispersal. Society was steadily disintegrating. Yet God the Creator did not abandon the human beings he had made in his own likeness (Gen. 9:6). Out of the prevailing godlessness he called one man and his family, and promised to bless not only them but through them the whole world. The scattering would not proceed unchecked; a grand process of ingathering would now begin.

The Promise

What then was the promise which God made to Abraham? It was a composite promise consisting of several parts.

First, it was the promise of a posterity. He was to go from his kindred and his father's house, and in exchange for the loss of his family God would make of him "a great nation." Later in order to indicate this, God changed his name from "Abram" ("exalted father") to "Abraham" ("father of a multitude") because, he said to him, "I have made you the father of a multitude of nations" (17:5).

Second, it was the promise of *a land*. God's call seems to have come to him in two stages, first in Ur of the Chaldees while his father was still alive (11:31; 15:7) and then in Haran after his father had died (11:32; 12:1). At all events he was to leave his own land, and in return God would show him another country.

Third, it was the promise of *a blessing*. Five times the words *bless* and *blessing* occur in 12:2-3. The blessing God promised Abraham would spill over upon all mankind.

A posterity, a land and a blessing. Each of these promises is elaborated in the chapters that follow Abraham's call.

First, *the land*. After Abraham had generously allowed his nephew Lot to choose where he wanted to settle (he selected the fertile Jordan valley), God said to Abraham: "Lift up your eyes, and look from the place where you are, northward and southward and eastward and westward; for all the land which you see I will give to you and to your descendants for ever" (13:14-15).

Second, *the posterity*. Sometime later God gave Abraham another visual aid, telling him to look now not to the earth but to the sky. On a clear, dark night he took him outside his tent and said to him, "Look toward heaven and number the stars." What a ludicrous command! Perhaps Abraham started, "1, 2, 3, 5,10, 20, 30...," but he must soon have given up. It was an impossible task. Then God said to him: "So shall your descendants be." And we read: "He believed the Lord." Although he was probably by now in his eighties, and although he and Sarah were still childless, he yet believed God's promise and God "reckoned it to him as righteousness." That is, because he trusted God, God accepted him as righteous in his sight.

Third, *the blessing*. "I will bless you." Already God has accepted Abraham as righteous or (to borrow the New Testament expression) has "justified him by faith." No greater blessing is conceivable. It is the foundation blessing of the covenant of grace, which a few years later God went on to elaborate to Abraham: "I will establish my covenant between me and you and your descendants after you...for an everlasting covenant, to be God to you and to your descendants after you...and I will be their God" (17:7-8). And he gave them circumcision as the outward and visible sign of his gracious covenant or pledge to be their God. It is the first time in Scripture that we hear the covenant formula which is repeated many times later: "I will be their God and they shall be my people."

A land, a posterity, a blessing. "But what has all that to do with mission?" For that let us turn now from the promise to the fulfillment.

The Fulfillment

The whole question of the fulfillment of Old Testament prophecy is a difficult one in which there is often misunderstanding and not a little disagreement. Of particular importance is the principle, with which I think all of us will agree, that the New Testament writers themselves understood Old Testament prophecy to have not a *single* but usually a *triple* fulfillment—past, present and future. The past fulfillment was an immediate or historical fulfillment in the life of the nation of Israel. The present is an intermediate or gospel fulfillment in Christ and his church. The future will be an ultimate or eschatological fulfillment in the new heaven and the new earth.

God's promise to Abraham received an immediate historical fulfillment in his physical descendants, the people of Israel.

God's promise to Abraham of a numerous, indeed of an innumerable, posterity was confirmed to his son Isaac (26:4, "as the stars of heaven") and his grandson Jacob (32:12, "as the sand of the sea"). Gradually the promise began to come literally true. Perhaps we could pick out some of the stages in this development.

The first concerns the years of slavery in Egypt, of which it is written, "The descendants of Israel were fruitful and increased greatly; they multiplied and grew exceedingly strong; so that the land was filled with them" (Ex. 1:7; cf. Acts 7:17). The next stage I will mention came several hundred years later when King Solomon called Israel "a great people that cannot be numbered or counted for multitude" (I Kings 3:8). A third stage was some three hundred fifty years after Solomon; Jeremiah warned Israel of impending judgment and captivity, and then added this divine promise of restoration: "As the host of heaven cannot be numbered and the sands of the sea cannot be measured so I will multiply the descendants of David my servant" (Jer. 33:22).

So much for Abraham's posterity; what about the land? Again we note with worship and gratitude God's faithfulness to his promise. For it was in remembrance of his promise to Abraham, Isaac and Jacob that he first rescued his people from their Egyptian slavery and gave them the territory which came on that account to be called "the promised land" (Ex. 2:24; 3:6; 32:13), and then restored them to it some seven hundred years later after their captivity in Babylon. Nevertheless, neither Abraham nor his physical descendants fully inherited the land. As Hebrews 11 puts it, they "died in faith *not* having received what was promised." Instead, as "strangers and exiles on the earth" they "looked forward to the city which has foundations, whose builder and maker is God" (see Heb. 11:8-16, 39-40).

God kept his promises about the posterity and the land, at least in part. Now what about the blessing? Well, at Sinai God confirmed and clarified his covenant with Abraham, and pledged himself to be Israel's God (for example, Ex. 19:3-6). And throughout the rest of the Old Testament God continued to bless the obedient while the disobedient fell under his judgment.

Perhaps the most dramatic example comes at the beginning of Hosea's prophecy, in which Hosea is told to give his three children names which describe God's awful and progressive judgment on Israel. His firstborn (a boy) he called "Jezreel," meaning "God will scatter." Next came a daughter "Lo-ruhamah," meaning "not pitied," for God said he would no longer pity or forgive his people. Lastly he had another son "Lo-ammi," meaning "not my people," for God said they were not now his people. What terrible names for the chosen people of God! They sound like a devastating contradiction of God's eternal promise to Abraham.

But God does not stop there. For beyond the coming judgment there would be a restoration, which is described in words which once more echo the promise to Abraham: "Yet the number of the people of Israel shall be like the sand of the sea, which can be neither measured nor numbered" (Hos. 1:10). And then the judgments implicit in the names of Hosea's children would be reversed. There would be a gathering instead of a scattering ("Jezreel" is ambiguous and can imply either), "not pitied" would be pitied, and "not my people" would become "sons of the living God" (1:10-2:1).

The wonderful thing is that the apostles Paul and Peter both quote these verses from Hosea. They see their fulfillment not just in a further multiplication of Israel but in the inclusion of the Gentiles in the community of Jesus: "Once you were no people but now you are God's people; once you had not received mercy but now you have received mercy" (I Pet. 2:9-10; cf. Rom. 9:25-26).

This New Testament perspective is essential as we read the Old Testament prophecies. For what we miss in the Old Testament is any clear explanation of just *how* God's promised blessing would overflow from Abraham and his descendants to "all families of the earth." Although Israel is described as "a light to lighten the nations," and has a mission to "bring forth justice to the nations" (Is. 42:1-4, 6; 49:6), we do not actually see this happening. It is only in the Lord Jesus himself that these prophecies are fulfilled, for only in his day are the nations actually included in the redeemed community. To this we now turn.

God's promise to Abraham receives an intermediate or gospel fulfillment in Christ and his church.

Almost the first word of the whole New Testament is the word Abraham. For Matthew's Gospel begins, "The book of the genealogy of Jesus Christ, the son of David, the son of Abraham. Abraham was the father of Isaac..." So it is right back to Abraham that Matthew traces the beginning not just of the genealogy but of the gospel of Jesus Christ. He knows that what he is recording is the fulfillment of God's ancient promises to Abraham made some two thousand years previously. (See also Lk. 1:45-55, 67-75.)

Yet from the start Matthew recognizes that it isn't just *physical* descent from Abraham which qualifies people to inherit the promises, but a kind of *spiritual* descent, namely, repentance and faith in the coming Messiah. This was John the Baptist's message to crowds who flocked to hear him: "Do not presume to say to yourselves, 'We have Abraham as our father,' for I tell you God is able from these stones to raise up children to Abraham" (Mt. 3:9; Lk. 3:8; cf. Jn. 8:33-40). The implications of his words would have shocked his hearers since "it was the current belief that no descendant of Abraham could be lost" (J. Jeremias, *Jesus' Promise to the Nations*, SCM Press, 1958, p. 48).

And God has raised up children to Abraham, if not from stones, then from an equally unlikely source, namely, the Gentiles! So Matthew, although the most Jewish of all four Gospel writers, later records Jesus as having said, "I tell you, many will come from east and west and sit at table with Abraham, Isaac, and Jacob in the kingdom of heaven, while the sons of the kingdom will be thrown into the outer darkness" (8:11-12; cf. Lk. 13:28-29).

It is hard for us to grasp how shocking, how completely topsy-turvy, these words would have sounded to the Jewish hearers of John the Baptist and Jesus. *They* were the descendants of Abraham; so *they* had a title to the promises which God made to Abraham. Who then were these outsiders who were to share in the promises, even apparently usurp them, while they themselves would be disqualified? They were indignant. They had quite forgotten that part of God's covenant with Abraham promised an overspill of blessing to *all* the nations of the earth. Now the Jews had to learn that it was in relation to Jesus the Messiah, who was himself seed of Abraham, that all the nations would be blessed.

The Apostle Peter seems at least to have begun to grasp this in his second sermon, just after Pentecost. In it he addressed a Jewish crowd with the words: "You are the sons...of the covenant which God gave to your fathers, saying to Abraham, 'And in your posterity shall all the families of the earth be blessed.' God, having raised up his servant [Jesus], sent him to you first, to bless you in turning every one of you from your wickedness" (Acts 3:25-26). It IS a very notable statement because he interprets the blessing in the moral terms of repentance and righteousness and because, if Jesus was sent "first" to the Jews, he was presumably sent next to the Gentiles, whose "families of the earth" had been "far off" (cf. Acts 2:39) but were now to share in the blessing.

It was given to the apostle Paul, however, to bring this wonderful theme to its full development. For he was called and appointed to be the apostle to the Gentiles, and to him was revealed God's eternal but hitherto secret purpose to make Jews and Gentiles "fellow heirs, members of the same body, and partakers of the promise in Christ Jesus through the gospel" (Eph. 3:6).

Negatively, Paul declares with great boldness, "Not all who are descended from Israel belong to Israel, and not all are children of Abraham because they are his descendants" (Rom. 9:6-7).

Who then are the true descendants of Abraham, the true beneficiaries of God's promises to him? Paul does not leave us in any doubt. They are believers in Christ of whatever race. In Romans 4 he points out that Abraham not only received justification by faith but also received this blessing *before he had been cir-*

cumcised. Therefore Abraham is the father of all those who, whether circumcised or uncircumcised (that is, Jews or Gentiles), "follow the example of [his] faith" (Rom. 4:9-12). If we "share the faith of Abraham," then "he is the father of us all, as it is written, 'I have made you the father of many nations'" (vv. 16-17). Thus neither physical descent from Abraham nor physical circumcision as a Jew makes a person a true child of Abraham, but rather faith. Abraham's real descendants are believers in Jesus Christ, whether racially they happen to be Jews or Gentiles.

What then is the "land" which Abraham's descendants inherit? The letter to the Hebrews refers to a "rest" which God's people enter now by faith (Heb. 4:3). And in a most remarkable expression Paul refers to "the promise to Abraham and his descendants, that they should *inherit the world* " (Rom. 4:13). One can only assume he means the same thing as when to the Corinthians he writes that in Christ "all things are yours, whether Paul or Apollos or Cephas or the world or life or death or the present or the future, all are yours" (I Cor. 3:21-23). Christians, by God's wonderful grace, are joint heirs with Christ of the universe.

Somewhat similar teaching, both about the nature of the promised blessing and about its beneficiaries, is given by Paul in Galatians 3. He first repeats how Abraham was justified by faith, and then continues: "So you see that it is men of faith who are the sons of Abraham" and who therefore "are blessed with Abraham who had faith" (vv. 6-9). What then is the blessing with which all the nations were to be blessed (v. 8)? In a word, it is the blessing of salvation. We were under the curse of the law, but Christ has redeemed us from it by becoming a curse in our place, in order "that in Christ Jesus the blessing of Abraham might come upon the Gentiles, that we might receive the promise of the Spirit through faith" (vv. 10-14). Christ bore our curse that we might inherit Abraham's blessing, the blessing of justification (v. 8) and of the indwelling Holy Spirit (v. 14). Paul sums it up in the last verse of the chapter (v. 29): "If you are Christ's, then you are Abraham's offspring, heirs according to promise."

But we have not quite finished yet. There is a third stage of fulfillment still to come. *God's promise to Abraham will receive an ultimate or eschatological fulfillment in the final destiny of all the redeemed.*

In the book of Revelation there is one more reference to God's promise to Abraham (7:9ff). John sees in a vision "a great multitude which no man could number." It is an international throng, drawn "from every nation, from all tribes and peoples and tongues." And they are "standing before the throne," the symbol of God's kingly reign. That is, his kingdom has finally come, and they are enjoying all the blessings of his gracious rule. He shelters them with his presence. Their wilderness days of hunger, thirst and scorching heat are over. They have entered the promised land at last, described now not as "a land flowing with milk and honey" but as a land irrigated from "springs of living water" which never dry up. But how did they come to inherit these blessings? Partly because they have "come out of great tribulation" (evidently a reference to the Christian life with all its trials and sufferings), but mostly because "they have washed their robes and made them white in the blood of the Lamb," that is, they have been cleansed from sin and clothed with righteousness through the merits of the death of Jesus Christ alone. *"Therefore* are they before the throne of God."

Speaking personally, I find it extremely moving to glimpse this final fulfillment in a future eternity of that ancient promise of God to Abraham. All the essential elements of the promise may be detected. For here are the spiritual descendants of Abraham, a "great multitude which no man could number," as countless as the sand on the seashore and as the stars in the night sky. Here too are "all the families of the earth" being blessed, for the numberless multitude is composed of people from every nation. Here also is the promised land, namely, all the rich blessings which flow from God's gracious rule. And here above all is Jesus Christ, the seed of Abraham, who shed his blood for our redemption and who bestows his blessings on all those who call on him to be saved.

Conclusion

Let me try to summarize what we learn about God from his promise to Abraham and its fulfillment.

First, he is the God of history. History is not a random flow of events. For God is working out in time a plan which he conceived in a past eternity and will consummate in a future eternity. In this historical process Jesus Christ as the seed of Abraham is the key figure. Let's rejoice that if we are Christ's disciples we are Abraham's descendants. We belong to his spiritual lineage. If we have received the blessings of justification by faith, acceptance with God, and of the indwelling Spirit, then we are beneficiaries today of a promise made to Abraham four thousand years ago.

Second, he is the God of the covenant. That is, God is gracious enough to make promises, and he always keeps the promise he makes. He is a God of steadfast love and faithfulness. Not that he always fulfils his promises immediately. Abraham and Sarah "died in faith *not* having received what was promised, but having seen it and greeted it from afar" (Heb. 11:13). That is, although Isaac was born to them in fulfillment of the promise, their seed was not yet numerous, nor was the land given to them, nor were the nations blessed. All God's promises come true, but they are inherited "through faith *and patience* " (Heb 6:12). We have to be content to wait for God's time.

Third, he is the God of blessing. "I will bless you," he said to Abraham (Gen. 12:2). "God...sent him [Jesus] to you first, to bless you," echoed Peter (Acts 3:26). God's attitude to his people is positive, constructive, enriching. Judgment is his "strange work" (Is. 28:21). His principal and characteristic work is to bless people with salvation.

Fourth, he is the God of mercy. I have always derived much comfort from the statement of Rev. 7:9 that the company of the redeemed in heaven will be "a great multitude which no man could number." I do not profess to know how this can be, since Christians have always seemed to be a rather small minority. But Scripture states it for our comfort. Although no biblical Christian can be a universalist (believing that all mankind will ultimately be saved), since Scripture teaches the awful reality and eternity of hell, yet a biblical Christian can—even must—assert that the redeemed will somehow be an international throng so immense as to be countless. For God's promise is going to be fulfilled, and Abraham's seed is going to be as innumerable as the dust of the earth, the stars of the sky and the sand on the seashore.

Fifth, he is the God of mission. The nations are not gathered in automatically. If God has promised to bless "all the families of the earth," he has promised to do so "through Abraham's seed" (Gen. 12:3; 22:18). Now we are Abraham's seed by faith, and the earth's families will be blessed only if we go to them with the gospel. That is God's plain purpose.

I pray that these words, "all the families of the earth," may be written on our hearts. It is this expression more than any other which reveals the living God of the Bible to be a missionary God. It is this expression too which condemns all our petty parochialism and narrow nationalism, our racial pride (whether white or black), our condescending paternalism and arrogant imperialism. How dare we adopt a hostile or scornful or even indifferent attitude to any person of another color or culture if our God is the God of "all the families of the earth?" We need to become global Christians with a global vision, for we have a global God.

So may God help us never to forget his four-thousand-year-old promise to Abraham: "By you and your descendants *all* the nations of the earth shall be blessed."

Study Questions

1. Why, according to Stott, is it important to know the grounds on which the Christian mission rests? For what other reasons could such foundational knowledge be important?

2. What was the context of God's promise to Abraham? How was the promise of a land, a posterity, and a blessing fulfilled in the past? How is the promise receiving fulfillment in the present? How will God's promise to Abraham receive its final fulfillment in the future?

3

Everyone's Question: What is God Trying to Do?

Stanley A. Ellisen

God's Eternal Kingdom

The Bible describes God as an eternal King: "The Lord is King forever" (Psa. 10:16). It also declares that He is sovereign over all things (Psa. 103:19). Being infinite, He is everywhere. So, at every time and place, in all the vast reaches of His universe, God has been in full control. He has never compromised this supreme prerogative of His Godhood. To do so would make Him less than God. It is essential to recognize His undiminished sovereignty if we are to have a proper view of His kingdom. His work of creation, with all the apparent risks involved, was the work of His sovereignty.

Primeval Rebellion

In the operation of His kingdom God rules by the principle of delegated authority. He organized the angels as a hierarchy, assigning levels of responsibility and spheres of service. To act as His supreme lieutenant in directing this kingdom, God endowed one specific archangel with striking beauty, wisdom, and power (Ezek. 28:12-17; Jude 9). He named him Lucifer and gave him a throne from which to rule (Isa. 14:12-14). This angel ruled as God's prime minister par excellence.

How long this harmonious arrangement continued in the distant past is not recorded. Endowed with freedom of choice, the crucial test of any creature was allegiance to the will of God. That crucial test came for Lucifer when he shifted his gaze to himself and his God-given features of splendor. Dazzled by his own greatness, he asserted independence and presumed himself to be "like the Most High" (Isa. 14:14). In that moment of decision he thrust himself outside the stabilizing axis of God's will and began the swirling catapult into the oblivion of a godless being. His decision was final and never repented of.

Stanley A. Ellisen is Professor of Biblical Literature and Chairman of the Division of Biblical Studies at Western Conservative Baptist Seminary in Portland, Oregon. The author of five books and numerous articles, Ellisen has also served in a number of pastorates in the Pacific Northwest and Southwest. Reprinted with permission from *Biography of a Great Planet*, Chapter 2, copyright 1975, Tyndale House Publishers, Inc., Wheaton, Illinois.

Lucifer, however, was not alone in this choice. He evidently had a following of one-third of the angels of heaven (Rev. 12:4-7), which also suggests the great allurement of his leadership. With this crowd of rebels he formed a kingdom of his own, a counterfeit kingdom of darkness. His name was changed to Satan (adversary), in keeping with his behavior. If God is sovereign, why didn't He immediately destroy this arch rebel? Why didn't He have a mass execution for the whole horde of disobedient angels? Or at least, why didn't He lock them up forever in the abyss of hell?

The answer is that God does have such a plan, but He is temporarily using these rebels to accomplish another purpose. In the outworking of His program, God was not locked in to a one-track plan, but was able to flex with the punches, so to speak. So deep is His sovereignty that He is able to make the wrath of men to praise Him and all His enemies to serve Him (Psa. 76:10). The devastating irony of it for His enemies is that they end up serving Him in spite of themselves. Some of the fallen angels He chained until judgment; others He has allowed a limited liberty until His further purpose is accomplished.

The central fact to observe is that God did allow the formation of a kingdom of darkness. This kingdom formed through voluntary forces led by Satan, not through God's creation, as such. It thus became an opposite pole to God's kingdom of light and an alluring option for all moral creatures in their exercise of moral freedom. It is a counterfeit kingdom running concurrently with the true kingdom of righteousness. Very often it seems to be dominant, not only coercing men and women but winning them. This is partly because of its modus operandi. Contrary to many naive opinions, the devil is not a red monster with a pitchfork, but often a do-gooder. His goal in life is to counterfeit the works of God. This has been his prized ambition ever since he went into business for himself. His first recorded intention ended with the words, "I will be like the Most High" (Isa. 14:14). This counterfeiting effort is his most effective ploy, for the more closely he can imitate God's work, the less likely will men be inclined to seek God or pursue His will.

God's Earthly Kingdom Inaugurated

After the fall of Satan, God began another creation: man. He likewise endowed this being with freedom of choice, dangerous though this second venture appears. Freedom of choice was essential to human personality, if man and woman were to be made in the image of God. God's grand design is to reproduce Himself in human personalities, especially His traits of love and holiness. And these divine characteristics can grow only in the soil of moral freedom. Fellowship involves moral choice.

By this freedom God sought to establish man and woman in a wholesome relationship to His sovereignty. He sought to relate to them by love, not coercion. The bond of love is infinitely stronger than that of muscle. With this in mind He made Adam and Eve partners in His rule. As an initial test they were forbidden to eat of the "tree of the knowledge of good and evil" (Gen. 2:17). They were given a choice of compliance or disobedience, clear and simple. The tree was not put there as a teaser or trap, but as an inevitable test. It gave the couple a choice as to whether they would be loyal to God or submit to enticing alternatives presented by the serpent. Had they turned from his evil suggestion to firm commitment to God, they might have eaten of the "tree of life" and been eternally confirmed in righteousness (Gen. 3:24; Rev. 22:2). But they each disobeyed the direct command of God, and the fall of the race took place.

By this deliberate action they declared their independence from the will of God and their affiliation with Satan's kingdom of darkness. The cause of this disaster was not the tree; nor was it the serpent or the devil behind the serpent (Rev. 12:9). These provided only an occasion for two individuals to express their freedom of choice with respect to the will of God. The cause of disaster was in their decision. In this test of allegiance they failed and fell, along with the previously fallen host of angels.

To all outward appearance, this second fall of God's creation seemed to dash God's high hopes of extending His kingdom in moral agents. Man was given cosmic responsibilities to have dominion over the earth—but he could not be trusted with a piece of fruit. Was the divine gift of free choice too risky? Would this endowment be the suicidal undoing of the whole race? It certainly seemed to be counterproductive to God's purpose, for sin appeared to be coming up the victor.

The two problems summarized

The dilemma at this point may be summarized as two problems which God acquired in the creative process. One was the fact that His trusted lieutenant, Lucifer, defected and started a counterkingdom, stealing also the allegiance of a large contingent of the angels. The second was that man, made in God's image, also defected and fell into a state of sin and personal disintegration. Thus God's kingdom was dissected and partially usurped.

The question is often raised as to why God bothered with a salvage operation. Why not destroy everything and start over? Of course this was not within His sovereign plan, nor would it have been a real solution to the deep challenge the double rebellion posed. God not only rose to the insidious challenge of sin, but His great heart of grace initiated an operation that would marvelously redeem sinners. In this plan He addressed Himself to two problems: 1) how to reclaim His usurped kingdom; and 2) how to provide redemption for mankind. The solution God sought could not deal with both problems separately; he thus devised a plan whereby the victory over the counterfeit kingdom would provide salvation for mankind. It could not be achieved by a mere display of divine muscle; the answer was not to crack the whip. Cataclysmic and inclusive judgment would be postponed. It would require action with the depth and power of His greatest attribute: love.

God's Kingdom and Redemptive Programs

When Adam and Eve first sinned, God began His judgment with the serpent (Gen. 3:14, 15). In this judgment He also gave the proto-evangel, announcing His redemptive purpose for men. To the serpent He said, "And I will put enmity between you and the woman, and between your seed and her seed; he shall bruise you on the head, and you shall bruise Him on the heel." This message was obviously for man as well as Satan, perhaps more so. In it God prophesied that, following a two-way enmity, two bruisings or crushings would take place. The serpent's head would be crushed by the woman's seed, and the heel of the woman's seed would be crushed by the serpent. The two figures in this conflict are later declared to be Christ, who was the seed born of a woman (Gal. 4:4), and Satan, called "the serpent of old" (Rev. 20:2).

By analyzing these two crushings we get a thumbnail sketch of God's program with respect to Satan and man. The first statement, "He shall bruise you on the head," was a prophecy that Christ would destroy the devil. Christ Himself spoke of His binding Satan, the "strong man" of this world system, and casting him out (Matt. 12:29; John 12:31). Christ's death on the cross provided the ground for Satan's final destruction, for "he who builds the scaffold finally hangs thereon." And with his final judgment, the counterfeit kingdom of his making will also be destroyed. This, of course, has not yet taken place, but will occur after Christ's millennial reign. This whole process by which God reclaims His authority in all realms and forever stops all rebellion can be thought of as God's "kingdom program."

The second crushing announced in Genesis 3:15 is the heel-crushing of the seed of the woman by the serpent. This devilish assault was fulfilled on the cross, where Satan was the driving force behind the crucifixion of Christ. The heel-crushing suggests the temporary nature of Christ's death in contrast to the head-crushing of the serpent. Christ's death on the cross then became the ground for God's redemptive program, the program by which He provided salvation for men.

Thus in this proto-evangel in Eden, God introduced in outline form His twofold program for His kingdom and man's redemption. He would ultimately reclaim His total kingdom by destroying Satan and Satan's kingdom, and would redeem believing men in the process by the death of Christ.

God's Twofold Program Unfolds

The rest of the Old Testament pictures the progressive development of this twofold purpose of God in the earth. The Lord chose two men of faith through whom He inaugurated these programs and set them in motion. The first was Abraham who lived about 2000 B.C. With him God made a covenant, promising among other things a seed that would bless all nations. This seed Paul identified as Christ, and the blessing which was to come through Him he identified as redemption or justification (Gal. 3:6-16). Abraham's seed would bring redemption to men, fulfilling the redemptive program.

To fulfill His kingdom purpose, God chose David out of the same line about 1000 B.C. and made a covenant about a kingdom and a royal seed (2 Sam. 7:12-16). This seed of David eventually would rule over the house of Israel forever. Besides ruling over Israel, it was later revealed that this anointed One would extend His rule over the whole world (Amos 9:12; Zech. 14:9). Through the seed of David, God would fulfill His kingdom program by destroying the rebels and governing the world in righteousness.

Two typical sons

It is interesting to note also that each of these two men was given a son who typified the seed he was promised. Abraham's son, Isaac, typified Christ in His redemptive function, being offered on Mount Moriah as a living sacrifice. David's son, Solomon, typified Christ in His royalty, being a king of glory and splendor. These two sons strikingly typified that seed of Abraham and of David who was looked for with such anticipation throughout the rest of the Old Testament period. In this light, it is no wonder that the Spirit of God begins the New Testament by introducing its central figure as "the son of David, the son of Abraham" (Matt. 1:1).

Two typical animals

The Old Testament also portrays the redemptive and kingdom functions of Christ by two symbolic animals. The sacrificial lamb typified Him in His redemptive work as the "Lamb of God who takes away the sin of the world" (John 1:29). It portrayed Him as the Lord's servant who was led "like a lamb...to slaughter" (Isa. 53:7).

The other animal typifying Christ in the Old Testament is the lion (Gen. 49:9,10). John, in Revelation 5:5, refers to this Old Testament metaphor when he describes Christ as the "Lion...from the tribe of Judah." As the king of the beasts, the lion represents kingly authority. The point is that out of the tribe of Judah would come a Ruler who would rule Israel and the world.

The two programs related

Although these two functions of Christ are inextricably related throughout the Bible, they are distinct in their purposes. The kingdom purpose is primarily for God, having to do with His reclaiming what was lost from His kingdom. The redemptive purpose relates primarily to man, providing the basis of His salvation. Though the kingdom purpose is broader, extending to the whole spiritual realm, it could not be accomplished without the redemptive program for man. Notice how John relates the two in his prophetic vision of Revelation 5. After seeing Christ as the Lion and Lamb, he hears the angelic throng loudly acclaim: "Worthy is the Lamb that was slain to receive power and riches and wisdom and might and honor and glory and blessing" (Rev. 5:12). He will have shown not only His right but His worthiness to rule as God's Lion, having been slain as God's Lamb. Before He moves in to destroy the kingdom of darkness with wrath, He had to walk the fires of judgment to salvage sinners, laying down His life as a lamb. These two roles then are interwoven, but they reach in two directions and demonstrate two qualities of God's nature.

This reclaimed kingdom Christ will finally present back to the Father (I Cor. 15:24). That presentation will constitute the fulfillment of His twofold commission from the Father in His role as the seed of the woman. And, of supreme importance, the process by which He will have reclaimed that kingdom will be through His redemptive love, not His coercive might. This redemptive grace is the genius of His twofold program, and it will also constitute the basis of His eternal fellowship with men. That divine-human fellowship will not be based on fear or force, but on love.

Study Questions

1. State God's two-fold problem in your own words.

2. Examine Ellisen's comments on the Redemptive and Kingdom programs. Does he imply that the two programs are distinct? Can you demonstrate an over-arching unity of God's purpose in dealing with creation?

4

Israel's Missionary Call

Walter C. Kaiser, Jr.

There is a rumor abroad that the Old Testament does not have a missionary message or vision. It is, so goes the popular adage, a book and a message dedicated solely to the Jews and their own nationalistic fortunes. But that rumor and view will not square with the claims that the Old Testament itself makes. Even if we limit our investigation to three key Old Testament texts, we will observe immediately that these three texts present three of the most powerful statements of a missionary call that can be given anywhere.

We would have been more hesitant in our suspecting that the Old Testament has no missionary challenge had we paid close attention to how the Old Testament begins. Certainly the message and scope of the earliest chapters in Genesis, namely Genesis 1-11, are universal in their appeal and international in their audience. Did God not deal with "all the families of the earth" when He moved in saving grace at three specific junctures in Genesis 1-11? To be specific, was it not true that after the Fall of Man, the flood of the earth and the failure of the tower of Babel that God gave the grand messages of salvation in Genesis 3:15, 9:27, and 12:1-3?

And should we doubt that the word to Abraham in Genesis 12:1-3 was international and universal in its offer, scope and intention, then let us quickly remind ourselves that it was painted against the backdrop of the table of the seventy nations of all the world in Genesis 10. The same "families of the earth" appears there and in Genesis 12:3.

Old Testament Gentiles Came to Faith

The phenomenon of Gentiles coming to faith in the coming "seed" or "Man of Promise" was not unknown or without constant reminders in the Old Testament. Consider Melchizedek (in Genesis 14), a priest-king over Salem (Jerusalem); this Gentile openly confessed his faith in Jehovah (Yahweh). Jethro, a Midianite and

Walter C. Kaiser, Jr. is Dean and Vice-President of Education as well as Professor of Semitic Languages and Old Testament at Trinity Evangelical Divinity School in Deerfield, Illinois. He previously taught at Wheaton College and served as a pastor. Adapted from an address given to the students of Trinity Evangelical Divinity School, Deerfield, Illinois, May 14, 1981. Used with permission of Walter Kaiser, Jr.

Moses' father-in-law, demonstrated his commitment to the same Lord espoused by Moses and Aaron by sitting down with them around a fellowship sacrificial meal in Exodus 18. No one could accuse Balaam of being pro-Jewish or chauvinistic in his attitude, for he badly wanted to oblige the king of Moab and curse the nation of Israel. Yet he was God's oracle of truth, even though he had a very rough start in which his donkey showed keener spiritual insight than he did. Nevertheless, Balaam gave us two fantastic chapters, including the great (and only) star prophecy of the Messiah, in Numbers 23-24.

Time fails me to remind us of whole cities that at times repented at the preaching of one Jewish prophet—for example, Jonah and the Ninevites. Even though God's servant was more than reluctant and became very "down-in-the-mouth" and had a "whale-of-an-experience" (literally) before he finally preached to dirty Gentiles who massacred Jews, the city came to know the Lord in grand proportions because Jonah *did* preach. Even then, he hoped this was one sermon in which no one would come forward.

But some may still doubt that the Old Testament explicitly enjoined believers and messengers in the Old Testament to *go* to the *Gentiles*. Did God, they ask, ever *send* an Israelite or the whole nation with the Great Commission?

Three Basic Texts

There are three basic texts that make it clear that God did do just that. These texts are: Genesis 12:1-3; Exodus 19:5-6; and Psalm 67. These three texts are so basic to our understanding of the missionary mandate that God had designed for the whole nation of Israel that it is impossible to view the Old Testament fairly without treating these texts in their missionary context. Israel had always, in the plan and purpose of God, been responsible for communicating the message of God's grace to the nations. Israel was meant to be a communicating nation.

Lest we think that these three Old Testament texts have no relevance to those of us who live in the Christian era and that their message is a B.C.-dated injunction, let it be plainly declared that they are also God's call to us. Put in outline form, their message is God's call to us:

I. To Proclaim His Plan to Bless the Nations—Gen. 12:3;

II. To Participate in His Priesthood as Agents of That Blessing—Exodus 19:4-6; and

III. To Prove His Purpose to Bless all the Nations—Psalm 67.

Genesis 1-11

No one can say that the Old Testament begins in a chauvinistic way or that the God of that testament was so pro-Jewish that missionary outreach did not occur until the time of the Gentiles arrived. Genesis 1-11, as we have stated, clearly argues for the reverse. The scope of that text is worldwide in its offer of salvation for all who would believe. The counter theme in those same chapters is the nations questing for a "name" for themselves. Both in Genesis 6:4 and Genesis 11:4, the sole object of mankind was to make a "name" for themselves and to advance their own reputation—but at the expense of the "name" of God.

Thus the "sons of God" (whom I believe to be tyrannical and polygamous despots in the context of Genesis 6) took to themselves this divine title along with its presumed prerogatives and distorted the very instrument of the state that God had set up for justice and abused it for their own desires and lusts. This constituted the second great failure of the pre-patriarchal era of Genesis 1-11. It had been preceded by the Fall of Man in Genesis 3 and it was climaxed in the third failure of the Tower of Babel in Genesis 11.

Genesis 12:1-3: Proclaim His Plan

Nevertheless, for each of these three failures, our Lord had a saving word of grace: Genesis 3:15; 9:27; and 12:1-3. It is this third gracious word that concerns us here, for it emphasizes God's word of grace over against the failures of men and their idolatrous questing for a "name" or reputation. Five times God said, "I will bless you," "I will bless you," "I will bless you," "I will bless those blessing you," and "In your seed all the nations of the earth shall be blessed."

No doubt the key word here is *bless* or *blessing*. That same word had characterized this whole section, beginning with the word to Adam and Eve—"He blessed them saying, 'Be fruitful and multiply'" just as He had also graciously promised to bless the animals.

And yet man continued to seek meaning on his own terms by questing for a "name." Over against the vacuum of that day (and ours), the vacuum of looking for human status, reputation and achievement devoid of God, Genesis 12:2 suddenly announces that God would give Abraham a "name" as a blessing from above rather than as an achievement of works which left God out of the picture.

The significance of this grandest of all missionary texts cannot be fully appreciated until we begin to realize that there are actually three promises of blessing in Genesis 12:2-3 in which God promises:

1. "I will make you a great nation,"
2. "I will bless you," and
3. "I will make your name great..."

But this is immediately followed by a purpose clause. It is "so that you may be a blessing." Not one of these three promises of blessing were to be for Abraham's self-aggrandizement. Indeed, he and his nation were to be blessed so that they might be a blessing. But to whom? How? For the answers to these questions, we must go on with two more promises.

There were to be two whole classes of people: the blessers of Abraham and the cursers of Abraham. The two additional promises were:

4. "I will bless those blessing you," and
5. "Those who curse you, I will curse."

Again, however, the writer of Genesis adds a purpose clause, while shifting the tense of the verb, so that a fuller statement of his purpose can be given. Now it was "so that in you all the families of the earth might be blessed."

That, then, explains why there was so much blessing. This man and his descendants were to be missionaries and channels of the truth from the very beginning. It is exceedingly important that we recognize that the Hebrew verb in this case must be translated as a passive verb ("the blessed") and not reflexively ("bless themselves") since all the earlier Hebrew grammars, versions, and New Testament understandings insist on it. It is a matter of grace, not of works or copy-catting!

The nations were to be blessed in this man's "*seed*." Indeed, the "seed" of the woman (Geneses 3:15), the "seed" of Shem in whose tents God would come to "tabernacle" or "dwell" (Genesis 9:27), and the "seed" of Abraham formed one collective whole, which was epitomized through its succession of representatives who acted as downpayments and earnests until Christ himself should come in that same line and as a part of that succession and corporate entity.

The recipients of this blessing initially were listed as none other than the seventy nations listed as all "the families" of the earth in Gensis 10. This chapter topically precedes man's third failure at Babel, which in turn leads in Genesis into the inbursting word of God's purpose and plan to bring all the nations of the world to Himself. The word to Abraham was meant to have a great impact on all the families on the face of the earth. This is indeed high and lofty missionary teaching.

Some may remain somewhat skeptical, saying that they cannot see any Gospel or good news in Genesis 12:2-3. Our answer is for those unconvinced doubters to observe that Paul named Abraham, in Romans 4:13, the heir of the whole world. That inheritance obviously must be spiritual in its nature. Moreover, Paul plainly stated in Galatians 3:8 that Abraham had the Gospel preached to him ahead of time when he received Genesis 12:3: "in you shall all the nations be blessed." That was and still is the Good News of the Gospel.

And if we today believe, then we are part of Abraham's "seed" (Galatians 3:29). The object of faith and trust is still the same; the focal point for Israel and the nations of the earth is that Man of Promise who was to come in Abraham and David's "seed" and is now come in Jesus Christ.

The message and its content, in fact the whole purpose of God, was that He would make a nation, give them a "name," bless them *so that* they might be light to the nations and thereby be a blessing to all the nations. To shrink back would be evil on Israel's part. Israel was to be God's missionary to the world—and so are we by virture of the same verses! The mission has not changed in our own day. Abraham and Israel were not intended to be passive transmitters of the "seed" any more than we are to be passive. They were to be a blessing so that they actually could communicate God's gift to the world.

The nations were viewed differently, but the way God dealt with them was always directly related to how they reacted to this Man of Promise who was to come through the nation God had made great and to which He had given this calling to bless and be a blessing. Israel's calling was not the occasion or basis for rejecting any of the nations of the world, but instead the very means of blessing them all. The quest for a "name," for fame, for reputation still goes on today, when God would give His own "name." He will still give His special "name" to those who will believe in that same "seed." It is the only means by which they and all their kindred upon the face of the earth will be blessed and made part of the family of God.

Some may agree that the object of faith was indeed to be the coming seed from Abraham's stock, but they may not agree that God thereby expected or demanded of Abraham and his successors anything like our missionary mandate. Perhaps they were meant to be entirely passive while God was the whole actor in the Old Testament.

Exodus 19:4-6: Participate in His Priesthood

Exodus 19:4-6, the second Old Testament text for our consideration, will not allow that interpretation. In Moses' famous "Eagle's Wings Speech," God reviews with Israel how he bore them along from Egypt like an eagle would transport her young learning how to fly. Since they were the recipients of this gift of deliverance, the text pointedly says, "Now therefore..." It implies a natural consequence ought to be forthcoming from God's miraculous aid in their escape from Egypt.

To begin reading Exodus 19:5 without the "now therefore", and to stress the "iffy-ness" of the words that follow, is to miss the emphasis of the text. This text, like Exodus 20:1, must begin in the environment of grace. "I am the Lord your God, who brought you up from out of the land of Egypt." The "now therefore..." follows because of the previous blessing of God.

Exodus 19:5-6 goes on to say: "...if you will obey my voice and keep my covenant, you shall be my *special possession* among all peoples; for all the earth is mine, and you shall be my *kingdom of priests* and a *holy nation* (italics mine)." Three ministries God specifies for Abraham's descendants.

In the first place, they were to be God's *special possession*, or as the older translations have it, "my peculiar people." The old English word "peculiar" came from the Latin word which meant valuables or any kind of moveable goods which were not, in contrast to real estate, attached to the land, such as jewels, stocks, or bonds. The fact was that Israel was to be God's Son, His people, His firstborn (Exodus 4:22), and now His special treasure. The emphasis here is on the *portability* of that message and the fact that God has placed such high value in *people*. This is exactly as Malachi 3:17 describes us: "jewels."

Another role Israel was to perform was that of being kings and priests for God. The genitive or construct form, "kingdom of priests," is better translated (based on six occurrences in prose texts) "kings and priests," "kingly priests," or "royal priests." It is here that Israel's missionary role became explicit, if any doubt had remained. The whole nation was to function on behalf of the kingdom of God in a mediatorial role in relation to the nations.

In fact, it was this passage that became the basis for our famous New Testament doctrine of the priesthood of believers (see I Peter 2:9; Revelation 1:6- 5:10). Unfortunately for Israel, they rejected this priesthood of all believers and urged Moses to go up to the mountain of Sinai on their behalf and as their representative. Nevertheless, even though God's original plan was for the moment frustrated and delayed until New Testament times, it was not defeated, substituted, or scrapped. It remained God's plan for believers. They were to have a mediatorial role!

Israel was to have a third function: a "holy nation." Holiness in the Bible is not just a form of ether that invades audiences on Sunday mornings and makes them somewhat listless and passive, but holiness is wholeness. To be "holy" is to be "wholly" the Lord's.

It is a shame that we had to divide the English word into two words: the one religious (holy) and the other secular (wholly), but the root was the same in Anglo-Saxon history. The same is true for the Hebrew root. Israel was to be given wholly over to the Lord as a nation. They were to be set apart not only in their lives, but also in their service. Their calling and election of God was for service and that service had been defined as early as the days of their ancestor Abraham.

As priests were to represent God and mediate his word to the nations, so Israel as a holy nation was to assume two relations: one side towards God their King and the other side towards the nations. They were to be a nation for all the times and for all the people—set apart. But instead, Israel began to act for herself, as we also often do, as a club of the pious, rather than remembering her call to be sharers of the blessings, truth, gifts and the "Seed" to the nations. In a sense, they carried a portfolio which read "Ambassadors of the Coming Man of Promise."

Now I have not forgotten the distinction between Israel and the Church. It is possible to distinguish between these two institutions, just as one can distinguish between male and female. Yet that middle wall of partition which demanded death for any Gentile that transgressed and passed its boundaries in the temple complex has now been knocked down by Christ's death. Maleness, femaleness, Jewishness, Gentileness, slave status or whatever no longer matter. All who believe are one "people of God." Indeed, that had been the continuity term to identify all who had belonged to the Saviour in all ages. And Peter makes it explicit by calling the Gentile believers of his day "a chosen race, a royal priesthood, a holy nation, God's own people" (I Peter 2:9). The use of Exodus 19 is very obvious and transparent. The point is, do we recognize the continuity in the purpose and plan of God?

Peter went on to make his point clear. God had called his people by these four titles (I Peter 2:9) "so that (they) might declare the wonderful deeds of Him who called (them) out of darkness into His marvelous light." The reason why Israel and now Gentile believers have been named a royal priesthood, a holy nation, the people of God, His chosen race, His special, moveable possession, is that we might announce, declare, and be His missionaries and witnesses.

None of these gifts were meant to be consumed on ourselves. They were not meant to be mere badges. They were for the purpose of declaring His wonderful deeds and calling people to His marvelous light. Once, says Peter in that same context (borrowing from Hosea's symbolic names for his children), we were: no people (Lo-Ammi), without mercy (Lo-Ruhamah). But now we are the people of God and now we have received God's mercy and grace.

Peter is trying to show us that the people of God in all ages have been one. Even though we can identify within the one people of God several aspects such as Israel and Church and even though we can list several aspects to the single plan and purpose of God that all the nations of the earth might be blessed, nevertheless the unity of all believers and the continuity of that program between Old and New Testaments is a certainty. And in both testaments we were all intended by God to participate in that priesthood who would be agents of blessing to all the nations of the earth. Exodus 19 has shown us that this was God's plan.

Psalm 67: Prove His Purpose

Our third and final text comes from Psalm 67. We have seen how God calls us all: 1) to *proclaim His plan* to the nations in Genesis 12, 2) to *participate in His priesthood* as agents of blessing to all the nations in Exodus 19, and now 3) to *prove His purpose* to bless all the nations in Psalm 67. This Psalm is derived from the Aaronic benediction found in Numbers 6:24-26:

> Now may the Lord bless you and keep you,
>
> May the Lord make his face shine upon you, and be gracious to you:
>
> May the Lord lift up his countenance upon you, and give you peace.

This word is often heard at the close of most Christian services today.

But look what the Psalmist does here. Rather than saying "Yahweh" (= LORD, Israel's covenantal and personal name for God), he substitutes Elohim (= God, the name used when God's relationship to all men, nations and creation is needed). The Psalmist prayed: "May God be gracious to us and bless us." Once more he changed the wording ever so slightly, using the words "among us" (literally) instead of "upon us": "And may he cause His face to shine among us."

It is significant that this missionary Psalm has applied what God gave through Aaron and the priests to all the peoples. The purpose for this enlarged blessing is given immediately in verse 2: "so that your way may be known upon the earth, your salvation among all the nations (or Gentiles)." That is why God had been gracious and blessed Israel and all who believed. This agrees, then, with Genesis 12:3.

The sentiment was: May God bless us, fellow Israelites. May He be pleased to benefit us. May our crops increase and may our flocks produce abundantly. May our families grow large and may we prosper spiritually, so that the nations may look at us and say that what Aaron prayed for, by way of God's blessing, has indeed happened. The very bounty of God demonstrates that God has blessed us. Therefore, may the rest of His purpose come to pass also that in blessing Israel all the nations of the earth might come to know Him as well.

This Psalm has been called the Old Testament *Pater Noster* ("Our Father"), or the Old Testament Lord's Prayer. It has three stanzas:

> vss. 1-3
>
> (ending with: "Let the people praise Thee, O Lord, let all the people praise thee.")
>
> vss. 4-5
>
> (ending with the same refrain)
>
> vss. 6-7

This Psalm was probably sung at the Feast of Pentecost. It is all the more remarkable that that is the event where God was to pour out his Spirit on all the nations and an unusual ingathering was to take place—greater than at any previous feast. Deliberately, the Psalmist refers to the ingathering of the harvest as an earnest, a downpayment, and a symbol of the spiritual harvest from every tribe, tongue and nation. So may the Lord indeed be gracious (full of grace) to us and bless us.

Three times this Psalm refers to the blessing from God: verse one, verse six and verse seven. The structure is almost an exact replica of Genesis 12:2-3. Bless us, bless us, bless us...*so that* all the nations might know the Lord.

The Psalmist calls us to prove and test God's purposes for three reasons. The reasons fit the structure we have already observed. The first is because God has been gracious to us (vss. 1-3). We have experienced the grace of God in his ways and manner of dealing with Israel. We have experienced that grace in the knowledge that His salvation has been extended to all nations. If only all the peoples of all the nations would personally come to know that same grace for themselves!

A second reason is because God rules and guides all nations (vss. 4-5). He is not a judge in a judicial, condemning or punishing sense in this context; instead, He is a royal ruler who judiciously rules in righteousness, as in Isaiah 11:3ff. He is a guide for the nations as the Great Shepherd of Psalm 23:3. Thus the refrain sounds again: Come on, all you peoples of the earth, let's hear it! It's about time you began praising the Lord.

Finally, a third reason is given: the very goodness of God (vss. 6-7). We ought to prove the purpose of God in blessing the nations because He has been so good to us. The land has yielded an abundant increase and our barns, grain bins, and silos are full to overflowing. Was this not an evidence that God answered the prayer of Aaron and the priests in Numbers 6:24-26? The power of God is evident in the very abundance of the harvest.

Now that same power and presence of God which brought the material increase is available for a spiritual increase. If this power were more evident in our lives and preaching, then the spiritual results abroad among the nations and in our own nation would be witnessed by everyone. The point is that the Psalmist did not mouth empty words and forms, but he gave the Psalm so that Israel and we might experience a real change in our lives. The blessing of God comes so that all the ends of the earth might receive spiritual benefit. What has happened materially was only to be an earnest of a blessing with much longer dimensions.

Yes, "God has blessed us; let all the ends of the earth fear Him" (v. 7). The word "fear" here does not mean terror or fright. There are two different usages of the word "fear." Exodus 20:20 urges us: "Fear not, but rather, fear the Lord." Don't be scared, but rather trust and put your whole soul's commitment on Him.

Hence, the fear of the Lord is the beginning of everything: of understanding, of living, of personal holiness, as well as of a vital personal relationship to Him. Fear is one of the Old Testament words for trust and belief. The goodness of God to Israel was meant to be one of God's ways of bringing all the nations on planet earth to fear Him, i.e., to believe the coming Man of Promise, our Lord Jesus Christ. Israel was to be a witnessing, proclaiming, and evangelizing nation. The Gentiles had to be brought to the light.

This purpose for Israel is seen even more clearly in a passage which is not part of this discussion; namely, the "Servant of the Lord" passages of Isaiah 42 and 49. Israel is that servant of the Lord even though the Messiah is the final representative of the whole group par excellence. As such, Israel was to be "a light to the nations," just as Abraham had been told, the writer of Exodus had exhorted, and the Psalmist had sung.

The Psalmist longed for and deeply desired that God, the King of Israel, might be acknowledged as Lord and Savior of all the families of the earth. Should we do less? Does God call us to anything less than also proving, along with Israel, His purpose in this passage of Psalm 67? God's challenge to Israel is also ours: we are to have a mediatorial role in proclaiming His name among the nations. That is still God's purpose. Is it happening in your life?

An Avalanche of Witnesses

May the flame of the Gospel, encapsulated in Genesis 12:2-3, and the call to be a holy nation and a royal priesthood fire us for proclaiming the Gospel in the days that lie ahead. May we announce, not only to North America but to every single nation on the face of the earth, that Jesus is Lord to the glory of God the Father. I trust that our schools and seminaries may do an excellent job in training men to preach as never before in the pulpits of North America, but I also trust and pray that there will come a mighty avalanche of men and women from our schools, seminaries and every walk of life who will literally circumvent the globe for the name above every other name, the name of our great God.

May God bless those of you who have already responded to this call. My only regret is that we don't have more going. May our Lord rebuke us and search us to see if we indeed should not be joining this grand group. I pray that we might support those who are going so that they might report back with such fulness of the power and blessing of the Spirit of God that another strong avalanche might be added to the first. And I pray that the funds that are needed might come as God speaks to each of us, that we might become generous to a Lord who has been very generous with us. So may it be. Amen.

Study Questions

1. Did God give a missionary mandate to the people of Israel in the Old Testament like He did to the church in the New Testament? Explain your answer with supporting Biblical references.

2. What continuity is there between the Old and New Testament mission of God?

5

The Story of His Glory

Steve Hawthorne

The story of the Bible is the story of his glory. The Bible is much more than a drawn-out sermon about how people get saved and behaved. It's basically a story about God. At the core of all other epics of people, and throughout all eras of the planet, God's story flows with steady continuity. It is a story that is even now unfolding. The story, too simply summarized, is God bringing glory to himself. It is the story of his glory.

Don't be thrown off by the rather religious word "glory." There are two amazing dimensions to glory. The first is that God *reveals* who he is. The second: God *receives* who people have become.

"Declare his glory...Give (him) glory"

Consider these two dimensions of glory as found in Psalm 96. First, the *revealing* of his glory:

> Sing to the Lord, bless his name. Proclaim good tidings of his salvation from day to day. Tell of his glory among the nations, his wonderful deeds among all the peoples (Psalm 96:2-3).

God isn't spreading rumors about himself. The record of what he has actually done is to be announced in every circle and setting of humanity.

Although the psalmist marvels that "the heavens declare the glory of God" (Psalm 19:1-3), God has not left the human race guessing about God in the subtle light of creation. He has spoken to people in speech and in actions, and supremely in the person of Jesus. God intends that this knowledge be passed on faithfully in every human language. When God speaks to the people in genuine, articulate language, telling them about what he has done or will do on earth, it's something special. It's special because God is saying more than what is obvious from the speechless light of created order. Some scholars call God's revealing of himself in

---

Steven C. Hawthorne is part of Hope Chapel in Austin TX and serves with the Antioch Network, helping churches with practical vision to plant new churches among the world's least evangelized peoples. He has led on-site research projects in Asia and the Middle East.

words "special revelation."

The heart of special revelation is the *name* of God. God does not go anonymous. He names himself, divulging wondrous matters that can be described in human speech. But the *name* of God is not to be confused with the *names* of God. There are many biblical names of God. He is pleased to be addressed by any of them. Usually, when scripture uses the phrase "the name of God," it is speaking of the entire record, or reputation about God, the body of truth that he has revealed of himself.

In every nation God wants to be *named*. This does not mean that he wants to be listed in the phone book under "G" for "God." He wants the truth about his history and his character made known amidst every people. Special revelation continues as people tell the story and divulge what God has spoken of himself. That's why Psalm 96, along with other Scriptures, calls for the proclamation of the record of God's dealings.[1]

But why is God so interested in getting himself proclaimed? Many believers have simply observed the eternal results and have concluded that God's uppermost passion must be salvation. Of course there is abundant biblical truth at this point. How astounding is God's love for the world! He cares for people's present predicaments as well as their eternal status. But the divine concern for people is not the whole story. Even more moves the heart of God.

As vast as God's love for the world, there is an even greater love. The Father loves the Son and gives everything into his hands as inheritance (John 3:35, Psalm 2:7-8). The Son loves the Father, revealing the Father and ultimately bringing all things to him again for his glory (John 14:31, Matthew 11:25-27, 1 Corinthians 15:24-28, Philippians 2:9-11). The Spirit of God searches and reveals the heart of God and glorifies the Son (1 Corinthians 2:10, John 16:13-15).

God desires to be glorified, to be revealed and recognized by all, and to be lovingly served by many from every people. God is worthy of such glory, but what is astounding to comprehend is that he desires the glory people can bring him. There is too much language about God being pleased with righteous worship to think otherwise.

Look at Psalm 96 again. Why the global proclamation? Why world evangelization? The reason is seen in the result of the gospel. God is praised, worshiped with the whole lives of entire families who live out righteousness and bring it to God as a personal love gift.

The basic rationale is that God *reveals* his glory *to* all peoples so that he may *receive* glory *from* all creation.

"For great is the Lord, and greatly to be praised" (Psalm 48:1). The reason given for a resounding declaration of the gospel of salvation is not the benefit to people; neither is it the rightful ascendancy of God over false gods, though both these things are wondrous. The reason for the world to be evangelized, like a song, is the praise that comes to God as a result.

Why does God have a penchant for praise? Does God have a public relations problem? A fool might conclude that the Most High has some kind of low self-image driving him to crave the adulation of people. Of course, this is not the case. God is to be praised simply because of his magnificent worthiness and beauty.

> Splendor and majesty are before him, strength and beauty are in his sanctuary. Give[2] to the Lord, O families of the peoples, give to the Lord glory and strength. Give to the Lord the glory of his name. Bring an offering, and come into his courts. Worship the Lord in the splendor of holiness (Psalm 96:6-9).

Every grouping of people with generational depth, the "families of the peoples," are beckoned to come near the royal presence of God. They are not to come empty-handed, but submissively extend a gift to God, a sampling of the unique glory and strength of their people. The peoples voice praise gifts to God in their many languages, but no people decides on their own what is sufficient praise. The truth God has revealed about himself, "the glory of his name," is the substance and true measure of worthy praise. While styles vary with the distinct flower of every culture, still each is to approach God according to the protocols of heaven's courts, with a radiant inner holiness only God can give. To evangelize the world is to labor that God be glorified by name in every people.

The Bible as God's Story

Let's return to the Bible as a single integrated story of his glory. Remember the basic thesis: God *reveals* his glory *to* all peoples so that he may *receive* glory *from* all creation. This double dimension of glory can help make sense out of an apparent jumble of ancient stories.

Abraham

When Abram finally completed the long sojourn from his ancestral homeland in Ur he didn't exactly succeed in a brilliant missionary career as we understand it. He's not on record as a great evangelist; instead he actually got thrown out of Egypt in disgrace. But I think he did the most missionary thing he could have done when he first arrived in the new land.

The first thing Abram did upon arrival was to establish ongoing public worship of God according to revealed truth. "He built an altar to the Lord and called upon the name of the Lord" (Genesis 12:7-8). Perhaps his household was the only one worshiping at that altar, but he explicitly worshiped God in some sort of continuing public way.

You know the story of Abram helping some of the neighboring peoples (Genesis 14). When windfall profits came his way because of his service, Abram was resolute to name God as the one who was blessing him. Abram was blessed to be a blessing to the nations, but in the words of Melchizedek, he was blessed to be a blessing "to God Most High" (Genesis 14:18-20)!

Significantly, what Abraham (now renamed) offered to God at that time was the wealth and glory of nations. He did not consume or keep any of the booty. Who then ended up serving as the surprise priest? Abraham! He helped the nations give a tithe (in biblical usage, not a church "tax" but rather a very significant gift of worship) to God.

The crucial, forming moment of Abraham's life was a worship event (Genesis

22). God tested him to find what kind of servant he really had. Would Abraham receive God's blessing but fail to render it to God again? Or would God find an obedient, priestly passion for God (literally, *a fearer of God*, Genesis 22:12)? You know the story. At that hour God reiterated with solemn oath his global purpose to bless the peoples of the earth through this family (22:18). If God has a worshiping people with their entire beings jealous for God, then God's intent to bless will ultimately not be dissipated in self-service.

The Exodus

God did more for his name than Abraham's early worship. God went global in a big way at the Exodus. Since then he has never ceased to deal with every people on earth according the truths he revealed at that time.

At first glance, the story of Exodus doesn't look like a great missionary event. Thousands of Egyptians dead. Grief in every Egyptian home. What was God doing?

The key passage is Exodus 9:13-16 in which Moses gives an ultimatum to Pharaoh, with a bold word about his purposes:

"Thus says the Lord, the God of the Hebrews, 'Let my people go, that they may serve me. For this time I will send all my plagues on you and your servants and your people, so that you may know that there is no one like me in all the earth. For if by now I had put forth my hand and struck you and your people with pestilence, you would then have been cut off from the earth. But indeed, for this cause I have allowed you to remain, in order to show you my power, and in order to proclaim my name through all the earth.'"

Take note that Moses never said, "Let my people go!" That's just half the sentence, without the purpose. Take care to hear the entire cry of salvation: "Let my people go, that they may *serve (worship) me!*" (Exodus 8:1, 20; 9:1, 13; 10:3)[3]

Pharaoh well understood the entire demand of Moses that the people be released to worship. Pharaoh probably thought that the appeal for a worship vacation was a ploy to escape. Perhaps many of the Hebrews made the same mistake. How many of them may have thought that the plans to worship God in the wilderness were but a ruse to dupe the authorities? Is it any wonder then that many of them remained fixated on matters of comfort, diet, safety, and entertainment? They were slow to comprehend that in their escape, God had a purpose for himself in the sight of the nations. They had turned salvation inside-out: They seriously thought that their rescue was the only ultimate concern of God. Instead, God was orchestrating a powerful plan to draw the nations to himself in worship.

God's purpose to be worshiped by the nations had to begin in pure simplicity with one people. God had rescued them to begin the worship festival on earth. Instead, for them, worship remained a perfunctory ritual along the way to their new homes and gardens. But God was resolute in making his worship the global issue.

God Brings Global Attention to His Name

God was singling himself out. He was making an "everlasting name" for himself at the Exodus (Isaiah 63:11-14 and Nehemiah 9:9-10). He wanted everyone in Egypt and beyond to know that there was absolutely no god like the living God. He wanted the world to watch a mob of slaves marching in procession to worship him. God established his reputation as one greater and absolutely different (truly holy, not just holier) than every other deity ever dreamed up by man—an exquisite, powerful, resplendent God. The Exodus was to be a reference point for all subsequent revelation to the world of his character, his holiness, and his power. How did chaos in Egypt reveal the everliving God?

Some scholars have noted that every one of the plagues of Egypt was either aimed against the false gods of Egypt or the oppressive power structures that were revered with fanatical zeal.[4] Some Egyptian deities, such as the Nile River, or the great sun god, were embarrassed directly by plagues of blood and darkness. Other deities were indirectly shamed by exposing their complete inability to do what they were supposed to do. There were gods who were revered as being able to deal with infestations of insects or protect cattle from disease. The powerful religious elite was shamed and diseased out of honor and power. The deeply revered military was summarily annihilated. Why was God wrecking Egypt like this before the watching world?

God was executing judgments "against all the gods of Egypt" (Exodus 12:12). He was not aimed at destroying people, but devastating one of the most highly regarded bunch of false gods in all the earth. If he wanted to destroy the people of Egypt he could have done it quickly. "For if by now I had put forth my hand and struck you…, you would then have been cut off from the earth. But indeed, for this cause I have allowed you to remain…to proclaim my name through all the earth."

Did it work? Did the world take notice of God making his name great? The devastation recorded in the book of Exodus didn't make headlines in Egyptian hieroglyphs, but understand that not many stories were chipped into stone which put Egypt in a bad light.

The waves of the Red Sea hadn't quite calmed down before Moses led the people in singing "The Lord is his name….Who is like you among the gods, O Lord? Who is like you, majestic in holiness?" Then they began to list some of the surrounding nations, stating clearly that: "The peoples have heard, and they tremble…." (Exodus 15:3, 11, 14)."

Jethro, married into Moses' family but a Gentile in every respect, had certainly heard about the God of the Hebrews for years from Moses. Perhaps many peoples and cities had heard something of this great God without trusting or worshiping him. But listen to Jethro after the plagues of Egypt. He was a leading priest of a foreign people with authority to evaluate such matters (Exodus 18:1). "Now I know that the Lord is greater than all the gods; indeed, it was proven when they dealt proudly against the people" (Exodus 18:11).

God showed himself as the "warrior" of which Moses sang, who "in the greatness of your excellence, you do overthrow those who rise up against you" (Exodus 15:3, 7). The Egyptian empire opposed God by dealing "proudly with the (Hebrew) people," and thus became his enemies.

For all of Pharaoh's concern about keeping the Hebrews as slaves, forced servitude is not the prominent issue. God does not take him to task about being a mean taskmaster. As Moses confronted ancient Egypt, it appeared to be just another a harsh empire. It turned out to be a complex of religious, economic, and military powers inextricably enmeshed with horrid spiritual evil. Instead God unraveled the system to show it for what it was at the core: dedicated to diverting or perverting worshipers coming to him. Egypt made itself an enemy of God.

This was not a cosmic extortion scheme to force worship from a kidnapped tribe. Just the reverse. It was very much a rescue mission. God dismantled the structures which had trapped people, hindering them from knowing, serving, and loving him.

His "judgments" of the plagues and the awesome Red Sea affair are not to be understood as overdone spankings for bad deeds. God's wrathful intervention ended up freeing people. Freed for what? "Let my people go, that they may *worship* me."

The Conquest

The conquest of the land is to be seen in the same light of God winning to himself a single, holy people of worship. To that people, and by their witness, he would draw every other people to revere and know him. The conquest of the promised land was a land grant, on the basis of ancient promises to Abraham's family, in order to unfold the purposes of blessing the nations.

The conquest doesn't seem more like a genocidal land grab than an imperial land grant. There is reference to the destruction of the peoples in the land because of their "wickedness" (Deuteronomy 9:5). But many more passages describe the likelihood that the people of the land would swiftly turn the Hebrews "away from following me to serve other gods" (Deuteronomy 4:15-24, 6:13-15, 7:1-8, for starters).

Joshua and Moses both voiced the same God-given rationale for the violence of the conquest: it was, at the core, an annihilation of false worship. God had mandated the destruction so that Israel would never "mention the name of their gods,...or serve them, or bow down to them" (Joshua 23:6-16). There are difficulties for anyone trying to understand this part of the story of God's people. However the conquest is understood, the overwhelming weight of biblical explanation for the conquest is worship, that God alone would be worshiped by this people.

Idolatry doesn't seem to threaten most believers today. Perhaps we think that idols could only attract the attention of so-called primitive peoples. Surely we moderns are beyond any kind of idolatry. Or so it may seem. But idolatry bores us. The first four commands of the ten commandments mystify us. Why was God so ferociously passionate about idolatry? Without grasping his global purposes for glory, it may seem that God is over-wrought about a nasty primitive habit.

But ponder idolatry from God's point of view. God had distinguished his name far above any other. Any kind of idolatry would, in effect, profane (bring down as common) God's name, the very name God had just sounded out to the world.

Look again at the conquest. The point of the invasion was not that Israel deserved someone else's homeland. God told Israel point blank that they weren't special or favored because of their intrinsic righteousness or their great nobility (Deuteronomy 7:6-7). Israel was told repeatedly that God would destroy them just as swiftly if they turned away from his worship to other gods.

The record is abundantly clear that the Hebrew people were at several points very early on precariously close to being destroyed. Why? Hadn't God specially loved and saved them? For all the special love God had promised the descendants of Abraham, God was resolute in dealing with the Hebrew nation; but God was not averse to taking a delay and working with another generation. The issue every time was the worship of the people to God and their witness to his glory.

One instance makes this constant purpose of God clear: The rebellion at Kadesh-Barnea. Israel had followed God through a divinely opened way, and stood on the threshold of fulfilling God's purposes. Spies were sent to check out the land and the people. You know the story. Ten of the spies spooked the whole people, touching off a hysterical rebellion for self-preservation (Numbers 13:17-14:10).

God was ready to vaporize the entire people and start over with Moses, making out of him another people "greater and mightier" than the Hebrews. The point is not that the people had done something so bad that God had become fatally angry. God simply required for his purposes a nation who would at least believe in him.

Moses actually argues with God, bringing up, as he had in a previous instance (Exodus 32:1-14), that the nations were watching; and that they had heard something of God's name which could be falsified by what God was about to do. "Now if you slay this people as one man, then the nations who have heard of your fame (literally "name") will say, 'Because the Lord could not bring this people (into the land)....'" Moses challenges God, telling him that the nations will conclude that the Hebrew God is a wimp—all beginnings but no finish.

Then Moses asks God to magnify himself according to how God himself had summarized his name: "The Lord is slow to anger and abundant in lovingkindness, forgiving iniquity and transgression...." [5] A long pause from heaven, and then God said that he had pardoned Israel according to the prayer of Moses. Then God raised his voice, I think, using some of the strongest expressions possible: "But indeed, as I live, all the earth will be filled with the glory of the Lord" (Numbers 14:11-21)!

What was God saying? That he would continue to use the nation, but wait for another generation. But though he was taking a delay, he remained everlastingly resolute to bring forth his purpose on earth which required an obedient, worshiping, witnessing people: to fill the earth with "the glory of the Lord."

The Temple

Perhaps the first clear mention of the temple is found in Deuteronomy 12, in context of destroying "all the places where the nations...serve their gods." Instead of remodeling any of the former places of worship, the shrines were to be completely wiped out in order to "obliterate their name." God's name was never to be equivocated with any other deity. Instead, a new and special place would be built, "to establish his name there for his dwelling" (Deuteronomy 12:2-14, especially verse 5).

Consider God's declaration of purpose for the temple: "to establish his name there for his dwelling." God wanted to do two things in this special place: first, to reveal himself by "his name." It would be a place of revelation. The stories and songs of his working and his character would be continually voiced.

But it would also be a place of encounter, of relationship, of dwelling. For God to "dwell" in a place does not mean that he has a mailing address, or that he wants to haunt a house with holiness. To "dwell" is a relational affair. God does not so much want to dwell *in* the building as he desires to dwell *with* his people.

Solomon knew that the temple was not God's domicile. As he dedicated the fabulous structure he prayed: "But will God indeed dwell with mankind on the earth? Behold, heaven and highest heaven cannot contain you; how much less this house which I have built" (2 Chronicles 6:18).[6]

David had designed the temple as a place of praise to God. Solomon installed the choirs and priestly musicians that his father had planned. These choirs were to continually "praise and glorify the Lord" using some of the Davidic songs, and no doubt using David's dedicatory hymn found in 1 Chronicles 16:23-33 (another rendition of Psalm 96, discussed above), which explicitly calls all nations to worship God.

According to Solomon's dedication, the house of the Lord is to be a place where God would see, hear, and answer his people. But not just Israel. Solomon makes special mention of the peoples. He knew that God's purpose for the temple was in keeping with his eternal purposes to reveal himself to all the earth.

Solomon recognized God's wisdom in making himself vastly famous and that God's purpose in this notoriety would be that the people of other nations would seek to know the God of Israel personally. Listen to Solomon's astounding prayer:

> Also concerning the foreigner who is not of your people Israel, when he comes from a far country for your name's sake (for they will hear of your great name and your mighty hand, and of your outstretched arm); when he comes and prays toward this house, hear in heaven your dwelling place, and do according to all for which the foreigner calls to you, in order that all the peoples of the earth may know your name, to fear you as do your people Israel... (1 Kings 8:41-43).

Solomon did not pray for some of the persons, but all of the peoples. He assumed that they would learn something about God through the witness of the people about God's greatness. Solomon prayed that the nations would meet God as they came to the house to pray and to worship. He did not ask that Gentiles know God in their own Gentile way, but rather to know God as Israel did. Solomon envisioned all peoples joining Israel in the same kind of humble, joyous worshipful walk with God that Israel enjoyed: "the fear of the Lord."

The Nations Begin To Come

Did the report of God's name go out the world? Did foreigners ever come to the house of the Lord and learn of the fear of the Lord? Did God answer Solomon's prayer? Yes and no to all the above.

The record shows that soon after the temple was complete (1 Kings 9:25), the Queen of Sheba "heard about the fame of Solomon *concerning the name of the Lord*" (1 Kings 10:1, my emphasis). She came to learn, she listened to Solomon's wisdom (10:8), and came away with understanding of the covenant-keeping God who "loved Israel forever." As only a royal potentate might see, she realized that God himself had established the power of Solomon, and the hope that through God's rulership, there might be "justice and righteousness" (1 Kings 10:9).

Was this an isolated instance? Apparently not. A few verses later it says that "All the earth was seeking the presence of Solomon, to hear his wisdom which God had put in his heart" (1 Kings 10:24). The world didn't honor Solomon for being brainy or clever with court cases. The world recognized that God had put wisdom in his heart. And what was lesson one of Solomon's wisdom? "The fear of the Lord is the beginning of wisdom" (Proverbs 1:7; 9:10). Solomon was introducing the world to the worship of God and the wisdom of God.

God's purposes were apparently being fulfilled. What could have possibly slowed the unfolding plan of God to draw the nations to himself? Only one thing. And it was the one matter about which God most stringently warned his people: Idolatry. And of all horrors, Solomon himself leads the way.

It is one of scripture's most bitter ironies. Imagine the brilliant hopes with the riches and the desires of the nations turning to Israel. Solomon had consecrated the temple in a spectacle of unimaginable glory. He had closed that event with a blessing of purpose on the building and nation: "so that all the peoples of the earth may know that the Lord is God; there is no one else" (1 Kings 8:60). Just three chapters after this, Solomon's heart was turned "away after other gods" and he actually constructs shrines within sight of the holy mountain of God (1 Kings 11:1-8). Can any believing reader of these verses not feel disappointment to the point of nausea? Can you feel a hint of grievous regret in these pages of the story that the global purposes of God had been so foolishly hindered? Was God's plan delayed? It's not wise to speculate. Perhaps we can never know what might have been had worship been pure and steady for another generation.

The Persistence of God

From what follows, it appears that God did not change his plan. He wanted to make his name great, and to welcome the nations to worship him personally through the witness of the people of Israel.

The story from this point turns to a prolonged up-and-down struggle with idolatry, with various episodes of revived fidelity to God's worship, followed by stunning new lows of profaning God's name.

If God delayed anything, it was his declared intention to destroy the people who falsified his testimony by worshiping other gods.

The disregard of the people for the worship of God became so advanced that at times generations would pass without the slightest attention to the simple regimens by which God had invited Israel to meet with him. The prophets exposed that at times, godly worship forms were followed, but were scandalously perverted by an entire lack of the justice and kindness that was supposed to have thrived behind every offering and prayer to God (Isaiah 1:11-15, Micah 6:6-8, Amos 5:21-24).

God delayed the great shaking of Israel and Judah, but finally the people were separated from the land which was to showcase the blessing of God; and the utmost tragedy—the house of God was burned and broken to rubble.

Near the end of the time of exile, Daniel cried out for God to enact his promise to restore the temple and people. Daniel was intensely aware of the entire saga, how God had brought his people "out of the land of Egypt with a mighty hand...(to) make a name for yourself, as it is this day" (Daniel 9:15). Daniel's bottom line was that the people of God and the wreck of intended glory on the holy mountain of the temple was reproach to God's glory to "all those around us." He prayed that God would restore the people and the city so that the glory of his name would be restored. Daniel did not base his request on the supposed greatness of Israel, but "For your own sake, O my God, do not delay, because your city and your people are called by your name" (Daniel 9:15-19).

Ezekiel, a near contemporary to Daniel, breathed the same themes. God had restrained his wrath at several junctures from destroying Israel, but God's restraint had been for the sake of his name (Ezekiel 20:5-22). The dealings of God with Israel were not at all a sickly favoritism, but solely for his glory among the nations:

> Thus says the Lord God, 'It is not for your sake, O house of Israel, that I am about to act, but for my holy name, which you have profaned among the nations where you went. And I will vindicate the holiness of my great name which has been profaned among the nations, which you have profaned in their midst. Then the nations will know that I am the Lord,' declares the Lord God, 'when I prove myself holy among you in their sight' (Ezekiel 36:22-23).

The Destiny of Israel: Glory From All Nations

The prophets and psalmists spoke of the destiny of Israel in terms of the nations being drawn to God by name, and worshiping him with diverse, lavish glory.

> All nations you have made shall come and worship before you, O Lord; and they shall glorify your name (Psalm 86:9).

> Shout joyfully to God, all the earth. Sing the glory of his name; make his praise glorious. Say to God, 'How awesome are your works!' Because of the greatness of your power your enemies will give feigned obedience to you. All the earth will worship you. And will sing praises to you; They will sing praises to your name (Psalm 66:1-4).

> For the earth will be filled with the knowledge of the glory of the Lord, as the waters cover the sea (Habakkuk 2:14).

> For then I will give to the peoples purified lips, that all of them may call on the name of the Lord, to serve him shoulder to shoulder. From beyond the rivers of Ethiopia my worshipers, my dispersed ones will bring my offerings (Zephaniah 3:9-10).

> For from the rising of the sun, even to its setting, my name will be great among the nations, and in every place incense is going to be offered to my name, and a grain offering that is pure; for my name will be great among the nations (Malachi 1:11).

These are but a sampling of the scores of prophetic words which tethered Israel's identity to the culmination of God's purposes: the glory of God on earth drawing the worship of all peoples.

The Glory of God in Christ

Is the theme of the glory of God from the nations merely that, a theme? Or is it something relegated to "Old Testament" times that has been superseded by some "New Testament" truth?

Of course, the person to look to is Jesus. What was his life all about? What did he teach? What did he mandate?

Jesus summed up his ministry in terms of glory to his Father: "I glorified you on the earth, having accomplished the work which you have given me to do." And what was the work? "I manifested your name to the men you gave me out of the world" (John 17:4, 6).

The prayer Jesus taught his disciples to pray can be easily misunderstood because of the antiquated English translation "Hallowed be Thy name." This prayer is not a statement of praise. It is explicitly a request in the original language: "Father...sanctify your name!" Or to paraphrase: "Father...lift up, single out, exalt, manifest, and reveal your name to the people of earth. Become famous for who you really are. Cause the people of earth to know and adore you." There is no reason not to understand the scope of the prayer as global: "on earth as it is in heaven." There is no question of the primacy of this prayer for all believers. There can be little doubt that Jesus is teaching the church to pray for the fulfillment of ancient purposes revealed in the law, the stories, the songs and the prophecies of Israel.

In one telling encounter with a non-Jewish Samaritan woman, Jesus declared God's future for her and other Gentile nations: "An hour is coming, and now is, when the true worshipers shall worship the Father in spirit and truth; for such people the Father seeks to be his worshipers" (John 4:23).

In his most dramatic challenge of the status quo, Jesus made the issue the worship of the peoples, echoing David's desire for the nations to come to God in his courts. As he cleansed the temple of excessive commercialism, he quoted Isaiah 56:7, "My house shall be called a house of prayer for all peoples." He and the religious leaders listening knew immediately the rest of the passage: "The foreigners who join themselves to the Lord, to minister to him, and to love the name of the Lord,...even those I will bring to my holy mountain, and make them joyful in my house of prayer. Their burnt offerings and their sacrifices will be acceptable on my altar."

At the hour of his greatest trouble of soul, just before going to his death, he pondered his life purpose, and the very purpose of the death he was about to die. Instead of asking to escape the pain, he cried out, "Father! Glorify your name!" To the bewildered amazement of those standing near him, God the Father himself spoke from heaven assuring them of the simple constancy of his purpose of glory. "I have both glorified it (my name), and will glorify it again." How would his death glorify God's name? "If I be lifted up, I will draw all men to myself."

Jesus was prompted into this public decision by the approach of a group of Greeks (Gentiles, not Jewish proselytes) who had come to the holy city to worship. They encountered Jesus at the crescendo of his ministry, his most public hour on earth, the grand worship procession we have come to call "Palm Sunday." The Pharisees looked on and could only say, perhaps with some measure of prophetic force, "Look, the world has gone after him" (John 12:19; see John 11:49-52 for an example of an inadvertent prophecy). The Gentiles asked to see Jesus. Though Jesus did not refuse to see them, he instead saw afresh his purpose, to be lifted up higher, by death and by exaltation, so that all people could be drawn to him (John 12:12-32).

Ministry of Surpassing Glory with Paul

Paul labored to "bring about the obedience of faith among all the nations *for his name's sake*" (Romans 1:5, emphasis mine). It appeared that Paul saw the entire world as divided into two categories, where Christ was "named" and where Christ was not yet named. Paul plainly prioritized his efforts so as to labor where Christ was not named (Romans 15:20).[7]

We can see the double direction of God's glory in Paul's ministry. He labored to glorify God by revealing Christ *to* the nations, getting Christ "named." But his deepest zeal, the very boast of his being, is in something that comes back again to God *from* the nations.

> Because of the grace that was given to me from God, to be a minister of Christ Jesus to the nations, priesting the gospel, that my offering of the nations might become pleasing, sanctified by the Holy Spirit. Therefore in Christ Jesus I have found reason for boasting in things pertaining to[8] God (Romans 15:15-17).

Paul's passionate ambition to "preach the gospel" was based on the far more fundamental commission (or in his language, a "grace that was given") which he had received from God to "priest the gospel." There's no mistaking the imagery. Paul sees himself before God, serving the nations as if he were a priest, instructing and ushering them near to God, helping them bring the glory of their people to God for his pleasure. Paul's job is not to change the societies and cultures. The Spirit of God was at work transforming and sanctifying the finest possible display of glory from the peoples.

Paul labored at great cost with a brilliant vision before him. It was something he knew was worth working and waiting for: "that with one voice" many different streams of believers, Jew and Gentile, weak and strong, would together "glorify the God and Father of our Lord Jesus Christ" (Romans 15:6).

The Hope of Glory

Then Paul quotes four Old Testament passages in Romans 15:9-12. Perhaps they might serve together as a rough outline of hope for the world:

First, in verse 9, the hope of Christ being declared by name to the nations: "I will give praise to you among the nations, and I will sing to your name." The word of God goes to the world as a song, giving clear testimony to the truth of his name.

Second, in verse 10, the hope of the nations joining with the people of God at the point of worship: "Rejoice, O nations, with his people." The peoples are welcomed to join the people of God, but not at a superficial point of uniformity. They remain the distinctive peoples they are, but profoundly at one with the singular point of joy: the God who is worshiped.

Third, in verse 11, the hope of culmination: "Praise the Lord, all you nations, and let all the peoples praise him." Somehow every one of the peoples come into the worship festival.

Fourth, in verse 12, the hope of the kingdom: "There shall come the root of Jesse, and he who arises to rule over the nations; in him shall the nations hope." Could the anticipated worship somehow instill a yearning to serve directly for the King? When the King of glory comes, will he not be the "desire of nations" meeting a rising hope from the nations?

This is not intended to work as a some scheme of the last days, but simply to show that there is abundant biblical warrant to expect and labor for the worship of all nations within history.

A Rehearsal for Eternal Glory

But beyond history, we will have found all of our love for God abundantly rewarded. We will have found something more, that all of the worshipful service of the many nations was a rehearsal for greater affairs of love and glory, still involving all the peoples of earth and history.

At the last God comes to his earth exulting in his ancient promise, now fulfilled: "Behold, the tabernacle of God is among men, and he shall dwell among them, and they shall be his peoples,[9] and God himself shall be among them."

The peoples endure everlastingly. God desires that the kings of the peoples continually bring the treasure and fruit of their lives to his throne (Revelation 21:22-26). Forever, with such honor and glory of the nations in our hands, we will be awed by having his very name on our faces. And gazing into his face, we shall serve him as priests (Revelation 22:1-5).

Labor Boldly for His Greater Glory

What shall we do now? Whatever God may grace us to do to glorify Jesus before the world in such a way that movements of obedient worship emerge. To use Paul's language in 2 Corinthians, may God give us a ministry of surpassing glory (3:10-11), and labor boldly toward a vast hope (3:12) because of the open access by the Spirit of God that men may now behold the very glory of God (3:17-18) in the face of Christ (4:6). Now is an hour for increased purity and encouragement of heart (4:1-3) to continue evangelization at great cost (4:7-14) in the face of satanic subversion that blinds people to "the gospel of the glory of Christ" (4:4). And what is the hope? That the sending, empowering grace[10] of God may multiply through the many who have believed to bring about a great "giving of thanks to abound to the glory of God" (4:15).

And though the story of his glory crescendos within history, with some from every people thankfully giving up to God what they are living out in their communities,[11] there is glory beyond. Lifetimes of labor for an earthly extravaganza of glory for God are altogether worthwhile. By such labor we lay hold of "a weight of glory far beyond all comparison" (4:17).

What is an Evangelized World For?

Until now we have cried "Let the earth hear his voice!" Let us never cease voicing his word to every creature. But soon comes the day when, by any reckoning, the earth will have heard. What then?

There is another cry, far more ancient. It is a shout for earth's destiny. It is to be lifted today more than ever: "Let all the peoples praise him!" We hear even now a growing praise from the nations. Now let us focus our deepest affections and boldest plans on the splendor of every people loving God with the sanctified best of their society. What a magnificent hope!

End Notes

1. Psalm 105:1 connects, by Hebrew parallel structure of poetry, the act of calling on God's name with making "known his deeds among the peoples." Psalm 145 and Isaiah 12 are among several other passages stressing the naming of God among the nations by the declaration of his deeds.

2. The Hebrew word often translated "ascribe" is a simple word meaning "give." I use the most literal translation "give" because "ascribe" could make it appear to be an entirely cognitive affair. The context describes this worship an affair involving gifts from people to God which far surpass mere mental ascriptions.

3. See as well the other variations of the appeal to release the Hebrews which reflect that the general Hebrew word translated *serve* is very much in the context of service of worship (Exodus 3:12; 4:23; 5:1; 7:16; 8:27, 29; 10:9). See especially Exodus 10:26 which makes it clear that to "serve" was to offer sacrificial gifts to God.

4. See *Moses and the Gods of Egypt* by John Davis (Grand Rapids: Baker Book House, 1971).

5. God had given this extensive summary of his dealings as his name at Sinai (Exodus 33:19, 34:6-8). It is good news in a capsule about how God does things with people. It is a very significant statement, and was recognized by later generations of Israel as a summary of what was to be proclaimed among the nations (Psalm 86:9-15; 145:1-2, 8-12, 21). Jonah himself recognized this package of truth as something that he knew, that he had withheld from the Ninevites (Jonah 3:9-4:2).

6. Don't take Solomon's question about God dwelling with people on earth as a word of despair of God ever dwelling with people. His prayer is not intended as a definitive map of the cosmos. It rather fits the self-effacing approach to the Most High. He follows with a profoundly humble appeal, in a most formal framework of courtly language, that the king of all the earth deign to turn his eyes toward a place of encounter and hold audience as he had promised (2 Chronicles 6:19-21). Compare 2 Chronicles 6:1-2 in which Solomon acknowledges the cloud of God's glory so filling the temple that no priest could endure the dreadful brilliance (2 Chronicles 5:13-14).

7. A close look at the context shows what Paul means by Christ being "named." It was not a matter of the message of Christ being preached once by a missionary, but rather a "foundation" being laid (Romans 15:20). Paul has just been speaking of specific regions in which the gospel is "fulfilled" or brought to a substantial closure (Romans 15:19).

Translations such as "fully preached" or "fully proclaimed" stress the cognitive transfer of gospel information far too steeply, especially in light of the full menu of gospel activities just reviewed in 15:18-19. In light of how Paul uses the idea of "foundation" elsewhere (particularly 1 Corinthians 3:8-15), I conclude that "Christ is named" when there is a growing movement of obedience to Christ established which has proven potential to articulate and demonstrate the life of Christ to its entire community. This is what many would consider a church.

8. The idea is "toward the face of God" as if in a temple.

9. Some variant manuscripts with good attestation keep the word "peoples" plural in this passage.

10. As much as half of Paul's usage of the word "grace" has more to do with God's empowering influence to co-labor with him in the advance of his purposes than with the familiar issue of personal salvation. A few examples: Romans 1:5, 15:15; 1 Corinthians 15:10; Galatians 2:9; Ephesians 3:2-8, 4:7; Philippians 1:7, 1:29; 1 Timothy 1:14; 2 Timothy 1:8-9. Most of the uses of the term "grace" in 2 Corinthians have to do with co-working with God by his power as in 6:1, 8:1-9, and 12:9-10.

11. Hebrews 13:15-16 reflects the simple fullness of the worship God desires to see in every community: his name being articulated, and his just love being demonstrated.

Study Questions

1. What were God's purposes for the Exodus, the conquest, and the Temple?

2. What were the goals of the Apostle Paul in his ministry?

3. According the Hawthorne, what would be the result of an evangelized world?

6

The Biblical Foundation for the Worldwide Mission Mandate

Johannes Verkuyl

THE SIGNIFICANCE OF THE OLD TESTAMENT

The twentieth century has produced a steady stream of literature which regards the Old Testament as an indispensable and irreplaceable base for the church's missionary task among the nations and peoples of this world. As one who has made frequent use of the literature, I wish to look at four motifs in the Old Testament which form the indispensable basis for the New Testament call to the church to engage in worldwide mission work: the universal motif, the motif of rescue and saving, the missionary motif, and the antagonistic motif.

The Universal Motif

The God who in the Old Testament identifies himself as the God of Abraham, Isaac and Jacob and who discloses to Moses his personal name, Yahweh, is the God of the whole world. The experience of a few partriarchs and later the one nation of Israel with this God expands to include the horizon of the entire world. We shall cite only a few of the Old Testament passages to illustrate this universal motif.

The table of nations in Genesis 10

Genesis 10, with its passage listing the table of nations, is important for understanding the universal motif of the Old Testament. Gerhard von Rad described it as the conclusion to the history of the Creation. All of the nations issue forth from the creative hand of God and stand under his watchful eye of patience and judgment. The nations are not mere decorations incidental to the real drama between God and man; rather, the nations—that is, mankind as a whole—are part of the drama itself. God's work and activity are directed at the whole of humanity.

This is one of the fundamental truths of Genesis 1-11, the record of history's

---

Johannes Verkuyl was formerly Professor and Head of the Department of Missiology and Evangelism at the Free University of Amsterdam. He is now retired. Excerpted from *Contemporary Missiology: An Introduction*, 1978. Used by permission of Wm B. Eerdmans Publishing Co.

beginning; it is also found in the moving account of history's end, the book of John's Revelation. The very God who revealed himself to Israel and dwelt among us in Jesus Christ identifies himself as the Alpha and Omega, the beginning and the ending. He does not lay down his work until "every tongue and nation" and "a multitude without number" have been gathered round his throne (Rev. 5:9-10 and 7:9-17). God is cutting a path directly through the weary and plodding activities of men in history in order to achieve his goals among the nations.

God's election of Israel with his eye on the nations

After the Bible finishes its account of God's judgment of the nations, so graphically described in the Genesis passage about the Tower of Babel, in chapter 12 it shifts to God's call to Abraham to leave Ur of the Chaldees. The "God of the whole earth" seems at first glance to narrow his interests to the private history of one family and tribe only, but in actuality nothing could be farther from the truth. In de Groot's words, "Israel is the opening word in God's proclaiming salvation, not the Amen."[1] For a time Israel, the "people of Abraham," is separated from the other nations (Ex. 19:3ff.; Deut. 7:14ff.), but only so that through Israel God can pave the way toward achieving his world-embracing goals. In choosing Israel as a segment of all humanity, God never took his eye off the other nations; Israel was a minority called to serve the majority.

God's election of Abraham and Israel concerns the whole world. He deals so intensely with Israel precisely because he is maintaining his personal claim on the whole world. To speak to this world in the fullness of time he needed a people. Countless recent studies are emphasizing this very point: God chose Israel in preparation for the complete unwrapping and disclosure of his universal intentions.

Whenever Israel forgot that God chose her with a view to speaking to the other nations and turned away from them in introverted pride, prophets like Amos, Jeremiah, and Isaiah lashed out at the people's ethnocentric pretension and charged them with subverting God's actual intentions (see especially Amos 9:9-10).

The breakthrough of the universal motif in the exile

Israel's experiences during the seventh and sixth centuries B.C. opened her eyes to God's universal intentions. As Israel passed through her catastrophic experience of being trounced by the Babylonians and carted off into exile, the prophets came to see how closely the career of Israel was tied in with the history of the nations. Out of the judgment which Israel was feeling there blossomed the eager hope of a new covenant, a new exodus, another Son of David. Jeremiah, Ezekiel and Isaiah all saw the horizon expanding and bore witness that all nations now fall within the spotlight of God's promises. The apocalyptic vision of Daniel predicts the coming of the Son of Man whose kingdom shall put an end to the brutish kingdoms of the world and whose domain shall include all peoples (Dan. 7:1-29).

The Motif of Rescue and Liberation

Yahweh, the redeemer of Israel

The soteriological theme of the Bible, that is, God's work of rescuing and saving both Israel and the other nations, is tied closely to the theme of universalism. Yahweh, the God of all the earth, displayed his love and kept his word to Israel by freeing her from the bonds of slavery with his strong and outstretched arm (see Deut. 9:26; 13:5; 15:15; 24:18). This was a basic part of Israel's credo and crucial to understanding the first commandment. This God—the one who saves and frees—alone is God. "You shall have no other gods before me" (Ex. 20). This credo transformed Israel from being merely one nation among others into the chosen community which owes its very existence to God's act of deliverance and returns its praises to him in psalms and prayers of thanksgiving.

Yahweh, the redeemer of the nations

The prophets of Israel grew increasingly aware that not only Israel would share in God's acts of redemption. God would break in to restore his liberating Lordship over the entire world of the nations.

In their studies Sundkler and Blauw point out that the prophets develop this theme centripetally; that is, after their rescue the other nations make their pilgrimage back to Zion, the mountain of the Lord. The prophets picture the people of the other nations as returning to Jerusalem, where the God of Israel shall appear as the God of all the peoples (see Isa. 2:1-4; Mic. 4:1-4; Jer. 3:17; Isa. 25:6-9; Isa. 60; Zech. 8:20ff).

Several psalms chant this theme, too. Psalm 87 proclaims Jerusalem as the ecumenical city whose citizens shall some day include inhabitants of the various nations, even from those nations who once most ardently opposed the God of Israel. They shall join in celebrating God's restored fellowship with the peoples.

God's method of achieving liberation

The Bible also describes the means God is using to bring salvation to Israel and the nations. No other Old Testament passage probes more deeply into this matter than the so-called "Servant" songs of Isaiah 40-55. These Servant songs make unmistakable reference to the spread of salvation through the whole world. The Servant shall carry it to the ends of the earth (Isa. 49:6), and he will not stop until righteousness prevails throughout the earth. The coastlands are awaiting his instruction (Isa. 42:4).

The fourth Servant song in chapter 53 uncovers the secret of *how* the Servant of the Lord shall discharge his mission. This deeply moving passage depicts the Servant becoming a victim of the most savage human butchery.

Every kind of mistreatment human minds can devise shall be done to him. However, the Servant also at that point shall be acting as a substitute who is incurring the judgment of God which was properly due not only to Israel but to all peoples and nations. As a substitute for both Israel and the nations, the Servant has to walk the path of suffering to bring them freedom. Moreover, this passage describes the nations as Yahweh's gifts to the Servant in return for his willing obedience to suffer death. He achieved the right to bring salvation and healing to all people.

In passing, we must note that Paul, the Apostle to the heathen Gentiles, grounds his call from God to engage in worldwide mission in these very Servant songs taken from the Old Testament (see Acts 13:47).

The Missionary Motif

Connected with the other two Old Testament motifs mentioned previously is the missionary motif. The prophets never tire of reminding Israel that her election is not a privilege which she may selfishly keep for herself; election is a call to service. It involves a duty to witness among the nations. Israel must be a sign to the other nations that Yahweh is both Creator and Liberator. One Servant song (Isa. 49:6) refers to Israel's mandate to become a light to the nations.

Virtually every author who attempts to explain this call to Israel comes up with the concept of presence. Chosen by God to become the special recipients of his mercy and justice, Israel now has the corresponding duty to live as the people of God among the other nations in order to show them his grace, mercy, justice, and liberating power. Time and time again the prophets recorded their deep disappointment over Israel's continual sabotage of her divine calling. But however hot their righteous anger burned against Israel's disobedience, the prophets kept on reminding Israel to the very end of her mandate to be present among the people as distinct people and a royal priesthood.

It is worth noting that since the Second World War a number of missiologists have urged Christian presence as one of the leading methods of engaging in today's mission work. For a variety of reasons and in a variety of manners, they claim that the most suitable form of witness lies in simply being a specific kind of people while living among other people. This is not the place to develop this idea further but only to point out that the idea that presence is witness has deep roots in the Old Testament. The prophets continually claimed that by her very act of living out her divine appointment to serve, Israel becomes a sign and bridge for the other nations.

However, I do not believe it is correct to view the missionary motif only in terms of the concept of presence. I simply do not understand why various writers make such a point of avowing that the Old Testament makes absolutely no mention of a missionary mandate.

In his book *Mission in the New Testament*, Hahn says, for example, that the Old Testament bears a "completely passive character." In my opinion this is an exaggeration. Bachli's book *Israel and die Volker* is closer to the truth by noting that the Exodus account and the Deuteronomic tradition distinguish between *am* ("people") and *qahat* ("the religious community") and expressly mention that already in the desert many individuals had joined the *qahat* who had not been original members of the *am*. The heathen people too who had come along with Israel and dwelt as strangers among God's people, participating in Israel's worship. They heard of God's mighty deeds and joined Israel in songs of praise.

Then there is that striking number of individuals who left their heathen origins and by word-and-deed witness were won over to trust and serve the living

God who had shown them mercy. The stories of Melchizedek, Ruth, Job, the people of Nineveh described in the book of Jonah, and many others in the Old Testament are windows, as it were, through which we may look out on the vast expanse of people outside the nation of Israel and hear the faint strains of the missionary call to all people already sounding forth.

The wisdom literature of the Old Testament is similar in both form and content to both Greek and Egyptian cultures. Without doubt, her own literature served Israel as a means of communicating her beliefs to the other nations.

Moreover there is no other way of explaining the powerful missionary impact of Judaism during the Diaspora than to affirm that those dispersed Jews *from their earliest days* had heard and understood their call to witness directly as well as by their presence.

The Motif of Antagonism

The above list of Old Testament missionary motifs is incomplete. Intricately connected with each of those mentioned above is the antagonistic motif, that is, Yahweh's powerful wrestling against those powers and forces which oppose his liberating and gracious authority.

The whole Old Testament (and the New Testament as well) is filled with descriptions of how Yahweh-Adonai, the covenant God of Israel, is waging war against those forces which try to thwart and subvert his plans for his creation. He battles against those false gods which human beings have fashioned from the created world, idolized, and used for their own purposes. Think, for example, of the Baals and the Ashtaroth, whose worshippers elevated nature, the tribe, the state and the nation to a divine status. God fights against magic and astrology which, according to Deuteronomy, bend the line between God and his creation. He contends against every form of social injustice and pulls off every cloak under which it seeks to hide (see Amos and Jeremiah, for example).

The whole of the Old Testament burns with a feverish desire to defeat these opposing powers. There are grand visions of that coming kingdom where every relationship is properly restored and when the whole of creation—people, animals, plants, and every other creature—will perfectly accord with God's intentions for it (see Isa. 2, Mic. 4, and Isa. 65). The Old Testament longs for this kingdom's final revealing and categorically states its promise that Yahweh shall indeed finally overcome. This too is a highly significant theme for missionary participation. To participate in mission is quite impossible unless one also wages war against every form of opposition to God's intentions wherever it be found, whether in churches, the world of the nations, or one's own life.

The Old Testament ties the antagonistic motif closely with the doxological theme: the glory of Yahweh-Adonai shall be revealed among all peoples. Then every human being shall come to know him as he really is, the "gracious and merciful God, slow to get angry, full of kindness, and always willing to turn back from meting out disaster" (Jon. 4:1-2).

The Book of Jonah

The book of Jonah is so significant for understanding the biblical basis of mission because it treats God's mandate to his people regarding the Gentile peoples and thus serves as the preparatory step to the missionary mandate of the New Testament. But it is also important for catching a glimpse of the deep resistance this mandate encounters from the very servant Yahweh has chosen to discharge his worldwide work.

Today there is much talk and writing about "educating the congregation" and "educating personnel" for mission. Jonah is a lesson in educating a person to be a missionary: it reveals the need for a radical conversion of one's natural tendencies and a complete restructuring of his life to make it serviceable for mission.

Background of the book

The title of the book is the personal name of the unwilling prophet, Jonah, and harks back to the days of King Jeroboam II (787-746 B.C.) when a prophet named Jonah ben Amittai was living. It is obvious, however, that this *midrash* is intended for reasons quite other than detailing the events of this prophet's life. The author uses this personal name to portray for his readers a missionary who has no heart for the Gentiles and who, like the later Pharisees, cannot tolerate a God who shows them mercy. In the words of the Dutch author Miskotte, "the writer intends to picture a person who is the exact opposite of an apostle." The author of Jonah warns his readers against this intolerant attitude and sets before each of them the question of whether he or she is willing to be transformed into a servant who works to accomplish the mandates of God.

As the author sees it, Israel has become so preoccupied with herself that she no longer directs her eyes toward the world of the nations. Israel, the recipient of all God's revelation, refuses to set foot in alien territory to tell the other peoples God's message of judgment and liberation. But the message of the book also is addressed to the New Testament congregation which tries various ways of evading her Lord's command to speak his message to the world.

Jonah's crafty evasion efforts represent a lazy and unfaithful church which does not heed its Lord's command. God has to wrestle against Israel's narrow ethnocentrism which tries to restrict his activity to the boundaries of Israel alone and against the church's ecclesiocentric refusal to go out into the world to proclaim God's message and do his work. The writer is bent on convincing his readers that the radius of God's liberating activity is wide enough to cover both Israel and the Gentiles.

It is a miracle that Jonah, with its strong warning against ethnocentrism, ever made its way into the canon of Scripture. It squarely sets forth man's attempt to sabotage God's worldwide plans so that its readers—Israel, the New Testament church, and us—can hear what the Holy Spirit through the medium of this little book is trying to tell them.

A short review of the book's eight scenes

The first scene opens with Jonah receiving the command to go to Nineveh. While the Old Testament usually appeals to the other nations to *come* to Zion, the mountain of God, Jonah, like the disciples of the New Testament (cf. Matt. 28:18-20), is told to *go*! The Septuagint translation of Jonah uses the word *porettomai* in 1:2-3 and again in 3:2-3, the very same verb used by Jesus in his Great Commission recorded in Matthew 28. Where must Jonah go? To Nineveh, of all places. Nineveh, a very center of totalitarianism, brutality, and warlike attitudes. To Nineveh, notorious for the shameful hounding, vicious torture, and imperialist brazenness it reserved for those who chose to oppose its policies. God wants his servant to warn Nineveh of impending judgment and to call her to repentance. He wants to save *Nineveh!*

But Jonah refuses. He prepares himself, to be sure, but only to *flee* from the face of God who is Lord over all.

In the second scene God responds to Jonah's flight by sending a mighty storm (1:4-16). The wind obeys Yahweh's commands, but the disobedient Jonah sleeps in the bottom of the boat, oblivious of the fact that the storm is directed at him. At times the church, too, sleeps right through the storm of God's judgment passing over the world, assuring herself that the wind outside has nothing to do with her. While the crew vainly searches for the storm's cause, Jonah confesses that he worships and fears the God who made both the sea and the dry land, the one God who is above all nations. This God, he claims, is bringing a charge against him, and the only way to quiet the waters is to throw him into the sea. In this scene the crew represents the Gentiles, a people for whom Jonah is totally unconcerned, and yet who themselves are interested in sparing his life. After a second order from Jonah they throw him overboard and the storm ceases. Scarcely able to believe their eyes, the sailors break forth in praise to the God of Jonah. Their obedience surpasses that of the saboteur Jonah: they are more open to God than the very prophet himself.

The third scene (1:17) describes a large fish which, at Yahweh's instructions, opens its mouth to swallow Jonah and spew him onto the shore at the appropriate time. Jonah simply cannot escape God's missionary mandate. The God who whipped up the stormy winds and directed the sailors to accomplish his purposes now guides a fish as part of his plan to save Nineveh. Yahweh continues his work of reforming and preparing his missionary to be a fit instrument in his plans.

In the fourth scene (2:1-10) Jonah implores God to rescue him from the belly of the fish. He who had no mercy on the Gentiles and refused to acknowledge that God's promises extended to them now appeals for Divine mercy, and by quoting lines from various psalms pants after those promises claimed by worshippers in God's temple.

Yahweh reacts. He speaks to the brute beast and Jonah lands on shore safe and sound. By his very rescue Jonah was unwittingly a witness of God's saving mercy. Though covered with seaweed, Jonah was nonetheless a testimony that God takes no delight in the death of sinners and saboteurs but rather rejoices m their conversion.

In the fifth scene (3:1-4) God repeats his order to the man whose very life affirms the truth of what he confessed in the belly of the fish: "Salvation is from Yahweh." The Septuagint uses the term *kerygma* in 3:1-2ff. That single word summarizes Jonah's mission: he must *proclaim* that Nineveh, however godless she may be, is still the object of God's concern, and unless she repents, she will be destroyed. His message must be one of threat as well as promise, of judgment as well as gospel.

In the sixth scene (3:5-10) Nineveh responds to Jonah's appeal to repent. The proud, despotic king steps down from his royal throne, exchanges his robes for dust and ashes, and enjoins every man and animal to follow his example. What Israel continually refused to do the heathen Gentiles did do: the cruel king of Nineveh stands as anti-type to the disobedient kings of Judah.

The people join the king in repenting. They cease all their devilish work and the terrifying and coercing engines of political injustice come to a halt. In deep penitence they turn away from idols to serve the God who is Lord of every nation and all creation. All this becomes possible because Yahweh is God. The world of the heathen is a potentially productive mission field for no other reason than this: He alone is God.

The curtain closes on this scene with these amazing words: "God saw what they did, and how they abandoned their wicked ways, and he repented and did not bring upon them the disaster he had threatened." Yahweh is faithful to his promises. Still today his will for Moscow and Peking, for London and Amsterdam, is no less "gracious and full of mercy" than it was for Nineveh. To borrow from Luther, who loved to preach from the book of Jonah, the left hand of God's wrath is replaced by his right hand of blessing and freedom.

The seventh scene (4:1-4) recounts the fact that the greatest hurdle to overcome in discharging the missionary mandate was not the sailors, nor the fish, nor Nineveh's king and citizenry, but rather Jonah himself—the recalcitrant and narrow-minded church. Chapter 4 describes Jonah, who has long since departed the city to find shelter east of the borders. The forty-day period of repentance has passed, but since God has changed his mind about destroying it, the city continues to be nourished by Yahweh's grace and mercy. Jonah is furious that God has extended his mercy beyond the borders of Israel to the Gentiles. He wanted a God cut according to his own pattern: a cold, hard, cruel nature-god with an unbending will set against the heathen. He cannot stand to think of the Gentiles as part of salvation history

This is Jonah's sin, the sin of a missionary whose heart is not in it. He who once pleaded with God for mercy from the desolate isolation of a fish's belly now is angry that this God shows mercy to the nations. He vents his fury in the form of a prayer found in 4:2, the key text of the whole book: "And he prayed to the Lord, 'This, O Lord, is what I feared when I was in my own country, and to forestall it I tried to escape to Tarshish: I knew that thou art a gracious and compassionate God, long-suffering and ever constant, and always willing to repent of the disaster.'" Part of the text comes from an ancient Israelite liturgy which every Israelite knew by heart and could rattle off in worship at the temple or synagogue while half asleep (cf. Ex. 34:6; Ps. 86:15: 103:8, 145:8, Neh. 9:17). But Jonah cannot stand to think that this liturgy is true not only for Jerusalem, the location of God's temple, but for other places as well—Nineveh, Sao Paulo, Nairobi, New York and Paris.

Why is Jonah really so angry? For no other reason than that God is treating those outside his covenant the same as he is those within. But Jonah's anger in effect is putting himself outside the covenant, for he obstinately refuses to acknowledge the covenant's purpose—to bring salvation to the heathen. He had not yet learned that Israel could not presume upon some special favors from God. Both Israel and the Gentiles alike live by the grace which the Creator gives to all of his creatures. So God comes to his prophet, but no longer as a covenant partner; he comes as the Creator and asks his creature: "Do you have a right to be so angry?"

In the eighth and last scene (4:5-11) one can see God still working to teach his thick-skulled missionary his lessons. He did not catch the point of the storm, the sailors, the fish, and Nineveh's conversion because he did not want to. Now Yahweh tries one more approach—the miraculous tree. A climbing gourd springs up quickly, offers Jonah protection against the beating sun, but as quickly withers and dies, the victim of an attacking worm. Jonah is peeved.

At that point God again turns to his missionary-student, using the tree as his object lesson. The very God who directs the whole course of history, rules the wind and wave and turned Nineveh's millions to repentance now asks tenderly: "Are you so angry over the gourd? You are sorry about the gourd, though you had nothing to do with growing it, a plant which came up in a night and withered in a night. And should not I be sorry for the great city of Nineveh, with its hundred and twenty thousand who cannot tell their right hand from their left, and cattle without number?"

God spares and rescues. Jerusalem's God is Nineveh's as well. Unlike Jonah, he has no "Gentile complex." And while he never forces any one of us, he tenderly asks us to put our whole heart and soul into the work of mission. God is still interested in transforming obstinate, irritable, depressive, peevish Jonahs into heralds of the Good News which brings freedom.

The book ends with an unsettling question which is never answered: "God reached his goal with Nineveh, but what about Jonah?" No one knows. The question of Israel and the church and their obedience is still an open one.

The question is one which every generation of Christians must answer for itself. Jacques Ellul closes his book *The Judgment of Jonah* with these words: "The Book of Jonah has no conclusion, and the final question of the book has no answer, except from the one who realizes the fulness of the mercy of God and who factually and not just mythically accomplishes the salvation of the world."[1]

The New Testament church must pay close heed to the message of Jonah's book. Jesus Christ is "One greater than Jonah" (Matt. 12:39-41, Luke 11:29-32). His death on the cross with its awful cry of God-forsakenness and his resurrection with its jubilant shout of victory are signs of Jonah for us, pointing to the profound meaning of his whole life and clearly attesting that God loved the whole world so much. If a person draws his lifeblood from the one greater than Jonah and yet declines to spread the good news among others, he in effect is sabotaging the aims of God himself. Jonah is father to all those Christians who desire the benefits and blessings of election but refuse its responsibility. Thomas Carlisle's poem "You Jonah" closes with these lines:

    And Jonah stalked
    to his shaded seat
    and waited for God

to come around
to his way of thinking.
And God is still waiting for a host of Jonahs
in their comfortable houses
to come around
to his way of loving.

THE INTERTESTAMENTAL PERIOD

Research into the period of the Jewish Diaspora has uncovered evidence of a Jewish effort to proselytize, which, in turn, definitely stamped later missionary work carried on by the Gentile as well as the Jewish Christians. The Septuagint (the Greek translation of the Old Testament) went through the whole of the civilized world and was explained in the synagogues. Diaspora Judaism's missionary impact was far greater than many realize. What is more, Judaism affected early Christianity, for the Jewish Christians kept close contact with the synagogue communities. The synagogue played a crucial role, for it attracted not only proselytes (Gentiles who adopted the complete range of Jewish beliefs and practices, including circumcision) but also a class it termed "God-fearers" (Gentiles who accepted most of Judaism's ethics and some of its cultus, but refused circumcision). In spite of the connection, however, the Jewish message was quite different from the New Testament gospel of God's kingdom and the Christian belief that Jesus was the Messiah. Palestinian Judaism required that the heathen be assimilated into the Jewish fellowship and made every effort to achieve this transfer. Jewish communities outside of Palestine, on the other hand, laid their emphasis on monotheism, a belief which the pagan world, weary with worshipping many gods, found highly attractive. They spiritualized the cultus and decried the decadent lifestyle of the Gentile world. Their message was to a great degree autosoteric—a person could save himself. Both the Sibylline oracles and book of Joseph and Asenath make the claim that a person, by properly maintaining the ethical and ritual requirements, can reconcile himself to God.

Jesus was quite possibly aiming his sharp words of Mathew 23:15 against these specific elements in the Jewish message when he lamented, "Alas for you, lawyers and Pharisees, hypocrites! You travel over sea and land to win one convert: and when you have won him you make him twice as fit for hell as you are yourselves." Paul joins Jesus in rebuking the Jewish legalism and efforts at self-justification in Romans 2:17-24.

Jesus and Paul were not opposing Jewish missions to the Gentiles per se. In fact Paul views his own work among them as continuing what the Jews in the Diaspora had already started among the Gentiles. But they do object to what the Jews said. Therefore, when Jesus began to proclaim his own message, he did not go back to late Jewish traditions for support, but back to the Old Testament itself.

THE NEW TESTAMENT: BOOK OF WORLD MISSION

From beginning to end, the New Testament is a book of mission. It owes its very existence to the missionary work of the early Christian churches, both Jewish and Hellenistic. The Gospels are, as it were, "live recordings" of missionary preaching, and the Epistles are not so much some form of missionary apologetic as they are authentic and actual instruments of mission work. We cannot discuss every detail which would underscore the New Testament's importance for the foundation and practice of mission, but we do nevertheless wish to examine a few of them.

Jesus, the Savior of the World

All the various Old Testament motifs converge in the person and work of Jesus of Nazareth. The half-Gentile Samaritan citizens of the town of Sychar are the first to speak of this when they say in John 4:42: "We know that this is indeed the Savior of the world."

The arrival of the all-embracing kingdom of God

At the outset of his ministry, Jesus came to his hometown of Nazareth. Having gone to the synagogue to worship on the Sabbath, the leaders accorded him the honor of reading the Scriptures. As he concluded his reading of the prophet Isaiah's message in chapter 61 and had set the scroll down, he added a comment which brings incalculable hope to many but at the same time deeply offends those who reject him. He said: "Today in your very hearing this Scripture has been fulfilled" (Luke 4:21).

The coming salvation to which the prophets bore witness came true in Jesus Christ. Salvation has arrived, and therefore the good news which Jesus proclaims describes a kingdom which had both *already come* and is *yet coming*. Applying the words of Isaiah 61 to himself, Jesus says the Spirit of the Lord is on him. He marks the beginning of God's kingdom and introduces the "acceptable year of the Lord" in all of its rich variety. The kingdom's first appearing was provisional and still awaits its final fulfillment, but when Jesus made his daring claim—"He has sent me to bring good news to the afflicted, to proclaim liberty to the captives, and recovery of sight to the blind, to set at liberty the oppressed, to proclaim the acceptable year of the Lord"—the kingdom had really come and the hour for decision had been reached. In Jesus Christ, God was holding before men his gracious saving work more directly and urgently than ever before. The shape of things to come, his kingdom, became exceptionally clear in the person, the words, and the deeds of the Messiah. He powerfully subdued those sinister forces which were destroying the souls and bodies of men and renewed those who were the victims and servants of those forces. He called people to repentance.

The whole of the New Testament speaks the language of fulfillment. God's gracious and saving work has *already appeared* for all people (see Titus 2:11; Eph 1:10; Gal. 4:4-5; Heb. 1:1-4). But it also affirms that the final appearing of this kingdom is *yet coming*. There is an air of expectation in the New Testament as well.

In the Gospels these motifs switch back and forth. The one presupposes the other. According to the Gospels we now live between the *already* of the kingdom which has come and the *not yet* of its final manifestation between the promise of Luke 4:21 ("Today in your very hearing this Scripture has been fulfilled") and the anticipation of Matthew 24:14 ("And this gospel of the Kingdom will be preached throughout the whole world, as a testimony to all nations: and then the end will come").

The manner of the kingdom's coming

Jesus' miracles and parables provide special help in understanding how the kingdom is revealed in this world. John's Gospel calls the miracles signs which point to the approaching kingdom and majestic character of the Messiah. These miracles address every human need: poverty, sickness, hunger, sin, demonic temptation, and the threat of death. By them Jesus is anticipating Easter. Each of them proclaims that wherever and whenever in God's name human needs and problems are being tackled and overcome, there God's kingdom is shining through. Likewise, the parables Jesus told—for example, the parables of the seed, the fishnet, the harvest, the mustard seed, and the leaven—tell how the message about this kingdom shall reach all nations and peoples (see Matt. 13; Luke 8; Mark 4).

"On the basis of Jesus' own preaching one may claim that the apostolic work of the Church throughout the whole world is the very reason for the interim period between Jesus' ascension and his return as the Son of Man."[2]

Jesus and Gentiles

In the encounters of Jesus with Gentiles I see Jesus itching with a holy impatience for that day when all the stops shall be pulled as the message goes out to the Gentiles. For a time he restricts his message to the lost sheep of the house of Israel, knowing that certain conditions must be met before the message goes out to the *goyim*. Israel must hear first (Matt. 10) and the blood of the Lamb must be poured out to bring forgiveness "to many" (Mark 10:45; 14:24).

Cross and resurrection—the foundation for world mission

On his cross Jesus vicariously endured God's judgment which was properly due to Israel and the Gentiles. His resurrection likewise brought about a liberating rule extended to reach the whole worldwide community of nations and peoples. Jesus' cross and resurrection are the bases for a worldwide mission. For this reason interspersed with reports of his cross and resurrection are the mandates to carry the message to all peoples. This mission will be accomplished only when the "fullness of the Gentiles has entered and the kingdom of God has fully come."

The Missionary Mandate in the Gospel of Matthew

New Testament scholars claim that Matthew's Gospel is composed of catechetical material gathered and organized mainly to instruct recent converts about Jesus' work, person, and coming kingdom but also to assist them in spreading the message to others.

To a great degree Matthew used Mark's Gospel as the source for his stories about Jesus' deeds, but his own unique contribution was to collect a ninefold series of Jesus' words. Matthew's Gospel thus becomes a textbook for missions.

Scholars disagree on the date the book was written, some claiming it comes from about A.D. 75 and others preferring a slightly later date, perhaps somewhere between the years 80 and 100. If they are right, we must then keep in mind that this Gospel reflects a period in the early church when both Jewish and Gentile Christians were powerfully broadcasting the good news. One can easily understand then that this Gospel issues a strong call to communicate the faith in Jesus the Messiah to both Israel and the non-Jewish nations and peoples.

Communication of the gospel to the people of Israel

Matthew 10 records Jesus' command to his disciples to proclaim the message to Israel. Note that the striking words of verse 5—"Go nowhere among the Gentiles and enter no town of the Samaritans, but go rather to the lost sheep of the house of Israel"—are from the very same book which in chapter 28 includes the Great Commission to go to *all* peoples. Matthew made no attempt to "reconcile" these two passages. As he saw it, none was necessary, for the two complement each other and remain equally valid. When the Gospel of Matthew was written, there were Jewish Christians living in Palestine who opposed any mission to the Gentiles because they anticipated certain other events happening first. The author-editor of this Gospel, quite possibly a member of the Jewish Christian community in Syria, wrote his textbook with the strong conviction that the call to proclaim the message to Israel had to be paired with a mission to the non-Israelite peoples. The synchronization, he believed, was an implication from the Lord Jesus' command. As the writer saw it, the pre-resurrection concentration on Israel was a matter of *strategic* significance.

A segment of Jewish Christendom played off the mission to the Jews against the mission to the Gentiles, believing that the second should not be undertaken until another event of eschatological importance had first transpired, namely, the gathering of "the sheep of the twelve tribes." Only then would the "way to the Gentiles" be open.

But the writer of Matthew 10 disagrees. For him the event which opened a way to the Gentiles was Jesus' resurrection. Prior to that, all the attention is focused on Israel, but the cross and resurrection are both the base for a worldwide mission and the signal to begin. Jesus' words recorded in Matthew 10:23— "Truly I say to you, you will not have gone through all the towns of Israel, before the Son of man comes"—are a covert reference to his resurrection. Ferdinand Hahn beautifully exegetes the relationship between Matthew 10 and 28. The two passages are concentric circles and synchronize the Christian mission to Jews and non-Jews. While the earthly Jesus, himself a messenger to Israel, called the church to continued contact with the old people of God, the risen and exalted Lord of the whole world issued the command to go to all peoples. What Matthew wants to assert in his own way is the priority of the mission to Israel and the permanent obligation towards it—for without Israel as the center there would indeed be no salvation. This mission, however, is only carried out rightly if at the same time the universal commission is observed by working among all nations.[3]

Chapters 10 and 28 in Matthew's Gospel are therefore not contradictory. On the contrary, they make clear the historical situation in the time after the resurrection when the disciples were called to engage in mission. Taken together, these two passages remind us that the doors are now open to everyone.

The Great Commission of Matthew 28

That only Matthew contains a mandate for engaging in worldwide mission is a popular and stubborn misconception. But there is no doubt about it: the concluding verses of Matthew's Gospel express it the most forthrightly. Not only is the conclusion to Matthew's Gospel extremely powerful compared to the other Gospels and Acts, but the final verses form a climax and present a summary of what was written before. They are the key to understanding the whole book.

In these concluding verses Jesus, the risen Lord, standing atop one of the mountains in Galilee—could it be the same one from which he delivered his Sermon on the Mount (Matt 5:1)?—proclaims a three-point message to his disclples.

(a) *Jesus' authority.* He mentions his authority in language reminiscent of Daniel 7:13-14 and of his own words before the Sanhedrin recorded in Matthew 26:64. No area, people, or culture now lies outside the domain of his power and authority. The missionary command which follows is directly connected to this report of the risen Lord's coronation. Having arisen, he now has exalted authority over the whole world. Thus, the mission mandate is not the basis for his enthronement. Rather, the reverse is true: the mandate *follows from* the fact of his authority. However the several recorded missionary mandates may vary, they all in unison proclaim this one truth: a saving and liberating authority proceeds from him, the victim who became a victor. He is the crucified Lord who now rules. His power is not that of a despot bent on destruction; instead he uses his power for our healing and liberation and accomplishes these goals by love, reconciliation, and patience.

(b) *Jesus' continuing mandate to mission.* After his enthronement the crucified and risen Lord issues his mandate to mission. The time between his resurrection and second coming is not simply an empty interim but rather a period during which the discharge of this command is included in the process of enthronement. Philippians 2:5-11 contains a strong parallel to this truth stated here.

What does the enthroned Lord command his disciples to do? He says, first of all, "Go therefore." The author chooses the Greek word *poreuthentes*, which means "to depart, to leave, to cross boundaries"—sociological boundaries, racial boundaries, cultural boundaries, geographic boundaries. This point is most important to one who carries on the task of communicating the gospel. It affects work done in his own area as well as in faraway places. The missionary must always be willing and ready to cross boundaries, whether they be at home or away. The word *poreuomai* in this text reminded the early Christian church of a peripatetic Jesus and his disciples who were continually crossing boundaries to reach out to the other person. Jesus also commands his followers to "make disciples of all nations." The author makes the Greek noun *mathetes* into a verb. The verbal form of this word occurs four times in the New Testament (in Matt. 13:52 and 27:57, in Acts 14:21, and here in Matt. 28:20). To become a disciple of Jesus involves sharing with him his death and resurrection and joining him on his march to the final disclosure of his messianic kingdom. He commands us to *make* disciples, that is, to move them to surrender to his liberating authority and to volunteer for the march already enroute to a new order of things, namely, his kingdom.

(c) *Jesus' promise.* When Jesus adds the concluding words of promise "Lo, I am with you always, even to the close of the age," he is reminding his disciples that he will be present among them in a new manner. The promise holds true for all time. Note in passing how often the word "all" occurs in this text: all power, all peoples, all the commandments, and finally, the word "always."

Christ promises to be with his church during "all of her days." As she discharges her missionary calling, the church must forever be asking "What kind of day is it today?", for no two days are alike in her history. But however much the days and ages may change as the church carries on her mission in the six continents, one fact never changes: Jesus Christ is urging on his church to complete her missionary calling as he guides her to her final destination And this missionary movement which emanates from him will not cease until the end of the world. Thus, even though the methods of carrying it out must be changed continually, the task itself remains the same.

End Notes

1. Jacques Ellul. *The Judgment of Jonah* (Grand Rapids: Eerdmans, 1971), p. 103.

2. "Report of the Netherlands Missionary Council on the Biblical Foundation for Mission," *De Heerban*, 4 (August 1951), pp. 197-221.

3. Ferdinand Hahn, *Mission in the New Testament* (London: SCM Press, 1965), pp. 127-128.

Study Questions

1. Why does Verkuyl disagree with various writers who claim the Old Testament makes absolutely no mention of a missionary mandate?

2. Jonah is a lesson in the need for a radical conversion of one's natural tendencies and a complete restructuring of one's life to make it serviceable for mission. What were the natural tendencies and restructuring that had to be done in Jonah's life? How was this same need typified in the nation of Israel?

3. How does Verkuyl reconcile the "disparity" between Matthew 10 and 28?

7

The Gospel of the Kingdom

George Eldon Ladd

In a day like this, wonderful yet fearful, men are asking questions. What does it all mean? Where are we going? What is the meaning and the goal of human history? Men are concerned today not only about the individual and the destiny of his soul but also about the meaning of history itself. Does mankind have a destiny? Or do we jerk across the stage of time like wooden puppets, only to have the stage, the actors, and the theatre itself destroyed by fire, leaving only a pile of ashes and the smell of smoke?

In ancient times, poets and seers longed for an ideal society. Hesiod dreamed of a lost Golden Age in the distant past but saw no brightness in the present, constant care for the morrow, and no hope for the future. Plato pictured an ideal state organized on philosophical principles; but he himself realized that his plan was too idealistic to be realized. Virgil sang of one who would deliver the world from its sufferings and by whom "the great line of the ages begins anew."

The Hebrew-Christian faith expresses its hope in terms of the Kingdom of God. This Biblical hope is not in the same category as the dreams of the Greek poets but is at the very heart of revealed religion. The Biblical idea of the Kingdom of God is deeply rooted in the Old Testament and is grounded in the confidence that there is one eternal, living God who has revealed Himself to men and who has a purpose for the human race which He has chosen to accomplish through Israel. The Biblical hope is therefore a religious hope; it is an essential element in the revealed will and the redemptive work of the living God.

Thus the prophets announced a day when men will live together in peace. God shall then "judge between the nations, and shall decide for many peoples; and they shall beat their swords into plowshares, and their spears into pruning hooks; nation shall not lift up sword against nation, neither shall they learn war any more" (Isa. 2:4). Not only shall the problems of human society be solved, but

George Eldon Ladd was Professor Emeritus of New Testament Exegisis and Theology at Fuller Theological Seminary. He died in 1982 at the age of 71. Taken from *The Gospel of the Kingdom,* Wm. B. Eerdmans Publishing Company, Grand Rapids, Michigan, 1959. Used by permission.

the evils of man's physical environment shall be no more. "The wolf shall dwell with the lamb, and the leopard shall lie down with the kid, and the calf and the young lion and the fatling together, and a little child shall lead them" (Isa. 11:6). Peace, safety, security—all this was promised for the happy future.

Then came Jesus of Nazareth with the announcement, "Repent, for the kingdom of heaven is at hand" (Matt. 4:17). This theme of the coming of the Kingdom of God was central in His mission. His teaching was designed to show men how they might enter the Kingdom of God (Matt. 5:20; 7:21). His mighty works were intended to prove that the Kingdom of God had come upon them (Matt. 12:28). His parables illustrated to His disciples the truth about the Kingdom of God (Matt. 13:11). And when He taught His followers to pray, at the heart of their petition were the words, "Thy kingdom come, thy will be done on earth as it is in heaven" (Matt. 6:10). On the eve of His death, He assured His disciples that He would yet share with them the happiness and the fellowship of the Kingdom (Luke 22:22-30). And He promised that He would appear again on the earth in glory to bring the blessedness of the Kingdom to those for whom it was prepared (Matt. 25:31, 34).

The Meaning of "Kingdom"

We must ask the most fundamental question: What is the meaning of "kingdom"? The modern answer to this question loses the key of meaning to this ancient Biblical truth. In our western idiom, a kingdom is primarily a realm over which a king exercises his authority. Not many kingdoms remain in our modern world with its democratic interests; but we think of the United Kingdom of Great Britain and Northern Ireland as the original group of countries which recognize the Queen as their sovereign. The dictionary follows this line of thought by giving as its first modern definition, "A state or monarchy, the head of which is a king; dominion; realm."

The second meaning of a kingdom is the people belonging to a given realm. The Kingdom of Great Britain may be thought of as the citizens over whom the Queen exercises her rule, the subjects of her kingdom.

We must set aside our modern idiom if we are to understand Biblical terminology. At this point Webster's dictionary provides us with a clue when it gives as its first definition: "The rank, quality, state, or attributes of a king; royal authority; dominion; monarchy; kingship. *Archaic.*" From the viewpoint of modern linguistic usage, this definition may be archaic; but it is precisely this archaism which is necessary to understand the ancient Biblical teaching. The *primary* meaning of both the Hebrew word *malkuth* in the Old Testament and of the Greek word *basileia* in the New Testament is the rank, authority and sovereignty exercised by a king. A *basileia* may indeed be a realm over which a sovereign exercises his authority; and it may be the people who belong to that realm and over whom authority is exercised; but these are secondary and derived meanings. First of all, a kingdom is the authority to rule, the sovereignty of the king.

This primary meaning of the word "kingdom" may be seen in its Old Testament use to describe a king's rule. Ezra 8:1 speaks of the return from Babylon "in the kingdom" of Artaxerxes, i.e., his reign. II Chronicles 12:1 speaks of the establishment of Rehoboam's kingdom or rule. Daniel 8:23 refers to the latter end of their kingdom or rule. This usage of "kingdom" as a human reign may also be found in such passages as Jeremiah 49:34; II Chronicles 11:17, 12:1, 36:20; 30-31; Ezra 4:5; Nehemiah 12:22, etc.

The Meaning of "the Kingdom of God"

When the word refers to God's Kingdom, it always refers to His reign, His rule, His sovereignty, and not to the realm in which it is exercised. Psalm 103:19, "The Lord has established his throne in the heavens, and his kingdom rules over all." God's Kingdom, His *malkuth*, is His universal rule, His sovereignty over all the earth. Psalm 145:11, "They shall speak of the glory of thy kingdom, and tell of thy power." In the parallelism of Hebrew poetry, the two lines express the same truth. God's Kingdom is His power. Psalm 145:13, "Thy kingdom is an everlasting kingdom, and thy dominion endures throughout all generations." The *realm* of God's rule is the heaven and earth, but this verse has no reference to the permanence of this realm. It is God's rule which is everlasting. Daniel 2:37, "You, O king, the king of kings, to whom the God of heaven has given the kingdom, the power, and the might, and the glory." Notice the synonyms for kingdom: power, might, glory—all expressions of authority. These terms identify the Kingdom as the "rule" which God has given to the king. Of Belshazzar, it was written, "God has numbered the days of your kingdom and brought it to an end" (Dan. 5:26). It is clear that the realm over which Belshazzar ruled was not destroyed. The Babylonian *realm* and *people* were not brought to an end; they were transferred to another ruler. It was the rule of the king which was terminated, and it was the rule which was given to Darius the Mede (Dan. 5:31).

One reference in our Gospels makes this meaning very clear. We read in Luke 19:11-12, "As they heard these things, he proceeded to tell a parable, because he was near to Jerusalem, and because they supposed that the kingdom of God was to appear immediately. He said therefore, 'A nobleman went into a far country to receive a *basileia* and then return.'" The nobleman did not go away to get a realm, an area over which to rule. The realm over which he wanted to reign was at hand. The territory over which he was to rule was this place he left. The problem was that he was no king. He needed authority, the right to rule. He went off to get a "kingdom," i.e., kingship, authority. The Revised Standard Version has therefore translated the word "kingly power."

This very thing had happened some years before the days of our Lord. In the year 40 B.C. political conditions in Palestine had become chaotic. The Romans had subdued the country in 63 B.C., but stability had been slow in coming. Herod the Great finally went to Rome, obtained from the Roman Senate the kingdom, and was declared to be king. He literally went into a far country to receive a kingship, the authority to be king in Judea over the Jews. It may well be that our Lord had this incident in mind in this parable. In any case, it illustrates the fundamental meaning of kingdom.

The Kingdom of God is His kingship, His rule, His authority. When this is once realized, we can go through the New Testament and find passage after passage where this meaning is evident, where the Kingdom is not a realm or a people but God's reign. Jesus said that we must "receive the kingdom of God" as little children (Mark 10:15). What is received? The Church? Heaven? What is received is God's rule. In order to enter the future realm of the Kingdom, one must submit himself in perfect trust to God's rule here and now.

We must also "seek first his kingdom and his righteousness" (Matt. 6:33). What is the object of our quest? The Church? Heaven? No; we are to seek God's righteousness—His sway, His rule, His reign in our lives.

When we pray, "Thy kingdom come," are we praying for heaven to come to earth? In a sense we are praying for this; but heaven is an object of desire only because the reign of God is to be more perfectly realized than it is now. Apart from the reign of God, heaven is meaningless. Therefore, what we pray for is, "Thy kingdom come; *thy will be done* on earth as it is in heaven." This prayer is a petition for God to reign, to manifest His kingly sovereignty and power, to put to flight every enemy of righteousness and of His divine rule that God alone may be King over all the world.

The Mystery of the Kingdom

The fourth chapter of Mark and the thirteenth chapter of Matthew contain a group of parables which set forth the "mystery of the kingdom of God" (Mark 4:11). A parable is a story drawn from the everyday experience of the people which is designed to illustrate the central truth of our Lord's message. This central truth is called "the mystery" of the Kingdom.

We must first establish the meaning of the term "mystery." A mystery in the Biblical sense is not something mysterious, nor deep, dark, profound and difficult. In modern English, the word may bear such connotations, but we cannot interpret the Bible by modern English. In Scripture, "mystery" is often a technical concept whose meaning is set forth in Romans 16:25-26. Paul writes, "Now to him who is able to strengthen you according to my gospel and the preaching of Jesus Christ, according to the revelation of the mystery which was kept secret for long ages but is now disclosed and through the prophetic writings is made known to all nations." Here is the Biblical idea of mystery: something which has been kept secret through times eternal but is now disclosed. It is a divine purpose which God has designed from eternity but has kept hidden from men. At last, however, in the course of His redemptive plan, God reveals this purpose, and by the Scriptures of the prophets makes it known to all men. A mystery is a divine purpose, hidden in the counsels of God for long ages but finally disclosed in a new revelation of God's redemptive work.

The parables set forth the mystery of the Kingdom—a new truth about the Kingdom of God which was not revealed in the Old Testament but which is at last disclosed in the earthly ministry of our Lord. What is this mystery?

The Old Testament perspective of the Kingdom

To answer this question, we must go back into the Old Testament and look at a typical prophecy of the coming of God's Kingdom. In the second chapter of Daniel, King Nebuchadnezzar was given a vision of a great image which had a head of gold, a chest of silver, thighs of bronze, legs of iron, and feet of iron and clay. Then he saw a stone, cut out without hands, which smote the image on the feet and ground it to powder. This dust was swept away by the wind "so that not a trace of them could be found." Then the stone which destroyed the image became a great mountain which filled the whole earth (Dan. 2:31-35).

The interpretation is given to us in verses 44 and 45. The image represents the successive nations which were to dominate the course of world history. The meaning of the stone is given in these words: "And in the days of those kings the God of heaven will set up a kingdom which shall never be destroyed, nor shall its sovereignty be left to another people. It shall break in pieces all these king-doms and bring them to an end, and it shall stand forever; just as you saw that a stone was cut from a mountain by no human hand, and that it broke in pieces the iron, the bronze, the clay, the silver, and the gold. A great God has made known to the king what shall be hereafter."

Here is the Old Testament perspective of the prophetic future. The Prophets look forward to a glorious day when God's Kingdom will come, when God will set up His reign on the earth. You will remember that we have discovered that the basic meaning of the Kingdom of God is God's reign. In that day when God sets up HIS reign it will displace all other reigns, all other kingdoms and authori-ties. It will break the proud sovereignty of man manifested in the rule of the nations which have dominated the scene of earthly history. God's reign, God's Kingdom, God's rule will sweep away every opposing rule. God alone will be King in those days.

In the Old Testament perspective, the coming of God's Kingdom is viewed as a single great event: a mighty manifestation of God's power which would sweep away the wicked kingdoms of human sovereignty and would fill all the earth with righteousness.

A new revelation of the Kingdom

We must now turn back to the Gospel of Matthew and relate this truth to our previous study. John the Baptist had announced the coming of the Kingdom of God (Matt. 3:2) by which he understood the coming of the Kingdom foretold in the Old Testament. The Coming One would bring a twofold baptism: Some would be baptized with the Holy Spirit and experience the Messianic salvation of the Kingdom of God, while others would be baptized with the fires of the final judgment (Matt. 3:11). That this is John's meaning is clear from the next verse. Messiah's work will be one of sifting and the separation of men. As the farmer threshes and winnows his harvest, preserving the good grain and discarding the chaff, Messiah will cleanse His threshing floor, gathering the grain into His barn (salvation for the righteous) but sending the wicked into the fiery judgment (v. 12). The phrase "unquenchable fire" shows that this refers to no ordinary human experience but to the eschatological judgment.

From his prison, John sent messengers to Jesus to ask if He really was the Coming One, or if they were to look for another. John's doubt has often been interpreted as a loss of confidence in his own mission and divine call because of his imprisonment. However, Jesus' praise of John makes this unlikely. John was no reed shaken by the wind (Matt. 11:7).

John's problem was created by the fact that Jesus was not acting like the Messiah whom John had announced. Where was the baptism of the Spirit? Where was the judgment of the wicked?

Jesus replied that He was indeed the Bearer of the Kingdom, that the signs of the Messianic Age of prophecy were being manifested. And yet Jesus said, "Blessed is he who takes no offence at me" (Matt. 11:6). "Lord, are you He who is to come, or shall we look for another?" Why did John ask that question? Because the prophecy of Daniel did not seem to be in process of fulfillment. Herod Antipas ruled in Galilee. Roman legions marched through Jerusalem. Authority rested in the hands of a pagan Roman, Pilate. Idolatrous, polytheistic, immoral Rome ruled the world with an iron hand. Although Rome exercised great wisdom and restraint in governing her subjects, granting concessions to the Jews because of religious scruples, yet only God possessed the right to rule His people. Sovereignty belongs to God alone. Here was John's problem; and it was the problem of every devout Jew, including Jesus' closest disciples, in their effort to understand and interpret Jesus' person and ministry. How could He be the bearer of the Kingdom while sin and sinful institutions remained unpunished?

Jesus answered, "Blessed is he who takes no offence at me." What Jesus meant is this. "Yes, the Kingdom of God is here. But there is a mystery—a new revelation about the Kingdom. The Kingdom of God is here; but instead of destroying human sovereignty, it has attacked the sovereignty of Satan. The Kingdom of God is here; but instead of making changes in the external, political order of things, it is making changes in the spiritual order and in the lives of men and women."

This is the mystery of the Kingdom, the truth which God now discloses for the first time in redemptive history. God's Kingdom is to work among men in two different stages. The Kingdom *is* yet to come in the form prophesied by Daniel when every human sovereignty will be displaced by God's sovereignty. The world will yet behold the coming of God's Kingdom with power. But the mystery, the new revelation, is that this very Kingdom of God has now come to work among men but in an utterly unexpected way. It is not now destroying human rule; it is not now abolishing sin from the earth; it is not now bringing the baptism of fire that John had announced. It has come quietly, unobtrusively, secretly. It can work among men and never be recognized by the crowds. In the spiritual realm, the Kingdom now offers to men the blessings of God's rule, delivering them from the power of Satan and sin. The Kingdom of God is an offer, a gift which may be accepted or rejected. The Kingdom is now here with persuasion rather than with power.

Each of the parables in Matthew 13 illustrates this mystery of the Kingdom; that the Kingdom of God which is yet to come in power and great glory is actually present among men in advance in an unexpected form to bring to men in the present evil Age the blessings of The Age to Come.

This is the mystery of the Kingdom: Before the day of harvest, before the end of the age, God has entered into history in the person of Christ to work among men, to bring to them the life and blessings of His Kingdom. It comes humbly, unobtrusively. It comes to men as a Galilean carpenter went throughout the cities of Palestine preaching the Gospel of the Kingdom, delivering men from their bondage to the Devil. It comes to men as His disciples went throughout Galilean villages with the same message. It comes to men today as disciples of Jesus still take the Gospel of the Kingdom into all the world. It comes quietly, humbly, without fire from heaven, without a blaze of glory, without a rending of the mountains or a cleaving of the skies. It comes like seed sown in the earth. It can be rejected by hard hearts, it can be choked out, its life may sometimes seem to wither and die. But it *is* the Kingdom of God. It brings the miracle of the divine life among men. It introduces them into the blessings of the divine rule. It is to them the supernatural work of God's grace. And this same Kingdom, this same supernatural power of God will yet manifest itself at the end of the age, this time not quietly within the lives of those who receive it, but in power and great glory purging all sin and evil from the earth. Such is the Gospel of the Kingdom.

When Will the Kingdom Come?

For this final study, we shall turn to a single verse in our Lord's teachings. The truth embodied in this verse is from one point of view the most important of this entire series of studies for the Church today. It is a text whose meaning can be grasped only against the background of the larger study of the Kingdom of God.

We have discovered that the Kingdom of God is God's reign defeating His enemies, bringing men into the enjoyment of the blessings of the divine reign. We have found that God's reign is accomplished in three great acts so that we might say that the Kingdom comes in three stages. The third and final victory occurs at the end of the Millennium when death, Satan, sin are finally destroyed and the Kingdom is realized in its ultimate perfection. A second victory occurs at the beginning of the Millennium when Satan is to be chained in the bottomless pit. Apparently, however, sin and death continue throughout this period, for death is not cast into the lake of fire until the end of the Millennium.

An initial manifestation of God's Kingdom is found in the mission of our Lord on earth. Before The Age to Come, before the millennial reign of Christ, the Kingdom of God has entered into This Present Evil Age here and now in the person and work of Christ. We may therefore now experience its power; we may know its life; we may enter into a participation of its blessings. If we have entered into the enjoyment of the blessings of God's Kingdom, our final question is, what are we to do as a result of these blessings? Are we passively to enjoy the life of the Kingdom while waiting for the consummation at the return of the Lord? Yes, we are to wait, but not passively. Perhaps the most important single verse in the Word of God for God's people today is the text for this study: Matthew 24:14.

This verse suggests the subject of this chapter, "When will the Kingdom come?" This of course refers to the manifestation of God's Kingdom in power and glory when the Lord Jesus returns. There is wide interest among God's people as to the time of Christ's return. Will it be soon, or late? Many prophetic Bible conferences offer messages which search the Bible and scan the newspapers to understand the prophecies and the signs of the times to try to determine how near to the end we may be. Our text is the clearest statement in God's Word about the time of our Lord's coming. There is no verse which speaks as concisely and distinctly as this verse about the time when the Kingdom will come.

The chapter is introduced by questions of the disciples to the Lord as they looked at the Temple whose destruction Jesus had just announced. "Tell us, when will this be and what shall be the sign of your coming, and of the close of the age?" (Matt. 24:3). The disciples expected This Age to end with the return of Christ in glory. The Kingdom will come with the inauguration of The Age to Come. Here is their question: "When will This Age end? When will you come again and bring the Kingdom?"

Jesus answered their question in some detail. He described first of all the course of This Age down to the time of the end. This evil Age is to last until His return. It will forever be hostile to the Gospel and to God's people. Evil will prevail. Subtle, deceitful influences will seek to turn men away from Christ. False religious, deceptive messiahs will lead many astray. Wars will continue; there will be famines and earthquakes. Persecution and martyrdom will plague the Church. Believers will suffer hatred so long as This Age lasts. Men will stumble and deliver up one another. False prophets will arise, iniquity abound, the love of many will grow cold.

This is a dark picture, but this is what is to be expected of an age under the world-rulers of this darkness (Eph. 6:12). However, the picture is not one of unrelieved darkness and evil. God has not abandoned This Age to darkness. Jewish apocalyptic writings of New Testament times conceived of an age completely under the control of evil. God had withdrawn from active participation in the affairs of man; salvation belonged only to the future when God's Kingdom would come in glory. The present would witness only sorrow and suffering.

Some Christians have reflected a similar pessimistic attitude. Satan is the "god of This Age"; therefore God's people can expect nothing but evil and defeat in This Age. The Church is to become thoroughly apostate; civilization is to be utterly corrupted. Christians must fight a losing battle until Christ comes.

The Word of God does indeed teach that there will be an intensification of evil at the end of the Age, for Satan remains the god of This Age. But we must strongly emphasize that God has not abandoned This Age to the Evil one. In fact, the Kingdom of God has entered into This Evil Age; Satan has been defeated. The Kingdom of God, in Christ, has created the Church, and the Kingdom of God works in the world through the Church to accomplish the divine purposes of extending His Kingdom in the world. We are caught up in a great struggle—the conflict of the ages. God's Kingdom works in this world through the power of the Gospel. "And this gospel of the kingdom will be preached throughout the whole world, as a testimony to all nations; and then the end will come."

The Gospel of the Kingdom

In this text I find three things. There is a message, there is a mission, there is a motive. The *message* is the Gospel of the Kingdom, this Good News about the Kingdom of God.

Some Bible teachers say that the Gospel of the Kingdom is not the Gospel of salvation. It is rather a gospel announcing the return of Christ which will be preached in the tribulation by a Jewish remnant after the Church is gone. We cannot deal at length with that problem, but we can discover that the Gospel of the Kingdom is the Gospel which was proclaimed by the apostles in the early Church.

We must first, however, notice a close connection between this verse and the Great Commission. At His Ascension, the Lord commissioned His disciples. "Go therefore and make disciples of all nations, baptizing them in the name of the Father and of the Son and of the Holy Spirit, teaching them to observe all that I have commanded you; and lo, I am with you always, to the close of the age" (Matt. 28:19-20). When one compares these verses, they speak for themselves. "What shall be the sign of your coming, and of the close of the age?" "This gospel of the kingdom will be preached throughout the whole world, as a testimony to all nations; and then the end will come." "Go therefore and make disciples of all nations...and lo, I am with you always, to the close of the age." Both verses speak about the same mission: world-wide evangelization until the end of the Age. This fact ties together Matt. 28:19 and Matt. 24:14.

The book of Acts relates that the apostles set out upon the fulfillment of this mission. In Acts 8:12, Philip went down to Samaria and preached the Gospel. The Revised Standard Version accurately describes his mission in these words: "he preached good news about the kingdom of God." Literally translated, the words are, "Gospeling concerning the kingdom of God." New Testament Greek has the same root for the noun, "gospel," and the verb, "to gospel" or "to preach the gospel." It is unfortunate for our understanding of this truth that we do not have the same idiom in English. Matthew 24:14 speaks of the "gospel of the kingdom," and Acts 8:12 speaks of "gospeling about the kingdom." This Gospel of the Kingdom must be preached in all the world. Philip went into Samaria, *gospeling* concerning the Kingdom of God, i.e., preaching the Gospel of the Kingdom. We have in Acts 8:12 the same phrases as that in Matt. 24:14, except that we have a verb instead of the noun with the preposition "about" inserted in the phrase.

When Paul came to Rome he gathered together the Jews, for he always preached the Gospel "to the Jew first." What was his message? "When they had appointed a day for him, they came to him at his lodging in great numbers. And he expounded the matter, from morning till evening, testifying to the kingdom of God and trying to convince them about Jesus" (Acts 28:23) The testimony about the Kingdom of God, the Gospel of the Kingdom, was the message Paul proclaimed to the Jews at Rome.

However, Paul met the same reaction as had our Lord when he appeared in Israel announcing the Kingdom of God (Matt. 4:17). Some believed, but the majority of the Jews rejected his message. Paul then announced the divine purpose for the Gentiles in the face of Israel's unbelief. "Let it be known to you then that this salvation of God has been sent to the Gentiles; they will listen" (Acts 28:28). Paul preached to the Jews the Kingdom of God; they rejected it. Therefore, "this salvation of God" was then offered to the Gentiles. The fact that the Gospel of the Kingdom of God is the same as the message of salvation is further proven by the following verses. "And he lived there two whole years at his own expense, and welcomed all who came to him, preaching the kingdom of God and teaching about the Lord Jesus Christ" (vv. 30-31). The Kingdom was preached to the Jews, and when they rejected it the same Kingdom was proclaimed to the Gentiles. The Good News about the Kingdom of God was Paul's message for both Jews and Gentiles.

Victory over death

We now turn again to the Scripture which most clearly and simply describes what this Gospel of the Kingdom is. In I Corinthians 15:24-25, Paul outlines the stages of our Lord's redemptive work. He describes the victorious issue of Christ's Messianic reign with the words, "Then comes the end, when he delivers the kingdom to God the Father after destroying every rule and every authority and power. For he must reign"—He must reign as King, He must reign in His Kingdom—"until he has put all his enemies under his feet. The last enemy to be destroyed is death."

Here is the Biblical description of the meaning of the reign of Christ by which His Kingdom shall attain its end. It is the reign of God in the person of His Son, Jesus Christ, for the purpose of putting His enemies under His feet. "The last enemy to be abolished is death." The abolition of death is the mission of God's Kingdom. God's Kingdom must also destroy every other enemy, including sin and Satan; for death is the wages of sin (Rom. 6:23) and it is Satan who has the power over death (Heb. 2:14). Only when death, sin, and Satan are destroyed will redeemed men know the perfect blessings of God's reign.

The Gospel of the Kingdom is the announcement of Christ's conquest over death. We have discovered that while the consummation of this victory is future when death is finally cast into the lake of fire (Rev. 20:14), Christ has nevertheless already defeated death. Speaking of God's grace, Paul says that it has now been "manifested through the appearing of our Saviour Christ Jesus, who abolished death and brought life and immortality to light through the gospel" (II Tim. 1:10). The word here translated "abolish" does not mean to do away with, but to defeat, to break the power, to put out of action. The same Greek word is used in I Corinthians 15:26, "The last enemy to be *destroyed* is death." This word appears also in I Corinthians 15:24, "Then comes the end, when he delivers the kingdom to God the Father after *destroying* every rule and every authority and power."

There are therefore two stages in the destruction—the abolition—the defeat of death. Its final destruction awaits the Second Coming of Christ; but by His death and resurrection, Christ has already destroyed death. He has broken its power. Death is still an enemy, but it is a defeated enemy. We are certain of the future victory because of the victory which has already been accomplished. We have an accomplished victory to proclaim.

This is the good news about the Kingdom of God. How men need this gospel! Everywhere one goes he finds the gaping grave swallowing up the dying. Tears of loss, of separation, of final departure stain every face. Every table sooner or later has an empty chair, every fireside its vacant place. Death is the great leveller. Wealth or poverty, fame or oblivion, power or futility, success or failure, race, creed, or culture—all our human distinctions mean nothing before the ultimate irresistible sweep of the scythe of death which cuts us all down. And whether the mausoleum is a fabulous Taj Mahal, a massive pyramid, an unmarked forgotten spot of ragged grass, or the unplotted depths of the sea, one fact stands: death reigns.

Apart from the Gospel of the Kingdom, death is the mighty conqueror before whom we are all helpless. We can only beat our fists in utter futility against the unyielding and unresponding tomb. But the Good News is this: death has been defeated; our conqueror has been conquered. In the face of the power of the Kingdom of God in Christ, death was helpless. It could not hold Him, death has been defeated; life and immortality have been brought to light. An empty tomb in Jerusalem is proof of it. This is the Gospel of the Kingdom.

Victory over Satan

The enemy of God's Kingdom is Satan; Christ must rule until He has put Satan under His feet. This victory also awaits the Coming of Christ. During the Millennium, Satan is to be bound in a bottomless pit. Only at the end of the Millennium is he to be cast into the lake of fire.

But we have discovered that Christ has already defeated Satan. The victory of God's Kingdom is not only future, a great initial victory has taken place. Christ partook of flesh and blood—He became incarnate—"that through death he might destroy him who has the power of death, that is, the devil, and deliver all those who through fear of death were subject to lifelong bondage" (Heb. 2:14-15). The word translated "destroy" is the same word found in II Tim. 1:10; I Cor. 15:24 and 26. Christ has nullified the power of death; He has also nullified the power of Satan. Satan still goes about like a roaring lion bringing persecution upon God's people (I Pet. 5:8); he insinuates himself like an angel of light into religious circles (II Cor. 11:14). But he is a defeated enemy. His power, his domination has been broken. His doom is sure. A decisive, *the* decisive, victory has been won. Christ cast out demons, delivering men from satanic bondage, proving that God's Kingdom delivers men from their enslavement to Satan. It brings them out of darkness into the saving and healing light of the Gospel. This is the Good News about the Kingdom of God. Satan is defeated, and we may be released from demonic fear and from satanic evil and know the glorious liberty of the sons of God.

Victory over sin

Sin is an enemy of God's Kingdom. Has Christ done anything about sin, or has He merely promised a future deliverance when He brings the Kingdom in glory? We must admit that sin, like death, is abroad in the world. Every newspaper bears an eloquent testimony of the working of sin. Yet sin, like death and Satan, has been defeated. Christ has already appeared to put away sin by the sacrifice of Himself (Heb. 9:26). The power of sin has been broken. "We know this, that our old self was crucified with him so that the body of sin might be destroyed, and we might no longer be enslaved to sin" (Rom 6:6). Here a third time is the word "to destroy" or "abolish." Christ's reign as King has the objective of "abolishing" every enemy (I Cor. 15:24, 26). This work is indeed future, but it is also past. What our Lord will finish at His Second Coming He has already begun by His death and resurrection. "Death" has been abolished, destroyed (II Tim. 1:10); Satan has been destroyed (Heb. 2:14); and in Rom. 6:6, the "body of sin" has been abolished, destroyed. The same word of victory, of the destruction of Christ's enemies, is used three times of this threefold victory: over Satan, over death, over sin.

Therefore, we are to be no longer in bondage to sin (Rom 6:6). The day of slavery to sin is past. Sin is in the world, but its power is not the same. Men are no longer helpless before it, for its dominion has been broken. The power of the Kingdom of God has invaded This Age, a power which can set men free from their bondage to sin.

The Gospel of the Kingdom is the announcement of what God has done and will do. It is His victory over His enemies. It is the Good News that Christ is coming again to destroy forever His enemies. It is a gospel of hope. It is also the Good News of what God has already done. He has already broken the power of death, defeated Satan, and overthrown the rule of sin. The Gospel is one of promise but also of experience, and the promise is grounded in experience. What Christ has done guarantees what He will do. This is the Gospel which we must take into all the world.

The Nature of Our Mission

In the second place, we find in Matthew 24:14 a *mission* as well as a message. This Gospel of the Kingdom, this Good News of Christ's victory over God's enemies, must be preached in all the world for a witness to all nations. This is our mission. This verse is one of the most important in all the Word of God to ascertain the meaning and the purpose in human history.

The meaning of history

The meaning of history is a problem which is today confounding the minds of thinking men. We do not need to be reminded that our generation faces potential destruction of such total proportions that few of us try to envisage the awful reality. In the fact of such threatening catastrophe, men are asking as they have never asked before, what is history all about? Why is man on this earth? Where is he going? Is there a thread of meaning, of purpose, of destiny, that will bring mankind to some goal? Or, to repeat a metaphor, are we simply a group of puppets jerking about on the stage of history, whose fate is to have the stage burn down, destroying the human puppets with it, leaving nothing behind but a handful of ashes and the smell of smoke? Is this to be the destiny of human history?

In a former generation, the philosophy of progress was widely accepted. Some thinkers charted the meaning of history by a single straight line which traced a gradual but steady incline from primitive savage beginnings upward to a high level of culture and civilization. The philosophy of progress taught that mankind, because of its intrinsic character, is destined to improve until it one day attains a perfect society, free from all evil, war, poverty, and conflict. This view has been shattered upon the anvil of history. Current events have made the concept of inevitable progress intolerable and unrealistic.

Another view interprets history as a series of cycles like a great spiral. There is movement both up and down. There are high points and low points on the spiral. But each ascent is a little higher than the last and each descent is not as low as the preceding. Even though we have our "ups and downs," the movement of the spiral as a whole is upward. This is a modification of the doctrine of progress.

Other interpretations have been utterly pessimistic. Someone has suggested that the most accurate chart of the meaning of history is the set of tracks made by a drunken fly with feet wet with ink, staggering across a piece of white paper. They lead nowhere and reflect no pattern of meaning. One of the greatest contemporary New Testament scholars, Rudolph Bultmann, has written, "Today we cannot claim to know the end and the goal of history. Therefore the question of meaning in history has become meaningless" *(History and Eschatology,* p. 120).

Many of the best minds of our generation are wrestling with this problem. The economic determinism of the Marxist system rests upon a philosophy of history which is materialistically grounded; but it *is* a philosophy of history and promises its adherents a destiny. Spengler believed that progress was impossible and that history was doomed to inevitable decline and degeneration. Toynbee has produced a massive study which attempts to find patterns and cycles of meaning in the history of civilizations.

On the other hand, such scholars as Niebuhr, Rust, and Piper have written learned studies which seek for the clue to the meaning of history in the Biblical truth of revelation. This is indeed a profound problem, and we do not wish to brush aside the complexities of the matter with a wave of the hand. However, it is the author's conviction that the ultimate meaning of history must be found in the action of God in history as recorded and interpreted in inspired Scripture. Here, Christian faith must speak. If there is no God, man is lost in a labyrinthine maze of bewildering experiences with no thread of meaning to guide him. If God has not acted in history, the ebb and flow of the tides of the centuries wash back and forth aimlessly between the sands of eternity. But the basic fact in the Word of God is that God has spoken, God has been redemptively at work in history; and the divine action will yet bring history to a divinely destined goal.

If there is no God who has His hand on the helm of history, I am a pessimist. But I believe in God. I believe God has a purpose. I believe God has revealed His purpose in history, in Christ and in His Word. What is that purpose? Where are its outlines to be traced?

One travels throughout the Near East and gazes with wonder upon the ruins which bear silent witness to once mighty civilizations. Massive columns still reach to the heavens, while elsewhere only huge mounds scar barren plains marking the accumulated debris of dead civilizations. The Sphinx and the pyramids of Gizeh, the pillars of Persepolis, the towers of Thebes, still bear eloquent testimony to the glory that was Egypt and Persia. One may still climb the Acropolis in Athens or tread the Forum in Rome and feel something of the splendour and glory of first-century civilizations which in some respects have never been surpassed. But today—ruins, toppled pillars, prostrate statues, dead civilizations.

What is the meaning of it all? Why do nations rise and fall? Is there any purpose? Or will the earth some day become a dead star, lifeless as the moon?

The divine purpose and the Chosen People

The Bible has an answer. The central theme of the entire Bible is God's redemptive work in history. Long ago, God chose a small, despised people, Israel. God was not interested in this people for their own sake; God's purpose included all mankind. God in His sovereign design selected this one insignificant people that through them He might work out His redemptive purpose which eventually would include the entire race. The ultimate meaning of Egypt, of the Assyrians, of the Chaldeans and of the other nations of the ancient Near East is found in their relationship to this one tiny nation—Israel. God set up rulers and cast them down that He might bring forth Israel. He raised up this people and preserved them. He had a plan, and He was working out this plan in history. We speak of this as Redemptive History. The Bible alone, of all ancient literatures, contains a philosophy of history, and it is a philosophy of redemption.

Then came the day when "in the fulness of time" appeared on earth the Lord Jesus Christ, a Jew, a son of Abraham after the flesh. God's purpose with Israel was then brought to a great fulfillment. This does not mean that God is done with Israel. But it does mean that when Christ appeared, God's redemptive purpose through Israel attained its initial objective. Up until that time, the clue to the meaning of the divine purpose in history was identified with Israel as a nation. When Christ had accomplished His redemptive work of death and resurrection, the divine purpose in history moved from Israel, who rejected the Gospel, to the Church—the fellowship of both Jews and Gentiles who accepted the Gospel. This is proven by our Lord's saying in Matthew 21:43 which is addressed to the nation Israel: "The kingdom of God will be taken away from you and given to a nation producing the fruits of it." The Church is "a chosen race, a royal priesthood, a holy nation" (I Peter 2:9); and it is in the present mission of the Church, as it carries the Good News of the Kingdom of God unto all the world, that the redemptive purpose of God in history is being worked out.

The ultimate meaning of history between the Ascension of our Lord and His return in glory is found in the extension and working of the Gospel in the world. "This gospel of the kingdom will be preached throughout the whole world, as a testimony to all nations; and then the end will come." The divine purpose in the nineteen hundred years since our Lord lived on earth is found in the history of the Gospel of the Kingdom. The thread of meaning is woven into the missionary programme of the Church. Some day when we go into the archives of heaven to find a book which expounds the meaning of human history as God sees it, we will not draw out a book depicting "The History of the West" or "The Progress of Civilization" or "The Glory of the British Empire" or "The Growth and Expansion of America." That book will be entitled, *The Preparation for and the Extension of the Gospel among the Nations.* For only here is God's *redemptive* purpose carried forward.

This is a staggering fact. God has entrusted to people like us, redeemed sinners, the responsibility of carrying out the divine purpose in history. Why has God done it in this way? Is He not taking a great risk that His purpose will fail of accomplishment? It is now over nineteen hundred years, and the goal is not yet achieved. Why did God not do it Himself? Why did He not send hosts of angels whom He could trust to complete the task at once? Why has He committed it to us? We do not try to answer the question except to say that such is God's will. Here are the facts: God has entrusted to us this mission; and unless we do it, it will not get done.

This is also a thrilling fact. The Christian Church today often has an inferiority complex. A few generations ago the pastor of a church was the most educated and respected leader in the community. There was a day when, because of this cultural situation, the Church exercised the predominant influence in the structure of Western community life. That day has long passed. We have often felt that the world has thrust the Church into a corner and passed us by. The Church does not count in the world at large. The United Nations is not calling upon the Church for advice in the solution of its problems. Our political leaders do not often depend upon leaders in the Church for their guidance. Science, industry, labour, education: these are the circles where wisdom and leadership are usually sought. The Church is brushed aside. Sometimes we get that feeling that we really do not count. We are on the margin of influence, we have been pushed over onto the periphery instead of standing squarely in the centre; and we pity ourselves and long for the world to pay attention to us. Thus we fall into a defensive attitude and attempt to justify our existence. Indeed, our main concern seems often to be that of self-preservation, and we assume a defeatist interpretation of our significance and of our role in the world!

Let this verse burn in our hearts. God has said this about no other group of people. This Good News of the Kingdom of God must be preached, if you please, by the Church in all the world for a witness to all nations. This is *God's* programme. This means that for the ultimate meaning of modern civilization and the destiny of human history, you and I are more important than the United Nations. What the Church does with the Gospel has greater significance ultimately than the decisions of the Kremlin. From the perspective of eternity, the mission of the Church is more important than the march of armies or the actions of the world's capitals, because it is in the accomplishment of this mission that the divine purpose for human history is accomplished. No less than this is our mission.

Let us be done with this inferiority complex. Let us forever lay aside this attitude of self-pity and lamentation over our insignificance. Let us recognize what we are as God sees us and let us be about our divinely appointed programme. This Good News about the Kingdom must be preached in all the world for a witness to all nations and then shall the end come. I am glad, indeed proud, to be a part of the Church of Christ because to us has been committed the most meaningful and worthwhile task of any human institution. This gives to my life an eternal significance, for I am sharing in God's plan for the ages. The meaning and destiny of history rests in my hands.

A Motive for Mission

Finally, our text contains a mighty *motive*. "Then the end will come." The subject of this chapter is, When will the Kingdom come? I am not setting any dates. I do not know when the end will come. And yet I do know this: When the Church has finished its task of evangelizing the world, Christ will come again. The Word of God says it. Why did He not come in A.D. 500? Because the Church had not evangelized the world. Why did He not return in A.D. 1000? Because the Church had not finished its task of world-wide evangelization. Is He coming soon? He is—if we, God's people, are obedient to the command of the Lord to take the Gospel into all the world.

What a sobering realization this is! It is so staggering that some people say, "I cannot believe it! It simply cannot be true that God has committed such responsibility to men." When William Carey wanted to go to India to take the Gospel to that country a century and a half ago, he was told, "Sit down, young man; when God wants to evangelize the heathen, He will do it without your help." But Carey had the vision and the knowledge of God's Word not to sit down. He rose up and went to India. He initiated the modern day of world-wide missions.

Our responsibility: to complete the task

God has entrusted to us the continuation and the consummation of that task. Here is the thing that thrills me. We have come far closer to the finishing of this mission than any previous generation. We have done more in the last century and a half in world-wide evangelization then all the preceding centuries since the apostolic age. Our modern technology has provided printing, automobiles, aeroplanes, radios, and many other methods of expediting our task of carrying the Gospel into all the world. Previously unknown languages are being reduced to writing. The Word of God has now been rendered, in part at least, into over 1,700 languages or dialects, and the number is growing yearly. Here is the challenging fact. If God's people in the English-speaking world alone took this text seriously and responded to its challenge, we could finish the task of world-wide evangelization in our own generation and witness the Lord's return.

Someone will say, "This is impossible. Many lands today are not open to the Gospel. We cannot get into China; the doors into India are closing. If the Lord's Return awaits the evangelization of the world by the Church, then Christ cannot possibly return in our lifetime, for so many lands are today closed to the Gospel that it is impossible to finish the task today."

Such an attitude fails to reckon with God. It is true that many doors are closed at the moment; but God is able to open closed doors overnight, and God is able to work behind closed doors. My concern is not with closed doors; my concern is with the doors that are open which we do not enter. If God's people were really faithful and were doing everything possible to finish the task, God would see to it that the doors were opened. Our responsibility is the many doors standing wide open which we are not entering. We are a disobedient people. We argue about the definition of world-wide evangelization and we debate the details of eschatology, while we neglect the command of the Word of God to evangelize the world.

Someone else will say, "How are we to know when the mission is completed? How close are we to the accomplishment of the task? Which countries have been evangelized and which have not? How close are we to the end? Does this not lead to date-setting?"

I answer, I do not know. God alone knows the definition of terms. I cannot precisely define who "all the nations" are. Only God knows exactly the meaning of "evangelize." He alone, who has told us that this Gospel of the Kingdom shall be preached in the whole world for a testimony unto all the nations, will know when that objective has been accomplished. But I do not need to know. I know only one thing: Christ has not yet returned; therefore the task is not yet done. When it is done, Christ will come. Our responsibility is not to insist on defining the terms of our task; our responsibility is to complete it. So long as Christ does not return, our work is undone. Let us get busy and complete our mission.

Becoming Biblical realists

Our responsibility is not to save the world. We are not required to transform This Age. The very paragraph of which this verse is the conclusion tells us that there will be wars and troubles, persecutions, and martyrdoms until the very end. I am glad these words are in the Bible. They give me stability. They provide sanity. They keep me from an unrealistic optimism. We are not to be discouraged when evil times come.

However, we have a message of power to take to the world. It is the Gospel of the Kingdom. Throughout the course of This Age, two forces are at work: the power of Evil, and the Kingdom of God. The world is the scene of a conflict. The forces of the Evil One are assaulting the people of God; but the Gospel of the Kingdom is assaulting the kingdom of Satan. This conflict will last to the end of The Age. Final victory will be achieved only by the return of Christ. There is no room for an unqualified optimism. Our Lord's Olivet Discourse indicates that until the very end, evil will characterize This Age. [The original form of the Olivet Discourse was concerned both with the fall of Jerusalem (Luke 21:20ff) and with the end of the Age. This, however involves critical problems which cannot be discussed here.] False prophets and false messiahs will arise and lead many astray. Iniquity, evil, are so to abound that the love of many will grow cold. God's people will be called upon to endure hardness. "In the world you have tribulation" (John 16:33). "Through many tribulations we must enter the kingdom of God" (Acts 14:22). We must always be ready to endure the tribulation as well as the kingdom and patience which are in Jesus (Rev. 1:9). In fact, our Lord Himself said, "He who endures to the end will be saved" (Matt. 24:13). He who endures tribulation and persecution to the uttermost, even to the laying down of his life, will not perish but will find salvation. "Some of you they will put to death...But not a hair of your head will perish" (Luke 21:16, 18). The Church must always in its essential character be a martyr church. As we carry the Gospel into all the world, we are not to expect unqualified success. We are to be prepared for opposition, resistance, even persecution and martyrdom. This Age remains evil, hostile to the Gospel of the Kingdom.

There is, however, no room for an unrelieved pessimism. In some prophetic studies, we receive the impression that the end of the Age, the last days, are to be characterized by *total* evil. Undue emphasis is sometimes laid upon the perilous character of the last days (II Tim. 3:1). The visible Church, we are told, is to be *completely* leavened by evil doctrine. Apostasy is so to pervade the Church that only a small remnant will be found faithful to God's Word. The closing days of This Age will be the Laodicean period when the entire professing Church will be nauseatingly indifferent to eternal issues. In such a portrayal of the last days, God's people can expect only defeat and frustration. Evil is to reign. The Church age will end with an unparalleled victory of evil. Sometimes so much stress is laid upon the evil character of the last days that we receive the impression (unintended, to be sure) that the faster the world deteriorates the better, for the sooner the Lord will come.

It cannot be denied that the Scriptures emphasize the evil character of the last days. In fact, we have already made this emphasis. The evil which characterizes This Age will find a fearful intensification at the very end in its opposition to and hatred of the Kingdom of God. This does not mean, however, that we are to lapse into pessimism and abandon This Age and the world to evil and Satan. The fact is, the Gospel of the Kingdom is to be proclaimed throughout the world. The Kingdom of God has invaded This present evil Age. The powers of The Age to Come have attacked This Age. The last days will indeed be evil days; but *"in these last days* (God) has spoken to us by a Son"* (Heb 1:2). God has given us a Gospel of salvation for the last days, a Gospel embodied in One who is Son of God. Furthermore, *"in the last days* it shall be,"* God declares, "that I will pour out my Spirit upon all flesh" (Acts 2:17). God has spoken for the last days; God has poured out His Spirit in the last days to give power to proclaim the divine Word. The last days will be evil, but not unrelieved evil. God has given us a Gospel for the last days, and He has given a power to take that Gospel into all the world for a testimony unto all the nations; then shall the end come.

This must be the spirit of our mission in This evil Age. We are not rosy optimists, expecting the Gospel to conquer the world and establish the Kingdom of God. Neither are we despairing pessimists who feel that our task is hopeless in the face of the evil of This Age. We are realists, Biblical realists, who recognize the terrible power of evil and yet who go forth in a mission of world-wide evangelization to win victories for God's Kingdom until Christ returns in glory to accomplish the last and greatest victory.

Here is the motive of our mission: the final victory awaits the completion of our task. "And then the end will come." There is no other verse in the Word of God which says, "And then the end will come." When will This Age end? When the world has been evangelized. "What will be the sign of your coming and of the close of the age?" (Matt. 24:3). "This gospel of the kingdom will be preached throughout the whole world as a testimony to all nation; and then, AND THEN, the end will come." When? *Then;* when the Church has fulfilled its divinely appointed mission.

"Go Ye Therefore"

Do you love the Lord's appearing? Then you will bend every effort to take the Gospel into all the word. It troubles me in the light of the clear teaching of God's Word, in the light of our Lord's explicit definition of our task in the Great Commission (Matt. 28:18-20) that we take it so lightly. "All authority in heaven and on earth has been given to me." This is the Good News of the Kingdom.

Christ has wrested authority from Satan. The Kingdom of God has attacked the kingdom of Satan; This evil Age has been assaulted by The Age to Come in the person of Christ. All authority is now His. He will not display this authority in its final glorious victory until He comes again; but the authority is now His. Satan is defeated and bound; death is conquered; sin is broken. All authority is His. "Go ye therefore." Wherefore? Because all authority, all power is His, and because He is waiting until we have finished our task. His is the Kingdom; He reigns in heaven, and He manifests His reign on earth in and through His church. When we have accomplished our mission, He will return and establish His Kingdom in glory. To us it is given not only to wait for but also to hasten the coming of the day of God (II Pet. 3:12). This is the mission of the Gospel of the Kingdom, and this is our mission.

Study Questions

1. What is "the mystery of the Kingdom?"

2. What relationship exists between the mission of the church and the coming of the Kingdom? Is it possible to affect the coming of the Kingdom?

3. Explain, specifically and concisely, the message of the Gospel of the Kingdom.

4. What is the ultimate meaning of history, according to the Bible?

5. Write an outline for the book mentioned on page 65: *The Preparation for and the Extension of the Gospel among the Nations.*

8

What if the Gospel is the Good News of the Kingdom?

Ron Sider

It is surely striking that social activists, charismatics and advocates of world evangelization often refer to the kingdom and sometimes even cite the same texts to support their different (frequently one-sided) concerns.[1] Social activists quote Luke 4:16ff to prove that faithful Christians, like Jesus, must meet the physical and social needs of the poor, blind, lame and oppressed. Charismatics quote Luke 4:16ff to demonstrate that faithful Christians, like Jesus, should be "filled with the power of the Spirit" and therefore perform miraculous signs and wonders. Proponents of world evangelization cite Luke 4:16ff (less often, however, until recently) to show that faithful Christians, like Jesus, will preach Good News to those who have not yet heard. Tragically, each group sometimes ignores or even rejects the concerns of the others.

The different interpretations of specific texts, of course, result from fundamentally divergent understandings of the kingdom. Medieval Catholicism tended to identify the kingdom with the institutional, visible church. Modern social activists, on the other hand, have viewed the kingdom largely as a socio-economic-political reality that human beings can create through politics—whether democratic politics in the Social Gospel movement or Marxist revolution in some liberation theology.

At the other extreme have been some twentieth century evangelicals who understand the kingdom largely as an inner spiritual reality in the souls of individual believers. Other conservative Christians (in the dispensationalist tradition of Darby and the Scofield Reference Bible) have seen the kingdom as entirely future.

What is the New Testament understanding of the kingdom?

Ron Sider is Professor of Evangelism and Culture at Eastern Baptist Theological Seminary. Committed to wholistic ministry, he helped organize Evangelicals for Social Action. He is also the author of several well-known books, including *Rich Christians in an Age of Hunger, Evangelicals and Development: Toward a Theology of Social Change, and Life-Style*. He received his PhD. in History from Yale University.

The Centrality of the Kingdom

Unless Matthew, Mark and Luke are totally wrong, all who want to preach and live like Jesus must place the "kingdom of God" at the center of their thought and action. This phrase (or Matthew's equivalent, the "kingdom of heaven") appears 122 times in the first three Gospels—most of the time (92) on the lips of Jesus himself.[2]

For Mark, the kingdom is the best summary of his entire Gospel: "After John was put in prison, Jesus went into Galilee, proclaiming the good news of God. 'The time has come,' he said. 'The kingdom of God is near. Repent and believe the Good News'" (Mark 1:14-15). Jesus explicitly defines his own mission in these terms: "I must preach the good news of the kingdom of God to the other towns also, because that is why I was sent" (Luke 4:43).

Jesus' response to John the Baptist demonstrates that Jesus viewed his preaching and healing as signs of the kingdom. In Luke 7:18-28, we read the story of the visit to Jesus by the disciples of John. They ask whether Jesus is the "one who was to come"—i.e. the long-expected Messiah who will usher in the messianic Kingdom of God. For his answer, Jesus points to his preaching, and his healing of the blind, the lame and even the socially ostracized lepers. Later, in his argument with the Pharisees, he makes the same claim, insisting that his miraculous casting out of demons is visible proof that the kingdom has begun (Matt. 12:28).

When Jesus sends out his disciples, he commands them to preach and demonstrate the kingdom in the same way. "As you go," he commissions the Twelve, "preach this message: 'The kingdom of heaven is near.' Heal the sick, raise the dead, cleanse those who have leprosy, drive out demons" (Matt. 10:7-8). The Seventy-Two receive the same instructions: "Heal the sick... and tell them, 'the kingdom of God is near you'" (Luke 10:9).

If anything is clear in Jesus, it is that the announcement and demonstration of the kingdom are at the very core of his message and life. Is it not astonishing that for decades those who have been most preoccupied with world evangelization have failed to define the Gospel the way Jesus did?

The kingdom Jesus announced was both present and future. It was decisively breaking into history in the person and work of Jesus the Messiah. But it would come in its fullness only at the return of the Son of Man on the clouds of heaven (Matthew 24:30).

Entering The Kingdom

Jesus' teaching differed sharply from that of his contemporaries. The Pharisees believed the Messiah would come if all Jews would obey the law perfectly for a day. The violent revolutionaries of the time thought the Messiah would come if all Jews would join in armed rebellion against Roman imperialism.[3] Jesus' way was radically different. The kingdom comes as sheer gift. We enter not by good deeds or social engineering, but only as we repent and accept God's forgiveness (Luke 18:9-14; Matt. 8:3).

The Kingdom Becomes Visible

Jesus was not a lone ranger. He did not travel around the countryside declaring God's forgiveness to isolated hermits. Jesus formed a new society. He gathered a new community of forgiven, forgiving disciples who challenged the evils of the status quo.

Zaccheus symbolizes Jesus' new community of forgiven sinners. As a tax collector for imperialistic Rome, Zaccheus was an affluent oppressor and a despised social outcast. But Jesus' astonishing acceptance and forgiveness overwhelmed him. In gratitude he offered the same love to others, making fourfold restitution for dishonest profit and giving half his goods to the poor (Luke 19:2-10).

A Disturbing Community

Jesus and his new community of disciples challenged the status quo wherever it was wrong. Nor was this merely some inward spiritual challenge or only a gauntlet thrown down to the religious leaders. To be sure, it included that. He denounced hypocrisy and blasted the religious leadership. But he also challenged the economic establishment, overturned social values and customs about women, and defied the political leadership. Precisely because Jesus knew how good the Creator intends culture and civilization to be, Jesus challenged surrounding society wherever sin had introduced brokenness.

Rich and poor. Jesus shocked the rich with his words about sharing. He told the rich young man who came enquiring about eternal life (and, probably, membership in Jesus' new circle as well) that he would have to sell his vast holdings and give all his wealth to the poor. As the wealthy youth turned away sadly, Jesus added a comment that still jars all of us who are rich: "It is easier for a camel to go through the eye of a needle than for a rich man to enter the kingdom of God" (Luke 18:18-25). When a different wealthy person responded in obedient repentance, he gave half of his vast riches to the poor (Luke 19:2-10). Jesus urged the rich to make loans to the poor, even if there was no reasonable hope of repayment (Luke 6:34-35). Those who do not feed the hungry and clothe the naked, he said, go to hell (Matthew 25:31-46). Jesus offered a radical challenge to an uncaring wealthy establishment.

It is very important to understand Jesus' teaching that his Messianic kingdom was especially for the poor.

> Blessed are you who are poor,
> for yours is the kingdom of God.
> Blessed are you who hunger now,
> for you will be satisfied (Luke 6:20-21).

When John the Baptist asked if he was the Messiah, Jesus pointed to the fact that he healed the sick and preached the Gospel of the kingdom to the poor (Luke 7:21-22). The inaugural address in the synagogue at Nazareth includes the same statement about preaching to the poor (Luke 4:18). One simply does not understand Jesus' teaching on the kingdom unless one sees that he was especially concerned that the poor realize that the kingdom breaking into history was particularly good news for them. Our proclamation of the Gospel is simply unbiblical unless we, like Jesus, focus special attention on the poor.

The heretical neglect of the poor by many affluent Christians is a flat rejection of the Lord of the Church. If Jesus is the norm, then faithful Christian sharing of the Gospel will make the poor one major priority in such a way that the poor in the world today are as convinced as the poor in Jesus' day that the Gospel is fantastic news for them—precisely because Jesus' new kingdom community embraces the poor, welcomes them into their fellowship, and shares economically so that, in the words of Acts, "there is no poor among them."

Jesus' special concern for the poor extended to all the marginalized, weak and socially ostracized. In sharp contrast to his contemporaries, Jesus demonstrated a special interest in the disabled, children, drunkards, prostitutes and lepers (cf. Luke 7:32-50; 19:1-10). In Jesus' day, lepers experienced terrible ostracism (Luke 17:12), living alone in awful poverty, shouting "unclean, unclean" lest anyone accidentally touch them. Jesus gently touched the lepers and miraculously healed them (Mark 1:41).

From the Dead Sea Scrolls, we learn that the Essenes, a Jewish religious group of Jesus' day, actually excluded the disabled from the religious community:

> No-one who is afflicted with any human impurity may come into the assembly of God.... Anyone who is...maimed in hand or foot, lame or blind or deaf or dumb or with a visible mark in his flesh.... These may not enter or take their place in the midst of the community.[4]

Jesus, by contrast, commands the members of his new messianic community to invite *precisely* these people: "When you give a banquet, invite the poor, the crippled, the lame, the blind" (Luke 14:13). In the parable of the Great Banquet, Jesus repeats the lesson, teaching that his kingdom is for "the poor, the crippled, the blind, and the lame" (Luke 14:32). Jesus was directly defying contemporary norms and social practices.

Women. Jesus' attitude toward women reflects the same sweeping challenge to the status quo. In Jesus' day, it was a scandal for a man to appear in public with a woman. A woman's word was considered useless in court.[5] It was better to burn a copy of the Torah (the first five books of the Old Testament) than allow a woman to touch it. Indeed, according to one first century statement, "if a man teach his daughter Torah, it is as though he taught her lechery."[6] Women were excluded from most parts of the temple. Nor did they count in calculating the quorum needed for a meeting in the synagogue. A widely used prayer by Jewish males thanked God they were not Gentiles, slaves or women: "I thank Thee Lord, that Thou hast not made me a Gentile...Thou has not made me a slave...Thou has not made me a woman."[7]

Jesus and his new community rejected centuries of male prejudice and treated women as equals. Jesus appeared with women in public (John 4:27), and taught them theology (Luke 10:38-42). He allowed a woman (Luke 7:36-50) that everybody knew was a sinner to wash his feet with her tears, wipe them with her tears, kiss and perfume them —all in public! When Mary abandoned her traditional role cooking food to listen to Jesus' theology lesson, Martha objected. But Jesus defended Mary (Luke 10:38-42). Jesus rejected Moses' teaching on divorce which allowed a man (but not a woman) to dismiss his wife if she did not find favor in his eyes (Deut. 24:1-2). Jesus called both husband and wife to live together in life-long covenant (Mark 10:1-12). It was surely no accident that Jesus granted the first resurrection appearance to women!

Luke 8:1-3 describes what Mortimer Arias calls the "first and most amazing evangelistic team ever assembled in the history of Christian mission."[8]

> Jesus travelled about from one town and village to another, pro-
> claiming the good news of the kingdom of God. The Twelve were
> with him, and also some women who had been cured of evil spir-
> its and diseases: Mary (called Magdalene) from whom seven
> demons had come out; Joanna, the wife of Cuza, the manager of
> Herod's household; Susanna; and many others. These women
> were helping to support them out of their own means (Luke 8:1-3).

What a shocking spectacle. This is not the normal homogeneous unit of a male rabbi with his male students but rather women and men together in public announcing the kingdom. One wonders what King Herod's budget director thought about his notorious wife's scandalous activity. And the women look more like breadwinners than cooks. "They were as heterogeneous as they could be: men and women, clergy and laity, fishermen, tax collectors, matrons, former prostitutes, the affluent and the poor!" [9] Centrally involved in this radical demonstration of Jesus' new kingdom community were women, publicly and actively ministering with him.

Jesus' challenge to current society did not end, however, with his approach to the poor and marginalized. Jesus also summoned the powerful to repent and change. Leaders should be servants. Love for enemies should replace vengeance. The religious leaders are snakes bound for hell unless they repent.

Political Leadership. Jesus must have infuriated Herod. When someone warned him that Herod wanted to kill him, Jesus shot back his response: "Go tell that fox..." (Luke 13:32). In Jesus' day, that word meant about the same thing as the slang use of the word "skunk" today.

In Jesus' time as today, rulers enjoyed dominating their subjects. Jesus was bluntly descriptive: "You know that those who are regarded as rulers of the Gentiles lord it over them." Jesus' kingdom model for leadership is servanthood (Mark 10:41-44).

Violent revolutionaries. Jesus also defied the violent liberation movement of his time. Most first century Jews expected the coming Messiah to be a military conqueror in the tradition of King David who would throw off the yoke of the oppressive Romans. Jesus rejected their whole approach. His messianic strategy was one of love for enemies not massacre of opponents. "You have heard that it was said, 'Love your neighbor and hate your enemy.' But I tell you: Love your enemies, and pray for those who persecute you, that you may be children of your Father in heaven" (Matthew 5:43-45). Jesus' peaceful path to Messianic shalom was a radical alternative and direct challenge to the popular, religious revolutionaries of his day.

Religious leaders. We have seen how Jesus' challenge to the status quo included economics, social life and politics. But he did not overlook the religious establishment. He denounced them as blind, hypocritical guides, whitewashed tombs, snakes and vipers. They meticulously tithe little things like mint and dill but neglect "the more important matters of the law—justice, mercy, and faithfulness" (Matthew 24:23).

It is important to see that the religious establishment moved to destroy Jesus for two reasons: both because of his radical socio-economic challenge to the status quo and because of his alleged blasphemy. It is quite understandable that the religious, economic and political establishment viewed Jesus' attack on the status quo as highly threatening. They obviously had to change their values and actions fundamentally or get rid of this disturbing prophet.[10] We simply misunderstand what led up to the cross if we miss the fact that Jesus' execution is "the punishment of a man who threatens society by creating a new kind of community leading a radically new kind of life."[11]

Jesus' theological claims also infuriated them. When he claimed divine authority to forgive sins, they objected (Mark 2:6-11). When he set his own authority above that of Moses, they were offended (Matthew 5:31-39). When he told the parable of the tenants who destroyed the master's vineyard and identified himself as the special Son sent by the Master (Luke 20:9-18), they began looking for a way to arrest him (v. 19). When he broke their rigid rules by healing on the Sabbath, they decided to destroy him (Matthew 12:9-12). When, at the trial, he acknowledged that he was "the Christ, the Son of the Blessed One," they tore their clothes and pronounced him a blasphemer (Mark 14:62-64).

Blasphemer, social radical and Messianic pretender. That was the charge. That is why the political and religious leadership conspired to kill him. When they forced Pilate to admit that Jesus' Messianic claims were a political threat to Rome (John 19:12-13), Pilate agreed to crucify him. The inscription on the cross ("King of the Jews") shows that the crime was Jesus' Messianic claim. Roman governors regularly crucified Jewish messianic pretenders in the first century.

In fact, Pilate and the priestly aristocracy were right. Jesus was a threat to their unjust, oppressive, unfaithful power and system. Jesus came, claiming to be the Messiah of the Jewish people. He urged the whole society to accept God's radical forgiveness and begin living his new kingdom values. But to do that, they would have to adopt Jesus' radical challenge to the way they exercised power and leadership and the way they treated the poor and marginalized. Equally serious, they would have to accept Jesus as God's Messiah and only Son. They preferred to kill him.

The Difference It Makes

Defining the Gospel as the Good News of the kingdom rather than merely the Good News of forgiveness or the Good News of personal salvation matters a great deal.[12] For one thing, people who confess Jesus as the way, the truth and the life ought to be careful not to abandon his central teaching! For another, understanding the central Christian message as the Gospel of the kingdom helps provide a comprehensive, holistic framework that transcends one-sided, partial perspectives.

Jesus' kingdom is clearly holistic in every sense. Thank God that it does bring forgiveness with God and personal, inner sanctification in the power of the

Spirit. But it also challenges and transforms the social order.[13] The kingdom impacts soul and body, individual and society. Full communication of the good news of Jesus' kingdom is possible only by word and deed, only by proclamation, miracles, acts of mercy and justice, and incarnational modeling.

The Good News of the kingdom precludes an inward-looking preoccupation with the church. Howard Snyder puts it pointedly: "Church people think about how to get people into the church; kingdom people think about how to get the church into the world. Church people worry that the world might change the church; kingdom people work to see the church change the world."[14]

The church, to be sure, is important. Indeed, so important that Jesus' new redeemed community is part of the Good News. God wants the church to be a little miniature now of the coming kingdom. For that reason, it should, like Jesus' first community, be a disturbing challenge to the status quo, rather than a comfortable club of conformity to the world. The church has learned the awesome secret of God's cosmic design to restore the whole creation to wholeness. Therefore Christians go forth into the world both to lead people to faith in Christ and also to erect signs of the coming kingdom within the broken kingdoms of the world, confident that the Messiah will one day return to complete the victory over the kingdom of darkness.

Few statements have captured the holistic, comprehensive meaning of Jesus' Good News of the kingdom as well as one from the first Lausanne Congress on World Evangelization:

> The **evangel** is God's Good News in Jesus Christ; it is Good News of the reign he proclaimed and embodies; of God's mission of love to restore the world to wholeness through the Cross of Christ and him alone; of his victory over the demonic powers of destruction and death; of his Lordship over the entire universe; it is Good News of a new creation of a new humanity, a new birth through him by his life-giving Spirit; of the gifts of the messianic reign contained in Jesus and mediated through him by his Spirit; of the charismatic community empowered to embody his reign of shalom here and now before the whole creation and make his Good News seen and known. It is Good News of liberation, of restoration, of wholeness, and of salvation that is personal, social, global and cosmic. Jesus is Lord! Alleluia![15]

End Notes

1. See the excellent discussion and citation of literature in Miroslav Volf, "Materiality of Salvation," *Journal of Ecumenical Studies*, Vol. 26, No. 3 (Summer, 1989), pp. 464-466.

2. Mortimer Arias, *Evangelization and the Subversive Memory of Jesus: Announcing the Reign of God* (Philadelphia: Fortress, 1984), p. 8. Arias' book is one of the best popular treatments of the kingdom of God.

3. Edward Schweitzer, *The Good News According to Matthew* (Atlanta: John Knox Press, 1975), p. 132 and John Piper, *Love Your Enemies* (Cambridge: Cambridge University Press, 1979), pp. 40-41.

4. Joachim Jeremias, *New Testament Theology* (London: SCM, 1971), p. 175-6.

5. See C.F.D. Moule, ed., "The Significance of the Message of the Resurrection for Faith in Jesus Christ," in *Studies in Biblical Theology*, No. 8 (London: SCM Press, 1968), p. 9.

6. Mishnah Sotah 3.4 quoted in Marcus J. Borg, *Jesus: A New Vision* (San Francisco: Harper-Collins, 1991), p. 146, n. 38.

7. Quoted in W. Ward Gasque, "The Role of Women in the Church, in Society and in the Home," *Priscilla Papers* , Vol. II, No. 2 (Spring, 1988), p. 9.

8. Arias, *Announcing the Reign of God*, p. 5.

9. *Ibid.*, p. 6.

10. Nor is it surprising that Jesus' contemporaries viewed this radical disturber of the status quo as a prophet like Elijah or Jeremiah. See the references in C. Rene Padilla, "The Politics of the Kingdom of God..." in Vinay Samuel and Albrecht Hauser, eds., *Proclaiming Christ in Christ's Way* (Oxford: Regnum Books, 1989), p. 187.

11. John Howard Yoder, *Politics of Jesus* (Grand Rapids: Eerdmans, 1972), p. 63.

12. See, for instance, Chris Sugden and Oliver Barclay, *Kingdom and Creation in Social Ethics* (Bramcote, Nottingham: Grove Books, 1990), especially, p. 19.

13. That does *not* mean that we should speak of the kingdom coming when justice emerges in secular society.

14. Howard Snyder, *Liberating the Church* (Downers Grove: Inter-Varsity, 1983), p. 11.

15. From the "Radical Discipleship" Statement; J. D. Douglas, ed., *Let The Earth Hear His Voice* (Minneapolis: WorldWide Publications, 1975), p. 1294.

Study Questions

1. Compare and contrast Sider's definition of the Kingdom with Ladd's definition of the Kingdom.

2. Why is this new community of disciples disturbing?

9

The Master's Plan

Robert E. Coleman

The plan of this study has been to trace the steps of Christ as portrayed in the Gospels to discern a motivating reason for the way He went about His mission. His tactics have been analyzed from the standpoint of His ministry as a whole, hoping thereby to see the larger meaning of His methods with men.

His Objective Was Clear

The days of His flesh were but the unfolding in time of the plan of God from the beginning. It was always before His mind. He intended to save out of the world a people for Himself and to build a church of the Spirit which would never perish. He had His sights on the day His Kingdom would come in glory and in power. This world was His by creation, but He did not seek to make it His permanent abiding place.

No one was excluded from His gracious purpose. His love was universal. Make no mistake about it. He was the "Saviour of the world" (John 4:42). God wanted all men to be saved and to come to a knowledge of the truth. To that end Jesus gave Himself to provide a salvation from all sin for all men. In that He died for one, He died for all. Contrary to our superficial thinking, there never was a distinction in His mind between home and foreign missions. To Jesus it was all world evangelism.

He Planned to Win

His life was ordered by His objective. Everything He did and said was a part of the whole pattern. It had significance because it contributed to the ultimate purpose of His life in redeeming the world for God. This was the motivating vision governing His behavior. His steps were ordered by it. Mark it well. Not

Robert E. Coleman is Director and Professor of Evangelism at the School of World Mission and Evangelism of Trinity Evangelical Divinity School. He serves as Director of the Billy Graham Institute of Evangelism at Wheaton, Illinois, and as Dean of the International Schools of Evangelism. He is a member of the Lausanne Committee for World Evangelization and has been Chairman of the North American Section. Coleman is the author of eight books, including *The Master Plan of Evangelism*. Excerpts from *The Master Plan of Evangelism* by Robert E. Coleman. Copyright 1972 by Fleming H. Revell Company. Used by permission.

for one moment did Jesus lose sight of His goal.

That is why it is so important to observe the way Jesus maneuvered to achieve His objective. The Master disclosed God's strategy of world conquest. He had confidence in the future precisely because He lived according to that plan in the present. There was nothing haphazard about His life—no wasted energy, not an idle word. He was on business for God (Luke 2:49). He lived, He died, and He rose again according to schedule. Like a general plotting His course of battle, the Son of God calculated to win. He could not afford to take a chance. Weighing every alternative and variable factor in human experience, He conceived a plan that would not fail.

Men Were His Method

It all started by Jesus calling a few men to follow Him. This revealed immediately the direction His evangelistic strategy would take. His concern was not with programs to reach the multitudes, but with men whom the multitudes would follow. Remarkable as it may seem, Jesus started to gather these men before He ever organized an evangelistic campaign or even preached a sermon in public. Men were to be His method of winning the world to God.

The initial objective of Jesus' plan was to enlist men who could bear witness to His life and carry on His work after He returned to the Father. Having called His men, Jesus made it a practice to be with them. This was the essence of His training program—just letting His disciples follow Him.

Jesus expected the men He was with to obey Him. They were not required to be smart, but they had to be loyal. This became the distinguishing mark by which they were known. They were called His "disciples" meaning that they were "learners" or "pupils" of the Master. It was not until much later that they started to be called "Christian" (Acts 11:26), although it was inevitable, for in time obedient followers invariably take on the character of their leader.

Jesus was always building up in His ministry to the time when His disciples would have to take over His work, and go out into the world with the redeeming Gospel. This plan was progressively made clear as they followed Him.

His Strategy

Why? Why did Jesus deliberately concentrate His life upon comparatively so few people? Had he not come to save the world? With the glowing announcement of John the Baptist ringing in the ears of multitudes, the Master easily could have had an immediate following of thousands if He wanted them. Why did He not then capitalize upon His opportunities to enlist a mighty army of believers to take the world by storm? Surely the Son of God could have adopted a more enticing program of mass recruitment. Is it not rather disappointing that one with all the powers of the universe at His command would live and die to save the world, yet in the end have only a few ragged disciples to show for His labors?

The answer to this question focuses at once the real purpose of His plan for evangelism. Jesus was not trying to impress the crowd, but to usher in a Kingdom. This meant that He needed men who could lead the multitudes. What good would it have been for His ultimate objective to arouse the masses to follow Him if these people had no subsequent supervision nor instruction in the Way? It had been demonstrated on numerous occasions that the crowd was an easy prey to false gods when left without proper care. The masses were like helpless sheep wandering aimlessly without a shepherd (Mark 6:34; Matt. 9:36; 14:14). They were willing to follow almost anyone that came along with some promise for their welfare, be it friend or foe. That was the tragedy of the hour—the noble aspirations of the people were easily excited by Jesus, but just as quickly thwarted by the deceitful religious authorities who controlled them. The spiritually blind leaders of Israel (John 8:44; 9:39-41; 12:40; cf., Matt. 23:1-39), though comparatively few in number, completely dominated the affairs of the people. For this reason, unless Jesus' converts were given competent men of God to lead them on and protect them in the truth, they would soon fall into confusion and despair, and the last state would be worse than the first. Thus, before the world could ever be permanently helped, men would have to be raised up who could lead the multitudes in the things of God.

Jesus was a realist. He fully realized the fickleness of depraved human nature as well as the Satanic forces of this world amassed against humanity, and in this knowledge He based His evangelism on a plan that would meet the need. The multitudes of discordant and bewildered souls were potentially ready to follow Him, but Jesus individually could not possibly give them the personal care they needed. His only hope was to get men imbued with His life who would do it for Him. Hence, He concentrated Himself upon those who were to be the beginning of this leadership. Though He did what He could to help the multitudes, He had to devote Himself primarily to a few men, rather than to the masses, in order that the masses could at last be saved. This was the genius of His strategy.

It all comes back to His disciples. They were the vanguard of His enveloping movement. "Through their word" He expected others to believe on Him (John 17:20), and these in turn to pass the word along to others, until in time the world might know Who He was and what He came to do (John 17:21,23). His whole evangelistic strategy—indeed, the fulfillment of His very purpose in coming into the world, dying on the cross, and rising from the grave—depended upon the faithfulness of His chosen disciples to this task. It did not matter how small the group was to start with so long as they reproduced and taught their disciples to reproduce. This was the way His Church was to win—through the dedicated lives of those who knew the Saviour so well that His Spirit and method constrained them to tell others.

Jesus intended for the disciples to produce His likeness in and through the Church being gathered out of the world. Thus His ministry in the Spirit would be duplicated many fold by His ministry in the lives of His disciples. Through them and others like them it would continue to expand in an ever enlarging circumference until the multitudes might know in some similar way the opportunity which they had known with the Master. By this strategy the conquest of the world was only a matter of time and their faithfulness to His plan.

Jesus had built into His disciples the structure of a church that would challenge and triumph over all the powers of death and Hell. It had started small like a grain of mustard seed, but it would grow in size and strength until it became a tree "greater than all the herbs" (Matt. 13:32; cf. Mark 4:32; Luke 13:18,19). Jesus did not expect that everyone would be saved (He recognized realistically the rebellion of men in spite of grace), but He did foresee the day when the Gospel of salvation in His Name would be proclaimed convincingly to every creature. Through that testimony His Church militant would someday be the Church universal even as it would become the Church triumphant.

It was not going to be an easy conquest. Many would suffer persecution and martyrdom in the battle. Yet no matter how great the trials through which His people would pass, and how many temporal skirmishes were lost in the struggle, the ultimate victory was certain. His Church would win in the end. Nothing could permanently prevail against it "or be strong to its detriment, or hold out against it" (Matt. 16:18, *Amplified New Testament*).

The principle of giving evangelistic work assignments to His disciples was conclusively demonstrated just before He returned to Heaven after His crucifixion and resurrection. On at least four occasions as He met with His disciples He told them to go out and do His work. It was first mentioned to the disciples, with the exception of Thomas, on the first Easter evening as they were assembled in the Upper Room. After Jesus had showed the astonished disciples His nail-scarred hands and feet (Luke 24:38-40), and had partaken of the meal with them (Luke 24:41-43), He then said: "Peace be unto you: as the Father hath sent Me, even so I send you" (John 20:21). Whereupon Jesus assured them again of the promise and authority of the Holy Spirit to do the work.

A little later as Jesus had breakfast with His disciples by the Sea of Tiberias, He told Peter three times to feed His sheep (John 21:15, 16,17). This admonition was interpreted to the big fisherman as the proof of his love to the Master.

On a mountain in Galilee He gave His great commission to, not only the eleven disciples (Matt. 28 16), but also to the whole church numbering then about 500 brethren (I Cor. 15:6). It was a clear proclamation of His strategy of world conquest. "All authority hath been given unto Me in heaven and in earth. Go ye therefore, and make disciples of all the nations, baptizing them into the Name of the Father and of the Son and of the Holy Ghost, teaching them to observe all things whatsoever I commanded you: and lo, I am with you always, even unto the end of the world" (Matt. 28:18-20; cf., Mark 16:15-18).

Finally, before He ascended back to the Father, Jesus went over the whole thing again with His disciples for the last time, showing them how things had to be fulfilled while He was with them (Luke 24:44-45). His suffering and death, as well as His resurrection from the third day, was all according to schedule (Luke 24:46). Jesus went on to show His disciples "that repentance and remission of sins should be preached in His Name unto all nations, beginning from Jerusalem" (Luke 24:47). And for the fulfillment of this divine purpose, the disciples were no less a part than their Master. They were to be the human instruments announcing the good tidings, and the Holy Spirit was to be God's personal empowerment for their mission. "Ye shall receive power, when the Holy Ghost is come upon you: and ye shall be my witnesses both in Jerusalem, and in all Judea and Samaria, and unto the uttermost part of the earth" (Acts 1:8; cf. Luke 24:48, 49).

Clearly Jesus did not leave the work of evangelism subject to human impression or convenience. To His disciples it was a definite command, perceived by impulse at the beginning of their discipleship, but progressively clarified in their thinking as they followed Him, and finally spelled out in no uncertain terms. No one who followed Jesus very far could escape this conclusion. It was so then; it is so today.

Christian disciples are sent men—sent out in the same work of world evangelism to which the Lord was sent, and for which He gave His life. Evangelism is not an optional accessory to our life. It is the heartbeat of all that we are called to be and do. It is the commission of the church which gives meaning to all else that is undertaken in the Name of Christ. With this purpose clearly in focus, everything which is done and said has glorious fulfillment of God's redemptive purpose.

Study Questions

1. Why did Jesus not use His reputation, power, and influence to enlist a mighty army of believers to take the world by storm?

2. What was the genius of Jesus' strategy? Do you think this should be followed today? Why or why not?

3. How do evangelistic strategies today compare with Jesus' strategy?

10
Jesus and the Gentiles

H. Cornell Goerner

We have tried to read our Bible as Jesus read his. This took us quickly through the Old Testament, the only Scriptures Jesus had. In all three sections of the Hebrew Bible, the books of Moses, the Prophets, and the Psalms, we found God's concern for all the nations and peoples of the earth, and his plan for dealing with them through the Messiah. We believe that Jesus mentally "underscored" these passages in his Bible, and planned deliberately to fulfill them by his life, his death, and his resurrection.

Turning now to the New Testament, we find in the Gospels that the words and actions of Jesus confirm this all-inclusive concept of his ministry. The New Testament flows right out of the Old, with unbroken continuity. In the distinctive title he chose for himself, in the strategy of his ministry, and in his clear teachings, it is obvious that Jesus undertook a mission for all mankind.

Malachi and Matthew

In our Bible the Gospel of Matthew comes immediately after Malachi, and appropriately so. Whatever the date of this last of the prophets, at least two or three centuries from God to his people is on record later than Malachi. Yet, as one closes the Old Testament and opens the New, it is as though just a few days intervened. Matthew begins right where Malachi ended. And no one was more conscious of that than Jesus was. He knew that he had come to fulfill what Malachi had predicted.

The four short chapters of Malachi are an unrelieved denunciation of the nation of Israel, the warning of an imminent day of judgment to be announced by a forerunner and then instituted by "the messenger of the covenant," who would come suddenly to the Temple and inaugurate a new era, not only for the people of Israel, but for the whole world.

After teaching missions and comparative religion at Southern Baptist Seminary for more than 20 years, in 1957 H. Cornell Goerner became Secretary for Africa, Europe, and the Near East for the Foreign Mission Board of the Southern Baptist Convention. He retired in 1976 as Secretary for West Africa, and now is a pastor of a church in a community near Richmond, Virginia. From *All Nations in God's Purpose* (Nashville: Broadman Press 1979), Chapter V. All rights reserved. Used by permission.

The coming judgment was called "the Day of the Lord." It would be "a great and terrible day" of testing, when the righteous would be separated from the wicked as gold is refined in a smelter, as dirt is removed from clothing by caustic lye soap, as chaff is separated from wheat at the threshing floor, and as an unfruitful tree is chopped down and consumed in a furnace (Mal. 3:2; 4:1, 5).

The judgment would be particularly severe on Israel and its leaders because of specific sins which are denounced: sham and hypocrisy in worship services (1:7-14); social injustice (2:10); pagan religious practices (2:11); divorce (2:16); withholding the tithe (3:8-10). But above all, the prophet declares, God's patience is coming to an end because the people who were supposed to exalt Yahweh and cause him to be reverenced and worshiped among the nations of the world have failed to do so. Instead, they have profaned his name and caused him to be dishonored (1:5-14). But God's purpose will not be defeated, for from east to west, all over the world, his name is to be exalted among the nations, and in every place prayers and worship are to be offered to him (1:11).

The keynote is sounded in Malachi 1:10:

> "Oh that there were one among you who would shut the gates, that you might not uselessly kindle fire on My altar! I am not pleased with you," says the Lord of hosts, "nor will I accept an offering from you." "For from the rising of the sun, even to its setting, My name will be great among the nations, and in every place incense is going to be offered to My name, and a grain offering that is pure; for My name will be great among the nations," says the Lord of hosts.

Because God is so concerned that he be exalted among the nations, he is about to act, Malachi warns. He will first send a messenger to prepare the way for him (Mal. 3:1). Then he will come himself, as the messenger of the covenant, who will inaugurate the time of judgment (Mal. 3:2-3). The forerunner will be an "Elijah," a fiery prophet of doom (Mal. 4:5). If he is not heeded, then fierce judgment and destruction will be certain.

All of these elements of Malachi are reflected in the third chapter of Matthew's Gospel. John the Baptist came preaching, "Repent, for the kingdom of heaven is at hand" (Matt. 3:2). This is the equivalent of "the Day of the Lord" in Malachi. The time of God's judgment is fast approaching! This is "the wrath to come" (Matt. 3:12). John uses the same figures of speech which are found in Malachi; the wheat and chaff are to be separated. To emphasize that the judgment is to be upon the Israelites, and not just the Gentiles, as some of the Jews believed, John declared in effect: "Don't think that you will escape because you are 'sons of Abraham'. I tell you, God is not dependent upon you. He can raise up 'sons of Abraham' from these stones, if he wishes. He will use others, if you are not worthy. You will be judged and punished, regardless of your Hebrew heritage" (Matt. 3:9, author's paraphrase).

Jesus picked up this message of warning to the nation of Israel. Immediately after his baptism we are told: From that time Jesus began to preach and say: "Repent, before it is too late. The time is short. The day of God's judgment is at hand."

Jesus identified John the Baptist as the Elijah whom Malachi had promised.

Just after John's imprisonment, Jesus declared: "For all the prophets and the Law prophesied until John; and if you are willing to accept it, he is Elijah who is to come. He who has ears to hear, let him hear" (Matt. 11:13-15, RSV).

Jesus was warning that a turning point in history was at hand. The last of the prophets had been sent to give a final warning before judgment came upon the nation of Israel. Some months later, after the death of John the Baptist, he again identified John as the Elijah foretold by Malachi:

> "But I say to you, that Elijah already came, and they did not recognize him, but did to him whatever they wished. So also the Son of Man is going to suffer at their hands." Then the disciples understood that He had spoken to them about John the Baptist (Matt. 17:12-13).

During his last week in Jerusalem as he taught in the Temple, Jesus was consciously fulfilling what is written in Malachi 3:1-2:

> "Behold, I am going to send My messenger, and He will clear the way before Me. And the Lord, whom you seek, will suddenly come to His temple, and the messenger of the covenant, in whom you delight, behold He is coming," says the Lord of hosts. "But who can endure the day of His coming? And who can stand when He appears? For He is like a refiner's fire and like fullers' soap."

John the Baptist had been sent as a messenger to prepare the way. He had done his work. Now the Lord himself had come to announce a New Covenant to replace the Old Covenant that had been broken. ("The Lord whom you seek" is not Yahweh, but the expected Messiah, indicated by *Adon* in the Hebrew. The Lord of hosts who is announcing the coming of the Lord [*Adon*] is Yahweh. Jesus with his knowledge of Hebrew understood this distinction.) The people had been seeking the coming of the Messiah, they thought, but actually they were not ready for his coming and the judgment which it brought. Only those who were spiritually prepared could endure his coming.

This is what it means to close the Old Testament and open the New Testament. Jesus knew that the covenant made at Sinai had been broken again and again by a disobedient people, and after a long line of prophets sent to win them back had failed, God's patience was approaching an end. A new covenant was to be sealed with a faithful remnant of Israel, who would then call the Gentile nations to repentance in the name of the Messiah, the judge of the living and the dead.

Judgment must begin with the house of Israel. It then must be proclaimed to all the nations. This was the note of urgency with which Jesus began his ministry. Matthew fulfills Malachi!

Son of Man

Nothing is more revealing than the personal title which Jesus chose for himself. We have seen that he did not like the term, "Son of David," the popular designation of the Messiah. He realized that he was indeed "the Son of God" referred to in Psalm 2:7, and during his trial before the Sanhedrin, he acknowledged this. But the title which he used throughout his ministry was, "Son of Man." More than forty times in the Gospels the term is used, always by Jesus referring to himself. The disciples never used the term, but called him "Lord," "Master," or "Teacher." For Jesus, the words were almost a substitute for the personal pronoun "I." Again and again he said it: "The Son of Man has nowhere to lay His head" (Matt. 8:20). "The Son of Man has authority on earth to forgive sins" (Matt. 9:6). "The Son of Man is Lord of the Sabbath" (Matt. 12:8). "Then they shall see the Son of Man coming in clouds with great power and glory" (Mark 13:26).

Jesus derived this term from two principal sources: the books of Ezekiel and Daniel. "Son of Man" is the distinctive title applied to the prophet Ezekiel by God, and occurs eighty-seven times. The Hebrew is *ben Adam*, literally, "Son of Adam," or "son of mankind." Originally it meant only "man," as opposed to God, and reminded Ezekiel of his humble status. But by the time of Jesus, the term had become an honorific title of the Messiah, and many passages in Ezekiel were idealized and interpreted messianically. As he read the book, Jesus must have heard God speaking directly to him: "Son of man, I am sending you to the sons of Israel, to a rebellious people" (Ezek. 2:3). "Son of man, I have appointed you a watchman to the house of Israel; whenever you hear a word from My mouth, warn them from Me" (3:17).

Especially significant for Jesus were the passages concerning a remnant to be spared (6:8); the new heart and spirit (11:19; 36:26-27); the new everlasting covenant (37:26); and the promise that the Gentile nations would come to know the Lord, God of Israel (37:28; 38:23; 39:7). All these were to be fulfilled by him, as Son of Man.

There can be no doubt that Daniel 7:13-14 was in the mind of Jesus when he used the title, "Son of Man." There it was an Aramaic term, *bar enash*, instead of *ben Adam*. But the meaning is similar, *enash* being the word for mankind in general, as against an individual male person. In rabbinical commentary and popular thought, the term had already been highly spiritualized, indicating the ideal man, almost divine in nature. The Book of Enoch, an apocalyptic discourse widely circulated during the first century, exalted the figure even beyond Daniel's vision.[1] But it is not necessary to assume that Jesus was influenced by Enoch. The words of Daniel are clear enough:

> I kept looking in the night visions,
> And behold, with the clouds of heaven
> One like a Son of Man was coming,
> And He came up to the Ancient of Days
> And was presented before Him.
> And to Him was given dominion,
> Glory and a kingdom,
> That all the peoples, nations, and men of every language
> Might serve him.
> His dominion is an everlasting dominion
> Which will not pass away;
> And His kingdom is one
> Which will not be destroyed (7:13-14).

Jesus knew that this would take place only after his suffering and glorification. He claimed the title for himself, thus identifying himself, not with the Hebrew people or the Jewish nation in any exclusive way, but with the whole human race, with all the families of mankind. He knew that he was the Son of Man and the Suffering Servant.[2]

From the Beginning

As we have already seen, the vision of a universal kingdom was integral to the plan of Jesus from the very beginning of his ministry. The fact that one of the wilderness temptations involved "all the kingdoms of the world and their glory" (Matt. 4:8) is conclusive. Jesus *did* aspire to world dominion. His ambition to rule over the nations was not wrong. The temptation was to take a short cut to that noble goal: to adopt the methods of the devil. In rejecting Satan's methods, Jesus did not give up his aim of worldwide authority. Rather, he chose the path of suffering and redemption which he found outlined in the Scriptures.

The first sermon at Nazareth demonstrates that his life purpose extended far beyond the nation of Israel. He was not surprised that his own people did not receive his message. "That's the way it has always been," he said. "The prophets have always found greater faith among foreigners than among their own people" (Luke 4:24, author's paraphrase). He then gave an example: "There were many widows in Israel in the days of Elijah…and yet [he] was sent to none of them, but only to Zarephath, in the land of Sidon, to a woman who was a widow" (Luke 4:25-26). His hearers knew the rest of the story told in I Kings 17. Received into a Gentile home, Elijah performed the remarkable miracle of replenishing the flour and oil, then later restored the widow's son to life—not a Jewish widow, but a Gentile!

Jesus did not stop with Elijah. He rubbed salt into the wounded feelings of his audience with the story of Elisha. For Naaman, the Syrian, was not only a Gentile, but a military leader—captain of the Syrian army which at that very time was at war with Israel and had almost eradicated the hapless little nation (2 Kings 5:1-14). Yet, although there were many lepers in Israel, "none of them was cleansed, but only Naaman the Syrian" (Luke 4:27). No more dramatic illustration could have been given that the grace of God was not limited to the people of Israel and that Gentiles often displayed greater faith than those who were considered "children of the kingdom." Small wonder that the proud citizens of Nazareth were infuriated at this brash young man, who insulted their nation and called in question their privileged status as God's "Chosen People"! But for his miraculous power, they would have hurled him to his death on the jagged rocks at the foot of a cliff (Luke 4:28-30).

To the Jews First

Jesus did have a deep conviction of a special mission to the Jewish nation. He expressed this so strongly that some have concluded that he envisioned no mission beyond Israel. But careful consideration of all his words and actions reveals that it was a question of strategy: As Paul later expressed it, his mission was "to the Jew first, and also to the Greek" (Rom. 1:16; 2:10).

Jesus' concern for Israel was shown in the instructions to the twelve disciples as he sent them out on their first preaching mission. "Do not go in the way of the Gentiles," he said, "and do not enter any city of the Samaritans; but rather go to the lost sheep of the house of Israel" (Matt. 10:5-6). The reason is obvious. The time was short, and doom was coming to the nation, if there was not speedy repentance. The need was urgent, more so for Israel than for the Gentile nations, whose time of judgment would come later. Indeed, in the very same context is the prediction that the preaching ministry of the disciples would be extended to the Gentiles; "You shall even be brought before governors and kings for My sake, as a testimony to the Gentiles" (v. 18). But they must concentrate upon the Jewish cities first, because their time of opportunity was short (v. 23).

Luke tells of a later preaching mission in which seventy others were sent out two by two (Luke 10:1). Just as the twelve apostles symbolically represent the twelve tribes of Israel, the seventy symbolize the Gentile nations. In Genesis 10, the descendants of Noah are listed, seventy in number.

Rabbinical tradition assumed that this was the total number of nations scattered over the earth after the Tower of Babel, and repeatedly referred to the seventy Gentile peoples. Jesus may have used this means of symbolizing his long-range purpose. The twelve were sent to warn the tribes of Israel of impending judgment. The seventy were sent later on a training mission in preparation for their ultimate mission to the whole world.[3]

Contacts with Gentiles

Most of the public ministry of Jesus was conducted in Jewish territory. Under the circumstances, the number of personal contacts with Gentiles recorded in the Gospels is surprising. He healed a Gadarene demoniac (Matt.8:28-34). Among ten lepers healed, one was a Samaritan, and Jesus remarked upon the fact that only the foreigner returned to thank him (Luke 17:12-19).

A Samaritan woman was the sole audience for one of Jesus' greatest sermons. She received the assurance that the time was near when God would be worshiped, not just in Jerusalem or at Mt. Gerizim, but all over the world, "in spirit and in truth" (John 4:5-42).

A Canaanite woman's faith was rewarded when her daughter was healed. Much has been made of Jesus' puzzling remark at the beginning of the encounter: "I was sent only to the lost sheep of the house of Israel" (Matt. 15:24). This may have been a deliberate rebuke of his disciples, who wanted to send her away with her request unanswered, and who shared the racial prejudice which was common at the time. The significant point is that Jesus *did* minister to this Gentile woman, and praised her faith in the presence of his disciples and the Jewish onlookers (v. 28).

The centurion whose servant was healed was almost certainly a Roman. Commander of a band of one hundred foreign soldiers quartered at Capernaum to keep the peace, he was despised by the Jews who resented this "army of occupation." Conscious of his own authority as a military man, he humbly assured Jesus that it would not be necessary for him to go to his house to heal the servant (and thus perhaps render himself unclean by entering a Gentile home). "Just say the word and my servant will be healed," he declared with genuine faith (Matt. 8:8). Jesus turned and announced to the Jewish crowd which was following him: "I tell you the truth: I have not found a single Hebrew who showed as much faith as this Gentile military leader" (Matt 8:10, author's paraphrase). He did not stop there, but continued with this solemn prediction: "I tell you, many such foreigners shall come from the east and the west to join Abraham, Isaac, and Jacob in the kingdom of heaven. But many others who thought they were 'sons of the kingdom' (the Chosen People of Israel) shall be shut out" (v. 11-12, author's paraphrase).

The coming of a group of Greeks precipitated the final crisis in the inner life of Jesus: his decision to move on to the cross. It is clear that these were not merely Hellenized Jews, but aliens, either inquirers or proselytes, who had accepted Judaism and thus were qualified to worship in the Temple area, at least in the court of the Gentiles. Their request for an audience caused Jesus to declare: "The hour has come for the Son of Man to be glorified" (John 12:23). The deep interest of the Greeks was evidence that the world was ready for his redemptive mission to be culminated by his atoning death: "And I, if I be lifted up from the earth, will draw all men to Myself." "All men"—Greeks as well as Jews; Gentiles and Hebrews alike—this is the clear implication of these profound words recorded by John (John 12: 32).

The Final Week

The events of that last week in Jerusalem bear eloquent testimony to the fact that Jesus, refusing to be a nationalistic Jewish Messiah, moved resolutely toward the cross, fully aware that he was to establish a new interracial, international people, the New Israel, destined to become worldwide in its scope as a spiritual kingdom. He entered the city on a donkey, in order to fulfill Zechariah's prediction of a king who would speak peace to the nations, and whose dominion would be from sea to sea (Zech. 9:9-10). He cleansed the court of the Gentiles, declaring sternly, "My house shall be called a house of prayer for all the nations" (Mark 11:17). Standing in the Temple, he denounced the chief priests and Pharisees, the official leaders of the Jewish nation, for having failed to be good stewards of the truths of the Kingdom which had been entrusted to the Chosen People, and solemnly declared, "Therefore, I say unto you, the kingdom of God will be taken away from you, and given to a nation producing the fruit of it" (Matt. 21:43) He predicted the fall of Jerusalem and the destruction of the Temple within that generation (Mark 13:30; Matt. 24:34; Luke 21:32); but when asked concerning the end of the age, he said, in effect: "Don't be misled. It will not be as soon as some think. For this gospel of the Kingdom shall be preached in the whole world for a witness to all nations, and after that the end shall come" (Matt. 24:4-14, author's paraphrase). Concerning his return in glory, he was purposely vague, declaring, "Of that day and hour no one knows, not even the angels of heaven, nor the Son, but the Father alone" (Matt. 24:36). But when he does come, he promised, *"all nations* will be gathered before Him, and He will separate them from one another, as the shepherd separates the sheep from the goats" (25:32, author's italics).

Just before the Passover, at a house in Bethany, an adoring woman anointed his body with costly ointment. When she was criticized for her extravagance, Jesus stoutly defended her with these words: "She did it to prepare Me for burial. Truly I say unto you, wherever this gospel is preached in the whole world, what this woman has done shall also be spoken of in memory of her" (26:13).

The next evening in the upper room with his disciples, he sealed the New Covenant with them, in anticipation of his death. He declared as he passed the cup, "This is My blood of the covenant, with is to be shed on behalf of many for forgiveness of sins" (v. 28). Only the eleven were present, and all were Jews. But Jesus knew that the small nucleus of a new Chosen People, the remnant of Israel, was soon to be enlarged, as the many for whom he died heard the good news and accepted him as Lord and Savior.

End Notes

1. William Manson, *Jesus The Messiah* (London: Hodder and Stoughton, 1943), pp. 102 f.

2. Alfred Edersheim, *The Life and Times of Jesus the Messiah* (Grand Rapids, MI: Eerdmans, 1950), 1:173.

3. *The Broadman Bible Commentary* (Nashville: Broadman Press, 1971), 1:149.

Study Questions

1. What events and statements could give the impression that Jesus came just for the nation of Israel?

2. Why does Goerner claim that Jesus' emphasis upon "the lost sheep of the house of Israel" was a strategic emphasis?

3. Describe some connections between the Old and New Testaments that give continuity to the Bible.

11
A Man for All Peoples

Don Richardson

Millions of Christians know, of course, that Jesus, at the end of His ministry, commanded His disciples to "go and make disciples of all [peoples]" (Matt. 28:19). We respectfully honor this last and most incredible command He gave with an august title—the Great Commission. And yet millions of us deep down in our hearts secretly believe, if our deeds are an accurate barometer of our beliefs (and Scripture says they are), that Jesus really uttered that awesome command without giving His disciples ample warning.

Read cursorily through the four Gospels and the Great Commission looks like a sort of afterthought paper-clipped onto the end of the main body of Jesus' teachings. It is almost as if our Lord, after divulging everything that was really close to His heart, snapped His fingers and said, "Oh yes, by the way, men, there's one more thing. I want you all to proclaim this message to everyone in the world, regardless of his language and culture. That is, of course, if you have the time and feel disposed."

Did Jesus hit His disciples with the Great Commission cold turkey? Did He just spring it on them at the last minute without fair warning and then slip away to heaven before they had a chance to interact with Him about its feasibility? Did He fail to provide reasonable demonstration on ways to fulfill it?

How often we Christians read the four Gospels without discerning the abundant evidence God has provided for an entirely opposite conclusion! Consider, for example, how compassionately Jesus exploited the following encounters with Gentiles and Samaritans to help His disciples think in crosscultural terms.

A Roman Centurion

On one occasion (Matt. 8:5-13), a Roman centurion, a Gentile, approached Jesus with a request on behalf of his paralyzed servant. Jews, on this occasion,

---

Don Richardson pioneered work for Regions Beyond Missionary Union (RBMU) among the Sawi tribe of Irian Jaya in 1962. Author of *Peace Child, Lords of the Earth,* and *Eternity in Their Hearts,* Richardson is now Minister-at-Large for RBMU. He speaks frequently at missions conferences and Perspectives Study Program classes. Taken from *Eternity in Their Hearts.* Copyright 1981, Regal Books, Ventura, CA 93003. Used by permission.

urged Jesus to comply. "This man deserves to have you do this, because he loves our nation and has built our synagogue," they explained.

In fact, walls and pillars of a synagogue built probably by that very centurion still stand two thousand years later near the north shore of the Sea of Galilee! But notice the implication of the Jews' reasoning. They were saying, in effect, that if the centurion had not thus helped them, neither should Jesus help the centurion or his pitifully paralyzed servant! How clannish of them! Little wonder Jesus could not help sighing occasionally, "O unbelieving and perverse genera- tion...how long shall I stay with you? How long shall I put up with you?" (Matt. 17:17).

Jesus responded to the centurion, "I will go and heal him." At that moment the centurion said something quite unexpected: "'Lord, I do not deserve to have you come under my roof. But just say the word, and my servant will be healed. For I myself am a man under authority, with soldiers under me....' When Jesus heard this, he was astonished," wrote Matthew. What was so astonishing? Simply this—the centurion's military experience had taught him something about authority. As water always flows downhill, so also authority always flows down an echelon (a chain of command). Whoever submits to authority from a higher level of an echelon is privileged also to wield authority over lower levels. Jesus, the centurion noticed, walked in perfect submission to God: therefore Jesus must have perfect authority over everything below Him on the greatest echelon of all—the cosmos! *Ergo!* Jesus must possess an infallible ability to command the mere matter of the sick servant's body to adapt itself to a state of health!

"I tell you the truth," Jesus exclaimed, "I have not found anyone in Israel with such great faith!" As in many other discourses, Jesus exploited the occasion to teach His disciples that Gentiles have just as great a potential for faith as Jews! And they make just as valid objects for the grace of God too!

Determined to maximize the point, Jesus went on to say: "I say to you that many will come from the east and the west [Luke, a Gentile writer, adds in his parallel account: 'and from the north and the south'] and will take their places at the feast with Abraham, Isaac and Jacob in the kingdom of heaven. But the sub- jects of the kingdom [this could only mean the Jews as God's chosen people] will be thrown outside, into the darkness, where there will be weeping and gnashing of teeth" (Matt. 8:7-12; Luke 13:28, 29).

Feasts are usually called to celebrate. What would you guess that future feast attended by Abraham and a host of Gentile guests will celebrate?

Intimations of the Great Commission to follow could hardly have been clearer! Wait, there is still much more!

A Canaanite Woman

Still later, a Canaanite woman from the region of Tyre and Sidon begged Jesus' mercy on behalf of her demon-possessed daughter. Jesus at first feigned indifference. His disciples, glad no doubt to see their Messiah turn a cold shoul- der to a bothersome Gentile, concurred at once with what they thought were His true feelings. "Send her away," they argued, "for she keeps crying out after us" (see Matt. 15:21-28).

Little did they know that Jesus was setting them up. "I was sent only to the lost sheep of Israel," He said to the woman. Having already manifested an apparent insensitivity toward the woman, Jesus now manifests an apparent inconsistency also. He has already healed many Gentiles. On what basis does He now reject this one's plea? One can imagine the disciples nodding grimly. Still they did not suspect. Undissuaded, the Canaanite woman actually knelt at Jesus' feet, pleading, "Lord, help me!"

"It is not right to take the children's bread." Then He added the crusher— "and toss it to their dogs!" "Dogs" was a standard epithet Jews reserved for Gentiles, especially Gentiles who tried to intrude upon Jewish religious privacy and privilege. In other words, Jesus now complements His earlier "insensitivity" and "inconsistency" with even worse "cruelty."

Was this really the Saviour of the world talking? No doubt His disciples thought His reference quite appropriate for the occasion. But just when their chests were swollen to the full with pride of race, the Canaanite woman must have caught a twinkle in Jesus' eye and realized the truth!

"Yes, Lord," she replied ever so humbly, not to mention subtly, "but even the dogs eat the crumbs that fall from their master's table!" (Matt. 15:21-27; see also Mark 7:26-30).

"Woman, you have great faith!" Jesus glowed. "Your request is granted!" No, He was not being fickle! This was what He intended to do all along. Immediately preceding this event, Jesus had taught His disciples about the difference between real versus figurative uncleanness. This was His way of driving the point home.

"And her daughter was healed from that very hour," Matthew records (v. 28).

A Samaritan Village

When on a later occasion Jesus and His band approached a certain Samaritan village, the Samaritans refused to welcome Him. James and John, two disciples whom Jesus nicknamed "sons of thunder" for their fiery tempers, were incensed. "Lord," they exclaimed indignantly (stamping their feet), "do you want us to call fire down from heaven to destroy them?"

Jesus turned and rebuked James and John. Some ancient manuscripts add that He said, "You do not know what kind of spirit you are of, for the Son of Man did not come to destroy men's lives, but to save them" (Luke 9:51-55, including footnote).

With those words, Jesus identified Himself as a Saviour for Samaritans!

Greeks at Jerusalem

Later on, some Greeks came to a feast at Jerusalem and sought audience with Jesus. Philip and Andrew, two of Jesus' disciples, relayed the request to Jesus who, as usual, exploited the occasion to get another wedge in for the "all-peoples perspective": "But I, when I am lifted up from the earth, will draw all men to myself" (John 12:32). This prophecy foreshadowed the manner of Jesus' death— crucifixion! But it also foretold the effect! All men—not merely in spite of Jesus' humiliation, but because of it—would be drawn to Him as God's anointed deliverer. On the surface this statement could be interpreted to mean that everyone in the world will become a Christian. Since we know that this is quite unlikely, the statement probably means instead that some of all kinds of men will be drawn to Jesus when they learn that His death atoned for their sins. And that is exactly what the Abrahamic Covenant promised—not that all people would be blessed, but that all peoples would be represented in the blessing. Jesus' disciples thus gained still another fair warning of the Great Commission soon to follow!

On the Road to Emmaus

Just as the disciples still did not believe Jesus' intimations of Gentile evangelism, so also they never really believed Him when He said He would rise from the dead. But He surprised them on both counts! Three days after His entombment He resurrected! And one of His first encounters after resurrection began in cognito fashion with two of His disciples on a road leading to Emmaus (see Luke 24:13-49). During the opening exchange the two disciples, still not recognizing Jesus, complained: "We had hoped that [Jesus] was the one who was going to redeem Israel" (v. 21); they did not add, "and make Israel a blessing to all peoples." A blind spot in their hearts still effectively obscured that part of the Abrahamic Covenant.

"How foolish you are," Jesus responded, "and how slow of heart to believe all that the prophets have spoken! Did not the Christ have to suffer these things and then enter his glory?" (vv. 25, 26).

Then, beginning with the five "books of Moses and all the Prophets, he explained to them what was said in all the Scriptures concerning himself." He had covered much of that ground before, but He went over it again—patiently (v. 27). And this time, the two disciples' hearts burned within them as He opened the Scripturues (see v. 32). Was a wider perspective at last winning its way into their hearts?

Later they recognized Jesus, but at the same moment He vanished from their sight! They retraced their steps at once to Jerusalem, found the Eleven (as the disciples were called for a while after Judas' defection) and recounted their experience. But before they finished talking, Jesus Himself appeared among them, and the Eleven experienced the end of the story for themselves!

As unerringly as a swallow returning to its nest, Jesus returned to the Scriptures and their central theme: "Then he opened their minds so they could understand the Scriptures. He told them, 'This is what is written: The Christ will suffer and rise from the dead on the third day, and repentance and forgiveness of sins will be preached in his name to all nations [*i.e., ethne*—peoples], beginning at Jerusalem. You are witnesses of these things'" (Luke 24:45-48).

Go and Make Disciples

Notice, however, that He still did not command them to go. That would come a few days later, on a mountain in Galilee where—as far as the disciples were concerned—it all started. And here is the working of the command which the Abrahamic Covenant had already foreshadowed for 2,000 years, and which Jesus for three long years had been preparing His disciples to receive: "All authority in heaven and earth has been given to me. Therefore go and make disciples of all nations, baptizing them in the name of the Father and of the Son and of the Holy Spirit, and teaching them to obey [note the limitation that follows] everything I have commanded you. And surely I will be with you always, to the very end of the age" (Matt. 28:18-20).

It was not an unfair command. The Old Testament foreshadowed it. Jesus' daily teaching anticipated it. His frequent prejudice-free ministry among both Samaritans and Gentiles had given the disciples a real-life demonstration of how to carry it out. Now He added the promise of His own authority bequeathed and His own presence in company—if they obeyed!

Still later, moments before He ascended back into heaven from the Mount of Olives (near Bethany), He added a further promise: "You will receive power when the Holy Spirit comes on you; and you will be my witnesses..." Then followed Jesus' famous formula for the exocentric progression of the gospel: "...in Jerusalem, and in all Judea and Samaria, and to the ends of the earth" (Acts 1:8).

It was Jesus' last command. Without another word, and without waiting for any discussion of the proposal, He ascended into heaven to await His followers' complete obedience to it!

Clannish Jews into Cross-Cultural Apostles?

Jesus knew of course that there was no hope of rescuing the majority of Jews in His time from blind self-centeredness any more than there is ever much hope of rescuing the majority of any people, for that matter, from the same plight! Throughout history, the majority of Jews focused so exclusively upon the top line of the Abrahamic Covenant that the bottom line became virtually invisible to them. It is probably not an exaggeration to describe their minds as hermetically sealed against any serious consideration of "the bottom line." That is why many Jews were determined to exploit Jesus' miraculous powers exclusively for their own benefit. But His covenant-based all-peoples perspective clashed constantly with their own "our people" mentality. Even one of His disciples, as we have seen, betrayed Him in the context of this issue! The only hope, then, lay with these other eleven. If only Jesus could win them to the all-peoples perspective the full promise of Abraham, and not just a truncated version, could still be fulfilled.

Question! Could even the Son of Man—without negating human free will—transform eleven men whose thought patterns were programmed from childhood to an extreme *ethnocentrism*? The question may seem silly. Could not the Son of Man, who is also the omnipotent Son of God, do anything? The answer is yes, but—human free will implies God's prior decision not to tamper with the metaphysical base of that free will. It also implies man's ability to reject the persuasion God uses to influence that free will while leaving its metaphysical base intact!

Persuasion, not compulsion, is what even He must rely upon! And persuasion, by its very definition, must be resistable! Yet the God who thus renders Himself resistable is so intelligent that He can overrule every consequence of His own self-limitation with ease! Working around and through human resistance as easily as through response, He still achieves His own eternal goals!

Ultimate suspense, then, does not hang upon the eventual success of God's design; for that success is assured. Ultimate suspense hangs rather upon questions like, *Who* among the sons and daughters of men will recognize the day of God's privilege when it dawns around them? And which men and women, among those who discern that privilege, will choose to scorn it as Esau scorned his birthright? And finally, just how will God accomplish His goal when even the men and women who love Him and make His purpose theirs turn out to be spiritually vulnerable, physically weak, and oh so limited in understanding?

Study Questions

1. On the basis of Matthew 10:5, 6 and 15:24, some say that Jesus came to offer the Jews a literal, physical kingdom, giving them exclusive dominion over the Gentiles then and there, and that He resorted to the Great Commission as a sort of "Plan B" only after the Jews rejected Him. Discuss this in the light of Matthew 10:18 and other such passages of Scripture.

2. Describe instances when Jesus used encounters with non-Jewish people to give His disciples an "all-peoples" perspective.

12

The Hidden Message of "Acts"

Don Richardson

Hundreds of millions of Christians think that Luke's Acts of the Apostles records the 12 apostles' obedience to the Great Commission. Actually it records their reluctance to obey it.

As the Eleven stood rooted to that hilltop, watching Jesus vanish into a cloud, did they really feel positive response to that last command? Surely Jesus' example of compassion for a Roman centurion, a Syrophoenician mother, a Samaritan leper, a Gadarene demoniac, a Syrian general like Naaman, the widow of Zarephath, the men of Nineveh who repented, and the people of Sodom and Gomorrah who perished without a clear call to repentance—must now prove sufficient to melt prejudice from their hearts, replace that prejudice with "peoples consciousness," and send them on their way to the ends of the earth!

Surely His sweeping survey of the Scriptures followed by His direct command, unveiling God's plan for the whole world, must now provide the disciples with adequate motivation! And finally—would not the promised bestowal of the Holy Spirit's power transform them into dynamic cross-cultural commandos?

Power for Evangelization

But wait—regarding that bestowal of the Holy Spirit's power—suppose God had hired you as a public relations expert to plan the event for Him! Suppose He had given you just one specification—it must happen in a manner which will make absolutely clear to even the dullest disciple that the power about to be bestowed is not merely for the personal blessing or exaltation of the recipients, but rather to enable them to take the gospel across the world to all peoples!

Even if you were the most ingenious public relations consultant of all time, you probably would not have fantasized a clearer way to get that point across than the following.

Don Richardson pioneered work for Regions Beyond Missionary Union (RBMU) among the Sawi tribe of Irian Jaya in 1962. Author of *Peace Child, Lords of the Earth,* and *Eternity in Their Hearts* , Richardson is now Minister-at-Large for RBMU. He speaks frequently at missions conferences and Perspectives Study Program classes.
Taken From *Eternity in Their Hearts.* Copyright 1981, Regal Books, Ventura, CA 93003. Used by permission.

When finally the power of the Holy Spirit came upon Jesus' disciples, the timing was perfect! God-fearing Jews from at least 15 different regions of the Near and Middle East had gathered in Jerusalem for a feast called Pentecost. In addition to their common knowledge of Hebrew and/or Aramaic, these strangers—often called Jews of the Diaspora, the "scattering"—spoke probably as many as several dozen Gentile languages.

The power of the Holy Spirit coming upon the apostles and other faithful followers of Jesus caused them to speak miraculously in the many Gentile languages represented by the throng of Diaspora Jews and Gentile converts then gathered in Jerusalem. Why?

Not merely to bless those who spoke. The bestowal of miraculous ability to speak *non-Jewish* languages was superfluous if only their own blessing was intended!

Further, it was not merely to bless the Diaspora Jews who understood those languages. If only their edification was intended either the Hebrew or the Aramaic language could have served as well.

Nor was the purpose to demonstrate the Holy Spirit's ability to perform amazing tricks.

Seen in the context of Jesus' ministry and His clearly articulated plans for the whole world, the bestowal of that miraculous outburst of *Gentile* languages could have only one main purpose: to make crystal clear that the Holy Spirit's power was and is bestowed with the specific goal of the evangelization of all peoples in view! Any attempt to exploit the power of the Holy Spirit for one's personal pleasure or aggrandizement, or to seek signs and miracles as ends in themselves, must appear to God as a misconstrual of His purpose.

Yet we sometimes still see Christians seek power and signs with no thought of committing themselves to the evangelization of all peoples!

Persecution and Scattering

But let us see if that first generation of Christians realized the significance of the Holy Spirit's gifts any better...

With the power of the Holy Spirit crackling through their witness, the apostles quickly crossed the first of the four thresholds Jesus mentioned— they evangelized Jerusalem—no problem! Their critics soon complained. "You have filled Jerusalem with your teaching" (Acts 5:28). The comment, "The number of disciples in Jerusalem increased rapidly" (Acts 6:7), was also soon recorded. By the end of the seventh chapter of the book of Acts we find, however, that all of the apostles and their thousands of converts are still clustered in Jerusalem. Twenty-five percent of the book of Acts was already history, and as far as the record shows, they were not even making plans to obey the rest of Jesus' last command!

Even God was getting impatient, if we understand correctly what follows. God, it appears, was willing to use extreme measures to keep his Son's gift to all mankind from ending up as the exclusive property of just one people—the Jews. God's solution was very simple, if painful: He scattered the Christians through persecution. The enemies who hounded Jesus' followers never dreamed they were fulfilling God's will: "A great persecution broke out against the church at

Jerusalem, and all except the apostles were scattered throughout Judea and Samaria" (Acts 8:1).

In the light of Jesus' last command, should not at least some of the apostles have led the way? Apparently even persecution could not dislodge them from home base. "Those who had been scattered preached the word wherever they went. Philip" (not the apostle Philip, but rather one of seven laymen appointed earlier to wait on tables for the thousands of believers in Jerusalem—Acts 6:5) "went down into a city of Samaria and proclaimed Christ there...So there was great joy in that city" (Acts 8:4-8).

Philip the Pioneer

After Philip, a "layman" on a working vacation from his catering service in Jerusalem (see Acts 6:1-5), had broken the Samaritan ice for them, the apostles decided to send two of their number—Peter and John—to add further blessing to the revival already in progress.

It could not have been an easy mission for Peter and John, and perhaps it was not easy for Philip either. Their own culture had trained Jews to be Class Samaritan-avoiders: "for Jews do not associate with Samaritans" (John 4:9). Samaritans, you see, worked from quite a different set of presuppositions. They did not even agree that Jerusalem—the Holy City of the Jews—was the center of the world! And their blood was mixed with Gentile blood! Straight Gentile would probably have been easier for Jews to stomach, but a mixture...how detestable!

Sumeria, perhaps even Siberia, might have presented an easier mission for men of Jewish background than distasteful Samaria.

Nevertheless, Peter and John began to feel enthused about cross-cultural ministry in the Samaritan city. So enthused were they that they "preached the gospel in many Samaritan villages" immediately afterward, but only on their way home to—guess where—Jerusalem (see Acts 8:25)!

Meanwhile, that same spunky layman named Philip was off like a first century Green Beret commando for the Holy Spirit on still another cross-cultural mission! "An angel of the Lord said to Philip, 'Go south to the road—the desert road—that goes down from Jerusalem to Gaza.' So he started out, and on his way he met an Ethiopian eunuch, an important official in charge of the treasury of Candace, queen of the Ethiopians. This man had gone to Jerusalem to worship" (vv. 26, 27).

Here is still another scriptural example of a Gentile person who worshiped the one true God. The record does not even say that he was a convert to Judaism, as it does earlier in the case of "Nicholas from Antioch, a convert to Judaism" (Acts 6:5).

Philip, traveling down "the desert road" noticed that the Ethiopian was "sitting in his chariot reading the book of Isaiah the prophet." Isaiah, incidentally, contains a directive concerning Cush—the upper Nile Valley— the very place where that Ethiopian eunuch was employed under Queen Candace: "Go, swift messengers, to a people tall and smooth-skinned" (the Dinka people of that region are among the tallest in the world, and the towering Watusi of Central Africa are believed also to originate from Cush), "to a people feared far and wide, an aggressive nation of strange speech, whose land is divided by rivers" (Isa. 18:2, 7).

Philip, as far as we know, was the first "swift messenger" who ever came close to fulfilling that strongly cross-cultural directive found in the very book from which the Ethiopian was reading.

The Ethiopian's attention, however, was riveted upon a different passage, one found in verse 7 of Isaiah 53: "He was led like a sheep to the slaughter, and as a lamb before the shearer is silent, so he did not open his mouth" (Acts 8:32).

The Ethiopian asked Philip, "'Tell me please, who is the prophet talking about, himself or someone else?' Then Philip began with that very passage of Scripture and told him the good news about Jesus" (Acts 8:34, 35).The Ethiopian believed, requested baptism that very day and "went on his way rejoicing" (v. 39). History indicated that he may have successfully prepared the way for the later establishment of thousands of Christian churches in the far-away Valley of the Nile.

Good work, Philip!

Parting from the eunuch, Philip went north on the "desert road," preaching along the sea coast from Azotus to Caesarea.

As far as we know, even Philip went no further. But, as he earlier blazed a trail for Peter and John into Samaria, so now his travels northward along the coast through Lydda, Joppa, and Caesarea also seem to have prepared the way again for Peter. For in Acts 9:32 to 11:18, we find Peter again following Philip's footprints. Peter was doing a great work to be sure, but he was still preaching Christ only where He had already been preached—with one outstanding exception!

Peter and Cornelius

While in Caesarea, Philip apparently missed a God-seeking Roman centurion named Cornelius. And so the mission to win Cornelius to faith in Christ fell to Peter. And what a trauma it was even for Spirit-filled Peter to try to convert a Roman! A vision intended to purge Peter of his anti-Gentile biases had to be repeated three times, but Peter got the point (see 10:9-23). His subsequent meeting with Cornelius is a poignant study of human prejudice gradually melting down through the sheer goodness of the gospel of Jesus Christ.

Peter summarized his preparation for encounter with a God-seeking Roman by saying, "I now realize how true it is that God does not show favoritism but accepts men from every nation who fear him and do what is right" (10:34, 35).

And yet, as he begins to preach to Gentile Cornelius and his household, Peter bumbled like a first-century Archi Bunker trying to be nice—but not too nice—to people who are "different." Peter described the gospel as a "message God sent to the people of Israel, telling the good news of peace through Jesus Christ" (v. 36). He didn't even go on to mention what Jesus so clearly specified—that it was also good news for all peoples. In the next breath, though, perhaps because he saw disappointment register on the faces of his Gentile listeners, Peter acknowledged that Jesus Christ does have some relationship with Gentiles. He is, Peter admitted, "Lord of all" (v. 36).

Still later Peter articulated Jesus' last command for his Gentile listeners; but oh, what a highly abridged version of the Great Commission it was! "He commanded us to preach to the people" (v. 42). It is not too hard to guess which "people" Peter instinctively meant.

Then, in spite of Peter's bias, the Holy Spirit finally got him to say it: "All the prophets testify about him that everyone (unqualified) who believes in him receives forgiveness of sins through his name" (v. 43).

And at that moment the Holy Spirit overwhelmed Peter's wistful Gentile audience just as He overwhelmed believing Jews on the day of Pentecost and outcasts of Samaria who were awakened first by deacon Philip's ministry.

But oh! The lesson of Jesus' world-wide cross-cultural imperative was so hard for even His own hand-picked apostles to learn! It still is for us today.

When Peter returned to Jerusalem, his fellow Christians of Jewish background criticized him—as he knew they would—saying, "You went into the house of uncircumcised men and ate with them" (Acts 11:3).

After Peter explained how God had practically compelled him to enter that Roman household, his critics changed their attitudes and said, "So then, God has even granted the Gentiles repentance unto life" (v. 18).

One wonders what—prior to that moment—they thought the purpose of Jesus' last command was! Or how they supposed it could be obeyed "to the ends of the earth" without a Jew ever having to eat with a Gentile!

The Antioch Church

Still other Christians of Jewish background, driven from Jerusalem by persecution, traveled as far north as Phoenicia, Cyprus and Antioch. They also proclaimed the gospel. But the record says they were careful to communicate it only to Jews.

Some of them, however, sent from Cyprus and Cyrene, decided to try giving the same message to Gentiles. At last! you cry, a breakthrough in their thinking has occurred! But wait a minute. They chose not to proclaim the gospel to Gentiles in their own home areas of Cyprus and Cyrene where they themselves were known. They did it in Antioch, where presumably they were not so well known. Why? Could it be that they wanted to preserve—if confronted by criticism such as Peter experienced—the option of fleeing away to their own regions, leaving the pot to boil behind them?

Once again the Spirit of the Lord broke through. One gets the impression from the book of Acts that He was constantly waiting to do just that wherever and as soon as He could find Christians who were willing to confront Gentiles with the gospel. And so we read: "The Lord's hand was with them, and a great number of people believed and turned to the Lord" (v. 21).

One can almost detect a note of mild sarcasm in the sentence that follows: "News of this reached the ears of the church at Jerusalem" (v. 22).

The inspired writer could as easily have said, "News of this reached the church in Jerusalem." The metaphor "ears of the church" may be a gentle hint of Luke's (and the Holy Spirit's) bemused impatience with the still-too-narrow vision of the church in Jerusalem. We must remember, too, that all 12 apostles (Matthias had replaced Judas) were still ensconced as heads of the church at Jerusalem. Hence the phrase "ears of the church" could as easily— but for Luke's gentle diplomacy—have been rendered "the ears of the apostles."

Nor did even one of the apostles venture to Antioch to see the great things happening among Gentile converts there. They sent a man named Barnabas.

Why a deputy to Antioch?

Could it be that Peter, John and the rest were suffering from a common human affliction called "headquarters fever"?

Apostles with Clay Feet

They will always be Christ's apostles. Their names are written forever upon the 12 foundation stones of the New Jerusalem (see Rev. 21:14). And yet, just as the four Gospels deliberately expose many of their human failings— bickering over rank, impetuosity, trying to steer Jesus away from the cross, etc., so the book of Acts reveals another error just as serious—their reticence to take Christ's last command seriously, at least during the early years following Pentecost.

Why did they linger in Jerusalem year after year, instead of going with the power God had given them on bold cross-cultural probes to more distant peoples?

Perhaps the best justification for their delay was the need to get their heads together—while Jesus' words and deeds were still fresh in their collective memory—and compile the data from which Matthew, Mark, the Gentile Luke, and John later wrote their four Gospels. This could have kept all of the apostles occupied for 5-10 years, and some of them perhaps longer. Evidence indicates, however, that 20 years or more passed before they began to move out. And even that evidence is open to question.

Did they also think that their continuing presence in Jerusalem was necessary to guarantee that the Holy City would always be central to the new faith, as it was to Judaism? If so, they had clearly forgotten what Jesus once said to the Samaritan woman beside that old well at Sychar: "Believe me, woman, a time is coming when you will worship the Father neither on this mountain nor in Jerusalem" (John 4:21).

Or was it the fact that they took wives (see I Cor. 9:5) who were limited as to the distances they could travel?

Or was it their old argument over who would be greatest that kept them concentrated in Jerusalem? To leave the large, well-established church in the Holy City and dirty one's hands in rough, potentially dangerous pioneer missionary work would be to step down in rank, wouldn't it? Did each apostle fear to leave Jerusalem in case one of the others might conspire during his absence to entrench himself as some sort of bishop of Jerusalem?

Whatever the answer or answers, clearly a new apostolic band was needed at once to rescue Jesus' last command from oblivion. Who on earth could qualify to do what Jesus' own hand-picked Spirit-filled apostles were in large measure failing to do?

The Conversion and Commissioning of Saul

"Saul, Saul...why do you persecute me?"

It was the voice of the newly ascended Jesus, speaking out of a light shining brighter than the sun. Suddenly blinded by the light, Saul of Tarsus fell to the ground.

"Who are you, Lord?" he asked.

"I am Jesus, whom you are persecuting," came the reply, notably without threat of retaliation for that persecution. Saul winced. Not long before, he had guarded the coats of those who stoned Stephen, one of Jesus' most impassioned witnesses, and his conscience had bothered him ever since. For he had personally consented to Stephen's death and cast many others of Stephen's persuasion into prison—only to find now, to his own awe and shame, that everything they had said about their Lord was valid! Jesus must truly be Lord!

"Now get up and go into the city," the voice continued, "and you will be told what you must do" (see Acts 9:4-6).

While Saul, still blinded, waited for three days in Damascus, Jesus appeared to a humble believer named Ananias and sent him to heal the eyes of that decade's most notorious persecutor of Christians. When Ananias hesitated, fearing for his own safety, Jesus said—note the words—"Go! This man is my chosen instrument to carry my name before the Gentiles and their kings and before the people of Israel. I will show him how much he must suffer for my name" (Acts 9:15).

Thus began the new apostolic band. Saul, admittedly, had certain advantages over the Palestine-born apostles for cross-cultural mission within the Roman Empire. He was raised in Tarsus, a predominantly Gentile city. He spoke not only Hebrew and Aramaic but also Greek and perhaps even Latin. He was born a Roman citizen. And his formal training in Old Testament Scriptures under the scholar Gamaliel enabled him to delineate the Old Testament moorings of Christian faith with unparalleled clarity and precision.

Churches for Gentiles

Later Saul helped Barnabas teach that host of Gentile converts for one year at Antioch. By the end of that year, Saul had apparently forged a new, clearly defined policy for extending the gospel cross-culturally to Gentiles. Gentile converts, he decided, under God need not be circumcised as the law of Moses required for Jews. Nor need they necessarily be identified with Jewish synagogues. They could form their own *ecclesia*—churches—wherein they could worship God through Jesus Christ without having to weather the disapproving frowns and ceremonial structures of rigorous Judaists. From now on it would be the moral content of the law and not the ceremonial framework that mattered!

This was a major breakthrough. Up until that time, Peter and the other apostles had wrestled with the problem of how to make Gentile converts conform to the standards for admission to what were regarded as "Nazarene" synagogues. After all, what else was there for Gentile converts to join? And since official synagogues were not set up to accommodate large numbers of Gentile converts, it was embarrassing if large numbers of them came asking for admission. If too many were admitted, they might even become a majority! It was simply easier not to win them in the first place!

Saul's idea, which Barnabas apparently accepted, that Gentile converts could form their own self-perpetuating authoritative ecclesia—churches led not necessarily by Christian Jews, but by themselves—cleared the way for large numbers of Gentiles to come to Christ. And so, after one year ministering together at Antioch, Saul and Barnabas journeyed to Jerusalem to present their new model for Gentile evangelism to the apostles. Cautiously they selected only Peter, James and John, who "seemed to be leaders," for their first audience. The other apostles apparently were judged by Saul and Barnabas to be perhaps too closed-minded.

Saul took with him Titus—a Greek believer who had never been circumcised—as a test case. Peter, James and John—as Saul hoped—did not insist that Titus be circumcised (see Gal. 2:1-5). Gradually, one degree at a time, their attitudes were swinging around. Saul later wrote: "[Peter, James and John] added nothing to my message. On the contrary, they saw that I had been given the task of preaching the gospel to the Gentiles...They agreed that we [Saul and Barnabas] should go to the Gentiles, and they to the Jews" (Gal. 2:6, 7, 9).

A Division of Labor

Notice the implication that none of the other apostles had yet ventured beyond the Jewish domain. Had any done so, Peter, James and John would hardly have spoken of Saul and Barnabas as the sole messengers of Christ to Gentiles.

How amazing! There were now at least 15 men generally recognized as apostles since Matthias, James the Lord's brother and Saul and Barnabas joined the original 11. And yet, out of the 15 only two are "commissioned" to evangelize the estimated 900 million Gentiles in the world at that time. The other 13 are convinced that they are all needed to evangelize only about three million Jews, among whom there were already tens of thousands of witnessing believers! Their unashamed willingness to let Paul and Barnabas take on the entire Gentile world boggles my mind.

Was this what the Lord Jesus intended?

Saul, who around this time began to favor his Roman name, Paul, was not altogether very impressed with the other apostles. Little wonder! Paul wrote: "As for [Peter, James and John] who seemed to be important—whatever they were makes no difference to me: God does not judge by external appearance" (Gal. 2:6).

Later Paul even had an open confrontation with Peter in Antioch. In spite of Peter's experience with Cornelius, the Roman centurion through which the Lord went to great pains to teach Peter that it was all right for him to eat with Gentiles, Peter—though he had digested Cornelius's food—had still not fully digested the lesson. Paul describes the problem: "Before certain men came from James [the Lord's own brother!], [Peter] used to eat with the Gentiles, but when they arrived he began to draw back and separate himself from the Gentiles because he was afraid of those who belonged to the circumcision group. The other Jews joined him in his hypocrisy...even Barnabas was led astray" (vv. 12, 13). That's how grim the struggle to maintain an "all-peoples perspective" was!

Paul took decisive action: "When I saw that they were not acting in line with the truth of the gospel, I said to Peter in front of them all, 'You are a Jew, yet you live like a Gentile and not like a Jew. How is it, then, that you force Gentiles to follow Jewish customs?'"(v. 14). Paul explained his logic: "I do not set aside the grace of God, for if righteousness could be gained through the law, Christ died for nothing!" (v. 21).

Free at Last

With the hammering out of these new concepts on the anvil of Paul's experiences in Antioch, Jerusalem and Tarsus, the way was now cleared. Free at last from the hindrance of Jewish particularism, the gospel now could spread to thousands of different peoples as a supra-cultural spiritual force. It was in fact a message far too magnificent and open-hearted to remain for long an ally of the bondage of pharisaic Judaism!

With the way thus cleared, "the Holy Spirit said, 'Set apart for me Barnabas and Saul for the work to which I have called them.' So after they had fasted and prayed, they placed their hands on them and sent them off" into the Gentile world (Acts 13:2, 3).

Paul and Barnabas were fully assured that Gentiles who believe became "heirs together with Israel, members together of one body, and sharers together in *the promise* in Christ Jesus...no longer foreigners and aliens, but fellow citizens with God's people and members of God's household...a dwelling in which God lives by his Spirit" (Eph. 3:6; 2:19, 22, italics added).

Paul would even dare to say, as he wrote later in his epistles, that in Christ "there is neither Jew nor Greek, slave nor free, male nor female...[but those who believe] are all one in Christ Jesus" (Gal. 3:28). For Christ "has destroyed the barrier, the dividing wall of hostility" (Eph. 2:14).

He and Barnabas later declared boldly: "We now turn to the Gentiles. For this is what the Lord has commanded us: 'I have made you a *light for the Gentiles* , that you may bring salvation to *the ends of the earth*'" (Acts 13:46, 47, italics added).

The lines were drawn. Christianity and Judaism were now separate religions! Peter, James and John had tried their utmost to keep them together, but the pressure of Jesus' last command was too strong. Spreading the blessing of Abraham to all peoples on earth was still the unchanging nature of his purpose. Once the Lord has bound Himself by an oath He cannot and will not change His mind.

Paul and Barnabas had returned to churches in Antioch and reported that God has "opened the door of faith to the Gentiles" (Acts 14:27).

Council at Jerusalem

Later those churches sent Paul and Barnabas to Jerusalem on still a second occasion to sit down with Peter, James and John and try to settle once and for all a question still vexing many Jewish believers—must Gentile converts, in order to be saved, submit to the ordeal of circumcision and obey all points of the Law of

Moses and its detailed rituals?

Peter, reconciled now to the inevitable, reminded the resulting council of his experience in Cornelius's household years earlier: "[God] made no distinction between us and them, for he purified their hearts by faith. Now then, why do you try to test God by putting on the necks of the disciples a yoke that neither we nor our fathers have been able to bear? No! We believe it is through the grace of our Lord Jesus that we are saved, just as they are" (Acts 15:9-11).

Later James, the Lord's brother, gave the last word: "[Peter] has described to us how God at first showed his concern by taking from the Gentiles a people for himself" (v. 14).

James put his finger on the main point—it was God's concern: it had to be, because they themselves could hardly have cared less! James continued: "The words of the prophets are in agreement with this, as it is written: 'After this I will return and rebuild David's fallen tent...that the remnant of men may seek the Lord, and all the Gentiles who bear my name'"(vv. 15-17).

Apostles as Missionaries

It is possible that some of the original apostles, Palestine-bound—at least until that conference—finally began to open their eyes at this point to the possibilities of ministry among far-away Gentiles. Hearing Paul and Barnabas report large scale response among Asian peoples may have forced them to realize at last that Jerusalem and Samaria were not the only places where the action was!

There is even a theory that Luke may have written his Acts of the Apostles as a subtly disguised handbook designed to encourage the other apostles and their Jewish converts to follow Paul's example in evangelizing the Gentiles!

In any case, Titus's destruction of Jerusalem in 70 A.D. must have scattered the apostles, since there was hardly a Jerusalem left to cloister in after that event.

Various traditions quoted by early church fathers and other sources indicate that James the Just—Jesus' physical brother—never did leave Palestine, but was martyred in Jerusalem. However, the apostle John extended the apostle Paul's ministry in Asia Minor and died in the region of Smyrna and Ephesus.

The apostle Peter extended his ministry into the Gentile world as far as Rome and was crucified upside down by pagan Romans in that city.

Thomas, tradition says, allowed that bottom line of the Great Commission to lead him into "India." In those days India meant anything east of Syria: yet evidence indicates that Thomas may have penetrated all the way to the region of Madras, near the southern tip of India proper. A large number of very ancient churches in that region call themselves the Mar Toma churches. *Toma* may trace back to Thomas's name.

Andrew reportedly traveled north of the Black Sea among the wild tribes of Scythia—forefathers of the modern Russian people . Other apostles apparently penetrated Ethiopia, North Africa, Syria and perhaps southern Arabia. Perhaps someday researchers will uncover ancient documents which will clarify with greater accuracy what finally happened in each apostle's final years.

What finally persuaded them to launch out in obedience to the bottom line of our Lord's last great command? Was it their reading of Luke's "how to" book—the Acts of the Apostles—that helped them to believe at last that they could indeed reach other peoples with the gospel, as Paul and Barnabas were doing?

Or was the destruction of Jerusalem by Titus in 70 A.D. the final persuasion that forced them out of their nest once and for all? Whatever the persuasion, they did move out. And ever since Christians have been moving out in obedience to that final command. Not all Christians, mind you. Only a small minority have obeyed the last great command in each generation.

But that small minority of Christians has been for 2,000 years the single most powerful determiner of human history!

Study Questions

1. Cite passages in Acts which show that the twelve apostles were still subliminally if not overtly reluctant to obey the "bottom line" of the Great Commission.

2. What was very probably Luke's barely-hidden motive for writing Acts? How does Luke reveal this in this writing?

13

The Missionary Task: An Introduction

Arthur F. Glasser

> As the Father has sent me, even so I send you (Jn. 20:21). Go into all the world and preach the gospel to the whole creation (Mk. 16:15). Repentance and forgiveness of sins should be preached in his name to all nations (Luke 24:47).

With these words the Lord Jesus Christ, on the evening of the day of his resurrection, commenced the revelation of his will for his Church in the world. Into all the world! To every creature! What Commander ever conceived so vast a campaign! What Leader ever confronted so small a band of followers with so formidable, so impossible a task! Truly, this is the command of Deity: this is the program of God! Such a gracious purpose—that the whole world of sinning men have the opportunity to hear the liberating good news of the grace of God and of the Kingdom (Acts 20:24, 25).

Our Lord had previously intimated that the future work of his disciples would be to evangelize the world (Mk. 14:9; Jn. 4:42; 10:16; Mt. 4:12-16; Lk. 4:18, 19). A most striking and significant statement was made on Tuesday evening of Passion Week, shortly after his last public appearance in the temple and final appeal to the leaders of Israel (Mt. 23:13-39; Jn. 12:44-50). In great grief he slowly left the temple, never to return (Mt. 24:1). While departing, in response to a casual remark from his disciples calling attention to its beauty and adornment, he solemnly predicted its coming destruction. Not one stone would be left upon another (Mt. 24:2, 3). The disciples were amazed and followed him in silence out of Jerusalem and on to the slopes of the nearby Mount of Olives. They sat down and looked across the valley over to the mighty city whose coming doom they had just heard announced. Finally, they could contain themselves no longer. In considerable confusion they blurted out several questions relating to the future.

Dean Emeritus and Professor Emeritus of the School of World Mission at Fuller Theological Seminary, Arthur F. Glasser served as a missionary in western China with the China Inland Mission (now Overseas Missionary Fellowship) and was also OMF's Home Secretary for North America for twelve years. Glasser is the editor of *Missiology: An International Review*, the official journal of the American Society of Missiology. With permission of the William Carey Library Publishers, P.O. Box 40129, Pasadena, CA, 91114. *Crucial Dimensions in World Evangelization*, Arthur F. Glasser, et al., 1976.

Christ's reply, known as the Olivet Discourse, constitutes his major prophetic utterance and consists of a panoramic sketch of future human history, from the Roman conquest of Jerusalem to the final consummation of the age. It is in this discourse that one finds our Lord saying: "The gospel must first be published among all nations." Then, and only then, would "the End" come.

Making Disciples

Several weeks later he amplified this mandate in the following fashion:

> Make disciples of all nations, baptizing them in the name of the Father and of the Son and of the Holy Spirit, teaching them to observe all that I have commanded you (Mt. 28:19, 20).

You will note that like a good teacher he first reviewed his initial instructions, before moving on to describe the new material. In restating the call to world evangelization, he deliberately replaced the basic verb "preach" ("to proclaim after the manner of a herald") with the imperative "make disciples" and adds that this is accomplished by "baptizing" and "teaching." At this point the scholars are needed to tell us how to fit all this together. Some argue that this merely means that we first enlist a man through our evangelistic witness. Later, we baptize him into the life and witness of a local congregation, and in the days ahead he becomes involved in the ongoing teaching that normally follows conversion. Others argue that one is not a disciple of Jesus until he has been baptized; and they reserve the teaching mandate for post-conversion education. In more recent days a third group of scholars feels that the grammar of the text forces them to conclude that both baptizing and teaching are directly related to making disciples. Baptism marks that the disciple has indeed placed himself under divine authority and become God's possession without qualification. And the teaching must refer to the initial communication of the gospel, especially in the area of making known what following the Lord truly means. We would agree to this, but feel that as a man receives Christ Jesus the Lord, so he is to live in him (Col. 2:6). The teaching that brings a man to his first commitment to Christ is to be given to him all the rest of his days.

Down through the ages the Church has found in this training aspect of the Great Commission ample authority for its program of education, ranging from primary church schools on through to theological seminaries. And God has used many a Christ-centered school to prepare young people for a life of usefulness in his service. Unfortunately, however, the training that is specifically designed to transform conduct is minimized, or altogether overlooked. The training of the mind is conceived as the central task. But the Great Commission is a call to evangelize the world and produce men and women who would be more than well-informed "believers" (not a common New Testament word). Jesus Christ wants disciplined disciples.

Planting Churches

But the Christian movement needs even more than strong, committed individuals. Christians need to be gathered together in communities. The missionary task is incomplete if it stops short of planting churches.

Our Lord did not reveal this added ministry until after Pentecost. Even then, it was unfolded only gradually by his Spirit. By his reference to "baptizing" in the Name of the Father, and of the Son, and of the Holy Spirit in the Great Commission, he had intimated this, but gave no further details. The disciples first needed to have individual, experiential knowledge of the great transformation wrought on the Day of Pentecost by the Holy Spirit. Until he descended, baptizing them "into one Body," bringing them into vital, mystical union with Christ, and making them members of his Church ("which is his Body"), the water baptism he had enjoined was devoid of full significance. The spiritual verities it represented had not as yet been accomplished. This Holy Spirit baptism had been promised frequently prior to Pentecost (by John the Baptist in Matt. 3:11 and by Jesus in Acts 1:5, etc.), was consummated on that Day (Acts 2:1-4) and described thereafter in the New Testament as a past, historical event (I Cor. 12:13).

When the Holy Spirit came on the Day of Pentecost, he endued the first disciples with power, and they began immediately under his direction to preach and witness. They won men and women to Christ and commenced meeting with them, leading them into a pattern of ongoing discipleship (Acts 2:5-47). It was then that they began to discover that God had given to them a corporate life quite distinct from their individual relationship to Christ. They started meeting together for worship, celebrating the Lord's Supper, and receiving instruction in the Word of God from the Apostles. The refreshing fellowship thus experienced was used by God's Spirit to draw them together, and they continued to sense, under his leadership, an obligation to continue their evangelistic outreach, an obligation that quickened their burden to pray together for the victory of God in the hearts of men.

Being all of Jewish background, this activity of public worship, reading the Scriptures, preaching and praying reminded them of the pattern they formerly had followed at their old synagogue services. It was natural for them to consider the probability that God wanted them to continue this pattern. It had a four-fold function. It was to be an assembly for worship, a family for fellowship, an organism for vigorous evangelistic outreach, and a school for training disciples. When the need arose for a pattern of organization, it was found that God's will embraced the use of deacons and elders, each with a distinct sphere of responsibility, whether material or spiritual. As to ministries, the Lord provided apostles, prophets, evangelists, pastors, and teachers.

Taking the Church at Corinth as an example, one notes that local churches developed at least three distinct types of meetings—one, for the purpose of instruction, coupled with prayer and exhortation, another for the purpose of thanksgiving and worship, beginning with a common fellowship meal and ending with the celebration of the Lord's Supper, and the third, a sort of congregational meeting to conduct the business of the local church.

God's program for the evangelization of the world involves the local church. Unless local congregations are firmly established in each population center that has been evangelized, there is no satisfactory way of conserving the results of evangelistic efforts. Without local churches new converts cannot be readily trained, for that training involves working in a group and participating in group worship as well as walking alone with God. Without the varied, extensive outreach of a spiritually-minded church, it is difficult to train young converts to discharge their responsibility under God to participate in gospel outreach. In fact, it is almost impossible to evangelize souls and train converts adequately without the healthy functioning of a local church.

Planting these churches, then, is ever the ultimate objective of all missionary work. Missionary labor, no matter how brilliant, will have little permanence unless this is accomplished. In the final analysis, it is the local congregations, rather than individual believers, that bring lasting changes to the spiritual life of a region. Only through the establishment and functioning of local churches scattered throughout the population centers, integrated in part to the culture of the area, and independent of all outside control and support, can an area originally designated as a "mission field" lose that title. "Mission fields" are areas where there are no churches. And the tragedy is that after more than 1900 years of Christianity there are still many dark places in the earth in which there are no indigenous churches witnessing to the true faith.

Conclusion

If one were asked to describe the relative importance of the different components of the missionary task, he would be obliged to confess that evangelism is 100% important: men are lost, and "the Coming of the Lord draws near." Training is 100% important: converts are babes, and God needs mature men, if his work is to go forward. Church-planting is 100% important: to ignore the Church and its corporate ministry is to remove all possibility of permanence from evangelistic or training efforts, and to violate a fundamental principle of the Word of God. No ministry is primary; no ministry is secondary. All are of fundamental importance. The program of God embraces all three.

Never has there been such a need to master and apply the principles of mission outlined in the New Testament. They are as true and workable now as when first applied: when a Roman world was won to Christ. They need to be used today if the cause of Christ is to advance in the teeth of the gathering storm.

Study Questions

1. Explain the relationship in the Great Commission between going, making disciples, teaching, and baptizing.

2. Why is the missionary task incomplete if it stops short of planting churches?

14

The Apostle Paul and the Missionary Task

Arthur F. Glasser

By the power of the Holy Spirit...I have fully preached the gospel of Christ...not where Christ has already been named, lest I build on another man's foundation, but as it is written, "They shall see who have never been told of him, and they shall understand who have never heard of him" (Rom. 15:19-21).

It is our task in this chapter to trace the Apostle Paul's approach to the task of evangelizing the nations. Obviously, we cannot examine in detail all the references in the New Testament record to his mission perspectives and labors. Before we review the calling of God that made him an apostle and set him apart "for the gospel of God...to bring about the obedience of faith for the sake of his name among all the nations" (Rom. 1:1, 5), we must review those earlier events which gave birth to the New Testament church and launched the missionary movement.

When John the Baptist announced that the coming One would baptize his people with the Holy Spirit and fire (Matt. 3:11), he was announcing the event that would preeminently mark the distinction between the Old and New Testaments. The Spirit would come upon the apostolic community Jesus had gathered and empower it to become a missionary movement. This climactic event took place on the morning of the Day of Pentecost. It was then that the Holy Spirit came upon a small company in an upper room (only 120) and "they began to speak" under his unction (Acts 2:4). Spirit and speech: by these the Church emerged as a witnessing community. From this time forward it was of her very essence to witness to the resurrected and glorified Christ. Out of this witness all

Dean Emeritus and Professor Emeritus of the School of World Mission at Fuller Theological Seminary, Arthur F. Glasser served as a missionary in western China with the China Inland Mission (now Overseas Missionary Fellowship) and was also OMF's Home Secretary for North America for twelve years. Glasser is the editor of *Missiology: An International Review*, the official journal of the American Society of Missiology. With permission of the William Carey Library Publishers, P.O. Box 128-C, Pasadena, CA, 91104. *Crucial Dimensions in World Evangelization*, Arthur F. Glasser, et al., 1976.

her other activities would arise.

The story of Pentecost is well known. A living organism was created (I Cor. 12:12, 13) and it soon demonstrated its capacity as a life-communicating presence among men. On that first day its numbers increased by 3,000. The flame went from heart to heart. In the weeks and months that followed, this living Church demonstrated its capacity to reach outward in a spontaneous fashion with the good news of Jesus Christ. In the early chapters of the Acts (2-12) we see evidence of the existing possibilities of what has been termed "near neighbor evangelism." Jerusalem, Judea, Samaria, Galilee—among the people of Palestine the devoted believers reaped the harvest where Jesus and his disciples had earlier sowed the good seed of the gospel of the Kingdom.

During this period, and scholars believe it lasted for some years, many things happened. The churches grew in size and number, the new "messianic Jews" faced courageously the persecution of their countrymen, many priests were converted, Stephen was stoned to death, revival broke out in Samaria and Peter took the gospel to Cornelius and his household, the first Gentile converts. But of central significance was the fact that God singled out a rabid persecutor of this new faith to be transformed into its greatest missionary.

Called to Be an Apostle

It is generally agreed that the first century of the Christian era was marked by intense missionary activity on the part of the Jews. We can well believe that Saul the Pharisee who later became Paul the Apostle was among those ardent Jews whose life was dedicated to bringing the blessings of the Jewish law to his contemporaries. Perhaps he was referring to this when he wrote: "I advanced in Judaism beyond many of my own age among my people, so extremely zealous was I for the traditions of my fathers" (Gal. 1:14). Incidentally, we should remember that although he had been born in Tarsus, a largely Gentile city in Cilicia, Asia Minor, Saul had been "brought up in Jerusalem at the feet of Gamaliel, educated according to the strict manner of the law" (Acts 22:3). This means he was no typical Jew of the Diaspora (the Jews scattered throughout the Mediterranean world). As a youth his direct contact with Gentiles had been minimal; some scholars feel he moved to Jerusalem with his parents shortly after his sixth birthday.

At any event, at his first appearance in the New Testament Saul is a young man, approving the stoning of Stephen (Acts 8:1) and persecuting the Church violently, even trying to destroy it (Gal. 1:13). But then, on the road to Damascus, he is chosen by Jesus Christ (Phil. 3:12). In those moments of initial encounter between Saul and Jesus, the divine call was given and received. As Paul later wrote: "It pleased God...to reveal his Son to me, in order that I might preach him among the Gentiles" (Gal. 1:16). Where previously he gave the law to men, now he had a person to share with them, Jesus Christ. From that time on Paul was possessed by one determination: to know Christ and to make him known.

Prepared for Missionary Service

The seven (or perhaps nine) years following his conversion and calling were

Paul's hidden years. During this time he apparently received little help from mature believers. In Damascus, Arabia, Jerusalem, Tarsus, the rural parts of Cilicia and finally Antioch, Paul went through a succession of experiences that have come to characterize the training period of many men of God. Note the succession: quiet fellowship, active witness, persecution, rejection by fellow-believers, enforced retirement, years of study, then active service under experienced leaders. Apparently this strange sequence was necessary. At first he fellowshiped with Christians in worship and ministry to the Lord (Damascus), then witnessed with them in the Jewish synagogues. A period of persecution followed, forcing Paul to turn to God for retirement, communion and divine instruction (Arabia). This meant separation from all his usual sources of strength and counsel and was apparently necessary so that Paul could find in God himself the sole source of all life and blessing. It is interesting to note that Paul was then sent back to his home environment (Tarsus, Syria and Cilicia) to serve, before being thrust out into ministry further afield. Finally, God deliberately called this man, destined for future leadership in his Church, to work under human authority for a time before giving him an independent ministry (Antioch). What seems amazing is that God spent such a long period training one who already knew the Jewish Scriptures so well. This suggests that it is unwise to push young believers too soon into active service, or even into places of responsibility and leadership in a local church or mission. Paul later wrote: "Do not be hasty in the laying on of hands:" (i.e., setting people apart to bear responsibilities in the local congregation—I Tim. 5:22). Perhaps he was putting into words his recognition that God was deliberately slow in sending him forth as a missionary to the Gentiles.

The Significance of the Apostolic Band

We have mentioned that Acts 2-13 describes the evangelistic possibilities for "near neighbor outreach" latent within the local congregation. We have referred to the manner in which the Christian movement expanded from Jerusalem to Judea to Samaria and from there to the edges of Jewish Palestine. Chapter 11 brings this story to a climax by showing how a largely Gentile church was planted in Antioch, the fourth largest city in the Mediterranean world. Its cluster of small congregations ("house churches") was so dynamic that Barnabas, who was sent from Jerusalem to supervise and aid in its ministry, became convinced that a more vigorous and able man was needed to prepare the new converts for incorporation into the life of the emerging congregations. He thought of Paul and set forth to Cilicia to seek him. Eventually he found him and the two men combined their strength to lead the church "for an entire year." It is impossible to speak of this church without using superlatives. It was noteworthy as a true cosmopolitan, most evangelistic, well-taught and outstandingly generous company of the Lord's people. And yet, in Acts 13:1-5 the church is described as burdened, and on its knees "worshiping the Lord and fasting."

Why so? What was the problem? The fact that the church was fasting conveys the impression that is was seeking guidance as it sensed its responsibility to take the gospel beyond Antioch to the diverse peoples of the Mediterranean world. Antioch's Christians had no doubt as to the suitability of the gospel for all men; what they lacked was a new method for sharing the gospel with them. The earlier method of near-neighbor, spontaneous outreach would only work within a homogeneous culture. What was now needed was a structured way of extending the knowledge of Christ, one that would surmount all the barriers, whether geographic, linguistic, cultural, ethnic, sociological or economic. So they prayed and fasted.

In response, the Holy Spirit led them to take a decisive step for which there was no precedent. The account twice refers to this, perhaps to underscore that the decision was in response to the Holy Spirit's presence and direction. They "organized what in later times would have been called a foreign mission" (Neill 1968:80). When Barnabas and Saul were designated as its charter members, the church merely "let them go" (vs. 3) because it was essentially the Holy Spirit whose authority and designation were behind his "sending them forth" (vs. 4).

From this, we cannot but conclude that both the congregational parish structure and the mobile missionary band structure are equally valid in God's sight. Neither has more right to the name "church" since both are expressions of the life of the people of God. Indeed, this record clearly challenges the widely held notion that "the local assembly is the mediating and authoritative sending body of the New Testament missionary" (Peters 1972:219). And, there is no warrant for the view that Paul, "for all his apostolic authority, was sent forth by the church (God's people in local, visible congregational life and in associational relationship with other congregations) and, equally important, felt himself answerable to the church" (Cook 1975:234 quoting Rees). This mobile team was very much on its own. It was economically self-sufficient, although not unwilling to receive funds from local congregations. It recruited, trained and on occasion disciplined its members. The Holy Spirit provided direction: like Israel in the wilderness, it had both leaders and followers .

The band was apostolic in the sense that its members regarded themselves as the envoys of God to the unbelieving world. They lived "under the continual constraint of crossing the border between belief and unbelief in order to claim the realms of unbelief for Christ" (Bocking 1961:24). Only when there are no more frontiers to be crossed—only when Jesus Christ has returned and subdued all peoples under his authority will it be possible to say that the need for such missionary bands has finally come to an end.

From this time on the Apostle Paul's missionary methodology was an expression of the activities of the apostolic band. It should be noted that the sodality is not biologically self-perpetuating, as the local congregation would be. One joins the band (or mission) by commitment to the Lord for full-time involvement with the extension of the Christian movement. Acts 14:21-23 describes the sequence of activities: preaching the gospel; making disciples; bringing converts to a sense of their corporateness as members of Christ and of one another and custodians of the gospel of the kingdom; and finally, organizing them into local congregations in which individual members commit themselves to one another and to the order and discipline of the Spirit of God. After a missionary journey was completed, the band returned to its base (Antioch) and rehearsed before the church all that God had accomplished through them (Acts 14:27).

The Strategy of the Apostolic Band

But what plan did the band follow in its missionary outreach? It seems to have had two general objectives. One, the band sought to visit all the Jewish synagogues scattered throughout the Roman Empire, beginning in Asia Minor. Since the gospel was "to the Jew first" (Rom. 1:16) this was natural. Indeed, Paul was very explicit on the subject. Only after the Jews in any one place rejected his message did he go out to the Gentiles. We recall his words in Pisidian Antioch:

> It was necessary that the word of God should be spoken first to
> you [Jews]. Since you thrust it from you, and judge yourselves
> unworthy of eternal life, behold we turn to the Gentiles. For so the
> Lord has commanded us, saying, "I have set you to be a light for
> the Gentiles, that you may bring salvation to the uttermost parts of
> the earth" (Acts 13:46, 47).

It should be noted that this initial outreach to the Jews was not "mission" in the modern sense of the term. Nor should it be. Mission implies reaching those without faith in God. In contrast, the Jews already possessed "the sonship, the glory, the covenants, the giving of the law, the worship, and the promises; to them belong the patriarchs, and of their race, according to the flesh, is the Christ" (Rom. 9:4, 5). The Jews of the synagogue, because they have rejected in principle the gospel, are said to be "made jealous." By this strategy Paul sought to "save some of them" (Rom. 11:11, 14). What does this mean? Probably, he felt that the Christian movement in the totality of its existence must convincingly demonstrate to the Jews that Jesus of Nazareth is attractive, desirable and illuminating as the Messiah who has already come. The Apostle Paul wanted to live with true Jewry. They were not people of another religion but remained the holy root to which the Gentile Church had been grafted. As a result he went wherever there were Jewish synagogues. It was only because they were largely to be found in the cities of the Empire that he went to the cities. God had unfinished business to complete with his ancient people. And this particular responsibility is still a priority task for the Church in our day. The gospel is "to the Jew first."

The second general objective that underlay Paul's missionary strategy was to plant Messianic synagogues or local congregations wherever he found people responsive to the gospel. Keep in mind that the first century of the Christian Era was *par excellence* the great century of Jewish missionary activity. Jesus referred to this when he reminded the Jewish leadership of his day that their scribes and Pharisees "traversed sea and land to make a single proselyte" (Matt. 23:15). This meant that circling virtually every synagogue was a ring of Gentiles, mostly Greek "God-fearers," who had been drawn by the witness of the Jews to the worship of one God and to a quality of life far surpassing anything practiced in the Roman world. Although compelled by Jewish moral strength, intellectual vigor, disciplined living and wholesome family life, these Gentiles stopped short of receiving circumcision and becoming Jews. Inevitably Paul was determined to win these spiritually hungry Gentiles to faith in Jesus and make them the nuclei of Messianic (generally Greek-speaking) synagogues (local congregations) of the emerging Christian movement. So then diaspora Judaism "ploughed the furrows for the gospel seed in the Western world" (Deissmann) and the Jews "were robbed of their due reward...and prevented from gathering in the harvest which they prepared"—all this by Paul and his team, "a generation of fanatics" (to borrow from the atheist Renan). When Luke wrote that "All the residents of Asia heard the word of the Lord, both Jews and Greeks" (Acts 19:10), he probably meant that the band's outreach from the Jewish presence in Ephesus extended throughout Asia, the southwestern portion of present-day Turkey, and that the new congregations of converted Jews and non-Jewish Greeks were uniformly involved in preaching the new faith. Inevitably, those Jews who remained deep within rabbinic Judaism were "made jealous." So it is today: the missionary obedience of the churches cannot but stir Jewish people to reflect on why they are unwilling to share their knowledge of the one God, the Creator of all men.

Spiritual Gifts and the Ministry

In his letters to the newly-founded congregations Paul frequently stressed the wonderful fact that God at Pentecost "gave gifts" to his people and thereby fully provided for their growth in grace and their participation in evangelistic witness. When he said that there were "varieties of service (ministry)" (I Cor. 12:5), he was underscoring the diversity which characterizes the service of Christians within the fellowship of local congregations and among the peoples of the world. To Paul the word "ministry" embraced the total range of Christian duties (Eph. 4:8, 12). All disciples of Christ are called to this ministry of service. When every part of the Body is "working properly" it grows in size, in spiritual depth and in extent (vs. 16).

Internal "service" embraces the local congregation's ministry to the Lord in worship (by prayer, praise, sacrament and the hearing of the word of God), the ministry of its members to one another "For their common good" (I Cor. 12:7; II Cor. 8:4), and the ministry of teaching by which the believing congregation is inculcated with the norms of the apostolic tradition (Acts 6:4; Rom. 12:7). These three: worship, sharing, and instruction are essential to the vitality of any local congregation's inner life—the "koinonia" of the people of God.

External "service" likewise has three components. They are frequently described as the "mission" of the Church since they embrace all that Christians have been sent into the world to accomplish. There is the specific calling to minister to those in special need: "the poor, the widow, the orphan, the prisoner, the homeless and the stranger within the gate." Paul clearly taught that God has equipped certain men and women for such works of mercy and relief (Rom. 12:8; Gal. 6: 10a). In addition, there is the ministry of reconciliation whereby Christians work for concord between men and for social justice within society. Since Paul preached a gospel which proclaimed that sinners could be reconciled to God through Christ's redemptive cross, he was also not indifferent to the obligation to work for the reconciliation of hostile groups within society (II Cor. 5:18-21). Finally, there is the ministry of evangelism whereby Christians confront men and women with the good news of redemptive salvation through Christ's death, burial and resurrection. Christians are to serve their unsaved contemporaries because they are the followers of the Great Servant. And their supreme service is to bring non-Christians to the Servant himself.

So then, we can conclude that through Paul's pointed instruction that all "born again" Christians have been given "the manifestation of the Spirit for the common good" (I Cor. 12:7), he was relaying the mandate of Christ's Great Commission to the churches. In this connection none of Paul's exhortations was more pointed than the challenge he pressed on Corinthian believers at the end of a lengthy discussion of spiritual gifts. He urged them to "covet earnestly the higher gifts" (12:31). His concern was that they should seek those gifts which concerned the oral ministry of the word of God. Covet the apostolic gift and become God's envoy, his evangelist, his church-planter in the unbelieving world. Covet the prophetic gift and become his spokesman, his revivalist to the professing Church. Covet the pastoral gift and become his teacher, his shepherd to the local congregation. As D. L. Moody used to say: "Covet usefulness! Make your plans big, because God is your Partner."

Church and Mission

"I was appointed a preacher and apostle (I am telling the truth, I am not lying), a teacher of the Gentiles in faith and truth" (I Tim. 2:7). Paul was determined to see the Church grow. Indeed, he regarded it her chief and irreplaceable task: to preach the gospel to all mankind and incorporate all those who believed into her communal life. He felt that only through the deliberate multiplication of vast numbers of new congregations would it be possible to evangelize his generation. As an apostle, a member of an apostolic band, he saw himself laboring on the fringes of gospel advance, doing this priority work.

This inevitably meant that Paul made crucial the relation between his band and the new congregations. Indeed, we cannot understand his preoccupation with gathering funds from the Gentile churches to bring relief to the Jewish churches, unless it was somehow related to his desire that the churches be one "that the world may believe" (John 17:21).

Furthermore, Paul also struggled to achieve and maintain a symbiotic relationship between his apostolic band and the churches it had planted. True, some of the churches promptly forgot him and displayed little interest in his evangelistic and missionary endeavors. Other churches opposed Paul and showed a surprising vulnerability to syncretistic thinking, false teaching and gross carnality. Still other churches remained so weak that he had to care for them as a nurse cares for little children. But there were churches, such as the one in Philippi, which loved him and expressed that love with sacrificial gifts. In turn, by his example, his teaching and his prayers, Paul constantly reminded the churches of their apostolic calling. They had been sent by God into the world to reach beyond their borders with the gospel. Their task was to bring into God's kingdom the nations for which Christ died and which had yet to acknowledge him as their king.

The most striking illustration of Paul's desire to establish this symbiotic relationship between local church and mobile mission is found in his epistle to the church in Rome. When he wrote this letter he was midway through his great missionary career: his work in the Eastern Mediterranean just completed. Indeed, he could state that "from Jerusalem and as far around as Illyricum" (present day Yugoslavia) he had "fully preached the gospel of Christ" (Rom. 15:19). However, the Western Mediterranean represented unrelieved darkness, with but one point of light: the church in Rome. Apparently, this solitary fact had been on Paul's mind for some years as he agonized in prayer and deliberated about his future ministry (15:22).

So, he took pen in hand and wrote this tremendous epistle. As a "task theologian" he carefully selected certain themes, and developed them to prepare the Roman Christians for his missionary strategy. They had to realize anew 1) the abounding sin of man, with all the world guilty before God (1:18-3:20); 2) the abounding grace of God to sinners, with justification offered to the believing because of Christ's redemptive work (3:21-5); 3) the abounding grace of God to Christians, with sanctification made possible through the Holy Spirit's indwelling presence and power (6:1-8:39); 4) the abounding grace of God to the nations, for although Israel had failed through unbelief, God was nonetheless determined to reach them with the gospel through the Church and restore Israel at his return (9:1-11:26); and 5) various practical matters such as the exercise of spiritual gifts (12:1-21), the relation of Church and State (13:1-7), and the importance of love to enable the diversity within the Church effectively to put united heart and conscience to reaching the nations (13:8-15:6). Only after this extensive review (15:15) does Paul reveal his strategy for the church at Rome: that it was to become a second Antioch, the new base of operations for his mission to Spain and the Western Mediterranean (15:22-24). It would have a significant role, providing Paul with experienced men and undertaking for their financial and prayer support. In other words, this epistle was written to give a strong cluster of house-churches in a great pagan city a sense of their missionary responsibility for peoples beyond their borders. Through its participating in the missionary obedience of Paul's apostolic band, the church at Rome would attain a new sense of its role as the "sent people" of God (1:11-15). We conclude: the local congregation needs the mobile team. Church needs mission that the "gospel of the kingdom will be preached throughout the whole world, as a testimony to all nations; and then the end will come" (Matt. 24:14).

The Strategy of Suffering

One final element remains. We cannot trace the Apostle Paul's missionary career without being impressed again and again with the fact that his whole life was marked by suffering. When the Lord Jesus called him to the apostolate he said: "I will show him how much he must suffer for the sake of my name" (Acts 9:16). Although set free by Christ, he knew that this freedom was only granted that he might take God's love to all, which meant that he would have to become the slave of all (I Cor. 9:19-23).

All this brings us to the deepest levels of Christian experience where life is lived in the tension of one's times and in spiritual encounter with the forces that seek to hinder the efforts of the people of God to liberate people with the gospel. Indeed, one cannot enter into the fabric of Paul's thought and experience without becoming aware that all his letters (with the possible exception of Philemon) make reference to Satan who constantly sought to thwart his plans (e.g., I Thess. 2:18). Paul writes of "the mystery of lawlessness," "the elemental spirits of the world," the "god of this age," "principalities and authorities"—indeed, these "world powers" penetrated every component of his thought, and although he knew they were vanquished by Christ at the cross, they still posed tremendous obstacles to his missionary obedience. And Paul knew these powers could only be overcome by faith, love, prayer and suffering. He wrote: "We are appointed unto afflictions" (I Thess. 3:3). This points up a cardinal principle: the gospel cannot be preached and the people of God cannot be gathered into one from the nations (John 11:52) without individuals here and there "completing what is lacking in Christ's afflictions" in order to accomplish this task (Col. 1:24). Apparently, one cannot become involved in proclaiming the gospel of the kingdom without paying a price for the privilege. And the privilege is extended to us as well.

The spirit world is always present and the demons are never friendly. This was Paul's experience. And he suffered in order to overcome them, using the weapons provided by his victorious Lord. Were he among us today he would call for our active resistance to all that hinders the ongoing purpose of God— the powers in religious structures, in intellectual structures ('ologies and 'isms), in moral structures (codes and customs) and in political structures (the tyrant, the market, the school, the courts, race and nation) (Yoder 1972:465). The good news our generation needs to hear today includes the breaking in of the kingdom of God by the One who rendered inoperative all opposing forces. But those who serve in his name will suffer. The cross is still the cross.

Study Questions

1. What were the crucial elements in the period of training in Paul's life before he became a missionary? What crucial elements do we stress in the preparation of missionaries today?

2. How is the notion that "the local assembly is the mediating and authoritative sending body of the New Testament missionary" challenged from the account in Acts 13:1-5?

15

The Church in God's Plan

Howard A. Snyder

To be biblical we must see the Church and the gospel within the context of God's cosmic plan.

I believe that God is saving souls and preparing them for heaven, but I would never accept that as an adequate definition of the Church's mission. It is much too narrow. It is not a biblical definition, for the Bible speaks of a divine master plan for the whole creation.

Master of a Great Household

What is this cosmic plan? It is stated most concisely in the first three chapters of Ephesians, and it is here I will begin my biblical analysis. Two striking facts emerge from these chapters. First, God has a plan and purpose. Second, this plan extends to the whole cosmos.

Paul speaks of "the will of God" (1:1), "his pleasure and will" (1:5), "the mystery of his will according to his good pleasure, which he purposed in Christ" (1:9). Paul repeatedly says God "chose," "appointed" and "destined" us according to his will. Paul wished to speak of the Church as the result of, and within the context of, the plan and purpose of God.

Note especially Ephesians 1:10. The word sometimes translated "plan" is oikonomia, which comes from the word for "house" or "household." It refers to the oversight of a household, or to the plan or arrangement for household management. The idea "is that of a great household of which God is the Master and which has a certain system of management wisely ordered by Him."[1] Here is an orderly, premeditated divine plan or design for salvation.[2] Paul's figure of speech is particularly apt since he elsewhere refers to the Church as "God's household," oikeios (Eph. 2:19), and the same figure sometimes extends to the whole inhabited world. (Ecumenical comes from the same root.) Thus the idea of

Howard A. Snyder, formerly Dean of the Free Methodist Seminary in Sao Paulo, Brazil, is currently the Heisel Professor of Evangelization and Church Renewal at United Theological Seminary in Dayton, OH. He was a major speaker at the 1974 Lausanne Congress on World Evangelization. Excerpts from Community of The King, copyright 1977, by Inter-Varsity Christian Fellowship of the USA and used by permission of Inter-Varsity Press.

a cosmic plan is implicit in Paul's wording here. Paul may even have had in mind Jesus' parables of God as a householder who will settle accounts in the Kingdom of God (Mt. 13:27; 20:1, 11; 21:33; Lk. 13:25; 14:21).

Secondly, Paul sees God's plan in cosmic perspective. God's plan is "to unite all things in him, things in heaven and things on earth" (1:10 RSV). Five times Paul speaks of "the heavenly realms." God is the "Father of all who is over all and through all and in all," and Christ has "ascended higher than all the heavens, in order to fill the whole universe" (4:6, 10). Particularly striking is 1:20-23, where Paul speaks of God's power *which he exerted in Christ when he raised him from the dead and seated him at his right hand in the heavenly realms, far above all rule and authority, power and dominion, and every title that can be given, not only in the present age but also in the one to come. And God placed all things under his feet and appointed him to be head over everything for the church, which is his body, the fullness of him who fills everything in every way.*

What a sublime starting point for understanding the Church and the Kingdom! We dare not hurry on to such favorite texts as Ephesians 2:8-9 or 4:11-12 or 6:10-20 without giving thorough attention to God's plan, hinging on Christ's victory. The Word of God is very clear: we begin to understand the Church and its mission as we see the Church as part of God's plan and purpose for the whole creation.

Not Just "Plan B"

But what is God's master plan? Simply this: *that God may glorify himself by uniting all things in Christ.* "God's plan is to unite and reconcile all things in Christ so that men can again serve their maker."[3]

The key idea is clearly that of reconciliation. God's plan is for the restoration of his creation, for over-coming, in glorious fulfillment, the damage done to persons and nature through the Fall. God's design for the reconciliation of all things in Christ reaffirms his original intention at creation now adjusted to the realities of the presence of sin in the world. But this is to speak humanly, from man's underside view of reality; we must not suppose that God's cosmic plan for reconciliation is "Plan B," a second-best, back-up plan that God thought up because he failed at creation. For God's eternal plan predates both the Fall and the creation; it existed in the mind of God "before the creation of the world" (Eph. 1:4).[4]

This plan includes not only the reconciliation of people to God, but the reconciliation of "all things in heaven and on earth" (Eph. 1:10). Or, as Paul puts it in Colossians 1:20, it is God's intention through Christ "to reconcile to himself all things, whether things on earth or things in heaven, by making peace through his blood, shed on the cross." Central to this plan is the reconciliation of persons to God through the blood of Jesus Christ. But the reconciliation won by Christ reaches to all the alienations that resulted from our sin—between man and his physical environment. As mind-boggling as the thought is, Scripture teaches that this reconciliation even includes the redemption of the physical universe from the effects of sin as everything is brought under its proper headship in Jesus Christ (Rom. 8:19-21). Or as the New International Version suggests in translating Ephesians 1:10, God's purpose is "to bring all things in heaven and on earth together under one head, even Christ."[5]

This is God's master plan as seen in Ephesians. The same perspective comes through in Paul's other writings, especially in the first two chapters of Colossians. In 2 Corinthians 5:17-21 we learn that "God was reconciling the world to himself in Christ" and has entrusted to the Church both the message (*logos*) and the ministry (*diakonia*) of reconciliation. Of similar importance is the teaching of Romans 8 that the salvation freedom of the Christian will, in God's plan, extend to the whole of creation, for "the creation itself will be liberated from its bondage to decay and brought into the glorious freedom of the children of God" (Rom. 8:21).

In all these passages, Paul begins with the fact of individual and corporate personal salvation through Christ. From this he goes on to place personal salvation in cosmic perspective. We are permitted no either/or here, no spiritual tunnel vision. The redemption of persons is the *center* of God's plan, but it is not the *circumference* of that plan. Paul switches from a close-up shot to a long-distance view. He uses a zoom lens for the most part, taking a close-up of personal redemption, but periodically zooming to a long-distance, wide-angle view which takes in "all things"—things visible and invisible; things past, present and future; things in heaven and things on earth; all the principalities and powers—in the cosmic/historical scene. To understand truly what God in Christ has done for and through man, we must step back and look at God's entire cosmic design.

This is the Pauline view of God's master plan. Is it also the larger biblical view? In other Scriptures we find in essence the same perspective, for all Scripture is God-breathed. All the promises of cosmic restoration in the Old Testament apply here, reaching their climax in Isaiah's sublime vision (Is. 11:6-9; 35:1-10; 65:17-25). The basic message of the book of Revelation is the harmonious uniting of all things under the lordship of Christ as all evil, all discord is destroyed. In a somewhat different context, this same "summing up" perspective is evident in Hebrews 1-2. Christ's parables of the Kingdom also point in this direction. And Isaiah, Peter and John speak of God creating a new heaven and a new earth (Is. 65:17; 66:22; 2 Pet. 3:13; Rev. 21:1). The testimony of Scripture is consistent: the same God who created the universe perfect, and sustains it in its fallen condition (Heb. 1:3), will restore all things through the work of Jesus Christ. As we shall see, it is Paul's particular task to emphasize the role of the Church in this cosmic redemption.

We cannot fully understand this cosmic design, this *oikonomia*, of God to unite all things in Christ. That is why Paul continually calls it a secret or hidden thing, a *musterion*.[6] But we can at least comprehend the basic outline of this plan and that this plan centers in Jesus' great reconciling, conquering work accomplished through his life, death and resurrection which is now being applied by the continuing work of the Holy Spirit.

Now or Then?

A very thorny problem here is the whole question of evil. If God is "reconciling all things to himself" through Jesus Christ, what is to become of those who reject Christ, and of Satan and his kingdom? Scripture does not answer all our questions here, but it does make plain that every alien authority and power will be destroyed (I Cor. 15:24-25). Jesus himself spoke forcefully of the eternal destruction of the wicked (for instance, in Mt. 25:31-46). Revelation tells that Satan and his followers will suffer eternal judgment (20:10; 21:8) and that nothing impure will enter the New Jerusalem (21:27). These Scriptures spell out what the Psalms repeatedly proclaim: God the King will conquer and destroy all his enemies. Our understanding of God's plan for reconciliation must be consistent with such scriptures, even if we cannot fully understand how this is possible.

When does God accomplish his reconciling work? Nearly all Christians admit that, in one sense or another, God is bringing history to a cosmic climax. But one branch of the Church has said, "Not now, *then!*" And in reaction, another group has said, "Not then, *now!*" The argument has centered on the nature of the Kingdom of God. Those who postpone any real presence of the Kingdom until after Christ's return ("Not now, *then!*") expect substantial renewal now only in the realm of individual religious experience, but not in politics, art, education or culture in general, and not even, really, in the Church. On the other side are those who so emphasize present social renewal that both personal conversion and the space-time future return of Christ are denied or overshadowed, and our deep sinfulness and rebellion are not taken seriously.

Our hope should be that orthodox Christians throughout the world can come to see that the Kingdom of God is neither entirely present nor entirely future. There should be no false antithesis between the presence and the future coming of the Kingdom. The Kingdom of God (the uniting of all things under Christ) is now here, is coming and will come. This is certainly one of the lessons of the parables of the Kingdom.

Francis Schaeffer expresses this more balanced view when he speaks of a "substantial healing" now in all areas of alienation caused by sin. Avoiding the extremes sometimes found both in premillennialism and in postmillennialism, Schaeffer says Christians should not put all real reconciliation off into an eschatological future, neither should they expect total perfection now. What God promises is a substantial healing now and a total healing after Christ's return.[7]

What this means is that God has already begun the reconciliation of all things in human history. The "fullness of time" has come (Gal. 4:4; Eph. 1:10), but not in total fullness. The decisive act of God's reconciling work has taken place in Jesus Christ. God's cosmic plan is now unfolding.

The Church is not the Kingdom but it is bound up with the Kingdom. It is the people of the Kingdom of God, the "eschatological community" which already lives under and proclaims God's rule.[8] Jesus' disciples are colaborers with him in revealing the Kingdom, for the head and body act together (2 Cor. 5:18-6:1; 1 Cor. 3:9). But even in its action the Church knows and confesses that the full coming of the Kingdom awaits Jesus' final revealing at his second coming.

We must now examine in more detail the question of the place of the Church in God's master plan.

What is the place of the Church in God's cosmic plan? What, in fact, is the Church?

A remarkable phrase occurs in Ephesians 3:10. God's cosmic plan, Paul says, is that "through the church, the manifold wisdom of God should be made known to the rulers and authorities in the heavenly realms."[9]

Let us look closely at this passage:

In reading this, then, you will be able to understand my insight into the mystery of Christ, which was not made known to men in other generations as it has now been revealed by the Spirit to God's holy apostles and prophets. This mystery is that through the gospel the Gentiles are heirs together with Israel, members together of one body, and sharers together in the promise in Christ Jesus...Although I am less than the least of all God's people, this grace was given to me: to preach to the Gentiles the unsearchable riches of Christ, and to make plain to everyone my administration [oikonomia] of this mystery, which for ages past was kept hidden in God, who created all things. His intent was that now, through the church, the manifold wisdom of God should be made known to the rulers and authorities in the heavenly realms, according to his eternal purpose which he accomplished in Christ Jesus our Lord (Eph. 3:4-6, 8-11).

The mystery, now made known, is that Gentiles as well as Jews may share in God's promised redemption. In fact Jew and Gentile are brought together into "one body." Through Jesus Christ, as Paul had explained already, God has "made the two one and has destroyed the barrier, the dividing wall of hostility." So all Christians are one body, "one new man." This was "through the cross, by which he put to death their hostility" (Eph. 2:14-16).

Note the two dimensions here. Jewish and Gentile believers are reconciled both to God and to each other. They have joined in a reconciling relationship to Jesus that transcends and destroys their old hostility toward each other. No longer enemies, they are now brothers and sisters.

What then is the mystery of God's plan? It is that in Christ God acts with such redemptive power that he is able to overcome hatreds and heal hostilities. The mystery is not merely that the gospel is preached to Gentiles; it is that through this preaching Gentile believers are now "heirs together" and "members of one body."

It is in this context that we can understand verse 10. God's "manifold wisdom" is now made known through Christ's reconciling love which brings Jew and Gentile together as brothers in the community of God's people, the Church. But Jew and Gentile only? Was the miracle of the gospel exhausted by the reconciliation of Jew and Gentile in the first century A.D.? Certainly not! There is more to the mystery of God's plan. The initial, historic reconciliation shows us that God reconciles alienated persons and peoples to himself through the blood of the cross. It started with the reconciliation of Jew and Gentile and extends to free and slave, man and woman, black and white, rich and poor (Col. 3:10-11; Gal. 3:28).

This is why Paul can say that now "through the church, the manifold wisdom of God" is "made known to the rulers and authorities in the heavenly realms." For it is precisely in the Church where such reconciliation takes place. The Church is the fruit of Christ's reconciling love, and thus the revelation of God's manifold wisdom. And the Church, as Christ's body, shares Christ's reconciling work.

It is in this sense that the Church is the agent of God's plan. This is why Peter,

Paul, James and John direct so many appeals to believers to be reconciled to each other, to watch carefully how they walk, to avoid all partiality, to walk in love and fellowship with the brothers and sisters. Their faithfulness, and ours, has kingdom significance.

The Church is more than God's agent of evangelism or social change, it is in submission to Christ, the agent of God's entire cosmic purpose. The Kingdom of God is coming, and to the extent that this coming of the Kingdom occurs in history before the return of Christ, God's plan is to be accomplished through the Church. This agrees beautifully with what we have already seen: God's plan is to sum up all things in Christ, and the Church is the body of Christ. What God is doing in Jesus Christ and what he is doing in and through the Church are part of one whole.

However we understand the Church, it must be seen as related to God's kingdom purposes. But to say the Church is the agent of the Kingdom of God can mean radically different, and even contradictory, things according to how the Church itself is understood. So we must look carefully at the biblical picture of the Church.

The Biblical Perspective

The Bible says the Church is nothing less than the body of Christ. It is the bride of Christ (Rev. 21:9), the flock of God (I Pet. 5:2), the living temple of the Holy Spirit (Eph. 2:21-22). Virtually all biblical figures for the Church emphasize an essential, living, love relationship between Christ and the Church. This underscores the key role of the Church in God's plan and reminds us that "Christ loved the church and gave himself up for her" (Eph. 5:25). If the Church is the *body* of Christ—the means of the head's action in the world—then the Church is an indispensable part of the gospel and ecclesiology is inseparable from soteriology. Therefore, to adopt what might be called an "anti-church stance" would be to dilute the very gospel itself and at the same time to demonstrate a misunderstanding of what the Bible means by "the church."

The Bible shows the Church in the midst of culture, struggling to be faithful but sometimes adulterated by unnatural alliances with paganism and Jewish legalism. In Scripture the earthly and heavenly sides of the Church fit together in one whole and do not leave us with two incompatible churches or with a split-level view of the Church. The Church is one; it is the one body of Christ that now exists both on earth and "in the heavenly realms" (Eph. 1:3; 2:6; 3:10). This view of the Church is sharply relevant for the modern age for reasons which are basic to the biblical view of the Church.[10]

First, *the Bible sees the Church in cosmic/historical perspective.* The Church is the people of God which God has been forming and through which he has been acting down through history. In this sense the Church has roots that go back into the Old Testament, back even to the Fall. Its mission stretches forward into all remaining history and into eternity. This horizontal line is the historical dimension.

The cosmic dimension reminds us that our space-time world is really part of a larger, spiritual universe in which God reigns. The Church is the body given to

Christ, the conquering Savior. God has chosen to place the Church with Christ at the very center of his plan to reconcile the world to himself (Eph. 1:20-23).

The Church's mission, therefore, is to glorify God by continuing in the world the works of the Kingdom which Jesus began (Mt. 5:16). This both justifies and demands the Church's broader ministry "to preach good news to the poor...to proclaim freedom for the prisoners and recovery of sight for the blind, to release the oppressed, to proclaim the year of the Lord's favor" (Lk.4:18-19).

Second, *the Bible sees the Church in charismatic, rather than in institutional, terms.* While the Church is, in a broad sense, an institution, it is more fundamentally a charismatic community. That is, it exists by the grace (*charis*) of God and is built up by the gifts of grace (*charismata*) bestowed by the Spirit. As seen biblically, it is not structured the same way a business corporation or university is, but is structured like the human body—on the basis of life. At its most basic level it is a community, not a hierarchy; an organism, not an organization (I Cor. 12; Rom. 12:5-8; Eph. 4:1-16; Mt. 18:20, 1 Pet. 4:10-11).

Third, *the Bible sees the Church as the community of God's people.* Here the cosmic and the charismatic are united, and we see the Church as both within the world and as transcending the world.

Since the Church is the people of God, it includes all God's people in all times and in all places, as well as those who have now crossed the space-time boundary and live in the immediate presence of God. But the people of God must have a visible, local expression, and at the local level the Church is the community of the Holy Spirit. As Samuel Escobar has said, "God calls those who become his people to be part of a community. So the new humanity that Christ is creating becomes visible in communities that have a quality of life that reflects Christ's example."[11]

The Church finds its identity in this unified, complementary rhythm of being a people and a community, both within a city or culture and within the larger worldwide context. People and community together constitute what the New Testament means by *ekklesia*, the called-out and called-together Church of God.

The biblical figures of body of Christ, bride of Christ, household, temple or vineyard of God, and so forth, give us the basic idea of the Church. Any contemporary definition must be in harmony with these figures or models. But these are metaphors and not definitions. I believe the most biblical definition is to say the Church is *the community of God's people.* The two key elements here are the Church as a people, a new race or humanity, and the Church as a community or fellowship—the *koinonia* of the Holy Spirit.[12]

The Community of God's People

These twin concepts emphasize that the Church is, in the first place, people—not an institutional structure. They emphasize further that the Church is no mere collection of isolated individuals, but that it has a corporate or communal nature which is absolutely essential to its true being. And finally, these truths show that being a community and a people is a gift from God through the work of Jesus Christ and the indwelling of the Holy Spirit. It is not produced by human techniques or plans. The Church is constituted the people of God by the action of

Jesus Christ, and this reality opens the door to the possibility of true and deep community. Here the figure of the body takes on added meaning, including both the fact of community and the fact of peoplehood.

This concept of peoplehood is firmly rooted in the Old Testament and underlines the objective fact of God's acting throughout history to call and prepare "a chosen people, a royal priesthood, a holy nation, a people belonging to God" (1 Pet. 2:9; compare Ex. 19:5-6). The Greek word for "people" is *laos*, from which comes the English "laity." This reminds us that the *whole* Church is a laity, a people. Here the emphasis is on the *universality* of the Church—God's people scattered throughout the world in hundreds of specific denominations, movements and other structures. It is the inclusive, worldwide, corporate reality of the multitude of men and women who throughout history, have been reconciled to God through Jesus Christ. This fact celebrates the moving of God in history to constitute a pilgrim people and is especially related to the concept of the covenant. *Seen in cosmic/historical perspective, the Church is the people of God.*

On the other hand, the Church is a community or fellowship, a *koinonia*. This emphasis is found more clearly in the New Testament and grows directly out of the experience of Pentecost. If peoplehood underlines the continuity of God's plan from Old to New Testament, community calls attention to the "new covenant," the "new wine," the "new thing" God did in the resurrection of Jesus Christ and the Spirit's baptism at Pentecost. The emphasis here is on the *locality* of the Church in its intense, interactive common life. *Seen as a charismatic organism, the Church is the community of the Holy Spirit.*

The Church as community emphasizes the local, temporal life of the Church in a given cultural context. Here we come down from the ethereal heights to the nitty-gritty business of Christians living together, sharing a common life. Here also we discover the basic fact that true community is essential for effective witness. And here too, as a result, we face the problem of wineskins—the necessity of dealing with practical structures in order to permit and encourage true community.

To speak of the Church as community is to take a somewhat more restricted view, since the Church is more than community. It is also the scattered people of God, the leaven of the gospel in the lump of the world, dispersed and working in every area of society. But community is essential, for where it is lacking, and where there are no working structures to nourish it, the leaven becomes inactive and the salt loses its savor.

It is critically important—especially in a worldwide, multicultural situation such as the Church faces today—to be clear that the essence of the Church is people, not organization; that it is a community, not an institution. The great divide in contemporary thinking about the Church is located precisely here. Biblically, the Church is the community of God's people, and this is a spiritual reality which is valid in every culture. But all ecclesiastical institutions—whether seminaries, denominational structures, mission boards, publishing houses or what have you—are not the Church. Rather, they are supportive institutions created to serve the Church in its life and mission.

They are culturally bound and can be sociologically understood and evaluated. But they are not themselves the Church. And when such institutions are confused with the Church, or seen as part of its essence, all kinds of unfortunate misunderstandings result, and the Church is bound to a particular, present cultural expression.

The Church is the body of Christ, the community of the Holy Spirit, the people of God. It is the community of the King and the agent in the world of God's plan for the reconciliation of all things. God's agent of the Kingdom must not be considered just one means among many. For from the cross to eternity it remains true that "Christ loved the church and gave himself up for her to make her holy...and to present her to himself as a radiant church, without stain or wrinkle or any other blemish" (Eph. 5:25-27).

End Notes

1. W. Robertson Nicoll, ed., *The Expositor's Greek Testament* (Grand Rapids: Eerdmans, 1961), 3:259. Thus our word *economic*. Note also the word *oikonomia*, and its various translations in Ephesians 3:2; Colossians 1:25; 1 Timothy 1:4; Luke 16:2-4.

2. Gerhard Kittel and Gerhard Friedrich, eds., *Theological Dictionary of the New Testament*, trans. G. Bromiley (Grand Rapids: Eerdmans, 1964-74), 5:151-52.

3. Bernard Zylstra, quoted in *Perspective* (newsletter of the Association for the Advancement of Christian Scholarship), 7, no. 2 (March/April, 1973), p. 141.

4. Note the recurrence of this significant phrase in Matthew 13:35; 25:34; John 17:24; Ephesians 1:4; Hebrews 4:3; 1 Peter 1:20; Revelation 13:8; 17:8. These passages make it clear that Christ was appointed as Savior from eternity and that God's kingdom plan is eternal.

5. See Kittel and Friedrich, *op. cit.*, 2:681-82.

6. A. A. Van Ruler, citing W. C. van Unnik, notes that the "Fathers use the word *mysterion* not only for the sacraments, but for all of God's action in history, the whole time filled by the Spirit in and from Jesus Christ. I think we should return to this broad and deep use of the term." *The Christian Church and the Old Testament*, pp.78-79.

7. Francis A. Schaeffer, *The God Who Is There* (Downers Grove, IL: Inter-Varsity Press, 1968), p. 152; and his *Pollution and the Death of Man* (Wheaton, IL: Tyndale, 1970), pp. 66-69.

8. John Bright, *The Kingdom of God* (Nashville: Abingdon Press, 1953), pp. 32-43.

9. The phrase *through the church* is ambiguously translated "by the church" in the AV, thus making the force of the fact that the Church is the *agent* of God's plan.

10. The three points which follow are summarized from Chap. 12 of Howard A. Snyder's *The Problem of Wineskins: church structure in a technological age* (Downers Grove, IL: Inter-Varsity Press, 1975).

11. Samuel Escobar, "Evangelism and Man's Search for Freedom, Justice, and Fulfillment" in *Let the Earth Hear His Voice*, compendium of the International Congress on World Evangelization, Lausanne, 1974, ed. by J. D. Douglas (Lausanne: World Wide Publications, 1975), p. 312.

12. Hans Kung similarly describes the Church as "the People of God...the community of the faithful"; the Church is "the community of the new people of God called out and called together." *Structures of the Church*, trans. Salvator Attanasio (London: Burns and Oates. 1964), pp. x, 11.

Study Questions

1. Restate God's cosmic plan. What is the role of the Church?

2. What distinguishes the Church from the Kingdom? What implications does this distinction have for missions?

3. Do you agree with Snyder that the Church is not so much an institution as a charismatic community? What practical implications does this have for planting churches?

16

Prayer: Rebelling Against the Status Quo

David F. Wells

You will be appalled by the story I am about to relate to you. Appalled, that is, if you have any kind of social conscience.

A poor black, living on Chicago's South Side, sought to have her apartment properly heated during the frigid winter months. Despite city law on the matter, her unscrupulous landlord refused. The woman was a widow, desperately poor, and ignorant of the legal system; but she took the case to court on her own behalf. Justice, she declared, ought to be done. It was her ill fortune, however, to appear repeatedly before the same judge who, as it turned out, was an atheist and a bigot. The only principle by which he abode was, as he put it, that "blacks should be kept in their place." The possibilities of a ruling favorable to the widow were, therefore, bleak. They became even bleaker as she realized she lacked the indispensable ingredient necessary for favorable rulings in cases like these—namely, a satisfactory bribe. Nevertheless, she persisted.

At first, the judge did not so much as even look up from reading the novel on his lap before dismissing her. But then he began to notice her. Just another black, he thought, stupid enough to think she could get justice. Then her persistence made him self-conscious. This turned to guilt and anger. Finally, raging and embarrassed, he granted her petition and enforced the law. Here was a massive victory over "the system"—at least as it functioned in his corrupted courtroom.

In putting the matter like this I have not, of course, been quite honest. For this never really happened in Chicago (as far as I know), nor is it even my "story." It is a parable told by Jesus (Luke 18:1-8) to illustrate the nature of petitionary prayer.

The parallel Jesus drew was obviously not between God and the corrupt judge, but between the widow and the petitioner. This parallel has two aspects.

David Wells is presently the Andrew Mutch Distinguished Professor of Historical and Systematic Theology at Gordon-Conwell Theological Seminary in South Hamilton, Massachusetts. Wells is the author of numerous articles and twelve books, including *The Person of Christ: A Biblical and Historical Analysis of the Incarnation, God the Evangelist, Turning to God,* and *No Place for Truth.* Adapted from "Prayer: Rebelling Against the Status Quo," *Christianity Today,* Vol. XVII (17), No. 6, November 2, 1979. Used by permission.

First, the widow refused to accept her unjust situation, just as the Christian should refuse to resign himself or herself to the world in its fallenness. Second, despite discouragements, the widow persisted with her case as should the Christian with his or hers. The first aspect has to do with prayer's *nature* and the second with its *practice*.

I want to argue that our feeble and irregular prayer, especially in its petitionary aspect, is too frequently addressed in the wrong way. When confronting this failing, we are inclined to flagellate ourselves for our weak wills, our insipid desires, our ineffective technique, and our wandering minds. We keep thinking that somehow our *practice* is awry and we rack our brains to see if we can discover where. I suggest that the problem lies in a misunderstanding of prayer's *nature* and our practice will never have that widow's persistence until our outlook has her clarity.

What, then, is the nature of petitionary prayer? It is, in essence, rebellion—rebellion against the world in its fallenness, the absolute and undying refusal to accept as normal what is pervasively abnormal. It is, in this its negative aspect, the refusal of every agenda, every scheme, every interpretation that is at odds with the norm as originally established by God. As such, it is itself an expression of the unbridgeable chasm that separates Good from Evil, the declaration that Evil is not a variation on Good but its antithesis.

Or, to put it the other way around, to come to an acceptance of life "as it is," to accept it on its own terms—which means acknowledging the *inevitability* of the way it works—is to surrender a Christian view of God. This resignation to what is abnormal has within it the hidden and unrecognized assumption that the power of God to change the world, to overcome Evil by Good, will not be actualized.

Nothing destroys petitionary prayer (and with it, a Christian view of God) as quickly as resignation. "At all times," Jesus declared, "we should pray" and not "lose heart," thereby acquiescing to what is (Luke 18:1).

The dissipation of petitionary prayer in the presence of resignation has an interesting historical pedigree. Those religions that stress quietistic acquiescence always disparage petitionary prayer. This was true of the Stoics who claimed that such prayer showed that one was unwilling to accept the existent world as an expression of God's will. One was trying to escape from it by having it modified. That, they said, was bad. A similar argument is found in Buddhism. And the same result, although arrived at by a different process of reasoning, is commonly encountered in our secular culture.

Secularism is that attitude that sees life as an end in itself. Life, it is thought, is severed from any relationship to God. Consequently the only norm or "given" in life, whether for meaning or for morals, is the world as it is. With this, it is argued, we must come to terms; to seek some other referent around which to structure our lives is futile and "escapist." It is not only that God, the object of petitionary prayer, has often become indistinct, but that his relationship to the world is seen in a new way. And it is a way that does not violate secular assumption. God may be "present" and "active" in the world, but it is not a presence and an activity that changes anything.

Against all of this, it must be asserted that petitionary prayer only flourishes where there is a twofold belief: first, that God's name is hallowed too irregularly, his kingdom has come too little, and his will is done too infrequently; second, that God himself can change this situation. Petitionary prayer, therefore, is the expression of the hope that life as we meet it, on the one hand, *can* be otherwise and, on the other hand, that it *ought* to be otherwise. It is therefore impossible to seek to live in God's world on his terms, doing his work in a way that is consistent with who he is, without engaging in regular prayer.

That, I believe, is the real significance of petitionary prayer in our Lord's life. Much of his prayer life is left unexplained by the Gospel writers (e.g., Mark 1:35; Luke 5:16; 9:18; 11:1), but a pattern in the circumstances that elicited prayer is discernible.

First, petitionary prayer preceded great decisions in his life, such as the choosing of the disciples (Luke 6:12); indeed, the only possible explanation of his choice of that ragtag bunch of nonentities, boastful, ignorant and uncomprehending as they were, was that he had prayed before choosing them. Second, he prayed when pressed beyond measure, when his day was unusually busy with many competing claims upon his energies and attention (e.g., Matt. 14:23). Third, he prayed in the great crises and turning points of his life, such as his baptism, the Transfiguration, and the Cross (Luke 3:21; 9:28-29). Finally, he prayed before and during unusual temptation, the most vivid occasion being Gethsemane (Matt. 26:36-45). As the "hour" of evil descended, the contrast between the way Jesus met it and the way his disciples met it is explained only by the fact that he persevered in prayer and they slept in faintness of heart. Each of these events presented our Lord with the possibility of adopting an agenda, accepting a perspective, or pursuing a course that was other than God's. His rejection of the alternative was each time signaled by his petitionary prayer. It was his means of refusing to live in this world or to do his Father's business on any other terms than his Father's. As such, it was rebellion against the world in its perverse and fallen abnormality.

To pray declares that God and his world are at cross-purposes; to "sleep," or "faint," or "lose heart" is to act as if they are not. Why, then, do we pray so little for our local church? Is it really that our technique is bad, our wills weak, or our imaginations listless? I don't believe so. There is plenty of strong-willed and lively discussion—which in part or in whole may be justified—about the mediocrity of the preaching, the emptiness of the worship, the superficiality of the fellowship, and the ineffectiveness of the evangelism. So, why, then, don't we pray as persistently as we talk? The answer, quite simply, is that we don't believe it will make any difference. We accept, however despairingly, that the situation is unchangeable, that what is will always be. This is not a problem about the practice of prayer, but rather about its *nature*. Or, more precisely, it is about the nature of God and his relationship to this world.

Unlike the widow in the parable, we find it is easy to come to terms with the unjust and fallen world around us—even when it intrudes into Christian institutions. It is not always that we are unaware of what is happening, but simply that we feel completely impotent to change anything. That impotence leads us, however unwillingly, to strike a truce with what is wrong.

In other words, we have lost our anger, both at the level of social witness and before God in prayer. Fortunately, he has not lost his; for the wrath of God is his opposition to what is wrong, the means by which truth is put forever on the throne and error forever on the scaffold. Without God's wrath, there would be no reason to live morally in the world and every reason not to. So the wrath of God, in this sense, is intimately connected with petitionary prayer that also seeks the ascendancy of truth in all instances and the corresponding banishment of evil.

The framework Jesus gave us for thinking about this was the Kingdom of God. The Kingdom is that sphere where the king's sovereignty is recognized. And, because of the nature of our king, that sovereignty is exercised supernaturally. In Jesus, the long-awaited "age to come" arrived; in him and through him, the Messianic incursion into the world has happened. Being a Christian, then, is not a matter of simply having had the right religious experience but rather of starting to live in that sphere which is authentically divine. Evangelism is not successful because our technique is "right," but because this "age" breaks into the lives of sinful people. And this "age to come," which is already dawning, is not the possession of any one people or culture. God's "age," the "age" of his crucified Son, is dawning in the whole world. Our praying, therefore, should look beyond the concerns of our private lives to include the wide horizon of all human life in which God is concerned. If the Gospel is universal, prayer cannot restrict itself to being local.

It is not beside the point, therefore, to see the world as a courtroom in which a "case" can still be made against what is wrong and for what is right. Our feebleness in prayer happens because we have lost sight of this, and until we regain it we will not persist in our role as litigants. But there is every reason why we should regain our vision and utilize our opportunity, for the Judge before whom we appear is neither an atheist nor corrupt, but the glorious God and Father of our Lord Jesus Christ. Do you really think, then, that he will fail to "bring about justice for his chosen ones who cry to him night and day? Will he keep putting them off?" "I tell you," our Lord declares, "he will see that they get justice, and quickly" (Luke 18:7-8).

Study Questions

1. What relationship exists between petitionary prayer and the mission of the church?

2. Wells states that we have two problem areas with petitionary prayer: its practice and its nature. Can you restate these problems? Which is the most important? Why?

3. Take note of Wells's interpretation of the "Lord's Prayer." How is this a "missions" prayer?

17

Lost

Robertson McQuilkin

Salvation is found in no one else, for there is no other name under heaven given to men, by which we must be saved (Acts 4:12).

Have you ever experienced the terror of being lost—in some trackless mountain wilderness, perhaps, or in the labyrinth of a great, strange city? Hope of finding your way out fades and fear begins to seep in. You have likely seen that fear of lostness on the tear-streaked face of a child frantically screaming or quietly sobbing because he is separated from his parent in a huge shopping center. Lost. Alone.

Equally terrifying and more common is the feeling of being hopelessly entangled or trapped in a frustrating personal condition or circumstance: alcoholism, cancer, divorce. Incredibly alone! Lost.

The Bible uses the word "lost" to describe an even more terrible condition. Those who are away from the Father's house and haven't found the way back to Him are "lost." Jesus saw the crowds of people surging about Him as sheep without a shepherd, helpless and hopeless, and He was deeply moved.

Worse than being trapped and not knowing the way out is to be lost and not even know it, for then one does not look for salvation, recognize it when it comes, nor accept it when it is offered. That's being lost.

How many are lost in our world? We are told there are 200 million Evangelicals. Some of these are lost no doubt, but at least that many people believe Jesus is the only way of salvation and that through faith in Him one is forgiven and made a member of God's family. Surely some who are not evangelical have saving faith. So let us double the number to a hypothetical 400 million. Those who remain number more than four billion people or nine of every ten on earth. These are the lost—longing for salvation but not finding it, or trusting some

Robertson McQuilkin was formerly the President and is now Chancellor at Columbia Biblical Seminary and Graduate School of Missions. He is the author of several books, including *Understanding and Applying the Bible*, and *The Great Omission*, from which this article was taken. Copyright, 1984, Baker Book House. Grand Rapids, MI. Used by permission.

other way to find meaning and hope.

The tragedy of this century of exploding population is that three of four people have never heard with understanding the way to life in Christ and, even more tragic, half the people of the world cannot hear because there is no one near enough to tell them. As we approach the end of the second millennium A.D., one of every two on planet earth lives in a tribe or culture or language group that has no evangelizing church at all. If someone does not go in from the outside they have no way of knowing about Jesus.

But are these people in the "dark half of the world" really lost? What of those who have never had a chance, who have never heard—are *any* of them lost? Are *all* of them lost?

Throughout church history there have been those who teach that none will finally be lost. The old universalism taught that all ultimately will be saved because God is good. Not much was heard of this position from the days of Origen in the third century until the nineteenth century when it was revived, especially by the Universalist Church. Simultaneously with the founding of the Universalist Church, which was honest enough to be up front about it and call itself by that name, the teaching began to spread in many mainline denominations.

There are problems with this position. Philosophically, such a teaching undermines belief in the atoning death of Christ. For if all sin will ultimately be overlooked by a gracious deity, Christ never should have died. It was not only unnecessary, it was surely the greatest error in history, if not actually criminal on the part of God for allowing it to happen. Universalism, therefore, philosophically demands a view of the death of Christ as having some purpose other than as an atonement for sin.

Another problem the Universalists faced is that Scripture consistently teaches a division after death between those who are acceptable to God and those who are not. This teaching and that concerning the atonement are so strong in the Bible that Universalists did not accept the authority of Scripture. Thus the marriage between the Universalist Church and the Unitarian Church was quite natural.

A New Universalism arose in the twentieth century which took the Bible more seriously. It was Trinitarian. Christ did die for sinners, and *all* will ultimately be saved on the basis of Christ's provision.

Karl Barth and many of his neo-orthodox disciples took such a position. All will be saved because God is all-powerful. His purposes will be accomplished. And He purposes redemption.

There were philosophical and biblical problems with this position also. Philosophically, if all will be saved eventually, for whatever reason, preaching the gospel is not really necessary. Why did Christ make this the primary mission of the church if all will ultimately find acceptance with God with or without the gospel? The more serious problem is biblical: Christ clearly taught of an eternal hell, of a great gulf between the saved and the lost (Luke 16:19-31). In fact, He clearly taught that the majority are on the broad road that leads to destruction (Matt. 7:13-14).

Because Universalism cannot be reconciled with biblical data, there were those who promoted what was called a "Wider Hope." Not all will be saved, but many who have not heard of Christ will be saved because God is just and will not condemn the sincere seeker after truth. The problem is that if sincerity saves in religion, it is the only realm in which it saves. For example, it does not save in engineering. The architect who designed the magnificent John Hancock building in Boston was sincere. The builder was sincere. The glassmaker was sincere. The owner, especially, was sincere. But when the giant sheets of glass began to fall on the streets below, sincerity did not atone for error. Neither does sincerity save in chemistry. We do not say, "If you drink arsenic, sincerely believing it to be Coca-Cola, according to your faith be it unto you." Sincerity does not alter reality. We shall consider the question of God's justice later.

The nineteenth-century doctrine of the Wider Hope has been superseded by what I have called the "New Wider Hope." According to this teaching those who live by the light they have may be saved on the merits of Christ's death through general revelation. Or, at least, they will be given a chance at death or after death. This is a more conservative version of the New Universalism. Richard Quebedeaux identifies this position as held by some "younger evangelicals," the New Left. A practical problem is that preaching the gospel seems almost criminal, for it brings with it greater condemnation for those who reject it, whereas they conceivably could have been saved through general revelation had they not heard the gospel. In any event, it certainly seems less urgent to proclaim the way of salvation to those who may well be saved without that knowledge. A mutation of this view is the idea that only those who reject the gospel will be lost. This viewpoint is not widespread because it makes bad news of the Good News! If people are lost only if they hear and reject, it is far better not to hear and be saved. On this view it would be better to destroy the message than to proclaim it!

For one committed to the authority of Scripture, our debate concerning the reasonableness of each position must yield to the authority of Scripture. What does Scripture teach concerning the eternal spiritual condition of those who have not heard the gospel?

> "For God so loved the world that he gave his one and only Son, that whoever believes in him shall not perish but have eternal life. For God did not send his Son into the world to condemn the world, but to save the world through him. Whoever believes in him is not condemned, but whoever does not believe stands condemned already because he has not believed in the name of God's one and only Son."

> "Whoever believes in the Son has eternal life, but whoever rejects the Son will not see life, for God's wrath remains on him" (John 3:16-18, 36).

Scripture teaches clearly that there are those who perish and those who do not. Notice that it is those who believe *on Christ*—not simply those who, through their encounter with creation and their own innate moral judgment, believe in a righteous creator—who receive eternal life. God's intent is to "save the world through him [Christ]" (3:17). The word "through" speaks of agency: it is by means of Jesus Christ that a person gains eternal life.

The passage does not deny other agencies, however. The Japanese proverb assures us that many roads lead up famed Mount Fuji but they all reach the top. This is the Japanese way of expressing the viewpoint that all religions will have a good outcome. But Jesus Christ Himself said, "No one comes to the Father except through me" (John 14:6). In other words, Jesus Christ is the *only* agency of salvation.

The New Wider Hope would affirm this. Salvation is by Jesus Christ alone. But, it would hold, that does not mean Jesus Christ must be known by a person for that person to be saved.

Jesus assures us that people will be judged because they have not believed on the *name* (John 3:18). Peter is even more explicit in telling us that there is no salvation in any other *name* given among men (Acts 4:12). Surely it is no accident that the name is so prominent in the Bible, especially in teaching on saving faith. Peter did not say, "in no other person." When a person is named, the identity is settled and ambiguity is done away. Peter does not make room for us to call on the Ground of Being or the great "all." You will be saved, he tells us, if you call on and believe in the name of Jesus of Nazareth, the Messiah. John, Jesus, and Peter are not the only ones with this emphasis. Paul also speaks to the issue:

> ..."Everyone who calls on the name of the Lord will be saved." How, then, can they call on the one they have not believed in? And how can they believe in the one of whom they have not heard? And how can they hear without someone preaching to them? And how can they preach unless they are sent? As it is written, "How beautiful are the feet of those who bring good news!" (Rom. 10:13-15).

The ones who call on *the name* are the ones who will be saved. But what of those who have not heard so they cannot call? Paul does not assure us that those who have not heard may simply believe on whatever they have heard. Rather, "faith comes from hearing the message, and the message is heard through the word of Christ" (Rom. 10:17).

Scripture is very clear that there are two kinds of people, both in life and in death: the saved and the lost. It is also very clear on the way of salvation. But still, for those who truly care, questions may remain: Is God loving, powerful, fair, just?

Is God loving? Yes, God is good and that is why men are lost. In love He created a being in His own image, not a robot programmed to respond as the Maker designed. In creating such a being to freely love and be loved, God risked the possibility of such a being rejecting His love in favor of independence or even self-love. Humankind did, in fact, choose this option. Still true to His character, God provided a way back even though the cost was terrible. But the way back must not violate the image of God in man, must not force an obedient response. Rather, the God of love chooses to wait lovingly for the response of love. Those who wish to reject Him may do so.

But is it fair and just for God to condemn those who have not had an opportunity to respond to His offer of grace? The Bible does not teach that God will judge a person for rejecting Christ if he has not heard of Christ. In fact, the Bible teaches clearly that God's judgment is based on a person's response to the truth he has received.

> "That servant who knows his master's will and does not get ready or does not do what his master wants will be beaten with many blows. But the one who does not know and does things deserving punishment will be beaten with few blows. From everyone who has been given much, much will be demanded; and from the one who has been entrusted with much, much more will be asked" (Luke 12:47-48).

> "When you enter a town and are welcomed, eat what is set before you. Heal the sick who are there and tell them, ' The kingdom of God is near you.' But when you enter a town and are not welcomed, go into its streets and say, 'Even the dust of your town that sticks to our feet we wipe off against you. Yet be sure of this: The kingdom of God is near.' I tell you, it will be more bearable on that day for Sodom than for that town. Woe to you, Korazin! Woe to you, Bethsaida! For if the miracles that were performed in you had been performed in Tyre and Sidon, they would have repented long ago, sitting in sackcloth and ashes. But it will be more bearable for Tyre and Sidon at the judgment than for you. And you, Capernaum, will you be lifted up to the skies? No, you will go down to the depths. He who listens to you listens to me; he who rejects you rejects me; but he who rejects me rejects him who sent me" (Luke 10:8-16).

Judgment is against a person in proportion to his rejection of moral light. All have sinned; no one is innocent. Therefore, all stand condemned. But not all have the same measure of condemnation, for not all have sinned against equal amounts of light. God does not condemn a person who has not heard of Christ for rejecting Him, but rather for rejecting the light he does have.

Not all respond to the light they have by seeking to follow that light. But God's response to those who seek to obey the truth they have is the provision of more truth. To him who responds, more light will be given:

> The disciples came to him and asked, "Why do you speak to the people in parables?"

> He replied, "The knowledge of the secrets of the kingdom of heaven has been given to you, but not to them. Whoever has will be given more, and he will have an abundance. Whoever does not have, even what he has will be taken from him. This is why I speak to them in parables:

> > "Though seeing, they do not see;
> > though hearing, they do not hear or understand.

> "In them is fulfilled the prophecy of Isaiah:

> > "'You will be ever hearing but never understanding;
> > you will be ever seeing but never perceiving.
> > For this people's heart has become calloused;
> > they hardly hear with their ears,
> > and they have closed their eyes.
> > Otherwise they might see with their eyes,
> > hear with their ears,
> > understand with their hearts

and turn, and I would heal them.'

But blessed are your eyes because they see, and your ears because they hear" (Matt. 13:10-16).

He said to them, "Do you bring in a lamp to put it under a bowl or a bed? Instead, don't you put it on its stand? For whatever is hidden is meant to be disclosed, and whatever is concealed is meant to be brought out into the open. If anyone has ears to hear, let him hear."

"Consider carefully what you hear," he continued. "With the measure you use, it will be measured to you—and even more. Whoever has will be given more; whoever does not have, even what he has will be taken from him" (Mark 4:21-25).

This repeated promise of additional light to those who obey the light they have is a basic and very important biblical truth concerning God's justice and judgment. Cornelius, the Roman officer, responded to the light he had with prayer and good deeds. God did not leave him in ignorance and simply accept him on the basis of his response to the initial light he had received. God sent Peter to him with additional truth (Acts 10). To him who had, more was given. Since this is revealed as God's way of dealing with men, we can be very sure that every person has received adequate light to which he may respond. God's existence and His power are made clearly evident to all people through creation (Rom. 1:18-21) and through each person's innate moral judgment or conscience (Rom. 2:14,15). To the one who responds obediently, God will send additional light.

Of course, His method for sending this light is a human messenger. Paul makes clear in his letter to the church at Rome (10:14, 15) that the solution to the terrible lost condition of men is the preacher who is sent, the "beautiful feet" of he who goes. Ultimately, then, the problem is not with God's righteousness, but with ours.

But suppose no one goes? Will God send some angel or some other special revelation? On this, Scripture is silent and, I believe, for good reason. Even if God did have such an alternative plan, were He to reveal that to us, we who have proved so irresponsible and disobedient would no doubt cease altogether obedience to the Great Commission.

But the question will not go away. How does one respond in a Japanese village when a new convert inquires, "What about my ancestors?" My response is simple: I am not the judge. "Will not the Judge of all the earth do right?" (Gen. 18:25). Abraham was pleading with God for the salvation of innocent people who did not deserve to be condemned and destroyed along with the guilty. He was appealing to God's justice, and God responded with grace more than Abraham dared ask. This crucial question recorded in the first book of the Bible is answered in the last: "Yes, Lord God Almighty, true and just are your judgments" (Rev. 16:7). We are not called as judge—either of God, whose ways we do not fully know, nor of man, whose destiny we are not called upon to settle. Rather, we are commissioned as His representatives to find the lost, declare amnesty to the captive, release the prisoner.

We may not be able to prove from Scripture with absolute certainty that no soul since Pentecost has ever been saved by extraordinary means without the knowledge of Christ. But neither can we prove from Scripture that a single soul has been so saved. If there is an alternative, God has not told us of it. If God in His revelation felt it mandatory not to proffer such a hope, how much more should we refrain from such theorizing. It may or may not be morally right for me to think there may be another way and to hope there is some other escape. But for me to propose it to other believers, to discuss it as a possibility, is certainly dangerous, if not immoral. It is almost as wrong as writing out such a hope so that those who are under the judgment of God may read it, take hope, and die. So long as the truth revealed to us identifies only one way of escape, this is what we must live by and proclaim.

Consider the analogy of a security guard charged with the safety of residents on the tenth floor of a nursing home. He knows the floor plan posted in a prominent place, and it is his responsibility in case of fire to get the residents to the fire escape which has been clearly marked. Should a fire break out and lives be put in jeopardy, it would be his responsibility to get those people to the fire escape. If he discusses with the patients or with a colleague the possibility of some other unmarked fire escape or recalls to them the news report he read of someone who had jumped from the tenth floor of a building and survived, he could surely be charged with criminal negligence. He must live and labor in obedience to the facts that are certain and not delay to act. He must not lead people astray on the basis of conjecture or logical deduction from limited information.

When all has been said that can be said on this issue, the greatest remaining mystery is not the character of God nor the destiny of lost people. The greatest mystery is why those who are charged with rescuing the lost have spent two thousand years doing other things, good things, perhaps, but have failed to send and be sent until all have heard the liberating word of life in Christ Jesus. The lost condition of human beings breaks the Father's heart. What does it do to ours?

In a dream I found myself on an island—Sheep Island. Across the island sheep were scattered and lost. Soon I learned that a forest fire was sweeping across from the opposite side. It seemed that all were doomed to destruction unless there were some way of escape. Although there were many unofficial maps, I had a copy of the official map and there discovered that indeed there is a bridge to the mainland, a narrow bridge, built, it was said, at incredible cost.

My job, I was told, would be to get the sheep across that bridge. I discovered many shepherds herding the sheep who were found and seeking to corral those who were within easy access to the bridge. But most of the sheep were far off and the shepherds seeking them few. The sheep near the fire knew they were in trouble and were frightened; those at a distance were peacefully grazing, enjoying life.

I noticed two shepherds near the bridge whispering to one another and laughing. I moved near them to hear the cause of joy in such a dismal setting. "Perhaps the chasm is narrow somewhere, and at least the strong sheep have opportunity to save themselves," said one. "Maybe the current is gentle and the stream shallow. Then the courageous, at least, can make it across." The other responded, "That may well be. In fact, wouldn't it be great if this proves to be no island at all? Perhaps it is just a peninsula and great multitudes of sheep are already safe. Surely the owner would have provided some alternative route." And so they relaxed and went about other business.

In my mind I began to ponder their theories: Why would the owner have gone to such great expense to build a bridge, especially since it is a narrow bridge, and many of the sheep refuse to cross it even when they find it? In fact, if there is a better way by which many will be saved more easily, building the bridge is a terrible blunder. And if this isn't an island, after all, what is to keep the fire from sweeping right across into the mainland and destroying everything? As I pondered these things I heard a quiet voice behind me saying, "There is a better reason than the logic of it, my friend. Logic alone could lead you either way. Look at your map."

There on the map, by the bridge, I saw a quotation from the first undershep-herd, Peter: "For neither is there salvation in any other, for there is no other way from the island to the mainland whereby a sheep may be saved." And then I dis-cerned, carved on the old rugged bridge itself, "I am the bridge. No sheep escapes to safety but by me."

In a world in which nine of every ten people is lost, three of four have never heard the way out, and one of every two cannot hear, the church sleeps on. "How come?" Could it be we think there must be some other way? Or perhaps we don't really care that much.

Study Questions

1. State and briefly describe the four different views of salvation reviewed in the article, as well as McQuilkin's own.

2. What scriptural support does McQuilkin give to his "correct Biblical" view?

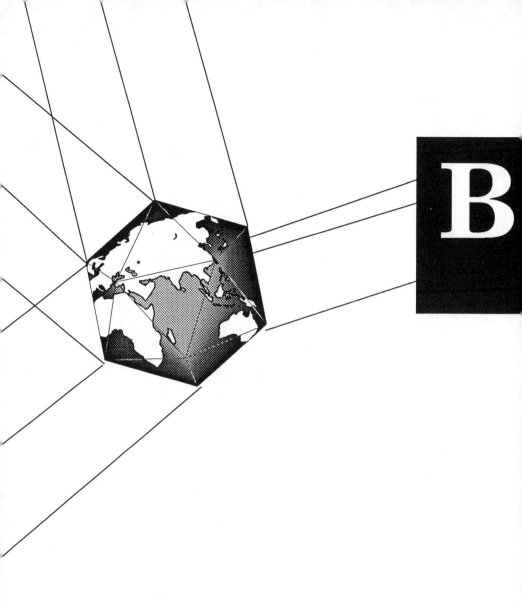

THE HISTORICAL PERSPECTIVE

1

The Kingdom Strikes Back: The Ten Epochs of Redemptive History

Ralph D. Winter

Man has virtually erased his own story. Human beings for as far back as we have any record have been pushing and shoving each other so much that they have destroyed well over 90 percent of their own handiwork. Their libraries, their literature, their cities, their works of art are mostly gone. Even what remains from the distant past is riddled with evidences of a strange and pervasive evil that has grotesquely distorted man's potential. This is strange because apparently no other species of life treats its own with such deadly malignant hatred. The oldest skulls bear mute witness that they were bashed in and roasted to deliver their contents as food for still other human beings.

We are not surprised then to find that the explanation for this strangeness comes up in the oldest, detailed, written records—surviving documents that are respected by Jewish, Christian and Muslim traditions, *whose adherents make up more than half of the world's population.* These documents, referred to by the Jews as "the Torah," by Christians as the "Books of the Law" and by Muslims as "the Taurat" not only explain the strange source of evil but also describe a counter-campaign and follow that campaign through many centuries.

To be specific, the first eleven "chapters" of Genesis constitute a trenchant introduction to the whole problem, indeed, to the Bible itself. These pages describe three things: 1) a glorious and "good" original creation; 2) the entrance of a rebellious, evil, superhuman power who is more than a force, actually a personality; and the result 3) a humanity caught up in that rebellion and brought under the power of that evil.

In the whole remainder of the Bible, we have a single drama: the entrance

After serving ten years as a missionary among Mayan Indians in western Guatemala, Ralph D. Winter spent the next ten years as a Professor of Missions at the School of World Mission at Fuller Theological Seminary. He is the founder of the U.S. Center for World Mission in Pasadena, California, a cooperative center focused on people groups still lacking a culturally relevant church. Winter has also been instrumental in the formation of the movement called Theological Education by Extension, the William Carey Library publishing house, the American Society of Missiology, the Perspectives Study Program and the International Society for Frontier Missiology. Since March of 1990 he has been the President of the William Carey International University.

into this enemy-occupied territory of the kingdom, the power and the glory of the living God. From Genesis 12 to the end of the Bible, and indeed until the end of time, there unfolds the single, coherent drama of "The Kingdom Strikes Back"—a good title for the Bible itself were it to be printed like a modern book. In this drama we see the gradual but irresistible power of God reconquering and redeeming His fallen creation through the giving of His own Son at the very center of the 4,000-year period we are now ending.

This counter-attack clearly does not await the appearance of the central Person in the center of the story. Indeed, there would seem to be five identifiable epochs before the appearance of the Christ. While the purpose of this article is mainly to describe the five epochs following His "visitation," in order for those to be seen as part of a single ten-epoch continuum, we will pause to give a few clues about the first five epochs.

The theme that links all ten epochs is that of the grace of God intervening into history in order to contest the enemy who temporarily is "the god of this world." God's plan for doing this is to reach all peoples by conferring an unusual "blessing" on Abraham and Abraham's children-by-faith. This "blessing" of God is in effect conditioned upon its being shared with other nations, since those who receive God's blessing are, like Abraham, men of faith who subject themselves to God's will, become part of His kingdom, and represent the extension of His rule throughout the world among all other peoples. The "blessing" is a key term. We see it where Isaac confers his "blessing" on Jacob and not on Esau. It was not "blessings" but "a blessing," the conferral of a family name, responsibility, obligation as well as privilege.

In the first epoch of roughly 400 years, Abraham was chosen and moved to the geographic center of the Afro-Asian land mass. The story of Abraham, Isaac, Jacob, and Joseph is often called the Period of the Patriarchs and displays only small breakthroughs of witness and sharing with the surrounding nations even though the central mandate (Gen. 12:1-3) is repeated twice again to Abraham (18:18, 22:18), and once to Isaac (26:4) and to Jacob (28:14,15). Joseph observed to his brothers, "You sold me, but God sent me," and was obviously a great blessing to Egypt. Even the Pharaoh recognized that Joseph was filled with the Spirit of God (Gen 41:38, Living Bible). But this was not the *intentional* missionary obedience God wanted. His brothers had not taken up an offering and sent him to Egypt as a missionary! God was in the missions business whether they were or not.

As we push on into the next four roughly 400-year periods: 2) the Captivity, 3) the Judges, 4) the Kings and 5) that of the second captivity and diaspora—the promised blessing and the expected mission (to share that blessing with all the nations of the world) often all but disappears from sight. As a result, where possible God accomplished His will through the voluntary obedience and godliness of His people, but where necessary, He did His will through involuntary means. Joseph, Jonah, the nation as a whole when taken captive represent the category of involuntary missionary outreach intended by God to force the sharing of the blessing. The little girl carried away captive to the house of Naaman the Syrian was able to share her faith. Naomi, who "went" shared her faith at a distance with her children and their non-Jewish wives . On the other hand, Ruth, her daughter-in-law, Naaman the Syrian and the Queen of Sheba all came voluntarily, attracted by God's blessing on Israel.

Note, then, the *four different* "mission mechanisms" at work whereby other peoples could be blessed: 1) going voluntarily, 2) going without missionary intent (involuntarily), 3) coming voluntarily, and 4) coming involuntarily (as with Gentiles settled forceably in Israel—II Kings 17).

We see in every epoch the active concern of God to forward His mission, with or without the full cooperation of His chosen nation. Thus, when Jesus appears, it is an incriminating "visitation." He comes to His own, and His own receive Him not. He is well received in Nazareth until He refers to God's desire to bless the Gentiles. Then a homicidal outburst of fury betrays the fact that this chosen nation—chosen to receive and to mediate the blessing (Ex. 19:5, 6; Ps. 67; Isa. 49:6)—has grossly departed from that. There was indeed a sprinkling of fanatical Bible students who "traversed land and sea to make a single proselyte." But their outreach was not so much to be a blessing to the other nations as it was to sustain and protect the nation Israel. They were not making sure that their converts were circumcised in heart (Jer. 9:24-26; Rom. 2:29).

In effect, under the circumstances, Jesus did not come to give the Great Commission but to take it away. The natural branches were broken off while other "unnatural" branches were grafted in (Rom. 11:13-24). Even so, despite the general reluctance of the chosen missionary nation, many people groups were in fact touched: Canaanites, Egyptians, Philistines (of the ancient Minoan culture), Hittites, the Moabites, the Phoenicians (of Tyre and Sidon), the Assyrians, the Sabeans (of the land of Sheba), the Babylonians, the Persians, the Parthians, the Medes, the Elamites, the Romans.

And now, as we look into the next 2,000 year period, it is one in which God, on the basis of the intervention of His Son, is making sure that the other nations are both blessed and similarly called "to be a blessing to all the families of the earth." Now, for them, "Unto whomsoever much is given, of him shall much be required" (Luke 12:48). Now the Kingdom strikes back in the realms of the Armenians, the Romans, the Celts, the Franks, the Angles, the Saxons, the Germans, and eventually even those ruthless pagan pirates, the Vikings. All were to be invaded, tamed and subjugated by the power of the gospel, and expected to share their blessing with still others.

But the next five epochs are not all that different from the first five epochs. Those that are blessed do not seem terribly eager to share that unique blessing. The Celts are the only nation in the first millenium who give an outstanding missionary response. As we will see, just as in the Old Testament, the conferral of this unique blessing brings sober responsibility, dangerous if unfulfilled. And we see repeated again and again God's use of the full range of his four missionary mechanisms.

The "visitation" of the Christ was dramatic, full of portent and strikingly "in due time." Jesus was born a member of a subjugated people. Yet in spite of her bloody imperialism, Rome was truly an instrument in God's hands to prepare the world for His coming. Rome controlled one of the largest empires the world has ever known, forcing the Roman peace upon all sorts of disparate and barbaric peoples. For centuries Roman emperors had been building an extensive communication system, both in the 250,000 miles of marvelous roads which stretched all over the empire, and in the rapid transmission of messages and documents somewhat like the Pony Express on the American frontier. In its conquests, Rome had enveloped at least one civilization far more advanced than her own—Greece—and highly educated artisans and teachers taken as slaves to every major city of the empire taught the Greek language. Greek was understood from England to Palestine. How else could a few gospels and a few letters from St. Paul have had such a widespread impact among so many different ethnic groups in such a short period of time?

Jesus came, lived for 33 years on earth, confronted the wayward missionary nation, was crucified and buried, rose again, underscored the same commission to all who would respond, and ascended once more to the Father. Today even the most agnostic historian stands amazed that what began in a humble stable in Bethlehem of Palestine, the backwater of the Roman Empire, in less than 300 years had taken control of the Lateran Palace of the emperors of Rome, a gift of Constantine to the church. How did it happen? It is truly an incredible story.

No Saints in the Middle?

Let us interrupt the story here briefly. We can do well at this point to confront a psychological problem. In church circles today we have fled, or feared, or forgotten these middle centuries. Let us hope evangelicals are not as bad in this respect as the Mormons. They seem to hold to a "BOBO" theory that the Christian faith somehow "blinked out" after the Apostles and "blinked on" again when Joseph Smith dug up the sacred tablets in the 19th century. The result of this kind of BOBO approach is that you have "early" saints and "latter-day" saints, but no saints in the middle. Many Protestants may have roughly the same idea. Such people are not much interested in what happened prior to the Protestant Reformation: they have the vague impression that before Luther and Calvin the church was apostate and whatever there was of real Christianity consisted of a few persecuted individuals here and there. In a series of twenty volumes on "Twenty Centuries of Great Preaching" only half of the first volume is devoted to the first *fifteen* centuries! In Evangelical Sunday Schools children are busy as beavers with the story of God's work from Genesis to Revelation, from Adam to the Apostles, and Sunday School publishers may even boast about their "all-Bible curriculum." But this only really means that the children do not get exposed at all to what God did *with the Bible* between the times of the Apostles and the Reformers, a period which is staggering proof of the uniqueness and power of the Bible! To all such people it is as if there were no saints in the middle.

In the space available, however, it is possible to trace only the Western part of the story of Christianity—and only its outline at that, but to do that we must recognize certain clear stages that make the whole story fairly easy to grasp.

Note the pattern in the chart following:

In Period I, Rome was won but did not reach out with the Gospel to the barbaric Celts and Goths. Almost as a penalty, the Goths invaded Rome and caved in the whole Western part of the empire.

In Period II, the Goths were added in, and they briefly achieved a new "Holy" Roman Empire. But they also did not effectively reach further north with the Gospel.

Thus, in Period III, again almost as a penalty, the Vikings invaded the area of these Christianized Celtic and Gothic barbarians, and the Vikings, too, became Christians in the process.

In Period IV, Europe, for the first time united by Christian faith, reached out in a sort of pseudo-mission to the Saracens and pointed further East in the aftermath of the great abortion of the Crusades.

In Period V, Europe now reached out to the very ends of the earth. In this period reaching out has been the order of the day, but with highly mixed motives; commercial and spiritual interests have been both a blight and a blessing. Yet, during this period, the entire non-Western world has suddenly been stirred into development. Never before have so few affected so many, and never before has so great a gap resulted between two halves of the world. What will happen before the year 2000? Will the non-Western world invade Europe and America like the Goths invaded Rome and the Vikings overran Europe? Will the "Third World" turn on us in a new series of barbarian invasions? Will the OPEC nations gradually buy us out and take us over? Clearly we face the reaction of an awakened non-Western world that now suddenly is beyond our control. What will the role of the Gospel be? Can we gain any light from these previous cycles of outreach?

Winning the Romans (0-400 A.D)

Perhaps the most spectacular triumph of Christianity in history is its conquest of the Roman Empire in roughly twenty decades. We know very little about this period. Our lack of knowledge makes much of it a mystery, and what happened to Christianity sounds impossible, almost unbelievable. Only the early part starts out blazoned in the floodlight of the New Testament epistles themselves. Let's take a glance at that. There we see a Jew named Paul brought up in a Greek city, committed to leadership in the Jewish tradition of his time. Suddenly he was transformed by Christ and saw that the faith of the Jews as fulfilled in Christ did not require Jewish garments but could be clothed in Greek language and customs as well as Semitic. In this one decisive struggle it should have once more been clarified that anyone could be a Christian, be transformed in the inner man by the living Christ—whether Jew, Greek, Barbarian, Scythian, slave, free, male or female. The Greeks didn't have to become Jews, undergo circumcision, take over the Jewish calendar of festivals or holy days nor even observe Jewish dietary customs, any more than a woman had to be made into a man to be acceptable to God.

Paul based his work on the radical biblical principle (unaccepted by many Jews to this day) that it is circumcision of the heart that counts (Jer. 9), and that the new believers of a new culture did not have to speak the language, wear the clothes, or follow all the customs of the sending church. This meant that for Greeks, the cultural details of the Jewish law were no longer relevant. Therefore, to the Jews Paul continued as one "under the law of Moses," but to those unfamiliar with the Mosaic law, he preached the "law of Christ" in such a way that it could be fulfilled dynamically and authentically in their particular circumstances. While to some he appeared to be "without law," he maintained that he was not without law toward God, and indeed, as regards the basic purpose of the Mosaic Law, the believers in the Greek church immediately developed the functional equivalent to it, in their own cultural terms, and they held on to the Old Testament as well.

We may get the impression that missions in this period benefited very little from deliberately organized effort. But Paul apparently worked within a "missionary team" structure, borrowed from the Pharisees. Paul's sending congregation in Antioch did undertake a definite responsibility. But they sent him off more than they sent him out. Let no one suppose that every new Christian in those days opened his Bible to the Great Commission and dutifully turned over his life to this objective. There is good reason to suppose, for example, that the Christian faith expanded in many areas by the "involuntary-go" mechanism, that is, merely because Christians were dispersed as the result of persecutions. We know that fleeing Arian Christians had a lot to do with the conversion of the Goths. We have the stories of Ulfilas and Patrick, whose missionary efforts were in each case initiated by the accident of their being taken captive. Furthermore, it is reasonable to suppose that Christianity followed the trade routes of the Roman Empire, and we know that there was a close relationship and correspondence between Christians in Gaul and Asia Minor. Yet we must face the fact that the early Christians of the Roman Empire (as are Christians today) were only rarely both willing and able to take conscious practical steps to fulfill the Great Commission. In view of the amazing results in these early decades, however, we are all the more impressed by the innate power of the Gospel itself.

One intriguing possibility of the natural transfer of the Gospel within a given social unit is the case of the Celts. Historical studies clarify for us the fact that the province of *Galatia* in Asia Minor was so called because it was settled by *Galatoi* from Western Europe (who as late as the fourth century still spoke both their original Celtic tongue and also the Greek of that part of the Roman Empire). Whether or not Paul's Galatians were merely Jewish traders living in the province of Galatia, or were from the beginning Celtic Galatoi who were attracted to synagogues as "God fearers," we note in any case that Paul's letter to the Galatians is especially wary of anyone pushing over on his readers the mere outward customs of the Jewish culture and confusing such customs with essential Christianity. A matter of high missionary interest is the fact that Paul's preaching had tapped into a cultural vein of Celtic humanity that may soon have included friends, relatives, and trade contacts reaching a great distance to the west. Thus Paul's efforts in Galatia may give us one clue to the surprisingly early penetration of the Gospel into the main Celtic areas of Europe—comprising a belt running across southern Europe, clear over into Galicia in Spain, Brittany in France and into the western and northern parts of the British Isles.

There came a time when not only hundreds of thousands of Greek and Roman citizens had become Christians, but Celtic-speaking peoples and Gothic tribes people as well had developed their own forms of Christianity both within and beyond the borders of the Roman Empire. It is probable that the missionary work behind this came about mainly through unplanned processes involving Christians from the eastern part of the Roman Empire. In any case this achievement certainly cannot readily be credited to Latin-speaking Romans in the West. This is the point we are trying to make. One piece of evidence is the fact that the earliest Irish mission compounds (distinguished from the Western Roman type by a *central* chapel) followed a ground plan derived from Christian centers in Egypt. And Greek, not Latin, was the language of the early churches in Gaul. Even the first organized mission efforts of John Cassian and Martin of Tours, for example, came from the East by means of commune structures begun in Syria and Egypt. Fortunately, these organized efforts carried with them a strong emphasis on literacy and literature and the studying and copying of Biblical manuscripts and ancient Greek classics.

As amazed pagan leaders looked on, the cumulative impact grew to prominent proportions by 300 A.D. We don't know with any confidence what personal reasons Constantine had in 312 for declaring himself a Christian. We know that his mother in Asia Minor was a Christian, and that his father, as a co-regent in Gaul and Britain, did not enforce the Diocletian edicts against Christians in his area. However, by this time in history the inescapable factor is that there were enough Christians in the Roman Empire to make an official reversal of policy toward Christianity not only feasible, but politically wise. According to Professor Lynn White, Jr. at U.C.L.A., one of the great medieval historians of the world today, even if Constantine had not become a Christian, the empire could not have held out against Christianity more than another decade or two! The long development of the Roman Empire had ended the local autonomy of the city-state and created a widespread need for a sense of belonging—he calls it a crisis of identity. Then as now, Christianity was the one religion that had no nationalism at its root. It was not the folk religion of any one tribe. In White's words it had developed "an unbeatable combination."

Thus, it is the very power of the movement which helps in part to explain why the momentous decision to tolerate Christianity almost inevitably led to its becoming (over 50 years later) the official religion of the Empire. Not long after the curtain rises on Christianity as an officially tolerated religion, the head of the Christian community in Rome turns out astonishingly to be the strongest and most trusted man around. Why else would Constantine, when he moved the seat of government to Constantinople, leave his palace (the famous Lateran Palace) to the people of the Christian community as their "White House" in Rome? Nevertheless, it is simply a matter of record that by 375 A.D. Christianity became the official religion of Rome. For one thing, of course, it couldn't have existed as just another type of tolerated Judaism since it had so much wider an appeal. If it had been merely an ethnic cult, it could not have been even a candidate as an official religion.

More important for us than the fact that Christianity became the official religion is the fact that western Roman Christianity made no special effort to complete the Great Commission, not in this period. This is not because the Romans were unaware of the vast mission field to the north. Their military and political leaders had had to cope with the Germanic tribespeople for centuries. We shall see how willingly those peoples became Christians.

Winning the Barbarians (400-800 A.D.)

Curiously, as the Barbarian tribes people became Christianized, they became a greater and greater threat to Rome. Somewhat unintentionally they wrecked the network of civil government in the West long before they were to try to rebuild it. In fact, the only reason the city of Rome itself was not physically devastated by the invasions, which began in 410, was that the Barbarians were, all things considered, really very respectful of life and property and especially the churches. Why? Because missionary efforts (for which Western Romans could claim little or no credit) had brought the Visigoths, the Ostrogoths, and the Vandals into at least a superficial Christian faith. Even secular Romans observed how lucky they were that the invaders held high certain standards of Christian morality.

We are tantalized by the reflection that this much was accomplished by the informal and almost unconscious sharing of the Gospel—e.g. the news of the blessing being extended to all Gentile nations. How much better might it have been for the Romans had that brief hundred years of official toleration of Christianity (310-410) prior to the first invasion been devoted to energetic, constructive missionary efforts. Even a little Christianity prevented the Barbarians from that total disregard of civilization which was to be shown by the Vikings in the third period. Perhaps a little more Christianity might have prevented the complete collapse of the governmental structure of the Roman Empire in the West. Today, for example, the ability of the new African states to maintain a stable government is to a great extent dependent upon their degree of Christianization (that is, both in knowledge and morality).

In any case, we confront the ominous phenomenon of a partially Christianized barbarian horde being emboldened and enabled to pour in upon a complacent, officially Christian empire that had failed effectively to reach out to them. This may remind us of our relation to the present-day colossus of China. The Chinese, like the Barbarians north of Rome, have been crucially affected by Christianity. In the past twenty years they have adopted extensively and profoundly a kind of superficial faith which embodies a number of distinctively Christian ingredients—despite the grave distortion of those Christian elements in the Communist milieu. Just as a modicum of Christian faith in some ways strengthened the hand of the Barbarians against the Romans, so the Chinese today are awesomely more dangerous due to the cleansing, integrating and galvanizing effect of the Communist philosophy and cell structure which is clearly derived from the West, and in many ways specifically from the Christian tradition itself. You can imagine the Barbarians criticizing the softness and degeneracy of the Roman Christians just as the Chinese today denounce the Russians for failing to live up to Communist standards.

Whether or not the Romans had it coming (for failing to reach out), and whether or not the Barbarians were both encouraged and tempered in their conquest by their initial Christian awareness, the indisputable fact is that, while the Romans lost the western half of their empire, the Barbarian world, in a very dramatic sense, gained a Christian faith.

The immediate result was that right in the city of Rome there appeared at least two "denominations," the one Arian and the other Athanasian. Also in the picture was the Celtic "church," which was more a series of missionary compounds than it was a denomination made up of local churches. Still less like a church was an organization called the Benedictines, which came along later to compete with the Celts in establishing missionary compounds all over Europe. By the time the Vikings appeared on the horizon there were, up through Europe, over 1,000 such mission compounds.

Protestants, and perhaps even modern Catholics, must pause at this point. Our problem in understanding these strange (and much misunderstood) instruments of evangelization is not so much our ignorance of what these people did, as our prejudice that has been developed against monks who lived almost a thousand years later. It is wholly unfair for us to judge the work of a traveling evangelist like Colomban or Boniface by the stagnation of the wealthy Augustinians in Luther's day—although we must certainly pardon Luther for thinking such thoughts.

It is indisputable that the chief characteristic of these "Jesus People" in this second period, whether they were Celtic peregrini or their parallel in Benedictine communes, was the fact that they loved the Bible, that they sang their way through the whole book of Psalms each week as a routine discipline, and that it was they, in any case, who enabled the Kingdom and the power and the glory to be shared with the Anglo-Saxons and the Goths.

It is true that many strange, even bizarre and pagan customs were mixed up as secondary elements in the various forms of Christianity that were active during the period of the Christianization of Europe. The headlong collision and competition between Western Roman and Celtic forms of Christianity undoubtedly eventuated in an enhancement of common biblical elements in their faith. But we must remember the relative chaos introduced by the invasions, and therefore not necessarily expect to see, dotting the landscape, the usual parish churches that are familiar in our day. Under the particular circumstances then (similar to many chaotic corners of the world today) the most durable structure around was the *order*—a fellowship much more highly disciplined and tightly knit than the usual American Protestant congregation today. We must admit, furthermore, that these Christian communities not only were the source of scholarship during the Middle Ages, but they also preserved the technologies of the

Roman tradesmen—tanning, dyeing, weaving, metal working, masonry skills, bridge building, etc. Their civil, charitable, and even scientific contribution is, in general, grossly underestimated. Probably the greatest accomplishment of these disciplined Christian communities is seen in the simple fact that almost our total knowledge of the ancient world is derived from their libraries, whose silent testimony reveals the appreciation they had, even as Christians, of the "pagan" authors of ancient times. In our secular age it is embarrassing to recognize that, had it not been for these highly literate "mission field" Christians who preserved and copied manuscripts (not only of the Bible but of ancient Christian and non-Christian classics as well), we would know no more about the Roman Empire today than we do of the Mayan or Incan empires, or many other empires that have long since almost vanished from sight. As a matter of fact, Barbarian Europe was won more by the witness and labors of Celtic and Anglo-Saxon converts than by the efforts of missionaries deriving from Italy or Gaul. This fact was to bear decisively upon the apparently permanent shift of power in Western Europe to the northern Europeans. Even as late as 596, when Rome's first missionary headed north (with great faintheartedness), he crossed the path of the much more daring and widely travelled Irish missionary Colomban, who had worked his way practically to the doorstep of Rome, and who was already further from his birthplace than Augustine was planning to go from his. Thus, while Constantinople was considered the "Second Rome" by people who lived in the East, and Moscow was later to become the "Third Rome" to the descendants of the newly Christianized Russians, neither Rome as a city nor the Italian peninsula as a region was ever again to be politically as significant as the chief cities of the daughter nations—Spain, France, Germany, and England.

Toward the end of the second period, or at the end of each of these periods, there was a great flourishing of Christianity within the new cultural basin. The rise of a strong man like Charlemagne facilitated communication throughout Western Europe to a degree unknown for three hundred years. Under his sponsorship a whole range of issues—social, theological, political—were soberly restudied in the light of the Bible and the writings of earlier Christian leaders in the Roman period. Charlemagne was a second Constantine in certain respects, and his political power was unmatched in Western Europe during a half a millenium. But he was much more of a Christian than Constantine and industriously sponsored far more Christian activity. Like Constantine, his official espousal of Christianity produced many Christians who were Christians in name only. There is little doubt that the great missionary Boniface was slain by the Saxons because his patron, Charlemagne (with whose policies he did not at all agree) had brutally suppressed the Saxons on many occasions. Then, as in our own recent past the political force of a colonial power not so much paved the way for Christianity, but as often as not turned people against the faith. Of interest to missionaries is the fact that the great centers of learning established by Charlemagne were copies and expansions of newly established mission compounds deep in German territory, outposts that were the work of British and Celtic missionaries from sending centers as far away as Iona and Lindisfarne in Britain.

Indeed, the first serious attempt at anything like public education was initiated by this great tribal chieftain, Charlemagne, on the advice and impulse of

Anglo-Celtic missionaries and scholars, such as Alcuin, whose projects eventually required the help of thousands of literate Christians from Britain and Ireland to man schools founded on the Continent. It is hard to believe, but Irish teachers of Latin (never a native tongue in Ireland) were eventually needed to teach Latin in Rome, so extensively had the tribal invasions broken down the civilization of the Roman Empire.

The Celtic Christians and their Anglo-Saxon and continental heirs especially treasured the Bible. A sure clue to their chief source of inspiration is the fact that the highest works of art during these "dark" centuries were marvelously "illuminated" biblical manuscripts and devoutly ornamented church buildings; manuscripts of non-Christian classical authors were preserved and copied, but not illuminated. Through the long night of the progressive breakdown of the Western part of the Roman Empire, when the tribal migrations reduced almost all of the life in the West to the level of the tribesmen themselves, the two great regenerating ideals were the hope of building anew the glory that was once Rome, and the hope of making all subject to the Lord of Glory. The one really high point, when these twin objectives were most nearly achieved, was during Charlemagne's long, vigorous career centered around the year 800. As one recent scholar puts it,

> In the long sweep of European history, from the decline of the Roman Empire to the flowering of the Renaissance nearly a thousand years later, his [Charlemagne's] is the sole commanding presence.

No wonder recent scholars call Charlemagne's period the Carolingian Renaissance, and thus discard the concept of "the dark ages" for a First Dark Ages early in this period, and a Second Dark Ages early in the next period.

Unfortunately, the rebuilt empire (later to be called the *Holy Roman Empire*) was unable to find the ingredients of a Charlemagne in his successor; moreover, a new threat now posed itself externally. Charlemagne had been eager for his own kind to be made Christian—the Germanic tribes. He offered wise, even spiritual leadership in many affairs, but did not throw his weight behind any kind of bold mission outreach to the Scandinavian peoples to the north. What was begun under his son was too little and too late. This fact was to contribute greatly to the undoing of the empire.

Winning the Vikings (800-1200 A.D.)

No sooner had the consolidation in Western Europe been accomplished under Charlemagne than there appeared a new menace to peace and propriety that was to create a second period of at least semi-darkness to last 250 years: the Vikings. These savages further north had not yet been effectively evangelized. While the tribal invaders of Rome, who created the First Dark Ages, were rough forest people who, for the most part, were nevertheless nominally Arian Christians, the Vikings, by contrast, were neither civilized nor Christian. There was another difference: they were men of the sea. This meant that key island sanctuaries for missionary training, like Iona, or like the off-shore promontory of Lindisfarne (connected to the land only at low tide), were as vulnerable to attacking seafarers as they had been invulnerable to attackers from the land. Both of these mission centers were sacked more than a dozen times, and their occupants slaughtered or sold off as slaves in middle Europe. It seems unquestionable that the Christians of Charlemagne's empire would have fared far better had the Vikings had at least the appreciation of the Christian faith that the earlier barbarians had when they overran Rome. The very opposite of the Visigoths and Vandals who *spared* the churches, the Vikings seemed attracted like magnets to the monastic centers of scholarship and Christian devotion; they took a special delight in burning churches, in putting human life to the sword, and in selling monks into slavery. A contemporary's words give us a graphic impression of their carnage:

> The Northmen cease not to slay and carry into captivity the Christian people, to destroy the churches and to burn the towns. Everywhere, there is nothing but dead bodies—clergy and laymen, nobles and common people, women and children. There is no road or place where the ground is not covered with corpses. We live in distress and anguish before this spectacle of the destruction of the Christian people (Christopher Dawson, *Religion and the Rise of Western Culture*, p. 87).

Once more, when Christians did not reach out to them, pagan peoples came where they were. And once more, the phenomenal power of Christianity manifested itself: the conquerors became conquered by the faith of their captives. Usually it was the monks sold as slaves or the Christian girls forced to be their wives and mistresses which eventually won these savages of the north. In God's eyes, their redemption must have been more important than the harrowing tragedy of this new invasion of barbarian violence and evil which fell upon God's own people whom He loved. (After all, he had not even spared His own Son in order to redeem us!)

In the previous hundred years, Charlemagne's scholars had carefully collected the manuscripts of the ancient world. Now the majority were to be burned by the Vikings. Only because so many copies had been made and scattered so widely did the fruits of the Charlemagnic (actually "Carolingian") literary revival survive at all. Once scholars and missionaries had streamed from Ireland across England and onto the continent, and even out beyond the frontiers of Charlemagne's empire. Thus the Irish volcano which had poured forth a passionate fire of evangelism for three centuries cooled almost to extinction. Viking warriors, newly based in Ireland followed the paths of the earlier Irish *peregrini* across England and onto the Continent, but this time ploughing with them waste and destruction rather than new life and hope.

There were some blessings in this horrifying disguise. Alfred the Great, King of Wessex, successfully headed up guerilla resistance and was equally concerned about spiritual as well as physical losses. As a measure of emergency, he let go the ideal of maintaining the Latin tongue as a general pattern for worship and began a Christian library in the vernacular—the Anglo-Saxon. This was a decision of monumental importance which might have been delayed several centuries had the tragedy of the Vikings not provided the necessity which was the mother of invention.

In any case, as Christopher Dawson puts it, the unparalleled devastation of England and the Continent was "not a victory for paganism." (p. 94) The Northmen who landed on the Continent under Rollo became the Christianized Normans, and the Danish who took over a huge section of middle England (along with invaders from Norway who planted their own kind in many other parts of England and Ireland) also were soon to become Christians. The Gospel was too powerful. One result was that a new Christian culture spread back into Scandinavia. This stemmed largely from England from which came the first monastic communities and early missionary bishops. What England lost, Scandinavia gained.

It must also be admitted that the Vikings would not have been attracted either to the churches or to the monasteries had not those centers of Christian piety to a great extent succumbed to luxury. The switch from the Irish to the Benedictine pattern of monasticism was an improvement in many respects, but apparently allowed greater possibilities for the development of the un-Christian opulence and glitter which attracted the greedy eyes of the Norsemen. Thus another side-benefit of the new invasions was its indirect cleansing and refinement of the Christian movement. Even before the Vikings appeared, Benedict of Aniane inspired a rustle of reform here and there. By 910, at Cluny, a momentous step forward was begun. Among other changes, the authority over a monastic center was shifted away from local politics, and for the first time (as dramatically and extensively) whole networks of "daughter" houses were related to a single, strongly spiritual "mother" house. The Cluny revival, moreover, produced a new reforming attitude toward society as a whole.

The greatest bishop in Rome in the first millenium, Gregory I, was the product of a Benedictine community. So, early in the second millenium, Hildebrand was a product of the Cluny reform. His successors in reform were bolstered greatly by the Cistercian revival which went even further. Working behind the scenes for many years for wholesale reform across the entire church, he finally became Pope Gregory VII for a relatively brief period. But his reforming zeal set the stage for Innocent III, who wielded greater power (and all things considered, greater power for good) than any other Pope before or since. Gregory VII had made a decisive step toward wresting control of the church from secular power—this was the question of "lay investiture." It was he who allowed Henry IV to wait for three days out in the snow at Knossis. Innocent III not only carried forward Gregory's reforms, but has the distinction of being the Pope who authorized the first of a whole new series of mission orders—the Friars.

Our first period ended with a barely Christian Roman Empire and a somewhat Christian emperor—Constantine. Our second period ended with a reconstitution of that empire under a christianized barbarian, Charlemagne, who was devoutly and vigorously Christian. Our third period ends with a pope, Innocent III, as the strongest man in Europe, made strong by the Cluny, Cistercian and allied spiritual movements which together are called the Gregorian Reform. The scene was not an enlarged Europe in which no secular ruler could survive without at least tipping his hat to the leaders in the Christian movement. It was not a period in which European Christians had reached out in missions, but they had at least with phenomenal speed grafted in the entire northern area, and had also deepened the foundations of Christian scholarship and devotion in the Europe of

Charlemagne. The next period would unfold some happy and unhappy surprises. Would Europe now take the initiative in reaching out with the Gospel? Would it sink in self-satisfaction? In some respects it would do both.

Winning the Saracens? (1200-1600 A.D.)

The fourth period began with a spectacular, new evangelistic instrument—the Friars, and it would end with the greatest reformation of all, but was meanwhile already involved for a hundred years in the most massive, tragic misconstrual of Christian mission in all of history. Never before had any nation or group of nations launched as energetic and sustained a campaign into foreign territory as did Europe in the tragic debacle of the Crusades. This was in part the carry-over of the Viking spirit into the Christian church. All of the major Crusades were led by Viking descendants. Yet while the Crusades had many political overtones (they were often a unifying device for faltering rulers), they would not have come about apart from the vigorous sponsorship of the Christian leaders. They were not only an unprecedented blood-letting to the Europeans themselves and a savage wound in the side of the Muslim peoples (a wound which is not at all healed to this day), but they were a fatal blow to the cause of Christian unity east and west and to the cultural unity of eastern Europe. In the long run, though they held Jerusalem for a hundred years, the Crusaders by default eventually gave the Byzantine inheritance over to the Ottoman sultans, and far worse, they established a permanent image of brutal, militant Christianity that alienates a large proportion of mankind to this day.

Ironically, the mission of the Crusaders would not have been so successfully negative had it not involved so high a component of abject Christian commitment. The great lesson of the Crusades is that good will, even sacrificial obedience to God, is no substitute for a clear understanding of His will. It was a devout man, Bernard of Clairvaux, to whom are attributed the words of the hymn, *Jesus the Very Thought of Thee*, who preached the first crusade. In all this period two Franciscans, Francis of Assisi and Raymond Lull, stand out as the only ones whose insight into God's will led them to substitute the gentle words of the evangel for warfare and violence as the proper means of extending the blessing God conferred on Abraham and and always had intended for all of Abraham's children of faith.

At this point we must pause for reflection. We may not succeed, but let us try to see things from God's point of view, treading with caution and tentativeness. We know, for example, that at the end of the First Period, after three centuries of hardship and persecution, just when things were apparently going great, invaders appeared and chaos and catastrophe ensued. Why? This is the period that could be called the "Constantinian Renaissance"—that is, it was both good and not so good. Just when Christians were translating the Bible into Latin and waxing eloquent in theological debate, when Eusebius was editing a massive collection of previous Christian writings (as the official historian of the government), when heretics were thrown out of the empire (and became, however reluctantly, the only missionaries to the Goths), when Rome finally became officially Christian...then suddenly God brought down the curtain. It was now time for a new cluster of people groups to be included in the "blessing," that is confronted with the claims, privileges, and obligations of the expanding Kingdom of Christ.

Similarly, at the end of the Second Period, after three centuries of chaos during which the rampaging Gothic hordes were eventually christianized, tamed and civilized, when Bibles and biblical knowledge proliferated as never before, when major biblical-missionary centers were established by the Celtic Christians and their Anglo-Saxon pupils, when, in this Charlemagnic renaissance, thousands of public schools led by Christians attempted mass biblical and general literacy, when Charlemagne dared even to attack the endemic use of alcohol, great theologians tussled with theological/political issues, and the Venerable Bede became Eusebius of this period (indeed, when both Charlemagne and Bede were much more Christian than Constantine and Eusebius), once again invaders appeared and chaos and catastrophe ensued. Why?

Strangely similar, then is the end of the Third Period. It only took two and a half centuries for the Vikings to capitulate to the "counter-attack of the Gospel."

The flourishing period was longer than a century and far more extensive than ever before. The Crusades, the cathedrals, the so-called Scholastic theologians, the universities, most importantly the blessed Friars, and even the early part of the Humanistic Renaissance make up this outsized 1050-1350 outburst of a Medieval Renaissance. And then suddenly, a new invader appeared, more virulent than ever, and chaos and catastrophe greater than ever occurred. Why?

Was God unsatisfied with incomplete obedience? That is, with the blessing being retained by those who received it and not sufficiently and determinedly shared with the other nations of the world? The plague that killed one third of the inhabitants of Europe killed a much higher proportion of the Franciscans (120,000 were laid still in Germany alone). Surely He was not trying to judge their missionary fire. Was He trying to judge the Crusaders, whose atrocities greatly outweighed the Christian devotional elements in their movement? If so, why did He wait so long to do that? And why did He inflict the Christian leadership of Europe so greatly rather than the Crusaders themselves? Why didn't the Crusaders die of the Plague?

Perhaps it was that Europe did not sufficiently listen to the saintly Friars; that it was not the Friars that went wrong but the hearers who did not respond. God's judgment upon Europe then, was to take the Gospel away from them, to take away the Friars and their message. Even though to us it seems like it was a judgment upon the messengers rather than upon the resistant hearers, is this not one impression that could be received from the New Testament as well? Jesus Himself came unto His own, and His own received Him not, and *Jesus* rather than the people was the one who went to the cross. God's judgment may often consist of the removal of the messenger.

In any case, the invasion of the Bubonic plague, first in 1346 and every so often during the next decade, brought a greater setback than either the Gothic or the Viking invasions. It first devastated parts of Italy and Spain, then spread west and north to France, England, Holland, Germany and Scandinavia. By the time it had run its course 40 years later, one third to one half of the population of Europe was dead. Especially stricken were the Friars and the truly spiritual leaders. They were the only ones who stayed behind to tend the sick and to bury the dead. Europe was absolutely in ruins. The result? There were three Popes at one point, the humanist elements turned menacingly humanistic, peasant turmoil (often based in justice and even justified by the Bible itself) ended up in orgies and excesses of violence. The poverty, confusion and lengthy travail led to the new birth of the greatest reform yet seen.

Once more, at the end of one of our periods, a great flourishing took place. Printing came to the fore, Europeans finally escaped their geographical cul de sac and sent ships for commerce, subjugation and spiritual blessing to the very ends of the earth. And as a part of the reform, the Protestant Reformation now loomed on the horizon: that great, permanent, cultural decentralization of Europe.

Protestants often think of the Reformation as a legitimate reaction against the evils of a monstrous Christian bureaucracy sunken in corruption. But it must be admitted that the Reform was not just a reaction against decadence in the Christian movement. This great decentralization of Christendom was in many respects the result of an increasing vitality which, unknown to most Protestants, was as evident in the return to a study of the Bible and to the appearance of new life and evangelical preaching in Italy, Spain, and France as in Moravia, Germany, and England.

In the Reformation, the Gospel finally succeeded in allowing Christians to be German, not merely permitting Germans to be Roman Christians. Unfortunately, the emphasis on justification by faith (which was preached as much in Italy and Spain as in Germany at the time Luther loomed into view) became identified with German nationalistic hopes and thus was suppressed as a dangerous doctrine by political powers in the South. But it is merely a typical Protestant misunderstanding that there was not as much a revival of deeper life, Bible study, and prayer in Southern Europe as in Northern Europe at the time of the Reformation. The issue may have appeared to the Protestants as faith versus law, or to the Romans as unity vs. division, but popular scales are askew because it was much more Latin uniformity vs. national diversity. The vernacular had to eventually conquer. Paul had not demanded that the Greeks become Jews, but the Germans had been obliged to become Roman. The Anglo-Saxons and the Scandinavians had at least been allowed their vernacular to an extent unknown in Christian Germany. Germany was where the revolt would have to take place. Italy, France, and Spain, formerly part of the Roman Empire and extensively assimilated culturally in that direction, had no nationalistic steam behind their reforming movements which became almost lost in the shuffle that ensued.

However, despite the fact that the Protestants won on the political front, and to a great extent gained the power to formulate anew their own Christian tradition, they did not even talk of mission outreach, and the period ended with *Roman* Europe expanding both politically and religiously on the seven seas. Thus, entirely unshared by Protestants, for at least two centuries, there ensued a worldwide movement of unprecedented scope in the annals of mankind in which there was greater Christian missionary presence than ever before.

To the Ends of the Earth (1600-2000 A.D.)

The period from 1600 to 2000 began with European footholds in the rest of the world. Apart from taking over what was almost an empty continent by toppling the Aztec and Inca empires in the Western hemisphere, Europeans had only tiny enclaves of power in the heavily populated portions of the non-Western world. By 1945, Europeans had virtual control over 99.5% of the non-Western world. Twenty-five years later, the Western nations had lost control over all but 5% of the non-Western population of the world. This 1945-1969 period of the sudden collapse of Western control, coupled by the unexpected upsurge of significance of the Christian movement in the non-Western world, I have elsewhere called "the twenty-five unbelievable years." If we compare this period to the collapse of the Western Roman Empire's domination over its conquered provinces of Spain, Gaul, and Britain, and to the breakdown of control over non-Frankish Europe under Charlemagne's successors, we can anticipate—at least by the logic of sheer parallelism—that by the year 2000 the Western world itself will be dominated by non-Westerners.

Indeed, ever since the collapse of Western power became obvious (during the "twenty-five unbelievable years"), there have been many who have decried the thought of any further missionary effort moving from the West to the non-Western world, perhaps confusing the absence of political control for the absence of the need for foreign missions. The true situation is actually very different. Rather, the absence of political control for the first time in many areas has now begun to allow non-Western populations to yield to the Kingdom of Christ without simultaneously yielding to the political Kingdoms of the Western world. Here we see a parallel to the Frankish tribes people accepting the faith of Rome only after Rome had become politically powerless, and the continued relative acceptability of the Roman faith among the Anglo-Saxons, Germans, and Scandinavians up until the point where the emergence of strong papal authority mixed with power politics became a threat to legitimate national ambitions, and led to a Reformation which allowed nationalized forms of Christianity.

The present spectacle of a Western world flaunting the standards of Christian morality in more obvious ways than ever is not as likely, therefore, to dissuade others from embracing the Christian faith in non-Christian lands as it is to disassociate the treasure of Christian ideals from a Western world which has, until this age, been their most prominent sponsor. When Asians accuse Western nations of immorality in warfare, they are appealing to Christian values, certainly not the values of their own pagan past. In this sense, Christianity has already conquered the world. No longer, for example, is the long-standing Chinese tradition of skillful torture likely to be boasted about in China nor highly respected anywhere else, at least in public circles.

But this world-wide change has not come about suddenly. Even the present, minimal attainment of world Christian morality on a tenuous public level has been accomplished only at the cost of a great amount of sacrificial missionary endeavor (during the four centuries of Period Five), labors which have been mightier and more deliberate than at any time in 2000 years. The first half (1600-1800) of this fifth period was almost exclusively a Roman show. By the year 1800, it was painfully embarrassing to Protestants to hear Roman missionaries writing off the Protestant movement as apostate simply because it was not sending missionaries. But by the year 1800, Roman missionary effort had been forced into sudden decline due to the curtailment of the Jesuits, and the combined effect of the French Revolution and ensuing chaos in the cutting of the European economic roots of Catholic missions.

However, the year 1800 marks the awakening of the Protestants from two and a half centuries of inactivity, if not actual slumber, in regard to missionary outreach across the world. The 1800 to 2000 year period is treated in the chapter on the Three Eras of Modern Missions. During this final period, for the first time, Protestants equipped themselves with structures of mission comparable to the Catholic orders and began to make up for lost time. Unheralded, unnoticed, all but forgotten in our day except for ill-informed criticism, Protestant missionary efforts in this period, more than Catholic missions, led the way in establishing all around the world the democratic apparatus of government, the schools, the hospitals, the universities and the political foundations of the new nations. Rightly understood, Protestant missionaries along with their Roman brethren are surely not less than *the prime movers* of the tremendous energy that is mushrooming in the Third World today. Take China, for example. Two of its greatest modern leaders, Sun Yat Sen and Chiang Kai-shek, were both Christians.

If the Western home base is now to falter and to fail as the tide is reversed by the new power of its partially evangelized periphery (as is the pattern in the earlier periods), we can only refer to Dawson's comment on the devastation wrought by the Vikings—that this will not be a "victory for paganism." The fall of the West will be due in part to a decay of spirit. It will be due in part to the pagan power in the non-Western world emboldened and strengthened by its first contact with Christian faith. It may come as a most drastic punishment to a Western world that has always spent more on cosmetics than it has on foreign missions—and lately ten times as much. From a secular or even nationalistic point of view, the next years may be a very dark period for the Western world, in which the normal hope and aspirations of Christian people for their own country may find only a very slight basis for optimism. But if the past is any guide at all, even this will have to be darkness before the dawn. While we may not be able to be sure about our own country we have no reason to suppose—there is no historic determinism that assures us—that the Christian faith will not survive. The entire Western world in its present political form may be radically altered.

For one thing, we can readily calculate, in regard to population trends, that by the year 2000 Westerners will constitute less than half as large a percentage of the world (8%) as they did in the year 1900 (18%). This does seem inevitable. But certainly, judging by the past, we cannot ultimately be pessimistic. Beyond the agony of Rome was the winning of the Barbarians. Beyond the agony of the Barbarians was the winning of the Vikings. Beyond the agony of the Western world we can only pray that there will be the winning of the "two billion" who have not yet heard. And we can only know that there is no basis in the past or in the present for assuming that things are out of the control of the living God.

If we in the West insist on keeping our blessing instead of sharing it, then we will, like other nations before us, have to lose our blessing for the remaining nations to receive it. God has not changed his plan in the last 4,000 years. But how much better not to focus on retaining but intentionally extend our "blessing," without reserve. That way "in you and in your descendants all of the peoples of the world will be blessed" That is the only way we can continue in God's blessing. The expanding Kingdom is not going to stop with us, "This gospel *must* be preached in the whole world as a testimony to all people groups, and then shall the end come (Matthew 24: 14).

Study Questions

1. Illustrate this thesis: "The conferring of the blessing brings sober responsibility, dangerous if unfulfilled."

2. Explain the cultural and social dynamics behind the Protestant Reformation.

3. Winter contends that history is a "single, coherent drama." What are the outlines of the "plot"? What themes are repeated? What major lessons are to be observed?

2

By Way of Inclusive Retrospect

Kenneth Scott Latourette

Latourette wrote A History of Christianity *as a Christian to other Christians. "By Way of Inclusive Retrospect" is his conclusion to this work in which he has ranged over 2000 years to gauge the impact of Jesus of Nazareth upon individuals and societies.*

It may be of help to take a backward glance over what has been traversed. To the reader to whom this book has been the first introduction to the history of Christianity, the sixty chapters through which he has made his toilsome way will probably seem so crowded with details, persons, and movements that he comes to their end with a bewildered sigh of relief. Although from time to time we have attempted to pause for perspective, it may be of help to conclude with an attempt at a comprehensive summary which, from the vantage of the mid-twentieth century, will survey the whole road over which we have travelled, point out its main stages, and essay some suggestions of its significance for our knowledge of man and of the universe.

Unpromising Beginnings

The beginning of Christianity, it will be remembered, seemed singularly unpromising. To be sure, Jesus had back of him the long religious development which had issued in the Judaism of his day and from which, humanly speaking, he was sprung. Moreover, his brief life was spent in a section of the Mediterranean world at the beginning of a period when the *pax Romana* was bringing administrative unity and material prosperity to that portion of mankind and when a profound and widespread religious ferment gave opportunity for the

---

Probably the premier historian of the Christian movement was Kenneth Scott Latourette. A member of the Student Volunteer Movement at Yale early in the twentieth century and very active in a vast network of student Bible study groups, Latourette sailed for China but returned after a year because of illness. He taught from 1921 to 1953 at Yale as Professor of Missions and Oriental History. Constantly active as a mission leader, Latourette was nevertheless a prolific author, recognized for his scholarship in East Asian Studies but best known for his seven-volume *History of the Expansion of Christianity*, five-volume Christianity in a Revolutionary Age, and two-volume *History of Christianity*. Chapter LXI, "By Way of Inclusive Retrospect," pages 1463-1477 in *A History of Christianity* by Kenneth Scott Latourette. Copyright, 1953, by Harper and Row Publishers, Inc. Reprinted by permission of the publisher.

successful dissemination of a new faith. However, in the few months of his public career Jesus wrote no book and created no elaborate organization to perpetuate his message and his work. His crucifixion appeared to mean complete frustration and his proclamation of the imminence of the kingdom of God seemed to be the futile dream of a well-meaning but quite unpractical visionary. At the outset his followers constitute merely one out of several Jewish sects and one of the feeblest of the many faiths which were competing in the Graeco-Roman world. Moreover, the Roman Empire occupied but a small fraction of the earth's surface and embraced only a minority of even the civilized portion of mankind. By the time that Christianity had begun to gain headway, the realm was giving indications of the illnesses which brought its demise. Its inhabitants were ceasing to say or to do much that was really new. The creative impulse seemed to be dying.

The First Five Centuries

Within its first five centuries Christianity won the professed allegiance of the large majority of the population of the Roman Empire and spread beyond it, chiefly but not entirely in contiguous territory. Christianity centered around Christ, but its theology, its organization, and its worship were developments which in part reflected the environment in which they took shape. Without Jesus, Christianity would not have been, and while some forms of the faith, especially those known collectively as Gnosticism, tended to belittle his historicity, the one which ultimately prevailed cherished the records of his earthly life and sought to make its theology take full account of it. So much creative vigour did Christianity possess that from it came the various churches. In theory there was only one Church, the "body of Christ," but in actuality there were several churches. One of them, which claimed to be catholic and the custodian of the faith as taught by Jesus and the apostles, was the largest.

There was that about Jesus, his life, teachings, death, and resurrection which stirred men to intense intellectual activity in an attempt to see their meaning and which, while inescapably utilizing some of the thought patterns of the day, issued in conclusions which were essentially new. Christian worship took much from Judaism, but at its core, especially in the Eucharist, it was a fresh creation. By its discipline the Catholic Church as well as some of the bodies which dissented from it attempted to bring the conduct of its members towards an approximation of what Jesus had taught. As hundreds of thousands flocked into the Church and, in spite of the efforts of many zealous clergy, the lives of most Christians were not much if any better than those of the adherents of the surviving remnants of paganism, monasticism arose. Negatively it was a protest against the laxity of the main body of Christians and positively it claimed to offer a way of becoming perfectly conformed to the teachings of Jesus. Although at first the monks on the one hand and many of the bishops and clergy on the other tended to look askance at each other, monasticism soon became an integral part of the life of the Church.

Christianity did not save the Roman Empire. In its first five centuries, except in the area of religion, it did not greatly alter the life and customs of the Graeco-Roman community. Nor did it reshape civilization. Death came slowly to the empire. Indeed, it never really arrived. There were prolonged illness and weakness and then transition to later stages of culture which continued much of the Graeco-Roman heritage. The decline of the empire was due to internal decay and to invasions from without. Christianity did not prevent either.

Disaster and Decline

From the Christian standpoint the most disastrous of the invasions was that of the Arabs. Inspired by a new religion, Islam, to which both Judaism and Christianity contributed, in the seventh and eighth centuries the Arabs made themselves masters of about half of Christendom, from Syria southward and westward to the Pyrenees. In that stretch of territory Islam was dominant, and while Christianity did not quickly disappear and in most places survived as the faith of a minority, the churches dwindled. In proportion to the area which it covered, through Islam Christianity suffered the greatest defeat in its history. Only in Spain, Portugal, and Sicily did it regain the ground then lost.

For some centuries it seemed that a similar fate might be overtaking Christianity in the territories which remained to it north of the Mediterranean. During five hundred years or more wave after wave of invaders, mostly non-Christian barbarians, poured in from the north and east.

Because of the decay of the realm and the culture with which it had become closely identified—the Roman Empire and its Graeco-Roman civilization—Christianity seemed to be on the way out. The churches which were its vehicles were dwindling in numbers and suffering from a loss in morale. A bulwark remained in the remnant of the empire which clustered around Constantinople and in the West Rome was the rallying centre of another wing of the faith. In the East, the Nestorians, although a minority, first under Zoroastrian and then under Moslem rulers, propagated the faith as far as the China Sea and South India. Yet the period roughly bounded by the years 500 and 950 was the most discouraging since the unpromising beginning in the first century. In the West the revival under the Carolingians in the eighth and ninth centuries was followed by a relapse which brought the Church of Rome to the lowest point it had thus far known and by 950 Nestorianism had died out on its easternmost frontier, China.

Fresh Achievements

Out of what looked like hopeless disaster and chiefly in what in the sixth century must have seemed the most unpromising areas and congeries of peoples came fresh achievements which were the preparation for the worldwide role which Christianity had in later centuries. The barbarian invaders of Eastern Europe were won, some of them during the darkest hours of the dark ages. From this apparently discouraging material and in a section of the world from which it seemed most unlikely that light would emerge, a civilization arose on which Christianity made a more profound impress and in which it had a larger creative part than it had had on that of Rome. In the formation of that civilization Christianity was by no means the only element. Pre-Christian Graeco-Roman culture, the Moslem Arabs, and Teutonic tradition all had a share. Nor was that civilization fully Christian. Yet it was continually challenged by Christianity and in it were many who were radiant because of the Gospel, who were honoured for their Christlikeness, and who were at once an inspiration and a rebuke to those about them. From Christianity came great theologies, vigorous new monastic movements, universities, noble art and architecture, daring political theories, and haunting ideals of peace. But much in the life of Western Europe from 950 to 1350, as later, was palpably, almost stridently non-Christian and in stark contrast to the faith to which almost all gave lip service.

While this culture was developing in Western Europe, Christianity persisted in the continuation of the Roman Empire which had Constantinople as its capital. From there it permeated some of the barbarians who had settled in the Balkans and spread into the vast plains of the later Russia. However, perhaps because the break with the Graeco-Roman past was not as marked, Christianity did not as nearly inform the eastern remnant of the Roman Empire as it did Western Europe, nor did as much creativity issue from it in the Balkans and Russia as in the West.

During the four centuries between 950 and 1350 the faith spread once more across Asia to the China coast, but, as before, it was represented only among small minorities.

A Second Period of Decline

There followed, approximately between 1350 and 1500, a period when Christianity again seemed moribund. In Asia it died out except westward from Persia to the Mediterranean and in South India. The Ottoman Turks, bearers of Islam, overwhelmed the remnants of the Byzantine Empire, long the bulwark of Christianity in Eastern Europe and Asia Minor, and turned the chief cathedral of the Greek Orthodox Church, Saint Sophia, into a mosque. They carried the crescent to the very walls of Vienna, threatening Western Europe. In Western Europe, the chief remaining stronghold of Christianity, the major official representative of the faith, the Roman Catholic Church, long suffered from debilitating division between rival Popes, and its hierarchy from the Popes down was shot through and through with moral corruption. The Renaissance came, in part having its source in Christianity. Yet in some of its aspects, notably in phases of humanism, it was in fact even though not ostensibly a departure from the faith. Towards the end of the period Western Europe entered on a breath-taking geographic expansion which at the outset was ruthless in its treatment of non-European peoples and upon which the professed faith of the explorers and conquerors appeared to have little effect.

Resurgence of Life

Then, beginning not far from 1500, there pulsed forth a great resurgence of life. It showed itself first in Western Europe, almost simultaneously in the Protestant and Roman Catholic Reformations. The Protestant Reformation was predominantly in North-western Europe, including the British Isles. It displayed great variety, but in general had as its distinctive principle salvation by faith. The Roman Catholic Church rejected it and Western Christendom was permanently divided.

The Roman Catholic Reformation began slightly before the Protestant Reformation. While to a large degree it was independent of the latter, it directed much of its energy against it, defined the position of the Roman Catholic Church on the issues at stake in such fashion as to leave no room for Protestantism, and sought, in some areas with success, to win back the territory which had been lost. By the middle of the seventeenth century it was clear that reconciliation between these two wings of Western Christianity was impossible, and that neither would eliminate the other. While neither was content to accept it as final, thereafter the geographic boundary between the two changed but little.

Somewhat later came movements in Russian Christianity which were indications of rising vigour, but at the outset they were quite distinct from those in Western Europe, nor did they have as widespread repercussions.

The fresh burst of life in European Christianity was followed by a territorial expansion of the faith which for magnitude had never been equalled, either by Christianity or by any other religion. It was closely associated with the amazing geographic discoveries, commerce, conquests, and migrations of European peoples. Precisely to what degree Christianity was responsible for these phenomena has never been determined. Similarly we do not know how far if at all the movements which we call the Protestant and Catholic Reformations and the abounding daring and vitality which led to this spread of European power were due to some factor or factors which were common to them all. However, in the sixteenth, seventeenth, and eighteenth centuries Christianity was planted in the Americas, on the fringes of Africa south of the Sahara, across the northern reaches of Asia, and in much of South and East Asia and its bordering islands. Most of this was by Roman Catholics, chiefly because predominatingly Roman Catholic lands, Spain and Portugal, were the main colonizing powers of the time. Some of it was by Protestants in connection with the colonies of Protestant peoples, and across Northern Asia it was by the Russian Orthodox.

The Christian communities which arose from this expansion varied greatly in vigour. The largest, in Spanish and Portuguese America, proved anemic and their continued life depended to no small degree upon unremitting transfusions of blood from Europe in the form of clergy and lay brothers. That in Canada, Roman Catholic, maintained itself even after the ties with France were severed. The one in Japan, also Roman Catholic, driven into hiding by persecution and cut off from the outside world, survived for about two hundred and fifty years with no contact with Christians of other lands. The Russian Orthodox communities, while spread over a large area, were small. The largest new Protestant communities, those in the British colonies in North America, were conspicuous for their vitality and propagating power. The small Protestant community in South Africa was also persistent and later experienced a rapid growth. Protestantism in the West Indies, India, Ceylon, and the East Indies, like the Roman Catholicism of Spanish and Portuguese America, was dependent upon that of Europe for its continued existence. In land after land, the presence of Christianity helped to soften the impact of European upon non-European peoples and to make the coming of the Occident a blessing rather than a curse.

A Combination of Adversities

The latter part of the eighteenth century brought a combination of adversities which to many of the intellectuals seemed to sound the death knell of Christianity. They were all the more serious because they largely centered in Western Europe, where Christianity had for several centuries shown its greatest vigour and because they bore heavily upon the Roman Catholic Church, through which most of the territorial expansion had been accomplished during the preceding several centuries. The dissolution of the Society of Jesus, the body through which much of the spread of the faith in the preceding two centuries had been made, was crippling. The growth of rationalism, partly sprung from a one-sided view of the conception of the dignity of man which had been derived from Christianity, but in which man's creatureliness and salvation through the act of God in Christ were ignored or discounted, undercut or destroyed the faith of many. A series of devastating wars and, above all, the French Revolution and the Wars of Napoleon shook Europe.

Yet, even while thousands were prepared to hail the demise of Christianity, movements were under way in Great Britain and the United States which were to issue in one of the most potent revivals that the faith had known. They were in Protestantism and were to rise to major proportions in the following century.

A Combination of Contrasts

The nineteenth century presented a combination of contrasts. On the one hand, much of the traditional Christendom was more prosperous than any large group of mankind had ever been. Science and the industrial revolution, to an undetermined degree outgrowths of Christianity, were enriching Western Europe and North America beyond anything previously seen. Compared with earlier eras, the age was peaceful. Knowledge of man's physical universe was expanding by breath-taking leaps and bounds. Optimism was mounting. Revolutionary ideas, partly derived from Christianity, envisioned a human society in which the humblest would share in the good things of life. These ideas contributed to revolutions which from time to time shook much of Christendom. European peoples were continuing at an accelerated pace the expansion which had begun at least as early as the fifteenth century. In that intoxicating atmosphere there were Christians who dreamed and planned for the complete remaking of mankind and civilization to bring them into conformation with the standards of their faith.

On the other hand, some features of the age appeared to threaten the very existence of Christianity. The materialism and secularism which were reinforced by the scientific and mechanical advances of the day dominated thousands and seemed to make Christianity irrelevant or a pleasant but optional adjunct to the good life. The patterns of the burgeoning industrial communities gave little room for the worship and parish life of the churches through which Christianity was perpetuated. At the outset they were a means of exploiting the labourers, with features which were a flat contradiction of Christian precepts and ideals. Some of the programmes offered for the reorganization of society, notably communism, were anti-Christian. Many who worked for better conditions of the labouring classes regarded the Church as one of the bulwarks of entrenched privilege and were critical of it and of the faith which it represented. Numbers of intellectuals and others who followed them believed, some regretfully, some gladly, that science had made Christianity untenable. The association of Christianity with Western imperialism proved a handicap: peoples upon whom that imperialism bore heavily either were critical because of the connection or were moved by it to look favourably upon Christianity, thus failing to understand the true genius of the faith.

In the face of these adverse factors Christianity displayed striking vitality and came to the end of the century more vigorous and more potent in the affairs of mankind than it had been at the outset of the century or at any previous time. This was true of all three of the main branches of the faith.

The Roman Catholic Church displayed notable resilience in recovering from the blows dealt it in the eighteenth century and especially during the French Revolution and the Napoleonic Wars. Old monastic orders renewed their strength and the Society of Jesus was revived and again became potent. Many new orders came into being. Anti-clericalism led to the separation of Church and state in France and in several other countries brought the confiscation of much ecclesiastical property and various restrictions on the Church. Partly because of the hostility of the governments of states which had once been friendly but which had sought to control the Church within their borders, the Roman Catholic Church became more tightly integrated under the Popes than ever before. The Pope was now formally declared to be infallible in matters of faith and morals. Administratively his power was markedly enhanced. The Papacy set itself against some of the major trends of the day. This also was in the direction of making the Roman Catholic church, especially its hierarchy, its monks and nuns, and its more loyal laity as distinguished from those to whom the connexion was mainly a social convention, a self conscious minority in an alien world and closely knit around the Pope. Yet the Roman Catholic Church was not merely on the defensive. It was expanding, both by emigration to the Americas and Australasia and through missions in Asia, Africa, and the Americas.

It was Protestantism which showed the greatest vigour of any of the branches of Christianity. From it issued many new movements and organizations. Within it there was a ferment of theological thought, a large proportion of it fresh and creative. There was also intensive study of the Bible, much of it courageously applying the new methods of historical scholarship. Protestantism moved in on the growing manufacturing and commercialized centres of industrialized Britain. Proportionately it spread more rapidly and widely than either the Roman Catholic Church or the Orthodox Churches. At the outset of the nineteenth century confined almost entirely to North-western Europe and the Atlantic seaboard of North America, by the dawn of the twentieth century it had spanned North America, was making a rapid growth in Latin America, was the dominant religion in Australasia, and had been planted in most of the countries of Africa and Asia.

The Orthodox Churches, especially that of Russia, were also on a rising tide, although not so strikingly as were the Roman Catholic Church and Protestantism. In the Balkans they emerged from under the Moslem Turkish yoke. In Russia there was access of vigour. While geographic expansion was not as spectacular as in the case of the other two major branches of the faith, it took place through migration to the Americas and Siberia and through a notable mission in Japan.

Challenges Faced and Met

The year 1914 opened a new and stormy stage in the course of Christianity. The contrasts were even greater than in the nineteenth century and the threats to the faith rose to larger proportions. Yet Christianity gave evidence of amazing vigour and continued its geographic spread.

The challenges to Christianity were many. Some were continuations of those of the nineteenth century, among them absorption in the pursuit of wealth, the growing industrialization of society, some of the programmes advocated for collective welfare, and adverse intellectual currents. To them were added two world wars and several lesser wars, the decline of Western Europe, revolutions which destroyed forms of government, social structures, and inherited ethical and religious convictions for at least a third of mankind, rebellion against the supremacy of Western European nations, the advance of pronouncedly anti-Christian communism, and a great groundswell among the masses in many lands demanding more of the good things of life. Significantly, and in the eyes of many observers ominously, most of these challenges originated and attained their most formidable dimensions in what had been regarded as the historic heart of Christendom.

Although it suffered losses, some of them serious, in general Christianity rose to the challenge. The Roman Catholic Church displayed features which had characterized it in the nineteenth century. Many of its hereditary constituency had their allegiance weakened or dissolved, but those who remained were more nearly consolidated under the Papacy. The See of Peter had a succession of able, upright men. There was fresh intellectual activity, especially in theology. The liturgical movement, Eucharistic congresses, and other developments stimulated piety. Catholic Action enlisted more and more of the laity. The geographic spread in Africa and Asia mounted. Also as in the nineteenth century, proportionately Protestantism flourished more pronouncedly than did the Roman Catholic Church. It experienced numerical decline in Europe, but it continued to gain in the United States, in Latin America (where its advance was chiefly among the nominally Roman Catholic population), in Africa, and in South and East Asia and its fringing islands. Even more than the Roman Catholic Church, it was stirred by theological ferment. Through the Ecumenical Movement it developed an expanding fresh approach towards Christian unity. The Eastern Churches were hard hit, especially the Russian Orthodox Church, but none of them died, and some exhibited sturdy vitality in the face of what looked like overwhelming disaster, especially from communism. Christianity came to the mid-twentieth century more nearly world-wide in its extent and influence than either it or any other religion had ever been.

The Effect of Christianity

In the relatively brief nineteen and a half centuries of its existence, in spite of its seemingly unpromising beginning, Christianity had spread over most of the earth's surface and was represented by adherents in almost every tribe and nation and in nearly every inhabited land. It had gone forward by pulsations of advance, retreat, and advance. Measured by the criteria of geographic extent, inner vigour as shown by new movements from within it, and the effect on mankind as a whole, each major advance had carried it further into the life of the world than the one before it and each major recession had been less severe than its predecessor. In spite of this spread, in the middle of the twentieth century Christianity was still the professed faith of only a minority of men, in some of the largest countries only a small minority. Of those who bore the Christian name, especially in lands where they were in the majority, only a minority made the thoroughgoing commitment required by the genius of the faith.

What effect had Christianity had across the centuries, operating as it did through this minority? Again and again in the preceding chapters we have sought to give data towards the answer. Often we cannot know whether Christianity was at all an element in a particular movement or action. In many other instances we can be reasonably sure that it entered as a factor but so compounded with other causes that we cannot accurately appraise the extent of its responsibility. Among these were the emergence of universities in the Middle Ages, the Renaissance, the rise of the scientific method, the geographic discoveries by Europeans in the fifteenth, sixteenth, and seventeenth centuries, democracy of the Anglo-Saxon kind, and communism. Whether in any of these it was determinative, so that but for it they would not have come into being, we are not and probably cannot be sure. We can be clear that in some movements Christianity was dominant. Such were the appearance and development of the various churches, monasticism in its several manifestations, the Protestant and Catholic Reformations, the formulation of the great creeds of the first few centuries, and the construction of most of the systems of theology. Yet in none of these was Christianity the only cause. Indeed, what we call Christianity changed from time to time. In most of its forms what came from Jesus and his apostles was regarded as primary and determinative, but other contributions entered, among them the cultural background of individuals and groups, the personal experiences of outstanding leaders, and inherited religions and philosophical conceptions.

The Fruits of the Faith

In spite of these uncertainties and complicating factors, we can be fully assured of some of the fruits of what constitutes the core of the Christian faith and of Christianity, namely, the life, teachings, death, and resurrection of Jesus. We can, of course, be clear that without this core Christianity and the churches would not have been. It is by no means responsible for all that was done in the guise of Christianity or under the aegis of the churches, and much was performed in its name which was quite contrary to it. However, the perversion of the Gospel is one of the facts of which an appraisal of the results of Christianity must take account. It is incontestable that from Christ issued unmeasured and immeasurable power in the life of mankind. We know that because of him across the centuries untold thousands of individuals have borne something of his likeness. Thousands have been so reared in the knowledge of him that from childhood and without striking struggle they have followed him and have increasingly shown the radiance of the faith, hope, and self-giving love which were in him. Other thousands have come to the same path and goal through deep sorrow, initial moral defeat, and soul-wrenching struggles. Some have been famous and have passed on to other thousands the light which has come from him. More have been obscure and have been known only to a limited circle, but within that circle they have been towers of strength.

Through Christ there has come into being the Church. The Church is never fully identical with ecclesiastical organizations. It is to be found in them, but not all of their members belong to it and it is greater than the sum of them all. Yet, though never fully visible as an institution, the Church has been and is a reality, more potent than any one or all of the churches. "The blessed company of all faithful people," it constitutes a fellowship which has been both aided and hampered by the churches, and is both in them and transcends them.

From individuals who have been inspired by Christ and from the Church has issued movement after movement for attaining the Christian ideal. That ideal has centered around the kingdom of God, an order in which God's will is done. It sets infinite value upon the individual. Its goal for the individual is to become a child of God, to "know the love of Christ which passeth knowledge" and to "be filled unto all the fulness of God"—God Who is Creator and Father, Who revealed His true nature, self-giving love, by becoming incarnate in Jesus Christ, and permitting the seeming defeat and frustration of the cross, and Who is ever active in history in individuals and the collective life of mankind. Its goal for the individual cannot be completely attained this side of the grave, but is so breathtaking that within history only a beginning is possible. Nor can it be reached in isolation, but only in community. In Christ's teaching, love for God, as the duty and privilege of man, is inseparably joined with love for one's neighbour.

The ideal and the goal have determined the character of the movements which have been the fruits of Christianity. Although men can use and often have used knowledge and education to the seeming defeat of the ideal, across the centuries Christianity has been the means of reducing more languages to writing than have all other factors combined. It has created more schools, more theories of education, and more systems than has any other one force. More than any other power in history it has impelled men to fight suffering, whether that suffering has come from disease, war, or natural disasters. It built thousands of hospitals, inspired the emergence of nursing and medical professions, and furthered movements for public health and the relief and prevention of famine. Although explorations and conquests which were in part its outgrowth led to the enslavement of Africans for the plantations of the Americas, men and women whose consciences were awakened by Christianity and whose wills it nerved brought about the abolition of Negro slavery. Men and women similarly moved and sustained, wrote into the laws of Spain and Portugal provisions to alleviate the ruthless exploitation of the Indians of the New World. Wars have often been waged in the name of Christianity. They have attained their most colossal dimensions through weapons and large scale organization initiated in Christendom. Yet from no other source have there come as many and as strong movements to eliminate or regulate war and to ease the suffering brought by war. From its first centuries the Christian faith has caused many of its adherents to be uneasy about war. It has led minorities to refuse to have any part in it. It has impelled others to seek to limit war by defining what, in their judgment, from the Christian stand-point is a "just war." In the turbulent middle ages of Europe it gave rise to the Truce of God and the Peace of God. In a later era it was the main impulse in the formulation of international law. But for it the League of Nations and the United Nations would not have been. By its name and symbol the most extensive organ-ization ever created for the relief of the suffering caused by war, the Red Cross, bears witness to its Christian origin. The list might go on indefinitely. It includes many other humanitarian projects and movements, ideals in government, the reform of prisons and the emergence of criminology, great art and architecture, and outstanding literature. In geographic extent and potency the results were never as marked as in the nineteenth and twentieth centuries.

Study Questions

1. Do you believe that Latourette overestimates, underestimates, or properly assesses the historical impact of Jesus Christ and Christianity? Why?

2. Describe some of the factors that can account for the geographical and cultural expansion of the Christian faith.

3
Four Men, Three Eras, Two Transitions: Modern Missions

Ralph D. Winter

College students around the world used to be bowled over by Marxist thought. One powerful reason was that Communism had a "long look." Communists claimed to know where history was heading, and that they were merely following inevitable trends.

Recently, evangelicals, too, have thought a lot about trends in history and their relationship to events to come. The massive response a while back to Hal Lindsey's books and films about possible events in the future has shown us that people are responsive to a "where are we going?" approach to life.

In comparison to the Communists, Christians actually have the longest look, backed up by a mass of hard facts and heroic deeds. Yet for some reason, Christians often make little connection between discussion of prophecy and future events, and discussion of missions. They see the Bible as a book of prophecy, both in the past and for the future. Yet, as Bruce Ker has said so well, "The Bible is a missionary book throughout...The main line of argument that binds all of it together is the unfolding and gradual execution of a missionary purpose."

Did I ever hear Ker's thought in Sunday School? Maybe. But only in later years have I come to a new appreciation of the fact that the story of missions begins long before the Great Commission. The Bible is very clear: God told Abraham he was to be blessed and be a blessing to all the families of the earth (Gen. 12:1-3). Peter quoted this on the day he spoke in the temple (Acts 3:25). Paul quoted the same mandate in his letter to the Galatians (3:8).

Yet some Bible commentators imply that only the first part of that verse could have happened right away. They agree that Abraham was to begin to be blessed

After serving ten years as a missionary among Mayan Indians in western Guatemala, Ralph D. Winter spent the next ten years as a professor of missions at the School of World Mission at Fuller Theological Seminary. He is the founder of the U.S. Center for World Mission in Pasadena, California, a cooperative center focused on people groups still lacking a culturally relevant church. Winter has also been instrumental in the formation of the movement called Theological Education by Extension, the William Carey Library publishing house, the American Society of Missiology, the Perspectives Study Program and the International Society for Frontier Missiology. Since March of 1990 he has been the President of the William Carey International University.

right away, but somehow they reason that two thousand years would have to pass before either Abraham or his descendants could begin "to be a blessing to all the families on earth." They suggest that Christ needed to come first and institute his Great Commission—that Abraham's lineage needed to wait around for 2,000 years before they would be called upon to go the ends of the earth to be a blessing to all the world's peoples (this could be called "The Theory of the Hibernating Mandate."). Worse still, one scholar, with a lot of followers in later decades, propounded the idea that in the Old Testament the peoples of the world were not expected to receive missionaries but to go to Israel for the light, and that from the the New Testament and thereafter it was the reverse, that is, the peoples to be blessed would not come but those already having received the blessing would go to them. This rather artificial idea gained acceptance partially by the use of the phrase, "Centripetal mission in the Old Testament and Centrifugal mission in the New Testament." Fact is, there is both in both periods, and it is very confusing to try to employ an essentially mickey mouse gimmick to explain a shift in strategy that did not happen. The existence of 137 different languages in Los Angeles makes clear that now, in the New Testament-and-after period, nations are still coming to the light.

A more recent and exciting interpretation (see Walter Kaiser's chapter four) observes that Israel, as far back as Abraham, was accountable to share that blessing with other nations. In the same way, since the time of the Apostle Paul, every nation which has contained any significant number of "children of Abraham's faith" has been similarly accountable (but both Israel and the other nations have mainly failed to carry out this mandate).

The greatest scandal in the Old Testament is that Israel tried to be blessed without trying very hard to be a blessing. However, let's be careful: *the average citizen of Israel was no more oblivious to the second part of Gen. 12:1-3 than the average Christian today is oblivious to the Great Commission!* How easily our study Bibles overlook the veritable string of key passages in the Old Testament which exist to remind Israel (and us) of the missionary mandate: Gen. 12:1-3, 18:18, 22:18, 28:14, Ex. 19:4-6, Deut. 28:10, 2 Chron. 6:33, Ps. 67, 96, 105, Isa. 40:5, 42:4, 49:6, 56:3, 6-8, Jer. 12:14-17, Zech. 2:11, Mal. 1:11.

Likewise, today, nations which have been singularly blessed by God may choose to resist and try to conceal any sense of their obligation to be a blessing to other nations. But that is not God's will. "Unto whomsoever much is given, of him shall much be required" (Luke 12:48).

Thus, how many times in the average church today is the Great Commission mentioned? Even less often than it comes up in the Old Testament! Yet the commission applies. It applied then, and it applies today. I believe it has been constantly applicable from the very moment when it was first given (Gen. 12:1-3). As individual Christians and as a nation we are responsible "to be a blessing to all the families of the earth."

This mandate has been overlooked during most of the centuries since the apostles. Even our Protestant tradition plugged along for over 250 years minding its own business and its own blessings (like Israel of old)—until a young man of great faith and incredible endurance appeared on the scene. In this chapter we are going to focus in on the A.D. 1800-2000 period which his life and witness kicked off. No other one person can be given as much credit for the vibrant new impetus of the last two hundred years. He was one of four such influential men whom God used, all of them with severe handicaps. Three great "eras" of new plunging forward into newly perceived frontiers resulted from their faith and obedience (it took two of them to launch the third and final era). Four stages of mission strategy characterized each of these eras. Two perplexing "transitions" of strategy inevitably appeared as the fourth stage of one era contrasted with the first stage of the next. It is easier to see this in a diagram. Better still, the story.

THE FIRST ERA

An "under thirty" young man, William Carey, got into trouble when he began to take the Great Commission seriously. When he had the opportunity to address a group of ministers, he challenged them to give a reason why the Great Commission did not apply to them. They rebuked him, saying, "When God chooses to win the heathen, He will do it without your help or ours." He was unable to speak again on the subject, so he patiently wrote out his analysis, "An Enquiry Into the Obligations of Christians to Use Means for the Conversion of the Heathens."

The resulting small book convinced a few of his friends to create a tiny missions agency, the "means" of which he had spoken. The structure was flimsy and weak, providing only the minimal backing he needed to go to India. However, the impact of his example reverberated throughout the English-speaking world, and his little book became the Magna Carta of the Protestant mission movement.

William Carey was not the first Protestant missionary. For years the Moravians had sent people to Greenland, America and Africa. But his little book, in combination with the Evangelical Awakening, quickened vision and changed lives on both sides of the Atlantic. Response was almost instantaneous: a second missionary society was founded in London; two in Scotland; one in Holland; and then still another in England. By then it was apparent to all that Carey was right when he had insisted that organized efforts in the form of missions societies were essential to the success of the missionary endeavor.

In America, five college students, aroused by Carey's book, met to pray for God's direction for their lives. This unobtrusive prayer meeting, later known as the "Haystack Prayer Meeting," resulted in an American "means"—the American Board of Commissioners of Foreign Missions. Even more important, they started a student mission movement which became the example and forerunner of other student movements in missions to this day.

In fact, during the first 25 years after Carey sailed to India, a dozen mission agencies were formed on both sides of the Atlantic, and the First Era in Protestant missions was off to a good start. Realistically speaking, however, missions in this First Era was a pitifully small shoe-string operation, in relation to the major preoccupations of most Europeans and Americans in that day. The idea that we should organize in order to send missionaries did not come easily, but it eventually became an accepted pattern.

Carey's influence led some women in Boston to form women's missionary prayer groups, a trend which led to women becoming the main custodians of mission knowledge and motivation. After some years women began to go to the field as single missionaries. Finally, by 1865, unmarried American women established women's mission boards which, like Roman Catholic women's orders, only sent out single women as missionaries and were run entirely by single women at home.

There are two very bright notes about the First Era. One is the astonishing demonstration of love and sacrifice on the part of those who went out. Africa, especially, was a forbidding continent. All mission outreach to Africa, prior to 1775, had totally failed. Of all Catholic efforts, all Moravian efforts, nothing remained. Not one missionary of any kind existed on the continent on the eve of the First Era. The gruesome statistics of almost inevitable sickness and death that haunted, yet did not daunt, the decades of truly valiant missionaries who went out after 1790 in virtually a suicidal stream cannot be matched by any other era or by any other cause. Very few missionaries to Africa in the first 60 years of the First Era survived more than two years. As I have reflected on this measure of devotion I have been humbled to tears, for I wonder—if I or my people today could or would match that record. Can you imagine our Urbana students today going out into missionary work if they knew that for decade after decade 19 out of 20 of those before them had died almost on arrival on the field?

A second bright spot in this First Era is the development of high quality insight into mission strategy. The movement had several great missiologists. In regard to home structure, they clearly understood the value of the mission structure being allowed a life of its own. For example, we read that the London Missionary Society experienced unprecedented and unequaled success, "due partly to its freedom from ecclesiastical supervision and partly to its formation from an almost equal number of ministers and laymen." In regard to field structure, we can take a note from Henry Venn who was related to the famous Clapham evangelicals and the son of a founder of the Church Missionary Society. Except for a few outdated terms, one of his most famous paragraphs sounds strangely modern:

> Regarding the ultimate object of a Mission, viewed under its ecclesiastical result, to be the settlement of a Native Church under Native Pastors upon a self-supporting system, it should be borne in mind that the progress of a Mission mainly depends upon the training up and the location of Native Pastors; and that, as it has been happily expressed, the "euthanasia of a Mission" takes place when a missionary, surrounded by well-trained Native congregations under Native Pastors, is able to resign all pastoral work into their hands, and gradually relax his superintendance over the pastors themselves, 'til it insensibly ceases; and so the Mission passes into a settled Christian community. Then the missionary and all missionary agencies should be transferred to the "regions beyond."

Note: no thought here of the national church launching its own mission outreach to new pioneer fields! Nevertheless, we see here something like *stages of mission activity*, described by Harold Fuller of SIM in the alliterative sequence:

Stage 1: A Pioneer stage - first contact with a people group.

Stage 2: A Paternal stage - expatriates train national leadership.

Stage 3: A Partnership stage - national leaders work as equals with expatriates.

Stage 4: A Participation stage - expatriates are no longer equal partners, but only participate by invitation.

MISSION-CHURCH RELATIONS:
FOUR STAGES OF DEVELOPMENT

STAGE I: PIONEER

Requires gift of leadership, along with other gifts. No believers- missionary must lead and do much of the work himself.

mission

STAGE II: PARENT

Requires gift of teaching. The young church has a growing child's relationship to the mission. But the "parent" must avoid "paternalism".

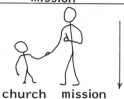

church   mission

STAGE III: PARTNER

Requires change from parent-child relation to adult-adult relation. Difficult for both to change, but essential to the church's becoming a mature "adult".

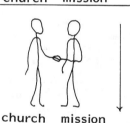

church   mission

STAGE IV: PARTICIPANT

A fully mature church assumes leadership. As long as the mission remains, it should use its gifts to strengthen the church to meet the original objectives of Matt. 28:19-20. Meanwhile the mission should be involved in Stage 1 elsewhere.

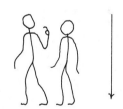

church   mission

Slow and painstaking though the labors of the First Era were, they did bear fruit, and the familiar series of stages can be observed which goes from no church in the pioneer stage to infant church in the paternal stage and to the more complicated mature church in the partnership and participation stages.

Samuel Hoffman of the Reformed Church in America Board puts it well: "The Christian missionary who was loved as an evangelist and liked as a teacher, may find himself resented as an administrator."

Lucky is the missionary in whose own career this whole sequence of stages takes place. More likely the series represents the work in a specific field with a succession of missionaries, or it may be the experience of an agency which in its early period bursts out in work in a number of places and then after some years finds that most of its fields are mature at about the same time. But rightly or wrongly, this kind of succession is visible in the mission movement globally, as the fever for change and nationalization sweeps the thinking of almost all executives at once and leaps from continent to continent, affecting new fields still in earlier stages as well as old ones in the latter stages.

At any rate, by 1865 there was a strong consensus on both sides of the Atlantic that the missionary should go home when he had worked himself out of a job. Since the First Era focused primarily upon the coastlands of Asia and Africa, we are not surprised that literal withdrawal would come about first in a case where there were no inland territories. Thus, symbolizing the latter stages of the First Era was the withdrawal of all missionaries from the Hawaiian Islands, then a separate country. This was done with legitimate pride and fanfare and fulfilled the highest expectations, then and now, of successful progress through the stages of missionary planting, watering and harvest.

THE SECOND ERA

A second symbolic event of 1865 is even more significant, at least for the inauguration of the Second Era. A young man, after a short term and like Carey still under thirty, in the teeth of surrounding counter advice established the first of a whole new breed of missions emphasizing the inland territories. This second young upstart was given little but negative notice, but like William Carey, brooded over statistics, charts and maps. When he suggested that the inland peoples of China needed to be reached, he was told you could not get there, and he was asked if he wished to carry on his shoulders the blood of the young people he would thus send to their deaths. This accusing question stunned and staggered him. Groping for light, wandering on the beach, it seemed as if God finally spoke to resolve the ghastly thought: "You are not sending young people in the interior of China. I am." The load lifted.

With only trade school medicine, without any university experience much less missiological training, and a checkered past in regard to his own individualistic behavior while he was on the field, he was merely one more of the weak things that God uses to confound the wise. Even his early antichurch-planting missionary strategy was breathtakingly erroneous by today's church-planting standards. Yet God strangely honored him because his gaze was fixed upon the world's least-reached peoples. Hudson Taylor had a divine wind behind him.

The Holy Spirit spared him from many pitfalls, and it was his organization, the China Inland Mission—the most cooperative, servant organization yet to appear—that eventually served in one way or another over 6,000 missionaries, predominantly in the interior of China. It took 20 years for other missions to begin to join Taylor in his special emphasis—the unreached, inland frontiers.

One reason the Second Era began slowly is that many people were confused. There were already many missions in existence. Why more? Yet as Taylor pointed out, all existing agencies were confined to the coastlands of Africa and Asia, or islands in the Pacific. People questioned, "Why go to the interior if you haven't finished the job on the coast?"

I am not sure the parallel is true today, but the Second Era apparently needed not only a new vision but a lot of new organizations. Taylor not only started an English frontier mission, he went to Scandinavia and the Continent to challenge people to start new agencies. As a result, directly or indirectly, over 40 new agencies took shape to compose the faith missions that rightly should be called frontier missions as the names of many of them still indicate: China Inland Mission, Sudan Interior Mission, Africa Inland Mission, Heart of Africa Mission, Unevangelized Fields Mission, Regions Beyond Missionary Union. Taylor was more concerned for the cause than for a career: at the end of his life he had spent only half of his years of ministry in China. In countless trips back from China he spent half of his time as a mobilizer on the home front. For Taylor, the cause of Christ, not China, was the ultimate focus of his concern.

As in the early stage of the First Era, when things began to move, God

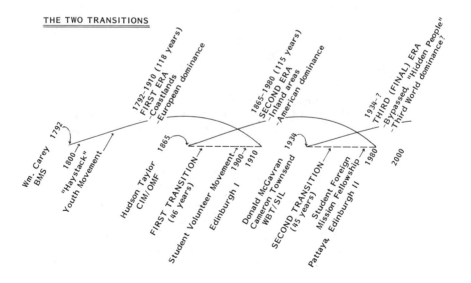

THE TWO TRANSITIONS

brought forth a student movement. This one was more massive than before—the Student Volunteer Movement for Foreign Missions, history's single most potent mission organization. In the 1880's and 90's there were only 1/37th as many college students as there are today, but the Student Volunteer Movement netted 100,000 volunteers who gave their lives to missions. Twenty-thousand actually went overseas. As we see it now, the other 80,000 had to stay home to rebuild the foundations of the missions endeavor. They began the Laymen's Missionary Movement and strengthened existing women's missionary societies.

However, as the fresh new college students of the Second Era burst on the scene overseas, they did not always fathom how the older missionaries of the First Era could have turned responsibility over to national leadership at the least educated levels of society. First Era missionaries were in the minority now, and the wisdom they had gained from their experience was bypassed by the large number of new college-educated recruits. Thus, in the early stages of the Second Era, the new college-trained missionaries, instead of going to new frontiers, sometimes assumed leadership over existing churches, not reading the record of previous mission thinkers, and often forced First Era missionaries and national leadership (which had been painstakingly developed) into the background. In some cases this caused a huge step backward in mission strategy.

By 1925, however, the largest mission movement in history was in full swing. By then Second Era missionaries had finally learned the basic lessons they had first ignored, and produced an incredible record. They had planted churches in a thousand new places, mainly "inland," and by 1940 the reality of the "younger churches" around the world was widely acclaimed as the "great new fact of our time." The strength of these churches led both national leaders and missionaries to assume that all additional frontiers could simply be mopped up by the ordinary evangelism of the churches scattered throughout the world. More and more people wondered if, in fact, missionaries weren't needed so badly! Once more, as in 1865, it seemed logical to send missionaries home from many areas of the world.

For us today it is highly important to note the overlap of these first two eras. The 45 year period between 1865 and 1910 (compare 1934 to 1980 today) was a transition between the strategy appropriate to the mature stages of Era 1, the Coastlands era, and the strategy appropriate to the pioneering stages of Era 2, the Inland era.

Shortly after the World Missionary Conference in Edinburgh in 1910, there ensued the shattering World Wars and the world-wide collapse of the colonial apparatus. By 1945 many overseas churches were prepared not only for the withdrawal of the colonial powers, but for the absence of the missionary as well. While there was no very widespread outcry, "Missionary Go Home," as some supposed, nevertheless things were different now, as even the people in the pews at home ultimately sensed. Pioneer and paternal were no longer the relevant stages, but partnership and participation.

In 1967, the total number of career missionaries from America began to decline (and it has continued to do so to this day). Why? Christians had been led to believe that all necessary beachheads had been established. By 1967, over 90 percent of all missionaries from North America were working with strong national churches that had been in existence for some time.

The facts, however, were not that simple. Unnoticed by most everyone, another era in missions had begun.

THE THIRD ERA

This era was begun by a pair of young men of the Student Volunteer Movement: Cameron Townsend and Donald McGavran. Cameron Townsend was in so much of a hurry to get to the mission field that he didn't bother to finish college. He went to Guatemala as a "Second Era" missionary, building on work which had been done in the past. In that country, as in all other mission fields, there was plenty to do by missionaries working with established national churches.

But Townsend was alert enough to notice that the majority of Guatemala's population did not speak Spanish. As he moved from village to village, trying to distribute scriptures written in the Spanish language, he began to realize that Spanish evangelism would never reach all Guatemala's people. He was further convinced of this when an Indian asked him, "If your God is so smart, why can't he speak our language?" He was befriended by a group of older missionaries who had already concluded the indigenous "Indian" populations needed to be reached in their own languages. He was just 23 when he began to move on the basis of this new perspective.

Surely in our time one person comparable to William Carey and Hudson Taylor is Cameron Townsend. Like Carey and Taylor, Townsend saw that there were still unreached frontiers, and for almost a half century he has waved the flag for the overlooked tribal peoples of the world. He started out hoping to help older boards reach out to tribal people. Like Carey and Taylor, he ended up starting his own mission, Wycliffe Bible Translators, which is dedicated to reaching these new frontiers. At first he thought there must be about 500 unreached tribal groups in the world. (He was judging by the large number of tribal languages in Mexico alone). Later, he revised his figure to 1,000, then 2,000, and now it is closer to 5,000. As his conception of the enormity of the task has increased, the size of his organization has increased. Today it numbers over 4,000 adult workers.

At the very same time Townsend was ruminating in Guatemala, Donald McGavran was beginning to yield to the seriousness, not of linguistic barriers, but of India's amazing social barriers. Townsend "discovered" the tribes; McGavran discovered a more nearly universal category he labeled "homogeneous units," which today are more often called "people groups." Paul Hiebert has employed the terminology of "horizontal segmentation" for the tribes which each occupied their own turf, and "vertical segmentation" for groups distinguished not by geography but by rigid social differences. McGavran's terminology described both kinds even though he was mainly thinking about the more subtle vertical segmentation.

Once such a group is penetrated, diligently taking advantage of that missiological breakthrough along group lines, the strategic "bridge of God" to that people group is established. The corollary of this truth is the fact that *until* such a breakthrough is made, normal evangelism and church planting cannot take place.

McGavran did not found a new mission (Townsend did so only when the existing missions did not properly respond to the tribal challenge). McGavran's active efforts and writings spawned both the church growth movement and the frontier mission movement, the one devoted to expanding within already penetrated groups, and the other devoted to deliberate approaches to the remaining unpenetrated groups.

As with Carey and Taylor before them, for twenty years Townsend and McGavran attracted little attention. But by the 1950's both had wide audiences. By 1980, 46 years from 1934, a 1910-like conference was held, focusing precisely on the forgotten groups these two men emphasized. The Edinburgh-1980 World Consultation on Frontier Missions was the largest mission meeting in history, measured by the number of mission agencies sending delegates. And wonder of wonders, 57 Third World agencies sent delegates. This is the sleeper of the Third Era! Also, a simultaneous youth meeting, the International Student Consultation on Frontier Missions, pointed the way for all future mission meetings to include significant youth participation.

As happened in the early stages of the first two eras, the Third Era has spawned a number of new mission agencies. Some, like the New Tribes Mission, carry in their names reference to this new emphasis. The names of others, such as Gospel Recordings and Mission Aviation Fellowship, refer to the new technologies necessary for the reaching of tribal and other isolated peoples of the world. Some Second Era agencies, like Regions Beyond Missionary Union, have never ceased to stress frontiers, and have merely increased their staff so they can penetrate further—to people groups previously overlooked.

More recently many have begun to realize that tribal peoples are not the only forgotten peoples. Many other groups, some in the middle of partially Christianized areas, have been completely overlooked. These peoples are being called the "Unreached Peoples" and are defined by ethnic or sociological traits to be people so different from the cultural traditions of any existing church that missions (rather than evangelism) strategies are necessary for the planting of indigenous churches within their particular traditions.

If the First Era was characterized by reaching coastland peoples and the Second Era by inland territories, the Third Era must be characterized by the more difficult-to-define, non-geographical category which we have called "Unreached Peoples"—people groups which are socially isolated. Because this concept has been so hard to define, the Third Era has been even slower getting started than the Second Era. Cameron Townsend and Donald McGavran began calling attention to forgotten peoples over 40 years ago, but only recently has any major attention been given to them. More tragic still, we have essentially forgotten the pioneering techniques of the First and Second Eras, so we almost need to reinvent the wheel as we learn again how to approach groups of people completely untouched by the gospel!

We know that there are about 11,000 people groups in the "Unreached Peoples" category, gathered in clusters of similar peoples, these clusters numbering not more than 3,000. Each individual people will require a separate, new missionary beachhead. Is this too much? Can this be done? Is there any realism in the slogan gaining currency, "A Church for Every People by the Year 2000?" The AD2000 Movement adds "and the Gospel for every person..." which, of course, cannot be accomplished unless each people is first penetrated.

Can We Do It?

The task is not as difficult as it may seem, for several surprising reasons. In the first place, the task is not an American one, nor even a Western one. It will involve Christians from every continent of the world. In 1980, we know of over 400 mission agencies in the non-western world, which are sending over 13,000 missionaries—and the number is increasing.

More significant is the fact that when a beachhead is established within a culture, the normal evangelistic process which God expects every Christian to be involved in replaces the missions strategy, because the mission task of "breaking in" is finished. Thus, establishing a beachhead in each "Unreached People" group by the year 2000 is a goal readily within our grasp.

Furthermore, "closed countries" are less and less of a problem, because the modern world is becoming more and more interdependent. There are literally no countries today which admit no foreigners. Many of the countries considered "completely closed"—like Saudi Arabia—are in actual fact avidly recruiting thousands of skilled people from other nations. And the truth is, they prefer devout Christians to boozing, womanizing, secular Westerners.

Thus certain exciting meetings in 1980—the COWE meeting in Thailand, the World Consultation on Frontier Missions in Edinburgh, and the Associated International Student Consultation on Frontier Missions in the same city—are all flash points of new departure in the heating-up of the Third Era.

Meanwhile, key Second Era mission agencies like the Sudan Interior Mission are turning their attention to new fields. SIM's Gerald Swank has located over a dozen new beachheads where SIM is seeking to begin again. The Missouri Synod Lutheran Church voted to triple its missionary force by 1990 in order to open ten major fields where they will reach Unreached Peoples. The Baptist General Conference, as a denomination chose Unreached Peoples to be its highest denominational priority. Dozens of examples could be given. More than 70 mission agencies are now working with the Adopt-A-People Clearinghouse. In well over half of all remaining 11,000 groups work has already begun or is soon to begin.

But our work in the Third Era has many other advantages. We have potentially a world-wide network of churches that can be aroused to their central mission. Best of all, nothing can obscure the fact that this could and should be the *final* era. No serious believer today dare overlook the fact that God has not asked us to reach every nation, tribe and tongue without intending it to be done. No generation has less excuse than ours if we do not do as He asks.

Study Questions

1. Describe the emphasis of each of the three eras and explain the tensions inherent in the transition from one era to another.

2. Name the key figure, approximate dates, and student movement associated with each era.

3. Explain the four stages of mission activity.

4. What factors make the year 2000 a realistic goal for the penetration of all remaining Unreached Peoples? What could thwart this hope?

4

The Two Structures of God's Redemptive Mission

Ralph D. Winter

In an address given to the All-Asia Mission Consultation in Seoul, Korea in August 1973 (the founding of the Asia Missions Association), Ralph Winter describes the forms that God's two "redemptive structures" take in every human society, and have taken throughout history. His thesis has two major implications: (1) We must accept both structures, represented in the Christian church today by the local church and the mission society, as legitimate and necessary, and as part of "God's People, the Church;" and (2) non-Western churches must form and utilize mission societies if they are to exercise their missionary responsibility.

It is the thesis of this article that whether Christianity takes on Western or Asian form, there will still be two basic kinds of structures that will make up the movement. Most of the emphasis will be placed on pointing out the existence of these two structures as they have continuously appeared across the centuries. This will serve to define, illustrate and compare their nature and importance. The writer will also endeavor to explain why he believes our efforts today in any part of the world will be most effective only if both of these two structures are fully and properly involved and supportive of each other.

Redemptive Structures in New Testament Times

First of all, let us recognize the structure so fondly called "the New Testament Church" as basically a Christian synagogue.[1] Paul's missionary work consisted primarily of going to synagogues scattered across the Roman Empire, beginning in Asia Minor, and making clear to the Jewish and Gentile believers in those synagogues that the Messiah had come in Jesus Christ, the Son of God; that in Christ

After serving ten years as a missionary among Mayan Indians in western Guatemala, Ralph D. Winter spent the next ten years as a professor of missions at the School of World Mission at Fuller Theological Seminary. He is the founder of the U.S. Center for World Mission in Pasadena, California, a cooperative center focused on people groups still lacking a culturally relevant church. Winter has also been instrumental in the formation of the movement called Theological Education by Extension, the William Carey Library publishing house, the American Society of Missiology, the Perspectives Study Program and the International Society for Frontier Missiology. Since March of 1990 he has been the President of the William Carey International University.

a final authority even greater than Moses existed; and that this made more understandable than ever the welcoming of the Gentiles without forcing upon them any literal cultural adaptation to the ritual provisions of the Mosaic Law. An outward novelty of Paul's work was the development eventually of wholly new synagogues that were not only Christian, but Greek.

Very few Christians, casually reading the New Testament (and with only the New Testament available to them), would surmise the degree to which there had been Jewish evangelists who went before Paul all over the Roman Empire—a movement that began 100 years before Christ. Some of these were the people whom Jesus himself described as "traversing land and sea to make a single proselyte." Saul followed their path; Paul built on their efforts and went beyond them with the new gospel he preached, which allowed the Greeks to remain Greeks and not be circumcised and culturally assimilated into the Jewish way of life. Paul had a vast foundation on which to build: Peter declared "Moses is preached in every City (of the Roman Empire)" (Acts 15:21).

Yet not only did Paul apparently go to every existing synagogue of Asia,[2] after which he declared, "...all Asia has heard the gospel," but, when occasion demanded, he established brand new synagogue-type fellowships of believers as the basic unit of his missionary activity. The first structure in the New Testament scene is thus what is often called the *New Testament Church*. It was essentially built along Jewish synagogue lines,[3] embracing the community of the faithful in any given place. The defining characteristic of this structure is that it included old and young, male and female. Note, too, that Paul was willing to build such fellowships out of former Jews as well as non-Jewish Greeks.

There is a second, quite different structure in the New Testament context. While we know very little about the structure of the evangelistic outreach within which pre-Pauline Jewish proselytizers worked, we do know, as already mentioned, that they operated all over the Roman Empire. It would be surprising if Paul didn't follow somewhat the same procedures. And we know a great deal more about the way Paul operated. He was, true enough, sent out by the church in Antioch. But once away from Antioch he seemed very much on his own. The little team he formed was economically self-sufficient when occasion demanded. It was also dependent, from time-to-time, not alone upon the Antioch church, but upon other churches that had risen as a result of evangelistic labors. Paul's team may certainly be considered a structure. While its design and form is not made concrete for us on the basis of remaining documents, neither, of course, is the structure of a New Testament congregation defined concretely for us in the pages of the New Testament. In both cases, the absence of any such definition implies the pre-existence of a commonly understood pattern of relationship, whether in the case of the congregational structure or the missionary band structure which Paul employed earlier as Saul the Pharisee, and later, at the time the Antioch congregation in Acts 13:2 released Paul and Barnabus for missionary work.

Thus, on the one hand, the structure we call the *New Testament church* is a prototype of all subsequent Christian fellowships where old and young, male and female are gathered together as normal biological families in aggregate. On the other hand, Paul's *missionary band* can be considered a prototype of all subsequent missionary endeavors organized out of committed, experienced workers who affiliated themselves as a second decision beyond membership in the first structure.

Note well the *additional* commitment. Note also that the structure that resulted was something definitely more than the extended outreach of the Antioch church. No matter what we think the structure was, we know that it was not simply the Antioch church operating at a distance from its home base. It was something else, something different. We will consider the missionary band the second of the two redemptive structures in New Testament times.

In conclusion, it is very important to note that neither of these two structures was, as it were, "let down from heaven" in a special way. It may be shocking at first to think that God made use of either a *Jewish* synagogue pattern or a *Jewish* evangelistic pattern. But this must not be more surprising than the fact that God employed the use of the pagan Greek language, the Holy Spirit guiding the biblical writers to lay hold of such terms as *kurios* (originally a pagan term), and pound them into shape to carry the Christian revelation. The New Testament refers to a synagogue dedicated to Satan, but this did not mean that Christians, to avoid such a pattern, could not fellowship together in the synagogue pattern. These considerations prepare us for what comes next in the history of the expansion of the gospel, because we see other patterns chosen by Christians at a later date whose origins are just as clearly "borrowed patterns" as were those in the New Testament period.

In fact, the profound missiological implication of all this is that the New Testament is trying to show us *how to borrow effective patterns*; it is trying to free all future missionaries from the need to follow the precise *forms* of the Jewish synagogue and Jewish missionary band, and yet to allow them to choose comparable indigenous structures in the countless new situations across history and around the world—structures which will correspond faithfully to the *function* of patterns Paul employed, if not their *form*! It is no wonder that a considerable body of literature in the field of missiology today underlies the fact that world Christianity has generally employed the various existing languages and cultures of the world-human community—more so than any other religion—and in so doing, has cast into a shadow all efforts to canonize as universal any kind of mechanically formal extension of the New Testament church—which is "the people of God" however those individuals are organized. As Kraft has said earlier, we seek *dynamic equivalence,* not formal replication.[4]

The Early Development of Christian Structures Within Roman Culture

We have seen how the Christian movement built itself upon two different kinds of structures that had pre-existed in the Jewish cultural tradition. It is now our task to see if the *functional* equivalents of these same two structures were to appear in later Christian cultural traditions as the gospel invaded that larger world.

Of course, the original synagogue pattern persisted as a Christian structure for some time. Rivalry between Christians and Jews, however, tended to defeat this as a Christian pattern, and in some cases to force it out of existence, especially where it was possible for Jewish congregations of the dispersion to arouse public persecution of the apparently deviant Christian synagogues. Unlike the Jews, Christians had no official license for their alternative to the Roman Imperial cult.[5] Thus, whereas each synagogue was considerably independent of the others, the Christian pattern was soon assimilated to the Roman context, and bishops became invested with authority over more than one congregation with a territorial jurisdiction not altogether different from the pattern of Roman civil government. This tendency is well confirmed by the time the official recognition of Christianity had its full impact: the very Latin word for Roman magisterial territories was appropriated—the *diocese*—within which parishes are to be found on the local level.

In any case, while the more "congregational" pattern of the independent synagogue became pervasively replaced by a "connectional" Roman pattern the new Christian *parish church* still preserved the basic constituency of the synagogue, namely, the combination of old and young, male and female—that is, a biologically perpetuating organism.

Meanwhile, the monastic tradition in various early forms, developed as a second structure. This new, widely proliferating structure undoubtedly had no connection at all with the missionary band in which Paul was involved. Indeed, it more substantially drew from Roman military structure than from any other single source. Pachomius, a former military man, gained three thousand followers and attracted the attention of people like Basil of Caesarea, and then through Basil, John Cassian, who labored in southern Gaul at a later date.[6] These men thus carried forward a disciplined structure, borrowed primarily from the military, which allowed nominal Christians to make a second-level choice—an additional specific commitment.

Perhaps it would be well to pause here for a moment. Any reference to the monasteries gives Protestants culture shock. The Protestant Reformation fought desperately against certain degraded conditions at the very end of the 1000-year medieval period. We have no desire to deny the fact that conditions in monasteries were not always ideal; what the average Protestant knows about monasteries may be correct for certain situations; but the popular Protestant stereotype surely cannot describe correctly all that happened during the 1000 years! During those centuries there were many different eras and epochs and a wide variety of monastic movements, radically different from each other, as we shall see in a minute; and any generalization about so vast a phenomenon is bound to be simply an unreliable and no doubt prejudiced caricature.

Let me give just one example of how far wrong our Protestant stereotypes can be. We often hear that the monks "fled the world." Compare that idea with this description by a Baptist missionary scholar:

> The Benedictine rule and the many derived from it probably
> helped to give dignity to labor, including manual labor in the
> fields. This was in striking contrast with the aristocratic conviction
> of the servile status of manual work which prevailed in much of
> ancient society and which was also the attitude of the warriors and
> non-monastic ecclesiastics who constituted the upper middle
> classes of the Middle Ages....To the monasteries...was obviously

due much clearing of land and improvement in methods of agriculture. In the midst of barbarism, the monasteries were centres of orderly and settled life and monks were assigned the duty of roadbuilding and road repair. Until the rise of the towns in the eleventh century, they were pioneers in industry and commerce. The shops of the monasteries preserved the industries of Roman times.... The earliest use of marl in improving the soil is attributed to them. The great French monastic orders led in the agricultural colonization of Western Europe. Especially did the Cistercians make their houses centres of agriculture and contribute to improvements in that occupation. With their lay brothers and their hired laborers, they became great landed proprietors. In Hungary and on the German frontier the Cistercians were particularly important in reducing the soil to cultivation and in furthering colonization. In Poland, too, the German monasteries set advanced standards in agriculture and introduced artisans and craftsmen.[7]

For all of us who are interested in missions the shattering of the "monks fled the world" stereotype is even more dramatically and decisively reinforced by the magnificent record of the Irish *peregrini*, who were Celtic monks who did more to reach out to convert Anglo-Saxons than did Augustine's later mission from the South, and who contributed more to the evangelization of Western Europe, even Central Europe, than any other force.

From its very inception this second kind of structure was highly significant to the growth and development of the Christian movement. Even though Protestants have an inbuilt prejudice against it for various reasons, as we have seen, there is no denying the fact that apart from this structure it would be hard even to imagine the vital continuity of the Christian tradition across the centuries. Protestants are equally dismayed by the other structure—the parish and diocesan structure. It is, in fact, the relative weakness and nominality of the diocesan structure that makes the monastic structure so significant. Men like Jerome and Augustine, for example, are thought of by Protestants not as monks but as great scholars; and people like John Calvin lean very heavily upon writings produced by such monks. But Protestants do not usually give any credit to the specific structure within which Jerome and Augustine and many other monastic scholars worked, a structure without which Protestant labors would have had very little to build on, not even a Bible.

We must now follow these threads into the next period, where we will see the formal emergence of the major monastic structures. It is sufficient at this point merely to note that there are already by the fourth century two very different kinds of structures—the diocese and the monastery—both of them significant in the transmission and expansion of Christianity. They are each patterns borrowed from the cultural context of their time, just as were the earlier Christian synagogue and missionary band.

It is even more important for our purpose here to note that while these two structures are *formally* different from—and historically unrelated to—the two in New Testament times, they are nevertheless *functionally* the same. In order to speak conveniently about the continuing similarities in function, let us now call the synagogue and diocese *modalities*, and the missionary band and monastery *sodalities*. Elsewhere I have developed these terms in detail, but briefly, a modality is a structured fellowship in which there is no distinction of sex or age, while a sodality is a structured fellowship in which membership involves an adult second decision beyond modality membership, and is limited by either age or sex or marital status. In this use of these terms, both the *denomination* and the *local congregation* are modalities, while a mission agency or a local men's club are sodalities.[8] A secular parallel would be that of a town (modality) compared to a private business (a sodality)—perhaps a chain of stores found in many towns. The sodalities are subject to the authority of the more general structures, usually. They are "regulated" but not "administered" by the modalities. A complete state socialism exists where there are no regulated, decentralized private initiatives. Some denominational traditions, like the Roman and the Anglican, allow for such initiatives. Many Protestant denominations, taking their cue from Luther's rejection of the sodalities of his time, try to govern everything from a denominational office. Some local congregations cannot understand the value or the need for mission structures. Paul was "sent off" not "sent out" by the Antioch congregation. He may have reported back to it but did not take orders from it. His mission band (sodality) had all the autonomy and authority of a "travelling congregation."

In the early period beyond the pages of the Bible, however, there was little relation between modality and sodality, while in Paul's time his missionary band specifically nourished the congregations—a most significant symbiosis. We shall now see how the medieval period essentially recovered the healthy New Testament relationship between modality and sodality.

The Medieval Synthesis of Modality and Sodality

We can say that the Medieval period began when the Roman Empire in the West started to break down. To some extent the diocesan pattern, following as it did the Roman civil-governmental pattern, tended to break down at the same time. The monastic (or sodality) pattern turned out to be much more durable, and as a result gained greater importance in the early Medieval period than it might have otherwise. The survival of the modality (diocesan Christianity) was further compromised by the fact that the invaders of this early Medieval period generally belonged to a different brand of Christian belief—they were Arians. As a result, in many places there were both "Arian" and "Catholic" Christian churches on opposite corners of a main street— something like today, where we have Methodist and Presbyterian churches across the street from each other.

Again, however, it is not our purpose to downplay the significance of the parish or diocesan form of Christianity, but simply to point out that during this early period of the Medieval epoch the specialized house called the *monastery*, or its equivalent, became ever so much more important in the perpetuation of the Christian movement than was the organized system of parishes, which we often call the church *as if there were no other structure making up the church.*

Perhaps the most outstanding illustration in the early Medieval period of the importance of the relationship between modality and sodality is the collaboration between Gregory the Great and man later called Augustine of Canterbury. While

Gregory, as the bishop of the diocese of Rome, was the head of a modality, both he and Augustine were the products of monastic houses—a fact which reflects the dominance even then of the sodality pattern of Christian structure. In any case, Gregory called upon his friend Augustine to undertake a major mission to England in order to try to plant diocesan structure there, where Celtic Christianity had been deeply wounded by the invasion of Saxon warriors from the continent.

As strong as Gregory was in his own diocese, he simply had no structure to call upon to reach out in this intended mission other than the sodality, which at this point in history took the form of a *Benedictine* monastery. This is why he ended up asking Augustine and a group of other members of the same monastery to undertake this rather dangerous journey and important mission on his behalf. The purpose of the mission, curiously, was not to extend the Benedictine form of monasticism. The remnant of the Celtic "church" in England was itself a network of sodalities since there were no parish systems in the Celtic area. No, Augustine went to England to establish diocesan Christianity, though he himself was not a diocesan priest. Interestingly enough, the Benedictine "Rule" (way of life) was so attractive that gradually virtually all of the Celtic houses adopted the Benedictine Rule, or *Regula* (in Latin).

This is quite characteristic. During a lengthy period of time, perhaps a thousand years, the building and rebuilding of the modalities was mainly the work of the sodalities. That is to say the monasteries were uniformly the source and the real focus point of new energy and vitality which flowed into the diocesan side of the Christian movement. We think of the momentous Cluny reform, then the Cistercians, then the Friars, and finally the Jesuits— all of them strictly sodalities, but sodalities which contributed massively to the building and the rebuilding of the *Corpus Cristianum*, the network of dioceses, which Protestants often identify as "the" Christian movement.

At many points there was rivalry between these two structures, between bishop and abbot, diocese and monastery, modality and sodality, but the great achievement of the Medieval period is the ultimate synthesis, delicately achieved, whereby Catholic orders were able to function along with Catholic parishes and dioceses without the two structures conflicting with each other to the point of a setback to the movement. The harmony between the modality and the sodality achieved by the Roman Church is perhaps the most significant characteristic of this phase of the world Christian movement and continues to be Rome's greatest organizational advantage to this day.

Note, however, that is not our intention to claim that any one organization, whether modality or sodality, was continuously the champion of vitality and vigor throughout the thousands of years of the Medieval epoch. As a matter of actual fact, there really is no very impressive organizational continuity in the Christian movement, either in the form of modality or sodality. (The list of bishops at Rome is at many points a most shaky construct and unfortunately does not even provide a focus for the entire Christian movement.) On the other hand, it is clear that the sodality, as it was recreated again and again by different leaders, was almost always the structural prime mover, the source of inspiration and renewal which overflowed into the papacy and created the reform movements which blessed diocesan Christianity from time to time. The most significant instance of this is the accession to the papal throne of Hildebrand (Gregory VII), who brought the ideals, commitment and discipline of the monastic movement right into the Vatican itself. In this sense are not then the papacy, the College of Cardinals, the diocese, and the parish structure of the Roman Church in some respects a secondary element, a derivation from the monastic tradition rather than vice versa? In any case it seems appropriate that the priests of the monastic tradition are called *regular priests*, while the priests of the diocese and parish are called *secular priests*. The former are voluntarily bound by a *regula*, while the latter as a group were other than, outside of ("cut off") or somehow less than the second-decision communities bound by a demanding way of life, a regula. Whenever a house or project or parish run by the regular clergy is brought under the domination of the secular clergy, this is a form of the "secularization" of that entity. In the lengthy "Investiture Controversy," the regular clergy finally gained clear authority for at least semi-autonomous operation, and the secularization of the orders was averted.

We may note that the same structural danger of *secularization* exists today whenever the special concerns of an elite mission sodality fall under the complete domination (e.g. administration not just regulation) of an ecclesiastical government, since the Christian modalities (congregations) inevitably represent the much broader and, no doubt, mainly inward concerns of a large body of all kinds of Christians, who, as "first-decision" members, are generally less select. Their democratic majority tends to move away from the high-discipline of the mission structures, and denominational mission budgets tend to get smaller across the decades as the church membership "broadens."

We cannot leave the medieval period without referring to the many unofficial and often persecuted movements which also mark the era. In all of this, the Bible itself seems always the ultimate prime mover, as we see in the case of Peter Waldo. His work stands as a powerful demonstration of the simple power of a vernacular translation of the Bible where the people were unable to appreciate either Jerome's classical translation or the celebration of the Mass in Latin. A large number of groups referred to as "Anabaptists" are to be found in many parts of Europe. One of the chief characteristics of these renewal movements is that they did not attempt to elicit merely celibate participation, although this was one of their traits on occasion, but often simply developed whole "new communities" of believers and their families, attempting by biological and cultural transmission to preserve a high and enlightened form of Christianity. These groups usually faced such strong opposition and grave limitations that it would be very unfair to judge their virility by their progress. It is important to note, however, that the average Mennonite or Salvation Army community, where whole families are members, typified the desire for a "pure" church, or what is often called a "believers" church, and constitutes a most significant experiment in Christian structure. Such a structure stands, in a certain sense, midway between a modality and a sodality, since it has the constituency of the modality (involving full families) and yet, in its earlier years, may have the vitality and selectivity of a sodality. We will return to this phenomenon in the next section.

We have space here only to point out that in terms of the durability and quality of the Christian faith, the 1000-year medieval period is virtually impossible to account for apart from the role of the sodalities. What happened in the city of Rome is merely the tip of the iceberg at best, and represents a rather superficial and political level. It is quite a contrast to the foundational well-springs of Biblical study and radical obedience represented by the various sodalities of this momentous millennium, which almost always arose somewhere else, and were often opposed by the Roman hierarchy.

The Protestant Recovery of the Sodality

The Protestant movement started out by attempting to do without any kind of sodality structure. Martin Luther had been discontented with the apparent polarization between the vitality he eventually discovered in his own order and the very nominal parish life of his time. Being dissatisfied with this contrast, he abandoned the sodality (in which, nevertheless, he was introduced to the Bible, to the Pauline epistles and to teaching on "justification by faith,") and took advantage of the political forces of his time to launch a full-scale renewal movement on the general level of church life. At first, he even tried to do without the characteristically Roman diocesan structure, but eventually the Lutheran movement produced a Lutheran diocesan structure which to a considerable extent represented the readoption of the Roman diocesan tradition. But, the Lutheran movement did not in a comparable sense readopt the sodalities, the Catholic orders, that had been so prominent in the Roman tradition.

This omission, in my evaluation, represents the greatest error of the Reformation and the greatest weakness of the resulting Protestant tradition. Had it not been for the so-called Pietist movement, the Protestants would have been totally devoid of any organized renewing structures within their tradition. The Pietist tradition, in every new emergence of its force, was very definitely a sodality, inasmuch as it was a case of adults meeting together and committing themselves to new beginnings and higher goals as Christians without conflicting with the stated meetings of the existing church. This phenomenon of sodality nourishing modality is prominent in the case of the early work of John Wesley. He absolutely prohibited any abandonment of the Parish churches. A contemporary example is the widely influential so-called *East African Revival*, which has now involved a million people but has very carefully avoided any clash with functioning of local churches. The churches that have not fought against this movement have been greatly blessed by it.

However, the Pietist movement, along with the Anabaptist new communities, eventually dropped back to the level of biological growth; it reverted to the ordinary pattern of congregational life. It reverted from the level of the sodality to the level of the modality, and in most cases, rather soon became ineffective either as a mission structure or as a renewing force.

What interests us most is the fact that in failing to exploit the power of the sodality, the Protestants had no mechanism for missions for almost three hundred years, until William Carey's famous book, *An Enquiry*, proposed "the use of means for the conversion of the heathen." His key word *means* refers specifically to the need for a sodality, for the organized but non-ecclesiastical initiative of the warmhearted. Thus, the resulting Baptist Missionary Society is one of the most significant organizational developments in the Protestant tradition. Although not the earliest such society, reinforced as it was by the later stages of the powerful "Evangelical Awakening" and by the printing of Carey's book, it set off a rush to the use of this kind of "means" for the conversion of the heathen, and we find in the next few years a number of societies forming along similar lines: the LMS and NMS in 1795, the CMS in 1799, the CFBS in 1804, the BCFM in 1810, the ABMB in 1814, the GMS in 1815, the DMS in 1821, the FEM in 1822, and the BM in 1824—twelve societies in thirty-two years. Once this method of operation was clearly understood by the Protestants, three hundred years of latent energies burst forth in what became, in Latourette's phrase, "The Great Century." By helping to tap the immense spiritual energies of the Reformation, Carey's book has probably contributed more to global mission than any other book in history other than the Bible itself!

The Nineteenth Century is thus the first century in which Protestants were actively engaged in missions. For reasons which we have not space here to explain, it was also the century of the lowest ebb of Catholic mission energy. Amazingly, in this one century Protestants, building on the unprecedented world expansion of the West, caught up with eighteen centuries of earlier mission efforts. There is simply no question that what was done in this century moved the Protestant stream from a self-contained, impotent European backwater into a world force in Christianity. Looking back from where we stand today, of course, it is hard to believe how recently the Protestant movement has become prominent.

Organizationally speaking, however, the vehicle that allowed the Protestant movement to become vital was the structural development of the sodality, which harvested the vital "voluntarism" latent in Protestantism, and surfaced in new mission agencies of all kinds, both at home and overseas. Wave after wave of evangelical initiatives transformed the entire map of Christianity, especially in the United States, but also in England, in Scandinavia and on the Continent. By 1840, the phenomenon of mission sodalities was so prominent in the United States that the phrase "the Evangelical Empire" and other equivalent phrases were used to refer to it, and now began a trickle of ecclesiastical opposition to this bright new emergence of the second structure. This brings us to our next point.

The Contemporary Misunderstanding of the Mission Sodality

Almost all mission efforts in the Nineteenth Century, whether sponsored by interdenominational boards or denominational boards, were substantially the work of initiatives that were mainly independent of the ecclesiastical structures to which they were related. Toward the latter half of the Nineteenth Century, there seemed increasingly to be two separate structural traditions.

On the one hand, there were men like Henry Venn and Rufus Anderson, who were the strategic thinkers at the helm of older societies—the Church Missionary Society (CMS) in England and American Board of Commissioners for Foreign

Missions (ABCFM), respectively. These men championed the semi-autonomous mission sodality, and they voiced an attitude which was not at first contradicted by any significant part of the leaders of the ecclesiastical structures. On the other hand, there was the centralizing perspective of denominational leaders, principally the Presbyterians, which gained ground almost without any reversal throughout the latter two-thirds of the Nineteenth Century, so that by the early part of the Twentieth Century the once-independent structures which had been merely *related* to the denominations gradually became *dominated* by the churches, that is *administered*, not merely *regulated*. Partially as a result, toward the end of the Nineteenth Century, there was a new burst of totally separate mission sodalities called the *Faith Missions*, with Hudson Taylor's CIM taking the lead. It is not widely recognized that this pattern was mainly a recrudescence of the pattern that had been established earlier in the century, prior to the trend toward denominational boards.

All of these changes took place very gradually. Attitudes at any point are hard to pin down, but it does seem clear that Protestants were always a bit unsure about the legitimacy of the second structure, the sodality. The Anabaptist tradition consistently emphasized the concept of a pure community of believers and thus was uninterested in a voluntarism that would involve only part of the believing community. The same is true of Alexander Campbell's "Restoration" tradition, and the Plymouth Brethren. The more recent sprinkling of independent "Charismatic Centers" with all their exuberance locally, tend toward sending out their own missionaries, and have not learned the lesson of the Pentecostal groups before them who employ mission agencies with great effect.

U.S. denominations, lacking tax support as on the Continent, have been generally a more selective and vital fellowship than the European state churches, and at least in their youthful exuberance, felt quite capable as denominations of providing all of the necessary initiative for overseas mission. It is for this latter reason that the many new denominations of the U.S. have tended to act as though centralized church control of mission efforts is the only proper pattern.

As a result, by the Second World War, a very nearly complete transmutation had taken place in the case of almost all mission efforts related to denominational structures. That is, almost all older denominational boards, though once semi-autonomous or very nearly independent, had by this time become part of unified budget provisions and so forth. At the same time, and partially as a result, a whole new host of independent mission structures burst forth again, especially after the Second World War. As in the case of the earlier emergence of the Faith Missions, these tended to pay little attention to denominational leaders and their aspirations for church-centered mission. The Anglican church with its CMS, USPG, etc., displays the Medieval synthesis, and so, almost unconsciously, does the American CBA with its associated CBFMS, CBHMS structures. Thus, to this day, among Protestants, there continues to be deep confusion about the legitimacy and proper relationship of the two structures that have manifested themselves throughout the history of the Christian movement.

To make matters worse, Protestant blindness about the need for mission sodalities has had a very tragic influence on mission fields. Protestant missions, being modality-minded, have tended to assume that merely modalities, e.g., churches, need to be established. In most cases where mission work is being pursued by what are essentially semi-autonomous mission sodalities, it is the planting of modalities, not sodalities, that is the only goal. That is to say, the mission agencies (even those that have been completely independent from denominations back home) have tended in their mission work very simply to set up churches and not to plant, in addition, mission sodalities in the so-called mission lands.[9] The marvelous "Third World Mission" movement has sprung up from these mission field churches, but with embarrassingly little encouragement from the Western mission societies, as sad and surprising as that may seem.

Thus, as we look back today, it is astonishing that most Protestant missionaries, working with (mission) structures that did not exist in the Protestant tradition for hundreds of years and without whose existence there would have been no mission initiative, have nevertheless been blind to the significance of the very structure within which they have worked. In this blindness they have merely planted churches and have not effectively concerned themselves to make sure that the kind of mission structure within which they operate also be set up on the field. As a matter of fact, many of the mission agencies founded after World War II, out of extreme deference to existing church movements already established in foreign lands, have not even tried to set up *churches*, and have worked for many years merely as auxiliary agencies in various service capacities trying to help the churches that were already there...

The question we must ask is how long it will be before the younger churches of the so-called mission territories of the non-Western world come to that epochal conclusion (to which the Protestant movement in Europe only tardily came), namely, that there need to be sodality structures, such as William Carey's "use of means," in order for church people to reach out in vital initiatives in mission, especially cross-cultural mission. There are already some hopeful signs that this tragic delay will not continue. We see, for example, the outstanding work of the Melanesian Brotherhood in the Solomon Islands.

Conclusion

This article has been in no sense an attempt to decry or to criticize the organized church. It has assumed both the necessity and the importance of the parish structure, the diocesan structure, the denominational structure, the ecclesiastical structure. The modality structure in the view of this article is a significant and absolutely essential structure. All that is attempted here is to explore some of the historical patterns which make clear that God, through His Holy Spirit, has clearly and consistently used another structure other than (and sometimes instead of) the modality structure. It is our attempt here to help church leaders and others to understand the legitimacy of *both* structures, and the necessity for both structures not only to exist but to work together harmoniously for the fulfillment of the Great Commission, and for the fulfillment of all that God desires for our time.

[Editor's note: This chapter, written at the founding of the Asia Missions Association in 1973, gives only hints of the exciting new wave of "Third World Mission" interest: the COMIBAM movement in Latin America, the Third World Mission

Association, the revitalized Missions Commission of the World Evangelical Fellowship, the growth not only of non-Western mission structures, but national level associations of missions, such as NEMA (Nigerian Evangelical Missions Association) and the IMA (India Mission Association), and all around the world dozens of training schools and programs for such missionaries. In 1992 it is estimated that there are well over 400 non-Western mission agencies. What an incredible change in 20 years!]

End Notes

1. One can hardly conceive of more providentially supplied means for the Christian mission to reach the Gentile community. Wherever the community of Christ went, it found at hand the tools needed to reach the nations: a people living under covenant promise and a responsible election, and the scriptures, God's revelation to all men. The open synagogue was the place where all these things converged. In the synagogue, the Christians were offered an inviting door of access to every Jewish community. It was in the synagogue that the first Gentile converts declared their faith in Jesus. (Richard F. DeRidder, *The Dispersion of the People of God* (Netherlands: J.H. Kok, N.V. Kampen, 1971), p. 87.

2. In Paul's day *Asia* meant what we today call Asia Minor, or present-day Turkey. In those days no one dreamed how far the term would later be extended.

3. That Christians in Jerusalem organized themselves for worship on the synagogue pattern is evident from the appointment of elders and the adoption of the service of prayer. The provision of a daily dole for widows and needy reflects the current synagogue practice (Acts 2:42, 6:1). It is possible that the epistle of James reflects the prevailing Jerusalem situation: in James 2:2 reference is made to a wealthy man coming *'into your assembly.'* The term translated 'assembly' is literally 'synagogue,' not the more usual word 'church.' Glenn W. Barker, William L. Lane and J. Ramsey Michaels, *The New Testament Speaks* (New York: Harper and Row Co., 1969), pp. 126-127.

4. "Dynamic Equivalence Churches," *Missiology: An International Review* , 1, no. 1 (1973), p. 39ff.

5. Christians, it said, resorted to formation of "burial clubs," which were legal, as one vehicle of fellowship and worship.

6. Kenneth Scott Latourette, *A History of Christianity* (New York: Harper & Brothers, 1953), pp. 181, 221-234.

7. Kenneth Scott Latourette, *A History of the Expansion of Christianity* , vol. 2, *The Thousand Years of Uncertainty* (New York: Harper & Brothers, 1938), pp. 379-380.

8. Ralph D. Winter, "The Warp and the Woof of the Christian Movement," in his and R. Pierce Beaver's, *The warp and woof: organizing for Christian mission* (South Pasadena, Calif.: William Carey Library, 1970), pp. 52-62.

9. Ralph D. Winter, "The Planting of Younger Missions," in *Church/Mission Tensions Today*, ed. by Peter C. Wagner (Chicago: Moody Press, 1972).

Study Questions

1. Define the terms "modality" and "sodality," and give examples of each.

2. Do you agree with Winter's thesis that sodality structures within the church are both legitimate and necessary? What practical significance does your answer suggest?

3. Explain the importance of being able to distinguish between *form* and *function*.

4. What does Winter claim was "the greatest error of the Reformation and the greatest weakness of the resulting Protestant tradition"?

5

The History of Mission Strategy

R. Pierce Beaver

Fifteen centuries of missionary action preceded the rise of Protestant world mission. Therefore, Protestant missionary action did not begin *de novo,* and with modern Roman Catholic theory makes up only the last chapter of a long story. These pages will present a capsule history of mission strategy before the rise of Protestant efforts, briefly trace the course of Protestant strategy, and unfortunately for lack of space, completely omit reference to modern Roman Catholic missions.

Boniface

The first instance of a well-developed mission strategy in the twentieth century understanding of the term is that employed in the English mission to the continent of Europe by Boniface in the eighth century. Boniface preached to Germanic pagans in a language so akin to their own that they could understand. He did use aggression: he defied their gods, demolished their shrines, cut down the sacred trees, and built churches on holy sites. But he made converts, and educated and civilized them. He founded monasteries which not only had academic schools but programs which taught people agriculture, grazing, and domestic arts. This made possible a settled society, a well-grounded church, and good Christian nurture. Into a second line of educational and domestic science institutions Boniface brought nuns from England. This is the first time that women were formally and actively enlisted in mission work. Clergy and monks were recruited from the people. All of this activity was supported by the church back "home" in England. Boniface sent reports and requests. He discussed strategy with people back home. The bishops, monks, and sisters in turn sent Boniface personnel, money, and supplies. They also undergirded the mission with intercessory prayer.

Unhappily such a true sending mission ceased to exist because of the ravages

R. Pierce Beaver was Professor Emeritus from the University of Chicago. He specialized in the history of missions in America, and was for fifteen years a formative director of the Missionary Research Library in New York City. Beaver authored, among other books, All Loves Excelling,, a description of the initiatives of American women in world evangelization. He died in 1982. Taken from Southwestern Journal of Theology, Volume XII, Spring 1970, No. 2, 1970. Used with permission.

which invaders wreaked on the people of England. Mission on the continent became too much an instrument of imperial expansion, both political and ecclesiastical, for it was employed by the Frankish kings, their German successors, the Byzantine emperor, and the Pope. Consequently the Scandinavian kings kept out missionaries from the continent and in the evangelization of their countries used English missionaries who were their own subjects or had no political connections.

The Crusades

The series of European wars against the Muslims, called the Crusades, can hardly be considered a form of true mission. They made mission to Muslims almost impossible down to the present because they left an abiding heritage of hatred in Islamic lands. Yet even before the Crusades had ended Francis of Assisi had gone in love to preach to the sultan and had created a missionary force which would preach in love and in peace. Ramon Lull, the great Franciscan tertiary, gave up his status as a noble high in the court of Aragon and devoted his life to mission to Muslims as "the Fool of Love." He would convince and convert by reason, using the instrument of debate. To this end he wrote his *Ars Magna*, which was intended to answer convincingly any question or objection which could be put by Muslim or pagan, and devised a kind of intellectual computer into which the various factors could be registered and the right answer would come forth. Lull for many decades before his martyrdom ceaselessly begged popes and kings to establish colleges for the teaching of Arabic and other languages and for the training of missionaries, and urged upon them many schemes for sending missionaries abroad.

Colonial Expansion

It was in the period of the sixteenth to eighteenth centuries that Christianity actually became a worldwide religion in connection with the expansion of the Portuguese, Spanish, and French empires. When the Pope divided the non-Christian lands of the earth already discovered or yet to be discovered between the crowns of Portugal and Spain, he laid upon the monarchs the obligation to evangelize the peoples of those lands, to establish the church, and to maintain it. Mission was thus made a function of government.

The Portuguese built a trade empire, and except in Brazil, held only small territories under direct rule. There they suppressed the ethnic religions, drove out the upper class who resisted, and created a Christian community composed of their mixed-blood descendants and converts from the lower strata of society.

Spain, on the other hand, endeavored to transplant Christianity and civilization, both according to the Spanish model. Ruthless exploitation killed off the Carib Indians and stimulated the heroic struggle for the rights of the remaining Indians by Bartholome de las Casas and other missionaries. Since then protection of primitive people against exploitation by whites and by colonial governments has been an important function of missions. After that mighty effort abolished slavery and forced baptism, the missionaries were made both the civilizers and protectors of the Indians. A mission would be established on a frontier with a central station about which a town was gathered and Indians brought into permanent residence. There was usually a small garrison of soldiers to protect both missionaries and Christian Indians. Satellite stations, smaller towns, were connected with the central one. The Indians were taught by catechists and supervised by priests in the cultic life of the church. They were actively enlisted in participation, serving as acolytes, singers, and musicians. Folk festivals were christianized, and the Christian feasts and fasts were introduced. Indian civil officers performed a wide range of supervisory functions under the careful oversight of the missionaries. Farms and ranches were developed and the Indians were taught all aspects of grazing and agriculture. Thus the Indians were preserved, civilized, and christianized, not killed off or displaced as would later be the case in the United States. Unfortunately, when the government decided that the missions had civilized the Indians, the missions were "secularized"; the missionaries replaced by diocesan clergy usually of low quality and too few in number; regular government officers came in as rulers in place of the missionaries and lacking their love for the people; the lands were parceled out among Spanish settlers; and the Indians were gradually reduced to peonage.

French policy in Canada was the opposite of the Spanish. Only a small colony was settled to be a base for trade and a bulwark against the English. The French wanted the furs and other products of the forests and consequently disturbed Indian civilization as little as possible. The missionaries had to develop a strategy consonant with this policy. Therefore, they lived with the Indians in their villages, adapting to conditions as well as they could, preaching, teaching, baptizing individuals, performing the rites of the church, allowing the converts still to be Indians. Some permanent towns with church and school were founded on the borders of French settlements, but most of the inhabitants were transients.

On the other side of the globe in what was to become French Indo-China, now Vietnam, where the region came under French rule only much later, a radical new evangelistic strategy was devised by Alexander de Rhodes. This was necessary because the French missionaries were persecuted and expelled from the region for long periods. Evangelization could only be achieved by native agents. Rhodes created an order of native lay evangelists living under rule who won converts by the thousands. Stimulated by this experience Rhodes and his associates founded the Foreign Mission Society of Paris dedicated to the policy of recruiting and training a diocesan clergy, who would be the chief agents in the evangelization of the country and the pastoral care of the churches, rather than missionaries. It was a policy marked by outstanding success.

Mission Strategists of the 17th Century

The first modern mission theorists appeared in the seventeenth century in connection with this great expansion of the faith, including Jose de Acosta, Brancati, and Thomas a Jesu. They wrote manuals of missionary principles and practice, described the qualifications of missionaries, and told them how to work with the people. In 1622 there was created in Rome the Sacred Congregation for the Propagation of the Faith which henceforth gave central direction to Roman Catholic missions and established colleges or institutes for the training of missionaries.

The great and courageous innovators in this period were the Jesuits who went to the Orient through Portuguese channels but defied Portuguese restrictions. They were of many nationalities. These were the modern pioneers in accommodation, acculturation, adaptation, or indigenization, whatever one may wish to call it. The first venture was in Japan where the missionaries adapted Japanese houses, costume, most customs, and the etiquette of social intercourse. They did not, however, make use of Shinto and Buddhist terms and concepts, forms, or rites in presentation of the gospel and establishing the church. They did make great use of the Japanese language in production of Christian literature printed on the mission press by Japanese converts. The heaviest burden in evangelism and teaching was borne by native deacons and catechists. A few were admitted to the priesthood. A large Christian community soon came into being. When the Shogun, fearing foreign aggression, closed Japan to all outsiders and persecuted Christianity in the seventeenth century many thousands suffered martyrdom. Christianity went underground and endured until Japan was opened to western intercourse two centuries later.

A second experiment at Madurai in South India went much farther. Robert de Nobili believed that the Brahmin caste must be won if Christianity were to succeed in India. Consequently he became a Christian Brahmin. He dressed like a *guru* or religious teacher, observed the caste laws and customs, and learned Sanskrit. De Nobili studied the major schools of Hindu philosophy and presented Christian doctrine as much as possible in Hindu terms. He is one of the very few evangelists who won many Brahmin converts.

The most noted attempt at accommodation was in China, where the strategy was set by Matteo Ricci and developed by his successors as head of the mission, Schall and Verbiest. Just as in Japan the missionaries adopted the national way of life and fundamentals of Chinese civilization, but they went much farther and gradually introduced Christian principles and doctrine through the use of Confucian concepts. They permitted converts to engage in ancestral and state rites regarding these as social and civil rather than religious in character. The missionaries gained tremendous influence as mathematicians, astronomers, cartographers, and masters of various sciences, thus introducing western learning to the Chinese, making friendships with influential persons, and finding opportunities personally to present the faith. They served the emperor in many capacities. All of this had one purpose—to open the way for the gospel. Success crowned the strategy, and a large Christian community developed, including influential persons in high places.

Other missionaries, however, were unable to appreciate anything that was not European and were absolutely wedded to traditional Roman Catholic terminology and practices. Motivated by nationalistic and party jealousies they attacked the Jesuits and laid charges against them in Rome. Ultimately Rome pronounced against the Jesuits' principles, banned their practices, and required that all missionaries going to the Orient take an oath to abide by that ruling. Christians were forbidden to practice family and state rites. It was henceforth impossible for any Christian to be a genuine Chinese and a Christian simultaneously. The profession of the Christian faith appeared to strike at the root of filial piety, which was the very foundation of Chinese society. Two centuries later the oath was abolished and modified rites permitted. The Jesuits lost the battle but ultimately won the war. Today almost all missionaries of all churches acknowledge the necessity of accommodation or indigenization.

New England Puritans: Missions to the American Indians

The participation of Protestants in world mission began early in the seventeenth century simultaneously with the evangelistic work of the chaplains of the Dutch East Indies Company and the New England missions to the American Indians. Mission was a function of the commercial company, but many of its chaplains were genuine missionaries. They had little influence on later mission strategy, but it was the Puritan missions to the red men that would provide the missions of a later day with inspiration and models. The aim of the missionaries was so effectively to preach the gospel that the Indians would be converted, individually receive salvation, and be gathered into churches where they would be nurtured in the faith under strict discipline. The intention was to make of the Indian a Christian man of the same type and character as the English Puritan member of a gathered Congregationalist church. This involved civilizing the Indian according to the British model.

Evangelism was the first item in the strategy. Preaching was the "grand means," supplemented by teaching. Most missionaries followed John Eliot in beginning with public preaching, although Thomas Mayhew, Jr., was very successful at Martha's Vineyard in beginning with a slow, individual, personal approach. Heavily doctrinal sermons stressing the wrath of God and the pains of hell, just like those given an English congregation, were addressed to the Indians. But David Brainerd, who like the Moravians preached the love of God rather than his wrath, was extremely effective in moving men and women to repentance.

The second point of the strategy was to gather the converts into churches, but the new Christians were at first put through long years of probation before the first churches were organized. On the contrary, when the second phase of the Indian mission opened in the 1730's this delay was no longer required and the churches were speedily gathered and organized. Both before and after the organization of the churches the converts were being instructed and disciplined in the faith.

A third strategic emphasis was the establishment of Christian towns. John Eliot and his colleagues in the mission believed that segregation and isolation were necessary to the converts' growth in grace. They must be removed from the baneful influence of their pagan brethren and of bad white men. It was thought that in purely Christian towns of "Praying Indians" the new members could live together under the strict discipline and careful nurture of the white missionaries and Indian pastors and teachers. This would insure what Cotton Mather called "a more decent and English way of living." Christianization and civilization would be simultaneous and indistinguishable. Eliot put his towns under a biblical form of government based on Exodus 18, but the General Court of Massachusetts, which gave the land and built the church and school, appointed English commissioners over the towns in 1658. Within the towns the Indians did live together under a covenant between them and the Lord, and both personal and community life were regulated by laws of a biblical flavor.

Most of the towns of the Praying Indians did not survive the devastation of King Philip's War in 1674, but the strategy of the special Christian town was again followed when John Sergeant established the Stockbridge mission in 1734. Stockbridge was not so closed a place as those earlier towns. There was constant movement between town and forest, even to great distances. Stockbridge Christians could, therefore, be evangelistic agents in their natural relationships.

Whatever may have been achieved in the development of Christian character in the early towns, no evangelistic influence could be exerted by the inhabitants, cut off as they were from other Indians. Throughout the nineteenth and early twentieth centuries missionaries to primitive people in Africa and the isles would continue to be enamoured of the idea of guaranteeing the purity of the converts' faith and conduct by segregating them in separate Christian villages or wards. The usual effect was to alienate the Christians from their people, to create a "mongrel" kind of society neither native nor European, and to prevent any evangelistic impact on others. A separated people cannot pass on the contagion of personal faith.

At the center of each town or mission station was a church flanked by a school house. Sermons on Sunday and in prayer meetings, catechization, and general elementary education all tended to nurture the convert in faith and civilization.

John Eliot's *Indian Catechism* was the first book ever to be published in an American Indian language. Both the vernacular and the English language were used. The English would enable the Indian better to adjust to white society, but his own tongue was more effective in imparting an understanding of Christian truth. Eliot produced textbooks in both languages. Reading, writing, and simple arithmetic were taught along with Bible study and religious instruction. Agricultural and domestic crafts were also introduced so that support in a settled and civilized way of life might be possible. In the second century of the mission, strategic considerations led John Sergeant to introduce the boarding school, so that youths could be entirely separated from the old life and brought up in the new. This institution, too, would become a primary strategic resource of the missions in the nineteenth century.

It is to the credit of the New England Puritans that they never doubted the transforming power of the gospel nor the potential ability of the Indians. They expected that some of them at least could attain the same standard as Englishmen. Therefore, more than the rudimentary schooling of the towns was required. Some promising youths were sent to the Boston Latin Grammar School, and a few were placed in the Indian College at Harvard College. Sergeant's boarding school at Stockbridge and Eleazer Wheelock's school at Lebanon, Connecticut, were better conceived efforts at a higher degree of education.

Worship, spiritual nurture, and education all demanded a vernacular literature of rather broad dimensions. Eliot produced the Massachusetts Bible and a library of other literature, to which a few of his colleagues added.

Absolutely fundamental to the entire plan of New England mission strategy was the recruiting and training of native pastors and teachers. Both the missionaries and their supporters realized that only native agents could effectively evangelize and give pastoral care to their people. In 1700 there were thirty-seven Indian preachers in Massachusetts. Unfortunately, the old Christian Indian towns declined under continuing white pressure and with them the supply of ministers and teachers also declined to the vanishing point.

Perhaps the most lasting effects of the Indian missions of the seventeenth and eighteenth centuries were two: first, they inspired numerous missionary vocations in a later day as men read the lives of Eliot and Brainerd; and second, they endowed the great overseas Protestant enterprise with its initial strategic program. This included evangelism through preaching, organization of churches, education aimed at Christian nurture and the attainment of civilization in European terms, Bible translation, literature production, use of the vernacular language, and the recruitment and training of native pastors and teachers.

The Danish-Halle Mission

The American missions to the indigenous population had been supported by missionary societies organized in England and Scotland, but missionaries had not been sent from Britain. The first sending mission from Europe was the Danish-Halle Mission. Beginning in 1705 the King of Denmark sent German Lutheran missionaries to his colony of Tranquebar on the southeast coast of India. The pioneer leader, Bartholomew Ziegenbalg, developed a strategy which was bequeathed to later generations of missionaries, although in some respects he was far ahead of his time. He stressed worship, preaching, catechization, education, translation work, and the production of vernacular literature. He blazed a trail in the study of Hindu philosophy and religion, discerning the great importance of such knowledge for evangelization and church growth, but the authorities in Germany decried such activity. This mission early added medical work to its program. It also pioneered in the use of Tamil lyrics in worship.

The most famous of the Halle missionaries after Ziegenbalg was one of the last, Christian Frederick Schwartz, who spent his life in ministry in the British-controlled portion of south India. He had a remarkable influence with Indians of all religions and with Europeans of several nationalities, both troops and civilians. His strategy was unique and unplanned. Although still a European to all appearances, Schwartz actually became in effect a *guru* or spiritual teacher, loved and trusted by all. Persons of all religions and castes could gather around him as his disciples regardless of the difference in their status. His ministry was essentially a remarkable kind of adaptation or accommodation to the culture.

Moravian Missions

The most distinctive strategy developed in the eighteenth century was that of the Moravian Church developed under the direction of Count Zinzendorf and Bishop Spangenberg. The Moravian missionaries, beginning in 1734, were purposely sent to the most despised and neglected people. These missionaries were to be self-supporting. That emphasis led to the creation of industries and business concerns which not only supported the work but brought the missionaries into intimate contact with the people. Such self-support could not be undertaken among the American Indians, however, and consequently communal settlements, such as Bethlehem in Pennsylvania and Salem In North Carolina, were founded with a wide range of crafts and industries, the profits of which supported the mission.

Moravian missionaries were told not to apply "the Herrnhut yardstick" (i.e., German home base standards) to other peoples and to be alert to the recognition of the God-given distinctive traits, characteristics and strong points of those people. Furthermore, the missionaries were to regard themselves as assistants to the Holy Spirit. They were to be primarily messengers, evangelists, preachers, who were not to stress heavy theological doctrines but rather tell the simple gospel story of God's loving act of reconciliation of men to himself in Christ our Savior, who lived and died for all men. In God's providence the time would come when the Holy Spirit would bring converts into the church in large numbers. Meanwhile the missionary messengers would gather the first fruits. If there should be no response they were to go elsewhere. Actually the missionaries left only when persecuted and driven out. They were remarkably patient and did not give up readily.

The Great Century of Protestant Missions

Out of all these earlier beginnings there came the great Protestant missionary overseas enterprise of the nineteenth century. It took initial form in Britain with the founding of the Baptist Missionary Society by William Carey in 1792. Organization had begun in the United States in 1787 and a score of societies came into being, all having a worldwide objective. However, the frontier settlements and the Indians absorbed all their resources. At length a student movement in 1810 broke the deadlock and launched the overseas mission through the formation of the American Board of Commissioners for Foreign Missions. The Triennial Convention of the Baptist Denomination for Foreign Missions was next organized in 1814 followed in 1816 by the United Foreign Missionary Society.

The new societies and boards began their work with the strategic presuppositions and methods inherited from the American Indian missions and the Danish-Halle Mission. For many years the directors at home thought that they understood fully how the mission was to be carried out and detailed instructions were handed each missionary when he sailed. After half a century or so it was discovered that the experienced missionaries on the field could best formulate strategy and policy, which might then be ratified by the board back home. There was in 1795 a conflict over strategy in the London Missionary Society between two strong personalities. One man wanted well-educated ordained missionaries sent to countries of high civilization and high religions. The other wanted artisan missionaries under an ordained superintendent to be sent to primitive peoples in the South Seas to christianize and civilize them. Both objectives were accepted.

Even in countries with a high culture, such as India and China, European missionaries stressed the "civilizing" objective as much as their brethren in primitive regions because they regarded the local culture as degenerate and superstitious—a barrier to christianization. During the early decades there was never debate about the legitimacy of the stress on the civilizing function of missions. Debate was only about priority; which came first, christianization or civilization? Some held that a certain degree of civilization was first necessary to enable a people to understand and accept the faith. Others argued that one should begin with christianization since the gospel inevitably produced a hunger for civilization. Most persons believed that the two mutually interacted and should be stressed equally and simultaneously.

India was soon receiving the greatest degree of attention from mission boards and societies, and the strategy and tactics developed there were copied and applied in other regions. The Baptist "Serampore Trio" of Carey, Marshman, and Ward was especially influential in the early period. Although Carey sought individual conversions, he wanted to foster the growth of a church that would be independent, well sustained by a literate and Bible-reading laity, and administered and shepherded by an educated native ministry. This self-educated genius was not content with establishing elementary schools, but founded a college. The King of Denmark (Serampore was a Danish colony) gave him a college charter which permitted the giving of even theological degrees. At Serampore there were schools for Indians and for foreign children. The vast program of Bible translation and printing, ranging beyond the Indian vernaculars even to the Chinese, established the high priority of such work among all Protestants. Other literature was produced for the churches. The Trio also demonstrated the importance of scholarly research for mission strategy and action, producing linguistic materials needed by all, and taking the leadership in the study of Hinduism.

Furthermore, this famous Trio worked for the transformation of society under the impact of the gospel, and they became a mighty force for social reform, bringing pressure on the colonial government and leading Hindus to enlightened views on old wrongs and their elimination. These men were influential in causing the abolition of *suttee* or widow-burning, temple prostitution, and other dehumanizing customs. Carey also introduced modern journalism, publishing both vernacular Bengali and English newspapers and magazines. He stimulated a renaissance of Bengali literature. It was a very comprehensive mission which was based at Serampore.

Much like Robert de Nobili before him, the Scotsman Alexander Duff believed that the Indian populace could be won for Christ only if the Brahmin caste were first brought to our Lord. He sought to win Brahmin youths through a program of higher education in the English language. Where he succeeded in large measure, others failed; but his venture led to tremendous emphasis being put on English language schools and colleges. They produced few converts, but they did give economic advancement which made for the welfare of the churches, and to the pleasure of the colonial establishment they produced English-speaking staff for the civil service and commercial houses. Such education soon consumed a large part of the resources of all the missions.

At the same time without any strategic planning there developed huge concentrated central mission stations where the converts clustered in economic and social dependence on the missionaries. Unless a convert came to Christianity with an entire social group, he was cast out of his family and lost his livelihood.

Simply to keep such persons alive they were given jobs as servants, teachers, and evangelists. The church became over-professionalized, laymen being paid to do what they should have done voluntarily. This bad practice passed on to missions in other regions. In such a main station there were the central church, the schools, the hospital, and often the printing press. A missionary was pastor and ruler of the community. Such a system had little place for a native pastor as William Carey had planned, and there were only preaching points, no organized churches, in the villages for fifty miles and more in the hinterland. Then in 1854-55 Rufus Anderson went on deputation to India and Ceylon. He caused the American Board missionaries to break up the huge central stations, to organize village churches, and to ordain native pastors over them. He decreed that education in the vernacular should be the general rule and education in English the exception.

Mission Strategists of the 19th Century

The two greatest mission theoreticians and strategists of the nineteenth century were also the executive officers of the largest mission agencies. Henry Venn was general secretary of the Church Missionary Society in London. Rufus Anderson was foreign secretary of the American Board of Commissioners for Foreign Missions. Anderson's mission strategy dominated American mission work for more than a century as did that of Venn in the British scene. The two men arrived independently at practically the same basic principles and in late years mutually influenced each other. Together they established as the recognized strategic aim of Protestant mission the famous "three-self" formula to which British and American missions gave assent from the middle of the nineteenth century until World War II: the goal of mission is to plant and foster the development of churches which will be self-governing, self-supporting, and self-propagating.

Rufus Anderson was a Congregationalist and Venn an Anglican Episcopalian, but both would build the regional church from the bottom upward. Venn wanted a bishop appointed as the crowning of the process of development when there was an adequate native clergy and a church supported by the people. Anderson protested the great stress on "civilization" and the attempt to reform society overnight, holding that such change would eventually result from the leaven of the gospel in the life of a nation. He based his strategy on that of Paul as he found it recorded in the New Testament.

According to Anderson, the task of the missionary was to preach the gospel and gather the converts into churches. He was always to be an evangelist and never a pastor or ruler. Churches were to be organized at once out of converts who showed a change of life towards Christ without waiting for them to reach the standard expected of American Christians with two thousand years of Christian history behind them. These churches were to be put under their own pastors and were to develop their own local and regional polity. The missionaries would be advisers, elder brothers in the faith to the pastors and people.

Both Anderson and Venn taught that when the churches were functioning well the missionaries should leave and go to "regions beyond" where they would begin the evangelistic process once again. The whole point of church planting was to be evangelism and mission. The churches would engage spontaneously in local evangelism and in a sending mission to other peoples. Mission would beget mission. In Anderson's view education in the vernacular would be for the sole purpose of serving the church, or raising up a laity of high quality and an adequately trained ministry. All ancillary forms of work were to be solely for evangelism and for the edification of the church.

The British missions resisted Anderson's views on vernacular education. American missions adopted his strategy officially and unofficially and in theory held to his system for more than a century. However, after his day they stressed secondary and higher education in English to an ever greater extent. This was partly due to the fact that social Darwinism had converted Americans to the doctrine of inevitable progress. This led to the replacement of the old eschatology with the idea that the Kingdom of God was coming through the influence of Christian institutions such as schools. Also by the end of the nineteenth century a second great strategic objective had been more or less explicitly added to the three-self formula, that is the leavening and transformation of society through the effect of Christian principles and the Christian spirit of service infused into the common life. High schools and colleges were essential to this aim.

John L. Nevius, Presbyterian missionary in Shantung, devised a strategy which somewhat modified that of Anderson, placing more responsibility on the layman. He advocated leaving the layman in his own craft or business and in his usual place in society. He was to be encouraged to be a voluntary, unpaid evangelist. Nevius advocated also constant Bible study and rigorous stewardship in combination with voluntary service and proposed a simple and flexible church government. His brethren in China did not adopt his system, but the missionaries in Korea did so with amazing success.

A Colonialist Mentality

Despite the avowed continued adherence to the Anderson-Venn formula, there was a great change in missionary mentality and consequently in strategy in the last quarter of the nineteenth century. Under Venn British missions in west Africa, for example, had aimed at (1) the creation of an independent church under its own clergy which would evangelize the interior of the continent, and (2) the creation of an African elite, i.e., an intelligentsia and middle class, which would produce the society and economy which could support such a church and its mission. Almost immediately after Venn's termination of leadership, mission executives and field missionaries took the view that the African was of inferior quality and could not provide ministerial leadership, which consequently would be furnished indefinitely by Europeans. The African middle-class businessman and intellectual was despised. This imperialist viewpoint was an ecclesiastical variant of the growing devotion to the theory of "the white man's burden," and it reduced the native church to a colony of the foreign planting church.

A very similar development occurred in India in the 1880's. Americans and others caught this colonialist mentality by contagion from the British. German missions, under the guidance of their leading strategist, Professor Gustav Warneck, were simultaneously aiming at the creation of *Volkskirchen*, national churches, but until their full development had been reached the churches were kept in bondage to the missionaries. Paternalism thwarted development. Thus all missions were paternalist and colonialist at the turn of the century. This unhappy state of affairs lasted until the studies and surveys made for the World Missionary Conference at Edinburgh in 1910 suddenly destroyed complacency and inertia. They revealed that the native church was really a fact and was restive under paternal domination. Consequently, following the Conference, there was a tremendous drive for "devolution" of authority from the mission organization to the church, and practically all boards and societies gave lip service, at least, to this ideal.

Evangelism, Education, and Medicine

Missionary strategy of the nineteenth century (down to Edinburgh 1910), in summary, aimed at individual conversions, church planting, and social transformation through three main types of action, which became known as evangelism, education, and medicine. Evangelism included preaching in all its forms, the organizing and fostering of churches, Bible translation, literature production, and the distribution of Bibles and literature.

In the realm of education, industrial schools were stressed in earlier times but generally abandoned because of the desire for an academic education. By the end of the century a vast educational system was in existence in Asian countries, ranging from kindergarten to college, and including medical and theological schools. Africa, however, was neglected with respect to secondary and collegiate education.

The first doctors sent abroad were sent primarily to take care of the families of other missionaries, but it was soon discovered that medical service to the general populace brought good will and provided an evangelistic opportunity. Thereupon, it was made a major branch of mission work. It was not until the middle of the twentieth century that it came to be realized that health services in the name and spirit of the Great Physician are in themselves a dramatic form of the preaching of the gospel. But at a very early date even the rural evangelistic missionary had taken to carrying a medicine bag with him on his travels.

It was the same spirit of general helpfulness and cultivation of good will, as well as out of a desire to improve the economic base of the church, that missionaries introduced improved poultry and livestock and better seeds along with new crops. The great orchard industry and the big peanut in Shantung were introduced in this manner.

With regard to the other religions, mission strategy was aggressive, seeking their displacement and total conversion of the peoples. This aggressive spirit declined towards the end of the century, and something of an appreciation of the work of God in the other faiths grew slowly until by 1910 many regarded them as "broken lights" which were to be made whole in Christ and as bridges to the gospel.

The customs of the Oriental peoples made it almost impossible for male missionaries to reach women and with them children in large numbers. Missionary wives endeavored to set up schools for girls and to penetrate the homes, zenanas, and harems, but they did not have enough freedom from home-making and child care and they could not itinerate. Realistic strategy demanded that adequate provision be made for women and children, but the boards and societies were stubbornly resistant to sending single women abroad for such work. Finally in desperation the women in the 1860's began organizing their own societies and sent forth single women. A whole new dimension was thus added to mission strategy: the vast enterprise to reach women and children with the gospel, to educate girls, and to bring adequate medical care to women.

When women came into the church, their children followed them. Female education proved to be the most effective force for the liberation and social uplift of women. The emphasis which the women placed on medical service led the general boards to upgrade the medical work, and greater stress was put on medical education. Out of these two great endeavors of American women, followed by the British and Europeans, there opened to women of the Orient what are today their most prestigious professions, medical service both as physicians and nurses, and teaching.

Comity

One more feature of nineteenth century missionary strategy must be listed. This was the practice of comity. Southern Baptists were among the founders and practitioners of comity. Good stewardship of men and money held a high priority among boards and societies. Waste was abhorred, and there was a strong desire to stretch resources as far as possible. The practice of comity was intended to make some agency responsible for the evangelism of every last piece of territory and every people. It was further intended to prevent double occupancy of a region (excepting big cities) and overlapping of mission programs, so that competition might be eliminated along with denominational differences which would confuse the inhabitants and thus hamper evangelism. Prior occupation of territory was recognized, the newcoming missions went to unoccupied areas. This custom produced "denominationalism by geography," but the general expectation was that when the missionaries left for the "regions beyond" the nationals would put the several pieces together into a national church which might be different from any of the planting churches.

Missions agreed on recognizing each other as valid branches of the one church of Christ, on baptism and transfer of membership, on discipline, on salaries, and on transfer of national workers. These agreements led to further cooperation in the establishment of regional and national boards for the arbitration of conflicts between missions and to union Bible translation projects, publication agencies, secondary schools and colleges, teacher training schools, and medical schools. Effective strategy called more and more for doing together all things which could be better achieved through a united effort. City, regional, and national missionary conferences in almost every country provided occasions for common discussion and planning.

Consultations and Conferences

Such cooperation on the mission fields led to increasing home base consultation and planning. The World Missionary Conference at Edinburgh in 1910 inaugurated the series of great conferences: Jerusalem 1928, Madras 1938, Whitby 1947, Willingen 1952, and Ghana 1957-58. In these the directions of strategy were largely determined, and then applied locally through further study and discussion in national and regional bodies. The International Missionary Council was organized in 1921, bringing together national missionary conferences (such as the Foreign Missions Conference of North America, 1892) and national Christian councils (such as the N.C.C. of China), and thus there was established a universal system at various levels for the voluntary study of problems and planning of strategy in common by a host of sovereign mission boards. In 1961 the I.M.C. became the Division of World Mission and Evangelism of the World Council of Churches.

From 1910 to World War II the most notable development of strategy was increasingly putting the national church in the central place, giving it full independence and authority, and developing partnership between the western churches and the young churches. "The indigenous church" and "partnership in obedience" were watchwords which expressed the thrust of prevailing strategy. The participants in the Jerusalem Conference in 1928 defined the indigenous church, underscoring cultural accommodation. The Madras Conference of 1938 restated the definition, emphasizing witness to Christ in "a direct, clear, and close relationship with the cultural and religious heritage of [the] country." Whitby, 1947, held up the ideal of "partnership in obedience."

Since World War II

A radically different mission strategy, based on Paul, was expounded by Roland Allen in his books *Missionary Methods: St. Paul's or Ours?* and *The Spontaneous Expansion of the Church*, but he gathered no following until after World War II, when the missionaries of the faith missions especially rallied to his standard. In barest essentials this is his strategy: the missionary communicates the gospel and transmits to the new community of converts the simplest statement of the faith, the Bible, the sacraments, and the principle of ministry. He then stands by as a counseling elder brother while the Holy Spirit leads the new church, self-governing and self-supporting, to develop its own forms of polity, ministry, worship, and life. Such a church is spontaneously missionary. Allen's theory applied to new pioneer beginnings. The old boards and societies were dealing with churches already old and set in their ways; they seldom sought untouched fields.

One after another, the mission organizations on the fields were dissolved. Resources were placed at the disposal of the churches and missionary personnel assigned to their direction.

The western boards and societies initiated very little that was new in the way of strategy, but much to develop new methods: agricultural missions or rural development, some urban industrial work, mass media communications, more effective literature. This was the final state of a mission which had been in progress for three hundred years. Now the world was no longer divided into Christendom and heathendom. There could no longer be a one-way mission from the West to the remainder of the world. The base for a mission was established in almost every land, for a Christian church and community with an obligation to give the gospel to the whole world existed there. The moment for a new world mission with a radical new strategy had arrived. The revolution which swept the nonwestern portions of the world during and after World War II unmistakably put an end to the old order of Protestant missions.

A new age of world mission has arrived, one in which other religions are now engaged in world mission also. A new understanding of mission, a new strategy, new organization, new ways, means, and methods are the demand of this hour in the central task of the church which shall never end until the Kingdom of God has come in all its glory. It will help as we pray, study, plan and experiment if we know the past history of mission strategy.

Study Questions

1. Since this article was written, evangelical Christians have convened a succession of consultations in acknowledgment that "a new age of world mission has arrived." Notable have been Berlin 1966, Lausanne 1974, Pattaya 1980, and Edinburgh 1980. What "new ways, means, and methods" would you expect from these gatherings? [The latter three consultations are represented elsewhere in this Reader.]

2. Describe, in your own words, the mission strategies employed by three individuals and by three organizations.

3. Beaver describes at length Puritan missions to New England Indians. What effects did these efforts have on later missionary endeavors?

6

Europe's Moravians: A Pioneer Missionary Church

Colin A. Grant

Sixty years before Carey set out for India and 150 years before Hudson Taylor first landed in China, two men, Leonard Dober, a potter, and David Nitschmann, a carpenter, landed on the West Indian island of St. Thomas to make known the gospel of Jesus Christ. They had set out in 1732 from a small Christian community in the mountains of Saxony in central Europe as the first missionaries of the Moravian Brethren, who in the next 20 years entered Greenland (1733), North America's Indian territories (1734), Surinam (1735), South Africa (1736), and the Samoyedic peoples of the Arctic (1737), Algiers and Ceylon, or Sri Lanka (1740), China (1742), Persia (1747), Abyssinia and Labrador (1752).

This was but a beginning. In the first 150 years of its endeavor, the Moravian community was to send no less than 2,158 of its members overseas! In the words of Stephen Neil, "This small church was seized with a missionary passion which has never left it."

The Unitas Fratum (United Brethren), as they had been called, have left a record without parallel in the post-New Testament era of world evangelization, and we do well to look again at the main characteristics of this movement and learn the lessons God has for us.

Spontaneous Obedience

In the first place, that *the missionary obedience of the Moravian Brethren was essentially glad and spontaneous,* "the response of a healthy organism to the law of its life," to use Harry Boer's words. The source of its initial thrust came as a result of a deep movement of God's Spirit that had taken place among a small group of exiled believers. They had fled the persecution of the anti-Reformation reaction in Bohemia and Moravia during the 17th century and had taken shelter on an estate at Berthesdorf at the invitation of Nicolas Zinzendorf, an evangelical Lutheran nobleman.

The first tree for their settlement, which was later to be named Herrnhut

Colin A. Grant was a missionary in Sri Lanka for twelve years with the British Baptist Missionary Society. He was chairman of the Evangelical Missionary Alliance and Home Secretary of the Evangelical Union of South America. Grant died in 1976. Reprinted with permission from the *Evangelical Missions Quarterly*, October 1976, Vol. 12, #4. Published by the Evangelical Missions Information Service, Box 794, Wheaton, Illinois 60187.

("The Lord's watch"), was felled by Christian David (himself to go overseas as a missionary at a later stage) in 1722 to the strains of Psalm 84. Five years later, so deeply ran the new tides of the grace and love of God among them that one of their number wrote: "The whole place represented truly a tabernacle of God among men. There was nothing to be seen and heard but joy and gladness."

This was God's preparation for all that was to follow. Challenged through meeting with Anton, an African slave from St. Thomas during a visit to Denmark for the coronation of King Christian VI, Dober and Nitschmann volunteered to go and were commissioned. To them it was a natural expression of their Christian life and obedience.

Dr. A. C. Thompson, one of the main nineteenth century recorders of the early history of Moravian missions, wrote: "So fully is the duty of evangelizing the heathen lodged in current thought that the fact of anyone entering personally upon that work never creates surprise....It is not regarded as a thing that calls for widespread heralding, as if something marvellous or even unusual were in hand."

What a contrast to the hard worked for interest that characterizes much of the missionary sending scene today! Rev. Ignatius Latrobe, a former secretary of the Moravian missions in the United Kingdom during the last century, wrote: "We think it a great mistake when, after their appointment, missionaries are held up to public notice and admiration and much praise is bestowed upon their devotedness to their Lord, presenting them to the congregations as martyrs and confessors before they have even entered upon their labours. We rather advise them quietly to set out, recommended to the fervent prayers of the congregation...." No clamor, no platform heroics, no publicity, but an ardent, unostentatious desire to make Christ known wherever his name had not been named. This became knit into the ongoing life and liturgy of the Moravian church, so that, for example, a large proportion of public prayer and subsequent hymnology was occupied with this subject.

Passion for Christ

In the second place, this surging zeal had as its prime motivation a *deep, ongoing passion and love for Christ*, something that found expression in the life of Zinzendorf himself. Born in 1700 into Austrian nobility, he came early under godly family influences and soon came to a saving knowledge of Christ. His early missionary interest was evidenced in his founding, with a friend, in his student days of what he called "The Order of the Grain of Mustard Seed" for the spread of Christ's kingdom in the world.

He became not only host to but the first leader of the Moravian believers and himself made visits overseas in the interests of the gospel. "I have one passion, and it is Him, only Him," was his central chord and it sounded through the more than 2,000 hymns he wrote.

William Wilberforce, the great evangelical English social reformer, wrote of the Moravians: "They are a body who have perhaps excelled all mankind in solid and unequivocal proofs of the love of Christ and ardent, active zeal in his service. It is a zeal tempered with prudence, softened with meekness and supported by a courage which no danger can intimidate and a quiet certainty no hardship can exhaust." Today, we need a full theological formulation of our motivation in mission and an adequate grasp of what we believe. But if there is no passionate love for Christ at the center of everything, we will only jingle and jangle our way across the world, merely making a noise as we go.

Courage in the Face of Danger

As Wilberforce indicated, a further feature of the Moravians was that *they faced the most incredible of difficulties and dangers with remarkable courage.* They accepted hardships as part of the identification with the people to whom the Lord had sent them. The words of Paul, "I have become all things to all men" (I Cor. 9:22) were spelled out with a practicality almost without parallel in the history of missions.

Most of the early missionaries went out as "tentmakers," working their trade (most of them being artisans and farmers like Dober and Nitschmann) so that the main expenses involved were in the sending of them out. In areas where white domination had bred the façade of white superiority, e.g. Jamaica, South Africa, the way they humbly got down to hard manual work was itself a witness to their faith. For example, a missionary named Monate helped to build a corn mill in the early days of his work in the Eastern Province of South Africa, cutting the two heavy sandstones himself. In so doing, he not only amazed the Kaffirs among whom he was working, but was enabled to "chat" the gospel to them as he worked!

To go to such places as Surinam and the West Indies meant facing disease and possible death; the early years took their inevitable toll. In Guyana, for instance, 75 out of the first 160 missionaries died from tropical fevers, poisoning and such. Men like Andrew Rittmansberger died within six months of landing on the island. The words of a verse from a hymn written by one of the first Greenland missionaries expresses something of the fibre of their attitude: "Lo through ice and snow, one poor lost soul for Christ to gain; Glad, we bear want and distress to set forth the Lamb once slain."

The Moravians resolutely tackled new languages without many of the modern aids, and numbers of them went on to become outstandingly fluent and proficient in them. This was the stuff, then, of which these men were made. We may face a different pattern of demands today, but the need for a like measure of God-given courage remains the same. Is our easy-going, prosperous society producing "softer" men and women?

Tenacity of Purpose

We finally note that *many Moravian missionaries showed a tenacity of purpose that was of a very high order,* although it must immediately be added that there were occasions when there was a too hasty withdrawal in the face of a particularly problematical situation (e.g., early work among the Aborigines in Australia in 1854 was abandoned suddenly because of local conflicts caused by a gold rush!).

One of the most famous of Moravian missionaries, known as the "Eliot of the West," was David Zeisberger. From 1735, he labored for 62 years among the

Huron and other tribes. On one occasion, after he had preached from Isaiah 64:8, one Sunday morning in August, 1781, the church and compound were invaded by marauding bands of Indians and in the subsequent burnings, Zeisberger lost all his manuscripts of Scripture translations, hymns and extended notes on the grammar of Indian languages. But like Carey, who was to undergo a similar loss through fire in India years later, Zeisberger bowed his head in quiet submission to the overruling providence of God and set his hand and heart to the work again.

Are we becoming short on missionary perseverance today? By all means let us acknowledge the value in short-term missionary assignments and see the divine purpose in many of them. But where are those who are ready to "sink" themselves for God overseas? Let us look at such problems as children's education and changing missionary strategy under the Lord's direction full in the face; but if men are to be won, believers truly nourished, and churches encouraged into the fullness of life in Christ, a great deal of "missionary staying power" of the right sort is going to be needed in some places.

Of course, these Moravians had their weaknesses. They concentrated more on evangelism than on the actual planting of local churches and they were consequently very weak on developing Christian leadership. They centered their approach on "the missionary station," even giving them a whole succession of biblical place names, such as Shiloh, Sarepta, Nazareth, Bethlehem, etc. Since most of the early missionaries went out straight from the "carpenter's bench" because of the spontaneous nature of their obedience, they were short on adequate preparation. In fact, it was not until 1869 that the first missionary training college was founded at Nisky, 20 miles from Herrnhut.

Despite all this, the words of J. R. Weinlick bring home the all-pervading lesson we have to learn from the Moravians today. "The Moravian church was the first among Protestant churches to treat this work as *a responsibility of the church as a whole* (emphasis mine), instead of leaving it to societies or specially interested people." True, they were a small, compact and unified community, and therefore it may be said that such a simple missionary structure as they possessed was natural. It is doubtful, however, if this can ever be made an excuse for the low level of missionary concern apparent in many sectors of God's church today, or for the complex and, often, competing missionary society system we struggle with at the present time. Have we ears to hear and wills to obey?

Study Questions

1. Which of the characteristics of the Moravians is most absent from the Christian church today? Which is most evident?

2. What is your answer to the question posed at the end of this article? Why?

7

Student Power in World Missions

David Howard

Why take time to read about the past? Why not get down to business to today's issues and planning for the future?

We learn from the past so that we can live effectively in the present and plan wisely for the future. He who will not learn from history is doomed to repeat her mistakes.

We learn about the Lord's working in past times so that we can understand him better and trust him more fully.

We turn to the Bible for basic information about those mighty deeds. But the Lord did not cease those glorious workings when he terminated the writing of the Bible. So we turn to later sources to learn of his subsequent deeds.

In particular, what has he been doing over the centuries in terms of work among college students in fulfilling the great Commission?

Earliest Traces

Perhaps the earliest traceable instance in which students had a definite part in promoting a world outreach is found in Germany in the early seventeenth century. Gustav Warneck, the great historian-theologian of missions, writes of seven young law students from Lubeck, Germany, who, while studying together in

David M. Howard, presently Senior Vice President of the David C. Cook Foundation, served for ten years as the International Director of the World Evangelical Fellowship based in Singapore. Prior to that he was Missions Director of Inter-Varsity Christian Fellowship and Director of the IVCF Urbana Conventions in 1973 and 1976. He also directed the Consultation on World Evangelization held in Pattaya, Thailand, in 1980 under the Lausanne Committee. Previously he spent fifteen years in Costa Rica and Colombia, where he was Assistant General Director of the Latin America Mission. He is the author of eight books including *Student Power in World Missions, The Great Commission for Today, What Makes a Missionary,* and *The Dream That Would Not Die.* Taken from *Student Power in World Missions,* by David M. Howard. Copyright 1979 by Inter-Varsity Christian Fellowship of the USA and used by permission of Inter-Varsity Press.

Paris, committed themselves to carry the gospel overseas. At least three of them finally sailed for Africa. All trace has been lost of two of these but the name of Peter Heiling has survived. After a two-year stay in Egypt, he proceeded to Abyssinia in 1634. He spent some twenty years in that land, where he translated the Bible into Amharic and finally died a martyr.

Heiling had no successors, and thus there was no continuation of what he began. But the translation of the Scriptures was a significant contribution that unquestionably made its impact.

The important thing to note here is that his original impetus to leave his own land and carry the gospel to another part of the world came when he banded together with fellow students to pray and work for the extension of the church overseas.

The Moravians

The name of Count Nicolaus Ludwig von Zinzendorf (1700-1760) stands high in missionary annals as a leader of the Moravian movement, one of the first, most effective and most enduring of missionary enterprises. Zinzendorf had the good fortune to know personally both Spener and Francke, the great leaders of the Pietists. The emphasis on a personal relationship to Jesus as Lord became the most influential factor in his early life. Before the age of ten he had determined that his lifelong purpose should be to preach the gospel of Jesus Christ throughout the world.

From 1710 to 1716, Zinzendorf studied in the Paedagogium founded by Francke in Halle, Germany. With five other boys he formed the Order of the Grain of Mustard Seed, whose members were bound together in prayer. The purposes were to witness to the power of Jesus Christ, to draw other Christians together in fellowship, to help those who were suffering for their faith, and to carry the gospel of Christ overseas. The same vision was carried over in his university days at Wittenberg and Utrecht. He never lost sight of this purpose.

In April, 1731, Zinzendorf attended the coronation of Christian VI of Denmark in Copenhagen. There he met Anthony Ulrich, from St. Thomas in the West Indies, who shared with the Count his deep desire that his brothers in the West Indies should hear the gospel. So deeply impressed was Zinzendorf that he saw the relationship between this and the commitments he had made as a student. By August, 1732, arrangements had been made for the first two Moravian missionaries to sail for St. Thomas.

Thus, the modern worldwide missionary movement (which traces parts of its roots to the Moravians of 1732) was actually born in the hearts of a group of students who joined together at Halle to pray for world evangelism.

The Wesleys

At the same time God was also moving among students in England, Charles Wesley entered Christ Church College, Oxford, in 1726, from which his brother, John, had just graduated. Because of his desire to know God better he formed a small society of students for the study of the classics and the New Testament. They became known as the "Holy Club" (in derision from their fellow students) and as the "Methodists" (because of their methodical approach to life). John Wesley returned as a teaching fellow to Lincoln College at Oxford and joined his brother in the activities of this group.

In addition to worship and study, the group translated their piety into an outreach to the poor, the hungry and the imprisoned. This facet of the activities became an increasingly important part of their club.

While John Wesley is usually known as an evangelist and theologian and Charles as a hymn writer, they both began their fruitful careers as overseas missionaries. In October, 1735, the two brothers sailed for the colony of Georgia with General Oglethorpe. John Wesley's journal indicated that he was not yet sure of his own salvation at this point and that his sailing for Georgia was partly a quest for knowing God better. At the same time, he had the desire to share what he knew of Christ with the Indians of America.

Shortly after Wesley arrived in Georgia, the English colonists there tried to persuade him to remain in Savannah as their pastor. However, his desire to preach the gospel to the unevangelized Indians caused him to write in his Journal:

> Tuesday, November 23 (1736)—Mr. Oglethorpe sailed for England, leaving Mr. Ingham, Mr. Delamotte, and me at Savannah, but with less prospect of preaching to the Indians than we had the first day we set foot in America. Whenever I mentioned it, it was immediately replied, "You cannot leave Savannah without a minister."
>
> To this indeed my plain answer was, "I know not that I am under any obligation to the contrary. I never promised to stay here one month. I openly declared both before, at, and ever since, my coming hither that I neither would nor could take charge of the English any longer than till I could go among the Indians."

This desire to share the message of Christianity with the Indians who did not know Jesus Christ was apparently a direct outgrowth of the fellowship of students at Oxford who sought to know God better through their "Holy Club."

Charles Simeon

No summary of the movement of God among students in England would be complete without reference to Charles Simeon. As a student at Cambridge University in 1779, Simeon came to know Christ. Following his graduation in 1782, he was appointed Fellow of King's College, ordained to the ministry and named incumbent of Holy Trinity Church at Cambridge. Thus began a remarkable ministry that was to span fifty-four years.

Students who came under Simeon's influence later became some of the great leaders of the church both in Great Britain and around the world. His informal gatherings of undergraduates in his home for Bible study and prayer were perhaps the most influential part of his work. Scores of students first came to a personal relationship to Jesus Christ. Here they began to understand the Word of God and its implications for their lives. And here they received their first visions of reaching out to others with that Word.

This outreach took very practical forms. In 1827 a group of five students, strongly influenced by Simeon's preaching at Holy Trinity Church, formed the Jesus Lane Sunday School in an attempt to reach the boys and girls of the community. Among those who taught in this Sunday School were men such at Conybeare, Howson, and Westcott, later to be known through the world for biblical scholarship.

Another example of outreach in which Simeon had direct influence was the forming of an auxiliary of the British and Foreign Bible Society at Cambridge in 1811. The purpose of the Society had always been to make available the Word of God throughout the world in the language of the people. The involvement of students in this auxiliary undoubtedly served to broaden their horizons and help them see how they could relate to world evangelization.

Simeon's influence continued long after his death in 1836. The "Simeonites" (as the students who attended his informal gatherings were dubbed) continued their activities in the Jesus Lane Sunday School and elsewhere in an outreach with the gospel. In 1848, the Cambridge Union for Private Prayer was formed and became a vital factor in the spiritual life and witness of many.

In 1857, David Livingstone visited Cambridge and delivered a moving missionary address. Partly as a result of this visit, the Cambridge University Church Missionary Union was established early in 1858 for the purpose of encouraging "a more extended missionary spirit by frequent meetings for prayer and the reading of papers, and for bringing forward an increased number of candidates for missionary employment."

The Inter-Varsity Fellowship of England traces its origins directly to the work begun by Charles Simeon. The Cambridge Inter-Collegiate Christian Union was formed in 1877. From small beginnings this movement soon spread to other British universities, then to other countries and finally around the world.

The Cambridge Seven

In 1882, the American evangelist, D. L. Moody, visited Cambridge during a tour of Britain. The results of one week of meetings were beyond expectations as great impact was made at the university. Immediately after his visit there was a rapid increase in the number of students who applied to the Church Missionary Society of the Anglican Church for service overseas.

About the same time there was a mounting interest in a new mission, the China Inland Mission, recently founded by J. Hudson Taylor. In 1883-84, a group of seven outstanding students (six of them from Cambridge) applied to the China Inland Mission. They were all brilliant and talented men with good background and upbringing and a variety of athletic and academic abilities.

Montagu H. P. Beauchamp, son of Sir Thomas and Lady Beauchamp, was a brilliant student. William W. Cassels was son of a businessman. Dixon Edward Hoste was converted under D. L. Moody. He held a commission in the Royal Artillery and was later to become the successor of Hudson Taylor as director of the China Inland Mission. Arthur Polhill-Turner was the son of a member of Parliament. Outgoing and quick, he played cricket and made friends easily at Cambridge. He, too, was converted under D. L. Moody. Arthur's brother, Cecil Polhill-Turner, was commissioned in the Dragoon Guards. Stanley P. Smith, son of a successful London surgeon, became captain of First Trinity Boat Club and stroke of the Varsity crew at Cambridge. Although he was brought up in a Christian home, he committed his life to Christ under the ministry of D. L. Moody. Charles Thomas Studd was the son of wealthy parents who knew every luxury of life. At Cambridge he was captain of the cricket team and generally considered the outstanding cricketer of his day.

In a variety of ways the Spirit of God began to move upon each of these men concerning going to China. Slowly but relentlessly the Spirit brought each one to a place of commitment and subsequently to an application for missionary service. Sensing a unity of purpose and outlook, these seven desired to share their vision with fellow students. Following graduation they traveled extensively throughout England and Scotland, visiting campuses and churches. Their impact for missionary work was far beyond the few months of time they invested in this tour. In February, 1885, the seven sailed for China, to be followed in subsequent years by scores of students who, under their influence, had given themselves to Jesus Christ to reach other parts of the world.

Thus the forward movement of the church continued to be inspired by youth. Whether it was among students at Halle with Zinzendorf, or at Oxford with the Wesleys, or at Cambridge with C. T. Studd and his fellows, the Holy Spirit continued to use students as spearheads in awakening the church to its worldwide responsibilities.

Samuel Mills

On the North American continent the beginnings of overseas interest on the part of the church can be traced directly to student influence, and more precisely, to the impact of one student, Samuel J. Mills, Jr. (1783-1818). Born in Connecticut as the son of a Congregational minister, Mills was brought up in a godly home. His mother reportedly said of him, "I have consecrated this child to the service of God as a missionary." This was a remarkable statement since missionary interest was practically unknown in the churches of that day and no channels (such as mission boards) for overseas service existed in America. Mills was converted at the age of seventeen as a part of the Great Awakening that began in 1798 and touched his father's church. His commitment to world evangelism seemed to be an integral part of his conversion experience. From the moment of conversion, on through the years of his study and for the rest of his public ministry, he never lost sight of this purpose.

The Haystack Prayer Meeting

In 1806, Mills enrolled in Williams College, Massachusetts. This school had been profoundly affected by the religious awakening of those years, and devout students on campus had a deep concern for the spiritual welfare of their fellow students. Mills joined with them in their desire to help others.

It was Mills' custom to spend Wednesday and Saturday afternoons in prayer with other students on the banks of the Hoosack River or in a valley near the college. In August, 1806, Mills and four others were caught in a thunderstorm while returning from their usual meeting. Seeking refuge under a haystack they waited out the storm and gave themselves to prayer. Their special focus of prayer that day was for the awakening of foreign missionary interest among students. Mills directed their discussion and prayer to their own missionary obligation. He exhorted his companions with the words that later became a watchword for them, "We can do this if we will."

Bowed in prayer, these first American student volunteers for foreign missions willed that God should have their lives for service wherever he needed them, and in that self-dedication really gave birth to the first student missionary society in America. Kenneth Scott Latourette, the foremost historian of the church's worldwide expansion, states, "It was from this haystack meeting that the foreign missionary movement of the churches of the United States had an initial impulse."[1]

The exact location of the haystack was unknown for a number of years. Then, in 1854, Bryan Green, one of those present in 1806, visited Williamstown and located the spot. A monument was erected on the site in 1867. Mark Hopkins, who was then president of the American Board of Commissioners for Foreign Missions, gave the dedicatory address in which he said, "For once in the history of the world a prayer meeting is commemorated by a monument."

The Society of Brethren

Back at Williams College students continued to meet for prayer. They were influential in leading a number of other students into a commitment for overseas service. In September, 1808, deciding to organize formally, they founded The Society of the Brethren for the purpose of giving themselves to extend the gospel around the world.

Desiring to extend the influence of this Society to other colleges, one of the members transferred to Middlebury College to found a similar society. In 1809, following his graduation from Williams College, Mills enrolled at Yale with the dual purpose of continuing theological studies and of imparting missionary vision to the students there.

Here he met Henry Obookiah, a Hawaiian, who encouraged him with the need of evangelizing the Hawaiian Islands. Obookiah did much in the next few years to stimulate student interest in evangelizing the Pacific Islands. He died prematurely before he was able to return to his homeland, but Latourette says of him, "The story of his life and missionary purpose was a major stimulus to the sending, in 1819, the year after his death, of the first missionaries of the American Board to Hawaii." (James Michener's caricature of Abner Hale as the first missionary to Hawaii, in his novel *Hawaii*, should not be allowed to obscure the commitment which led Obookiah, Mills and other students to be concerned for the evangelization of those who had never heard of Christ.)

The American Board of Commissioners for Foreign Missions

In June, 1810, the General Association of Congregational Churches met in Bradford, Massachusetts, in annual meeting. Samuel Mills (then studying at Andover Theological Seminary), with several fellow students, including Adoniram Judson, presented a petition requesting the formation of a society which could send them out as foreign missionaries. On June 29, the Association recommended to the assembly "That there be instituted by this General Association a Board of Commissioners for Foreign Missions, for the purpose of devising ways and means, and adopting and prosecuting measures for promoting the spread of the Gospel to heathen lands." Although not legally incorporated until 1812, the Board began activities immediately. It was interdenominational in character, enjoying the support of numerous church bodies. Volunteers were recruited and prepared.

On February 19, 1812, Adoniram Judson and Samuel Newell and their wives sailed for India, and five days later Samuel Nott, Gordon Hall and Luther Rice also embarked on another ship for India. These first American missionaries joined hands with the great English pioneer, William Carey, who since 1793 had been evangelizing in India. Judson and Rice subsequently persuaded the Baptists of North America to form their own missionary society, which became the second foreign board in the United States.

Thus, within four years of the haystack prayer meeting, these students had been influential in the formation of the first North American missionary society, and a year and a half later the first volunteers were on their way to Asia.

The Student Volunteer Movement

In the history of modern missions, probably no single factor has wielded a greater influence in the world-wide outreach of the Church than the Student Volunteer Movement. The names of its great leaders—men of the stature of John R. Mott, Robert C. Wilder, Robert E. Speer, to name a few—stand high in the annals of the foreign missionary movement. Its watchword, "The evangelization of the world in this generation," was so profoundly influential in motivating students for overseas service that John R. Mott could write, "I can truthfully answer that next to the decision to take Christ as the leader and Lord of my life, the watchword has had more influence than all other ideals and objectives combined to widen my horizon and enlarge my conception of the Kingdom of God."

The SVM had its distant roots in the famous Haystack Prayer Meeting held at Williams College in 1806. Out of that meeting grew two very influential developments. First was the Society of Brethren at Andover Theological Seminary. Second was the American Board of Commissioners for Foreign Missions, the first North American foreign mission agency. One of the members of the Society of Brethren in later years was Royal Wilder, who sailed for India under the ABCFM in 1846. Returning to the U.S. for health reasons in 1877, he settled in Princeton, NJ, where his son, Robert, soon formed the "Princeton Foreign Missionary Society." The members of this Society declared themselves "willing and desirous, God permitting, to go to the unevangelized portions of the world." Their prayers and activities bore fruit in the summer of 1886.

At the invitation of D. L. Moody, 251 students gathered at Mt. Hermon, Mass., for a month-long Bible conference in July 1886. A great burden for world evangelization was gripping some of these students. A memorable address given by one of the Bible teachers, Dr. A. T. Pierson, contained the seed form of the

"The Mount Hermon One Hundred"

SVM watchword, and he is generally credited with having originated it. As a result of Pierson's challenge, plus other motivations, including "The meeting of the Ten Nations" and lengthy prayer meetings, 100 students volunteered for overseas service during the conference.

The foundations of the SVM were laid that summer, and the movement was formally organized in 1888. During the school year 1886-87, Robert G. Wilder and John Forman, both of Princeton, travelled to 167 different schools to share the vision they had received of world evangelization. During that year they saw 2,106 students volunteer for missionary work. Among these were Samuel Zwemer and Robert E. Speer, whose influence in missions during the next decades is almost incalculable.

The SVM was formally organized in 1888 with John R. Mott as its chairman. A fivefold purpose was developed:

> The fivefold purpose of the Student Volunteer Movement is to lead students to a thorough consideration of the claims of foreign missions upon them personally as a lifework; to foster this purpose by guiding students who become volunteers in their study and activity for missions until they come under the immediate direction of the Mission Boards; to unite all volunteers in a common, organized, aggressive movement; to secure a sufficient number of well-qualified volunteers to meet the demands of the various Mission Boards; and to create and maintain an intelligent, sympathetic and active interest in foreign missions on the part of students who are to remain at home in order to ensure the strong backing of the missionary enterprise by their advocacy, their gifts

and their prayers.[2]

Taking a cue from the Princeton Foreign Missionary Society with its "pledge," the SVM developed a declaration card. The purpose of the card was to face each student with the challenge of the "evangelization of the world in this generation." The card stated: "It is my purpose, if God permit, to become a foreign missionary." When a student signed this, it was understood as his response to the call of God. Every student was expected to face the issue and either to respond to it in the affirmative or else show that God was clearly leading him elsewhere.

Growth and Outreach

The growth of the SVM in the following three decades was nothing short of phenomenal. In 1891, the first international student missionary convention sponsored by SVM was held in Cleveland, Ohio. It was decided that such a convention should be held every four years in order to reach each student generation. Until the 1940's, this became a pattern, interrupted only by World War I. The first convention at Cleveland was attended by 558 students representing 151 educational institutions, along with 31 foreign missionaries and 32 representatives of missionary societies.[3]

By the time of the Cleveland convention, there were 6,200 Student Volunteers from 352 educational institutions in the United States and Canada. And 321 volunteers had already sailed for overseas service. In addition, 40 colleges and 32 seminaries were involved in financial support of their alumni who had gone overseas as Volunteers.[4] All of this had taken place in just five years since the Mt. Hermon conference. The Movement had also reached out and planted seeds of similar movements in Great Britain, Scandinavia, and South Africa.

An educational program in the schools was initiated and spread rapidly. Mott could later write that "At one time before the war the number in such circles exceeded 40,000 in 2,700 classes in 700 institutions."[5]

These efforts on the local campuses, the quadrennial conventions, plus literature, speaking tours and other activities, resulted in thousands of students volunteering for overseas service. "By 1945, at the most conservative estimate, 20,500 students from so-called Christian lands, who had signed the declaration, reached the field, for the most part under the missionary societies and boards of the Churches."[6]

In 1920 (the peak year statistically) 2,783 students signed the SVM decision card, 6,890 attended the quadrennial convention in Des Moines, and in 1921, 637 Volunteers sailed for the field, this being the highest number in any single year. The motivations were genuine, the grounding in biblical principles was solid, and the leadership had a burning vision for world evangelism.

Confusion and Decline

But in 1920 an ominous change began to take place. "The Missionary Review of the World" (a journal founded by Royal Wilder in 1887) analyzed the SVM convention at Des Moines as follows:

The Des Moines Volunteer Convention...was marked by a revolt against the leadership of the "elder statesman." That convention was large in number but the delegates were lacking in missionary vision and purpose and were only convinced that a change of ideals and of leadership was needed. They rightly believed that selfishness and foolishness had involved the world in terrible war and bloodshed and they expressed their intention to take control of Church and State in an effort to bring about better conditions. The problems of international peace, social justice, racial equality and economic betterment obscured the Christian foundations and ideals of spiritual service.

From the high point of 1920, the SVM experienced a rapid decline. Thirty-eight Volunteers sailed for the field in 1934 (as compared with 637 in 1921). Twenty-five Volunteers enrolled in SVM in 1938 (as compared with 2,783 in 1920). In 1940, 465 delegates attended the quadrennial convention in Toronto (as compared with the 6,890 at Des Moines in 1920).

Here was a movement whose influence on students and the world mission of the church had been incalculable. Yet it could be said of SVM that "by 1940 it had almost ceased to be a decisive factor either in student religious life or in the promotion of the missionary program of the churches."[7]

What had happened to precipitate, or to allow, such a drastic decline?

Dr. William Beahm has highlighted the following factors, while stating that no one reason by itself is an adequate explanation of the steady decline.

1. Many changes of leadership broke the continuity of its life and left the subtle impression of a sinking ship from which they were fleeing.

2. There was increasing difficulty in financing its program. This was closely related to the depression and the loss of Mott's leadership.

3. The program tended to become top-heavy. In 1920 the Executive Committee was expanded from six to thirty members.

4. Its emphasis upon foreign mission seemed to overlook the glaring needs in America, and so the Movement appeared to be specialized rather than comprehensive.

5. When the interest of students veered away from missions, it left the Movement in a dilemma as to which interest to follow—student or missionary.

6. There was a great decline in missionary education. One reason for this was the assumption that discussion of world problems by students was an improvement over the former types of informative procedure. The Conventions came to have this discussional character.

7. Their emphasis shifted away from Bible study, evangelism, lifework decision and foreign mission obligation on which the SVM had originally built. Instead they now emphasized new issues such as race relations, economic injustice and imperialism.

8. The rise of indigenous leaders reduced the need for western personnel.

9. The rise of the social gospel blotted out the sharp distinction between Christian America and the "unevangelized portions of the world."

10. Revivalism had given way to basic uncertainty as to the validity of the Chris-

tian faith, especially of its claim to exclusive supremacy. Accordingly the watchword fell into disuse and the argument for foreign missions lost its force.[8]

By the 1924 convention, attention was turning rapidly from world evangelism to the solution of social and economic problems. "The Missionary Review" stated that in 1924 "They failed to make much impression or to reach any practical conclusions."

Termination of the SVM

After 1940, its activities moved steadily away from an emphasis on overseas missions as SVM became more involved in political and social matters. In 1959, the SVM merged with the United Student Christian Council and the Interseminary Movement to form the National Student Christian Federation (NSCF). This in turn was allied with the Roman Catholic National Newman Student Federation and other groups in 1966 to form the University Christian Movement (UCM). The purpose of the UCM at its inception was threefold: "to provide an ecumenical instrument for allowing the church and university world to speak to each other, to encourage Christian response on campuses to human issues, and to act as an agent through which sponsors could provide resources and services to campus life."[9] It is obvious that these purposes, while legitimate in themselves, show little relationship to the original objectives of the SVM as spelled out at Mt. Hermon and in subsequent developments.

On March 1, 1969, the General Committee of the University Christian Movement at its meeting in Washington, D. C., took action in the form of an affirmative vote (23 for, 1 against, 1 abstention) of the following resolution: "We the General Committee of the UCM, declare that as of June 30, 1969, the UCM ceases to exist as a national organization..."[10]

Thus, the final vestiges of the greatest student missionary movement in the history of the church were quietly laid to rest eighty-three years after the Spirit of God had moved so unmistakably upon students at Mt. Hermon.

No human movement is perfect, nor can it be expected to endure indefinitely. But the great heritage left by the SVM can still speak to our generation. The reasons for its decline can serve as warning signals. Its principal emphases can redirect our attention to the basic issues of today: emphasis on personal commitment to Jesus Christ on a lifelong basis; acceptance of the authority of the Word of God and emphasis on personal Bible study; sense of responsibility to give the gospel of Christ to the entire world in our generation; reliance on the Holy Spirit; emphasis on student initiative and leadership to carry out these objectives.

Recent Advances

Yet God does not leave himself without a witness. By the mid-1930s with the decline in missionary interest, with the Great Depression taking its toll, with war clouds rising again in Europe, with the liberal-fundamentalist controversy raging, the church was deeply discouraged. But once again God moved upon students who would not be deterred from fulfilling God's call, in spite of surrounding circumstances.

In 1936 at Ben Lippen Bible Conference grounds in North Carolina a group of students shared their concern that SVM seemed to have changed its original purposes. Convinced that they could not sit idly by and watch the church give up its missionary outreach, they decided to act. The following week a delegation from Ben Lippen went to Keswick, N.J., to share with a similar student conference the burden God had given to them. After careful consultation with some SVM leaders, and feeling that their purposes were now different, they decided to form a new organization.

Thus, the Student Foreign Missions Fellowship was organized in 1938 and SFMF was formally incorporated under student leadership, and chapters were formed throughout the country. Rapid growth was experienced, and once again the church was awakened through students who refused to be daunted by the circumstances for their times.

In 1939 Inter-Varsity came to the U.S. from Canada. It was soon evident that one of its purposes, that of fomenting missionary interest among students, overlapped directly with the purposes of SFMF. After several years of prayer and consultation, both groups felt led by God to a merger that was consummated in November, 1945, the SFMF becoming the Missionary Department of IVCF.

In December, 1946, the newly merged SFMF and IVCF sponsored their first international missionary convention, attended by 575 students, at the University of Toronto. In 1948 the first convention was held at the University of Illinois, Urbana, where it has been held since that time.

Following World War II there was a great upsurge of missionary concern. Veterans who had fought in the Pacific and Europe returned to the campuses deeply desirous to go back and share the gospel with the people who so recently had been their enemies. These veterans had seen the world, life, and death in a way few students before or since had seen it. God used them to lead others into an understanding of mission obligation. From many campuses in the late 1940s and early 1950s more students went overseas in missionary endeavor than at any other comparable period in history.

However, during the 1950s it seemed as though the human race was begging for a breather. This general lull took its toll in missionary interest as well. Once again there was a decline in the churches and among students.

In sharp contrast, the student world of the 1960s was marked by activism, violent upheavals, and negative attitudes. The anti-government, anti-establishment, anti-family, anti-church attitudes were also expressed in anti-missions reactions. Seldom have missions been looked upon with less favor by students than during that decade.

However, early in the next decade a sudden, unexpected change took place. Apparently recognizing that negativism was not going to solve the problems of the world, students began to take a more positive attitude and to work for change from within "the system." Nowhere was this more dramatically seen than at the Urbana student missionary conventions. Inter-Varsity uses world evangelism decision cards at these conventions as a regular part of the process of stimulating student responses to missions. In 1970 seven percent of the students at Urbana signed these cards. Three years later, 28 percent signed the card. The number grew to 50 percent by the 1976 convention. This percentage has remained above 50 percent since then.

Now, in the 1990s, we are still riding the crest of a great wave of student interest and activism in missions. Summer programs and short-term assignments overseas have increased dramatically in recent years. The Perspectives Study Program of the U.S. Center for World Mission's Training Division, and similar programs of missionary preparation, have been attracting steady streams of candidates.

Today's students have the great privilege of standing on the shoulders of their forebears to view with thanksgiving what God has done in the past and to look ahead to the future with hope.

End Notes

1. Kenneth Scott Latourette, *These Sought a Country* (New York: Harper and Brothers, 1950), p. 46.

2. John R. Mott, *Five Decades and a Forward View* (New York: Harper and Brothers, 1939), p. 8.

3. Robert P. Wilder, *The Student Volunteer Movement: Its Origin and Early History* (New York: The Student Volunteer Movement, 1935), p. 58.

4. Watson A. Omulogoli, *The Student Volunteer Movement: Its History and Contribution* (master's thesis, Wheaton College, 1967), p. 73.

5. Mott, *Op. cit..*, p. 12.

6. Ruth Rouse and Stephen C. Neill, *A History of the Ecumenical Movement, 1517- 1948* (Philadelphia: Westminster Press, 1967), p. 328.

7. William H. Beahm, *Factors in the Development of the Student Volunteer Movement for Foreign Missions*, unpublished Ph.D. dissertation, University of Chicago, 1941.

8. *Ibid.*, pp. 14-15.

9. Report of Religious News Service, April 1, 1969.

10. *News Notes*, Department of Higher Education, National Council of the Churches of Christ in the U.S.A., New York, XV, No. 3, March, 1969.

Study Questions

1. Trace the roots of the Student Volunteer Movement.

2. If another student missions movement were to arise today, how do you think it would be similar to and different from the SVM in its origin, characteristics, and effects? What factors would promote the development of such a movement? What factors would hinder its development?

3. In your own words, explain the decline of the SVM and the lessons to be learned by contemporary students.

8

The Laymen's Missionary Movement

J. Campbell White

J. Campbell White was a leader in the Student Volunteer Movement during its early years and became the first secretary of the Laymen's Missionary Movement, founded in 1906. White here describes, in a 1909 publication, a brief history, statement of principles, and significance of this latter movement, which successfully engaged thousands of laymen in mission as study, prayer, and financial support of existing missionary boards and new volunteers in the first two decades of the twentieth century.

One hundred years ago, at the famous Haystack Prayer Meeting, the first organized foreign missionary work in North America was inaugurated. A small group of college students at Williamstown, Massachusetts voiced the keynote of the new enterprise in the now historic phrase, "We can do it if we will."

During the last twenty years the missionary spirit has had a marvelous development among the colleges of the United States and Canada. The Student Volunteer Movement, born at Northfield in 1886, has swept through the colleges with its inspiring watchcry, "The Evangelization of the World in This Generation," familiarizing students with world conditions and leading thousands of strong men and women to live with a dominating missionary life purpose.

As volunteers went into various mission fields they found very few, even among their fellow-workers, who were living in the hope of seeing the world evangelized in this generation. Largely under their influence this conception of the Church's present duty has taken hold of the missionaries abroad and the missionary leaders at home, until now it has become a part of the prayers and earnest hopes of nearly all the important missionary societies of Christendom.

Every four years there is a great convention of the Student Volunteer Movement, bringing together some thousands of the students of North America to consider the progress of the kingdom throughout the world. The last of these conventions was held at Nashville, in February-March, 1906. It was at this convention that the seed-thought of the Laymen's Missionary Movement was planted by the Spirit in the mind of a young businessman of the City of Washington. As he saw over three thousand students considering for several days their relation to the evangelization of the world, this thought came to him—if the

---

Taken from Laymen's Missionary Movement Publication, October 1909. "The Genesis and Significance of the Laymen's Missionary Movement," J. Campbell White.

laymen of North America could see the world as these students are seeing it, they would rise up in their strength and provide all the funds needed for the enterprise.

A Laymen's Movement is Founded

The providential opportunity for testing this idea came a few months later. The one hundredth anniversary of the Haystack Prayer Meeting was to be celebrated in New York City by a series of interdenominational missionary meetings. It was arranged that one of these meetings should be for laymen and should take the form of a prayer meeting. This meeting was held on November 15, 1906, in the Fifth Avenue Presbyterian Church. The afternoon was very stormy, and only about seventy-five laymen were present. Mr. Samuel B. Capen, of Boston, presided. It was really a prayer meeting, most of the time from 3 to 6 p.m. being spent in actual prayer. After an intermission of an hour for supper, the meeting continued in the evening, consisting mainly of discussion as to what practical steps should be taken. Out of this discussion a series of resolutions was adopted, calling into existence the Laymen's Missionary Movement.

Organization and Goals

From the first, the whole idea of the movement has been to co-operate with the regular missionary agencies of the churches in the enlargement of their work. It does not divert any missionary offerings from congregational or denominational channels. Nor does it promote the organization of separate Men's Missionary Societies within the congregations. All the organization asked for is a Missionary Committee of men in each congregation to work with the pastor in enlisting all members and adherents in the intelligent and adequate support and extension of missionary work.

The Movement itself has no organization apart from a General Committee, which meets twice a year, and an Executive Committee of twenty-one members, which meets every month. Five secretaries give their whole time to the work of the general Movement.

At least twelve denominational Laymen's Missionary Movements have already been organized. As a rule, these follow the practice of the general Movement and consist merely of a series of committees. Ten secretaries of denominational Movements have now been secured, and others are about to be appointed.

As the Movement is "an inspiration, not an administration," it has been chiefly occupied with the presentation of an adequate missionary policy to influential groups of men, and also with the exploitation of methods of missionary finance, which have produced the best results.

The Movement stands for investigation, agitation and organization; the investigation by laymen of missionary conditions, the agitation of laymen of an adequate missionary policy, and the organization of laymen to co-operate with the ministers and Missionary Boards in enlisting the whole Church in its supreme work of saving the world.

It has been found of enormous advantage to present the missionary operations of the Church in the large to men of all the churches together. Only in this way is it possible to secure the full inspiration from past success and to plan on a comprehensive basis for the completion of the work that has been so splendidly begun.

It is noteworthy that wherever the Movement has been presented, in scores of cities of the United States and Canada, it has received the enthusiastic commendation and co-operation of representative men. A Commission of six laymen from the United States and Canada presented the Movement in Great Britain, where it was at once taken up and National Committees organized both in England and Scotland. It has since spread to Germany and to Australia. We are rapidly approaching the time when the Christian men of all nations will be federated for co-operative action in behalf of mankind.

While the Movement has already resulted in enlisting large numbers of men in the active promotion of missionary interest and has been one of the main factors in adding hundreds of thousands of dollars to the receipts of Missionary Boards, it is not to be expected that the whole church can be aroused suddenly to its missionary responsibility. If during the next five or ten years the whole Church can be filled with the missionary spirit and fired with enthusiasm for world evangelization, it will be a marvelous triumph of grace.

The Significance of the Movement

What explains the power of this Movement in the lives of men? What is its significance in the life of the Church? To these questions, at least partial answer is found in the following considerations:

1. The Movement presents to men the greatest possible spiritual challenge. The greatest thing in the world is the world. If the world's needs are not great enough to arrest a man's attention and command his help, he is incapable of being moved by the most imperative challenge with which God has confronted men. That man had the right conception of life who said, "I would rather save a million men than save a million dollars." Men are awakening to their opportunity to enter as influential constructive factors into the currents of human history and leave the whole world better because they lived.

2. This Movement makes the largest possible demands upon men. It strives simply to voice to them God's call for a life whose dominant purpose is to establish the reign of Christ in human relationships. It reminds men that all life is a sacred trust, involving the stewardship of opportunity, of influence, of time, and of treasure; that spiritual values are the only permanent values; that selfishness is suicidal while service of others brings to the soul the supremest possible satisfaction.

It has been truly said that we must either ask more of men or less. They are not satisfied with what they have been doing. The Laymen's Movement believes that we can only be true to the call of the world and of Christ by asking of men all they have and are, that the Kingdom may come and God's will may be done on earth as it is in heaven.

3. The effort to evangelize the world presents to every man the largest opportunity of service which can come to him in this life. It includes the man nearest to us, and also the one furthest away. It asks for the best which any man has of

intelligence and ability to help solve the supreme problem of the world. This is an enterprise into which the most resourceful of men can put all they possess of life and possessions, and then wish that they had manifold more to invest. No man can live the large life which God has planned for him unless he enters with his whole soul into the program of Christ for the redemption of the race. Many of our best pastors and lay workers at home have been developed by the missionary spirit.

4. The life-purpose being emphasized by the Laymen's Movement, when followed, satisfies the deepest spiritual ambitions of men. Most men are not satisfied with the permanent output of their lives. Nothing can wholly satisfy the life of Christ within His followers except the adoption of Christ's purpose toward the world He came to redeem. Fame, pleasure and riches are but husks and ashes in contrast with the boundless and abiding joy of working with God for the fulfillment of His eternal plans. The men who are putting everything into Christ's undertaking are getting out of life its sweetest and most priceless rewards.

5. The effort to evangelize the world presents the speediest and surest methods of saving the Church. Our material resources are so stupendous that we are in danger of coming to trust in riches rather than in God. "If a man is growing large in wealth, nothing but constant giving can keep him from growing small in soul." The evangelization of the world is the only enterprise large enough and important enough to provide an adequate outlet for the Church's wealth.

Another of the subtle modern foes of the Church is rationalism. The final answer to this dangerous enemy is the standing miracle of modern missions. In the aggressive missionary operations of the Church lies her fairest hope of salvation from formalism, from materialism, from rationalism, from selfishness and from indifference to the will of God.

6. As all branches of the Church co-operate to accomplish the evangelization of the world, there are multiplying evidences that the unity of the Church itself may be restored. In the mind of Christ, the union of His Church was associated with the salvation of mankind. He prayed "that they all may be one that the world may believe." Men believe in the Laymen's Movement because it is actually associating men of all churches in cooperative work for the accomplishment of Christ's one great purpose through His Church. Professor Bosworth says that there are four things that bind men together: 1. A common hope; 2. A common work; 3. Deliverance from common peril; and, 4. Loyalty to a common friend. On this quadrilateral, men of all communions may unite to make Christ known and loved to earth's remotest bound.

Study Questions

1. Describe the relationship between the Laymen's Missionary Movement and the Student Volunteer Movement.

2. Are the *functions* of the Laymen's Missionary Movement being fulfilled today? Explain.

9

An Enquiry into the Obligation of Christians to Use Means for the Conversion of the Heathens

William Carey

In 1792 an impoverished and youthful English pastor, part-time teacher, and shoe-maker undertook the task of setting down his convictions in a small pamphlet, counter-acting the prevailing view in his day that the Great Commission no longer applied to Christians. He possessed few literary graces. He avoided the limelight. He even belonged to one of the smaller bodies of dissenting churches of that day. Yet, William Carey's Enquiry *and personal example over the next 40 years resulted in a major revolution in outlook and outreach of the Christian Church, primarily as his emphasis established for Protestants the validity and necessity of mission "order" structures.*

Carey and a colleague, under the newly formed Baptist Missionary Society, sailed for India in 1793, eventually settling in Serampore, a Danish enclave near Calcutta. Carey, Joshua Marshman, and William Ward, the "Serampore Trio", translated and printed parts of the Bible into several Asian languages and founded a school for the training of Indian Christians. With little formal education but possessing extraordinary persever-ance and conviction, Carey weathered financial crises, natural disasters, family illness, and criticisms from England to make advances in evangelism, philology, the natural sci-ences, and education. He exhorted others and himself to "Expect great things from God; attempt great things for God."

Today, Carey is recognized as the "father of Protestant missions," since historians date the modern era of Protestant missions back to the publishing date of his Enquiry. *Dr. Ernest A. Payne observes, "He who reads the* Enquiry *today is struck, first of all, by its sober matter-of-factness and its modernity. More than a fourth of the pages are taken up with schedules detailing the different countries of the world, their length and breadth, the number of their inhabitants and the religions there represented. Throughout there is a clear division into sections and the points are numbered. The contents are brief, logical, precise, more like a Blue Book or a committee's report than a prophetic call to the Church of Christ. There is here no appeal to eloquence or sentiment, no elaborate building up of proof-texts from the Bible, no involved theological argument, but a careful setting down of facts. The very title is characteristic of the author...." George Smith, writing in 1885, called it "the first and still the greatest missionary treatise in the English language." It has not yet been surpassed in simplicity or cogency.*

Excerpted from *An Enquiry Into the Obligations of Christians to Use Means for the Conversion of the Heathens*, William Carey, New Facsimile Ed., Carey Kingsgate Press, London, (1792), 1962.

What follows is a composition of extracted paragraphs from Carey's original 87-page Enquiry.

As our blessed Lord has required us to pray that his kingdom may come, and his will be done on earth as it is in heaven, it becomes us not only to express our desires of that event by word, but to use every lawful method to spread the knowledge of his name. In order to do this, it is necessary that we should become in some measure acquainted with the religious state of the world; and as this is an object we should be prompted to pursue, not only by the gospel of our Redeemer, but even by the feelings of humanity, so an inclination to conscientious activity therein would form one of the strongest proofs that we are the subject of grace, and partakers of that spirit of universal benevolence and genuine philanthropy, which appear so eminent in the character of God himself.

Sin was introduced amongst the children of men by the fall of Adam, and has even since been spreading its baneful influence. By changing its appearances to suit the circumstances of the times, it has grown up in ten thousand forms, and constantly counteracted the will and designs of God. One would have supposed that the remembrance of the deluge would have been transmitted from father to son, and have perpetually deterred mankind from transgressing the will of their Maker; but so blinded were they, that in the time of Abraham gross wickedness prevailed wherever colonies were planted, and the iniquity of the Amorites was great, though not yet full. After this, idolatry spread more and more, till the seven devoted nations were cut off with the most signal marks of divine displeasure. Still, however, the progress of evil was not stopped, but the Israelites themselves too often joined with the rest of mankind against the God of Israel.

Yet God repeatedly made known his intention to prevail finally over all the power of the Devil, and to destroy all his works, and set up his own kingdom and interest among men, and extend it as universally as Satan had extended his. It was for this purpose that the Messiah came and died, that God might be just, and the justifier of all that should believe in him. When he had laid down his life, and taken it up again, he sent forth his disciples to preach the good tidings to every creature, and to endeavor by all possible methods to bring over a lost world to God. They went forth according to their divine commission, and wonderful success attended their labours; the civilized Greeks, and uncivilized barbarians, each yielded to the cross of Christ, and embraced it as the only way of salvation. Since the apostolic age many other attempts to spread the gospel have been made, which have been considerably successful, notwithstanding which a very considerable part of mankind are still involved in all the darkness of heathenism. Some attempts are still being made, but they are inconsiderable in comparison to what might be done if the whole body of Christians entered heartily into the spirit of the divine command on this subject. Some think little about it, others are unacquainted with the state of the world, and others love their wealth better than the souls of their fellow-creatures.

In order that the subject may be taken into more serious consideration, I shall enquire, whether the commission given by our Lord to his disciples be not still binding on us—take a short view of former undertakings—give some account of the present state of the world, consider the practicability of doing something more than is done—and the duty of Christians in general in this matter.

An Enquiry Whether the Commission Given by Our Lord to His Disciples Be Not Still Binding On Us

Our Lord Jesus Christ, a little before his departure, commissioned his apostles to *Go, and teach all nations;* or, as another evangelist expresses it, *Go into all the world, and preach the gospel to every creature.* This commission was as extensive as possible, and laid them under obligation to disperse themselves into every country of the habitable globe, and preach to all the inhabitants, without exception, or limitation. They accordingly went forth in obedience to the command, and the power of God evidently wrought with them. Many attempts of the same kind have been made since their day and which have been attended with various success, but the work has not been taken up or prosecuted of late years (except by a few individuals) with that zeal and perseverance with which the primitive Christians went about it. It seems as if many thought the commission was sufficiently put in execution by what the apostles and others have done; that we have enough to do to attend to the salvation of our own countrymen; and that, if God intends the salvation of the heathen, he will some way or other bring them to the gospel, or the gospel to them. It is thus that multitudes sit at ease, and give themselves no concern about the far greater part of their fellow-sinners, who to this day, are lost in ignorance and idolatry. There seems also to be an opinion existing in the minds of some, that because the apostles were extraordinary officers and have no proper successors, and because many things which were right for them to do would be utterly unwarrantable for us, therefore it may not be immediately binding on us to execute the commission, though it was so upon them. To the consideration of such persons I would offer the following observations.

FIRST, If the command of Christ to teach all nations be restricted to the apostles, or those under the immediate inspiration of the Holy Ghost, then that of baptizing should be so too; and every denomination of Christians, except the Quakers, do wrong in baptizing with water at all.

SECONDLY, If the command of Christ to teach all nations be confined to the apostles, then all such ordinary ministers who have endeavoured to carry the gospel to the heathens, have acted without a warrant, and run before they were sent. Yea, and though God has promised the most glorious things to the heathen world by sending his gospel to them, yet whoever goes first, or indeed at all, with that message, unless he have a new and special commission from heaven, must go without any authority for so doing.

THIRDLY, If the command of Christ to teach all nations extend only to the apostles, then, doubtless, the promise of the divine presence in this work must be so limited; but this is worded in such a manner as expressly precludes such an idea. *Lo, I am with you always, to the end of the world....*

It has been objected that there are multitudes in our own nation, and within our immediate spheres of action, who are as ignorant as the South-Sea savages, and that therefore we have work enough at home, without going into other countries. That there are thousands in our own land as far from God as possible, I readily grant, and that this ought to excite us to ten-fold diligence to our work, and in attempts to spread divine knowledge amongst them is a certain fact; but that it ought to supersede all attempts to spread the gospel in foreign parts seems to want proof. Our own countrymen have the means of grace, and may attend on the word preached if they choose it. They have the means of knowing the truth, and faithful ministers are placed in almost every part of the land, whose spheres of action might be much extended if their congregations were but more hearty and active in the cause; but with them the case is widely different, who have no Bible, no written language (which many of them have not), no ministers, no good civil government, nor any of those advantages which we have. Pity therefore, humanity, and much more Christianity, call loudly for every possible exertion to introduce the gospel amongst them.

A Short Review of Former Undertakings for the Conversion of the Heathen

...Thus far the history of the acts of the Apostles informs us of the success of the word in the primitive times; and history informs us of its being preached about this time, in many other places. Peter speaks of a church at Babylon; Paul proposed a journey to Spain, and it is generally believed he went there, and likewise came to France and Britain. Andrew preached to the Sythians, north of the Black Sea. John is said to have preached in India, and we know that he was at the Isle of Patmos, in the Archipelago. Philip is reported to have preached in upper Asia, Sythia, and Phrygia; Bartholomew in India, on this side of the Ganges, Phrygia, and Armenia; Matthew in Arabia, or Asiatic Ethiopia, and Parthia; Thomas in India, as far as the coast of Coromandel, and some say in the island of Ceylon; Simon, the Canaanite, in Egypt, Cyrene, Mauritania, Libya, and other parts of Africa, and from thence to have come to Britain; and Jude is said to have been principally engaged in the lesser Asia, and Greece. Their labours were evidently very extensive, and very successful; so that Pliny, the younger, who lived soon after the death of the apostles, in a letter to the emperor, Trajan, observed that Christianity had spread, not only through towns and cities, but also through whole countries. Indeed before this, in the time of Nero, it was so prevalent that it was thought necessary to oppose it by an Imperial Edict, and accordingly the proconsuls, and other governors, were commissioned to destroy it...

A Survey of the Present State of the World

In this survey I shall consider the world as divided, according to its usual division, into four parts, Europe, Asia, Africa, and America, and take notice of the extent of the several countries, their population, civilization, and religion...The following Tables will exhibit a more comprehensive view of what I propose, than anything I can offer on the subject. *(Editor's note: the following charts are just 4 of 24 charts Carey included in the "Enquiry".)*

EUROPE.

Countries.	EXTENT. Length. Miles.	EXTENT. Breadth. Miles.	Number of Inhabitants.	Religion.
Great-Britain . . .	680	300	12,000,000	Proteſtants, of many denominations.
Ireland	285	160	2,000,000	Proteſtants, and Papiſts.
France	600	500	24,000,000	Catholics, Deiſts, and Proteſtants.
Spain	700	500	9,500,000	Papiſts.
Portugal	300	100	2,000,000	Papiſts.
SWEDEN, including Sweden proper, Gothland, Shonen, Lapland, Bothnia, and Finland . .	800	500	3,500,000	The Swedes are ſerious Lutherans, but moſt of the Laplanders are Pagans, and very ſuperſtitious.
Iſle of Gothland . .	80	23	5,000	
—— Oeſel . . .	45	24	2,500	
—— Oeland . . .	84	9	1,000	
—— Dago	26	23	1,000	

AMERICA.

Countries.	EXTENT. Length. Miles.	EXTENT. Breadth. Miles.	Number of Inhabitants.	Religion.
Peru	1800	600	10,000,000	Pagans and Papiſts.
Country of the Amazons	1200	900	8,000,000	Pagans.
Terra Firma . . .	1400	700	10,000,000	Pagans and Papiſts.
Guiana	780	480	2,000,000	Ditto.
Terra Magellanica . .	1400	460	9,000,000	Pagans.
Old Mexico . .	2220	600	13,500,000	Ditto, and Papiſts.
New Mexico . . .	2000	1000	14,000,000	Ditto.
The States of America	1000	600	3,700,000	Chriſtians, of various denominations.
Terra de Labrador, Nova-Scotia, Louiſiana, Canada, and all the country inland from Mexico to Hudſon's-Bay .	1680	600	8,000,000	Chriſtians, of various denominations, but moſt of the North-American Indians are Pagans.

AFRICA.

Countries.	EXTENT. Length. Miles.	EXTENT. Breadth. Miles.	Number of Inhabitants.	Religion.
Biledulgerid . .	2500	350	3,500,000	Mahometans, Chriſtians, and Jews.
Zaara, or the Deſart .	3400	660	800,000	Ditto.
Abyſſinia . . .	900	800	5,800,000	Armenian Chriſtians.
Abex	540	130	1,600,000	Chriſtians and Pagans.
Negroland . . .	2200	840	18,000,000	Pagans.
Loango	410	300	1,500,000	Ditto.
Congo	540	220	2,000,000	Ditto.
Angola	360	250	1,400,000	Ditto.
Benguela . . .	430	180	1,600,000	Ditto.
Mataman . . .	450	240	1,500,000	Ditto.
Ajan	900	300	2,500,000	Ditto.
Zanguebar . . .	1400	350	3,000,000	Ditto.
Monoemugi . .	900	660	2,000,000	Ditto.

ASIA.

Countries.	EXTENT. Length. Miles.	EXTENT. Breadth Miles.	Number of Inhabitants.	Religion.
Ifle of Ceylon . . .	250	200	2,000,000	Pagans, except the Dutch Chriftians.
—— Maldives . .	1000 *in number.*		100,000	Mahometans.
—— Sumatra . . .	1000	100	2,100,000	Ditto, and Pagans.
—— Java	580	100	2,700,000	Ditto.
—— Timor . .	2400	54	300,000	Ditto, and a few Chriftians.
—— Borneo . . .	800	700	8,000,000	Ditto.
—— Celeoes . .	510	240	2,000,000	Ditto.
—— Boutam . .	75	30	80,000	Mahometans.
—— Carpentyn . .	30	3	2,000	Chriftian Proteftants.
—— Ourature . . .	18	6	3,000	Pagans.
—— Pullo Lout . .	60	36	10,000	Ditto.

Befides the little Iflands of Manaar, Aripen, Caradivia, Pengandiva, Analativa, Nainandiva. and Nindundiva, which are inhabited by Chriftian Proteftants.

This, as nearly as I can obtain information, is the state of the world; though in many countries, as Turkey, Arabia, Great Tartary, Africa, and America, except the United States, and most of the Asiatic Island, we have no accounts of the number of inhabitants, that can be relied on. I have therefore only calculated the extent, and counted a certain number on an average upon a square mile; in some countries more, and in others less, according as circumstances determine.... All these things are loud calls to Christians, and especially to ministers, to exert themselves to the utmost in their several spheres of action, and to try to enlarge them as much as possible.

The Practicability of Something Being Done, More Than What is Done, for the Conversion of the Heathen

The impediments in the way of carrying the gospel among the heathen must arise, I think, from one or other of the following things;—either their distance from us, their barbarous and savage manner of living, the danger of being killed by them, the difficulty of procuring the necessities of life, or the unintelligible- ness of their languages.

FIRST, *As to their distance from us,* whatever objections might have been made on that account before the invention of the mariner's compass, nothing can be alleged for it, with any colour of plausibility in the present age. Men can now sail with as much certainty through the Great South Sea as they can through the Mediterranean, or any lesser Sea. Yea, and providence seems in a manner to invite us to the trial, as there are to our knowledge trading companies, whose commerce lies in many of the places where these barbarians dwell....

SECONDLY, *As to their uncivilized and barbarous way of living,* this can be no objection to any, except those whose love of ease renders them unwilling to expose themselves to inconveniences for the good of others.

It was no objection to the apostles and their successors, who went among the barbarous *Germans* and *Gauls,* and still more barbarous *Britons!* They did not wait for the ancient inhabitants of these countries to be civilized before they could be christianized, but went simply with the doctrine of the cross and Tertullian could boast that "those parts of Britain which were proof against the Roman armies were conquered by the gospel of Christ." It was no objection to an Elliot, or a Brainerd, in later times. They went forth, and encountered every difficulty of the kind, and found that a cordial reception of the gospel produced those happy effects which the longest intercourse with Europeans without it could never accomplish. It *is* no objection to commercial men. It only requires that we should have as much love to the souls of our fellow-creatures, and fellow-sinners, as they have for the profits arising from a few otter-skins, and all these difficulties would be easily surmounted...

THIRDLY, *In respect to the danger of being killed by them,* it is true that whoever does go must put his life in his hand, and not consult with flesh and blood; but do not the goodness of the cause, the duties incumbent on us as the creatures of God, and Christians, and the perishing state of our fellow men, loudly call upon us to venture all and use every warrantable exertion for their benefit? Paul and Barnabas, who *hazarded their lives for the name of our Lord Jesus Christ,* were not blamed as being rash, but commended for so doing, while John Mark who through timidity of mind deserted them in their perilous undertaking was branded with censure. After all, as has been already observed, I greatly question whether most of the barbarities practiced by the savages upon those who have visited them have not originated in some real or supposed affront, and were therefore, more properly, acts of self-defence than proofs of ferocious disposi- tions. No wonder if the imprudence of sailors should prompt them to offend the simple savage, and the offence be resented; but *Elliot, Brainerd,* and the *Moravian missionaries,* have been very seldom molested. Nay, in general the heathen have showed a willingness to hear the word, and have principally expressed their hatred of Christianity on account of the vices of nominal Christians.

FOURTHLY, *As to the difficulty of procuring the necessaries of life,* this would not be so great as may appear as first sight; for though we could not procure Euro- pean food, yet we might procure such as the natives of those countries which we visit subsist upon themselves...

It might be necessary, however, for two, at least, to go together, and in gen- eral I should think it best that they should be married men, and to prevent their time from being employed in procuring necessaries, two, or more, other persons, with their wives and families, might also accompany them, who should be wholly employed in providing for them. In most countries it would be necessary for them to cultivate a little spot of ground just for their support, which would be a resource to them whenever their supplies failed. Indeed a variety of methods may be thought of, and when once the work is undertaken, many things will sug- gest themselves to us, of which we at present can form no idea.

FIFTHLY, *As to learning their languages,* the same means would be found nec- essary here as in trade between different nations. In some cases interpreters might be obtained, who might be employed for a time; and where these were not to be found, the missionaries must have patience, and mingle with the people, till they have learned so much of their language as to be able to communicate their ideas to them in it. It is well known to require no very extraordinary talents to learn, in the space of a year, or two at most, the language of any people upon earth, so much of it at least, as to be able to convey any sentiments we wish to their understandings.

An Enquiry into the Duty of Christians in General, and What Means Ought to be Used, in Order to Promote this Work

If the prophecies concerning the increase of Christ's kingdom be true, and if what has been advanced, concerning the commission given by him to his disciples being obligatory on us, be just, it must be inferred that all Christians ought heartily to concur with God in promoting his glorious designs, for *he that is joined to the Lord is one spirit.*

One of the first, and most important of those duties which are incumbent upon us, is *fervent and united prayer....*I trust our *monthly prayer-meetings* for the success of the gospel have not been in vain. It is true a want of importunity too generally attends our prayers; yet unimportunate and feeble as they have been, it is to be believed that God has heard, and in a measure answered them....If an holy solicitude had prevailed in all the assemblies of Christians in behalf of their Redeemer's kingdom, we might probably have seen before now, not only an *open door* for the gospel, but *many running to and fro, and knowledge increased*; or a diligent use of those means which providence has put in our power, accompanied with a greater blessing than ordinary from heaven.

Many can do nothing but pray, and prayer is perhaps the only thing in which Christians of all denominations can cordially, and unreservedly unite; but in this we may all be one, and in this the strictest unanimity ought to prevail....

We must not be contented however with praying, without *exerting ourselves in the use of means* for the obtaining of those things we pray for. Were *the children of light* but *as wise in their generation as the children of this world* they would stretch every nerve to gain so glorious a prize, nor ever imagine that it was to be obtained in any other way.

When a trading company has obtained their charter they usually go to its utmost limits; and their stocks, their ships, their officers, and men are so chosen, and regulated, as to be likely to answer their purpose; but they do not stop here, for encouraged by the prospect of success, they use every effort, cast their bread upon the waters, cultivate friendship with everyone from whose information they expect the least advantage....

Suppose a company of serious Christians, ministers and private persons, were to form themselves into a society, and make a number of rules respecting the regulation of the plan, and the persons who are to be employed as missionaries, the means of defraying the expense, etc., etc. This society must consist of persons whose hearts are in the work, men of serious religion, and possessing a spirit of perseverance; these must be a determination not to admit any person who is not of this description, or to retain him longer than he answers to it.

From such a society a *committee* might be appointed, whose business it should be to procure all the information they could upon the subject, to receive contributions, to enquire into the characters, tempers, abilities and religious views of the missionaries, and also to provide them with necessaries for their undertakings.

If there is any reason for me to hope that I shall have any influence upon any of my brethren, and fellow Christians, probably it may be more especially amongst them of my own denomination. I would therefore propose that such a society and committee should be formed amongst the *particular baptist denomination*.

I do not mean by this, in any wise to confine it to one denomination of Christians. I wish with all my heart, that everyone who loves our Lord Jesus Christ in sincerity would in some way or other engage in it. But in the present divided state of Christendom, it would be more likely for good to be done by each denomination engaging separately in the work than if they were to embark in it conjointly.

In respect to *contributions* for defraying the expenses, money will doubtless be wanting...If congregations were to open subscriptions of *one penny*, or more per week, according to their circumstances, and deposit it as a fund for the propagation of the gospel, much might be raised in this way.

We are exhorted *to lay up treasure in heaven, where neither moth nor rust doth corrupt, nor thieves break through and steal*. It is also declared that *whatsoever a man soweth, that shall he also reap*. These Scriptures teach us that the enjoyments of the life to come bear a near relation to that which now is a relation similar to that of the harvest, and the seed. It is true all the reward is of mere grace, but it is nevertheless encouraging what a *treasure*, what an *harvest* must await such characters as Paul, and Elliot, and Brainerd, and others, who have given themselves wholly to the work of the Lord. What a heaven will it be to see the many myriads of poor heathens, of Britons amongst the rest, who by their labours have been brought to the knowledge of God. Surely a *crown of rejoicing* like this is worth aspiring to. Surely it is worthwhile to lay ourselves out with all our might in promoting the cause and kingdom of Christ.

Study Questions

1. Note the prominence in Carey's pamphlet of statistics, "...loud calls to Christians, and especially to ministers, to exert themselves to the utmost in their several spheres of action...." Are Christians *today* moved to action by statistics? Why or why not?

2. Carey concludes the pamphlet with a brief description of the "means" he advocates. Summarize his definition of "means."

10

The Call to Service

J. Hudson Taylor

James Hudson Taylor, founder of the China Inland Mission, was herald of a new era in Protestant missions. "A Retrospect" provides further autobiographical details. In "The Call to Service," Taylor describes his spiritual, academic, and practical preparations for missionary service in China. After seven years in China with the Chinese Evangelization Society, he was compelled by failing health to return home to England in 1860. "A New Agency Needed" details Taylor's growing convictions over the next five years that God was calling him to take personal responsibility for the millions in China's inland provinces by forming a mission agency exclusively focused on them. Carrying the weight of widespread opposition from contemporary mission leaders, but equally haunted by the "accusing map" of China in his study, Taylor came to a decision while wandering the beaches of Brighton on a summer Sunday in 1865.

The Call to Service

The first joys of conversion passed away after a time, and were succeeded by a period of painful deadness of soul, with much conflict. But this also came to an end, leaving a deepened sense of personal weakness and dependence on the Lord as the only Keeper as well as Saviour of His people. How sweet to the soul, wearied and disappointed in its struggle with sin, is the calm repose of trust in the Shepherd of Israel.

Not many months after my conversion, having a leisure afternoon, I retired to my own chamber to spend it largely in communion with God. Well do I remember that occasion. How in the gladness of my heart I poured out my soul before God; and again and again confessing my grateful love to Him who had done everything for me—who had saved me when I had given up all hope and even desire for salvation—I besought Him to give me some work to do for Him, as an outlet for love and gratitude; some self-denying service, no matter what it might be, however trying or however trivial; something with which He would be pleased, and that I might do for Him who had done so much for me. Well do I remember, as in unreserved consecration I put myself, my life, my friends, my all, upon the altar, the deep solemnity that came over my soul with the assurance that my offering was accepted. The presence of God became unutterably real and blessed; and though but a child under sixteen, I remember stretching myself on

"The Call to Service," from *A Retrospect*, Overseas Missionary Fellowship, n.d.

the ground, and lying there silent before Him with unspeakable awe and unspeakable joy.

For what service I was accepted I knew not; but a deep consciousness that I was no longer my own took possession of me, which has never since been effaced. It has been a very practical consciousness. Two or three years later propositions of an unusually favourable nature were made to me with regard to medical study, on the condition of my becoming apprenticed to the medical man who was my friend and teacher. But I felt I dared not accept any binding engagement such as was suggested. I was not my own to give myself away; for I knew not when or how He whose alone I was, and for whose disposal I felt I must ever keep myself free, might call for service.

Within a few months of this time of consecration the impression was wrought into my soul that it was in China the Lord wanted me. It seemed to me highly probable that the work to which I was thus called might cost my life; for China was not then open as it is now. But few missionary societies had at that time workers in China, and but few books on the subject of China missions were accessible to me. I learned, however, that the Congregational minister of my native town possessed a copy of Medhurst's *China*, and I called upon him to ask a loan of the book. This he kindly granted, asking me why I wished to read it. I told him that God had called me to spend my life in missionary service in that land. "And how do you propose to go there?" he inquired. I answered that I did not at all know; that it seemed to me probable that I should need to do as the Twelve and the Seventy had done in Judea— go without purse or scrip, relying on Him who had called me to supply all my need. Kindly placing his hand upon my shoulder, the minister replied, "Ah, my boy, as you grow older you will get wiser than that. Such an idea would do very well in the days when Christ Himself was on earth, but not now."

I have grown older since then, but not wiser. I am more than ever convinced that if we were to take the direction of our Master and the assurances He gave to His first disciples more fully as our guide, we should find them to be just as suited to our times as to those in which they were originally given.

Medhurst's book on China emphasized the value of medical missions there, and this directed my attention to medical studies as a valuable mode of preparation.

My beloved parents neither discouraged nor encouraged my desire to engage in missionary work. They advised me, with such convictions, to use all the means in my power to develop the resources of body, mind, heart, and soul, and to await prayerfully upon God, quite willing should He show me that I was mistaken, to follow His guidance, or to go forward if in due time He should open the way to missionary service. The importance of this advice I have often since had occasion to prove. I began to take more exercise in the open air to strengthen my physique. My feather bed I had taken away, and sought to dispense with as many other home comforts as I could in order to prepare myself for rougher lines of life. I began to also to do what Christian work was in my power, in the way of tract distribution, Sunday-school teaching, and visiting the poor and sick, as opportunity afforded.

After a time of preparatory study at home, I went to Hull for medical and surgical training. There I became assistant to a doctor who was connected with the Hull school of medicine, and was surgeon also to a number of factories, which brought many accident cases to our dispensary, and gave me the opportunity of seeing and practising the minor operations of surgery.

And here an event took place that I must not omit to mention. Before leaving home my attention was drawn to the subject of setting apart the first fruits of all one's increase and proportionate part of one's possessions to the Lord's service. I thought it well to study the question with my Bible in hand before I went away from home, and was placed in circumstances which might bias my conclusions by the pressure of surrounding wants and cares. I was thus led to the determination to set apart not less than one-tenth of whatever moneys I might earn or become possessed of for the Lord's service. The salary I received as medical assistant in Hull at the time now referred to would have allowed me with ease to do this. But owing to changes in the family of my kind friend and employer, it was necessary for me to reside out of doors. Comfortable quarters were secured with a relative, and in addition to the sum determined on as remuneration for my services I received the exact amount I had to pay for board and lodging.

Now arose in my mind the question, Ought not this sum also to be tithed? It was surely a part of my income, and I felt that if it had been a question of Government income tax it certainly would not have been excluded. On the other hand, to take a tithe from the whole would not leave me sufficient for other purposes; and for some little time I was much embarrassed to know what to do. After much thought and prayer I was led to leave the comfortable quarters and happy circle in which I was now residing, and to engage a little lodging in the suburbs—a sitting-room and bedroom in one—undertaking to board myself. In this way I was able without difficulty to tithe the whole of my income; and while I felt the change a good deal, it was attended with no small blessing.

More time was given in my solitude to the study of the Word of God, to visiting the poor, and to evangelistic work on summer evenings than would otherwise have been the case. Brought into contact in this way with many who were in distress, I soon saw the privilege of still further economizing, and found it not difficult to give away much more than the proportion of my income I had at first intended.

About this time a friend drew my attention to the question of the personal and pre-millennial coming of our Lord Jesus Christ, and gave me a list of passages bearing upon it, without note or comment, advising me to ponder the subject. For a while I gave much time to studying the Scriptures about it, with the result that I was led to see that this same Jesus who left our earth in His resurrection body was so to come again, that His feet were to stand on the Mount of Olives, and that He was to take possession of the temporal throne of His father David which was promised before His birth. I saw, further, that all through the New Testament the coming of the Lord was the great hope of His people, and was always appealed to as the strongest motive for consecration and service, and as the greatest comfort in trial and affliction. I learned, too, that the period of His return for His people was not revealed, and that it was their privilege, from day to day and from hour to hour, to live as men who wait for the Lord; that thus living it was immaterial, so to speak, whether He should or should not come at any particular hour, the important thing being to be so ready for Him as to be able, whenever He might appear, to give an account of one's stewardship with joy, and not with grief.

The effect of this blessed hope was a thoroughly practical one. It led me to look carefully through my little library to see if there were any books there that were not needed or likely to be of further service, and to examine my small wardrobe, to be quite sure that it contained nothing that I should be sorry to give an account of should the Master come at once. The result was that the library was considerably diminished, to the benefit of some poor neighbours, and to the far greater benefit of my own soul, and that I found I had articles of clothing also which might be put to better advantage in other directions.

It has been very helpful to me from time to time through life, as occasion has served, to act again in a similar way; and I have never gone through my house, from basement to attic, with this object in view, without receiving a great accession of spiritual joy and blessing. I believe we are all in danger of accumulating— it may be from thoughtlessness, or from pressure of occupation—things which would be useful to others, while not needed by ourselves, and the retention of which entails loss of blessing. If the whole resources of the Church of God were well utilized, how much more might be accomplished! How many poor might be fed and naked clothed, and to how many of those as yet unreached the Gospel might be carried! Let me advise this line of things as a constant habit of mind, and a profitable course to be practically adopted whenever circumstances permit.

A New Agency Needed

"My thoughts are not your thoughts, neither are your ways my ways, saith the Lord. For as the heavens are higher than the earth, so are my ways higher than your ways, and my thoughts than your thoughts" (Isaiah 55:8, 9). How true are these words! When the Lord is bringing in great blessing in the best possible way, how oftentimes our unbelieving hearts are feeling, if not saying, like Jacob of old, "All these things are against me." Or we are filled with fear, as were the disciples when the Lord, walking on the waters, drew near to quiet the troubled sea, and to bring them quickly to their desired haven. And yet mere common-sense ought to tell us that He, whose way is perfect, *can* make no mistakes; that He who has promised to "perfect that which concerneth" us, and whose minute care counts the very hairs of our heads, and forms for us our circumstances, *must* know better than we the way to forward our truest interests and to glorify His own Name.

> "Blind unbelief is sure to err
> And scan His work in vain;
> God is His own Interpreter,
> And He will make it plain."

To me it seemed a great calamity that failure of health compelled my relinquishing work for God in China, just when it was more fruitful than ever before; and to leave the little band of Christians in Ningpo, needing much care and teaching, was a great sorrow. Nor was the sorrow lessened when on reaching

England, medical testimony assured me that return to China, at least for years to come, was impossible. Little did I then realize that the long separation from China was a necessary step towards the formation of a work which God would bless as He has blessed the China Inland Mission. While in the field, the pressure of claims immediately around me was so great that I could not think much of the still greater needs of the regions farther inland; and, if they were thought of, could do nothing for them. But while detained for some years in England, daily viewing the whole country on the large map on the wall of my study, I was as near to the vast regions of Inland China as to the smaller districts in which I had laboured personally for God; and prayer was often the only resource by which the burdened heart could gain any relief.

As a long absence from China appeared inevitable, the next question was how best to serve China while in England, and this led to my engaging for several years, with the late Rev. F. F. Gough of the C.M.S., in the revision of a version of the New Testament in the colloquial of Ningpo for the British and Foreign Bible Society. In undertaking this work, in my short-sightedness I saw nothing beyond the use that the Book, and the marginal references, would be to the native Christians; but I have often seen since that, without those months of feeding and feasting on the Word of God, I should have been quite unprepared to form, on its present basis, a mission like the China Inland Mission.

In the study of that Divine Word I learned that, to obtain successful labourers, not elaborate appeals for help, but, *first*, earnest *prayer to God to thrust forth labourers*, and, *second*, the deepening of the spiritual life of the Church, so that *men should be able to stay at home*, were what was needed. I saw that the apostolic plan was not to raise ways and means, but *to go and do the work*, trusting in His sure Word who has said, "Seek ye *first* the kingdom of God and His righteousness, and all these things shall be added unto you."

In the meantime the prayer for workers for Chehkiang was being answered. The first, Mr. Meadows, sailed for China with his young wife in January 1862, through the kind co-operation and aid of our friend Mr. Berger. The second left England in 1864, having her passage provided by the Foreign Evangelization Society. The third and fourth reached Ningpo on July 24th, 1865. A fifth soon followed them, reaching Ningpo in September 1865. Thus the prayer for the five workers was fully answered; and we were encouraged to look to God for still greater things.

Months of earnest prayer and not a few abortive efforts had resulted in a deep conviction that *a special agency was essential* for the evangelisation of Inland China. At this time I had not only the daily help of prayer and conference with my beloved friend and fellow-worker, the late Rev. F. F. Gough, but also invaluable aid and counsel from Mr. and Mrs. Berger, with whom I and my dear wife (whose judgment and piety were of priceless value at this juncture) spent many days in prayerful deliberation. The grave difficulty of possibly interfering with existing missionary operations at home was foreseen; but it was concluded that, by simple trust in God, suitable agency might be raised up and sustained without interfering injuriously with any existing work. I had also a growing conviction that God would have *me* to seek from Him the needed workers, and to go forth with them. But for a long time unbelief hindered my taking the first step.

How inconsistent unbelief always is! I had no doubt that, if I prayed for workers, "in the name" of the Lord Jesus Christ, they would be given me. I had no doubt that, in answer to such prayer, the means for our going forth would be provided, and that doors would be opened before us in unreached parts of the Empire. But I had not then learned to trust God for *keeping* power and grace for myself, so no wonder that I could not trust Him to keep others who might be prepared to go with me. I feared that in the midst of the dangers, difficulties, and trials which would necessarily be connected with such a work, some who were comparatively inexperienced Christians might break down, and bitterly reproach me for having encouraged them to undertake an enterprise for which they were unequal.

Yet, what was I to do? The feeling of blood-guiltiness became more and more intense. Simply because I refused to ask for them, the labourers did not come forward—did not go out to China—and every day tens of thousands were passing away to Christless graves! Perishing China so filled my heart and mind that there was no rest by day, and little sleep by night, till health broke down. At the invitation of my beloved and honoured friend, Mr. George Pearse (then of the Stock Exchange), I went to spend a few days with him in Brighton.

On Sunday, June 25th, 1865, unable to bear the sight of a congregation of a thousand or more Christian people rejoicing in their own security, while millions were perishing for lack of knowledge, I wandered out on the sands alone, in great spiritual agony; and there the Lord conquered my unbelief, and I surrendered myself to God for this service. I told Him that all the responsibility as to issues and consequences must rest with Him; that as His servant, it was mine to obey and follow Him—His, to direct, to care for, and to guide me and those who might labour with me. Need I say that peace at once flowed into my burdened heart? There and then I asked Him for twenty-four fellow-workers, two for each of eleven inland provinces which were without a missionary, and two for Mongolia; and writing the petition on the margin of the Bible I had with me, I returned home with a heart enjoying rest such as it had been a stranger to for months, and with an assurance that the Lord would bless His own work and that I should share in the blessing. I had previously prayed, and asked prayer, that workers might be raised up for the eleven then unoccupied provinces, and thrust forth and provided for, but had not surrendered myself to be their leader.

About this time, with the help of my dear wife, I wrote the little book, *China's Spiritual Need and Claims*. Every paragraph was steeped in prayer. With the help of Mr. Berger, who had given valued aid in the revision of the manuscript, and who bore the expense of printing an edition of 3000 copies, they were soon put in circulation. I spoke publicly of the proposed work as opportunity permitted, specially at the Perth and Mildmay Conferences of 1865, and continued in prayer for fellow-workers, who were soon raised up, and after due correspondence were invited to my home, then in the East of London. When one house became insufficient, the occupant of the adjoining house removed, and I was able to rent it; and when that in its turn became insufficient, further accommodation was provided close by. Soon there were a number of men and women under preparatory training, and engaging in evangelistic work which tested in some measure their qualifications as soul-winners.

Study Questions

1. Can you see any connection between Taylor's "call to service" and his later conclusion that "a new agency is needed"?

2. In your own words, state the reasons for Taylor's hesitancy to assume responsibility for a new missions agency.

11

China's Spiritual Need and Claims

J. Hudson Taylor

As mentioned in the previous article, Taylor wrote China's Spiritual Needs and Claims *in keeping with his crucial decision made at Brighton to recruit workers for the China Inland Mission. Further editions were printed in the succeeding years, and the following excerpts are from one of these later editions. Taylor here concludes with a backward glance at the effects of the first edition of the pamphlet and at the first years of the China Inland Mission. His own life and that of the agency he formed gave testimony to his frequent assertion, "There is a living God. He has spoken His word. He means just what He says, and will do all that He has promised."*

If thou forbear to deliver them that are drawn unto death,
And those that are ready to be slain;
If thou sayest, Behold, we knew it not;
Doth not He that pondereth the heart consider it?
And He that keepeth thy soul, doth not He know it?
And shall not He render to every man according to his works?
Prov. 24: 11, 12.

It is a solemn and most momentous truth that our every act in this present life—and our every omission too—has a direct and important bearing both on our own future welfare, and on that of others. And as believers, it behoves us to do *whatsoever* we do in the name of our Lord Jesus Christ. In His name, and with earnest prayer for His blessing, the following pages are written; in His name, and with earnest prayer for His blessing, let them be read. The writer feels deeply that, as a faithful steward he is bound to bring the facts contained in these pages before the hearts and consciences of the Lord's people. He believes, too, that these facts must produce *some* fruit in the heart of each Christian reader. The legitimate fruit will undoubtedly be—not vain words of empty sympathy, but—effectual fervent prayer, and strenuous self-denying effort for the salvation of the benighted Chinese. And if in any instance they fail to produce this fruit, the writer would urge the consideration of the solemn words at the head of this page,—"If thou forbear to deliver them that are drawn unto death, and those that

---

Taken from *China's Spiritual Needs and Claims*, by Hudson Taylor, 1895.

are ready to be slain; if thou sayest, Behold, we knew it not; doth not He that pondereth the heart consider it? and He that keepeth *thy* soul, doth not He know it? and shall not He render to every man according to his works?"

Very early in the course of His ministry, the Lord Jesus taught His people that they were to be *the light*—not of Jerusalem, not of Judea, nor yet of the Jewish nation, but—*of the world*. And He taught them to pray—not as the heathen, who use vain and unmeaning repetitions; nor yet as the worldly-minded, who ask first and principally (if not solely) for their own private benefit and need: "For," said He, "*your* Father knoweth what things *ye have need of before ye ask Him. After this manner therefore pray ye:*"

Our Father which art in heaven,
Hallowed be Thy name;
Thy kingdom come;
Thy will be done; as in heaven, so in earth.

And it was only after these petitions, and quite secondary to them, that any personal petitions were to be offered. Even the very moderate one, "Give us *this day* our daily bread," followed them. Is not this order too often reversed in the present day? Do not Christians often really feel, and also act, as though it was incumbent upon them to *begin* with, "Give us this day our daily bread;" virtually *concluding* with "If consistent with this, may Thy name be hallowed too?" And is not Matt. 6:33, "Seek ye *first* the kingdom of God, and His righteousness; and all these things shall be *added* unto you;" practically read, even amongst the professed followers of Christ, seek first all *these things* (food and clothing, health, wealth, and comfort), and then the kingdom of God and His righteousness? Instead of honouring Him with the first-fruits of our time and substance, are we not content to offer Him the fragments that remain after our own supposed need is supplied? While we thus refuse to bring the tithes into His storehouse and to prove the Lord therewith, can we wonder that He does not open the windows of heaven, and pour us our the fulness of blessing that we desire?

We have a striking exemplification of the manner in which we should seek first the kingdom of God and His righteousness, in the life and in the death of our Lord Jesus Christ. And when risen from the dead, ere He ascended on high, He commissioned His people to make known everywhere the glad tidings of salvation—full and free—through faith in His finished work. This duty He enjoined on us; enjoined in the most unmistakable form, and to the most definite extent; saying, "*Go Ye,* into *all* the world, and preach the gospel to every creature." Grievously has the Church failed in fulfilling this command. Sad it is to realize that so near to the close of the nineteenth century of the Christian era, there are immense tracts of our globe either wholly destitute of, or most inadequately provided with, the means of grace and the knowledge of salvation.

In order to enable our readers to realize the vast extent of the outlying districts of the Chinese empire, we would suggest a comparison of them with those countries which are nearer home.

The whole continent of Europe has an area of 3,797,256 square miles; Manchuria, Mongolia, the Northwestern Dependencies, and Thibet, together, have an area of 3,951,130 square miles. These extensive regions contain many millions of our fellow-creatures, but except the four missionaries in Newchwang, they have *no missionary*. They are perishing, and they are left to perish. Among them *no missionary* resides to make known that wisdom, the merchandise of which "is better than the merchandise of silver, and the gain thereof than fine gold." Throughout this immense territory, larger than the whole continent of Europe, with the exception noted above, there is not a single ambassador for Christ from all the Protestant churches of Europe and America to carry the word of reconciliation, and to pray men in *Christ's* stead, "Be ye reconciled to God." How long shall this state of things be allowed to continue?

Think of the over eighty millions beyond the reach of the Gospel in the seven provinces, where missionaries have longest laboured; think of the over 100 millions in the other eleven provinces of China Proper, beyond the reach of the few missionaries labouring there; think of the over twenty millions who inhabit the vast regions of Manchuria, Mongolia, Thibet, and the Northwestern Dependencies, which exceed in extent the whole of Europe—an aggregate of over 200 millions beyond the reach of all existing agencies—and say, how shall

God's name be hallowed by them,
His kingdom come among them, and
His will be done by them?

His name, His attributes they have never heard. His kingdom is not proclaimed among them. His will is not made known to them!

Do you *believe* that each unit of these millions has a precious soul? And that "there is none other name under heaven given amongst men whereby they must be saved" than that of *Jesus*? Do you *believe* that He *alone* is "the Door of the sheepfold"; is the "Way, the Truth, and the Life"? that "*no man* cometh unto the Father but by Him?" If so, think of the state of these unsaved ones; and solemnly examine yourself in the sight of God, to see whether you are doing *your utmost* to make Him known to them.

We have now presented a brief and cursory view of the state and claims of China. To have entered into them at all in detail would have required for each province more time and space that we have devoted to the consideration of the whole empire. We have shewn how *God* has blest the efforts which have been put forth; and have endeavoured to lay before you the facilities which at present exist for the more extensive evangelization of this country. We have sought to press the great command of our risen *Savior*, "Go ye, into all the world, and preach the gospel to *every creature:*" and would point out that the parable of our *Lord*, contained in Matt. 25, it was not a *stranger*, but a *servant*; not an *immoral*, but an *unprofitable* one who was to be cast into outer darkness, where there is weeping and gnashing of teeth. "If ye love me," said our master, "keep my commandments;" and one of these was, "Freely ye have received, freely give." We have shewn that in seven provinces of China Proper after allowing far more than they can possibly accomplish to the Protestant missionaries and their native assistants, there still remains an overwhelming multitude altogether beyond the sound of the gospel. We have further shewn that there are eleven other provinces in China Proper still more needy,—eleven provinces, the very smallest of which exceeds Burmah in population, and which average each the population of both Scotland

and Ireland combined! And what shall we say of the vast regions of Tartary and Thibet,—more extensive than the whole continent of Europe, all without any Protestant missionary save the four in Newchwang? The claims of an empire like this should surely be not only admitted, but realized! Shall not the eternal interests of one-fifth of our race stir up the deepest sympathies of our nature, the most strenuous efforts of our blood-bought powers? Shall not the low wail of helpless, hopeless misery, arising from one-half of the heathen world, pierce our sluggish ear, and rouse us, spirit, soul, and body, to one mighty, continued, unconquerable effort for China's salvation? That, strong in God's strength, and in the power of His might, we may snatch the prey from the hand of the mighty, may pluck these brands from the everlasting burnings, and rescue these captives from the thraldom of sin and Satan, to grace the triumphs of our sovereign King, and to shine for ever as stars in His diadem!

We cannot but believe that the contemplation of these solemn facts has awakened in many the heartfelt prayer, "Lord, what wilt thou have *me* to do, that Thy name may be hallowed, Thy kingdom come, and Thy will be done in China?" It is the prayerful consideration of these facts, and the deepening realisation of China's awful destitution of all that can make man truly happy, that constrains the writer to lay its claims as a heavy burden upon hearts of those who have experienced the power of the blood of Christ; and to seek, first from the Lord, and then from His people, the men and the means to carry the gospel into every part of this benighted land. We have to do with Him who is the Lord of all power and might, whose arm is not shortened, whose ear is not heavy; with Him whose unchanging word directs us to ask and receive, that our joy may be full; to open our mouths wide, that He may fill them. And we do well to remember that this gracious God who has condescended to place His almighty power at the command of believing prayer, looks not lightly upon the blood-guiltiness of those who neglect to avail themselves of it for the benefit of the perishing; for He it is who has said, "If thou forbear to deliver them that are drawn unto death, and those that are ready to be slain; if thou sayest, Behold, we knew it not, doth not He that pondereth the heart consider it? and He that keepeth *thy* soul, doth not He know it? And shall not He render to every man according to his works?"

Such considerations as the foregoing caused the writer in 1865 so to feel the overwhelming necessity for an increase in the number of labourers in China that, as stated in the first edition of this appeal, he did not hesitate to ask the great Lord of the harvest to call forth, to *thrust* forth, twenty-four European, and twenty-four native evangelists, to plant the standard of the cross in all the unevangelized districts of China Proper and of Chinese Tartary.

The same considerations lead us today to cry to God for many more. Those who have never been called to prove the faithfulness of the covenant-keeping God, in supplying, in answer to prayer, the pecuniary need of His servants, might deem it a hazardous experiment to send evangelists to a distant heathen land, with "*only* God to look to." But in one whose privilege it has been for many years past to prove the faithfulness of God, in various circumstances—at home and abroad, by land and by sea, in sickness and in health, in necessities, in dangers, and at the gates of death,—such apprehensions would be wholly inexcusa-

Proportion of Missionaries to the Population in the Eighteen Provinces of China Proper.

Province.	Population.*	No. of Missionaries.†	Proportion to Population.	Or, One Missionary to a Population exceeding that of
KWANG-TUNG	17½ millions	100	1 to 170,000	Huddersfield and Halifax (166,957).
FUH-KIEN	10 ,,	61	1 to 163 000	Newcastle (155,117).
CHEH-KIANG	12 ,,	58	1 to 206,000	Hull (191,501).
KIANG-SU	20 ,,	85	1 to 227,000	Bristol (220,915).
SHAN-TUNG	19 ,,	60	1 to 316,000	Sheffield (310,957).
CHIH-LI	20 ,,	68	1 to 294,000	Newcastle and Portsmouth (291,395).
HU-PEH	20½ ,,	43	1 to 476,000	Nottingham and Edinburgh (472,324).
KIANG-SI	15 ,,	12	1 to 1,250,000	New York (1,207,000).
GAN-HWUY	9 ,,	15	1 to 600,000	Liverpool (586,320).
SHAN-SI	9 ,,	30	1 to 300,000	Salford and Huddersfield (299,911).
SHEN-SI	7 ,,	13	1 to 530,000	Glasgow (521,999).
KAN-SUH	3 ,,	9	1 to 333,000	Sheffield (310,957).
SI-CHUEN	20 ,,	17	1 to 1,176,000	Glasgow and Liverpool (1,108,319).
YUN-NAN	5 ,,	10	1 to 500,000	Sheffield and Newcastle (466 074).
KWEI-CHAU	4 ,,	2	1 to 2,000,000	{ Glasgow, Liverpool, Birmingham, Manchester (1.919,595).
KWANG-SI	5 ,,	0	0 to 5 millions	Ireland (no Missionary).
HU-NAN	16 ,,	3 itinerating	0 to 16 ,,	Four times Scotland.
HO-NAN	15 ,,	3	1 to 5 ,,	London.

* The estimate of population is that given in the last edition of "China's Spiritual Need and Claims."
† The number of Missionaries is according to an account corrected to March, 1887.

ble. The writer has seen God, in answer to prayer, quell the raging of the storm, alter the direction of the wind, and give rain in the midst of prolonged drought. He has seen Him, in answer to prayer, stay the angry passions and murderous intentions of violent men, and bring the machinations of His people's foes to nought. He has seen Him, in answer to prayer, raise the dying from the bed of death, when human aid was vain; has seen Him preserve from the pestilence that walketh in darkness, and from the destruction that wasteth at noonday. For more than twenty-seven years he has proved the faithfulness of God in supplying the pecuniary means for his own temporal wants, and for the need of the work he has been engaged in. He has seen God, in answer to prayer, raising up labourers not a few for this vast mission-field, supplying the means requisite for their outfit, passage, and support, and vouchsafing blessing on the efforts of many of them, both among the native Christians and the heathen Chinese in fourteen out of the eighteen provinces referred to.

Study Questions

1. As with Carey, Taylor is deeply moved by the statistics before him. What "fruit" does he insist must result from consideration of the "facts"?

2. What observations does Taylor make about the nature and purpose of prayer?

12

Tribes, Tongues, and Translators

Wm. Cameron Townsend

William Cameron Townsend founded Wycliffe Bible Translators and its sister agency, the Summer Institute of Linguistics. Starting out as a student to distribute portions of the Bible in Spanish, he was overtaken by the conviction that Spanish Bibles were inadequate for the Indian tribes of Guatemala. He completed a translation of the New Testament into Cakchiquel in 1931 and then turned his attention to other tribes. Others soon joined him. Using linguistics and technological advances, Wycliffe translators have fanned out across the globe in the last 50 years, reducing languages to writing, translating portions of the Bible, and enriching tribal societies as well as facilitating their response to the pressures of majority peoples. "Uncle Cam" has been recognized and appreciated by kings and presidents as well as by the "little people" of the world, and growing numbers of Christians are joining his vision to take the Scriptures to 3,000 further languages that are an essential key to 5,000 tribal groups. He died in 1982 at the age of 85.

"Don't be a fool," friends told me fifty years ago when I decided to translate the Word for the Cakchiquel Indians, a large tribe in Central America. "Those Indians aren't worth what it would take to learn their outlandish language and translate the Bible for them. They can't read anyhow. Let the Indians learn Spanish," they said.

My friends used these same arguments fourteen years later, when, after having seen the transformation the Word brought to the Cakchiquels, I dreamed of reaching all other tribes. When I included even the small primitive groups in Amazonia in my plan, my friends added other arguments: "They'll kill you," said one old, experienced missionary. "Those jungle tribes are dying out anyway. They kill each other as well as outsiders with their spears, or bows and arrows. If they don't kill you, malaria will get you, or your canoe will upset in the rapids and you'll be without supplies and a month away from the last jumping-off place. Forget the other tribes, and stay with the Cakchiquels."

"Tribes, Tongues, and Translators," adapted from *Who Brought the Word*, with permission of Wycliffe Bible Translators, Inc., Huntington Beach, CA 92648, 1963.

But I couldn't forget them. And one day God gave me a verse that settled the matter for me. He said: "The Son of Man is come to save that which was lost. How think ye? If a man have a hundred sheep, and one of them be gone astray, doth he not leave the ninety and nine, and goeth into the mountains and seeketh that which is gone astray (Matt. 18:11-12)?"

That verse guided me; I went after the "one lost sheep," and four thousand young men and women have followed suit.

We call ourselves the "Wycliffe Bible Translators," in memory of John Wycliffe who first gave the whole Bible to the speakers of English. Half our members are dedicated to linguistic and translation work among the tribespeople, bringing them the Word. The other half are support personnel; teachers, secretaries, pilots, mechanics, printers, doctors, nurses, accountants and others who man the supply lines, keeping oatmeal, cooking oil, milk for the babies, and other necessities moving toward the front lines. Our tools are linguistics and the Word, administered in love and in the spirit of service to all without discrimination.

The tribes are being reached. Geographical barriers once so formidable are surmounted today by our planes and short-wave radios. The newly-developed science of descriptive linguistics breaks the barriers of strange tongues. Witchcraft, killings, superstition, ignorance, fear and sickness are giving way before the Light of the Word, literacy, medicine and contact with the best in the outside world. Tribesmen formerly lost to the lifestream of their respective nations are being transformed by the Word. And whether the transformation occurs in the mountains of Southern Mexico, the jungles of Amazonia or the desert plains of Australia, it is a spectacular leap out of the old into the new.

Doors into the tribes are rapidly opening to our type of approach. The way the Bible translation program has moved forward during the past fifty years encourages us to expect the completion of the task by the turn of the century. In order to take the Word to 3,000 more Bibleless tribes, many more translators and support personnel are needed. The pace must be accelerated. Each translation may take from five to 25 or more years and involves not only the linguist we send to each tribe but also one or more tribal informants.

Politically, this seems to be the day of neglected countries and neglected tribes. Spiritually this may be their day as well. The man of Luke 14:16 invited many to the great supper he had prepared but they declined. Then he sent messengers into the cities and invited the masses on the streets but still there was room. Finally he sent his messengers to the country trails to bring in guests. They came. Perhaps at long last a special day of opportunity has come for the out-of-the-way tribes who have never had the slightest chance.

We know that all of them *must* hear the message of God's love, for they are included in both the Great Commission and in the prophetic vision of the vast throng of the redeemed recorded in Revelation 7:9, "After this I beheld and lo, a great multitude which no man could number of all nations and kindreds and peoples and TONGUES, stood before the throne and before the Lamb, clothed with white robes and palms in their hands." They can get there only if they hear the Word in a language they can understand. How else could they be saved?

May God stir the hearts of many to join us in completing our God-given task of reaching every tribe.

Study Questions

1. What similarities do you observe between Carey, Taylor, and Townsend?
2. What prompted Townsend to turn from the completion of the Cakchiquel New Testament to the completion of the Great Commission among tribal peoples?

13

The Glory of the Impossible

Samuel Zwemer

When Robert Wilder visited Hope College in 1887 on behalf of the Student Volunteer Movement, Samuel Zwemer was completing his senior year. Responding to Wilder's appeal, Zwemer became a volunteer and soon organized a mission to Arabia with other students. After 23 years with the Arabian Mission in Basrah, Bahrain, Muscat, and Kuwait, and service as the first candidate secretary of the SVM, Zwemer began a career of speaking and writing that radiated out to the Muslim world from an interdenominational study center in Cairo. A prolific and gifted author, Zwemer wrote books and articles to challenge the church in Muslim evangelism, provided scholarly studies on historical and popular Islam, and produced writings and tracts in Arabic for Muslims and Christians in the Middle East. For 36 years he edited The Muslim World, *an English quarterly review of current events in the Muslim world and a forum for missionary strategy among Muslims, complementing this service with personal evangelism among the students and faculty of Al-Azhar, Cairo's famous training center for Muslim missionaries. Zwemer was an outstanding evangelical leader, an honored speaker in SVM gatherings, and the driving force behind the Cairo 1906 and Lucknow 1911 conferences which inaugurated a less confrontational and more positive approach to Muslims. James Hunt observed of this statesman, "He may be said to have been a man of one idea. While his interests and knowledge were wide, I never talked with him ten minutes that the conversation did not veer to Islam...." "The Glory of the Impossible" is taken from an SVM publication of 1911.*

The challenge of the unoccupied fields of the world is one to great faith and, therefore, to great sacrifice. Our willingness to sacrifice for an enterprise is always in proportion to our faith in that enterprise. Faith has the genius of transforming the barely possible into actuality. Once men are dominated by the conviction that a thing must be done, they will stop at nothing until it is accomplished. We have our "marching orders," as the Iron Duke [Arthur Wesley, Duke of Wellington] said, and because our Commander-in-Chief is not absent, but with us, the impossible becomes not only practical but imperative. Charles Spurgeon, preaching from the text, "All power is given unto Me...Lo I am with you always," used these words: "You have a factor here that is absolutely infinite,

---

Taken from *The Unoccupied Mission Fields of Africa and Asia*, Student Volunteer Movement for Foreign Missions, Chapter 8, pp. 215-231, 1911.

and what does it matter as to what other factors may be. 'I will do as much as I can,' says one. Any fool can do that. He that believes in Christ does what he can not do, attempts the impossible and performs it." [1]

Frequent set-backs and apparent failure never disheartened the real pioneer. Occasional martyrdoms are only a fresh incentive. Opposition is a stimulus to greater activity. Great victory has never been possible without great sacrifice. If the winning of Port Arthur required human bullets,[2] we cannot expect to carry the Port Arthurs and Gibraltars of the non-Christian world without loss of life. Does it really matter how many die or how much money we spend in opening closed doors, and in occupying the different fields, if we really believe that missions are warfare and that the King's glory is at stake? War always means blood and treasure. Our only concern should be to keep the fight aggressive and to win victory regardless of cost or sacrifice. The unoccupied fields of the world must have their Calvary before they can have their Pentecost. Raymond Lull, the first missionary to the Moslem world, expressed the same thought in medieval language when he wrote: "As a hungry man makes dispatch and takes large morsels on account of his great hunger, so Thy servant feels a great desire to die that he may glorify Thee. He hurries day and night to complete his work in order that he may give up his blood and his tears to be shed for Thee." [3]

"An Inverted Homesickness"

The unoccupied fields of the world await those who are willing to be lonely for the sake of Christ. To the pioneer missionary the words of our Lord Jesus Christ to the apostles when He showed them His hands and His feet, come with special force: "As my Father hath sent Me, even so send I you" (John 20:21). He came into the world, and it was a great unoccupied mission field. "He came unto His own, and His own received Him not" (John 1:11). He came and His welcome was derision, His life suffering, and His throne the Cross. As He came, He expects us to go. We must follow in His footprints. The pioneer missionary, in overcoming obstacles and difficulties has the privilege not only of knowing Christ and the power of His resurrection, but also something of the fellowship of His suffering. For the people of Tibet or Somaliland, Mongolia or Afghanistan, Arabia or Nepal, the Sudan or Abyssinia, he may be called to say with Paul, "Now I rejoice in my sufferings for you and fill to the brim the penury of the afflictions of Christ in my flesh for His body's sake which is the Church" (Greek text, Col. 1:24; cf. Luke 21:4 and Mark 12:44). What is it but the glory of the impossible! Who would *naturally* prefer to leave the warmth and comfort of hearth and home and the love of the family circle to go after a lost sheep, whose cry we have faintly heard in the howling of the tempest? Yet such is the glory of the task that neither home-ties nor home needs can hold back those who have caught the vision and the spirit of the Great Shepherd. Because the lost ones are *His* sheep, and He has made us His shepherds and not His hirelings, we must bring them back.

> Although the road be rough and steep
> I go to the desert to find my sheep.

"There is nothing finer nor more pathetic to me," says Dr. Forsyth, "than the way in which missionaries unlearn the love of the old home, die to their native land, and wed their hearts to the people they have served and won; so that they cannot rest in England, but must return to lay their bones where they spent their hearts for Christ. How vulgar the common patriotisms seem beside this inverted home-sickness, this passion of a kingdom which has no frontiers and no favored race, the passion of a homeless Christ!" [4]

James Gilmour in Mongolia, David Livingstone in Central Africa, Grenfell on the Congo, Keith Falconer in Arabia, Dr. Rijnhart and Miss Annie Taylor in Tibet, Chalmers in New Guinea, Morrison in China, Henry Martyn in Persia, and all the others like them had this "inverted home-sickness," this passion to call that country their home which was most in need of the Gospel. In this passion all other passions died; before this vision all other visions faded; this call drowned all other voices. They were the pioneers of the Kingdom, the forelopers of God, eager to cross the border-marches and discover new lands or win new empire.

The Pioneer Spirit

These forelopers of God went not with hatchet and brand, but with the sword of the Spirit and with the fire of Truth they went and blazed the way for those that follow after. Their scars were the seal of their apostleship, and they gloried also in tribulation. Like the pioneer Apostle, "always bearing about in the body the dying of the Lord Jesus," and approving themselves "as ministers of God in stripes, in imprisonments, in tumults, in watchings, in fasting."

Thomas Valpy French, Bishop of Lahore, whom Dr. Eugene Stock called "the most distinguished of all Church Missionary Society missionaries," had the real pioneer spirit and knew the glory of the impossible. After forty years of labors abundant and fruitful in India, he resigned his bishopric and planned to reach the interior of Arabia with the Gospel. He was an intellectual and spiritual giant. "To live with him was to drink in an atmosphere that was spiritually bracing. As the air of the Engadine [a favorite tourist ground in Switzerland] is to the body, so was his intimacy to the soul. It was an education to be with him. There was nothing that he thought a man should not yield—home or wife or health if God's call was apparent. But then every one knew that he only asked of them what he himself had done and was always doing." And when Mackay, of Uganda, in his remarkable plea for a mission to the Arabs of Oman called for "half a dozen young men, the pick of the English universities, to make the venture in faith," [5] this lion-hearted veteran of sixty-six years responded alone. It was the glory of the impossible. Yet from Muscat he wrote shortly before his death:

> If I can get no faithful servant and guide for the journey into the interior, well versed in dealing with Arabs and getting needful common supplies (I want but little), I may try Bahrein, or Hodeidah and Sana, and if that fails, the north of Africa again, in some highland; for without a house of our own the climate would be insufferable for me—at least during the very hot months—and one's work would be at a standstill. But I shall not give up, please God, even temporarily, my plans for the interior, unless, all avenues being closed, it would be sheer madness to attempt to carry them out. [6]

"I shall not give up"—and he did not till he died. Nor will the Church of

Christ give up the work for which he and others like him laid down their lives in Oman. It goes on.

The Apostolic Ambition

The unoccupied provinces of Arabia and the Sudan await men with the spirit of Bishop French. For the ambition to reach out from centers already occupied to regions beyond, even when those very centers are undermanned and in need of reinforcement, is not Quixotic or fantastic, but truly apostolic. "Yes, so have I been ambitious," said Paul, "to preach the Gospel not where Christ was already named, lest I should build on another man's foundation; but as it is written, they shall see to whom no tidings of Him came, and they who have not heard shall understand" (Romans 15:20-21). He wrote this when leaving a city as important as Corinth, and goes on to state that this is the reason why he did not yet visit Rome, but that he hopes to do so on his way to Spain! If the uttermost confines of the Roman Empire were part of his program who had already preached Christ from Jerusalem to Illyricum in the first century, we surely, at the beginning of the twentieth century, should have no less ambition to enter every unoccupied field that "they may see to whom no tidings came and that those who have not heard may understand."

> There is no instance of an Apostle being driven abroad under the compulsion of a bald command. Each one went as a lover to his betrothed on his appointed errand. It was all instinctive and natural. They were equally controlled by the common vision, but they had severally personal visions which drew them whither they were needed. In the first days of Christianity, there is an absence of the calculating spirit. Most of the Apostles died outside of Palestine, though human logic would have forbidden them to leave the country until it had been Christianized. The calculating instinct is death to faith, and had the Apostles allowed it to control their motives and actions, they would have said: "The need in Jerusalem is so profound, our responsibilities to people of our own blood so obvious, that we must live up to the principle that charity begins at home. After we have won the people of Jerusalem, of Judea and of the Holy Land in general, then it will be time enough to go abroad; but our problems, political, moral and religious, are so unsolved here in this one spot that it is manifestly absurd to bend our shoulders to a new load." [7]

It was the bigness of the task and its difficulty that thrilled the early Church. Its apparent impossibility was its glory, its world-wide character its grandeur. The same is true today. "I am happy," wrote Neesima of Japan, "in a meditation on the marvelous growth of Christianity in the world, and believe that if it finds any obstacles it will advance still faster and swifter even as the stream runs faster when it finds any hindrances on its course." [8]

Hope and Patience

He that ploweth the virgin soil should plow in hope. God never disappoints His husbandmen. The harvest always follows the seed time. "When we first came to our field," writes missionary Hogberg from Central Asia, "it was impossible to gather even a few people to hear the glad tidings of the Gospel. We could not gather any children for school. We could not spread gospels or tracts. When building the new station, we also had a little chapel built. Then we wondered, Will this room ever be filled up with Moslems listening to the Gospel? Our little chapel has been filled with hearers and still a larger room! Day after day we may preach as much as we have strength to, and the Moslems no longer object to listen to the Gospel truth. 'Before your coming hither no one spoke or thought of Jesus Christ, now everywhere one hears His name,' a Mohammedan said to me. At the beginning of our work they threw away the Gospels or burnt them, or brought them back again—now they buy them, kiss the books, and touching it to the forehead and pressing it to the heart, they show the highest honor that a Moslem can show a book." [9]

But the pioneer husbandman must have long patience. When Judson was lying loaded with chains in a Burmese dungeon, a fellow prisoner asked with a sneer about the prospect for the conversion of the heathen. Judson calmly answered, "The prospects are as bright as are the promises of God." [10] There is scarcely a country today which is not as accessible, or where the difficulties are greater, than was the case in Burma when Judson faced them and overcame.

Challenge of the Closed Door

The prospects for the evangelization of all the unoccupied fields are "as bright as the promises of God." Why should we longer wait to evangelize them? "The evangelization of the world in this generation is no play-word," says Robert E. Speer. "It is no motto to be bandied about carelessly. The Evangelization of the World in this Generation is the summons of Jesus Christ to every one of the disciples to lay himself upon a cross, himself to walk in the footsteps of Him who, though He was rich, for our sakes became poor, that we through His poverty might be rich, himself to count his life as of no account, that He may spend it as Christ spent His for the redemption of the world." [11] Who will do this for the unoccupied fields?

The student volunteers of to-day must not rest satisfied until the watchword, peculiarly their own, finds practical application for the most neglected and difficult fields, as well as the countries where the harvest is ripe and the call is for reapers in ever increasing numbers. The plea of destitution is even stronger than that of opportunity. Opportunism is not the last word in missions. The open door beckons; the closed door challenges him who has a right to enter. The unoccupied fields of the world have, therefore, a claim of peculiar weight and urgency. "In this twentieth century of Christian history there should be no unoccupied fields. The Church is bound to remedy the lamentable condition with the least possible delay." [12]

Make a Life, Not a Living

The unoccupied fields, therefore, are a challenge to all whose lives are unoccupied by that which is highest and best; whose lives are occupied only with the weak things or the base things that do not count. There are eyes that have never been illumined by a great vision, minds that have never been gripped by an unselfish thought, hearts that have never thrilled with passion for another's wrong, and hands that have never grown weary or strong in lifting a great burden. To such the knowledge of these Christless millions in lands yet unoccupied should come like a new call from Macedonia, and a startling vision of God's will for them. As Bishop Brent remarks, "We never know what measure of moral capacity is at our disposal until we try to express it in action. An adventure of some proportions is not uncommonly all that a young man needs to determine and fix his manhood's powers." [13] Is there a more heroic test for the powers of manhood than pioneer work in the mission field? Here is opportunity for those who at home may never find elbow-room for their latent capacities, who may never find adequate scope elsewhere for all the powers of their minds and their souls. There are hundreds of Christian college men who expect to spend life in practicing law or in some trade for a livelihood, yet who have strength and talent enough to enter these unoccupied fields. There are young doctors who might gather around them in some new mission station thousands of those who "suffer the horrors of heathenism and Islam," and lift their burden of pain, but who now confine their efforts to some "pent-up Utica" where the healing art is subject to the law of competition and is measured too often merely in terms of a cash-book and ledger. They are making a living; they might be making a life.

Bishop Phillips Brooks once threw down the challenge of a big task in these words: "Do not pray for easy lives; pray to be stronger men. Do not pray for tasks equal to your powers; pray for powers equal to your tasks. Then the doing of your work shall be no miracle, but you shall be a miracle." [14] He could not have chosen words more applicable if he had spoken of the evangelization of the unoccupied fields of the world with all their baffling difficulties and their glorious impossibilities. God can give us power for the task. He was sufficient for those who went out in the past, and is sufficient for those who go out today.

Face to face with these millions in darkness and degradation, knowing the condition of their lives on the unimpeachable testimony of those who have visited these countries, this great unfinished task, this unattempted task, calls today for those who are willing to endure and suffer in accomplishing it.

No Sacrifice, But a Privilege

When David Livingstone visited Cambridge University, on December 4, 1857, he made an earnest appeal for that continent, which was then almost wholly an unoccupied field. His words, which were in a sense his last will and testament for college men, as regards Africa, may well close this book:

> For my own part, I have never ceased to rejoice that God has appointed me to such an office. People talk of the sacrifice I have made in spending so much of my life in Africa. Can that be called a sacrifice which is simply paid back as a small part of a great debt owing to our God, which we can never repay? Is that a sacrifice which brings its own blest reward in healthful activity, the consciousness of doing good, peace of mind, and a bright hope of a glorious destiny hereafter? Away with the word in such a view, and with such a thought! It is emphatically no sacrifice. Say rather it is a privilege. Anxiety, sickness, suffering, or danger, now and then, with a foregoing of the common conveniences and charities of this life, may make us pause, and cause the spirit to waver, and the soul to sink, but let this only be for a moment. All these are

nothing when compared with the glory which shall hereafter be revealed in and for us. I never made a sacrifice.

I beg to direct your attention to Africa. I know that in a few years I shall be cut off in that country, which is now open; do not let it be shut again! I go back to Africa to try to make an open path for commerce and Christianity; do you carry out the work which I have begun. *I leave it with you.* [15]

End Notes

1. Sermon on "Our Omnipotent Leader," in *The Evangelization of the World* (London, 1887).

2. *Human Bullets*, a novel by Tadayoshi Sakurai. The experience of a Japanese officer at Port Arthur and a revelation of Japanese patriotism and obedience.

3. Raymond Lull's "Liber de Contemplations in Deo," in Samuel M. Zwemer's *Raymund Lull: first missionary lo the Moslems* (New York and London: Funk and Wagnalls, 1902), p. 132.

4. P.T. Forsyth, *Missions in State and Church: Sermons and Addresses* (New York: A. C. Armstong, 1908), p. 36.

5. Mrs. J. W. Harrison, *Mackay of Uganda*, pp. 417-430.

6. S. M. Zwemer, *Arabia: The Cradle of Islam; studies in one geography people and politics of one peninsula with an account of Islam and mission work...*(New York: F. H. Revell, 1900), p. 350.

7. Charles H. Brent, *Adventure for God* (New York: Longmans, Green, 1905), pp. I 1-12.

8. Robert E. Speer, *Missionary Principles and Practice: a discussion of Christian missions and of some criticisms upon them* (New York: Fleming H. Revell, 1902), p. 541.

9. Letter to Commission No. 1, World Missionary Conference, Edinburgh, 1910.

10. Arthur Judson Brown, *The Foreign Missionary: an incarnation of a world movement* (New York: Fleming H. Revell, 1932), p. 374.

11. Speer, *op. cit.*, p. 526.

12. Report of World Missionary Conference, Edinburgh, 1910, Vol. 1.

13. Brent, *op. cit.*, p. 135.

14. Phillips Brooks, *Twenty Sermons* (New York: E. P. Dutton & Co., 1903), p. 330.

15. William Garden Blaikie, *Personal Life of David Livingstone...* (New York: Harper & Bros., 1895?), pp. 243-244.

Study Questions

1. Answer Zwemer's question: "Is there a more heroic test for the powers of manhood than pioneer work in the mission field?" Explain.

2. Are the challenges in this article an inspiration or a disturbance to you? Restate the challenge in this article in your own words.

14

The Responsibility of the Young People for the Evangelization of the World

John R. Mott

John R. Mott was a sophomore at Cornell when, tardily entering a lecture room where J. K. Studd was speaking, he heard Studd say as if to him, "Young man, seekest thou great things for thyself? Seek them not! Seek ye first the kingdom of God." Mott's subsequent conversion and commissioning began him down a path that led to attendance at the Mt. Hermon Conference in 1886, where the Student Volunteer movement was born and where he became a volunteer and leader. He served on the SVM's original executive committee and was its chairman over 30 years, simultaneously providing able leadership for what at that time was a highly evangelistic YMCA and World's Student Christian Federation. Latourette comments, "Combining a simple faith issuing from a complete commitment to Christ with a commanding platform presence, world-wide vision, skill in discerning and enlisting young men of ability, and the capacity to win the confidence of men of affairs, and reaching out across ecclesiastical barriers to unite Christians of many traditions in the endeavor to win all mankind to the faith, Mott became one of the outstanding leaders in the entire history of Christianity." To the day he died he classified himself simply as an evangelist. The following address, given in April 1901 but vibrant with relevance today, gives a glimpse of his heart and mind.

It is a most inspiring fact that the young people of this generation do not apologize for world-wide missions. It would seem that that Christian who in these days would apologize for missions is either ignorant or thoughtless, because a man who apologizes for missions apologizes for all enduring religion; for, as Max Muller has said, "The non-Christian religions are either dying or are dead." He apologizes manifestly for Christianity, because that is essentially a missionary enterprise. He apologizes for the Bible, because missions constitute its central theme. He apologizes for the prayer of his Lord and for the Apostles' Creed; and he need only repeat their familiar phrases to be humiliated with the thought. He apologizes for the fatherhood of God, and in doing so also for the brotherhood of man. If he is a Christian, he apologizes for every whit of spiritual life that is in himself; and, worst of all, he apologizes for Jesus Christ, who is the Propitiation not for our sins only but for the sins of the world. I repeat, he is either ignorant or thoughtless.

Taken from *Missionary Issues of the Twentieth Century* (Reprint), 1901.

Grounds of Belief in World Evangelization

Not only do the students and other young people of our day, however, not apologize for this world-wide enterprise, but they believe in it as has no preceding generation of young people. They are believing in it with a depth of conviction, and manifesting their belief with a practical sympathy and purpose and action, such as has never been witnessed in any preceding age in the history of the Church. If you ask me tonight to give you the grounds of their belief, and in this way to define their responsibility for the world's evangelization, I would place at the threshold the fundamental reason that they feel their obligation to preach Christ because all people need Christ.

All People Need Christ

The need of the non-Christian world is an extensive need. South of this country we have not less than fifty millions of people in Mexico, the West Indies, Central America, and the South American republics. In the Levant there are tens of millions of others. In the Dark Continent, at the most conservative estimate, there are over one hundred and fifty millions; in the East Indies and the other islands of the Southern seas, fifty millions more; in India, Burma, Ceylon, and Siam, not less than three hundred millions; in the Sunrise Kingdom of Japan, over forty millions; and not less than four hundred millions in China and the states that fringe upon her, Korea, Manchuria, Mongolia, and Tibet.

Over one thousand millions! Can we grasp the number? No, indeed! It is indeed an extensive need. It is not only an extensive need, but it is an intensive one; and the intensive need of the non-Christian world is indescribably great. The Scriptures maintain this much. They show us most vividly the condition of men apart from Jesus Christ. They present today, as every world traveler will tell you, an unexaggerated picture of the moral and spiritual condition of over two-thirds of the human race. Not only the Scriptures but scientific observation proves to be a demonstration that those peoples without Christ have a need which is very deep. Think of them tonight, living in darkness and ignorance, steeped in superstition and idolatry, in degradation and corruption; see them, under what a load of shame and sorrow and sin and pain and suffering, as they live and move on in silence to the tomb; notice the fearful inroads and onslaughts of the forces of evil. And remind yourselves that they do not have those powers of resistance which we have as the result of Christian heredity, Christian environment, and the domination of Christian ideas and ideals. They fight a losing battle. If I could take every one of you on a long journey of nearly two years, through those great sections of the non-Christian world, that you might see what I have seen, that you might hear what I have heard, that you might feel what I have felt, the last iota of skepticism which may linger in the mind of any one here as to the need of these people of knowing Christ would vanish. Truly their need is indescribably great. It comes back to haunt me in the watches of the night; and if God spares my life and my plans can be properly shaped, I want in a few months hence to put my life once more alongside those young men who are fighting their losing fight.

We need not to be world travelers; we need not to be missionaries; no, we need not to be profound students of the Bible to be convinced that men need Christ. Look only into your own heart. If you and I know that we need Jesus Christ, that he has been and is essential to us, is it not presumptuous to suppose that people living in less favored lands, without the ennobling and inspiring forces and associations with which we are familiar, can get along without him? Moreover, it should be emphasized that the non-Christian religions are inadequate to meet this need. Over fifteen thousand four hundred Protestant missionaries, scattered throughout the world, present a united front on this question. There is no division of opinion among them. Standing face to face with the need itself, and, therefore, in a position to make a thorough study of the problem, they say with one voice that, unless Christ is borne to these regions, these people are without hope. I used to doubt that, Mr. Chairman, when I was studying comparative religion, and when I went as a delegate to the Parliament of Religions in Chicago several years ago. But when I had opportunity to make a scientific study of the problem (and a scientific study takes account of all the facts, and not simply of theories) all my skepticism vanished. As I went up and down densely populated provinces and presidencies and native states, as I conversed with over thirteen hundred missionaries, representing some eighty missionary societies (and I know of no university education that means more to a man than to sit at the feet of missionaries), as I talked with hundreds of civilians and native students and priests, as I visited countless shrines and temples and holy places, as I witnessed the superstitions, the abominations, the cruelties, the injustices, within the immediate confines of these sacred places, so called, the conviction became ever deeper and stronger that these nations without Christ are without hope. Yes, I believe to the core of my being that Christ some day must have sway over this whole world. He is not going to divide the World with Buddhism and Confucianism and Hinduism and Mohammedanism; he is going to have complete sway. It takes no prophet in our time to see that that Church which conquered the Roman Empire, which cast the spell of the matchless Christ over the nations of Western and Northern Europe, which has moved with giant strides among the nations and is shaking them today—that that Church will prevail. He shall reign from sea to sea. When He girds on his conquering sword all the ends of the earth shall see the salvation of our God.

We Owe Christ to All Men

I would note also that this obligation which is felt so deeply by the young people of our day is intensified by a further consideration, not only that all men need Christ, but that we owe Christ to all men. To have a knowledge of Christ is to incur a tremendous responsibility to those that have it not. You and I have received this great heritage, not to appropriate it to our own exclusive use, but to pass it on to others. It concerns all men. We are trustees of the gospel, and in no sense sole proprietors. Every Chinese, every East Indian, every inhabitant of the Southern seas, has the right to know of the mission of Jesus Christ; and you and I violate the eighth commandment if we keep this knowledge from them. You may show me the very best disciple of any one of these religions—and I have seen men living noble lives who are devotees of those religions—I say he has a right to know of the life and death and resurrection of Jesus Christ, and of his mission to mankind. What a colossal crime against two-thirds of the human race to with-hold this surpassing knowledge!

The weight of responsibility becomes still greater when we stop to ask our-selves the question: If we do not take this knowledge of Christ to these people, who will? What should move us, fellow young men, and what should move the young women here, and those whom we all represent, to fling ourselves into this enterprise and bear Christ to these people? It would seem that the claims of our common humanity and of universal brotherhood would be sufficient to inspire us to go ourselves or to send substitutes. If that is not sufficient, the golden rule of Jesus Christ, by which I take it every one of us desires to fashion conscien-tiously his life, would lead us logically and irresistibly to do so. If that does not move us, the example of our Lord in this practical age ought to stir us to action, because those who say they abide in him ought themselves so to walk even as he walked. If that does not move us, then every thoughtful and reflecting person, it would seem, should be moved by the Great Commission or the marching orders of the Church of God. The last commandment of Christ is operative until it is repealed. We have had no intimation that it has been repealed. It is not optional, as some would assume, but obligatory. It awaits its fulfillment by a generation which shall have the requisite faith and courage, and audacity and the purpose of heart, to do their duty to the whole world. It would seem to me that every Christian who is a Christian of reality ought to be a missionary Christian; for, as Archbishop Whately has said—mark his language, note it well: "If my faith be false, I ought to change it; whereas if it be true, I am bound to propagate it." There is no middle ground; either abandon my religion or be a missionary in spirit.

World evangelization essential to our own best life

There is yet a third consideration; and that is, that the young people of our day should seek to evangelize the world because it is essential to their own best life. If all men need Christ, and if we owe a knowledge of Christ to all men, mani-festly it is our duty to take that knowledge to them. To know our duty and to do it not is sin. Continuance in the sin of neglect and disobedience necessarily weak-ens the life and arrests the growth. What loss of spiritual life, what loss of energy and of faith, the Church of Christ has already suffered from a fractional obedi-ence to the last command of our Lord!

The young people's movements of our day, like our own Epworth League, the Baptist Young People's Union, the Young People's Society of Christian Endeavor, the St. Andrew's Brotherhood, the Young Men's and the Young Women's Christian Associations, need nothing so much as some mighty objec-tive to call out the best energies of mind and heart. We find precisely such an objective in the sublime enterprise of filling the earth with a knowledge of the Lord as the waters cover the deep. If we would save our Christian young people's movements from their perils of ease and luxury and selfishness and slothfulness and unreality, we must necessarily take up some great and scrip-tural object like this, and give ourselves to it with holy abandon.

This point comes to mean more when we remember that the largest manifes-tation of the presence of Christ is to those that are obedient to his missionary command. Have you ever reflected upon it that the baptism of the Holy Spirit is invariably associated with testimony and witness-bearing? Therefore we can do nothing which will mean so much to the home Church as to develop this foreign missionary spirit. If we would have the Holy Spirit working with mighty power in all our communities—and is this not our greatest need?—we shall have this experience as we walk in the pathway of our missionary Leader in obedience to his command.

An Urgent Obligation

The obligation to evangelize the world, which presses in upon the young people of our day, is also a most urgent obligation. The Christians who are now living must preach Christ to the non-Christians who are now alive, if they are ever to hear of Christ. The Christians of a past generation cannot do it; they are dead and gone. The Christians of the next generation cannot do it; by that time the present non-Christians will be dead and gone. Obviously, each generation of Christians must make Christ known to its own generation of non-Christians, if they are to have the knowledge of Christ. But we might just as well get the Christians who come after us to love God for us, or get them to love our neighbors for us, as to be obedient for us. Moreover (and I am now speaking to those of my own generation), we are living in a time of unexampled crisis. It is also a time of marvelous opportunity. The world is better known and more accessible than in any other generation which has ever lived. The need of the world is more articulate and intelligible than it has ever been, and the resources of the Church are far greater today, as well as her ability to enter these open doors, than has been the case in any preceding generation. It would seem that this would impose a great burden of responsibility upon our generation; greater than upon any other generation. You and I cannot excuse ourselves by doing what our fathers did. The world is smaller today to us than this country was to our fathers. We have the opportunity to do larger things, and we are going to be judged by our talents and the use of them. God forbid that we should lack vision in these days to take advantage of the tide that is rising to sweep multitudes into the all-embracing kingdom of Jesus Christ.

The forces of evil are not putting off their work until the next generation. When I was in Japan I found that militarism and materialism said: "Let us engulf Japan in this generation, and we shall not be so much concerned about subsequent generations." Commerce and avarice and international jealousies say: "Give us China in this generation." In India I discovered that rationalism said: "Let us have the right of way in the Indian universities for this one generation, and we will hold that great continent for several generations." In the Turkish Empire lust and cruelty said: "Let us go unchecked in this generation." Why should not the Church of God rise in her might, and give herself to this task as no preceding generation has done?

Examples of Heroism and Consecration

It would seem that the enterprises of a secular or non-Christian character might stir us from our lethargy and inspire us to undertake larger things. The different governments of the world have recently united to make a magnetic survey of the whole world and complete their survey by the year 1910.

Stanley, before starting on his last trip to Africa, wanted some thirty European helpers, and advertised for that number. They were to go into the most deadly parts of Africa. Within two weeks, how many responded? Over twelve hundred young men, ready to face African fever and other perils known and unknown, that they might extend the domain of knowledge. We have read of the great rushes for gold in the Northwest in the last two or three years. You remember that there went over the difficult passes (and they were very difficult in the early days) within fourteen months over one thousand young men to the Klondike. It meant not only a great risk to them, but in a great number of cases death—and all for the love of gold. Down in the Philippines we have had at one time over sixty thousand troops. They have gone, regiment after regiment, without any particular strain upon the country. And when these regiments have returned they have met with a constant ovation from the Golden Gate until they passed to the different sections of the North, South, or East to which they were journeying. In South Africa the British army has grown steadily until now they have there not less than 250,000 men, and they have blocked off that part of the world into squares, and are sweeping over those squares every few days in their work of cornering up the forces of the Boers. We have been impressed with the wonderful spectacle presented of the unity and loyalty of the British Empire. Doubtless we were even more impressed to see not only the young men, but also the old men and the boys, go out from the two little mountain republics to fight the battles of their country. In recent months an international army has been assembled in China from Europe and Asia and America. But the world takes it as a matter of course. They say that these are precisely the things to do if certain purposes are to be accomplished. And yet when somebody suggests that a few tens of thousand of young men and young women living in this favored generation rise up and, in obedience to the last command of Christ, go out into the places where he has not been named, we are told that it would be too great a strain on the resources of the Church, and that it would handicap the activities of the Church at home. They forget the law of God: "There is that scattereth, and yet increaseth; and there is that holdeth more than is meet, but it tendeth to poverty" [Proverbs 11:34].

The Mormon Church has 250,000 members, and they have over 1,700 missionaries—that is, men working outside of the Mormon community proselyting. They also have a law by which they can increase their number of workers to between seven and eight thousand if they so desire, and their young men respond obediently whenever the call comes for a larger reenforcement.

When I was in the little island of Ceylon I reviewed its history, and was deeply stirred as I thought that from that little island there went forth, centuries ago, not hundreds but thousands of Buddhist missionaries. They stormed the whole Asiatic coast; and as the result, largely of their labors, there are today hundreds of millions of adherents to that great incomplete and false religion.

When I was in Cairo I visited the famous university of El Azar. As I remember, there are some three hundred and seventy pillars, and around many of them I found classes of Mohammedan students seated on the pavement with a teacher in the center of each group. One of the students said to me: "We have between eight and nine thousand students here." I asked him what books they were studying, and he said that they were studying only one and the commentaries on it— the Koran. I said, "What is your object?" and he said, "We are all studying here to go out as missionaries of Mohammed." These men had come from regions reaching all the way from the Pillars of Hercules down to the island of the East Indies to prepare themselves to be emissaries of the false prophet.

As we think of examples like these, are not our hearts moved within us? I am looking day by day for young men and young women of like heroism and of greater consecration, touched by the spirit of the ascended Christ, who will show like loyalty in carrying out his final wishes with reference to the world for which he died.

Keep Ourselves Informed

How can the young men and young women of our day best discharge their obligation to the world's evangelization? Well, manifestly we must keep ourselves informed concerning the great enterprise of world-wide missions.

The words of Christ, in an entirely different connection, suggest themselves to me now: "Ye do err, not knowing the Scriptures, nor the power of God." If there is any place where the power of God is being manifested today more than elsewhere, it is in the non-Christian world where the arm of God has been made bare and where we are witnessing such marvelous triumphs of the gospel of the Son of God.

We do ourselves an injustice if we do not keep in vivid touch with this wonderful missionary movement. To do the will of God, we must know the needs of man. I fail to see how any young men or young women can be perfectly sure that they are doing what God wants them to do, if they are not carrying on a thorough study of this great world. Every young Christian in the Church ought to have an ambition to know the kingdom of Jesus Christ, its great fields, its marvelous triumphs, its problems, its inspiring opportunities, and its transcendent resources. We can have no better creed than the creed of St. Augustine: "A whole Christ for my salvation, a whole Bible for my staff, a whole Church for my fellowship, and a whole world for my parish." Let us be satisfied with nothing less than the world-wide horizon of Jesus Christ our Lord.

Each band of young people should also be a center for disseminating information concerning the work of God in the world. There is a shocking amount of ignorance and of flimsy excuses and objections concerning world-wide missions, which will be banished only by an educational campaign. Therefore, let me endorse with strong conviction everything that has been said on this platform from this morning until tonight, and which has been so ably stated by the different advocates, on the inestimable importance of educating on missions beginning even with the child at the mother's knee, reaching up through the Sunday school and the Junior Department of the Epworth League, and the Senior Department, up to the ministrations of the pastor, so that we will have a generation who will have knowledge adequate to meet the opportunity that confronts this generation. There is no subject, unless it be the study of the Life of Christ, the study of which is more broadening, more deepening, more elevating, more inspiring than the subject of world-wide missions. No subject more broadening; it embraces all mankind. No subject more deepening; it takes us down to the very depths of the designs of God. Surely no subject more elevating. I can think of nothing that so lifts a man out of himself. And can anything be more inspiring than that enterprise which commanded the life and death and resurrection of our Lord? I repeat it, therefore, that we do our fellow young men and young women in the Epworth League, the Sunday school, and Churches a grave injustice if we keep out of their lives this sublime enterprise as a special study.

Bands of Intercession and Sacrifice

Each one of our bands of young people, whether it be large or small, should also be a band of intercession. There is an old Jewish proverb that "He prays not at all in whose prayers there is no mention of the kingdom of God." Everything vital to missions hinges upon prayer. This is one of my strongest convictions, but I pass it at this time, as I shall have an opportunity to enlarge upon it fully tomorrow night.

Every one of our organizations of young people should be a school of self-sacrifice. Believe me, there is need in our day of more heroic and self-denying giving. We need to teach young men and young women that they are the stewards, not simply of a tenth, but of all they possess, and that we are responsible, not alone for the good use of our money, whether it be little or great, but for its best possible use. Let every one of us be guided by that scriptural principle which governed the life of Livingstone, that we will place no value upon anything we have or may possess, except in its relation to the kingdom of God. This would revolutionize the habits of giving of the Christian Church.

Wesley at one time received a salary of sixty pounds ($300) a year, and was able to live upon it and to give quite a little of it to Christian work. As his salary and income increased, he still lived on less than sixty pounds, and gave all the remainder to the extension of Christ's kingdom. Not many months ago a young man in Canada (not a very wealthy young man, you would not count him wealthy at all if I could give you the estimated figures of his possessions, but a young man prosperous in his business) came to me and said that he would like to support a representative on the foreign field, and he gave $1,200 toward the salary and expenses of a foreign worker. A few weeks ago, when I was at Princeton College, I received a message telling me that I should go to New York City and see this young man. He was to take the boat on the following day for Europe. When I met him in New York he said: "I have been so much blessed by helping to support that man in Japan that I should like to have a hand, if you can find an equally good man, in supporting another." I did not find it very difficult to suggest a man equally good. I held out before him two men. I said, "Here is one man that it will take about $1,200 to send, and this one about $800;" and he decided that he would improve the $1,200 opportunity. He took his boat, and less than two days ago, since I have been at this Conference, I received a letter from him, written in England, saying that as he was praying about it on the ocean he decided that he wanted to take the $800 man also. He said: "God has prospered me in my business, and as I extend my business I want to enlarge my cooperation in the propagation of the gospel of Jesus Christ. I do not need any more expensive house or furniture." That man has the idea of Christ; and if that idea can take possession of a sufficient number of young men, we shall have money sufficient to evangelize the world in a generation, with ease so far as money is concerned.

An Offering of Young People

We need not only more money, but also more of our best young men and young women for this work. We were all impressed by the magnificent offering of $50,000 by the delegates here last night. But there is still needed, in order to make this convention reach its highest climax, a great offering of the most consecrated young men and women of this convention, and, through the many pastors who shall go back from here, hundreds of equally consecrated young men and young women in the different spiritual centers of the South. This is needed because of the great opportunity before us. I was told by Dr. Lambuth tonight that the Missionary Society of the Methodist Episcopal Church, South, have decided that with God's blessing they will send out the next five years one hundred new missionaries. This is a direct leading of the Spirit of God, who leads us to do large things. Where are all these missionaries coming from? I cannot conceive of any riper harvest field than the one right here, prepared by many months of patient prayerfulness. Here we have hundreds of consecrated Christians from all over this favored Church. Where have we the right to look with greater confidence for reenforcements? May we not have many here who, as the result of fighting to the end of self, shall say with glad abandonment of self: "Here am I, send me"? Remember the German proverb: "The good is the enemy of the best." Let us be satisfied with nothing else than leaving the deepest mark on our generation. And remember also that if it is a good thing to go where we are needed, it is more Christlike to go where we are needed the most. Is there anything which reason and conscience can summon which would take issue with that position? God grant that we may step into the footsteps of our Lord, to go to the most destitute fields of our own country and the great open places beyond! May God move the parents here tonight not only not to interfere and hinder, but rather to facilitate the favorable decision of our own sons and daughters to enter upon this exalted service! O, it is a solemn responsibility for any father or mother in these days to do anything by word, or other expression or attitude, to keep a son or daughter who is qualified from entering upon this unutterably important work of preaching Christ where he is not known. What a responsibility! I misinterpret the spirit of this gathering if there is any father or mother here who would do this. Rather, in the spirit of God, who spared not his only Son, but delivered him up for us all, we shall be willing to make this sacrifice for the sake of Christ, who has done so much for us.

Each Congregation a Force to be Wielded

I have one word of appeal to the pastors here. You have a unique opportunity to go back and influence the young men and the young women in your Churches to devote their lives to foreign missionary service. When I was in England last year I learned of a Church of three hundred members that within ten years had furnished thirty-two missionary volunteers, and of that number twenty had finished preparation and were already on the mission field, while others were still preparing themselves. I envied their pastor. Think how he has multiplied his life. Think what we also may do to help support missionaries and to influence individual members in our congregations to go to those much burdened secretaries of our Mission Boards, our dearly beloved brothers, with gifts to the Lord of a thousand dollars, or five hundred dollars, or any other amount they are able to give to the cause to build up the fight on monetary lines as well as on lines of offering for life service.

Let each pastor have the true conception of his Church as not merely a field to be cultivated, but also as a force to be wielded on behalf of the world's evangelization. And my final word is to us all. Whether God calls us to go or to stay, O my friends, let each one of us resolve that he will act as if he were the only Christian to act. That has never led the Christian into error. Act in such a way that if a sufficient number of men and women would do the same thing we could take the knowledge of Christ with faithfulness and thoroughness to the hearing of every creature on this earth. Let each one act for himself. Forget the others. If you feel the pressure of the facts and the pulse of the spirit of the living God, be serious and be obedient. It is a great thing to have dealings with the living God. Responsibility is individual, untransferable, urgent. Some day every man of us must pass before the judgment seat of Christ, and at that time we shall be judged not by what some one else did, but by what we did to serve our own generation by the will of God. Responsibility is not only individual and untransferable; it is urgent.

> The work which centuries might have done
> Must crowd the hour of setting sun.

Live or Die for the Evangelization of the World

"I must work the works of Him that sent me, while it is day: the night cometh, when no man can work." Therefore, friends, in view of the awful need of men who tonight are living without Christ; in view of the infinite possibilities of the life related to Christ as mighty Saviour and risen Lord; in view of the magnitude of the task which confronts the Church of this generation; in view of the impending crisis and the urgency of the situation; in view of the conditions which favor a great onward movement within the Church of God, in view of the dangers of anything less than a great onward movement; in view of the great cloud of witnesses who gathered around us last night, of those who subdued kingdoms and wrought righteousness—yes, in view of the constraining memories of the Cross of Christ and the love wherewith he hath loved us, let us rise and resolve, at whatever cost of self-denial, that live or die, we shall live or die for the evangelization of the world in our day.

Study Questions

1. What grounds does Mott put forward for placing the responsibility of world evangelization on young people?

2. Identify the statement in this address that you feel might have been the greatest catalyzing force in challenging young people of his day to evangelize the world in their generation.

15

The Bridges of God

Donald A. McGavran

The Bridges of God appeared in 1954, and it has since become known as the classic summons for missionaries to utilize the "bridges" of family and kinship ties within each people group thereby prompting "people movements" to Christ. This is contrasted with the "Mission Station Approach," dominant in missionary strategy of the nineteenth century, whereby individual converts are gathered into "colonies" or compounds isolated from the social mainstream. McGavran claims that whereas the latter approach was necessary and useful in the nineteenth and early twentieth centuries, "a new pattern is at hand, which, while new, is as old as the Church itself."

The Crucial Question in Christian Missions

How do peoples become Christian?

Much study has been devoted to world evangelization. We know the answers to many questions about the propagation of the Gospel. But what is perhaps the most important question of all still awaits an answer. That question is: *How do Peoples become Christian?*

This article asks how clans, tribes, castes, in short how *Peoples* become Christian. Every nation is made up of various layers of strata of society. In many nations each stratum is clearly separated from every other. The individuals in each stratum intermarry chiefly, if not solely, with each other. Their intimate life is therefore limited to their own society, that is, to their own people. They may work with others, they may buy from and sell to the individuals of other societies, but their intimate life is wrapped up with the individuals of their own people. Individuals of another stratum, possibly close neighbours, may become Christians or Communists without the first stratum being much concerned. But when individuals of their own kind start becoming Christians, that touches their very lives. How do chain reactions in these strata of society begin? *How do Peoples*

Known worldwide as perhaps the foremost missiologist, Donald McGavran was born in India of missionary parents and returned there as a third-generation missionary himself in 1923, serving as a director of religious education and translating the Gospels in the Chhattisgarhi dialect of Hindi. He founded the School of World Mission of Fuller Theological Seminary, and was formerly Dean Emeritus. McGavran died in 1990 at the age of 93. McGavran was the author of several influential books, including *The Bridges of God, How Churches Grow,* and *Understanding Church Growth.* Excerpts from *The Bridges of God* (Revised Edition), 1981. Used by permission.

become Christian?

Here is a question to which not speculation but knowledge must urgently be applied. The question is how, in a manner true to the Bible, can a Christian movement be established in some class, caste, tribe or other segment of society which will, over a period of years, so bring groups of its related families to Christian faith that the whole people is Christianized in a few decades? It is of the utmost importance that the Church should understand how peoples, and not merely individuals, become Christian.

The Unfamiliar in People Movements

Individualistic Westerners cannot without special effort grasp how peoples become Christian. The missionary movement is largely staffed by persons from the West or by nationals trained in their ideas, and while evangelization has been carried on with correct enough views on how individuals have become Christian, there have been hazy or even erroneous views on how peoples become Christian.

Western individualism obscures group processes

In the West, Christianization is an extremely individualistic process. This is due to various causes. For one thing, in Western nations there are few exclusive subsocieties. Then too, because freedom of conscience exists, one member of a family can become Christian and live as a Christian without being ostracized by the rest of the family. Furthermore, Christianity is regarded as true, even by many who do not profess it. It is considered a good thing to join the Church. A person is admired for taking a stand for Christ. There have been no serious rivals to the Church. Thus individuals are able to make decisions as individuals without severing social bonds.

Again, with the disruption of clan and family life following upon the industrial revolution, Westerners became accustomed to do what appealed to them as individuals. As larger family groupings were broken up through migration, the movement of rural folk to the cities, and repeated shifts of homes, people came to act for themselves without consulting their neighbours or families. A habit of independent decision was established. In the Christian churches this habit was further strengthened by the practice of revival meetings appealing for individual decisions to the accompaniment of great emotion. Indeed, the theological presupposition was not merely that salvation depended on an individual act of faith in Christ (which is unquestioned), but also that this act was somehow of a higher order if it were done against family opinion (which is dubious). Separate individual accessions to the Church were held by some to be not only a better, but the only valid, way of becoming a Christian. Had the question arisen as to how peoples became Christian, the answer would have been given that it was by individual after individual becoming soundly converted.

Of the social organism which *is* a people, or of the desirability of preserving the culture and community life, indeed, of enhancing them through the process of conversion, there tended to be little recognition. Peoples were thought of as aggregates of individuals whose conversion was achieved one by one. The social factor in the conversion of peoples passed unnoticed because peoples were not identified as separate entities.

However, a people is not an aggregation of individuals. In a true people intermarriage and the intimate details of social intercourse take place within the society. In a true people individuals are bound together not merely by common social practices and religious beliefs but by common blood. A true people is a social organism which, by virtue of the fact that its members intermarry very largely within its own confines, becomes a separate race in their minds. Since the human family, except in the individualistic West, is largely made up of such castes, clans and peoples, the Christianization of each nation involves the prior Christianization of its various peoples as peoples.

Because of the intense battle against race prejudice, the concept of separate races of men is discredited in many circles. Missionaries often carry this antipathy to race into their work in tribes and castes who believe themselves to be separate races, marry within their people and have an intense racial consciousness. But to ignore the significance of race hinders Christianization. It makes an enemy of race consciousness, instead of an ally. It does no good to say that tribal peoples ought not to have race prejudice. They do have it and are proud of it. It can be understood and should be made an aid to Christianization.

What to do and what not to do

To Christianize a whole people, the first thing not to do is snatch individuals out of it into a different society. Peoples become Christians where a Christward movement occurs *within that society.* Bishop J. W. Pickett, in his important study *Christ's Way to India's Heart,* says:

> The process of extracting individuals from their setting in Hindu or Moslem communities does not build a Church. On the contrary it rouses antagonism against Christianity and builds barriers against the spread of the Gospel. Moreover, that process has produced many unfortunate, and not a few tragic results in the lives of those most deeply concerned. It has deprived the converts of the values represented by their families and friends and made them dependent for social support to the good life and restraint on evil impulses upon men and women, their colleagues in the Christian faith, with whom they have found it difficult to develop fellowship and a complete sense of community. It has sacrificed much of the convert's evangelistic potentialities by separating him from his People. It has produced anaemic Churches that know no true leadership and are held together chiefly by common dependence on the mission or the missionary.

Equally obviously the Christianization of a people requires reborn men and women. A mere change of name accomplishes nothing. While the new convert must remain within his people, he must also experience the new birth. "If ye then be risen with Christ, set your affection on things above, not on things on the earth." The power of any People Movement to Christ depends in great measure on the number of truly converted persons in it. We wish to make this quite clear. The Christianization of peoples is not assisted by slighting or forgetting real personal conversion. There is no substitute for justification by faith in Jesus Christ or for the gift of the Holy Spirit.

Thus a Christward movement within a people can be defeated either by extracting the new Christians from their society (i.e. by allowing them to be squeezed out by their non-Christian relatives) or by the non-Christians so dominating the Christians that their new life in Christ is not apparent. An incipient Christward movement can be destroyed by either danger.

The group mind and group decision

To understand the psychology of the innumerable subsocieties which make up non-Christian nations, it is essential that the leaders of the Churches and missions strive to see life from the point of view of a people, to whom individual action is treachery. Among those who think corporately only a rebel would strike out alone, without consultation and without companions. The individual does not think of himself as a self-sufficient unit, but as part of the group. His business affairs, his children's marriages, his personal problems, or the difficulties he has with his wife are properly settled by group thinking. Peoples become Christian as this group-mind is brought into a lifegiving relationship to Jesus as Lord.

It is important to note that the group decision is not the sum of separate individual decisions. The leader makes sure that his followers will follow. The followers make sure that they are not ahead of each other. Husbands sound out wives. Sons pledge their fathers. "Will we as a group move if so-and-so does not come?" is a frequent question. As the group considers becoming Christian, tension mounts and excitement rises. Indeed, a prolonged informal vote-taking is under way. A change of religion involves a community change. Only as its members move together, does change become healthy and constructive.

Groups are usually fissured internally. This has a definite bearing on group decision. If in some town or village there are seventy-six families of a given people, they may be split into several sub-groups. Often such divisions are formed by rivalries between prominent men. Often they are geographical: the lower section of the village as against the upper section. Often they are economic: the landed as opposed to the landless. Often they depend on education, marriage relationships, or attitudes toward customs. Group thinking usually occurs at its best within these sub-groups. A sub-group will often come to decision before the whole. Indeed, a sub-group often furnishes enough social life for it to act alone.

Peoples become Christian as a wave of decision for Christ sweeps through the group mind, involving many individual decisions but being far more than merely their sum. This may be called a chain reaction. Each decision sets off others and the sum total powerfully affects every individual. When conditions are right, not merely each sub-group, but the entire group concerned decides together.

Terms defined

We call this process a "People Movement." "People" is a more universal word than "tribe", "caste" or "clan." It is more exact than "group." It fits everywhere. Therefore in this article we shall speak of People Movements to Christ.

The Characteristic Pattern of the Great Century

Dr. Latourette has given the name "the Great Century" to the time between 1800 and 1914. He says: "When consideration is given to the difficulties which faced it, in the nineteenth century, Christianity made amazing progress all around the world. It came to the end of the period on a rapidly ascending curve. Its influence on culture was out of all proportions to its numerical strength. It had an outstanding role as a pioneer in new types of education, in movements of the relief and prevention of human suffering and in disseminating ideas."

How did Christianization proceed during the Great Century? This is a most important question because most of our present thinking is coloured by the missionary effort of that century. When we think of missions today, we think of those with which we are familiar, and which prevailed in China, Africa, India and other countries during the Great Century. Since this century produced a radically new and different approach, the older kind of missions which existed for 1,800 years have tended to be forgotten. The missionary and the Churches tend to think that the only kind of missions and the only kind of Christianization possible is that used with greater or lesser effect during the past 150 years. The Great Century created a new method to meet a new situation. Both situation and method are worthy of our closest study.

The new situation described: the gulf of separation

Missions were carried on from the ruling, wealthy, literate, modern countries, which were experiencing all the benefits of political and religious freedom, an expanding production, and universal education. In the year 1500, European visitors to India and China described countries which compared favourably with their own. But by the nineteenth century the West had progressed while the East had stood still, so that there was a great gap between them. Western missionaries went to poor, illiterate, medieval and agricultural countries. The gap widened with the passage of the years, for the progress of the West continued to be greater than that of the East. While it is true that missionaries tried to identify themselves with the people, they were never able to rid themselves of the inevitable separateness which the great progress of their home lands had imposed upon them.

This gulf became very clear in the living arrangements which European and American missionaries found necessary. Their standard of living at home was many times higher than that of the average citizen on the mission fields, though it could not compare with that of the few wealthy Chinese, Japanese and Indians. Modern medicine was unknown. Health demanded big bungalows on large sites. Servants were cheap and saved much domestic labour. The people of the land generally walked, but the missionary was accustomed to a conveyance and so he used one. The colour of his skin also set him apart. He could not melt into the generality of the inhabitants of the land as Paul could. He was a white man, a member of the ruling race. To this day in the rural sections of India, seven years after independence, the white missionary is frequently addressed as *Sarkar* (Government). The missionary was an easy victim not only to malaria but to intestinal diseases. He had to be careful about what he ate. The Western style of cooking agreed with him, whereas the Eastern style did not. So in matters of food also there came to be a great gulf between him and the people of the land.

There were practically no bridges across this gulf. There was nothing even remotely similar to the Jewish bridge over which Christianity marched into the

Gentile world. Staggering numbers of people lived on the fertile plains of Asia, but not one of them had any Christian relatives! Even in the port cities there were none. *Més alliances* between white soldiery, rulers or commercial people and the women of the various lands were so resented on the one hand and despised on the other that they served as barriers rather than bridges. The normal flow of the Christian religion simply could not take place. Separated by colour, standard of living, prestige, literacy, mode of travel, place of residence, and many other factors, the missionary was, indeed, isolated from those to whom he brought the message of salvation.

The missionaries did learn the languages of the country and learned them well. They served the people with love, taught their children, visited in their homes, went with them through famines and epidemics, ate with them, bought from them and sold to them, and, more than any other group of white men in the tropics, were at one with them. Thus, it will be said, this emphasis on the separateness of the missionary is exaggerated. To the student of the growth and spread of religions, however, it is apparent that these casual contacts described above are just that—casual contacts. They are not the living contacts, the contacts of tribe and race and blood, which enable the non-Christian to say, as he hears a Christian speak: "This messenger of the Christian religion is one of my own family, my own People, one of us." Casual contacts may win a few individuals to a new faith, but unless these individuals are able to start a living movement within their own society, it does not start at all.

The separateness we describe seemed likely to last a long time. It existed in an unchanging world, where the dominance of the West and the dependence of the East seemed to be permanent. Missionaries thought, "There will be centuries before us, and, in a 400-year relationship like that of Rome to her dependent peoples, we shall gradually bring these peoples also into the Christian faith."

This grave separateness faced Christian missions during the Great Century. When the churches and their missionaries have no relations, no contacts and no bridges over inter-racial gulfs, what do they do? How do they carry out the command of their Lord? When there is no living approach, how do they go about the Christianization of peoples?

The new method evolved: the exploratory mission-station approach

If there is any aspect that is typical of modern missions, it is the mission station with its gathered colony. Missionaries facing the gulf of separation built mission stations and gathered colonies of Christians.

They acquired a piece of land, often with great difficulty. They built residences suitable for white men. Then they added churches, schools, quarters in which to house helpers, hospitals, leprosy homes, orphanages and printing establishments. The mission station was usually at some centre of communication. From it extensive tours were made into the surrounding country-side. It was home to the missionary staff and all the activities of the mission took place around the station.

Together with building the station, the missionaries gathered converts. It was exceedingly difficult for those hearing the Good News for the first time, knowing nothing of Christians, or of Christianity save that it was the religion of the invading white men, to accept the Christian religion. Those who did so were usually forced out of their own homes by fierce ostracism. They came to live at the mission colony, where they were usually employed. Orphans were sheltered. Slaves were bought and freed. Women were rescued. Some healed patients became Christian. Many of these usually came to live at the mission station. They were taught various means of earning a livelihood and directed into various forms of service. They formed the gathered colony.

This kind of mission approach took shape out of the individualistic background typical of much Protestantism in the eighteenth and nineteenth centuries. To be a Christian was to come out and be separate. For converts to leave father and mother invested their decisions with a particular validity. To gather a compound full of Christians out of a non-Christian population seemed a good way to proceed. Frequently it was also the only possible way. The universal suspicion and often the violent hostility with which Christianity was regarded would have forced into the gathered colony pattern even those who consciously sought integration.

This, then, was the pattern which was characteristic of most beginnings in the Great Century. We call it the exploratory mission station approach, but from the point of view of the resulting churches, it was the exploratory gathered colony approach.

It was excellent strategy in its day. It was a probe to ascertain which peoples were ready to become Christian. Christianity must be seen to be stable before it will be accepted as a way of salvation. Peoples are not going to commit their destinies to a faith which is here to-day and gone to-morrow. Men must see over a period of years what the Christian life means and what Christ does to persons and to groups. While the Good News is first being presented and the Christian life demonstrated the mission station and the gathered colony are essential. As we look back over the last hundred years it seems both necessary and desirable for there to have been this approach. With all its limitations, it was the best strategy for the era. This approach has been no mistake. It fitted the age which produced it. It was inevitable.

The road branches according to response

This beginning, adopted by practically all missions, may be considered as a road running along a flat and somewhat desolate plain and then dividing, one branch to continue along the plain, the other to climb the green fertile hills. Whether missions continued on the flat accustomed road (of the gathered church approach) or ascended the high road by means of the People Movement Approach depended on the response given to the Christian message by the population and on the missionaries' understanding of that response.

Where the number of conversions remained small decade after decade, there the mission remained the dominant partner and the Mission Station Approach continued and, indeed, was strengthened. It was strengthened because the gathered colony furnished Christian workers so that the mission could expand mission healing, mission teaching and mission preaching. Where the number of conversions mounted steadily with every passing decade, there the Church became the dominant partner and the mission turned up the hill road. It started using the People Movement Approach. Scores of thousands became Christians.

These two roads, these two ways of carrying on mission work, are distinct and different. Clear thinking about missions must make a sharp differentiation between them. Each must be described separately. The People Movements, the hill road, will be described in the next section. The remainder of this section will be devoted to describing the widening road on the plain, the way in which the exploratory phase gradually turned into the permanent Mission Station Approach or gathered colony approach.

Small response was not expected by the early missionaries. The exploratory Mission Station Approach was not launched as an accommodation to a hard-hearted and irresponsive population. It was regarded as *a first stage after which great ingathering would occur.* Even after the Basel Mission had lost eight of its first ten missionaries in nine years, the heroic Andreas Riis wrote back from the Gold Coast in Africa, "Let us press on. All Africa must be won for Christ. Though a thousand missionaries die, send more." The exploratory gathered colony approach was adopted with the expectation that the Christian faith would sweep non-Christian lands bringing them untold blessings.

But these expectations were often frustrated by meagre response. In the light of the event Professor Latourette can now serenely write:

> The advanced cultures and faiths of Asia and North Africa did not yield so readily as did those of the primitive folk, either to Western civilization or to Christianity. This was to be expected. It has usually been characteristic of advanced cultures and their religions that they have been much slower to disintegrate before an invading civilization.

But the meagre response was not expected by the early messengers of the Church. It was disappointing.

A factor in the small response, whose importance cannot be overestimated, is that, partly because of the individualistic bias of the missionaries and partly because of the resistance of the hearers, conversions were mainly *out* of the nation. Converts felt that they were joining not merely a new religion, but an entirely foreign way of living—proclaimed by foreigners, led by foreigners and ruled by foreigners. Converts came alone. Often even their wives refused to come with them. Naturally conversions were few. A vicious circle was established: the few becoming Christian one by one set such a pattern that it was difficult for a Christward movement to be started, and by the lack of a movement converts continued to come one by one and in very small numbers. In many parts of the field it was psychologically difficult for a person to become a Christian as it would be for a white man in South Africa to join a Negro Church knowing that his children would intermarry with the black children. The person not only became a Christian, but he was generally believed to have "joined another race." When, among peoples which intermarry only amongst themselves, a man becomes a Christian, his old mother is likely to reproach him, saying, "Now whom will your sons marry? They cannot get wives from amongst us any more."

The exploratory approach becomes permanent: terms defined

Where meagre response continued, there gathered colony missions gradually accommodated themselves to carrying on mission work among populations which would not obey the call of God. Once this occurred we may say that the mission, which had started its road-building on the plain, with the intention of reaching high fertile land as soon as possible, settled down to road-building on the barren plain as its God-given duty. It found plenty of good work to do. It never admitted, even to itself, that it had really given up hope of reaching the hills; but that is what had actually happened.

The churches born of the mission station approach

The first aim of missions is the establishment of churches. So, as we start to examine the results of the Mission Station Approach we turn to an inspection of the kind of churches which mission stations have fathered. These we shall call Mission Station churches or gathered colony churches.

They have some favourable characteristics. They are composed of greatly transformed individuals. The membership is literate. They come to church with hymn-books. They can read their Bibles. Many among them are specially trained beyond the ordinary school. In some stations there are many high school and college graduates on the church rolls. The membership contains a goodly proportion of day labourers and artisans, household helps and casual labourers, as well as teachers, preachers, medical workers, clerks, and other white-collar workers. In some places factory and railway employees form a considerable part of the membership. On the whole the Mission Station Churches are made up of people who are soundly Christian. There is not much superstition among them and not much temptation to revert to the old non-Christian faiths. The membership is proud of being Christian, and feels that it has gained tremendously by belonging to the Christian fellowship. There are, of course, many nominal Christians and some whose conduct brings shame on the church. But even these are likely to send their children to Sunday School and church!

They are organized into strong congregations. They have good permanent church buildings on land indubitably theirs. The pastors and ministers are usually qualified people. The services or worship are held regularly. The elders, deacons and other elected members form church councils and govern the church. The giving would probably compare favourably in regard to percentage of income with that in the Western churches, though often most of it is provided by those in mission employ. In some churches the giving is exemplary and there are many tithers. All told, the impression is that of small, tight, well-knit communities, buttressed by intermarriage and considering themselves to be a part of world Christianity.

On the debit side, these mission station churches are lacking in the qualities needed for growth and multiplication. They are, in truth, gathered churches, made up of individual converts, or "brands snatched from the burning", or famine orphans, or a mixture of all three. The individual converts and rescued persons have usually been disowned by their non-Christian relatives. The famine orphans have no close connection with loving brothers and sisters and uncles and aunts. Furthermore, the lives of these Christians have been so changed, and they find such satisfaction in the fellowship of their own sort (i.e. other mission station Christians) that they feel immeasurably superior to their own unconverted relatives.This is particularly true when they come from the oppressed classes. The second generation of Christians is even farther removed from their non-Christian relatives than the first, while in the third generation, in the very land where they live, the gathered church members know as a rule no non-Christian relatives at all. The precious linkages which each original member had as he came from non-Christian society and which are so needed for reproduction are all gone. A *new people* has been established which intermarries only within itself and thinks of itself as a separate community.

The Christians of the gathered colony approach have a vivid realization of the power of education. It has been education, they feel, that has lifted them out of the depths. They are keen for their children to receive as much education as possible. They skimp and scrape that their boys and girls may go on to school and proceed as far as possible on the road to a B.A. or an M.A. But they do not always have a vivid experience of the power of God. Many would grant that it was Christian education which had lifted them—an education given to them in the name of Jesus Christ. But on such experiences as the power of the Spirit, the forgiveness of sins and the blessedness of faith, many mission station Christians are likely to have a weak witness. "Become Christians and educate your children," they are likely to say. "It won't do you much good but it will be wonderful for your sons and daughters."

Gathered colony churches usually have a vivid consciousness of the mission as their parent. The churches tend to feel that it is the business of the missionary to head up a wealthy social service agency, designed to serve the Christian community. It sometimes happens that the members of a mission station church, sensing the obvious fact that there is only limited employment in a mission station, look on new converts as a labour union would on immigrants. They draw the easy conclusion that if more people become Christians, the resources of the mission will be spread thinner and there will be less for each of the existing Christians. Cases have occurred where they have actually discouraged possible converts from becoming Christian.

Gathered colony churches are often over-staffed. They are too richly served by foreign missions. Their members acquire a vested interest in the *status quo*. In one typical mission station church of 700 souls we find a missionary in charge of two primary schools and one middle school for day pupils, another in charge of a middle boarding school for girls, a missionary doctor and his nurse wife who run a hospital, and an evangelistic missionary who gives half his time to the Christian community. Then there is a national minister who is a high school graduate with theological training, five high school graduates who teach the older boys and seven high school graduates who teach the older girls, four evangelists, five Bible women and a primary school staff of six. Missionaries, who, with less than half these resources, are shepherding large numbers of Christians who have come to Christ in some People Movement, may gasp with unbelief that such heavy occupation could occur. Yet both the national and the missionary leaders of such mission station churches consider that they really are managing with a minimum degree of foreign aid!

But—the era is drawing to a close

However, as Latourette points out, the era is passing. The days in which the mission stations can exert a major influence on the affairs of Eastern nations are drawing to a close. The sleeping nations are now awake. At the headquarters of the provincial and national governments are whole departments, amply provided with millions of money raised by taxes, whose chief duty it is to plan for the future of the nations. The tens of thousands of students who journey to the West for education, the flood of publications in all the major languages of the land, the advent of the movie, the loudspeaker and programmes of social education, the sensitiveness to foreign criticism, the intense desire to prove their own nation the equal of any on earth, and the resentment felt at foreign leadership— all these presage the end of an era in which mission stations in the urban centres exerted an influence out of all proportion to their numbers.

Mission schools in Asia and North Africa no longer have the influence which they once had. In the beginning they were the only schools. But now they form a small percentage of the total, and are being crowded into the background. It is still true that there are a few outstanding Christian schools in most countries, mission schools, convent schools, which are known as the best in the land. Even so, they do not get 1 per cent of the students. There was a day when they had 50 per cent of the sons of the leading families. Mission educationists cannot dodge the plain fact that mission schools cannot expect to wield the influence which they did in the days when Western cultures were first arriving in Asia and Africa.

What is true of schools is also true of mission station hospitals. Up till 1945 the Central Provinces of India had not produced a single qualified doctor. Its university had no standard medical school. The only fully qualified doctors were a few immigrants from other provinces and missionary doctors from abroad. But to-day there are four hundred students in the medical college of its university. As this flood of physicians flows out over the cities and towns and eventually the villages of this province, the present near monopoly of the Christian hospitals is likely to be destroyed. The same sort of thing is taking place in one awakened nation after another.

Non-Christian nations are impatient with foreign tutelage. They believe it is demeaning to their national pride to admit to the need for guidance from any Western nation. The East, particularly India, honestly believes that, except for mechanization and industrialization, the West has little to give to the "spiritual East." The excoriations heaped upon Western nations by their own prophets, crying out against race prejudice, economic injustice and recurrent wars, are taken at their face value by the nations of the East. The West comes to be looked upon as soul-less, materialistic, unjust, money-mad, and moved by none but ulterior motives. The temper of these days in the East is not that of humbly sitting at the feet of missionary tutors.

It would be giving a distorted impression if the last few paragraphs were to imply that Christian missions have no more usefulness as cultural "hands across the sea." In the days ahead when nations are forced into closer and closer co-operation, all friendly efforts to interpret nations to each other will be of value. The continued residence of Westerners in the East will doubtless do good. But the days of great secular influence of foreign mission stations apart from great national Churches are probably about over.

They should be over for a further reason: there is now a use for mission resources which will do more for nation building, more for international peace, and more for the Church than the further penetration of non-Christian faiths and cultures from the vantage point of a mission station.

Salute and farewell

So has run the characteristic pattern of the Great Century. An age of tremendous mission expansion in terms of geography and influence; an age of heroism and devotion and self-sacrifice; an age of the meeting of two cultures separated by a wide gulf which, through the mission stations, outposts of goodwill and faith, has slowly drawn closer to the point where one world is in sight; an age when there is hardly a race or nation in which there is not found the Church.

So has run its pattern. But that age is now over. A new age is upon us. A new pattern is demanded. A new pattern is at hand, which, while new, is as old as the Church itself. It is a God-designed pattern by which not ones but thousands will acknowledge Christ as Lord, and grow into full discipleship as people after people, clan after clan, tribe after tribe and community after community are claimed for and nurtured in the Christian faith.

The God-given People Movements

While the typical pattern of missionary activity has been that of the Mission Station Approach, occasionally People Movements to Christ have resulted. These have not as a rule been sought by missionaries—though in Oceania, Indonesia and Africa there have been some exceptions. The movements are the outcome of the mysterious movement of the Spirit of God. Their pattern of growth is very different from that described in the last chapter. They have provided over 90 per cent of the growth of the newer Churches throughout the world. The great bulk of the membership and of the congregations of the younger Churches consist of converts and the descendants of converts won in People Movements.

In spite of this, we maintain that People Movements were the exception and that the typical approach of the last century was the Mission Station Approach. The number of mission stations from which Christian movements have started is small compared with the number serving static churches. Mission enterprises are, for the most part, those which serve non-Christians and gathered colony churches. The leadership of many conferences on missions comes largely from those who know and are immersed in the Mission Station Approach. And, as Dr. Hendrik Kraemer writes: "Missionary thinking and planning in this revolutionary period are still overwhelmingly influenced by the Mission Station Approach." The Mission Station Approach must then be taken as the typical outcome of the past years, and the People Movements as the exceptions.

In dividing mission work into these two varieties—that operating through the Mission Station Approach and that operating through the People Movements—it is recognized that some mission work cannot be classified under either head. For example, the translation and printing of the Scriptures. We are not attempting an exhaustive classification, but a practical one into which more than 90 per cent of missionary activity can be placed.

Some people movements described

Adoniram Judson went to Burma as a missionary to the cultured Buddhist Burmese. But he took under his wing a rough character, by name Ko Tha Byu, a Karen by race. The Karens were among the backward tribes of Burma. They were animistic peasants and were supposed by the Burmese to be stupid inferior people. "You can teach a buffalo, but not a Karen," was the common verdict. Judson spent six months trying to teach this former criminal, now his servant, the meaning of the redemptive death of our Lord Jesus Christ, and made such little progress that he was inclined to take the common verdict as true. However, he persisted, and a few months later Ko Tha Byu became a convinced, if not a highly illuminated, Christian.

As Judson toured Burma, speaking to the Burmese of that land, Ko Tha Byu, the camp follower, spoke to the humble Karen in each vicinity. The Karens started becoming Christian. Here a band of ten families, there one or two, and yonder a jungle settlement of five families accepted the Lordship of Christ. We do not have the data to prove that those who came were interrelated, but it is highly probable that connected families were coming in. A chain reaction was occurring. We can reasonably assume that among his close relatives alone, to say nothing of cousins and second cousins, Ko Tha Byu had a host of excellent living contacts. The early converts doubtless came from among these, and their relatives.

Judson, translating the Bible into Burmese, was concerned with more important matters than a Christian movement among a backward tribe. For years he considered the Karen converts a side issue. However, the next generation of missionaries included some who were veritable Pauls, expanding the movement as far along the paths and across the rice paddies as possible. Today there is a mighty Christian Movement among the Karens and their related tribes in Burma, numbering hundreds and thousands of souls. The Christian Karens are the educated Karens and will provide the leadership for the mixed population of Karens, Kachins and other tribes which predominate in parts of Burma. The Christward Movement among the Karens may well be the source of a Church numbering millions, and exercising a decisive influence upon the history of all South-East Asia.

By contrast, the Mission Station Approach to the Buddhist Burmese has yielded its ordinary quota of small, static mission station churches with a membership of perhaps 20,000 souls for all Burma.

The Karen Christians are good Christians. In a hundred sections of Burma there are communities of Christian Karens with their own church building, their own pastor, their own tradition of regular worship, their own Sunday school, and a Christian tribal life which augurs well for the permanence of the Christian Churches of Burma. The Karens, discipled through a People Movement, and now in the process of perfecting, are not under the delusion that a nominal Christianity is worth anything to God. The thousands of churches scattered across the country contain a normal proportion of earnest Spirit-filled Christians. They are "reborn Baptists" who will compare favourably with the reborn Baptists of any land.

We stress this because it is a mistake to assume that People Movement Christians, merely because they have come to the Christian faith in chains of families, must inevitably be nominal Christians. Such an assumption is usually based on prejudice, not fact. All Churches face the problem of how to avoid creating nominal Christians. Even Western Churches, made up of only those individual converts who testify to regeneration, soon come to have a second and third generation who easily grow up to be nominal Christians. The policies of the Churches vary in their ability to produce Christians vividly conscious of their own salvation. People Movements in themselves do not encourage the production of nominal Christians.

Up in the north of Pakistan there was a lowly people called Churas. They were the agricultural labourers in a mixed Muslim and Hindu civilization. They formed about 7 per cent of the total population, and were Untouchables. They were oppressed. They skinned dead cattle, cured the skins, collected the bones and sold them. They had been largely overlooked by the missionaries preaching Christ to the respectable members of the Hindu and Muslim communities, and organizing their few hard-won converts into mission station churches. Then a man named Ditt from among the Churas turned to Christ, continued to live among his people, despite their attempts at ostracism, and gradually brought his relatives to the Christian faith. The missionaries were at first dubious about admitting to the Christian fellowship these lowest of the low, lest the upper castes and the Muslims take offence and come to think of the Christian enterprise as an "untouchable" affair. But those who became Christians were pastored and taught and organized into churches. Because the converts came as groups without social dislocation the efforts of the pastors and the missionaries could be given largely to teaching and preaching. Attention did not have to be diverted to providing jobs and wives, houses and land for individual converts. The Mission to whom God had entrusted this Movement was made up of devout men and women and they gave themselves to the task. The outcome was at the end of about eighty years there are no more Churas in that section of India. *They have all become Christians.*

Whereas the Church in mission station areas often numbers no more than one-tenth of 1 per cent of the total population, in the Chura area *the Church numbers 7 per cent of the population.* There are congregations in many of the villages and a Christian witness is maintained, not by foreign missionaries, but by the citizens of Pakistan.

In Indonesia there is a large mission work. In addition to static gathered colonies there have been also a comparatively large number of God-given People Movements. In the north of Sumatra there is a flourishing Batak People Movement, numbering hundreds of thousands. In 1937, on the island of Nias, off the north-west coast of Sumatra, there were 102,000 Christians: in 1916 there were none. In the northern parts of the Celebes the Minahasa tribes were by 1940 fairly solidly Christian and in the centre the growth of People Movements was rapid. There were tribal movements toward Christ in the Moluccas, the Sangi and the Talaud Islands. Around the year 1930 between eight and ten thousand a year were being baptized in Dutch New Guinea. By 1936 the number of Protestant Christians was reported to be 1,610,533. The Roman Church also has increased by numerous People Movements. In 1937 there were 570,974 members of the Roman Catholic Church. After 1950 new large People Movements in Sumatra and after 1960 in Irian and Kalimantan have taken place.

The only instance in the entire world of a hundred thousand Muslims being won to Christ occurs in Indonesia, in the midst of these numerous People Movements. It is also interesting that in Indonesia there is apparently a bridge between the natives and the Chinese immigrants, a bridge over which Christianity can cross. If this were strengthened it might well happen that more Chinese would become Christian indirectly *via* the People Movements of Indonesia than have been won in China itself.

In Africa there have been a large number of People Movements. The day is not far off when most of Africa south of the Sahara will have been discipled.

There is an instructive case of People Movements in the Gold Coast. These have grown into a great Presbyterian Church. For nineteen years (1828-47) the Basel Mission of Switzerland battled to establish a foothold in the Gold Coast. Of the sixteen missionaries sent out ten died shortly after arrival. The daring expedient had to be adopted of bringing in eight West Indian families to demonstrate that black men could read the white man's Book, and to provide missionaries less susceptible to the ravages of the climate. During this time there had not been a single baptism. The first four baptisms were in 1847 among the Akim Abuakwa tribe. The following table shows how the Church grew.

Year	Church members	Year	Church members
1847	4	1864	12,000
1858	365	1918	24,000
1868	1581	1932	57,000
1890	9000	1953	137,000

Till about 1870 the records show evidence of the exploratory Mission Station Approach. Slaves were purchased, freed, and employed at the mission stations for instruction. Run-away slaves were given shelter. Labourers on mission buildings were settled on mission land. In 1868 there was one missionary for each thirty Christians. The Basel Mission had a gathered colony at each of its nine mission stations. But in the decade 1870 to 1880 outlying chains of families started becoming Christian, and several stations among the Tsui-speaking tribes began to be surrounded by small Christian groups in scattered villages. Schools were established in each and the groups gradually became churches. An important feature of this movement, like many other African People Movements, was that pagan parents frequently sent their children to Christian schools, desiring them to become Christians. The school thus had enormous influence.

Early growth was tribe-wise. Teacher-preachers, the slightly educated first generation Christian workers on whom so much of the discipling of the tribes of Africa has depended, were usually recruited from each tribe in which a Christian movement started. They were then trained and sent back to that tribe to teach others, shepherd the Christians and win others to Christ. Later, as Christian movements arose in practically all the tribes, they became a uniting factor in the life of the nation, and workers were appointed more or less regardless of tribal relationships.

The churches born of people movements

The most obvious result of Christian missions which have been fathering and furthering Christward movements is a tremendous host of Christian churches. It has been calculated that there are well over a hundred thousand congregations of Christians brought to a knowledge of God through recent Christian People Movements. These exist in most of the non-Christian countries.

Let us consider the unexpectedly large number of People Movements. The islands of the Pacific have been largely discipled by People Movements. India has its extensive list of movements from the Malas and Madigas, the Nagas and Garas, the Mahars and Bhils, and many others. Indonesia and Burma total well over a score of People Movements of some power. Africa has numerous tribes in which the churches are growing in tribe-wise fashion. Two new People Movements are being reported in 1980: One in Mindanao and one in Mexico. Our list might be made much larger. Each of these hundreds of People Movements is multiplying Christian congregations as it grows.

These scores of thousands of congregations have many features in common. Many members of the churches are illiterate. In some lands the percentage of illiteracy in the People Movement churches is over eighty. The pastors of the churches are usually men with about seven years of schooling plus some seminary training. The church buildings are often temporary adobe or wattle buildings, though there are many well-built churches among the older congregations. In new People Movements, the missionary usually plays an important role— starting, funding, and developing them. The pastoring of the congregations is almost entirely in the hands of the nationals however. In older, larger People Movements to-day national ministers head the Church, while missionaries work as assistants directed by the church council. The services to Christians, so marked in the Mission Station Approach, are very much curtailed. The numbers of children are so great that, aside from small unsatisfactory primary schools, few children get a chance at education. In the mission station churches it is common practice for every child to be sent, largely at mission expense, through school as far as his intelligence will allow him to go. But in the People Movement churches the bulk of the Christian population has available to it only such educational advantages as the average non-Christian shares. This makes for an illiterate and ignorant church membership.

In some African countries, the school picture is totally different. Government does its education through missions. In such lands the children of the People Movements have excellent educational opportunities and the membership of the churches is growing up largely literate.

Scattered as the congregations are it is difficult to reach them with medical aid. Cholera and small-pox epidemics, sudden death from cerebral malaria, infant maladies which carry off children like flies, and health conditions which are a scandal to the human race, are characteristic of these myriad rural churches.

Yet People Movement Churches are remarkably stable. There are reversions, specially in the early days, but on the whole, once a *people* has become Christian, it stays Christian even in the face of vigorous persecution. In addition to the faith of each individual and the courage which comes from world-wide fellowship, the very bonds of relationship and social cohesion keep weak individuals from denying the faith.

Unvalued pearls

One of the curious facts about People Movements is that they have seldom been sought or desired. Pickett records, in *Christian Mass Movements in India*, that most People Movements have actually been resisted by the leaders of the Church and mission where they started. These leaders often had grave doubts whether it was right to take in groups of individuals, many of whom seemed to have little ascertainable personal faith. Nevertheless, despite a certain degree of repression, movements did occur. One wonders what would have happened had missions from the beginning of the "Great Century" been actively searching and praying for the coming of Christward marches by the various peoples making up the population of the world.

Those People Movements which did occur were seldom really understood. The way of corporate decision was obscured by the Western preference for individual decision. The processes of perfecting the churches were confused with the process by which a people turns from idols to serve the living God. Even where there has been great growth, as in parts of Africa, faulty understanding of People Movements has resulted in much less than maximum growth and has caused needless damage to tribal life.

Christward movements of peoples are the supreme goal of missionary effort. Many who read this book will not agree with this, and, indeed, it has never been generally accepted. Yet we not only affirm it, but go further and claim that the vast stirrings of the Spirit which occur in People Movements are God-given. We dare not think of People Movements to Christ as merely social phenomena. True, we can account for some of the contributing factors which have brought them about; but there is so much that is mysterious and beyond anything we can ask or think, so much that is a product of religious faith, and so much evident working of divine Power, that we must confess that People Movements are gifts of God. It is as if in the fulness of time God gives to His servants the priceless beginning of a People Movement. If that succeeds, the Church is firmly planted. If it fails, the missionary forces are back to the preliminary stages of exploration. Yet the essential recognition that the People Movements to Christ is the supreme goal is not often made by Christian leaders. Gifts of God come and go unrecognized; while man-directed mission work is carried faithfully, doggedly forward.

It is time to recognize that when revival really begins in China, Japan, Africa, the Muslim world, and India, it will probably appear in the form of People Movements to Christ. This is the way in which Evangelical Christianity spread in Roman Catholic Europe at the time of the Reformation. It is the best way for it to spread in any land.

Five great advantages

People Movements have five considerable advantages. First, they have provided the Christian movement with permanent churches rooted in the soil of hundreds of thousands of villages. For their continued economic life they are quite independent of Western missions. They are accustomed (unfortunately too accustomed) to a low degree of education. Yet their devotion has frequently been tested in the fires of persecution and found to be pure gold. They are here to stay. They are permanent comrades on the pilgrim way.

They have the advantage of being naturally indigenous. In the Mission Station Approach the convert is brought in as an individual to a pattern dominated by the foreigner. The foreigner has set the pace and the style, often to his own dismay. But such denationalization is a very minor affair in true People Movements. In them the new Christians seldom see the missionary. They are immersed in their own cultures. Their style of clothing, of eating and of speaking continues almost unchanged. Their churches are necessarily built like their houses—and are as indigenous as anyone could wish. They cannot sing or learn foreign tunes readily, so local tunes are often used. Thus an indigenous quality, highly sought and rarely found by leaders of the Mission Station Approach churches, is obtained without effort by the People Movement churches. Church headquarters, however, need to make special efforts to keep thoroughly indigenous their training of People Movement youth and leadership.

People Movements have a third major advantage. With them "the spontaneous expansion of the Church" is natural. The phrase "spontaneous expansion" sums up the valuable contribution to missionary thinking made by Roland Allen and World Dominion. It requires that new converts be formed into churches which from the beginning are fully equipped with all spiritual authority to multiply themselves without any necessary reference to the foreign missionaries. These might be helpful as advisers or assistants but should never be necessary to the completeness of the Church or to its power of unlimited expansion. Spontaneous expansion involves a full trust in the Holy Spirit and a recognition that the ecclesiastical traditions of the older Churches are not necessarily useful to the younger Churches arising out of the missions from the West. New groups of converts are expected to multiply themselves in the same way as did the new groups of converts who were the early churches. Advocates of spontaneous expansion point out that foreign directed movements will in the end lead to sterility and antagonism to their sponsors, and that therefore the methods now being pursued, here called the Mission Station Approach, will never bring us within measurable distance of the evangelization of the world.

Desirable as spontaneous expansion is, it is a difficult ideal for the Mission Station Approach churches to achieve. They might be freed from all bonds to the Western Churches, they might be convinced that they had all the spiritual authority needed to multiply themselves, they might be filled with the Holy Spirit and abound in desire to win others to Christ, and yet—just because they form a separate people and have no organic linkages with any other neighbouring people—they would find it extremely difficult to form new churches. In People Movement churches, on the contrary, spontaneous expansion is natural. Both the desire to win their "own fold" and the opportunity to bear witness in unaffected intimate conversation are present to a high degree. There is abundant contact through which conviction can transmit itself. True, in People Movements this natural growth can be and, alas, sometimes has been, slowed down by the atmosphere and techniques of the all-pervading gathered colony approach. But once these are recognized and renounced by the leaders of the People Movement churches, it becomes comparatively easy for spontaneous expansion to occur. Missions can then, like Paul, deliberately attempt to use the relatively unplanned expansion of a Christward People Movement to achieve still greater and more significant enlargement. Thus we come to the most marked advantage of these movements.

Enormous possibilities of growth

These movements have enormous possibilities of growth. That these possibilities are to-day largely ignored and unrecognized even by the leader of the churches does not diminish either the truth or the importance of this fact.

The group movements are fringed with exterior growing points among their own peoples. As Paul discovered, the Palestinian movement had growing points in many places outside that country. Just so, every Christward movement has many possibilities of growth on its fringes. For example, the Madigas have become Christians in large numbers. They are the labourers of South India. They have migrated to many places in India and even abroad. One cannot help wondering whether a fervent proclamation by a modern Madiga St. Paul carrying the news that "We Madigas are becoming Christian by tens of thousands each year: we have found the Saviour and have as a people come into possession of the unsearchable riches of Christ," might not start Madiga Movements in many parts of the world.

People Movements also have internal growing points; that is, the unconverted pockets left by any such sweeping movement. Here the leaders of the Christian forces must be alert to see to it that strategic doorways are entered *while they are open*. Doorways remain open for about one generation. Then they close to the ready flow of the Christian religion. Until the discipling of the entire people, there will be both internal and external growing points. Both will yield large returns if cultivated.

Of rarer occurrence are the bridges to other communities, such as that over which St. Paul launched his Gentile movements. In order to be called a bridge, the connection must be large enough to provide not merely for the baptism of individuals, but for the baptism of *enough groups in a short enough time and a small enough area to create a People Movement* in the other community. More of these bridges would be found if they were assiduously sought. More would be used for the expansion of the Christian faith if leaders could be led to understand them and become skilled in their use.

The possibilities for growth in People Movements are not by any means confined to developing new movements. Leaders of People Movement churches find that after the Church has attained power and size the normal process of growth, including the baptism of individual seekers on the fringes of the congregations, often produce more quiet regular in-gatherings year after year than was the case during the period of the greatest exuberance of the movement. One might conclude that once a People Movement Church has gained a hundred thousand converts, and has become indigenous to the land and forms a noticeable proportion of the population, it is likely to keep on growing. A moderate amount of missionary assistance, at places where the churches feel their need, produces results far beyond that which those accustomed to the mission station tradition would consider possible.

Providing the normal pattern of Christianization

The fifth advantage is that these movements provide a sound pattern of becoming Christian. Being a Christian is seen to mean not change in standard of living made possible by foreign funds, but change in inner character made possible by the power of God. In well-nurtured People Movement Churches, it is seen to mean the regular worship of God, the regular hearing of the Bible, the giving to the church, the discipline of the congregation, the spiritual care exercised by the pastor, habits of prayer and personal devotion and the eradication of un-Christian types of behaviour. This life, centering in the village church, often built by the Christians themselves, is seen to be the main feature of the Christian religion. There are no impressive institutions to divert attention from the central fact. Christians become "people with churches, who worship God" rather than "people with hospitals who know medicine," or "people with schools who get good jobs." The health of the Christian movement requires that the normal pattern be well known, not merely to the non-Christian peoples, but to the leaders of Church and mission and to the rank and file of members. The People Movement supplies the pattern which can be indefinitely reproduced. It is the pattern which with minor variations has obtained throughout history.

Study Questions

1. Briefly define the term "the bridges of God" and explain the significance of these bridges for mission strategy.

2. Are group decisions valid? Why or why not? Explain the strategic importance of encouraging "multi-individual" decisions.

16

The New Macedonia:
A Revolutionary New Era in Mission
Begins

Ralph D. Winter

*Donald McGavran commented, "At the International Congress on World Evangeli-
zation, Dr. Ralph Winter proved beyond any reasonable doubt that in the world today
2,700,000,000 men and women cannot hear the Gospel by 'near neighbor evangelism.'
They can hear it only by E-2 and E-3 evangelists who cross cultural, linguistic and geographical barriers, patiently learn that other culture and language, across the decades
preach the Gospel by word and deed, and multiply reproductive and responsible Christian
churches." The following article is the text of this address, given at the July 1974 Lausanne Congress. McGavran added, "Nothing said at Lausanne had more meaning for the
Expansion of Christianity between now and the year 2000."*

In recent years, a serious misunderstanding has crept into the thinking of
many evangelicals. Curiously, it is based on a number of wonderful facts: the
Gospel has now gone to the ends of the earth. Christians have now fulfilled the
Great Commission in at least a geographical sense. At this moment of history we
can acknowledge with great respect and pride those evangelists of every nation
who have gone before us and whose sacrificial efforts and heroic accomplish-
ments have made Christianity by far the world's largest and most widespread
religion, with a Christian church on every continent and in practically every
country. This is no hollow victory. Now more than at any time since Jesus
walked the shores of Galilee, we know with complete confidence that the Gospel
is for all men, that it makes sense in any language and that it is not merely a religion of the Mediterranean or of the West.

This is all true. On the other hand, many Christians as a result have the

After serving ten years as a missionary among Mayan Indians in
western Guatemala, Ralph D. Winter spent the next ten years as a
Professor of Missions at the School of World Mission at Fuller Theological Seminary. He is the founder of the U.S. Center for World Mission in Pasadena, California, a cooperative center focused on people
groups still lacking a culturally relevant church. Winter has also
been instrumental in the formation of the movement called Theological Education by Extension, the William Carey Library publishing
house, the American Society of Missiology, the Perspectives Study
Program and the International Society for Frontier Missiology. Since
March of 1990 he has been the President of the William Carey International University.

impression that the job is now nearly done and that to finish it we need only to forge ahead in local evangelism on the part of the now worldwide church reaching out wherever it has already been planted. Many Christian organizations ranging widely from the World Council of Churches to many U.S. denominations, even some evangelical groups, have rushed to the conclusion that we may now abandon traditional missionary strategy and count on local Christians everywhere to finish the job.

This is why *evangelism* is the one great password to evangelical unity today. Not everyone can agree on foreign mission strategies, but more people than ever agree on *evangelism* because that seems to be the one obvious job that remains to be done. All right! There is nothing wrong with evangelism. Most conversions must inevitably take place as the result of some Christian witnessing to a near neighbor and that is evangelism.

The awesome problem is the additional truth that most non-Christians in the world today are not culturally near neighbors of any Christians and that it will take a special kind of "cross-cultural" evangelism to reach them.

CROSS-CULTURAL EVANGELISM: THE CRUCIAL NEED

Examples of the Need

Let us approach this subject with some graphic illustrations. I am thinking, for example, of the hundreds of thousands of Christians in Pakistan. Almost all of them are people who have never been Muslims and do not have the kind of relationship with the Muslim community that encourages witnessing. Yet they live in a country that is 97 per cent Muslim! The Muslims, on their part, have bad attitudes toward the stratum of society represented by the Christians. One group of Christians has boldly called itself *The Church of Pakistan*. Another group of Christians goes by the name *The Presbyterian Church of Pakistan*. While these are "national" churches in the sense that they are part of their countries, they can hardly be called *national* churches if this phrase implies that they are culturally related to that vast bloc of people who constitute the other 97 per cent of the country, namely, the Muslims. Thus, although the Muslims are geographically near neighbors of these Christians they are not *cultural near-neighbors* and thus *normal evangelism* will not do the job.

Or take the Church of South India, a large church which has brought together the significant missionary efforts of many churches over the last century. But while it is called *The Church of South India*, 95 per cent of its members come from only five out of the more that 100 social classes (castes) in South India. Ordinary evangelism on the part of existing Christians will readily persuade men and women of those same five social classes. However, it would be much more difficult—it is in fact *another kind of evangelism*—for this church to make great gains within the 95 other social classes which make up the vast bulk of the population.

Or take the great Batak church in Northern Sumatra. Here is one of the famous churches of Indonesia. Its members have been doing a great deal of evangelism among fellow Bataks of whom there are still many thousands whom they can reach without learning a foreign language, and among whom they can work with the maximum efficiency of direct contact and understanding. But at the same time, the vast majority of all the people in Indonesia speak other languages and are of other ethnic units. For the Batak Christians of Northern Sumatra to win people to Christ from other parts of Indonesia will be a distinctly different kind of task. It is *another kind of evangelism.*

Or take the great church of Nagaland in Northeast India. Years ago, American missionaries from the plains of Assam reached up into the Naga hills and won some of the Ao Nagas. Then these Ao Nagas won practically their whole tribe to Christ. Next thing, Ao Nagas won members of the nearby Santdam Naga tribe that spoke a sister language. These new Santdam Naga Christians then proceeded to win almost the whole of their tribe. This process went on until the majority of all fourteen Naga tribes became Christian. Now that most of Nagaland is Christian—even the officials of the state government are Christian—there is the desire to witness elsewhere in India. But for these Nagaland Christians to win other people in India is as much a foreign mission task as it is for Englishmen, Koreans or Brazilians to evangelize in India. This is one reason why it is such a new and unprecedented task for the Nagas to evangelize the rest of India. Indian citizenship is one advantage the Naga Christians have as compared to people from other countries, but citizenship does not make it easier for them to learn any of the hundreds of totally foreign languages in the rest of India.

In other words, for Nagas to evangelize other peoples in India, they will need to employ a radically different kind of evangelism. The easiest kind of evangelism, when they used their own language to win their own people, is now mainly in the past. The second kind of evangelism was not a great deal more difficult—where they won people of neighboring Naga tribes, whose languages were sister languages. The third kind of evangelism, needed to win people in far-off parts of India, will be much more difficult.

Different Kinds of Evangelism

Let's give labels to these different kinds of evangelism. Where an Ao Naga won another Ao, let us call that *E-1 evangelism.* Where an Ao went across a tribal language boundary to a sister language and won the *Santdam,* we'll call it *E-2 evangelism* . (The E-2 task is not as easy and requires different techniques.) But then if an Ao Naga goes to another region of India, to a totally strange language, for example, Telegu, Korhu or Bhili, his task will be considerably more difficult than E-1 or even E-2 evangelism. We will call it *E-3 evangelism.*

Let us try out this terminology in another country. Take Taiwan. There, also, there are different kinds of people. The majority are Minnans, who were there before a flood of Mandarin-speaking people came across from the mainland. Then there is the huge bloc of Hakka-speaking people who came from the mainland much earlier. Up in the mountains, however, a few hundred thousand aboriginal peoples speak Malayo-Polynesian dialects entirely different from Chinese. Now if a Mainlander Chinese Christian wins others from the mainland, that's E-1 evangelism. If he wins a Minnan Taiwanese or a Hakka, that's E-2 evangelism. If he wins someone from the hill tribes, that's E-3 evangelism, and remember, E-3 is a much more complex task, performed at a greater *cultural* distance.

Thus far we have only referred to language differences, but for the purpose of defining evangelistic strategy, any kind of obstacle, any kind of communication barrier affecting evangelism is significant. In Japan for example, practically everybody speaks Japanese, and there aren't radically different dialects of Japanese comparable to the different dialects of Chinese. But there are social differences which make it very difficult for people from one group to win others of a different social class. In Japan, as in India, social differences often turn out to be more important in evangelism than language differences. Japanese Christians thus have not only an E-1 sphere of contact, but also E-2 spheres that are harder to reach. Missionaries going from Japan to other parts of the world to work with non-Japanese with totally different languages are doing an evangelistic task on the E-3 basis.

Lastly, let me give an example from my own experience. I speak English as a native language. For ten years, I lived and worked in Central America, for most of the time in Guatemala, where Spanish is the official language, but where a majority of the people speak some dialect of the Mayan family of aboriginal languages. I had two languages to learn. Spanish has a 60 per cent overlap in vocabulary with English, so I had no trouble learning that language. Along with the learning of Spanish, I became familiar with the extension of European culture into the New World, and it was not particularly difficult to understand the lifeways of the kind of people who spoke Spanish. However, because Spanish was so easy by comparison, learning the Mayan language in our area was, I found, enormously more difficult. In our daily work, switching from English to Spanish to a Mayan language made me quite aware of the three different "cultural distances." When I spoke of Christ to a Peace Corpsman in English, I was doing E-1 evangelism. When I spoke to a Guatemalan in Spanish, it was E-2 evangelism. When I spoke to an Indian in the Mayan language, it was the much more difficult E-3 evangelism.

Now where I live in Southern California, most of my contacts are in the E-1 sphere, but if I evangelize among the million who speak Spanish, I must use E-2 evangelism. Were I to learn the Navajo language and speak of Christ to some of the 30,000 Navajo Indians who live in Los Angeles, I would be doing E-3 evangelism. Reaching Cantonese-speaking refugees from Hong Kong with the Good News of Christ would also be, for me, an E-3 task. Note, however, that what for me is E-3 could be only E-2 for someone else. American-born Chinese would find Hong Kong refugees only an E-2 task.

Everyone who is here in this Congress has his own E-1 sphere in which he speaks his own language and builds on all the intuition which derives from his experience within his own culture. Then perhaps for almost all of us there is an E-2 sphere—groups of people who speak languages that are a little different, or who are involved in culture patterns sufficiently in contrast with our own as to make communication more difficult. Such people can be reached with a little extra trouble and with sincere attempts, but it will take us out of our way to reach them. More important, they are people who, once converted, will not feel at home in the church which we attend. In fact, they may grow faster spiritually if they can find Christian fellowship among people of their own kind. More significant to evangelism: it is quite possible that with their own fellowship, they are more likely to win others of their own social grouping. Finally, each of us here in Lausanne has an E-3 sphere: most languages and cultures of the world are totally strange to us; they are at the maximum cultural distance. If we attempt to evangelize at this E-3 distance, we have a long uphill climb in order to be able to make sense to anyone.

In summary, the master pattern of the expansion of the Christian movement is first for special E-2 and E-3 efforts to cross cultural barriers into new communities and to establish strong, on-going, vigorously evangelizing denominations, and then for that national church to carry the work forward on the really high-powered E-1 level. We are thus forced to believe that until every tribe and tongue has a strong, powerfully evangelizing church in it, and thus, an E-1 witness within it, E-2 and E-3 efforts coming from outside are still essential and highly urgent.

CROSS-CULTURAL EVANGELISM: THE BIBLICAL MANDATE

At this point, let us ask what the Bible says about all this. Are these cultural differences something the Bible takes note of? Is this something which ought to occupy our time and attention? Is this matter of cultural distance something which is so important that it fits into a Congress like this? Let us turn to the Bible and see what it has to say.

Acts 1:8: An Emphasis on Cultural Distance

Let us go to that vital passage in the first chapter of Acts, so central to this whole Congress, where Jesus refers his disciples to the worldwide scope of God's concern—"in Jerusalem, in all Judea, and in Samaria and unto the uttermost part of the earth." If it were not for this passage (and all the other passages in the Bible which support it), we would not even be gathered here today. Without this biblical mandate, there could not have been a Congress on World Evangelization. It is precisely this task—the task of discipling all the nations—which includes all of us and unifies all of us in a single, common endeavor. Notice, however, that Jesus does not merely include the whole world. He distinguishes between different parts of that world and does so according to the relative distance of those people from his hearers. On another occasion he simply said, "Go ye into all the world," but in this passage he has divided that task into significant components.

At first glance you might think that he is merely speaking geographically, but with more careful study, it seems clear that he is not talking merely about *geographical* distance, but about *cultural* distance. The clue is the appearance of the word *Samaria* in this sequence. Fortunately, we have special insight into what Jesus meant by *Samaria*, since the New Testament records in an extended passage the precise nature of the evangelistic problem Jews faced in trying to reach the Samaritans. I speak of the well-known story of Jesus and the woman at the well. Samaria was not far away in the geographical sense. Jesus had to pass there whenever he went from Galilee to Jerusalem. Yet when Jesus spoke to this Samaritan woman, it was immediately obvious that he faced a special cultural obstacle. While she was apparently close enough linguistically for him to be able to understand her speech, her very first reply focused on the significant difference between the Jews and the Samaritans— they worshipped in different places.

Jesus did not deny this profound difference, but accepted it and transcended it by pointing out the human cultural limitations of both the Jewish and the Samaritan modes of worship. He spoke to her heart and by-passed the cultural differences.

Meanwhile, the disciples looking on were mystified and troubled. Even had they understood that God was interested in Samaritans, they probably would have had difficulty grappling with the cultural differences. Even if they had tried to do so, they might not have been sensitive enough to by-pass certain differences and go directly to the heart of the matter—which was the heart of the woman.

Paul acted on the same principle when he sought to evangelize the Greeks, who were at an even greater cultural distance. Just imagine how shocked some of the faithful Jewish Christians were when they heard rumors that Paul by-passed circumcision, one of the most important cultural differences to the Jews, even Christian Jews, and went to the heart of the matter. He was reported to them as saying, "Neither circumcision nor uncircumcision is worth anything in comparison to being in Christ, believing in him, being baptized in his name, being filled with his Spirit, belonging to his body."

At this point we must pause long enough to distinguish between cultural distance and walls of prejudice. There may have been high *walls of prejudice* involved where Jews encountered Samaritans, but it is obvious that the Greeks, who did not even worship the same God, were at a far greater *cultural distance* from the Jews than were the Samaritans, who were close cousins by comparison. It is curious to note that sometimes those who are closest to us are hardest to reach. For example, a Jewish Christian trying to evangelize would understand a Samaritan more easily than he would understand a Greek, but he would be more likely to be hated or detested by a Samaritan than by a Greek. In Belfast today, for example, the problem is not so much cultural distance as prejudice. Suppose a Protestant who has grown up in Belfast were to witness for Christ to a nominal Belfast Catholic and an East Indian. He would more easily understand his Catholic compatriot, but might face less prejudice from the East Indian. Generally speaking, then, cultural distance is more readily traversed than high walls of prejudice are climbed.

But, returning to our central passage, it is clear that Jesus is referring primarily neither to geography nor walls of prejudice when he lists *Judea, Samaria,* and *the ends of the earth.* Had he been talking about prejudice, Samaria would have come last. He would have said, "in Judea, in all the world, and *even in Samaria."* It seems likely he is taking into account cultural distance as the primary factor. Thus, as we today endeavor to fulfill Jesus' ancient command, we do well to be sensitive to *cultural distance* . His distinctions must underlie our strategic thinking about the evangelization of the whole world.

Evangelism in the Jerusalem and Judea sphere would seem to be what we have called *E-l evangelism,* where the only barrier his listeners had to cross in their proposed evangelistic efforts was the boundary between the Christian community and the world immediately outside, involving the same language and culture. This is "near neighbor" evangelism. Whoever we are, wherever we live in the world, we all have some near neighbors to whom we can witness without learning any foreign language or taking into account any special cultural differences. This is the kind of evangelism we usually talk about. This is the kind of evangelism most meetings on evangelism talk about. One of the great differences between this Congress and all previous congresses on evangelism is its determined stress on *crossing cultural frontiers where necessary* in order to evangelize the whole earth. The mandate of this Congress does not allow us to focus merely on Jerusalem and Judea.

The second sphere to which Jesus referred is that of the Samaritan. The Bible account shows that although it was relatively easy for Jesus and his disciples to make themselves understood to the Samaritans, the Jew and the Samaritan were divided from each other by a frontier consisting of dialectal distinctions and some other very significant cultural differences. This was *E-2 evangelism*, because it involved crossing a *second* frontier. First, it involved crossing the frontier we have referred to in describing E-1 evangelism, the frontier between the church and the world. Secondly, it involved crossing a frontier constituted by significant (but not monumental) differences of language and culture. Thus we call it *E-2 evangelism*.

E-3 evangelism, as we have used the phrase, involves even greater cultural distance. This is the kind of evangelism that is necessary in the third sphere of Jesus' statement, "to the uttermost part of the earth." The people needing to be reached in this third sphere live, work, talk, and think in languages and cultural patterns utterly different from those native to the evangelist. The average Jewish Christian, for example, would have had no head start at all in dealing with people beyond Samaria. If reaching Samaritans seemed like crossing two frontiers (thus called E-2 evangelism), reaching totally different people must have seemed like crossing three, and it is reasonable to call such a task *E-3 evangelism*.

One Christian's Judea is Another Christian's Samaria

It is very important to understand the full significance of the distinctions Jesus is making. Since he was not talking about geographical, but cultural distance, the general value of what he said has striking strategic application today. Jesus did not mean that all down through history Samaria specifically would be an object of special attention. One Christian's Judea might be another Christian's Samaria. Take Paul, for example. Although he was basically a Jew, he no doubt found it much easier to traverse the cultural distance to the Greeks than did Peter, because unlike Peter, Paul was much better acquainted with the Greek world. Using the terminology we have employed, where an E-1 task is near, E-2 is close, and E-3 is far (in cultural, not geographical distance), we can say that reaching Greeks meant working at an E-2 distance for Paul; but for Peter it meant working at an E-3 distance. For Luke, who was himself a Greek, reaching Greeks was to work only at an E-1 distance. Thus what was distant for Peter was near for Luke. And vice versa: reaching Jews would have been E-1 for Peter, but more likely E-3 for Luke. It may well be that God sent Paul rather than Peter to the Gentiles partially because Paul was closer culturally. By the same token, Paul, working among the Greeks at an E-2 distance, was handicapped by comparison with E-1 "nationals" like Luke, Titus, and Epaphroditus; and, as a matter of evangelistic strategy, he wisely turned things over to "national" workers as soon as he possibly could. Paul himself, being a Jew, often began his work in a new city in the Jewish synagogue where he himself was on an E-1 basis and where, with the maximum power of E-l communication, he was able to speak forcefully without any non-Jewish accent.

Let us straightforwardly concede right here that, all other things being equal, the national leader always has a communication advantage over the foreigner. When the evangelists went from the plains of Assam up into the Naga hills, it must have been very much harder for them to win Ao Nagas than it was for Ao Naga Christians to do so, once a start had been made. When the first German missionaries preached to the Bataks, they must have had a far greater problem than when the faith, once planted, was transmitted from Batak to Batak. E-l evangelism—where a person communicates to his own people—is obviously the most potent kind of evangelism. People need to hear the Gospel in their own language. Can we believe God intends for them to hear it from people who speak without a trace of accent? The foreign missionary communicator may be good, but he is not good enough. If it is so important for Americans to have thirty translations of the New Testament to choose from, and even a "Living Bible," which allows the Bible to speak in colloquial English, then why must many peoples around the world suffer along with a Bible that was translated for them by a foreigner, and thus almost inevitably speaks to them in halting phrases?

This is why the easiest, most obvious surge forward in evangelism in the world today will come if Christian believers in every part of the world are moved to reach outside their churches and win their cultural near neighbors to Christ. They are better able to do that than any foreign missionary. It is a tragic perversion of Jesus' strategy if we continue to send missionaries to do the job that local Christians can do better. There is no excuse for a missionary in the pulpit when a national can do the job better. There is no excuse for a missionary to be doing evangelism on an E-3 basis, at an E-3 distance from people, when there are local Christians who are effectively winning the same people as part of their E-l sphere.

In view of the profound truth that (other things being equal) E-l evangelism is more powerful than E-2 or E-3 evangelism, it is easy to see how some people have erroneously concluded that E-3 evangelism is therefore out-of-date, due to the wonderful fact that there are now Christians throughout the whole world. It is with this perspective that major denominations in the U.S. have at some points acted on the premise that there is no more need for missionaries of the kind who leave home to go to a foreign country and struggle with a totally strange language and culture. Their premise is that "there are Christians over there already." With the drastic fall-off in the value of the U.S. dollar and the tragic shrinking of U.S. church budgets, some U.S. denominations have had to curtail their missionary activity to an unbelievable extent, and they have in part tried to console themselves by saying that it is time for the national church to take over. In our response to this situation, we must happily agree that wherever there are local Christians effectively evangelizing, there is nothing more potent than E-l evangelism.

However, the truth about the superior power of E-1 evangelism must not obscure the obvious fact that E-1 evangelism is literally *impossible* where there are no witnesses within a given language or cultural group. Jesus, as a Jew, would not have had to witness directly to that Samaritan woman had there been a local Samaritan Christian who had already reached her. In the case of the Ethiopian eunuch, we can conjecture that it might have been better for an Ethiopian Christian than for Philip to do the witnessing, but there had to be an initial contact by a non-Ethiopian in order for the E-1 process to be set in motion. This kind of initial, multiplying work is the primary task of the missionary when he rightly understands his job. He must decrease and the national leader must increase. Hopefully Jesus' E-2 witness set in motion E-1 witnessing in that Samaritan town. Hopefully Philip's E-2 witness to the Ethiopian set in motion E-1 witnessing back in Ethiopia. If that Ethiopian was an Ethiopian Jew, the E-1 community back in Ethiopia might not have been very large, and might not have effectively reached the non-Jewish Ethiopians. As a matter of fact, scholars believe that the Ethiopian church today is the result of a much later missionary thrust that reached, by E-3 evangelism, clear through to the ethnic Ethiopians.

Thus, in the Bible, as in our earlier illustrations from modern mission history, we arrive at the same summary:

E-1 Powerful, but E-3 Essential

The master pattern of the expansion of the Christian movement is first for special E-2 and E-3 efforts to cross cultural barriers into new communities and to establish strong, on-going, vigorously evangelizing denominations, and then for that national church to carry the work forward on the really high-powered E-1 level. We are thus forced to believe that until every tribe and tongue has a strong, powerfully evangelizing church in it, and thus an E-1 witness within it, E-2 and E-3 efforts coming from outside are still essential and highly urgent. From this perspective, how big is the remaining task?

CROSS-CULTURAL EVANGELISM: THE IMMENSITY OF THE TASK

Unfortunately, most Christians have only a very foggy idea of just how many peoples there are in the world among whom there is no E-1 witness. But fortunately, preparatory studies for this Congress have seriously raised this question: Are there any tribal tongues and linguistic units which have not yet been penetrated by the Gospel? If so, where? How many? Who can reach them? Even these preliminary studies indicate that cross-cultural evangelism must still be the highest priority. Far from being a task that is now out-of-date, the shattering truth is that at least four out of five non-Christians in the world today are beyond the reach of *any* Christian's E-1 evangelism.

"People Blindness"

Why is this fact not more widely known? I'm afraid that all our exultation about the fact that every *country* of the world has been penetrated has allowed many to suppose that every *culture* has by now been penetrated. This misunderstanding is a malady so widespread that it deserves a special name. Let us call it "people blindness"—that is, blindness to the existence of separate *peoples* within *countries*—a blindness, I might add, which seems more prevalent in the U.S. and among U.S. missionaries than anywhere else. The Bible rightly translated could have made this plain to us. The "nations" to which Jesus often referred were mainly ethnic groups within the single political structure of the Roman government. The various nations represented on the day of Pentecost were for the most part not *countries* but *peoples*. In the Great Commission as it is found in Matthew, the phrase "make disciples of all *ethne* (peoples)" does not let us off the hook once we have a church in every country—God wants a strong church within every people!

"People blindness" is what prevents us from noticing the sub-groups within a country which are significant to development of effective evangelistic strategy. Society will be seen as a complex mosaic, to use McGavran's phrase, once we recover from "people blindness." But until we all recover from this kind of blindness, we may confuse the legitimate desire for church or national unity with the illegitimate goal of uniformity. God apparently loves diversity of certain kinds. But in any case this diversity means evangelists have to work harder. The little ethnic and cultural pieces of the complex mosaic which is human society are the very subdivisions which isolate four out of five non-Christians in the world today from an E-1 contact by existing Christians. The immensity of the cross-cultural task is thus seen in the fact that in Africa and Asia alone, one calculation has it that there are 1,993 million people virtually without a witness. The immensity of the task, however, lies not only in its bigness.

Need for E-2 Evangelism in the United States

The problem is more serious than retranslating the Great Commission in such a way that the peoples, not the countries, become the targets for evangelism. The immensity of the task is further underscored by the far greater complexity of the E-2 and E-3 task. Are we in America, for example, prepared for the fact that most non-Christians yet to be won to Christ (even in our country) will not fit readily into the kinds of churches we now have? The bulk of American churches in the North are middle-class, and the blue-collar worker won't go near them. Evangelistic crusades may attract thousands to big auditoriums and win people in their homes through television, but a large proportion of the newly converted, unless already familiar with the church, may drift away simply because there is no church where they will feel at home. Present-day American Christians can wait forever in their cozy, middle-class pews for the world to come to Christ and join them. But unless they adopt E-2 methods and both *go out after these people and help them found their own churches*, evangelism in America will face, and is already facing, steadily diminishing returns. You may say that there are still plenty of people who don't go to church who are of the same cultural background as those in church. This is true. But there are many, many more people of differing cultural backgrounds who, even if they were to become fervent Christians, would not feel comfortable in existing churches.

If the U.S.—where you can drive 3,000 miles and still speak the same language—is nevertheless a veritable cultural mosaic viewed evangelistically, then surely most other countries face similar problems. Even in the U.S., local radio stations employ more than forty different languages. In addition to these language differences, there are many equally significant social and cultural differences. Language differences are by no means the highest barriers to communication.

The need, in E-2 evangelism, for whole new worshipping groups is underscored by the phenomenon of the Jesus People, who have founded hundreds of new congregations. The vast Jesus People Movement in the U.S. does not speak a different language so much as it involves a very different life-style and thus a different style of worship. Many American churches have attempted to employ the guitar music and many of the informal characteristics of the Jesus Movement, but there is a limit to which a single congregation can go with regard to speaking many languages and employing many life-styles. Who knows what has happened to many of the "mods" and "rockers" who were won as a result of Billy Graham's London Crusades? On the one hand, the existing churches were understandably culturally distant from such people, and on the other hand, there may not have been adequate E-2 methods employed so as to form those converts into whole new congregations. It is this aspect of E-2 evangelism which makes the cross-cultural task immensely harder. Yet it is essential. Let us take one more well-known example.

When John Wesley evangelized the miners of England, the results were conserved in whole new worshipping congregations. There probably would never have been a Methodist movement had he not encouraged these lower-class people to meet in their own Christian gatherings, sing their own kind of songs, and associate with their own kind of people. Furthermore, apart from this E-2 technique, such people would not have been able to win others and expand the Christian movement in this new level of society at such an astonishing rate of speed. The results rocked and permanently changed England. It rocked the existing churches, too. Not very many people favored Wesley's contact with the miners. Fewer still agreed that miners should have separate churches!

A Clear Procedural Distinction

At this point we may do well to make a clear procedural distinction between E-1 and E-2 evangelism. We have observed that the E-2 sphere begins where the people you have reached are of sufficiently different backgrounds from those of people in existing churches that they need to form their own worshipping congregations in order best to win others of their own kind. John, chapter four, tells us that "many Samaritans from that city believed in him (Jesus) because of the woman's testimony." Jesus evangelized the woman by working with great sensitivity as an E-2 witness; she turned around and reached others in her town by efficient E-1 communication. Suppose Jesus had told her she had to go and worship with the Jews. Even if she had obeyed him and gone to worship with the Jews, she would on that basis have been terribly handicapped in winning others in her city. Jesus may actually have avoided the issue of where to worship and with what distant Christians to associate. That would come up later. Thus the Samaritans who believed the woman's testimony then made the additional step of inviting a Jew to be with them for two days. He still did not try to make them into Jews. He knew he was working at an E-2 distance, and that the fruits could best be conserved (and additional people best be won) if they were allowed to build *their own fellowship of faith.*

A further distinction might be drawn between the kind of cultural differences Jesus was working with in Samaria and the kind of differences resulting from the so-called "generation gap." But it really does not matter, in evangelism, whether the distance is cultural, linguistic, or an age difference. No matter what the reason for the difference or the permanence of the difference, or the perceived rightness or the wrongness of the difference, the procedural dynamics of E-2 evangelism techniques are quite similar. The E-2 sphere begins whenever it is necessary to found a new congregation. In the Philippines we hear of youth founding churches. In Singapore we know of ten recently established youth break-away congregations. Hopefully, eventually, age-focused congregations will draw closer to existing churches, but as long as there is a generation gap of serious proportions, such specialized fellowships are able to win many more alienated youth by being allowed to function considerably on their own. It is a good place to begin.

Whatever we may decide about the kind of E-2 evangelism that allows people to meet separately who are different due to temporary *age differences*, the chief factors in the immensity of the cross-cultural task are the much more profound and possibly permanent *cultural differences*. Here, too, some will always say that true cross-cultural evangelism is going too far. At this point we must risk being misunderstood in order to be absolutely honest. All around the world, special evangelistic efforts continue to be made which often break across culture barriers. People from these other cultures are won, sometimes only one at a time, sometimes in small groups. The problem is not in winning them; it is in the cultural obstacles to proper follow-up. Existing churches may cooperate up to a point with evangelistic campaigns, but they do not contemplate allowing the evangelistic organizations to stay long enough to gather these people together in churches of their own. They mistakenly think that being joined to Christ ought to include joining existing churches. Yet if proper E-2 methods were employed, these few converts, who would merely be considered somewhat odd additions to existing congregations, *could* be infusions of new life into whole new pockets of society where the church does not now exist at all!

The Muslim and Hindu Spheres

A discussion of the best ways to organize for cross-cultural evangelism is beyond the scope of this paper. It would entail a great deal of space to chart the successes and failures of different approaches by churches and by para-church organizations. It may well be that E-2 and E-3 methods are best launched by specialized agencies and societies working loyally and harmoniously with the churches. Here we must focus on the nature of cross-cultural evangelism and its high priority in the face of the immensity of the task. Aside from the Chinese mainland sector, the two greatest spheres in which there is a tragic paucity of effective cross-cultural evangelism are the Muslim and the Hindu. Our concluding words will center in these two groups, which, in aggregate, number well over one billion people.

As we have earlier mentioned, a converted Muslim will not feel welcome in the usual Presbyterian Church in Pakistan. Centuries-old suspicions on both sides of the Muslim-Hindu fence make it almost impossible for Muslims, even converted Muslims, to be welcomed into the churches of former Hindu peoples. The present Christians of Pakistan (almost all formerly Hindu) have not been at all successful in integrating converted Muslims into their congregations. Furthermore, it is not likely even to occur to them that Muslims can be converted and form their own separate congregations. The enormous tragedy is that this kind of impasse postpones serious evangelism along E-2 lines wherever in the world there are any of the 664 million Muslims. Far to the east of Mecca, in certain parts of Indonesia, enough Muslims have become Christians that they have not been forced one by one to join Christian congregations of another culture. Far to the west of Mecca, in the middle of Africa on some of the islands of Lake Chad, we have reports that a few former Muslims, now Christians, still pray to Christ five times a day and worship in Christian churches on Friday, the Muslim day of worship. These two isolated examples suggest that Muslims can become Christians without necessarily undergoing serious and arbitrary cultural dislocation. There may be a wide, new, open door to the Muslims if we will be as cross-culturally alert as Paul was, who did not require the Greeks to become Jews in order to become acceptable to God.

Vast *new* realms of opportunity may exist in India, too, where local prejudice in many cases may forestall effective "near-neighbor" evangelism. Indians coming from a greater distance might by E-2 or E-3 methods be able to escape the local stigmas and establish churches within the 100 or so social classes as yet untouched. It is folly for evangelists to ignore such factors of prejudices, and their existence greatly increases the immensity of our task. Prejudice of this kind adds to cultural distance such obstacles that E-2 evangelism, where prejudice is deep, is often more difficult than E-3 evangelism. In other words, scholarly, well-educated Christians from Nagaland or Kerala might possibly be more successful in reaching middle-class Hindus in South India with the Gospel than Christians from humble classes who have grown up in that area and speak the same language, but are stigmatized in local relationships. But who dares to point this out? It is ironic that national Christians all over the non-Western world are increasingly aware that they do not need to be Westernized to be Christian, yet they may in some cases be slow to sense that the challenge of cross-cultural evangelism requires them to allow other people in their own areas to have the same liberty of self-determination in establishing culturally divergent churches of their own.

In any case, the opportunities are just as immense as the task. If 600 million Muslims await a more enlightened evangelism, there are also 500 million Hindus who today face monumental obstacles to becoming Christians other than the profound spiritual factors inherent in the Gospel. One keen observer is convinced that 100 million middle-class Hindus await the opportunity to become Christians—but there are no churches for them to join which respect their dietary habits and customs. Is the kingdom of God meat and drink? To go to the special efforts required by E-2 and E-3 evangelism is not to let down the standards and make the Gospel easy—it is to disentangle the irrelevant elements and to make the Gospel clear. Perhaps everyone is not able to do this special kind of work. True, many more E-1 evangelists will eventually be necessary to finish the task. But the highest priority in evangelism today is to develop the cross-cultural knowledge and sensitivities involved in E-2 and E-3 evangelism. Where necessary, evangelists from a distance must be called into the task. Nothing must blind us to the immensely important fact that at least *four-fifths* of the non-Christians in the world today will never have any straightforward opportunity to become Christians unless the Christians themselves go more than halfway in the specialized tasks of cross-cultural evangelism. Here is our highest priority.

QUESTIONS ABOUT THE THEOLOGICAL NATURE OF THE TASK

The main theological question, raised more often than any other, is so profound that I feel I must devote my remaining time to it. The question was stated in many ways in your response papers, but is basically this: "Will not our unity in Christ be destroyed if we follow a concept of cross-cultural evangelization which is willing to set up separate churches for different cultural groups within the same geographical area?" It is only with humble dependence upon the Holy Spirit to honor the Word of God above the secular influences to which we all are subject, that I dare to proceed with a perspective which I myself could not understand nor accept until several years ago. I was brought up in the United States, where for many people integration is almost like a civil religion, where such people almost automatically assume that eventually everyone will speak English and really shouldn't speak any other language. To me cultural diversity between countries was a nuisance, but cultural diversity within a country was simply an evil to be overcome. I had no thought of excluding anyone from *any* church (and I still do not), but I did unconsciously assume that the best thing that could happen to Black, White, Chicano, etc., was that they all would eventually come to the White, Anglo-Saxon, Protestant church and learn to do things the way that I felt was most proper.

Following this kind of American culture-Christianity, many missionaries have assumed that there ought to be just one national church in a country—even if this means none at all for certain sub-groups. Such missionaries, in all earnestness, have assumed that the denominational pluralism in their own home country is simply a sin to be avoided. They have assumed that *Southern* Baptists aren't necessary in *Northern* India, even though, as a matter of fact, in Boston today most of the Anglo churches have been sitting around waiting for the Arabs and the Japanese to come to their churches, and it has taken Southern Baptists to go into Northern United States and plant Arab churches and Japanese churches, and Portuguese churches, and Greek churches, and Polish churches, right under the nose of hundreds of good-willed Anglo churches which have been patiently waiting for these people to assimilate to the Anglo way of life. With one or two fine exceptions, the Anglo churches, with all their evangelistic zeal, simply did not have the insight to do this kind of E-2 and E-3 evangelism.

Christian Unity and Christian Liberty

For my own part, after many years of struggling with this question, I am now no less concerned than before about the unity and fellowship of the Christian movement across all ethnic and cultural lines, but I realize now that Christian unity cannot be healthy if it infringes upon Christian liberty. In terms of evangelism, we must ask whether the attempt to extend, for example in Pakistan, an external form into the Muslim culture is more important than making the Gospel clear to such peoples within their own culture. Can we not condition our desire for uniformity by an even greater desire for effective preaching of the Gospel? I personally have come to believe that unity does not have to require uniformity, and I believe that there must be such a thing as healthy diversity in human society *and in the Christian world church.* I see the world church as the gathering together of a great symphony orchestra where we don't make every new person coming in play a violin in order to fit in with the rest. We invite the people to come in to play the same score—the Word of God—but to play their own instruments, and in this way there will issue forth a heavenly sound that will grow in the splendor and glory of God as each new instrument is added.

The example of the apostle Paul

But some of you have said, "OK, if that is what you mean, what about the Apostle Paul? Did he set up separate congregations for masters and slaves?" I really don't know. I don't think so. But that does not mean that didn't happen. In a recent monograph by Paul Minear entitled *The Obedience of Faith,* the author suggests that in Rome there were probably five separate congregations of Christians, who numbered a total 3000, and that Paul's letter to the Romans was written actually to a cluster of churches in the city of Rome. He also suggests that these churches were very different from each other, some being composed almost entirely of Jewish Christians, and others (the majority) almost entirely of Gentile Christians. "Instead of visualizing a single Christian congregation, therefore, we should constantly reckon with the probability that within the urban area were to be found forms of Christian community which were as diverse, and probably also as alien, as the churches of Galatia and those of Judea." But whatever the case in Rome, Paul in his travels was usually dealing with the phenomenon of house churches, where whole households, masters and slaves, quite likely worshipped together. We cannot believe he ever separated people. However, we do know that he was willing to adopt in different places a radically different approach, as he put it, "for those under the law and for those not under the law." When, for example, he established an apparently non-Jewish congregation among the Galatians, it was obviously different, perhaps radically different from that of the Jewish congregations elsewhere. We know this because Jewish Christians followed Paul to the Galatians and tried to make them conform to the Jewish Christian pattern. Galatia is a clear case where it was impossible for Paul to submit simultaneously both to the provisions of the Jewish Christian way of life and at the same time to the patterns of an evidently Greek (or perhaps Celtic) congregation.

Paul's letter to the Galatians, furthermore, shows us how determined he was to allow the Galatian Christians to follow a different Christian life-style. Thus, while we do not have any record of his forcing people to meet separately, we do encounter all of Paul's holy boldness set in opposition to anyone who would try to *preserve a single normative pattern* of Christian life through a cultural imperialism that would *prevent* people from employing their own language and culture as a vehicle for worship and witness. Here, then, is a clear case of a man with cross-cultural evangelistic perspective doing everything within his power to guarantee liberty in Christ to converts who were different from his own social background.

This same thing is seen when Paul opposed Peter in Antioch. Peter was a Galilean Jew who was perhaps to some extent bi-cultural. He could have at least been able to understand the predominantly Greek life-style of the Antioch church. Indeed, he did seem to fit in until the moment other Jewish Christians came to the door. At this point Peter also discovered that in a given situation he had to choose between following Jewish or Greek customs. At this point he wavered. Did he lack the Spirit of God? Did he lack the love of God? Or did he fail to understand the way of God's love? Peter did not question the validity of a Greek congregation. Peter had already acknowledged this before his Jewish compatriots walked in the door. The point was that Peter was pained for others to know him as one who could shift from one community to the other. What this means to us today is quite clear. There were in fact in the New Testament period two significantly different communities of believers. Peter was regarded the apostle to the circumcision and Paul to the uncircumcision. Peter identified more easily with the Jews, and no doubt had a hard time explaining to Jews his experience at Cornelius' household, namely his discovery that Greek congregations were to be considered legitimate. Paul, on the other hand, was able to identify more closely with the Greek congregations. They were perhaps eventually his primary missionary target, even though in a given locality he always began with the Jews.

The equality of diversity

One clue for today is the fact that where Paul found some Christians to be overly scrupulous about certain foods, he counseled people in those situations to abide by the stricter sensibilities of the majority. However, it is always difficult to make exact parallels to a modern situation. The New Testament situation would compare more easily to modern India today were it the case that the only Christians in India were Brahmins (and other members of the middle castes) with their highly restrictive diet. Then we would envision Brahmin Christians finding it hard to allow the less restrictive meat-eating groups to become Christian; but the actual situation is very nearly the reverse. In India today it is those who eat meat who are Christians, and the problem is how to apply Paul's missionary strategy to this situation. In regard to food restrictions, it is as though the Brahmins are "under the law," not the present Christians. In this situation can we imagine Paul saying, "To those under the law I will go as under the law if by all means I may win some"? Can we hear him say as an E-2 or E-3 evangelist, "If meat makes my brother offended, I will eat no meat"? Can we hear him defending worshipping groups among the Brahmins against the suggestion *or expectation* that they should change their diet or join congregations of very different life-style in order to be accepted as Christians? Against the accusation that he was dividing the church of Christ, can we hear Paul insist that "in Christ there is neither Jew nor Greek, low caste nor high caste"? Is this not the actual force of his oft repeated statement that these different kinds of people, following their different cultural patterns, are all equally acceptable to God? Was he really announcing a policy of local integration, or was he insisting on the equality of diversity?

Note very carefully that this perspective does not enforce (nor even allow) a policy of segregation, nor any kind of ranking of Christians in first- and second-class categories. It rather guarantees equal acceptability of different traditions. It is a clear-cut apostolic policy against forcing Christians of one life-style to be proselytized to the cultural patterns of another. This is not a peripheral matter in the New Testament. True circumcision is of the heart. True baptism is of the heart. It is a matter of faith, not works, or customs, or rites. In Christ there is freedom and liberty in this regard—people must be free either to retain or abandon their native language and life-style. Paul would not allow anyone to glory either in circumcision or in uncircumcision. He was absolutely impartial. He was also widely misunderstood. Paul's problem ultimately was in gaining acceptance by the Jews, and it was Asian Jews, possibly Christians, who pointed him out in the temple and thus finally caused his martyrdom for his belief in the separate liberty of the Greek Christian tradition. Let no one who seeks to be a missionary in the tradition of the Apostle Paul expect that working between two cultures will be easy to do. But he can take heart in the fact that the hazards of the profession are more than justified by the urgent missionary purposes of the cross-cultural evangelist.

If, for example, a cross-cultural evangelist encourages members of a Brahmin family to begin worship services in their own home, does he insist that they invite people from across town to their very first meeting? On the other hand, any Brahmin who becomes a Christian and who begins to understand the Bible will soon realize, whether it was entirely clear before or not, that he now belongs to a world family within which there are many tribes and tongues—indeed, according to the Book of Revelation (Rev. 7:9), this kind of diversity will continue right down to the end of time. When the cross-cultural evangelist allows the development of a Brahmin congregation, he is not thereby proposing Brahmin segregation from the world church. He is not suggesting that the Brahmin Christians shun other Christians, but that Brahmins be included within the world church. He is merely affirming their liberty in Christ to retain those elements of their life-style that are not inimical to the Gospel of Christ. He is not increasing their alienation. He is giving them the Word of God which is the passkey to the ultimate elimination of all manner of prejudices, and is already signing them into a world Christian family which embraces all peoples, tribes and tongues as equals.

Unity and Uniformity

Now, I regret that this subject is so delicate, and I would not embark upon it if it were not so urgently significant for the practical evangelistic strategies which we must have if we are going to win the world for Christ. I would not even bring it up. Yet I must say I believe this issue is the most important single issue in evangelism today.

Many people asked me what I meant by the strategic value of the establishment of youth churches. It is important to realize the youth situation is highly parallel to the situation we have just discussed. It is by no means a case where we are suggesting that young people not be allowed in adult services. We are not suggesting segregation of the youth. Youth churches are not ends, but means. We are not abandoning the thought that young people and older people should often be in the same service together. We are merely insisting, with what I pray is apostolic intuition, that young people have the freedom in Christ to meet together by themselves if they choose to, and *especially if this allows them to attract other young people who would likely* not come to Christ in an age-integrated service.

It is a curious fact that the kind of culturally sensitive evangelism I have been talking about has always been acceptable wherever people are geographically isolated. No one minds if Japanese Christians gather by themselves in Tokyo, or Spanish-speaking Christians gather by themselves in Mexico, or Chinese-speaking Christians gather by themselves in Hong Kong. But there is considerable confusion in many people's minds as to whether Japanese, Spanish and Chinese Christians should be allowed or encouraged to gather by themselves in Los Angeles. Very specifically, is it good evangelistic strategy to found separate congregations in Los Angeles in order to attract such people? Do Cantonese-speaking non-Christians need a Cantonese-speaking congregation to attract them to Christian faith and fellowship? If you talk to different people, you will get different answers. In my opinion, this question about evangelistic strategy in the forming of separate congregations must be considered an area of Christian liberty, and is to be decided purely on the basis of whether or not it allows the Gospel to be presented effectively to more people—that is, whether it is evangelistically strategic. Some go as far as granting separate *language* congregations, but hesitate when the differences between people are social and non-linguistic. Somehow they feel that people may be excused for meeting separately if their language is different, but that the Gospel urges us to ignore all other cultural differences. Many people are literally outraged at the thought that a local congregation would deliberately seek to attract people of a certain social level. And yet, while no one should be excluded from any church under any circumstances, it is a fact that where people can choose their church associations voluntarily, they tend to sort themselves out according to their own way of life pretty consistently. But this absolutely must be their own free choice. We are never suggesting an enforced segregation. Granting that we have this rich diversity, let us foster unity and fellowship between *congregations* just as we now do between *families* rather than to teach everyone to worship like Anglo-Americans. Let us glory in the fact that the *world* Christian family now already includes representatives of more different languages and cultures than any other organization or movement in human history. Americans may be baffled and perplexed by world diversity. God is not. Let us glory in the fact that God has allowed different life-styles to exist in different forms, and that this flexibility has been exercised throughout history. Let us never be content with mere isolation, but let us everlastingly emphasize that the great richness of our Christian tradition can only be realized as these differing life ways maintain creative contact. But let us be cautious about hastening to uniformity. If the whole world church could be gathered into a single congregation, Sunday after Sunday, there would eventually and inevitably be a loss of a great deal of the rich diversity of the present Christian traditions. Does God want this? Do we want this?

Jesus *died* for these people around the world. He did not die to preserve our Western way of life. He did not die to make Muslims stop praying five times a day. He did not die to make Brahmins eat meat. Can't you hear Paul the Evangelist saying we must go to these people within the systems in which they operate? True, this is the cry of a cross-cultural evangelist, not a pastor. We can't make every local church fit the pattern of every other local church. But we must have radically new efforts of cross-cultural evangelism in order to effectively witness to 2387 million people, and we cannot believe that we can continue virtually to ignore this highest priority.

Study Questions

1. Explain the difference between E-1, E-2, and E-3 evangelism. Which of the three does Winter consider most powerful? Why? Which does he consider most urgent? Why?

2. "Christian unity cannot be healthy if it infringes upon Christian liberty." Do you agree? What significance does this issue have for "practical evangelistic strategies"?

17

The Task Remaining: All Humanity in Mission Perspective

Ralph D. Winter

No perspective on the entire human race can be brief without tending to be simplistic. When God chose Abraham and his lineage both for a special blessing and for special responsibility to extend that authority and that blessing to "all the families of the earth" (Gen. 12:3; 18:18, etc.), Abraham mercifully did not understand how big and complex the task was.

Now however, 4,000 years later, the predominant majority of the people living in over half of "all the families of the earth" are at least superficially what Toynbee calls "Judaic" in religion and have certainly received at least some direct blessing through people with faith like Abraham's and through the redemptive work of the One to whom Abraham looked (John 8:56). If we take into account indirect influences, it would be possible to estimate that nine-tenths of all humanity has by now received some of that blessing, even if mixed with other elements.

Nations and Countries

In today's world we tend to think "political entity" or "country" when we see the word "nation." Unfortunately, this is not the concept expressed in the Bible. A closer translation comes directly from the Greek word "ethnos," which has not only been translated "nation" but also "ethnic unit," "people," or (as in the New Testament) "heathen" or "Gentiles." In no case does it refer to a country as we think of a political unit today. A more correct usage would be as in the phrase "the Cherokee nation," referring to the tribe of American Indians known as the Cherokee. Even in the Old Testament this same concept holds true. Two words

After serving ten years as a missionary among Mayan Indians in western Guatemala, Ralph D. Winter spent the next ten years as a professor of missions at the School of World Mission at Fuller Theological Seminary. He is the founder of the U.S. Center for World Mission in Pasadena, California, a cooperative center focused on people groups still lacking a culturally relevant church. Winter has also been instrumental in the formation of the movement called Theological Education by Extension, the William Carey Library publishing house, the American Society of Missiology, the Perspectives Study Program and the International Society for Frontier Missiology. Since March of 1990 he has been the President of the William Carey International University.

are used in the Old Testament. *Gam*, which occurs 1821 times, refers to a people, a single race or tribe, or to a specific lineage of mankind, as in Deut. 4:6 and 28:37. The other word, *mishpahgheh*, occurs only 267 times and is mainly used to refer to a smaller entity of kindred or relatives. This smaller entity, *mishpahgheh*, is the word used in Gen. 12:3, "In thee shall all the *families* of the earth be blessed." (The Biblical word "house" approximates our modern English word, *family*.) The concept of "country" or a politically defined nation is totally absent

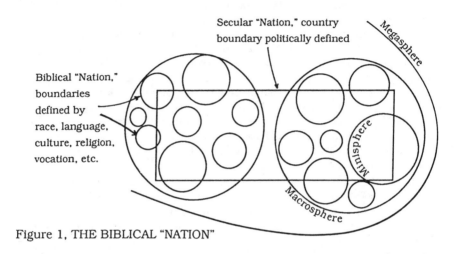

Figure 1, THE BIBLICAL "NATION"

in both of these cases. The fact that not countries, but rather ethnic units or people groups is what is implied is made even more pointed when in a number of places (e.g., Rev. 5:9, 10:11, etc.) not only is the word "nation" used, but it is further spelled out as peoples, tribes, tongues and kindreds.

Paul knew himself as the apostle to the Gentiles (read "peoples" or "nations"). He was one of the first of the new church to conclude that God wanted to use the marvelous diversity of the cultural mosaic of mankind. He came to see that God did not require a Gentile to commit cultural suicide to become a believer. Paul spoke of this as a mystery long hidden, but now made plain (Eph. 3:4). There was nothing new about a Gentile becoming a Jew and joining the community of faith of the people of God. A few hardy proselytes in Paul's day did this, though they had a hard time. Most Gentiles would not have gone that far. (Did they sense instinctively that such a shift could not in itself be salvific?) They needed a Paul to establish a synagogue of, by, and for their own people, that is, a Gentile synagogue. The new thing was unity without uniformity. Gentiles could follow Jesus without becoming culturally Jewish.

Many Americans in particular tend to assume that all who live in China are racially Chinese, by which they probably mean "Han" Chinese. Or they may assume all the people of the Soviet Union are ethnically Russian. However, even the unity-seeking government of the People's Republic of China recognizes a number of ethnic minorities, that is, distinctly non-Han groups of people who were born and have lived in China for hundreds of years. Furthermore, there are a great many varieties of Han Chinese. There are at least 100 mutually unintelligible varieties of the Chinese family of languages! India is a country of 3,000 nations, only 100 of which have any Christians at all. The former Soviet Union also has widely diverse peoples with practically nothing in common except the political glue that binds them together.

For example, one major mission organization states its purpose as "multiplying laborers in every nation," yet for many years it only kept track of how many *countries* it worked in, not how many biblical *nations* it was touching, nor whether such nations already have a well established work or not. Another outstanding mission agency has produced a book entitled *The Discipling of a Nation*, which speaks of needing one church for every thousand people in a "nation." The thinking of the leaders of that mission is clear, but the book title is ambiguous since most people would understand it to mean countries, not biblical nations. Yet, strange as it may at first sound, it is perfectly possible to reach the goal of having planted one church per thousand people in, say, the *country* of India and not have touched even half of the 3,000 different biblically-defined nations in that country.

Thus to look at the world from the "peoples" concept is not only biblical, it is also highly strategic, for there is one kind of cross-cultural evangelism and church planting that is far more strategic than all the others. Moreover, the "peoples" concept stresses the need to look at people as part of their own culture, not merely as individuals, and to see them, when converted as individuals, as strategic, natural bridges to the rest of their society. To give a diagrammatic example of the significance of the "peoples" concept for mission strategy, let us look at one small sector of the world.

Megaspheres, Macrospheres, and Minispheres

Figure 2 shows some people groups within two large cultural blocs, or "megaspheres"—the Muslim megasphere and the Han Chinese megasphere. Within these megaspheres we find three large circles filled with a number of smaller circles. Each large circle represents a "cultural macrosphere"—a group of societies that have certain cultural similarities both within and between them. The middle macrosphere consists of Cantonese-speaking people, most of whom are found in a single country, the People's Republic of China, and they number in the millions of people. The smaller circles, which I will call "minispheres," represent groups of people which speak divergent dialects of Cantonese mutually unintelligible to each other. People from two such sub-groups can be understood by each other only if they learn a "trade language" variety of Cantonese. Either the macrosphere or the minisphere could be considered a *nation* in biblical terms, but note that neither is a *country*. (Still smaller "microspheres" could be defined by clan or family or vocational differences too small to require separate churches for maximally effective outreach.)

E-1, E-2, and E-3 Evangelism

Note further that in some of the minispheres—the smaller circles—there is a

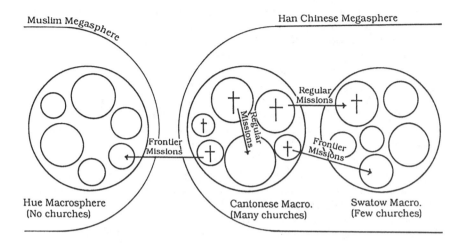

Figure 2, REGULAR MISSIONS/FRONTIER MISSIONS

cross, representing an indigenous church that has been planted within that culture sometime in the past. These churches, if they are vital and witnessing, are readily able to win the remaining non-Christians in that dialect group by normal, near-neighbor evangelism. We call this E-1 evangelism. There is only one barrier to be crossed in near-neighbor evangelism, the "stained glass barrier." Should that barrier get too thick, the believing community then becomes an enclave that is essentially a different minisphere and must be treated as such.

Some of the smaller circles, however, have no cross. Those minispheres obviously need someone from somewhere else to do that initial evangelizing and to plant the first church. That kind of evangelism from the outside is much more difficult than near-neighbor evangelism, for it requires the evangelist from the outside to learn another language, or at least another dialect of Cantonese. Also, he will find out that some of the cultural assumptions will be different. In other words, ordinary evangelism will not do the task that is required to pioneer in this frontier area. This type of evangelism we call E-2 or E-3. The evangelist must penetrate significant cultural barriers.

Looking again at Figure 2, you will notice that schematically we show only six of the many minispheres in the Cantonese macrosphere, and that five have a cross, meaning an indigenous church. The Swatow macrosphere, by contrast, has only one minisphere with an indigenous church, and the Muslim Hue macrosphere, which pertains to an entirely different Muslim megasphere, has no Christian church at all in any of its minispheres. Each of these macrospheres numbers millions of people; indeed, even some of the minispheres may number over a million people. The job of the ordinary evangelist is to plant churches in his own minisphere. That we call E-1, near neighbor evangelism.

But where there is no church—no indigenous community of believers— there is not the evangelism potential to reach the entire minisphere. In fact, there may be a number of individual believers who (like the New Testament "God-fearers") worship outside their culture. There may even be some believers from that group who have left their minisphere and become "proselytized" to another. But there is still no viable, indigenous church. By viable church we mean a minimum, yet sufficiently developed indigenous Christian tradition, capable of evangelizing its own people without cross-cultural help. This implies that there would be a cluster of indigenous evangelizing congregations and a significant part of the Bible translated by the people themselves. Minispheres which do not have that cluster of indigenous, growing, evangelizing congregations can be considered "unreached." These people groups require cross-cultural evangelism.

A people group can be considered "reached" if there is a body of Christians with the potential to evangelize its own people such that outside, cross-cultural efforts can be "safely" terminated. This potential may be roughly predicted by measuring the percentage of practicing Christians. The figure of 20 percent has been established by the Lausanne Committee for World Evangelization, to be on the "safe side," but this figure is not absolutely crucial if in a given case it is known that the indigenous church shows every indication that it can and will evangelize its entire minisphere. Where there is no viable church it takes a Paul, or someone from outside that language group and culture, to go to that people and plant a church there. Or it takes a Luther within the culture to wake up and go indigenous. In any case, the Cantonese evangelist in Figure 2 who goes to a Swatow dialect where there is no church is doing a missionary type of evangelism. In Paul's words, he is "going where Christ is not named."

Evangelism and Missions

If, however, a Cantonese evangelist goes from his Cantonese-speaking church to a Swatow minisphere where there already is an indigenous church, to help those believers to evangelize their own non-Christian Swatows, remaining in the same minisphere, he may very well be making a "missionary trip," but he is doing evangelism, not missions. We have defined as evangelism the activity of reaching out from an existing church within the same minisphere, working to its fringes. The people back home in his Cantonese minisphere may very likely call such a person their "missionary," but technically speaking, even in the biblical and classical sense, he is an evangelist who happens to be working at a cultural distance from his own background. The main point is that winning people into a church that is already within their own minisphere is the work of an evangelist, even if the "missionary" comes from a great distance. We must admit that this is the usual pattern of so-called "missions" today. Most "missionaries," whether from the U.S.A., Europe, Asia or Africa, go from their own cultures to work in another culture where a church is already established. We may have to concede the term "Regular Missions" to such activity, just because of social pressure; in that case we fall back to the term "Frontier Missions" for the other activity. Some workers are incorrectly called "missionaries" even when they go to work with Christians from their own culture who have moved to a foreign country. In that case, such people are not even evangelists but rather "transplanted pastors."

Regular Missions and Frontier Missions

We can distinguish "Frontier Missions" from "Regular Missions" by considering the matrix in Figure 3. The quadrants on the left side are concerned with *reached* people groups and the quadrants on the right side are concerned with *unreached* or *hidden* people groups. Thus the horizontal axis effectively measures the *cultural* distance between the people and the culturally nearest potential wit-

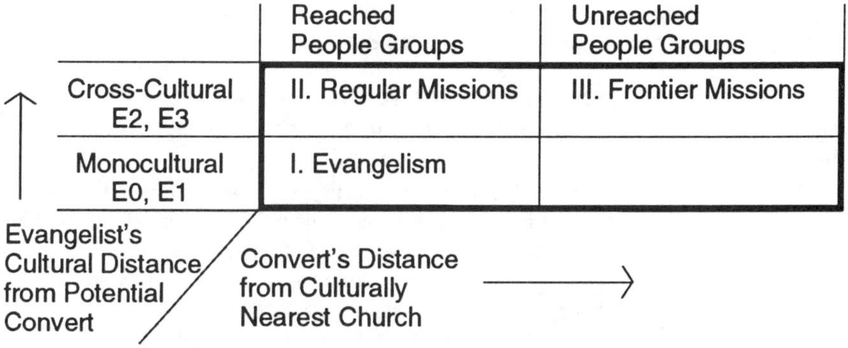

	Reached People Groups	Unreached People Groups
Cross-Cultural E2, E3	II. Regular Missions	III. Frontier Missions
Monocultural E0, E1	I. Evangelism	

Evangelist's Cultural Distance from Potential Convert / Convert's Distance from Culturally Nearest Church $\longrightarrow$

I. Evangelism: by a same-culture worker, where the missiological breakthrough of a viable church has taken place.

II. Regular Missions: cross-cultural evangelism by a different-culture worker, in association with same-cultural workers if possible, where a missiological breakthrough has taken place.

III. Frontier Missions: here is where cross-cultural evangelism (by a different-culture worker) is essential, since no missiological breakthrough has yet been made.

Figure 3

ness embodied in a church, while the vertical axis is the *evangelist's* cultural distance from the potential convert. The bottom two quadrants designate *monocultural* work. The top two quadrants specify *cross-cultural* evangelism.

Quadrant I is classic near-neighbor evangelism. An evangelist makes disciples within his own minisphere, where there is already a vibrant growing fellowship. But it is quite possible for this same Christian worker to work in what is for him a radically different culture (E-3 evangelism) and yet be working among an essentially reached group (Quadrant II). This is "missions" only in the sense that the worker is away from his own home. The converts have all the advantages of those in Quadrant I. But if our evangelist does E-3 evangelism in a people group without a viable church (Quadrant III), then he must work for the "missiological breakthrough" of establishing the first indigenous church. This is the crucial task of "Frontier Missions." We trust that the term "Regular Missions" highlights the strategic priority of "Frontier Missions" without diminishing the value of cross-cultural workers in reached people groups.

The convert and the cultural distance of an indigenous church

A closer look at the evangelism/mission dichotomy will help us decide whether, in a given case, E-2 or E-3 work is frontier missions or not. That is, instead of making distinctions merely on the basis of the cultural distance the evangelist must go, suppose we also make distinctions in reference to the degree of transformation that is necessary for the culturally nearest church to become indigenous to the minisphere of the new convert.

In other words, how far do the people have to come to become Christian if there were *no* effort to evangelize them? Referring again to Figure 3, notice that people within a "reached" people group (on the left side of the matrix) need suffer little cultural dislocation in becoming Christians. Unreached people on the right can only become Christians by abandoning their cultural ties, unless the gospel is brought near by cross-cultural workers.

Thus it would be helpful to know not only how far the evangelist has gone to take the church, but also how far—the minimum cultural distance—the potential convert would have to go to find the church. To state this in more graphic terms, Cornelius apparently didn't go the necessary distance to become a Jewish proselyte. He attended a Jewish synagogue, but as a "God-fearer," he only witnessed a believing group representing a distinctly foreign culture. The cultural distance was so great even Peter had extreme reluctance coming the other direction to visit him. But when the whole household of Cornelius turned to Christ, an indigenous church was formed to which his Roman friends could now have gone a much shorter cultural distance to find accountable fellowship with Christian believers.

The job of Peter, the evangelist, (or rather, the "missionary" in this case), is probably E-3 on our scale above. The problem of Cornelius, in whose Roman culture there was no indigenous church, would be measured on the "Peoples" or P Scale. It was P-3 to begin with, but P-1 when the new congregation was formed, if indeed one survived. The family of P distinctions is similar, almost a mirror image of the E scale.

P-O: These are nominal Christians, not yet real believers who are nevertheless participating to some extent in a local church. Yet they face no problem of cultural distance in understanding the Gospel from the closest church.

P-1: These people consciously do not consider themselves Christians, but they are, nevertheless, part of the same minisphere within which an indigenous, evangelizing church is to be found, and can thus, on this score at least, be readily won into existing congregations. Note that a Christian community within a minisphere usually forms a microsphere of its own. Over a period of time, if few additional members are won from the surrounding minisphere, and the religious sub-culture becomes sufficiently strange so that strategically whole new congregations must be formed in order to win new people, then the earlier church community has to become ghetto-ized into its own minisphere, and the minisphere from which it has withdrawn becomes a separate, P-2 minisphere.

P-2: These people are not the same but only similar culturally to a cultural minisphere possessing an indigenous church. They are in the same cultural macrosphere, but are part of a sufficiently different minisphere so as not to be easily incorporated into an existing church. (It may be useful to conceive of a P-2.5 distance in which the closest indigenous church is in the same megasphere but in a different macrosphere.)

P-3: These people belong to groups that are very, very different from any of the cultural spheres which have an indigenous church. That is, not even their megasphere has been penetrated.

The Task in the Third Era

I believe we are in the third and final era of Protestant missions. I don't think this way because of general turmoil in our world. Many times in history there have been wars, rumors of wars, persecution, famine, and distress on all sides. I believe that the most determinative arena of events in the world today is what is happening in missions. Jesus said (Matt. 24:14) that before He would return the gospel would first be preached to every tribe, tongue, and people. For the first time in history it is physically possible for this to be true. Not by satellite—for then all people could not hear in their own language, as this verse implies. For the first time in history it is possible for there to be a church within the language and social structure of every people group on earth, and it can literally be done by the year 2000.

At first glance, the task seems enormous—impossible, really! Figures 4 and 5 show the number of individuals in the world today who still need a viable witness. But this great possibility will never be an actuality apart from a serious and sustained gaze at the dimensions of the task. A glance at Figure 4 will show humanity divided into the categories of reached—requiring evangelism and Regular Missions, and unreached—requiring Frontier Missions. Easily noticeable are the millions of nominal Christians (1,260 million) and non-Christians (1,600 million) who live in "reached" societies. All of these can be won by E-0 and E-1 near-neighbor, ordinary evangelism. Church members in every country can reach out to these people and win them without any specialized cross-cultural training.

The much more difficult task is that of reaching the Unreached People groups—those as yet unpenetrated by the church of Jesus Christ. As Figure 4 shows, there are 2,101 million individuals in the Hidden People category still to be evangelized by E-2 and E-3 methods. Figures 5 and 6 graphically portray the number of individuals within the unreached people groups of the major cultural blocs. Carefully note the plight of those within five major blocs or megaspheres: Muslim, Buddhist, Hindu, Han Chinese and Tribal.

Figure 4
ALL HUMANITY IN MISSION PERSPECTIVE

		A. REACHED PEOPLES					
			INDIVIDUALS (in millions)				
		PEOPLE GROUPS	True Christians (TCR): Reached Individuals as a work force.	Nominal "Christians" (P0, P.5): Needing Renewal Evangelism (E0 to E3).	Non-Christians (P1): needing E1 to E3 Outreach Evangelism.	TOTAL	NORTH AMERICAN PROTESTANT MISSIONARIES
MAJOR CULTURAL BLOCS	Muslim	200	3	0	100	103	600
	Tribal	3,300	33	32	30	95	13,000
	Hindu	1,500	15	10	156	181	400
	Han Chinese	2,300	95	10	867	972	3,000
	Buddhist	120	6	1	65	72	2,000
	Subtotal	7,420	152	53	1,218	1,423	19,000
OTHER CATEGORIES	Other African	3,050	105	145	45	295	15,400
	Other Asian	1,300	70	94	110	274	10,400
	Other Western	700	140	795	192	1,127	26,000
	U.S.A. and Canada	500	72	173	35	280	5,200
	Subtotal	5,550	387	1,207	382	1,976	57,000
	Grand Total	12,970	539	1,260	1,600	3,399	76,000
		EVANGELISM AND "DOMESTIC" MISSIONS					

Notes

Evangelism within the same cultural group.
{
E0: Renewal evangelism of church members.
E.5: Evangelism of those on the fringe.
E1: Evangelism of non-Christians with no contact with the church.
}

Evangelism external to one's own cultural group.
{
E2: Evangelism of non-Christians in a similar but different culture.
E2.5: Evangelism of non-Christians in a similar but quite different culture.
E3: Evangelism in a completely different culture.
}

B. UNREACHED PEOPLES / WORLD TOTALS

PEOPLE GROUPS	True Christians (TCU):* Reached Individuals living within Unreached People Groups.	Non-Christians (P2): needing E2 to E3 Cross-Cultural Evangelism.	Non-Christians (P2.5): needing E2.5 to E3 Cross-Cultural Evangelism.	Non-Christians (P3): needing E3 Outreach.	TOTAL	NORTH AMERICAN PROTESTANT MISSIONARIES	LANGUAGES	PEOPLE GROUPS	INDIVIDUALS (millions)	NORTH AMERICAN PROTESTANT MISSIONARIES	THIRD WORLD MISSIONARIES**	OTHER WESTERN MISSIONARIES**
			INDIVIDUALS (in millions)									
3,800	.01	306	585	0	891	800	580	4,000	994	1,400	1,200	500
2,700	.01	30	40	20	90	4,500	3,000	6,000	185	17,500	8,200	5,000
1,800	.6	484	75	0	560	200	500	3,300	741	600	4,200	200
900	.01	135	15	0	150	300	200	3,200	1,122	3,300	2,500	700
900	.01	120	141	0	261	600	100	1,020	333	2,600	3,000	2,300
10,100	.64	1,075	856	20	1,952	6,400	4,380	17,520	3,375	25,400	19,100	8,700
400	.14	17	8	15	40.1	400	300	3,450	335	15,800	14,300	12,300
300	.08	17	16	8	41.1	800	700	1,600	315	11,200	10,600	10,000
150	.01	40	16	6	62	400	100	850	1,189	26,400	5,300	3,700
50	.001	4	1	1	6	1,000	30	550	286	6,200	1,700	300
900	.231	78	41	30	149	2,600	1,130	6,450	2,125	59,600	31,900	26,300
11,000	.871	1,153	897	50	2,101	9,000	5,510	23,970	5,500	85,000	51,000	35,000

FRONTIER MISSIONS

The numbers given above for remaining unreached peoples are significantly smaller than those listed in the previous edition of this book. Most of the change, however, reflects requests from the Lausanne Statistics Task Force rather than great successes in reaching groups. Note also that the round numbers in this chart reflect the degree of guess work that is essential when dealing with the concept of "Unreached Groups." See the definitions in the text to note how unusually difficult it is to count these groups before they are reached.

Certain statistics are derived from *The World Christian Encyclopedia* by David Barrett (Oxford Univ. Press, New York), and from Barrett's *Annual Statistical Table on Global Mission* (January 1992, *International Bulletin of Missionary Research*) projected to the end of 1992.

*This column has not been incorporated into the world totals lest a false impression of accuracy be implied.

**Neither Third World nor "other Western" missionary forces are plotted in the following Diagrams because we have not found studies indicating their distribution by our categories. In the case of the Third World forces we at least have a total (projected forward to the end of 1992 from the total given by Larry Pate in *From Every People* (MARC, 1989) and have made guesses as to the breakdown.

Figure 5

THE GLOBE AT A GLANCE

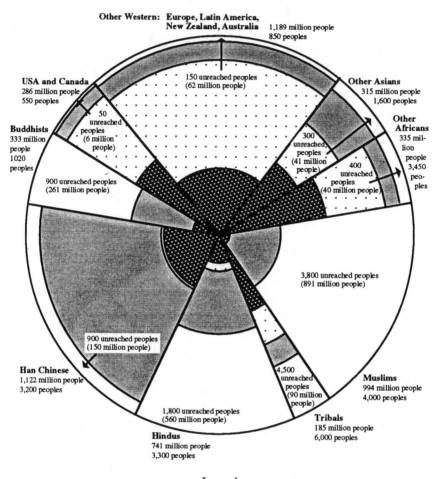

Other Western: **Europe, Latin America, New Zealand, Australia** 1,189 million people 850 peoples

USA and Canada 286 million people 550 peoples

Buddhists 333 million people 1020 peoples

150 unreached peoples (62 million people)

50 unreached peoples (6 million people)

900 unreached peoples (261 million people)

Other Asians 315 million people 1,600 peoples

Other Africans 335 million people 3,450 peoples

300 unreached peoples (41 million people)

400 unreached peoples (40 million people)

3,800 unreached peoples (891 million people)

900 unreached peoples (150 million people)

Han Chinese 1,122 million people 3,200 peoples

4,500 unreached peoples (90 million people)

Muslims 994 million people 4,000 peoples

1,800 unreached peoples (560 million people)

Tribals 185 million people 6,000 peoples

Hindus 741 million people 3,300 peoples

Legend

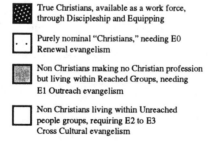

True Christians, available as a work force, through Discipleship and Equipping

Purely nominal "Christians," needing E0 Renewal evangelism

Non Christians making no Christian profession but living within Reached Groups, needing E1 Outreach evangelism

Non Christians living within Unreached people groups, requiring E2 to E3 Cross Cultural evangelism

Figure 6

People, Peoples, Missionaries: Graphically Portrayed

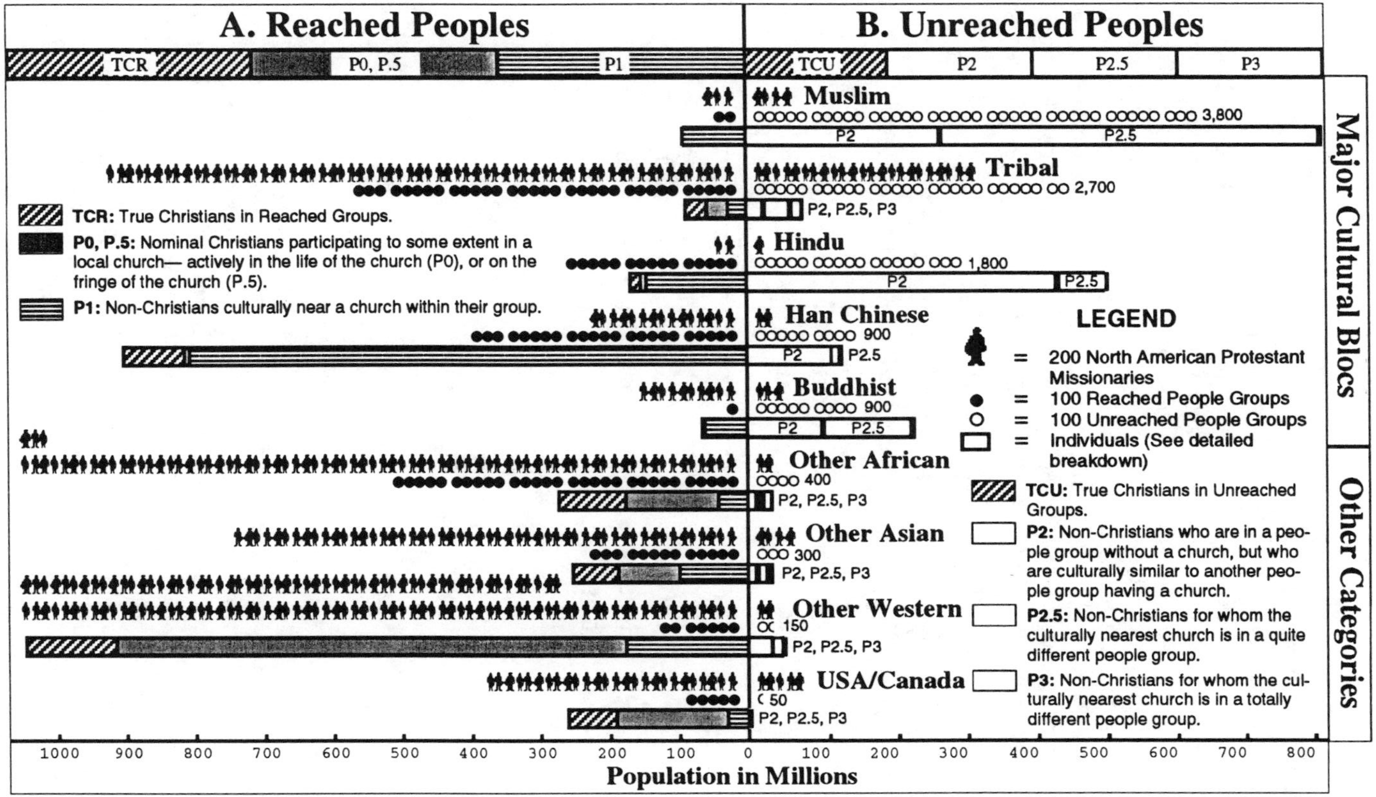

| Major Cultural Blocs | Other Categories |

A. Reached Peoples

B. Unreached Peoples

TCR | P0, P.5 | P1 | TCU | P2 | P2.5 | P3

Muslim
ooooo ooooo ooooo ooooo ooooo ooooo 3,800
P2 | P2.5

Tribal
ooooo ooooo ooooo oo 2,700
P2 | P2.5

Hindu
ooooo ooooo ooooo ooo 1,800
P2 | P2, P2.5, P3

Han Chinese
ooooo ooooo 900
P2 | P2.5

Buddhist
ooooo ooooo 900
P2 | P2.5

Other African
ooooo 400
P2, P2.5, P3

Other Asian
ooo 300
P2, P2.5, P3

Other Western
150
P2, P2.5, P3

USA/Canada
50
P2, P2.5, P3

LEGEND

= 200 North American Protestant Missionaries
= 100 Reached People Groups
= 100 Unreached People Groups
= Individuals (See detailed breakdown)

TCR: True Christians in Reached Groups.

P0, P.5: Nominal Christians participating to some extent in a local church— actively in the life of the church (P0), or on the fringe of the church (P.5).

P1: Non-Christians culturally near a church within their group.

TCU: True Christians in Unreached Groups.

P2: Non-Christians who are in a people group without a church, but who are culturally similar to another people group having a church.

P2.5: Non-Christians for whom the culturally nearest church is in a quite different people group.

P3: Non-Christians for whom the culturally nearest church is in a totally different people group.

Population in Millions
800 700 600 500 400 300 200 100 0 100 200 300 400 500 600 700 800 900 1000

What an imbalance!

The task seems impossible. Complicating the picture is the fact that most missionaries are not now concentrating on this task. Rather, where the church is well established, missionaries and Christian workers tend mainly to seek to win nominal Christians to a real faith in the Lord rather than to evangelize unreached people groups. Carefully scrutinize Figure 7. This graph shows the current mission deployment against the "reachedness" of the world's individuals and the world's people groups. Note that only 9,000 North American workers (at best) are concentrating on 11,000 people groups (2.1 billion people), while over eight times that number of workers are working among reached people groups. What

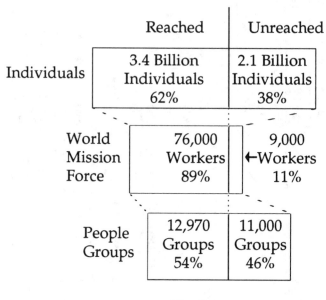

Figure 7

an imbalance! For every one person who professes the name of Christ, there is at least *one* person who has no access to the gospel in their own culture. For every one missionary bringing the Gospel to these Unreached Peoples, there are *more than eight* Christian workers evangelizing individuals in reached groups!

This fact was very poignantly pointed out to me at the Lausanne Consultation in Switzerland in 1974. I had just come down from the platform, where I had delivered an address stressing the necessity of going beyond our own culture and our present mission fields, when I met George Samuel of India. Keep in mind now that George is a former nuclear physicist, a brilliant scientist, who doesn't make mistakes with numbers. He said to me with tears in his eyes, "Ralph, I have just completed a very careful study of all the evangelizing efforts being undertaken in India, whether by missionaries or by national leaders, and I have concluded that 98% of all evangelization in India is focused upon winning back to the church the nominal Christians. Not even the non-Christians within those same cultures where the church is found receive much attention."

I was stunned. I finally stuttered out the words, "But, George, what are the 2% doing? Surely they, at least, are working among the unreached!"

"No," he said, "the 2% are reaching within the same societies, doing E-1 work."

"You surely don't mean to tell me that no one is crossing frontiers in India," I insisted.

"Well, of course American missionaries are crossing frontiers."

"But is it not true," I answered, "that while they are indeed working cross-culturally, they are for the most part not crossing mission frontiers? They're crossing frontiers to get to Madras and to learn the Tamil language. But they're only going where there is already a church. To my knowledge they are rarely crossing any mission frontiers." He agreed.

I believe it is different today, perhaps partly because of the many voices that stress reaching further out. There are some agencies, the Friends Missionary Prayer Band for one, that are working cross-culturally and in some cases are going into cultures where there is no church.

More recruits needed!

The task is not as impossible as it might seem. We must adjust our thinking so that we focus on penetrating people groups and planting evangelizing, indigenous churches. Then, instead of talking of evangelizing 2.1 billion individuals, we will talk of penetrating 11,000 Unreached People groups.

If we were to assign one missionary to each of these unreached people groups, we would need at least 11,000 recruits, but this is only one new missionary from every 49,000 True Christians! Some frontiers involve millions of people, and obviously require more than one missionary or one couple. Yet today we have the potential of missionaries from all parts of the globe.

The job is large, but not too large for the church around the world. We are in a new era. Now every church in the world ought to be involved with the frontiers. New missionary recruits cannot come just from the West, nor just from Asia, Africa or Latin America. We must all work together to do this task.

Abraham's Commission and Abraham's Children

Abraham persistently believed that God would fulfill His purposes through Abraham's descendants. He was fully convinced that what God had promised, He was able also to perform. This kind of faith enabled him to become a "father of many nations." Cannot we, the descendants of Abraham through Jesus Christ, believe God's promise that *"all* the families of the earth shall be blessed"? God's promise is certain, His ability unquestioned, His intention sure. Only our response is in question; will *we* become spiritual fathers to the yet unreached nations? Or will we miss participation in the fulfillment of the promise, as did a generation of Abraham's physical descendants on the edge of the "promised land?" They balked in unbelief, even though they had sent ahead for a perspective on the frontiers. God forgave them but banished them to a wilderness, saying, "As I live, all the earth will he filled with the glory of the Lord" (Num. 14:21). He would fulfill His purpose with or without *their* obedience. But finishing the remaining task will take *someone's* obedience. Will it be ours?

Study Questions

1. Try applying the distinctions between megasphere, macrosphere, and minisphere. Name a macrosphere and a corresponding minisphere within the *Muslim* megasphere.

2. Of the cross-cultural missionaries you know, which are engaged in "regular missions?"Which are engaged in "frontier missions?"

3. Describe the activity represented by the quadrant not marked in Figure 3 (mono-cultural evangelism in unreached peoples). How could this activity be important for frontier missions?

4. Carefully consider the "imbalance" evidenced in Figure 7. Suggest possible reasons for the imbalance. Suggest possible solutions to the imbalance.

18

The 2.4 Billion: Why are We Still So Unconcerned?

David A. Fraser

The number falls off our lips so easily: 2.4 billion. That's 2,400,000,000 people! The best Christian researchers of the present say that's how many people live outside the circle of effective gospel witness.

Lurking in the shadows of our suspicious minds must be a feeling that such a figure just *cannot* be true. Else how can we explain our real lack of concern? We find it difficult not only to conceive of so many people, but even to believe that such an astronomical figure could be true. We don't want it to be true. What is it about us and our current generation of Christians that permits us to live so comfortably in an age when there are more lost people than ever before in human history?

The first thing to discount is the idea that that number is purely an illusion. Of course it is true that the Church is more widespread and deeply rooted than ever before in its history, that there are 55,000 Protestant missionaries in over a hundred countries of the world, that North America alone invests $700 million a year in overseas ministries, that there are Third World mission agencies sending missionaries, and so forth. The past 25 years have been ones of unbelievable advance. Successes can be listed from every continent of the world. But the more carefully one looks, country-by-country, people-by-people, the more obvious it becomes that there are geographic, political, linguistic and cultural barriers that seal off major groups of peoples from the gospel. It is not an illusion to conclude that there is an enormous spiritual famine that circles the globe. The Bread of Life is simply not available to hundreds and hundreds of millions of people. There is no viable church, no Christian witness, in their midst.

But if it isn't an illusion, then we get back to ourselves. What is it about us that allows us to repeat the number so casually, so scientifically, so easily? There

David Fraser is currently Chair of the Department of Biblical and Theological Studies and Associate Professor of Sociology at Eastern College in Wayne, PA. Fraser was formerly a professor at Columbia Bible College in Columbia, South Carolina. Reprinted from *MARC Newsletter*, January 1979. Copyright 1979 MARC. Used with permission.

are probably dozens of reasons. But as we look inside our own experience and that of those around us, the following seem important:

1. *We live in "gospel affluent" areas.* We find it hard to imagine a situation where the radio or TV cannot be turned on and the evangelist be heard in a culturally appropriate format, or a city without churches on dozens of street corners.

2. *We hide from ourselves the true dimensions of the larger world we live in.* We don't even understand the reasons for poverty or the reality of how many people starve to death each day. The real physical world depresses us, makes us feel guilty and embarrassed. This is even more true for the real spiritual world in which we live.

3. *We have heard the statistic too often.* After a while it becomes a cliche, then a bore, and finally we no longer hear it and are no longer moved by the magnitude of need it expresses.

4. *We are a visual generation.* We find it difficult to dramatize to ourselves or others the spiritual tragedy of lost, unreached peoples. We have no camera that can penetrate to the spirit world and portray spiritual malnourishment or the spiritual death of people starving for the Bread of Life. And, increasingly, what we cannot see on our television screens, what we are not seeing regularly, we perceive as unreal and probably not true.

5. *Many of us are "closet" universalists.* We really believe that God in the end will save everyone, that He will turn out to be a "jolly good fellow" who will allow everyone into His heaven after a stern talking to about the mischief they got into on earth. Or, perhaps we hope (even though the Bible doesn't suggest it) that God is already saving the Hindus, Muslims and others apart from the proclamation of the Good News. Everyone is really a "Christian" even if they don't know it yet!

There may be many reasons beyond these. But none of them count as much as the 2.4 billion reasons why we should not be at ease in Zion. We may not like to admit it to ourselves. We may not like what implications it has for our current unimaginative, puny efforts for world evangelization. But there are 2,400,000,000 who are alive now, whose opportunities to hear or not to hear will be largely created by us.

Study Questions

1. What is your response to this article? Do any of the items listed particularly apply to you?

2. Review the statistics presented in this section. What was new to you? What was disturbing? Reflect on the implications for action.

19

World Mission Survey

Ralph D. Winter and David A. Fraser

Is This "Post-Christian" Europe?

For much of the 20th Century, it seemed like Christian Europe may have given its faith to the rest of the world but had failed to keep the faith itself.

The movement sparked by William Carey certainly produced a stupendous spread of God's light. Vast parts of Africa, Asia and the Pacific Islands have lit up as the result of tens of thousands of missionaries mainly from the Western World.

Yet the flames of Christendom in the heartlands of Europe and the Soviet Union for 70 long years seemed to flicker and gradually grow dim. The faith of millions seemed to decay like a radioactive element into a powerful secularism. Some people even began speaking of a "post-Christian" Europe in the 1950's. However, even before the collapse of European Communism there were many evidences of continuing Christian vitality.

What was happening during the 20th century was not the snuffing out of Christianity so much as the *disestablishment* of a Christendom in which certain denominations were official (like the Church of England, the Church of Sweden,

After serving ten years as a missionary among Mayan Indians in western Guatemala, Ralph D. Winter spent the next ten years as a professor of missions at the School of World Mission at Fuller Theological Seminary. He is the founder of the U.S. Center for World Mission in Pasadena, California, a cooperative center focused on people groups still lacking a culturally relevant church. Winter has also been instrumental in the formation of the movement called Theological Education by Extension, the William Carey Library publishing house, the American Society of Missiology, the Perspectives Study Program and the International Society for Frontier Missiology. Since March of 1990 he has been the President of the William Carey International University. The substantial changes in this chapter in this edition are entirely the work of Winter.

David Fraser is currently Chair of the Department of Biblical and Theological Studies and Associate Professor of Sociology at Eastern College in Wayne, PA. Fraser was formerly a professor at Columbia Bible College in Columbia, South Carolina. Reprinted from *MARC Newsletter*, January 1979. Copyright 1979 MARC. Used with permission.

etc.). Your membership was formed at birth. In the 20th century the rapid decline of vigor of such "state churches" was linked with the rise of secular communism in Eastern Europe and secularism in Western Europe and the United States, and it looked like Europe and the entire Western world was becoming "post Christian." Centralized Christendom could be quelled by central, totalitarian governments. Many of the surface indicators of "establishment Christendom" waned: membership registrations, church weddings, perfunctory attendance all decreased. Formerly hidden nominal Christians became much more evident.

Similarly, in the formation of the United States of America the official religion was so clearly Christianity that it would have been unthinkable to have to say so in the U.S. Constitution, which merely prohibited any specific denomination being set up as the official "established" church: "Congress shall make no law respecting the establishment of religion nor prohibiting the free exercise thereof." This clause, however, due to the same secularization process occurring in Europe, has been interpreted to mean the banning of any State or Federal activity favorable to religion itself, a gross (and intentional) misunderstanding of the text of the Constitution on the part of anti-Christian secular forces.

Meanwhile, due to the the massive revolution in Europe in the late 1980's, many places where Christianity had been most prohibited became the least restricted. Communist official proscription of religion in many cases gave way to great freedom of religion—the showing of the "Jesus" film in public schools, for example. In the same period that could not have occurred in the United States where there had developed a strident "freedom *from* religion" movement.

However, it is probable that at no time in the 20th Century did a grass-roots Christian movement give way. Whether in the Soviet Union, where Christianity was officially opposed, or in the United States where it was subtly opposed in the media, the schools, and the courts, actual faith on a completely voluntary basis may likely have steadily increased at every point. By the time of Glasnost, there were more recognized Christians in the Soviet Union than there had been in total population at the time of the Communist Revolution, and church members outnumbered Communist party members about ten to one.

In the United States, formal church membership steadily climbed through the century as well. In both spheres a smoldering reality of Christian conviction at the grass roots has eventually turned out to be a veritable conflagration of new Christian movements.

Missions to Europe and the Soviet Union

During the years that Christianity was pummeled in Eastern Europe and the Soviet Union by political disapproval and ideological warfare, the church trimmed down and discovered a new inner strength. Restrictions limited outside missions to occasional preaching tours, Bible smuggling, radio programs and a few quiet missionaries. But from within renewal and revival generated movements of witness and mission. In fact, startling as it may seem, even before the collapse of communism, there were more devout believers behind the Iron Curtain than in Western Europe!

Even during the many years of oppression, the persecuted Baptist church of

Romania was the fastest growing church of Europe, adding thousands of converts each year, mostly from Orthodox or secularized Christian background, while within the Orthodox church the "Lord's Army" appeared as a renewal movement encompassing hundreds of thousands of devout people whose existence would not likely make it into a Western press as prejudiced in its "free" secularism as any of the more predicably prejudiced totalitarian media. Even before Glasnost, in Poland, where Catholicism and nationalism have been virtually synonymous, proportionately more people (over 50 percent of adults) attended church weekly than in the U.S.A. The Protestant community of East Germany was pushed down from 80 percent to 60 percent of the population by government pressure. But even by 1975 there were probably a million highly committed Christians (6 percent of the population at the most), a larger committed minority than at any previous time.

Western Europe has long been the focus of a growing influx of missionaries from the English-speaking West. Focused largely on converting nominal Christians to active faith in Jesus Christ, these missionaries have peppered Europe with Bible institutes, seminaries, conferences, and evangelistic crusades. "Glasnost" and the dissolution of the USSR has released these energies to be extended Eastward. Now the vast ethnic diversity of the former USSR and the dozens of autonomous ethnically diverse republics within the Russian Federation itself suddenly became open to a degree not known for 70 years.

However, the non-European guest workers such as the Turks in West Germany are only being marginally evangelized. The traditional churches are struggling to survive and have long been introverted. Where evangelism is occurring, it is often being done by "diaspora" missionaries. Hundreds of Korean missionaries have followed the Korean influx to Europe. Filipino, Chinese and Indian pastors are working in Europe with their fellow kinsmen. But there remain large groups of unreached peoples, e.g., making up Europe's millions of Muslims.

Missions from Europe and the Soviet Union

While only one in five of the current Protestant mission force in the world comes *from* Europe and the Soviet Union, the percentage may increase greatly in view of the dramatic changes of the breakdown of the USSR.

An examination of the work of some of the older European overseas missions, as in America, reveals a pattern of success-stagnation: a great deal of effort is concentrated on strengthening the existing churches that have resulted from past evangelism, not on reaching the large blocs of unreached peoples. And, many of the missions from other traditions are found largely in diaspora situations (Russian Orthodox missionaries have largely followed settlements of Russians).

The picture is nevertheless a bright one. Europe's churches must cope with massive numbers of nominal Christians, but where the church is being reborn there are now no restrictions holding back any surge of new missions. The marvelous "AD2000 Movement" has gone around the world galvanizing national forces to reach out to the unreached peoples within their own sphere. This movement has, with great vision, included the incredible spiritual resources of the many new Eastern European countries, so long held back by atheistic totalitarian forces.

Latin America—No Longer Slow To Accept the Challenge of Missions

Five miles of pews (or benches) in a single church building! Does that seem too many for the church you attend?

Yet this was only the first shipment of wooden benches for the auditorium rising in Sao Paulo, Brazil. If ultimately they were in fact to seat 25,000 in that auditorium, my calculations showed that they would need about two more miles of pews.

Right there you see one difference between Nordic and Latin America. Even Robert Schuller's Crystal Cathedral isn't supposed to seat 25,000 people. And there are more new churches (about 3,000) in Brazil each year than in any other country in the world. For a decade Brazil has had more missionaries from North America than any other country (over 2,000 today). Three out of five of the largest cities in the Western Hemisphere are in Latin America. Flying into Sao Paulo on a clear day confronts you with so many high rise buildings that New York and Chicago will never look the same again.

Missions to Latin America

But as a *mission field* Latin America is widely and vastly misunderstood. It is not really a mission field in the classic sense of "where Christ is not known." Latin America may in some ways be slightly less religious than Europe, but it is also more religious in other respects. The main thing to recognize is that non-

English speaking Europe and Latin America are not all that different.

Mexico, with its numerous large Indian populations, is the least typical country of Latin America—the rest of Latin America has for the most part very little awareness of the so-called American Indians that live in that hemisphere. Only four countries other than Mexico have sizeable numbers of Indians: Guatemala, which shares with Mexico the descendants of the Maya (spread out in 33 languages in Guatemala alone), and then the three countries in South America which sit astride the majestic Andes (Ecuador, Bolivia and Peru). Thus, more than 20 million "American Indians" lie largely forgotten in Latin America by the majority of what is the world's largest concentration of missionaries (over 10,000). One reason is instantly obvious: it is incredibly more difficult for a North American missionary to learn to love and live with and make sense to these aboriginal populations than it is to plunge into the swim of Spanish or Portuguese-speaking Latin America where there is something like a two-thirds overlap of vocabulary (between English and Spanish or Portuguese). Parkinson's fifth law should be: "Missionary work always seems plenty hard even if it is relatively easy compared to some other kind of mission work."

But Latin America is constantly exciting. After a decade in Latin America our family came back to an America which, quite honestly, was drab, gray, slow-moving and really pretty dull by comparison. Visits back to Latin America display extravagant, dizzying change, wild contrasts, high-minded idealism sand-bagged by a hopelessness and aimlessness endemic to large sectors of the population. But the evangelical movement is virile, valiant, growing many places between two and three times the general population growth rate. When this author left Latin America in 1967 Guatemala was 5% evangelical. Now it is more like 30%.

Missions from Latin America

Can Latin America be a *mission base*? Here comes Parkinson's sixth law: "If you convince people they need help, you may convince them that they cannot help others." Latin believers can become missionaries only to the extent that they no longer see themselves as dependent on missionaries.

Latin Americans are super-rich by comparison to citizens of India. The Friends Missionary Prayer Band (of which Dr. Samuel Kamalesan is president) in India is so determined to send missionaries to other parts of India, without any foreign help, that they once turned down an offer of one million dollars from outside India. Yet those desperately poor families which are sending the FMPB's hundreds of missionaries to northern India are far poorer than most Latin Americans, who for many years were slow in accepting their logical role in sending missionaries to other parts of the world. They may indeed not be the best ones to reach their own American Indian populations due to centuries of suspicion on both sides, but Latin Americans are now eagerly sending missionaries to Europe. Buenos Aires is 60% Italian; southern Brazil is heavily German. If Latin America seems to be more open to the gospel than Europe, then it logically can be a springboard for penetrating Europe.

An astonishing and almost wholly unexpected transformation swept Latin

America during the late '80s. In the most sudden turn-about of any continent, Latin America is now seething with new interest in Latin Americans becoming missionaries to the ends of the earth.

Latin Americans are discovering that they are as able as anyone else to organize mission societies! Indeed, in the inevitable logic of mission strategy on a global level, Latin America *is now rapidly tranforming itself into a major mission base* to reach Asia's millions—Muslims, Hindus and Chinese. Asia is where most of the non-Christians of today's world are. Latins feel especially close to the Muslims of the world because Spain was occupied by Muslims for seven centuries and tens of thousands of Spanish words are derived from Arabic. Let's take a closer look at the Muslims.

"Muslims for Jesus" Strategy Explored

Imagine you're a geographer. But in the world in which you live continents move several miles a year. Earthquakes weekly thrust up new islands or level mountain ranges. Lakes vanish overnight, their waters gulped by thirsty cracks in the earth.

What headaches in trying to draw a map! Every year the atlases and textbooks would have to be rewritten and relearned. A place known to be located at one point this year would have to be repositioned next year because of how much it had moved.

Such is the Muslim world. Not just because of the Gulf War. That brief war merely gives us a clue to what has massively modified the dynamics of the entire Middle East: oil. Titanic changes are affecting everything we thought we once

knew about Islam's nearly one billion people. It is no longer the world Samuel Zwemer tried to reach with the good news. What used to be major features of its landscape are being transformed overnight. New maps must be drawn if the Christian is to discover passable highways to use in carrying the gospel to responsive Muslim peoples.

Muslims are on the move. While there are 42 countries with Muslim majorities, 40 other countries contain significant minorities. Petro-migration is thrusting Muslims out of traditional isolation. Six million reside in Western Europe. The USA boasts a dozen cities with more than 50,000 Muslims (and more than 70 Muslim sects competing for allegiance)! $15 million was spent on a mosque in Chicago. Yet the largest populations of Muslims are not found in oil-rich countries or the West but in Indonesia, Pakistan, Bangladesh, India, the People's Republic of China and Turkey.

More Christians are flooding into the heartlands of Islam around Mecca than ever before. Professionals, technicians, and skilled laborers are being imported from dozens of countries to modernize sheikdoms and help the deserts bloom. 50,000 Arab Christians are employed in Saudi Arabia. 13,000 foreign Christians work in Qatar. Foreigners outnumber the citizens in the United Arab Emirates (240,000 to 225,000) and no one has counted how many Christians there are among these Western technicians. Modernization is revolutionizing the atmosphere and opportunity for Christian-Muslim relationships.

There is a creeping optimism emerging in Christian circles. The long glacial age that began with the Christian Crusades in the Middle Ages appears to be thawing as traditionally icy attitudes towards Christianity seem to be melting. Not that there aren't places where Muslim conversion is met with death or where there are purgatories of hatred such as Lebanon with Christian and Muslim struggling in a death grip. But there are signs of new receptivity to the gospel. And promising developments are appearing on the horizon:

1. The Ancient Christian Churches in Muslim lands (17 million members in the Middle East and Northern Africa) are being shown that they can break out of their ethnic and cultural defensiveness and win Muslims to Jesus. The Orthodox Egyptian Coptic Church has been undergoing a steady, massive revival for the past 30 years and now it is resulting in 30 to 40 baptisms of Muslim converts a week. But this is still the exception rather than the rule. Centuries of turmoil and battering have made the ancient churches generally ingrown enclaves whose cultural difference from the Islamic community is so great that it is almost impossible for a Muslim convert to join them without betraying his own cultural heritage or without remaining a "foreigner" to the Christian community with centuries of cultural divergence.

2. Cross-cultural ministry is finding explosive response where greater cultural sensitivity is being used in evangelistic approaches. The enrollment in one non-Arab country correspondence course added 3900 Muslims in the first six months. A high percentage continued on to completion and advanced courses. Significant numbers evidenced new-found faith in letters and testimonies. Yet the Church is barely exploiting the tremendous opportunity of the Muslim world. There are about 500 North American Protestant missionaries engaged in

Muslim evangelization, a bare 1% of the missionary force for 25% of the world's unreached population. Note the imbalance between workers and need in the charts on pages B—186 to B—188.

3. Secret believers and Christian sympathizers have multiplied. Muslim followers of Jesus still hesitate to take any step such as public baptism since it would send all kinds of wrong signals to their own people. Islam has formidable social and economic barriers for anyone leaving its fold. Apostasy is the supreme betrayal. Yet there are thousands secretly believing in Jesus who long for some new, creative form of Christian movement that would not appear to be treason to their own people and blasphemy to God.

4. New strategies are being explored to see if a "Muslims for Jesus" movement could not be a viable reality in a manner similar to the "Jews for Jesus" movement. Just as the apostle Paul suggested that he be a Greek to the Greeks and a Jew to the Jews, so such principles might suggest being a Muslim to the Muslims. Some evangelical evangelists to Islam are saying that Muslims might truly become believers in Jesus Christ as Savior and Lord without calling themselves Christian, even as the "Messianic Jews" did. In some situations what may be needed is the encouragement of new Christian congregations with a Muslim cultural orientation, churches centered on Jesus Christ but with Islamic cultural forms, where, in fact, the word "Christian" is not even employed.

5. The old malaise and paralysis characteristic of Christian attitudes toward Muslim evangelization seems to be vanishing. Quiet conferences and consultations are forging new concepts and organizations. Hundreds of turned-on mission candidates ought to reconsider the enormous gap between the opportunity and the actual staffing of culturally sensitive approaches to Muslims. The believing followers of Christ are now at the very edge of what could be the most significant advance in reaching unreached Muslims in history—especially if we don't think we have to make them into "Christians" any more than Paul felt he had to make Greeks into Jews. In several places around the world there are movements running into the thousands which consist of blood-washed followers of Christ, whose Koran is now the Christian's Bible, but who do not refer to themselves as Christians.

6. Some scholars feel that illuminating parallels can be drawn between the major cultural streams flowing out of the Incarnation, Death and Resurrection of Jesus Christ: Islam being an Arabic movement, but then there are the cultural synergies of Russian Orthodoxy, Greek Orthodoxy, Ethiopian Orthodoxy, Eastern-Rite Roman Catholicism, Latin-Rite Roman Catholicism, German Lutheranism, English Anglicanism, the variety of American sects. As well thousands of even more strange cultural traditions have evolved among the mission field believers of the world.

In each case, the Gospel has put on "native" dress. The pre-Christian English sunrise service in honor of their spring goddess of fertility, named Eostre, is now our Easter service (which benefits only if we keep our minds and hearts on the Biblical meaning assigned to it).

The pagan Roman practice of giving and receiving gifts on the 25th of December caught on in Latin-speaking countries but not in the Greek and Russian speaking countries, understandably. But the Christian adaptation of this pagan holiday, although the same day of the year does not say anything about the meaning of Saturn, after which this day in the Roman pagan calendar was named (the Saturnalia).

The Assyrian Church of the East (hundreds of thousands of these Christians live in Iraq) had an interesting custom of praying 7 times a day. It was borrowed by Muhammed for Islam (but he cut it down to 5 times a day so as to avoid awaking believers in the dead of night).

Even the Christian Syriac and Arabic word, Allah, which Christians had been using for God for centuries was adopted by Muhammed for Islam. It is still the word for God in the Christian Bibles in those languages.

Bethlehem's Star Over China

The attics of Western memory are stuffed with an incredible array of pictures of China: weather-beaten junks, pagodas with upturned eaves on mist-enshrouded mounts, Dr. Fu Manchu, firecrackers and gaudy dragons, Kung Fu, Stillwell and Chiang Kai Shek, missionary graves, hordes of fanatics waving little Red Books. China has been one of the great obsessions of the West.

And well she might be! The major tides of history indicate that a major wave of the future may be from China. Across the centuries she has been weak only to have the tide of affairs reverse and carry her back to preeminence as the most advanced, powerful, albeit isolated nation on the face of the earth, a position she has held more often and longer than any other society. Christianity will have to sail that tide if she is to be part of China's future.

The church contemplates her more than a billion citizens as the largest single unified bloc of humanity, one which has a very widespread Christian element. At the height of missionary activity in Mainland China, nearly 10,000 Catholic and Protestant missionaries were active. When the Communists took over in 1949 one tangible result of a century and a half of effort was a formal Christian community of 3.2 million Catholics and 1.8 million Protestants, a bare one-percent of the whole of China.

The Christian movement under the People's Republic has experienced a radical change and some shrinkage due to the loss of nominal members, some martyrdom, and minor migration. The pressures of successive waves of repression interspersed with brief periods of toleration for many years robbed the church of its more visible organized expressions. "Institutionless" Christianity is what began expanding at an astounding rate. The Communists tried to rid China once and for all of Christians during the dread ten-year "Cultural Revolution," but only succeeded in refining and spreading the faith. Due to many factors the government began to allow certain buildings to re-open as "official" churches where the government could monitor events. One hundred were allowed. They were immediately but unexpectedly packed. Then, a few more, and more, and soon it was over 6,000 "official" churches. No one can hazard a guess at the church's real size, though one frequent figure quoted is that there may be more than 50 million believers, and more than 50 thousand "house" churches. The latter are without full-time clergy, denominational structure, church buildings, budgets, or seminaries. Their meetings are informal and semi-clandestine.

Some have held out hope that this scattered church under pressure will repeat the story of the early church, gradually leavening the whole of China. And the church is experiencing some growth through healings and exorcism, moving along the lattice work of family relationships with which a Chinese screens himself in a hostile world.

Restrictions continue to be stringent so that open proclamation is forbidden. Those who believe missionaries or Chinese evangelists as such will soon enter the People's Republic cannot easily conclude this from current events in 1992. Millions of people go in and out of China each year but not openly as evangelists or Christian witnesses.

Radio waves do reach behind the bamboo curtain. Government presses actually print Bibles—perhaps due to outside pressures and the sheer economic profit from the world's most sought book. There are reports of greater Christian freedom and activity in South East China and conversions in areas such as Northern Thailand where crossing the border is possible. Despite the tightening following the Tienanmen Square incident, there is nothing so sure, so extensive, so durable, as Christianity in China.

Outside Mainland China the picture is even more hopeful. Overall five to seven percent of some 40 million profess faith in Christ. Of course there are striking variations. In some cases there is burgeoning growth. Six hundred churches serve the one of eight in Hong Kong who follow Christ. Taiwan's AD 2000 Movement committee, the first to unite all of Taiwan's Protestants, has determined to go from 2,000 churches to 10,000 by the year 2000. About ten percent of the 600,000 Chinese in the USA are Protestant or Catholic. In other instances the

Christian presence has only begun to penetrate Chinese populations. Thailand's 3.6 million Chinese have only a tiny church among them with only 4,000 Protestants. Restaurant workers in Europe, such as those in the 50 Chinese restaurants of Vienna, are virtually without a Christian fellowship.

More importantly there are indications that the Chinese church is taking major strides as a maturing body. Rapid and soaring increases are reported in many of the 70 countries with significant Chinese minorities. With that growth has come a new awareness of world mission. From Chinese churches and sending agencies there are now over 300 Chinese missionaries throughout the world. The majority of them, however, are not in cross-cultural ministry but are serving Chinese churches.

It may well be that this new movement of God's Spirit will equip the Christians of the diaspora for an as yet unforeseen opportunity to reach into Mainland China sometime in the near future, but it may also be that when that day comes, as in the case of the opening of the USSR, it will be a two-way street as the believers whose faith has endured hardship become a blessing to those outside of their former prisons.

If the door to China were to open next year, what would happen? Many American-born Chinese Christians no longer speak any Chinese dialects. To evangelize in traditional fashion would require a relearning of their roots, their languages and cultures. English-speaking Chinese would be in real demand to again enter their homeland and through language teaching be ambassadors for Christ. Other parts of the Chinese diaspora are similar. Seventy percent of Indonesia's 3.6 million Chinese are Indonesian born. They speak Indonesian and live like Indonesians.

It is clear that China now contains one of the world's largest numbers of devout, praying Christians. Probably no people group, unreached or not, is very far removed, culturally, from another Chinese group within which the Gospel is now strong.

Any Hope, India?

Remember "Wrong Way Corrigan?" He took off in a small plane from the New York airport and flew across the Atlantic in the repetition of Lindbergh's feat. He had filed a legal flight pattern to some nearby spot in the U.S. and then calmly flew across the Atlantic, pretending he had gone the wrong way. "They let Lindbergh do it. Why not me?"

God played a trick something like that with William Carey, that brilliant young rural schoolteacher in England in the late 1700's. He had plotted and planned for years to go to those islands in the Pacific newly discovered by Captain Cook. (Those islands today are 75% Christian in at least nominal church membership.) He landed instead in India which is still 97% non-Christian. God had the best idea because East India is the closest thing to a crossroads of the world's great blocs of non-Christians—Chinese, Hindus and Muslims. Hindus alone are over 750 million in 1992 and are mainly in India, that amazing country.

Why is India so amazing? Although smaller in size than Argentina, it has twenty-five times the population (more than the whole world in the days of

Columbus), plus 800 distinct languages and dialects, and the world's largest democracy. It is the largest non-Christian country that is at all open to the Gospel.

India is also amazing to even exist as a functioning nation. When the British were forced out in 1947, and literally millions were killed in the bloodshed that later separated Pakistan from a reduced India, many despaired that India could ever pull itself together and survive. Yet today India is in many ways doing magnificently. Only 25% literate, it nevertheless has fifty times as many radios as it did at independence and for many years has boasted the world's largest motion picture industry.

What staggers the imagination is the human diversity of India. Most countries are stratified with layers of people ranging from the downtrodden to the aristocracy. But India is not merely vertically stratified by the world's most rigidly defined social caste system, it is also horizontally cut up due to the linguistic and racial differences that chop India into at least a thousand pieces. Nowhere in the world are cultural differences more difficult to ignore. The most astonishing thing of all is that the Christian church of India has valiantly tried to ignore those distinctions. The church lives outside the caste system but almost entirely on the bottom level of society. Therefore, most Indians who join a Christian church must virtually part ways, downward from all their social and family relationships. Instead of determinedly taking the gospel into the thousands of social compartments of India, the prevailing strategy, insofar as there is one, at the grass roots level is to tear down the social fabric, not just the prejudices embodied therein.

Thus the Church of South India braved all prejudices by sending a lower class bishop to an upper class segment of their church in Kerala, thereby tweaking the nose of the caste system in India. This is all right for a bishop at his level, but the practical requirements of evangelism at the grass roots level of local churches are something else. This is a very delicate subject since at first glance there seems to be a collision between the demands of Christian unity and the freedoms of Christian liberty.

But do Hindus want to become Christians, if they are *not* forced to join a different caste? Some estimates indicate that about 100 million Hindus— people who have been in contact with Christians of other castes for many years—would become Christians tomorrow if someone would take the necessary pains to establish a believing fellowship within their own social grouping. Isn't that a fantastic challenge?

What, pray tell, are missionaries and Indian Christians doing if they are not trying to penetrate one by one the thousands of sub-cultures of India? The answer is, they are doing other things. Aren't they evangelizing at all? Wouldn't it be great if the twenty five million Christians in India would get out there and really evangelize?

Yes, certainly, but two-thirds of the Christians in India need themselves to be evangelized, just as is true in America today. The real shocker is that according to one study 98% of the evangelism in India is devoted to rewinning nominal Christians rather than to penetrating the frontiers that effectively wall off 500 million people.

One of the great marvels of history is the impact of missions on the course of India. While less than 3% of the population is Christian, over half of all the nurses are Christian (it was once 90%); 600 hospitals are there because of missions; and thousands of schools of all kinds. Hinduism itself has significantly changed. The subtle impact of the missionary movement is a story that may never fully be told. Missionaries introduced not just hospitals and schools, but invented khaki colored clothing (it wouldn't show the village dust) and a special and superior kind of tile roofing used now all over India. They brought an end to the custom of widow burning. And the fact that many states of India even today prohibit all liquor is mute testimony of an impact far larger than church statistics. In South India, where most of the Christians are to be found, their presence is felt strongly. In the states of northeast India where 50 to 70 to 95% of the population of the mountain peoples are Christians, the transformation is even more spectacular —from being headhunters as late as 1934, now to being devout Christians, some with Ph.D's. The stories behind all of these achievements almost defy comparison for sheer excitement.

For many years it was rare when mission agencies sprouted from Indian soil itself. Now there is the India Mission Association which includes over 60 different mission agencies, although many others also exist to make India one of the leading countries for "Third World" mission societies.

The Indian Missionary Society followed by the National Missionary Society and then the Indian Evangelical Mission and the Friends Missionary Prayer Band (in 1903, 1905, 1965, 1968, respectively) were early examples of the simple fact that Indians who believe the gospel are willing and able to do both home and foreign mission work. Three of these four early societies determinedly refuse to accept any foreign funds (one was offered a million dollars of foreign money), feeling that the development of sacrificial outreach among their people is as important as the outreach itself. India's strict rules against sending currency out of the country may require collaboration with other countries in order for some opportunities to be grasped. But the Friends Missionary Prayer Band sends its missionaries from south India to north India where there are very few Christians. Indeed north India contains by far the largest block of reachable non-Christians. Pioneer missionary techniques are by no means out of date where the world's largest presently reachable mission field is still to be found.

Tribes: An Endangered Species

The race is on! Tribes are vanishing faster than we are succeeding in translating Scripture into their languages. Technology is leveling the tropics, immobilizing the nomads, dispossessing the weak, deculturizing the alien, and decimating the primitive. Tribes fall prey to epidemics, economic exploitation, modern weaponry and nationalism. In Brazil alone an Indian population of 3 million in 1500 A.D. at the first European contact was reduced to 200,000 by 1968 and to 80,000 since then.

Yet, in many areas of the world the strongest, most aggressive churches are found among tribal peoples. At present, even excluding Africa, thanks in part to

the world's largest mission, the Wycliffe Bible Translators, there are at least 10,000 Protestant missionaries who focus on tribal peoples.

It is virtually impossible to generalize about over 3,000 cultural groups ranging from several million people to miniscule groups of a few dozen individuals. Living in every imaginable habitat, following a mind-boggling array of different customs and experiencing radically different fates, tribal groups vividly express the range and complexity of the unfinished task. But there are several patterns that are apparent from a broad, sweeping overview.

Receptivity

In general, tribal groups are refugees, living in perpetual fear of aggression from other tribes or more powerful civilizations. Often they are able to survive by finding out how to live where no one else would want the land, in incredibly mountainous areas as in West Cameroon, or South China, or Northeast India, or the precipitous highlands (or gigantic swamps of the coastlands) of the great island of New Guinea, the tiny atolls of the South Pacific, or the swamps and jungles of the upper Amazon.

This is one reason they have been the most highly responsive peoples to modern missions, more so than the more secure peasant peoples which constitute the great world religions of Islam, Buddhism, Hinduism and Confucianism.

Also, tribal peoples, characterized by beliefs called "animism" (each group having its own distinctive religious system and worldview) have found conversion to Jesus Christ and His book easier than those who already have their own religious book and literary tradition. Tremendous successes can be illustrated in Oceania, where 70 to 90 percent are Christian; Burma, where 97 percent of all Burmese Christians are tribal; and northeast India, where among the tribal peoples the Nagas are now 70 percent Christian, the Garos and Khasis, 50 percent, and the Mizos, virtually 99 percent! Though the tribal population is only seven percent of India, it represents 15 percent of all Christians in India.

But it must be admitted that within certain types of tribal peoples the Church has made little impact. Nomadic peoples have almost never been reached until and unless they became settled. Hunters and gatherers, like the Pygmies of Africa, and the pastoral peoples who exploit the enormous arid belt running from Morocco to Manchuria, still are solidly outside the faith. Bedouins, shepherds, reindeer and cattle herders await a new creative strategy to give the gospel mobility and vitality for them.

Privilege

At least with the major segments of tribal peoples, the Western Church and mission agencies have had the greatest interest and heaviest involvement. Where there has been receptivity and success, further resources and personnel have followed. Papua New Guinea boasted 3388 missionaries or one missionary for every 800 people. The harvest gathered there has been great: 80 percent of the population of some 500 tribes profess Christ! It does not seem unreasonable to mount a parallel commitment to the major blocs of unreached peoples, the Muslims, Hindus, Chinese and Buddhists. While those blocs are incredibly larger in the number of individual human beings, if you are counting the number of missionary breakthroughs that are necessary, it is fascinating to note that there are only 3 or 4 times as many to deal with because each breakthrough is into a much larger group.

Of course we are not advocating any lessening of commitment to tribal peoples. But who knows what the impact might be and how the numbers of churches might multiply if those other parts of God's vineyard were to receive equal attention and care?

Change

It is impossible to keep tribal peoples isolated and "safe" from modern society. For good and mostly for bad, the tribal groups are being transformed. Where the faith of Jesus Christ has been potent, it has eased the impact of the modern world. Missionaries have been among the most ardent defenders of the rights and dignity of the tribals. Their voices have been heard against multi-national corporation land seizures, local hostilities, and governmental neglect. Missionaries have been in the forefront of those resisting making tribal peoples into jungle slum dwellers. Where whole tribes have become Christian, economic and educational uplift has been enormous. But new problems of survival and finding a place in the modern world system put even greater demands on mission agencies.

Opportunity

Evangelization remains a basic task in many areas. India's 35 million tribals, concentrated in the north central hills, need to be evangelized. Indian Christians in the south and the tribal Christians of the northeast are beginning the task, just as Navajo Christians are sending missionaries to the Laplanders and to Mongolia (where the people have a number of similar customs!). Reconversion is needed in regions where second and third generation "Christians" are growing up with no vital experience with Christ or where tribes have left their first love for a syncretistic revival of traditional religion. Economic and educational developments cry out with enormous needs, which evangelical missions are now more responsibly meeting.

350 Million Asians: Latent or Blooming

First, there are those who live in "Christianized" areas such as the Philippines and Oceania. Overall 80-95% of these regions would nominally claim to be Christians.

Here the dominant problem is the need to convert "Christians" to Christ. That is quite a different matter than converting peoples with no professed allegiance or knowledge to the Savior. Missionaries tackle the situation in large numbers; although the population of the Christianized areas make up only 15% of the 350 million people, fully 50% of the Protestant missionaries in these countries as in Latin America are seeking to make active believers out of nominal Christians.

Second, there are those who live in areas where vigorous, dynamic Christian movements are thriving. This brings us to the first law of these peoples: Where Buddhism has prevailed, the gospel has languished. Dynamic Christian movements are found largely in tribal animists such as the 3 million Karen of Burma and Thailand or among large ethnic groups such as the Koreans where Buddhism is weak. But Korea shows that Buddhists can grasp the significance of Jesus. About one out of four people in South Korea are Christians. It is said that when the border to North Korea opens there will be a million "evangelists" flowing northward to share their joy in Christ as at least that many split-up families attempt to reunite. With Billy Graham's visit, the beginning of the end of the hermit kingdom of the North draws closer, and sits astride a peninsula with the strongest concentration of active Christians anywhere in Asia.

Third, there are those who live in areas with sizable Christian minorities that are currently static or stymied. These are the Roman Catholic showplaces of Sri Lanka (Catholics outnumbered Protestants 9 to 1) and Vietnam (where the ratio is 13 to 1) with approximately 7% of the populace in each country professing some form of Christianity. Sri Lanka sees itself as the haven of "pure" Buddhism. Missions from the outside are limited. The Church is ineffective in reaching the Sinhala Buddhist majority and grows only out of biological necessity. Revival is the only hope at present. Vietnam's evangelical Church was experiencing significant growth especially among the tribal peoples, when the war ended. Little reli-

able information is known but the few indications coming out of Vietnam reveal the Church is continuing even though activities are greatly restricted. Vietnam's 3 million Catholics are a large and influential group but their numbers were not growing by conversion before the war ended.

Fourth, there are those who live in areas where a tiny church is well established, the gospel is regularly proclaimed, but the growth of the Christian movement is negligible. Half of Asia's Christians live in this situation.

Burma exhibits such a pattern. Three percent profess Christ, but the majority of them are not the ethnic Burmese but the tribal animists who have come into the Church in large movements. They are of a different culture and social order than the Burmese Buddhists who will not be easily or readily evangelized by them.

Japan is a unique case. The Western Church has sent large numbers of missionaries. Prominent and influential Japanese have followed Christ resulting in major cultural impacts upon Japanese life. Popular surveys say Jesus Christ is the most admired religious leader in Japan. Yet a tiny percent of Japan's people is willing to identify with the well established but slow growing church. The one exception is among Japanese who have migrated to other countries. Brazil's nearly one million Japanese now profess Christ in the main and best estimates indicate at least 8% regularly participate in Christian congregations.

Fifth, there are areas and peoples where the Church is at best precarious and where evangelization is either restricted or neglected. The tiny countries of Bhutan and Sikkim perched on the Himalayas have few known Christians. The only known church in Bhutan was established in 1971. Nepal suddenly turned a corner and thousands of Christians greeted that change with new, bold plans. Cambodia's tiny church of 5,000 Protestants was exploding with growth when the country fell to the Khmer Rouge. Indications are not hopeful concerning the fate of that church.

Laos had a much larger missionary presence and church before it too closed to the West. But it was largely a tribal church and many members fled to Thailand. Mongolia, on the edge of China, has long been one of the few areas of the earth where there were no Christians present; now like Albania, it is an almost totally new picture. Hundreds of English language teachers are being requested. These gospel-poor regions should drive the Church to her knees in prayer that the Lord of the universe will show his love to these long restricted areas.

God's African Story Filled With Harvest

Someday there will be more Christians in Africa than on any other continent in the world! By the year 2000, the African followers of Jesus Christ in all their diversity will number 350 million.

Africa's century-old missionary story is filled with astounding miracles and sacrifices. Kenya in 1900 had less than 2,000 Christians; today there are more than six million. If we could somehow whisk into the present the two Protestant missionaries who opened up Zaire (formerly Belgium Congo) in 1880, they would hardly comprehend that nearly 60 percent of the citizens identify with Christian traditions.

Some would call this rapid growth alarming because the Church has hardly been able to keep pace in teaching and caring for those coming to Christ. But that is only part of the picture.

If we were to conceive Africa as a village with a population of 1000, the religious make-up would show 417 Muslims, living in the north. The Christians would claim 406, with 162 Roman Catholics and 244 Protestants, Orthodox, Anglicans and Independents. Not all of them would practice their faith. Many would not be evangelical. Many would still practice elements of traditional African religions.

But they would represent an enormous pool of favorable responses to Jesus Christ, and they would have some of the most dynamic revival forces to be found in Christendom. The remainder of the village would be 177 residents who maintain their involvement in traditional African religions.

At first glance it might seem that Muslims and Christians compete in a close race for followers with the Muslims forging ahead.

Oil money is establishing Muslim universities in Black Africa, and in some Muslim places, such as Sudan and Uganda, the Christians have been harried and killed. But since as long ago as 1950 Islam has made few solid advances below the imaginary "Muslim line," 100 miles south of the Sahara. The Church is growing more rapidly than Islam in most parts of black Africa where the large group of unevangelized tribes remain.

The law of sowing and reaping has worked well here. The Western church has sent enormous amounts of personnel and money. Schools and hospitals are to be found in all parts of Africa because Christians have cared. The top political and business elite in country after country received training from missionary schools. There are literally hundreds of Bible schools and seminaries. Over 470 languages have the Bible or portions of scriptures.

Even at the present, the high level of concern of the Western church can be symbolized by the fact that Africa with 10 percent of the world's population contains nearly 27 percent of the Western missionaries. The relatively lavish involvement of the Church with Africa (though even here it has been small in face of need) has resulted in a large harvest. If there could be an equal involvement of the Church with the Muslim world, 27 missionaries would be added for each one now at work!

Does this mean there is no need for missionaries in Africa? Some of the African church leaders have been calling for a halt to Western church money and missionaries. This would give the growing churches of Africa time to develop their own strength and initiative. But there are 260 tribes that remain largely unevangelized. Although Zaire may be nearly 60 percent Christian, there are still 13 major tribal groups that are less than one percent Christian.

But cannot the African churches reach the remaining peoples? In some cases they are. The evangelical churches of West Africa trained and sent 15 missionaries into the Maguzawa of Nigeria in 1976, and a church has already begun to grow. That same church is training and sending medical missionary personnel into the Sudan to evangelize the Muslims. The Anglican diocese of Mt. Kenya East has set up an evangelists' training school and has been busy evangelizing the seven large unreached tribes found in northeastern Kenya.

It would be difficult to begin to catalog the hundreds of missionaries that proclaim the gospels of some 6,000 African independent churches which have split off from mission churches to develop a more African form of Christianity. Nonetheless, there still are neglected groups who will be reached only when a Western mission agency catches the vision.

A number of crucial tasks remain before the Church. Millions are streaming into Africa's crowded cities. The churches have a great responsibility to shepherd the Christians who seek a better life there. In Kinshasa, some 750,000 claim to be Protestants, but no more than 100,000 are actually involved with a local fellowship. Most were reared in rural areas, became Christians in mission schools and then were baptized. Now they drift toward secularism and nominalism. Who will care for their future?

There are titanic transformations taking place all over Africa. Nation building is barely keeping pace with tyranny. In country after country, like a bomb with a delayed-action fuse, events have led to gruesome civil wars and destabilized governments, in part a reaction to the massive breakdown of traditional authority in the former USSR. Even without the atrocities of war, there are the lingering atrocities of a darkened human society, which, for example, has produced the 80 women alive today in Africa who have undergone "female circumcision," a mindless traditional ceremony at puberty which, in all three variations inflicts serious maiming. This kind of thing, protected as it is by powerful cultural forces, can only be seen as a tragic distortion of God's creative intent.

Africa provides only two percent of the world's production and faces tremendous problems in economic and social development. Western mission agencies and churches are heavily involved in fostering this transformation. Christianity itself is undergoing Africanization. New worship forms, new approaches to polygamy, new theologies are all being developed in a serious attempt to incorporate Christianity in less Western garb. Africa may be the next Christian continent but there will be hardly anything drab or staid about it.

Study Questions

1. What opportunities for and which obstacles to missions advancement are apparent from each of the areas surveyed in this article?

2. What is the dominant impression left by these articles? guarded optimism? caution? skepticism? enthusiasm?

20

Missions in the Modern Milieu

J. Herbert Kane and Ralph R. Covell

THE NEW DAY OF CHRISTIAN MISSIONS

Steven Neill in his book *Colonialism and Christian Mission* writes: "One age has died; another is striving to be born. We stand in the time of birthpangs, in which the future is still obscure." [1] There is no doubt about it; we are living in a new day as far as the Christian mission is concerned. The last thirty years have seen more changes in the political configuration of the world than any previous period of similar length. Colonialism, the most powerful force in the world in the 19th century, has given way to nationalism, by far the greatest force in the 20th century. With the end of the Vasco da Gama era, the missionary movement now finds itself in a political atmosphere sometimes favorable, sometimes unfavorable—at times downright hostile.

One problem is that we had it too good in the 19th century. In those days the Christian missionary could come and go as he pleased. Passports were seldom required and visas were unknown. The great European powers imposed their peace on whole continents, and the missionaries enjoyed the protection of their respective colonial authorities.

Drawing on fifteen years of missionary experience in central China with the China Inland Mission, J. Herbert Kane taught for many years in the School of World Mission and Evangelism at Trinity Evangelical Divinity School, and was Professor Emeritus before his death in 1989. Kane was the author of a number of missions textbooks, among them *Christian Missions in Biblical Perspective* and *A Global View of Christian Missions*..

Having served as a missionary with the Conservative Baptist Foreign Missionary Society in China for one term, Ralph R. Covell spent the next fourteen years in Taiwan, where he translated the New Testament into the Sediq language and developed a Bible institute into a seminary for training Christian leaders. From 1966 to 1990 he was a professor of missions at Denver Conservative Baptist Seminary and he is currently an Adjunct Professor of World Mission. Reproduced by permission from *Trinity World Forum*, Vol. 3, No. 3, Spring 1978.

The New Situation

Today the situation is different. The United Nations began in 1945 with 51 charter members. Now the membership has reached 149 [Ed. note: 166 as of 1991; N. Korea, S. Korea, Micronesia, and Latvia all added in 1991.] and it is still climbing. Most of the new members are ex-colonies that have reached their independence since 1960. Naturally they have every intention of enjoying and exercising their new-found sovereignty.

Every sovereign state has the right to exclude or expel anyone deemed undesirable. Communist countries have historically closed their doors to the Christian missionary. Many Muslim countries have done the same. Other countries, acting in national self-interest, have passed laws banning or restricting missionary activities. Not only visas, but residence and work permits are required. Sometimes they are granted; at other times they are either withheld or interminably delayed, to the utter frustration of the missionary.

Thailand, always considered friendly to Christian missions, has shown signs of tightening up on its immigration laws. The Overseas Missionary Fellowship submitted 54 applications during the first six months of 1977. Of these, 41 were refused and none had been granted by August 1. Similar difficulties and delays have been experienced from time to time in Nigeria, Malaysia, Guyana, Peru, India and other countries.

Independence, which promised to solve all their problems, has turned out to be a mirage, and the long-suffering people involved are, in many cases, worse off than before. The white *sahibs* have been replaced by black and brown *sahibs*. Worse still, economic stagnation and political instability continue to plague the dictatorships. In some parts of the world, governments rise and fall almost overnight. The American missionary, with his tradition of an open society with multi-party politics and freedom of speech, press, and assembly, finds life and work under a dictatorship very irksome.

Mass murders have occurred in Cambodia, Sudan, Ethiopia, Chad, Uganda, and Burundi. The situation in other African countries remains highly explosive. Two Christian radio stations have been taken over by government action—Radio Voice of the Gospel in Ethiopia and Radio Cordac in Burundi.

Today's world is divided into two groups: the *"have"* and the *"have-not"* nations. The *have* nations, for obvious reasons, are quite content with the status quo. The *have-not* nations, for equally obvious reasons, are determined to bring about change. They are in a state of ferment—intellectual, political, economic and social, which slowly but surely is rising to the point where it will boil over in what Adlai Stevenson called a *"revolution of rising expectations."*

Most nationalists prefer peaceful revolution; but if peaceful revolution proves impossible, then violent revolution becomes inevitable. Many of the countries of Latin America, though politically independent for over 150 years, are wracked with social unrest. In the summer of 1977, some fifty Roman Catholic missionaries in Guatemala were threatened with death because of their efforts to secure social justice for the poverty-stricken people of that country. Guerrilla fighters in Thailand, Ethiopia, and Rhodesia have kidnapped and killed missionaries in an effort to embarrass the powers that be. Today's missionary is a guest in the host country; as such he has no "rights," only privileges, and these are not always forthcoming. If he gets into trouble there is little the U.S. government can do about it.

The Missionary's Response

The missionary should honestly face up to the realities of the new situation.

It will help him immensely if he will take a second look at the teachings of Christ in Matthew 10, where Jesus lays down three principles. (1) *Conflict in the Christian mission is inevitable.* "Do not think that I have come to bring peace on earth; I have not come to bring peace, but a sword." (v. 34) (2) *Conflict will involve the disciples in personal danger—perhaps death.* "Beware of men, for they will deliver you up to councils, and flog you in their synagogues, and you will be dragged before governors and kings for my sake." (vv. 17-18) (3) *Neither danger nor death should deter the missionary.* "Do not fear those who kill the body but cannot kill the soul....When they persecute you in one town, flee to the next." (vv 28, 23) These are among the *"hard sayings"* of Jesus to which we have paid little heed in the past. They are eminently appropriate tor the new day in which we are living.

The missionary should remember that he is an ambassador for Jesus Christ, not for Uncle Sam.

He is not interested in exporting the American way of life, the capitalist system, or Western democracy, though he may be persuaded that all three are highly desirable. He is a world citizen and his chief task is to build the Kingdom of God on earth. This being so, he is under no obligation to support, much less defend, all the foreign policy pronouncements of the U.S. government. Certainly he will abhor the approach which says, *"My country, right or wrong."* When his country is right, he will in all sincerity try to explain and defend it. When it is wrong, he should have the courage and candor to say so.

The missionary must not equate the Kingdom of God with any particular political, economic and social system.

All human systems, including his own, are under the judgment of God and should be evaluated in the light of the Holy Scripture. In today's pluralistic world, the missionary must be prepared to live and labor under alien systems of various kinds without trying to undermine or overthrow them. He must resist the temptation to jump on every passing bandwagon that promises to solve the political problems of the day.

The missionary must not assume that Western democracy is for everyone.

Democracy to be effective must be supported by other institutions: a free press, a multi-party system, a universal franchise, and a secret ballot. But what is the use of these things if the majority of the electorate is illiterate and the common man has no burning desire to be part of the decision-making process? For centuries he has lived a communal life, with others, often the tribal chief or elders, making his decisions for him. The same is true of the peasant in his paddy field. He could not care less about free elections and a secret ballot. All he wants is to be left alone with his family and his fields.

The missionary must be prepared to work and witness under political and social conditions that are not to his liking.

It was assumed that the demise of the colonial system would bring a full measure of freedom to the oppressed peoples of the Third World, but it has not worked out that way. Very few countries are genuine democracies. Human rights, taken for granted in the West, simply do not exist. They started out well. Democracy was tried but found wanting. One by one, duly elected governments were overthrown, political parties were banned, constitutions were scrapped, and dictatorships were established. Of the 158 nations in the world, only 40 enjoy complete freedom, 53 are partially free, and 65 have few if any civil rights;[2] and the vast majority of missionaries are living in the countries listed in the last two categories.

The missionary must be content with whatever freedom is permitted.

He is not likely to be accorded more liberty, religious or civil, than is granted to the nationals. It is both foolish and futile for him to demand what the government is not prepared to give. Under a repressive regime he has two options. He can mind his own business and continue his work, or he can speak out against the regime and be expelled. Each missionary must make up his own mind what to do in a given situation. If he elects to stay, his role will not be an easy one. Like Lot in Sodom, his righteous soul will be tormented day after day by the lawless deeds he will have to witness. If he cannot remain silent and live with his conscience, he will have to speak out. In that case he is almost sure to be expelled.

If he is expelled, what will happen to the people left behind, Christians and non-Christians, who depend on him for medical and educational facilities? Will the church and the community be better off or worse off without him? If he happens to be the only doctor in a 100-bed hospital, what will become of his patients when he is gone? It may require more wisdom and courage to remain at his post under very difficult and dangerous conditions than to sound off and be expelled from the country.

What About The Future?

Conditions in the Third World are not likely to improve in the near future.

It is going to take time for these new nations to set their house in order and to achieve political stability, economic prosperity, and social justice. In the meantime, coups and counter-coups will occur, dictators and demagogues will hold office, and the jails will be filled with political prisoners.

Today, the cry for freedom is heard all over the world. The missionary, however, must be on his guard lest he be tempted to join the chorus, shout the slogans, and wave the banners with all the "freedom fighters" of the world. When it comes to the highly complex and often doubtful issues of politics, the missionary should hesitate to take sides. He need not assume that his allegiance to Jesus Christ requires him to join the picket line every time an opposition newspaper is banned or a local politician goes to jail.

Changing conditions in the West call for sober reflection.

Supporting churches in the West must come to terms with reality. From Constantine to World War II, Church and state were closely identified. The Church supported the political, economic and social status quo; and in return received preferential treatment by both government and society. But the situation is changing rapidly. One by one the props are being removed. If the Church is to stand at all, she will have to stand on her own feet. In the very near future, we shall have come full circle and be back where the Church was in the first century. We may even be in for a period of persecution, and this may not be all bad.

In spite of her vast military and economic power, the U.S. is in for hard sledding in the days ahead. Faced with the colossal power of the Soviet Union, plagued with an energy crisis and a plunging dollar, burdened with a horrendous deficit in our balance of trade, and embarrassed by crime in the streets, corruption in politics, and vandalism in the pubic schools, Uncle Sam is no longer regarded as the undisputed leader of the world. This melancholic fact has immediate and enormous influence on the Christian mission still based largely in the West.

In the days ahead, our *message* will remain unchanged; but most other things will be different. Methods, motives, attitudes, understanding, programs, and priorities—all will undergo change. One can only hope that the Western missions and their supporting churches, reading aright the signs of the times, will be given the wisdom to pray intelligently and the courage to act decisively in the challenging days ahead.

Church and mission do well to remember that world mission is God's work, not theirs.

Before Jesus gave the Great Commission, He reminded His disciples that all power in heaven and on earth belongs to Him. At the same time, He promised to be with them to the end of the age. Stephen Neill has described missionary work as "the most difficult thing in the world." [3] He is right. Missionary work has always been difficult, dangerous, and discouraging. We have no reason to believe that the future will be any different from the past. If the missionary enterprise is to remain true to its own genius and realize its high destiny, it must continue to operate within the context of world history, however turbulent it might become.

Jesus Christ is not only the Head of the Church. He is also the Lord of history. He has both the will and the power to achieve His purpose in and through His Church. He knows the end from the beginning and is working all things after the counsel of His own will. Dictators come and go; kingdoms rise and fall; civilizations wax and wane; but the worldwide mission of the Church will continue to the end of the age.

When Jesus gave His disciples their marching orders, He pulled no punches. He told them exactly what to expect at the hands of a hostile world. He promised neither easy victory nor immediate success. He spoke of opposition, tribulation, and persecution. The enterprise was to be fraught with all kinds of difficulties and dangers. His messengers would be hunted and hounded from pillar to post. They would be scourged by the Jews and flogged by the Romans. Indeed, some of them would be called upon to seal their testimony with their blood.

But the mandate would never be rescinded or the mission aborted. They were taught to believe that they were engaged in a holy war with an implacable foe. Casualties would occur and reverses come; but they were to press on in full assurance that the Captain of their salvation would be with them to the end of the age. Many battles would be lost, but the war would be won. He would see to that.

AN APOLITICAL GOSPEL OR THE GOSPEL OF THE KINGDOM?

Kane has reminded us of the unfriendly political milieu in which modern missions must often work. Not that this hostility is really a new phenomenon. Roman Catholic missionaries suffered at the hands of oppressive rulers in many places, particularly Japan and China, long before the modern Protestant missionary put in his appearance. The first American Protestant missionaries sailed for British-controlled India at the height of the war of 1812. Hundreds of missionaries and Chinese Christians, Protestant and Roman Catholic alike, lost their lives in the Boxer Rebellion of 1900. The thousands of missionaries who remained in China in 1949-51, after the advent of a new regime, chose priorities of the Kingdom of God over personal safety. But the present scene is different. The American missionary, at least, has been reared in the *"no risk"* atmosphere of a soft Christianity and finds it easy to forget these past sacrifices. Furthermore, as Dr. Kane points out, the demise of colonialism has left the missionary exposed and powerless, seemingly at the whim of political forces beyond his control.

Attitudes in the "New Situation"

My own twenty years of missionary experience, some of it under extreme political adversity, leads me to agree with much of what Dr. Kane has written. Beyond his message, however, there seems to lurk a *"para-message"* implying that the missionary does well not to be involved in socio-political matters. I am concerned with several attitudes that I see in some evangelical missionaries confronted with this *"new situation."*

1. The gospel they preach is not Paul's gospel of the kingdom. Their pietistic heritage, experience and education have programmed them to believe that socio-political issues at home or abroad, are not within the purview of the gospel. They are hesitant to affirm with the Lausanne Covenant that *"evangelism and socio-political involvement are both part of our Christian duty"* and that they *"should not be afraid to denounce evil and injustice wherever they exist."*

2. That to not speak out on such issues assures they are preaching a pure, apolitical gospel. Many evangelical Third World leaders are reminding us that American missionaries are not able to see, let alone understand, the oppression under which their people live. Silence signals acquiescence.

3. That we are expelled from countries because we do not *"mind our own business"* and preach the simple gospel. If, however, the mission is God's mission, are missionaries not subject to the

demands of the gospel of the kingdom, and all that it teaches with respect to sin (personal and corporate), God's righteousness, and His justice?

Involvement as a Guest

It goes without saying that a missionary is a *"guest"* in the host country. He must carefully choose his battlefields. Cultural sensitivity, disengagement from purely American values and attitudes, humility, deference to the desires of the national church, low-profile types of informal action, and concerted attempts to keep lines of communication open with those he must criticize would be required in whatever is done. Assuming, however, that the missionary chooses to do nothing to oppose basic social, economical, or political injustices, are there other alternatives? Let me suggest two.

1. Using proper channels he can seek to modify or alter policies of his own government that may contribute to these injustices. Such action puts feet to his belief that the systems of his own government are *"under judgment of God and should be evaluated in the light of Holy Scripture ."* Missionaries often urge our government to stand up against leftist totalitarianism. May we not also oppose the oppressive exploitation in many countries of totalitarianism of the right?

2. He must use Biblical principles to educate local Christians on God's norms for human society. Unfree himself to speak out or act, his Christian education will include all the *"counsel of God."* Amos, as well as Romans, will be his curriculum. Local Christians will learn how, by the leading of the Holy Spirit, to contextualize the gospel. The result may well be something like the Koinonia Declaration issued by Christians in South Africa.

The holy war in which we are engaged is a *"no holds barred"* battle with the enemy and his strongholds. The hostility will increase as we wage our struggle *on all fronts* rather than limiting ourselves, in the fashion of the traditional Eastern religions, to a religious vacuum.

End Notes

1. Neill, Stephen, *Colonialism and Christian Missions* (New York: McGraw-Hill 1966), p. 422.

2. *U.S. News and World Report*, January 19, 1976.

3. Neill, Stephen, *Call to Mission* (Philadelphia: Fortress Press, 1971), p. 24.

Study Questions

1. Why does Kane claim that "the missionary should hesitate to take sides" in political issues of the Third World? Do you agree? Why or why not?

2. In what areas might American missionaries be tempted to equate the Kingdom of God with a particular political, economic, or social system?

21

The Hope of a Coming World Revival

Robert E. Coleman

We go forth in the confidence that someday the harvest will be gathered from the ends of the earth. This promise certainly accentuates the possibility of a mighty cosmic revival before the end of the age. Is this hope realistic? If so, it gives us reason to walk on tiptoes.

An Exciting Prophecy

Considering the convulsive struggles of our civilization, any discussion of last things seems relevant today. The growing concern for the world's unreached billions, and how the church will reach them, makes the subject even more pertinent.

Scripture does point to some kind of a climactic spiritual conflagration, though the time and extent of its coming can be variously understood. Most of the references to this coming world revival are bound up with other historical situations, such as the return of the Jews from captivity and the restoration of their nation. How one understands the millennium, tribulation, and rapture must also be taken into account. Obviously those who see Christ returning to take away his church before his millennial reign will look at the awakening from a different perspective than those who view it as an aspect of the millennium. Notwithstanding the differences, nothing in the varying positions necessarily precludes a coming world revival.

Let us admit that the complexity of the biblical prophecies makes any conclusion tentative. Yet, recognizing that we now only see through the glass darkly, it is possible to discern an outline of a future movement of revival that will make anything seen thus far pale by comparison.

Robert E. Coleman is a professor at the School of World Mission and Evangelism of Trinity Evangelical Divinity School. He serves as Director of the Billy Graham Institute of Evangelism at Wheaton, Illinois, and a Dean of the International Schools of Evangelism. He is a member of the Lausanned Committee for World Evangelization and has been Chairman of the North America Section. Excerpted from The *Spark that Ignites*. Used by permission of Worldwide Publications, Minneapolis, MN, 1989.

A Universal Outpouring of the Holy Spirit

The day is envisioned when the church in all parts of the world will know the overflow of God's presence. No one will be excluded, as Joel prophesied, "And it shall come to pass afterward, that I will pour out my spirit upon all flesh; and your sons and your daughters shall prophesy, your old men shall dream dreams, your young men shall see visions: And also upon the servants and upon the handmaids in those days will I pour out my spirit." (Joel 2:28, 29), a statement clearly indicating that all classes of people from around the world will feel the impact of this spiritual rejuvenation. Peter associated this promise with the coming of the Holy Spirit at Pentecost (Acts 2:16, 17). Yet the universal dimension of the prophecy of Joel was not experienced fully, in that the Spirit did not then come upon God's people from all over the world. Of course, potentially the first Pentecostal visitation reached to "all flesh," even to them that "are afar off" (Acts 2:39). This was typified by the Spirit-filled disciples' witness to the people present that day from "every nation under heaven" (Acts 2:5). But in actual extent that outpouring was confined to the city. As the church gradually moved out in the strength of the Holy Spirit, the flame spread to Judea, to Samaria, and finally to many distant places of the civilized world. The message is still going out. But complete fulfillment of the prophecy awaits a glorious day to come.

Certainly a spiritual awakening around the world would be in keeping with the all-embracing love of God (John 3:16). In a dramatic way, it would give notice of the gospel mandate to reach "the uttermost part of the earth" (Acts 1:8; cf. Mark 16:15; John 20:21; Matthew 28:19), fulfilling at last the promise to Abraham that in him all peoples on the earth shall be blessed (Genesis 12:3; 22:18). The worship of God by all the families of the nations, so long foretold, would then be a reality (see Psalms 22:27; 86:9; Isaiah 49:6; Daniel 7:14; Revelation 15:4), and God's name would be great among the Gentiles, "from the rising of the sun even unto the going down of the same" (Malachi 1:11).

According to this reasoning, the church age began and will end in a mighty spiritual baptism. What happened at the first Pentecost may be seen as the "early" display of the refreshing rain from heaven, while the closing epic is the "latter rain" (Joel 2:23; Hosea 6:3; Zechariah 10:1; James 5:7). Water or rain, it will be remembered, is often symbolic of the Holy Spirit (John 7:37-39).

Strange Demonstrations of Power

In describing the Spirit's outpouring, Joel foretells "wonders in the heavens and in the earth, blood, and fire, and pillars of smoke. The sun shall be turned into darkness, and the moon into blood, before the great and the terrible day of the Lord come" (Joel 2:30, 31; cf. Acts 2:19, 20). Yet these phenomena are not mentioned as happening in the account of the first Pentecost, so apparently they are yet to occur.

Jesus spoke of days immediately "after the tribulation" in similar terms, adding that "the stars shall fall from heaven, and the powers of the heavens shall be shaken" (Matthew 24:29; cf. Revelation 6:12,13). It seems that God will summon the forces of nature to bear witness to what is happening on the earth.

Adding to the spectacle, some persons will have the power to perform wondrous deeds, such as turning water to blood (Revelation 11:6; cf. Galatians 3:5). Naturally Satan will do what he can to counterfeit that which he knows is real. We are warned of "false Christs" and "false prophets" of this time who will show "great signs and wonders to deceive the elect (Matthew 24:24; cf. Exodus 7:10-12; Matthew 7:15-20; 2 Thessalonians 2:9, 10). The sensory appeal is always fraught with danger, which is all the more reason why we are exhorted to try the spirits. If they are not Christ-exalting, then they are not of God (1 John 4:1-3).

Unprecedented Trouble

Those fearful conditions of the last days described in Matthew 24 and intermittently in Revelation 6 to 17 also seem to characterize this period. And things will get worse as the end approaches (cf. 2 Timothy 3:12; 2 Thessalonians 2:1-3).

Famines, pestilence, and earthquakes of staggering proportions will occur. Wars and intrigue will fill the earth. Hate will bind the hearts of men. No one will feel secure. As moral integrity breaks down, apostasy in the church will increase. Those who do not conform to the spirit of the age will be hard pressed, and many will be martyred. Clearly, the cost of discipleship will be high.

Yet amid this terrible adversity, Scripture indicates that revival will sweep across the earth. When God's "judgments are in the earth, the inhabitants of the world will learn righteousness" (Isaiah 26:9). Dreadful calamities will mingle with awesome displays of salvation—the terrors will actually create an environment for earnest heart searching. Not everyone will turn to God, of course. Some persons will remain unrepentant and become even more brazen in their sin. But the world will be made to confront, as never before, the cross of Jesus Christ.

How it will all end is not clear. Possibly the revival will close and there will be "a falling away" before the Lord returns (2 Thessalonians 2:3). Some Bible students believe that the worst tribulation will come after the church is caught up. Others think that Christians will be taken out of the world midway through this dreadful period.

However viewed, Scripture gives us no reason to think that the last great revival will avert the coming catastrophe. The line of no return will have already been passed. Judgment is certain. Revival may delay, but it will not prevent, the final day of reckoning.

Cleansing of the Church

Through the purging of revival God's people will be brought to the true beauty of holiness. Our Lord expects to present his bride unto himself "a radiant church, without stain or wrinkle or any other blemish, but holy and blameless" (Ephesians 5:27, NIV; cf. 1 John 3:2, 3; 2 Corinthians 7; 1 Peter 1:13-16; 3:4). The trials of the last days will serve as fires to refine the gold of Christian character. Out of them the bride of Christ, "arrayed in fine linen, clean and white," will emerge ready for the marriage supper of the Lamb (Revelation 19:7-9; cf. Daniel 12:10). To this end, the "latter rain" of the Spirit is intended to bring "the precious fruit" of the church to maturity in preparation for the Lord's return (James 5:7; cf. Song of Solomon 2).

The church should not fear affliction, though it cause anguish and even death. Suffering may be necessary to convince us that we do not live by bread alone. When received as an expression of God's trust, our suffering can be a means of helping us comprehend more of the love of Christ, who "suffered for us, leaving us an example, that ye should follow his steps" (1 Peter 2:21; cf. Heb. 2:10; 5:8). Without hardship, probably few of us would learn much about the deeper life of grace.

A purified church will be able to receive unhindered the power of the out-poured Spirit, and thereby more boldly enter into the mission of Christ. It is also reasonable to believe that this greater concurrence with God's program will multiply the manifestation of ministry gifts in the body (Ephesians 3:7-15; cf. Romans 12:6-8; 1 Corinthians 12:4-11; 1 Peter 4:10-11). This would further call attention to the momentous awakening on earth.

Tremendous Ingathering of Souls

The coming world revival will naturally result in multitudes calling upon the name of the Lord for salvation (Joel 2:32; Acts 2:21; cf. Romans 10:13). And the same revival will also prepare workers for that great harvest of souls. People who are full of the Holy Spirit are committed to God's work. They want to be where laborers are needed most, and there is no more pressing need than bringing the gospel to hell-bound men and women.

Significantly, Jesus said that the fulfillment of his preaching mission would precede his return "This gospel of the kingdom will be preached in the whole world as a testimony to all nations, and then the end will come" (Matthew 24:14, NIV; cf. Luke 12:36, 37; 14:15-23). Doubtless the passion to get out the message while there is yet time will increase with the revival, even as the witnesses multiply. That the gospel will eventually penetrate "every nation, tribe, people and language" is clear from the description of the innumerable multitude of the white-robed saints gathered around the throne of God in heaven (Revelation 7:9, NIV; cf. 5:9). The Great Commission will finally be fulfilled.

Many believe that Jews will be among the lost who turn to Christ at that time. At least, there are prophecies which speak of their general repentance and acceptance of the Messiah (see Ezekiel 20:43, 44: Jeremiah 31:34; Romans 11:24), and of God's pardon and blessing (see Jeremiah 31:27-34; 32:37-33:26; Ezekiel 16:60-63; 37:1-28; Hosea 6:1, 2; Amos 9:11-15; Revelation 7:1-17). The world revival seems a logical time for this to happen. Pretribulationists might put the Jewish awakening after the rapture of the church, making a great deal of Romans 11:25-26, which speaks of Israel's being saved when the fulness of the Gentiles is come. This passage, however, could serve equally well to support the idea of revival before Christ comes again.

Whatever position one might hold, there can be little question that the greatest day of evangelism is before us. The harvesting may be short in duration, and may require enormous sacrifice, but it will be the most far-reaching acceptance of the gospel this world has ever seen.

Preparing for Christ's Return

The massive turning to Christ by people from the four corners of the earth will prepare the way for the coming of the King. Our Lord's return may be waiting now on this spiritual revolution. "Behold, the husbandman waiteth for the precious fruit of the earth, and hath long patience for it, until he receive the early and latter rain. Be ye also patient; stablish your hearts: for the coming of the Lord draweth nigh" (James 5:7, 8).

The fact that our Lord has not already returned to establish his kingdom is evidence of his desire to see the church perfected and the gospel presented to every person for whom he died. God is "longsuffering toward us, not willing that any should perish, but that all should come to repentance" (2 Peter 3:9). But we dare not presume upon his patience. None of us can be so sure of our understanding of prophecy as to preclude his return at any moment. Every day we should be ready to meet the Lord, the more so as we see the night approaching.

Anticipation of our Lord's return is a summons to action. We must cast off anything that blocks the flow of the Holy Spirit and commit ourselves to being about the Father's business. World evangelization now is the responsibility around which our lives should be centered. Whatever our gifts, we are all needed in the witness of the gospel.

Uniting in Prayer

As we anticipate the coming world revival prayer is our greatest resource. The prophet reminds us, "Ask ye of the Lord rain in the time of the latter rain" (Zechariah 10:1). "When the tongue faileth for thirst," God says, "I will open rivers in high places, and fountains in the midst of the valleys" (Isaiah 41:18; cf. 44:3). Surely it is time to "seek the Lord, till he come and rain righteousness" upon us (Hosea 10:12; cf. Joel 2:17; Acts 1:14). There is no other way to bring life to the church and hope to the barren fields of the world.

As the first Great Awakening was sweeping America in 1748, Jonathan Edwards, responding to a proposal from church leaders in Scotland, published *A Humble Attempt to Promote Explicit Agreement and Visible Union of God's People in Extraordinary Prayer, for the Revival of Religion and the Advancement of Christ's Kingdom on Earth, Pursuant to Scripture Promises and Prophecies Concerning the Last Time*. It was an appeal for the church to unite in earnest intercession for world revival, based on the text of Zechariah 8:20, 21:

> It shall yet come to pass, that there shall come people, and the inhabitants of many cities: And the inhabitants of one city shall go to another, saying, Let us go speedily to pray before the Lord, and to seek the Lord of hosts: I will go also. Yea, many people and strong nations shall come to seek the Lord of hosts.

About this passage Edwards said:

> From the representation mode in this prophecy, it appears...that it will be fulfilled something after this manner; first, that there shall be given much of a spirit of prayer to God's people in many places, disposing them to come into an express agreement, unitedly to pray to God in an extraordinary manner, that he would appear for the help of his church, and in mercy to mankind, and to pour out his Spirit, revive his work, and advance his spiritual kingdom in the world as he has promised; and that this disposi-

tion to such prayer, and union in it, will spread more and more, and increase in greater degrees; with which at length will gradually be introduced a revival of religion, and a disposition to greater eagerness in the worship and service of God, amongst his professing people; that this being observed, will be the means of awakening others, making them sensible of the wants of their souls, and exciting in them a great concern for their spiritual and everlasting good, and putting them upon earnest crying to God for spiritual mercies, and disposing them to join with God's people ... and that in this manner religion shall be propagated, until the awakening reaches these that are in the highest stations, and until whole nations be awakened, and there be at length an accession of many of the chief nations of the world to the church of God.... And thus that shall be fulfilled "O thou that hearest prayer, unto thee shall all flesh come" (Psalm 65:2).[1]

Edwards's plea for God's people to come together in fervent and constant prayer for revival still speaks with urgency. Not only does it call us to our most essential ministry of intercession, but it also reminds us of the way God has ordained to quicken his church and to disseminate her witness until finally the nations of the earth shall come and worship before the Lord.

Living in Expectancy

Billy Graham in his last message at the Lausanne Congress in 1974 expressed succinctly both the realism and the hope we have in awaiting "the climactic movement and the total fulfillment of what was done on the Cross." Then, reflecting upon the future, he added:

I believe there are two strains in prophetic Scripture. One leads us to understand that as we approach the latter days and the Second Coming of Christ, things will become worse and worse. Joel speaks of "multitudes, multitudes in the valley of decision!" The day of the Lord is near in the valley of decision. He is speaking of judgment.

But I believe as we approach the latter days and the coming of the Lord, it could be a time also of great revival. We cannot forget the possibility and the promise of revival, the refreshing of the latter days of the outpouring of the Spirit promised in Joel 2:28 and repeated in Acts 2:17. That will happen right up to the advent of the Lord Jesus Christ.

Evil will grow worse, but God will be mightily at work at the same time. I am praying that we will see in the next months and years the "latter rains," a rain of blessings, showers falling from heaven upon all the continents before the coming of the Lord.[2]

All of us should join in this prayer, even as we look expectantly to what lies ahead. Something great is on the horizon. You can almost feel it in the air. Though forces of evil are becoming more sinister and aggressive, there is a corresponding cry for spiritual awakening. Across the world never has there been more yearning by more people for spiritual reality, nor has the church ever had the means it now has to take the glad tidings of salvation to the lost, unreached peoples of the earth. What a day to be alive!

Certainly this is not a time for despair. The King's coming is certain. And in preparation for his return we may be the very generation that will see the greatest movement of revival since the beginning of time.

End Notes

1. Jonathan Edwards, *A Humble Attempt...,The Works of President Edwards*, Vol. 3 (New York: Leavitt, Trow and Co., 1818), 432, 433. The full discourse, encompassing pages 423-508, lifts up the promise of world revival, and the need to pray unitedly for it, more than any other writing in the English language. The appeal for concerts of prayer also comes out in George Whitefield's ministry during this same period, and, indeed, continued in revival efforts through the nineteenth century. In recent years it has been picked up again by such international voices as the Lausanne Committee for World Evangelization. For a contemporary exposition of the movement, and practical direction in how you can become involved, see David Bryant's *With Concerts of Prayer* (Ventura: Regal Books, 1984); or his more recent, *Operation: Prayer* (Madison: Inter-Varsity Christian Fellowship, 1987); historical background is given by J. Edwin Orr in *The Eager Feet: Evangelical Awakenings, 1790-1830* (Chicago: Moody Press, 1975).

2. Billy Graham, "The King is Coming," in *Let the Earth Hear His Voice*, Official Reference Volume for the International Congress on World Evangelization, Lausanne, Switzerland, ed. J. D. Douglas (Minneapolis: World Wide Publications, 1975), 1466.

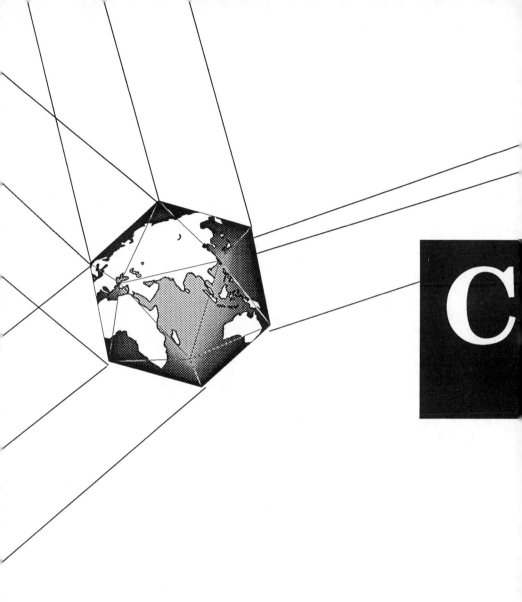

THE CULTURAL PERSPECTIVE

1

Understanding Culture

Lloyd E. Kwast

What is a culture, anyway? For the student just beginning the study of missionary anthropology, this question is often a first response to a confusing array of descriptions, definitions, comparisons, models, paradigms, etc. There is probably no more comprehensive word in the English language than the word "culture," or no more complex a field of study than cultural anthropology. Yet, a thorough understanding of the meaning of culture is prerequisite to any effective communication of God's good news to a different people group.

The most basic procedure in a study of culture is to become a master of one's own. Everyone has a culture. No one can ever divorce himself from his culture. While it is true that anyone can grow to appreciate various different cultures, and even to communicate effectively in more than one, one can never rise above his own, or other cultures, to gain a truly supra-cultural perspective. For this reason, even the study of one's own culture is a difficult task. And to look objectively at something that is part of oneself so completely is nearly impossible.

One helpful method is to view a culture, visualizing several successive "layers," or levels of understanding, as one moves into the real heart of the culture. In doing so, the "man from Mars" technique is useful. In this exercise one simply imagines that a man from Mars has recently landed (via spaceship), and looks at things through the eyes of an alien space visitor.

The first thing that the newly arrived visitor would notice is the people's *behavior*. This is the outer, and most superficial, layer of what would be observed by an alien. What activities would he observe? What is being done? When walking into a classroom, our visitor may observe several interesting things. People are seen entering an enclosure through one or more openings. They distribute themselves throughout the room seemingly arbitrarily. Another person enters dressed quite differently than the rest, and moves quickly to an obviously prear-

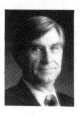

Lloyd Kwast taught for eight years in a college and theological school in Cameroon, West Africa under the North American Baptist General Missionary Society. He has been chairman of the Department of Missions at Talbot Theological Seminary, and is currently a Professor of BIOLA University School of Intercultural Studies and is Director of the Doctor of Missiology Program there.

ranged position facing the others, and begins to speak. As all this is observed, the question might be asked, "Why are they in an enclosure? Why does the speaker dress differently? Why are many people seated while one stands?" These are questions of *meaning*. They are generated by the observations of behavior. It might be interesting to ask some of the participants in the situation why they are doing things in a certain way. Some might offer one explanation; others might offer another. But some would probably shrug and say, "It's the way we do things here." This last response shows an important function of culture, to provide "the patterned way of doing things," as one group of missionary anthropologists defines it. You could call culture the "super-glue" which binds people together and gives them a sense of identity and continuity which is almost impenetrable. This identity is seen most obviously in the way things are done— behavior.

In observing the inhabitants, our alien begins to realize that many of the behaviors observed are apparently dictated by similar choices that people in the society have made. These choices inevitably reflect the issue of cultural *values*, the next layer of our view of culture. These issues always concern choices about what is "good," what is "beneficial," or what is "best."

If the man from Mars continued to interrogate the people in the enclosure, he might discover that they had numerous alternatives to spending their time there. They might have been working or playing instead of studying. Many of them chose to study because they believed it to be a better choice than play or work. He discovered a number of other choices they had made. Most of them had chosen to arrive at the enclosure in small four-wheel vehicles, because they view the ability to move about quickly as very beneficial. Furthermore, others were noticed hurrying into the enclosure several moments after the rest had entered, and again moving out of the room promptly at the close of the meeting. These people said that using time efficiently was very important to them. Values are "pre-set" decisions that a culture makes between choices commonly faced. It helps those who live within the culture to know what "should" or "ought" to be done in order to "fit in" or conform to the pattern of life.

Beyond the questions of behavior and values, we face a more fundamental question in the nature of culture. This takes us to a deeper level of understanding, that of cultural *beliefs*. These beliefs answer for that culture the question: "What is true?"

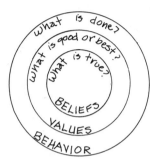

Values in culture are not selected arbitrarily, but invariably reflect an underlying system of beliefs. For example, in the classroom situation, one might discover upon further investigation that "education" in the enclosure has particular significance because of their perception of what is true about man, his power to reason, and his ability to solve problems. In that sense culture has been defined as "learned and shared ways of perceiving," or "shared cognitive orientation."

Interestingly, our alien interrogator might discover that different people in the enclosure, while exhibiting similar behavior and values, might profess totally different beliefs about them. Further, he might find that the values and behaviors were opposed to the beliefs which supposedly produced them. The problem arises from the confusion within the culture between operating beliefs (beliefs that affect values and behavior) and theoretical beliefs (state creeds which have little practical impact on values and behavior).

At the very heart of any culture is its *world view*, answering the most basic question: "What is real?" This area of culture concerns itself with the great "ultimate" questions of reality, questions which are seldom asked, but to which culture provides its most important answers. Few of the people our man from Mars questions have ever thought seriously about the deepest assumptions about life, which result in their presence in the classroom. Who are they? Where did they come from? Is there anything or anyone else occupying reality that should be taken into consideration? Is what they see really all there is, or is there something else, or something more? Is right now the only time that is important? Or do events in the past, and the future, significantly impact their present experience? Every culture assumes specific answers to these questions, and those answers control and integrate every function, aspect, and component of the culture.

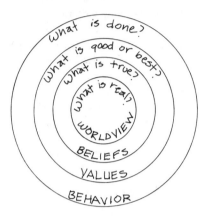

This understanding of world view as the core of every culture explains the confusion many experience at the level of beliefs. One's own world view provides a system of beliefs which are reflected in his actual values and behavior. Sometimes a new or competing system of beliefs is introduced, but the world view remains unchallenged and unchanged, so values and behavior reflect the old belief system. Sometimes people who share the gospel cross-culturally fail to take the problem of world view into account, and are therefore disappointed by the lack of genuine change their efforts produce.

This model of culture is far too simple to explain the multitude of complex components and relationships that exist in every culture. However, it is the very simplicity of the model which commends it as a basic outline for any student of culture.

Study Questions

1. What relationships exist between the "layers" of culture?

2. What is the practical value of this model of culture?

2
Christ and Culture

David J. Hesselgrave

When God created man and man's environment, He pronounced everything "very good" (Gen. 1:31). God gave man a *Cultural Mandate* which entailed certain rulership over his environment (Gen. 1:26-30). God, however, did not withdraw from the scene. Nor did He cease to be God. Rather, He continued to provide for, and fellowship with, His creatures. How long that blissful state continued we do not know, but it was interrupted by the Fall. And the Fall left its mark on creation, creature, and culture (Gen. 3:14-19). Man's hope rested on the promise of the "Seed of woman" who would bruise the Serpent's head.

Subsequently, mankind collectively failed as miserably as Adam and Eve had failed individually with the result that God pronounced judgment upon man, beast, and land (Gen. 6:6-7). Following the Flood, Noah and his family received promises and a *Social Mandate* that was to apply to them and their progeny down through the generations (Gen. 8:21-9:17).

The significance of this simple and sublime story in the first chapters of Genesis must be carefully probed but can never be completely fathomed. It forms the basis of a theology of culture that is amplified throughout sacred Scripture. Man's relationship to God precedes and prescribes all other relationships. In this sense true religion is prior to culture, not simply a part of it. In listening to the usurper and choosing to disobey God, man invited the impress of sin upon all that he was and all he touched. The Fall did not result in the eradication of the image of God in the creature nor in the countermanding of all cultural prerogatives. But it did interpose another and false authority over man and it did mar man's person and productions. Only under Christ can man be redeemed and his culture renewed.

After twelve years' service in Japan under the Evangelical Free Church, David J. Hesselgrave became Professor of Missions at the School of World Mission and Evangelism at Trinity Evangelical Divinity School in Deerfield, Illinois. He later served as Director of the School of World Mission and Evangelism, and is now the Professor Emeritus of Mission. He is the executive director of the Evangelical Missiological Society. Hesselgrave is the author of *Planting Churches Cross-Culturally* and *Communicating Christ Cross-Culturally*. From *Communicating Christ Cross-Culturally* by David J. Hesselgrave. Copyright 1978 by David J. Hesselgrave. Used by permission of Zondervan Publishing House.

The *Gospel Mandate* (Matt. 28:18-20) requires that missionaries teach other men to observe all that Christ has commanded. In teaching, missionaries touch culture and happily so for *all culture needs transformation in motivation if not in content*. If anything at all is apparent in our world, it is that God has ordained culture but has not been allowed to order culture. Satan is indeed "the god of this world" (2 Cor. 4:4). Therefore, as Calvin insisted, believers must work to make culture Christian (i.e., under Christ) or at least conducive to (i.e., allowing the maximum opportunity for) Christian living. As J. H. Bavinck puts it, the Christian life *takes possession* of heathen forms of life and thereby makes them new.

> Within the framework of the non-Christian life, customs and practices serve idolatrous tendencies and drive a person away from God. The Christian life takes them in hand and turns them in an entirely different direction; they acquire an entirely different content. Even though in external form there is much that resembles past practices, in reality everything has become new, the old has in essence passed away and the new has come. Christ takes the life of a people in his hands, he renews and re-establishes the distorted and deteriorated, he fills each thing, each word, and each practice with a new meaning and gives it a new direction.[1]

The missionary is involved in this process directly and indirectly. He may attempt to stay above the culture line and deal only with matters of the soul. But that effort is as hopeless as is the effort of the social scientist to eliminate God from his world and explain Christianity in cultural terms only. In the first place, the missionary cannot *communicate* without concerning himself with culture because communication is inextricable from culture. Just as Christ became flesh and dwelt among men, so propositional truth must have a cultural incarnation to be meaningful. In the second place, the missionary cannot communicate *Christianity* without concerning himself with culture because, though Christianity is supracultural in its origin and truth, it is cultural in its application.

End Notes

I. John Herman Bavinck, *An Introduction to The Science of Missions*, trans. David H. Freeman (Grand Rapids: Baker, 1969), p. 179.

3

Culture and Cross-Cultural Differences

Paul G. Hiebert

One of the first shocks a person experiences when he or she leaves his home country is the foreignness of the people and their culture. Not only do they speak an incomprehensible language, but also dress in strange clothes, eat unpalatable foods, organize different kids of families and have unintelligible beliefs and values. How do these differences affect the communication of the Gospel and the planting of churches in other societies?

The Concept of Culture

In ordinary speech we use the term "culture" to refer to the behavior of the rich and elite. It is listening to Bach, Beethoven and Brahms, having the proper taste for good clothes, and knowing which fork to use when at a banquet.

But anthropologists in their study of all humankind, in all parts of the world and at all levels of society, have broadened the concept and freed it from value judgments, such as good or bad. There has been a great deal of discussion on how to define the term. For our purposes we will define culture as *the integrated system of learned patterns of behavior, ideas and products characteristic of a society.*

Patterns of learned behavior

The first part of this definition is "learned patterns of behavior." We begin learning about a culture by observing the behavior of the people and looking for patterns in the behavior. For example, we have all seen two American men on meeting grasp each other's hand and shake it. In Mexico we would see them embrace. In India each puts his hands together and raises them towards his fore-

Paul G. Hiebert is Professor of Missions and Anthropology and Chairman of the Missions and Evangelism Department at Trinity Evangelical Divinity School. He previously taught Anthropology and South Asian Studies at Fuller Theological Seminary's School of World Mission in Pasadena, California. Hiebert served as a missionary in India with the Mennonite Brethren Board and has also been a professor of anthropology at the University of Washington in Seattle. He is the author of *Cultural Anthropology, Anthropological Insights for Missionaries,* and *Case Studies in Mission* with Frances H. Hiebert.
Reprinted with permission of the William Carey Library Publishers, P. O. Box 40129, Pasadena, CA 91114. Updated from *Crucial Dimensions in World Evangelization,* Arthur F. Glasser, et al.

head with a slight bow of the head—a gesture of greeting that is efficient, for it permits a person to greet a great many others in a single motion, and clean, for people need not touch each other. The latter is particularly important in a society where the touch of an untouchable used to defile a high caste person and force him to take a purification bath. Among the Siriano of South America, men spit on each other's chests in greeting.

Probably the strangest form of greeting was observed by Dr. Jacob Loewen in Panama. On leaving the jungle on a small plane with the local native chief, he noticed the chief go to all his fellow tribesmen and suck their mouths. When Dr. Loewen inquired about this custom, the chief explained that they had learned this custom from the white man. They had seen that every time he went up in his plane, he sucked the mouths of his people as magic to insure a safe journey. If we stop and think about it a minute, Americans, in fact, have two types of greeting, shaking hands and sucking mouths, and we must be careful not to use the wrong form with the wrong people.

Like most cultural patterns, kissing is not a universal human custom. It was absent among most primitive tribesmen, and considered vulgar and revolting to the Chinese who thought it too suggestive of cannibalism.

Not all behavior patterns are learned. A child touching a hot stove jerks his hand away and yells "Ouch!" His physical reaction is instinctive, but the expletive is culturally learned.

Ideas

Culture is also the ideas people have of their world. Through their experience of it, people form mental pictures of maps of this world. For instance, a person living in Chicago has a mental image of the streets around his home, those he uses to go to church and work, and the major arteries he uses to get around town. Obviously, there are a great many streets not on his mental map and as long as he does not go to these areas, he has no need for knowing them. So also people develop conceptual schemes of their worlds.

Not all our ideas reflect the realities of the external world. Many are the creations of our minds, used to bring order and meaning in our experiences. For example, we see a great many trees in our lifetime, and each is different from all others. But it would be impossible for us to give a separate name to each of them, and to each bush, each house, each car—in short, to each experience we have. In order to think and speak we must reduce this infinite variety of experiences into a manageable number of concepts by generalization. We call these shades of color red, those orange, and that third set yellow. These categories are the creations of our mind. Other people in other languages lump them into a single color, or divide them into two, or even four colors. Do these people see as many colors as we? Certainly. The fact is we can create as many categories in our minds as we want, and we can organize them into larger systems for describing and explaining human experiences.

In one sense, then, a culture is a people's mental map of their world. This is not only a map of their world, but also a map for determining action (Geertz 1972:169). It provides them with a guide for their decisions and behavior.

Products

A third part of our definition is "products." Human thought and actions often lead to the production of material artifacts and tools. We build houses, roads, cars and furniture. We create pictures, clothes, jewelry, coins and a great many other objects.

Our material culture has a great effect on our lives. Imagine, for a moment, what life in America was like a hundred years ago when there were no cars or jets. The invention of writing, and more recently of computers, has and will have an even more profound effect upon our lives, for these permit us to store up the cultural knowledge of past generations and to build upon it.

Form and meaning

Behavior patterns and cultural products are generally linked to ideas or meanings. Shaking hands means "hello." So does kissing in certain situations. We also assign meaning to shaking our fists, to frowning, to crying, to letters of the alphabet, to crosses and to a great many other things. In fact, human beings assign meaning to almost everything they do and make.

It is this linkage between an experienceable *form* and a mental *meaning* that constitutes a symbol. We see a flag, and it carries the idea of a country, so much so that men in battle will even die to preserve their flags. A culture can be viewed as the symbol systems, such as languages, rituals, gestures and objects, that people create in order to think and communicate.

Integration

Cultures are made up of a great many patterns of behavior, ideas and products. But it is more than the sum of them. These patterns are integrated into larger cultural complexes, and into total cultural systems.

To see this integration of cultural patterns we need only observe the average American. On entering an auditorium to listen to a musical performance, he looks until he finds a chair on which to perch himself. If all these platforms are occupied, he leaves because the auditorium is "full." Obviously there are a great many places where he can sit on the floor but this is not culturally acceptable, at least not at the performance of a symphony orchestra.

At home the American has different kinds of platforms for sitting in the living room, at the dining table and at his desk. He also has a large platform on which he sleeps at night. When he travels abroad his greatest fear is being caught at night without a platform in a private room, so he makes hotel reservations well ahead of time. People from many parts of the world know that all you need is a blanket and a flat space in order to spend the night, and the world is full of flat places. In the airport, at three in the morning, the American traveler is draped uncomfortably over a chair rather than stretched out on the rug. He would rather be dignified than comfortable.

Not only do Americans sit and sleep on platforms, they build their houses on them, hang them on their walls, and put fences around them to hold their children. Why this obsession with platforms? Behind all these behavior patterns is a basic assumption that the ground and floor are dirty. This explains their obsession for getting off the floor. It also explains why they keep their shoes on when they enter the house, and why the mother scolds the child when it picks a potato chip off the floor and eats it. The floor is "dirty" even though it has just been washed, and the instant a piece of food touches it, the food becomes dirty.

On the other hand, in Japan the people believe the floor is clean. Therefore they take their shoes off at the door, and sleep and sit on mats on the floor. When we walk into their home with our shoes on, they feel much like we do when someone walks on our couch with their shoes on.

At the center, then, of a culture are the basic assumptions the people have about the nature of reality and of right and wrong. Taken together, they are referred to as the people's *world view*.

This linkage between cultural traits and their integration into a larger system have important implications for those who seek to introduce change. When changes are made in one area of culture, changes will also occur in other areas of the culture, often in unpredictable ways. While the initial change may be good, the side effects can be devastating if care is not taken.

Cross-Cultural Differences

In their study of various cultures, anthropologists have become aware of the profound differences between them. Not only are there differences in the ways people eat, dress, speak and act, and in their values and beliefs, but also in the fundamental assumptions they make about their world. Edward Sapir pointed out that people in different cultures do not simply live in the same world with different labels attached, but in different conceptual worlds.

Edward Hall points out just how different cultures can be in his study of time (1959). When, for example, two Americans agree to meet at ten o'clock, they are "on time" if they show up from five minutes before to five minutes after ten. If one shows up at fifteen after, he is "late" and mumbles an unfinished apology. He must simply acknowledge that he is late. If he shows up at half past, he should have a good apology, and by eleven he may as well not show up. His offense is unpardonable.

In parts of Arabia, the people have a different concept or map of time. If the meeting time is ten o'clock, only a servant shows up at ten—in obedience to his master. The proper time for others is from ten forty-five to eleven fifteen, just long enough after the set time to show their independence and equality. This arrangement works well, for when two equals agree to meet at ten, each shows up, and expects the other to show up, at about ten forty-five.

The problem arises when an American meets an Arab and arranges a meeting for ten o'clock. The American shows up at ten, the "right time" according to him. The Arab shows up at ten forty-five, the "right time" according to him. The American feels the Arab has no sense of time at all (which is false), and the Arab is tempted to think Americans act like servants (which is also false).

Culture shock

Our first reaction to the prospect of going overseas is one of excitement and anticipation. The flight, the new sights and strange customs—is this really happening to me? The market place is colorful with its bargains, if only the vendors could speak English. The village is fascinating. Is there a drugstore where I can get some medicine for my stomach pains? Not until next week when I return to the city?! The food is interesting, to say the least. I like to try new dishes, but I suppose I couldn't stand this as a steady diet. You mean to say the people here eat it twice a day, every day? And so will I when I move to the village? For three years? In this house with no running water? No doctor? No one who can talk decent English? How did I get into this anyway?

Our first confrontation with cultural differences is culture shock, the sense of confusion and disorientation we face when we move into another culture This is not a reaction to poverty or the lack of sanitation, for foreigners coming to the U.S. experience the same shock. It is the fact that all the cultural patterns we have learned are now meaningless. We know less about living here than even the children, and we must begin again to learn the elementary things of life—how to speak, to greet one another, to eat, to market, to travel, and a thousand other things.

We never really enter culture shock as tourists, for then we launch out daily from our little American-style hotels to see the people, but not to settle down among them and build stable relationships. It is when we realize that this now is going to be our life, and for a long time to come, that the shock comes. Disorientation, disillusionment and depression strike, and we would go home if only we did not have to face the folks there.

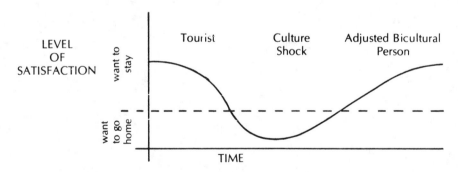

Culture shock is a sense of cultural disorientation in a different society.

But this reaction is perfectly normal. As we learn to speak the new language, make a few friends, find out that we can travel by bus, learn to count the now not so strange coins, and realize that we can keep our health, we begin to fit into the new cultural setting. We need to avoid the temptation to withdraw into ourselves and our houses, or to try to return in part to our old culture by creating a little America in which we live. We can get out and learn to live in the new culture, and, in time, we will feel as at home in it as our own, possibly even more so.

Something happens to us when we adapt to a new culture: we become bicultural people. Our parochialism, based on our unquestioned feeling that there is really only one way to live, and our way is it, is shattered. We must deal with cultural variety with the fact that people build cultures in different ways, and that they believe their cultures are better than ours. Aside from some curiosity at our foreignness, they are not interested in learning our ways.

But to the extent we identify with the people and become bicultural, to that extent we find ourselves alienated from our kinsmen and friends in our homeland. This is not reverse culture shock, although we will experience that when we return home after a long stay abroad. It is a basic difference in how we now look at things. We have moved from a philosophy that assumes uniformity to one that has had to cope with variety, and our old friends often don't understand us. In time we may find our closest associates among other bicultural people.

In one sense, bicultural people never fully adjust to one culture, their own or their adopted one. Within themselves they are part of both. When Americans are abroad, they dream of America, and need little rituals that reaffirm this part of themselves—a food package from home, a letter, an American visitor from whom they can learn the latest news from "home." When in America, they dream of their adopted country, and need little rituals that reaffirm this part of themselves—a visitor from that country, a meal with its food. Bicultural people seem happiest when they are flying from one of these countries to the other.

Cross-cultural misunderstandings

Some missionaries in Zaire had trouble in building rapport with the people. Finally, one old man explained the people's hesitancy to befriend the missionaries. "When you came, you brought your strange ways," he said. "You brought tins of food. On the outside of one was a picture of corn. When you opened it inside was corn and you ate it. Outside another was a picture of meat, and inside was meat, and you ate it. And then when you had your baby, you brought small tins. On the outside was a picture of babies, and you opened it and fed the inside to your child."

To us the people's confusion sounds foolish, but it is all too logical. In the absence of other information, they must draw their own conclusions about our actions. But we do the same about theirs. We think they have no sense of time when, by our culture, they show up late. We accuse them of lying when they tell us things to please us rather than as they really are (although we have no trouble saying "Just fine!" when someone asks "How are you?"). The result is cultural misunderstanding, and this leads to poor communication and poor relationships.

Cultural misunderstandings often arise out of our subconscious actions. Hall illustrates this (1959) in the way people use physical space when they stand around talking. North Americans generally stand about four or five feet apart when they discuss general matters. They do not like to converse by shouting to people twenty feet away. On the other hand, when they want to discuss personal matters, they move in to about two or three feet and drop their voices. Latin Americans tend to stand about two or three feet apart in ordinary conversations and even closer for personal discussions.

Misunderstandings arise only when a North American meets a Latin American. The latter subconsciously moves in to about three feet. The former is vaguely uneasy about this and steps back. Now the Latin American feels like he is talking to someone across the room, and so he steps closer. Now the North American is again confused. According to his spacial distance, the Latin American should be discussing personal matters, like sharing some gossip or arranging a bank robbery. But, in fact, he is talking about public matters, about the weather and politics. The result is the North American thinks Latin Americans are pushy and always under his nose; the Latin American concludes that North Americans are always distant and cold.

Misunderstandings are based on ignorance about another culture. This is a problem of knowledge. The solution is to learn to know how the other culture works. Our first task in entering a new culture is to be a student of its ways. Even later, whenever something seems to be going wrong, we must assume that the people's behavior makes sense to them, and reanalyze our own understandings of their culture.

Ethnocentrism

Most Americans shudder when they enter an Indian restaurant and see the people eating curry and rice with their fingers. Imagine going to a Thanksgiving dinner and diving into the mashed potatoes and gravy with your hand. Our response is a natural one, to us. Early in life each of us grows up in the center of our own world. In other words, we are egocentric. Only with a great deal of difficulty do we learn to break down the circle we draw between I and You, and learn to look at things from the viewpoint of others We also grow up in a culture and learn that its ways are the right ways to do things. Anyone who does differently is not quite "civilized." This ethnocentrism is based on our natural tendency to judge the behavior of people in other cultures by the values and assumptions of our own.

But others judge our culture by their values and assumptions. A number of Americans went to a restaurant with an Indian guest, and someone asked the inevitable question, "Do people in India really eat with their fingers?" "Yes, we do," the Indian replied, "but we look at it differently. You see, we wash our hands carefully, and besides, they have never been in anyone else's mouth. But look at these spoons and forks, and think about how many other people have already had them inside their mouths!"

If cross-cultural misunderstandings are based on our knowledge of another culture, ethnocentrism is based on our feelings and values. In relating to another people we need not only to understand them, but also to deal with our feelings that distinguish between "us" and "our kind of people," and "them" and "their kind of people." Identification takes place only when "they" become part of the circle of people we think of as "our kind of people."

Premature Judgments

We have misunderstandings on the cognitive level and ethnocentrism on the affective level, but what can go wrong on the evaluative level? The answer lies in premature judgments (see Figure 15). When we relate to other cultures we tend to judge them before we have learned to understand or appreciate them. In so doing, we use the values of our own culture, not of some metacultural framework. Consequently, other cultures look less civilized.

Cultural Relativism. Premature judgments are usually wrong. Moreover, they close the door to further understanding and communication. What then is the answer?

As anthropologists learned to understand and appreciate other cultures, they came to respect their integrity as viable ways of organizing human life. Some were stronger in one area such as technology, and others in another area such as family ties. But all "do the job," that is, they all make life possible and more or less meaningful. Out of this recognition of the integrity of all cultures emerged the concept of cultural relativism: the belief that all cultures are equally good–

that no culture has the right to stand in judgment over the others.

The position of cultural relativism is very attractive. It shows high respect for other people and their cultures and avoids the errors of ethnocentrism and premature judgments. It also deals with the difficult philosophical questions of truth and morality by withholding judgment and affirming the right of each culture to reach its own answers. The price we pay, however, in adopting total cultural relativism is the loss of such things as truth and righteousness. If all explanations of reality are equally valid, we can no longer speak of error, and if all behavior is justified according to its cultural context, we can no longer speak of sin. There is then no need for the gospel and no reason for missions.

What other alternative do we have? How can we avoid the errors of premature and ethnocentric judgments and still affirm truth and righteousness?

Beyond Relativism. There is a growing awareness that no human thought is free from value judgments. Scientists expect one another to be honest and open in the reporting of their findings and careful in the topics of their research. Social scientists must respect the rights of their clients and the people being studied. Businessmen, government officials, and others also have values by which they live. We cannot avoid making judgments, nor can a society exist without them.

On what basis, then, can we judge other cultures without being ethnocentric? We have a right as individuals to make judgments with regard to ourselves, and this includes judging other cultures. But these judgments should be well informed. We need to understand and appreciate other cultures *before* we judge them. Our tendency is to make premature judgments based on ignorance and ethnocentrism.

As Christians we claim another basis for evaluation, namely, Biblical norms. As divine revelation they stand in judgment on all cultures, affirming the good in human creativity and condemning the evil. To be sure, non-Christians may reject these biblical norms and use their own. We can only present the gospel in a spirit of redemptive love and let it speak for itself. Truth, in the end, does not depend on what we think or say, but on reality itself. When we bear witness to the truth, we do not claim a superiority for ourselves, but affirm the truth of the gospel.

But what is to keep us from interpreting the Scripture from our own cultural point of view, and so imposing many of our own cultural norms on the people? First, we need to recognize that we have biases when we interpret the Scriptures, and thus be open to correction. We also need to let the gospel work in the lives of new Christians and through them in their culture, recognizing that the same Holy Spirit who leads us is at work in them and leading them to the truth.

Second, we need to study both the values of the culture in which we minister and those of our own. By this approach, we can develop a metacultural framework that enables us to compare and evaluate the two. The process of genuinely seeking to understand another system of values goes a long way in breaking down our monocultural perspectives. It enables us to appreciate the good in other systems and be more critical of our own.

Since even in the formulation of a metacultural system of values our own cultural biases come into play, we need to involve Christian leaders from other cultures in the process. They can detect our cultural blind spots better than we can, just as we often see their cultural prejudgments better than they.

The critical hermeneutics that involve a dialogue between Christians of different cultures can help us all to develop a more culture-free understanding of God's moral standards as revealed in the Bible. On the one hand, it keeps us from the legalism of imposing foreign norms upon a society without taking into account its specific situations. On the other, it keeps us from a situational ethics that is purely relativistic in nature.

Interestingly enough, we cannot reach such a transcultural understanding of the Bible without first experiencing the shattering of our monocultural perspectives of truth and righteousness. Our temptation, when we first realize that other cultures have different norms, is to reject them without examination and to justify our own as biblical. But this only closes the door for us to deal biblically with the problems of another culture. Moreover, it makes the gospel seem foreign to other cultures.

In a sense, to free ourselves from our monocultural biases, we need to face the relativism that comes when we realize that our cultural values are not absolute and then we begin to view all cultures with greater appreciation. But we can develop such a perspective only if we avoid premature judgments and seek to understand and appreciate another culture deeply before we evaluate it. As we enter into another culture, the control our own has on us is weakened. Interestingly enough, when we become bicultural people, we are more appreciative of other cultures and more critical of our own.

Having experienced the shattering of our own cultural absolutes and faced the abyss of relativism, we can move beyond monoculturalism and relativism, to an affirmation of cultures and of the transcultural norms of the Scriptures. A truly metacultural perspective can also help us to be more biblical on our understanding of reality.

Evaluation in the three dimensions. As humans we pass judgment on beliefs to determine whether they are true or false, on feelings to decide likes and dislikes, and on values to differentiate right from wrong. As missionaries we are faced with evaluating other cultures and our own along each of these dimensions.

On the cognitive level, we must deal with different perceptions of reality, including diverse ideas about hunting, farming, building houses, human procreation, and diseases. For example, in South India, villagers believe illnesses are caused by local goddesses when they become angry. Consequently, sacrifices must be made to them to stop the plague. We must understand the people's beliefs in order to understand their behavior, but if we want to stop illness, we may decide that modern theories of disease are better. On the other hand, after examining their knowledge of hunting wild game, we may conclude that it is better than our own.

We need to evaluate not only the people's folk sciences but their religious beliefs, for these affect their understanding of Scripture. Although they already have such concepts as God, ancestors, sin, and salvation, these may or may not be adequate for an understanding of the gospel.

On the affective level, we may find that much is a matter of "taste." People in some cultures like their food hot, in other cultures sweet or salty. In one culture they prefer red clothes, houses with steep roofs, eating with their fingers, and entertaining themselves with dramas. In another they choose dark clothes, flat-roofed houses, eating with spoons, and entertaining themselves with mournful songs. Even on this level, however, cultures that prefer peace and compassion may be better than those that emphasize hatred and revenge.

On the evaluative level, a great many of the norms in other cultures are "good." A high value is often placed on loving children, caring for the aged, and sharing with the needy. On the other hand, there may be norms that conflict with biblical values, such as slavery, head-hunting, burning of widows on the funeral pyres of their husbands, or oppression of the poor.

We will find that there is much in every culture that is worthwhile and should not only be retained but encouraged. For instance, most cultures are much better than ours in human relationships and social concern, and we can learn much from them. Much, too, is "neutral" and need not be change. In most settings wood houses serve as well as mud or brick ones, and a dress is not better than a sari or sarong. Some things in all cultures, however, are false and evil. Since all people are sinners, we should not be surprised that the social structures and cultures they create are affected by sin. It is our corporate sins, not only our individual sins, that God seeks to change.

Now to the discussion of translation. Beginning in Genesis we read, "In the beginning God. . ." The question is, how shall we translate the word "God"? In Telugu, a south Indian language, we can use the words "Isvarudu," "Devudu," "Bhagavanthudu," or a number of others. The problem is that each of these carries the Hindu connotation that gods have exactly the same kind of life as human beings, only more of it. They are not categorically different from people. There is no word that carries the same connotations as the Biblical concept of God.

This also raises the problem of translating the Biblical concept of "incarnation." In the Biblical setting incarnation is seen as an infinite God crossing the great gulf between Himself and human beings, and becoming a person. In other words, He crossed from one category to another. In the Indian setting gods constantly become incarnate by moving down within the same category to the level of people. Obviously this concept of incarnation is fundamentally different from the Christian one. To use it is to lose much of the meaning of the Christian message. But how then can we translate the Biblical concepts of God and incarnation in Telugu or other Indian languages?

We might coin a new word for "God" or "incarnation," but then the people will not understand it. Or we can use one of the Telugu words, but then we face the danger that the Biblical message will be seriously distorted. Often the best we can do is use a word with which the people are familiar, but then to teach them the meaning we are giving to it. It may take years and even generations before the people understand the new meanings and the total Biblical world view within which these meanings make sense.

This process may seem to take too long. What about the illiterate peasant who accepts Christ at an evening service? Do not his concepts and world view change

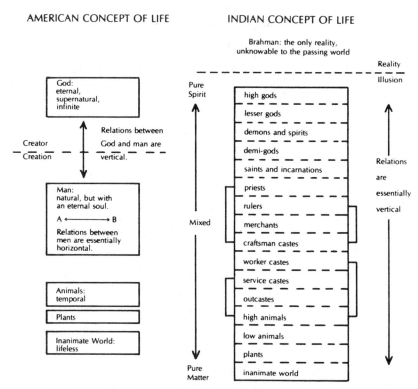

A comparison of American and Indian views of life.

immediately? Obviously not. But his salvation is not dependent on whether he has a Christian world view or not, but on whether he accepts Christ's salvation however he understands it, and becomes His follower. However, for the long range building of the church, the people and their leaders must have an understanding of the Biblical concepts and world view if the message is to be preserved over the generations.

Implications of Cultural Differences for Missions

It is clear that cultural differences are important to a missionary who must go through culture shock, learn to overcome misunderstandings and ethnocentric feelings, and translate his message so that it is understood in the local language and culture. But there are a number of other important implications that need to be touched briefly.

The Gospel and culture

We must distinguish between the Gospel and culture. If we do not, we will be in danger of making our culture the message. The Gospel then becomes democracy, capitalism, pews and pulpits, Robert's Rules of Order, clothes, and suits and ties on Sunday. One of the primary hindrances to communication is the foreignness of the message, and to a great extent the foreignness of Christianity has been the cultural load we have placed upon it. As Mr. Murthi, an Indian evangelist, put it, "Do not bring us the Gospel as a potted plant. Bring us the seed of the Gospel and plant it in our soil."

The distinction is not easy to make, for the Gospel, like any message, must be put into cultural forms in order to be understood and communicated by people. We cannot think without conceptual categories and symbols to express them. But we can be careful not to add to the Biblical message our own.

A failure to differentiate between the Biblical message and other messages leads to a confusion between cultural relativism and Biblical absolutes. For example, in many churches where it was once considered sinful for women to cut their hair or wear lipstick, or for people to attend movies, these are now acceptable. Some, therefore, argue that today premarital sex and adultery are thought to be sinful, but that in time they too will be accepted.

It is true that many things we once considered sin are now accepted. Are there then no moral absolutes? We must recognize that each culture defines certain behavior as "sinful," and that as the culture changes, its definitions of what is sin also change. There are, on the other hand, certain moral principles in the Scriptures that we hold to be absolute. However, even here we must be careful. Some Biblical norms, such as leaving the land fallow every seventh year and not reaping the harvest (Lev. 25) or greeting one another with a holy kiss (I Thess. 5:26) seem to apply to specific cultural situations.

Syncretism versus indigenization

Not only must we separate the Gospel from our own culture, we must seek to express it in terms of the culture to which we go. The people may sit on the floor, sing songs to native rhythms and melodies, and look at pictures of Christ who is Black or Chinese. The Church may reject democracy in favor of wise elders, or turn to drama to communicate its message.

But, as we have seen, translation involves more than putting ideas into native forms, for these forms may not carry meanings suitable for expressing the Christian message. If we, then, translate it into native forms without thought to preserving the meaning, we will end up with *syncretism*—the mixture of old meanings with the new so that the essential nature of each is lost.

If we are careful to preserve the meaning of the Gospel even as we express it in native forms we have *indigenization*. This may involve introducing a new symbolic form, or it may involve reinterpreting a native symbol. For example, bridesmaids, now associated with Christian weddings, were originally used by our non-Christians ancestors to confuse the demons whom, they thought, had come to carry off the bride.

Conversion and unforeseen side effects

Since cultural traits are linked together into larger wholes, changes in one or more of them lead often to unforeseen changes in other areas of the culture. For example, in one part of Africa, when the people became Christians, their villages also became dirty. The reason for this was that they were now not afraid of evil spirits which they believed hid in the refuse. So they no longer had to clean it up.

Many cultural traits serve important functions in the lives of the people. If we remove these without providing a substitute, the consequences can be tragic. In some places husbands with more than one wife had to give up all but one when they became Christians. But no arrangements were made for the wives who were put away. Many of them ended up in prostitution or slavery.

Theological autonomy and world Christianity

As Christianity becomes indigenous in cultures around the world, the question of the unity of the church arises. There is an increasing stress that the church in each cultural setting become autonomous: self-supporting, self-administering and self-propogating. But how do we cope with theological variety? How do we react when the churches we help plant want theological autonomy and call for a socialist or even Marxist evangelical Christianity?

It is clear that cultures vary a great deal. As the Gospel becomes indigenous to them, their theologies—their understandings and applications of this Gospel— will also vary. What, then, does it mean to be a Christian? And how can Christians who disagree in some points of theology have true fellowship with one another?

Here we must remember two things. In the first place, we need to understand the nature of human knowledge and recognize its limitations. People experience an infinitely varied world around them and try to find order and meaning in their experiences. In part they discover the order that exists in the world itself, and in part they impose a mental order on it. They create concepts that allow them to generalize, to lump a great many experiences into one. They also act like a movie editor, linking certain experiences with certain other ones in order to make sense of them. For example, experiences in the same classroom on a number of different days are put together and called Introduction to Anthropology. A different set is thought of as "church activities."

When we read the Scriptures, we must remember that we interpret them in terms of our own culture and personal experiences. Others will not interpret them in exactly the same way. We must, therefore, distinguish between the Scriptures themselves, and our theology or understanding of them. The former is the record of God's revelation of Himself to humankind. The latter is our partial, and hopefully growing, understanding of that revelation. If we make this distinction, we can accept variations in interpretation, and yet find fellowship with those who are truly committed followers of Christ.

In the second place, we must never forget that the same Holy Spirit who helps us to understand the Scriptures, is also interpreting it to believers in other cultures. Ultimately it is He and not we who is responsible for preserving divine truth and revealing it to us. We must make certain that we are committed follow-ers of Jesus Christ and open to the instruction of His Spirit.

Study Questions

1. Give an example of two forms that could carry the same meaning. Give another example of two meanings that could be understood from the same form.

2. Briefly explain the different components of "culture."

3. How do you think that culture shock can be minimized?

4

Social Structure and Church Growth

Paul G. Hiebert

People are social beings, born, raised, married, and usually buried in the company of their fellow humans. They form groups, institutions and societies. Social structure is the ways in which they organize their relationships with one another and build societies.

Societies can be studied on two levels: that of interpersonal relation, and of the society as a whole. A study of missions at each of these levels can help us a great deal to understand how churches grow.

Interpersonal Relationships: The Bicultural Bridge

When a missionary goes overseas and settles down, what does he do? Whatever his specific task, he is involved in interpersonal relationships with a great many people. Many of these are not Christians, but, most likely, he will spend much of his time with Christian converts. He will go to the market, or preach in the village square, but his closest relationships will be with national pastors, evangelists, teachers and other Christians. What are the characteristics of these various relationships?

It is clear that in most cases communication across cultures is multistepped. The missionary received the message in his family, church and school. He communicates it to national Christian leaders who in turn pass it on to local Christians and non-Christians in the cities and villages. With few exceptions, the greatest share of the mission work in a country is done by these unheralded nationals.

Paul G. Hiebert is Professor of Missions and Anthropology and Chairman of the Missions and Evangelism Department at Trinity Evangelical Divinity School. He previously taught Anthropology and South Asian Studies at Fuller Theological Seminary's School of World Mission in Pasadena, California. Hiebert served as a missionary in India with the Mennonite Brethren Board and has also been a professor of anthropology at the University of Washington in Seattle. He is the author of *Cultural Anthropology, Anthropological Insights for Missionaries*, and *Case Studies in Mission* with Frances H. Hiebert. Reprinted with permission of the William Carey Library Publishers, P. O. Box 40129, Pasadena, CA 91114. *Crucial Dimensions in World Evangelization*, Arthur F. Glasser, et al.

Here, in order to see how a structural analysis is used, we will look at one link in this chain of communication—the relationships between the missionary and his national counterpart. This has sometimes been called the bicultural bridge, and is the critical step in which much of the translation of the message into a new culture occurs.

The bicultural bridge is a set of relationships between people from two cultures. But it is more. It is itself a new culture. The missionary rarely can "go native." He will set up housing, institutions and customary ways of doing things that reflect his home culture, in part, and, in part, are adapted from the culture in which he finds himself. His national counterparts do the same. It is true that they have not moved out of their own culture, but their interaction with the missionary exposes them to a great many foreign influences that can potentially alienate them from their home culture.

A great deal of energy in the bicultural setting is spent on defining just how this new culture should operate. Should the missionary have a car in a society where most of the people do not? If so, should his national counterparts have them too? Where should the missionary send his children to school—to the local schools, to a school for missionary children, or to those in North America? What food should the missionary eat, what dress should he wear and what kind of house should he and the national workers have? These and a thousand more questions arise in the bicultural setting.

Status and role

The term "status" has a number of common meanings, but anthropologists use it in a specific sense, defining it as the "positions in a social system occupied by individuals." At the level of interpersonal relationships, a social organization is made up of a great many such positions: teachers, priests, doctors, fathers, mothers, friends and so on.

Each status is associated with certain behavioral expectations. For example, we expect a teacher to act in certain ways towards his students. He should show up for class and lead it. He should not sleep in class, or come in a dressing gown. A teacher should also act in certain ways vis-a-vis his administrators, the parents of the students, and the public.

All interpersonal relationships can be broken down into complimentary role pairs: teacher-student, pastor-parishioner, husband-wife, etcetera. The nature of the relationship between two individuals is based very much on the statuses they choose.

The Missionary and the Nationals. "What are you?" This question is repeatedly asked of a person who goes abroad to settle. The people ask because they want to know how to relate to the newcomer.

Missionaries generally answer, "We are missionaries." In stating this they are naming a status with its associated roles, all of which are perfectly clear to themselves. They know who "missionaries" are, and how they should act. But what about the nationals, particularly the non-Christians who have never met a missionary before. What do they think of these foreigners?

Here we must come back to cultural differences, again. Just as languages differ, so also the roles found in one culture differ from those found in another culture. "Missionary" is an English word, representing a status and role found in the West. In most other cultures it does not exist. When a missionary shows up in these cultures, the people must observe him and try to deduce from his behavior which of their roles he fits. They then conclude that he is this type of person and expect him to behave accordingly. We, in fact, do the same thing when a foreigner arrives and announces that he is a "sannyasin." From his looks we might conclude he is a hippie, when, in fact, he is a Hindu saint.

How have the people perceived the missionaries? In India the missionaries were called "dora." The word is used for rich farmers and small-time kings. These petty rulers bought large pieces of land, put up compound walls, built bungalows, and had servants. They also erected separate bungalows for their second and third wives. When the missionaries came they bought large pieces of land, put up compound walls, built bungalows, and had servants. They, too, erected separate bungalows, but for the missionary ladies stationed on the same compound.

Missionary wives were called "dorasani." The term is used not for the wife of a dora for she should be kept in isolation away from the public eye, but his mistress whom he often took with him in his cart or car.

The problem here is one of cross-cultural misunderstanding. The missionary thought of himself as a "missionary," not realizing that there is no such thing in the traditional Indian society. In order to relate to him, the people had to find him a role within their own set of roles, and they did so. Unfortunately, the missionaries were not aware of how the people perceived them.

A second role into which the people often put the missionary in the past was "colonial ruler." He was usually white, like the colonial rulers, and he sometimes took advantage of this to get the privileges given the rulers. He could get railroad tickets without waiting in line with the local people, and he could influence the officials. To be sure, he often used these privileges to help the poor or oppressed, but by exercising them, he became identified with the colonial rulers.

The problem is that neither of the roles, rich landlord or colonial ruler, permitted the close personal communication or friendship that would have been most effective in sharing the Gospel. Their roles often kept the missionaries distant from the people.

But what roles could the missionaries have taken? There is no simple answer to this, for the roles must be chosen in each case from the roles in the culture to which he goes. At the outset he can go as a "student," and request that the people teach him their ways. As he learns the roles of their society, he can choose one that allows him to communicate the Gospel to them effectively. But when he chooses a role, he must remember that the people will judge him according to how well he fulfills their expectations of that role.

The Missionary and National Christians. The relationship between a missionary and national Christians is different from that between him and non-Christians. The former, after all, are his "spiritual children" and he their "spiritual father."

This parent-child relationship is vertical and authoritarian. The missionary is automatically in charge. He is the example that the people must imitate, and their source of knowledge. But people soon become tired of being children, particularly when they are older and in many ways wiser than their parents. If not permitted to be responsible for themselves, they will never mature, or they will rebel and leave home.

The missionary is also imprisoned by this parental role. Not only is it difficult for him to form close relations with the people, with them as his equals, but also he feels he can admit to no wrong. If he were to confess personal sins and weaknesses to the people, he fears that they will lose their faith in Christ. But he is also their model for leadership roles, and they soon come to believe that no leader should admit to sin or failure. Obviously the missionary and the national leaders do sin, and because of their roles, they have ways of confessing sin and experiencing the forgiveness of the Christian community without destroying their ministry.

Another role into which missionaries can slip, often unawares, is that of "empire builders." Each of us needs to feel that we are part of an important task. From this it is only a small step to seeing ourselves as the center of this task and indispensable. We gain personal followers and build large churches, schools, hospitals and other institutions that prove our worth.

However, this role, like the first, is not the best for effective communication. From a structural perspective, it is a vertical role in which communication proceeds from the top down. There is little feedback from the bottom up. People below comply with the orders from above, but often do not internalize the message and make it their own. From a Christian perspective, this role does not fit the example of Christ. On the contrary, it can lead to an exploitation of others for our own personal gain.

What roles can the missionary take? Here, because the missionary and the nationals are Christians, we can turn to a Biblical model—that of brotherhood and servanthood. As members of one body we must stress our equality with our national brothers and sisters. There is no separation into two kinds of people, "we" and "they." We trust the nationals just as we trust our fellow missionaries, and we are willing to accept them as colleagues and as administrators over us. Assignments of leadership within the church are not based on culture, race or even financial power. They are made according to God-given gifts and abilities.

There is leadership in the Church, just as there must be in any human institution if it is to function. But the Biblical concept of leadership is servanthood. The leader is one who seeks the welfare of the others and not himself (Matt. 20:27). He is dispensable, and in this sense the missionary is most dispensable of all, for his task is to plant the church and to move on when his presence begins to hinder its growth.

Identification

Good relationships involve more than choosing suitable roles. Within a role the individual expresses different attitudes that show his deep feelings toward the other person.

If we feel that somehow we are a different kind of people from those with whom we work, this will be communicated to them in a number of subtle ways. We may live apart from them, allow them only into our living rooms which are public space, and not permit our children to play with theirs. Or we may allow no nationals on mission committees.

When we identify with the people, we will do so in formal ways—at an annual feast given to the staff of the school or hospital, in their homes, but only on formal invitation, and on the committees by allowing a few to participate. We may even wear the native dress on certain occasions. But formal identification is identification at arms length. It stresses the basic difference between people, even as it demonstrates their superficial oneness.

The real test of identification is not what we do in formal, structured situations. It is how we handle our informal time, and our most precious belongings. When the committee meeting is over, do we go aside with fellow Americans to discuss cameras, and thereby exclude our national colleagues by our use of space and the topic of discussion? Do we frown on our children playing with the local children?

But is it possible for a missionary ever to "go native?" Obviously not. It takes immigrants from Northern Europe three or four generations to assimilate into American culture, and where the cultural differences are greater, it takes even longer.

The basic issue in identification is not formal equivalence—living in the same houses, eating the same food and wearing the same dress. We can do so and still communicate to people the mental distinction we make between them and us. The issue is one of mental maps and basic feelings. If we indeed, see and feel ourselves to be one of them, this message will come through, even if we have different life styles. A national gives us his best food, lets us sleep in his guest room and use his oxcart, and we share with him our best food, guest room and car. The principle is not formal equality but true love and mutual reciprocity.

A sense of oneness with the people creates in us an interest in learning more about them, and in sharing in their culture. Our example is Christ who, because of His love, became incarnate among us in order to bring us God's good news.

The Organization of Societies and Church Growth

Another way of looking at social structures is to see how societies as wholes are put together. What are the various social groups and institutions within a given society, how do these articulate with one another, and how does change occur? Here, again, two or three illustrations can show best the application and usefulness of the concept.

Tribal societies

In many tribes, social groups play an important role in the life of an individual, more so than they do in our own society with its strong emphasis on individualism and freedom. In a tribe a person is born and raised within a large kinship group or lineage made up of all the male descendants of some remote ancestor, plus all the families of these males. To get something of a feel for this type of society, imagine, for a moment, living together with all of your relatives who share your last name, on a common farm, and sharing responsibilities for one another. All the men one generation older than you would be your "fathers" responsible for disciplining you when you deviate from the tribal rules and customs. All the women of that generation would be your "mothers" who care for you. All in your lineage of your own age would be "brothers" and "sisters," and all the children of all your "brothers" would be your "sons" and "daughters."

In some tribes, a lineage is made up of all the female descendants of a remote ancestress, together with their families. But, again, the authority of and responsibility to the group remains central in the life of the person.

Strong kinship groups in a tribe provide the individual with a great deal of security. They provide for you when you are sick or without food, support you when you go away to school, contribute to your purchasing a field or acquiring a bride, and fight for you when you are attacked. In turn, the group makes many demands on you. Your lands and your time are not strictly your own. You are expected to share them with those in your lineage who need them.

TRIBAL SOCIETIES

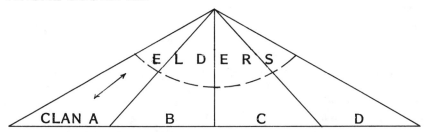

- Stress on kinship as basis for social bonding
- Strong group orientation with mutual responsibility and group decision-making processes
- Minimal social hierarchy
- Vertical communication

Important decisions in these tribes are generally made by the elders—the older men who have had a great deal of experience with life. This is particularly true of one of the most important decisions of life, namely, marriage. Unlike in our society where young people are all too ready to get married when they "fall in love" (analogous to "falling into a mud puddle"?) without carefully testing the other person's social, economic, mental and spiritual qualifications, in most tribes weddings are arranged by the parents. From long experience they know the dangers and pitfalls of marriage, and they are less swayed by the passing emotional attachments of the present. The parents make the match only after a long and careful examination of all the prospective partners. Love grows in these marriages as in any marriage by each partner learning to live with and to love the other.

Lineage and tribal decisions are also made by the elders. Family heads have their say, but they must comply with the decisions of the leaders if they want to remain a part of the tribe.

This type of social organization raises serious questions for Christian evangelism. Take, for example, Lin Barney's experience. Lin was in Borneo when he was invited to present the Gospel to a village tribe high in the mountains. After a difficult trek he arrived at the village and was asked to speak to the men assembled in the long house. He shared the message of the Jesus Way well into the night, and, finally, the elders announced that they would make a decision about this new way. Lineage members gathered in small groups to discuss the matter, and then the lineage leaders gathered to make a final decision. In the end they decided to become Christians, all of them. The decision was by general consensus.

What should the missionary do now? Does he send them all back and make them arrive at the decision individually? We must remember that in these societies no one would think of making so important a decision as marriage apart from the elders. Is it realistic, then, to expect them to make an even more important decision regarding their religion on their own?

Should the missionary accept all of them as born again? But some may not have wanted to become Christian and will continue to worship the gods of their past.

Group decisions do not mean that all of the members of the group have converted, but it does mean that the group is open to further Biblical instruction. The task of the missionary is not finished, it has only begun, for he must now teach them the whole of the Scriptures.

Such people movements are not uncommon. In fact, much of the growth of the church in the past has occurred through them, including many of the first Christian ancestors of most of the readers of this book.

Peasant societies

The social organization of peasant societies is quite different from that of tribal societies. Here we often have the weakening of extended kinship ties and the rise of social classes and castes. Power is often concentrated in the hands of an elite that is removed from the commoners.

We can turn to India for an illustration of how peasant social structure influences church growth. Villages are divided into a great many *jatis* or castes. Many of these, such as the Priests, Carpenters, Ironsmiths, Barbers, Washermen, Potters and Weavers, are associated with certain job monopolies. Not only does a person inherit the right to perform his caste's occupation, he must marry someone from within his own caste. A rough analogy would be for American high school teachers to marry their children to other high school teachers, for preachers to marry their children to other preachers' children, and for each other occupation to do the same. One can see, therefore, the need to begin marriage negotiations early.

Castes are also grouped into the clean castes and the untouchables. The latter are ritually polluting and their touch, in the past, polluted clean-caste folk who had to take a purification bath to restore their purity. Consequently, the untouchables formerly had to live in hamlets apart from the main villages, and were forbidden to enter the Hindu temples.

When the Gospel came, it tended to move in one of the group of castes or the other, but not in both. Some of the first converts were from the clean castes. But when many of the untouchables accepted Christ, the clean-caste people objected. They did not want to associate with the folk from the wrong part of town. The missionaries continued to accept all who came and required that they all join the same church. Consequently, many of the clean-caste people reverted back to Hinduism.

PEASANT SOCIETIES

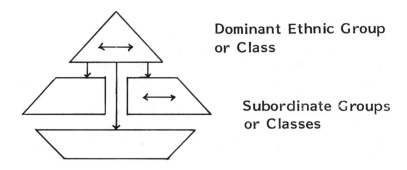

Dominant Ethnic Group
or Class

Subordinate Groups
or Classes

- Stress on kinship as basis for social bonding
- Strong group orientation with group decision-making processes
- Intergroup hierarchs
- Communication horizontal within groups, vertical between them

The problem here is not a theological one. Many of the high-caste converts sincerely believed the gospel, and even today many are secret believers. It is a social problem. The high-caste folk did not want to associate with the untouchables. Before we judge them, let us stop and look at the churches and denominations in America. In how many of them do we find a wide mixture of people from different ethnic groups and social classes? How long has it taken them to break down the last remnants of racial segregation? In how many of them have differences in wealth, social class and political power become unimportant in the fellowship and the operation of the churches?

The dilemma is that theologically the church should be one, but, in fact, people are socially very diverse. Moreover, they find it hard to associate closely and intermarry with people markedly different from themselves. Can we expect people to change their deep-seated social ways at the moment of their conversion—in other words, should we expect them to join the same church? Or is changing our social customs a part of Christian growth— should we allow them to form different churches with the hope that with further teaching they will become one? The question is similar to one many American churches face; is giving up smoking or drinking alcohol or any other behavior defined as sinful essential to salvation, or is it a part of Christian growth?

There have been some in India who have held that the peoples' salvation is not tied to their joining a single church, and they have, therefore, started different churches for the clean castes and the untouchables. They have had a much greater success in winning people from the clean castes, but they have also faced a great deal of criticism from those who argue that this is contrary to the will of God.

The Urban Scene

The recent growth of cities has been phenomenal. In 1800 no city in the world had a population of a million, and fewer than twenty-five had more than 100,000 inhabitants. By 1950 forty-six cities had more than a million residents. The New York metropolitan area, which had over fifteen million people in 1970, may reach twenty-two million by 1985.

This rapid urbanization of the world raises many questions for those concerned with church growth. What is the social structure of a city and how does this structure influence communication and decision making? How do changes take place in the highly mobile and varied city society?

URBAN INDIVIDUALISTIC SOCIETIES

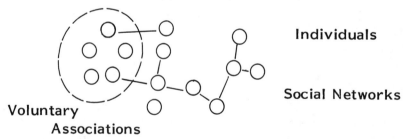

Individuals

Social Networks

Voluntary Associations

- Stress on individualism and personal decision-making
- Organization on basis of voluntary associations, networks and geographical groupings
- Heterogenents and hierarchs
- Use of mass media in addition to networks

The social processes affecting church growth in tribal and peasant societies are less evident in urban societies. Large people movements in which people come to Christ on the basis of group decisions, or in which the message is shared through caste and kinship ties, seem almost absent. On the other hand, there are new forces at work. City folk are often caught up in rapid change. Their ideas are molded by mass media, educational institutions and voluntary associations. Communication often follows networks of people who are mutually acquainted. In other words, a friend tells a friend, who, in turn, tells another friend.

What methods should missions use in the city? So far no clear-cut strategy has emerged. Mass media, friendship, neighborhood and apartment evangelism, large educational and medical institutions and mass rallies have all been tried, and with mixed success. There is no simple formula that will bring success—there never has been. Building churches is a difficult and long-range task.

Cities also offer tremendous opportunity. They are the centers for world communication, and the source from which ideas spread to the countryside. One reason for the rapid spread of early Christianity was its movement through the cities. We desperately need to look more closely at modern urban dynamics in order to understand how change takes place, and then to apply these insights to today's mission planning.

Study Questions

1. Explain the development and function of the "bicultural bridge."

2. Hiebert describes some roles assumed by missionaries that were inappropriate for communication of the gospel. What types of roles *are* appropriate?

5

The Role of Culture in Communication

David J. Hesselgrave

There was a time in history of man (and it was not long ago!) when the barriers between the earth's peoples seemed to be mainly physical. The problem was one of transporting men, messages, and material goods across treacherous seas, towering mountains, and trackless deserts. Missionaries knew all too well how formidable those challenges were. Today, thanks to jumbo jets, giant ocean vessels, and towering antennae, those earlier problems have been largely resolved. We can deliver a man, or a Bible, or a sewing machine anywhere on the face of the earth within a matter of hours, and we can transmit a sound or a picture within seconds. This does not end the matter, however. To quote Robert Park:

> One can transport words across cultural boundaries (like bricks)
> but interpretation will depend on the context which their different
> interpreters bring to them. And that context will depend more on
> past experience and present temper of the people to whom the
> words are addressed than on the good will of the persons who
> report them.[1]

Park goes on to assert that the traits of material culture are more easily diffused than those of nonmaterial culture. He illustrates his point by citing the example of the African chief whose immediate response upon seeing a plow in operation was "It's worth as much as ten wives!" One wonders how much prayer and how many hours of study and patient instruction would have been necessary to convince that chief that Christ is infinitely more valuable than plows or wives or fetishes and false gods! Yes, the barriers are, after all, very real and challenging. But they are no longer essentially physical—if, indeed, they ever were.

The Cultural Barrier to Missionary Communication

There is a very real danger that, as our technology advances and enables us to cross geographical and national boundaries with singular ease and increasing frequency, we may forget that *it is the cultural barriers which are the most formidable.* The gap between our technological advances and our communication skills is perhaps one of the most challenging aspects of modern civilization. Western diplomats are beginning to realize that they need much more than a knowledge of their message and a good interpreter or English-speaking national. Many educators have come to the position that cross-cultural communication is a *sine qua non* for citizenship in this new world. Missionaries now understand that much more than a microphone and increased volume is involved in penetrating cultural barriers.

Unfortunately, intercultural communication is as complex as the sum total of human differences. The word "culture" is a very inclusive term. It takes into account linguistic, political, economic, social, psychological, religious, national, racial, and other differences. Communication reflects all these differences, for, as Clyde Kluckhohn says, "Culture is a way of thinking, feeling, believing. It is the group's knowledge stored up for future use." [2] Or, as Louis Luzbetak writes:

> Culture is a design for living. It is *a plan according to which society adapts itself to its physical, social, and ideational environment.* A plan for coping with the physical environment would include such matters as food production and all technological knowledge and skill. Political systems, kinships and family organization, and law are examples of social adaptation, a plan according to which one is to interact with his fellows. Man copes with his ideational environment through knowledge, art, magic, science, philosophy, and religion. Cultures are but different answers to essentially the same human problems.[3]

Missionaries must come to an even greater realization of the importance of culture in communicating Christ. In the final analysis, they can effectively communicate to the people of any given culture to the extent that they understand that culture (language being but one aspect of culture). Before missionaries go to a foreign country the first time, they tend to think primarily of the great distance they must travel to get to their field of labor. Often it means traveling thousands of miles from their homes. But once they arrive on the field, they begin to realize that in this modern age it is nothing to travel great distances. The great problem to be faced is the last eighteen inches! What a shock! The missionary has studied for many years. He has traveled ten thousand miles to communicate the gospel of Christ. He now stands face-to-face with the people of his respondent culture and he is unable to communicate the most simple message! Ask experienced missionaries about their frustrating experiences on the field and most of them will respond by telling of their problems in communication.

Missionaries should prepare for this frustration. They have been preoccupied with their message! By believing it they were saved. By studying it they have been strengthened. Now they want to preach it to those who have not heard it, for that is a great part of what it means to be a missionary! But before they can do so effectively, they must study again—not just the language, but also the audi-

ence. They must learn before they can teach, and listen before they can speak.
They need to know the message for the world, but also the world in which the
message must be communicated.

A Three Culture Model of Missionary Communication

Eugene Nida of the American Bible Society has made important contributions
toward an understanding of the communication problems of the missionary. The
discussion and diagram in his chapter on "Structure of Communication" furnish
the basis for our consideration of a "three-language model" of missionary communication.[4] Though modifications have been made in order to further our
present objectives, the reader will greatly benefit by a reading of Nida's text.

As a communicator, the missionary stands on middle ground and looks in
two directions (see figure). In the first place, he looks to the Scriptures. The message is not really his. He did not originate it. He was not there when it was first
given. His own words are not "inspired" in the biblical sense. He cannot say as
could the apostle,

> What was from the beginning, what we have heard, what we have
> seen with our eyes, what we beheld and our hands handled, con-
> cerning the Word of life—and the life was manifested and we have
> seen and bear witness and proclaim to you the eternal life, which
> was with the Father and was manifested to us. (I John 1:1-2).

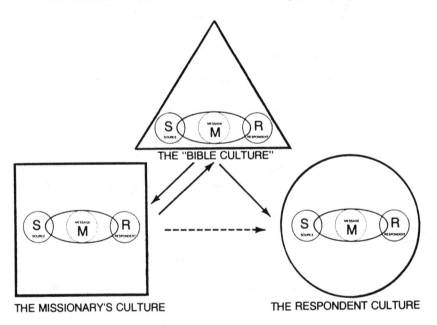

A THREE-CULTURE MODEL
OF MISSIONARY COMMUNICATION

He knows that he must be diligent to present himself "approved to God as a workman who does not need to be ashamed, handling accurately the word of truth" (2 Tim. 2:15). He knows that he must study and obey the Word of God. He is aware that there are some very solemn warnings to be absolutely faithful to that original message:

> I testify to everyone who hears the words of the prophecy of this book: if anyone adds to them, God shall add to him the plagues which are written in this book; and if anyone takes away from the words of the book of this prophecy, God shall take away his part from the tree of life and from the holy city, which are written in this book (Rev. 22:18-19).

In summary, in relationship to the biblical message, the missionary is simply a messenger, an ambassador—a secondary, never a primary source.

In the second place, when the missionary lifts up his eyes and looks to the fields, he sees people—millions of them—who need the message. If only they could understand their real need! If only their worship were directed to the true God! If only their faith were to be placed in the one Savior and Lord. If only they could be reached, instructed, and persuaded to repent. It is these of whom his Lord spoke when He said, "All authority has been given to Me in heaven and in earth. Go, therefore, and make disciples of all the nations, baptizing them in the name of the Father and the Son and the Holy Spirit, teaching them to observe all that I commanded you" (Matt. 28:18-20). But looking at his respondent culture, he realizes that he will never be an indigenous source. The language of that culture will always have an element of strangeness. That culture will always be his *adopted culture*, never his *native culture*.

It is this intermediate position, this looking in two directions, that constitutes the special challenge and unusual opportunity of the missionary as an ambassador of Christ. It is a special challenge because of the comprehensive and demanding nature of the task. It is an unusual opportunity because it means giving the one needful message to those who have not understood or believed it.

Let's take another look at what is involved from the perspective of communication. At the primary level the missionary message is the message of the Bible. It was given by God through the apostles and prophets in the languages and cultural contexts of the Bible. For the sake of simplification we will say that "Bible culture" includes all cultural contexts in which the message of the Bible was originally given, whether Judah at the time of Ezra, Jerusalem at the time of Christ, or Athens at the time of Paul. In those cultural contexts there were sources (Ezra, our Lord Christ, or Paul), messages and respondents. The sources of the messages were identified with the cultures we have labeled "Bible culture." They encoded the messages in forms that were understandable in those cultures to respondents who were members of those cultures.

At the secondary level, the missionary is a citizen of a quite different culture, whether his home address is in London, Chicago, or even Tokyo. He has been brought up in his own culture and has been schooled in its language world view, and value system. He has received the Christian message in the context of culture as it was communicated by a source (or sources) who most likely was a citizen of the culture. We will label that culture the "missionary's culture."

At the tertiary level, there are people in still another culture with its own sources, messages and respondents. We will label this third culture the "respondent culture" (and, occasionally, the "target culture"). In relationship to this respondent culture the missionary has immediate and ultimate objectives. First, he desires to communicate Christ in such a way that the people will understand, repent, and believe the gospel. Second, he wants to commit the message to "faithful men who will be able to teach others" (2 Tim. 2:2) in culturally relevant terms that only they, in the final analysis, can command.

The missionary task can now be seen in clearer perspective. Starting from the missionary's culture, cultural boundaries must be traversed in two directions. The missionary's first responsibility is to study the Scriptures, in the original languages if possible, but always in terms of the "Bible culture context." Any sound system of hermeneutics must take into account the cultural context in which the message was originally communicated, the background and syntax and style, the characteristics of the audience, and the special circumstances in which the message was given. This process is essential to Bible exegesis. The important thing, after all, is not what the Bible reader or interpreter feels the meaning to be; the important thing is what the source intended that his respondents should understand by his message! The Bible interpreter is constantly tempted to project the meanings of his own cultural background into the exegetical process with the result that the original meaning is missed or perverted. This temptation is heightened by the fact that, for the most part, all of us learn our own culture quite unconsciously and uncritically. Therefore, there is the ever-present tendency to generalize from our own experience.

Most Bible readers and interpreters will find sufficient reason for confessing to their weakness in this area. For example, a friend of mine recently joined a tour group in Palestine. While walking under a tree in the Jordan Valley, the guide reached up, picked some fruit, peeled away the husk and ate the fruit. As he did so, he turned to the group and said, "According to the Bible, John the Baptist's diet consisted of this fruit and wild honey. This is the locust." Almost to a person the members of the group expressed astonishment. They had always supposed that the locusts mentioned in Matthew and Mark were grasshoppers! As a matter of fact, they probably were correct. The point is that they had not thought of this second possibility because in their own culture "grasshopper locusts" are prevalent while "locust fruit" is not!

Another example of this tendency to interpret the Word of God through cultural glasses related to the Authorized Version's translation of our Lord's instructions to His disciples at the Passover meal, "Drink ye all of it" (Matt. 26:27 KJV). Perhaps most Protestant congregations in America (and not a few ministers) understand this to mean that all the wine is to be consumed though little significance is attached to the phrase in view of the fact that the elements usually come in such minuscule proportions that consuming all is not a very challenging task! How much more significant is the original meaning which, properly translated would be: "Drink from it, all of you" (NASB), or "All of you drink some of it" (*Williams*). Two facts of American culture militate against this original meaning, however. First, most of us do not drink from a common cup in the manner to which the disciples were accustomed. And second, the syntax of the English language as spoken by most Americans makes it unlikely that they will decode the message in accordance with the original meaning.

Proper exegesis, however, is but the beginning of missionary responsibility. The missionary must now look in another direction—the direction of the respondent culture with its own world view, value system, and codes of communication. He must remember that respondents in *that* culture have imbibed as deeply of its particular ideas and values as he has of his. It is likely that they will be more ignorant of the "Bible culture" than non-Christian members of the "missionary's culture" are. Further, they will exhibit the same tendency to generalize and project their own cultural understandings into the message of the Bible culture. The missionary task, therefore, is to properly exegete (decode) the biblical message. With minimal intrusion of his own cultural understanding, he must encode the message in a culturally relevant form in the target culture so that the respondents will understand as much as possible of the original message. This is not the simple task that many have supposed. Consider what is involved in translating Revelation 3:20 in terms which are meaningful to the Zanaki people.

> One cannot say to the Zanaki people along the winding shores of sprawling Lake Victoria, "Behold, I stand at the door and knock" (Rev. 3:20). This would mean that Christ was declaring Himself to be a thief, for in Zanaki land thieves generally make it a practice to knock on the door of a hut which they hope to burglarize; and if they hear any movement of noise inside, they dash off into the dark. An honest man will come to a house and call the name of the person inside, and this way identify himself by his voice. Accordingly, in the Zanaki translation it is necessary to say, "Behold, I stand at the door and call." This wording may be slightly strange to us, but the meaning is the same. In each case Christ is asking people to open the door. He is no thief and He will not force an entrance; He knocks and in Zanaki "He calls." If anything, the Zanaki expression is a little more personal than our own. [5]

Or, consider the strangeness of the phrase "devours widows' houses" in a still different respondent culture.

> To understand a strange culture one must enter as much as possible into the very life and viewpoint of the native people. Otherwise, a person will not realize how ridiculous it is to talk to Indians of southern Mexico about scribes who "devour widows' houses" (Mark 12:40). Their houses are often made with cornstalk walls and grass roofs, and farm animals do eat them when fodder gets scarce, so that people guard against hungry cows breaking in to eat down a house. "Devouring widows' houses" is no bold metaphor in some places, but a real danger. Hence the native reader wonders. "What were these 'scribes' anyway? Was this just a name for starved, ravenous cattle?" In such cases one must translate "destroy widows' houses." [6]

There remains still another important aspect of missionary communication. We said that the ultimate goal of the missionary is to raise up effective sources of the Christian message from within the target culture. Missionary communication that does not keep this goal in mind is myopic. The world mission of the church has been greatly weakened by lack of vision at this point. It is not so much that missionaries have been remiss in encouraging the emergence of Christian leadership in the Third World. *But it has been all too easy to encourage (perhaps unconsciously) those leaders to become Western in their thinking and approach.* After a course in cross-cultural communication, a national pastor of five years of experience confessed that throughout his ministry he had preached "Western sermons" to Asian audiences. After all, he had learned the gospel from American missionaries: he had studied his theology, homiletics and evangelism from English and German textbooks; and the great percentage of his Christian training had been in the language and other patterns of Western culture. No wonder his Christian communication lacked "respondent cultural relevance" even though the respondent culture in this case was his own culture!

Furthermore, for the most part, *missionaries have not communicated Christ's concern for the people of still other respondent cultures.* As a result many Christians in Hong Kong have little vision for Indonesia, and many Christians in Venezuela exhibit little concern for unbelievers in Peru. When missionary vision is born (and it has been born in many churches in the Third World), it seldom occurs as a result of the ministry of the North American or European missionary. Though the state of affairs is ironic and deplorable, it is understandable. The missionary's own missionary concern has been expressed in terms of *his* target culture. Unless he keeps his eyes on the fields, unless he sees the whole world as the object of God's love, and unless he communicates this to national Christians, *their vision will tend to be limited by his own!*

In Summary

It is now possible to summarize the missionary communication task by resorting to a hypothetical illustration. Imagine the case of a missionary from New York who goes to Nagoya, Japan. His short-range objective will be to take the truths communicated in the biblical terms *Theos, hamartia* and *soteria* [7] (and related synonyms) and communicate them in terms of *Kami, tsumi* and *sukui.* [8] Ideally he will encode these truths with as little intrusion of the North American cultural accretions attached to the terms "God," "sin," and, "salvation" as possible. This is no easy task, for by virtue of his enculturation he is better equipped to understand the terms *Theos, hamartia* and *soteria* . And he is certainly better prepared to understand *Kami, tsumi* and *sukui* !

Moreover, his long-range objective must be to encourage Japanese Christian converts to become "sources" and communicate Christ in culturally relevant terms within their own culture and in still other respondent cultures—Javanese culture, for example. In that culture, Japanese missionary "sources" will be called upon to communicate the meaning of *Theos, hamartia* and *soteria* in terms of *Allah, dosa* and *keselamatan* . [9] The way in which missionaries communicate Christian truth to Japanese in forms available within Japanese culture may have a salutary effect on the way in which Japanese missionaries present these same truths to Javanese Muslims. After all, Allah is defined by the Javanese Muslim in such a way as to make the Incarnation impossible. Sin is defined in such a way as to make the Incarnation unnecessary. And as for salvation, Muslims view God as merciful and sovereign and are quite willing to let it go at that. Whether or not the Japanese missionary is prepared to deal with these cultural differences may well depend upon the communication he has received from missionary tutors and models in Japan.

End Notes

1. Robert Parks, "Reflections on Communication and Culture," in *Reader in Public Opinion and Communication* , ed. Bernard Berelson and Morris Janowitz, 2nd ed. (New York: Free Press, 1966), p. 167.

2. Clyde Kluckhohn, *Mirror for Man* (New York: Whittlesev, 1949), p. 23.

3. Louis J. Luzbetak, *The Church and Cultures* (Techny, Ill.: Divine Word, 1963), pp. 60-61.

4. Eugene A. Nida, *Message and Mission: The Communication of the Christian Faith* (New York: Harper and Row, 1960), pp. 33-58.

5. Eugene A. Nida, *God's Word in Man's Language* (New York: Harper and Row, 1952), pp. 45-46.

6. *Ibid..*, p.45.

7. The Greek words corresponding to God, sin and salvation.

8. The Japanese words corresponding to God, sin and salvation.

9. The Javanese words corresponding to God, sin and salvation.

Study Questions

1. Summarize the three-culture model of missionary communication.

2. What other examples can you suggest of Bible interpretation through American "cultural glasses"?

6

World-view and Contextualization

David J. Hesselgrave

During a visit to an American southwestern university you are invited by a friend who is preparing for service in the Peace Corps to attend a class with him.[1] In his lecture, the instructor explains the kind of problems that may be encountered in introducing more efficient methods or machines to (for example) Indian nationals or Amerindians. He explains that the problems may well stem from the fact that representatives of the Peace Corps and representatives of these other cultures understand the notion of "progress" in very different ways. The Indian peasant may well ask "What is progress?" and inquire as to why he should adopt a method of rice-growing simply because it is more efficient. The American white sees the exchange of horse and wagon for a pickup truck as a case of unquestioned progress, but for the Navajo Indian it is simply a desirable substitute, not "progress."

The instructor goes on to explain that the different ideas of "progress" are understandable when one stops to reconstruct the fundamental perspectives of the three cultures:

> Here in the U.S. he would be able to assume that if he could demonstrate the practical superiority of a certain technique or practice people would adopt it. Elsewhere in the world, such a proof might fall on deaf ears and uncomprehending minds. An American sees a pickup truck as an absolute advance over a horse and wagon. It is more efficient and faster and, all in all, totally in keeping with his notion of progress. To the Navajo Indian the pickup truck is no less desirable, but it is not progress—it is simply a substitute for a horse and wagon.

> This is a difficult idea to put into illustrative words. Perhaps it will

After twelve years' service in Japan under the Evangelical Free Church, David J. Hesselgrave became Professor of Missions at the School of World Mission and Evangelism at Trinity Evangelical Divinity School in Deerfield, Illinois. He later served as Director of the School of World Mission and Evangelism, and is now the Professor Emeritus of Mission. He is now the executive director of the Evangelical Missiological Society. Hesselgrave is the author of *Planting Churches Cross-Culturally* and *Communicating Christ Cross-Culturally*.

help to compare the Navajo's overall view of history with our own. The Navajo believes that his people were created in mythic times through various miraculous adventures, each of which gave rise to the ancestor of one of the tribe's many clans. To him those times are not really past. By singing the proper songs and carrying out certain rituals, the Navajo medicine man brings those events of the creation myths back to life and uses them to cure illnesses. Similarly the Hopi Indian, dancing in his elaborate masks and costume, becomes to a degree one of the beings who created the earth and to whom the Hopi owe allegiance.

In the day-to-day life of the Christian, however, there is no such circularity of existence. The earth was created and will remain so until it ends. Christ was born, lived, preached, and was crucified. If he is to come again it will be a second coming, not the same one. Adam and Abraham, Moses and Saul are historical as well as sacred figures and our theologians and historians have spent much time establishing their precise place in history. From Adam's fall to the present is an expanse of time which will never be repeated.

The Hindu, by contrast, lives in a universe that remains essentially the same and man moves through it a life at a time. Man's status may rise toward godliness, or escape from life, or it may descend through the lower orders of existence as a consequence of the way he lives each life, but through it all the universe remains the same. Such a man does not live in a universe that constantly changes or progresses—rather, he changes within a changeless universe. Little wonder then that he seems fatalistic to westerners and uninterested in progress as we see it. He is interested in improvements in his life—better living conditions, more money, healthier children—but each of these things in his eyes is a separate and distinct condition, not an aspect of something called progress.

The caveat remains. Don't expect all people to view as you do this thing called progress or even to understand the idea. Remembering this can save a great deal of frustrating misunderstanding.[2]

Perhaps the foregoing illustration will serve as a cue to our starting point in the study of intercultural communication per se. It illustrates several all important facts about men in culture. In the first place, men in certain large cultural groupings tend to share certain fundamental commonalties in defining the reality around them. This commonality is a part of culture. Any given culture is made up of folkways, modes and mores, language, human productions, and social structures. It is all of these and more than these. It is also the larger significance of men and things in relation to which these aspects of culture take on meaning. One might compare culture to a large and intricate tapestry. The tapestry is made up of numberless threads, various colors, larger shadings and lines all of which go to make up the overall mosaic or pattern which in turn serves in interpreting any part. *Culture is also this wholeness, this larger reality.*

In the second place, people are born and reared "into" culture. They are *enculturated*, to use the term of the anthropologists. By this process culture is made to be uniquely their own—the *cultural* reality becomes *their* reality over a period of time. As James Downs says,

> Men living in coherent groups...define the world around them, deciding what is real and how to react to this reality. Failure to grasp this simple fact about culture—that is, culture, not rocks or trees or other physical surroundings, is the environment of man dooms any attempt to work in a cross-cultural context.[3]

In the third place, since people of a culture tend to take this culturally determined view of reality with utmost seriousness, the missionary communicator must take it with utmost seriousness also. To fail to do so may render the missionary incapable of effective communication. This does not mean that every way of looking at reality is valid. It is obvious that certain cultural views cancel out certain other cultural views. It is this process of cancellation that fosters cultural relativism by rendering many students of culture incapable of subscribing to *any* view as having universal validity. But the point to be stressed here is that the way of looking at reality which prevails in any respondent culture is valid for the members of that culture. It is *that* validity that must be taken with utmost seriousness by the missionary if he wants to communicate Christ in the respondent culture. Since respondents will decode messages within the framework of a reality provided by their own culture, the missionary must encode his message with that reality in mind. To put this in terms of that part of culture with which we are now concerned, the communication of most people is circumscribed by the perspective provided by their own world view. This is true of the missionary also. Moreover, it will be true of him until he makes that herculean effort required to understand the world view of his respondents in their culture and speaks within that framework. At that point true missionary communication begins.

Norman Geisler correctly contends,

> The Christian accepts as axiomatic that his task is to communicate Christ to the world. That sounds simple enough, but in fact it is very complex. It is complex for at least three reasons: first, there are many views of "Christ"; secondly, there are many ways to "communicate"; and thirdly, there are many "worlds" to which Christ must be communicated.[4]

He then goes on to liken the various world views to colored glasses through which people see themselves and the universe around them. Everything is given the "tint" or "hue" of whatever particular "world view glasses" the person happens to be wearing. Moreover, since the vast majority of people are used to one pair of glasses from the time of their earliest recollections, they are not predisposed even were they able to lay those glasses aside (even temporarily) in order to look at the world through another pair of glasses.

The analogy is a good one as we shall see!

The way people see reality can be termed their world view. It is instructive that in Latin, Greek, Sanskrit, English, and certain other languages, one meaning for the word "see" is "know." A world view is the way people see or perceive the world, the way they "know" it to be. What men see is in part what is there. It is partly who we are. But these combine to form one reality, one world view.

Adapting the Message to World View

From a communication point of view it is imperative that we analyze the world views of our respondent cultures. It is in the context of these world views that our message will be decoded and evaluated. One reason why much missionary communication has been monological (one way—missionary to respondent) is that missionaries have not been conversant enough with world views other than their own. In ignorance of what is happening in the decoding process, they have simply "related" (!) the gospel. One gets the distinct impression that in some cases the motivation is to deliver the soul of the missionary rather than to save the souls of those who hear him. But it was not so with Christ and the apostles.

Though our Lord ministered within the confines of the world view of Judaism, He nevertheless adapted to interests, needs, and "points of view" within various contexts. He did not communicate with the rich young ruler in terms of the new birth, or with the woman of Samaria in terms of "selling what she had and following Him," or with Nicodemus in terms of the Water of life. All three approaches would have been valid as concerns God's eternal truth, but they would not have been valid as adaptations within the respective contexts.

In the same way, Peter and Paul adapted their message to the world views of their respondents. A comparison of Peter's message on Pentecost (Acts 2:14-36) and in the house of Cornelius (10:34-43), and of Paul's messages in the synagogue of Antioch in Pisidia (13:16-41) and on Mars' hill in Athens (17:22-31) will reveal a profound appreciation for the differences between monotheistic Jews and Gentile God-fearers, and between Jews and polytheistic heathen. How can missionaries communicate from their world view into other world views? How can they persuade non-Christian respondents who see everything through the glasses of their respective world views? Only three ways are logically possible.

First, missionaries can invite their non-Christian respondents to lay aside their own world view and temporarily adopt the Christian world view in order to understand the message. But while this approach is theoretically possible, it is highly impractical, as we have indicated previously. Why? The reason is that comparatively few non-Christian respondents are *able* to do this. They have never been called upon to do so—much less are they prepared to do so. It is as though their glasses have become a part of their eyes. Of the few who by virtue of education or association are *able* to change glasses, there are only a few of them who are *willing* to do so. Their reticence may be due to pride or disinterest or other causes. Whatever the cause, the result is the same and is in evidence everywhere.

Second, missionaries can temporarily adopt the world view of their non-Christian respondents. Then, by reexamining their message in the light of the respondent world view, they can adapt the message, encoding it in such a way that it will become meaningful to the respondents. This approach is not easy, but it is both possible and practical. Complete communication may not be attainable. Perfection seldom is. But effective communication is possible if missionaries take the initiative and pay the price. And true missionary motivation is to communicate a message, not simply dispense it.

Third, missionaries can invite their respondents to meet them halfway, to exchange one lens and try looking through one eye, so to speak. This has been a rather popular approach to the problem. Traditionally, the study of comparative religion has been undertaken by many missionaries in order to find points of contact or establish common ground between religious world views. Many such points and places turn out to be mirages upon closer examination, however. Others seem to have some kind of reality to commend them, but upon close examination the "reality" turns out to be a kind of religious quicksand. That is why Hendrik Kraemer insists that one must have a "totalitarian" understanding of religion.[5] In other words, the separate parts of any religion must be understood in terms of the whole of it. To return to our former analogy, we need both lenses. Otherwise we risk distortion.

If we grant limited validity and practicality to approaches one and three above, it seems apparent that approach number two, the contextualization of the message by the missionary into the world view of his respondents, is in keeping with the missionary calling and the realities of culture. The missionary is the evangel to men only when they understand something about the God of whom he speaks and the true nature of the human condition. With *God's ends* in view he begins with *their starting point*. What they believe concerning the existence and nature of reality, the world around them, and man in relationship to the whole is of the essence. Adaptation to those beliefs is one of the first requirements of missionary communication. This process will affect the source, substance, and style of the missionary message.

The Missionary as Source of the Message

Identification is not so much a matter of adopting this or that kind of dress or food as it is a matter of entering into the experiences of a people with understanding. To do this one must know what lies behind those experiences; one must take their world view seriously. We take other world views seriously, in the first place, when we study them and demonstrate an understanding of them. An understanding of their respective world views enables the missionary to account for the attraction which neutrality holds for the Indian, the fatalism of the Muslim, the affection which Ibero-Americans have for the Virgin Mary, the ethnocentrism of the Japanese, and the inclination of many peoples to downgrade sin, or add another deity, or honor the ancestors.

A very careful study of the Chinese world view, for example, enables the missionary to Chinese people to understand why they objected that the Japanese occupation forces were "killing" the earth. (According to the Chinese myth, the man-god Pán-Ku was born from the *Yin* and *Yang*. He sacrificed himself and thus became the substance of creation. His head became the mountains, his hair the trees, his breath the clouds, his veins the rivers, and his voice the thunder.) Careful study enables the missionary to Chinese people to understand why a corpse is laid out in a direct line toward the door, and why bridal parties take a circuitous route to the marriage ceremony. (The traditional belief was that evil spirits cannot turn corners. Therefore the bridal couple taking a devious route cannot be followed by evil spirits. In the case of the corpse, if the spirit were to become a werewolf, it would walk straight through the door and not remain in the house.)

By demonstrating some understanding of such beliefs, the missionary gains *integrity* and *credibility* before his audience. His purpose is not to impress or entertain the people. Instead, he seeks to demonstrate that he has considered indigenous alternatives to God's revelation in Christ and that he is not a religious huckster who is simply hawking God's Word (cf. 2 Cor. 2:17 LB). On the contrary, he is someone who can be trusted, someone who understands. This kind of missionary insight may be even more important when the rationale for a custom or ritual has been forgotten by the people while the custom itself remains.

We take other world views seriously when, in the second place, we make every effort to empathize with their adherents. Missionary communication is not enhanced by an arrogant show of superiority, or by ridiculing or downgrading other views, or by repeatedly pointing out their inconsistencies. There comes to my mind the case of the missionary who carefully studied the Shinto myth in order to hold it up to ridicule. Then he pointed to the slanted eyes and rounded features of indigenous gods while laughing at their provinciality. This approach may serve the ego but it betrays the kingdom. The weaknesses, inconsistencies, and inadequacies of false systems of philosophy and religion are not to be overlooked. But missionaries must also deal with them at the points of their strength. Examples of strength are numerous. The contributions of Buddhism to the arts of China and Japan are a matter of record. The attraction of Hindu inclusivism in a divided world is incontrovertible. The fascination with which many view mysticism and transcendental experience is evident in the West as well as the East. The fact that adherents of some other religions are much more appreciative of the world around them than are many Christians who ostensibly accept that world as a gift of Almighty God is plain to see. That many a Communist exhibits much less of materialistic outlook than many Christians goes without saying. We must learn to deal with the best case that non-Christians can make, not with their weakest case, lest we succeed only in pricking balloons and knocking down straw men. *To honestly and sympathetically deal with the best case that any form of unbelief can make, and then show the desperate need that still remains and how it can only be met by the true God and his redeeming Son—this is the more excellent way.*

Furthermore, when we take this approach we find it easier to identify with men in their searching. We too are sinners. It is possible that we too gave our best efforts and thought to these perplexing questions of life only to discover that our best was unavailing and that we were poor sinners in need of the only Savior and Lord. We must remember that millions of the world's people believe they have "never seen a sinner." Their own world views do not really allow for such a category. And when the missionary comes to them, he comes as a "saint" who is somehow better than other men. He comes as a "religious man" whose record of past sins has been wiped out and whose present sins are as invisible as the missionary can make them.

Again, there is a better way. The missionary in his new situation is a sinner saved by grace. He sinned against God in his own world view by rejecting the Creator and Redeemer of men. Yet he was captivated by God's truth and love. Such a context makes the missionary a more faithful communicator of the Christian message. Moreover, he is recognized as a person of *goodwill* who has the best interests of his respondents at heart.

These are some of the ways the missionary wins a hearing and authenticates his message. This approach takes us beyond sympathy to empathy, but it has its price.

World View and the Substance of the Missionary Message

The Christian message is universal. It is for all men irrespective of race, language, culture, or circumstance. Some have therefore naively assumed that this ends the matter. If one knows what the gospel is, all that remains is the motivation to deliver it. There is, of course, "one Lord, one faith, one baptism, one God and Father of all" (Eph. 4:5, 6). But without betraying that unique message in any way, the gospel writers and preachers of the New Testament demonstrated a remarkable variegation in their communication of it, not only in style but in substance.

Let us return to our previous examples in the ministries of Christ, Peter, and Paul. In each case the missionary communication included a pointed reference to the basic spiritual need of man in his natural state of sin and alienation from God. In each case, however, this universal need was particularized somewhat differently. Nicodemus had had but one birth; the Samaritan woman was practicing immorality and false worship; Peter's audience at Pentecost had delivered Christ to be crucified; Cornelius and his friends needed to know that remission of sins was available by believing in the name of Christ; the congregation of the synagogue in Antioch of Pisidia needed to beware lest they refuse the very One of whom the prophets had testified and whom the Father had appointed as Savior; the Greeks of Athens needed to know that the true God would no longer overlook their ignorant worship now that He had raised Christ from the dead.

It would seem that in the New Testament, missionary communication involved either making a case for Christian claims from the Old Testament in the case of those who held to the Judeo-Christian world view, or filling in the information concerning God, His world, man, and history which the Old Testament affords in the case of those who had non-Judeo-Christian world views. Notice that in the partially recorded discourses of Paul at Lystra (Acts 14:15-17) and on Mars' hill (17:22-31) Paul begins with the Creator God who was unknown to those Gentile polytheists. Paul's approach is elaborated in the first chapters of Romans.

We conclude, therefore, that while certain general statements can be made concerning the substance of the gospel (e.g., I Cor. 15:1-9) and the spiritual need of man as a sinner (e.g., Rom. 3:9-18), the communication of these truths in specific situations involves a contextualization process which includes *definition, selection, adaptation,* and *application.*

1. *Definition.* One of the disastrous aspects of man's sin was that he did not retain God in his knowledge. As a result man's understanding has been perverted in precisely those areas where divine revelation is crystal clear. The true God is excluded, but false gods abound. Men distinguish between good and evil in some way, but not in accordance with the biblical view. A majority of men

believe themselves to be immortal in some sense of the term, but the forms of immortality vary greatly with world views. Geoffrey Bull's reflections on presenting Christ to Tibetan Buddhists illustrates the point well.

The expansion of the Tibetan language came with the growth of Buddhist philosophy; thus words used often represent two distinct concepts. We take up and use a word in Tibetan, unconsciously giving it a Christian content. For them, however, it has a Buddhist content. We speak of God. In our minds this word conveys to us the concept of the supreme and Eternal Spirit, Creator and Sustainer of all things, Whose essence is Love, Whose presence is all holy, and Whose ways are all righteous. For them, the Tibetan word god means nothing of the kind. We speak of prayer, the spiritual communion between God our Father and His children. For them prayer is a repetition of abstruse formulae and mystic phrases handed down from time immemorial. We speak of sin. For them the main emphasis is in the condemnation of killing animals.

When I was at Batang I saw an open-air performance of a Buddhist play. One of the chief sins depicted there was the catching of fish. When I asked the special significance of the "transgression" I was told, "Oh, fishes mustn't be killed, they can't speak," meaning, I presume, that they utter no sound. It is a common sight to see a man, when killing a yak, at the same time muttering his "prayers" furiously. Gross immorality is also condemned by the most thoughtful lamas, but rarely publicly. We speak of the Savior. They think of Buddha or the Dalai Lama. We speak of God being a Trinity. They will say: "Yes, god the buddha, god the whole canon of Buddhist scripture, and god the whole body of the Buddhist priesthood." We speak of man's spirit being dead in sin and his thus being cut off from God. They cannot understand. A person, they say, is only soul and body. What do you mean by the third concept, a man's spirit? When a man dies, they believe his soul escapes by one of the nine holes in his body: we know nothing of his spirit, they say. We speak of a revelation from God, His own Word which we are commanded to believe, and they know no word but the vast collection of Buddhist sayings, which only one in a thousand even vaguely understands. Those who have studied them believe that only in the exercise of the human intellect, in meditation and contemplation over a very long period, can one begin to enter into the deep things of the "spirit." What "spirit" though, perhaps few of them realize.

We, of course, speak of the Holy Spirit as a gift of God to the believer in Christ. They say. "What nonsense! As if a man could obtain the Holy Spirit as easily as that." Of course, I would point out the other aspect; that it is not so much our possessing the Spirit, as the Spirit possessing us. On acceptance of Christ the believer is born of the Spirit, yet it may be but slowly that He will obtain full sovereignty of the heart and will. This is dismissed as being contrary to the concept of God being a Spirit. We speak of the Almighty power of God and yet of man being responsible to Him, particularly in his acceptance or rejection of His way of salvation. I was told this was a "lower doctrine," cause and effect as a fatalistic law being widely propounded by the lamas.[6]

The missionary who takes the Fall seriously, then, must stop to define his terms as we have seen. Which terms? He must define those terms dictated by the distance between divine truth and cultural error. The definitional process must proceed by comparison and contrast. If this process seems too painstaking for the Western missionary who is used to instant everything—from instant cake to instant coffee to instant conversion—so be it. But he should know that to build Christian conversion on non-Christian world views is like building skyscrapers on sand. The mission fields are well populated with men and women who have been ushered into the heavenlies without knowing why they got on the elevator. Once back on earth they have no intention of being taken for another ride.

2. *Selection.* The previous point may become more understandable if we realize that the missionary must always give a partial message in the particular situation. Christ commanded us to teach men to observe *all things* which He commanded (Matt. 28:20), but certainly He did not intend that we deliver everything in one sitting! As a matter of fact, Christ never did that Himself, nor did the apostles. The world could not contain all the books that could be written about Christ and truth of God (John 21:25). Selection has always been necessary! Thus while the missionary communicates nothing but the truth, he communicates the whole truth only over a period of time. Priorities are essential. Understanding comes with precept taught upon precept and line upon line.

It was an awareness of the need for selection that prompted many early missionaries to avoid Old Testament passages concerning the wars of the Israelites. Their rationale was that the people were already too warlike. Of course, it would be both fallacious and faithless to think that the exploits of Israel could be forever neglected. But in every case care should be exercised in selecting culturally appropriate expressions of God's message to man. Let the polytheist be told of the power of Christ, not just to save souls, but to subdue all things to himself. Let him hear that the "unknown God" has revealed Himself to men. Let the Confucianist know that the only superior Man is the Son of God and Savior of men who recreates men and makes them into better husbands, wives, children, friends, and citizens. Let the Muslim see that God is love and hear why God can be just and the Justifier of the one who believes in Jesus. Let our Jewish friend hear once again that Christians believe that God still has a great future for them as a people and that a new day will dawn for any Jew who will look long enough at Jesus of Nazareth to see who He really is. All of this is, of course, oversimplified and somewhat redundant. But if it is also suggestive, it serves a purpose.

3. *Adaptation.* The sensitive missionary source of gospel communication defines his terms and makes a careful selection of content from the larger revelation of God. He also carries on a closely related and continual process of adaptation. He notes the special concerns occasioned by the particular world view and adjusts to those concerns.

For example, in the Hindu-Buddhistic or Taoist contexts, there is little point in attempting to demonstrate the sinfulness of man initially by showing that men are liars. Where all propositional statements (and especially those of a religious nature) are mere approximations, lying becomes *in one sense* a necessary concomitant of communication itself! But selfishness and covetousness are already matters of great concern. Is there any *biblical* ground for labeling these fundamental human weaknesses as sin? There most assuredly is such a basis. Then we can *all* agree that selfishness and covetousness are indeed evil. And we can point out how God looks upon these evils and deals with them.

The missionary does well to answer problems posed but not answered in the false systems. When problems of an other-worldly nature were put to Confucius, he answered very matter-of-factly that he hardly understood this world and should not be expected to know about another world. On the basis of their own world view, Communists are hard-pressed to give a satisfactory answer as to why extreme sacrifices should be made by the present generation of men for the generations yet unborn. Many Hindus must recoil in utter despair when faced with the seemingly numberless existences required to effect their final emancipation from the wheel of existence. Christ has real answers for these problems if only His ambassadors will deliver them.

Adaptation also requires that we answer objections that respondents can be expected to raise vis-a-vis the Christian message. The literature of Nichiren Buddhism, for example, makes much of the point that a man who knows the truth will die peacefully and with happiness apparent in his very facial expression. That Christ died on a cross while raising the anguished cry, "My God, my God, why hast thou forsaken me?" (Matt. 27:46 KJV) raises for these Buddhists a serious question as to whether Christ Himself knew the truth. A brief apologetic *before* the problem is articulated will go far to disarm the objector.

Finally, the missionary should also be alert to watch for special entries to these non-Christian systems. Confucius said,

> A holy man I shall not live to see; enough could I find a gentleman! A good man I shall not live to see; enough could I find a steadfast one! But when nothing poses as something, cloud as substance, want as riches, steadfastness must be rare.[7]

Lao-tze said that "he who bears the sins of the world is fit to rule the world."[8] These quotations furnish the Christian communicator with communication opportunities that should not be overlooked.

4. *Application.* As is the case in all communication, the missionary message becomes most compelling when it ceases to be general and becomes personal. We are not in the final analysis speaking to world views but to the minds and hearts of men of flesh and blood who live out these world views in their decisions and actions. Can we make the message of Christ compelling to *them*? We can and we must. It is in application that we say, "Thou art the man" (2 Sam. 12:7 KJV).

Of course, ultimately the Holy Spirit must apply the Word. Geoffrey Bull illustrates that truth in his illustration of a Tibetan Buddhist military governor who refused to be moved by the most obvious refutation of his own faith.

> I was surprised how even a man like the Dege Sey believed in reincarnation. There was rather an amusing incident. He was saying to me how they had to be very careful, for even one of the domestic animals might be his grandmother. I was about to make some mildly humorous comment as to the general treatment of dogs in Tibet, when the words were taken out of my mouth and

far more eloquent sounds fell on our ears. From the courtyard came the piercing squeals of some pitiful canine, which had just been either kicked or battered with a brick bat. The Dege Sey, generally quick to see a joke, sat quite unmoved. Incarnation as a doctrine itself is readily accepted by the Tibetans, but when we assert there is but one incarnation of the Living and True God, "The Word made flesh," it is totally unacceptable to them.[9]

If application is a function of knowledge, it is also a function of faith. It is not according to the usual bent of human nature to admit that one is wrong or to agree with God that we are sinners—especially helpless sinners whose only hope is in divine grace. When God's truth is faithfully and lovingly applied, however, there will be a response throughout Adam's race if that truth is presented intelligently and in dependence upon the Spirit.

World View and the Style of the Missionary Message

A "contextualized content" requires the accompaniment of a "contextualized style." Style can best be thought of as the personal imprint of the source upon his message. Its ingredients vary with the communication code, whether linguistic or nonlinguistic, and therefore we can speak of style as it relates to sermons, lectures, magazine articles, books, drawings, or films and even to the way in which one lives out his Christian faith before other people. It can be studied in relation to the source, message, code, and respondents. It should be evaluated as to correctness, clarity, and appropriateness. Style is that part of missionary communication in which the source's understanding of his respondent culture, his powers of imagination, and his skill in the manipulation of symbols are given most reign and can be put to great service for the kingdom. At the same time, a style that is out of keeping with the respondent culture does the kingdom a disservice.

Think for a moment in terms of the respondent culture the author knows best—Japan. To contemporary Japanese much missionary communication (as reflected not only by missionaries but by national pastors and workers who often simply duplicate Western patterns) must seem to exhibit a great lack of style, though it is not so much a lack of style as a foreignness of style that is at the root of the problem. There are numerous aspects of the Judeo-Christian world view *as it has come through the Western mold* that must stamp missionary communication as un-Japanese. Some of these would be directness, brusqueness, matter-of-factness, lack of awe and a sense of mystery, oversimplification, narrow scope of interest, aloofness from everyday concerns, and insensitivity to the feelings of the audience.

On the other hand, the missionary who by his demeanor and speech communicates the greatness and holiness of God, a deep appreciation for the beauty of God's world, and the mystery of Christian teachings such as the Trinity, the incarnation and the atonement will find that his audience will be much more "at home" with his message.

In Summary

The Christian message is, indeed, abiding and universal. It is for all men of every time in history and of every culture on earth. But the cultural contexts in which God revealed it and the missionary delivers it are distinct and different. They cannot be superimposed upon one another. If Christian meaning is not to be lost in the communication process, contextualization is required. There are many facets of contextualization but at the very least it involves appropriate responses to cultural differences in local perceptions of the missionary source and in the substance and style of the missionary's message.

End Notes

1. The imagined experience is based on a discussion by James F. Downs, who served as an instructor in the training programs of the Peace Corps and VISTA. Cf. James I. Downs, *Cultures in Crisis* (Beverly Hills: Glencoe, 1971), pp. 128-29.

2. *Ibid.*

3. *Ibid.*, pp. 36-37.

4. Norman L. Geisler, "Some Philosophical Perspectives on Missionary Dialogue," in *Theology and Mission*, ed. David J. Hesselgrave (Grand Rapids: Baker, 1978), p. 241.

5. Hendrick Kraemer, *The Christian Message in a Non-Christian World* (Grand Rapids: Kregel, 1963), pp. 135-41.

6. Geoffrey T. Bull, *When Iron Gates Yield* (London: Hodder and Stoughton, 1967), pp. 97-99.

7. "Selections from the Analects," in *Readings in Eastern Religious Thought*, ed. Ollie M. Frazier, 3 vols. (Philadelphia: Westminster, 1963), 3:74.

8. *The Book of Tao*, trans. Frank J. MacHovee (Mt. Vernon, N.Y.: Peter Pauper, 1962), Sutra 78, p. 17.

9. Bull, *op. cit.*, p. 63.

Study Questions

1. Explain how world view can determine beliefs, values, and behavior. Give an example from your own experience.

2. Hesselgrave states that "the missionary should…be alert to watch for special entries to…non-Christian systems." Would you expect to find few or many such "special entries?" Why?

3. Define "contextualization."

4. Can you identify an occasion from your own experience (mono-cultural or cross-cultural) in which you may have used Hesselgrave's four parts of contextualization?

7

Pachacutec's Mini-Reformation

Don Richardson

We Christians err whenever we too readily assume that pagans know nothing of God. In fact, a startling number of pagan peoples possess amazingly clear concepts about a Supreme God who created all things. Also, several passages of Scripture warn us to expect pagan peoples to have some awareness of God. For example:

1. "Since the creation of the world," wrote Paul the Apostle. "God's invisible qualities—His eternal power and divine nature—have been clearly seen, being understood from what has been made, so that men are without excuse" (Romans 1:20 NIV).

This belief that men already know something about God even before they hear of either Jewish law or the Christian Gospel was a cornerstone of Paul's theology of evangelism. He expressed it also in an Asian town called Lystra, where he once confronted a formidable cross-cultural communication barrier, proclaiming:

2. "In the past, He (God) let all nations go their own way; yet *He has not left Himself without testimony* "(Acts 14:16, 17 NIV).

3. In his famous letter to Roman Christians, Paul wrote: "...when Gentiles...do by nature things required by the law...they show that the requirements of the law are *written on their hearts* " (Romans 2:14,15 NIV).

4. John the Apostle declared that Jesus Christ is "the true Light that gives light to *every* man" (John 1:9 NIV).

5. King Solomon wrote that God has *"set eternity in the hearts of men,"* and then added the cautionary statement that man of himself still "cannot fathom what God has done from beginning to end" (Ecclesiastes 3:11 NIV). According to Hebrew scholar Gleason Archer, Solomon's statement means that mankind has a

---

Don Richardson pioneered work for Regions Beyond Missionary Union (RBMU) among the Sawi tribe of Irian Jaya in 1962. Author of *Peace Child, Lords of the Earth,* and *Eternity in Their Hearts,* Richardson is now Minister-at-Large for RBMU. He speaks frequently at missions conferences and Perspectives Study Program classes. From *Today's Mission Magazine,* since renamed *World Christian Magazine,* 21150 Oxnard St.. Suite 860, Woodland Hills, CA Used with permission.

God-given ability to grasp the concept of eternity, with all its unsettling implications for moral beings like himself.[1]

6. It was, however, Solomon's father, King David, who penned an even more eloquent appreciation of God's universal testimony to Himself through creation: "The heavens declare the glory of God; the skies proclaim the works of His hands. Day after day they pour forth speech; night after night they display knowledge. There is no speech or language where their voice is not heard. Their voice goes out into all the earth, their words to the end of the world" (Psalm 19:1-4 NIV).

David then focuses upon the sun, describing it as a "bridegroom coming forth from his pavilion" and as a "champion rejoicing to run his course" (Psalm 19:5, 6 NIV). This, perhaps more than any other Scripture, fittingly introduces Pachacutec.

Pachacutec's Mini-Reformation

Pachacutec is probably history's finest example of what Paul and John and Solomon and David meant in the above quotations. Pachacutec was an Inca who lived between 1400 and 1448 A.D.[2] He was also the entrepreneur who designed and built Macchu Picchu, which was perhaps the first mountain resort in the New World. After the Spanish invasion of Peru, Macchu Picchu became a last sanctuary for the Inca upper class.

Pachacutec and his people worshipped the sun, which they called Inti. But Pachacutec became suspicious of Inti's credentials. Like King David, King Pachacutec studied the sun. It never did anything, as far as Pachacutec could tell, except rise, shine, cross the zenith and set.

Next day, same thing: rise, shine, cross the zenith, set.

Unlike David, who likened the sun to a bridegroom or a champion, Pachacutec said, "Inti seems to be but a laborer who has to perform the same chores daily. And if he is merely a laborer, surely he cannot be God! If Inti were God, Inti would do something original once in a while!"

The King mused again. "Any mist dims the light of Inti," he observed. "Surely if Inti were God, nothing could dim his light!"

Thus did Pachacutec tumble to a crucial realization—he had been worshipping a mere *thing* as creator!

But if Inti wasn't God, to whom could Pachacutec turn?

Then he remembered a name his father had once extolled—*Viracocha!*

Viracocha, according to his father's claims, was none other than a god who created all things. All things including Inti!

Pachacutec came to a brisk decision: this Inti-as-God nonsense had gone far enough! He called an assembly of the priests of the sun—a sort of pagan equivalent of a Nicene Council. Standing before the assembly, Pachacutec explained his reasoning about the supremacy of Viracocha. Then he commanded that Inti, from that time forward, be addressed "as kinsman only." Prayer, he said, must be directed to Viracocha, supreme God.

To put Pachacutec's action in perspective, let me point out that scholars, while generally ignoring him, have widely acclaimed Akhenaten, an Egyptian King (1379-1361 B.C.), as a man of rare genius because he attempted to replace the grossly confused idolatry of ancient Egypt with the purer, simpler worship of the sun as sole God.[3]

Pachacutec, however, was leagues ahead of Akhenaten in his realization that the sun, which could merely *blind* human eyes, was no match for a God too great to be seen by human eyes! If Akhenaten's sun worship was a step above idolatry, Pachacutec's choice of an invisible God was a leap into the stratosphere!

Why have scholars—religious as well as secular—virtually ignored this amazing man?

Perhaps it was because Pachacutec stopped short of an even greater achievement...

One important measure of a man of genius is his ability to communicate his insight to "common" people. Great religious leaders from Moses to Buddha to Paul to Luther have all excelled in this skill.

Pachacutec never even tried.

Deeming the masses of his people too ignorant to appreciate the worth of an invisible God, he deliberately left them in the dark about Viracocha. That is why Pachacutec's reformation, amazing as it was, became a *mini* reformation, limited to upper classes only. Upper classes are notoriously short-lived social phenomena. Less than a century after Pachacutec's death, ruthless conquistadors obliterated the upper classes of Pachacutec's empire. His reformation ended.

Is Viracocha Yahweh?

Now for an evaluation—was Viracocha really the true God, the God of creation? Or was he merely a figment of Pachacutec's imagination, hence an impostor? In other words, if Paul the Apostle had lived in Pachacutec's day, and if one of his missionary journeys had swept him all the way to Peru, would he have denounced Pachacutec's insight as a delusion? Or would he have said, "Very well, Yahweh's name in this land is Viracocha."

It is really not difficult to deduce Paul's attitude toward questions of this sort. When Paul preached the Gospel among Greek-speaking peoples, he did not impose a Jewish name for God—Jehovah, Yahweh, Elohim, Adonai, or El Shaddai—upon them. Rather he placed his Apostolic seal upon a 200-year old decision of the translators of the Septuagint version of the Old Testament. They had given the God of the Jews a totally Greek name—*Theos*. Paul followed suit.

Interestingly, translators of the Septuagint did not try to equate the Greek god Zeus with Yahweh. Nor did Paul. Although Greeks esteemed Zeus as "king of the gods," he was also viewed as the offspring of two other gods, Cronus and Rhea. Hence the name Zeus could not qualify as a synonym for Yahweh, the uncreated. This was true even though the Latin cognate of Zeus—Deus—was later accepted as the equivalent of Yahweh for Roman Christians!

In fact, it is probable that even "Theos" sprang from the same linguistic root as both "Zeus" and "Deus."

Further, when Paul preached the Gospel at Athens, he boldly equated

Yahweh with an "unknown God" associated with a certain altar in the city, saying: "What you worship as something unknown I am about to proclaim to you!"

A principle emerges: there is nothing sacred—contrary to Jehovah's Witness' belief—about any particular combination of sounds or letters as a name for the Almighty. He may have ten thousand aliases, if need be, in ten thousand languages. It is impossible to talk about an uncreated Creator without meaning HIM, and anyone capable of protesting: "But all His attributes are missing!" is responsible to fill them in! Any theological vacuum surrounding the concept of God is a communicator's opportunity, not an obstacle!

Let pagan theologians try to fill the vacuum and almost invariably they botch it, as they did, for example, when they made Zeus an offspring of other gods, disqualifying what was probably at one time a valid name for the Almighty.

A Supreme God in a Thousand Human Traditions

Christianity, spreading around the world, has continued from Paul's time to confirm, rather than ignore, the concept of a Supreme God in a thousand human traditions. When Celtic missionaries reached my pagan forefathers in northern Europe, they did not impose upon them Jewish or Greek names for Deity, but used Anglo-Saxon words such as Gött, God or Gut. American Baptist missionaries, George and Sarah Boardman, in 1828 found the Karen people of southern Burma believing that a great God named Y'wa (shades of Yahweh) had long ago given their forefathers a sacred book! Alas, the forefathers, rascals that they were, went and lost it! But one day "a white brother," said a persistent Karen tradition, "would restore the lost book to the Karen people, bringing them back into fellowship with Y'wa!" Boardman became the white brother, and 100,000 Karen people became baptized believers within a few decades!

Norwegian Lutheran missionary, Lars Skrefsrud, found in 1867 thousands of Santal people in India wistfully regretting their forefather's rejection of Thakur Jiu, the Genuine God. Skrefsrud proclaimed that Thakur Jiu's Son had come to earth to reconcile estranged humanity to himself.

The result: within a few decades more than 100,000 Santal received Jesus Christ as their Savior!

Presbyterian pioneers in Korea discovered a Korean name for God— Hananim, the Great One. Rather than sweeping Hananim aside and imposing a foreign name for God, they proclaimed Jesus Christ as the Son of Hananim. Within some 80 years, more than two and one-half million Koreans have become followers of Jesus Christ.

During the 1940's, Albert Brant of the Sudan Interior Mission found thousands of Dorsa tribesmen in Ethiopia believing that Magano, the Creator, would one day send a messenger to camp under a certain sycamore tree. Unsuspectingly, Albert camped under that tree and an awesome response to the Gospel began, bringing 250 churches to birth in less than three decades!

Breakthrough narratives of this sort can be multiplied by the hundreds from the history of missions! Truly Paul and John and Solomon and David were right! God has not left Himself without witnesses. And yet, tragically, an earlier generation of our fellow believers, ignoring the Great Commission, allowed a man like Pachacutec to die without finding in the Gospel of Jesus Christ the blessed and only fulfillment of that which he—because eternity was in his heart—knew must be true.

How many other Pachacutecs are we allowing to die unconfirmed?

How many generations of Pachacutecs will rise up in the judgment to join Nineveh and the Queen of Sheba in condemning indifferent believers? Let us strive to be—for our generation—the Boardmans, the Skrefsruds, and the Albert Brants who care enough to go and tell!

End Notes

1. From a personal interview with Gleason Archer.

2. From *Indians of the Americas* (Wash., D.C.: National Geographic Society, 1955), pp. 293-307.

3. From *The Horizon Book of Lost Worlds* (New York: American Heritage Publishing, 1962), p. 115.

Study Questions

1. Do you agree with Richardson's assertion that "it is impossible to talk about an uncreated Creator without meaning HIM"? What significance would your answer have, for example, for missions to Muslims, who worship Allah?

2. What biblical rationale does Richardson put forward in explanation of Pachacutec's discovery?

8

Concept Fulfillment

Don Richardson

When a missionary enters another culture, he is conspicuously foreign, and that is to be expected. But often the gospel he preaches is labeled foreign. How can he explain the gospel so it seems culturally right?

The New Testament way seems to be through concept fulfillment. Consider:

—The Jewish people practiced lamb sacrifice. John the Baptist proclaimed Jesus as the perfect, personal fulfillment of that sacrifice by saying, "Behold the *Lamb of God*, who takes away the sin of the world!"

This is concept fulfillment.

—Nicodemus, a Jewish teacher, knew that Moses had lifted up a serpent of brass upon a pole, so that Jews when dying of snakebite could look at it and be healed.

Jesus promised: "As Moses lifted up the serpent in the wilderness, even so must the Son of Man be lifted up, that whoever believes in Him should not perish, but have everlasting life."

This too is concept fulfillment.

—A Jewish multitude, recalling that Moses had provided miraculous manna on a six-day-a-week basis, hinted that Jesus ought to repeat His miracle of the loaves and fishes on a similar schedule.

Jesus replied, "Moses gave you not the *true* bread from heaven. The true bread from heaven is He who comes down from heaven and gives life to the world...I am that Bread of Life!"

Once again, concept fulfillment.

When some charged that Christianity was destroying the Jewish culture, the writer to the Hebrews showed how Christ actually fulfilled all the central ele-

---

Don Richardson pioneered work for Regions Beyond Missionary Union (RBMU) among the Sawi tribe of Irian Jaya in 1962. Author of *Peace Child, Lords of the Earth,* and *Eternity in Their Hearts,* Richardson is now Minister-at-Large for RBMU. He speaks frequently at missions conferences and Perspectives Study Program classes. From *Moody Monthly.* Vol. 9, 1976, pp. 54 ff. Used by permission of Don Richardson.

ments of Jewish culture—the priesthood, tabernacle, sacrifices, and even the Sabbath Rest. Let's call these *redemptive analogies*—looking for their fulfillment in Christ. Their God-ordained purpose was to pre-condition the Jewish mind to recognize Jesus as Messiah.

Application Today

The strategy of concept fulfillment can be applied by missionaries today—if only we learn to discern the particular redemptive analogies of each culture.

Consider the advantage: when conversion is accompanied by concept fulfillment, the individuals redeemed become aware of the spiritual meaning dormant within their own culture. Conversion does not deny their cultural background, leaving them disoriented. Rather they experience heightened insight into both the Scriptures and their own human setting, and are thus better prepared to share Christ meaningfully with other members of their own societies. See how concept fulfillment has worked in other cultures:

Examples in Other Cultures

The Damal and "Hai"

Less than one generation ago, the *Damal* people of Irian Jaya were living in the Stone Age. A subservient tribe, they lived under the shadow of a politically more powerful people called the Dani.

What hope could there be, you may ask, of finding a redemptive analogy in such a Stone Age setting?

And yet the Damal talked of a concept called *hai*. *Hai* was a Damal term for a long anticipated golden age, a Stone Age utopia in which wars would cease, men would no longer oppress one another, and sickness would be rare.

Mugumenday, a Damal leader, had yearned to see the advent of *hai*. At the end of his life, Mugemenday called his son Dem to his side and said: "My son, *hai* has not come during my lifetime: now you must watch for *hai*. Perhaps it will come before you die."

Years later, Gordon Larson, John Ellenburger, Don Gibbons and their wives entered the Damal valley where Dem lived. After tackling the Damal language they began to teach the gospel.

The people, including Dem, listened politely. Then one day...

"O my people!" Dem, now a mature adult, had risen to his feet. "How long our forefathers searched for *hai*. How sadly my father died without seeing it. But now, don't you understand, these strangers have brought *hai* to us! We must believe their words, or we will miss the fulfillment of our ancient expectation."

A breakthrough began. Virtually the entire population welcomed the gospel. Within a few years congregations sprang up in nearly every Damal village.

But that was not the end.

The Dani and "Nabelan-Kabelan"

The Dani, haughty overlords of the Damal, were intrigued by all the excitement. Curious, they sent Damal-speaking representatives to inquire. Learning that the Damal were rejoicing in the fulfillment of their ancient hope, the Dani were stunned. They too had been waiting for the fulfillment of something they called *nabelan-kabelan*—the belief that one day immortality would return to mankind.

Was it possible that the message which was *hai* to the Damal could also be *nabelan-kabelan* to the Dani?

By then Gordon and Peggy Larson had been assigned to work among the Dani. Dani warriors now recalled that they often mentioned "words of life," and a man named Jesus who not only could raise the dead but also rose again Himself.

Suddenly everything fell into place for the Dani as it had for the Damal. The word spread. In valley after valley the once barbarous Dani listened to the words of life. A church was born.

Concept fulfillment.

The Karen and a black book

The Karen tribe in Burma had a legend that one day a teacher of truth would appear, and he would carry a black object tucked under his arm. This first missionary to come among them always carried a black, leather-covered Bible tucked under his arm. The Karen listened with rapt attention every time he took the Bible out from under his arm and preached.

Triggered by this catalyzing cultural element, a great moving of the Spirit of God soon swept thousands of Karen into the Church of Jesus Christ. Yet some studies of the phenomenal growth of the church among the Karen fail to mention this detail.

The Asmat and a new birth

When Jesus told Nicodemus he must be born again, Nicodemus was astounded. Even though he was well educated he met Jesus' assertion with a naively literal, almost childish objection:

"How can a man be born when he is old? Can he enter into his mother's womb a second time and be born?"

Surely if a theologian like Nicodemus had that hard a time comprehending the meaning of "new birth," then a naked, illiterate, stone-age cannibal would have a thousand times more difficulty.

On the contrary, one part of Irian Jaya's Asmat tribe have a way of making peace which requires representatives from two warring villages to pass through a symbolic birth canal formed by the bodies of a number of men and women from both villages. Those who pass through the canal are considered *reborn* into the kinship systems of their respective enemy villages. Rocked, lullabied, cradled, and coddled like new-born infants, they become the focus of a joyful celebration. From then on they may travel freely back and forth between the two formerly warring villages, serving as living peace bonds.

For no one knows how many centuries, this custom has impressed deeply upon the Asmat mind a vital concept: *True peace can come only through a new birth experience!*

Suppose God called you to communicate the gospel to these Asmat people. What would be your logical starting point? Let us assume you have learned their language and are competent to discuss the things dear to their hearts.

One day you visit a typical Asmat man—let's call him Erypeet—in his long-house. First you discuss with him a former period of war and the new birth transaction which brought it to an end. Then...

"Erypeet, I too am very interested in new birth. You see, I was at war with an enemy named God. While I was at war with God, life was grim, as it was for you and your enemies.

"But one day my enemy God approached me and said, 'I have prepared a new birth whereby I can be born in you and you can be born again in Me, so that we can be at peace....'"

By this time Erypeet is leaning forward on his mat, asking,

"You and your people have a new birth too?" He is amazed to find that you, an alien, are sophisticated enough to even *think* in terms of a new birth, let alone *experience* one!

"Yes," you reply.

"Is it like ours?"

"Well, Erypeet, there are some similarities, and there are some differences. Let me tell you about them...."

Erypeet understands.

What makes the difference between Erypeet's and Nicodemus's responses? Erypeet's mind has been pre-conditioned by an Asmat redemptive analogy to acknowledge man's need for a new birth. Our task is simply to convince him that he needs *spiritual* rebirth.

Do redemptive analogies like these occur by mere coincidence? Because their strategic use is foreshadowed in the New Testament, and because they are so widespread, we discern the grace of God working. Our God, after all, is far too sovereign to be merely lucky.

But has anyone found a culture lacking concepts suitable for redemptive analogies?

The Yali and "Osuwa"

A formidable candidate for this grim distinction was the cannibal Yali culture of Irian Jaya. If ever a tribe needed some Christ-foreshadowing belief a missionary could appeal to, it was the Yali.

By 1966 missionaries of the Regions Beyond Missionary Union had succeeded in winning about twenty Yali to Christ. Priests of the Yali god Kembu promptly martyred two of the twenty. Two years later they killed missionaries Stan Dale and Phillip Masters, driving about one hundred arrows into each of their bodies. Then the Indonesian government, also threatened by the Yali, stepped in to quell further uprisings. Awed by the power of the government, the Yali decided they would rather have missionaries than soldiers. But the missionaries could find no analogy in Yali culture to make the gospel clear.

Last year another missionary and I conducted a much belated "culture probe" to learn more about Yali customs and beliefs. One day a young Yali named Erariek shared with us the following story from his past:

"Long ago my brother Sunahan and a friend named Kahalek were ambushed by enemies from across the river. Kahalek was killed, but Sunahan fled to a circular stone wall nearby. Leaping inside it, he turned, bared his chest at his enemies, and laughed at them. The enemies immediately lowered their weapons and hurried away."

I nearly dropped my pen. "Why didn't they kill him?" I asked.

Erariek smiled. "If they had shed one drop of my brother's blood while he stood within that sacred stone wall—we call it an *osuwa*—their own people would have killed them."

Yali pastors and the missionaries working with them now have a new evangelistic tool. Christ is the spiritual *Osuwa*, the perfect place of refuge. For Yali culture instinctively echoes the Christian teaching that man needs a place of refuge. Ages earlier they had established a network of osuwa in areas where most of their battles took place. Missionaries had noticed the stone walls, but had never ferreted out their full significance.

Redemption and Resistance

Concepts like the Damal's *hai*, the Dani's *nabelan-kabelan*, the Asmat new birth, and the Yali *osuwa*, form the very heart of their cultural life. When outsiders obliterate distinctives like these, something dies within the hearts of the people. But the gospel preserves these concepts. Converts among such tribes then find, along with their personal redemption, that they become resistant to *apathy*, the great destroyer of indigenous peoples overcome by culture shock.

Hundreds of areas remain where response to the gospel has been unsatisfactory or even non-existent. In many of these areas, sensitive culture probes may discover undreamed-of possibilities for spiritual penetration through concept fulfillment. Discouraged missionaries or national pastors may gain fresh confidence in their ability to make the gospel understood.

Study Questions

1. What explanation does Richardson suggest for the prevalence of redemptive analogies in human societies?

2. What connection does Richardson make between the discovery of redemptive analogies and the preservation of tribal societies?

9

Finding the Eye Opener

Don Richardson

In Acts 26:17,18, the Apostle Paul articulated before King Agrippa the formula that Jesus Christ—appearing to Paul in a vision on the road to Damascus—gave as a basis for ministering the Gospel. Follow carefully to see if I quote it correctly. I might make a mistake.

Jesus said to Paul, "...I am sending you to turn them from darkness to light and from the power of Satan to God, so that they may receive forgiveness of sins and a place among those who are sanctified by faith in me."

Notice that I omitted an entire phrase: "...to open their eyes." At first glance, the formula seems complete without the missing phrase. And indeed many missionaries have set out without ever thinking of the importance of opening people's eyes so that they can see the difference between darkness and light. "Opening their eyes" means establishing a beachhead for the truth in the understanding. It's the equivalent of getting to first base in the game of baseball. Of course, getting to first base doesn't count as a run, but it is a necessary first step if a run is to be scored.

In baseball, it's not enough merely to touch all four bases. You have to touch them in the right order, first base first, second base second, third base third. I know of some missionaries who have gone out full of zeal into cross-cultural situations and have started in right away rebuking people for their sins. They were intent upon turning people from darkness to light but without *first* having opened their eyes to see the difference between darkness and light.

Often, when eyes are not opened first, people get their back up; they take offense and they start trying to avoid this obnoxious foreigner with his ministry of rebuke. The missionary soon finds he is not getting anywhere. Years pass and no church is established. There will be some who will take it and respond, but usually the majority will not. And then he will say, "Lord, what am I doing

Don Richardson pioneered work for Regions Beyond Missionary Union (RBMU) among the Sawi tribe of Irian Jaya in 1962. Author of *Peace Child, Lords of the Earth*, and *Eternity in Their Hearts*, Richardson is now Minister-at-Large for RBMU. He speaks frequently at missions conferences and Perspectives Study Program classes. Used by permission of Don Richardson.

wrong? You want me to preach against sin, don't you? They need to be turned from darkness to light, don't they? I've preached faithfully against sin. I've rebuked evil. I upheld that which was good and the people don't respond."

But there is a missing element. He has not found the eye-opener that clears the way for that sort of ministry. What, then, do we need to "open their eyes"? You don't know? What do you need to open a tin can? A can-opener! What do you need to open someone's eyes? An eye-opener! And don't you think that the God who commands us to open people's eyes is responsible to provide the eye-openers we need to fulfill his command?

The Example of Jesus

In chapter 4 of John's Gospel, the Lord Jesus himself "touched first base first." In John 4, he's experienced what you might call a "close encounter of a cross-cultural kind." Jesus came to a town in Samaria called Sychar, near the plot of ground that Jacob gave to his son Joseph. Jacob's well was there.

That well was to Sychar what Valley Forge is to Philadelphia. If you had gone to visit someone in Sychar back in those days, you wouldn't have been in the home of your host and hostess very long before they would take you around to show you Jacob's Well. And they would give you the "tour guide's pitch" concerning how their forefather Jacob had dug it himself. So Jesus sat down by that very significant well—the thing that put Sychar on the map more than probably anything else.

His disciples had gone into the town to buy food. A Samaritan woman came to draw water. Jesus said to her, "Will you give me a drink?" The Samaritan woman said to him, "You are a Jew and I am a Samaritan." There's that cultural chasm. She was ever so much aware of the cultural barrier between him and her. "How can you ask me for a drink?" And here is the parenthesis—"for Jews do not associate with Samaritans." Jesus answered her, "If you knew the gift of God and who it is who asked you for a drink, you would have asked him and he would have given you living water."

"Sir," the woman said, "You have nothing to draw with and the well is deep. Where can you get this living water? Are you greater than our father, Jacob, who gave us this well and drank from it himself, as did also his sons, flocks, and herds?" That's the tour guide's pitch. Hear her civic pride coming through! She was determined that this strange Jew should be duly impressed with the fact that *that* was actually Jacob's Well and that it was given to her forefathers. But, notice that Jesus made her civic pride in the well to be his ally.

Jesus answered, "Everyone who drinks this water will get thirsty again. Even though your forefather Jacob dug it himself and drank from it, as did his children and his herds and his cattle, it is still ordinary water. You drink it and you get thirsty again. But, whoever drinks the water that I give him will never thirst. Indeed, the water I give him will become inside him a well of water springing up into everlasting life!"

Now, how many wells are in the picture? Two. The external, physical, historically significant well and the internal, eternal, spiritually satisfying well of living water! He used this object of her civic pride as *an analogy* to talk about a well that can be inside a person. That was his eye-opener! And it worked !

"Sir," the woman said, "Give me this water so I won't get thirsty and have to keep coming here to draw water." He told her, "Go, call your husband and come back." "I have no husband," she said. Jesus said to her, "You are right when you say you have no husband. The fact is, you have had five husbands and the man you now have is not your husband. What you have just said is quite true."

The conversation has turned in a new direction! He used the eye opener to reach first base by awakening spiritual thirst. But what stood in the way of her receiving that living water? The sin in her life; thus, he had proceeded now towards "second base," turning her from darkness to light! The problem of her loose morals had to be dealt with early. He was following the same formula he would outline later for the Apostle Paul in that remarkable vision on the road to Damascus.

And notice how positive the Lord is! When she said, "I have no husband," some of us, if we had the insight into her history that Jesus had, would have pounced at once, saying "You liar! You are hiding your sin behind a half-truth! The fact is, you are living with a man out of wedlock." But Jesus said—so positively, gently, and delicately—"What you have just said is quite true. You have had five husbands. The man you have now is not your husband. So you are quite right when you say you have no husband." He could have crushed her, but he didn't.

I think that's the kind of spirit he wants us to have. And I've seen many missionaries fail for lack of that kind of a spirit of love. At the same time, you must be careful not to become sentimental. The *sentiments* of human nature can easily revert to the *sediments* of fallen human nature. You may have been through a secular university or college course where you have been told that there is no such thing as guilt or real evil. If someone goes out and shoots somebody else or rapes somebody's wife or burns down somebody's house, he does it because society hasn't treated him right; you have to correct society and then the behavior of the individual will be corrected.

That philosophy is humanistic, not theistic. There is *real* evil out there, and it lies *within* human nature. And you have to be *against* it, and if you are not *against* it, the Spirit of God will not be *for* you. You will lose his blessing. The Son of Man has come to destroy the works of the devil and to deliver people from sin in whatever form it occurs.

You need to maintain this crucial balance of loving the sinner while hating the sin. And it's not always going to be easy to come into confrontation with evil without becoming obnoxious, unloving, or unwise in your approach to people. On the other hand, there is a danger of finding the eye opener and securing a beachhead of understanding in the minds of the people who need Christ and then be so delighted when they tell you that they understand that you stop right there and think that your job is done. It isn't! You've still got to "round first" and "head for second." They've got to be turned from darkness to light and from the power of Satan to God, etc.

Yes, even then, when the person begins to see that he needs to make certain changes in his lifestyle in order to live consistent with the will of God, he's going to find that there is a power trying to keep him from making those changes. This is the power of the evil one himself and of his hosts of demons. Winning the victory against the unseen forces who are "behind the sins" in a person's life will bring you around to "third base." But a run is not scored until he himself "touches home plate." And that occurs only when that person receives from God the forgiveness of sins and a place among those who are sanctified by faith in Him. What a beautiful formula—if only we can remember it! *Touch all four bases!*

The Example of Paul

I want to look at yet another example of an eye opener, found in Acts 17. First, here is some historical background to this story of Paul at Mars Hill.

Three ancient Greek writers, Diogenes Laertius, Philostratus, and Pausanias, referred to a plague that struck the City of Athens and began to decimate the population around 600 B.C. The people of Athens offered sacrifices to their thousands of gods, asking them to intervene and halt the plague. You would think that 30,000 gods could do something, but the sacrifices were futile. The plague persisted.

In desperation, the elders of the city sent messengers to summon a Greek hero known as Epimenedes. He came in response and they said to him, "There is terror in our city. No one knows who will be struck down next. We have done all that we know to do. We have offered thousands of sacrifices to our gods and the plague persists. Will you please apply your wisdom to our desperate situation and save our city? We have heard that you have rapport with the gods."

Epimenedes took stock of the situation, and then took a course of action based on two premises. First, he reasoned that there must be another god who did not consider himself represented by any of the thousands of idols in the city but who was hopefully good enough and great enough to do something about the plague. They had to contact him and enlist his help.

For those who replied, "What if we don't know his name? How can we contact him?", Epimenedes was ready with premise number two: *Any god who is great enough and good enough to do something about the plague is probably also great enough and good enough to smile upon us in our ignorance if we openly acknowledge our ignorance of him.*

Epimenedes called for the people to bring a flock of sheep to Mars Hill, a plot of sacred ground in the City of Athens. He specified that the sheep had to be of more than one color, reasoning that since they did not know which color of sheep that god might prefer, they would give him a choice. Then he commanded that this multicolored flock be released on Mars Hill.

Sheep so released on a grassy knoll will normally begin to graze. But as the sheep meandered, grazing across the hill, Epimenedes, first commanding the men of the city to follow the sheep, called upon any god concerned in the matter of the plague to cause the sheep to lie down on the spot where that god wanted that sheep offered as a sacrifice to him. This they would take as a sign of the god's willingness to help.

We do not know how many sheep lay down upon the ground, but at least one and perhaps several did so. Wherever a sheep lay down upon the ground, the Athenians built an altar there and inscribed upon its side, "To an Unknown God." And then those sheep were offered as sacrifices to the unknown god.

All three writers confirm the plague was lifted immediately. The city was delivered. The people of Athens quickly returned to the worship of those thousands of futile gods, but they left at least one of those altars standing on Mars Hill.

Six centuries later, while the Apostle Paul was waiting for his friends in Athens, he was greatly distressed to see that the city was full of idols. If I can read between the lines a little bit, I can imagine what had happened. If six centuries earlier they had 30,000 gods probably by Paul's time they had 40,000, still equally as futile, but still drawing the attention of the people away from the true God.

This glut of gods in the city of Athens is confirmed by another writer named Patronius, who visited Athens in ancient times, came away shaking his head, and wrote sarcastically in one of his books that in Athens it was easier to find a god than it was a man! Athens was a byword in the ancient world for this surfeit of gods.

And what is Paul's emotional reaction at the sight of thousands of Athenians prostituting the image of God that is in them by bowing down to false gods? He was greatly distressed and obviously determined to do something about it.

I fear for anyone who can go out to the mission field and confront such things as widows flinging themselves on the funeral pyres of their husbands, or little children being forced into prostitution in temples, or ritualized wife trading as we find in some cultures in the southern part of Irian Jaya, or whatever else and not feel something of the distress, the anguish that Paul felt over the idols in Athens. We cannot go forth on a mission energized by the Holy Spirit without feeling anguish over evil and sin. We must be able to look upon sin with something of the perspective that God has.

Paul was in anguish. So he reasoned day by day with those who happened to be there. A group of Epicurean and Stoic philosophers began to dispute with him. Some of them asked, "What is this babbler trying to say?," and you can hear the scorn behind the words. Others remarked, "He seems to be advocating foreign gods." In other words, Paul, whoever you are, we already have 30,000 gods here in Athens, and you are bringing us the message of still another god? We need another god like we need a hole in our heads! We've got so many gods here in Athens we can't keep track of them all!

Who would have the audacity to proclaim another god in that context? Paul, of course. And how does he respond to the charge that he's advocating some superfluous or nuisance god in the city already afflicted with 30,000 or more of them? He stood up in the meeting of the Aeropagus, another name for Mars Hill, and said, "Men of Athens, I see that in every way you are very religious [Doesn't that remind you of Jesus at the well, saying to the woman "You're quite right when you say you have no husband."?]. For as I walked around and observed your objects of worship, I even found an altar with this inscription, 'To the Unknown God'. Now what you worship as someone unknown, I am going to proclaim to you." Paul, in effect, was saying: "Foreign God? No! The God I proclaim is that God who did not consider himself represented by any of the idols in the city so many hundreds of years ago, but who delivered your city from the plague when you simply acknowledged your ignorance of him. But why be ignorant of him any longer, if you can know him?"

In this way Paul used that familiar Athenian altar as an eye-opener to get to first base. Then he went on to try to turn his listeners from the darkness of idolatry to the light of God's truth. He reminded the people of their gross ingratitude to that delivering, prayer-answering God. He found a residual testimony, didn't he, in this unexpected form? And he appropriated it. This was part, at least, of the testimony that God had reserved to himself in that pagan context. And this unknown God has left a witness to Himself in hundreds of other cultures around the world.

The Principle Defined

The principle that I have been talking about comes down to this: the reason that an analogy based upon a Peace Child ideal in the Sawi cultures works for the Sawi, or a reference to a place of refuge has special appeal to a Yali mind, or

new birth attracts an Asmat mind, is because the people of each of these respective cultures cherish that particular idea or concept or ceremony. They see these things as the best in their world. When you start talking about something new in reference to this cherished, familiar thing, you have an automatic interest.

So we need to ask ourselves, what is it that my neighbor, my fellow student on campus, my professor, my associate in business, or my friend of another culture cherishes in this world. You may know someone who has no time for God at all. But he loves his wife. There are some unsaved men who really do love their wives. They find meaning in the marriage relationship. Doesn't the Bible have a lot to say about the parallels between marriage and redemption?

You may find someone else who doesn't love his wife and who may be on the edge of divorce, but see if he loves his children. The parent-child relationship has often been paralleled with redemption. Or he may neglect his kids or be a child abuser, but perhaps he really cherishes his job.

You just never know what sort of a spiritual chain reaction you are going to be a part of, maybe today or tomorrow or the next day, maybe in your own culture or in another culture, as you ask God to make you a communicator of good news. God can give us an instinct, an ability to sniff out, to sense in the hearts and minds of people that which they are committed to and which may yield an analogy which will give us a handle on their hearts. And if you try it and get rebuffed, don't give up; try again. It takes time to learn, doesn't it?

You're like a law student: the more case histories you can absorb and meditate on, the more your imagination will be stretched to anticipate what God may be waiting to do. And sometimes it will not so much be what you say, it will be the timing. And God will arrange the timing.

So don't ever allow yourself to say, "This is an absolutely impossible situation; there is no way." God is the God who makes ways where there are no ways. And he is the One, after all, who is sending you out there and going ahead of you.

Study Questions

1. What criteria does Richardson suggest for the discovery and use of "eye-openers?"

2. What additional perspective does the story of Epimenedes give to the biblical account of Paul at Mars Hill?

10

What kind of encounters do we need in our Christian witness?

Charles H. Kraft

We're hearing more about power encounter these days among non-charismatics. We are more open and less afraid of spiritual power than we used to be. Several missionary training institutions now include courses on power encounter. But there are extremes we want to avoid. My task in this article is to offer an approach to power encounter that is biblically balanced with two other encounters that evangelicals have always emphasized.

The Basic Concept

The term "power encounter" comes from missionary anthropologist Alan Tippett. In his 1971 book, *People Movements in Southern Polynesia*, Tippett observed that in the South Pacific the early acceptance of the gospel usually occurred when there was an "encounter" demonstrating that the power of God is greater than that of the local pagan deity. This was usually accompanied by a desecration of the symbol(s) of the traditional deity by its priest or priestess, who then declared that he or she rejected the deity's power, pledged allegiance to the true God, and vowed to depend on God alone for protection and spiritual power.

At such a moment, the priest or priestess would eat the totem animal (e.g., a sacred turtle) and claim Jesus' protection. Seeing that the priest or priestess suffered no ill effects, the people opened themselves to the gospel.[1] These confrontations, along with those classic biblical power encounters (e.g., Moses vs. Pharoah, Ex. 7-12, and Elijah vs. the prophets of Baal, 1 Ki. 18) formed Tippett's view of power encounter.

More recently, the term has been used more broadly to include healings, deliverances, or any other "visible, practical demonstration that Jesus Christ is more powerful than the spirits, powers, or false gods worshiped or feared by the members of a given people group."[2] The concept of "taking territory" from the

Charles Kraft has been professor of anthropology and intercultural communication at Fuller Theological Seminary, School of World Mission, since 1969. Prior to that he was a missionary in Nigeria for 13 years. Used by permission from "What kind of encounters do we need in our Christian witness?", *Evangelical Missions Quarterly* (July 1991), pp. 258-265.

enemy for God's kingdom is seen as basic to such encounters.

According to this view, Jesus' entire ministry was a massive power confrontation between God and the enemy. The ministry of the apostles and the church in succeeding generations is seen as the continuing exercise of the "authority and power over all demons and all diseases" given by Jesus to his followers (Lk. 9:1). Contemporary stories about such encounters come from China, Argentina, Europe, the Muslim world, and nearly everywhere else where the church is growing rapidly.

Tippett observed that most of the world's people are power-oriented and respond to Christ most readily through power demonstrations.[3] Gospel messages about faith, love, forgiveness, and the other facts of Christianity are not likely to have nearly the impact on such people as the demonstrations of spiritual power. My own experience confirms Tippett's thesis. Therefore, cross-cultural workers ought to learn as much as possible about the place of power encounter in Jesus' ministry and ours.

Additional Encounters

Of course, missionaries face several questions about power encounter. One of the basic ones is how to relate power concerns and approaches to our traditional emphases on truth and salvation. Let me suggest that we need to use a three-pronged approach to our witness.

Jesus battled Satan on a broader front than simply power encounters. If we are to be biblically fair and balanced, we must give two other encounters equal attention—commitment encounters and truth encounters. We need to focus on the close relationship in the New Testament between these three encounters. Here's an outline that will help:

JESUS CHRIST CONFRONTS SATAN

1. *Concerning power.* This results in power encounters to release people from satanic captivity and bring them into freedom in Jesus Christ.

2. *Concerning commitment.* This results in commitment encounters to rescue people from wrong commitments and bring them into relationship to Jesus Christ.

3. *Concerning truth.* This results in truth encounters to counter error and to bring people to correct understandings about Jesus Christ.

Throughout the world many Christians who have committed themselves to Jesus Christ, and who have embraced much Christian truth, have not given up their pre-Christian commitment to and practice of what we call spiritual power. The powers of darkness which they formerly followed have not been confronted and defeated by the power of Jesus. So they live with a "dual allegiance" and a syncretistic understanding of truth.

Therefore, some mistakenly assume that if they confront people with healing and deliverance campaigns to show them Christ's power, they will turn to him in droves. They assume that those who experience God's healing power will automatically commit themselves to the source of that power.

However, I know of several such campaigns that have produced few, if any, lasting conversions. Why not? Because little attention was paid to leading the people from an experience of Jesus' power to a commitment to him. These people are accustomed to accepting power from any source. Therefore, they see no greater compulsion to commit themselves to Jesus than to any of the other sources of power they regularly consult.

I believe Jesus expects power demonstrations to be as crucial to our ministries as they were to his (Lk. 9:1, 2). However, any approach that advocates power encounter without giving adequate attention to the other two encounters—commitment and truth—is not biblically balanced. Many people who saw or experienced power events during Jesus' ministry did not turn to him in faith. This should alert us to the inadequacy of power demonstrations alone as a total evangelistic strategy.

A Balance of Encounters

We can see the three kinds of encounters outlined above in Jesus' ministry. Typically, he started by teaching, followed by a power demonstration, then a return to teaching, at least for the disciples (e.g., Lk.4:31ff.; 5:1ff., 17ff.; 6:6ff., 17ff., etc.). Appeals for commitment to the Father or to himself appear both implicitly and explicitly throughout his teaching. Jesus seems to have used power demonstrations more when interacting with people who had not yet become his followers, focusing more on the teaching of truth with those already committed to him.

His appeal for commitment to at least the first five apostles (Peter, Andrew, James, John—Lk 5—and Levi—Lk. 5:27-28) occurred after significant power demonstrations. Once his followers had successfully negotiated their commitment encounter, their subsequent growth was primarily a matter of learning and practicing more truth.

First century Jews, like most people today, were very concerned about spiritual power. Paul said they sought power signs (1 Cor. 1:22). Jesus' usual practice of healing and deliverance from demons soon after entering a new area (e.g., Lk. 4:33-35, 39; 5:13-15; 6:6-10, 18-19, etc.) may be seen as his way of approaching them at the point of their concern. When he sent out his followers to the surrounding towns to prepare the way for him, he commanded them to use the same approach (Lk. 9:1-6; 10:19).

Jesus' reluctance to do miraculous works merely to satisfy those who wanted him to prove himself (Mt. 12:38-42; 16:1-4) would, however, seem to indicate his power demonstrations were intended to point to something beyond the mere demonstration of God's power. I believe that he had at least two more important goals. First, Jesus sought to demonstrate God's nature by showing his love. As he said to Philip, "If you have seen me, you have seen the Father" (Jn. 14:9). He freely healed, delivered, and blessed those who came to him and did not retract what he had given, even if they did not return to thank him (Lk. 17:11-19). He used God's power to demonstrate his love.

Second, Jesus sought to lead people into the most important encounter, the commitment encounter. This is clear from his challenge to the Pharisees when they demanded a miracle, that the people of Nineveh who repented would accuse the people of Jesus' day who did not do likewise (Mt. 12:41). Experiencing

God's power may be both pleasant and impressive, but only a commitment to God through Christ really saves.

The Nature and Aims of the Encounters

The three encounters—power, commitment, and truth—are not the same, but they are each intended to initiate a process crucial to the Christian experience aimed at a specific goal.

1. The concern of the truth encounter is understanding. The vehicle of that encounter is teaching.

2. The concern of the commitment encounter is relationship. The vehicle of that encounter is witness.

3. The concern of the power encounter is freedom. Its vehicle is spiritual warfare.

Truth and understanding have a lot to do with the mind; commitment and relationship rest primarily in the will; and freedom is largely experienced emotionally.

1. *Truth encounters.* Truth encounters in which the mind is exercised and the will is challenged seem to provide the context within which the other encounters take place and can be interpreted. Jesus constantly taught truth to bring his hearers to ever greater understandings about the person and plan of God. To teach truth, he increased their knowledge. However, in Scripture, knowledge is grounded in relationship and experience; it is not simply philosophical and academic. The truth encounter, like the other two, is personal and experiential, not merely a matter of words and head knowledge.

When we focus on knowledge and truth, we enable people to gain enough understanding to be able to accurately interpret the other two encounters. For example, a power demonstration has little, or wrong, significance unless it is related to truth. Knowledge of the source of, and the reason for, the power are essential for proper interpretation of a power event. The need for such knowledge is probably why Jesus used his power demonstrations in the context of teaching his disciples.

A diagram of what I have been saying about the nature and aim of truth encounters looks like this:

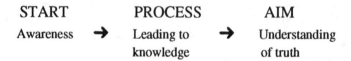

START	PROCESS	AIM
Awareness →	Leading to knowledge →	Understanding of truth

2. *Commitment encounters.* Commitment encounters, involving the exercise of the will in commitment and obedience to the Lord, are the most important of the encounters. For without commitment and obedience to Jesus, there is no spiritual life.

The initial commitment encounter leads a person into a relationship with

God. Through successive encounters between our will and God's, we grow in intimacy with and likeness to him, as we submit to his will and practice intimate association with him. Initial commitment and the relationship that proceeds from it are tightly linked to truth, both because they are developed within the truth encounter and because a relationship with God is the true reason for human existence.

Implied in the commitment encounter is the cultivation of the fruits of the Holy Spirit, especially love toward God and man. We are to turn from love of (or, commitment to) the world that is under the control of the evil one (1 Jn. 5:19) to God who loved the world and gave himself for it. As we grow in our relationship with him, we become more like him, conforming to the image of Christ (Rom. 8:29).

The commitment encounter looks like this:

START		PROCESS		AIM
Committment	➔	Growth in	➔	Character
to Jesus		relationship		of Jesus Christ

3. *Power encounters.* Power encounters contribute a different dimension to Christian experience. They focus on freedom from the enemy's captivity. Satan is the blinder (2 Cor. 4:4), restricter, hinderer, crippler—the enemy who attempts to keep people from commitment to God and truth. Though he works on all human faculties, the enemy seems particularly interested in crippling people emotionally. If people are to move into commitment to Christ they need emotional freedom.

The power encounter process may be diagrammed as follows:

START		PROCESS		AIM
Healing,	➔	Increasing	➔	Victory over
deliverance, etc.		freedom, etc.		Satan

For the one who is healed, delivered, blessed, or otherwise freed from the enemy's grip, the major payoff is freedom. However, for an observer, the impact is likely to be quite different. If properly interpreted, the encounter communicates basic truths about God's power and love. The observer sees that God is worthy of his trust because he is willing and able to free people from Satan's destructive hold, as we see in this diagram:

START		PROCESS		AIM
Attract	➔	Demonstration	➔	Trust
attention				God

Although we do not call them power encounters, our demonstrations of love, acceptance, forgiveness, and peace in troubled times—plus a number of other Christian virtues—play the same role of attracting attention and leading people to trust God. These all witness to the presence of a loving God willing to give abundant life and bring release from the enemy.

The Encounters Work Together

Our missionary witness needs to use all three encounters together, not separately, as we can see in this three-part circle:

People need freedom from the enemy to (1) open their minds to receive and understand truth (2 Cor. 4:4), and (2) to release their wills so they can commit themselves to God. However, they can't understand and apply Christian truth, nor can they exercise power, without a continuing commitment to God. Nor can they maintain the truth and their commitment without freedom from the enemy won through continual power encounters. We constantly need each of these dimensions in our lives.

The diagram below shows the interworkings of these three aspects of Christian life and witness in more detail.

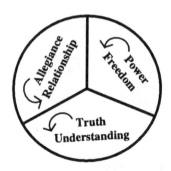

There are three stages in the process, the third of which results in witness to those at the start of Stage 1. At the start (Stage 1), people are under Satanic captivity in ignorance and error and are committed to some non-Christian allegiance. Through power encounters, they gain freedom from that captivity, moving from the blindness and will-weakening of the enemy into openness to the truth. Through truth and commitment encounters, they receive enough understanding to act on, plus enough challenge to induce them to commit themselves to Christ.

In the second stage, having made their commitment to Jesus, people need continued spiritual warfare to attain greater freedom from the enemy's continued efforts to harass and cripple them. They also need continued teaching and challenges to greater commitment and obedience. They grow in their relationship to God and his people through continued encounters in all three areas.

In the third stage, this growing relationship results in power encounters through prayer to break the enemy's power to delude, harass, cause illness,

	START	NEED	PROCESS	RESULT
STAGE I	Satanic captivity	Freedom to understand	Power encounter	
	Ignorance /error	Enough Commitment to	Truth encounter understanding	Committment to Jesus Christ
	Non-Christian commitment	Challenge to commit to Christ	Commitment encounter	
STAGE II	Commitment to Jesus Christ	Spiritual warfare to provide protection, healing, blessing, deliverance	Power encounter	Growing relationship to God and his people
		Teaching	Truth encounter	
		Challenges to greater commit- ment and obedience	Commitment encounter	
STAGE III	Growing relationship to God and his people	Authoritative prayer	Power encounter	Witness to those at the beginning of Stage I
		Teaching	Truth encounter	
		Challenges to commitment	Commitment encounter	

demonize, and the like. These encounters are accompanied by truth and commitment encounters, so that believers are challenged to greater commitment and obedience, especially in witness to those in the first stage.

Beyond our own Christian growth lies our witness. At the end of his ministry, Jesus taught much about his relationship to his followers and theirs to each other (e.g., Jn 14-16), as well as about the authority and power he would give them (Acts 1:8). He carefully related power and authority to witness (e.g., Mt. 28:19, 20; Mk. 16:15-18; Acts 1:8).

He told the disciples to wait for spiritual power before they embarked on witness (Lk. 24:49; Acts 1:4), just as Jesus himself had waited to be empowered at his own baptism (Lk. 3:21, 22). We are not fully equipped to witness without the freedom-bringing, truth-revealing power of the Holy Spirit (Acts 1:8).

Some Guidelines for Evangelicals

Because Satan is a master at deceit and counterfeiting, we must encounter or confront him, rather than simply ignore him. And we know as we confront him that greater is he who is in us than he who is in the world (1 Jn. 4:4), and we thank God that Jesus has "stripped the spiritual-rulers and authorities of their power" (Col. 2:15). But we are still at war and we are commanded to put on armor and fight against the "wicked spiritual forces in the heavenly world" (Eph. 6:11-12). So, although we know how this war will end, many battles remain and we need to know our enemy and how to fight him.

As we survey the world's mission fields, we find many places where Christians still have dual allegiances. Many believers, including pastors, still go to shamans, priests, and other spirit mediums. At the same time, charismatic and Pentecostal churches specializing in power encounter evangelism and witness are growing rapidly in most parts of the world.

Many of us evangelicals grew up with a knowledge-truth brand of Christianity, that pays little if any attention to power encounters. But we go out to witness and evangelize among people who have grown up in spirit-oriented cultures and often find that solid, lasting conversions to Christ are hard to achieve with our knowledge-truth approach alone.

Satan counterfeits truth, instills damning allegiances, and provides power. He has, as it were, three arrows in his quiver. However, generally, evangelical missionaries have only two, so their work often founders on the rocks of dual allegiance and nominalism.

We encounter commitment to other gods and spirits with the challenge to commitment to Jesus Christ. But when the people need healing, or seek fertility, or when there isn't enough rain, or there are floods, too often our answer is the hospital, the school, and modern agriculture. We provide secular answers to what to them (and the Bible) are basically spiritual issues.

We have encountered Satan's counterfeit "truths" with the exciting truths of Christianity, but often in such an abstract way that our hearers have seen little verification of that truth in our lives. In most cases, both missionaries and the local Christians are more impressed with scientific than with biblical truth.

The missing element for them and for us is the "third arrow," genuine New Testament power, the continual experience of the presence of God, who every day does things the world calls miracles. We must encounter Satan's counterfeit power with God's effective power. Truth and commitment alone won't do. We need all three kinds of biblical encounters, if we are to succeed in our world mission.

End Notes

1. Alan Tippett, *People Movements in Southern Polynesia* (Chicago: Moody Press, 1971), p. 206.

2. C. Peter Wagner, *How to Have a Healing Ministry* (Ventura, Calif.: Regal Books, 1988), p. 150. See also John Wimber, *Power Evangelism* (New York: Harper-Row, 1985), pp. 29-32, and Charles Kraft, *Christianity With Power* (Ann Arbor: Servant, 1989).

3. Tippett, *op. cit.*, p. 81.

11

Communication and Social Structure

Eugene A. Nida

Therefore its name was called Babel, because there the Lord confused the language of all the earth; and from there the Lord scattered them abroad over the face of all the earth (Gen. 11:9).

Communication never takes place in a social vacuum, but always between individuals who are part of a total social context. These participants in the communicative event stand in a definite relationship to each other; for example, as boss to employee, son to father, policeman to offender, and child to baby-sitter. Moreover, in every society there are definite rules about what types of people say what kinds of things to certain classes of persons. On the other hand, what is quite proper for one class to say may be unbecoming for another, and even the same remarks from different persons may be quite differently interpreted. The same behavior interpreted as offensive arrogance in an underling may be considered charming insouciance on the part of the boss, and what is squirming subservience in the lower middle class may be interpreted as lovable modesty in the upper class.[1] Whatever different classes of people say is inevitably influenced by their respective positions in society. For man is more than an individual; he is a member of a very large "family," whether clan, tribe, or nation, and there are always important, though usually unformulated, rules that apply to all interpersonal communication.

This aspect of communication within the social structure is particularly important from the religious point of view. For wherever there are tribal or national gods, these deities inevitably occupy special positions of importance in the social structure, either as mythical ancestors or as guardians of the social patterns and mores of the people. One thing is sure, these deities can usually be depended upon to conserve the *status quo* and in this way help to regulate the

Eugene A. Nida has been translations secretary of the American Bible Society and Director of the Translations Program of the United Bible Societies. A foremost linguist, he has worked in some 85 countries helping translators in over 200 languages. Dr. Nida has written 22 books on translation, anthropology, and missions, among them *Customs and Cultures, Message and Mission,* and *God's Word in Man's Language.* Reprinted with permission of the William Carey Library Publishers, P. O. Box 128-C, Pasadena, CA 91104. *Message and Mission,* Eugene A. Nida, 1972.

traditional relations between people. For this reason religion is often in opposition to any breach with the past, any breaking away of individuals from the "faith," and any presumed undermining of the prestige of traditional leadership. More often than not, a new convert to Christianity in a predominantly pagan society will feel very much like one Hopi Indian who returned to his own village after having been away at school, where he had been baptized a Christian. The first day of his return, when all the villagers went off to a dance and left him sitting in the shadow of the mission wall, he felt, as he described it later, "like a man without a country."

Unfortunately, some missionary approaches to non-Christians have involved the creation of a Christian caste or subculture. Almost unconsciously some well-meaning missionaries in India, before that nation's independence, felt that new converts, in order to become truly Christian and remain faithful to their new stand, needed full identification with the missionaries and the foreign community. But the result in some instances was the development of a wholly artificial, "hothouse" environment, where Christian converts might be protected, but could never really grow. In a sense they were being taught to be square pegs in round holes.

Well-intentioned missionary work has sometimes failed to communicate the gospel because the source adopted a role completely incompatible with any effective identification with those to be reached. In one mission to Indians in South America the role of the communicators is that of a rich landowner. Such a person can accomplish a good deal on the basis of this prestige. He cannot, however, effectively relate the Good News to the people he seeks to reach because the roles of the participants in communication block effective understanding. These missionaries have unselfishly done much *for* the people, but they have never been able to do anything *with* the people. Given the roles of landowner and peon, there is never a two-way traffic of meaningful communication about the real issues of life, and without two-way communication there can be no identification.

Types of Social Structures

Social structures, together with the networks of communication they represent, are very diverse. We shall attempt neither a detailed analysis of all the various types of social structures nor a discussion of the many factors that give rise to different patterns of social life. Here we are concerned only with a particular aspect of social structure—namely, that which is significant in terms of interpersonal communication. For this purpose two primary types of distinctions, intersecting on various levels, may be distinguished. First, we must distinguish between the urban (or so-called "metropolitan" society) and the rural (or "face-to-face" society) types of structures. Second, we must analyze these types of structures in terms of their homogeneous or heterogeneous character. The urban society is characteristic of the typical city dweller in large urban centers, whether in New York, London, or Calcutta, and the rural society is characteristic of the peasant community, whether it is an Indian village near Mexico City or a mountain hamlet in northern Thailand.

By a homogeneous society we mean one in which most or all of the people participate in the common life in more or less the same way. Such groups may have class differences and distinctions of leadership and positions of authority, but the society is nevertheless an integrated whole, sharing much the same system of values; it is not merely an aggregate of subcultures which operate along quite different lines. Sweden, for example, may be regarded as a more or less homogeneous society, in contrast to the United States with its large, heterogeneous population in varying degrees of "assimilation." It may be contrasted also with a country like Peru, which maintains an Ibero-American culture in its cities, but has a distinctly different culture in the villages of the altiplano and the eastern jungle.

Diagrammatic Models of Social Structure

In order to understand more clearly certain of the essential features of social structure, it is convenient to diagram such social patterns, using as a general base an "inverted" diamond jewel shape.

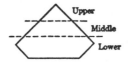

In this generalized and schematic diagram we indicate not only the relative positions and sizes of the different classes—upper, middle, and lower—but also something of the total configuration. This configuration suggests that the upper class tapers off into a relatively limited number of top leaders and that the lower class (which might be called the indigent section of the population) are generally fewer in number at the very bottom than are those somewhat higher in the social structure.

We have arbitrarily chosen to represent social structure in three classes. In some societies, however, one must recognize four, five, six, or even more classes. In such a case it is customary to speak of such distinctions as upper upper, lower upper, upper middle, lower middle, upper lower, and lower lower. Haitian society, for example, can be described as having five principal classes. The elite, who constitute the upper class, are divided into two groups, called "first-class elite" and "second-class elite." The middle class, a relatively small group, is growing rapidly. The lower class is divided into (1) an upper-lower class consisting of the better-to-do tradesmen and farmers who own their own land, and (2) an indigent class who eke out a bare existence as tenant farmers and common laborers.

It would be wrong, however, to leave the impression that all societies differ radically in structural configuration. As a result, it is possible to describe diagrammatically certain of the over-all "impressionistic" features of certain societies in the following contrastive manner:

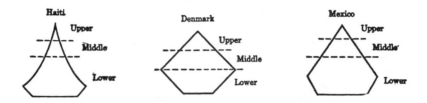

The forms of these diagrams are not based upon statistical data, for such data are not available in terms of class criteria. They are obviously impressionistic, but very useful.

It should be noted, for example, that in Haitian society the upper class constitutes a very narrow, stratified group, while the society almost bulges at the base. In the diagram of Denmark, the upper class does not tower proportionately so much above the rest of the structure, the middle class is rather large, and the lower tapers off to a very restricted indigent base. Mexico, on the other hand, represents a somewhat more "typical" structure, with a growing middle class, a somewhat attenuated upper class, and the bulk of the society in the lower class, though not with the proportionately heavy concentration at the bottom that characterizes Haiti.

Communication within Social Structures

The significance of social structure for communication can be summarized in two basic principles: (1) people communicate more with people of their own class; that is, interpersonal communication of a reciprocal nature is essentially horizontal; and (2) prestigeful communication descends from the upper classes to the lower classes, and this vertical communication is primarily in one direction and tends to be principally between adjacent groups.

Truly effective communication, however, is not unidirectional. There must be reciprocity in communication (which we may call "social feedback"), or the results may be unsatisfactory.

Both in the ministry and in missionary work it is usual for the religious professional to do most of the talking. Too often the minister or missionary regards himself solely as intermediary of a superior message from God, and hence not aware of or dependent upon the feedback which should come from the congregation. He has gone forth to tell people the truth, not to listen to other people's ideas about the truth. If this attitude is pushed to an extreme, the message inevitably will become irrelevant. Even though it may be true, it does not reach its receptor, for the "master of the household" does not know the conditions under which the servants live and work. And even if he does know, his communication will be immeasurably strengthened, provided those to whom he speaks are convinced of the fact that he knows and understands.

Communicative Approach to Urban Society

In communicative approaches to various societies there have been, in the recent past, three main types of orientation. These can be called generally Roman Catholic, Communist, and Protestant, though one must immediately raise a caution against a tendency to identify a "missionary approach" with a particular institutional structure. Nevertheless, these distinctions, as we shall see, reflect in general the manner in which for the most part Roman Catholics, Communists, and Protestants have set out to influence significantly the social structures.

In the Roman Catholic approach to a new society, primary consideration has usually been given to the upper class, though a number of instances can be cited in which a broad segment of the society has been approached. The tendency, however, has been for the Roman Church to identify itself with the leadership of the society and through it to influence the lower classes. In exchange for partnership in controlling the society, the Church always provides the upper class with many benefits, including the best professional religious services and facilities for the education of children. Moreover, the leadership of the Church is generally drawn from the upper class (Pope John XXIII was a notable exception).

The typical Roman Catholic approach may be schematically diagrammed as follows:

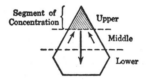

The shaded area indicates the class with which the Church has primarily identified itself, and the arrows indicate both the direction of control (downward) and the pressures of opposition (upward).

In Latin America, where the Roman Church has traditionally dominated the social and political structure of society, most of the opposition to the joint control of society by the upper class, who see in the coalition of the rich landed aristocracy and the Church a threat to their ambition to improve their status. Hence, thwarted middle-class leaders often compete for the loyalties of the lower classes, especially the more aggressive elements of the upper-lower class, and by means of revolutions have from time to time overthrown clerical control. Such a revolution has occurred at one time or another in almost all the independent Roman Catholic countries of Latin America. However, it has often happened that after winning the revolution the leaders of liberal movements have failed to reorganize society with a new set of values. Because of the resulting vacuum, the Church has consistently returned, though usually not with the same degree of control, and often making a broader appeal to the masses who deserted their earlier masters.

Since Vatican II the sociological orientation of Roman Catholic churches in many parts of the world has changed considerably. Much greater concern is expressed for the poor and disenfranchised people, and in a number of instances remarkably creative work has been undertaken on behalf of people who for so long have been neglected and exploited.

The Communist technique in approaching a society is to draw out a segment from the middle and lower classes, usually the lower-middle class and the upper-lower classes. In this segment there is usually a small nucleus of frustrated middle-class intellectuals, who may have been thwarted in their attempts at social climbing or who represent minority group disabilities. These intellectuals then combine with the economically, socially, or politically disenfranchised lower-class elements and by revolution capture the leadership. The former upper class must then be liquidated, either by confiscation to destroy its economic power, or by physical destruction, or by brainwashing. The main features of this development may be diagrammed as follows:

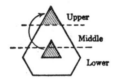

Having taken over leadership, the new upper class of party members and certain technicians then establish a heavy barrier between themselves and the middle classes. Leadership is not recruited from the middle classes (except in so far as certain experts may work for the state); the decisions and the control of communication continue to be exerted by an elite drawing its membership from the lower-middle and upper-lower classes. For example, in East Germany during the last few years the often brilliant sons of professionals are discriminated against in obtaining advanced educational opportunities, while the less intelligent sons of working men are given preferential treatment.

Persons who have been selected according to this system, and catapulted by means of party membership from a lower-class status to one of the highest priority, naturally owe all they are to the party, and not primarily to personal achievement or background. They are thus far more obedient to the party than would otherwise be the case; for expulsion from it means not a somewhat horizontal movement, as in our society, but a severe loss of all privileges and status. All this centralized control is made possible in our modern society because of the highly specialized nature of communication and transportation, by means of which a relatively small group of people can control millions. There is no longer any possibility of successful pitchfork rebellions.

The present Protestant approach to society, especially in its missionary aspects, is quite different from the Roman Catholic and Communist orientations. It must be recognized that, in the past, Protestant developments were closely related to broad political and social movements in northern Europe, in which significant changes in church affiliation were considerably influenced by the loyalties of certain princes and rulers. However, it is also possible to read too much significance into the actions of individual kings and to forget that they reflected as well as molded the events that precipitated the break with the Roman Church.

If, however, we are to judge the Protestant approach to society as evidenced both in the mission field and in certain aspects of important Protestant movements in England and America (e.g., the development of Methodism), we may say that Protestants concentrated their efforts on the diagrammatic bulge in society, that is, on the lower-middle and upper-lower classes even as, in a sense, Communists have done. In such areas as Latin America, for example, persons of the lower-middle and upper-lower classes often have little to lose by identifying themselves with the Protestant cause, since they belong largely to a socially "disinherited" group. On the contrary, they often feel that they have much to gain, quite apart from the benefits they believe are derived from a direct personal relationship to God rather than a relationship through some mediating person or institution. These supplementary benefits often involve educational opportunities for their children, medical assistance for themselves and their families, and a new sense of dignity and "belongingness" in a fellowship which is highly interdependent and mutually helpful. The major aspects of this development may be diagrammed as follows (but note that on this diagram the arrow indicates direction of mobility):

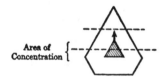

Area of Concentration

It should be noted that the constituency thus formed tends to have an upward movement. This upward mobility results almost inevitably from a greater sense of personal responsibility, accumulation of capital (for the convert does not spend so much money as formerly on certain forbidden "pleasures"), increased concern for and appreciation of education, a new attitude toward work as virtue (part of the "Protestant ethic"), and opportunities for the expression of leadership within the Protestant fellowship.

However, this same upward mobility tends to separate those concerned from the very groups out of which they have come. The Methodist movement in England was a typical Protestant approach to the lower bulge of the social structure. It came as a reaction against the more or less authoritarian structure of the British religious system, which had been inherited from Roman Catholicism. The principal appeal was made to the lower-middle and upper-lower classes, including some of the very lowest classes, especially the miners. This movement is now, however, distinctly upper-middle class and even lower-upper class. In the United States, Methodism has experienced the same type of upward movement, but with an interesting series of successive waves of related movements. These "waves" have progressively sought to reach out to bring in those who were being left behind or neglected, and who, as they were included, have in turn moved up in the social structure. As Methodists moved up, such groups as the Nazarenes came in to reach those "left behind," and as the Nazarenes in turn moved up, the various types of Pentecostals made their special appeal to the lower classes.

Protestant missionary programs to reach the intelligentsia in various countries are of course very worthy, and most certainly the upper classes should not be neglected, for they are likewise objects of God's constraining love. Nevertheless, it must also be clearly recognized that not infrequently the leaders adopt the religion of the masses, even as Donald McGavran has pointed out,[2] basing his observations on Arnold Toynbee's analyses.

To our thesis that Protestants generally approach the lower-middle and upper-lower classes there is one seeming exception; namely, that in India, Protestant missionaries have concentrated their attention upon the outcastes and have had a notable response from them. There are two important reasons for missionary success among such groups and for the high quality of leadership displayed by so many of these people. First, these people usually have had everything to gain and nothing to lose by identifying themselves with a foreign religion, since for all practical purposes they have been excluded from Hinduism itself. At the same time, however, the outcastes must not be regarded as merely an accumulation of indigent people (the equivalent of "poor white trash" in the United States) who, having never made good at anything, finally drifted into the outcaste groups. On the contrary, many of these people came from indigenous groups forced into various types of occupations that made them ceremonially unclean and hence outside the pale of Hindu ritual. Other persons became outcastes because they violated taboos. These outcastes, despite their miserable lot, are thus not just the dregs of society, but rather a religiously excluded class that included many persons of unusual gifts and capacities, as they have shown, once they were given an opportunity.

One reason for Protestantism's lack of appeal to many elements in the strictly indigent class—which is not only poor, but content with its status—is that it demands too high a standard of personal accountability, while at the same time failing to adjust its approach to different constituencies. Moreover the Protestant church has had from the strictly indigent, drifting classes few who could provide leadership to reach out to bring in other persons of the same groups.

The Structure of Face-to-Face Societies

To the structure of urban societies, the rural, peasant, and primitive face-to-face societies present certain striking contrasts. There are, of course, many important differences between, for example, a small rural community in the hills of Kentucky and a village in the northern part of Zaire. Nevertheless, certain significant features are particularly relevant to the problems of communication.

In general, there are two main types of face-to-face societies: (1) folk and (2) primitive. The first is a dependent type of society which looks toward the urban center, derives considerable benefits from it, and also contributes much to it, especially by way of raw materials. The primitive society, on the other hand, is also a strictly face-to-face grouping, whether loosely or tightly organized, but its economy and orientation are almost completely independent of outside influences. Such a group, with its own laws, is quite homogeneous, with little division of labor, except as between sexes. Actually, strictly primitive groups—in this sense of the term—are now few. They consist primarily of small tribelets in Amazonia and New Guinea, as well as certain more isolated parts of Africa. Societies often spoken of as primitive, e.g., Indian tribes in Mexico and the altiplano of South America, are basically "peasant" or dependent societies; and many African tribes south of the Sahara and indigenous groups in India, Southeast Asia and the Islands of the Sea, are rapidly becoming such, though at present they are in a transitional state. The rapid development of transportation and communications and the economic exploitation of so-called primitive areas and peoples have in many instances changed these people from independent to dependent societies.

A typical folk or peasant society is not only economically dependent upon the urban center, whether it looks to the mining area around Lubumbashi in Zaire or sends its produce into a *ladino* town such as Cuzco in Peru; it also exists in cultural dependency to the prestigeful urban center from which so many cultural influences radiate. In contrast to the large, often heterogeneous and impersonal city society, with its lax morals, softer life, secular attitudes, and aggressive manner, the peasant, folk society is generally small, usually quite homogeneous, and intimate, with a milder, more passive manner, and with emphasis upon strong concepts of traditional morality, capacity for physical endurance, and deep religious sentiments. In such a face-to-face society, everyone knows everyone else, and also knows almost everyone's business, including a good deal about everyone's private life—in fact nothing is hidden from the prying and watchful eyes of neighbors. There is very little formal codification of law, but the customs are generally adhered to with an almost fanatical loyalty. By and large the people are more honest, especially within the in-group (the rural society with which the people identify themselves); but they are also more defensive against outside influences, and hence more likely to suspect ulterior motives and to react with blind stupidity and recalcitrance. In some ways long-established folk societies (though not "transitional societies") are more resistant to change than are strictly primitive groups, to which the outside world is less familiar. Furthermore, the folk society has generally discovered that the only defense against being overwhelmed by the outside world is to resist, passively but stubbornly, any changes sponsored by the out-group (the social grouping of which they are not members). This fact partly explains why Protestant missionaries have generally been more successful in dealing with primitive societies, for example, those in Africa, rather than with such a society as the Andean Indians of South America, whose patterns of resistance have been crystallized in opposition to the threats of domination by the white-sponsored culture of the urban centers.

In contrast to the inverted diamond structure with horizontal class cleavage which is typical of urban cultures, folk societies and, to a considerable extent, primitive societies as well may be diagrammatically described as broad-based, pyramidal forms, with roughly parallel rather than cross-sectional divisions:

communication in a face-to-face society

The pyramid in this instance is quite broad-based, for in general the distinctions between those who lead and those who are led are not great. At the same time, there are no simple higher, middle, and lower classes, or elaborations of these distinctions. Rather, the structure of the society breaks down essentially into family groups related by birth or marriage, and consisting of clans, tribelets, phratries, or moieties, depending upon the particular form which any particular social structure may take.

The apex of the diagram indicates the leadership of a small group, the elders of the society, who form an oligarchical control, but who also, as suggested by the dotted lines, individually represent their family affiliations. Such a society has a strong sense of cohesion and presents a more or less uniform front against intrusion. It must be conservative in orientation in order to preserve itself. By and large it makes collective decisions, not by any formal parliamentary techniques but by the kind of informal discussion and interchange of opinions that characterize most types of "family decisions." The effective spread of information in such a society is not describable as along either horizontal or vertical axes (as in our previous diagrams), but rather primarily along family and clan lines. McGavran makes a point of the necessity of using these effective channels of communication as the "bridges of God." [3]

Communicative Approach to a Face-to-Face Society

The methods by which we can best reach people in an urban type of society are quite evident to us, because most of us belong to such a social grouping. But the best type of approach to people living in a face-to-face society is for the same reason strange to most of us, since the social and communicational lines and structures are unfamiliar. However, once we have recognized the fundamental structure of such societies, we can see that the approaches which have proved to be most successful in them are the ones that make optimum use of the natural flow of communication. The basic principles in such an approach are four: (1) effective communication must be based upon personal friendship, (2) the initial approach should be to those who can effectively pass on communication within their family grouping, (3) time must be allowed for the internal diffusion of new ideas, and (4) the challenge for any change of belief or action must be addressed to the persons or groups socially capable of making such decisions.

In a face-to-face society it is essential to establish a personal basis of friendship and acceptance before communication can become effective. An outstanding early missionary in Peru, John Ritchie, instrumental in establishing more than two hundred congregations among the Indian population, made it an invariable rule never to go into a village except by personal invitation. He went to the home of the villager who had invited him and there remained during his visit of two or three days. In other words, he never went unannounced and unexpected into any Indian community to "evangelize," for he had concluded on the basis of years of experience that this course was simply not to be followed in an Indian community. Indians who were Christians might do so, for they could always establish some "family or clan" connection with the inhabitants, but the missionary, a stranger to the group, always felt that his message could be made acceptable to the people only if he was personally "sponsored" by someone belonging to the village. His host, though not necessarily a Christian, must be someone sufficiently interested in the Good News to invite the missionary to come as his personal guest. Such an approach also meant that there was little or no danger that other villagers would organize an attack to drive out the missionary, for as a guest of a member of the face-to-face community he was relatively immune from the overt opposition of hostile religious elements. The primary purpose of this invited approach, however, was not self-protection, but effective communication.

For this missionary invitations to visit new villages were not difficult to obtain, since interested persons, whether or not they had become believers, had relatives and friends in other villages who would invariably pass on the word about this remarkable new message. Moreover, the people learned that the missionary would not impose himself upon anyone, but in typical Indian fashion approached them only on the basis of friendship, and not as a campaigning politician or a dubiously motivated rabble-rouser. It then became a matter of distinction for the leading men in various villages to invite the missionary to come and stay with them, while he shared his personal message of what God had done for all people, including the Quechua speaking Indians of the altiplano.

The second and perhaps the most important principle to be followed in approaching such a community is to make the initial approach to those able effectively to pass on the communication. In some instances, the missionary is able to appeal to the chief of the tribe. In the United States, the rural "missionary" may be able to get the backing of the richest farmer in the region where he works. Usually, however, the unqualified support of the "top man" cannot be obtained immediately, for the leaders in a face-to-face society are generally slow to move ahead of their people. In fact, a man's position of leadership in a face-to-face society depends more upon the intimate and knowledgeable support of his followers than is true of a leader in an impersonal, urban society, where "money talks" more successfully. Thus the chief or headman in such a society is likely to be cautious about accepting any new thing; for the society itself is highly conservative and the leader is usually even more traditional in orientation than the majority of the people. In such a society strength lies in conservatism. Accordingly, those successful in reaching people in folk societies have usually approached a key person near the top, but not quite at the top—someone who, though respected within his own family and clan, has not yet assumed responsibility as an elder of the people. This person is usually a strong personality, well liked by the people. Not infrequently he feels that sponsorship of new ideas may be to his social benefit. However, a word of caution should be added here. It must be recognized that a truly "marginal person" in the cult will not prove satisfactory for this purpose. Such a person's status may mean that he has been ostracized by his own society because of some affront to traditional leadership, or because he has violated the ethical standards of the people. It may mean that he is really an outsider in the face-to-face society, but hangs on in parasitical fashion because he derives economic benefit from exploiting the folk society.

Whereas in our own churches we often think in terms of high-pressure dynamic programs intended to reap results overnight, the approach to face-to-face societies must be of quite a different order. Traditionalists living within the comfortable emotional security of their "extended family" which maintains itself primarily by resistance to ideas from the outside world cannot be pushed into making quick decisions. Such people, confronted by a "crash program", will be inclined to reject it at once. Just as a family must be given time to make up its mind, so a face-to-face society must be carefully nursed along until the people are ready to act. At this point, an acute problem arises, for the missionary's tendency is to encourage some especially responsive persons to step out, repudiate the traditions of their tribe, and declare themselves for Christ. Such a procedure often causes the people as a whole to reject the message. For until a people are able to make what seems to them a valid decision, any pulling out of members from the ranks of the closed society immediately raises the fear of loss of solidarity. An instinctive resistance to assault upon the tight-knit social structure follows. By far the most effective work among folk societies has been done by those sensitive to the "timing" of the first converts. Allowing sufficient time for the making of decisions is the indispensable third principle in communicating with face-to-face societies.

In one unusually fine piece of work among Indians in Latin America, I was personally surprised to find, on visiting the region, that the missionary never extended public invitations to people to "accept Jesus Christ." I had more or less expected that the missionary's background would prompt this type of approach. When I asked why he did not use such a method, he explained frankly that he never gave such an invitation because he was certain that a number of Indians would then make a public "confession"—not so much because of personal conviction, but because of their desire to please him. Moreover, he explained, he tried to keep close to these people so that he would know when the Spirit of God was dealing with them. Then they would either come to him of their own accord, or he would provide an opportunity whereby, in a natural context of friendly conversation and without the evangelistic trimmings of group pressure, they could be led to an effective decision for Christ. This work, though not spectacular, is well founded and growing rapidly. It will continue to expand for years to come, for it has won its way into the very life of the tribe.

The fourth principle in approaching face-to-face societies is to present the challenge for change of belief to persons socially capable of making valid decisions. We who do not know the meaning of clan life, since we are not ourselves members of such a society, can rarely imagine the pressures upon the individual in such an organization. We take it for granted that anyone can and should make up his own mind about what he believes and what he should do. But this is not true in all cultures. Members of such a society feel an instinctive loyalty to the extended family unit. The individual derives his personal and social security from it, and usually gives it his complete and often unthinking support. Even an adult man may find it impossible to break with such a family unit. It is as though we invited a neighbor child to go to the beach for a day with our family, without consulting his parents. In general, his first response will be, "I'll go ask my mother." In fact, if we handle such an invitation rightly we would ask his mother for him, so that she would recognize the conditions as well as the genuineness of the invitation. Something of the same situation exists in face-to-face cultures, where individuals do not act on their own, but respond as members of families, clans, and tribes.

This group response to the gospel message lies at the core of the so-called "mass movement," called "people's movements" by McGavran. He pleads, and rightly so, for a more intelligent appreciation of the structure of societies in which people normally act as groups. He, therefore, insists that the process of Christianization must be divided between initial "discipling" and later instruction, and that the importance of initial commitment by the people to a new way of life must be fully recognized and built upon. The motives of such a people in mass response should no more be suspect that are the often mixed motives that prompt many individuals in an urban society to declare themselves for Christ, only to find later that they have committed themselves to more than they had earlier thought. In either case the initial commitment of either group or individual provides the basis by which instruction in the faith may be given and through which full maturity of Christian discipleship may be reached.

The Problem of Heterogeneous Societies

Heterogeneous societies are primarily of two types: (1) urban societies that contain urban-structured minority groups, similar, for example, to the Negro subculture within American life; and (2) urban societies that include face-to-face subsocieties.

In the first type one must recognize three factors: (1) the basic differences, which mean that one cannot, for all his idealism, use identically the same approaches to the various groups; (2) the immense prestige differential, which means that the people in the less prestigeful groups try to follow, or think that they are following the norms of the higher group; and (3) the priority of intra-group communication, if effective communication is to be attained. The relation between two urban-structured groups in a single society can be diagrammatically represented as follows:

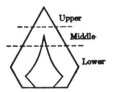

In the second principal type of heterogeneous society the dominant urban structure includes a minority group having a face-to face type of society. A typical situation of this kind may be illustrated by the following diagram:

a face-to-face minority group within a heterogeneous society in an urban context

Several significant features of this diagram should be recognized. First, the included face-to-face group may penetrate into the middle class, if one takes into account economic resources and general prestige. Second, the base of the included face-to-face group is usually not so low as that of the urban culture for in general the poor people of the urban slums are in far worse circumstances than are the poor people of the smaller rural communities. This is certainly true, for example, of the poor Indians of the altiplano in South America as compared with the indigent urban population. Sociologists in Mexico also regard the poor people of the slums around Mexico City as in much more desperate circumstances, and often less amenable to effective help, than are the Indians of many tribes living in remote areas of the country.

Included folk societies have always been recognized as in some degree different from their urban neighbors, especially if they happen to speak another language and wear different types of clothing. But, rarely is it recognized that such folk societies have fundamentally different orientations toward life and are usually structured along quite different lines from the urban society, so that any communication to them must be specially formulated and transmitted if it is to be relevant.

Frequently missionary effort fails to recognize the need of devising different approaches to the urban and folk societies, but lumps them together without regard to their different structures. The probable reasons for this lack of discrimination are that American missionaries mistakenly think that the urban and rural areas abroad are equivalent to the corresponding areas in the United States. Even though Americans living in small towns and rural communities have a number of characteristics typical of a face-to-face community, farmers in the United States are by no means "peasants." Except for people in certain very isolated communities in mountainous areas, their world view, standard of values, general orientation toward life, and educational opportunities are substantially the same as those of the city dweller. There are of course differences between the "hayseed" and the "city slicker," but except for certain very restricted cases, in American life there is no peasant culture, with its emphasis upon family structure and clan relationships, and its highly traditional and resistant attitudes. Certain of these tendencies do exist, but they are by no means so pronounced or so significant as in a true peasant culture.

When an American goes to a foreign country, however, he tends to judge all situations by what he has known at home. He does not appreciate the significance of the existing contrasts, because his eyes have not been opened to them. He, therefore, lumps all groups together and proceeds without reference to basic differences. If, however, he is to be successful in communicating, he must recognize the distinctions that exist between various classes of people and make his message applicable to their circumstances and transmittable by means of their traditional networks of communication. Each class or subculture must be reached within the contexts of its own life, and in so far as they are interdependent, the Christians among them must be helped to recognize their mutual responsibilities.

Principles of Communication and the Social Structure

Obviously in view of the fact that the social context not only affects the ways in which messages are transmitted, but also involves the manner in which they are decoded, the encoding of messages can be done effectively only when these social factors in communication are considered. The basic principles which may be derived from this study of social structure can perhaps best be summarized as follows:

1. The response to the preaching of the Good News may at times reflect a social situation, even more than a religious conviction.
2. Opposition to the communication of the Christian message may be in many instances more social than religious.
3. Changes in social structure may alter the religious view of behavior.
4. Effective communication follows the patterns of social structure.
5. A relevant witness will incorporate valid indigenous social structures.

The fact that effective communication within any social context must inevitably follow the social structure seems quite evident. However, what has happened in a particular instance in the Huichol tribe of Mexico may add certain significant insights. A young man, Roman Diaz, who became a Christian a few years ago, has become interested in evangelizing his neighbors. With the instruction of the missionary, he has made himself particularly useful to his own people by learning some simple remedies for easily diagnosed illnesses. He dispenses medicines for such ailments and has developed quite a reputation as a new kind of "medicine man." When people come to him for medicines, he follows the standard routine used by the traditional medicine man, who never treats a patient unless, after conversation of an hour or more, he and his patient have established just how they are related through birth or marriage. The Huichols are a relatively small tribe, with a long tradition of marriage only within their group and great emphasis upon genealogies, so that sooner or later one can establish his relationship to virtually every other member of the tribe. After thus establishing social ties, the new medicine man diagnoses the illness and prescribes the medicines, which he then dispenses. The patients almost always arrange to stay around for a few days to see how they fare and whether they need further treatment. During this period the "Christian medicine man" takes a good deal of time to chat informally with all those who wish to hear. Moreover, much of this instruction he gives in traditional forms of chanting which have a high theological and didactic content. Little by little he is making a significant impact upon a highly "defensive" group of people. From the point of view of communication his methods are more effective than those of a typical foreign medical doctor, who would set up a clinic and as a specialist leave all the religious instructions to the "theologically trained personnel." For in Huichol culture healing and religion go together, and religious instruction should be given by the medicine man himself if it is to be given credence.

An effective church always incorporates into its structure the valid indigenous forms of social organization. This is not syncretism, but indigenization, the invariable and necessary means of making the Good News relevant in any community. Marie F. Reyburn, in an analysis of one area in Ecuador, South America, outlines a number of social features of the Quechua culture which can be incorporated with profit into an evangelistic witness to the total community:[4] (1) the use of kinship groups (by incorporating the systems of godfathers and godmothers into the Protestant church); (2) the election of heads of families as church leaders (this is the present pattern of Indian life, in which the male heads of families are responsible for various community functions and affairs, including fiestas); (3) the use of more elaborate ceremonies, e.g., in baptism and marriage (since these are at present so important in the Christo-pagan religious system); (4) the sponsorship of liquor-free fiestas (as a legitimate means for social expression and community solidarity); and (5) the development of cooperatives for group enterprises (this is a traditional pattern of Indian community life, and could be effectively carried out by Christian congregations).

People are such an integral part of the social structure in which they live that only in and through this structure can they be reached and live out their faith.

End Notes

1. David Riesman, *Individualism Reconsidered* (Garden City, N.Y.: Doubleday & Co., Inc., 1954), p. 46.

2. Donald A. McGavran, *The Bridges of God* (London: World Dominion Press, 1955), p. 120.

3. *Ibid.*

4. Marie F. Reyburn, "Applied Anthropology among the Sierra Quechua of Ecuador," *Practical Anthropology*, 1(1953), p. 21.

Study Questions

1. Compare both the patterns of decision-making and the communication approaches needed in urban and face-to-face societies.

2. Nida claims that the average expatriate American "lumps all groups together and proceeds without references to basic differences." What are some possible explanations for this tendency?

12

From Every Language

Barbara F. Grimes

"After this I looked and there before me was a great crowd that no one could count, from every nation, tribe, people and language, standing before the throne and in front of the Lamb." Rev. 7:9

Which Language?

We have been commanded to make disciples of all peoples. Every person who wants to communicate across language boundaries needs to decide what language he will use. This is as true for evangelists, teachers, and preachers, as it is for Bible translators.

Too often the choice is made on the basis of what is easiest for the communicator, rather than what communicates best to the hearers. This does not count the cost of miscommunication, producing churches of nominal Christians who are not equipped to carry on their ministry, to sustain spiritual depth into succeeding generations, to answer false teaching, wage spiritual warfare, reach out to others, and avoid syncretism; or having people completely fail to recognize that the Christian God is the universal God to whom they must answer.

Making Disciples

A lot of what a disciple is commanded to do involves language. Being a disciple of Jesus Christ involves getting to know Him personally. That requires adequate comprehension of the Good News and of God's Word. Understanding and knowledge are repeatedly emphasized throughout the Scriptures. The Apostle Paul said it was his responsibility to make the message clear (Col. 4:4).

But being a disciple involves more than passive comprehension. He is commanded to witness to his faith, encourage other Christians, exhort those who

Barbara F. Grimes has been a member of the Summer Institute of Linguistics and the Wycliffe Bible Translators since 1951, working with her husband Joseph among the Huichol Indians of Mexico for sixteen years. She has been editor of the *Ethnologue* since 1971, and was a topic editor for the *Oxford International Encyclopedia of Linguistics*. Since 1989 she and her husband have been working with speakers of Hawaii Creole English to translate the Scriptures into that language. From "Reached" Without the Scriptures?, *International Journal of Frontier Missions* 7:2.41-47.

need it, pray, give praise, give thanks, sing, memorize God's Word, teach his own children, older women to teach younger women, instruct one another, meditate; exercise gifts of the Spirit given to him that involve verbal behavior, such as the utterance of wisdom, utterance of knowledge, prophecy, interpretation of tongues, fulfilling the functions of appointed messengers, evangelists, pastors, and teachers. Some persons are to read Scripture publicly, to teach, preach, and interpret any foreign language used in church.

The mother tongue is the language people learn first at their mother's knee; in which they learn to think and talk about the world around them, to interact with people closest to them, to acquire and express their values, the language which becomes part of their personality and identity, and which expresses ethnicity and solidarity with their people. People can handle the verbal skills required for adequate comprehension of the Good News and functioning as a disciple in their mother tongue; the question is whether or not they can do those things in their second language.

'Adequately Bilingual?'

Careful study of how different languages are used in multilingual societies has given important insights to sociolinguists in recent decades. Multilinguals use each of their languages in different circumstances, with different people, to talk about different topics, with varying degrees of success in speaking and understanding, and with different psychological connotations. It is important for those who want to communicate the most important message in the world to be aware of these factors, lest both they and their message be misunderstood or rejected.

Spread Across the Population

Because the second language is learned in certain situations, and depends on the amount of contact an individual has had with it, and his desire and need to learn it, there are differences in fluency across a population. It is not possible to judge the bilingual proficiency of a population by looking at only a small sample of the population. It is necessary to investigate how different age groups, both sexes, people in different regions or with different educational levels use their languages, and to study any other factors which may influence contact with the second language in that culture. The importance of reaching everyone for Christ, including women, older people, the uneducated, and those in remote areas, justifies the time and effort needed to carry out a reliable investigation of these differences.

Levels of Bilingual Proficiency

A useful scale to describe levels of bilingual proficiency has been developed by the United States Foreign Service Institute. It describes six levels of proficiency, from memorized ability all the way to the equivalent of an educated native speaker.

What Threshold is Needed?

The question of what threshold of bilingual proficiency is needed for adequate understanding of the Good News and use of Scripture is crucial. It includes the kinds of discourse involved, and the kind of comprehension needed for those kinds of discourse. It is also necessary for each disciple to be able to use the language actively if that language is to be the means of communication for a group.

There are at least four reasons why an advanced proficiency level is needed as the threshold for adequate long term use of Scripture and verbal activity as a disciple.

(1) *Domain.* Sociolinguists identify classes of situations, or domains, in which different forms of speech are used in multilingual situations; such as home and family, close friends, traditional culture, religion, school, work, trade, and outside culture. A second language is learned through contact in certain domains, and a speaker's vocabulary, at least, is often limited to functioning in those domains in that language.

The last domain in which speakers usually learn to use the second language is the interpersonal domain; yet that is the most crucial domain in Scripture. The understanding of reconciliation as an interpersonal relationship between God and man, rather than as the result of the religious performance of certain prescribed acts, and the extending of that reconciliation to human relationships which affects every domain of life, is basic to Christianity. Christian faith is personal and intimate as well as corporate and public. If the second language is not learned and used extensively in interpersonal relationships, its effective use by a disciple will be very limited.

(2) *Unfamiliar information.* Scripture has much unfamiliar information to convey, and much of it is cross-culturally unfamiliar. This involves not just material culture, but basic concepts, such as the nature of God, evil, forgiveness, and reconciliation.

(3) *Complex structure and discourse.* A person who lacks advanced proficiency is not able to handle the kind of complex structure in the Scriptures, and especially in the Epistles. He may understand the words, but not really understand how they fit together.

(4) *Abstract speech.* The kinds of discourse in Scripture include not only narrative, but exhortations, expositions, and explanations; not only events and simple propositions, but complex concepts and arguments.

Brewster and Brewster also point out that anyone involved as a cross culture change agent needs to have advanced proficiency to be effective.[1]

The Language Broker Model

The language broker model has been used extensively in missions, in which a bilingual person hears the message or reads Scripture in his second language, and then is expected to transfer the meaning into his first language for the benefit of those who do not understand the other language. Unfortunately, few people are able to do that kind of transferring without extensive training and experience in that skill. Most bilingual speakers of minority languages have learned their second language through direct oral contact outside a classroom, and lack training in language transfer.

The Scriptures are often available to those churches only in the second language. This model avoids having to translate the Scriptures into the first language, but assumes that spontaneous paraphrases of Scripture are adequate. There is no guarantee that such impromptu paraphrases done repeatedly by various speakers in different situations are at all accurate.

The language broker model often results in a bilingual elite in the church being the only ones eligible to become leaders. Others to whom God may have given the gifts of teaching, preaching, and other gifts involving using language may be hindered from exercising those gifts by lack of sufficient bilingual proficiency to function in the second language.

Conclusion

Can a group be considered truly reached if they have been contacted only through their second language, and there are few, if any, highly bilingual people in the group? Can they be considered reached if they do not have the Scriptures in a language they understand adequately? We have to conclude that ministry in the mother tongue and mother tongue Scriptures are two of the prerequisites for nearly all peoples in order for them to be accurately described as 'reached'.

End Note

1. Brewster, E. Thomas and Elizabeth S. Brewster, *Language Acquisition Made Practical* (Colorado Springs: Lingua House, 1976).

Study Question

1. How do you respond to Grimes' conclusion that Scriptures and ministry in the mother tongue are necessary for a group to be 'reached?'

13

The Viable Missionary: Learner, Trader, Story Teller

Donald N. Larson

When my interest in the mission of the Christian Church first awakened, I was too old to be acceptable to my denomination as a candidate. But for the past twenty years I have worked behind-the-scenes in mission, helping people to deal with the problems of language and culture learning. From this position off-stage, I have observed missionaries, sending agencies, local missionary communities, and national Christians and non-Christians in several fields. From these observations I have concluded that there is often a wide gap in the missionary's conception of his role and how it is viewed by the non-Christians of his adopted community. The purpose of this paper is to examine this gap and propose ways and means of closing it.

By way of example, I recently met a young man heading for a short-term of missionary service in southeast Asia and asked him what he was going to be doing there. He replied in all seriousness that he was "going to teach the natives to farm." I pressed him with a question: "Don't they know how to farm there?" He thought for a moment and then replied, "Well, I really don't know. I haven't got a very clear picture of things yet." Imagine what the non-Christian of his adopted community would think of him if they should hear him say such things! Whether this young man knows it or not, these Asians were farmers long before the Pilgrims landed at Plymouth Rock and even long before there were Christians anywhere.

Unfortunately, such statements as those made by the young man are not limited to short-termers. Career missionaries are sometimes unaware of the experience, background and world view of the members of their host communities and how they themselves are viewed. This gap between missionaries and non-Christians in their local communities generates communication problems of many different kinds.

Donald N. Larson is Senior Consultant for Cross-Cultural Learning at Link Care Missions. He was professor of Anthropology and Linguistics at Bethel College in St. Paul, Minnesota and Director of the Toronto Institute of Linguistics. He formerly served as Director of the Inter-Church Language School in the Philippines. Reprinted from *Missiology: An International Review*, Arthur F. Glasser, ed., April 1978. Used with permission.

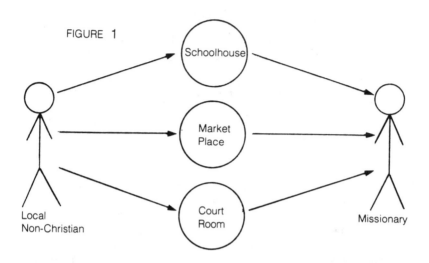

FIGURE 1

Schoolhouse

Market Place

Court Room

Local Non-Christian

Missionary

Typical Encounter Models

In an encounter with the missionary, whom he views as an outsider, the local non-Christian tends to view their relationship in one of three ways. He uses the schoolhouse, the market place and the court room as backdrops to his encounters with the missionary. As if they were at school, he sees the missionary as teacher and himself as student. The purpose of their encounter is to transmit information to be learned. As if they were in the market place, he sees the missionary as seller and himself as buyer. The purpose of their encounter is to buy and sell something. As if in the court room, he sees the missionary as an accuser and himself as the accused. Their encounter deals with judgment. In the schoolhouse the teacher says, "I will teach you something." In the market place the merchant says, "I have something to sell you." In the court room the judge says, "I will measure you by this standard." Depending on the scene, the national views his need differently. In the schoolhouse he asks himself whether he needs to learn what the teacher has to teach. In the market place he asks himself whether he needs to buy what the merchant has to sell. In the court room he asks himself whether he needs to take the judge's accusation seriously.

But can an outsider teach or sell or accuse an insider? Does the non-Christian need what the missionary presents? Is the missionary able to communicate the Gospel through the roles of seller, teacher or accuser? Are they effective? These are serious questions.

Of course, there are other ways to look at the non-Christian's encounter with the missionary than through the three analogies used above.

Viable Role Dimensions

The typical missionary today may be paying too little attention to the *viability* of his role. If I were volunteering for missions today and hoped to be productive and happy, I would make certain that my role were viable from four perspectives: (1) the community in which I reside, (2) its missionary residents, (3) the agency that sends me and (4) myself.

To elaborate, my role must allow me to be myself; to be my own person. It must also be viable in the local missionary community. If the local missionary community doesn't recognize my role and its importance, I won't be able to survive for long. My role must also be viable from the standpoint of the sending agency. I need their support and encouragement. I cannot survive for long if they do not give me an important place in their community. Finally, my role must be viable from the point of view of the local community. I do not want to parade myself around in this community as some kind of a freak, or a misfit, or a spy, or useless. This matter of community viability is often overlooked. It should not be. It is important, for I must have positive experiences in order to continue. Local residents must feel good about my presence in their community. My contribution must reinforce and complement the ongoing missionary program. The sending agency must have a solid rationale underlying its programs and the opportunities it provides for me.

So the new missionary must look for roles that are simultaneously legitimate to these four parties: me, my host community, its missionary community and the sending agency.

To the non-Christian, the roles of teacher, seller or accuser may or may not be viable. The non-Christian may expect the outsider to learn the insider's viewpoint before he can teach effectively about the outside. He may expect him to survive on the level of insiders and depend on the local market before he can sell important goods. He may expect him to measure himself by their own laws before he accuses insiders in terms of an outside standard.

A principle of order seems to be important: learner before teacher, buyer before seller, accused before accuser. An outsider may have to follow this order before he can be viable in these roles to the insider.

Outsiders cannot live on the edge of a community without coming to the attention of insiders in a negative way. The term "outsider" has negative connotations. So the missionary must become an insider, at least to some extent, if he hopes to avoid these negative reactions to his presence and become a valuable person in the community.

If the insider is reluctant to learn from an outside teacher or buy from an outside seller or accept the accusations of an outside accuser, the outsider cannot hope to accomplish much until he finds new roles or redesigns the old ones.

Three Roles

As I see it, there are three roles that the missionary can develop in order to establish viability in the eyes of the national non-Christian: learner, trader and story teller. I would first become a learner. After three months I would add another: trader. After three more months, I would add a third: story teller. After three more months, while continuing to be learner, trader and story teller, I would begin to develop other roles specified in my job description.

Let me elaborate. From his position as an outsider, the missionary must find a way to move toward the center if he hopes to influence people. Some roles will help him to make this move. Others will not. His first task is to identify those which are most appropriate and effective. Then he can begin to develop ways and means of communicating his Christian experience through these roles in which he has found acceptance.

Learner

More specifically, as learner, my major emphasis is on language, the primary symbol of identification in my host community. When I try to learn it, they know that I mean business—that they are worth something to me because I make an effort to communicate on their terms. I learn a little each day and put it to use. I talk to a new person every day. I say something new every day. I gradually reach the point where I understand and am understood a little. I can learn much in three months.

I spend my mornings with a language helper (in a structured program or one that I design on my own) from whom I elicit the kinds of materials that I need to talk to people in the afternoons. I show him how to drill me on these materials and then spend a good portion of the morning in practice. Then in the afternoon I go out into public places and make whatever contacts are natural with local residents, talking to them as best I can with my limited proficiency—starting the very first day. I initiate one conversation after another, each of which says both verbally and non-verbally, "I am a learner. Please talk with me and help me." With each conversation partner, I get a little more practice and a little more proficiency, from the first day on.

At the end of my first three months, I have established myself with potentially dozens of people and reached the point where I can make simple statements, ask and answer simple questions, find my way around, learning the meaning of new words on the spot, and most importantly, experience some measure of "at-homeness" in my adopted community. I cannot learn the "whole language" in three months, but I can learn to initiate conversations, control them in a limited way and learn a little more about the language from everyone whom I meet.

Trader

When my fourth month begins, I add a role—that of trader, trading experience and insight with people of my adopted community—seeing ourselves more clearly as part of mankind, not just members of different communities or nations. I prepare for this role by periods of residence in as many other places as I can, or vicariously, through course work in anthropology and related fields. I also come equipped with a set of 8 x 10 photos illustrating a wide range of ways to be human.

During the second three months I spend mornings with my language helper learning to talk about the photos in my collection. Thus I build on the language proficiency developed in the first month. I practice my description of these pictures and prepare myself as best I can to answer questions about them. Then in the afternoon I visit casually in the community, using the photos as part of my "show and tell" demonstration. I tell as much as I can about the way others live, how they make their livings, what they do for enjoyment, how they hurt, and how they struggle for survival and satisfaction.

At the end of this second phase, I establish myself not only as a learner but as one who is interested in other people and seeks to trade one bit of information for another. My language proficiency is still developing. I meet many people. Depending upon the size and complexity of the community, I establish myself as a well-known figure by this time. I become a bridge between the people of the local community and a larger world—at least symbolically.

Story Teller

When I begin my seventh month, I shift emphasis again to a new role. Now I become a story teller. I spend mornings with my language helper. Now it is to learn to tell a very simple story to the people whom I meet and respond to their inquiries as best I can. The stories that I tell are based on the wanderings of the people of Israel, the coming of Christ, the formation of God's new people, the movement of the Church into all the world and ultimately into this very community, and finally, my own story of my encounter with Christ and my walk as a Christian. During the mornings I develop these stories and practice them

intensively. Then in the afternoon I go into the community, as I have been doing for months, but now to encounter people as story teller. I am still language learner and trader, but I have added the role of story teller. I share as much of the story with as many people as I can each day.

At the end of this third phase, I have made acquaintances and friends. I have had countless experiences that I will never forget. I have left positive impressions as learner, trader and story teller. I am ready for another role, and another and another.

Viability Reconsidered

With this profile in mind, let's examine this activity in the light of our earlier discussion of viability. Figure 2 helps to focus on the issues: In Figure 2, the plus sign (+) means that the role is unquestionably viable. The question mark (?) means that some further discussion and clarification is probably necessary before viability can be established.

FIGURE 2

		DIMENSIONS		
ROLES	Local Residents	Missionary Community	Sending Agency	Missionary
Learner	+	?	?	+
Trader	+	?	?	?
Story Teller	+	+	+	+

From the standpoint of local residents, an outsider who is ready, willing and able to learn probably has an entree. Furthermore, the average person in these communities probably has a natural curiosity about people in other places. This curiosity can probably be tapped and traded by a sensitive approach. Finally, story telling and the reporting of incidents is common in every community. Everyone does it. Of course, there are rules which must be respected. I assume that someone who has already established himself as learner and trader can share stories and experiences of his own with other people. Local residents will probably listen and perhaps even help him to get it told.

I find these roles viable. I enjoy learning and know how to go about it. I have a general understanding of different ways that people live and appreciate the possibilities inherent in the trader role. I love to tell stories and enjoy listening to them, especially when the teller is deeply involved in them himself.

But from the standpoint of the sending agency and the local community, these roles may be questionable. Of the three, the story teller role is perhaps the easiest one to develop, though one often finds missionaries to be sermonizers, theologizers or lecturers, not story tellers. The viability of the learner role is open to question. A new missionary, expected to be a learner as far as the affairs of his local missionary organization are concerned, is not always given the time or encouraged to get to know local residents intimately. The viability of the trader role is largely untested, though I believe that sending agencies and local missionary communities should consider its importance carefully.

Why not exploit the learner role to the fullest? Most people who live as aliens sooner or later realize its importance. Why not get the new missionary off on the right foot—especially if it has increasing payoff in his second and third phases? Furthermore, the learner role symbolizes a number of important things to local residents that are important in the communication of the Gospel. The learner's dependence and vulnerability convey in some small way the messages of identification and reconciliation that are explicit in the Gospel. Coming to be known as a learner can certainly do the local missionary community no harm. It may be able to do some good.

The viability of the trader role is perhaps more difficult to establish—partly because of its newness. It seems to be too "secular." Yet from the community's standpoint, a secular role may be much more natural and acceptable for the alien. Coming as some sort of "sacred specialist," the outsider generates all sorts of questions, objections and barriers. But there is still another consideration: this role reinforces the idea of the Gospel as something for all people. Except for anthropologists, demographers and a few other specialists, Christians probably have a wider understanding of human variation than any other group of people, simply because of our multi-ethnic, multi-racial and multi-lingual characteristics. The trader role complements the more formal presentation of the Gospel through the sharing of essentially "secular knowledge" about peoples of the world.

There are obvious implications here for the selection, orientation and evaluation of missionaries. A discussion of them however is beyond the scope of this paper.

Conclusion

We face a difficult situation today as the star of colonialism continues to fall, and as the star of maturing national churches continues to rise. Missionaries become more and more frustrated as the viability of their role is questioned. We must take this situation seriously. The biblical mandate challenges the Christian to become one with those to whom he brings the Word of Life. Furthermore, history shows that vulnerability and flexibility are themselves powerful witnesses to the working of the Spirit within man. Finally, if the mission movement is to continue, new roles must be added and old ones must be redesigned.

Any new missionary can prepare himself in rather simple and straightforward fashion to meet the demands of these three roles. Insofar as these roles are viable from the point of view of the local community, the new missionary should begin with them. Unfortunately, sending agencies and local missionary communities may not be ready to buy these ideas. The let's-get-on-with-the-job mentality militates against getting bogged down in learning, trading and story telling. But this get-on-with-the job mentality needs to be challenged; for if it implies roles that insulate the missionary from local residents, alternatives must be developed.

Some months ago at a language and culture learning workshop in East Africa, a missionary asked me if I knew anything about elephants. When I replied that I did not, she asked more specifically if I knew what happens when a herd of elephants approaches a water hole that is surrounded by another herd. I replied that I did not know what would happen. She then proceeded to explain that the lead elephant of the second group turns around and backs down toward the water hole. As soon as his backside is felt by the elephants gathered around the water hole, they step aside and make room for him. This is then the signal to the other elephants that the first herd is ready to make room for them around the hole.

When I asked what point she was trying to make, she stated simply and powerfully, "We didn't back in." The continuing movement of mission in the world today may require missionaries to "back in" to their host communities. The roles of learner, trader and storyteller may not be appropriate in a headfirst approach, but they may be necessary in an approach which emphasizes "backing in."

Study Questions

1. Why does Larson claim that the learner, trader, and storyteller roles are "viable" for missionaries?

2. Why would Larson's suggested roles possibly be "questionable" to the sending agency and the local missionary community?

14

Bonding and the Missionary Task: Establishing a Sense of Belonging

E. Thomas and Elizabeth S. Brewster

And the Word became flesh and dwelt among us. John 1:14

We have a new little boy who was born into our home just a few months ago. In preparing for his natural childbirth at home we were introduced to the concept of bonding.

In the animal world it is called imprinting. Most of us remember the picture in our college psychology books of the psychologist Konrad Lorenz being followed by ducklings. At the critical time, right after hatching, Lorenz and the ducklings were alone together and, from then on, they responded to him as though he were their parent. The imprinted duck experiences a sense of belonging to the man.

More recent studies supporting the concept of bonding have been carried out with a variety of animals, including goats, calves and monkeys. In each case, the infant and mother have an early period of sensitivity right after birth. If mother and infant are together at that time, a close bond results which can withstand subsequent separations.

But, if infant and mother are separated immediately after birth, the infant can become attached to a surrogate—a cloth doll, a different adult animal or even a human. If infant and mother are later reunited, one or both may reject the other

E. Thomas and Elizabeth S. Brewster have been a husband-wife team specializing in helping missionaries develop effective techniques for learning any language and adapting to the broader culture of which the language is a part. Tom was teaching at Fuller Theological Seminary when he died in 1985. Betty Sue is part-time Assistant Professor for Language and Culture Learning at Fuller's School of World Mission. Their work has taken them to more than 75 countries and they have helped train over 2,500 missionaries. Their textbook *Language Acquisition Made Practical (LAMP)* has been widely acclaimed for its innovative approach and pedagogical creativity. Revised from, "Bonding and the Missionary Task," E. Thomas and Elizabeth S. Brewster. Lingua House. Used by permission.

or at least not respond to the other with normal attachment.

Studies of human infants and mothers show the importance of bonding. Apparently, just after birth, divinely-designed psychological and physiological factors in the newborn uniquely prepare him to become bonded with his parents. Certainly the excitement and adrenaline levels of both the child and his parents are at a peak. The senses of the infant are being stimulated by a multitude of new sensations. The birth is essentially an entrance into a new culture with new sights, new sounds, new smells, new positions, new environment and new ways of being held. Yet, at that particular time, he is equipped with an extraordinary ability to respond to these unusual circumstances.

People who support home birth are concerned about the bonding process between parents and the infant. An important collection of research studies on human bonding published in *Maternal Infant Bonding* by Klaus and Kennell (Mosby Co., St. Louis, 1976) is widely read. It is pointed out that the non-drugged newborn is more alert during the first day than at any time during the next week or two. This was our experience as our son was full of interest and curiosity for his first six hours, then, after sleeping, he continued very alert for a few more hours.

These alert hours are the critical time for bonding to occur—for a sense of belonging to be established.

Typical American hospital birth is not conducive to normal bonding for two reasons. Hospital-born babies are usually drugged—groggy from a variety of medications typically given to the laboring mother. Neither the baby nor mother, then, has an opportunity to experience the period of acute alertness immediately after birth.

The other reason normal bonding does not occur within the hospital establishment is that the baby is typically snatched away from his family and straightway placed in the isolation of the nursery.

When normal bonding does not occur, rejection can result. It has been demonstrated, for example, that child abuse occurs far more frequently with children who were born prematurely and then isolated from the mother for even a few days while being kept in incubators (Klaus and Kennell, pp. 2-10).

Our desire to be intimately together as a family and away from institutional commotion in order to maximize the bonding opportunity for all three of us (father included) was a major reason for choosing home birth.

The Missionary Analogy

There are some important parallels between the infant's entrance into his new culture and an adult's entrance into a new, foreign culture. In this situation the adult's senses, too, are bombarded by a multitude of new sensations, sights, sounds, and smells—but he, too, is able to respond to these new experiences and even enjoy them. Just as the participants in the birth experience, his adrenaline is up and his excitement level is at a peak. Upon arrival, he is in a state of unique readiness, both physiologically and emotionally, to become a belonger in his new environment. But then...

Just as the infant is snatched away by the hospital establishment and put into the isolation of the nursery, so the newly-arrived missionary is typically snatched away by the expatriate missionary contingency and thus isolated from his new language community.

He is ready to bond—to become a belonger with those to whom he is called to be good news. The timing is critical. Ducklings do not become imprinted at any old time. Imprinting occurs at the critical time. Bonding best occurs when the participants are uniquely ready for the experience.

The way the new missionary spends his first couple of weeks in his new country is of critical importance if he is to establish a sense of belonging with the local people.

It is not uncommon for a baby to become bonded with hospital personnel instead of with his own parents. The baby then cries when with the mother, and is comforted by the nurse. New missionaries, too, tend to become bonded to the other expatriates rather than to the people of the new society. It happens subtly, maybe while the newcomer is subject to the hospitality of an orientation time.

When his sense of belonging is established with the other foreigners, it is then predictable that the missionary will carry out his ministry by the "foray" method—he will live isolated from the local people, as the other foreigners do, but make a few forays out into the community each week, returning always to the security of the missionary community. Without bonding he does not have a sense of feeling at home within the local cultural context. Thus, he does not pursue, as a way of life, significant relationships in the community. When normal bonding is not established, rejection of the people, or even abuse, can occur. It is often reflected in the attitude behind statements like, "Oh, these people! Why do they always do things this way?" or "Somebody ought to teach them how to live!" or "Won't these people ever learn?"

Implications of Bonding for the Missionary Task

A missionary is one who goes into the world to give people an opportunity to belong to God's family. He goes because he, himself, is a belonger in this most meaningful of relationships. His life should proclaim: "I belong to Jesus Who has given me a new kind of life. By my becoming a belonger here with you, God is inviting you through me to belong to Him."

The missionary's task thus parallels the model established by Jesus Who left heaven, where He belonged, and became a belonger with humankind in order to draw people into a belonging relationship with God.

We are convinced that the normal missionary newcomer is ready physiologically, emotionally and spiritually to become bonded with the people of his new community. Fulfillment of this unique readiness must be initiated at the time of arrival.

The timing is critical.

During his first couple of weeks, the newcomer is uniquely able to cope with and even enjoy the newness of a foreign country and its language. There have been months or even years of planning, and his anticipation, excitement and adrenaline are now at a peak.

The newcomer who is immediately immersed in the local community has many advantages. If he lives with a local family, he can learn how the insiders organize their lives, how they get their food and do their shopping and how they get around with public transportation. During the first couple of months, he can learn much about the insiders' attitudes and how they feel about the ways typical foreigners lives. As he experiences an alternative lifestyle, he can evaluate the value of adopting it for himself and his own family. On the other hand, the missionary whose first priority is to get settled can only settle in his familiar Western way, and once this is done he is virtually locked into a pattern that is foreign to the local people.

Culture shock is predictable for the missionary who has not bonded with the local people of his new community, but is much less likely for the bonded person. The one who feels at home does not experience culture shock.

In our first culture it comes naturally for us to do things in a way that works. We know which way to look for traffic as we step off the curb, how to get a bus to stop for us, how to pay a fair price for goods or services, how to get needed information, etc., etc.

But, in a new culture, the way to do things seems to be unpredictable. As a result, newcomers experience a disorientation which can lead to culture shock.

The new missionary who establishes his sense of belonging with other missionary expatriates has his entry cushioned by these foreigners. It is generally thought that this cushioning is helpful for the adjustment of the newcomer, whose arrival is often planned to coincide with a field council pow-wow.

We would like to suggest, however, that this cushioning is an unfortunate disservice, because during the first two or three weeks the newcomer would have been especially able to cope with the unpredictable situations encountered in the new culture. Indeed, he might even revel in all the variety. But the critical first few days are the only time such a response is likely. The way these days are spent is, therefore, of crucial importance—and cushioning is the *last* thing he needs.

The first prayer letter the cushioned missionary sends from the field will typically describe his airport meeting with the local missionaries, the accommodations provided by them, and the subsequent orientation by these expatriates. After writing about how he has been accepted by the other missionaries (one of his high priorities) he will invariably close with something like: "Our prayer request at this time is that we will be accepted by the local people." A noble desire, but a concern that is being expressed about three weeks too late!—and now without a viable strategy to achieve the goal. The initial blush of life in the new environment is now gone.

The individual who hopes to enter another culture in a gradual way will probably fail to do so, and he may never enjoy the experience of belonging to the people or having them care for him.

Better to plunge right in and experience life from the insiders' perspective. Live with the people, worship with them, go shopping with them and use their public transportation. From the very first day it is important to develop many meaningful relationships with local people. The newcomer should early communicate his needs and his desire to be a learner. People help people who are in need! Then, when potentially stressful situations come up he can, as learner, secure help, answers, or insight from these insiders. (The one who is being cushioned gets outsiders' answers to insiders' situations and his foreignness and alienation are thereby perpetuated.)

A couple who has chosen to be isolated from Western people during their first months in a Muslim context wrote us about the victories they have experienced:

> My husband and I knew before we left that we would have different types of adjustments. I knew the hardest time for me would be at first and he felt that his hard times would occur after he had been here a while. So it has been. I really had a hard time leaving our family. But after I started getting out with the people here, my homesickness faded. The local community has so warmly received us. At Christmas, 125 of these friends came to our Christmas celebration. And during that season, the closeness of our interpersonal relationships amazed us.
>
> I'm not exactly sure why my husband just recently went through a depression. Christmas for us was different than it has been. Plus he was laid up for a week with the flu. During that time, he yearned for familiar things. And he says he was tired of always trying to be sensitive as to how he is coming across. The Lord has blessed our work here, and two Muslim converts that he is discipling are what is helping him get over this. We really have been alone in many ways. We supported each other but at times the burdens seemed so big and we didn't have anyone else to talk to or look to for advice. But I suppose that is why we have such good national friends.

Bonding is the factor that makes it possible for the newcomer to belong to "such good national friends." Of course there will be stressful situations, but the bonded newcomer, experiencing the wonder of close relationships, is able to derive support from the network of the local friendships he has developed. This in turn facilitates the acquisition of the insiders' ways and gives a sense of feeling at home. The one who feels at home may feel discouraged or even melancholy for a time and some cultural stress is to be expected, but it may not be necessary to experience culture shock. Culture shock, like severe postpartum blues, may be a problem of the structure more than a problem of individuals.

It is significant to note that the new Muslim converts mentioned in the letter above are the result of the ministry of relative newcomers. At a time when other missionaries might typically be experiencing the cushioning and isolation of a language school, those who are bonded and carrying out their language learning in the context of relationships in the new community also have the opportunity to pursue the development of their new ministry from the earliest days of language learning. A few years ago the authors supervised the initial language learning for a team of eleven newcomers in Bolivia. We published an article describing that project, in the April, 1978, *Evangelical Missions Quarterly*:

> ...Over 30 people came to know Christ as a result of the involve-

ment ministry that these new language learners were able to develop during those (first) three months. Many of these were either members of families with whom we were living, or were on a route of regular listeners. In both cases, as a result of the personal relationships that they had developed, they were able to follow up and disciple the new believers. Little wonder that this was a fulfilling experience for these new language learners. (pg. 103)

Insights gained through relationships can help to ensure, right from the beginning, that the wheels of ministry are not only turning but that they are on the ground and moving in a direction that makes sense to the local people.

Bonding and effective interpersonal ministry are realistic even for short-termers, and should be encouraged and facilitated. (The rapid international expansion of Mormonism is virtually all being carried out by short-termers, most of whom immediately move in with a local family and become belongers in the community. We were recently told by a Cantonese man from Hong Kong that the missionaries there who have learned the language best are Mormons!)

Only a minimum of the target language is needed to initiate bonding relationships. For example, we recently received a letter with the following comment: "The best thing that happened to me was on the first day when you challenged us to take the little we knew how to say and go talk with fifty people. I didn't talk with fifty, I only talked with forty-four. But I *did* talk with forty-four." (The "text" she was able to say that first day was limited to a greeting and an expression of her desire to learn the language; then she could tell people that she didn't know how to say any more but she would see them again. She then closed with a thank you and a leave-taking.) The ice was broken on her very first day and, from then on, she was able to begin to feel at home in her new community.

Having local friendships is essential for feeling at home. A report developed by a mission for whom we recently consulted on a language learning project compared the 18 maximally-involved learners with a control group of missionaries who had been through language school. The report revealed that the individuals of the control group (the resident missionaries) each had an average of one close national friend, while each of the learners—after only eleven weeks—had a minimum of 15 close local friendships. Since each learner had contacts with dozens of local people, there were at least 1000 nationals who had positive experiences with the learners during the weeks of the project. The report continued: "Who knows how all of this low-level public relations will ultimately benefit (the mission); it is highly improbable that it will be detrimental. 'Maximum involvement' language learning is where it's at."

Language acquisition is essentially a social activity, not an academic one. As a result, gaining proficiency in the language is normal for the person who is deeply contexted and has his sense of belonging in the new society. But language study will often be a burden and frustration for the one who is bonded to other foreign missionaries.

It is therefore important to facilitate an opportunity for new missionaries to become bonded with (and hence belongers in) their new community. New missionaries should be challenged with the bonding objective and prepared to respond to the opportunity to become a belonger.

Preparation should include an orientation to the importance of bonding, with a commitment to do so. A few sentences of the new language that will be helpful for entry purposes could be learned. Also, skills should be developed in how to carry on language learning in the context of community relationships. [A recent study by Stephen M. Echerd (an in-house mission report, p. 3) included a comparison between learners that had been trained in advance and others who developed skills after arriving in the country: "Those in the group who had previous exposure to *LAMP (Language Acquisition Made Practical)* made 11.78 time units of progress compared to 5.82 time units of those who had no previous exposure—more than double!"]

Then, most important, from his first day he should be encouraged to totally immerse himself in the life of the new community. He should be permitted to choose to remain in isolation from other missionaries for his first few months. He should seek to worship with the people, away from churches where missionaries lead or congregate. (Our observation is that experienced but non-bonded missionaries can be a primary obstacle to the new missionary who wishes to pursue the bonding goals. We have therefore occasionally recommended that a new missionary arrive about three weeks before the other missionaries expect him.)

If a newcomer is going to successfully establish himself as a belonger, live with a local family and learn from relationships on the streets, a prior decision and commitment to do so is essential. Without such a prior commitment it doesn't happen.

When we have accompanied missionary learners at the time of their entry into other countries we have found that a prior preparation of perspectives and expectations is helpful. We therefore expect all participants in projects we supervise to meet four conditions:

1) Be willing to live with a local family,

2) Limit personal belongings to 20 kilos,

3) Use only local public transportation, and

4) Expect to carry out language learning in the context of relationships that the learner himself is responsible to develop and maintain.

A willingness to accept these conditions tells a lot about an individual's attitude and flexibility.

With a prepared mentality, a newcomer is freed to creatively respond to the bonding and learning opportunities that surround him. We have seen that with a prior decision to do so, it is almost always possible to live with a local family (though non-bonded senior missionaries are typically pessimistic). Our experience is that the new missionary—whether single, married, or even with children—can successfully live with a local family immediately upon arrival. (Live-in options may be multiplied with sleeping bags.) We have seen newcomers find their own families by learning to say something like: "We want to learn your language. We hope to find a family to live with for about three months, and we will pay our expenses. Do you know of a possible family?" It would be unusual to say this 'text' to fifty people without getting at least some positive response—a mediator to help you or a family to live with.

We do not intend to imply that immediate and total immersion in a new culture is without risk. There is no other time with so much stress and danger as birth; and entry into a new culture has its own accompanying stress and risk factors. It is likely, however, that the stress and risk components themselves are essential to the formation of the unique chemistry that makes imprinting and bonding possible.

And there is another side to the risk question. If one doesn't take the initial risk and seek to establish himself comfortably with the new society, then he is opting for a long-term risk. It seems that one or the other cannot be avoided. The problem of missionary casualties suggests that there is a heavy price to be paid by those who fail to become belongers—probably half do not return for a second term, and some who stay despite ineffectiveness may be greater casualties than those who go back home.

Indeed it is not easy to live with a family, make friends with numerous strangers and learn the language, but neither is it easy to continue as a stranger without close friendships and without knowing cultural cues, living a foreign lifestyle with all the time, effort, and alienation that entails.

Once the new learner is securely established as a belonger he need not relate exclusively with the local people—he has not rejected either America nor Americans. (The bi-cultural apostle Paul ministered primarily to Gentiles, but when he was back among the believing Jews in Jerusalem (Acts 21) he did not reject them, but readily shaved his head, took a vow, and purified himself in readiness for a sacrifice.) The bonded missionary will probably continue to live and minister with the local people, but after the first few weeks it might not be detrimental from the bonding perspective for him to participate in occasional activities with other expatriates. It might even be helpful for him to spend Saturday evenings with other learners or a supervisor (and, of course, he may seek to listen to the Super Bowl with other Americans).

[The question has been raised: "What about missionaries who go to the field as a team?" A team is a team because its members share certain commitments. As a group they can decide that each will become bonded in the local culture, and they can encourage each other in the pursuit of that goal. For the initial months, a sharing time each week or so should be sufficient to maintain their commitments to each other.]

The concept of bonding implies a bi-cultural individual with a healthy self-image. Bonding and "going native" are not the same thing. "Going native" generally implies the rejection of one's first culture—a reaction which is seldom seen and which may not be possible for normal, emotionally stable individuals. Nor is being bi-cultural the same as being schizophrenic. The schizophrenic is a broken, fragmented self. But the bi-cultural person is developing a new self—a new personality.

The development of this new personality, adapted to the new culture, can be facilitated and symbolized by taking on a new, insider's name. (The Scriptures give various examples of individuals whose names were changed to symbolize changed roles and relationships.) The new personality, with its new name, does not have an established self-image to protect, and it can therefore be free to behave in uninhibited, creative, and child-like ways; it can make mistakes and try, try again. The newly developing personality enables the individual to feel at home in a second culture.

For the Christian missionary, the process of becoming bi-cultural can begin with the recognition that God in His sovereignty does not make mistakes in creating us with our first ethnicity. Yet in His sovereignty He may step in and touch us on the shoulder, as it were, and call us to go and be good news to a people of a different ethnicity.

To become a belonger in a legal sense, through formal immigration, might also be considered by some serious missionaries. Immigration need not imply a rejection of one's first country, but rather acceptance of a new one. Throughout history, people have immigrated for political, economic, religious and marriage reasons. The challenge of reaching a people for Christ should have the potential to similarly motivate some of Christ's bond-servants. The missionary's heavenly citizenship should lift him above the provincialism and ethnocentrism of a continuing allegiance to a country where, in obedience to Christ, he no longer lives. This "recovered pilgrim spirit" was the challenge presented by Joseph F. Conley in a recent *Regions Beyond* editorial (December 1979):

> For most North American missionaries, North America is *home* . That is where he goes when he's sick, and when the going gets too rough he can always return to blend in with the scenery. Tomorrow the quick retreat may be cut off. We may be forced to relive those days when missionaries went abroad, never expecting to return. Many governments which refuse entry to missionary expatriates, hold the door open to naturalized citizens of colonizing communities. The Moravians led the way in this as they set up Christians colonies around the world.

> Surrender of treasured U.S. or Canadian citizenship admittedly calls for a rare variety of commitment. But is that unthinkable? To such our Lord's words will find new and glowing exegesis, "He that hath forsaken lands,...for My sake...shall receive an hundred-fold and shall inherit everlasting life."

Belated Bonding

Can a missionary who has lived overseas for a time without becoming a belonger and without learning the language very well change his course? Is bonding possible after the first critical months have passed? In the past decade our work has carried us to almost seventy countries, giving us opportunity to observe missionary activity in many places. Only a small percentage of these missionaries manifest the kinds of relationships with local people that would demonstrate that bonding had occurred. It is not too difficult to tell the difference—the bonded missionaries are typically the ones who feel that even their social needs are fulfilled in their relationships with local people.

"Happiness is belonging, not belongings." Yet the lifestyle of the majority of Western missionaries is a major deterrent to bonding. It is hard to devote time to pursuing the meaningful relationships with local people when concerned about getting barrels of stuff through customs and unpacked and settled. This sense of belonging to one's belongings is a bonding of the worse kind—bondage. Unfortunately, it is a subtle bondage that is difficult to throw off. "When the farmer has got his house, he may not be the richer but the poorer for it, and it be the house that has got him...a man is rich in proportion to the number of things which he can afford to let alone." (Thoreau, *Walden*)

Is it possible for an established non-bonded missionary to experience a belated bonding so that his life and ministry are then characterized by a sense of belonging with local people? The answer must be yes because it is a normal human process to establish belonging relationships. But we must confess that we have seldom seen overseas Americans shift their sense of belonging for their expatriate community to the people of the local culture.

Yet we believe that potential missionary effectiveness is so greatly affected by the bonding factor and by being truly bilingual and bicultural that the issue must be pursued. Again we seek an analogy with another divinely ordained relationship of intimacy—the marriage relationship. This model may be helpful, for in it adult participants achieve a belonging relationship with each other. In our culture, readiness for bonding is established during courtship; with the honeymoon, the bonding is culminated.

The analogy would suggest that an established but non-bonded missionary might release the potential of his ministry with steps paralleling the marriage model: acknowledge the potential and desirability of a belonging relationship with the local people; implement a decision to make such a commitment to the people; then set a date and inform the missionary community of the scope and implications of the potential change in his relationships. In all cultures, times of major life transition, like puberty, graduation, marriage and death, can be facilitated through festivities at the peak of emotion. The festival itself can serve to intensify the emotion which in turn can help facilitate the transition.

The commitment to belatedly join a new community might successfully be initiated by a festive transition celebration. When the date arrives, the honeymoon analogy suggests the necessity of becoming established with the local people by moving in with a local family (maybe in another community) and adopting a Learner role.

The mutual ownership of assets by a married couple might suggest the need to heed Jesus' instructions to the rich young ruler. The minimum would seem to be a need for a means of reciprocity with the people. Bonding, like marriage, implies a radical adjustment of lifestyle.

The Dilemma of the Bonded Missionary

It must be pointed out that the new missionary who pursues the bonding objective may find himself in a dilemma: his non-bonded colleagues and superiors may be threatened by the initiative he takes in pursuing his ministry through a lifestyle of relationships with the local people. His total involvement lifestyle of ministry may contrast all too sharply with the foray ventures of other missionaries.

A few years ago we became friends with an African while he was in North America. We later had opportunity to visit him on the mission station where he worked in Kenya. In the course of our conversation he related a dilemma he was experiencing. A new missionary had arrived a few months earlier who loved the Kenyans and demonstrated it by his lifestyle. Our friend liked the new missionary and wanted to encourage him in his identification with Kenyans, but he was afraid to do so. Over the years he had observed that the missionaries who had not learned Swahili or the tribal language—and hence did not relate to the Africans—were the ones who were then advanced to administrative positions on the station and in the mission. It was his experience that new missionaries who loved Kenyans became an unacceptable threat to these administrators and did not last; and he did not want to hasten the termination of a man whose missionary approach he valued.

The bonded missionary is invariably viewed with suspicion by non-bonded colleagues. At best they may think him to be a maverick, at worst a traitor. We know those who have even been accused of losing their faith because of their efforts to make sense to the local people.

Time and again we have received feedback from new missionaries describing the resistance they experience in their efforts toward a total lifestyle approach to language learning and ministry. This resistance is expressed by other missionaries in at least four ways: rejection, jealousy, guilt and fear.

> Rejection may result if the bonding behavior and motives of the newcomer are misunderstood or misinterpreted. The missionary community may feel that the newcomer has rejected them. But what he has rejected is the foray approach.

> Jealousy can arise if an established missionary observes that the newcomer has many close friendships with local people while he doesn't.

> Guilt may occur if an established missionary recognizes that the newcomer's bonding approach may have more potential for effectiveness, particularly if he feels that he, too, should become a belonger, yet remains unable to make such a commitment.

> Fear may surface if it appears that familiar, secure ways are going to be complicated by this new mentality. Change from traditional ways in which missionaries relate to nationals can be viewed as a movement into slippery, uncharted areas. Change implies risk and potential failure. Missionaries may also fear the newcomer's well-being, fearing that his involvement with the people could cause him to lose the theological distinctives of their group, his own orthodoxy, or even his faith. There may be fear that he will go too far or lose his cultural identity.

Some of their fears may come true. The bonded newcomer could cause raised eyebrows in mission circles through his nonconformity. But it should be pointed out that through his bonding, and even his nonconformity, this bicultural missionary has the potential of an added dimension of cultural sensitivity. It could be the very thing that might enable him to discover a redemptive analogy within the culture and pursue its implications (see Don Richardson's *Peace Child*). His ability to gain an insider's perspective might also be a means of reducing the likelihood of syncretism among new believers.

Pioneer missionaries on most fields may have established belonging relationships with the people, but too often those who came after them have not followed their example and now there are few models for young missionaries to follow. If the concept of bonding has validity for the present-day missionary task, then it seems that established missions must find ways to affirm and encourage newcomers who choose to become bonded with the local people.

The quality of relationships between new missionaries and their senior colleagues is, of course, a primary concern for all parties involved. Open lines of communication are needed. Maybe discussion about the bonding issue could give potential missionaries information that would be helpful in developing these relationships, or even in selecting a missionary agency. Prospective missionaries might initiate this interaction with both the home and field leadership of missions they consider joining. The new missionary must communicate his concerns in an attitude of love, and refrain from condemning or being judgmental of his predecessors who have ministered faithfully according to insights available to them. The fact is that he would have probably done things in much the same way. But new options are now open to him due to fresh insights and perspectives. A possible approach might be for him to request permission to personally experiment with a bonding strategy.

It could be that individuals who desire to become belongers within a new community might best be able to maximize their missionary potential by volunteering for service among an unreached, or hidden, people group rather than where missions have already established traditions of non-involvement. Indeed, the present practice of many established missions in regard to bonding could be the stimulus that might propel a significant number of young North American missionaries into the thousands of remaining groups of unreached peoples.

Conclusion

In summary, we have observed that the newcomer goes through a critical time for establishing his sense of identity and belonging during his first few weeks in a new country. If he becomes a belonger with expatriates he may always remain a foreigner and outsider. But at this crucial time he has the unique opportunity to establish himself as a belonger with insiders, in order to live and learn and minister within their social context.

The bonded missionary, because he is a belonger, has the opportunity to gain an empathetic understanding of insiders' ways, their feelings, desires, attitudes and fears. He can listen with sensitivity to their otherwise hidden values, concerns and motives. Thus he can acquire insights and adopt habits of lifestyle and ministry that will enable him to be good news from the perspective of local people in order to draw them into a belonging relationship with God.

Bonding is therefore a perspective many missionaries may choose to value and a goal they may choose to pursue. Making this kind of significant cultural adjustment is not easy but it is possible, especially if initiated at the critical time for bonding.

Study Questions

1. Explain why timing is critical in bonding.

2. "Language acquisition is essentially a social activity, not an academic one." Describe the relationship between bonding and language acquisition.

3. What connections do the Brewsters make between bonding and the discovery of redemptive analogies? Between bonding and pioneer missions?

4. How can language learning be considered as a ministry?

15

Identification in the Missionary Task

William D. Reyburn

A steady downpour of rain had been falling from late afternoon until long after dark. A small donkey followed by a pair of men slowly made its way down the slippery sides of the muddy descent which wound into the sleepy town of Baños, high in the Ecuadorean Andes. No one appeared to pay any attention as the two dark figures halted their burro before a shabby Indian hostel. The taller of the two men stepped inside the doorway where a group of men sat at a small table drinking *chicha* by candle light. No sooner had the stranger entered the room than a voice from behind the bar called out, *"Buenas noches, meester."* The man in the rain-soaked poncho turned quickly to see a fat-faced woman standing half concealed behind the counter. *"Buenas noches, señora,"* he replied, lifting his hat slightly. Following a short exchange of conversation the man and barmaid reappeared outside and led the donkey through a small gate to a mud stable. The two men removed their load and carried it to a stall-like room beside the stable where they were to spend the night.

I sat down on the straw on the floor and began pulling off my wet clothes. I kept hearing the word *meester* which I had come to dislike intensely. Why had that funny little woman there in the semi-darkness of the room addressed me as *meester*? I looked at my clothes. My hat was that of the poorest *cholo* in Ecuador. My pants were nothing more than a mass of patches held together by still more patches. On my dirty mud-stained feet I wore a pair of rubber tire *alpargatas* the same as any Indian or *cholo* wore. My red poncho was not from the high class Otavalo weavers. It was a poor man's poncho made in Salcedo. It had no fancy tassels and in true *cholo* fashion there were bits of straw dangling from its lower edge, showing that I was a man who slept with his burro on the road. But why then did she call me *meester*, a term reserved for Americans and Europeans? At least she could have addressed me as *señor*, but no, it had to be *meester*. I felt as

William D. Reyburn has served the United Bible Societies as a translations consultant in South and Central America, Africa, Europe, and the Middle East. During 1968-72 he served as translations coordinator of the UBS based in London, England. Used with permission of the William Carey Library Publishers, P. O. Box 40129, Pasadena, CA 91114. *Readings in Missionary Anthropology II*, edited by William A. Smalley, 1978.

though my carefully devised disguise had been stripped from me with the mention of that word. I kept hashing it over and over in my mind. It wasn't because she detected a foreign accent, because I had not as yet opened my mouth. I turned to my Quechua Indian companion, old Carlos Bawa of Lake Colta. "Carlos, the lady knew I am a *meester*. How do you think she knew, Carlitos?"

My friend sat huddled in the corner of the room with his legs and arms tucked under his two ponchos. "I don't know, *patroncito*." Looking up quickly at Carlos I said, "Carlos, for three days I have been asking you not to call me *patroncito*. If you call me that people will know I am not a *cholo*." Carlos flicked a finger out from under the collar of his woolen poncho and touching his hat brim submissively replied, "I keep forgetting, *meestercito*."

Disgusted and aching in my rain-soaked skin I felt like the fool I must have appeared. I sat quietly watching the candle flicker as Carlos dozed off to sleep in his corner. I kept seeing the faces of people along the road we had walked for the past three days. Then I would see the face of this woman in Baños who had robbed me of what seemed like a perfect disguise. I wondered then if perhaps I hadn't been taken for a European even earlier. I was hurt, disappointed, disillusioned, and to make things worse I was dreadfully hungry. Reaching into our packsack I pulled out the bag of *machica* flour my wife had prepared for us, poured in some water and stirred the brown sugar and barley mixture with my finger and gulped it down. The rain was letting up now and from a hole in the upper corner of the room I could see the clouds drifting across the sky in the light of the moon. A guitar was strumming softly out in the street and in the stall next to us a half dozen Indians had just returned from the stable and were discussing the events of their day's journey.

Blowing out the candle I leaned up against the rough plank wall and listened to their conversation, then eventually fell asleep. It was some hours later when I was startled awake from the noise of our door creaking open. I got to my feet quickly and jumped behind the opening door waiting to see what was going to happen. The door quietly closed and I heard old Carlos groan as he settled down onto his mat to sleep. Carlos was returning, having gone out to relieve himself. My companion had been warning me for several days that Indians often rob each other and I should always sleep lightly. It was quiet now, deathly silent. I had no idea what time it may have been, as a watch was not suitable for my *cholo* garb. I lay on the floor thinking about the meaning of identification. I asked myself again and again what it meant to be identified with this old Quechua Indian who was so far removed from the real world in which I lived.

I was traveling the Indian markets of the Ecuadorean Andes in order to know what really lay hidden in the hearts of these Quechua Indians and Spanish-speaking *cholos*. What was the real longing in their hearts that could be touched? I wanted to know what it was that drunkenness seemed to satisfy. Was the Quechua Indian really the sullen withdrawn personality that he appeared to be before his *patrón*? Was he so adjustable to life conditions that his attitude could incorporate most any conflict without upsetting him seriously? Was he really a good Catholic, a pagan, or what kind of a combination? Why underneath was he so opposed to outward change? What was he talking about and worrying over when he settled down at night in the security of his own little group? I was after the roots that lay behind the outward symbols which could respond to the claims of Christ. The answer to questions like these would form the basis for a missionary theology, a relevant communication to these people's lives. I could see no purpose in putting the Christian proposition before a man unless it was made in such a way that it forced him to struggle with it in terms of surrender to the ultimate and most basic demand that could be placed upon him. In order to know what had to be addressed to the depths of his being I had to wade down to it through what I was convinced were only outward displays of a deeper need in his heart.

A major aspect of the missionary task is the search for what in German is called *der Anknüpfungspunkt*, connection or point of contact. The proclamation of the gospel aside from such a contact point is a proclamation which skirts missionary responsibility. This is simply the process in which the one who proclaims the good news must make every effort to get into touch with his listener. Man's heart is not a clean slate that the gospel comes and writes upon for the first time. It is a complex which has been scrawled upon and deeply engraved from birth to death. The making of a believer always begins with an unbeliever. Clearly this is the job of the Holy Spirit. However this does not remove man from his position of responsibility. It is man in his rational hearing and understanding that is awakened to belief. It is the conquering of man's basic deceit that allows the Holy Spirit to lay claim to him and to make of him a new creature. A man must be aware that he stands in defiance of God's call before he can be apprehended by God's love. Before an enemy can be taken captive he must stand in the position of an enemy.

The Forms of Identification

Missionary identification may take on many different forms. It may be romantic or it may be dull. It may be convincing or it may appear as a sham. The central point is that identification is not an end in itself. It is the road to the task of gospel proclamation. Likewise the heart of the controversial matter of missionary identification is not how far one can go but rather what one does with the fruits of identification. Going native is no special virtue. Many missionaries in the humdrum of their daily routine about a school or hospital have awakened men's hearts to the claim of the gospel.

Some so-called identification is misoriented and tends to create the impression that living in a native village or learning the native tongue is automatically the "open sesame" of the native's heart. It is not the sheer quantity of identification that counts; it is rather the purposeful quality that comprehends man as a responsible being seeking to be in touch with his reality. The limitations for knowing what is this contacted reality are great. The practical obstacles for missionary identification are many. In the pages that follow we shall attempt to outline some of these as we have lived in them and to evaluate the effects of the lack of missionary identification and participation.

Strength of Unconscious Habit

Without doubt the nature of the obstacle to identification is the fact that one has so well learned one's own way of life that he practices it for the most part without conscious reflection. In the case described above the old Quechua Indian Carlos Bawa, the donkey and I had been traveling across the plateau of the Andes spending the days in the markets and the nights cramped into tiny quarters available to itinerant Indians and *cholos* for approximately 10 cents U.S. We had made our way from Riobamba to Baños, a three-day trek by road, and no one except an occasional dog appeared to see that all was not quite normal. It was not until stepping into the candle-lit room of the inn at Baños that I was taken for a foreigner (at least it so appeared). I suspect that it bothered me a great deal because I had created the illusion for a few days that I was finally on the inside of the Indian-*cholo* world looking about and not in the least conspicuous about it. When the innkeeper addressed me as *meester* I had the shock of being rudely dumped outside the little world where I thought I had at last gained a firm entrance.

The following morning I went to the lady innkeeper and sat down at the bar. "Now, tell me, *señora*," I began, "how did you know I was a *meester* and not a local *señor* or a *cholo* from Riobamba?" The fat little lady's eyes sparkled as she laughed an embarrassed giggle. "I don't know for sure," she replied. I insisted she try to give me the answer, for I was thoroughly confused over it all. I went on. "Now suppose you were a detective, *señora*, and you were told to catch a European man dressed like a poor *cholo* merchant. How would you recognize him if he came into your inn?" She scratched her head and leaned forward over the counter. "Walk outside and come back in like you did last night." I picked up my old hat, pulled it low on my head, and made for the door. Before I reached the street she called out, "Wait, *señor*, I know now what it is." I stopped and turned around. "It's the way you walk." She broke into a hearty laugh at this point and said, "I never saw anyone around here who walks like that. You Europeans swing your arms like you never carried a load on your back." I thanked the good lady for her lesson in posture and went out in the street to study how the local people walked. Sure enough the steps were short and choppy, the trunk leaning forward slightly from the hips and the arms scarcely moving under their huge ponchos.

Knowing that the squatting position with the poncho draped from ears to the hidden feet was more natural I squatted on the street corner near a group of Indians and listened to them chat. They continued with their conversation and paid no attention to my presence. Two missionaries whom I knew very well emerged from a hotel doorway nearby. I watched them as they swung their cameras about their shoulders and discussed the problem of overexposure in the tricky Andean sunlight. A ragged *cholo* boy sitting beside me scrambled to his feet, picked up his shoe shine box and approached the pair. He was rebuffed by their nonchalant shaking of the head. As they continued to survey the brilliant market place for pictures the shoe-shine boy returned to his spot beside me. Sitting down he mumbled, "The *señores* who own shoes ought to keep them shined." I leaned toward the boy and beckoned for his ear. He bent over his shoe box as I whispered to him. The boy then jumped back to his feet and started after the pair who were crossing the street. On the other side they stopped and turned to him as he said, "The evangelicals are not respected here unless we see their shoes are shined." One man lifted a foot and rubbed his shoe on his pants cuff, while the other settled down for a toothbrush, spit and polish shine.

I arose, passed within three feet of my friends and took up a listening post in the heart of the busy market where I sat until my legs began to ache. As I got up to my feet I yawned and stretched, and as I began to walk away I noticed I had drawn the attention of those sitting about me. Again I had behaved in a way that felt so natural but in a way which was not like the local folks do. In front of me an old woman dropped a bag of salt. I unthinkingly reached down to help her, and it was only by a bit of providential intervention that I was saved from being hauled off to jail for attempting to steal.

This extremity of identification or disguise may appear as one way of overdoing a good thing. However, only a missionary among the withdrawn highland Quechuas can really appreciate how difficult it is to talk with these people in a situation of equality. I simply could not accept the Quechua's response as being valid and representing his real self as long as he was talking to the *patrón*. I wanted to hear him without a *patrón* present and I wanted to be addressed stripped of that feudal role which I was sure completely colored our relationship. I found that the submissive, sluggish Indian whom I had known in my role of *patrón* became a scheming, quick-witted person who could be extremely friendly, helpful or cruel depending upon the situation.

Limits of Identification

Perhaps the most outstanding example in which I was reminded of the limitations of identification occurred while we were living in a mud-and-thatch hut near Tabacundo, Ecuador. We had moved into a small scattered farming settlement near the Pisque river about a kilometer from the United Andean Mission for whom we were making a study. My wife and I had agreed that if we were to accomplish anything at the U.A.M. we would have to settle among the people and somehow get them to accept us or reject us. We were accepted eventually but always with reservations. We wore nothing but Indian clothes and ate nothing but Indian food. We had no furniture except a bed made of century plant stalks covered with a woven mat exactly as in all the Indian houses. In fact, because we had no agricultural equipment, weaving loom, or granary, our one-room house was by far the most empty in the vicinity. In spite of this material reduction to the zero point the men addressed me as *patroncito*. When I objected that I was not a *patrón* because I owned no land they reminded me that I wore leather shoes. I quickly exchanged these for a pair of local made *alpargatas* which have a hemp fiber sole and a woven cotton upper. After a time had passed I noticed that merely changing my footwear had not in the least gotten rid of the appellation of *patroncito*. When I asked again, the men replied that I associated with the Spanish townspeople from Tabacundo. In so doing I was obviously identifying myself with the *patrón* class. I made every effort for a period to avoid the townspeople but the term *patroncito* seemed to be as permanently fixed as it was the day we moved into the community.

The men had been required by the local commissioner to repair an impassable road connecting the community and Tabacundo. I joined in this work with the Indians until it was completed two months later. My hands had become hard and calloused. One day I proudly showed my calloused hands to a group of men while they were finishing the last of a jar of fermented *chica*. "Now, you can't say I don't work with you. Why do you still call me *patroncito*?" This time the truth was near the surface, forced there by uninhibited alcoholic replies. Vicente Cuzco, a leader in the group, stepped up and put his arm around my shoulder and whispered to me. "We call you *patroncito* because you weren't born of an Indian mother." I needed no further explanation.

Ownership of a Gun

Living in an African village caused us to become aware of the effect of other formative attitudes in our backgrounds. One of these in particular is the idea of personal ownership. While living in the south Cameroun village of Aloum among the Bulu in order to learn the language, we had been received from the first day with intense reception and hospitality. We were given Bulu family names; the village danced for several nights and we were loaded with gifts of a goat and all kinds of tropical foods.

We had been invited to live in Aloum and we were not fully prepared psychologically to understand how such an adoption was conceived within Bulu thinking. Slowly we came to learn that our possessions were no longer private property but were to be available for the collective use of the sub-clan where we had been adopted. We were able to adjust to this way of doing because we had about the same material status as the others in the village. Their demands upon our things were not as great as their generous hospitality with which they provided nearly all of our food.

Then one night I caught a new vision of the implication of our relation to the people of Aloum. A stranger had appeared in the village and we learned that Aloum was the home of his mother's brother. It was the case of the nephew in the town of his maternal uncle, a most interesting social relationship in the patrilineal societies in Africa. After dark when the leading men in the village had gathered in the men's club house, I drifted over and sat down among them to listen to their conversations. The fires on the floor threw shadows which appeared to dance up and down on the mud walls.

Finally silence fell over their conversations and the chief of the village arose and began to speak in very hushed tones. Several young men arose from their positions by the fires and moved outside to take up a listening post to make sure that no uninvited persons would overhear the development of these important events. The chief spoke of the welcome of his nephew into his village and guaranteed him a safe sojourn while he was there. After these introductory formalities were finished the chief began to extol his nephew as a great elephant hunter. I was still totally ignorant of how all this affected me.

I listed as he eulogized his nephew's virtue as a skilled hunter. After the chief finished another elder arose and continued to cite cases in the nephew's life in which he had displayed great bravery in the face of the dangers of the jungles. One after another repeated these stories until the chief again stood to his feet. I could see the whites of his eyes which were aimed at me. The fire caused little shadows to run back and forth on his dark face and body. "Obam Nna," he addressed me. A broad smile exposed a gleaming set of teeth. "We are going to present our gun to my nephew now. Go get it."

I hesitated a brief moment but then arose and crossed the moonlit courtyard to our thatch-covered house where Marie and some village women sat talking. I kept hearing in my ears: "We are going to present *our* gun...our gun..." Almost as if it were a broken record stuck on the plural possessive pronoun. It kept repeating in my ears, "...*ngale jangan...ngale jangan....*" Before I reached the house I had thought of half a dozen very good reasons why I should say no. However I got the gun and some shells and started back to the club house. As I re-entered the room I caught again the sense of the world of Obam Nna. If I were to be Obam Nna I should have to cease to be William Reyburn. In order to be Obam Nna I had to crucify William Reyburn nearly every day. In the world of Obam Nna I no longer owned the gun as in the world of William Reyburn. I handed the gun to the chief and, although he didn't know it, along with it went the surrender of a very stingy idea of private ownership.

Symbolic Value of Food

Another problem in village participation is the matter of food and water. However, this is not the problem most people think it is. We found while living in Paris that our French friends were often scandalized at the things which we ate. One of the most offensive of these was cheese with pie. I have seen Frenchmen grimace as if in agony upon seeing us combine these two foods.

I have stayed among the Kaka tribe on the open grasslands of the eastern Cameroun, and have made studies among them. The life of these people is quite different from the jungle Bulu of the south. Life on the savanna is more rigorous and results in a different adjustment to natural conditions. Food is much less abundant and cassava is the main staple. Unlike the Bulu who have adopted many European ways the Kaka are more under the influences of Islam which filter down from their cattle-raising Fulani neighbors to the north.

I had gone into the village of Lolo to carry out some studies relative to the translation of the book of Acts and had taken no European food, determined to find what the effects of an all-Kaka diet would be. I attempted to drink only boiled water, but often this was entirely impossible. I found that the simple mixture of cassava flour and hot water to form a mush was an excellent sustaining diet. On one occasion over a period of six weeks on this diet I lost no weight, had no diarrhea, and suffered no other ill effects. All of this food was prepared by village women and I usually ate on the ground with the men wherever I happened to be when a woman would serve food. On several occasions when I was not in the right place at the right time it meant going to bed with an empty stomach. I carefully avoided asking any woman to prepare food especially for me, as this had a sexual connotation which I did not care to provoke.

Once I had been talking most of the afternoon with a group of Kaka men and boys about foods people eat the world over. One of the young men got his Bulu Bible and read from the 10th chapter of Acts the vision of Peter who was instructed to kill and eat "all manner of four-footed beasts of the earth, and wild beasts, and creeping things, and fowls of the air." This young Kaka who had been a short while at a mission school said, "The Hausa people don't believe this because they won't eat pigs. Missionaries, we think don't believe this because they don't eat some of our foods either." I quite confidently assured him that a missionary would eat anything he does.

That evening I was called to the young man's father's doorway, where the old man sat on the ground in the dirt. In front of him were two clean white enamel pans covered by lids. He looked up at me and motioned for me to sit. His wife brought a gourd of water which she poured as we washed our hands. Then flicking wet fingers in the air to dry them a bit, the old man lifted the lid from the one pan. Steam arose from a neatly rounded mass of cassava mush. Then he lifted the lid from the other pan. I caught a glimpse of its contents. Then my eyes lifted and met the unsmiling stare of the young man who had read about the vision of Peter earlier in the afternoon. The pan was filled with singed caterpillars. I swallowed hard, thinking that now I either swallowed these caterpillars, or I swallowed my words and thereby proved again that Europeans have merely adapted Christianity to fit their own selfish way of life. I waited as my host scooped his shovel-like fingers deep into the mush, then with a ball of the stuff he pressed it gently into the caterpillar pan. As he lifted it to his open mouth I saw the burned and fuzzy creatures, some smashed into the mush and other dangling loose, enter between his teeth.

My host had proven the safety of his food by taking the first portion. This was the guarantee that he was not feeding me poison. I plunged my fingers into the mush but my eyes were fixed on the caterpillars. I wondered what the sensation in the mouth was going to be. I quickly scooped up some of the creeping things and plopped the mass into my mouth. As I bit down the soft insides burst open and to my surprise I tasted a salty meat-like flavor which seemed to give the insipid cassava mush the ingredient that was missing

We sat silently eating. There is no time for conversation at the Kaka "table" for as soon as the owner has had his first bite male hands appear from every direction and the contents are gone. As we sat eating quickly the old man's three wives with their daughters came and stood watching us from their kitchen doorways. They held their hands up and whispered busily back and forth "White man Kaka is eating caterpillars. He really has a black heart." The pans were emptied. Each one took a mouthful of water, rinsed his mouth and spat the water to one side, belched loudly, said "Thank you, Ndjambie" (God), arose and departed into the rays of the brilliant setting sun. My notes on that night contain this one line: "An emptied pan of caterpillars is more convincing than all the empty metaphors of love which missionaries are prone to expend on the heathen."

Ideological Insulation

There are other obstacles to missionary participation in native life which arise from background as well as local Christian tradition. It does not take a folk or primitive people long to size up the distance which separates themselves from the missionary. In some cases this distance is negligible but in others it is the separation between different worlds. Missionaries with pietistic backgrounds are prepared to suspect that everything the local people do is bad and that therefore, in order to save them, they must pull them out and set up another kind of life opposed to the original one. This process seldom if ever works, and when it does the result is the creation of a society which consists of converted souls, but no converted life. The missionary under these circumstances takes the path of least resistance, keeps himself untouched by the world and of course does not get into touch with the world in order to save it.

It is not surprising to find that American missionaries make a tradition of this mistake more than do their European colleagues. The missionary who has been brought up in a closed environment in his home town, has gone away to a church college, and proceeded then to a seminary, is usually still blissfully ignorant of the very life of his own country. He carries this wall of insulation from the world to the mission field and surreptitiously invites anyone who dares to slip inside with him. For this poor soul political questions are dangerous, sex is evil, and academic thought is suspect. This is the Christian expression which drives the man to hard work and no play because again relaxation is an evil pulling of the world from which he must remain isolated at all costs.

So extreme does this loss of touch with the world become that missions have been guilty of making demands on people that tend to separate them from any hope of living the Christian witness among their own people. An outstanding missionary, who spent fifteen years in the French Cameroun and was awarded the French Legion of Honor for his contribution as director of an industrial school, remarked, "When I was getting ready to go to Africa, a dear old Christian woman said, 'Well, whatever you do, Mr. C, get those black people to wear shoes.'"

The children of catechists in one mission in Central Africa are required by the mission rules to wear clothes. The fact that this puts them into a special socio-economic class where they demand more and more money to buy clothes and live up to the class they have been forced into appears to the mission as wanton

materialism. In another mission in French Equatorial Africa all catechists were required recently to sign a statement that if they joined a political party they would lose their jobs. These same missionaries most likely never voted themselves in an election and now they are asking their converts to take up the same ignorant attitude toward the State which they have.

It is little wonder therefore that the French administration conceives of much Protestant mission work in Africa as the attempt to form *un état dans l'état*, 'a state within a state.'

Freedom to Witness

The Christian church sealed off from the world becomes unintelligible to the world it attempts to reach. It is like the father who can never remember how to be a child and therefore is looked upon as a foreigner by his children. Missionary participation and identification are not produced by a study of anthropology but by being freed through the Spirit of the Lord to witness to the truth of the gospel in the world.

Christianity calls men into a brotherhood in Christ, but at the same time Christians often negate that call by separating mechanisms which run the gamut from food taboos to racial fear. The Christian gospel is foreign enough to the self-centeredness of man's view of the universe. However, before this misconception of the self can be corrected, there is a barrier that must be penetrated. In Christian terminology it is the cross which leads man from his walled-up self out into the freedom for which he was intended. There is yet another foreignness which must be overcome through sacrifice of one's own way of thinking and doing things. Christianity cannot be committed to one expression of civilization or culture. The missionary task is that of sacrifice. Not the sacrifice of leaving friends and comfortable situations at home, but the sacrifice of reexamining one's own cultural assumptions and becoming intelligible to a world where he must *not* assume that intelligibility is given.

A missionary theology asks this question: "At what points in this man's heart does the Holy Spirit challenge him to surrender?" The missionary task is to ferret out this point of contact through identification with him. The basis of missionary identification is not to make the "native" feel more at home around a foreigner nor to ease the materialistic conscience of the missionary but to create a *communication* and a *communion* where together they seek out what Saint Paul in II Corinthians 10:5 calls the "arguments and obstacles"—"We destroy arguments and every proud obstacle to the knowledge of God, and take every thought captive to obey Christ." This is the basis for a missionary science, the Biblical foundation of a missionary theology and the *raison d'être* of the missionary calling in which one seeks, even in the face of profound limitations, to identify oneself in the creation of new creatures in a regenerate communion.

C—130 IDENTIFICATION IN THE MISSIONARY TASK

Study Questions

1. Explain both the necessity and the limits of identification for missionary communication.

2. "An emptied pan of caterpillars is more convincing than all the empty metaphors of love which missionaries are prone to expend on the heathen." Can you suggest other "caterpillar" tests that might confront the Western missionary?

16

God's Communicator in the 90's

Phil Parshall

It is a great calling and privilege to be a missionary. It is my joy to have rubbed shoulders with hundreds of foreign missionaries over the past three decades. By and large, they impress me very positively.

The missionary calling has unique features. The missionary must be reasonably well-educated, cross geographical boundaries, leave loved ones behind, sacrifice financially (though not always), adjust to another language and culture, and work on a closely-knit team. At the same time, missionaries must open themselves to criticism, both from friend and foe. They must be willing to reevaluate sacrosanct methodology. "Change" must not be a dreaded word, as we consider the qualifications and methods of missionaries for the coming decade. I speak from a heart of love and concern—from within the camp.

Dr. Saeed Khan Kurdistani was an outstanding Iranian Christian who died in 1942. In 1960, a man went to the area where Dr. Saeed had lived and ministered. An aged man of the community was asked by the visitor if he had known Dr. Saeed. The elderly man caught his breath and whispered: "Dr. Saeed was Christ himself!" Reverently, it can be said that this is our goal. But as we head into the 1990's we need to take a hard look at such practical matters as missionary finances, housing, intellectual life and ministry with churches.

Finances

There is an overwhelming difference of opinion on this subject. Some feel it is imperative to "go native" and to denounce all who do not meet their standard. Others feel strongly that they must live on a western standard for the sake of their family's mental and physical health. They defend their position by saying the nationals will understand their needs. Between these two extremes will be found every conceivable view.

Phil Parshall is a missionary in the Philippines serving as Director of SIM's Asian Research Center. He has authored five books, the latest of which is *The Cross and the Crescent* (Tyndale House). Reprinted with permission from the October 1979 issue of *Evangelical Missions Quarterly*, published by Evangelical Missions Information Service, Box 794, Wheaton, Illinois 60187.

Many Third World countries are economically depressed. This fact sets the stage for the conflict between the living standard of the western missionary and the national. Chaeok Chun, a Korean missionary in Pakistan, comments on this tension. "I think it is significant that today's image of the Christian missionary endeavor from the Asian receptor's point of view is an image of comfort and privilege. Hence, Asians tended to reject the missionary and misunderstand his message." [1]

The Irish monks of the seventh and eighth centuries were well-known for their asceticism. Their entire outfit consisted of a pilgrim's staff, a wallet, a leather water bottle and some relics. When they received money from the wealthy, they quickly gave it away to the needy. [2] Is this a proper model for the contemporary missionary? In this vein, Dr. Donald McGavran suggested that "the missionary from affluent countries lives on a standard far higher than he needs to. What is called for—if we are to meet this problem head on—is an order of missionaries, celibate or married without children, who live in Bangladesh on three hundred rupees a month (*i.e.*, ten dollars). *But any such move is at present unthinkable, alas.*" [3]

I would, at the risk of being controversial, like to pull some thoughts together on this very important issue.

1. It *does* matter what nationals think about the financial profile of the missionary community. Generally, they are appalled at the gap between the living standard of themselves and the western missionary. If we turn away from this concern with indifference, we are in danger of being insensitive to Paul's clear teaching about being a stumbling block to others.

2. Singles and couples without children can more easily make the adjustment to a simple life style. This should be encouraged but not legislated.

3. Experimentation should be allowed. One couple with a newborn infant is living in a bamboo hut with a mud floor in a Muslim rural village. They should be supported, but at the same time, not made to feel embarrassment when at any time they feel withdrawal advisable.

4. Each family should be open before the Lord on this subject. They should prayerfully evaluate their own physical and emotional needs. The goal is to live as closely as possible to the style of life of their target people without adverse results to anyone in the family. Balance is a key word.

5. Often the missionary can reside in stark simplicity in a rural area and then take an occasional week-end trip to a nearby city for relaxation and necessary shopping. This accommodation to our cultural backgrounds is not, in my view, an act of hypocrisy. We must be realistic concerning our needs and various levels of capacity to endure deprivation within foreign culture.

6. It is permissible to consider this a moot issue with missionaries, but idle criticism, a judgmental attitude, and self-righteousness must be studiously avoided. Often, missionaries living in extreme poverty or those living in great affluence are the most opinionated and self-defensive. For the sake of unity in the body, it may be wise to avoid entering into heavy discussions with these particular missionaries on this subject.

Housing

The day of the "mission compound" is by no means over. These western enclaves are still found throughout the developing world. They are often misunderstood and, in some cases, despised by the nationals. A convert questioned their existence by asking, "Am I wrong if I say that mission bungalows are often a partition wall between the hearts of the people and the missionaries?" [4]

It is my personal conviction that remaining mission compounds should be dismantled. This would free the missionary to move into the community and share his incarnational testimony among them, rather than being shut off in a large plot of land that has a very negative appraisal in the minds of the people. It is preferable also for the Christians to scatter out among their non-Christian townspeople rather than live in a sealed-off community. Light must be diffused to be of any benefit. Our first five-year term living in a small town in Bangladesh was a great learning and sharing experience. Just outside the bedroom window of our rented home lived a Muslim lady who was separated from her husband. Her two young daughters lived with her. Quickly we became very intimate friends. The girls were always coming over to borrow a spice or an egg. We felt free to do the same. When the youngest daughter had a raging fever, we brought her over and nursed her. From our bedroom window, we learned more about Muslim culture than scores of books could ever have taught us. A mission compound experience would not have made such a life style and involvement in the community possible.

There needs to be some latitude as regards city, town or village life. The main concern is to relate to the group with whom one is working. Student work in a university area would demand facilities quite different from a rural village setting.

Intellectual Life

Missionary work has undergone a radical transformation since the end of the colonial era. New approaches and attitudes have been demanded. Pioneers like Dr. Donald McGavran have popularized the science of missiology. Hundreds of case studies and textbooks are now on the market that can be utilized as resource material. Outstanding graduate schools with mission studies include Fuller, Trinity, Columbia, Dallas, Wheaton and Asbury. Extension study for the missionary on the field is offered through Fuller, Columbia, and Wheaton. Journals like *Evangelical Missions Quarterly* and *Missiology* keep the missionary abreast of fast-breaking concepts and practical outreaches around the world.

One relevant bit of advice to missionaries is that they should "keep an open mind, realizing that times change and one must make adjustments. Tactics of ten years ago will not work and even those of five years ago are outdated." [5] It is always sad to see older missionaries become rutted and inflexible. Their orientation and allegiance to traditional methodology makes it seem to them to be almost a denial of truth to move carefully into new areas of sensitive experimentation. Younger missionaries arriving on the field become frustrated. Their ideas and zeal are often lost in a patronizing "Keep it under your hat for a few years. Experience will mellow you and mature your input." There must develop a fresh and non-threatening relationship between the senior and junior missionary. One adds experience and the other brings the latest in theory and enthusiasm. United, they are almost unbeatable. Divided, they are a catastrophe, not only to the inner team of missionaries, but also to the perceptive onlooking national community.

Our commitment to Jesus Christ means that we want to be the best servant possible for his glory. It means stretching, not only in spirit, but also in intellect. True academic excellence leads to greater effectiveness, not to pride or snobbery. We must beware of vegetating on the mission field. Both our hearts and our minds must stay alive and alert.

Attitudes

Still fresh in my mind are the words Harold Cook, for many years professor of missions of Moody Bible Institute, told his missions class, in 1959: "Students, the single most important area of your life and ministry will be in the realm of attitudes. It is here you will either succeed or fail as a missionary. Attitudes touch every nerve end of life. Your relationship to Christ, fellow missionary, national believer and non-Christian will be deeply affected by proper or improper attitudes."

There are a number of ingredients to a positive attitude toward nationals. One is empathy. Let me illustrate. Each morning at sunrise, a Hindu neighbor in our village would rise up, wash, and go out and stand near his cow. He would then look up at the sun, fold his hands and go through a ceremony which involved worship of both the sun and the cow. I watched our Hindu friend perform this ritual scores of times. One day the cow became ill and died suddenly. Grief struck the Hindu household. It was indeed a tragic loss to them. I personally disagreed with worshiping a cow, but I had somehow entered into the world view of that Hindu. He hurt and I hurt. Quickly I learned a few appropriate phrases (as we were new in the country) and went along to his shop. I stuttered out a few incorrectly pronounced words about being sorry that his cow had died. My Hindu friend was deeply touched. Though we were worlds apart in culture and religion, yet I cared. I had for a brief moment stepped into his life.

There is an old adage that contains a great deal of truth. "The gift without the giver is bare." Missionaries are giving people. Their job demands that role. They may be engaged in relief, teaching, medical work, or some other ministry that necessitates the act of sharing. But the act of giving is inadequate in itself. What is the force behind the action? Is there love? Is there a deep concern for the other person? Has giving become a professional obligation? Have the poor or the heathen become a product to sell? These are heavy questions.

Ministry

It is time now to consider the ministerial focus of the missionary. When we turn to New Testament missions, we find that Paul's involvement was exceedingly temporary. He came, stayed a few weeks or months, or at most a few years, and left to go into new areas. The churches he planted did not remain in his control. Even if a heretical influence came into the churches, Paul could only exhort the Christians to walk in truth. He had no funds to cut off. The believers were totally free. Certainly the contemporary picture of missions is different from

Paul's day.

Leslie Newbegin writes of Paul totally entrusting leadership into local hands. He pungently comments that Paul didn't do what modern missionaries have done, "He does not build a bungalow." [6] George Peters maintains Paul could have rightfully said, "Here is enough work for me to do. This is where I am." Paul resisted the temptation and kept on the move.[7] Roland Allen points out that Paul didn't neglect the churches. He continued to visit and correspond with them. But the basic leadership responsibility was all put in local hands.[8]

Now, western missionaries have a very difficult time completely turning over control to the younger churches. At times, missionaries may be withdrawn as denominational budgets flounder. Even in these cases, funds continue to go directly to the churches, thus perpetuating dependence. And worst of all, the missionaries are not deployed in a virgin area in the task of church planting. Rather, they are brought home under the camouflage that now the emerging church can take care of its own evangelistic responsibility.

In other situations, missionaries have been content to be resident in one mission station working among a small cluster of churches for a full missionary career of thirty-five years. In many ways, the ministry is fulfilling. One experiences joy in seeing children born, later becoming Christians, getting married and on to settling into good professions. There is a continuity and routine about such a life. National Christians, too, feel good about having a foreign missionary around to assist them in their times of need. However, this is inadequate strategy for the 90's.

The missionary must move on as soon as possible after worshiping groups have been established. Converts must not transfer their dependence onto the missionary and away from the Lord.

> Having travailed, given birth, and cared for young churches the missionaries (whether Tamilian or Naga or American or Australian) should turn over authority to indigenous leaders. Travail

must not go on too long. It must be followed by weaning and pushing out of the nest. Then the missionary goes on and repeats the process. [9]

The missionary must keep before him constantly the imperative of pressing out to new frontiers.

Conclusion

I am an optimist concerning the decade of challenge that lies just before us. There will surely be opening doors, closing doors, and revolving doors within the great challenge of reaching the nations for Christ in the 90's. A beautiful picture of a ship on an ocean in the midst of a storm graces my bedroom door. The inscription reads, "A ship in a harbor is safe, but that is not what ships are built for." The front line of a battle is risky, but no victory has ever been registered in the annals of history as having been won solely by those supportive people who linger far behind the range of enemy gunfire. Our task calls for reflection, decision and engagement.

End Notes

1. Chaeok Chun, "An Exploration of the Community Model for Muslim, Missionary Outreach by Asian Women," an unpublished D. Miss. dissertation. Fuller Theological Seminary, Pasadena, CA 1977.

2. Sister Mary Just, *Digest of Catholic Mission History* (Maryknoll, N.Y.: Maryknoll Publications, 1957), p. 22.

3. Donald McGavran, letter to the author, March, 1979.

4. D. A. Chowdhury, "The Bengal Church and the Convert," *The Moslem World* no. 29 (1939), p. 347.

5 Joseph A. McCoy, *Advice From the Field* (Baltimore: Helicon Press, 1962), p. 144.

6. Lesslie Newbegin, *The Open Secret* (London: SPCK, 1978), p. 144.

7. George W. Peters, "Issues Confronting Evangelical Missions," *Evangelical Missions Tomorrow* (Pasadena, CA: William Carey Library, 1977), p. 162.

8. Roland Allen, *Missionary Methods: St. Paul's or Ours?* (Grand Rapids: Eerdmans, 1962), p. 151.

9. Donald McGavran, *Ethnic Realities and the Church* (South Pasadena, CA: William Carey Library, 1979), p. 130.

Study Questions

1. Why is the issue of missionary living standards so emotionally charged?

2. *Should* remaining mission compounds be dismantled? Why or why not?

17

Do Missionaries Destroy Cultures?

Don Richardson

When Fray Diego de Landa, a Catholic missionary accompanying Spanish forces in the New World, discovered extensive Maya libraries, he knew what to do. He burned them all, an event, he said, the Maya "regretted to an amazing degree, and which caused them much affliction." The books, in his opinion, were all of "superstition and lies of the devil." And so, in 1562, the poetry, history, literature, mathematics, and astronomy of an entire civilization went up in smoke. Only three documents survived de Landa's misguided zeal.

Magnificent totem poles once towered in Indian villages along Canada's Pacific coast. By 1900 virtually all such native art had been chopped down, either by missionaries who mistook them for idols, or by converts zealously carrying out the directives of missionaries.

These incidents and many more show that we missionaries have sometimes acted in a culture-destroying manner. Whether through misinterpreting the Great Commission, pride, culture shock, or simple inability to comprehend the values of others, we have needlessly opposed customs we did not understand. Some, had we understood them, might have served as communication keys for the gospel!

The world has been quick to notice our mistakes. Popular authors like Herman Melville, Somerset Maugham, and James Michener have stereotyped missionaries as opinionated, insensitive, neurotic, sent to the heathen because they were misfits at home.

Michener's austere Abner Hale, a missionary in the novel *Hawaii* , became the archetype of an odious bigot. Hale shouts hellfire sermons against the "vile abominations" of the pagan Hawaiians. He forbids Hawaiian midwives to help a missionary mother at the birth of "a Christian baby." The mother dies.

Don Richardson pioneered work for Regions Beyond Missionary Union (RBMU) among the Sawi tribe of Irian Jaya in 1962. Author of *Peace Child, Lords of the Earth,* and *Eternity in Their Hearts,* Richardson is now Minister-at-Large for RBMU. He speaks frequently at missions conferences and Perspectives Study Program classes. Adapted and reprinted with permission from three publishers: *Moody Monthly,* Vol. 8, 1976; *The Washington Post,* August 3, 1976; and *Wherever* Magazine, a publication of TEAM.

Hale even forbids Hawaiians to help his wife with housework lest his children learn the "heathen Hawaiian language." His wife works herself into an early grave.

When Buddhist Chinese settle in Hawaii, Michener has Hale barging into their temples to smash their idols.

Interesting literary grist, to be sure.

Unfortunately for naive readers, "Abner Hale" came to mean "missionary." We've been carrying him on our backs ever since.

Anthropologist Alan Tippett of the Fuller Seminary School of World Mission once researched hundreds of early missionary sermons stored in the Honolulu archives. None had the ranting style Michener suggests as typical. Critics seem to suggest, naively, that if only missionaries stayed home, primitive people would be left undisturbed to fulfill the myth of Rousseau's "noble savage."

The fact is, commercial exploiters or other secular forces have already wrought havoc with indigenous cultures on an awesome scale. Livingstone was preceded by Arab slave traders. Amy Carmichael was preceded by victimizers who dragged boys and girls away to temples, where they faced the terrors of child prostitution.

Secular forces such as these have sometimes destroyed entire peoples. In North America not only the famous Mohicans but also the Hurons and possibly as many as twenty other Indian tribes were pushed into extinction by land-hungry settlers. Pioneers on one occasion sent a tribe wagonloads of gift blankets known to be infected with smallpox.

In Brazil only 200,000 Indians remain from an original population estimated at 4 million. In the past seventy-five years more than one tribe per year has disappeared.

Readers may assume that Brazil's missing tribes have been absorbed into society, but this is not the case. Thousands have been brutally poisoned, machine-gunned, or dynamited from low-flying aircraft. Other thousands succumbed to a slower, more agonizing death by *apathy*. As encroachment caused their cultures to disintegrate, Indian men have even been known to cause their wives to miscarry. They refused to bring children into a world they could no longer understand.

Prior to 1858, India's *Andaman Islands* were the home of at least 6,000 pygmy negritoes. Then the British established a penal colony in the islands and victimization began. Today a scant 600 negritoes remain.

Similar tragedies are unfolding throughout the Philippines, Asia, and Africa.

Concern is widespread today—and justly so—for endangered animal species. But hundreds of our own human species are in even greater danger! A yearly loss of ten linguistically distinct tribes may be a conservative figure.

Only a few of the world's governments have established agencies to protect their ethnic minorities. Brazil, the Philippines, and India, are three examples.

Secular agencies, however, suffer from severe budget restrictions. Furthermore, other arms of government may interfere with the programs.

For example, not long after Brazil's National Foundation for the Indian established Xingu National Park as a reserve for endangered tribes, roadbuilders obtained permission to blast a modern highway through the center of it! As a result two of Xingu's "protected" tribes were destroyed by measles and influenza introduced by construction crews.

Clearly, the "enlightened" policy of "leave-them-alone" isn't working.

What then, can halt their march toward extinction?

Grants, land, and secular welfare programs may help on the physical level (though sometimes godless officials introduce alcoholism or other vices, undermining whatever good their programs may accomplish).

But the greatest danger to aboriginals is one that such programs cannot deal with—the breakdown of the aboriginal's sense of "right" relationship with the supernatural. Every aboriginal culture acknowledges the supernatural and has strict procedures for "staying right" with it. When arrogant outsiders ridicule a tribe's belief, or shatter its mechanisms for "staying right," severe disorientation sets in. Tribesmen believe they are under a curse for abandoning the old ways. They become morose and apathetic, believing they are doomed to die as a people.

Materialistic social workers or scientists cannot help such people. The tribesmen *sense* even an unspoken denial of the supernatural, and become even more depressed.

Who then can best serve such people as spiritual ombudsmen?

None other than the very ones popularly maligned as the number one enemy: the Bible-guided, Christ-honoring missionary.

Consider some case histories:

Less than a generation ago, according to Robert Bell of the Unevangelized Fields Mission, Brazil's Wai Wai tribe had been reduced to its last sixty members. This had come about largely through foreign diseases, and by the Wai Wai custom of sacrificing babies to demons to try to prevent those diseases.

Then a handful of UFM missionaries identified themselves with the tribe, learned their language, gave it an alphabet, translated the Word of God, and taught Wai Wai to read. Far from denying the supernatural world, the missionaries showed the Wai Wai that a God of love reigned supreme over it. And that God had prepared for them a way of "staying right" on a far deeper level than they had ever dreamed of.

The Wai Wai now had a rational—even delightful—basis for *not* sacrificing babies to demons, and the tribe began to grow. Today the Wai Wai are fast becoming one of Brazil's most populous tribes. And optimistic Wai Wai Christians are teaching other dwindling groups of Indians how to cope with the twentieth century through faith in Jesus Christ.

Repentance and faith in Jesus Christ *can* solve many of the survival problems of endangered peoples.

The help given to the Wai Wai, furthermore, is only a very recent example of a long heritage of helping beleaguered peoples.

Near Stockbridge, in what is now Massachusetts, early American missionary John Sargent and his associates established a community to preserve Indian rights, preparing them for survival among encroaching Europeans.

Before ethnocentrism was named as a social evil, and before the birth of anthropology as a science, Sargent and his helpers unpatronizingly tilled the soil side by side with their Indian friends. Practicing what anthropologists now call "directed change," they also shared their Christian faith. The Indians received it as their own.

That faith, and the love of their spiritual paracletes, sustained the tribe through more than a century of suffering. Greedy settlers soon decided that the land was too good for "mere Indians" and evicted them. After protesting unsuccessfully, Sargent obtained guarantees of land further west.

A few years later the community was uprooted again by other settlers. And again. Fifteen times they were forced to move. Each time the missionaries moved with them, wresting concessions for new land and holding the community together.

At last the community settled in Michigan, where it was allowed to rest, and survives to this day. As a side benefit, such missionary experiments helped convince scholars that a science of anthropology was necessary.

In both cases just cited, missionaries introduced culture change, but not arbitrarily and not by force. They brought only changes required by the New Testament or required for the survival of the people. Often the two requirements overlap (for example, the cessation of Wai Wai child sacrifices).

Once an interviewer regaled me (perhaps facetiously) for persuading the Sawi tribe in Indonesia to renounce cannibalism.

"What's wrong with cannibalism?" he asked. "The Sawi practiced it for thousands of years. Why should they give it up now?"

I replied, "Can a people who practice cannibalism survive in the World today? No, they cannot. The Sawi are now citizens of the Republic of Indonesia. The Indonesian Republic does not permit its citizens to eat other people. Therefore, part of my task was to give the Sawi a rational basis for *voluntarily* renouncing cannibalism before the guns of the police decided the issue."

On another level Sawi culture entertained a dark compulsion to venerate dead relatives by handling, or even *eating*, the rotting flesh of their corpses. Yet when the Sawi received the Christian teaching of the resurrection, they immediately abandoned such procedures, almost with a sigh of relief. The gospel cured them of this strange compulsion.

The Sawi are among perhaps 400 black-skinned Melanesian tribes just emerging from the stone age in Irian Jaya. Thirteen years ago the Netherlands ceded Irian Jaya (then New Guinea) to Indonesia. Today, an estimated one hundred thousand Indonesians have migrated to Irian Jaya. Will the tribal people be prepared to cope with their more enterprising migrant neighbors? Or will they become extinct?

Scattered throughout Irian Jaya, more than 250 evangelical missionaries (all too few) are ministering the gospel to both races. Knowledgeable in Indonesian as well as many of Irian's 400 tribal languages, they are helping members of clashing cultures understand each other. With the sympathetic help of the Indonesian government, they are optimistic that major culture shock may be averted.

Already, through faith in Christ, tens of thousands of Irianese have begun a smooth transition into the twentieth century.

Surely ethnic crises of this magnitude are far too sensitive to be left to the dubious mercy of purely commercial interests. Missionaries whose hearts overflow with the love of Christ are the key.

CULTURAL IMPERIALISM: GUILTY AS CHARGED

Are missionaries cultural imperialists? You decide. Consider this journalist's charges against missionaries, made after he visited Irian Jaya to cover the effects of a severe earthquake in June 1976. Hamish McDonald quickly turned his attention to the relationship between tribespeople and missionaries, and the resulting article appeared in the Washington Post *on August 3, 1976.*

JAYAPURA, Irian Jaya—Fundamentalist Christian missionaries are provoking hostile and occasionally murderous reactions from primitive tribespeople in mountain areas south of here. In the most savage of recent incidents, about eighteen months ago, thirteen local assistants of a mission were killed and eaten as soon as the European missionary went away on leave.

The missionaries are also coming under attack by anthropologists and other observers for attempting the almost total destruction of local cultures in the areas they evangelize. This is seen as the basic cause of recent violent outbreaks, and is contrasted with the more adaptive policies of Roman Catholic and mainstream Protestant missionary groups.

The fundamentalists are working in the remote Jayawijaya mountains where they are now carrying the brunt of relief work following recent severe earthquakes believed to have killed as many as a thousand people.

They belong to five missionary groups—the Christian and Missionary Alliance, the Unevangelized Fields Mission, the Regions Beyond Missionary Union, The Evangelical Alliance Mission, and the Asia-Pacific Christian Mission—banded together in an organization called The Missionary Alliance. They are joined by a technical missionary group, the Missionary Aviation Fellowship, an efficient air service with fifteen light aircraft and a helicopter—essential in a territory where the longest paved road is the 25-mile drive from Jayapura, the provincial capital, to the airport. They are well backed by Congregationalist, Baptist, and nondenominational Bible groups in North America, Europe, and Australia, although most members and funds come from the United States.

Sometimes rejecting the label "fundamentalist," they describe themselves as "orthodox" or "faith" Christians. Their central characteristic is belief in the literal truth of the Bible.

In recent years they have set up several missions in the Jayawijaya mountains, an unmapped and little-known area that had its first outside contact only about twenty years ago. The Melanesian people there learned the use of metal only recently. They live on sweet potatoes, sugar cane, and bananas, supplemented by pork and occasional small marsupials or birds that they hunt with bows and arrows.

Their only domestic animals are their pigs, which they regard as having souls. When I asked an anthropologist there why they ate such close friends, he said: "It doesn't matter. They eat people, too."

The men wear only the *koteka*, a penis gourd, and the women small tufts of grass fore and aft. Divided by rugged terrain and language from even close neighbors, they feud periodically in set-piece confrontations.

Although their culture recognizes personal and family property, they are remarkable for their willingness to share. Tobacco is their only vice, imported from the coast somehow in the forgotten past. Cowrie shells are the only currency resembling money.

Their culture and traditional religion express the most basic human concepts. They and the other 900,000 people in Irian Jaya produce dazzling works of art in traditional carvings and handicrafts.

Typically, a new missionary arriving builds his house by itself, next to a grass airstrip. One told me: "The first thing is to move in and live with the people. You must prove that you want to help them, by giving them food, medicine, and shelter, teaching them, and learning their language. Often it takes two to four years to learn the language. I guess what you are looking for is the cultural key, the key that unlocks the culture and opens the way for the gospel."

But many missionaries appear to regard the gospel as totally incompatible with the traditional culture, in which they see no deep value. One missionary from the Papua-New Guinea border region referred to the old men who stayed aloof from his mission as "having no interest in spiritual things." The first action of a missionary who stayed awhile recently in Valley X was to hand out shirts to tribesmen. At Nalca Mission, women have been persuaded to lengthen their grass skirts to knee length, apparently to satisfy missionary modesty.

Smoking tobacco is condemned and forbidden as sinful. Until recently, the mission air service searched baggage and refused to fly anyone found carrying tobacco or alcohol.

In 1968 two Western missionaries were killed on the south slope of the Jayawijaya range. Three months ago an American missionary was virtually chased out of the Fa-Malinkele Valley because of his manner.

The incident of cannibalism occurred at a mission called Nipsan, where the Dutch missionary had been using local Irianese assistants from the longer evangelized area near Wamena, further west. When the missionary went on leave, the tribespeople turned on fifteen assistants, killing and eating thirteen. Two escaped to the jungle. An Indonesian army unit later entered but dropped the case because of the baffling problems of law involved.

The Dutch missionary subsequently made a fund-raising tour of Europe and North America to buy a helicopter from which he proposed to conduct aerial evangelization through a loudspeaker. But the first time this was tried, a month ago, volleys of arrows reportedly greeted the airborne preacher.

The fundamentalists are compared unfavorably with the Roman Catholic missionaries who operate on the southern side of Irian Jaya under a territorial division initiated by the Dutch and maintained by the Indonesians after the 1963 transfer of administration.

"The difference between them is quite simple," said one source at Jayapura. "The Protestants try to destroy the culture. The Catholics try to preserve it."

At a mission called Jaosakor near the southern coast, the Catholics recently consecrated a church largely designed by the local people and incorporating traditional Asmat carvings around the walls. Bishop Alphonse Sowada, of the Nebraska-centered Crosier Fathers, carried out the ceremony in Episcopal robes accompanied by local leaders in full regalia of paint, tooth necklaces, and nosebones. The method of dedication was to scatter lime, made from fired seashells, from bamboo containers over walls, floors, and altars in the way the Asmat people inaugurate their own communal buildings.

Nearly all Catholic missionaries in Irian Jaya are required to hold degrees in anthropology before beginning their calling. Many have published articles and writings on the local peoples. "The basis of our approach is that we believe God is already working through the existing culture, which follows from the belief that God created all things and is present in all of them," one priest said.

VINDICATED ON ALL COUNTS

How would you respond to McDonald's assertions? On September 21, 1976, I sent a letter to the Post, *but it never appeared in its "letters to the editor" column. Here, slightly condensed, is my open letter.*

Dear Sirs:

A few weeks ago journalist Hamish McDonald arrived in Irian Jaya to report on the earthquake which recently devastated a mountainous region here. At least that's what he told the missionaries whose help he needed to reach the area.

The earthquake was of particular interest because it struck the habitat of a number of the earth's last remaining stone age tribes, some of whom still practice cannibalism. Triggering literally thousands of landslides, the upheaval wiped out fifteen tribal villages, killed more than a thousand people, and left 15,000 survivors with only 15 percent of their gardens. The missionaries McDonald approached were busy staging an urgent food airlift. Still, they graciously offered him space on one of their overloaded mercy flights from Jayapura into the interior...

The world might never have known that these tribes exist, nor would relief agencies have been informed of their plight, had not a dozen or more evangelical Protestant missionaries explored their uncharted mountainous habitat during the past fifteen years. At risk to their own lives, the evangelicals succeeded in befriending several thousand of these highly suspicious, unpredictable tribesmen. Meticulously, they learned and analyzed unwritten tribal languages, a task so agonizing that less motivated persons would have no time for it. They also carved out the four airstrips which now made relief operations possible and, as a sidelight, enabled McDonald to carry out his assignment on location.

The missionary aircraft taxied to a halt on one of these airstrips. McDonald leaped out and began snapping pictures...

C—144 DO MISSIONARIES DESTROY CULTURES?

There are reasons why the missionaries had to go into isolated areas like Irian Jaya as soon as they could. History has taught them that even the most isolated minority cultures must eventually be overwhelmed by the commercial and political expansion of majority peoples. Naive academics in ivy-covered towers may protest that the world's remaining primitive cultures should be left undisturbed, but farmers, lumbermen, land speculators, miners, hunters, military leaders, road builders, art collectors, tourists, and drug peddlers aren't listening.

They are going in anyway. Often to destroy. Cheat. Exploit. Victimize. Corrupt. Taking, and giving little other than diseases for which primitives have no immunity or medicine.

This is why, since the turn of the century, more than ninety tribes have become extinct in Brazil alone. Many other Latin American, African, and Asian countries show a similar high extinction rate for their primitive minorities. A grim toll of five or six tribes per year is probably a conservative worldwide estimate.

We missionaries don't want the same fate to befall these magnificent tribes in Irian Jaya. We risk our lives to get to them first because we believe we are more sympathetic agents of change than profit-hungry commercialists. Like our predecessor John Sargent, who in 1796 launched a program which saved the Mohican tribe from extinction, and like our colleagues in Brazil who just one generation ago saved the Wai Wai from a similar fate, we believe we know how to precondition tribes in Irian Jaya for survival in the modern world. The question, "Should anyone go in?" is obsolete because obviously someone *will*.

It has been replaced by a more practical question: "Will the most sympathetic persons get there first?" To make the shock of coming out of the stone age as easy as possible. To see that tribals gain new ideals to replace those they must lose in order to survive. To teach them the national language so they can defend themselves in disputes with "civilizados." And yet produce literature in their own language so it will not be forgotten. To teach them the value of money, so that unscrupulous traders cannot easily cheat them. And better yet, set some of them up in business so that commerce in their areas will not fall entirely into the hands of outsiders. To care for them when epidemics sweep through or when earthquakes strike. And better yet, train some of them as nurses and doctors to carry on when we are gone. We go as ombudsmen who help clashing cultures understand each other.

We missionaries are advocates not only of spiritual truth, but also of physical survival. And we have enjoyed astonishing success in Irian Jaya and elsewhere. Among the Ekari, Damal, Dani, Ndugwa, and other tribes, more than 100,000 stone agers welcomed our gospel as the fulfillment of something their respective cultures had anticipated for hundreds of years. The Ekari called it *aji*. To the Damal, it was *hai*. To the Dani, *nabelan-kabelan*—an immortal message which one day would restrain tribal war and ease human suffering.

The result: cultural fulfillment of the deepest possible kind. And it opened the door to faith in Jesus Christ for tens of thousands.

Along with our successes, there have been setbacks. Nearly two years ago one of our colleagues from a European mission, Gerrit Kuijt, left some coastal helpers in charge of a new outpost while he returned to Holland. In his absence, a few of the coastals began to molest the surrounding tribespeople for private reasons. Thirteen coastals were killed in retaliation.

Sympathize. Sometimes it is not easy to find responsible helpers willing to venture with us into these wild areas. At times you have to trust someone; you have no choice.

Earlier, in 1968, two of our buddies, Phil Masters and Stan Dale, died together while probing a new area of the Yali tribe. But then Kusaho, a Yali elder, rebuked the young men who killed them, saying: "Neither of these men ever harmed any of us, nor did they even resist while you killed them. Surely they came in peace and you have made a terrible mistake. If ever any more of this kind of men come into our valley, we must welcome them."

And so a door of acceptance opened through the wounds of our friends. It was a costly victory. Stan's and Phil's widows were each left with five small children to raise alone. Yet neither widow blamed anyone for the death of her husband, and one of them still serves with us in Irian Jaya today.

Ours is a great work, and a very difficult one. It is not subsidized by any government, and can succeed only as it has sympathetic support from churches, private individuals, and the public in general. That is where correspondent McDonald could have helped. Instead...

McDonald now transferred to a Mission Aviation Fellowship helicopter loaded with sweet potatoes contributed by Christians from the Dani tribe and rice from Indonesian government stores. Pilot Jeff Heritage thought McDonald seemed surprisingly uninterested in the many tribal hamlets stranded like islands in the midst of uncrossable landslides, their inhabitants on the edge of starvation. After only a few hours in the interior, he returned to the coast and wrote his report.

Wielding the cliché "fundamentalist" with obvious intent to stigmatize and nettle us, McDonald launched a scathing yet baseless attack which appeared as a major article in the *Washington Post* and was relayed by wire service to hundreds of newspapers around the world. Citing the loss of Gerrit Kuijt's thirteen helpers and the murder of Phil and Stan eight years ago, he made the absurd accusation that we are "provoking hostile and occasionally murderous reactions from primitive tribesmen." He continues: "The missionaries are also coming under attack by anthropologists and other observers for attempting the almost total destruction of cultures..."

Who are the anthropologists and other observers? Within our ranks we have a number of men who hold degrees in anthropology, and they have not warned us of any such attack by members of their discipline. We have cooperated with a number of anthropologists in Irian Jaya over the past twenty years, and have had good mutual understanding with them.

Perhaps McDonald is referring to the three remaining members of a German scientific team he met on one of his helicopter stops in the interior. Some of them, reportedly, have been critical toward us, not on the basis of wide knowledge of our work, but because of anti-missionary sentiments they brought with them to Irian Jaya.

C—146 DO MISSIONARIES DESTROY CULTURES?

Their problem is that they hold to an old school of anthropology, still current in some areas, which favors isolating primitive tribes from all change in zoo-like reserves. A new school, now rising in America, has at last recognized the futility of this approach, and advocates instead that primitive tribes be exposed to survival-related "directed change," in order that they may learn to cope with encroachment, now seen as inevitable.

Directed change is exactly what evangelical missionary John Sargent practiced back in 1796 and what we are practicing in 1976. In fact, missionaries are virtually the only persons who do. Anthropologists don't remain with tribesmen long enough. And humanists aren't sufficiently motivated. But if, indeed, we are under attack, a careful reporter should have asked us for our defense, if any. McDonald did not do this, though he had opportunity. What evidence does he present for his charge that we are "attempting the almost total destruction of local cultures" in Irian Jaya? He writes: "The first action of a missionary…in Valley X recently was to hand out shirts to the tribesmen."

The tribesmen concerned had just lost most of their homes in the earthquake. Indonesian officials had provided shirts to help them stay warm at night in their crude temporary shelters at mile-high elevations. No one wanted a rash of pneumonia cases complicating the relief operation. Johnny Benzel, the missionary, cooperated with the government directive by handing out the shirts.

Nowhere have we ever provided Indonesian or Western-style clothing until demand for it arose among the tribal people themselves. This usually took from seven to fifteen years. Tribal church elders preached in the open or under grass-roofed shelters, wearing their penis gourds, and no one thought anything of it. Even today the vast majority of men still wear gourds and women wear grass skirts.

It is the Indonesian government, not missionaries, which tries to shame tribals into exchanging gourds and grass skirts for shorts and dresses under *Operation Koteka*. But they do it for understandable reasons. They want the tribesmen to become part of Indonesian society as soon as possible, find employment, etc.

At Nalca, McDonald snapped a photo of a native with a ball-point pen stuck through the pierced septum of his nose. This photo appeared in some newspapers with the ludicrous caption: "Ball-point pen replaces nosebone; fundamentalist preachers destroy culture." A native forages a used ball-point pen out of Johnny Benzel's wastepaper basket, sticks it through his nose, and presto! Johnny is accused of destroying culture. Very tricky, McDonald.

McDonald slams Johnny again: "At Nalca mission, women have been persuaded to lengthen their grass skirts to knee-length…" What actually happens is that families of the Dani tribe follow missionaries to places like Nalca, and over a period of years the Nalca women begin to imitate the style of their Dani counterparts, which happens to be longer.

Do we, then, approve of everything in the local cultures? No, we do not, just as no one in our own Western culture automatically approves of everything in it.

We are out to destroy cannibalism, but so also is the Indonesian government. The difference is, we use moral persuasion, and if we fail, the government will eventually use physical force. Our task is to give the tribals a rational basis for giving it up voluntarily before the guns of the police decide the issue with traumatic effect.

We also want to stop the intertribal warfare that has gone on for centuries. In view of all they have to go through in the next fifty years, it is imperative that the tribes stop killing and wounding each other *now*. Often we are able to stop the fighting by emphasizing little-used peace-making mechanisms within the cultures themselves. Or we simply provide the third-person presence which enables antagonists to see their problems in a new light.

We are against witchcraft, suspicion of which is a major cause of war. Killing by witchcraft is contrary, not only to Christian concepts of goodness, but also to the humanist's, isn't it?

We are against sexual promiscuity, and not for religious reasons only. In 1903, Chinese traders seeking bird-of-paradise plumes landed on the south coast of Irian Jaya. They introduced a venereal disease called lymphogranuloma venereum among the 100,000-member Merind tribes. Since group sex was widely accepted, the disease spread like wildfire. It wiped out 90,000 lives in ten years.

McDonald attempts to antagonize us still further by comparing our methods unfavorably with "the more adaptive policies of Roman Catholic and mainstream Protestant groups."

Only one "mainstream" Protestant mission works in interior Irian Jaya, and they have experienced the same problems McDonald uses as grounds to incriminate us. For example, that mission's director was seriously wounded with three arrows eight years ago, and eight of his carriers were killed, while trekking through a wild area. Such incidents are merely an occupational hazard, and should not be used to levy blame.

As far as I know, Roman Catholic missionaries have not been wounded or slain by tribals in Irian Jaya. This is due, not to "more adaptive policies," but to the fact that they limit their work mainly to areas already well-controlled by the government. But they have counted their martyrs across the border in Papua New Guinea, and this is no shame to them.

If McDonald had taken time to visit Roman Catholic and evangelical Protestant areas of operation and compare them, he would have found the degree of culture change at least as great if not greater in the Roman Catholic areas. For example, in all Roman Catholic areas primitives are expected to give up their tribal names and take Latin names like Pius or Constantius, whereas in evangelical Protestant areas they still use their Irianese name, like Isai or Yana. But here again, if it is survival-related directed change, it cannot be faulted on anthropological grounds.

McDonald continues, "Nearly all Roman Catholic missionaries in Irian Jaya are required to hold degrees in anthropology." Actually, the percentage of Roman Catholic and evangelical Protestant missionaries holding degrees in anthropology is approximately equal, and when it comes to prowess in learning tribal dialects, the evangelicals excel by far. The majority of Roman Catholic priests teach in Indonesian even where it is not understood.

McDonald describes the lime-scattering dedication of a new Catholic church at Jaosakor. Surely if this is the limit of their cultural penetration, our Catholic friends must be far from satisfied. Cultural penetration, to be effective, must go far deeper than mere externals like scattering lime. Not until you come to grips with internal concepts in the category of the Ekari tribe's *aji* or the Dani tribe's *nabelankabelan*, are you getting close to the heart of a people. And in matters of this category, we evangelicals have been spot on. As one of our members said to McDonald, "What we are looking for is the cultural key..." McDonald quoted his words, yet failed totally to appreciate them.

Another point of McDonald's article calls for refutation: Gerrit Kuijt raised funds for a helicopter for general service to all tribal peoples in Irian Jaya, not for "aerial evangelism." In fact, it was this helicopter which was on hand just in time to help in the earthquake relief operation and which bore McDonald on his reporting mission. Thank you, Gerrit, for your foresight. The rest of us are not unappreciative like McDonald.

McDonald, your article was erroneous, inept, and irresponsible. You have made a perfect nuisance of yourself. You and the *Washington Post* owe us a printed apology.

Do missionaries destroy cultures? We may destroy certain things "in" cultures, just as doctors sometimes must destroy certain things "in" a human body, if a patient is to live. But surely as we grow in experience and God-given wisdom, we must not and will not destroy cultures themselves.

Study Questions

1. What variations on McDonald's criticisms have you read or heard? Do you think them justified or not? Why?

2. Does Richardson adequately answer McDonald's criticisms? What would you add to or subtract from Richardson's response?

3. Do you agree with the policy of "directed change" in tribal societies? Why or why not?

18

Cultural Implications of an Indigenous Church

William A. Smalley

Over the past generation, a large amount of thought concerning the strategy of modern missions has gone into the question of the relation of the new churches (which have resulted from missionary work) to the missionary body and to the society (the non-Christian culture) around them. It is not my purpose here to go into the extensive literature dealing with this subject, but a classic work, often referred to and widely read, is Roland Allen's *Missionary Methods, St. Paul's or Ours?* [1] The burden of a great deal of this discussion has been the well-taken observation that modern missions have all too often resulted in churches which are tied to the supporting home church in the West, protected by the mother denomination, and unable to stand alone in their society. This is an over-simplification, but I am in substantial agreement with a great deal of it. There are some anthropological problems which have not always been faced in such discussions, however, although many writers have at points touched upon them and Roland Allen seems well aware of many of them.

A False Diagnosis

It seems to have become axiomatic in much missionary thinking that a church which is "self-governing, self-supporting, and self-propagating" is by definition an "indigenous church." It further seems to follow in the thinking of many people that such an indigenous church (and so defined) is the goal of modern missions. There are some very serious reservations which may be made to this point of view, however, and it is a point of view which may be very misleading

---

William A. Smalley is Professor Emeritus of Linguistics at Bethel College in St. Paul, Minnesota. Smalley worked for 23 years for the United Bible Societies and continues as a consultant to the Bible societies in his retirement. He helped found the Toronto Institute of Linguistics. He was editor of the journal *Practical Anthropology* from 1955 to 1968 and is editor of *Readings in Missionary Anthropology* and numerous other articles. He has also written *Translation as Mission* and *Mother of Writing: the Origin and Development of a Hmong Messianic Script*. With permission of the William Carey Library Publishers, P. 0. Box 128-C, Pasadena, CA 91104. *Readings in Missionary Anthropology II*, William Smalley, edited by William A. Smalley.

as it molds policy for the development of a church, if we look at some of its cultural implications.

It seems to me, first of all, that the criteria of "self-governing, self-supporting, and self-propagating" are not necessarily diagnostic of an indigenous movement. The definition of such a movement has to be sought elsewhere, and, although these three "self" elements may be present in such a movement, they are essentially independent variables. The three "selfs" seem to have become catch phrases which can be stamped without any particular understanding on one church or on another. Yet it is evident on an examination of the facts that they are not necessarily relevant at all.

Misinterpretation of Self-government

It may be very easy to have a self-governing church which is not indigenous. Many presently self-governing churches are not. All that is necessary to do is to indoctrinate a few leaders in Western patterns of church government, and let them take over. The result will be a church governed in a slavishly foreign manner (although probably modified at points in the direction of local government patterns), but by no stretch of imagination can it be called an indigenous church.

It is further possible for a genuinely indigenous Christian movement to be "governed" to a degree by foreigners. Even in the large-scale Christward movements which have taken place in the world, movements which have been so extensive that the foreign body has had more difficulty in controlling them than what it has had in most of its mission work, the mission body has often exerted its governing influence upon the upper level of society, at least, where it was related in any way to the movement. This may have been by the direct action of missionaries or by the action of church leaders who were trained in the foreign patterns of government. Although such government may be unfortunate in many cases, it does not in the least detract from the indigenous nature of such a Christward movement on the part of a group of people.

Misapplication of Self-support

It is unlikely that there would be any disagreement with the idea that the Jerusalem church in the first century was an indigenous church. The Jerusalem Christians were so strongly Jewish in their attitudes that they resented the conversion of Gentiles unless they joined the Jewish ritualistic performance of the law. That church, however, in its time of need received gifts from abroad, from Europe—in modern-day terminology, from the West. Paul himself carried some of those gifts to Jerusalem. No one would argue that the receiving of such gifts infringed upon the indigenous nature of the Jewish church.

Neither can one argue, I believe, that the receiving of such gifts by the younger churches today will necessarily infringe upon their indigenous character. This is true in spite of the very real dangers which exist in the subsidy of the younger churches by the mission bodies.

I was in Indo-China as a missionary during some of the years of civil war. Those were days when the whole country was badly upset, when church congregations could be cut off from the mission without more than a few hours notice as the battle line shifted, when groups which had been under mission subsidy could suddenly lose their mission help and be placed in a fearful economic position. Together with most of my colleagues, I felt the tremendous weakness of a missionary program which was based upon the foreign financing of its national workers. In a time of crisis such as that we worked hard to see to it that the church was placed on a footing of self-support.

Self-support is, wherever possible, really the soundest method of church economics. It is healthy for the church and for the mission, but there certainly are situations in which it is not possible, or where it is not advisable, where self-support can make church growth nearly impossible, and in such situations its presence does not necessarily imply the lack of an indigenous church. It is an independent variable within the pattern of the mission and church. All depends on how the problems are handled, and how the temptation to control church life through the manipulation of funds is resisted by the mission body. If foreign funds are handled in an indigenous way, they may still have their dangers, but they do not preclude an indigenous church.

Examples of areas in which the younger churches can usually not be expected to be self-supporting are publication, Bible translation, education, health and medicine, and many other fields entirely outside the range of their economy. These are not indigenous activities, but they are valuable activities for many churches in the modern world. Whether or not such things enter into the life of a church in an "indigenous manner" is entirely dependent upon the way in which the changes take place, not the source of income. If the changes in the younger church society take place as the result of the fulfillment of a strongly felt need, and in a manner planned and executed by them for their own purposes and in their own way, the simple presence of foreign funds in the project does not destroy its indigenous character.

The richness of Western economy makes it possible for many Western church groups not to need to seek for funds elsewhere. However, even in the rich West many groups have to seek for funds from foundations or other institutions. This does not destroy their indigenous character in the least; it is simply a part of the Western economic scene. Such economic possibilities are usually not open to the younger churches except as they seek their help from the mission body. It is the way the funds are administered, the way the decisions are made, and the purposes to which they are put, that are diagnostic of an indigenous church, not the presence or absence of such foreign funds.

It would be hard to think of any more fiercely or self-consciously independent country than India today, yet it receives large sums from abroad to bolster its economy and to do things which badly need to be done for its people. On the other hand, it would be very easy to find many examples of self-supporting churches in which the basic indigenous character is not present. There is, for example, a church which is advertised by its founding mission as a great indigenous church, where its pastors are completely supported by the local church members, yet the mission behind the scenes pulls the strings and the church does its bidding like the puppets of the "independent" iron curtain countries. This colonial manipulation may even be quite unconscious on the part of the missionaries. If the church makes its own decisions, without outside interference, as to how its funds shall be used and does so on the basis of economic patterns natural to it in its own cultural setting, this church may be considered indigenous, even if funds are provided by an outside source.

Misunderstanding of Self-propagation

Of the three "selfs," it seems to me that that of self-propagating is the most nearly diagnostic of an indigenous church, but here again the correlation is by no means complete. In a few areas of the world it may be precisely the foreignness of the church which is the source of attraction to unbelievers. There are parts of the world where aspirations of people lead them toward wanting to identify themselves with the strong and powerful West, and where the church provides such an avenue of identification.[2] Self-propagation in such a case may be nothing more than a road to a non-indigenous relationship.

I very strongly suspect that the three "selfs" are really projections of our American value systems into the idealization of the church, that they are in their very nature Western concepts based upon Western ideas of individualism and power. By forcing them on other people we may at times have been making it impossible for a truly indigenous pattern to develop. We have been Westernizing with all our talk about indigenizing.

The Nature of an Indigenous Church

What, then, is an indigenous church? It is a group of believers who live out their life, including their socialized Christian activity, in the patterns of the local society, and for whom any transformation of that society comes out of their felt needs under the guidance of the Holy Spirit and the Scriptures. There are several basic elements in this tentative formulation. For one thing, the church is a *society*. As society, it has its patterns of interaction among people. If it is an indigenous society, an indigenous church, those patterns of reaction will be based upon such patterns existing in the local society. This is true simply because people learn to react with each other in their normal process of enculturation, of growing up, and those normal habits are carried over into church structure. If other patterns are forced upon a church by missionaries, consciously or unconsciously, such a church will not be an indigenous one.

The presence of the Holy Spirit, however, is another basic factor in the indigenous church, and the presence of the Holy Spirit implies transformation both of individual lives and of society. But, as I have tried to point out in another article on the nature of culture change,[3] such transformation occurs differently in different societies, depending on the meaning which people attach to their behavior and the needs which they feel in their lives. Missionaries generally approve of and strive for culture change which makes people more like themselves in form (and this is true even though they may overlook the meaning of this form). An indigenous church is precisely one in which the changes which take place under the guidance of the Holy Spirit meet the needs and fulfill the meanings of that society and not of any outside group.

Many have said things like this, and such a statement should and could be elaborated considerably to provide a more adequate description of the nature of an indigenous church. Sometimes in our search for an understanding of the nature of the church we turn to the New Testament (as we rightly should) and seek for it there. But it is not in the formal structure and operation of the churches in the New Testament that we find our answer. As a matter of fact, the church of Jerusalem was apparently different even in operational matters from the churches in Europe, and it was certainly different in the outlook on the basic cultural issues which were so important to the Jews. In the New Testament we do find the picture of the indigenous church. It is that of a church in which the Holy Spirit has worked its transformation within the society. And where that society differs from another (as the Greek world is different from the Jewish world) the church resulting is different.

Missionaries Do Not Like It

But having said this much, we would now like to stress some of the implications of an "indigenous church," implications which have often not been realized. One is that missionaries often do not like the product. Often a truly indigenous church is a source of concern and embarrassment to the mission bodies in the area.

An example of this is that of the Toba Indians as reported by Dr. William D. Reyburn.[4] The mission was disturbed and unhappy about the indigenous church which spread so rapidly among the Toba people because it assumed a form so different from that of the mission group. It was not until they saw something of the nature of the church in the sense in which we are discussing it here and of the working of the Holy Spirit in societies other than their own, that the missionaries not only became reconciled to the indigenous church's existence, but sought to harmonize their program with it, to the strengthening of that church and to the greater glory of God.

There have been indigenous movements which missionaries have approved of. This approval was sometimes due to the unusual insight and perception of the missionaries who saw beyond the limitations of their own cultural forms and recognized the movement of the Holy Spirit among other people. At other times the general value systems of the new church group so nearly coincided with our own that the result was a church which reflected many of the things that we hold very valuable. Movements in China such as the Jesus Family displayed outstanding personal qualities of frugality, cleanliness, thrift, and other virtues which rate so highly in our own society and which were considered to be the fruits of the Christian movement. These are, however, ideals present in non-Christian Chinese life. A transformed life in such a case resulted in the perfection of such value systems already in existence in the culture. But that was not the case among the Tobas, where the giving away of possessions, the sharing with one's relatives and neighbors, and the joining in of emotional expressions of religion characterized the group because it was in these ways that their values were expressed.

However, as Dr. William D. Reyburn put it some time ago, most of us want to join in the jury as God in making his judgments upon people and cultures, yet we don't even understand the meaning of the trial. We are quick to make our evaluations and quick to decide what course the new church should follow or what course a new Christian individual should take, but we simply are neither competent nor qualified to make such decisions, having little or no real knowledge of the cultural background of the people or individual.

It is our work first of all to see the Bible in its cultural perspective, to see God dealing with men through different cultural situations. It is our responsibility to see God change in dealing with people as the cultural history of the Jews changes, to recognize that God has always, everywhere dealt with people in terms of their culture. It is next our responsibility to take new Christians to the Bible and to help them see in the Bible God interacting with other people, people whose emotions and problems were very similar to their own so far as their fundamental nature is concerned, but also at times very different from their own in the specific objective or working of their forms of life. It is our responsibility to lead them in prayer to find what God would have them do as they study His Word and seek the interpretation and leadership of the Holy Spirit.

It is the missionary task, if the missionary believes in "the indigenous principle," to preach that God is in Christ Jesus, reconciling the world unto Himself. That message is supercultural. It applies to all cultures and all places. The faith it engenders is supercultural, but the medium of its communication and the outworking of its faith in individual lives is not supercultural, it is bound in with the habits and values of every people. It is to deliver that message, the message that turned the world upside down and continues to do so, that the missionary is called.

It is, furthermore, the missionary's responsibility to be a source of cultural alternatives for people to select if they want and need them. Missionaries with their knowledge of history, their understanding of the Scriptures, and their knowledge of the church in their own land and in other missionary areas, can often suggest to local groups that there are ways out of their dilemma, that there are ways of a better life in Christ than what they are now living. This is certainly a legitimate missionary function, their role in cultural change. But if genuine change is to take place, the decision, the selection, has to be made by the people themselves, and if the church is to be an indigenous one, we can know that the selection will be made in the light of the needs and problems, the values and outlooks, those people have.

It is the church which will have to decide whether boiling water, abstinence from alcohol, the wearing of clothes and monogamy are the proper expressions of a Christian in that society. It is the church under the leadership of the Holy Spirit which will have to determine the best ways of fostering its own growth, spreading its own witness, and supporting its own formal leadership (if it should have any formal leadership at all).

As we have already suggested, the problem of the implications of the indigenous church are as old as the Judaizers of Jerusalem. Those Judaizers saw Greek Christianity through Hebrew eyes. They are like many missionaries in that, if they were content that any Gentile should be converted at all, they saw conversion in the light of filling of a formal mold.

The New Testament, however, clearly repudiated that view and sets up the church as a group of believers within its own society, working a chemical change within the society like salt in a dish, rather than cutting the society to pieces as the Judaizers would. This is not to gainsay the exclusiveness of Christianity. The church is a separate group, but it is separate in spiritual kind, in relationship to God. It is in the indigenous church that the relationship between the Holy Spirit and society comes into being. This is the New Testament church.

The converts of an indigenous movement are not necessarily cleaner than their neighbors, not necessarily more healthy, not necessarily better educated. It is, furthermore, often the moment at which they become cleaner, more healthy, more educated that the barrier begins to grow which makes their indigenous interaction with their neighbors less likely and the growth of the movement begins to taper off. As Dr. McGavran has pointed out in his tremendously significant book *The Bridges of God*, missions have traditionally poured their funds not into the people's movements but into the station churches, into the huge mission compounds, into the churches which are their satellites, rather than into the grass roots growing development of an embarrassing indigenous church.

Not only do many missionaries not like some of the outstanding examples of indigenous church movements, but to an even greater degree their supporting home constituencies are likely not to approve of them. Our cultural values as applied to our churches are so strong that we feel that a corporate structure, a profit motive, individualism, and thrift are *ipso facto* the expressions of Christianity. That God should work in any other forms than our own is inconceivable to most of us.

An implication of the indigenous church which I think is very unwelcome to many missionaries is that the missionary can make no cultural decisions for the Christians. By this I do not mean that the missionary does not make value judgments. Individual missionaries cannot help doing so, nor should they wish not to do so. Their value judgments, if they are to be worth while, have to be cross-culturally oriented, but they will be there. Neither do I mean by this that missionaries cannot exercise an important measure of guidance, of suggestion, on the younger church as they fulfill their functions of teaching and preaching and, in many respects, advising.

An Indigenous Church Cannot be "Founded"

The next implication which has often not fully penetrated into the thinking of missionaries who discuss indigenous movements is that it is impossible to "found" an indigenous church. The Biblical figure of planting and harvesting is far more realistic than our American figure based on our American values and expressed in the idea of the "establishment" or "founding" of a church.

No, indigenous churches cannot be founded. They can only be planted, and the mission is usually surprised at which seeds grow. Often they have the tendency to consider the seeds which do grow in any proliferation to be weeds, a nuisance, a hindrance in their carefully cultivated foreign mission garden, and all the time the carefully cultivated hothouse plants of the mission "founded" church are unable to spread roots and to derive their nurture either from the soil of their own life or from the Word of God in the root-confining pots of the mission organization and culture.

Indigenous Churches Start Apart from Missions

Another implication of the whole idea of an indigenous church is that the great indigenous movements are often not the result of foreign work in any direct way. Sometimes they are the result of the witness of someone who was converted by the efforts of foreign missionaries, but usually it is not the foreign missionary whose witness brings about the establishment or beginning of an indigenous movement. Saint Paul was not a foreigner to the Greek world. He was a bi-cultural individual, one who was as much at home in the Greek world as he was in the Hebrew world and whose preaching carried to the Greek world the message which came to him from the Christians of the Hebrew world.

Prophet Harris, who wandered along the west coast of Africa preaching about the men who would come with a Book, was not a foreign missionary. The men from whom the Tobas heard the gospel as it came to them in its pentecostal form were not foreigners. True, they were not Tobas, but they were the poorer-class Latin-Americans and mixed Spanish-Indian inhabitants of the areas where the Tobas lived. They were very much a part of the cultural picture in which the Tobas found themselves; they were not foreign missionaries. The people's movements in China were usually the result of the energetic faithful work of a Chinese Christian, not the result of foreign missionary evangelism except as he may have been a convert of missionaries.

The Hmong movement described by G. Linwood Barney was not brought about through the preaching of a missionary, but through the cooperative work of a Hmong shaman who had been converted (under a missionary) and who took another tribesman of the area with whom the Hmong were very familiar from village to village, preaching from town to town. Our distance from most other cultures is so great, the cultural specialization of the West is so extreme, that there are almost no avenues of approach whereby the work which we do can normally result in anything of an indigenous nature. It is an ironical thing that the West, which is most concerned with the spread of Christianity in the world today, and which is financially best able to undertake the task of world-wide evangelism, is culturally the least suited for its task because of the way in which it has specialized itself to a point where it is very difficult for it to have an adequate understanding of other peoples.

Conclusion

Denominationalism is in many cases a result of the development of more or less indigenous churches in various subgroups or social levels of Western society. Usually they start in the lower brackets, fossilizing in their cultural forms as they move up in society and on through time. Until we are willing for the church to have its different manifestations in different cultures as between the Jewish Christians and the various kinds of Greeks, rather than export the denominational patterns rooted in our history and often irrelevant to the rest of the world, we will not have indigenous churches, whether they are "self-governing, self-supporting, and self-propagating" or not. It is not until we are willing to let churches grow also that we have learned to trust the Holy Spirit with society. We are treating the Spirit as a small child with a new toy too complicated and dangerous to handle. Our paternalism is not only a paternalism toward other peoples; it is also a paternalism towards God.

End Notes

1. Roland Allen, *Missionary Methods: St. Paul's or Ours?* (Chicago: Moody Press, 1956).

2. William D. Reyburn, "Conflicts and Contradictions in African Christianity."

3. William A. Smalley, "The Missionary and Culture Change," *Practical Anthropology*, 4, no. 5 (1957), pp. 231-237.

4. Donald McGavran, *The Bridges of God* (London: World Dominion Press, 1955).

Study Questions

1. What constitutes an "indigenous" church, according to Smalley?

2. Why cannot the missionary "found" an indigenous church?

19

The Missionary's Role in Culture Change

Dale W. Kietzman and William A. Smalley

That missionaries have historically been agents of culture change in non-Western societies, no informed, thinking person would deny. Their role of initiating culture change has often been seriously misunderstood, however, in different ways by missionaries themselves, their supporters, and their critics. The basic attitudes of missionaries on this matter, and fundamental missionary policy in an area with respect to it, will inevitably influence profoundly the successful communication of the gospel and the possible development of an "indigenous" expression of Christianity.

Some critics of the missionary enterprise have grossly exaggerated missionary influence in their condemnation of the "rape" of non-Western cultures, with destruction of values, detribalization, apathy, or conflict resulting. There certainly have been some such direct cases of unnecessary and damaging cultural disturbance in missionary history, but for the most part the missionary's part has been very minor relative to the impact of Western business, politics, and education, not to speak of the often unsavory influences of motion pictures and printed matter. There have also been some outstanding cases where the gospel and

Dale W. Kietzman, a member of Wycliffe Bible Translators since 1946, worked with the Amahuaca Indians of Peru. He served in a number of administrative roles, including United States Division Director. He also served as President of World Literature Crusade/Every Home for Christ and more recently as Chairman of the Communications Division at the William Carey International University. Kietzman is author of numerous articles and books on mission subjects and on the Indians of South America.

William A. Smalley is Professor Emeritus of Linguistics at Bethel College in St. Paul, Minnesota. Smalley worked for 23 years for the United Bible Societies and continues as a consultant to the Bible societies in his retirement. He was also active in the formation of the Toronto Institute of Linguistics. He was editor of the journal *Practical Anthropology* from 1955 to 1968 and is editor of *Readings in Missionary Anthropology* and numerous other articles. Used with permission of the William Carey Library Publishers, P. O. Box 40129, Pasadena, CA 91114. *Readings in Missionary Anthropology II*, Dale W. Kietzman and William Smalley, edited by William A. Smalley, 1978.

C—158

resulting culture change have provided an opportunity for the reintegration of a segment of a culture already in rapid change.

Many supporters of Christian missions, on the other hand, have gauged the success of their whole program in terms of some overt, symbolic types of culture change. These may be anything from monogamy to haircuts, from attendance at church to the disappearance of scarification, but missionaries see in them signs that their ministry is taking effect. Missions and missionaries which declare that they are not going out to introduce Western culture, but only to preach the gospel, are no different in this respect from those with whom they contrast themselves. It is usually institutionalism (hospitalization, education, agricultural mission, etc.) which they are rejecting by such statements, not really their roles as agents of Westernization. They, too, are thrilled when Ay Blah learns to bathe with Ivory soap, brush his teeth with Crest, and cut his hair in "civilized" fashion. And if Ta Plooy does not give up his second and third wives or contribute to the church treasury, this is a matter for deep concern, for Ta Plooy obviously is not following the "gospel teaching" which he has been getting.

The Motivation for Culture Change

Culture change comes only as an expression of a need felt by individuals within a society. People do not change their behavior unless they feel a need to do so. The need may be trivial, as that for some new excitement or amusement, or it may be profound, as for security in a disintegrating world. Usually it is relatively unconscious. Peoples have not analyzed it or given it a name, but it motivates behavior. Something which no missionary who senses culture change going on round him should ever forget, however, is that the need being satisfied by a change very likely is not the need which the casual observer from our Western culture might see.

Among some of the tribal peoples of Laos and Vietnam, for example, the missionary sees the need for clothing. Many missionaries would feel the people need clothing for reasons of modesty (as in cases where women habitually wear nothing above the waist) or for warmth in the chilly season for the year. The second need is one which is felt by the people themselves to some degree, but it is strongly overshadowed by the other needs which they feel and which will be discussed in a moment. The need for modesty in the use of additional clothing is not felt at all, because people consider themselves adequately dressed from that point of view.

When the missionary barrel arrives and the clothes are given out, or when the missionary gives away an old shirt, or when some individual buys a new piece of clothing, what are the needs which he is meeting? One is the need to look respectable in the sight of outsiders—the need for being accepted by people who have prestige. This is why women will often not wear blouses in the village, but will wear them into town or put them on when the missionary shows up. Thus clothing may be a symbol of acceptance by the missionaries, of status and prestige in relation to them. Another is the desire to look well among one's equals, to wear something difficult to obtain, something impossible for one's neighbors to buy.

A case in point is a preacher from one of the tribes of Southeast Asia after he had been given a topcoat out of the missionary barrel. This was the only topcoat in the lot; he was the only tribesman who possessed a topcoat. It never got so cold in the area that a missionary ever wore a topcoat, although a woolen suit was comfortable in the evening for two or three months of the year. On a trip over rather rugged, mountainous jungle, when people in T-shirts and cotton trousers were perspiring profusely because of the heat, our friend with the topcoat was, of course, wearing it. How else would people see him with a topcoat on unless he wore it?

Then there was the woman who wore nothing above the waist but a substantial pink bra...

A man who starts to wash his clothes after his conversion is probably not doing so because of his love for Christ, even though this seems to the missionary to be vindication of the view that cleanliness is next to godliness. What are the needs being expressed in a change from polygamy to monogamy, in church attendance, in church government, in learning to read, in sending children to school? We would be the last to say that the need of man for God is never involved in some of these, in some places, but even then, as in all human situations, motives are mixed.

Clearly, the typical missionary reaction to culture change is to approve of that which makes other peoples more like themselves in *form*, in the outward aspects of behavior, whether the meaning of the behavior is the same or not. It is quite possible to give encouragement to the development of a form which is expressing a meaning, fulfilling a need, which the missionary would seriously deplore.

The Role of the Church in Culture Change

Culture is constantly changing, and what is vital for our purpose, it is constantly changing from within. While a good bit is said and written about acculturation, seldom has the role of the innovator, the nonconformist, the rebel been described. Yet all societies have them, and they have their place in bringing about the constant change that is characteristic of culture. The important thing for the missionary to note is that change is almost always initiated by someone within the cultural community. Even though the idea may have been sparked by contact with another culture, it still must be introduced from within to be accepted. The alternative to this scheme is change forced upon a people through superior might, whether moral or physical. This is the sort of change that missions have often been responsible for, and that resulted in such unfortunate reaction.

The real agent of the Holy Spirit in any society for the changes in the culture of that society is the church, the body of believers (*not* necessarily the organized church of any particular denomination). The church is the salt working through the whole dish. It is that part of the society which has a new relationship to God yet it reacts in terms of the attitudes and presuppositions of that society. It understands, in an intuitive, unanalyzed way, motives and meanings as the missionary cannot. It must make the decisions.

The Missionary's Part

What, then, can missionaries do about culture change? Are they only to be evangelists preaching a noncultural gospel without making value judgments? This is an impossibility, even if it were desirable. There cannot be preaching except in cultural terms, and no human being can or should try to escape value judgments. Missionaries cannot legitimately force or enforce any culture change. Nor do they have an adequate basis for advocating specific changes in a culture unless they have a profound knowledge of the culture.

Missionaries do, however, have an extremely important function in the tactful, thoughtful, serious presentation of alternate forms of cultural behavior to the Christians in a society. On the basis of their knowledge of history, their understanding of the church elsewhere, and above all, their knowledge of the tremendously varied ways in which God deals with people, as recorded in the Scriptures, they can make it clear to them that there are alternative ways of behavior to their own, and help them in prayer and study and experiment to select those cultural forms which would be the best expression for their relationship to God in their culture.

The missionary's basic responsibility is to provide the material upon which the native Christian and church can grow "in grace and knowledge" to the point where they can make reliable and Spirit-directed decisions with regard to their own conduct within the existing culture. This involves a complete freedom of access to the Word of God, with such encouragement, instruction and guidance in its use as may be necessary to obtain a healthy and growing Christian community.

The missionary's role in culture change, then, is that of a catalyst and of a source of new ideas, new information. It is the voice of experience, but an experience based on his own culture for the most part and therefore to be used only with care and understanding. Part of the value of anthropological study, of course, is that it gives at least vicarious experience in more than one cultural setting, for by study in this field missionaries can gain awareness of the much wider choice of alternatives than their own culture allows.

It is the church which is the legitimate agency in which the missionary should work. It is the people who must make the decisions based on the new ideas which they have received. It is they who must reinterpret old needs and expressions, examined now in the light of their relationship to God and to their fellow men in Christ Jesus.

Study Questions

1. What role in culture change is here suggested for the missionary? For the national church? To what extent should missionaries become engaged in political activities in their host countries?

2. How can the underlying motivation for culture change be discerned?

20

The Willowbank Report

The Lausanne Committee for World Evangelization

The Willowbank Report is the product of a January 1978 consultation on "Gospel and Culture," sponsored by the Lausanne Committee for World Evangelization and conducted in Willowbank, Somerset Bridge, Bermuda. Some 33 theologians, anthropologists, linguists, missionaries, and pastors attended. The report reflects the content of 17 written papers circulated in advance, summaries of them and reactions to them made during the consultation, and viewpoints expressed in plenary and group discussions.

1. The Biblical Basis of Culture

"Because man is God's creature, some of his culture is rich in beauty and goodness. Because he is fallen, all of it is tainted with sin and some of it is demonic." (Lausanne Covenant, para. 10).

God created mankind male and female in his own likeness by endowing them with distinctive human faculties—rational, moral, social, creative and spiritual. He also told them to have children, to fill the earth and to subdue it (Gen. 1:26-28). These divine commands are the origin of human culture. For basic to culture are our control of nature (that is, of our environment) and our development of forms of social organization. Insofar as we use our creative powers to obey God's commands, we glorify God, serve others and fulfill an important part of our destiny on earth.

Now, however, we are fallen. All our work is accompanied by sweat and struggle (Gen. 3:17-19), and is disfigured by selfishness. So none of our culture is perfect in truth, beauty or goodness. At the heart of every culture—whether we identify this heart as religion or world-view—is an element of self-centeredness, of man's worship of himself. Therefore a culture cannot be brought under the Lordship of Christ without a radical change of allegiance.

For all that, the affirmation that we are made in God's image still stands (Gen. 9:6; James 3:9), though the divine likeness has been distorted by sin. And still God expects us to exercise stewardship of the earth and of its creatures (Gen. 9:1-3, 7), and in his common grace makes all persons inventive, resourceful and fruitful in their endeavors. Thus, although Genesis 3 records the fall of humanity, and

"The Willowbank Report," used with permission of the Lausanne Committee for World Evangelization, 1978.

Genesis 4 Cain's murder of Abel, it is Cain's descendants who are described as the cultural innovators, building cities, breeding livestock, and making musical instruments and metal tools (Gen. 4:17-22).

Many of us evangelical Christians have in the past been too negative towards culture. We do not forget the human fallenness and lostness which call for salvation in Christ. Yet we wish to begin this Report with a positive affirmation of human dignity and human cultural achievement. Wherever human beings develop their social organization, art and science, agriculture and technology, their creativity reflects that of their Creator.

2. A Definition of Culture

Culture is a term which is not easily susceptible of definition. In the broadest sense, it means simply the patterned way in which people do things together. If there is to be any common life and corporate action, there must be agreement, spoken or unspoken, about a great many things. But the term "culture" is not generally used unless the unit concerned is larger than the family—unitary or extended.

Culture implies a measure of homogeneity. But, if the unit is larger than the clan or small tribe, a culture will include within itself a number of subcultures, and subcultures of subcultures, within which a wide variety and diversity is possible. If the variations go beyond a certain limit, a counterculture will have come into being, and this may prove a destructive process.

Culture holds people together over a span of time. It is received from the past, but not by any process of natural inheritance. It has to be learned afresh by each generation. This takes place broadly by a process of absorption from the social environment, especially in the home. In many societies certain elements of the culture are communicated directly in rites of initiation, and by many other forms of deliberate instruction. Action in accordance with the culture is generally at the subconscious level.

This means that an accepted culture covers everything in human life.

At its center is a world-view, that is, a general understanding of the nature of the universe and of one's place in it. This may be "religious" (concerning God, or gods and spirits, and of our relation to them), or it may express a "secular" concept of reality, as in a Marxist society.

From this basic world-view flow both standards of judgment or values (of what is good in the sense of desirable, of what is acceptable as in accordance with the general will of the community, and of the contraries) and standards of conduct (concerning relations between individuals, between the sexes and the generations, with the community and with those outside the community).

Culture is closely bound up with language, and is expressed in proverbs, myths, folk tales, and various art forms, which become part of the mental furniture of all members of the group. It governs actions undertaken in community—acts of worship or of general welfare; laws and the administration of law; social activities such as dances and games; smaller units of action such as clubs and societies, associations for an immense variety of common purposes.

Cultures are never static; there is a continuous process of change. But this should be so gradual as to take place within the accepted norms; otherwise the culture is disrupted. The worst penalty that can be inflicted on the rebel is exclusion from the culturally defined social community.

Men and women need a unified existence. Participation in a culture is one of the factors which provide them with a sense of belonging. It gives a sense of security, of identity, of dignity, of being part of a larger whole, and of sharing both in the life of past generations and in the expectancy of society for its own future.

Biblical clues to the understanding of the human culture are found in the threefold dimension of people, land, and history on which the Old Testament focuses attention. The ethnic, the territorial, and the historical (who, where and whence we are) appear there as the triple source of economic, ecological, social and artistic forms of human life in Israel, of the forms of labor and production, and so of wealth and well-being. This model provides a perspective for interpreting all cultures.

Perhaps we may try to condense these various meanings as follows: Culture is an integrated system of beliefs (about God or reality or ultimate meaning), of values (about what is true, good, beautiful and normative), of customs (how to behave, relate to others, talk, pray, dress, work, play, trade, farm, eat, etc.), and of institutions which express these beliefs, values and customs (government, law courts, temples or churches, family, schools, hospitals, factories, shops, unions, clubs, etc.), which binds a society together and gives it a sense of identity, dignity, security, and continuity.

3. Culture in the Biblical Revelation

God's personal self-disclosure in the Bible was given in terms of the hearers' own culture. So we have asked ourselves what light it throws on our task of cross-cultural communication today.

The biblical writers made critical use of whatever cultural material was available to them for the expression of their message. For example, the Old Testament refers several times to the Babylonian sea monster named "Leviathan," while the form of God's "covenant" with his people resembles the ancient Hittite Suzerain's "treaty" with his vassals. The writers also made incidental use of the conceptual imagery of the "three-tiered" universe, though they did not thereby affirm a pre-Copernican cosmology. We do something similar when we talk about the sun "rising" and "setting."

Similarly, New Testament language and thought-forms are steeped in both Jewish and Hellenistic cultures, and Paul seems to have drawn from the vocabulary of Greek philosophy. But the process by which the biblical authors borrowed words and images from their cultural milieu, and used them creatively, was controlled by the Holy Spirit so that they purged them of false or evil implications and thus transformed them into vehicles of truth and goodness. These undoubted facts raise a number of questions with which we have wrestled. We mention five:

The nature of biblical inspiration

Is the biblical author's use of the words and ideas of their own culture incompatible with divine inspiration? No. We have taken note of the different literary genres of Scripture, and of the different forms of the process of inspiration which they imply. For instance, there IS a broad distinction in form between the work of the prophets, receiving visions and words of the Lord, and historians and writers of letters. Yet the same Spirit uniquely inspired them all. God used the knowledge, experience and cultural background of the authors (though his revelation constantly transcended these), and in each case the result was the same, namely God's word through human words.

Form and meaning

Every communication has both a meaning (what we want to say) and a form (how we say it). The two—form and meaning—always belong together, in the Bible as well as in other books and utterances. How then should a message be translated from one language into another?

A literal translation of the form ("formal correspondence") may conceal or distort the meaning. In such cases, the better way is to find in the other language an expression which makes an equivalent impact on the hearers now as did the original. This may involve changing the form in order to preserve the meaning. This is called "dynamic equivalence. " Consider, for example, the RSV translation of Rom. 1:17, which states that in the gospel "the righteousness of God is revealed through faith for faith." This gives a word-for-word rendering of the original Greek, that is, a "formal correspondence" translation. But it leaves the meaning of the Greek words "righteousness" and "from faith to faith" unclear. A translation such as TEV—"the gospel reveals how God puts people right with himself: it is through faith from beginning to end"—abandons the principle of one-to-one correspondence between Greek and English words; but it expresses the meaning of the original sentence more adequately. The attempt to produce such a "dynamic equivalence" translation may well bring the translator to a deeper understanding of Scripture, as well as make the text more meaningful to people of another language.

Some of the biblical forms (words, images, metaphors) should be retained, however, because they are important recurring symbols in Scripture (e.g., cross, lamb, or cup). While retaining the form, the translators will try to bring out the meaning. For example, in the TEV rendering of Mark 14:36—"take this cup of suffering away from me"—the form (i.e., the "cup" image) is retained, but the words "of suffering" are added to clarify the meaning

Writing in Greek, the New Testament authors used words that had a long history in the secular world, but they invested them with Christian meanings as when John referred to Jesus as "the Logos." It was a perilous procedure because "logos" had a wide variety of meanings in Greek literature and philosophy, and non-Christian associations doubtlessly clung to the word. So John set the title within a teaching context, affirming that the Logos was in the beginning, was with God, was God, was the agent of creation, was the light and life of men, and became a human being (John 1:1-14). Similarly some Indian Christians have taken the risk of borrowing the Sanskrit word "avatar" (descent), used in Hinduism for the so-called "incarnations" of Vishnu, and applied it, with careful explanatory safeguards, to the unique incarnation of God in Jesus Christ. But others have refused to do so, on the ground that no safeguards are adequate to prevent misinterpretation.

The normative nature of Scripture

The Lausanne Covenant declares that Scripture is "without error in all that it affirms" (para. 2). This lays upon us the serious exegetical task of discerning exactly what Scripture is affirming. The essential meaning of the biblical message must at all costs be retained. Though some of the original forms in which this meaning was expressed may be changed for the sake of cross-cultural communication, we believe that they too have a certain normative quality. For God himself chose them as wholly appropriate vehicles of his revelation. So each fresh formulation and explanation in every generation and culture must be checked for faithfulness by referring back to the original.

The cultural conditioning of Scripture

We have not been able to devote as much time as we would have liked to the problem of the cultural conditioning of Scripture. We are agreed that some biblical commands (e.g., regarding the veiling of women in public and washing one another's feet) refer to cultural customs now obsolete in many parts of the world. Faced by such texts, we believe the right response is neither a slavishly literal obedience nor an irresponsible disregard, but rather first a critical discernment of the text's inner meaning and then a translation of it into our own culture. For example, the inner meaning of the command to wash each other's feet is that mutual love must express itself in humble service. So in some cultures we may clean each other's shoes instead. We are clear that the purpose of such "cultural transposition" is not to avoid obedience but rather to make it contemporary and authentic.

The controversial question of the status of women was not debated at our Consultation. But we acknowledge the need to search for an understanding which attempts with integrity to do justice to all the biblical teaching, and which sees the relations between men and women as being both rooted in the created order and at the same time wonderfully transformed by the new order which Jesus introduced.

The continuing work of the Holy Spirit

Does our emphasis on the finality and permanent normativeness of Scripture mean that we think the Holy Spirit has now ceased to operate? No, indeed not. But the nature of his teaching ministry has changed. We believe that his work of "inspiration" is done, in the sense that the canon of Scripture is closed, but that his work of "illumination" continues both in every conversion (e.g., 2 Cor. 4:6) and in the life of the Christian and the church. So we need constantly to pray that he will enlighten the eyes of our hearts so that we may know the fulness of God's purpose for us (Eph. 1:17ff) and may be not timorous but courageous in making decisions and undertaking fresh tasks today.

We have been made aware that the experience of the Holy Spirit revealing the application of God's truth to personal and church life is often less vivid than it should be: we all need a more sensitive openness at this point.

Questions for discussion

1. The commands of Genesis 1:26-28 are sometimes referred to as "the cultural mandate" which God gave to mankind. How responsibly is it being fulfilled today?

2. In the light of the definition of culture above, what are the main distinctive elements of your own culture?

3. If you know two languages, make up a sentence in one and then try to find a "dynamic equivalence" translation of it into the other.

4. Give other examples of "cultural transposition" which preserve the biblical text's "inner meaning" but transpose it into your own culture.

4. Understanding God's Word Today

The cultural factor is present not only in God's self-revelation in Scripture, but also in our interpretation of it. To this subject we now turn. All Christians are concerned to understand God's word, but there are different ways of trying to do so.

Traditional approaches

The commonest way is to come straight to the words of the biblical text, and to study them without any awareness that the writer's cultural context differs from the reader's. The reader interprets the text as if it had been written in his own language, culture and time.

We recognize that much Scripture can be read and understood in this way, especially if the translation is good. For God intended his word for ordinary people; it is not to be regarded as the preserve of scholars; the central truths of salvation are plain for all to see; Scripture is "useful for teaching the truth, rebuking error, correcting faults, and giving instruction for right living" (2 Tim. 3:16, TEV); and the Holy Spirit has been given to be our teacher.

The weakness of this "popular" approach, however, is that it does not seek first to understand the text in its original context; and, therefore, it runs the risk of missing the real meaning God intends and of substituting another.

A second approach takes with due seriousness the original historical and cultural context. It seeks also to discover what the text meant in its original language, and how it relates to the rest of Scripture. All this is an essential discipline because God spoke his word to a particular people in a particular context and time. So our understanding of God's message will grow when we probe deeply into these matters.

The weakness of this "historical" approach, however, is that it fails to consider what Scripture may be saying to the contemporary reader. It stops short at the meaning of the Bible in its own time and culture. It is thus liable to analyze the text without applying it, and to acquire academic knowledge without obedience. The interpreter may also tend to exaggerate the possibility of complete objectivity and ignore his or her own cultural presuppositions.

The contextual approach

A third approach begins by combining the positive elements of both the "popular" and the "historical" approaches. From the "historical" it takes the necessity of studying the original context and language, and from the "popular" the necessity of listening to God's word and obeying it. But it goes further than this. It takes seriously the cultural context of the contemporary readers as well as of the biblical text, and recognizes that a dialogue must develop between the two.

It is the need for this dynamic interplay between text and interpreters which we wish to emphasize. Today's readers cannot come to the text in a personal vacuum, and should not try to. Instead, they should come with an awareness of concerns stemming from their cultural background, personal situation, and responsibility to others. These concerns will influence the questions which are put to the Scriptures. What is received back, however, will not be answers only, but more questions. As we address Scripture, Scripture addresses us. We find that our culturally conditioned presuppositions are being challenged and our questions corrected. In fact, we are compelled to reformulate our previous questions and to ask fresh ones. So the living interaction proceeds.

In this process of interaction our knowledge of God and our response to his will are continuously being deepened. The more we come to know him, the greater our responsibility becomes to obey him in our own situation, and the more we respond obediently, the more he makes himself known.

It is this continuous growth in knowledge, love and obedience which is the purpose and profit of the "contextual" approach. Out of the context in which his word was originally given, we hear God speaking to us in our contemporary context, and we find it a transforming experience. This process is a kind of upward spiral in which Scripture remains always central and normative.

The learning community

We wish to emphasize that the task of understanding the Scriptures belongs not just to individuals but to the whole Christian community, seen as both a contemporary and a historical fellowship.

There are many ways in which the local or regional church can come to discern God's will in its own culture today. Christ still appoints pastors and teachers in his church. And in answer to expectant prayer he speaks to his people, especially through the preaching of his word in the context of worship. In addition, there is a place for "teaching and admonishing one another" (Col. 3:16) both in group Bible studies and in consulting sister churches, as well as for the quiet listening to the voice of God in the Scriptures, which is an indispensable element in the believer's Christian life.

The church is also a historical fellowship and has received from the past a rich inheritance of Christian theology, liturgy and devotion. No group of believers can disregard this heritage without risking spiritual impoverishment. At the same time, this tradition must not be received uncritically, whether it comes in the form of a set of denominational distinctives or in any other way but rather be tested by the Scripture it claims to expound. Nor must it be imposed on any church, but rather be made available to those who can use it as a valuable resource material, as a counterbalance to the spirit of independence, and as a link with the universal church.

Thus the Holy Spirit instructs his people through a variety of teachers of both the past and the present. We need each other. It is only "with all the saints" that we can begin to comprehend the full dimensions of God's love (Eph. 3:18, 19). The Spirit "illumines the minds of God's people in every culture to perceive its (that is, the Scripture's) truth freshly through their own eyes and thus discloses to the whole Church ever more of the many-coloured wisdom of God" (Lausanne Covenant, para. 2, echoing Eph. 3:10).

The silences of Scripture

We have also considered the problem of Scripture silences, that is, those areas of doctrine and ethics on which the Bible has nothing explicit to say. Written in the ancient Jewish and Graeco-Roman world, Scripture does not address itself directly, for example, to Hinduism, Buddhism, or Islam today, or to Marxist socio-economic theory, or modern technology. Nevertheless, we believe it is right for the church guided by the Holy Spirit to search the Scriptures for precedents and principles which will enable it to develop the mind of the Lord Christ and so be able to make authentically Christian decisions. This process will go on most fruitfully within the believing community as it worships God and engages in active obedience in the world. We repeat that Christian obedience is as much a prelude to understanding as a consequence of it.

Questions for discussion

1. Can you recall any examples of how either of the two "traditional approaches" to Bible reading had led you astray?

2. Choose a well known text like Matthew 6:24-34 (anxiety and ambition) or Luke 10:25-38 (the Good Samaritan) and use the "contextual approach" in studying it. Let a dialogue develop between you and the text, as you question it and it questions you. Write down the stages of the interaction.

3. Discuss some practical ways of seeking the guidance of the Holy Spirit today.

5. The Content and Communication of the Gospel

Having thought about God's communication of the gospel to us in Scripture, we now come to the very heart of our concern, our responsibility to communicate it to others, that is, to evangelize. But before we consider the communication of the gospel, we have to consider the content of the gospel which is to be communicated. For "to evangelize is to spread the good news..." (Lausanne Covenant, para. 4). Therefore there can be no evangelism without the evangel.

The Bible and the gospel

The gospel is to be found in the Bible. In fact, there is a sense in which the whole Bible is gospel, from Genesis to Revelation. For its overriding purpose throughout is to bear witness to Christ, to proclaim the good news that he is life-giver and Lord, and to persuade people to trust in him (e.g., John 5:39, 40; 20:31; 2 Tim. 3:15).

The Bible proclaims the gospel story in many forms. The gospel is like a multi-faceted diamond, with different aspects that appeal to different people in different cultures. It has depths we have not fathomed. It defies every attempt to reduce it to a neat formulation.

The heart of the gospel

Nevertheless, it is important to identify what is at the heart of the gospel. We recognize as central the themes of God as Creator, the universality of sin, Jesus Christ as Son of God, Lord of all, and Savior through his atoning death and risen life, the necessity of conversion, the coming of the Holy Spirit and his transforming power, the fellowship and mission of the Christian Church, and the hope of Christ's return.

While these are basic elements of the gospel, it is necessary to add that no theological statement is culture-free. Therefore, all theological formulations must be judged by the Bible itself, which stands above them all. Their value must be judged by their faithfulness to it as well as by the relevance with which they apply its message to their own culture.

In our desire to communicate the gospel effectively, we are often made aware of those elements in it which people dislike. For example, the cross has always been both an offense to the proud and folly to the wise. But Paul did not on that account eliminate it from his message. On the contrary, he continued to proclaim it, with faithfulness and at the risk of persecution, confident that Christ crucified is the wisdom and the power of God. We too, although concerned to contextualize our message and remove from it all unnecessary offense, must resist the temptation to accommodate it to human pride or prejudice. It has been given to us. Our responsibility is not to edit it but to proclaim it.

Cultural barriers to the communication of the gospel

No Christian witness can hope to communicate the gospel if he or she ignores the cultural factor. This is particularly true in the case of missionaries. For they are themselves the product of one culture and go to people who are the products of another. So inevitably they are involved in cross-cultural communication, with all its exciting challenge and exacting demand. Two main problems face them.

Sometimes people resist the gospel not because they think it false but because they perceive it as a threat to their culture, especially the fabric of their society, and their national or tribal solidarity. To some extent this cannot be avoided. Jesus Christ is a disturber as well as a peacemaker. He is Lord, and demands our total allegiance. Thus, some first-century Jews saw the gospel as undermining Judaism and accused Paul of "teaching men everywhere against the people, the law, and this place," i.e., the temple (Acts 21:28). Similarly, some first-century Romans feared for the stability of the state, since in their view the Christian missionaries, by saying that "there is another King, Jesus," were being disloyal to Caesar and advocating customs which were not lawful for Romans to practice (Acts 16:21; 17:7). Still today Jesus challenges many of the cherished beliefs and customs of every culture and society.

At the same time, there are features of every culture which are not incompatible with the lordship of Christ, and which therefore need not be threatened or discarded, but rather preserved and transformed. Messengers of the gospel need to develop a deep understanding of the local culture, and a genuine appreciation of it. Only then will they be able to perceive whether the resistance is to some unavoidable challenge of Jesus Christ or to some threat to the culture which, whether imaginary or real, is not necessary.

The other problem is that the gospel is often presented to people in alien cultural forms. Then the missionaries are resented and their message rejected because their work is seen not as an attempt to evangelize but as an attempt to impose their own customs and way of life. Where missionaries bring with them foreign ways of thinking and behaving, or attitudes of racial superiority, paternalism, or preoccupation with material things, effective communication will be precluded.

Sometimes these two cultural blunders are committed together, and messengers of the gospel are guilty of a cultural imperialism which both undermines the local culture unnecessarily and seeks to impose an alien culture instead. Some of the missionaries who accompanied the Catholic *conquistadores* of Latin America and the Protestant colonizers of Africa and Asia are historical examples of this double mistake. By contrast, the apostle Paul remains the supreme example of one whom Jesus Christ first stripped of pride in his own cultural privileges (Phil. 3:4-9) and then taught to adapt to the cultures of others, making himself their slave and becoming "all things to all men" in order by all means to save some (I Cor. 9:19-23).

Cultural sensitivity in communicating the gospel

Sensitive cross-cultural witnesses will not arrive at their sphere of service with a pre-packaged gospel. They must have a clear grasp of the "given" truth of the gospel. But they will fail to communicate successfully if they try to impose this on people without reference to their own cultural situation and that of the people to whom they go. It is only by active, loving engagement with the local people, thinking in their thought patterns, understanding their world-view, listening to their questions, and feeling their burdens, that the whole believing community (of which the missionary is a part) will be able to respond to their need. By common prayer, thought and heart-searching, in dependence on the Holy Spirit, expatriate and local believers may learn together how to present Christ and contextualize the gospel with an equal degree of faithfulness and relevance. We are not claiming that it will be easy, although some Third World cultures have a natural affinity to biblical culture. But we believe that fresh creative understandings do emerge when the Spirit-led believing community is listening and reacting sensitively to both the truth of Scripture and the needs of the world.

Christian witness in the Islamic world

Concern was expressed that insufficient attention had been given at our Consultation to the distinctive problems of the Christian mission in the Islamic world, though there are approximately 600 million Muslims today [Ed. note: amost 1 billionin 1992]. On the one hand, a resurgence of Islamic faith and mission is taking place in many lands; on the other hand, there is a new openness to the Gospel in a number of communities which are weakening their ties to traditional Islamic culture .

There is a need to recognize the distinctive features of Islam which provide a unique opportunity for Christian witness. Although there are in Islam elements which are incompatible with the gospel, there are also elements with a degree of what has been called "convertibility." For instance, our Christian understanding of God, expressed in Luther's great cry related to justification, "Let God be God," might well serve as an inclusive definition of Islam. The Islamic faith in divine unity, the emphasis on man's obligation to render God a right worship, and the utter rejection of idolatry could also be regarded as being in line with God's purpose for human life as revealed in Jesus Christ. Contemporary Christian witnesses should learn humbly and expectantly to identify, appreciate and illuminate these and other values. They should also wrestle for the transformation—and, where possible, integration—of all that is relevant in Islamic worship, prayer, fasting, art, architecture, and calligraphy.

All this proceeds only within a realistic appreciation of the present situation of the Islamic countries characterized by technological development and secularization. The social liabilities of new wealth and traditional poverty, the tensions of political independence, and the tragic Palestinian dispersion and frustration—all of these afford areas of relevant Christian witness. The last has given birth to much passionate poetry, one note in which is the paradigm of the suffering Jesus. These and other elements call for a new Christian sensitivity and a real awareness of the habits of introversion under which the church has for so long labored in the Middle East. Elsewhere, not least in sub-Sahara Africa, attitudes are more flexible and possibilities more fluid.

In order to fulfill more adequately the missionary challenge, fresh attempts are needed to develop ways of association of believers and seekers, if need be outside the traditional church forms. The crux of a lively, evangelizing sense of responsibility towards Muslims will always be the quality of Christian personal and corporate discipleship and the constraining love of Christ.

An expectation of results

Messengers of the gospel who have proved in their own experience that it is "the power of God for salvation" (Rom. 1:16) rightly expect it to be so in the experience of others also. We confess that sometimes, just as a Gentile centurion's faith put to shame the unbelief of Israel in Jesus' day (Matt. 8:10), so today the believing expectancy of Christians in other cultures sometimes shows up the missionary's lack of faith. So we remind ourselves of God's promises through Abraham's posterity to bless all the families of the earth and through the gospel to save those who believe (Gen. 12:1-4; I Cor. 1:21). It is on the basis of these and many other promises that we remind all messengers of the gospel, including ourselves, to look to God to save people and to build his church.

At the same time, we do not forget our Lord's warnings of opposition and suffering. Human hearts are hard. People do not always embrace the gospel, even when the communication is blameless in technique and the communicator in character. Our Lord himself was fully at home in the culture in which he preached, yet he and his message were despised and rejected, and his Parable of the Sower seems to warn us that most of the good seed we sow will not bear fruit. There is a mystery here we cannot fathom. "The Spirit blows where he wills" (John 3:8). While seeking to communicate the gospel with care, faithfulness and zeal, we leave the results to God in humility.

Questions for Discussion

1. In the above text, the Report refuses to give a "neat formulation" of the gospel, but identifies its "heart." Would you want to add to these "central themes," or subtract from them, or amplify them?

2. Clarify the "two cultural blunders." Can you think of examples? How can such mistakes be avoided?

3. Think of the cultural situation of the people you are wanting to win for Christ. What would "cultural sensitivity" mean in your case?

6. Wanted: Humble Messengers of the Gospel!

We believe that the principal key to persuasive Christian communication is to be found in the communicators themselves and what kind of people they are. It should go without saying that they need to be people of Christian faith, love, and holiness. That is, they must have a personal and growing experience of the transforming power of the Holy Spirit, so that the image of Jesus Christ is ever more clearly seen in their character and attitudes.

Above all else we desire to see in them, and especially in ourselves, "the meekness and gentleness of Christ" (2 Cor. 10:1), in other words, the humble sensitivity of Christ's love. So important do we believe this to be that we are devoting the whole of this section of our Report to it. Moreover, since, we have no wish to point the finger at anybody but ourselves, we shall use the first person plural throughout. First, we give an analysis of Christian humility in a missionary situation, and secondly, we turn to the Incarnation of God in Jesus Christ as the model we desire by his grace to follow.

An analysis of missionary humility

First, there is the humility to acknowledge the problem which culture presents, and not to avoid or over-simplify it. As we have seen, different cultures have strongly influenced the biblical revelation, ourselves, and the people to whom we go. As a result, we have several personal limitations in communicating the gospel. For we are prisoners (consciously or unconsciously) of our own culture, and our grasp of the cultures both of the Bible and of the country in which we serve is very imperfect. It is the interaction between all these cultures which constitutes the problem of communication; it humbles all who wrestle with it.

Secondly, there is the humility to take the trouble to understand and appreciate the culture of those to whom we go. It is this desire which leads naturally into that true dialogue "whose purpose is to listen sensitively in order to understand" (Lausanne Covenant, para. 4). We repent of the ignorance which assumes that we have all the answers and that our only role is to teach. We have very much to learn. We repent also of judgmental attitudes. We know we should never condemn or despise another culture, but rather respect it. We advocate neither the arrogance which imposes our culture on others, nor the syncretism which mixes the gospel with cultural elements incompatible with it, but rather a humble sharing of the good news—made possible by the mutual respect of a genuine friendship.

Thirdly, there is the humility to begin our communication where people actually are and not where we would like them to be. This is what we see Jesus doing, and we desire to follow his example. Too often we have ignored people's fears and frustrations, their pains and preoccupations, and their hunger, poverty, deprivation or oppression, in fact their "felt needs," and have been too slow to rejoice or to weep with them. We acknowledge that these "felt needs" may sometimes be symptoms of deeper needs which are not immediately felt or recognized by the people. A doctor does not necessarily accept a patient's self-diagnosis. Nevertheless, we see the need to begin where people are, but not to stop there. We accept our responsibility to gently and patiently lead them on to see themselves, as we see ourselves, as rebels to whom the gospel directly speaks with a message of pardon and hope. To begin where people are not is to share an irrelevant message; to stay where people are and never lead them on to the fulness of God's good news, is to share a truncated gospel. The humble sensitivity of love will avoid both errors.

Fourthly, there is the humility to recognize that even the most gifted, dedicated and experienced missionary can seldom communicate the gospel in another language or culture as effectively as a trained local Christian. This fact has been acknowledged in recent years by the Bible Societies, whose policy has changed from publishing translations by missionaries (with help from local people) to training mother-tongue specialists to do the translating. Only local Christians can answer the questions, "God, how would you say this in our language?" and "God, what will obedience to you mean in our culture?" Therefore, whether we are translating the Bible or communicating the gospel, local Christians are indispensable. It is they who must assume the responsibility to contextualize the gospel in their own languages and cultures. Would-be cross-cultural witnesses are not on that account necessarily superfluous; but we shall be welcome only if we are humble enough to see good communication as a team enterprise, in which all believers collaborate as partners.

Fifthly, there is the humility to trust in the Holy Spirit of God, who is always the chief communicator, who alone opens the eyes of the blind and brings people to new birth. "Without his witness, ours is futile" (Lausanne Covenant, para. 14).

The Incarnation as a model for Christian witness

We have met for our Consultation within a few days of Christmas, which might be called the most spectacular instance of cultural identification in the history of mankind, since by his Incarnation the Son became a first-century Galilean Jew.

We have also remembered that Jesus intended his people's mission in the world to be modeled on his own. "As the Father has sent me, even so I send you," he said (John 20:21; cf. 17:18). We have asked ourselves, therefore, about the implications of the Incarnation for all of us. The question is of special concern to cross-cultural witnesses, whatever country they go to, although we have thought particularly of those from the West who serve in the Third World.

Meditating on Philippians 2, we have seen that the self-humbling of Christ began in his mind: "he did not count equality with God a thing to be grasped." So we are commanded to let his mind be in us, and in humility of mind to "count" others better or more important than ourselves. This "mind" or "perspective" of Christ is a recognition of the infinite worth of human beings and of the privilege it is to serve them. Those witnesses who have the mind of Christ will have a profound respect for the people they serve, and for their cultures.

Two verbs then indicate the action to which the mind of Christ led him: "he emptied himself...he humbled himself..." The first speaks of sacrifice (what he renounced) and the second of service, even slavery (how he identified himself with us and put himself at our disposal). We have tried to think what these two actions meant for him, and might mean for cross-cultural witnesses.

We began with his *renunciation*. First, the renunciation of status. "Mild he laid his glory by," we have been singing at Christmas. Because we cannot conceive what his eternal glory was like, it is impossible to grasp the greatness of his self-emptying. But certainly he surrendered the rights, privileges, and powers which he enjoyed as God's Son. "Status" and "status symbols" mean much in the modern world, but are incongruous in missionaries. We believe that wherever missionaries are they should not be in control or work alone, but always with— and preferably under—local Christians who can advise and even direct them. And whatever the missionaries' responsibility may be they should express attitudes "not of domination but of service" (Lausanne Covenant, para. 11) .

Next the renunciation of independence. We have looked at Jesus—asking a Samaritan woman for water, living in other people's homes and on other people's money because he had none of his own, being lent a boat, a donkey, an upper room, and even being buried in a borrowed tomb. Similarly, cross-cultural messengers, especially during their first years of service, need to learn dependence on others.

Thirdly, the renunciation of immunity. Jesus exposed himself to temptation, sorrow, limitation, economic need, and pain. So the missionary should expect to become vulnerable to new temptations, dangers and diseases, a strange climate, an unaccustomed loneliness, and possibly death.

Turning from the theme of renunciation to that of *identification*, we have marvelled afresh at the completeness of our Saviour's identification with us, particularly as this is taught in the Letter to the Hebrews. He shared our "flesh and blood," was tempted as we are, learned obedience through his suffering and tasted death for us (Heb. 2:14-18; 4:15; 5:8). During his public ministry Jesus befriended the poor and the powerless, healed the sick, fed the hungry, touched untouchables, and risked his reputation by associating with those whom society rejected.

The extent to which we identify ourselves with the people to whom we go is a matter of controversy. Certainly it must include mastering their language, immersing ourselves in their culture, learning to think as they think, feel as they feel, do as they do. At the socio-economic level we do not believe that we should "go native," principally because a foreigner's attempt to do this may not be seen as authentic but as play-acting. But neither do we think there should be a conspicuous disparity between our life style and that of the people around us. In between these extremes, we see the possibility of developing a standard of living which expresses the kind of love which cares and shares, and which finds it natural to exchange hospitality with others on a basis of reciprocity, without embarrassment. A searching test of identification is how far we feel that we belong to the people, and still more—how far they feel that we belong to them. Do we participate naturally in days of national or tribal thanksgiving or sorrow? Do we groan with them in the oppression which they suffer and join them in their quest for justice and freedom? If the country is struck by earthquake or engulfed in civil war, is our instinct to stay and suffer with the people we love, or to fly home?

Although Jesus identified himself completely with us, he did not lose his own identity. He remained himself. "He came down from heaven...and was made man" (Nicene Creed); yet in becoming one of us he did not cease to be God. Just so, "Christ's evangelists must humbly seek to empty themselves of all but their personal authenticity" (Lausanne Covenant, para. 10). The Incarnation teaches identification without loss of identity. We believe that true self-sacrifice leads to true self-discovery. In humble service there is abundant joy.

Questions for Discussion

1. If the main key to communication lies in the communicators, what sort of people should they be?
2. Give your own analysis of the humility which all Christian witnesses should have. Where would you put your emphasis?
3. Since the Incarnation involved both "renunciation" and "identification," it was obviously very costly for Jesus. What would be the cost of "incarnation evangelism" today?

7. Conversion and Culture

We have thought of the relations between conversion and culture in two ways. First, what effect does conversion have on the cultural situation of converts, the ways they think and act, and their attitudes to their social environment? Secondly, what effect has our culture had on our own understanding of conversion? Both questions are important. But we want to say at once that elements in our traditional evangelical view of conversion are more cultural than biblical and need to be challenged. Too often we have thought of conversion as a crisis, instead of as a process as well; or we have viewed conversion as a largely private experience, forgetting its consequent public and social responsibilities.

The radical nature of conversion

We are convinced that the radical nature of conversion to Jesus Christ needs to be reaffirmed in the contemporary church. For we are always in danger of trivializing it, as if it were no more than a surface change, and a self-reformation at that. But the New Testament authors write of it as the outward expression of a regeneration or new birth by God's spirit, a recreation, and resurrection from spiritual death. The concept of resurrection seems to be particularly important. For the resurrection of Jesus Christ from the dead was the beginning of the new creation of God, and by God's grace through union with Christ we have shared in this resurrection. We have therefore entered the new age and have already tasted its powers and its joys. This is the eschatological dimension of Christian conversion. Conversion is an integral part of the Great Renewal which God has begun, and which will be brought to a triumphant climax when Christ comes in his glory.

Conversion involves as well a break with the past so complete that it is spoken of in terms of death. We have been crucified with Christ. Through his cross we have died to the godless world, its outlook, and its standards. We have also "put off" like a soiled garment the old Adam, our former and fallen humanity. And Jesus warned us that this turning away from the past may involve painful sacrifices, even the loss of family and possessions (e.g., Lk. 14:25ff).

It is vital to keep together these negative and positive aspects of conversion, the death and the resurrection, the putting off of the old and the putting on of the new. For we who died are alive again, but alive now with a new life lived in, for, and under Christ.

The lordship of Jesus Christ

We are clear that the fundamental meaning of conversion is a change of allegiance. Other gods and lords—idolatries every one—previously ruled over us. But now Jesus Christ is Lord. The governing principle of the converted life is that it is lived under the lordship of Christ or (for it comes to the same thing) in the Kingdom of God. His authority over us is total. So this new and liberating allegiance leads inevitably to a reappraisal of every aspect of our lives and in particular of our world-view, our behavior, and our relationships.

First, our world-view. We are agreed that the heart of every culture is a "religion" of some kind, even if it is an irreligious religion like Marxism. "Culture is religion made visible" (J. H. Bavinck). And "religion" is a whole cluster of basic beliefs and values, which is the reason why for our purposes we are using "world-view" as an equivalent expression. True conversion to Christ is bound, therefore, to strike at the heart of our cultural inheritance. Jesus Christ insists on dislodging from the center of our world whatever idol previously reigned there, and occupying the throne himself. This is the radical change of allegiance which constitutes conversion, or at least its beginning. Then once Christ has taken his rightful place, everything else starts shifting. The shock waves flow from the center to the circumference. The convert has to rethink his or her fundamental convictions. This is *metanoia*, "repentance" viewed as a change of mind, the replacement of "the mind of the flesh" by "the mind of Christ." Of course, the development of an integrated Christian world-view may take a lifetime, but it is there in essence from the start. If it does grow, the explosive consequences cannot be predicted.

Secondly, our behavior. The lordship of Jesus challenges our moral standards and whole ethical life style. Strictly speaking, this is not "repentance" but rather the "fruit that befits repentance" (Matt. 3:8), the change of conduct which issues from a change of outlook. Both our minds and our wills must submit to the obedience of Christ (cf. II Cor. 10:5; Matt. 11:29, 30; John 13:13).

Listening to case studies of conversion we have been impressed by the primacy of love in the new convert's experience. Conversion delivers both from the inversion which is too preoccupied with self to bother about other people and from the fatalism which considers it impossible to help them. Conversion is spurious if it does not liberate us to love.

Thirdly, our relationships. Although the convert should do his utmost to avoid a break with nation, tribe and family, sometimes painful conflicts arise. It is clear also that conversion involves a transfer from one community to another, that is, from fallen humanity to God's new humanity. It happened from the very beginning on the Day of Pentecost: "Save yourselves from this crooked generation," Peter appealed. So those who received his message were baptized into the new society, devoted themselves to the new fellowship, and found that the Lord continued to add to their numbers daily (Acts 2:40-47). At the same time, their "transfer" from one group to another meant rather that they were spiritually distinct than that they were socially segregated. They did not abandon the world. On the contrary, they gained a new commitment to it, and went out into it to witness and to serve.

All of us should cherish great expectations of such radical conversions in our day, involving converts in a new mind, a new way of life, a new community, and a new mission, all under the lordship of Christ. Yet now we feel the need to make several qualifications.

The convert and his culture

Conversion should not "de-culturize" a convert. True, as we have seen, the Lord Jesus now holds his or her allegiance, and everything in the cultural context must come under his Lord's scrutiny. This applies to every culture, not just to those of Hindu, Buddhist, Muslim, or animistic cultures but also to the increasingly materialistic culture of the West. The critique may lead to a collision, as elements of the culture come under the judgment of Christ and have to be rejected. At this point, on the rebound, the convert may try to adopt the evangelist's culture instead; the attempt should be firmly but gently resisted.

The convert should be encouraged to see his or her relation to the past as a combination of rupture and continuity. However much new converts feel they need to renounce for the sake of Christ, they are still the same people with the same heritage and the same family. "Conversion does not unmake; it remakes." It is always tragic, though in some situations it is unavoidable, when a person's conversion to Christ is interpreted by others as treachery to his or her own cultural origins. If possible, in spite of the conflicts with their own culture, new converts should seek to identify with their culture's joys, hopes, pains, and struggles.

Case histories show that converts often pass through three stages: (1) "rejection" (when they see themselves as "new persons in Christ" and repudiate everything associated with their past); (2) "accommodation" (when they discover their ethnic and cultural heritage, with the temptation to compromise the new-found Christian faith in relation to their heritage); and (3) "the re-establishment of identity" (when either the rejection of the past or the accommodation to it may increase, or preferably, they may grow into a balanced self-awareness in Christ and in culture).

The power encounter

"Jesus is Lord" means more than that he is Lord of the individual convert's world-view, standards and relationships, and more even than that he is Lord of culture. It means that he is Lord of the powers, having been exalted by the Father to universal sovereignty; principalities and powers having been made subject to him (I Peter 3:22). A number of us, especially those from Asia, Africa, and Latin America, have spoken both of the reality of evil powers and of the necessity to demonstrate the supremacy of Jesus over them. For conversion involves a power encounter. People give their allegiance to Christ when they see that his power is superior to magic and voodoo, the curses and blessings of witch doctors, and the malevolence of evil spirits, and that his salvation is a real liberation from the power of evil and death.

Of course, some are questioning today whether a belief in spirits is compatible with our modern scientific understanding of the universe. We wish to affirm, therefore, against the mechanistic myth on which the typical western world-view rests, the reality of demonic intelligences which are concerned by all means, overt and covert, to discredit Jesus Christ and keep people from coming to him. We think it vital in evangelism in all cultures to teach the reality and hostility of demonic powers, and to proclaim that God has exalted Christ as Lord of all and that Christ, who really does possess all power, however we may fail to acknowledge this, can (as we proclaim him) break through any world-view in any mind to make his lordship known and bring about a radical change of heart and outlook.

We wish to emphasize that the power belongs to Christ. Power in human hands is always dangerous. We have called to mind the recurring theme of Paul's two letters to the Corinthians—that God's power, which is clearly seen in the cross of Christ, operates through human weakness (e.g., I Cor. 1:18-2:5; II Cor. 4:7; 12:9, 10). Worldly people worship power; Christians who have it know its perils. It is better to be weak, for then we are strong. We specially honor the Christian martyrs of recent days (e.g., in East Africa) who have renounced the way of power, and followed the way of the cross.

Individual and group conversions

Conversion should not be conceived as being invariably and only an individual experience, although that has been the pattern of western expectation for many years. On the contrary, the covenant theme of the Old Testament and the household baptisms of the New should lead us to desire, work for, and expect both family and group conversions. Much important research has been undertaken in recent years into "people movements" from both theological and sociological perspectives. Theologically, we recognize the biblical emphasis on the solidarity of each *ethnos*, i.e., nation or people. Sociologically, we recognize that each society is composed of a variety of subgroups, subcultures or homogeneous units. It is evident that people receive the gospel most readily when it is presented to them in a manner which is appropriate—and not alien—to their culture, and when they can respond to it with and among their own people. Different societies have different procedures for making group decisions, e.g., by consensus, by the head of the family, or by a group of elders. We recognize the validity of the corporate dimension of conversion as part of the total process, as well as the necessity for each member of the group ultimately to share in it personally.

Is conversion sudden or gradual?

Conversion is often more gradual than traditional evangelical teaching has allowed. True, this may be only a dispute about words. Justification and regeneration, the one conveying a new status and the other a new life, are works of God and instantaneous, although we are not necessarily aware when they take place. Conversion, on the other hand, is our own action (moved by God's grace) of turning to God in penitence and faith. Although it may include a conscious crisis, it is often slow and sometimes laborious. Seen against the background of the Hebrew and Greek vocabulary, conversion is in essence a turning to God, which continues as all areas of life are brought in increasingly radical ways under the lordship of Christ. Conversion involves the Christian's complete transformation and total renewal in mind and character according to the likeness of Christ (Rom 12:1,2).

This progress does not always take place, however. We have given some thought to the sad phenomena called "backsliding" (a quiet slipping away from Christ) and "apostasy" (an open repudiation of him). These have a variety of causes. Some people turn away from Christ when they become disenchanted with the church; others capitulate to the pressures of secularism or of their former culture. These facts challenge us both to proclaim a full gospel and to be more conscientious in nurturing converts in the faith and in training them for service.

One member of our Consultation has described his experience in terms of turning first to Christ (receiving his salvation and acknowledging his lordship), secondly to culture (rediscovering his natural origins and identity), and thirdly to the world (accepting the mission on which Christ sends him). We agree that conversion is often a complex experience, and that the biblical language of "turning" is used in different ways and contexts. At the same time, we all emphasize that personal commitment to Jesus Christ is foundational. In him alone we find salvation, new life, and personal identity. Conversion must also result in new attitudes and relationships, and lead to a responsible involvement in our church, our culture, and our world. Finally, conversion is a journey, a pilgrimage, with ever-new challenges, decisions, and returnings to the Lord as the constant point of reference, until he comes.

Questions for Discussion

1. Distinguish between "regeneration" and "conversion" according to the New-Testament.

2. "Jesus is Lord." What does this mean for you in your own culture? What are the elements of your cultural heritage which you feel (a) you must, and (b) you need not, renounce for the sake of Christ?

3. What is sudden and what is (or may be) gradual in Christian conversion?

8. Church and Culture

In the process of church formation, as in the communication and reception of the gospel, the question of culture is vital. If the gospel must be contextualized, so must the church. Indeed, the sub-title of our Consultation has been "the contextualization of Word and Church in a missionary situation."

Older, traditional approaches

During the missionary expansion of the early part of the 19th century, it was generally assumed that churches "on the mission field" would be modeled on churches "at home." The tendency was to produce almost exact replicas. Gothic architecture, prayer book liturgies, clerical dress, musical instruments, hymns and tunes, decision-making processes, synods and committees, superintendents and archdeacons—all were exported and unimaginatively introduced into the new mission-founded churches. It should be added that these patterns were also eagerly adopted by the new Christians, determined not to be at any point behind their western friends, whose habits and ways of worship they had been attentively watching. But all this was based on the false assumptions that the Bible gave specific instructions about such matters and that the home churches' pattern of government, worship, ministry, and life were themselves exemplary.

In reaction to this monocultural export system, pioneer missionary thinkers like Henry Venn and Rufus Anderson in the middle of the last century and Roland Allen earlier in this century popularized the concept of "indigenous" churches, which would be "self-governing, self-supporting and self-propagating." They argued their case well. They pointed out that the policy of the apostle Paul was to plant churches, not to found mission stations. They also added pragmatic arguments to biblical ones, namely that indigeneity was indispensable to the church's growth in maturity and mission. Henry Venn confidently looked forward to the day when missions would hand over all responsibility to national churches, and then what he called "the euthanasia of the mission" would take place. These views gained wide acceptance and were immensely influential.

In our day, however, they are being criticized, not because of the ideal itself, but because of the way it has often been applied. Some missions, for example, have accepted the need for indigenous leadership and have then gone on to recruit and train local leaders, indoctrinating them (the word is harsh but not unfair) in western ways of thought and procedure. These westernized local leaders have then preserved a very western-looking church, and the foreign orientation has persisted, only lightly cloaked by the appearance of indigeneity.

Now, therefore, a more radical concept of indigenous church life needs to be developed, by which each church may discover and express its selfhood as the body of Christ within its own culture.

The dynamic equivalence model

Using the distinctions between "form" and "meaning," and between "formal correspondence" and "dynamic equivalence," which have been developed in translation theory and on which we have commented, it is being suggested that an analogy may be drawn between Bible translation and church formation. "Formal correspondence" speaks of a slavish imitation, whether in translating a word into another language or exporting a church model to another culture. Just as a "dynamic equivalence" translation, however, seeks to convey to contemporary readers meanings equivalent to those conveyed to the original readers, by using appropriate cultural forms, so would a "dynamic equivalence" church. It would look in its culture as a good Bible translation looks in its language. It would preserve the essential meanings and functions which the New Testament predicated of the church, but would seek to express these in forms equivalent to the originals but appropriate to the local culture.

We have all found this model helpful and suggestive, and we strongly affirm the ideals it seeks to express. It rightly rejects foreign imports and imitations, and rigid structures. It rightly looks to the New Testament for the principles of church formation, rather than to either tradition or culture, and it equally rightly looks to the local culture for the appropriate forms in which these principles should be expressed. All of us (even those who see limitations in the model) share the vision which it is trying to describe.

Thus, the New Testament indicates that the church is always a worshipping community, "a holy priesthood to offer spiritual sacrifices to God through Jesus Christ" (I Pet. 2:5), but forms of worship (including the presence or absence of different kinds of liturgy, ceremony, music, color, drama, etc.) will be developed by the church in keeping with indigenous culture. Similarly, the church is always a witnessing and a serving community, but its methods of evangelizm and its program of social involvement will vary. Again, God desires all churches to have pastoral oversight, but forms of government and ministry may differ widely, and the selection, training, ordination, service, dress, payment, and accountability of pastors will be determined by the church to accord with biblical principles and to suit the local culture.

The questions which are being asked about the "dynamic equivalence" model are whether by itself it is large enough and dynamic enough to provide all the guidance which is needed. The analogy between Bible translation and church formation is not exact. In the former the translator controls the work, and when the task is complete it is possible to make a comparison of the two texts. In the latter, however, the original to which an equivalent is being sought is not a detailed text but a series of glimpses of the early church in operation, making the comparison more difficult, and instead of a controlling translator, the whole community of faith must be involved. Further, a translator aims at personal objectivity, but when the local church is seeking to relate itself appropriately to the local culture, it finds objectivity almost impossible. In many situations it is caught in "an encounter between two civilizations" (that of its own society and that of the missionaries). Furthermore, it may have great difficulty in responding to the conflicting voices of the local community. Some clamor for change (in terms of literacy, education, technology, modern medicine, industrialization, etc.) while others insist on the conservation of the old culture and resist the arrival of a new day. It is asked whether the "dynamic equivalence" model is dynamic enough to face this kind of challenge.

The test of this or any other model for helping churches develop appropriately, is whether it can enable God's people to capture in their hearts and minds the grand design of which their church is to be the local expression. Every model presents only a partial picture. Local churches need to rely ultimately on the dynamic pressure of the Living Lord of history. For it is he who will guide his people in every age to develop their church life in such a way as both to obey the instructions he has given in Scripture and to reflect the good elements of their local culture.

The freedom of the church

If each church is to develop creatively in such a way as to find and express itself, it must be free to do so. This is its inalienable right. For each church is God's church. United to Christ, it is a dwelling place of God through his Spirit (Eph. 2:22). Some missions and missionaries have been slow to recognize this and to accept its implications in the direction of indigenous forms and an every-member ministry. This is one of the many causes which have led to the formation of Independent Churches, notably in Africa, which are seeking new ways of self-expression in terms of local culture.

Although local church leaders have also sometimes impeded indigenous development, the chief blame lies elsewhere. It would not be fair to generalize. The situation has always been diverse. In earlier generations there were missions which never manifested a spirit of domination. In this century some churches have sprung up which have never been under missionary control, having enjoyed self-government from the start. In other cases missions have entirely surrendered their former power, so that some mission-founded churches are now fully autonomous, and many missions now work in genuine partnership with churches.

Yet this is not the whole picture. Other churches are still almost completely inhibited from developing their own identity and program by policies laid down from afar, by the introduction and continuation of foreign traditions, by the use of expatriate leadership, by alien decision-making processes, and especially by the manipulative use of money. Those who maintain such control may be genuinely unaware of the way in which their actions are regarded and experienced at the other end. They may be felt by the churches concerned to be a tyranny. The fact that this is neither intended nor realized illustrates perfectly how all of us (whether we know it or not) are involved in the culture which has made us what we are. We strongly oppose such "foreignness," wherever it exists, as a serious obstacle to maturity and mission, and a quenching of the Holy Spirit of God.

It was in protest against the continuance of foreign control that a few years ago the call was made to withdraw all missionaries. In this debate some of us want to avoid the word "moratorium" because it has become an emotive term and sometimes betrays a resentment against the very concept of "missionaries."

Others of us wish to retain the word in order to emphasize the truth it expresses. To us it means not a rejection of missionary personnel and money in themselves, but only of their misuse in such a way as to suffocate local initiative. We all agree with the statement of the Lausanne Covenant that "a reduction of foreign missionaries and money...may sometimes be necessary to facilitate the national church's growth in self-reliance..." (para. 9).

Power structures and mission

What we have just written is part of a much wider problem, which we have not felt able to ignore. The contemporary world does not consist of isolated atomic societies, but is an interrelated global system of economic, political, technological, and ideological macro-structures, which undoubtedly results in much exploitation and oppression.

What has this got to do with mission? And why do we raise it here? Partly because it is the context within which the gospel must be preached to all nations today. Partly also because nearly all of us either belong to the Third World, or live and work there, or have done so, or have visited some countries in it. So we have seen with our own eyes the poverty of the masses, we feel for them and with them, and we have some understanding that their plight is due in part to an economic system which is controlled mostly by the North Atlantic countries (although others are now also involved). Those of us who are citizens of North American or European countries cannot avoid some feeling of embarrassment and shame, by reason of the oppression in which our countries in various degrees have been involved. Of course, we know that there is oppression in many countries today, and we oppose it everywhere. But now we are talking about ourselves, our own countries, and our responsibility as Christians. Most of the world's missionaries and missionary money come from these countries, often at great personal sacrifice. Yet we have to confess that some missionaries themselves reflect a neo-colonial attitude and even defend it, together with outposts of western power and exploitation such as Southern Africa.

So what should we do? The only honest response is to say that we do not know. Armchair criticism smacks of hypocrisy. We have no ready-made solutions to offer to this worldwide problem. Indeed, we feel victims of the system ourselves. And yet we are also part of it. So we feel able to make only these comments.

First, Jesus himself constantly identified with the poor and weak. We accept the obligation to follow in his footsteps in this matter as in all others. At least by the love which prays and gives we mean to strengthen our solidarity with them.

Jesus did more than identify, however. In his teaching and that of the apostles the corollary of good news to the oppressed was a word of judgment to the oppressor (e.g., Luke 6:24-26; Jas. 5:1-6). We confess that in complex economic situations it is not easy to identify oppressors in order to denounce them without resorting to a shrill rhetoric which neither costs nor accomplishes anything. Nevertheless, we accept that there will be occasions when it is our Christian duty to speak out against injustice in the name of the Lord who is the God of justice as well as of justification. We shall seek from him the courage and wisdom to do so.

Thirdly, this Consultation has expressed its concern about syncretism in Third World churches. But we have not forgotten that western churches fall prey to the same sin. Indeed, perhaps the most insidious form of syncretism in the world today is the attempt to mix a privatized gospel of personal forgiveness with a worldly (even demonic) attitude to wealth and power. We are not guilt-less in this matter ourselves. Yet we desire to be integrated Christians for whom Jesus is truly Lord of all. So we who belong to, or come from, the West will exam-ine ourselves and seek to purge ourselves of western-style syncretism. We agree that "the salvation we claim should be transforming us in the totality of our per-sonal and social responsibilities. Faith without works is dead" (Lausanne Cove-nant, para. 5).

The danger of provincialism

We have emphasized that the church must be allowed to indigenize itself, and to "celebrate, sing and dance" the gospel in its own cultural medium. At the same time, we wish to be alert to the dangers of this process. Some churches in all six continents go beyond a joyful and thankful discovery of their local cultural heritage, and either become boastful and assertive about it (a form of chauvin-ism) or even absolutize it (a form of idolatry). More common than either of these extremes, however, is "provincialism," that is, such a retreat into their own cul-ture as cuts them adrift from the rest of the church and from the wider world. This is a frequent stance in western churches as well as in the Third World. It denies the God of creation and redemption. It is to proclaim one's freedom, only to enter another bondage. We draw attention to the three major reasons why we think this attitude should be avoided.

First, each church is part of the universal church. The people of God are by his grace a unique multi-racial, multi-national, multi-cultural community. This community is God's new creation, his new humanity, in which Christ has abol-ished all barriers (see Ephesians 2 and 3). There is therefore no room for racism in the Christian society, or for tribalism—whether in its African form, or in the form of European social classes, or of the Indian caste system. Despite the church's fail-ures, this vision of a supra-ethnic community of love is not a romantic ideal, but a command of the Lord. Therefore, while rejoicing in our cultural inheritance and developing our own indigenous forms, we must always remember that our pri-mary identity as Christians is not in our particular cultures but in the one Lord and his one body (Eph. 4:3-6).

Secondly, each church worships the living God of cultural diversity. If we thank him for our cultural heritage, we should thank him for others' also. Our church should never become so culture-bound that visitors from another culture do not feel welcome. Indeed, we believe it is enriching for Christians, if they have the opportunity, to develop a bi-cultural and even a multi-cultural existence, like the apostle Paul who was both a Hebrew of the Hebrews, a master of the Greek language, and a Roman citizen.

Thirdly, each church should enter into a "partnership...in giving and receiv-ing" (Phil. 4:15). No church is, or should try to become, self-sufficient. So churches should develop with each other relationships of prayer, fellowship, interchange of ministry and cooperation. Provided that we share the same central truths (including the supreme lordship of Christ, the authority of Scripture, the necessity of conversion, confidence in the power of the Holy Spirit, and the obligations of holiness and witness), we should be outgoing and not timid in seeking fellowship; and we should share our spiritual gifts and ministries, knowledge, skills, experience, and financial resources. The same principle applies to cultures. A church must be free to reject alien cultural forms and develop its own; it should also feel free to borrow from others. This way lies maturity.

One example of this concerns theology. Cross-cultural witnesses must not attempt to impose a ready-made theological tradition on the church in which they serve, either by personal teaching or by literature or by controlling seminary and Bible college curricula. For every theological tradition both contains elements which are biblically questionable and have been ecclesiastically divisive and omits elements which, while they might be of no great consequence in the country where they originated, may be of immense importance in other contexts. At the same time, although missionaries ought not to impose their own tradition on others, they also ought not to deny them access to it (in the form of books, confessions, catechism, liturgies and hymns), since it doubtless represents a rich heritage of faith. Moreover, although the theological controversies of the older churches should not be exported to the younger churches, yet an understanding of the issues, and of the work of the Holy Spirit in the unfolding history of Christian doctrine, should help to protect them from unprofitable repetition of the same battles.

Thus we should seek with equal care to avoid theological imperialism or theological provincialism. A church's theology should be developed by the community of faith out of the Scripture in interaction with other theologies of the past and present, and with the local culture and its needs.

The danger of syncretism

As the church seeks to express its life in local cultural forms, it soon has to face the problem of cultural elements which either are evil or have evil associations. How should the church react to these? Elements which are intrinsically false or evil clearly cannot be assimilated into Christianity without a lapse into syncretism. This is a danger for all churches in all cultures. If the evil is in the association only, however, we believe it is right to seek to "baptize" it into Christ. It is the principle on which William Booth operated when he set Christian words to popular music, asking why the devil should have all the best tunes. Thus many African churches now use drums to summon people to worship, although previously they were unacceptable, as being associated with war dances and mediumistic rites.

Yet this principle raises problems. In a proper reaction against foreigners, an improper flirtation with the demonic element of local culture sometimes takes place. So the church, being first and foremost a servant of Jesus Christ, must learn to scrutinize all culture, both foreign and local, in the light of his lordship and God's revelation. By what guidelines, therefore, does a church accept or reject culture traits in the process of contextualization? How does it prevent or detect and eliminate heresy (wrong teaching) and syncretism (harmful carry-overs from the old way of life)? How does it protect itself from becoming a "folk church" in which church and society are virtually synonymous?

One particular model we have studied is that of the church in Bali, Indonesia, which is now about 40 years old. Its experience has provided the following guidelines:

The believing community first searched the Scriptures and learned from them many important biblical truths. They then observed that other churches (e.g., round the Mediterranean) used architecture to symbolize Christian truth. This was important because the Balinese are very "visual" people and value visible signs. So it was decided, for example, to express their affirmation of faith in the Trinity in a Balinese-style three-tiered roof for their church buildings. The symbol was first considered by the council of elders who, after studying both biblical and cultural factors, recommended it to local congregations.

The detection and elimination of heresy followed a similar pattern. When believers suspected an error in life or teaching, they would report it to an elder, who would take it to the council of elders. Having considered the matter, they in their turn passed their recommendations to the local churches who had the final word.

What was the most important safeguard of the church? To this question the answer was: "we believe that Jesus Christ is Lord and Master of all powers." By preaching his power, "the same yesterday and today and forever," by insisting at all times on the normative nature of the Scriptures, by entrusting elders with the obligation to reflect on Scripture and culture, by breaking down all barriers to fellowship, and by building into structures, catechism, art forms, drama, etc., constant reminders of the exalted position of Jesus Christ, his church has been preserved in truth and holiness.

Sometimes, in different parts of the world, a cultural element may be adopted which deeply disturbs oversensitive consciences, especially those of new converts. This is the problem of the "weaker brother" of whom Paul writes in connection with idol-meats. Since idols were nothing, Paul himself had liberty of conscience to eat these meats. But for the sake of "weaker" Christians with a less well-educated conscience, who would be offended to see him eat, he refrained, at least in specific situations in which such offense might be caused. The principle still applies today. Scripture takes conscience seriously and tells us not to violate it. It needs to be educated in order to become "strong," but while it remains "weak" it must be respected. A strong conscience will give us freedom; but love limits liberty.

The church's influence on culture

We deplore the pessimism which leads some Christians to disapprove of active cultural engagement in the world, and the defeatism which persuades others that they could do no good there anyway and should therefore wait in inactivity for Christ to put things right when he comes. Many historical examples could be given, drawn from different ages and countries, of the powerful influence which—under God—the church has exerted on a prevailing culture, purging, claiming, and beautifying it for Christ. Though all such attempts have had defects, they do not prove the enterprise mistaken.

We prefer, however, to base the church's cultural responsibility on Scripture rather than on history. We have reminded ourselves that our fellow men and women are made in God's image, and that we are commanded to honor, love, and serve them in every sphere of life. To this argument from God's creation we add another from his kingdom which broke into the world through Jesus Christ. All authority belongs to Christ. He is lord of both universe and church. And he has sent us into the world to be its salt and light. As his new community, he expects us to permeate society.

Thus we are to challenge what is evil and affirm what is good; to welcome and seek to promote all that is wholesome and enriching in art, science, technology, agriculture, industry, education, community development and social welfare; to denounce injustice and support the powerless and the oppressed; to spread the good news of Jesus Christ, which is the most liberating and humanizing force in the world; and to actively engage in good works of love. Although, in social and cultural activity as in evangelism, we must leave the results to God, we are confident that he will bless our endeavors and use them to develop in our community a new consciousness of what is "true, noble, right, pure, lovely, and honorable" (Phil. 4:8, TEV). Of course, the church cannot impose Christian standards on an unwilling society, but it can commend them by both argument and example. All this will bring glory to God and greater opportunities of humanness to our fellow human being whom he made and loves. As the Lausanne Covenant put it, "churches must seek to transform and enrich culture, all for the glory of God" (para. 10).

Nevertheless, naive optimism is as foolish as dark pessimism. In place of both, we seek a sober Christian realism. On the one hand, Jesus Christ reigns. On the other, he has not yet destroyed the forces of evil; they still rampage. So in every culture Christians find themselves in a situation of conflict and often of suffering. We are called to fight against the "cosmic powers of this dark age" (Eph. 6:12, TEV). So we need each other. We must put on all God's armor, and especially the mighty weapon of believing prayer. We also remember the warnings of Christ and his apostles that before the end there will be an unprecedented outbreak of wickedness and violence. Some events and developments in our contemporary world indicate that the spirit of the coming Antichrist is already at work not only in the non-Christian world, but both in our own partially Christianized societies and even in the churches themselves. "We therefore reject as a proud, self-confident dream the notion that man can ever build a utopia on earth" (Lausanne Covenant, para. 15), and as a groundless fantasy that society is going to evolve into perfection.

Instead, while energetically laboring on earth, we look forward with joyful anticipation to the return of Christ, and to the new heavens and new earth in which righteousness will dwell. For then not only will culture be transformed, as the nations bring their glory into the New Jerusalem (Rev. 21:24-26) but the whole creation will be liberated from its present bondage of futility, decay and pain, so as to share the glorious freedom of God's children (Rom. 8:18-25, TEV). Then at last every knee will bow to Christ and every tongue openly proclaim that he is Lord, to the glory of God the Father (Phil. 2:9-11).

Questions for Discussion

1. Is your local church "free" to develop its own selfhood? If not, what forces are hindering it?

2. Some hard things have been said in this text about "power-structures." Do you agree? If so, can you do anything about it?

3. "Provincialism" and "syncretism" are both mistakes of a church which is trying to express its identity in local cultural forms. Is your church making either mistake? How can they be avoided without repudiating indigenous culture?

4. Should the church in your country be doing more to "transform and enrich" its national culture? If so, in what way?

9. Culture, Christian Ethics and Life Style

Having considered some of the cultural factors in Christian conversion, we come finally to the relations between culture and Christian ethical behavior. For the new life Christ gives his people is bound to issue a new life style.

Christ-centerdness and Christ-likeness

One of the themes running right through our Consultation has been the supreme Lordship of Jesus Christ. He is Lord of the universe and the church; he is Lord of the individual believer also. We find ourselves gripped by the love of Christ. It hems us in and leaves us no escape. Because we enjoy newness of life through his death for us, we have no alternative (and desire none) but to live for him who died for us and rose again (2 Cor. 5:14, 15). Our first loyalty is to him, to seek to please him, to live a life worthy of him, and to obey him. This necessitates the renunciation of all lesser loyalties. So we are forbidden to conform ourselves to this world's standards, that is, to any prevailing culture which fails to honor God, and are commanded instead to be transformed in our conduct by renewed minds which perceive the will of God.

God's will was perfectly obeyed by Jesus. Therefore, "the most outstanding thing about a Christian should not be his culture, but his Christlikeness." As the mid-second century *Letter to Diognetus* puts it: "Christians are not distinguished from the rest of mankind by country or by speech or by customs...they follow the customs of the land in clothing and food and other matters of daily life, yet the condition of citizenship which they exhibit is wonderful...in a word, what the soul is in the body, that Christians are in the world."

Moral standards and cultural practices

Culture is never static. It varies both from place to place and from time to time. And throughout the long history of the church in different countries, Christianity has, in some measure, destroyed culture, preserved it, and in the end created a new culture in place of the old. So everywhere Christians need to think seriously about just how their new life in Christ should relate to contemporary culture.

In our Consultation's preliminary papers two rather similar models were set before us. One suggested that there are several categories of customs which need to be distinguished. The first includes those practices which the convert will be expected to renounce immediately as being wholly incompatible with the Christian gospel (e.g., idolatry, the possession of slaves, witchcraft and sorcery, head hunting, blood feuds, ritual prostitution, and all personal discriminations based on race, color, class or caste). A second category might comprise institutionalized customs which could be tolerated for a while but would be expected to disappear gradually (e.g., systems of caste, slavery, and polygamy). A third category might relate to marriage traditions, especially questions of consanguinity, on which the churches are divided, while into a fourth category would be put the "matters indifferent" which relate only to customs and not to morals, and therefore may be preserved without any compromise (e.g., eating and bathing customs, forms of public greeting to the opposite sex, hair and dress styles, etc.).

The second model we have considered distinguishes between "direct" and "indirect" encounters between Christ and culture, which correspond approximately to the first and second categories of the other model. Applied to 19th century Fiji in the case-study presented to us, it was assumed that there would be "direct encounter" with such inhuman practices as cannibalism, widow-strangling, infanticide, and patricide, and that converts would be expected to abandon these customs upon conversion. "Indirect" encounter would take place, however, either when the moral issue was not so clear-cut (e.g., some marriage customs, initiation rites, festivals and musical celebrations involving song, dance and instruments) or when it becomes apparent only after the convert has begun to work out his or her new faith in the applied Christian life. Some of these practices will not need to be discarded, but rather to be purged of unclean elements and invested with Christian meaning. Old customs can be given new symbolism, old dances can celebrate new blessings, and old crafts can serve new purposes. To borrow an expression from the Old Testament, swords can be hammered into ploughs and spears into pruning knives.

The Lausanne Covenant said: "The Gospel does not presuppose the superiority of any culture to another, but evaluates all cultures according to its own criteria of truth and righteousness, and insists on moral absolutes in every culture" (para. 10). We wish to endorse this, and to emphasize that even in this present age of relativity moral absolutes remain. Indeed, churches which study the Scriptures should not find it difficult to discern what belongs to the first or "direct encounter" category. Scriptural principles under the guidance of the Holy Spirit will also guide them regarding the category of "indirect encounter." An additional test proposed is to ask whether a practice enhances or diminishes human life.

It will be seen that our studies have focused mainly on situations where younger churches have to take up a moral stance against certain evils. But we have been reminded that the church needs to confront evil in western culture too. In the 20th century West, often more sophisticated but no less horrible examples of the evils which were opposed in 19th century Fiji exist. Parallel to cannibalism is social injustice which "eats" the poor; to widow-strangling, the oppression of women; to infanticide, abortion; to patricide, a criminal neglect of senior citizens; to tribal wars, World Wars I and II; and to ritual prostitution, sexual promiscuity. In considering this parallelism, it is necessary to remember both the added guilt adhering to the nominally Christian nations, and also the courageous Christian protest against such evils, and the immense (though incomplete) successes which have been won in mitigating these evils. Evil takes many forms, but it is universal, and wherever it appears Christians must confront and repudiate it.

The process of cultural change

It is not enough for converts to make a personal renunciation of the evils in their culture; the whole church needs to work for their elimination. Hence the importance of asking how cultures change under the influence of the gospel. Of course, the evil and the demonic are deeply entrenched in most cultures, and yet Scripture calls for national repentance and reform, and history records numerous cases of cultural change for the better. In fact, in some cases culture is not as resistant to necessary change as it may appear. Great care is needed, however, when seeking to initiate it.

First, "people change as and when they want to." This seems to be axiomatic. Further, they want to change only when they perceive the positive benefits which change will bring them. These will need to be carefully argued and patiently demonstrated, whether Christians are advocating in a developing country the benefits of literacy or the value of clean water, or in a western country the importance of stable marriage and family life.

Secondly, cross-cultural witnesses in the Third World need to have great respect for the in-built mechanisms of social change in general, and for the "correct procedures of innovation" in each particular culture.

Thirdly, it is important to remember that virtually all customs perform important functions within the culture, and that even socially undesirable practices may perform "constructive" functions. That being so, a custom should never be abolished without first discerning its function and then substituting another custom which performs the same function. For example, it may be right to wish to see abolished some of the initiatory rites associated with the circumcision of adolescents and some of the forms of sex education which accompany it. This is not to deny that there is much of value in the processes of initiation; great care must be taken to see that adequate substitutes are provided for the rites and forms of initiation which the Christian conscience would desire to see abolished.

Fourthly, it is essential to recognize that some cultural practices have a theological undergirding. When this is so, the culture will change only when the theology changes. Thus, if widows are killed in order that their husbands may not enter the next world unattended, or if older people are killed before senility overtakes them, in order that in the next world they may be strong enough to fight and hunt, then such killings, because founded on a false eschatology, will be abandoned only when a better alternative, the Christian hope, is accepted in its place.

Questions for Discussion

1. Can "Christ-likeness" be recognized in every culture? What are its ingredients?

2. In your own culture, what would you expect a new convert to renounce immediately?

3. Take some "institutionalized custom" in your country which Christians hope will "disappear gradually" (e.g., polygamy, the caste system, easy divorce, or some form of oppression). What active steps should Christians be taking to work for change?

Conclusion

Our Consultation has left us in no doubt of the pervasive importance of culture. The writing and the reading of the Bible, the presentation of the gospel, conversion, church and conduct—all these are influenced by culture. It is essential, therefore, that all churches contextualize the gospel in order to share it effectively in their own culture. For this task of evangelization, we all know our urgent need of the ministry of the Holy Spirit. He is the Spirit of truth who can teach each church how to relate to the culture which envelops it. He is also the Spirit of love, and love is "the language—which is understood in every culture of man." So may God fill us with his Spirit! Then, speaking the truth in love, we shall grow up into Christ who is the head of the body, to the everlasting glory of God (Eph. 4:15).

NOTE: Unattributed quotations in this report have been drawn from various papers presented at this Consultation.

D

THE STRATEGIC PERSPECTIVE

1

Today's Task, Opportunity, and Imperative

Donald A. McGavran

The Task

It is difficult to speak about today's task when hundreds of tasks lie before the Church and God calls her to every one of them. Internal tasks abound— raising church budgets, helping Christians grow in grace, holding educated youth, erecting new buildings, training lay leaders, teaching the Bible, and many more. External tasks abound—building brotherhood in the midst of racial strife, giving underprivileged youth a chance, working for peace and justice, reaching unevangelized men and women with the Gospel, establishing new churches in suitable locations, and scores of others. The calls from across the seas were never more numerous or clamant. Great numbers of persons die each year of hunger and malnutrition. Yet there are still refugees to house, illiterates to teach, the sick to heal—and *three billion who have never heard the name of Christ* to flood with knowledge of their Savior.

In spite of all, the thesis of this chapter is that—for the welfare of the world, for the good of mankind—according to the Bible, one task is paramount. Today's supreme task is effective multiplication of churches in the receptive societies of earth.

The other good and urgent things to do, far from contradicting this thesis, reinforce it. The many tasks that lie at hand should be done—there can be no two opinions about that. Preaching good sermons, teaching illiterates to read, working at planned parenthood or the world's food supply, administering churches skillfully, applying Christianity to all of life, using mass media of communication, and hundreds of other activities are not sinful. They are good. Some are urgent.

Known worldwide as perhaps the foremost missiologist, Donald McGavran was born in India of missionary parents and returned there as a third-generation missionary himself in 1923, serving as a director of religious education and translating the Gospels in the Chhattisgarhi dialect of Hindi. He founded the School of World Mission of Fuller Theological Seminary, and was formerly Dean Emeritus. McGavran died in 1990 at the age of 93. McGavran was the author of several influential books, including *The Bridges of God*, *How Churches Grow*, and *Understanding Church Growth*. Taken from *Understanding Church Growth*. Used by permission of Wm. B. Eerdman's Publishing Co., Grand Rapids, Michigan, 1970.

But are they all of equal importance? Even if the mission of the Church is defined as everything she does outside her four walls, are all these activities of equal value? Does mission consist in a large number of parallel thrusts between which Christians may not discriminate? Does it make no difference which comes first, or which is omitted?

If a man stands upon this planet with no other guidance than to follow what seems reasonable to him, in the Bible or out of it, then if there is any mission at all it consists in countless parallel thrusts, each having no more authority than that of the man who advocates it. If he is a man of genius or has seized control of some powerful Christian organization or apparatus, his project will achieve temporary importance. To enhance this and persuade other men, he may quote such random verses of Scripture as support his purposes. Soon, however, others who also hold his position on "guidance" will come to power and quote other Bible verses which support *their* thrusts in mission, since it depends on what seems reasonable to man. The guidance becomes confusion.

In contradistinction to such chaos, Christians accept the authority of the Bible in its total impact and, believing that God's revelation in Christ and the Bible establishes guidelines for all men, find sure guidance concerning the relative importance of various courses of conduct. They are not left to human wisdom, with some maintaining that man is a responsible being and some that he is an automaton. They do not have to wonder whether the highest good is ethical achievement or being in Christ. Their path is illumined by God's revelation. Such Christians can and should draw the distinction between root and fruit, and base their policies in mission upon it. Those who prepare mission budgets and spend mission funds should never be in doubt as to the ultimate outcome they desire, the ultimate goal to which God directs them. They will carry on innumerable activities; they will take innumerable steps. But they should be certain what that ultimate goal is. The Church does not vacillate between sending missionaries to preach the Gospel when that is popular and distributing "the pill" when that is "in." In her supreme duty, led by the Holy Spirit, the Church obediently engages in God's mission according to Scripture.

We must not oversimplify the situation, as if Christians could do one task and leave all others undone. They can and should do many tasks together. When Nehemiah built the wall, some carried stone, some brought water, some mixed mortar, and some laid the stones in place. All were controlled, however, by the overriding purpose—all were building the wall. The supreme aim guided the entire enterprise. Stones and mortar arrived at the wall in the right proportions at the right time to guarantee maximum wall-building.

In mission today, many tasks must be carried on together, yet the multiplicity of good activities must contribute to, and not crowd out, maximum reconciliation of men to God in the Church of Jesus Christ. God desires that men be saved in this sense: that through faith they live in Christ and through obedience they are baptized in His name and live as responsible members of His Body. God therefore commands those of His household to go and "make disciples of all nations." Fulfilling this command is the supreme purpose which should guide the entire mission, establish its priorities, and coordinate all its activities.

The Church today faces deep cleavage among her members at just this point. Some are so deeply impressed by the physical needs of man—and who can deny them urgency?—that meeting these needs becomes for them the highest present purpose of God and the Church.

In 1977, my *Conciliar Evangelical Debate: The Crucial Documents 1964-76* presented the writings of 15 spokesmen of the Conciliar and 15 of the Evangelical Wing of the Church. Sharply differing opinions as to ends and means mark the volume. In the rough and tumble of vigorous disagreement, the writers spoke of the basic questions of evangelism and mission. The convictions of major thinkers were weighed in the balance of reason and revelation and, when found adequate, embraced and, when found wanting, rejected.

In 1979, Dr. Harvey Hoekstra, then president of the Reformed Church in America, published his well-researched book *The WCC and the Demise of Evangelism* , showing how the leaders of the Conciliar Churches and Mission Boards, following the theory and theology of "New Mission," had all but abandoned evangelism as they sought to minister to the physical needs of mankind and to rectify the basic injustices of the global social order.

Deeply as I sympathize with the problem and long as I have ministered to desperate physical needs—for years I superintended a leprosy home—I cannot ally myself on this point with those who put social action first. On the contrary, my conviction is that the salvation granted to those who believe on Jesus Christ is still the supreme need of man, and all other human good flows from that prior reconciliation to God.

The Lord Jesus put it succinctly when He said, "Seek first the kingdom of God and His righteousness and all these things shall be added to you." He spoke of food and clothing, the simplest necessities of life, but the passage will bear much added freight: safety, health, education, comfort, production—even justice, peace, and brotherhood. As we try to help men to achieve these, the longest first step we can lead them to take is to believe in Christ as Lord and Savior and become dependable members of His Church. Enormous liberation of the human spirit and extension of righteousness among men will become possible as sound churches of Christ are multiplied among the three billion who now yield Him no allegiance. Such liberated persons and congregations will become in their own cultures and communities the most effective and permanent sources of "good works" as well as of true cooperation toward solving the bitter practical problems of the world.

Some earnest Christians, who readily grant the above, nevertheless reject multiplication of churches as today's chief task, because they pin their hopes on quality rather than quantity. What use, they ask, to make more Christians unless they are *better* Christians? Throughout much of Africasia [Africa, Latin America, and Asia—ed.] they affirm that education of Christians is more important than evangelism. In America they assert that brotherhood or church unity is more important than church extension.

No doubt the Church must win on both educational and brotherhood fronts. Both are important sectors of the ceaseless battle against the powers of darkness. Christians should be able to read the Bible, and should speed the spread of the marvelous learning God has granted us in our age. Race pride, too, which refuses equal opportunity to people of other groups and customs, and seems to doubt that God is the Father of all mankind, must be very firmly rejected.

But we must not throw out the baby with the bath. As C. S. Lewis, I believe, once said, you *cannot* (my italics) have the brotherhood of man without the fatherhood of God. Nothing can advance learning and brotherhood more in the long run than for men of every tribe and tongue and kindred and nation to become disciples of Christ in whom there is no Jew or Greek.

Furthermore, we must inspect closely this attractive plea for quality. As soon as we separate quality from the deepest passion of our Lord—to seek and save the lost—it ceases to be Christian quality. No amount of sophistication can change this very simple fact. To fight for brotherhood is good; but to proclaim that brotherhood is more important than salvation is misguided. If in Africasia we rear Christians who shine with a high polish, speak beautiful English, have an advanced education, but care nothing whatever about their unconverted kinsmen being reconciled to God, then their vaunted quality as Christians is ashes. Even if we produce Christians who live as full brothers with men of other races, but do not burn with desire that those others may have eternal life, their "quality" is certainly in doubt.

Any who seriously plead for this kind of quality are in effect advocating works righteousness and substituting ethical achievement, the fruit of the Spirit, for the Gospel. Christians, when true to the Scriptures and to Christ, reject such legalism and insist that ethical achievement *grows out of life in Christ* and must not be made a prerequisite for faith in Him.

On a practical plane, church leaders have continually to choose between pressing tasks, all good. They would do well to listen to Dr. Ralph Winter, who writes:

> I used to be an expert in the gadgets and the gimmicks—the various means and types of ministries common to most missions. Recently it has become steadily clearer to me that the most important activity of all is the implanting of churches. The care, feeding and reproduction of congregations is the central activity to which all the gimmicks and means must be bent.

The chief task: often left undone

Christian mission should take serious account of the many Africasian Churches marked by slight growth. Specialists in carrying water abound, but there are few masons. Tons of mortar arrive, but few stones. The wall does not go up. Slight church growth characterizes many whole denominations, both liberal and conservative. Worse, the lack of growth is taken as natural and unavoidable.

In the state of Sinaloa in the west of Mexico, the Congregational Church, now the United Church of Christ, has been at work for over half a century. During all these years its dedicated missionaries have labored earnestly; yet in 1962 it had only "300 members in 9 small static churches."[1]

Scores of denominations both large and small in North America have plateaued or declined. For example, three large denominations—the United Presbyterians, the United Church of Christ, and the United Methodists—lost 10 to 12 per cent of their membership between 1965 and 1975. The Oregon Yearly Meetings of Friends is a typical small denomination. In 1961 the average figure for church membership, Sunday School membership and Sunday morning attendance in its sixty-one congregations was 5,300. In 1968 the average figure was 5,400.[2]

In Taiwan, where the Presbyterian Church has registered great growth, trebling in twelve years from 57,407 in 1952 to 176,255 in 1964,[3] and the Baptists who came over from the mainland in 1948 with a few hundred numbered 21,783 in 1967,[4] the Methodists in 1967—despite the fact that Methodist Chiang Kai Shek and Madame Chiang were ardent Christians—numbered only 4,553. The Methodist Church in Taiwan demonstrates that it is quite possible to miss church growth in receptive populations.

In Chile, where Pentecostal denominations in the last forty years have grown from nothing to a total communicant membership of 360,000, one North American mission with thirty missionaries, at work for about 30 years, in 1965 counted less than 300 Chilean Christians in its congregations. It believes that Chile has "an almost Islamic population."

The secretary of a large conservative missionary society said recently, "We have spent $3,000,000 in Japan in the last thirty years; and our churches there now have less than 500 full members."

My interest in church growth was first roused when Pickett's survey showed that 134 mission stations in mid-India (where I was a missionary) had experienced an average church growth of only 12 per cent per decade, or about 1 per cent per year.[5] The ten stations of my own mission, the India Mission of the Disciples of Christ, were not significantly different from the other 124. They had a staff of over 75 missionaries and a "great work"—but had been notably unsuccessful in planting churches. In the town of Harda where my wife and I with six other missionaries worked from 1924 to 1930, not one baptism from outside the church occurred between 1918 and 1954, a period of thirty-six years.

Lack of church growth is part of my own experience. I present these few instances as typical of much mission effort. The churches and missions cited are not more blameworthy than others; indeed, I hesitate to call them blameworthy at all. They do good work. They pour out life. They bear witness to Christ. They teach and heal men, distribute powdered milk, and demonstrate improved agricultural methods. But they do all these things, and much more, while their churches grow, if at all, by baptizing their own children. It may be truly said that the ambiguous cliché "splendid church and mission work, whether the Church grows or not" characterizes most churches and missions today—in America and elsewhere.

It is not fair to take examples from brief periods of nongrowth. Even rapidly growing Churches have occasional plateaus. So it is specially instructive to consider the following century-long graph of growth of the combined membership of four notable Churches in Jamaica.

In 1850 the Baptist, Methodist, Moravian, and Presbyterian Churches in Jamaica had a total membership of 54,000 communicants or full members (see the left bottom corner of the graph). During the next hundred years the member-ships increased to 60,000—that is, over a full century, during which they were continuously assisted by missionaries and funds from England, they added a total of only 6,000 members, or 15 members per year per denomination !

Meanwhile, the population of the island rose from 400,000 to 1,400,000. The communicants of these four denominations formed 13 per cent of the island population in 1850 and 4 percent in 1950.[6]

Since Jamaica was an advanced field, where missions turned authority over to the Churches between 1840 and 1880, its record in church growth is a sober warning to those who like to believe that when nationals are in charge of Africasian Churches, all will be well.

CHURCH GROWTH IN JAMAICA

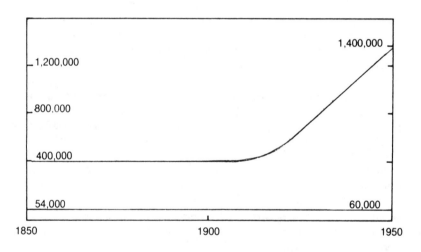

These cases of little growth have been taken from lands where the Church *can* grow, as proved by the fact that some branches are growing. They are significant because in populations where the Church *can* grow, some missions and mission-aries, Churches and ministers engaged in witness for Christ and "many good works," nevertheless seem content with little or no growth. Faced with a general population in which some segments are accepting Christ, they try to propagate the Gospel either among gospel rejecters or by methods which obviously are not blessed of God to the increase of the Church. This is the predicament of a consid-erable portion of the Church today in England, America and elsewhere.

Illustrations of lack of growth in receptive populations could be multiplied indefinitely. Most missionary societies, both conservative and liberal, if they would chart accurately the growth of the Africasian Churches they assist, would find many cases of small growth. For example, leaders of the Foursquare Gospel Church—a vigorous Church of the Pentecostal family— recently had occasion to study the development of ten of its younger Churches. They found one greatly growing Church of 25,000, three moderately growing Churches of around 10,000 and six static Churches of less than 2,000 each.

In a few cases, nongrowth or slight growth is irremediable. It can be truly ascribed to the hard, rebellious hearts of those to whom the Gospel is proclaimed. Resistance is too high, hostility too great, for men to obey or even "hear" the Gospel. There are counties and cities in almost every nation in which Christians can preach, teach, and heal for decades with practically no one accepting Christ. Such resistant populations exist. Remembering our Lord's command that the Gospel must be preached to every creature, the Church should not bypass these.

In most cases, however, the situation is remediable. Arrested growth can be ascribed to faulty procedures. Sometimes, when a shepherd returns empty-handed, it is because the sheep refuse to be found and flee at his approach. Sometimes, however, empty-handedness becomes a habit and is caused by peering into ravines where there are no sheep, resolutely neglecting those who long to be found in favor of those who refuse to be. Sometimes it is a question of sticking for decades to methods which have proved ineffective. Suffice it to say that lack of church growth is an unnecessary trait, or experience, of many branches of the Church and many missionary societies.

Today's Opportunity: Receptive Populations

The urgency of church growth is heightened by the fact that the Church now faces a most responsive world. Together with many little growing Churches, some are growing moderately and a few with great vigor. Together with lack of growth in far too many instances goes an amazing amount of real, sometimes spectacular growth in other cases. When it is realized that much of the standstill is unnecessary and can be replaced by a steady, healthy increase among those who have become new creatures in Christ, the extent of today's opportunity can be better assessed.

North America is commonly held to be a difficult field. Indifference to Christ marks its secular pluralistic populations. Denominations decline. Church growth is most unlikely. Why strive for it? Thus it appears to the leaders of static Churches. Yet in this very land, the General Conference Baptists grew from 40,000 in 1940 to 125,000 in 1978. The fact is that ripe harvests abound in North America—but men with scythes are needed. Conviction that the Lord of the harvest has sent them in to work is essential if the fields are to be reaped.

Overseas, comparison with conditions a hundred years ago heightens appreciation of today's responsiveness. Then, a chief goal of most missions was to get into closed lands and manage to stay there. Dread diseases killed off many Westerners. Non-Christian rulers and governments with the power of life and death considered missionaries the advance agents of Western imperialism and often prohibited entry as long as they could. When the missionaries got in, it was to encounter incredible difficulties.

Today in countless areas all this has changed. Danger to health has been dramatically reduced. Missionaries come and go, harassed by nothing more than delays and paper work. It is true that some countries present hindrances to mission—China, India, Egypt, Russia—but by contrast with earlier days the world is full of mission opportunities and eager populations, with relatively little risk to life and limb. Six-month journeys on foot are rare. Missionaries arrive by jet to find large and flourishing Churches glad to receive them. If they know where to look and want to evangelize the people whom God has prepared, they can generally find hundreds or thousands who, like the common people in the day of our Lord, will hear the Gospel gladly and obey it.

The responsiveness of peoples to the Gospel is sometimes obscured by adjustment to the post-colonial era. Inside Africasian Churches, transfer of authority to nationals has been painful in many cases. Friction between church and mission leaders has not been pleasant for either side. Outside the Churches, newly independent nations have sometimes treated missionaries from Eurica [Europe and America—ed.] as Euricans once treated Africasians. Entry has been denied. Missionaries have been sent home. Yet all this, which gains headlines, is more than balanced by the great cordiality with which most missionaries are treated in the fields where they work. The incontrovertible fact that the number of missionaries working abroad was never larger than it is today is a tremendous testimonial to open doors.

Probably a greater cause for pessimism concerning church growth in Africasia lies in domestic conditions in Europe and, to a lesser extent, in America. European powers have seen their empires fade away. Public and private worship has declined. The disaster and disruption of two world wars have torn the Church. The inability of state Churches to evangelize their own nominal members, and their determination to prevent free Churches from doing so (lest they multiply "sects" in the land), have denied them the greatest single source of renewal. The new religion of secularism, arrayed in beautiful Christian clothing which it did not make, has seemed particularly attractive. All these factors have contributed to a feeling that the advance of the Church is no longer a tenable hope for intelligent men.

The failure of nerve at home cast a black pall across the estimate of things abroad. Avant-garde Eurican Christians came to feel that the Church ought to renounce a "sociological triumphalism" and espouse the "humble and much more Christian role" of servant in the house of common humanity. Inevitably such feelings in Eurica obscured the spiritual hunger of millions in both Eurica and Africasia and their readiness for change. Responsiveness to the Gospel was burgeoning, but Christians, absorbed in their own troubles, could not see it.

Responsiveness, to be sure, must not be overstated. Of the 160 million Americans who have little actual connections with the Church—though of these possibly eighty million have their names on a church roll somewhere—at least thirty million are hard-core pagans born of pagans. No denomination gains many of these. This block of Americans is not notably responsive.

Well over half of the rest of the world is still indifferent or even hostile to the Good News. Millions have set their faces like flint against Christ. Christian missionaries have been thrown out of Russia, China, Cuba, and other Communist lands. A few million souls in Afghanistan and Arabia are still closed to evangelization. All this and more must be taken into account. Nevertheless, many lands *are* responsive, many populations *are* receptive. Compared to a time when everyone was hostile, now only some are.

Outside the Communist blocks, it is a rare land where there is not some receptive segment of the population. The upper and middle classes in Chile are probably as scornful of Evangelical Christianity as they were in 1900, but the Chilean masses, as the rise of large Pentecostal denominations testifies, are abundantly able to hear the Good News and obey it. Most touchable castes in India have yet to ripen, but since 1947, in two Indian Methodist conferences alone, that Church has grown from 100,000 to 200,000.[7] When the British left, many denominations in India—including the great united Churches of North India and South India—decided to lie low and not court persecution by active evangelization. These two sections of the Methodist Church, however—enduring persecution joyfully—doubled from among the lower castes. In short, the Methodist Church, rejecting the counsels of the fainthearted that the Church cannot grow in independent India, established a multitude of congregations in receptive segments of the population.

In Ethiopia (before the Communist takeover), missions which had evangelized the responsive groups saw great church growth. The Sudan Interior Mission was in 1967 assisting a Church of 100,000 baptized believers[8] despite the fact that most of its missionaries still worked in resistant sections of the country. Had the mission concentrated its efforts on those who were responsive, it would have seen a still greater increase.

In country after country, the number of ripe or ripening sections of the population is amazing. One last illustration must suffice. In the first decades of this century, southern Brazil was flooded by hundreds of thousands of Italian immigrants. Most were cool toward the Church of Rome. They came from the laboring section of the Italian population which later became Communist. The first generation or two spoke Italian. They were highly responsive to the Evangelical message. The Methodists, Presbyterians, Lutherans, and Baptists, however, were busy among Portuguese-speaking Brazilians. The leaders of their Churches knew nothing but Portuguese and did not even glimpse the Italian opportunity.

An Italian convert from Chicago, however, totally without financial resources, moved from North America to Brazil and preached Christ. The Church he founded, which until 1936 conducted its services in Italian, by 1965 had grown to 400,000 baptized believers. Its Mother Church in Sao Paulo is a beautiful structure seating 4,000. In general it may be said that responsive segments exist in many lands, but they are not always found by missionaries or national church leaders.[9]

More winnable people live in the world today than ever before. There are far more winnable men and women in Illinois or Canada than there were a hundred years ago. The general population in many states and regions is more favorable to Christ and more open to conversion.

India has far more now than in the days of Carey or Clough. Africa has myriads who can be won. Latin America teems with opportunity. For the Gospel, never before has such a day of opportunity dawned. These populations have not become receptive by accident. In their responsiveness to the Evangel, he who has eyes to see can discern God at work. His sunshine and rain, His providence and Holy Spirit, have turned population after population responsive. One hears a great deal today about the Lord of history and His action in the affairs of men. Christians, sensitive to the oppressions of the masses by feudal lords, *hacenderos* and *malguzars* (landowners), and longing for revolutions which will rectify age-old injustices, speak much about God at work in history. No doubt even among those who reject Him, God does work in many ways to bring about righteousness and justice. Is it not equally reasonable to believe that He works among them to bring about a tremendous responsiveness to His Son Jesus Christ?

Since it is true that the most democratic nations today are those with the largest proportions of Evangelical Christians, may we not say that as God works to bring about the rule of justice, one of the first things He does is to touch men's ears so they can hear His apostle say, "Among those who have put on Christ, there is neither Greek nor Jew, Barbarian, Scythian, bond or free" (Col. 3:11)? It takes new creatures to make democracy work. Only in Christ do men of any nation become new creatures.

This amazing responsiveness is well known. Bishop Neill, the noted authority on missions, says, "On the most sober estimate, the Christian is reasonably entitled to think that by the end of the twentieth century, Africa south of the Sahara will be in the main a Christian continent."[10] If even half this forecast—with which I am in substantial agreement—comes to pass, during the next four decades we shall witness the greatest accessions to the Church that have ever taken place. The few millions who slowly became Christian in Europe in the eight hundred years between A.D. 200 and 1000 constituted, we may say, a small pilot project in God's strategy for His world. In the last third of the twentieth century He is preparing the peoples of Africa, Korea, Taiwan, Assam, and other lands to journey out of Egypt into the Promised Land. In Europe and North America, millions can be and, we are convinced, will be led to become responsible followers of Jesus Christ and members of His Church. Great movements lie ahead.

One thing can delay a vast discipling of the peoples of earth. If, in the day of harvest the most receptive day God has yet granted His Church—His servants fail Him, then the ripened grain will not be harvested. If slight church growth persists, then the winnable will not be won. If missions and Churches continue content with little growth, God's preparations for the feast may be wasted.

The specialist and church growth

The propagation of the Gospel is often hindered and often helped by the specialist. It is helped because the work of the Church is complex and men and women of different gifts are needed. It is hindered because it is so easy for specialists to forget that the central task of the Church is evangelism. As the International Congress on World Evangelization said, "*Evangelism* and the *salvation of souls* is the *vital mission* of the Church" (31). Specialist duties exempt no one from this primary thrust. All Christians should witness to Christ. They ought not take shelter in specialist roles any good humanist could play. These may never be substituted for consciously seeking to bring others into a personal relationship to Jesus Christ.

Specialist in Eurica

Christians in Europe and America, and long established Christian communities in other continents too, playing specialist roles are often tempted to neglect intentional evangelism. They neither pray that others may come to Christ nor take deliberate steps to bring this about. Such work, Satan teaches them, is what the pastor is paid to do. Specialists who teach in Sunday School, sing in the choir, usher at worship services, or cook church suppers sometimes are evangelistically influential; but often they do nothing to lead the unsaved home.

Specialists in Africasia

The great number of missionary specialists going abroad in this day of opportunity increases the danger that just this will happen there also. None can doubt the need of specialist missionaries. They are here to stay and may increase in number, if not in proportion. With added learning, life grows more and more complex, and hundreds of full-time employments undreamed of fifty years ago occupy the lives of thousands of men and women. Each specialization enriches life. For example, in medicine, X-ray technique is a narrow specialization which greatly assists accurate diagnosis: today many missionaries go abroad as X-ray specialists. Hundreds of other illustrations come to mind. It is precisely the enrichment of life made possible by missionary specialization that creates the danger that such enrichment may come to take the place of strong church growth. The missionary specialist should beware lest he help church growth to remain slight. So should the specialist in American denominations.

I speak as a specialist. My professional training is in education. For many years my chief responsibility in India was schools. I approach the growth of churches not as a trained evangelist, but from the viewpoint of a missionary who was trained in and spent most of his time in an auxiliary aspect of the chief undertaking.

The great temptation of the specialist—in North American churches as well as on mission fields—is to hope that someone else will proclaim the Evangel and persuade men to become disciples of Christ. The pastor of the church should do it—he is prepared for it. Or, thinks the specialist missionary, national Christians should proclaim Christ.

"Was I right," he queries, "in allowing them to think the missionary is going to evangelize? Furthermore, if missionaries are to preach the Gospel, it should certainly not be lay missionaries. Preaching is what ordained men do. Let educators teach, medical men heal, and evangelistic missionaries evangelize."

Finally, the specialist takes refuge in theology. "I cannot win others to Christ—that is the prerogative of the Holy Spirit. I but bear witness teaching Sunday School or singing in the choir, by the service I render, the relief goods I distribute, the classes in English I teach, and the kindly acts I perform. The Holy Spirit convicts men of sin and brings them to the Savior. But not I, Lord! I am too busy. I have important assigned work to do." This is the temptation of the specialist. Since there are many specialists today, it is a widespread temptation.

The result is that, while much good work is done, there is little church growth. All sorts of useful services are performed and necessary tasks completed; but churches remain barren. One looks in vain for their daughter congregations. Barrenness was a reproach in biblical times and, despite the population explosion, still is in many parts of the world. Specialists often increase the likelihood that the congregations in which they work will be barren.

Abroad, when specialist missionaries go home, small clusters of unreproductive congregations, grown accustomed to good works done by foreign helpers with large budgets from abroad, are left. These are unable to continue such works, and furthermore are quite unaccustomed to discipling their neighbors.

The specialist, however, does not need to increase barrenness. He can help make his churches fruitful, mothers of many sons and daughters. With the same eagerness with which he took up his specialty, he can learn how churches are growing in his own and other denominations in the country to which God has sent him. Educators, radio technicians, literacy experts, agricultural demonstrators, and builders can become as knowledgeable as ordained men about the processes of church growth. Several physicians and educators while on furlough have studied at the Fuller Institute of Church Growth and returned to their fields to bring added insight to bear on the communication of Christ to an entire countryside.

Perhaps the most immediately practical thing for the specialist is to devote regular time each week to church planting—proclamation and persuasion with the intent that unbelievers should accept Christ and be baptized and added to the Lord in new and old congregations. Some specialists already do this. Many more should.

In a large town in Ohio, I saw one of the most striking cases of church growth ever to come to my attention. One specialist who earned his living selling hardware also had a conscience on personal evangelism. Year after year, he was the chief cause for dozens of additions to his church.

The Anglican Church of Ruanda for many years owed much to several missionary physicians, who in addition to their hospital duties were fountainheads of new spiritual life for multitudes. A Baptist physician in India gave two nights a week to proclamation, often in areas where he had no former patients, and in addition commended Christ to every patient in his hospital. Because of him many on the hospital staff became active lay evangelists. A new people movement which brought a thousand a year into the Church owed much to him. Principal Miller of Madras Christian College in the early years of this century was the means under God of leading many of his upper-caste students to Christian commitment and baptism. About 1884, when the Churahs of the Punjab were coming like a flood, all the missionaries of the United Presbyterian mission, whatever their specialty, turned for a season to preaching, teaching, baptizing, and shepherding the new village congregations.

The Church expects every Christian—housewife, peasant, carpenter, mechanic, truck driver, or teacher—to do personal evangelism. How much more should she expect that every missionary of the Gospel, whatever branch of mission he may be in, to whatever special task assigned, will exercise his sacred privilege to bring men and women to the feet of the Lord. So should every ordained person and seminary professor.

THE IMPERATIVE OF MISSION TODAY

Today's task and opportunity reinforce the biblical imperative. This is the day par excellence to reconcile men to God in the Church of Jesus Christ. We must not be limited by the small expectations of our forefathers, nor measure tomorrow's advances by yesterday's defeats. Modes of mission which suited a hostile population should not be continued when that population (or some other in the neighborhood) turns receptive. Concepts of what God desires our Church to do, formed during the frozen decades when our predecessor did well merely to hang on, must not deter us from planning to double the churches when, for at least some segments of the population, the climate moderates.

Verse 5 of the first chapter of the Epistle to the Romans gives direction here. One can call this the Great Commission as given to Paul. In the light of the last verses of Matthew and the redemptive purposes of God as portrayed in the entire Bible, it also speaks to the whole Church. The commission is found in three places in the epistle, but I quote it from 16:25, 26 as it appears in the New English Bible. "The Gospel I brought you...[is] now disclosed and...by Eternal God's command made known to all nations, to bring them to faith and obedience." For exact rendering of the Greek words *panta ta ethne*, "all nations" should read "all peoples." The apostle did not have in mind modern nations-states such as India or America. He had in mind families of mankind—tongues, tribes, castes, and lineages of men. That is exactly what *ta ethne* means both here and in Matthew 28:19.

In a day when few nations as wholes are turning responsive, but many segments of them are, an exact rendition is vital to understanding. When peoples are turning responsive as social classes, as peasants moving into cities, as minorities, tribes, castes, tongues, and numerous other *ethne*, the biblical mandate to bring the *ethne* to faith and obedience falls on our ears with particular force. Not only is there the command, but God has provided the opportunity. Christians might be excused for neglecting the divine directive in ages when all peoples were hostile to the Gospel; but when many segments of society at home and abroad are ready for change, can hear the Gospel, and can be won, what answer shall we give to God if we neglect the work of reconciling them to Him? What answer shall we make to men, if while providing them with all the lesser furnishings of the banquet of life, we withhold from them the bread and meat we know is true nourishment?

Thus today's paramount task, opportunity, and imperative is to multiply churches in the increasing numbers of receptive peoples of all six continents.

End Notes

1. Donald A. McGavran, *Church Growth in Mexico* (Grand Rapids: Eerdmans, 1963), p.45.

2. J.L.Willcuts, *Friends in the Soaring Seventies*(NewbergOR: Oregon Yearly Meeting of Friends) p. 27.

3. Taiwan Presbyterians Synodical Office, *Announcing the Second Century—Basic Facts and Discussion Materials* (Taipei: Taiwan Presbyterians Synodical Office, 1966), pp. 76, 80.

4. H. Wakelin Coxill and Kenneth Grubb, ed., *World Christian Handbook* (London: Lutterworth, 1968), p. 181.

5. Jarrell Waskom Pickett, *Church Growth and Group Conversion* (Lucknow: Lucknow Publishing House, 1962), p. ix.

6. Donald A. McGavran, *Church Growth in Jamaica* (Lucknow: Lucknow Publishing House, 1962), p. 20.

7. J. T. Seamands, "Growth of the Methodist Church in South India" (Dissertation, Asbury Theological Seminary, 1968), p. 121.

8. Coxill and Grubb, *Op. cit.*, p. 67.

9. William R. Read, *New Patterns of Church Growth in Brazil* (Grand Rapids: Eerdmans, 1965), pp. 20-44.

10. Stephen Neill, *A History of Christian Missions* (Baltimore: Penguin Books, 1964), p. 568.

Study Questions

1. Suppose the mission of the Church is defined as everything she does outside her four walls. You are responsible for overseeing a church's activities. Would you consider them all of equal value? Would you prioritize them? Does it matter what activities the church engages in so long as it's helping people? Explain your reasoning.

2. Why is the "chief task" often left undone?

3. How can increasing specialization sidetrack the church from the primary mission?

2
Mission and the Church

Edward R. Dayton and David A. Fraser

The Church has been given numerous commands and models to reveal what it ought to be and do. It is not difficult to catalogue a large number of specific commands given to the early Christians and their churches, commands to engage in caring, nurturing, witnessing, worshipping, studying and giving. All these ministries were ignited with enthusiasm by the early Christians as they began to see themselves as part of the movement of the Spirit of God. Somehow in the midst of all these words and portraits the modern Church must seek its essential identity and dynamic for carrying out its business in the twentieth century.

Think of all the metaphors and images found in the New Testament that reveal the nature and mission of the Church: light, salt, leaven, a pillar holding up the truth, an ambassador for God, a farmer sowing seed, a temple of worship, a servant carrying a cross. The list goes on and on!

There are so many important and necessary things that the Church is to be and do that the center about which they all revolve can be lost if one aspect or facet is considered apart from the others. In the end all these images and commands are rooted in the reality that the Church is a result of and a participant in the mission of God. God is acting in history to bring about His redemption and reign over a creation in rebellion. God has miraculously revealed Himself by acting in history in the person of Jesus Christ and through His people. The Church is both a result of and a copartner with God in the process of effecting the

Edward R. Dayton is a management consultant helping mission agencies. He served with World Vision International for 25 years, most recently as Vice-President for Missions and Evangelism and as the founding director of World Vision's Missions and Advance Research and Communications Center (MARC). He has written extensively on management and mission strategy.

David Fraser is currently Chair of the Department of Biblical and Theological Studies and Associate Professor of Sociology at Eastern College in Wayne, PA. Fraser was formerly a professor at Columbia Bible College in Columbia, South Carolina. Reprinted from *MARC Newsletter*, January 1979. Copyright 1979 MARC. Used with permission.

Kingdom of God here on earth.

To express and define the essence of the mission of the Church is to delineate the *Missio Dei*. *The Church's mission is its participation in and cooperation with what God is graciously doing redemptively here on the earth.* It is to be a sign of the presence of the Kingdom in word and deed. It is to be a partial answer to the prayer, "Thy Kingdom come, thy will be done on earth as it is in heaven." It is to understand the Church in its reality as the new creation of God, the body of Christ, the temple of the Spirit. The mission of the Church must be understood and defined in terms of the triune God whose creation and agent in the world is the Church of Jesus Christ.

However mission is imaged, it must be rooted and centered in the reality and power of a loving, gracious God who so loved the world that he sent his unique Son to liberate and open us to the life of his kingly rule in the company of his people. The movement outward to seek and save the lost, to deliver those who live in the fear of death, to feed the hungry and to clothe the naked, to set at liberty those that are oppressed, is rooted in the movement of God in sending the Son and the Spirit. "As the Father sent me, so send I you" (Jn. 20:21).

The Debate Over Evangelization

The whole Church, in facing the whole world in the totality of its historical, social, and spiritual development, must embody all of the meanings connected with mission. However, current debates over the mission of the Church have led to polarization between the ecumenical and evangelical wings of the Protestant churches. We want to consider a number of issues concerning mission and evangelization in the light of that polarization.

From the outset we want to make clear that we consider the extremes in both camps of the contemporary debate to be unfortunate and a needless divorcing of elements of the mission of the Church from one another. There are a host of issues that are successfully mediated within the life of the Church only when they are kept in tension and not allowed to become exclusive preoccupations. One thinks of such issues as personal vs. social gospel, the Kingdom present vs. the Kingdom to come, the inward journey of discipleship vs. the outward journey of evangelism, word vs. deed, and so on. In this connection we empathize with Carl Braaten's words:

> We refuse to take sides in the polarization between evangelical-minded and ecumenical-minded theologians who needlessly restrict the gospel either to its vertical dimension of personal salvation through faith in Jesus Christ or its horizontal dimension of human liberation through the creation of a just social order. It is painful to hear leading evangelicals sneer at the concerns of the ecumenical people who connect mission to liberation, revolution, humanization, dialogue, secularization, socialization, and the like. For the deepest human longings and profoundest social needs are gathered up and reflected in such slogans. To dismiss them to a place of secondary importance is to pass by on the other side while modern man lies in the ditch bleeding to death. It is equally disturbing when ecumenical voices fail to find the language to underscore the permanent relevance of gospel proclamation in sermon

and sacraments, in words of witness as well as deeds which lead to personal conversion and the spread of Christianity. In stressing now the social dimensions of the gospel we do not diminish one bit its depth dimension in personal life and the *koinonia* of faith and worship. A theology of the gospel includes both forgiveness and freedom, both faith and food.[1]

The current polarization is an expression of deep differences over a number of crucial questions. On the one hand, there are those who advocate a new understanding of mission and evangelization in the light of all that has been discovered about other religions and the principles articulated in modern theology. They have stressed a more this-worldly interpretation of Christianity with emphasis on the servant role of the Church in relating to the dire social and political needs of millions of people. Salvation is seen as essentially the humanization of humanity and its world. J .C. Hoekendijk is a representative of this trend. He interprets salvation by the Old Testament idea of "shalom" (an order of peace, integrity, justice, community, and harmony). Evangelism is *not* the planting of churches or the use of confessional propaganda to convince people to believe what Christians have confessed down through the centuries. Salvation is the liberation of oppressed peoples from structures and institutions that dehumanize.

Christ is seen as already present in all the religions as well as the regional and ethnic histories of humanity. People can find salvation without direct contact with or belief in the distinctive Christian gospel. Traditional religions are the "ordinary ways of salvation," whereas explicit commitment to Christian faith is God's "extraordinary way of salvation." In some cases this is joined with the idea that the crucifixion and resurrection of Jesus Christ brought about the reconciliation of all people so that all are born again irrespective of their knowledge or attitude toward the historical saving activity of God in the particular people of Israel or his Messiah, Jesus of Nazareth. Evangelization is the announcement of this fact and the "conscientization" of people in regard to their real social situation so as to bring about the shalom which God desires on this earth. The traditional views and practice of mission are rejected as inadequate, as masks for the ideology and extension of influence of ecclesiastical institutions. Traditional evangelism in these terms is seen as "often little else than a call to restore 'Christendom,' the *Corpus Christianum*, as a solid, well-integrated cultural complex, directed and dominated by the church."[2]

On the other hand, there are those who take a more traditional approach to the nature and task of evangelization. An example is the Frankfurt Declaration of 1970 where several German theological professors and missiologists registered their affirmation of traditional understandings of mission and their rejection of the developing new approaches.

> Christian mission discovers its foundation, goals, tasks, and the content of its proclamation solely in the commission of the resurrected Lord Jesus Christ and His saving acts as they are reported by the witness of the apostles and early Christianity in the New Testament. Mission is grounded in the nature of the gospel...
>
> The first and supreme goal of mission is the *glorification* of the name of the one *God* throughout the entire world and the proclamation of the Lordship of Jesus Christ, His Son.

We therefore oppose the assertion that mission today is no longer so concerned with the disclosure of God as the manifestation of a new man and the extension of a new humanity into all social realms. *Humanization* is not the primary goal of mission. It is rather a product of our new birth through God's saving activity in Christ within us, or an indirect result of the Christian proclamation in its power to perform a leavening activity in the course of world history...

Jesus Christ our Savior, true God and true man, as the Bible proclaims Him in His personal mystery and His saving work, is the basis, content, and authority of our mission. It is the goal of this mission to make known to all people in all walks of life the Gift of His salvation.

We, therefore, challenge all non-Christians, who belong to God on the basis of creation, to believe in Him and to be baptized in His name, for in Him alone is eternal salvation promised to them...

Mission is the witness and presentation of eternal salvation performed in the name of Jesus Christ by His Church and fully authorized messengers by means of preaching, the sacraments, and service. This salvation is due to the sacrificial crucifixion of Jesus Christ, which occurred once for all and for all mankind.

The appropriation of this salvation to individuals takes place first, however, through proclamation, which calls for decision, and through baptism, which places the believer in the service of love. Just as belief leads through repentance and baptism to eternal life, so unbelief leads through its rejection of the offer of salvation to damnation...

The primary visible task of mission is to *call out the messianic, saved community* from among all people.

Missionary proclamation should lead everywhere to the establishment of the Church of Jesus Christ, which exhibits a new, defined reality as salt and light in its social environment...

The offer of salvation in Christ is directed without exception to all men who are not yet bound to him in conscious faith. The adherents to the non-Christian religions and world views can receive this salvation only through participation in faith. They must let themselves be freed from their former ties and false hopes in order to be admitted by belief and baptism into the Body of Christ...

The Christian world mission is the decisive, continuous saving activity of God among men between the time of the Resurrection and the Second Coming of Jesus Christ. Through the proclamation of the gospel, new nations and people will progressively be called to decision for or against Jesus Christ...

We do, however, affirm the determined advocacy of justice and peace by all churches, and we affirm that 'assistance in development' is a timely realization of the divine demand for mercy and justice as well as of the command of Jesus: 'Love thy neighbor.'

We see therein an important accompaniment and verification of mission. We also affirm the humanizing results of conversion as signs of the coming Messianic peace.[3]

Both sides have some areas of agreement. Both argue that a more humane and non-oppressive social order and a more just distribution of resources are important concerns of the Church. Both want to see discipleship have its expression in concrete, this-worldly concerns that result in the extension of God's kingdom into spheres where humanity is oppressed and exploited. But there is disagreement over the priority of the various elements involved in carrying out mission, over what is means and what is end, over the very understanding of the concepts of the Bible as they are utilized to build the foundation for a theology and practice of mission. These differences clearly lead to different prescriptions for the kinds of actions and allocation of resources in mission.

The Kingdom of God and Mission

We are convinced that only a theology of the Kingdom of God can bring coherence and order to the debate. Jesus' proclamation of the good news of the Kingdom of God is the basis and content of mission. God is bringing about the extension of his rule over an unruly world. The *Missio Dei* is the Kingdom of God and the integrating aim of mission.

The problems that exist within the new as well as the traditional understanding of mission lie in the degree to which they truncate or lose contact with this dynamic reality. Those who have come to stress humanization as the encompassing image of mission have tended to eliminate the tension between the Kingdom as present and the Kingdom as coming. They have been prone to separate the gospel deed from its necessary proclamation in word, to confuse human political action with the acts of God in establishing his Kingdom, to erase the line between the Church as the community of the subjects of that Kingdom and the world as those being called to enter the Kingdom, to neglect the importance of the call to explicit discipleship in a personal sense. The degree to which the political and social dimensions of the Kingdom are stressed to the exclusion of the other equally important dimensions is the measure to which humanization as an ideal narrows the nature of the Kingdom and makes it less than what Jesus proclaimed.

The traditionalists have also often narrowed the scope of the Kingdom. They too have tended to eliminate the tension between the Kingdom present and the Kingdom coming, only in the other direction. They have been prone to eliminate the political and social implications of the gospel, to stress the word over the deed, to offer a discipleship that is only personal and individualistic, to break the connection between the Church as participant in the Kingdom of God and God's action in the world, and to identify the mission of the Church only with proclamation. The degree to which they have stressed a personal-spiritual salvation to the exclusion of the political-social dimensions of the Kingdom is the measure to which they have narrowed the nature of the Kingdom and made it less than what Jesus proclaimed.

Johannes Verkuyl is right in the way in which he sketches the various elements of mission as implicated in the Kingdom of God:

The Kingdom to which the Bible testifies involves a proclamation and a realization of a total salvation, one which covers the whole range of human needs and destroys every pocket of evil and grief affecting mankind. Kingdom in the New Testament has a breadth and scope which is unsurpassed, it embraces heaven as well as earth, world history as well as the whole cosmos.[4]

Thus mission involves confronting people with the urgency and importance of responding to that Kingdom. They are addressed by Jesus to repent and enter through the forgiveness of sins and the accepting love of a heavenly Father. Conversion is imperative if they are to leave the kingdom of darkness and enter into the eternal life and light offered by God. It is a personal, though not an individualistic, call to discipleship: to take up one's own cross and follow Jesus the Messiah. Mission is all this and more. It is the process by which a community of the people of God is formed from all the peoples of the earth. Conversion is not an end in itself but leads to the participation in the people of God with a mission. In the support and nurture of that worshipping community the Christian finds himself or herself called to participate in the struggle against every form of human ill and evil. The whole of human life falls under the Lordship of Christ, and the mission of the Church finds its wholeness in that comprehensive Lordship.

For years we have debated "social action or evangelism?" Social action dealt with mankind's human needs, while evangelism dealt with spiritual needs. We thus neatly carved people into physical and spiritual beings. Try as we might, we could not bring these two together, nor could we abandon one for the other. The Bible was clear in demanding that we do both. The pendulum often swung back and forth. At times the mission of the Church to non-Christians was confined to doing good to people in need without "interfering" with their values. For others, a people's "ultimate destiny" was the key concern, for what good would it do to help people in this life if they were left "outside Christ" in the next?

As is often the case, the two sides often talk past one another. They fail to see that "social action or evangelism?" is a non-question. It has meaning only when put into context: "Social action or evangelism where? When?" Christian social action and evangelism are actions carried out by Christians. Social action that is not anchored in a biblical theology or a Christian value system is adrift. To speak of liberation apart from the Liberator, of peace but not the Prince of Peace, is to offer something that is sub-Christian. Likewise an evangelism that does not hold men and women accountable for their actions toward one another announces a truncated gospel. The gospel Jesus preached calls people to be more human, to become more what God wants them to be, not only in the hereafter, but in the here and now.

Mission, Evangelism, and Development

In this generation, with more mission agencies and churches becoming explicitly involved in various development projects, it is important to address the nature of that expression of mission and its relationship to evangelism. Development is the process of forging new values and enabling a community to have a part in determining its own destiny. *Christian* development makes a statement about what those values should be. It sees value in two dimensions: people interacting with people, and people finding ultimate meaning and value in the person of Jesus Christ. Christian development believes that men and women can be free only when they find freedom in Christ. Christian development always has the *intention* of evangelization, because it offers the only true basis of effective human relationships without which development cannot be fully achieved.

Biblical evangelism starts at the point of need of a people. Christian love demands that we reach out to all the needs of a people in compassionate service. Development is not a sub-Christian response that acts as a substitute for the real task of evangelism. It is part of the Christian's commitment to communicate the gospel in word and deed. By its very nature it is limited in scope. Who has the resources to carry out effective development in every poor community of a country? Christian development models what the local church should be, a community of people helping one another, able to love because they are loved by the Maker of the universe.

Christian development, therefore, has large potential to establish a church that has the capacity to carry the gospel to the edge of its cultural boundaries. One can imagine what a vital force such a church can become! A church that sees Christianity not just as a system of belief with a creedal religious practice, but rather as a joyous desire to share its life in every dimension will quickly become a missionary church. It also will become a community that sees all of life under the Lordship of Christ and continually seeks ways to relate the Kingdom of God in its midst to all the needs of humanity.

Christian development has a number of components. First, it is carried out by Christians, people who have had their own personal encounter with the person of Jesus Christ, people who know that there is something more to life than bread. The gospel contains more than the content of the message. If the receptor does not see any evidence of a desirable transformation in the life of the one who offers the gospel, why should he or she be attracted to it?

Second, Christian development attempts to integrate into the process a new world view that results from knowing Christ in such a way that it is seen as part of all that is being offered, that it has a wholeness that encompasses all of life. At the same time, Christian development seeks to avoid the charge that it creates "rice Christians" by its integral and unconditional concern for all of life.

Third, Christian development adopts a stance as learner as well as teacher. Christians engaging in development are themselves undergoing the same process. They are moving toward a more human existence and will learn new dimensions of it from every community they help. This is not to suggest that the Christian becomes a missionary to find a better religion, but rather that he or she expects that the Holy Spirit will have something unique to say when the gospel penetrates a new culture or subculture. Christians discover a beauty and dignity in the pre-Christian culture which also serves as an example of authentic humanness. Christians come as enablers, enablers of other people who have an equal potential to be Spirit-filled, God-led leaders of their own communities.

Fourth, Christian development plans to give the knowledge of the gospel and the outward opportunity to the community so that the community can confront Jesus Christ and who He claims to be. Whether this event should happen is not at question. When and how it will happen are the questions. To enable a community to see how its life is lived in reference to its Maker and Redeemer is not an easy task. It means helping it to realize the immediate relationship between physical, social, cultural, and spiritual dimensions as it confronts Christ.

Fifth, Christian development is just as concerned with measuring a community's movement toward the Savior as it is in measuring progress in food production and health care. In measuring the "quality of life," it includes the spiritual dimension. It is not necessary to be limited only to measuring "decisions for Christ" or church membership.

If the goal of biblical evangelism is to make disciples who will communicate Christ's love to others, Christian development can be a powerful means of evangelism. It crystallizes the dimensions of the Kingdom of God as they infiltrate the life of a particular community. Whether through health care, clean water (more than a cup of it!), agricultural improvement, education, training for income production, or the creation of new social structures, people come to discover that the Christian faith is an incarnated and embodied faith.

Abraham Maslow pointed out that people have a hierarchy of needs: food, safety, social interaction, esteem, and what he called "self-actualization." These are the dimensions of human life. As Christians, we understand that each must be satisfied if life is to be as full as God intended it to be. To love a people is to respond to their need. All the levels described by Maslow's hierarchy are valid human needs. Christian love demands that we do everything within our power to go to another people, not with set solutions as to what we imagine may be their need, but rather with minds and hearts open to what *they* perceive to be their need.[5]

To those with few material needs we offer not only more satisfying interpersonal relationships and feelings of self-worth, but we point them to the One in whom can be found true "self-actualization," a self-actualization experienced by the indwelling of the Holy Spirit and centered upon a suffering Savior. To those in material need we offer what we can, not because it is their ultimate need, but because Christian love demands it. We cannot call people to a "new life in Christ" unless we are willing to demonstrate that new life.

We may not always be able to do that. We may be called to live and proclaim Christ among a people whose needs overwhelm us. Our vial of oil and our purse may be quickly emptied. To cease to announce the possibility of reconciliation with God, to refuse to meet the need for a new allegiance or a new set of values just because we cannot meet all the needs of hunger and safety and self-esteem is sub-Christian. But to refuse to give what we are able to give is just as sub-Christian.

End Notes

1. Carl E. Braaten, *The Flaming Center* (Philadelphia: Fortress Press, 1977), pp. 3-4.

2. J. C. Hoekendijk, "A Call to Evangelism," reprinted in Donald McGavran, *The Conciliar-Evangelical Debate* (South Pasadena, Calif.: William Carey Library, 1977), pp. 42-43.

3. Peter Beyerhaus, *Missions—Which Way?* (Grand Rapids: Zondervan, 1971), pp. 113-120.

4. Johannes Verkuyl, *Contemporary Missiology* (Grand Rapids: Eerdmans, 1978), pp. 197-198.

5. Abraham Maslow, *Motivation and Personality*, 2nd ed. (New York: Harper and Row, 1970).

Study Questions

1. How does the alleviation of suffering and injustice relate to the priorities of the Kingdom of God? How does evangelization, in the sense of gospel proclamation, relate to the priorities of the Kingdom?

2. In what ways can a theology of the Kingdom of God overcome some of the contemporary polarizations in the debate about the proper mission of the Church?

3

By the Year 2000: Is God Trying to Tell Us Something?

Thomas Wang

What is God trying to say to us today? Are we listening—with discernment?

Recently, as we are drawing near to the close of this century, significant things are happening around us. Gigantic plans of evangelism on a global scale are being creatively conceived, planned, and to a degree executed by different groups and orders within Christendom. So much so that I think if only one or two of them succeed in all their objectives, they would truly turn the world upside down.

What is equally noteworthy is that most of these movements take AD 2000 as their target year for an unprecedented world ingathering of harvest for the Kingdom. These are overwhelmingly significant happenings. What is God trying to say to us through them all?

Let me share with you a number of movements of evangelism that are currently either in the planning stage or are already in operation.

The World by 2000

By the year 2000 the entire world will have the opportunity to hear the gospel through radio broadcast. This goal was set by a historic meeting between leaders of three major Christian broadcasting groups in the fall of 1985; they were Ron Cline (HCJB), Bob Bowman (FEBC) and Paul Freed (TWR).

A statement was jointly signed by the three presidents saying, "We are committed to provide every man, woman and child on earth the opportunity to turn on their radio and hear the gospel of Jesus Christ in a language they can understand, so they can become followers of Christ and responsible members of His church. We plan to complete this task by the year 2000."

"Technology is already in place to reach virtually every corner of the earth since short wave signals can literally travel thousands of miles," Cline explained.

The Rev. Thomas Wang is founder and chairman of the AD 2000 Movement, Inc. He is the founding president of the Great Commission Theological Seminary. He previously served as the International Director of the Lausanne Committee for World Evangelization. This article first appeared in May 1987 in *World Evangelization*, the magazine of the Lausanne Committee.

"Our signals can already reach the remote 'hidden peoples.'"

The three major Christian broadcasters are spreading the gospel in more than 100 languages. Cline estimates that more than 90 percent of the world's population can now hear the good news in a language they understand.

Bold Mission Thrust

This is the Southern Baptist denominational strategy on world evangelization which gives adequate emphasis to both discipling and evangelizing.

It is a "massive movement involving scores of denominational agencies, thousands of churches and millions of church members at home and around the world. Its program emphasizes the importance of discipling, centered on the phrase 'evangelism that results in churches.'" Indeed, it has been labelled as "one of history's most extensive, most organized, most detailed and most determined evangelistic plans."

Its pronounced objectives include:

—To reach every living person in the world with the gospel by the year 2000.

—To provide every person on earth the opportunity to hear the gospel by the close of the century.

—To enable every person in the world to have an opportunity to hear and respond to the gospel of Christ by the year 2000.

Charismatic Initiatives

1. *Singapore Consultation* (February 9-11,1987)

Organized by Larry Christianson, Director of the Lutheran Renewal Center, St. Paul, Minnesota, the Consultation took place in Singapore. It was attended by 30 charismatic leaders from a wide spectrum of denominations, including Roman Catholics, from many parts of the world.

A consensus was reached among the conferees that the Singapore Consultation is to be a "Consultation to consider a 1990 World Conference that would usher in a Decade of Evangelization leading up to the year 2000."

2. *General Congress on the Holy Spirit and World Evangelization* (July 22-26, 1987)

The Charismatic conference attended by 50,000 in Kansas City in 1977 was followed by "New Orleans '86: Leaders Congress" attended by 10,000 and sponsored by the North America Renewal Service Committee. This again was followed by another huge gathering in July of 1987—the North America Congress on the Holy Spirit and World Evangelization.

According to Congress Director, Vinson Synan, "Between 35 to 50 thousand members of over 40 denominations, ministries, and fellowships are coming to New Orleans in July to worship and to learn how they can work together to preach the gospel to all nations by the year 2000."

DAWN Movement

As a youth, Jim Montgomery had specific calling to commit himself to world evangelization. He served as a missionary for twenty-two years with Overseas Crusades in several overseas posts. In July of 1984 he had a clear calling from God to launch the DAWN (Discipling A Whole Nation) movement worldwide.

DAWN's concern is that the whole church in every country work at the discipling of the whole nation, including all its people groups.

DAWN's nation-by-nation strategy is to communicate the DAWN vision to national leaders, identify the "John Knoxes" of a nation (Give me my country or I die!), and serve as a consultant to him to fulfill the task.

The whole nation approach of DAWN has enjoyed successes in the Philippines and Guatemala. More national churches are requesting their service. Their recent status sheet said, "Worldwide movement is taking shape! Twenty-seven countries now involved!" [Ed. note: Today 122 countries are impacted by DAWN and 56 countries have DAWN projects underway.]

Evangelization 2000

Roman Catholics are planning a one-billion-dollar project called "Evangelization 2000," as reported by Julia Duin in the News Section of *Christianity Today* (February 6, 1987). "The ten-year project will culminate with a worldwide satellite telecast on Christmas Day in the year 2000 when Pope John Paul II or his successor will speak to a potential audience of at least 5 billion people."

Tom Forrest, the Redemptorist priest who is in charge of "Evangelization 2000," said, "The project is to give Jesus Christ a 2,000th birthday gift of a world more Christian than not."

"Evangelization 2000," by using numerous portable satellite-receiving dishes, will convey "a papal message to Catholic missionaries around the world who will record the transmission on videotapes, then translate the audio into the local languages."

Forrest is also planning a retreat for the world's Catholic bishops in 1989. The conference will inform them about "Evangelization 2000" and provide them with books on evangelization. A worldwide conference for 7,000 priests is planned for 1990 with the same goals in mind.

EXPLO '90

On December 31, 1985, at the closing day of EXPLO '85 in Mexico City, Dr. Bill Bright, President of Campus Crusade for Christ, announced that a similar but expanded event will take place in 1990.

"There is a great worldwide excitement that EXPLO '85 will accelerate the fulfillment of the Great Commission," Bright stated. "Because of this overwhelming response...(we) have decided to announce to you...our plans for a greatly expanded EXPLO '90."

EXPLO '85 leaders were encouraged with the success of a worldwide video conference through 18 commercial satellites, linked up with almost all the 94 sites in 54 countries. Simultaneous translation was provided in more than 30 languages. A continent-by-continent follow-up training course is being conducted.

Pentecost '87

This is called "A National Satellite Celebration of Catholic Evangelization," scheduled to take place across America on June 6, 1987. It is developed by the Paulist National Catholic Evangelization Association and sponsored by over 75

Archdioceses and Dioceses in America.

Using Pope Paul VI's "On Evangelization In The Modern World" as a guideline, Pentecost '87 will give special focus to (a) evangelizing the 75 million unchurched of America, (b) evangelizing the 15 million inactive Catholics, and (c) evangelizing 52 1/2 million active Catholics in America.

The event will use the Catholic Telecommunications Network of America's (CTNA) satellite to offer training courses to the 60,000 Catholic evangelizers in one day.

This carefully designed media event, partially pre-recorded and partially live, will be aired with new and expanded contents on every Pentecost Saturday until the year 2000.

Mission 2000

For discussion purposes, the U.S. Center for World Mission has proposed a 15-year plan called "Mission 2000" to chart the course of cooperative mission effort (as reported by Missionary News Service, February 1, 1985).

Director Ralph Winter spelled out the underlying convictions of Mission 2000 (Mission Frontiers, April-June, 1985) as follows:

"1. We believe that those who are blessed by God are automatically obligated to be a blessing to all the other peoples of the world (Gen. 12:1-3).

"2. We believe that 'to be a blessing' means to spread the news of the saving power and sanctifying lordship of Jesus Christ.

"3. We believe that the best way to do this is to plant the church within each and every one of the world's peoples.

"4. We believe that this unique, 'pioneer' church-planting activity is the most fundamental goal of missions. We are encouraged by the fact that a broad consensus of mission scholars and leaders is in agreement with this conviction.

"5. We believe there are ample evangelical resources in the world community (i.e., 147 congregations per group to be reached!) to make a serious attempt to plant the church within every people by the year 2000, and that such a goal for the year 2000 is therefore a reasonable goal to work and pray for.

"6. We believe this task is thus more readily within our grasp than ever in history, and that the very end of history may therefore be near."

What Is God Trying To Say?

The above is an impressive list. But it is only a portion of the whole. Some are still in the embryo stage pending further decision, such as the International Satellite Mission of the Billy Graham Evangelistic Association. Some are in the early planning stage, such as the book distribution plan of the World Literature Crusade of putting two books on salvation and Christian growth in the hands of every home on earth in their own language before the year 2000.

To these tremendous happenings David Barrett, author of *World Christian Encyclopedia*, and his friends have coined a new term: Global Evangelization Movement (GEM). But Barrett also gave his caution here. Throughout the history of the church there have been at least 300 plans of world evangelization. Most of them have fizzled out and about 30 of them are still in existence today.

What were the reasons for these failures? Barrett has this to say:

> Perhaps the major reason for the failure has been the absence of
> any attempt either to structure the objective or to deal realistically
> with the major obstacles...Pious hopes have been allowed to sub-
> stitute for determined organizational and logistical investigation
> and action on the part of thoroughly well-informed global mis-
> sions leaders meeting and acting regularly together, with all the
> facts in front of them. We need to structure this global movement
> somewhat more realistically.

He further added, "The extraordinary thing is that most of these plans are operating in comparative isolation and in virtual ignorance of the existence of the other 30 or so plans."

Now, coming closer home, what do all of these mean to the Lausanne movement? What is God saying to us as leaders and partners of the LCWE? We are catalysts. We are networkers. Our most up-to-date definition for ourselves is, "a movement of people in Christ who covenant together for biblical world evangelization."

With the current world evangelization happenings before us, what should be our role? How should we chart the course of the Lausanne movement for the next decade, or "unto the year 2000," in order to be more creatively useful and instrumental to the total task of world evangelization?

More urgently, how should we plan the program for Lausanne's '89 Congress so that it would not be a mere repetition or near repetition of 1974, but a dynamic and creative encounter of 6,000 "evangelizers" (and millions more around the world if satellite communications are to be used) whom God has destined to use for the ultimate fulfillment of spreading His redemption plan?

What is God trying to say to you and me?

Scientists and astronomers have built clusters of giant listening devices called the "Big Ear" to listen to radio signals from outer space in order to probe the mysteries of the universe. Are we today tuning our "big ears" to the Creator of the universe who is the Keeper of all mysteries?

We are all busy preaching, speaking, teaching, researching, writing, publishing, broadcasting and telecasting. But are we listening? Has our frantic way of life made our relation to God a one-way street? Again, what is He trying to say to you and me through all these happenings around us today?

Perhaps we should all come before the Lord like young prophet Samuel did and say to God, "Speak, Lord, for thy servant is listening."

I will be most happy to hear from you and to know if God has something to say through you to the church, to the parachurch, to the Lausanne movement, and to us all. I welcome your response.

Study Questions

1. Do you believe God is trying to tell us something? What could that be?

2. How could you help your church listen to the works of God like the prophet Samuel did, "Speak, Lord, for thy servant is listening."?

4

The Work of Evangelism

J. Herbert Kane

Purpose of Evangelism

Evangelism has a two-fold purpose, one immediate and the other remote. The immediate purpose is the conversion of the individual and his incorporation into the Christian church. The remote purpose is the proclamation of the Lordship of Christ over all creation and the extension of the Kingdom of God throughout the earth. The first is emphasized in Mark's account of the Great Commission. "Go ye into all the world, and preach the gospel to every creature. He that believeth and is baptized shall be saved, but he that believeth not shall be damned" (Mark 16:15-16, KJV). The second is found in Matthew's version of the Great Commission. "All power is given unto me in heaven and in earth. Go ye therefore, and teach [make disciples of] all nations, baptizing them in the name of the Father, and of the Son, and of the Holy Ghost" (Matt 28:18-19, KJV).

It is quite impossible to exaggerate the importance of conversion. One of the strongest statements on the subject comes from Stanley Jones, who gave sixty years to the evangelization of India.

> We divide humanity into many classes—white and colored, rich and poor, educated and uneducated, Americans and non Americans, East and West...But Jesus drew a line down through all these distinctions and divided humanity into just two classes— the unconverted and the converted, the once-born and the twice-born. All men live on one side or the other of that line. No other division matters—this is a division that divides; it is a division that runs through time and eternity.[1]

Unfortunately, "conversion" is a dirty word in some circles. It is anathema among the Hindus of India. Gandhi inveighed against the missionaries for attempting to convert Hindus to the Christian faith. "If you come to India to

---

Drawing on fifteen years of missionary experience in central China with the China Inland Mission, J. Herbert Kane taught for many years in the School of World Mission and Evangelism at Trinity Evangelical Divinity School, and was Professor Emeritus until his death in 1990. Kane is authored a number of missions textbooks, among them *Christian Missions in Biblical Perspective* and *A Global View of Christian Missions*. From *Life and Work on the Mission Field* by J. Herbert Kane. Copyright 1980 by Baker Book House. Used by permission.

make us better Hindus, fine; but don't try to convert us to Christianity." During the 1960s, two states in India passed anti-conversion laws; they were later repealed by the Supreme Court. Others in the Third World regard conversion as an act of cultural imperialism—all right for the nineteenth century but completely out of keeping with the more sophisticated mood of the twentieth century.

Even in the West we find an aversion to the idea of conversion. Some theologians are embarrassed by the term and would like to get rid of it. J. G. Davies says: "I would be glad if the term conversion could be dropped from the Christian vocabulary." [2] Those who believe in baptismal regeneration obviously have no need of conversion; baptism has already made them a "child of God, a member of Christ, and an inheritor of the Kingdom of God." Others regard conversion as a spiritual experience appropriate to skid row but hardly acceptable in more refined circles.

Some equate conversion with proselytism, which has always been in disrepute in respectable circles. Missionaries in India, Uganda and other places have been accused of "buying" converts by giving them money, famine relief, educational advantages, and medical services, or by according them other kinds of preferential treatment. Because of the humanitarian character of their work these charges seem to be substantiated. If a government wanted to press charges it could easily produce the required "evidence." Some governments have forbidden young people under the age of eighteen to accept Christian baptism.

In spite of the difficulties and dangers involved, however, the Christian missionary has no choice. His aim is to make converts, and if pressed to do so, he would have to acknowledge that such is the case, even in Muslim countries. At the same time he would vigorously deny that he engages in proselytizing. Such reprehensible conduct is beneath the dignity of the Christian missionary. He will not use force, nor will he offer inducements. He will present the claims of Christ and hope that the listener will voluntarily acknowledge Jesus Christ as his Savior. Beyond that he will not go; to do so would be to violate the freedom and integrity of the individual.

Conversion, to be genuine, must involve a complete change of heart and life. The root meaning of the word is "to turn." It was said of the Thessalonian believers that they "turned to God from idols" (1 Thess. 1:9, KJV). It is therefore a threefold turning: *from* sin *to* righteousness, *from* death *to* life, *from* idols *to* God. It is morally impossible to embrace sin and righteousness at the same time. Paul asks: "What fellowship hath righteousness with unrighteousness? And what communion hath light with darkness? And what concord hath Christ with Belial?" (2 Cor. 6:14-15, KJV). By conversion the person becomes a "new creature, old things are passed away; all things are become new" (2 Cor. 5:17, KJV). The convert is then a "new man," with a new center of gravity, a new system of values, a new standard of morality, a new frame of reference, and a new purpose in life. The outstanding example of conversion in the New Testament is Zacchaeus in Luke 19. When this dishonest tax collector had a personal encounter with Jesus Christ, he was immediately and completely turned around. His confession is noteworthy. "Behold, Lord, the half of my goods I give to the poor; and if I have taken anything from any man by false accusation, I restore him fourfold." That is genuine conversion.

Following conversion, the convert does not remain in isolation. He becomes a member of the universal church, the Body of Christ, by the baptism of the Holy Spirit. By an act of his own he joins a local congregation and becomes part of its fellowship, work and witness.

The second purpose of evangelism is the proclamation of the Lordship of Jesus Christ over all creation and the extension of the Kingdom into all parts of the world. The church's earliest creed was "Jesus Christ is Lord" (Phil. 2:11, KJV). There is a direct connection between the Lordship of Christ and the world mission of the church. This comes out clearly in Matthew's account of the Great Commission. It is precisely because all authority in heaven and on earth has been given by God the Father to God the Son that the church has the responsibility to make disciples of all nations. The Kingdom of God becomes a reality only as the peoples of the world respond to the gospel and become part of the Kingdom (Acts 26:18; Col. 1:13).

Varieties of Evangelism

There are three kinds of evangelism: presence evangelism, proclamation evangelism, and persuasion evangelism. The first is the kind most strongly advocated in ecumenical circles. The second is most widely practiced by evangelicals. The third has supporters and detractors in both camps.

Presence evangelism

In spite of widespread aversion of this kind of evangelism on the part of evangelicals, it is a valid, even a necessary, kind to use. We dare not preach a gospel that we are not prepared to live by. Bishop Azariah of Dornakal attributed the mass movement in the Telugu country to the quality of life manifested by the Christians.

> It is universally admitted by all missions and churches that the reason most often given by the converts for accepting the Christian way of life is the impression produced upon them by the changed lives of the Christian community.[3]

Not all Christians have this kind of testimony. Dr. Ambedkar was for many years the leader of the Untouchables in India. Realizing that Hinduism had nothing to offer his followers, Ambedkar decided to study the other religions with a view to joining one of them. After examining the claims of Christianity with Bishop Pickett, he remarked: "When I study the life of Christ in the Gospels I think that I and my people should become Christians; but when I see the lives of the Christians here in Bombay, I say to myself, 'No, Christianity is not for us.'" Some time later, at an open-air service in Nagpur, Dr. Ambedkar and 70,000 of his followers renounced Hinduism and became Buddhists. Let no one say that presence evangelism is not important. We have the same problem here in the West. It was the German philosopher Nietzsche who said: "I could more readily believe in your Savior if I could find more people who had been saved by Him."

If we insist on talking about the transforming power of the gospel, we had better be sure that we and our converts have really been transformed. Otherwise our words will have a hollow ring.

Proclamation evangelism

In spite of its importance, presence evangelism is not enough to lead a person to saving faith in Christ. At best it can only create within him a desire to know more. To be really effective it must be accompanied by proclamation evangelism.

This is the form most frequently referred to in the New Testament. John the Baptist came "preaching," Jesus came "preaching." The apostles in the Book of Acts preached; Paul said: "Jesus Christ sent me not to baptize but to preach" (I Cor. 1:17, KJV). Certain things belong together. You ride a horse, you play a game. You preach the gospel. God has ordained that men should be saved through preaching (I Cor. 1:21).

The gospel contains certain propositional truths that must be understood before saving faith can be exercised. These include the truths concerning God, man, sin, and salvation, and the facts concerning the life, death, and resurrection of Christ. These truths must be preached with all the clarity we can muster.

It is rather strange that proclamation evangelism, which occupied such a large place in the preaching and teaching of the early church, should have fallen into disrepute. The Billy Graham type of evangelism, which is based on "the Bible says" and directed to the salvation of the individual, is totally unacceptable in certain quarters today. When Billy spoke to the National Council of Churches in Miami several years ago he was chided for his simplistic approach to the complex problems of present-day society. They said, "Billy, you'll have to give up this kind of preaching. You're taking us back to the nineteenth century." To which Billy replied, "I thought I was taking you back to the first century."

Alan Walker, a well known Australian evangelist, does not share their point of view. He said: "I confess I cannot understand the current depreciation of the preaching ministry. Some protest against an over-verbalizing of the Gospel is justified, but the effectiveness of a man, a woman standing up to preach with conviction is undoubted." [4]

Persuasion evangelism

Persuasion goes one step beyond proclamation and tries to induce the hearer to *believe* the message for himself. There are those who repudiate this method, declaring that the evangelist is not responsible for results. He should be content to preach the gospel and leave the results with the Lord.

There is something to be said for both sides. It is possible to overstep the bounds of propriety and bring undue pressure to bear until the person accepts the gospel under duress. It should be categorically stated that this approach is both wrong and harmful. The results of such a method can be disastrous. It has no sanction in Scripture and should be studiously avoided.

On the other hand, the word "persuasion" is not foreign to the New Testament; Paul said, "Knowing therefore the terror of the Lord, we *persuade* men" (2 Cor. 5:11, KJV). The New English Bible refers to Paul as "trying to *convince* Jews and Greeks" (Acts 18:4, NEB). In Ephesus, before moving over to the school of Tyrannus, Paul spent three months in the synagogue, "using argument and *persuasion* in his presentation of the gospel" (Acts 19:8, NEB). Preaching the gospel is serious business, fraught with eternal consequences for good or evil (2 Cor. 2:16). Paul was never guilty of presenting the gospel on a take-it-or-leave-it basis. He pled with men to be reconciled to God (2 Cor. 5:20). The apostles did not use force to win converts, but they did call for a response. Moreover, they expected results and when they did not get them they turned to other people more willing to receive the message (Acts 13:46).

End Notes

1. E. Stanley Jones, *Conversion* (New York: Abingdon Press, 1959), p. 5.

2. J. G. Davies, *Dialogue with the World* (London SCM Press, 1967), p. 54.

3. C. Rene Padilla, ed., *The New Face of Evangelism* (Downers Grove, Ill.: Inter-Varsity Press, 1976), p. 80.

4. *Evangelism, The Madras Series* (New York: International Missionary Council, 1939), 3:42.

Study Questions

1. What is the difference between conversion and proselytism? Give illustrations of both in the New Testament.

2. Explain the possible consequences if a missionary among a people were *only* involved in (a) presence evangelism, (b) proclamation evangelism, or (c) persuasion evangelism.

5
Strategy

Edward R. Dayton and David A. Fraser

What does *strategy* mean?

> Strategy differs from tactics. One has to do with the general plan
> of a campaign and the principles on which it is based; the other
> deals with the carrying out of the plan in its details, the various
> instrumentalities, agencies and methods. Tactics must be the con-
> stant study of those responsible for the conduct of the missionary
> enterprise. It is indispensable, but quite different from the study of
> the principles on which the world mission is built, the rationale of
> the enterprise as a whole. (Soper, 1943, p. 235)

In one sense everyone and every organization has a strategy, a way of
approaching problems or achieving goals. Many organizations do this quite
unconsciously. Others have developed their strategies into almost fixed, standard approaches.

The apostle Paul had a strategy. We read in Acts 17:2 that on the Sabbath he
went into the synagogue *as was his custom*. Paul's strategy was to arrive at a
major city, visit the synagogue if there was one, proclaim Jesus, and then let
events take their course.

A strategy is an overall approach, plan, or way of describing how we will go
about reaching our goal or solving our problem. Its concern is not with the small
details. Paul's ultimate goal was to preach Christ throughout the world. His own

Edward R. Dayton is a management consultant helping mission
agencies. He served with World Vision International for 25 years,
most recently as Vice-President for Missions and Evangelism and as
the founding director of World Vision's Missions and Advance
Research and Communications Center (MARC). He has written
extensively on management and mission strategy.

David Fraser is currently Chair of the Department of Biblical and
Theological Studies and Associate Professor of Sociology at Eastern
College in Wayne, PA. Fraser was formerly a professor at Columbia
Bible College in Columbia, South Carolina.

Excerpted from *Planning Strategies for World Evangelization*.
Used by permission of Wm. B. Eerdman's Publishing Co., Grand
Rapids, Michigan, 1980.

calling motivated frontier evangelism, preaching Christ where there were no communities of Christians (Rom. 15:20). His day-to-day plans would differ, but his strategy remained the same.

Strategy looks for a range of possible "means and methods" and various "operations" that will best accomplish an objective. Strategy is a way to reach an objective. It looks for a time and place when things will be different from what they are now. For the military it might be capturing a key town or city. For a business person it might mean achieving a desired volume in a particular market. For a Christian organization it may mean everything from deciding in what country to serve to the overall approach to reaching a particular group of people.

Why Have A Strategy?

As Christians, a strategy forces us to seek the mind and will of God. Strategy is an attempt to anticipate the future God wants to bring about. It is a *statement of faith* as to what we believe that future to be and how we can go about bringing it into existence.

Strategy is also a means of communication to fellow Christians so they can know where we think we should concentrate our efforts. It thus gives us an overall sense of direction and helps to generate cohesiveness. Because it tells us and others what we *will* do, it tells others what we have decided *not* to do.

Types of Strategies

There are many different approaches to strategies for evangelism. Some are based on past success. That is, a particular way of doing things worked so well in the past that the pattern became a "Standard Solution Strategy." Standard Solution Strategies are assumed to be universally applicable. Their advocates use them in all parts of the earth with only cosmetic modifications.

The problem with these strategies is that they assume all people everywhere are basically the same. Cultural and social differences are not thought to play important roles in evangelism strategies.

Other strategies come from the notion that the Holy Spirit will provide serendipitous guidance in the moment of action. "Being-in-the-Way" strategies assume that Christian partnership with God's activity does not require human planning. In fact, planning is sometimes seen as against the Holy Spirit.

The net effect of this approach eliminates failure. Whatever happens is God's responsibility. Anything that happens is God's will. But it runs into the problem that when two or more Christians appeal to the direct, inspired leading of the Holy Spirit "in-the-Way," they may be in each other's way. A hidden assumption of this approach is that proper spirituality cuts out the need for human forethought.

We are proponents of the "Unique Solution" approach to strategy. Like the Standard Solution approach, it recognizes that we learn from the way God has led people in the past. The successes of the Spirit are a real resource. We can and must learn as much as possible about what God has done and use it where it is indeed applicable.

But this approach argues that the differences between the situations and cultures of various people groups are also important. People and culture are not like standardized machines that have interchangeable parts. We cannot simply use an evangelism approach that has worked in one context in another and expect the same results. Strategies must be as unique as the peoples to whom they apply.

Further, the Unique Solution approach recognizes with the Being-in-the-Way Strategy that God has new surprises for us. Strategies must be open to new insight and new developments and cannot be rigidly standardized once and for all. Yet it also argues that we risk the sin of sloth (laziness) in not using all we have and are. We are to offer to God our best human efforts.

When God calls us to preach, we do not suppose we violate the leading of the Holy Spirit in carefully planning a sermon: researching the text until we have confidence we understand the author's intention, developing a clear outline to follow, praying for illustrations and examples that will communicate the point of God's word in contemporary terms. We *plan* the sermon carefully *because* we seek to speak about and for God. We can take the Lord's name in vain by invoking the Holy Spirit over our inattention, lack of discipline and forethought, or even laziness.

Just so, while remaining constantly open to God's surprises and extraordinary leadings, the Unique Solution approach believes that we can sketch the outline of a well-thought-out "Solution" to the question of how a given people could be effectively evangelized. We are not ruling out visions, dreams, or sudden convictions. Planning uses whatever resources are authentically given to us by the Spirit of God. The idea that the Holy Spirit does not use good human preparation in doing the work of the kingdom is inadequate to Scripture and experience.

The Unique Solution Strategy thus seeks to avoid what we see as the two extremes in some Christian approaches to strategy. On the one hand, the Standard Solution approach supposes we need only one basic strategy, that God has revealed the universal pattern once and for all, that success is "in the plan." The Being-in-the-Way approach, on the other hand, turns out to be an antistrategy dressed up in a rigid portrait of the Holy Spirit as guiding only when human beings do the least.

The Unique Solution approach argues that God has given us some universal *goals* and *guidance* as to what we are about in evangelism. Yet how and when and where and many other components are as variable as are the cultures and social groups God sends us out to evangelize. This is not to say that we do not use the experience of the past. Rather, we combine past experience with that which lies ahead.

Is Our Strategy "Western"?

If you are new to this idea of strategy, you may logically ask: "Isn't all this just a Western technological approach? Doesn't this substitute modern human methods for God's work?" These are valid questions.

We can never be complacent or arrogant about any of our approaches to doing God's will. There is a constant tension here. Often we do not know which ideas are purely our own and which indeed come from the wisdom of God. We never grow beyond the childlike dependence upon God, even when we have done our very best planning. However, childlike does not mean childish. When we act without forethought we risk the sin of tempting God (Matt. 4:7).

Planning and strategies, while greatly refined and strengthened in the modem industrial world, are not a modern or even Western invention. Joshua followed a strategy in his capture of the city of Ai. The building of the Great Wall of China or the pyramids of Egypt show the signs of careful planning and forethought.

However, in the most refined and technical sense of planning and strategy development (which we advocate in this book), we are following a pattern that has its roots and strength in Western developments. Yet it is also related to the Christian worldview. Because a loving and rational Creator created our world, early science was convinced it was a lawful world. And if the world is to some degree lawful, then we can anticipate it and plan for its future. The more we understand how the world and history works, the more we can plan for the future.

So on the one hand we must say: this is a Western approach. Yet, on the other, we must say that developing strategies is not incompatible with the Christian mission. Planning is a way we can be "as wise as serpents, and as harmless as doves" (Matt. 10:16).

Strategies take God's commission and goals seriously. They do so by showing how we plan to carry out God's commission. They also show how we seek to be wise in our evangelism. They help us insure that we are not harmful to God's intentions or to the people he sends us to evangelize.

In the ten years since the concepts in this book were first developed, thousands of First- and Two-Thirds World missionaries have been exposed to them. Non-Western missionaries in Nepal, Indonesia, Chad, Taiwan, Singapore, Argentina, Chile, India, the Philippines, Kenya, Uganda, and a host of other countries have expressed joy in using them. They say that the Holy Spirit *focused* their thinking with these concepts and made them more effective for the Lord.

Study Question

1. What is a preferred strategy approach? Why?

6

The Challenge Before Us

Luis Bush

How can we describe the challenge before us at the Lausanne II Congress in Manila? Perhaps it can be described by something we have experienced. This was true for me one day right here in Manila, when I met Andrew. For two years, he had been proclaiming Christ in a community of some seven thousand people who made their living off the garbage dump of Manila.

We put on boots, and as we walked to the dumps, I saw a group of people swimming in the river that flows out to the Manila Bay and to the Pacific. As in other cities around the world, the water is completely polluted. The houses are one-room shacks where entire families live.

While we were in the area, a woman approached us. She was crying. In her hand, she carried a bag which contained the remains of her infant baby who had died only a short while before. She did not have the money needed to give the baby a decent burial, and had approached Andrew for help.

Trucks daily unload the garbage onto a smoldering heap of refuse. At the top of the dump, which smokes six months out of the year, it was a shock to see young and old scavenging—picking up broken bottles and old tin cans to sell to recyclers.

As I looked over the smoking dump on the one side and the community of people on the other with the river in the distance leading out to the Manila Bay, I thought, *What a graphic picture of the world in which we live. What a graphic picture of the challenge before us.*

The challenge before us is to work together with understanding, in a rapidly growing urban world which is increasingly unfriendly. We need to work together in an attitude of dependence on the Lord Jesus Christ and the Holy Spirit, to mobilize all the forces within the body of Christ in every country of the world to fulfill the Great Commission. We must strive to proclaim the gospel to

Luis Bush is the International Director of the AD 2000 and Beyond Movement. He formerly was the International President of Partners s International. Bush is a citizen af Argentina. He introduced the concept of the "10/40Window" at Lausanne 2, and has written several articles, including "Getting to the Core of the Core," and "The Challenge Before Us." Adapted from his address at Lausanne 2.

every people group, and to obey the Great Commandment by demonstrating love for the whole person as we approach the year 2000 and until He comes.

"To Work Together With Understanding"

During my time at the dump community in Manila, I was moved by what I saw. There was a team of about twenty people working together in harmony. They proclaimed the gospel and sacrificially served the community. Among them were young and old, men and women, charismatics and non-charismatics. Over half of the workers were national Christians from the Philippines. There were people from six different countries and from a number of different Christian organizations working together to share Christ's love. This is the kind of cooperation needed.

The challenge before us is to build new bridges of understanding. We must build a strong bridge of understanding between the younger, rapidly growing churches in the Two-Thirds World countries and the matured and financially blessed churches in the West.

We need to build a bridge which brings together the younger generation and the older generation of Christian leaders. While younger leaders are looking for ways to have meaningful involvement in Christian work by horizontal networking, older leaders, used to working with "top-down" authority lines, need to look for creative ways to support the developing gifts of younger leaders. This requires new and creative styles of leadership.

We must build a bridge to unite the rapidly growing charismatic movement with the more traditional forms of Christianity. The one emphasizes the supernatural power of God operating in spiritual gifts and signs and wonders, while the other underscores the Word of God. We need *both* the power of God and the Word of God.

The fourth bridge would bring together with understanding the call of God for both evangelism and social responsibility, sacrificial service in the world and preaching the gospel of Christ to the world, of both word and deed, proclamation and presence.

Our goal is to build bridges of understanding during the next ten days in our national delegation meetings, in the different tracks, over meals, and when we all meet together. The spirit of cooperation we experience in the next ten days could well be a foretaste of the kind of cooperation we will enjoy over the next ten years.

"In a Rapidly Growing Urbanizing World"

The world is moving to the cities. In 1900, a little more than one out of ten people were urban dwellers. One hundred years later, in the year 2000, almost eight out of ten will be urban dwellers, according to United Nations statistics. The world is becoming one gigantic city.

Moody said, "If we reach the cities we reach the nation. But if we fail in the cities, they will become a cesspool that will infect the entire country."

For all the "human family," this is an increasingly unfriendly world. Major threats to the earth's environment drive one hundred species of plants and animals to extinction every day because of the gases from automobiles, factories and power plants, toxic and household waste, and overpopulation. One out of every five people in the world go to bed hungry every night.

It is also an increasingly unfriendly world for Christians. In the year 1900, virtually every country was open to expatriate missionaries of one tradition or another. This is no longer true. Major changes are taking place in the ability of expatriate missionaries, particularly from the West, to move into unreached areas. By the year 2000, at present trends, over eight out of ten people of the world will be living in countries with restricted access to traditional missionaries.

"In an Attitude of Dependence"

It is Jesus who is Lord. It was Jesus who said: "All authority in heaven and on earth has been given to me. Therefore go.... And surely I am with you always, to the very end of the age" (Matthew 28:18-20). "The horse is made ready for the day of battle, but victory rests with the Lord" (Proverbs 21:31).

It is the Holy Spirit who empowers the church. We have experienced three mighty waves of worldwide Pentecostal/Charismatic renewal in this century. There is a fourth wave of those of us who desire to hear what the Spirit is saying to the churches through these other waves and join them in the task of spreading the kingdom of God throughout the earth to the year 2000 and until He comes.

"To Mobilize the Body of Christ"

There is a shift in the center of gravity in Christianity from the West to the East and from the North to the South. This growing, global church is becoming mobilized for world evangelization. As John Stott wrote in his commentary on the Lausanne Covenant, "Unless the whole church is mobilized, the whole world is not likely to be reached."

In the Lausanne Covenant, embedded within fourteen other affirmations, one stands out like a precious jewel because it is the only article which speaks of rejoicing. It is article 8, titled "Churches in Evangelistic Partnership," which begins: "We rejoice that a new missionary era has dawned."

The dawn of partnership with missions movements around the world has become at least mid-morning of a new day in Christianity—a day in which the responsibility for world evangelization is being taken up by the "whole body of Christ." More Christians from more countries are seeking to fulfill the Great Commission than at any time in history. The internationalization of missions is the great new fact of our time. Our challenge is to encourage the new world-evangelization initiatives from Africa, Asia, and Latin America, which at the present rate will place more than one hundred thousand missionaries in the field by the year 2000.

But not only that, we are challenged by the need to unleash all the forces within the church in this mobilization. Particularly, we need to see women, young people, and laypeople within our churches renewed, moved into action, and growing as they discover and fulfill their role in world evangelization.

Andrew described to me the tremendous ministry a single laywoman had at the Manila dump over the years. I was also impressed that a man as young as

Andrew had such compassion and vision. When we got to the top of the dump and saw those children bent over, picking up garbage, he said two things that I will never forget: "These are beautiful people." And then he added, "It is a privilege to work here."

How much he was like Andrew, the brother of Peter, who kept on bringing people to Jesus. And this Andrew was only twenty-one years old. We need to give the youth of our generation room to grow, and even allow them to make mistakes, and release them in ministry along with other people. All these vital forces need to be released in order to achieve our goal.

"To Fulfill the Great Commission"

This means going beyond "near neighbor" evangelism. This means we need to take the gospel cross-culturally to those groups of unreached people who have never had an adequate internal witness. Cross-cultural evangelism to the unreached is our highest priority. These people groups have never had an indigenous church movement in their midst.

This point was highlighted at Lausanne I. Fifteen years ago there were an estimated seventeen thousand unreached people groups, defined by dialect and subculture which needed to be reached. Today, that number has been reduced to some twelve thousand. Most of these people groups live in a belt that extends from West Africa across Asia, between ten degrees north of the equator to forty degrees north of the equator. This includes the great Muslim bloc, the Hindu bloc, and the Buddhist bloc. And today, only seven of every one hundred missionaries are working among these peoples.

We must refocus our efforts in evangelization. We must redeploy our missionaries. We must think of new creative ways of partnership. And we must not forget the need for the re-evangelization of Europe.

"To Obey the Great Commandment"

A recent study indicated that a great deal of the lost are poor and a great deal of the poor are lost. It also became evident that those in greatest need are living in the midst of Muslim contexts in the Third World.

By the year 2000, one out of every four people will be urban poor. Our challenge is incarnational missions—to respond to the needs of the whole person as we proclaim new life in Christ.

Andrew and his team have learned to minister to the whole person. There is a food program for the children under five living in the community. Many of the workers are trained in primary health care and lovingly minister to the sick and suffering. While I was there they were preparing a room that was to be used as a Christian preschool.

"Until He Comes"

As Christians approach the end of this century, many groups within the worldwide body of Christ are setting the year 2000 as a symbolic milestone for humankind. This milestone year serves both as a focal point for evangelization plans and as a transition time into a new century of world evangelization.

Several countries, including the Philippines, already have a "2000 Plan" and national A.D. 2000 task forces. Others, like Costa Rica in Central America, have already planned their meetings. They are expecting over one thousand Christian leaders in San Jose, Costa Rica in August for what they have called *Alcance 2000*, "reaching out to the year 2000."

Other remarkable national initiatives are taking place. There will be time during this Congress for delegations to come together and discuss what can be done in their country as we approach the year 2000 and beyond.

Preliminary rough-draft plans setting goals by the year 2000 are being laid out and considered by leaders in the continents of Southeast Asia, South Asia, Africa, Latin America, the Middle East, and North America.

The challenge at this Congress is to see those plans mature and expand so every country and continent will have aggressive faith goals for the last ten years of this century and millennium.

As you gather in your national meetings, begin to think of the mandate of Scripture, the context and the issues facing the church in your country, the unreached people groups, the great cities, and the twenty-five most unevangelized countries that your national church can reach. And seek to answer the question: *What can be done by the year 2000?* Set a date for yourself—December 31, 1999. Prepare to involve the wider Christian constituency from your country. Over the next three years, we would like to see 150 countries have national consultations to set faith goals and discover national strategies.

There are also local and global plans focused on the year 2000 by Christian organizations, local churches, denominations, Christian movements, and affinity groups. The challenge before us is to set significant goals. Ten year goals can become steps of faith that take us from present limitations to future possibilities—goals that are specific, measurable, and achievable. Let us trust God together to do great things.

At the Manila dump community, I also observed signs of joy and peace in the midst of all the agony. Children could be seen playing soccer on the dirt streets and were laughing. An older woman with a big smile came up and gave Andrew a loving embrace.

I also learned something as I heard from others outside of the team. The community had gone through a transformation over the previous two years. Signs of the presence of God among His people were everywhere: in the fourteen home Bible studies, in the church filled with children at mid-morning, and throughout the community as Christians became salt and light.

Brothers and sisters in Christ, if it can be done in a dump community, then why can we not strive to proclaim the whole gospel to the whole world with the whole church by the year 2000 and until He comes?

Study Question

1. What do you want your church to accomplish by the year 2000?

7

On the Cutting Edge of Mission Strategy

C. Peter Wagner

Mission strategy has taken a sharp new focus today. No longer is it enough to say we are "faithful" missionaries—we must also be "successful" in evangelizing and discipling all nations. This is abundantly clear in the parable of the talents. If evangelism is our highest priority in mission, then we need to understand what the task involves—and that power encounters are a crucial factor in missions today.

Today's cutting edge issues in missions fall under three general headings: (1) mission principles—thinking clearly about our task, (2) mission practices—planning strategically as we move out, and (3) mission power—ministering supernaturally as we encounter the enemy. Much of what we do emerges from what we think. Thus, I have no hesitation in starting with some aspects of missiological theory. I believe that an important starting point is understanding what mission is, what evangelism is, what the task is, and what is actually happening on the field.

The Mission—No Options Here!

The definition of mission has been a topic of constant debate for the past one hundred years. It revolves chiefly around the relationship of what have been called the cultural mandate and the evangelistic mandate.

The cultural mandate, which some refer to as Christian social responsibility, goes as far back as the Garden of Eden. After God created Adam and Eve, He said to them: "Be fruitful and multiply; fill the earth and subdue it; have dominion over the fish of the sea, over the birds of the air, and over every living thing

Peter Wagner has been Professor of Church Growth in the Fuller Seminary School of World Mission for over 20 years. Donald McGavran, founder of both the Church Growth Movement and the School of World Mission, picked Wagner as his successor at Fuller. Previous to joining the Fuller faculty, Wagner, along with his wife, Doris, served the Lord in Bolivia in evangelism, church planting, seminary teaching, and mission administration. While there he began writing books and now has authored over 30 volumes on missions and church growth. Since 1980, Peter Wagner has specialized in the spiritual aspects of church growth, writing such books as *Wrestling with Dark Angels*, *Spiritual Power and Church Growth*, and *Warfare Prayer*. In addition to teaching at Fuller Seminary, he coordinates the United Prayer Track of the AD 2000 Movement.

that moves on the earth" (Gen. 1:21). As human beings, made in the image of God, we are held accountable for the well-being of God's creation. In the New Testament we are told that we are to love our neighbors as ourselves (Matt. 22:39). The concept of neighbor, as the parable of the Good Samaritan teaches, includes not only those of our own race or culture or religious group, but all of humanity. Doing good to others, whether our efforts are directed toward individuals or to society as a whole, is a biblical duty, a God-given cultural mandate.

The evangelistic mandate is also first glimpsed in the Garden of Eden. For a period of time, whenever God went to the Garden, Adam and Eve were waiting for Him and they had fellowship. But sin entered into the picture. The very next time that God went to the Garden, Adam and Eve were nowhere to be found. Fellowship had been broken. Humans had been alienated from God. God's nature, in light of the events, was made clear by the first words which came out of His mouth, "Adam, where are you?" (Gen. 3:9). He immediately began seeking Adam. The evangelistic mandate involves seeking and finding lost men and women, alienated from God by sin. Romans 10 tells us that whoever calls on the name of the Lord will be saved. But they cannot call if they have not believed and they cannot believe if they have not heard and they cannot hear without a preacher. "How beautiful are the feet of those who preach the gospel of peace" (Rom. 10:15). Bearing the gospel which brings people from darkness to light is fulfilling the evangelistic mandate.

Both the cultural mandate and the evangelistic mandate are essential parts of biblical mission, in my opinion. Neither is optional. There is a growing consensus on this point in Evangelical circles.

This was not true as early as twenty-two years ago when the Berlin World Congress on Evangelism was held in 1966. Not only was virtually no mention made there of the cultural mandate (Paul Rees of World Vision was a minor exception), but such a prominent Evangelical spokesman as John R. W. Stott defined mission as including only the evangelical mandate, and not the cultural mandate, although he did not use that precise terminology. One of the first Evangelicals to stress the cultural mandate in a public forum was Horace Fenton of the Latin America Mission at the Wheaton Congress on the Church's Worldwide Mission, also held in 1966. Following that, the social consciousness generated by the social upheavals of the 1960's brought the cultural mandate to prominence until it was given a relatively high profile on the platform of the International Congress on World Evangelization at Lausanne in 1974. By then John Stott himself had changed his views, recognizing that mission included both the cultural and the evangelistic mandates. The Lausanne Covenant makes a strong statement on the cultural mandate in Article 5, and on the evangelistic mandate in Article 6.

The current debate involves four positions: (1) those who would prioritize the cultural mandate over the evangelistic, (2) those who would give equal weight to both—even arguing that it is illegitimate to divide them by using such terminology, (3) those who would prioritize the evangelistic mandate, and (4) those who would hold the pre-Lausanne view that mission is the evangelistic mandate, period.

My personal view is that of the Lausanne Covenant. But I spend little time fussing with those who hold that mission should be understood as evangelism and that social ministry should be termed a Christian duty or an outcome of mission rather than part of mission itself. I see either of these positions as contributing more positively to the evangelization of the world than the other options. But I do not accept the prioritization of evangelism solely on pragmatic grounds. I believe it best reflects the New Testament doctrine of mission. Jesus came to seek and to save the lost (Lk. 10:10), and we move out in Jesus's Name to do the same. While we must not neglect our Christian social responsibility, in my opinion, it must never get in the way of soul-winning evangelism.

Evangelism—Making Disciples

If evangelism is the highest priority in mission, it is extremely important that we clearly understand what evangelism is.

Among the best contemporary books on evangelism is Joe Aldrich's *Lifestyle Evangelism*. One of the things I like about it is that he, unlike many other authors of books on evangelism, begins by defining clearly what he means by evangelism. He realizes that the way we think about evangelism will ultimately influence the way we do evangelism and consequently the final result.

The three prominent ways of defining evangelism in the Christian world today can be labeled presence, proclamation and persuasion. Presence holds that evangelism is helping people to fulfill their needs. It is giving a cup of cold water in the Name of Jesus. It is lending a helping hand. Proclamation recognizes that presence is necessary, but goes beyond it and says that evangelism is making known the message of Jesus so that people hear it and understand it. But once people are exposed to the gospel message they are evangelized whether they accept it or not according to a strict proclamation definition. Persuasion argues that presence and proclamation are both necessary, but that biblical evangelism goes beyond that and insists on making disciples.

My view of evangelism affirms both presence and proclamation, but neither as adequate definitions of evangelism in themselves. But I believe that a person should not be considered evangelized until he or she has become an ongoing disciple of Jesus Christ.

This is rooted in the Great Commission. While the Great Commission appears in all four Gospels and Acts, the Matthew account is the most complete for understanding it in context. "Go, therefore, and make disciples of all the nations, baptizing them in the name of the Father and of the Son and of the Holy Spirit, teaching them to observe all things that I have commanded you" (Matt. 28:19-20). Three of the four action verbs in the Great Commission are participles in the original Greek: "go," "baptize," and "teach." They are helping verbs. The one imperative is "make disciples." If the Great Commission is the key text for evangelism, its goal, exegetically speaking, is to make disciples.

If making disciples is that important, what then is a disciple? Theologically, a disciple is one who has been regenerated by the Holy Spirit, a new creature in Christ Jesus (see 2 Cor. 5:17). Empirically, a disciple is one who is known by the fruit. When true regeneration takes place, visible fruit inevitably follows. Those of us who identify with the Church Growth Movement agree that, while there are many, many legitimate fruits of regeneration, one which is an excellent indicator is responsible church membership. In order to be counted as a disciple, a person should be committed not only to Jesus Christ, but also to the body of Christ.

Field research increasingly indicates that evangelistic efforts based on presence or proclamation alone are considerably less effective in terms of resulting church growth than those seeing evangelism as persuasion.

The Task—Reaching the 78% Outside

Jesus said that the good shepherd who has a flock of 100 sheep and discovers that one is lost, leaves the 99 who are safe in the fold and searches for the lost sheep until it is found. This is another indicator of where God's priorities lie. We must spend time nurturing existing Christians. We must strive for healthy churches. We must stress quality as well as quantity. But we also must be good shepherds and never rest so long as there are human beings who are lost. Christ died for them and He wants them to be reconciled to the Father. Today we do not have 99 in the fold and one outside. It is more like 30 in the fold and 70 outside, at the best.

In the world today over three billion people are outside the fold. Of them, about 850 million can be reached by ordinary evangelism within a given culture. We missiologists call it E-1. That is a massive task in itself, and one for which large amounts of human, financial and technological resources are being invested. But far overshadowing that task are the 2.3 billion people who as yet do not have a viable, evangelizing church within their own culture. These 2.3 billion, comprising 78 percent of those outside the fold, will be reached only through what we ordinarily call missions. Someone will have to leave the comforts of their own culture, learn a new language, learn how to eat new food, live a different lifestyle, love people who may appear to be unlovely, and share the gospel of Christ with them. This is cross-cultural evangelism, E-2 and E-3, and as Ralph Winter of the U.S. Center for World Mission showed in the Lausanne Congress of 1974, it is the highest priority for planning the task of world evangelization.

The Field—Third World Missionaries Go Out

We are in the springtime of Christian missions. The spread of the gospel and the growth of Christian churches around the world far outstrips anything that has been known throughout history. The age of modern missions began roughly in 1800 when William Carey went to India. More people have been won to Christ and more Christian churches have been planted in the 185 years since then than in the total of 1800 years previously. Every day of the year sees an estimated 78,000 new Christians and every week there are 1,600 new Christian churches worldwide.

Time will not permit me to go into detail about church growth in different parts of the world. Flash points of growth include Central America, Korea, the Philippines, Nigeria, Brazil, Ethiopia, China, and many other places. Thirty percent of the Korean population is now Christian and the percentage is rising rapidly. Leaders are projecting that by 1990 Guatemala will be 50 percent Evangelical. There were one million Chinese believers in 1950 when Marxism took over. With all the persecution, many of us on the outside thought they must have been obliterated. Instead, we now know that they have grown to a conservative 50 million, probably many more. It is believed that most of the growth occurred since 1970, which means that for the rest of the century China may well continue to be the greatest harvest field in the world, evangelistically speaking.

To meet the challenge of reaping the tremendous harvest which God has ripened, He is calling forth large numbers of workers here in the United States and abroad. Not since the decade following World War II has there been such a vital interest in missions among Christian young people. The vision of Robertson McQuilkin's book, *The Great Omission*, is coming true. I'm sure that many of you recall the doldrums of the 1960s and early 70s when interest in missions was dismally low among college and seminary students. Toward the end of the 70s God began doing a new thing, and it has not yet peaked. Young people are ready to serve God wherever He calls them. New and exciting mission agencies have been created such as Youth With a Mission, Frontiers, the Mission Society for United Methodists, and many others.

Churches in Asia, Africa and Latin America are also mobilizing their forces for cross-cultural missions. In 1972, 3,400 Third World missionaries were identified. By 1980 the figure had risen to 13,000 and researchers such as Larry Keyes of O.C. Ministries are estimating that there may be 18,000 on the field today. By the end of the century there may be as many or more missionaries on the field from the two-thirds world as from our one-third world. As we recruit an increasing number of missionaries worldwide, we are seeing an answer to the prayer that the Lord of the harvest will send forth laborers into the harvest fields.

Thinking clearly about our task is an essential starting point for mission strategy. It gives us a base for sound and effective practice.

Mission Practice—Planning Strategically

One of the most significant missiological works of our time is *Planning Strategies for World Evangelization* by Edward Dayton and David Fraser. I have used it as a textbook ever since it was first published in 1980. It does a great deal in helping to shape a positive Evangelical attitude toward strategy. They say, "As Christians, a strategy forces us to seek the mind of God and the will of the Holy Spirit. What does God desire? How can we conform to the future that He desires?" I agree with Dayton and Fraser who argue that setting goals and developing a strategy to reach them is a statement of faith. It is putting substance on things hoped for, as Hebrews 11:1 recommends. Since it is impossible to please God without faith according to Hebrews 11:6, I believe that planning strategy according to the will of God is pleasing to Him.

Planning strategy must not be seen as a substitute for the work of the Holy Spirit. Jesus said, "I will build My church" and we do well to emphasize the "I." He has been building His church for 2,000 years, and He will continue to build it until He returns—with or without the help of any of us. But He cordially invites each of us to join Him in the worldwide task of building that church. And if we accept the invitation, we become instruments in Jesus' hands for the accomplishment of His task. All that I am advocating here is that we do whatever is necessary to become the best servants possible as the Master uses us to do His work.

Thus, I see obedience to the Master as a starting point for formulating our attitudes toward mission strategy. The Great Commission is a clear commandment. We are to go into the world, preach the gospel to every creature, and make disciples of all nations—*panta ta ethne*. God is not willing that any should perish (see 2 Peter 3:9). As servants we need have no doubt as to the will of the Master.

We must be willing to be New Testament stewards. And we are told explicitly that we are stewards of the mysteries of God—a parallel expression to the gospel (see 1 Cor. 4:1). What is the gospel for? It is the power of God for salvation (see Romans 1:16).

We are also told that stewards are required to be found faithful (see 1 Cor. 4:2). It is important to understand what is meant by "faithful," here. I have heard some say, "God, I thank you that you do not require me to be successful, only faithful." But the central passage on stewardship, the parable of the talents in Matthew 25, makes no distinction between the two. It tells us that the stewards who did their master's will and turned two talents and five talents into four and ten respectively were regarded as good and faithful servants. Here success and faithfulness go hand in hand. The steward who buried the talent and made no money, not even bank interest, from it was considered unfaithful.

The foundational principle of New Testament stewardship is that the steward takes the resources given by the Master, uses them for the Master's purpose, and returns to give glory to the Master.

This has a direct application to mission strategy. Since we know that the Master's will is to make disciples of all nations, we are responsible, as good stewards, to use what resources He has given us to accomplish that task. To the degree that we are successful, we will be called faithful.

Setting goals for world evangelization and planning strategies to accomplish those goals require a degree of pragmatism. I realize that pragmatism can be carnal, but here I am speaking of consecrated pragmatism. I am not suggesting pragmatism concerning doctrine or ethics. But I am advocating pragmatism as to methodology. If we are investing resources of time, personnel and money in programs which are supposed to make disciples but are not, we need to reconsider them and be willing to change the program if needed. Jesus' parable suggests that if the fig tree does not bear fruit after an appropriate lapse of time, it should be cut down and the ground used for something more productive (see Luke 13:6-9).

The Targets For Strategy

If we agree to take a positive attitude toward strategy planning for world missions, the precise targets of our activity then become highly important. Much research is being carried out these days in many parts of the world to help us get a clear picture of exactly what we are aiming for. I will mention but three here: the unreached peoples, the cities, and whole nations.

Unreached Peoples: The concept of unreached peoples as target groups for mission strategy first surfaced prominently in the International Congress on World Evangelization in Lausanne, Switzerland in 1974. Edward Dayton on the MARC division of World Vision distributed the first Unreached Peoples Directory to all the participants. Then Ralph Winter, now director of the U.S. Center for World Mission, highlighted the concept of people groups in a plenary session address.

Subsequently the Lausanne Committee for World Evangelization was formed and its Strategy Working Group focused its attention on unreached peoples research, contracting MARC as its research agency. I had the privilege of chairing the Strategy Working Group for its first four years, and more recently Dayton himself had been the chairperson. The U.S. Center for World Mission has concentrated its research on the unreached peoples as well, calling them at times hidden peoples or frontier peoples. Much of this research has been reported in the series of *Unreached Peoples Annuals* beginning with *Unreached Peoples '79.* A Global Mapping Project is now in place under the direction of Bob Waymire *[Ed. note: now Global Mapping International under Mike O'Rear],* applying computer technology to unreached peoples research with a view of producing computer-generated maps showing, in color, the harvest fields and the harvest forces for any given part of the world.

For several years a spirited discussion was carried on among the leaders of unreached peoples research as to the definition of an unreached people group. A blow by blow account of this is given in Ralph Winter's chapter, "Unreached Peoples: The Development of the Concept," in Harvie Conn's recent book, *Reaching the Unreached.* By the way, I highly recommend this book for those who wish an introduction to the subject. As Winter points out, the definition now agreed upon by all concerned is:

> An unreached people is a people group among which there is no indigenous community of believing Christians with adequate numbers and resources to evangelize this people group without outside (cross-cultural) assistance.

An estimated 75 percent of the world's non-Christians find themselves in unreached people groups. That means that over two billion individuals for whom Christ died will not hear of His love unless someone follows the call of God, leaves their own culture, learns a new language, eats new food, adjusts to a new lifestyle, loves new peoples who may appear unlovely, and shares the gospel message with them. This is mission, pure and simple. The age of missions is far from over. On the contrary, cross-cultural service for Christ is the most massive and most exciting challenge for Christians today.

It is yet unclear exactly how many unreached people groups exist. Many of us have been using the figure 16,750, rounded to 17,000 *[Ed. note: now 11,000]* which is Ralph Winter's somewhat symbolic estimate. Some say the number may turn out to be 100,000 or more. Time will tell. Whatever the final number, over 5,000 have been identified and listed in the *Unreached Peoples Annuals* so far. Happily, some originally classified as unreached have now become reached over the past few years. But my point is that among missiologists there is a wide agreement that this unit, namely, people groups, is the most useful primary target for planning mission strategy.

Cities: Many people groups find themselves clustered in close proximity to each other in the cities of the world. A major socio-demographic phenomenon of our age, especially post-World War II, is the urban explosion. At the time of World War II only New York and London had over 10 million inhabitants. Now there are more than ten such megacities, and the projection for the end of our century is twenty-five. Mexico City had fewer than three million people during World War II, but it is expected to contain over 30 million by the end of the century, the largest city in the world.

Raymond Bakke, the outstanding Evangelical urbanologist who has been carrying on research under the Lausanne Strategy Working Group and MARC for the past few years, has identified over 250 of what he calls "world class cities," and he has visited most of them. A world class city is one which has over one million persons (form or structure), and international influence (function or role). The number of world class cities is expected to rise to 500 by the end of the century.

Bakke explains how the dual targets of unreached peoples and world class cities relate to each other by making the helpful distinction between (1) the geographically distant unreached peoples and (2) the culturally distant unreached peoples. Granted, there is a cultural distance in both cases, but in the first there is also a significant geographical barrier. Traditionally, geographically distant peoples have been the chief target of those we send to the mission field. But in today's cities, culturally distant peoples may be living right next door or a block or two away, but we may be blind to their existence as targets for sharing the gospel. Bakke says, "They will not be reached for Jesus Christ unless existing churches become multicultural by intention or unless user-friendly churches are started by and for them."

Many are picking up the challenge of the cities. Let me mention two examples out of any others which could be highlighted. Under the creative leadership of Harvie Conn and Roger Greenway, Westminster Seminary in Philadelphia has become a strategic Evangelical training center for urban ministry. A new journal, *Urban Mission*, is being edited by Greenway.

Recently, a new mission agency was created to target one particular urban population—the poverty-stricken squatter settlements now popping up all over the world. Sparked by Tom and Betty Sue Brewster of the Fuller School of World Mission, and Viv Grigg of New Zealand, the organization is called Servants Among the Poor. It is challenging a new breed of missionaries not only to live among the squatters, but to agree to share their standard of living over the long haul in order to evangelize and plant churches. We are experiencing a healthy trend among Evangelicals as we target research, training, and deployment of workers toward the urban areas.

Whole Nations: While cities are increasingly important as evangelistic targets, the politically-defined nations of the world continue to maintain the highest profile in the national and international media. They also are extremely prominent in international social psychology. With all the necessary emphasis on people groups and urbanization, our strategy planning for missions must not ignore the geo-political countries of the world. At this point in time, the cutting-edge leader who, I believe, has seen this most clearly and who has taken aggressive action to implement it is James Montgomery. Montgomery left Overseas Crusades in the early 80s to form a new mission agency called DAWN Ministries. DAWN is an acronym for "Discipling a Whole Nation."

The aim of DAWN is to mobilize the entire body of Christ in a given nation for a determined effort to complete the Great Commission by working towards the goal of providing an Evangelical congregation for every village and urban neighborhood in the country. Montgomery believes in the people group concept, but argues that concentration on the people groups located within given countries is the most practical way of reaching all the unreached.

The DAWN program is long term, extending over several years. It begins with an extensive research project on the status of evangelism and church growth in the country, with the results published in a book in the national language. Christian leaders are organized into task forces to provide coordination of activities and accountability for results. A major national DAWN congress is held for motivation, inspiration, training and goal setting. This is either preceded or followed by regional DAWN conferences over a period of time.

DAWN is more than just an idea. The pilot project was undertaken in the Philippines where DAWN-type congresses were held in 1974, 1980, and 1985. The results have been amazing. I cannot take time to list them here, but I will mention as an example that the Christian and Missionary Alliance planted as many new churches in the five years after becoming involved in DAWN as they had in the previous 75 years of ministry. The Conservative Baptists doubled their membership from 10,000 to 20,000 in five years (1981-85) and have now set a goal of 90,000 members by 1990. The second effort was Guatemala with the national congress held in 1984. At that time Evangelicals formed about 25 percent of the population and the annual growth rate was 12.5 percent. They projected raising the annual growth rate to 17 percent and look forward to the Evangelical community becoming 50 percent of the population by 1990. Plans are now underway for DAWN programs in several other countries, and I recommend them with enthusiasm.

Three Tools For Strategy

We live in an era of an explosion of missiological technology. New tools for completing the Great Commission are constantly being developed. Any missions professor could readily compile a list of a dozen or more areas of significant advance in our knowledge of how missions can be conducted more efficiently.

Research is multiplying. I have already mentioned the research on unreached peoples at World Vision and the U.S. Center for World Mission. I have mentioned Ray Bakke's work on world class cities. In my institution alone, we now have 486 graduate theses and dissertations written by students which have been indexed and annotated in a volume called Missiological Abstracts. Similar reports could be given from the missiology faculties of Trinity, Columbia, Biola, Dallas, Asbury, Southwestern, and a dozen other Evangelical institutions. Strategic, specialized research centers such as the Samuel Zwemer Institute are springing up.

Contextualization is another cutting-edge missiological tool. For over a decade now, Evangelicals have become increasingly aware of the cultural demands for a relevant gospel message. Don Richardson's seminal contributions in the area of the redemptive analogy have changed the thinking of many. The scholarly centerpiece of this activity has been my colleague Charles Kraft's *Christianity in Culture,* in my opinion one of the three Evangelical missiological classics of our time. Current quarrels as to whether Kraft is an Evangelical are ludicrous, as Harvie Conn's book *Eternal Word and Changing Worlds* testifies.

Contextualization raises important questions such as what should our approach be to peoples who worship ancestors? We need to help them in the struggle to reconcile the first commandment: "You shall have no other gods before me" with the fifth: "Honor your father and your mother." How do we approach Muslims who sincerely believe that we Christians are tritheists? What about people groups which practice polygamy? Where is the line between orthodoxy and syncretism in the African Independent churches? Our answers to these and similar questions are highly important for the spread of the gospel.

In many parts of the world, the rapid growth of churches is raising the issue of adequate leadership selection and training. Conversions and new churches are multiplying much more rapidly than are pastors to care for the flocks. We at Fuller consider this a central issue and are concentrating on ways and means of providing tools for greatly accelerated leadership training. We are just adding our twelfth full-time missions professor, Eddie Elliston, to join Bobby Clinton in the area of leadership. Trinity Evangelical Divinity School has added Ted Ward to their faculty this year. The Theological Education by Extension movement has made significant contribution to this problem over the past decade or two. But a new generation of educational technology, relating both to formal and non-formal structures, is now being added to what has already been done.

Mission Power—Ministering in the Spirit

We have looked briefly at the mission principles which help us think more clearly about our task. We have examined cutting-edge mission practices which are enabling us to reach out more efficiently than ever before. Now, finally, I want to consider what I am calling "mission power."

Many of us who come from non-Pentecostal and non-Charismatic backgrounds have not known as much about the workings of the supernatural and the miraculous in the world today as we should have. But one of the cutting edges of contemporary mission strategy has been a relatively new manifestation of the Holy Spirit among more traditionally straight line Evangelicals. I have found myself playing an increasingly active role in this during the decade of the 80s. I see what is happening as the "third wave" of the Spirit of God in the 20th century. The first was the Pentecostal movement at the beginning of the century. The second was the Charismatic movement at the mid-point of the century. Both of these continue strong and I see them expanding vigorously throughout the rest of the century.

The third wave involves those of us—and I include myself—who, for one reason or another, do not personally wish to identify with either the Pentecostals or the Charismatics. We love, respect and admire our friends in those movements and we pray God's blessing on them in all their work. We recognize that currently they represent the most rapidly growing segment of the body of Christ worldwide. We have learned a great deal from them and desire to learn more. But our style is slightly different. We minister in very similar ways, but explain what we do in alternate theological terminology. We serve the same Lord and are involved in the same task of world evangelization. I believe that we Evangelicals need a fresh look at supernatural power, a fresh awareness of worldview, and a fresh examination of the theology of the Kingdom.

A Fresh Look At God's Supernatural

Jesus sent his disciples out with "power over unclean spirits, to cast them out, and to heal all kinds of sickness and all kinds of diseases" (Mt. 10:1). The apostle Paul testified that he preached the Gospel to the Gentiles from Jerusalem to Illyricum "in mighty signs and wonders, by the power of the Spirit of God" (Rom. 15:19). Hebrews records that salvation has come through God's witness "both with signs and wonders, with various miracles, and gifts of the Holy Spirit...." (Heb. 2:4).

While we do not deny the validity of the Word of God, many of us have not experienced this kind of New Testament power in our personal ministries. I for one never saw it at all during my 16 years as a missionary to Bolivia. To me the power of God was to save souls and help us live a good Christian life. I now see that as correct, but only a partial view of God's power. It is some consolation for me that all of my colleagues on the Fuller School of Mission faculty look on their missionary careers with similar observations.

As Timothy Warner of the Trinity School of World Mission and Evangelism says: "The issue of encounter with demonic forces is one which has understandably been avoided by large segments of the church. For most of my life, I was among those who steered clear of such involvement." But, he goes onto say, "We can no longer afford this luxury." Warner believes that power and the power encounter is a crucial factor in today's mission. As he looks out on the unreached peoples he observes that "In many parts of the world...people are much more power-conscious than they are truth-conscious. We may preach a very logical and convincing message by Western standards, but our hearers remain unimpressed. Let them see Christian power displayed in relation to the spirit world in which they live with great fear, however, and they will 'hear' the message more clearly than our words alone could ever make it."

A similar concern is expressed by Richard De Ridder of Calvin Theological Seminary in his book *Discipling the Nations*. De Ridder reflects on his missionary experience in Sri Lanka in these words:

> One thing deeply impressed me: how irrelevant so much of traditional Reformed Theology was to these people and their situation, and how seldom this theology spoke to their real needs. E.g., the questions that concern Satan, demons, angels, charms, etc., are not of great concern, nor do they receive much attention in the West. These are living issues to the Christians of these areas, surrounded

as they were by animism and the continual fear of the spiritual realm. Among the greatest joys that we experienced was to proclaim to men the victory of Christ over the powers and see the shackles of slavery to elemental spirits broken by Christ. This is a chapter of Reformed Theology that has still not been written by the West. When the "Five Points of Calvinism" were preached to these people, they often responded with the question, "What's the issue?" Missionaries and pastors were scratching where it didn't itch.

I receive a large number of letters, both form letters and personal letters, from missionaries around the word. Since this was a personal letter and I do not have permission to cite the writer, I will disguise the identity of the person and the mission agency in my paraphrase of the letter, but suffice it to say that the writer is a traditionally and impeccably Evangelical mission executive:

As you know, we are committed to planting churches in the Muslim world. We are face to face with a power encounter of gigantic proportions. I am convinced that there is a demonic base to Islam that is much greater than most of us have ever dared admit. Of course, it doesn't make good copy to say these things or write them, and we are all rather embarrassed by our ineptitude in facing Islam today. Why does the Christian church have to lie down and let the Islamic horde sweep over us as so many tanks?

This is an increasing cry. Large numbers of missionaries and international church leaders in our school at Fuller are asking the same questions and we are beginning to provide them with some answers, however elementary at this stage. Two of our students, serving with the Latin America Mission in Costa Rica, wrote of several experiences with supernatural power in a recent newsletter. Among them was this:

Since our return to Costa Rica in January, we have been operating in a new power we never knew in our previous six years here. We have ministered to a person that had been diagnosed to be epileptic only to be freed by the expulsion of demons. This person had an experience early in life with witchcraft, through contact with a Ouija board. Her mother also had been very much involved in the occult. Now after 46 years of torment, she is totally free.

These missionaries lamented the fact that "Christianity has all too often been presented as a religion of the textbook and the head." They now see how distant this is from the Christianity of the New Testament where "worship was alive and meaningful, prayer was an avid encounter, and signs and wonders drew people to faith."

An O.M.F. missionary to Singapore recently wrote that he witnessed to a man there who said, "No point in becoming a Christian. My brother is a pastor. When my mother got ill, he couldn't do anything to help. We took her to the temple and she was healed." Another woman, a Hindu, said, "The trouble with you Christians is that you have no power!" My friend comments, "How tragic when people get the idea that Christianity is a matter of mere intellectual conviction, a religion of words largely devoid of power."

An increasing number of our Evangelical seminary missions faculties and our Evangelical mission agencies have begun to raise issues of spiritual power. I am convinced that it is an area which requires some fresh study and some discerning implementation if we are to participate fully in contemporary world evangelization.

A Fresh Awareness of Worldview

Due to the pervasive influence of cultural anthropology in our current missiological research, the concept of worldview has gained a great deal of prominence. We are able to talk about worldview and to understand its implications for daily life much more freely and accurately than we used to. One of the more disturbing things we are beginning to discover is that, in more cases than we would care to think, our missionary message in the Third World has been having a secularizing influence.

I first realized this when I read an article by my colleague, Paul G. Hiebert, called "The Flaw of the Excluded Middle" in 1982. He begins the article by citing the question that John the Baptist had his disciples ask Jesus: "Are you the Coming One, or do we look for another?" (Lk. 7:20). Hiebert emphasized that Jesus' reply was not a carefully reasoned argument, but rather a demonstration of power in healing the sick and casting out of evil spirits.

"When I read the passage as a missionary in India, and sought to apply it to missions in our day," says Hiebert, "I had a sense of uneasiness. As a Westerner, I was used to presenting Christ on the basis of rational arguments, not by evidence of His power in the lives of people who were sick, possessed and destitute." He goes on to point out that the worldview of most non-Westerners is three-tiered. There is a cosmic tier on top, an everyday life tier on the bottom, and a large middle zone where the two constantly interact. This is a zone largely controlled by spirits, demons, and ancestors, goblins, ghosts, magic, fetishes, witches, mediums, sorcerers, and such powers. The common reaction of Western missionaries, whose worldview does not contain such a middle zone, is to attempt to deny the existence of the spirits rather than claim the power of Christ over them. As a result, says Hiebert, "Western Christian missions have been one of the greatest secularizing forces in history."

Most of us are aware that secular humanism has deeply influenced our culture in America. But relatively few of us have understood how profoundly this has permeated even our Christian institutions including churches, colleges and seminaries. The more we realize it, however, and the more we recognize that our secularized worldview is significantly different from those of the Jews and the Greeks in the New Testament context, the more we can become open to what is called a paradigm shift. This paradigm shift is very helpful in bringing missionaries more in touch with the worldview of the men and women to whom they are attempting to communicate the gospel.

A Fresh Examination of the Theology of the Kingdom

In the Lord's prayer we say, "Thy kingdom come, Thy will be done on earth as it is in heaven." I must confess that up until recently those words had very little meaning for my life. I repeated them by rote memory without much spiritual processing taking place as I did. For one thing, my understanding was that the Kingdom was something that was future so my assumption was that I was praying for the return of the Lord. An accompanying assumption was that, because God is sovereign, His will is in fact being done on earth today and that we can rather passively accept what happens as something which God directly or indirectly approves of.

I now see the theology of the Kingdom in a different light. I now believe that when Jesus came, He introduced the Kingdom of God into the present world.

This was a direct confrontation or invasion of the kingdom of darkness ruled by Satan who is called "the god of this age" (2 Cor. 4:4). I take Satan more seriously than I used to, recognizing that some things which occur today do so because of the will of the enemy, not because they are the will of God. The era between the first and second comings of Christ is an era of warfare between the two kingdoms. Two strong powers are occupying the same territory.

Let me say quickly that I still believe in the sovereignty of God who, for His own reasons, has allowed this spiritual warfare to take place for almost 2,000 years now. And there is no doubt as to the outcome. Satan and all his demonic forces were defeated by the blood of Jesus on the cross. His is, at best, a holding action, but a ferocious, destructive and dehumanizing action which God expects us, as His servants, to actively oppose.

What are some things clearly out of God's will which are happening today? In heaven there is not one poor, at war, oppressed, demonized, sick or lost. As Evangelicals we understand the last one best. Even though it is not God's will that any should perish according to 2 Peter 3:9, the world today is full of those who are perishing, as I have previously mentioned. There are three billion of them out there and our task, as instruments of God's hands, is to reach out to them and bring them into the Kingdom through the new birth (see Jn. 3:3). This is the great missiological challenge.

We do the best we can to reach the lost for Christ knowing full well ahead of time, on both biblical and experiential grounds, that we are not going to win them all. That knowledge does not discourage us, even though we know the reason why some do not respond. We learn from 2 Corinthians 4:3-4 that it is essentially because Satan has succeeded in blinding their eyes to the light of the gospel. We weep knowing that each year millions of people die and go into a Christless eternity, and we know that it is not God's will that they should perish.

If this is true about the lost, it may well be true about the poor, those at war, the oppressed, the demonized and the sick. So long as Satan is the god of this age, they will all be with us. But meanwhile, as citizens of the Kingdom of God, we must reflect the values of the Kingdom and combat these evils as strenuously as possible. For example, we must heal the sick knowing ahead of time that not all will be healed. I was pleased when this was recognized at a high level Evangelical conference in 1982. At that time the Lausanne Committee sponsored a consultation on the relationship of evangelism to social responsibility in Grand Rapids, and recognized in its report that among the signs of the Kingdom were "making the blind see, the deaf hear, the lame walk, the sick whole, raising the dead, stilling the storm, and multiplying loaves and fishes." The report mentions that "Demon possession is a real and terrible condition. Deliverance is possible only in a power encounter in which the name of Jesus is invoked and prevails." This is what missiologists, such as Timothy Warner, are also saying to us.

At least two missiological faculties that I am aware of now consider this an important enough cutting edge issue to introduce it explicitly into their curriculum. Professor Warner of Trinity Evangelical Divinity School began a course on power encounter last summer. In 1982 our Fuller missions faculty invited Pastor John Wimber to teach an experimental course on the miraculous and church growth, which he did for four years. It is now being reorganized under two of Wimber's disciples, Professor Charles Kraft and myself. I agree with Kraft, who once said in a faculty meeting, "We can no longer afford to send missionaries and national church leaders back to their fields or to send young people to the missions field for the first time without teaching them how to heal the sick and cast out demons." We are still at the beginning stages of this, and we are not yet satisfied with the way we are doing the job, but we are trusting God to continue to teach us so that we can in turn teach others.

I feel that one of the callings that God has given me is to be an encouragement to traditional Evangelical non-Pentecostal and non-Charismatic institutions so that they will begin to take a new look at mission power—ministering supernaturally as we encounter the enemy.

References

Bakke, Raymond J. "Evangelization of the World's Cities," *An Urban World: Churches Face the Future,*.Nashville: Broadman.

Dayton, R. Edward. *Planning Strategies for World Evangelization*. Grand Rapids: Eerdmans, 1980, p. 16.

De Ridder, Richard R. *Discipling The Nations*. Grand Rapids: Baker, 1975, p. 222.

Hiebert, Paul G. "The Flaw of the Excluded Middle," *Missiology: An International Review*, Vol.X, Number 1, Jan. 1982, pp. 35-47.

Hinton, Keith and Linnet. Singapore: May 20, 1985 Newsletter.

Lausanne Committee for World Evangelization and the World Evangelical Fellowship. *Evangelism and Social Responsibility: An Evangelical Commitment*, 1982. p. 31.

Wagner, Doris M. ed. *Missiological Abstracts*. Pasadena, CA. Fuller School of World Mission, 1984.

Warner, Timothy "Power Encounter in Evangelism," *Trinity World Forum*, Winter 1985, pp. 1, 3.

Weinand, George and Gayle. San Jose, Costa Rica. May 1985 Newsletter.

Winter, Ralph D. "Unreached Peoples: The Development of a Concept," *Reaching the Unreached*. Phillipsburg, New Jersey: Presbyterian and Reformed Publishing Company, 1984.

Study Questions

1. Explain what is the highest priority for the task of world evangelization. Why?

2. How does the "fear of the excluded middle" affect your evangelistic approach and strategy?

8

A Church for Every People

Bradley A. Gill

Down through history certain men have been captivated by a sense of God's holy purpose for their lives. And down through the years certain words have been to them a guiding light. In the late 1800's tens of thousands of young college students in the United States were flung out across the world in response to one such call. Their watchword was "The Evangelization of the World in this Generation."

Their goal was stupendous—more stupendous than they could ever know. For a few short years the world was relatively at peace; then it erupted again in first one and then another major world war, preceded and followed by hundreds of smaller local ones. Yet these volunteers left growing, healthy Christian churches scattered around the globe by the thousands.

Did they evangelize the world in their generation? They certainly got to places where Americans had rarely gone before—and they usually stayed for the rest of their lives. Yet the world has grown larger. Now we know that we cannot just reach to the 250 nations of the world. Our courses in anthropology teach us that the world is not made up of geographical boundaries so much as of peoples within those boundaries. And all too often those closest to each other hate each other the most.

Just a few weeks ago I was in a small meeting with seven other young people and two veteran missionary couples: Dr. and Mrs. Donald McGavran, members of that early Student Volunteer band, and Dr. and Mrs. Ralph Winter. We were gathered around a book printed in 1891 which discussed the dreams of those early volunteers. In the heart of each of us present was the cry, "Lord, do it again!" We knew the need now was just as great as then. We had all grappled with the fact there are still two-and-a-half billion people beyond the reach of any mission or church anywhere in the world. *What would it take for the Lord to send*

After doing graduate study at Gordon-Conwell Theological Seminary, Brad Gill joined the staff of the U. S. Center for World Mission, and has served as chairman of the Training Division. Gill was a coordinator of the 1980 International Student Consultation on Frontier Missions, held in Edinburgh, Scotland, and is now doing work among Muslims. Taken with permission from *Global Church Growth Bulletin*. Copyright July 1979, Santa Clara, California.

forth again young people, like us, by the thousands? What could be the watch word for our day that would grip their hearts? We knew that to follow Christ's example, it would not only be necessary to evangelize, but gather those won into living fellowships of mutual support and commitment. Only then could they grow and as a body reach out to win the rest of their tribe, their language group, their "people."

"How about A CHURCH FOR EVERY PEOPLE BY THE YEAR 2000?" one of those gathered suggested. The task it outlined was tremendous. Could we do it? The task would belong to us, the young, but we knew there were thousands like us around the world who loved our Lord just like we did who would want to share in that harvest. They only needed to be touched by that certain spark!

So we examined that watchword. Did it say all we wanted it to say? What would following it require of us?

This Watchword Requires a Sensitivity to Culture

I stood recently in the great Hall of Crucifixion and Resurrection at Forest Lawn in Glendale, California and viewed there the mural which covers one entire wall. The central mural of three, standing 50 feet high, is a graphic representation of the millions of people who will greet their Lord at His second coming. There stand the Anglo-Saxons, the Scandinavians, the Latins, the Gauls and other European peoples. The splintered peoples of Africa join the Indian, Dorean and Oriental peoples of Asia. As I looked on all those faces, so enrapt at seeing their Lord return, I thought of John the Apostle's description of a similar scene in Revelation where people from every tribe, tongue and nation would be gathered in front of the throne (Rev. 7:9). Surely, if we understand what John was saying, how sensitive we should be in reaching people within their own cultures. The bride of the Lamb will not be complete until there are some from every tribe, tongue and nation who call him Lord.

My mind went back through history. I thought of the many times when against extreme odds the Gospel had managed to penetrate a culture and change its people from Celtic head-hunters to Irish saints, slave hunters to hymn writers, careless, idle youth to flaming wandering evangelists. Throughout the expanse of time and space, across geographical boundary and successive generation, the gospel had managed to cross the threshold of culture again and again and in amazing power to make of that culture what it could never dream of becoming.

Yes, the gospel was effective. The Holy Spirit could be counted on to be faithful. How about us?

Just recently, in a discussion with one of the foremost missionary thinkers, Dr. Alan Tippett, I was fascinated with the story of the Fiji Islands. Once a place of many tribal factions, it has experienced a fascinating metamorphosis as a result of the penetration of the gospel. The Church has become established in many of these societies. I inquired as to whether there were any more frontiers of any kind in Fiji. He told me of the 260,000 people from India, 30,000 of whom are most likely Muslim. Also, he said, massive urbanization has created a severe stratification of the original social structure. Fiji is now grappling with the problems of suburbia!

Applying this same cultural filter to the rest of the word, we find that 11,000 peoples have yet to hear the gospel in their own cultures. The watchword of this generation must articulate that only as we are equipped with a cultural sensitivity can we objectively recognize the frontiers that lie before us.

This Watchword Requires a "Strategy of Closure"

The church must continually define its purpose as that of working toward the completion of the Great Commission. It is very easy for Christians to feel we are accomplishing this end when we are broadcasting the seed by radio, by television, by literature, by whatever method, without perhaps ever going back to see whether some of that seed has taken root and grown. Yet it would be foolhardy to cross new cultural frontiers if we do not have a definite, measurable plan for bringing new converts into churches of their own kind which on their own will reach out even further to others within that same language group. *"Closure strategy" says that it is not enough for us today to go across the world and do a good job. We must work toward finishing the task,* toward bringing all the sheaves in, toward completing the full count of the bride of Christ.

When Hudson Taylor turned his eyes to the inland areas of China, it was not because these coastal areas were fully evangelized. He saw that to complete the Great Commission, those beyond had to be reached. He had a plan and a measurable objective and set out to reach all of China. In so doing, he was following a "strategy of closure."

Fifty years later in 1910 at the World Missionary Conference in Edinburgh, Scotland, most of the known missionary societies of the world joined together in an effort to strategize the completion of the world evangelization. Essential to the basic fabric of this meeting of hearts and minds was a "strategy of closure." Only recently have plans been developed at another conference of this same sort. The World Consultation for Frontier Missions, in Edinburgh in 1980, drew together all the known mission agencies of the world, both Western and non-Western, in order to strategize between themselves how to go about reaching those 11,000 still unreached peoples of the world. This again is a "strategy of closure."

I do not believe that we can be content with "vague generalizations" when dealing with the Great Commission. *These 11,000 ethnic groups still need a viable church planted within their societies.* India alone has over 1500 such unchurched peoples. By the year 2000 we must attempt a final push across these remaining frontiers. *What will be the response of the Church to this challenge?* This, I believe, is the final condition inherent in our watchword.

This Watchword Requires a Sacrificial Commitment

In an age of specialization, when academia and the various media encourage young people to pursue profitable careers arising from their personal interests, *one wonders if this generation can ever really link up with a task as costly to self-interest as the Great Commission.* Can their priorities be shifted? Can their small ambitions be shelved in light of the mandate which confronts us? In the words of John Wesley, our watchword—"A Church for Every People by the Year 2000"—can provide the "explosive power of a new affection" which will wipe all small ambitions from their hearts.

Who will be required to make this sacrificial commitment? Is it only U.S. and European students? No, now there are resources worldwide. In conferences in Singapore, Korea, India, and other countries in the Third World, students are considering the claims of the Great Commission on their lives. The watchword today is made in the context of an international thrust.

There must also be an intergenerational thrust. Young men will see visions but old men will dream dreams! Without the resources and commitment of those who remain and fortify the base, the ability of many young people to launch into service will be hampered. The entire generation, both young and old, must take up the challenge.

Our watchword, then, like that almost a hundred years ago, must not be too weak to demand our best. It must not be so limited that it fails to work toward completing the task. And it must be wise enough to reach people within their own cultures and languages, no matter how many that may involve. "A CHURCH FOR EVERY PEOPLE BY THE YEAR 2000" requires all three of these. May we find it within ourselves, fueled by the facts and consumed by the Holy Spirit and by our love for the Lord of the harvest, to give ourselves to this great mandate.

Study Questions

1. What might you envision as major tasks to be done to fulfill the goal of "a church for every people by the year 2000"?

2. Can you think of another watchword that might capture the imagination of young people today for the Great Commission? If so, what would it be?

9
Quantifying the Global Distribution of Evangelism and Evangelization

David B. Barrett

In this article, we tackle the toughest nut of all, if we want to measure or monitor frontier mission—how to quantify all the varieties of evangelization, including the organized activity—individual or collective—that we term evangelism. What follows is an exploratory attempt to define the boundaries and to stake out the territory. We solicit the reader's assistance or feedback on this subject, especially if it is mathematical or methodological.

This essay constructs, compiles, and then interprets two new global diagrams in our 10-year ongoing series of 49 diagrams to date. The first, Global Diagram 48 deals with the quantifying of evangelization as an overall concept, under which we have identified and described 300 different dimensions and 700 different verbal facets (these are all listed in *AD 2000 Global Monitor*, No. 16, page 3).

The second, Global Diagram 49, then extends the analysis to the measurement of evangelism itself, the actual giving of opportunities to people to become Christ's disciples.

I. QUANTIFYING EVANGELIZATION

Global Diagram 48

Evangelization is contact with Christ. It is being faced with or confronted with the person and work of the Savior. It is being given an opportunity to follow Christ, to become his disciple. Ultimately, therefore, what the quantification of evangelization boils down to (at the human level) is—measuring the various modes of contact that persons or populations have had with evangelizers, that is with Christian believers and all their varieties of influences. In short, it means enumerating the duration, quality, and intensity of all conversations and awarenesses resulting from this contact with Christians, Christianity, Christ and the gospel.

David B. Barrett, his wife Pam, and their three children live in Richmond, Virginia, U.S.A. He works as a world evangelization research consultant for the Foreign Mission Board of the Southern Baptist Convention. "Quantifying the Global Distribution of Evangelism and Evangelization," *International Journal of Frontier Missions* (April 1992), pp. 71-76.

Quantifying evangelization results from monitoring the interactions of 3 quite separate and distinct categories of people or roles. First there are the activities of *Christian evangelizers* themselves, proclaiming the Good News in season and out of season. These activities can be measured as "witness-hours", or "evangelism-hours", the number of man-hours or woman-hours spent on varieties of evangelizing. (The exact definitions of all neologisms used here are given at the top of Global Diagram 48). Second, this witness results in them functioning as *Christian opportunity-givers* (a sub-role or sub-variety of evangelizers), who give to others numbers of clear, unambiguous, specific opportunities or offers or invitations to become Christ's disciples; these events or occasions can be termed "disciple-opportunities". Third, the recipients of these occasions then become *opportunity-receivers*. These are all those who willingly or unwillingly find themselves faced with these opportunities to become Christ's disciples, whether knowingly or unwittingly, as well as whether for the first time, second time, or even multiple times. Note carefully that we are not at this point measuring their *response* (which may range from hostility and rejection to acceptance, conversion, and baptism). Measuring response is a separate subject and needs its own separate quantification; we have explored this earlier in Global Diagrams 14, 19, 24, 46, et alia.

How long does it take to evangelize a person?

To understand the process and this terminology better, consider 7 cases in the New Testament where Jesus, the master Evangelizer, gives 7 individuals each one single, individual, personal "disciple-opportunity". In descending order of brevity, here they are, with the biblical reference and the amount of time that each encounter took, or takes to read: (a) Nicodemus (John 3:1-21; perhaps an hour or two); (b) Herod (Luke 23:7-12; about an hour); (c) the Samaritan Woman at the Well (John 4:7-29; probably under an hour); (d) Pontius Pilate (John 18:28-19:16; 3 brief interviews—probably half an hour or so); (e) Blind Bartimeus (Mark 10:46-52; about 20 minutes); (f) the Rich Young Ruler (Matthew 19:16-22; 40 seconds); and (g) Matthew the Tax-Gatherer (Matthew 9:9; "Follow me"—1 second). Here we see Jesus contacting and then evangelizing 7 persons in an hour or less each (under one "witness-hour"), creating and then giving them 7 disciple-opportunities, and watching as the 7 each receives his or her opportunity or offer or invitation and then reacts to it.

How much time is enough to make such a contact into an adequate "disciple-opportunity"? This list of 7 brief biblical narratives suggests 15 minutes each may often be enough, everything else being in place. Generalizing to the whole world, across 20 centuries and up to 1992, and being very conservative we could say that one whole hour is needed. During this hour, on average some 6,000 words will be spoken, and heard. To be even more on the safe side, we could elaborate on this to say that before we would consider an individual to have become "adequately" evangelized, he or she needs to have received at least one clearly-focused evangelism-hour producing one disciple-opportunity, or a variety of other more general evangelizing activities producing up to 10 disciple-opportunities or offers or invitations. Note also that although individuals can avoid contact with Christ, once confronted by Christ he evangelizes them whether they want to be evangelized or not.

Global Diagram 48. **QUANTIFYING THE ORIGIN, CREATION, AND GLOBAL DISTRIBUTION OF EVANGELIZATION: 18,700 TRILLION CHRISTIAN WITNESS-WORDS PER YEAR, RESULTING IN 505 BILLION DISCIPLE-OPPORTUNITIES OFFERED TO THE GLOBE PER YEAR.**

The table below enumerates and totals per year every form of evangelizing activity at the global level. It measures how many hours evangelizers work, and how many hours are then heard by audiences under differing media circumstances. The following definitions are used:

evangelizing activity. This refers to all activity spreading the gospel or demonstrating new life in Christ; quantified as the number of Christians involved multiplied by the number of hours each is involved or the number of evangelizing words uttered.

Hours spent by evangelizers:

presence-hours (column 3). "Presence" means a Christian's indirect witness to Christ by life-style, quality of life, relationships, prayer, ethics; quantified as *presence-hours*, the number of person-hours engaged in by all Christians in this mode.

witness-hours (column 4). "Witness" means a Christian's direct spoken testimony to the Risen Christ, naming the Name, in unstructured situations as

they occur; quantified as *witness-hours*, the number of person-hours engaged in particularly by Great Commission Christians in this mode.

evangelism-hours (column 5). "Evangelism" means a Christian's or a church's deliberate, structured, organized endeavour to present Christ and his gospel; quantified as *evangelism-hours*, the number of person-hours engaged in, particularly by professional Christians—evangelists, pastors, full-time workers, missionaries. Note that, as we are defining them, statistics of evangelism-hours are also included in witness-hours, and both form part of the presence-hours figures.

Received by audiences:

hearer-hours (column 7). This means the number of person-hours received (heard, viewed, read, perceived) by the audience being evangelized, this being enumerated as the total number of hours spent by evangelizers on evangelism (column 5) multiplied by a media factor (column 6).

witness-words (column 8). This measure gives the total number of all person-words of the 2 main evangelizing types (witness, evangelism) disseminated to and received (heard, viewed, read, perceived) by those being evangelized; enumerated as columns 7 plus 4 multiplied by our standard rate of 6,000 words spoken per hour.

evangelism-words (column 9). These are the numbers of explicitly evangelistic person-words disseminated to and received (heard, viewed, read, perceived) by those being evangelized; enumerated as evangelism-hours (column 5), multiplied by the media factor (column 6), then multiplied by our standard rate of 6,000 words spoken per hour per individual.

disciple-opportunities ("offers") (column 10). Specific opportunities (offers, invitations) given to individuals to become Christ's disciples; quantified here as conferred by at least one evangelism-hour each person (column 5 multiplied by column 6, or column 9 divided by 6,000). Also equivalent to *opportunity-receivers.*

DISTRIBUTION OF EVANGELIZATION by end of the 1980s (below):

GLOBAL EVANGELIZATION MOVEMENT

to encourage fair distribution throughout the 1990s to Worlds A and B of the current 95 offers (disciple-opportunities) per global inhabitant per year

World A

World B

World C

To World A:
0.3% of all witness-words
1.3 billion offers p.a.

To World B:
7.9% of all witness-words
40.1 billion offers p.a.

To World C:
91.8% of all witness-words
463 billion offers p.a.

KEY TO MINIDIAGRAM (left):
The segmented world is shown trichotomized into World C (all who are Christians), World B (all evangelized non-Christians), and World A (all who are unevangelized). On the left, evangelizing activity is 92% directed only at Christians in World C. The large white arrow represents the efforts of the Global Evangelization Movement to secure for World A a fair share of each year's enormous output of evangelism and witness.

KEY TO TABLE 1 (below):
Column 1. Seven types of contact or modes or varieties of offering disciple-opportunities.
Column 2. Basic statistics of showings, persons, copies, items.
Columns 3-5. Three main levels of evangelizing activity (see top). Column 3 also includes pages and broadcast hours.
Columns 3 & 4. These include presence or witness by all participants during preparation of materials, production, publicity, logistics, follow-up.

Column 6. Media factor, to be multiplied by column 5 to get column 7. For the last 8 lines, this is derived by dividing column 7 by column 5. **Column 7.** Hours as received by audiences. **Column 8.** Words of witness through the 2 main levels of evangelizing activity, including media multiplication. **Column 9.** Explicitly evangelistic words received by audiences. **Column 10.** Specific offers, invitations, opportunities made per year. (By definition, similar in size to column 7).

Table 1. EVANGELIZING HOURS SPENT EACH YEAR, HOURS RECEIVED BY HEARERS, WORDS DISSEMINATED, AND OFFERS OF DISCIPLESHIP MADE PER ANNUM.

Column groups: columns 3–5 = *HOURS SPENT EVANGELIZING p.a.*; column 7 = *RECEIVED p.a.*; columns 8–9 = *WORDS DISSEMINATED p.a.*; column 10 = *OFFERS MADE p.a.*

Column 1	2	3	4	5	6	7	8	9	10
1. HIDDEN WORDS									
Intercession (columns 4-10 not quantifiable)	—	*Presence-hours* 256 billion	—	—	—	—	—	—	—
2. VISUAL WORDS (audiovisuals)	*Showings p.a.*	*Presence-hours*	*Witness-hours*	*Evangelism-hours*	*Media*	*Hearer-hours*	*Witness-words*	*Evangelism-words*	*Disciple-opportunities*
Christians' lifestyle	1.8 billion	5.2 trillion	—	—	—	—	—	—	—
"Jesus" Film (in 200 languages)	900,000	100 million	25 million	2,250,000	50	113 million	768 billion	678 billion	113 million
Other Bible/Christian films	20 million	4 billion	900 million	60 million	50	3 billion	23.4 trillion	18.3 trillion	3 billion
Other audiovisual ministries	250 million	15 billion	5 billion	500 million	20	10 billion	90 trillion	60 trillion	10 billion
3. PERSONAL WORDS	*Persons*	*Presence-hours*	*Witness-hours*	*Evangelism-hours*	*Media*	*Hearer-hours*	*Witness-words*	*Evangelism-words*	*Disciple-opportunities*
Personal work and evangelism by:									
Christians (of all kinds)	1.8 billion	10.5 trillion	2.6 trillion	327 billion	1	327 billion	17,562 trillion	1,962 trillion	327 billion
Great Commission Christians	530 million	3.1 trillion	775 billion	96.5 billion	2	193 billion	5,808 trillion	1,158 trillion	193 billion
4. PROCLAIMED WORDS	*Professionals*	*Presence-hours*	*Witness-hours*	*Evangelism-hours*	*Media*	*Hearer-hours*	*Witness-words*	*Evangelism-words*	*Disciple-opportunities*
Full-time workers	4,200,000	24.5 billion	6.1 billion	766 million	10	7.7 billion	82.8 trillion	46.2 trillion	7.7 billion
Foreign missionaries	285,000	1.7 billion	416 million	52 million	100	5.2 billion	33.7 trillion	31.2 trillion	5.2 billion
Evangelists	700,000	4.2 billion	1.0 billion	126 million	200	25.6 billion	160 trillion	154 trillion	25.6 billion
5. WRITTEN WORDS (Scriptures)	*Copies p.a.*	*Pages p.a.*	*Witness-hours*	*Evangelism-hours*	*Media*	*Hearer-hours*	*Witness-words*	*Evangelism-words*	*Disciple-opportunities*
Bibles (1300 pages)	51.4 million	66.8 billion	10 million	5 million	10	50.0 billion	300 trillion	300 trillion	50.0 billion
New Testaments (300 p)	76.9 million	23.1 billion	5 million	2.3 billion	5	11.5 billion	69 trillion	69 trillion	11.5 billion
Portions (gospels) (25 p)	120 million	3.0 billion	600 million	300 million	2	3.6 billion	3.6 billion	3.6 billion	600 million
Selections (4 p)	1.1 billion	4.4 billion	300 million	146 million	1	146 million	876 billion	876 billion	146 million
6. PRINTED WORDS (literature)	*Pieces p.a.*	*Pages p.a.*	*Witness-hours*	*Evangelism-hours*	*Media*	*Hearer-hours*	*Witness-words*	*Evangelism-words*	*Disciple-opportunities*
Christian books (100 p)	3.0 billion	300 billion	25 million	20 billion	1	20 billion	120 trillion	120 trillion	20 billion
Christian periodicals (30 p)	1.0 billion	30 billion	3 billion	2 billion	5	10 billion	60 trillion	60 trillion	10 billion
Tracts (3 p)	4.0 billion	12 billion	500 million	400 million	1	400 million	2.4 trillion	2.4 trillion	400 million
7. ELECTRONIC WORDS (broadcasting)	*Items*	*Hours a day*	*Witness-hours*	*Evangelism-hours*	*Media*	*Hearer-hours*	*Witness-words*	*Evangelism-words*	*Disciple-opportunities*
Christian radio programs	1,000	10,000	5 million	365,000	50,000	18.2 billion	109 trillion	109 trillion	18.2 billion
Christian TV programs	400	4,000	2 million	146,000	100,000	14.6 billion	88 trillion	88 trillion	14.6 billion
Christian-owned computers	119 million	250 million	3 million	100,000	10	1.0 billion	6 trillion	6 trillion	1.0 billion
TOTAL HOURS, WORDS, AND OFFERS		*Presence-hours*	*Witness-hours*	*Evangelism-hours*	*Media*	*Hearer-hours*	*Witness-words*	*Evangelism-words*	*Disciple-opportunities*
7 varieties of evangelizing words:									
Hidden words		256 billion							
Visual words		5.2 trillion	5.9 billion	562 million	23	13.1 billion	114.1 trillion	79 trillion	13.1 billion
Personal words		10.5 trillion	2.6 trillion	327 billion	1	327 billion	17,562 trillion	1,962 trillion	327.0 billion
Proclaimed words		24.5 billion	6.1 billion	766 million	50	38.5 billion	276 trillion	231 trillion	38.5 billion
Written words		30 billion	15.9 billion	7.7 billion	8	62.2 billion	374 trillion	374 trillion	62.2 billion
Printed words		60 billion	28.5 billion	22.4 billion	1.3	30.4 billion	182 trillion	182 trillion	30.4 billion
Electronic words		20 billion	10 billion	611,000	55,300	33.8 billion	203 trillion	203 trillion	33.8 billion
Grand totals per year		**10.5 trillion**	**2.6 trillion**	**327 billion**	**1.5**	**505.0 billion**	**18,711 trillion**	**3,031 trillion**	**505.0 billion**
Grand totals per year per global inhabitant		1,980	491	62	1.5	95	3,530,400	571,890	95

Source: World Evangelization Database

AD 2000 Global Monitor, January 1992, No. 15, revised 3/92.

Seven varieties of offering disciple-opportunities

In the Palestinian ministry of Jesus, we note 5 main modes or types of contact through words producing disciple- opportunities. These can be catalogued as follows: (1) *hidden words* (his private hopes and prayers): his intercessory words and plans to extend the Good News to those around him; (2) *visual words* (what people saw of his person, his life, his lifestyle, his deeds, his actions): everything implied in the Incarnation of the Word of God; (3) *personal words* (personal evangelism): face-to-face meetings with an individual, with conversation, the spoken word, shared words, dialogue, challenge; (4) *proclaimed words* (public proclamation): Jesus' face-to-face preaching and teaching of the proclaimed word to groups, crowds, even multitudes; and (5) *written words*: use of the written Word of God, in this case Jesus' use of scrolls of the Old Testament (later to become hand-copied scriptures). Two millennia later, disciples of Jesus can add 2 additional modes: (6) *printed words*: print media, apologetics, and other literature, tracts, magazines, books; and (7) *electronic words*: electronic media, broadcasting, radio/TV, also via cassettes, CD-ROM, and computers. We will shortly quantify these 7 modes of evangelization. But first we will discuss how to enumerate hours spent on evangelizing in general.

Three levels of evangelizing activity (Table 1, columns 3-5)

Let us now sharpen enumeration by defining exactly all the terms involved. In Jesus' ministry, he evangelized at 3 levels: (A) by his presence (who he was and what he did each day), (B) by his witness—mainly unstructured situations as occasion arose (such as that before Pilate), and (C) by his evangelism—structured preaching, pro-clamation, and teaching (such as the Sermon on the Mount, or his parables). In the same way, we can recognize that these 3 synonyms of the term "evangelization" represent for us as disciples 3 different levels of evangelizing activity: our Christian *presence*, our *witness*, and our *evangelism*. These 3 will then enable us to measure by means of hours and words. The best way to understand all these neologisms is to keep them constantly before us as a series of defini-tions, as is done at the top of Global Diagram 48.

Quantifying hours spent by evangelizers (columns 3-5)

With these definitions, we can now enumerate the situation of a people, an ethnic group, a language community, a city, a country, or any other population. We therefore ask: How many hours or minutes of evangelizing contact with Christianity, Christ, and the gospel has this population had? And, how many such hours does this population have each day, and how many per capita per year? To understand our method and our results, study Table 1 as you read on below.

Let's assume the average Christian's conscious day is 16 hours (during the day's other 8 hours we're all asleep). That's 5,840 waking hours a year (p.a., per annum). In these, the normal Christian is expected to live as a disciple of Jesus, in 3 modes: to be firstly, (1) a Christian *presence*, incarnating his Lord and Master, actively in contact with people (we call the time he spends "presence-hours" to represent the widest form of witnessing and evangelizing); secondly as a Great Commission Christian to be (2) a *martys* (a witness to Jesus and his Resurrection, spending active "witness-hours"); and thirdly to be (3) an *evangelizer* or an evangelist, actively spreading the Good News and passing on the gospel of Christ ("evangelism-hours"). Note that, as we are defining them, evangelism-hours are also included in witness- hours (evangelism being a specific form of witness), and both form part of the presence-hours category.

Let's assume next that the average Christian's actively witnessing day (witness by life and by word) is 4 hours in contact with other people, and his actively evangelistic day is 30 minutes. The 5,840 waking presence-hours thus include 1,460 active witness-hours a year, and both include 182 evangelism- hours a year.

Now let's quantify this for the entire Christian world. There are 1.8 billion Christians across the globe. Together they spend 10.5 trillion presence-hours a year (see Table 1, column 3, row 3 under "Christians", also the bottom 2 rows). Dividing by the total world population of 5.3 billion, this becomes 1,980 Christian presence-hours ex-pended per inhabitant of the globe per year (5.4 presence-hours a day). Dividing instead by the world's 3.5 billion non-Christians, this is 3,000 presence-hours per non-Christian per year. Dividing instead by the 1,254 million unevangelized, this is 8,380 presence-hours per World A inhabitant per year. This should be enough to ensure evangelizing the world! Like the global supply of food and water, it's entirely adequate—*if it's properly shared and distributed.*

Let's sharpen our definitions by talking next about our globe's 530 million active, committed, Great Commission Christians. They put in 775 billion Great Commission "witness- hours" a year (see Table 1, column 4) which is 146 per global inhabitant a year (0.4 hours a day), or 221 Great Commission witness-hours per non- Christian per year. Specifically on evangelism, these Great Commission Christians each do 182 evangelism- hours a year which totals to 96.5 billion evangelism-hours a year (column 5). This can also be stated as 18.2 evangelism-hours per global inhabitant a year.

An even sharper approach ensues when we consider full-time Christian workers, who number 4.2 million today (see Table 1, row 4). As full-time evangelizers they put in 766 million evangelism-hours a year. This is 8.7 evangelism-minutes per global in-habitant a year.

Finally, let's consider the world's 285,000 foreign missionaries. They put in 1.7 billion presence-hours per year which is 0.48 presence-hours per non-Christian per year. Further, they also engage in 416 million witness-hours per year which is 0.12 witness- hours per non-Christian per year (7.1 minutes of contact each year, 1.2 seconds every day, or 8.3 seconds a week). Lastly, they do 52 million active evangelism-hours per year.

To see what this means for a country, consider the world's most-evangelized country, the United States of America with its 170 million church members. These produce 993 billion presence- hours p.a., which is 3,970 hours per USA inhabitant p.a. This includes 1,200 Great Commission witness-hours per USA inhabitant p.a. And the USA also produces the remarkable number of 124 evangelism-hours per capita each year (7 times the global average). This means that the average USA Christian continues year after year to be saturated with 124 additional disciple-opportunities which (because he is already a disciple) he does not need. It's exactly analogous to wasted food.

Global Diagram 49. **THE PROBLEM OF UNEQUAL DISTRIBUTION: THE CASE FOR INITIATING A PROPERLY BALANCED SHARING OF THE CHURCH'S EVANGELISM (EVANGELISTIC OFFERS) ACROSS THE GLOBE, TOTALING 1,383 MILLION DISCIPLE-OPPORTUNITIES EVERY DAY.**

This diagram continues the analysis in Global Diagram 48, which quantified the differing ministries and modes of the churches' evangelization. Here we zero in on that diagram's final column quantifying the churches' *evangelism* as "disciple-opportunities" (evangelistic offers). Table 1 below then expands that column into 10 new ones, columns 4-13, showing how these are distributed among Worlds A, B, and C.

The grand total of all such offers made by the churches every day is startlingly high: 1,383 million directly-evangelistic offers, opportunities, or invitations per day.

Several other surprising findings may be observed in the analysis below by the 3 worlds (columns 5 to 13). Comparisons can be made horizontally along a particular row, or vertically down a column.

The main problem at present can be seen to be the grossly unequal distribution of offers. World C gets 91.8% of all the churches' evangelism, while

World A gets only 0.3%. Obviously this latter figure is woefully inadequate. But what would a "fair share" look like? Here is a short miniglossary of the central terms on this subject.

adequacy. This term refers to the evangelistic situation among a population which has received enough preaching and evangelizing to give its peoples sufficient chance to become disciples if they so wish.

balance. A missionary situation in which adequate evangelistic attention is paid not only to Worlds B and C but also to World A. Or, the situation when all the globe's non-Christians are receiving numerically the same fair share of the daily offers generated.

disciple-opportunities. These are specific opportunities, offers, or invitations given to individuals to become Christ's disciples. (For further details, see *AD 2000 Global Monitor*, No. 15, pages 2-3).

fair share. This refers to a situation in which no one population or individual continues to receive multiple disciple-opportunities while other populations or individual in World A has received at least one such opportunity or a first chance. Numerically, a "fair share" would be 23% of the global total, that is, 318 million offers a day for World A's populations (which number 1.2 billion). This is 91 times larger than the present grossly unfair "share".

offers. Evangelistic offers; synonymous with disciple-opportunities.

proper balance. The situation of a mission agency which has adjusted its resources so that non-Christians and all the unevangelized get equal opportunities to learn about and follow Christ as disciples.

DISTRIBUTION OF DAILY OFFERS in the early 1990s (below):

To persons in World A: 3.5 million offers p.d.

To persons in World B: 110 million offers p.d.

To persons in World C: 1,268 million offers p.d.

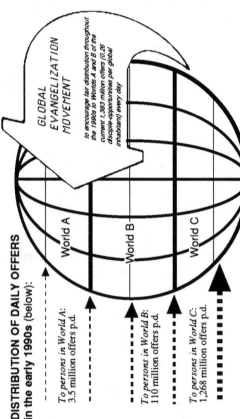

GLOBAL EVANGELIZATION MOVEMENT

to encourage fair distribution throughout the 1990s to Worlds A and B of the current 1,383 million offers (0.26 disciple-opportunities per global inhabitant) every day

World A

World B

World C

KEY TO MINIDIAGRAM (left):
The segmented world is shown trichotomized into World C (all who are Christians), World B (all evangelized non-Christians), and World A (all who are unevangelized). On the left, daily offers (evangelizing activities) are 92% directed only at Christians in World C. The large white arrow represents the efforts of the Global Evangelization Movement to secure for World A a fair share of each day's enormous output of specific opportunities, offers, and invitations to become Christ's disciples.

KEY TO TABLE 1 (below): *Column 1*. Seven types of contact, modes, or varieties of offering disciple-opportunities, subdivided into 20 kinds of ministries. Note that the statistical row "Great Commission Christians" is included in the row above it and so is ignored in all vertical totaling; the same with 3 other rows. *Column 2*. Basic statistics of persons, copies, items. *Columns 3*. Specific offers, invitations, opportunities made each day (per day, per diem, p.d.). *Column 4*. Column 3 as % of global total of 1,383 million. *Columns 5-7* describe World A; *8-10* World B; and *11-13* World C. *Columns 5,8,11*. Column 3 divided among Worlds A, B, C. *Columns 6,9,12*. Preceding column as % of column 3, adding up horizontally to 100%. *Columns 7,10,13*. Offers as % of each world's total (at bottom of column 5, 8, or 11), adding up vertically to 100%.

Table 1. **DISCIPLE-OPPORTUNITIES OFFERED DAILY TO PERSONS IN 3 WORLDS BY MEANS OF 20 MINISTRIES. (Note: "p.d."=per diem, per day, daily)**

	Column 1	2	3	4	5	6	7	8	9	10	11	12	13
			DISCIPLE-OPPORTUNITIES (OFFERS) MADE DAILY TO THE GLOBE AND ITS 3 CONSTITUENT WORLDS										
			Whole globe	%	World A	%	%	World B	%	%	World C	%	%
1.	**HIDDEN WORDS**												
	Intercession (not quantifiable)												
2.	**VISUAL WORDS** (audiovisuals)	*Showings p.d.*											
	Christians' lifestyle	1.8 billion											
	"Jesus" Film (in 200 languages)	2,460	310,000	0.0	3,100	1.0	0.1	24,800	8.0	0.0	282,100	91.0	0.0
	Other Bible/Christian films	54,800	8.2 million	0.6	8,200	0.1	0.2	164,000	2.0	0.1	8 million	97.9	0.6
	Other audiovisual ministries	684,930	27.4 million	2.0	27,400	0.1	0.8	520,600	1.9	0.5	26.9 million	98.0	2.1
3.	**PERSONAL WORDS**	*Persons*											
	Personal evangelism by:	1,800 million	895 million	64.7	26,000	0.0	0.7	45 million	5.0	40.9	850 million	95.0	67.0
	Christians (of all kinds)	530 million	529 million	38.2	20,000	0.0	0.6	37 million	7.0	33.7	492 million	93.0	38.8
	Great Commission Christians												
4.	**PROCLAIMED WORDS**	*Professionals*											
	Full-time workers	4.2 million	21 million	1.5	147,000	0.7	4.2	1 million	4.8	0.9	20 million	94.5	1.6
	Foreign missionaries	285,000	14 million	1.0	168,000	1.2	4.8	1.2 million	8.5	1.1	12.6 million	90.3	1.0
	Evangelists	700,000	70 million	5.1	1.4 million	2.0	40.0	6.3 million	9.0	5.7	62.3 million	89.0	4.9
5.	**WRITTEN WORDS** (Scriptures)	*Copies p.d.*											
	Bibles	140,800	137 million	9.9	959,000	0.7	27.4	41 million	30.0	37.3	95 million	69.3	7.5
	New Testaments	210,700	31 million	2.2	310,000	1.0	8.9	11.5 million	37.0	10.5	19.2 million	62.0	1.5
	Portions (gospels)	328,800	1.6 million	0.1	24,000	1.5	0.7	640,000	40.0	0.6	936,000	58.5	0.1
	Selections	3 million	400,000	0.0	6,400	1.6	0.2	140,000	35.0	0.1	253,600	63.4	0.0
6.	**PRINTED WORDS** (literature)	*Pieces p.d.*											
	Christian books	8.2 million	55 million	4.0	110,000	0.2	3.1	550,000	1.0	0.5	54.3 million	98.8	4.3
	Christian periodicals	2.7 million	27 million	2.0	270,000	1.0	7.7	1.8 million	6.7	1.6	24.9 million	92.3	2.0
	Tracts	10.9 million	1.1 million	0.1	3,300	0.3	0.1	49,500	4.5	0.0	1 million	95.2	0.1
7.	**ELECTRONIC WORDS** (broadcasting)	*Items*											
	Christian radio programs	1,000	50 million	3.6	5,000	0.01	0.1	45,000	0.09	0.0	50 million	99.9	3.9
	Christian TV programs	400	40 million	2.9	0	0.0	0.0	40,000	0.1	0.0	40 million	99.9	3.2
	Christian-owned computers	119 million	2.7 million	0.2	0	0.0	0.0	27,000	1.0	0.0	2.7 million	99.0	0.2
	TOTALS OF ALL KINDS OF OFFERS												
	7 varieties of offering disciple-opportunities:												
	Hidden words		35.9 million	2.6	38,700	0.1	1.1	709,400	2.0	0.6	35.2 million	98.0	2.8
	Visual words		895 million	64.7	26,000	0.0	0.7	44.8 million	5.0	40.9	850 million	95.0	67.0
	Personal words		105 million	7.6	1.7 million	1.8	48.6	8.5 million	8.1	7.7	95 million	90.3	7.5
	Proclaimed words		170 million	12.3	1.3 million	0.8	37.1	53.4 million	31.4	48.6	115 million	67.9	9.1
	Written words		83 million	6.0	383,300	0.5	11.0	2.4 million	2.9	2.2	80 million	96.6	6.3
	Printed words		92.7 million	6.7	5,000	0.0	0.1	112,000	0.1	0.1	92.6 million	99.9	7.3
	Electronic words												
	Grand totals per day		**1,363 million**	**100.0**	**3.5 million**	**0.3**	**100.0**	**109.9 million**	**7.9**	**100.0**	**1,269 million**	**91.8**	**100.0**
	Grand totals per day per global inhabitant		0.26		0.00			0.02			0.24		

Source: World Evangelization Database

AD 2000 Global Monitor, March 1992, No. 17, revised.

Quantifying hours received by those being evangelized (column 7)

Now comes a staggering increase in order of magnitude. We can illustrate it from the Argentina Crusade of November 13-17, 1991. For it, evangelist Billy Graham preached the gospel for some 10 hours—that is, he expended 10 of our "evangelism-hours". But for 5 nights his words were received by a radio/TV audience of 70 million each night throughout Latin America. So his 10 evangelism-hours instantly became 700 million "hearer-hours". Admittedly, this is an unusually massive case. In Table 1, column 6 gives the much lower average media factor we use to compute column 7 for all such evangelism in general (= column 5 x column 6).

Quantifying words disseminated (columns 8-9)

Words mean power and action. The city of Washington D.C. is known to produce every day 100 billion official words—spoken, written, telegraphed, faxed, broadcast, or published. That's 36 trillion words p.a. In the same way we can assess the huge effect of evangelization by measuring its output of words.

We return therefore to enumerating words, as a refinement of hours. This results in a somewhat different way of quantifying the amount of evangelization by counting the number of "witness-words" (our blanket term for all person-words spoken by Christian disciples in both witness and evangelism) and "evangelism-words". These are words heard or received by the target individual or population and which then proceed to evangelize them. The totals depend particularly on the different communication modes em-ployed. Table 1 in Global Diagram 48 lists the 7 varieties of words (modes of contact) and the 3 levels of evangelizing activity, and then tabulates the number of copies of the various media, number of standardized pages or broadcasts or showings involved, number of words involved, and the equivalent number of "hearer-hours" through which these words reach their targets.

Quantifying offers made (column 10)

The final column of Table 1 refers to the related number of disciple-opportunities. This gives the number of persons who have had an offer of discipleship made to them. It is derived by dividing column 9 by the average number of words required for a disciple-opportunity, earlier defined as 6,000. (By definition, the numbers are similar in size to those in column 7). A brief illustration is: evangelist Billy Graham preaches for only 10 hours (10 "evangelism-hours"), but the 70 million who hear him actually get 4.2 trillion evangelism-words. Altogether these offer the audiences some 700 million disciple-opportunities.

"e" as a measure of extent of opportunity

The extent to which a people or population has received adequate disciple-opportunities can be easily enumerated as e=total all disciple- opportunities received per capita, per year. Allowance has to be made, of course, for uneven distribution and the probability that many persons in the population will have had not one but multiple opportunities. But it's a beginning in precise enumerating and accounting. This e, it should be noted, is a similar variable to our 27-year-old scale of demographic evangelization, E%, in which E=the number of individuals in the population who have each received at least one disciple-opportunity and so have become adequately evangelized and are now aware of Christianity, Christ, and the gospel (expressed as a percentage of the population).

Summary: "human rights" must include the gospel

This diagram and its table allow us to make some general observations.

As Christians we affirm the whole range of the human rights of every individual, every people, and every population on Earth. In a plentiful world, everyone has the right to a fair share of food, water, shelter, clothing, energy, electricity, health, literacy, literature, education, money, and also to their spiritual counterparts—salvation in Christ, the Good News, the gospel, scriptures, missions, literature, broadcasts, churches, evangelism, witness, witness-hours, witness-words, evangelism-hours, evangelism-words, disciple-opportunities. Everyone has the fundamental, inalienable, basic right to at least one chance to become a disciple—an absolute minimum of one definitive evangelism-hour and one disciple-opportunity, perhaps 10 times that number as an immediate practical target toward the eventual goal of a fair share, and then an ongoing right to the average global individual share of 62 evangelism-hours and 95 disciple- opportunities a year per capita.

The basic problem is the same as with world hunger and starvation—the supply is vastly more than adequate but distribution is criminally inadequate. Current distribution of the benefits of Christianity, Christ, and the gospel is uneven, unfair, unplanned, chaotic, counterproductive. Over a billion Christians in World C get everything Christianity has to offer and 95% of all its tangible benefits; over a billion non-Christians in World A get nothing. Yet we as missionary-minded Christians continue to direct 92% of all our evangelizing activity at other Christians. Who will fight to change this?

II. QUANTIFYING EVANGELISM

Global Diagram 49

The first part of this article has developed the quantification of evangelization, defining the term as consisting of *presence, witness,* and *evangelism.* Now in this second part we will zero in for a closer look at the third component, evangelism. By expanding the last column in Global Diagram 48 we are able to produce the detailed analysis by Worlds A, B, and C that is presented here in Global Diagram 49.

With this second diagram opposite, our series of 49 global diagrams arrives at the heart of the problem confronting world evangelization today—unequal distribution. In a nutshell, this problem has two aspects, the first satisfactory, the second unsatisfactory. These are: (1) The church worldwide is evangelizing—spreading the Good News of Jesus Christ—far and wide, creating every day the startlingly high total of over one billion offers or opportunities for others to become Christ's disciples. But, (2) 99.7% of all of this evangelistic effort is directed only at people who have already been evangelized earlier, including

91.8% at people who are Christians and so already are disciples.

The second diagram shows the distribution of all this effort among the 3 worlds of our mission trichotomy, Worlds A, B, and C. Table 1 shows the relevant figures, all given per day (per diem, p.d.). Some figures are surprisingly high. This analysis into 3 worlds (columns 5-13) reveals the following trends.

World A: local evangelists predominate

Far and away the largest percentage of daily offers in the unevangelized world is contributed by local evangelists (such as Palestinian free-lance evangelists across the Arabian peninsula). Such evangelists are responsible for some 40% of all 3.5 million disciple-opportunities each day in World A (see columns 5 and 7). Second in size comes circulation of complete Bibles. These give World A dwellers opportunities at the rate of nearly one million a day (column 5). This is much more effective than circulation there of scripture selections, portions, or even of New Testaments; it is also far more effective than any other forms of literature.

World B: scripture circulation works best

Column 10 shows that scripture circulation again is the largest single evangelistic mode in evangelizing World B peoples (48%). Personal evangelism by Christians themselves has become almost as significant (41%). Local evangelists are still very important but have fallen to under 6%.

World C: personal evangelism tops the list

Column 13 shows that in the Christian world by far the largest generator of offers comes through personal evangelism (67%). By contrast, professional circulation of complete Bibles has dropped in effectiveness to only 7%. So once again we see that the key to winning the world for Christ lies not with full-time professional workers but with ordinary lay disciples. Proper training and equipping of the laity for this task are therefore paramount.

How should one assess these findings? Let's return to our earlier illustration. There is a close parallel with the problem of world hunger today. Enough food is produced every day to feed the whole world. Yet 1.8 billion persons across the globe are undernourished, 950 million go hungry every night, and 400 million live on the verge of starvation. Agencies distributing food cannot supply every need but must reach a balance involving need, priorities, adequate supply, equal opportunity, fair shares. And the already well-fed should not be allowed to divert such supplies to their own use.

Likewise, our diagram (in Table 1's final 2 lines) shows that the average Christian in World C receives every day 360 times more invitations than an unevangelized non-Christian in World A. This is clearly an unbalanced situation. Proper balance must mean that at least as much attention is given to the individual in World A as in Worlds B or C.

What is a "fair share" for the inhabitants of World A? Numerically, it should be over one fifth of the global whole, since the 1.2 billion unevangelized amount today to some 22% of the globe. This would be some 304 million offers a day given to World A—87 times as large as its present share—resulting on average in one offer being made every 4 days for every individual in World A.

But it is not only a question of fair shares or equal distribution of evangelism across the globe. There is the question of why most persons in World C should be getting primary evangelism at all. To serve 3 parallel but different types of analysis, our definition of World C takes 3 alternate forms: (1) all persons or *individuals* who individually are Christian disciples; or (2) all ethnolinguistic *peoples* whose populations are each over 60% Christians and 95% evangelized; or (3) all *countries* over 60% Christians and 95% evangelized. Whichever of the 3 definitions we find most helpful in understanding, it is obvious that persons in World C both are heavily evangelized already and also are mostly Christian disciples already. Why therefore are they still being continuously deluged with 1,269 million opportunities/invitations/offers to be-come disciples every day?

A personal illustration may help. Every week I find myself, as an ordinary Christian disciple, sitting in services or meetings large or small (or listening on radio or television) in which for an hour or so I hear a preacher explaining the gospel and inviting his audience to accept Jesus Christ as Lord. If his audience is 100 persons, then, in our terminology, he has produced one evangelism-hour and 100 disciple-opportunities. But I am a disciple already; I belong to World C. I do not need such additional offers (I need to be told how to be a better disciple, but that's not the issue here). This overlap in resources may be trivial in my case, but it assumes enormous importance when it escalates to its present level of one billion such redundant "wasted" offers every day, as it has done and as it continues to do.

Any serious solution to this problem will depend on deliberate attempts by agencies to increase the abysmally small figures in column 6, the percentage of each variety of evangelism which actually gets to World A. In particular, agencies could be challenged to zero in each on one specific low percentage in that column and could determine to double it, treble it, or even quadruple it within the next 12 months.

There are 18 such percentages in that column in the diagram. So it only needs 18 mission agencies to take action, and then this entire situation—stagnant over the last 100 years—could at last begin to be transformed.

10

The Spontaneous Multiplication of Churches

George Patterson

Our Lord Jesus Christ commands us to look on the fields that are ready for harvest (John 4:35). So—let's do it. How many men and women and children, persons with feelings like ours, still know nothing of Jesus' sacrificial death and life-giving resurrection? At least 2.2 billion persons! To shake their hands, at a rate of 60 a minute or 3,600 an hour, for 8 hours each day of the week, would take over 200 years! How painful to see so many unaware of God's pardon!

Our Lord sends us to disciple every "nation" (people group) by training them to obey all His commands—which include, of course, discipling *others* (Matt. 28:18-20). This means that we disciple a "nation" only when it is permeated by obedient disciples who also disciple other unevangelized peoples. So we don't simply go and start a church among a people. We, or those we send, must start the kind of church that grows and reproduces spontaneously as churches will, in daughter churches, granddaughter churches, great-granddaughter churches and so on. *Spontaneous* reproduction of churches means the Holy Spirit moves a church (yours?) to reproduce daughter churches on its own, without outsiders pushing it (Acts 13:1-3).

I began training pastors in Honduras in a traditional theological institution and had the traditional problems for the traditional reasons. I assumed the bright young men I trained were dedicated because they came to our resident Bible school. Our plan was for them to return to their home towns as pastors. But the graduates found the gold lettering on their diplomas did not go well with the white-washed adobe walls back home. It enabled them, however, to earn more in the office of the Dole Banana Co.

My raspy supervisor had the gall to blame us teachers; he told us, "Close the school; start discipling the people."

"No," I argued, "they're too hard."

In 1965 George Patterson began working in northern Honduras with the Conservative Baptist Home Mission Society. He adapted theological education-by-extension to "obedience oriented discipling." He trained Honduran pastoral students on the job as they raised up and pastored over 100 churches. Patterson continues to work with the CBHMS and now trains missionaries for church reproduction. He also directs a ministry called Cultural Adaptation Training (CAT).

"Excuses! They're poor, semi-literate, subsistence farmers but you teach as though they were educated, middle class Americans."

I wrote my missionary buddies from language school, now spread all over Latin America, fishing for sympathy. They had the same problem!

"I'm a teacher without a classroom!" I complained.

"So," my supervisor rasped, "teach by extension."

"What's that?"

He handed me a smelly old saddle, explaining, "You're promoted. This is the Chair of Evangelism and Church Planting in your new extension Bible institute."

After a few weeks of blisters on my south side I learned to communicate with the mission mule and announced, "Hey, I can do this TEE stuff. It's great."

My supervisor warned me, "Then your students had better raise up and pastor their own churches or we'll close down this Theological Education by Extension, too."

I took the pastoral studies to family men (Biblical "elder" types) in the poverty-ridden villages, mountains and cities. Unlike their single young sons, they had crops, jobs or family responsibilities that kept them from going off to our resident Bible school. They also lacked the education to absorb its intensive teaching. But these older men, with roots in their villages and barrios, could begin pastoring with the respect of their people easier than the single young men could. By God's mercy I slowly learned to evangelize and disciple these *elders* in a way that enabled them to raise up and pastor their small village churches. As will be the case in many of today's remaining unreached fields, we began to see growth not through any one church growing big or fast, but through the slow, steady reproduction of many small churches.

I could have avoided years of sour stomach groping for principles of church reproduction had I looked first in the operator's manual. New Testament discipling principles, conscientiously applied, are enabling churches to reproduce in Honduras and many other fields. We must distinguish between these general *principles* and culture-specific *applications*. Some of the methods cited below, for example, will not fit in your golf bag if you work in Tokyo. But the Biblical principles themselves, if applied with culturally relevant methods, should enable churches to reproduce wherever there is plenty of "good soil." Theologically speaking, good soil for the gospel seed to take root in and multiply is *bad people*, and lots of them (Rom. 5:20-21; Matt. 13:18:23; Eph. 2:1-10). Field testing of programs based on these principles give consistently good results in Latin America and Asia, including hostile fields where evangelism is illegal.

The simplicity of the principles disappoints some educators. They expect something more sophisticated, at least new or expensive. Missionary or not, one can multiply disciples doing these four simple things:

1. *KNOW AND LOVE THE PEOPLE YOU DISCIPLE* (just as Jesus emptied Himself of His heavenly glory and power to become a man, take on Jewish culture and draw near to the publicans and sinners.

2. *MOBILIZE YOUR DISCIPLES TO EDIFY IMMEDIATELY THOSE THEY ARE DISCIPLING* (Don't not just educate for some vague future).

3. TEACH AND PRACTICE OBEDIENCE TO JESUS' BASIC COMMANDS, IN LOVE, BEFORE AND ABOVE ALL ELSE.

4. ORGANIZE YOUR CHURCH OR PROGRAM BY BUILDING LOVING, EDIFYING ACCOUNTABILITY RELATIONSHIPS BETWEEN DISCIPLES AND CHURCHES.

If you are already doing these basics effectively, you may now take a nap. Otherwise, read prayerfully the explanations below and record the details you plan to make a part of your ministry:

1.   KNOW AND LOVE THE PEOPLE YOU DISCIPLE

We must know and love a people before we can disciple them. When Jesus told His disciples to "Look at the fields" they were finding it hard to love the Samaritans around them; they could not see them receiving God's grace.

Limit Your Area of Responsibility to One People or Community.

We must focus on one people group, the one God has given us. Paul knew his area of responsibility before God (II Cor. 10:12-16; Acts 16:6-10; Gal. 2:8). He knew what kind of churches to plant and where. For a *movement of church reproduction* a church planting team needs a clear focus from God. My area was "the Spanish speaking people of the Aguan Valley and surrounding mountains." It helps to be exact.

At home or abroad every discipler needs to ask: "For whom am I responsible?" If a missionary fails to do this the geographic and ethnic limits of his ministry remain blurred. He will jump from opportunity to opportunity. I asked one of these wandering gold prospectors in Central America what his area of responsibility was. "Oh," he said, "I am winning the country for Christ." He goes from city to city preaching in prisons and army camps; he bombs villages with tracts from his Cessna. It's fun and folks back home eagerly finance it. But he will never plant a reproductive church until he learns to hold the people of a community in his heart.

Choosing your people in a new field needs study and prayer. Confer with other missionaries, nationals and God Himself for guidance. I found a map of my area made by Texaco (I don't know why; the average town only had two cars, one of which ran). But it showed where the villages were and kept me from getting lost so often. So, find the population centers, where you can buy safe milk, where others are not discipling and—even before the milk—where folks want to know God and enjoy Him forever.

Knowing a people means more than finding how many tons of figs they exported last year, that the average adult male has 7.4 children or that their legislature has two chambers. It means touching the heart of individuals. Laughing with those who laugh. Weeping with those who weep. Playing marbles with 2-year old Chimbo and checkers with his grandpa (or whatever they play in the town square). It may help if you let him beat you. This applies to arguing religion, too. It's dangerous always to be "right" when you're the new kid on the block. Learn to appreciate the people and their ways, even the toothless old men. Listen and learn until you have discovered those things in their folk religion or culture that help communicate the gospel.

Once you know your area and people, discern which segment among them is most receptive to you and to Jesus Christ. To penetrate restricted, resistant fields, aim *first* at the working class or an oppressed minority. This contradicts some popular church growth theories. We are not dealing with second generation growth in Pasadena, California, however, but the *initial beachhead* where people get a curved blade in their ribs for witnessing. Jesus did not begin His public ministry among the influential middle class and natural leaders in the political nerve centers of Rome or Jerusalem, but with the working class upriver in Galilee where they spoke Hebrew with a backwoods accent—otherwise He would have been crucified prematurely.

Let the Church Be of the People.

Like most inexperienced church planters I started "preaching points" at first, instead of genuine New Testament churches. Someone went every week to a community where a group gathered to hear their pulpit oratory and sing (well, at least to sing). Converts were not baptized. Local leaders were not trained. The Lord's Supper was neglected. No one knew for sure who were Christians. Obedient, sacrificial discipling gave way to entertaining (a tradition brought by American missionaries). Preaching points develop a personality of their own; they stubbornly refuse to evolve into obedient, giving, reproductive churches. They become sponges soaking up the time and efforts of outside workers and producing nothing—except where God's sheer mercy overrides our routine.

Find what a church's people can do and plan that, before planning its structure, forms and organization. I hope it takes you less time than it took me, to learn that formal pulpit preaching is ineffective (often illegal) in many of today's remaining unreached fields. You can preach the Word with power in many other ways, if you know your people. We used dramatic Bible reading, songs with music and lyrics composed by nationals, poems, symbols and story telling. They sang with more enthusiasm when they composed songs in the local style. Bach would have croaked (so would the average director of contemporary church music). But the music was *theirs*. I'd spend days preparing an evangelistic sermon for our first trip to a distant village. They'd listen politely. Then I learned to let them dramatize Bible stories in their own way (one rehearsal fifteen minutes beforehand). They let local non-Christians play the fatted calf and other minor roles in the Prodigal son and the whole community complained for weeks. Not about the terrible acting but about the jerk who was too greedy to wait for his old man to die, to get his hands on his inheritance! Which all lead to more conversions than a year of my sermons.

Let the new church's self-identity be evident. Know exactly what you are aiming at within the community: a well defined body of obedient disciples of Jesus Christ. Once I made the mistake of allowing more outside helpers to be present than members of the community during the first baptism and celebration of the Lord's Supper.The church died at birth. There must be a majority from the community itself, especially at the first Baptism or worship meetings, or the church is not born as a distinct entity within the community. Our converts felt that they had simply been added to some organization of the outsiders. I robbed them of the thrill of looking at each other and saying, "*We* are now the church here!" They must see the new church being born as a part of their community.

List What You Will Do to Reproduce Disciples among a People.

What you do first often determines the direction of your work, for good or bad, for years to come. Will it lead to reproductive churches? The right steps will vary for each field but will always include teaching the converts first to obey Jesus' basic commands (Matt. 28:18-20). Take the shortest route possible to start a real church: a group of believers in Christ dedicated to obey His commands. In a pioneer field let it start small, perhaps with only three or four members. It will grow if you disciple the people as Jesus said.

The first question you ask about an unreached people group is, "*Who* can best reach them?" The answer is often, "Church planters from a people that is culturally closer than we." You, or the missionaries you send, may need to train and mobilize church planting team members from another people group that is more similar to your target group in race, politics, economic level, educational, lifestyle and world view.

Let's assume you research well all the factors: race, culture, logistics, urban versus rural backgrounds, language similarities, education and economic levels, etc. You learn the language. Then you go in a crowded bus to your new field, with a team of church planters as similar to the local people as possible in every aspect. Some or all of them may be from another developing country. You are happy because they do not have to make that long cultural leap that delays church planting by years (the less responsive the people are to missionaries, the more crucial this cultural fit). Now you finally arrive, unpack your toothbrush, take a deep breath, pray, step out the door and find fifty thousand people living around you who think Jesus was John Wayne's cousin. Now what?

Avoid institutions if possible at this beachhead stage (community development programs unrelated to church planting, schools, clinics, etc.); they will come later. In Honduras we developed community development work but it grew out of the churches, not vice versa. We taught obedience to the great commandment of loving our neighbor in a practical way. A poverty program can aid church planting if the two are integrated by the Holy Spirit. But churches dependent on charitable institutions are almost always dominated by the foreign missionary and seldom reproduce. Your local missiologist may point to celebrated exceptions here and there, perhaps in a southern suburb of outer Myitkyina, or some place where a freak with fifteen fingers was also born in 1967. But we don't build broad movements for Christ on exceptions.

To start a church that will multiply in the normal way in a *pioneer* field with no experienced pastors nor organized churches, take the following steps (change them where local circumstances require it):

1) Witness first to male heads of households. We often told them Bible stories they could pass on immediately, even before saved, to their own family and friends. We went with them to show them how. But why *male* heads of families? We worked in a macho culture (right where the word Macho came from,

where men carried sharpened machetes and used them readily). Female leadership, right or wrong, limited the outreach of brand new works. Later, when a church was established with male pastor and elders, women could take a higher profile. Be sensitive to your community's norms, especially in the first impressions you give of the church.

2) Baptize all repentant believers without delay (entire families when possible). At first I acted as though a big buzzard were perched on my shoulder just waiting to pounce on our converts that fell way; I delayed baptism to make sure they were "safe." But I soon saw that the very reason many fell away was my distrust. That's the funny thing about God's grace; He wants us to let it slop over on the unworthy (Rom 5:20-21).

3) Provide a style of worship that new elders-in-training can lead and teach to others. Don't invite the *public* until local leaders can lead the services. Celebrate the Lord's Supper weekly as the center of worship, especially until local men are mature enough to preach in an edifying, humble way.

4) Organize a provisional board of elders as soon as mature men are converted. Show them how to win and pastor their own people right away. Remember, this is for pioneer fields with no experienced pastors nor well organized churches. We, like Paul, must use the best men God gives us as the churches multiply, or the new disciples have no leadership at all (Acts 14:23).

5) Enroll these new elders in pastoral training on the job. Don't remove them from their people for training. Meet with them every two or three weeks (moreoften if possible until they are mobilized).

6) Provide a list of activities planned for the congregation, starting with the commands of Christ and His Apostles. Let everyone know where he is going and what he needs to learn for each activity. Use this as a check list to monitor the progress of the elders you train, in both their studies and pastoral work, as they mobilize their own people in ministry.

Decide How You Can Best Use your Ministry Gifts with the People.

Define your own ministry. What spiritual gifts has the Holy Spirit given you? Before I turned over leadership to the Honduran nationals, my own job was: *To help the Honduran churches train their own leaders.* I could say it in one sentence. My ministry now is: "To train missionaries to reproduce churches in pioneer fields." What is your ministry? Be concise. If you don't know, ask for help. You may work in a field for a year or two before you can pin it down. If you have been working hard in the same church for several years and still cannot briefly define your ministry, you probably have taken on too much. Trim your job down so that you can't help but do it well; then God may open new doors.

Since my preparation came primarily from books and classrooms, I failed to use my gift of teaching in proper harmony with other spiritual gifts. Like most recent seminary graduates, I used my superior knowledge of God's Word to "pull rank" on those who knew less. My teaching stifled their use of the gifts of servant leadership, evangelism and other gift-based ministries. I had to do some painful repenting before I could work in harmony with a ministry team in which the Holy Spirit harmonized the use of several spiritual gifts.

2. MOBILIZE YOUR DISCIPLES IMMEDIATELY TO EDIFY THOSE THEY ARE DISCIPLING.

To build up the church as a living, reproducing body, Paul instructs pastors and teachers to train the members of the church for the ministry, to edify the Body of Christ (Eph. 4:11-12).

Build Edifying Relationships with the Leaders you Disciple.

Like most new missionaries, I took myself too seriously. I worried about what my disciples were up to. It took me years to learn to sit back with my coconut milk, laugh at my own goofs and trust the Holy Spirit to do His work in my students. How can we enable the leaders we train to edify each other and their people through personal, loving relationships?

Paul left his pastoral disciple Timothy behind to work with the elders in newly planted churches with these instructions: "The things you have heard from me...these entrust to faithful men who will be able to teach others also" (II Tim. 2:2). How dynamic and reproductive this loving "Paul-Timothy" relationship between teacher and student! If you have not yet tried to teach the way Jesus and His Apostles did, you are in for a blessing. If it frightens you, start with just one or two potential leaders. Train them on the job; take responsibility for their effective ministry. Personal discipling does not mean "one-on-one" (Jesus taught twelve), nor is it just to deal with personal needs (Jesus spent most of His time personally discipling the top level leaders of the Church, the very Apostles).

In Honduras I usually taught from one to three students, in a way they could imitate and pass on to others immediately. I helped each one have an effective ministry. I taught and modeled what he would pass on to his own people and his own pastoral trainees in the daughter or granddaughter churches. These taught other elders who taught still others as Paul instructed Timothy. The chain grew to over a hundred pastors in training, all elders of churches. As soon as a new church was born, the outside worker enrolled a local leader, normally an elder highly respected by his people, and began passing on to him the same doctrine and materials as he was receiving himself. This new "Timothy" taught the rest of the new elders in his young church. It kept multiplying as long as each discipler did *everything* in a way his students could imitate immediately. I stopped teaching and preaching in the professional way in which I was used to (they admired it, but could not imitate it). I stopped using electronic equipment including movies, and anything else that was not available to all our workers. That's hard on a gadget-oriented westerner used to gadgets conditioned to using the very latest technology for the glory of Christ.

Once we developed loving, Paul-Timothy discipling relationships we seldom had to discuss church planting. The Holy Spirit channeled the Word of God through these relationships to mobilize the Timothies and church reproduction took care of itself. At first I failed to trust the Holy Spirit and pushed the men myself. I dictated rules and prerequisites to keep the doctrine and the church pure and to make sure the men did their job. It stifled the work; one bitter failure

A PASSIVE, PASTOR-CENTERED CHURCH:

A weak pastor dominates his church.

INTERACTION IN A DYNAMIC CHURCH:

A strong pastor promotes ties between all members.

New nuclei of leadership readily form both within the mother church and in daughter churches.

Teach your converts from the beginning to edify one another in love. Building a network of strong relationships provides for the large number of ministries required in the local church in order for it to grow and reproduce daughter churches.

followed another. I prayed, "Lord, I don't want a big ministry of my own; just let me help the Hondurans have a good ministry." God answered this prayer. I also learned through disappointments to let the people themselves decide on their own leaders, using I Timothy 3:1-7.

We learned not plant the churches first then train the leaders for them; nor did we train the leaders first then tell them to raise up their churches. We married the two efforts in one ministry. My American culture pushed me at first to compartmentalize our organization, isolating its ministries. But I learned to let the Holy Spirit integrate diverse ministries and gifts in the united body (I Cor. 12:4-26).

I also began with education objectives that focused on educating the man. But according to Ephesians 4:11-16, our education should seek only to edify the *church* in love. I had to discipline myself to keep my student's people in view as I taught, and not focus only on my student and the teaching content.

Before I learned to imitate the way Christ and His Apostles discipled, I was satisfied if my student answered test questions correctly and preached good sermons in the classroom. I neither saw nor cared what he did in his church with what he was learning. I slowly learned to see beyond my student to his ministry with his people. I responded to the needs of his church by listening at the beginning of each session to the reports of my students. Then I often set aside what I had prepared and taught rather what each student's people needed at that time.

It was hard at first to let the developing churches' needs and opportunities dictate the order of a functional curriculum. In time much of my discipling, like the teaching of the Epistles, became *problem solving*. Yes, if we start reproductive churches we will have problems. The Apostles did, too. To avoid problems, don't have children and don't have churches.

Build Edifying Teaching Relationships between Elders and Disciples.

The pastor or leading elder sets the example for all the leaders. They in turn enable all the members of an infant congregation to minister to each other in love. A weak pastor dominates his congregation. He tries to do everything, or delegates it in a demanding way. He herds rather than leads (both Jesus and Peter prohibit herding in a demanding way: Matt. 20:25-28; I Peter 5:1-4). Where do you suppose pastors on the mission field pick up the bad practice of herding others? It's not all cultural; they learned it from us missionaries. I furnished the only model the new pastors had in our pioneer field. Because of my superior education and resources, I made the decisions for my less educated colleagues. At the same time, like most new missionaries, I felt insecure and overprotected the first churches. A strong missionary, like a strong pastor, does not fear to give authority and responsibility to others. He does not force gifted, willing workers into existing slots in his organization, but rather builds ministries around them.

3. TEACH AND PRACTICE OBEDIENCE TO JESUS' COMMANDS IN LOVE, ABOVE AND BEFORE ALL ELSE

Jesus, after affirming His deity and total authority on earth commissioned His Church to make disciples who obey all His commands (Matt. 28:18-20). So His commands take priority over all other institutional rules (even that hallowed *Church Constitution and Bylaws*). This obedience is always in love. If we obey God for any other reason, it becomes sheer legalism; God hates that.

Start Right Out with Loving Obedience to Jesus' Basic Commands.

To plant churches in a pioneer field, aim for each community to have **a group of believers in Christ committed to obey His commands**. This definition of a church might get a D minus where you studied theology; but *the more you add to it, the harder it will be for the churches you start to reproduce* . We asked our converts to memorize the following list of Christ's basic commands:
1. Repent and believe: Mark 1:15
2. Be baptized (and continue in the new life it initiates): Matt. 28:18-20; Acts 2:38; Rom. 6:1-11
3. Love God and neighbor in a practical way: Matt. 22:37-40
4. Celebrate the Lord's Supper: Luke 22:17-20
5. Pray: Matt. 6:5-15
6. Give: Matt. 6:19-21; Luke 6:38
7. Disciple others: Matt. 28:18-20

Memorize them; you can neither be nor make obedient disciples, unless they are basic to your Christian experience. They are the ABC's of both discipling and church planting.

Define Evangelism Objectives in terms of Obedience.

Do not simply preach for "decisions;" make obedient disciples. Only disciples produce a church that multiplies itself spontaneously within a culture. Consider the two commands: "Repent and believe" and "Be baptized." In western culture a man stands alone before his God and "decides" for Christ. But in other cultures sincere conversion needs interaction with family and friends. Faith, repentance and immediate baptism of the entire family or group—no invitation to make a decision—is the norm (Acts 2:36-41; 8:11; 10:44-48; 16:13-15, 29-34; 18:8). Repentance goes deeper than a decision; it is a permanent change wrought by God's Spirit. We are born all over again. Few purely intellectual decisions in any culture lead to permanent, obedient discipleship.

We found that when we baptized repentant believers reasonably soon, without requiring a long doctrinal course first, the great majority then responded to our training in obedient discipleship. The detailed doctrine came later. Teaching heavy theology *before* one learns loving, childlike obedience is dangerous. It leaves him assuming that Christianity is having Scripturally correct doctrine and he leaves it at that. He becomes a passive learner of the Word rather than an active disciple. Balanced discipling activates mind, heart and hands. It integrates Word, Care, Task. It learns, loves, serves. Emphasizing one of the three at the expense of the others yields spiritually unbalanced believers, not disciples.

The new members of the first New Testament church in Jerusalem obeyed *all* of the basic commands of Christ from the very beginning. After repentance and baptism they learned the Apostle's doctrine (Word), broke bread, prayed and fellowshipped (Care), and give and witnessed, adding new members every day (Task): Acts 2:41-47. We also must teach each new convert from the very beginning to obey all these commands in love (John 15:15). Don't wait to start obeying Christ! The first few weeks of their new life in Christ are the most impressionable; they will determine more than any other time of teaching whether or not they are (and make) Bible centered, active, loving *disciples*.

Define Theological Education Objectives in Terms of Obedience.

God does not bless methods; He blesses obedience . How can we help a student to train his congregation to do the things Christ orders us to do? One way is to combine *Theological Education by Extension with Biblical discipling, orienting it to loving obedience to Jesus' commands*. Many criticized our TEE in Honduras it because it violated their institutional rules (not on Biblical grounds).

God's Word commands the pastor to "do the work of an evangelist" (II Tim. 4:5). A pastor does many other things but evangelism is basic. Education and evangelism married to each other in one extension ministry became an effective church planting tool for us; one reinforced the other. Isolating pastoral training from the other ministries of the body violates Scripture. God teaches that all spiritual gifts (including teaching) *must edify the body in loving harmony with the exercise of the other gifts* (Romans 12:3-11, Ephesians 4:1-16 and I Corinthians chapters 12-13).

Orient your Teaching to Loving Obedience.

We taught our pastors to orient all church activity to New Testament commands. As they taught the Word of God, they accustomed their people to discern three levels of authority for all that they did as a body of disciples:

1) NEW TESTAMENT COMMANDS. These carry all the authority of heaven. They include the commands of Jesus' inspired the Apostles in the Epistles which apply only to baptized, more mature Christians who are already members of a church. We don't vote on them nor argue about doing them. They always take precedent over any human organization's rules.

2) APOSTOLIC PRACTICES (NOT COMMANDED). We cannot enforce these as laws because Christ alone has authority to make laws for His own church, His Body. Nor can we prohibit their practice because they have apostolic precedent. Examples include: holding possessions in common, laying hands on converts, celebrating the Lord's Supper frequently in homes using one cup, baptizing the same day of conversion, Sunday worship.

3) HUMAN CUSTOMS. Practices not mentioned in the New Testament have only the authority of a group's voluntary agreement. If it involves discipline, the agreement is recognized in heaven (but only for that congregation; we do not judge another congregation by the customs of our own: Matt. 18:15-20).

Nearly all church divisions and quarrels originate when a power hungry person seeking followers puts mere apostolic practices or human customs (levels 2 or 3 above) at the top level as law.

We developed a "Congregation Activities Register" listing 49 activities for the churches , based on the seven general commands of Christ listed above, and other commands in the Epistles. Under each activity in this chart we listed related studies. It became our pastoral training curriculum guide. We brought in all major areas of Bible, doctrine and church history, precisely where they best aided a church activity. Theological education paralleled church development. The activities, besides the basic commands of Jesus, include: counsel, mobilize youth for ministry, train elders in the daughter church, develop public worship, etc. Each activity includes reading in the relevant areas of Bible, doctrine, church history and pastoral work (all the essential elements of a traditional pastoral training curriculum) as well as questions to verify that the practical work was done. (An example of materials using this functional discipling curriculum is SEAN's *Train and Multiply* program, Casilla 561, Viña DelMar, Chile.)

Extension teachers use this chart every two weeks or so when they meet with their pastoral student, to register his progress and decide which of the activities they should begin next. In each leadership discipling session we do the following (to remember it think of LEAP—Listen, Evaluate, Assign, Pray):

L) Listen as each student reports his field work done and plans what to do next. Write down his plans down with a carbon copy to review at the next session when he reports his work; always listen first to report: he will have something good or bad to tell you (either way he will not listen well to your teaching or counsel until he has mentioned it).

E) Evaluate what he has learned. Ask questions about the content of reading he has done, scan his written answers in workbooks, listen to a brief talk on the subject just studied (especially to help him prepare to give it to his church or group).

A) Assign reading related to his pastoral work plans. Assign chapters in the Bible or other books (use only books on the level of his people, even if you have to write summaries of the essentials of a subject). Do not assign so much reading that he lacks time for his pastoral work. Do not lecture on things that you expect him to learn from his reading (enable him to be an active learner and doer rather than a passive listener: James 1:22).

P) Pray. Each participant prays for the work of another.

Don't forget. LEAP!

4.   ORGANIZE YOUR CHURCH OR PROGRAM BY BUILDING LOVING, EDIFYING ACCOUNTABILITY RELATIONSHIPS BETWEEN INDIVIDUAL DISCIPLES AND CHURCHES

Healthy daughter churches need loving, edifying discipling relationships within themselves and with the mother church (Acts 11:19-30; 14:21-28 and 15:1-2, 28-31). If your church, church planting or training organization is already formed, add this personal discipling to it; don't insist on ruthless changes.

Help Each New Church to Reproduce.

Each church should send extension workers to reproduce daughter churches, as did the Antioch church (Acts 13:1-3). The longer you wait to mobilize a church for multiplication, the harder it is to reprogram its thinking. Teach your elders the joy of sacrificing to separate their strongest tithers and leaders, in the power of the Holy Spirit as in Antioch, to extend Christ's kingdom. After prayer, perhaps fasting, a formal separation service with laying on of hands, as they did. Remember, it is not the individuals that reproduce, but *congregations* that pray and are moved by the Holy Spirit. Let each new church be a link in the chain. The individual extension worker is only an arm of his church.

Ask the new church leaders to chart their own plans. They must take the initiative (don't push your plans on them; simply teach them what the Word says about their task and let them respond). For example, we asked our pastors to draw a large map, with arrows to the villages which they planned for their church to reach directly or through their daughter or granddaughter churches. Their church workers then signed their names by those towns or neighborhoods for which they would pray and plan.

Show Each New Believer How to Witness to Friends and Relatives.

The Holy Spirit flows readily through the bonds that exist between family members and close friends (Acts 10:24, 44). Keep new converts in a loving relationship with them (don't pull them out of their circle to put them in a safe Christian environment, or those very bonds which aid the spread of the gospel become barriers).

We prepared simple gospel studies (mostly Bible stories) that even illiterates could use at once to share their new faith. We accompanied them to show them how to do it, modeling it all in a way they could immediately imitate.

Build Edifying Inter-church Discipling Relationships.

At first I applied church "body life" only to local congregations. Then I learned to build inter-church discipling relationships with accountability. Elders in one church sacrificially discipled less experienced pastors in the daughter or granddaughter churches.

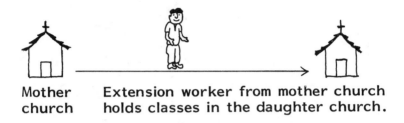

Mother   Extension worker from mother church
church   holds classes in the daughter church.

Sometimes travel was difficult for an older elder, and the main worker from the daughter church rode his horse to the mother church every two weeks or so.

Mother   Extension student–worker from the
church   daughter church studies in the mother
            church.

Where the churches were one or two days' walk apart the teacher and student took turns slogging through the muddy trails.

Beware of the bad strategy of a mother church sending workers to several daughter churches at once, as though she were the only church with God's reproductive power.

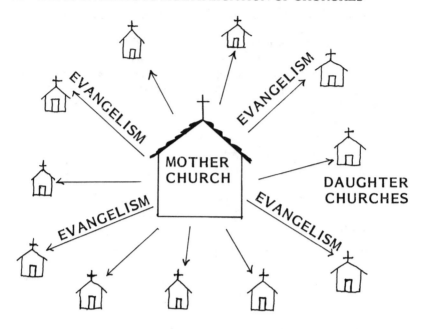

The above "hub" strategy wears out the workers and discourages the mother church. God's power, inherent in all churches in which His Spirit dwells, enables a mother church to start a daughter church and train its new elders to help it develop *and* reproduce in granddaughter churches. Just disciple the disciplers and watch it happen! The primary links in the chain of churches in Honduras were volunteer extension teachers from the mother church.

The chain was not a hierarchy to control; volunteer teachers with no organizational authority worked with volunteer students. It took sweat and guts to build these loving ties between churches, helping men to know, love and train each other for immediate pastoral ministry. In the process men were shot, put to death by machete, weakened by disease and almost drowned. It was worth it.

The modern western missionary's most common sin is controlling the national churches. I had to learn to keep out of the way and let the Spirit's power inherent in the churches produce the ministries by which the churches were edified and reproduced. I guided, encouraged, taught the Word and counseled, but I no longer pushed. Then we saw the chain reaction; one of the extension networks produced five generations and over twenty churches.

We met occasionally to reaffirm our plans and decide which church would reach certain villages or communities. We divided our entire area of responsibility into nine regions and planned the steps to start a daughter church that would

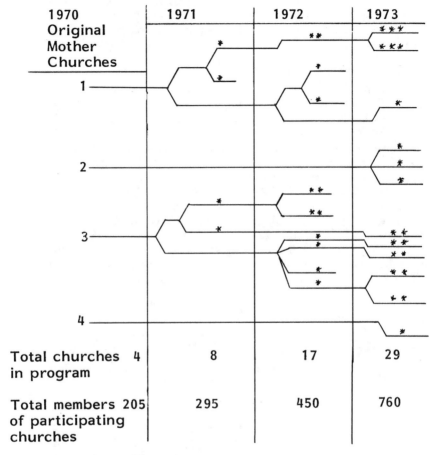

	1970	1971	1972	1973
Total churches in program	4	8	17	29
Total members of participating churches	205	295	450	760

* Daughter Churches
** Granddaughter Churches
*** Great-Granddaughter Churches

By the end of 1979, the program had produced:

Great-great-granddaughter churches	8
Great-great-great granddaughter churches	4
Total churches in program	64
Total baptized members (approx.)	2020

reproduce in each region. The pastoral students of the Honduras Extension Bible Institute have for many years been starting an average of five new churches a year, each of which has from one to three new pastors in training. After turning the leadership of this program to Hondurans, it has continued to reproduce in spite of other missionaries' pressure to revert to traditional pastoral training methods.

Pray for Reproduction Power.

Christ's parables in Matthew 13, Mark 4 and John 15 compare the growth and reproduction of His churches to that of plants. Like all other living creatures God has created, the church has her own seed in herself to reproduce after her own kind. Every time we eat, we eat the fruit of God's tremendous reproduction power given to plants and animals. Look around out of doors; it's everywhere— grass, trees, birds, bees, babies and flowers. All creation is shouting it! This is the way God works! Reproduction is His *style* . Pray for it! (God in His infinite wisdom acts a bit lazy when we don't ask Him to move; He limits His absolute power to our weak faith!) We ourselves don't make the church grow or reproduce, any more than pulling on a stalk of corn would make it grow. Paul plants, Apollos waters, God gives the growth. We sow, water, weed, fertilize and fence the crop, but rely on the church's own God-given potential to reproduce. An obedient, Spirit-filled church *has* to reproduce at home or abroad. It's her very nature; she is the Body of the risen, life-giving Son of God.

One of the several extension chains we have in Honduras has reproduced over five generations and twenty churches.

Each new church in a chain, like a grain of wheat, has the same potential to start the reproduction all over again. When a chain gets too long for good communication, simply reorganize the teaching relationships. Don't assume that doctrine will get watered down the longer the chain. Each Spirit-filled teacher in the chain has the same love for the Word and will rejuvenate the flow. I discovered that the strongest churches were usually one or two links removed from me, the foreign missionary. The key to maintaining the chains is loving communication in both directions. Accurate student reports from each daughter church are essential, for his teacher to respond applying the Word accurately to its life, needs and opportunities.

Pray for protection from traditions that hamper this spontaneous reproduction. We have mentioned teaching that neglects discipleship, and failure to mobilize newly repentant converts to obey beginning with baptism. Another almost universal impediment to reproduction are missionary subsidies that stifle nationals' own giving and build a dependent spirit. Don't rob poor believers of the blessing of sacrificial giving! God multiplies their mite by special celestial mathematics that will prosper them now and for eternity. Paying national pastors with outside funds nearly always stifles spontaneous reproduction and eventually leads to deep resentment when the source no longer equals the demand.

Most impediments come from rules that well meaning men make, who in weakness of faith fear the spontaneous and won't let the Holy Spirit to surprise them:

"But our By-laws state clearly that our church must wait at least 5 years and have 100 members, to start its daughter church."

"We need a strong home base before we can send missionaries."

"We can't do it until it's gone through the committee and budgeted."

"We can't baptize you even though you've met the Bible requirements of repentance and faith, until you take our 6 month's disciple's course; baptism is the graduation ceremony."

"You can't officiate Holy Communion; you're not duly ordained."

"What? Jesus commands it? Well, we'll vote on it and see."

"We can't allow everything the Apostles did; times have changed."

"Discipling is for lay leaders; a real pastor needs seminary."

"You can't train other pastors until you finish the whole program."

"You must get your pastoral training in a formal seminary."

"We more experienced pastors will run our Association of churches."

"You can't obey Christ until you know the whole Word of God."

Sooner or later all such "can't do" laws without Biblical basis replace simple obedience to Christ and stifle reproductive discipleship. They sound spiritual but contradict what the Spirit of God does did in Scripture and does today where men do not limit Him. Our weak faith fears the spontaneous; we don't want God to surprise us.

Here's how the reproduction occurred in Honduras once it got its initial impetus between 1970 and 1973 (see next page):

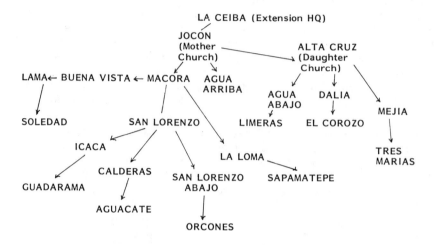

Study Questions

1. Traditional theological objectives focus on educating a man while Biblical education objectives aim to edify the church. Explain the difference in the way a typical theological professor teaches, from the way a discipler of pastors works.

2. How would you start and develop an extension chain from yourself to a great-granddaughter church in a new field? Explain the role of everyone involved: yourself, trainers in the daughter church, the congregations, elders, new converts, and pastors in training.

3. What is a "preaching point" and how do you avoid it?

4. What are the basic commands of Christ? How will you make sure your disciples, and those they disciple, obey all of them?

5. What do we build into our organization to assure reproduction?

11

Evangelization of Whole Families

Chua Wee Hian

Year: 1930

Locality: Northwest China

Case studies:

1. The approach and strategy of two single European lady missionaries.

2. The approach and strategy of the Little Flock Assembly of Chefoo, Shantung.

Objectives: Identical—to plant local churches and to engage in extensive village evangelism.

Case study 1

Two gifted and dedicated lady missionaries were sent by their missionary society to Northwest China. Their mandate was to evangelize and plant congregations in a cluster of villages. They spoke fluent Chinese; they labored faithfully and fervently. After a decade, a small congregation emerged. However, most of its members were women. Their children attended the Sunday School regularly. The visitor to this small congregation would easily detect the absence of men.

In their reports and newsletters, both missionaries referred to the "hardness of hearts" that was prevalent among the men. References were made also to promising teenagers who were opposed by their parents when they sought permission for baptism.

Case study 2

In 1930 a spiritual awakening swept through the Little Flock Assembly in Shantung. Many members sold their entire possessions in order to send seventy *families* to the Northwest as "instant congregations." Another thirty *families*

Chua Wee Hian is General Secretary Emeritus of the International Fellowship of Evangelical Students (IFES). An Asian from Singapore, he has served as an associate secretary for IFES in East Asia and as editor of *The Way*, a quarterly magazine for Asian students. Taken by permission from *Let The Earth Hear His Voice*, copyright 1975, World Wide Publications, Minneapolis, MN, U.S.A.

migrated to the Northeast. By 1944, forty new assemblies had been established, and all these were vitally involved in evangelism.

Now, in terms of dedication and doctrinal orthodoxy, both the Europeans and the Little Flock Assembly shared the same commitment and faith. But why the striking contrasts in results and in their strategies of church-planting?

Consider the case of the two single lady missionaries. Day by day, the Chinese villagers saw them establishing contacts and building the bridges of friendships with women, usually when their husbands or fathers were out working in the fields or trading in nearby towns. Their foreignness (dubbed "red hair devils") was enough to incite cultural and racial prejudices in the minds of the villagers. But their single status was something that was socially questionable. It was a well-known fact in all Chinese society that the families constitute basic social units. These units insure security. In Confucian teaching, three of the five basic relationships have to do with family ties— father and son, older brother and younger brothers, husband and wife. The fact that these ladies were making contacts with individual women and not having dialogues with the elders would make them appear to be foreign agents seeking to destroy the fabric of the village community. A question that would constantly crop up in the gossip and discussion of the villagers would be the fact of the missionaries' single state. Why aren't they married? Why aren't they visibly related to their parents, brothers and sisters, uncles and aunts and other relatives? So when they persuaded the women or the youth to leave the religion of their forefathers, they were regarded as "family-breakers."

By contrast, the Little Flock Assembly in sending out Chinese Christian families sent out agents that were recognizable socio-cultural entities. Thus the seventy families became an effective missionary task force. It is not difficult to imagine the heads of these families sharing their faith with the elders of the villagers. The grandmothers could informally transmit the joy of following Christ and of their deliverance from demonic powers to the older women in pagan villages. The housewives in the markets could invite their counterparts to attend the services that were held each Sunday by the "instant congregations." No wonder forty new assemblies were established as a result of this approach to church-planting and evangelism.

Evangelizing Families in Other Cultures

The strategy of evangelizing whole families is applicable not only in Chinese communities. It is also effective in other Asian communities, African villages and tribes, Latin American *barrio* and societies. Writing on the rapid spread of the Christian faith in Korea, Roy Shearer observed: "One most important factor governing how the church grew is the structure of Korean society. In Korea, we are dealing with a society based on the family, not the tribe. The family is strong even today. The soundest way for a man to come to Christ is in the setting of his own family."

He went on to relate repeated situations when heads of families returned to their clan villages and were successful in persuading their relatives and kinsmen to "turn from idols to serve the living God." He concluded: "The Gospel flowed along the web of family relationships. This web is the transmission line for the current of the Holy Spirit that brought men and women into the church."

In her book *New Patterns for Discipling Hindus*, Miss B.V. Subbamma categorically asserted that the Hindu family might be the only social institution through which the Gospel could be transmitted and received. Not all would agree with this assertion, because there are evidences of university students who have professed faith in Christ in the great university centers of India. Some could take this step of faith because they were free from parental pressures. However, as a general rule, Miss Subbamma's observation and deduction are correct.

Evangelizing whole families is the pattern of current missionary outreach in parts of Latin America. There in the Roman Catholic culture of web relationships, family structures are strong. Exploiting this social pattern, the Chilean Pentecostals, like the Little Flock Assembly in Shantung forty years ago, dispatch *families* from among their faithful to be agents and ambassadors of church expansion. Through these evangelizing families, many assemblies and congregations have been planted in different parts of that continent. The phenomenal growth of the Pentecostal movement in Latin America reflects the effectiveness of using families to evangelize families.

At times it is difficult for individualistic Westerners to realize that in many "face to face" societies religious, decisions are made corporately. The individual in that particular type of society would be branded as a "traitor" and treated as an outcast if he were to embrace a new religious belief. After the Renaissance, in most Western countries, identity is expressed by the Cartesian dictum *Cogito ergo sum*: I think, therefore I am. Man as a rational individual could think out religious options for himself and is free to choose the faith that he would like to follow. This dictum does not apply in many African tribal communities. For the Africans (and for many others) the unchanging dictum is, *I participate, therefore I am*. Conformity to and participation in traditional religious rites and customs give such people their identity. So if there is to be a radical change in religious allegiance, there must be a corporate or multi-individual decision.

This is particularly true of Muslim families and communities. The one-by-one method of individual evangelism will not work in such a society. A lecturer friend of mine who teaches in the multi-racial university of Singapore once made this significant remark, "I've discovered that for most Malay students (who are nearly all Muslims) Islam consists not of belief in Allah the supreme God—it is *community*." Ambassadors for Christ in Islamic lands should cope not only with theological arguments concerning the unity and nature of God, they should consider the social and cultural associations of Muslims. Where sizable groups of Muslims had been converted, their decisions were multi-individual. An excellent illustration would be that of Indonesia. During the past fifteen years, wise missionaries and national pastors had been engaging in dialogues and discussions with the elders and leaders of local Muslim communities. When these decision-makers were convinced that Christ is the only way to God and that he alone is the Savior of the world, they returned to their villages and towns, and urged all members to turn to Christ. So it was not surprising to witness whole communities being catechized and baptized together.

Such movements are termed as "people movements," and many years before the Indonesian happening, Ko Tha Byu, a remarkable Burmese evangelist, was instrumental in discipling whole Karen communities and villages. Today the Karen church is one of the strongest Christian communities in Southeast Asia.

The Biblical Data

When we turn to the biblical records, we shall discover that families feature prominently both as the recipients as well as the agents of salvation blessing.

To begin with, the family is regarded as divinely instituted by God (Eph. 3:15). In fact, all families owe their descent and composition to their Creator. By redemption, the church—God's own people, is described as "the household of God" (Eph. 2:19) and the "household of faith" (Gal. 6:10).

In the Pentateuch, great stress is laid on the sanctity of marriage, the relation between children and parents, masters and slaves. This emphasis is underscored in the New Testament (see Col. 3:18-4:1; Eph. 5:22-6:9; 1 Pet. 2: 1:8-3:7).

It is the family or the household that pledges its allegiance to Yahweh. Joshua as head of his own household could declare, "As for me and my house, we will serve the Lord" (Jos. 24:15). Through Joshua's predecessor Moses, Yahweh had taught his people to celebrate His mighty acts by sacred meals and festivals. It is interesting to observe that the feast of the Passover (Exod. 12:3-4) was a family meal. The head of the family was to recite and reenact the great drama of Israel's deliverance at this family gathering. Through Israel's history, even until New Testament days, family feasts, prayer, and worship were regularly held. Thus the Jewish family became both the objects of God's grace and the visual agents of his redemptive actions. Their monotheistic faith expressed in terms of their family solidarity and religion must have created a tremendous impression on the Gentile communities. One of the results was that large numbers of Gentiles became proselytes, "associate members" of the Jewish synagogues. Jewish families made a sizable contribution to the "missionary" outreach.

The apostolic pattern for teaching was in and through family units (Acts 20:20). The first accession of a Gentile grouping to the Christian church was the family of the Roman centurion Cornelius in Caesarea (Acts 10:7, 24). At Philippi, Paul led the families of Lydia and the jailer to faith in Christ and incorporation into his Church (Acts 16:15, 31-34). The "first fruits" of the great missionary apostle in Achaia were the families of Stephanas (1 Cor. 16:15), Crispus and Gaius (Acts 18:8; 1 Cor. 1:16; Rom. 16:23). So it was clear that the early church discipled both Jewish and Gentile communities in families.

It was equally clear that households were used as outposts of evangelism. Aquila and Priscilla used their home in Ephesus and Rome as a center for the proclamation of the Gospel (1 Cor. 16:19; Rom. 16:5). Congregations met in the homes of Onesiphorus (2 Tim. 1:16; 4:19) and Nymphas (Col. 4:15).

Study Questions

1. What are the consequences for an individual in a face-to-face society (family and community-oriented) if he becomes a Christian?

2. What kind of missionary strategy has to be followed to work in face-to-face societies? How might this be developed today?

12

A Church in Every People:
Plain Talk About a Difficult Subject

Donald A. McGavran

In the last eight years of the twentieth century, the goal of Christian mission should be to preach the Gospel and by God's grace to plant in every unchurched segment of mankind—what shall we say—*"a church"* or *"a cluster of growing churches?"* By the phrase "segment of mankind" I mean an urbanization, development, caste, tribe, valley, plain, or minority population. I shall explain that the steadily maintained long range goal should never be the first; but should always be the second. The goal is not one small sealed-off conglomerate congregation in every people. Rather, the long range goal (to be held constantly in view in the years or decades when it is not yet achieved) should be *"a cluster of growing congregations in every segment."*

As we consider the question italicized above, we should remember that it is usually easy to start one single congregation in a new unchurched people group. The missionary arrived. He and his family worship on Sunday. They are the first members of that congregation. He learns the language and preaches the Gospel. He lives like a Christian. He tells people about Christ and helps them in their troubles. He sells tracts and gospels or gives them away. Across the years a few individual converts are won from this group and that. Sometimes they come for very sound and spiritual reasons; sometimes from mixed motives. But here and there a woman, a man, a boy, a girl do decide to follow Jesus. A few employees of the mission become Christian. These may be masons hired to erect the buildings, helpers in the home, rescued persons or orphans. The history of mission in Africa is replete with churches started by buying slaves, freeing them and employing such of them as could not return to their kindred. Such as chose to could accept the Lord. A hundred and fifty years ago this was a common way of starting a church. With the outlawing of slavery, of course, it ceased to be used.

Known worldwide as perhaps the foremost missiologist, Donald McGavran was born in India of missionary parents and returned there as a third-generation missionary himself in 1923, serving as a director of religious education and translating the Gospels in the Chhattisgarhi dialect of Hindi. He founded the School of World Mission of Fuller Theological Seminary, and was formerly Dean Emeritus. McGavran died in 1990 at the age of 93. McGavran was the author of several influential books, including *The Bridges of God, How Churches Grow,* and *Understanding Church Growth.*

One single congregation arising in the way just described is almost always a conglomerate church—made up of members of several different segments of society. Some are old, some young, orphans, rescued persons, helpers and ardent seekers. All seekers are carefully screened to make sure they really intend to receive Christ. In due time a church building is erected; and lo, "a church in that people." It is a conglomerate church. It is sealed off from all the people groups of that region. No segment of the population says, "That group of worshippers is *us*." They are quite right. It is not. It is ethnically quite a different social unit.

This very common way of beginning the process of evangelization is a slow way to disciple the peoples of earth—note the plural, "the peoples of earth." Let us observe closely what really happens as this congregation is gathered. Each convert, as he becomes a Christian, is seen by his kin as one who leaves "us" and joins "them." He leaves our gods to worship their gods. Consequently his own relations force him out. Sometimes he is severely ostracized; thrown out of house and home; his wife is threatened. Hundreds of converts have been poisoned or killed. Sometimes, the ostracism is mild and consists merely in severe disapproval. His people consider him a traitor. A church which results from this process looks to the peoples of the region like an assemblage of traitors. It is a conglomerate congregation. It is made up of individuals, who one by one have come out of several different societies, castes or tribes.

Now if anyone, in becoming a Christian, is forced out of, or comes out of a tightly-structured segment of society, the Christian cause wins the individual but loses the family. The family, his people, his neighbors of that tribe are fiercely angry at him or her. They are the very men and women to whom he cannot talk. You are not of us, they say to him. You have abandoned us, you like them more than you like us. You now worship their gods not our gods. As a result, conglomerate congregations, made up of converts won in this fashion, *grow very slowly*. Indeed, one might truly affirm that where congregations grow in this fashion, the conversion of the ethnic units (people groups) from which they come is made doubly difficult. "The Christians misled one of our people," the rest of the group will say; "We're going to make quite sure that they do not mislead any more of us."

One-by-one, is relatively easy to accomplish. Perhaps 90 out of every 100 missionaries who intend church planting get only conglomerate congregations. I want to emphasize that. Perhaps 90 out of every 100 missionaries who intend church planting, get only conglomerate congregations. Such missionaries preach the Gospel, tell of Jesus, sell tracts and gospels and evangelize in many other ways. They welcome inquirers, but whom do they get? They get a man here, a woman there, a boy here, a girl there, who for various reasons are willing to become Christians and patiently to endure the mild or severe disapproval of their people.

If we are to understand how churches grow and do not grow on new ground, in untouched and unreached peoples, we must note that the process I have just described seems unreal to most missionaries. "What," they will exclaim, "could be a better way of entry into all the unreached peoples of that region than to win a few individuals from among them? Instead of resulting in the sealed-off church you describe, the process really gives us points of entry into every society from which a convert has come. That seems to us to be the real situation."

Those who reason in this fashion have known church growth in a largely Christian land, where men and women who follow Christ are not ostracized, are not regarded as traitors, but rather as those who have done the right thing. In that kind of a society every convert usually can become a channel through which the Christian Faith flows to his relatives and friends. On that point there can be no debate. It was the point I emphasized when I titled my book *The Bridges of God*.

But in tightly-structured societies, where Christianity is looked on as an invading religion, and individuals are excluded for serious fault, *there* to win converts from several different segments of society, far from building bridges to each of these, erects barriers difficult to cross.

Now let us contrast the other way in which God is discipling the peoples of Planet Earth. My account is not theory; but a sober recital of easily observable facts. As you look around the world, you see that while most missionaries succeed in planting only conglomerate churches by the "one-by-one out of the social group" method, here and there clusters of growing churches arise by the people movement method. They arise by tribe-wise or caste-wise movements to Christ. This is in many ways a better system. In order to use it effectively, missionaries should operate on seven principles.

First, they should be clear about the goal. The goal is not one single conglomerate church in a city or a region. They may get only that, *but that must never be their goal*. That must be a cluster of growing, indigenous congregations every member of which remains in close contact with his kindred. This cluster grows best if it is in one people, one caste, one tribe, one segment of society. For example, if you were evangelizing the taxi drivers of Taipei, then your goal would be to win not some taxi drivers, some university professors, some farmers and some fishermen, but to establish churches made up largely of taxi drivers, their wives and children, and their assistants and mechanics. As you win converts of that particular community, the congregation has a natural, built-in social cohesion. Everybody feels at home. Yes, the goal must be clear.

The second principle is that the national leader or the missionary and his helpers, should concentrate on one people. If you are going to establish *a cluster of growing congregations* amongst, let us say, the Nair people of Kerala, which is the southwest tip of India, then you would need to place most of your missionaries and their helpers so that they can work among the Nairs. They should proclaim the Gospel to Nairs; and say quite openly to them, we are hoping that within your great caste there soon will be thousands of followers of Jesus Christ, who also remain solidly in the Nair community. They will, of course, not worship the old Nair gods; but then plenty of Nairs don't worship their old gods. Plenty of Nairs are Communist and ridicule their old gods.

Nairs whom God calls, who choose to believe in Christ, are going to love their neighbors more than they did before, and walk in the light. They will be saved and beautiful people. They will remain Nairs, while at the same time they become Christians. To repeat, concentrate on one people group. If you have three missionaries, don't have one evangelizing this group, another that, and a third 200 miles away evangelizing still another. That is a sure way to guarantee that any churches started will be small, non-growing, one-by-one churches. The social dynamics of those sections of society will work solidly *against* the eruption of any great growing people movement to Christ.

The third principle is to encourage converts to remain thoroughly one with their own people in most matters. They should continue to eat what their people eat. They should not say, my people are vegetarians, but now that I have become a Christian I'm going to eat meat. After they become Christians they should be more rigidly vegetarian than they were before. In the matter of clothing, they should continue to look precisely like their kinsfolk. In the matter of marriage, most peoples are endogamous, they insist that "our people marry only our people." They look with very great disfavor on our people marrying other people. And yet when Christians come in one-by-one, they cannot marry their own people. None of them have become Christian. Where only a few of a given people become Christians there, when it comes time for them or their children to marry, they have to take husbands or wives from other segments of the population. So their own kin look at them and say, "Yes, become a Christian and mongrelize your children. You have left us and have joined them."

All converts should be encouraged to bear cheerfully the exclusion, the oppression, and the persecution that they are likely to encounter from their people. When anyone becomes a follower of a new way of life, he is likely to meet some disfavor from his loved ones. Maybe it's mild; maybe it's severe. He should bear such disfavor patiently. He should say on all occasions,

> I am a better son than I was before; I am a better father than I was before; I am a better husband than I was before; and I love you more than I used to do. You can hate me, but I will not hate you. You can exclude me, but I will include you. You can force me out of our ancestral house; but I will live on its veranda. Or I will get a house just across the street. I am still one of you, I am more one of you than I ever was before.

Encourage converts to remain thoroughly one with their people in most matters.

Please note that word "most." They cannot remain one with their people in idolatry, or drunkenness or obvious sin. If they belong to a segment of the society that earns its living by stealing, they must "steal no more." But, in most matters (how they talk, how they dress, how they eat, where they go, what kind of houses they live in) they can look very much like their people, and ought to make every effort to do so.

The fourth principle is to try to get group decisions for Christ. If only one person decides to follow Jesus do not baptize him immediately. Say to him, "You and I will work together to lead another five, or ten, or God willing, fifty of your people to accept Jesus Christ as Saviour so that when you are baptized, you will be baptized with them." Ostracism is very effective against one lone person. But ostracism is weak indeed when exercised against a group of a dozen. And when exercised against two hundred it has practically no force at all.

The fifth principle is this: Aim for scores of groups of that people to become Christians in an ever flowing stream across the years. One of the common mistakes made by missionaries eastern as well as western all around the world is that when a few become Christians, perhaps 100, 200 or even 1,000, the missionaries spend all their time teaching them. They want to make them good Christians and they say to themselves, if these people become good Christians, then the Gospel will spread. So for years they concentrate on a few congregations. By the time, ten to twenty years later, that they begin evangelizing outside that group, the rest of the people no longer want to become Christians. That has happened again and again. This principle requires that from the very beginning the missionary keeps on reaching out to new groups. But, you say, "Is not this a sure way to get poor Christians who don't know the Bible? If we follow that principle we shall soon have a lot of 'raw' Christians. Soon we shall have a community of perhaps five thousand people who are very sketchily Christian."

Yes, that is certainly a danger. At this point, we must lean heavily upon the New Testament, remembering the brief weeks or months of instruction Paul gave to his new churches. We must trust the Holy Spirit, and believe that God has called those people out of darkness into His wonderful light. As between two evils, giving them too little Christian teaching and allowing them to become a sealed-off community that cannot reach its own people, the latter is much the greater danger. *We must not allow new converts to become sealed off.* We must continue to make sure that a constant stream of new converts comes into the ever-growing cluster of congregations.

Now the sixth point is this: The converts, five or five thousand, ought to say or at least feel:

> We Christians are the advance guard of our people, of our
> segment of society. We are showing our relatives and neighbors a
> better way of life. The way we are pioneering is good for us who
> have become Christians, and will be very good for you thousands
> who have yet to believe. Please look on us not as traitors in any
> sense. We are better sons, brothers and wives, better tribesmen
> and caste fellows, better members of our labor union, than we ever
> were before. We are showing ways in which, while remaining
> thoroughly of our own segment of society, we all can have a better
> life. Please look on us as the pioneers of our own people entering a
> wonderful Promised Land.

The last principle I stress is this: Constantly *emphasize brotherhood.* In Christ there is no Jew, no Greek, no bond, no free, no Barbarian, no Scythian. We are all one in Christ Jesus. But at the same time let us remember that Paul did not attack all imperfect social institutions. For example, he did not do away with slavery. Paul said to the slave, be a better slave. He said to the slave owner, be a kindlier master.

Paul also said in that famous passage emphasizing unity, "There is no male or female." Nevertheless Christians in their boarding schools and orphanages continue to sleep boys and girls in separate dormitories!! In Christ, there is no sex distinction. Boys and girls are equally precious in God's sight. Men from this tribe, and men from that are equally precious in God's sight. We are all equally sinners equally saved by grace. These things are true; but at the same time there are certain social niceties which Christians at this time may observe.

As we continue to stress brotherhood, let us be sure that the most effective way to achieve brotherhood is to lead ever increasing numbers of men and women from every ethnos, every tribe, every segment of society into an obedient relationship to Christ. As we multiply Christians in every segment of society, the possibility of genuine brotherhood, justice, goodness and righteousness will be enormously increased. Indeed, the best way to get justice, possibly the only way to get justice is to have very large numbers in every segment of society become committed Christians.

As we work for Christward movements in every people, let us not make the mistake of believing that "one-by-one out of the society into the church" is a bad way. One precious soul willing to endure severe ostracism in order to become a follower of Jesus, one precious soul coming all by himself is a way that God has blessed and is blessing to the salvation of mankind. But it is a slow way. And it is a way which frequently seals off the converts' own people from any further hearing of the Gospel.

Sometimes one-by-one is the only possible method. When it is, let us praise God for it, and live with its limitations. Let us urge all those wonderful Christians who come bearing persecution and oppression, to pray for their own dear ones and to work constantly that more of their own people may believe and be saved.

One-by-one is one way that God is blessing to the increase of his Church. The people movement is another way. The great advances of the Church on new ground out of non-Christian religions have *always* come by people movements, never one-by-one. It is equally true that one-by-one-out-of-the-people is a very common beginning way. In the book, *Bridges of God*, which God used to launch the Church Growth Movement, I have used a simile. I say there that missions start out proclaiming Christ on a desert-like plain. There life is hard; the number of Christians remains small. A large missionary presence is required. But, here and there, the missionaries or the converts find ways to break out of that arid plain and proceed up into the verdant mountains. There large numbers of people live; there great churches can be founded; there the Church grows strong; that is people movement land.

I commend that simile to you. Let us accept what God gives. If it is one-by-one, let us accept that and lead those who believe in Jesus to trust in Him completely. But let us always pray that, after that beginning, we may proceed to higher ground, to more verdant pasture, to more fertile lands where great groups of men and women, *all of the same segment of society*, become Christians and thus open the way for Christward movements in each people on earth. Our goal should be Christward movements within each segment. There the dynamics of social cohesion will advance the Gospel and lead multitudes out of darkness into His wonderful life. We are calling people after people from death to life. Let us make sure that we do it by the most effective methods.

Study Questions

1. "Indeed, the best way to get justice, possibly the only way to get justice, is to have very large numbers in every segment of society become committed Christians." Do you agree? Why or why not?

2. Why does McGavran insist that "a cluster of growing churches" rather than "a church" is the proper goal in pioneer church planting?

13

The Evangelization of Animists

Alan R. Tippett

The title given to me seems to imply the existence of a concrete religious system, called *Animism*—something which might be set over against say, Hinduism or Buddhism, not only for purposes of description and study, but also as a subject requiring a strategy for evangelistic approach. Because the greatest number of currently open doors for the Gospel are among animist people, the inclusion of the topic is certainly appropriate in spite of any intellectual problems the title may raise. Therefore to avoid the loss of time in debating semantics in our sessions, the preamble seems desirable.

Animism

Some scholars prefer to subdivide Animism and to deal with the subunits—Shamanism, Fetishism, Ancestor Worship, and so on treating each as a religion in its own right, thus avoiding Animism altogether. This may have some descriptive advantages, until one discovers that the sub-units are not discrete: several may be found interwoven together, and their practitioners may have multi-functional roles. The "religious systems" are thus found to be merely functional distinctions within what certainly looks like a general religious system, with no more diversity than Hinduism or Buddhism; and now we are back again to the notion of Animism.

The term Animism is certainly to be preferred to *Tribal Religion(s)* because Animism is active in great cities like Los Angeles, New Orleans or Sao Paulo, and has many non-tribal aspects. It is preferable also to *Primitive Religion(s)*, as it is neither chronologically nor conceptually primitive; indeed, it is currently much alive, and frequently quite sophisticated. Nevertheless, we should recognize that we are using the word as a term of convenience to provide a frame of reference

An ordained minister of the Methodist Church of Australia, Alan R. Tippett spent over 20 years as a missionary in the Fiji Islands. His *Solomon Islands Christianity* has been acclaimed as a classic by missiologists and anthropologists alike. Perhaps the world's leading authority on animism, Tippett was Professor Emeritus of Anthropology and Oceanic Studies at Fuller Theological Seminary's School of World Mission before his death in 1988 at the age of 77. Taken by permission from *Let the Earth Hear His Voice*, copyright 1975, World Wide Publications Minneapolis, MN.

for our discussions, presupposing that Animism is a discrete enough philosophical "system" among the religious to warrant our consideration of an evangelistic strategy for winning its followers to Christ. This is precisely the same position the members of our other groups will find themselves in, for Hinduism, Islam and Buddhism may also be manifested in a great diversity of systematic forms.

The popular use of the term Animism comes down to us from E. B. Tylor (1871). He did not give it the technical meaning it acquired from the comparative religionists, of a "kind of religion," but used it to signify "the deep-lying doctrine of Spiritual Beings, which embodies the very essence of Spiritualistic as opposed to Materialistic philosophy." It was for him a "minimum definition of religion" which saw the animistic way of life as accepting the reality of spiritual force(s) and beings over against the materialist outlook on life. "In its full development," Taylor agreed, it formulated concrete beliefs in such notions as the soul(s), the future state, controlling deities and subordinate spirits, especially when these beliefs result in "some kind of active worship."

I believe this is a realistic approach, because it permits us to talk about animism and biblical religion in the same philosophical or conceptual structure, and to weigh one over against the other, and therefore to understand the meaning of commitment when a present-day animist comes to his "moment of truth" and makes his decision for Christ. Thus the very term "evangelizing animists" puts us into an identifiable category of communication and response. We are not dealing with secularists or scientific agnostics, whom we would need to approach by means of a different path in order to witness. But Animists and Christians have one thing in common— they accept the spiritual view of life. They do not need to be convinced of the existence of the supernatural. This opens many ways for dialogue; even though, at the same time it exposes us to many problems and dangers, which we shall examine in a moment.

In spite of the wide range of categories, forms, and functions that may be identified in the study of animistic communities, and which compel us to admit that perhaps every animist community is different from every other one, I firmly believe that Animism can be examined as a cohesive thing, and that enough universals can be identified to permit us to discuss the evangelization of this kind of community in general terms. I believe we should be able to deal with tribes in the forests of Africa, in the highlands of New Guinea, or in the hogans on the mesas of New Mexico under this head— and to a large extent also the drug cults of Hollywood. My purpose, therefore, is to generalize as far as I can, and to delineate some common problem areas for discussion, rather than diversify one form of Animism as over against another. But I hope the diversity will be apparent in our discussions.

Whether the evangelist be from an old or a young church, if he is witnessing cross-culturally he will be hoping to leave some kind of an indigenous church behind him. The fellowship group will have to be the Body of Christ ministering the mind, touch and heart of Christ in its cultural and animist world; for evangelism is not merely the winning of individuals, but also their incorporation into relevant local fellowship groups. Therefore, before I enumerate my common problem areas, I must examine the biblical data base from which I operate.

The Biblical Theology of Animism

From the biblical point of view there is really no such thing as a taxonomy of religions for comparative study. Not even Hinduism or Buddhism has any biblical standing as a religion. For the people of God there is only one God, and all those who do not serve him are grouped together in a single category. Although there is sufficient data in the biblical narrative for a whole textbook on Animism, the common practice of classifying religions, with Animism at one end and Christianity at the other, as if in an evolutionary scale of development, is not in tune either with Scripture or with the anthropological data.

Of course, I may turn to the Scriptures and read about the deities with whom the people of God came into contact from time to time on their pilgrimage—of Dagon, of Chemosh, of Molech, of Tammuz, and of Bel. I also learn of their confrontations with fertility cults, of heathen sacrifices and libations of ceremonial inhumanity like infanticide, of making cakes to the Queen of Heaven, and of worshipping the smooth round stones of the valley. We have everything—from individual and domestic ritual acts to national assemblies and the worship of national war gods—rites performed in fields, by the wayside, in groves and high places, and in great temples. We have divination, necromancy, and sorcery, and numerous other ideas covered by the biblical word "idolatry." We could break down the whole animistic system of the biblical word into categories for study, but in the last analysis the Bible disposes of them as a *single category* in the first two commandments (Exod. 20:2-6)—anything that would usurp the Lord's place in the life of his people and set itself in God's place is grouped together as "over against Him" and idolatrous.

Nevertheless, when we consider the world of biblical times—the first two millennia before Christ and the first Christian century afterwards—we find it very similar to that of our own. The people of God stood over against all the forms we meet in Christian mission today, on all the various levels—private individual, domestic, peasant, and national. The characteristics of each of these levels recur through history with the kind of lives people live on those respective levels, and do not fit into a chronological evolutionary scale from the simple to the sophisticated. The Bible deals with both tribal and great religions, with both simple and complex, with both oral and written religious traditions—and it treats them all under one rubric both in the Old and New Testaments (Exod. 20:2-6; Rom. 1:19-25).

In this paper I wish to speak of evangelization in a somewhat wider sense than just bringing individuals to an act of "decision for Christ." It is this, of course—but more. It involves both a step of commitment and an experience of consummation, in which the Spirit witnesses with the convert's spirit that he is now a son of the Father, and if a son, then an heir through Christ (Gal. 4:6-7)—that the blessing of Abraham might come to the Gentiles, or heathen, through Christ, receiving the promise of the Spirit through faith (Gal. 3: 14). This is a process, bringing folk out of heathenism—here defined by Paul as "worshipping not-gods" (Gal. 4:8). The picture we have here of conversion from heathenism is that of a *process*—an *on-going experience*.

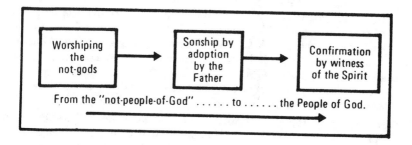

Adoption into the household of God brings the convert into a *group experience*. Some kind of incorporation into the fellowship group is always part of the evangelization process. This comes out clearly in the opening verses of I John, where witness (vv. 1-2) leads up to joining in the fellowship (v. 3), and from that verse on, John is dealing not with an individual in isolation, but one in context, i.e., in a state of fellowship (vv. 6-7).

Now, as we consider the evangelization of animists, it should be remembered that we are not dealing with individuals in isolation, but with men brought from death unto life *within a fellowship group*. We cannot escape the truth, that to give a man the Gospel of personal salvation demands incorporation into a fellowship group as a concomitant. Evangelization implies the existence of, or planting of, a church.

The Evangelization of Animists

The conversion of animists and their incorporation into fellowship groups involves us in each of the following problems, which I have conceptualized anthropologically because I think that such a treatment best opens up the subject for our discussions. I am reminded of the question of Henri Maurier, "Does not every theology have to be accompanied, in counterpoint, by as concrete an anthropology as possible? It is not enough for the apostle to learn what God has said; he also has to understand the men to whom he is bringing the Word."

Pay attention to the problem of encounter

Animists cannot just *drift* into the Christian faith. True, they may attach themselves to the fringe of some congregation as interested spectators, and maybe even become what we sometimes call "sympathizers," and it may well be that by so doing they will fall under the influence of the Spirit of God and be brought to vigorous commitment; but the passage from heathenism to the Christian faith is a definite and clear-cut act, a specific change of life, a "coming out of something" and an "entry into something quite different," a change of loyalty—or in the biblical analogy, a change of citizenship (Eph. 2:12-13).

The notion of making a definite act of commitment to the Lord is a biblical concept in both the Old and New Testaments, and was normally accompanied by some kind of ocular demonstration of the commitment. The book of Joshua ends with such an episode (24:14-15)—"Choose you this day whom you will serve; whether the gods your fathers served in the region beyond the river, or the gods of the Amorites in whose land you dwell; but as for me and my house, we will serve the Lord." Here, there is a definite encounter of religions. There are three options—the ancestral animism, or the current environmental animism of the land, or the Lord God. Then, after the public discussion (for no pressure is brought to bear on them) the decision is made, and Joshua then demands a demonstration of that decision. "Then, *put away* the foreign gods and incline your hearts to the Lord" (v. 23). A covenant is made at Shechem, and a stone is set up as a *witness* to the act of commitment (vv. 26-27).

Was it not the same in the days of New Testament Ephesus? The people movement among the workers of magic led to the public burning of their magical literature—and so large a bonfire it was that the value of the books burned was recorded as 50,000 pieces of silver (Acts 19:18-19). Be it noted that this demonstration was both an *act of commitment* and an *act of rejection*, a spiritual encounter. Indeed, the anthropologist, Van Gennep, would have called it a *rite of separation* , because it marked a precise cutoff from an old life and status, before entering into a new one. Was it not to these same Ephesians that Paul so articulated it? Put off the old man (4:22), and put on the new man (4:24)—"put off" and "put on," as one changing clothes.

The biblical evidence of this demand for commitment to Christ in some form of dramatic encounter shows the convert(s) demonstrating that the old way no longer has power over him (them), and henceforth he is "God's man" (the collective, "people of God"). Thus Paul, seeking to encourage the young man Timothy, addresses him, "O man of God," committed now to fight the good fight of faith, and to strive for Christian perfection (I Tim. 6:11; II Tim. 3: 17).

In the animist world today the public demonstration, or *rite of separation*, varies with the cultural climate—fetish-burning, burial of ancestral skulls, casting the sacred paraphernalia into the sea or river, eating the forbidden totem fish or animal, according to the pattern of their animism. These are cultural equivalents of Joshua setting up the stone of witness, and the Ephesian magicians burning their books. This is symbolism, but more than symbolism. Psychologically, men are strengthened to keep their covenant by having made a public confession and having done it as a *company of converts*. "Let the redeemed of the Lord say so!" said the Psalmist (107:2).

The symbolic rejection of the old way not only involves a religious encounter, but thereafter it serves as a continual reminder of the act of rejection that alone can save the convert from syncretism or polytheism. It was just at this point that Paul had trouble with the Corinthian Christians, who found it easier to incorporate Christ into their heathen pantheon, than reject that pantheon for Christ. "No way!" says Paul, "Ye cannot drink the cup of the Lord and the cup of devils" (I Cor. 10:21). And it is precisely at this same point that the modern mission among animists is really Christian or just another kind of Animism.

Pay attention to the problem of motivation

Animists may be interested in Christianity for many and varied reasons—some good, others bad. Many factors may bring a field to ripen unto harvest. Of course, we are interested in all inquirers, but problems are bound to arise if the evangelist accepts all such inquiry at its face value without really evaluating the basic motivation; which may be for as materialistic a reason, for example, as the fact that the power of western armies and navies in war surely makes the religion of these powerful foreigners better to have on your side than against you.

Many supposed converts misunderstand both Christianity itself and the salvation it proclaims. They misunderstand their own needs also. The book of Acts (Ch. 8) supplies us with a good example of the problem. On the surface, the conversion of Simon, the sorcerer, at Samaria was quite genuine when he came to Philip (vv. 9-13) and believed. However, shortly afterwards, when confronted with Peter's ministry and the gift of the Spirit, it is immediately apparent that Simon had a complete misunderstanding of the nature of the Gospel due to his wrong motivation: he thought he could buy the gift of God with money (vv. 18-24).

Animists sometimes respond because the Christian mission offers a ministry of healing which seems to be more effective than that of their own shamans and medicine-men. Animist chiefs have even invited missionaries to live in their midst in order to have a trade store in their community—this meaning a regular supply of steel knives, fishhooks, nails and axe-heads, all of which are not only utilitarian, but are also symbols of wealth and status for both this chief among other chiefs, and this tribe among other tribes.

The motivation for accepting Christianity naturally affects their view of Christianity, the character of the Gospel, the nature of their Christian ethics, and their concept of Christian responsibility.

Let me give you an example of the problem as I met it repeatedly in Papua, New Guinea. One of the real problems there is that of the Cargo Cult. It even occurs where there have been prolonged pre-baptismal training programs. Indeed, perhaps the unduly long period of training has itself made baptism appear as a goal rather than an entry into an experience of nurture and growth. It gives the impression that converts "have arrived," as it were. They came enthusiastically in the first place, but now they want to "back out" in syncretistic cults which deny much that they have been taught. I met a young New Guinean who put it this way to me, "A few years ago I became a Christian because I wanted to achieve the white man's status and wealth. I wanted a good job, with a good wage and a house like the white men have. I worked hard in mission educational institutions, and I was baptized. But now it is all empty and worth nothing." The young man was thoroughly disillusioned with Christianity because his motivation had been wrong in the first place. His spiritual advisers had not detected this. They had interpreted his industry as a behavior-change due to conversion, and now he is a potential trouble-maker.

I also picked up a report from a missionary who had shared his all with a New Guinea colleague—a national pastor—whom he trusted implicitly. After many years, the pastor, recognizing this missionary's openness, asked, "Now we have shared everything, won't you tell me the secrets Jesus gave you?" The missionary was staggered to discover that even his pastoral colleague had what they call "the cargo mentality," which must have been there in his mind from the very motivation of his first attraction to Christianity. One major cause of Cargo Cults is the wrong expectation converts have had of Christianity.

I do not want to give the impression that all conversions from Animism are like this—that would not be true. There are thousands and thousands of wonderful warm-hearted Christians who really know Jesus as Lord. But, nevertheless, it remains quite true that we have never really faced up to the problem of motivation when the convert first comes for instruction. We ought to be asking the question—what is the role of the pastoral counselor when the would-be convert first moves forward to respond to the Gospel?

Pay attention to the problem of meaning

Paul and Barnabas cured the cripple at Lystra in the name of the Gospel after proclaiming the Word, thinking, thereby, that the name of God would be praised. The people took the incident to mean that the two evangelists were the Greek gods, Mercury and Jupiter, anthropomorphized; and they brought forth their approved religious paraphernalia and the sacrifice, to worship them—the very last thing Paul and Barnabas wanted (Acts 14:8-13)—and, indeed, the people could hardly be restrained from this intention (v. 18). Here we are confronted with the problem of meaning. The proclamation, no doubt, was faithfully given, but alas, quite misunderstood.

Anthropology has a number of suggestions to offer the evangelist in this area of communication—at least to indicate why this kind of thing can happen. Let me enumerate a few, for purposes of discussion.

The biblical case I have just cited represented a confusion which arose from the *world view of the listeners*. Seeing the miracle, which was beyond the normal powers of science as they knew it, and, therefore, had to be due to supernatural factors, they interpreted it in terms of their own mythology. Every cross-cultural missionary runs into this problem sooner or later. It is the problem of translation and of Scripture interpretation. Every word selected—the word for God, for the Spirit, for the Son of God, for sin, for love, for prayer, for forgive comes from a non-biblical world view, and is a potential for misunderstood meaning. If it is a problem for the evangelist who speaks in the language of his listeners it is doubly so for the evangelist who does not learn the language, but uses a third party to come between him and his audience.

The meaning of the message can be distorted also by *the image of the evangelist* in the eyes of his audience. It was for this reason that western missionaries to China before the Communist days, were often heard as imperialists and capitalists, even though they did not think of themselves in that way. As one scholar put it, they became essential to the Revolution, so that Christianity could be rejected. I know the documents of one place where missionaries worked for sixteen years without a convert, living devout, industrious lives, and by their very industry giving the impression that salvation was merely a Gospel of hard work and trade—the very last thing they desired to do.

Then again the *evangelist's conceptualization of his message* can condition the meaning ascribed to it. Is he proclaiming a faith prophetically, or teaching philosophically? Does the teaching of Scripture come through in a foreign or denominational garment? Is it presented as a moral, legal code, or oriented to the joy of the Lord and the glory of God? Is it directed to the problems of the evangelist, or to the felt needs of the listeners? The animists have come from a world of power encounter and presumably they, therefore, need a God who speaks and demonstrates with power. The preaching of a purely ethical Gospel is hardly likely to inspire such a people; but a life transformed by a God of power will lead to a new ethic. Why do the charismatic figures of so many nativistic movements retain the use of the Bible in their cultic practices? Several prophets have spoken on the point. Recognizing the power of the Word, they have pointed that the missionaries of each denomination interpret the Word in their own way, and asked, "Why cannot we do it in our way?" And this they then do—in terms of their mythology.

Thus there are three points where the message of the Word may be blurred in communication: (i) *at the "advocate end"* (evangelist), (ii) *at the "accepter end"* (convert), and (iii) *in the message itself* (the theological emphasis of the evangelist). We can no longer run the risk of sending out missionaries (westerners or nationals) without some cross-cultural training, and, of course, it follows also that they should be competent interpreters of the Word.

Pay attention to the problem of social structure

At first thought we may wonder what social structure has to do with evangelization. This is because many of us are individualists, and we assume that everyone should do things the way we do. But the peoples of the world do not have identical social behavior patterns, and this creates problems when evangelization is cross-cultural. The people to whom the evangelist goes may organize their daily life very differently from him, and he should remember that the process of evangelization should lead to the formation of fellowship groups, and that these should be indigenous and not foreign in structure. At least, the evangelist ought to be aware of social structure, and reckon on the Holy Spirit being able to use ways of life different from his own. Let me cite two examples of the importance of social structure for evangelization.

Most animist societies are communally orientated: i.e., they tend to operate in homogeneous groups. These groups, of course, do not ignore the individual; but he is always an individual within a group context. Groups are multi-individual. Discussions of important issues for decision go on and on until a *consensus* is reached. This may take a long time, but it eliminates the problem created by "majority decision" which denies some of the rights of the minority that is outvoted. These communal societies have a high degree of social responsibility, and often the individualistic foreign evangelist has trouble with group decision making. Groups exist at different levels of social organization, and authority for decisions may lie at different levels—e.g., decision-making in domestic affairs, agriculture, religion, politics, and war may be the responsibility of household, extended-family, village, or clan. It is important for the evangelist to identify these because the manifest behavior of the multi-individual group in turning from heathenism to Christ will have the appearance of *group movements*—

households, villages, age-grades, extended families or clans, according to their normal social organization. Unless it is so, it will not be meaningful to the people.

There is nothing strange or unbiblical about this. The apostles found that the rural villages and townships of Palestine often "turned to the Lord" as whole communities, like Sharon and Lydda (Acts 9:35), whereas, in other cases, like that of the centurion at Philippi (Acts 16:30-34) and Crispus, the chief of the synagogue at Corinth (Acts 18:8), the groups became Christian as households. They were acting within the regular operative social mechanisms of daily life.

In the same way those who respond in these group movements have to be formed into fellowship groups or churches; and the operating character of these should either reflect or, at least, be compatible with their familiar structures. This applies especially to any leadership patterns introduced. For example, a common blunder in church-planting across cultures has been to appoint a young Christian leader (on the grounds that he can read and has had some education) over a new Christian community in a gerontocratic society, normally led by a council of elders, where the basic values are maturity, experience, and gray hairs. In this way the evangelization of these people brings an unfortunate and unnecessary bone of contention.

These two illustrations, at the levels of decision-making and leadership, will serve to make the point that effective evangelization requires a church indigenous from the beginning; and the more foreign organizational structures imposed on a church-planting situation the more problems will be created for the subsequent generation which has to find the passage "from mission to church," which can be a painful experience.

Pay attention to the problem of incorporation

One of the tests of valid biblical evangelism is the provision of a way for incorporating converts into the fellowship of believers. The Bible demonstrates this in several ways. First, there are passages, like the introduction of John's first letter, wherein, the notion of *witness* (vv. 1-2) is associated with that of fellowship (v. 3); and the Great Commission itself which does not end with "Go and make disciples," but continues "baptize and teach." For the purpose of study, we take these texts separately, but in reality they are wholes. The analysis must be adjusted by synthesis, or our evangelization is only partial.

Second, the notion of the fellowship is crucial in biblical argument. True, we can speak of evangelism as bringing individual men face to face with Christ, but we cannot leave it there, because the New Testament did not leave it there. Christ is, of course, the Ultimate, and in that sense we need no more than to be with him. But for this present point of time in which he has been born, the convert has to be incorporated into some precise fellowship group, the Church, which is Christ's Body. In the records of the early Church (Acts) and the letters which tell us so much of its inner life, the configuration which holds it all together structurally is the church—be it theologically the Church Universal, or practically the local church. Remove that concept from the New Testament and look for a disembodied collection of isolated people who had met Christ, and you will soon be disillusioned. Christian activity and theology are always spoken of in collective figures—Christians are "fellow citizens," "members of the household of God," a "priesthood," a "nation," a "flock," a "fellowship," the "members of the Body," or "the church which is at..."

Fellowship-forming or church-planting is thus part of evangelization. Right at the beginning of Acts (1:13-14), we have a fellowship group in prayer, and immediately a worshipping, witnessing, growing body (Acts 2:46-47), meeting for instruction, fellowship, breaking of bread and prayer (v.24). Thus is the Church his Body, fulfilling his ministry in this world in this day, and if evangelization does not mean that, it is defective.

To pass from this biblical base to the situation in the animist world, where men are being won to Christ in communities completely different in both social life and values perhaps from that to which the evangelist belongs, the latter has to consider what a convert from animism needs to find in the fellowship group into which he is incorporated. How does he get his new experience of Christian *belonging*, so that he becomes a participating, worshipping, witnessing, and serving member of the Body of Christ *in his own kind of world*? I hope for a profitable discussion of this issue, not only to provide us with some worthwhile directions for ministry in such situations, but also to help cross-cultural evangelists at large to appreciate a problem which many of them have never thought about at all.

Pay attention to the problem of the cultural void

Over the last ten years I have been able to visit a great many young churches whose members have come to Christ out of animist backgrounds. Apart from their wide range of cultural differences, there are also manifest spiritual differences. Some of them, though quite strange to me culturally and linguistically, have nevertheless been obviously vibrant with life, creative in their worship, using their own indigenous forms of music and art with enthusiasm, and performing significant service ministries in the animist world about them. On the other hand, others have been the very opposite. They have tried to worship according to patterns more familiar in the West, and sing hymns in Western music and to have many quite obvious accouterments of European denominationalism. These churches have been misfits in their own worlds. They limp along as if almost ready to die; as if trying to be what they really are not. In some cases they are even led entirely by a foreigner, and there is little, if any, congregational participation; and financially their work is possible only with the aid of foreign funds. If they have a national pastor, he is a little replica of the foreign missionary. How is this church ever going to see itself as the Body of Christ, ministering the mind and heart and Word of Christ to the animist world outside? In a hundred years of history it has no more than a hundred members, and is currently static. The truth remains that the Christian programs of evangelization used over the last century of Christian missions produced these two kinds of churches. And I believe that in each case their characters were, more often than not, formed in the early periods when the first fellowship groups were being formulated. I believe that the majority (I did not say all) of our second generation problems have their roots in faulty follow-up of the original religious awakenings. In church growth parlance we say, "The people movement has to be effectively consummated."

One of the problems of following up a great movement of the Spirit of God in bringing many persons to Christ, is not just to incorporate them into a Christian group, but to be sure that it is an indigenously structured and meaningful group, in which they can participate in their own way. Thus, for example, a New Guinea convert should not have to become American or Australian to be a Christian: linguistically and culturally he should be a *New Guinea* Christian. Likewise the fellowship group should be New Guinean. The members' participation, praying, worship, and service ministry should be New Guinean. A gifted New Guinean animist musician, on becoming Christian, should be a *New Guinean* Christian musician—and so on.

If we get into this kind of a situation where evangelists dispose of all cultural values and creative arts on the presupposition that they are all incompatible with Christianity because they have been used previously for heathen purposes (as many evangelists do argue), we find ourselves with creative people who can no longer create, and would-be participators who become non-participant, and before long the cultural voids we have created begin to be felt. Cargo Cults are only partly due to foreign domination; they are also due to cultural voids. Those who believe they are called to evangelism should remember that evangelization does not take place in a vacuum.

The problem of *maintenance* (as the anthropologist, F. E. Williams called the preservation of traditional techniques and values in a situation of changing culture), of course, involves a value judgment—can this or that element be preserved and be made truly Christian? Or will its maintenance involve the church in syncretism? The New Testament warns us that we are bound to meet this problem and that it must be faced squarely. This is why I began this statement with "The Problem of Encounter." But, even so, when the basic commitment to Christ has been effectively faced, there will yet remain an indigenous way of life which is also worth winning for Christ. It should be possible for a tribal man from, say, Africa or New Guinea, to be a Christian without having to reject his tribe. It must be so or we could hardly hope for the "great multitude which no man can number of all nations, and kindreds, and peoples and tongues (standing) before the throne and before the Lamb" in that day.

I asked a tribal man whose people had come into Christianity from animism, but whose Christian life was largely innocuous and foreign, making little impact on its surrounding world, "What happened to your tribal skills?" He told me sadly that they had "melted away" and that life was empty because of it. He was feeling the cultural void. Something within him was crying out to be creative. He had discovered another Christian church in his country which utilized the indigenous arts and crafts to the glory of God, and he felt his own tribe had been robbed of something precious. A basic question recurs: What does it mean to a Christian convert from animism to be a Christian in an animist world, and to be a participating member in a fellowship group of converted animists? This applies to more than arts and crafts. How does the converted animist meet the physical and spiritual needs that spring from the tribal way of life—problems of danger, of death, of sickness, or sorcery—and how does one discover the will of God for him?

D—118 THE EVANGELIZATION OF ANIMISTS

Evangelization does not end with an offer of the Gospel, or with the conversion of an individual, but with the coming into being of an ongoing fellowship, which is the Body of Christ in that kind of world.

Study Questions

1. Suppose you were to visit a first-generation group of believers from an animistic background in Irian Jaya. You can sense that their expression of Christianity as a fellowship is not very authentic. How would you determine whether they are experiencing one of the six problems Tippett describes in the "Christianization" of animistic people?

2. Explain the "Cargo Cult" mentality.

14

Christian Witness to Hindus

The Lausanne Committee for World Evangelization

HISTORICAL SKETCH AND CONTEMPORARY SITUATION

The Hindu Population

The Aryans from Central Asia entered India in the 3rd century B.C. and set-tled on the banks of the river Indus. Their search for God resulted in the writing of the Vedas. Based on the Vedic scriptures, the Aryan religion was born, which evolved into Hinduism. It absorbed everything, covering tribals and Dravidians. Hinduism dominated and built a strong sense of community in the Indian society, stratifying it into different castes. Wherever the Indian was taken, either to serve in plantations or in the British army, Hinduism followed, spreading far and wide.

Generally speaking, a Hindu is born, not made. Except for recent trends of conversion to Hinduism, by and large the growth of Hinduism has been biological. The world population is said to be 4.3 billion*[Ed. Note: now well over 5 billion]*, of which Hindus make up over 565 million or 13 per cent of the total population. Of that number, 527 million live in India and 38 million have moved to places such as the Middle East, United Kingdom, the United States, South Africa, East Africa, Malaysia, Fiji, Singapore, and Sri Lanka. In India, 83 per cent of the total population are Hindus (527 million), whereas the Christian popula-tion in India is only 2.9 per cent (19 million).

The Hindu Religion

There is no one definition which explains Hinduism in its entirety. In fact, it is a conglomeration of ideas, beliefs, convictions, and practices—varying from people to people and from region to region. For example, Aryan Hinduism of North India is radically different at many points from Dravidian Hinduism of South India. However, Hinduism can be understood in the following ways:

Philosophic Hinduism

This form of Hinduism is dominated by the authority of the Vedas and Upan-ishads (scriptures). Concerning the understanding of the Ultimate Reality, there are three popular schools of thought:

Taken from "Christian Witness to Hindu People," *Lausanne Occasional Paper #14.* Lausanne Committee for World Evangelization, 1980.

Advaita— non-dualism
Dvaita— dualism
Visishtadvaita— modified dualism

They teach from the ancient Vedas that there is a spark of divinity in man, and hence to call a man a sinner is blasphemous; there is, then, no need for a savior.

Religious Hinduism

Adherents to this type believe in the Puranas (epics) and in the Mahabharatha, Ramayana, and Bhagavadgita, saying these epics are revelations from God. There is a strong belief in avatars (incarnations of gods). Their theology is syncretistic. Man is at liberty to choose his own god from among a pantheon of 33 *crores* (330 million), and to worship any number of gods. Salvation may be attained in one of three ways:—

Gnanamarga— (way of knowledge)
Bhaktimarga— (way of devotion)
Karmamarga— (way of good deeds)

Popular Hinduism

This form of Hinduism is far removed from philosophy and Brahmanism. The followers of this form are influenced by ancestral tradition, animal worship, temple cults, magic, exorcism, etc. They are indifferent to the authority of the Vedas and are concerned only about a god who protects them, blesses them, and makes them prosperous. The majority of Hindus adhere to this form.

Mystic Hinduism

Gurus with mysterious personal experiences are drawing many to themselves. The claims of these gurus are sensational, often asserting that they are avatars and that they have supernatural gifts of healing, ability to perform miracles, to read the inner thoughts of people, and to prophesy the future. Prominent among the gurus who have a mass following are Satya Sai Baba, Bal Yogeshwar, and Acharya Rajnesh. The Transcendental Meditation of Mahesh Yogi has drawn many disciples from India and other countries.

Tribal Hinduism

This type is very much influenced by animism, spiritism, the occult, necromancy, and animal worship. The fear of the unknown exercises its instinctive dread over followers' minds.

Secular Hinduism

Those who belong to this group are generally nominal in their beliefs and indifferent to religious practices. Even the few religious customs that they follow are motivated by materialistic tendencies.

Modern trends in Hinduism

Although the Christian faith is claimed to have been brought to India in the first century A.D. by the Apostle Thomas, resulting in the formation of a Christian church, it remained introverted and did not spread. In the 16th century,

Catholic missionaries, such as Francis Xavier and Robert de Nobili, brought the gospel to the Hindus. After them came the Protestants in a floodstream, with various mission societies establishing churches, as people movements spread mostly into the lower category of Hindu community. The emphasis on higher education by Alexander Duff and succeeding missionaries led to a Hindu renaissance giving birth to Hindu Reform Movements such as Brahma Samaj, Arya Samaj, and Prarthana Samej. The formation of Hindu Missionary Movements, such as the Rama Krishna Mission, followed.

A concept of mission is not one of the main tenets of Hinduism. But Hindu theologians, such as Vivekananda and Aurobindo, by their interpretation of the main teaching of Hinduism, have added this new missionary dimension. The missionary vision of some Hindus is posing a threat to Christian evangelistic activities. We now hear of cases of nominal Christians, as well as Hindu converts to Christianity, reverting to Hinduism. Further, western converts to Hinduism are being sent as Hindu missionaries to some parts of the world. The Hare Krishna Movement has a notable impact in many Western countries. This movement has a big appeal to young people. In some Western countries it has established centers for the propagation of this movement.

In conclusion, modern trends in Hinduism find expression in the Harijan Movement [Harijans, often called "untouchables," were called "children of God" by Mahatma Gandhi] initiated and propagated by Mahatma Gandhi, in the missionary movement designed by Vivekananda, in a secular socialist ideology advocated by Jawaharlal Nehru, and in the militant communal sectarian groups such as Rashtriya Swayam Sevak (RSS).

The post-independence Indian society has developed into a secular democracy. The agnostic leadership emphasized industrialization, resulting in rapid secularization, modernization and westernization. The urban population developed popular nominal Hinduism which leaves it open to new influences. The rural Hindu, oppressed by poverty and corruption, seeks a liberating gospel. The unrest caused by several philosophies and a weak political structure has softened the Hindus within India for the gospel, even though the above varieties of Hinduism continue to prevail. Overseas Hindus are in a very unsettled, fluid state. In some countries of the world they are undergoing a period of great strain and change, which may influence their receptivity to the gospel.

BIBLICAL FRAMEWORK FOR HINDU EVANGELIZATION

Jesus Christ, the Son of God, became flesh within an Asian context. During the days of His flesh, He lived within a Hebraic cultural framework within this Asian context. He was poor. He walked among the villages and wept over the cities. He accepted social rejects and understood the fluctuating fortunes of leadership within a tangible human society. The Hindu can understand him.

Before such an understanding can be effected, however, Jesus Christ must be made known to the Hindu. In this effort to communicate Jesus Christ to the Hindu, the Indian Christian faces the tension between being faithful to the content of the Bible and relating this content to the theological, philosophical, and religious context of the Hindu.

The resolution of this problem does not lie in interfering with the content of biblical truth, but in the proper use of the crucible of Hindu categories and needs in the process of communicating that truth.

This is not the first time for such an effort to be attempted because, as early as the 19th century A.D., many Christian congregations existed in South India within a culturally Hindu environment. Jesus Christ, the Son of God, is relevant and relates to all human cultures. He can be made known to a Hindu in a traditionally Hindu culture in India, likewise to Hindus living outside of India.

Theological Perspective

The gospel is never proclaimed within a vacuum. India provides a particular context which influences the kind of communication we should pursue. Thus we need to examine the Indian context in the light of the scriptures and see which aspects warrant our careful consideration in Christian communication. The following are some crucial factors which will influence Hindu evangelism:

Spirituality

Hindus are a very religious people. An aura of holiness characterizes every man who claims to be spiritual. They identify externals to be reflective of holiness. The Bible calls us to live a holy life (I Peter 1:16; Rom. 12:1, 2) and to keep our behavior excellent among unbelievers so that they may glorify God (I Peter 2:12; Matt. 5:16). The power of God through a transformed holy life will be a powerful influence on the Hindu.

Community

Human dignity stems from man being made in the image of God (Gen. 1:26, 27) and is reinforced by Christ's death for all (I John 2:2). Christians are a human community. However, their equality before God is not affirmed within Indian society. Although people like to become Christians without crossing cultural boundaries, we believe that scripture demands spiritual unity of all believers. It is here that the functioning of the community of Jesus Christ in biblically relevant ways can be a formidable witness to the dignity that is restored in Christ. When true community is practised within the church it will prove to the world (John 13:35) our discipleship. Further, when the church participates in the lives of people through genuine love, our verbal messages will be validated (James 2:4, 26).

Poverty

Perhaps the starkest reality of populous India is her poverty. While we will do everything humanly possible to rectify this situation, in God's eyes a man's worth is not determined by poverty—because he is made in the image of God. Christ not only identified with the poor; He was poor (2 Cor. 8:9; Phil. 2:7). Elsewhere, it is seen that God has a special heart for the poor (Prov. 14:31). This message has special relevance to the Hindu within the Indian context.

Theological Blocks

Four particular theological barriers to effective communication with Hindus should be highlighted:

Hindus in general are syncretistic

They believe that all religions lead to God, implying thereby that there is therefore no need to change from one religion to another. Indeed, Hindus find the very mention of change of religion by the Christian highly objectionable. Such demands must be presented with clarity and respect.

The concept of sin

The Hindu understanding of the concept of sin varies from group to group and even from individual to individual (e.g., to some, sin is just committing bad deeds; to others, it is disobedience to one's conscience; to still others, it is mere selfishness; and to some, sin is just non-existent. Vivekananda said, "It is sin to call anyone a sinner.").

The doctrine of Karma

You reap what you sow. Behavior in the past determines fate in the present, and deeds in the present determine the future. The cycles of rebirths keep recurring till finally "moksha" (salvation) is attained. However, just as karma is a block, it is also a bridge.

The doctrine of Salvation

This highlights the difficulty of terminology. Although the concept of salvation exists within Hinduism, its understanding as liberation from the cycle of rebirth is radically different from the Christian viewpoint.

Theological Bridges: Introduction

We must recognize that Hinduism revolves around a different center than does Christianity, asking fundamentally different questions and supplying different answers. The use of any theological bridge, therefore, is fraught with difficulty, particularly if we attempt to use a specific term or concept to demonstrate that Christ is the fulfillment or crown of Hinduism.

No concept of Hinduism can be accepted into Christianity without change. By way of illustration, the following bridges can be grouped into two categories:

Points of Contact

Those concepts which require radical change of content:

The concept of God. In evangelism among Hindus we are speaking into a pantheistic world view, and although clarification and re-definition are required, it is not necessary to defend the existence of God.

Respect for Scripture. The Hindu respect for the sacred writings can be developed in the context of the unique authority of the Bible. Unlike any other religious community, Hindus will listen attentively to an exposition of Scripture. The sole authority of the Bible must be stressed without any compromise whatsoever.

The person of Christ. The quality of Christ's relationship with people, his teachings (particularly the Sermon on the Mount), and his unique vicarious self-giving and suffering have a strong appeal to the Hindu. As the Christian communicator fills this respect for Christ with an understanding of the unique and absolute claim to be "the Word made flesh," a significant bridge may be built.

The doctrine of karma. While this doctrine is a barrier in terms of defining moksha (salvation), it also can serve as a bridge while communicating the gospel to the Hindu. The Hindu seeks to get free from the cycle of rebirth which his sin causes. He must be told of the Savior Jesus Christ, who by his vicarious suffering and death on the cross triumphed over sin, and has taken upon himself the penalty of the sins of mankind.

Points of Caution and Clarification

Concepts which require a radical conceptual redefinition:

Christianity and Hinduism differ radically in their understanding of history. We should use this dissimilarity as a bridge, stressing the purposes of God in time, creation, the historical resurrection, and the coming judgment.

Hindu spirituality. There is a deep desire in the Hindu for spiritual experience (anubhava). This is noticeable, for example, among the Bhakti Margis. The emphasis on meditation, austerity, and the willingness to accept physical suffering are commendable aspects of the Hindu way of life. At the same time, however, the Christian communicator must stress the degree of personal freedom that comes in Christian worship, and the Christian understanding that spirituality is not an end in itself, nor is it merely by spiritual exercises that one inherits the Kingdom. Essentially, the value of this bridge lies in the importance of the spiritual qualities of the evangelist or communicator of the gospel in gaining credibility.

Incarnation. Hindu beliefs in the intervention of God in human history through avatars must be radically redefined in Christian communication. Avatars enter the world to destroy sinners, and this requires repeated avatars. The incarnation of Christ is unique, historical, sufficient for all time, and is rooted in the love of God, saving sinners.

HINDRANCES TO EVANGELIZATION OF HINDUS

Socio-Cultural Issues

Western culture has been injected into Indian culture as an acceptable form of Christianity; thus, it appears to non-Christians, this alienates them to a large extent. The following are some of the issues that have alienated Hindus and proved a hindrance to evangelism:

1. Food habits among Christians which are totally contrary to Hindu religious sentiments—i.e., beef eating.

2. The Christian way of worship which is predominantly non-Indian.

3. Excessive social mingling of boys and girls in Christian families and in religious activities.

4. The practice of Christians in forbidding the use of vermillion [a red spot on the forehead].

5. Christianity appears as a foreign religion—i.e., western.

6. Christianity is seen as a threat to Indian culture and identity, because of the prevailing thought that "Indian" means "Hindu."

7. The wrong notion that Christians are not patriotic.

8. The wrong notion that only "untouchables" (Harijans) embrace Christianity.

9. The fact that caste is the Hindu's strongest forte of social security. Conversion to Christianity destroys this, leading to: excommunication from the community, damage to family reputation, termination of marital prospects, and physical assault and persecution.

10. *Superstition:* Many Hindus live under the constant fear of invoking the wrath of the Kula Devata (family god), if they accept the gods of other religions.

Economic Issues

1. The fear of loss of property upon conversion to Christianity.

2. Loss of privileges and position in society, because of the non-recognition of caste distinction in the Christian faith.

3. The misunderstanding that Christians are a middle-class people. Hence low-caste people hesitate to mingle with Christians even socially.

4. The wrong understanding that the Indian church is quite rich, supported by the influx of foreign money. This notion is partly due to the huge, widely publicized gospel crusades conducted by foreign evangelists in Indian cities.

5. The loss of economic privileges—e.g., withdrawal of financial aid by the government to Harijan students converted to Christianity.

Methodological Issues

1. We should enunciate theology in Indian categories so that the Hindu can understand the gospel.

2. We must develop a truly Christian world view consistent with the Indian context.

3. While presenting the gospel, we must be aware of the fact that the Hindu understands the doctrine of God, man, sin, and salvation in a way entirely different from the biblical doctrine.

4. We need to review our communications approaches. In our presentation of the gospel we must:

   (a) Speak to the context of the listener.

   (b) Be deeply involved in the life of the listener.

   (c) Grapple openly with the problems, questions, and needs of our listener.

   (d) Present our message in such a way that it answers those problems, questions and needs.

   (e) Speak in such a way that we demonstrate love and a deep respect for the listener, and his questions. There is no room in our evangelism for a condescending attitude.

(f) Recognize that the response of a person to the gospel has both intellectual and emotional elements. Much gospel communication in the past has emphasized a rational response and has failed to appeal to the heart. This statement must not be interpreted as an endorsement of emotional gospel appeals, but a recommendation that our message must speak to the whole person, mind and heart.

(g) Recognize the fact that our listener lives in a particular social context. The response of an individual is undoubtedly affected by the attitudes of those around him. As we become aware of the specific social environment in which we communicate, principles of evangelism will emerge. Our concern must go beyond the individual response to understand the broader questions related to the acceptance of Christ by the entire society.

(h) Communicate the gospel through indigenous methods such as bhajans, drama, dialogue, discourse, Indian music, festival processions, etc.

(i) Be loving and compassionate, and adopt a life-style that is contextualized and communicative.

(j) Recognize what Hindus consider essential qualities in a spiritual leader (guru) that authenticate a person to be: willing to wait, willing to mortify his body and desires, willing to suffer pain, and willing to fast. Christian leaders with this type of spiritual qualification are a powerful means of communication.

CONCLUSION

The Hindu Quest

The Hindu quest for peace (shanti) and bliss is so overwhelming that he is willing to exert extreme effort in a relentless search to find this. Christ, as the author and giver of peace, with the promise of heavenly bliss, provides ample incentive for the Hindu to look into the Christian gospel of peace with God.

Love Dynamic

Principles of love, to become meaningful, must be personalized within a given context. The incarnation is the model for this (John 3:16). The communicator to the Hindu must first feel and know and respond to this intense love of God for the Hindu. The love of God for the Hindu provides the reason for the relentless search to understand the Hindu and identify with him. The communicator's love for Jesus Christ is the rationale for continued obedience to love, even when it seems unreasonable to do so. You cannot question the intentions behind the demands of Calvary love (John 15:14).

The reaching of the Hindu is one of the greatest challenges to the people of God in this generation. To this end we call for:

1. Personal and corporate intercession for the evangelization of Hindu people groups all over the world.

2. Personal and corporate sacrificial giving to support this evangelization.

3. The acceptance of Christ's call to personal involvement at every opportunity for such evangelism.

4. The mobilization of the loving concern, intercession, and financial resources from the worldwide body of Christ.

Closing Concern

We have waited on the Lord and have used the best insights among us to produce the preceding statements. They are not in any way exhaustive nor adequate, but they do seek to alert the earnest Christian, seeking to reach unreached Hindu people groups, concerning some points of contact and concern.

Having said that, we know that reaching any "people group" for Christ cannot be merely academic; and we cannot, and must not, place our total confidence in correct words and statements, but upon the living Lord who seeks all Hindus. We must be aware that the Holy Spirit who has gone before us, is alongside us and guides us, and alone can reveal Jesus Christ (I Cor. 12:3). Without Him we cannot succeed (John 15:5).

Study Questions

1. Which characteristics of Hinduism are bridges and which are barriers to communication of the gospel?

2. How must incarnation be "redefined" if Christians are to bear witness to the Incarnation of Jesus among Hindu peoples?

15
Strategy for India

Ezra Sargunam

Several forces at work in India today need to be counteracted with the gospel message. From one angle, if we look at them, they might appear as great barriers to the Gospel, but if we approach them from another angle, the same stumbling blocks can be turned into stepping stones.

Stumbling Blocks or Stepping Stones

People's capacity for religion

Indians at large have a great capacity for belief and religion. They are prepared to believe anything and everything. This is where, perhaps, the great danger lies and this is where a non-Christian begins. Christ has already been accepted in India as one of the gods. While this is not what we want to happen, it is how sometimes the "leavening" takes place.

It is a real danger that we will not recognize the inherent values God has already placed in their hearts—a capacity to believe things. It is also equally dangerous to recognize these values in paganism to the extent of minimizing the uniqueness of Christ and Christianity and thus falling into syncretism or relativism.

After a Hindu has already given a place for Christ, it is our duty to continue to persuade the man to accept Christ as the Lord, the only Avatar, and the only Saviour of mankind.

Secularism

There is no real danger with secularism in India. As a matter of fact, it is nothing but a great surprise and the providence of God that India is today a secular and democratic country. This secularism can very well be traced in large part to Christian teaching. This being the case, the Christian in India doesn't reject secu-

Ezra Sargunam is President and Bishop-elect for the Evangelical Church of India, with 700 churches and a community of 250,000. Sargunam has been a participant or speaker at Lausane, Amsterdam '83 and '86. He has written a number of articles, including "Multiplying Churches in India," "Strategy for India," From *Multiplying Modern Churches in India*, 1974. Used with permission.

larism as something entirely ungodly but helps formulate a theology out of it.

The duty of the Christian is to baptize every system into Christ "according to God's good pleasure which He hath purposed in Himself; that in the fullness of time He might gather in one all things in Christ, both which are in heaven, and which are on earth" (Eph. 1:9-10). The fullness of time for India has come and secularism, which helps to break away traditional beliefs, is one sign of it. Secularism is not a march backward but forward. Christ is a symbol of progress and he is already in it with his presence.

The caste

Is caste a stumbling block or a stepping stone? Can caste be used for the propagation of the Gospel?

There is a good side and a bad side to caste. It is the prime duty of the Christian to know both sides of it. Let us first look at the apparently good side of caste. For centuries the missionaries could not properly understand the caste system. Let me narrate here an embarrassing situation in which a young missionary found himself because of this issue.

Early in 1963, in one of the summer camps at the Sat Tal Ashram of Dr. E. Stanley Jones in India, they had a seminar on "Caste and Christianity." In one of the sessions a certain young missionary gave his talk on the subject. He vehemently attacked the caste system in India and went on to condemn the Indian Christians among whom the caste feelings were much prevalent. He further suggested that at least the Christians must set an example in mixing with other caste Christians through intermarriages and other possible union. The missionary thought that he had really delivered his goods.

But, during question hour, the first question came from the floor from one gentleman, whose name, incidentally, was Brave. Mr. Brave wanted to know which country the missionary came from and how many children he had. The missionary replied politely that he came from the U.S.A., and that he had three daughters. Then Mr. Brave came out with a most personal and trying question when he asked the missionary, "Will you let your daughters marry black youth in your country?" The missionary mumbled along and finally came out with "I don't know what I would do under those circumstances." Mr. Brave replied kindly, "We know what you would do; you would never allow your daughters to marry Negroes—not necessarily because of your racial prejudice—you may even love the Negroes, but you wouldn't encourage mixed marriages for certain social and cultural reasons." He went on to say, "You are not the first missionary who has picked on us. Please try to have a sympathetic understanding of the caste situation in this country."

On the other hand, this caste system may be compared to the class or racial institutions found among other societies. But by its own merits or demerits, there is nothing parallel to caste in any other society anywhere else in the world. There have been some missionaries who have made correct judgment on the caste situation. John Grant makes this valuable observation:

> In the West, caste is commonly misunderstood and undervalued.
> First-hand contact inspires considerable respect for the values

inherent in caste. The caste serves in many ways as a brotherhood, exercising a moral discipline among its members and providing economic support for those who are in need. It offers the security that goes with a sense of belonging. It gives many of the satisfactions that North Americans seek by joining fraternal orders or service clubs. Exclusion from his caste is the worst disaster that can befall an Indian, for it robs him not only of his material security but also moral sanctions that mold him into accepted patterns of social living. The sudden disintegration of the caste system would probably result in moral chaos, for an Indian is not accustomed to making decisions as a self-contained individual.[1]

Rev. J. W. Grant points out very clearly the tragic state of an individual when he is "suddenly" detached from his particular caste and community. This is something the church planters in India must constantly bear in mind.

I would partly agree with Rev. Canjanan Gamaliel, who thinks that caste is the "divine order of preservation in society in India until the Gospel can transform society and create a new order of preservation."[2] But I hesitate to call caste wholly and solely a *divine* order. There is too much evil in it. Though untouchability has been made illegal, it is very prevalent in villages even to this day. Yet I would like to say that caste is a necessary evil for the function of society in India. I prefer to think that man made it. It is part of culture. Man made it and man can change it and is changing it. People movements and web movements could be well organized within castes. Caste helps a society to make collective decisions. So let us learn to accept this "order" rather than to declare a war against it.

Syncretism

Syncretism is a commonly accepted philosophy of life among most of the Hindus. Even an average Hindu would say that all religions are one and we are going to the same place, just as the rivers that flow from different sources finally get to the same ocean. It is hard to convince a Hindu of the supremacy of Christ and Christianity.

The Hindus have now gone a step further and have taken the offensive. Dr. Radhakrishnan, who is hailed as the saviour of Hinduism, with his extraordinary knowledge of Christian thought and philosophy makes "plain" to Christians and Hindus alike the superiority of Hinduism as a way of life, characterized as it is by that width of outlook which makes it so much better fitted to be a universal religion than Christianity with its narrowness, its dogmas, and its "intolerance." He calls his religion "Sanatanadharma" (the eternal religion).

Dr. Radhakrishnan, as a typical Brahmin, with all his "cleverness," does not realize that he is trying to hatch an egg much bigger than he is. We could understand that he is attempting to redefine Hinduism, which has been dubbed as a "pagan" and "primitive" religion with all the numerous gods and the "evil" system of caste. I would like to pose a question to the eminent scholar, philosopher, and former President of India: what has he got in his philosophical system that is going to ultimately relieve the sufferings of the depressed community in India? Who cares for his "Sanatana Dharma?" People are looking for something—anything—which can liberate them from the four-thousand-year-old Brahmin oppression.

Bishop Stephen Neil, commenting on Dr. Radhakrishnan's neo-Hinduism, says:

> It is unlikely that these threats will grow any less between now and the end of the century. It is probable that the churches will find the world situation increasingly unfavorable to them. In this, there is no special reason for discouragement. The Church has often been here before, and has made difficulty the stepping stone to recovery.[3]

I see here a key thought for the success of Christian religion in India. The future of mission in India lies in our ability to make the most of stumbling blocks as stepping stones.

With this brief sketch on the present state of affairs of the various forces that are at work in India, I go on to make these following proposals.

Ten Proposals

These ten proposals might become the tools to disciple the responsive populations of India.

Let the church in India be a "waiting" church

By that I mean let the Indian church be a church that is waiting on God for an outpouring of the Holy Spirit. A great spiritual awakening among the Christians can result in passion for souls and sacrifices for the cause of evangelism in India.

Go, preach, disciple, teach

With this fourfold ideal strategy, we not only go to the people and preach to them, but when they put their trust in Christ we disciple them by baptizing them in the name of the Father, the Son, and the Holy Spirit. Then we continue to teach them to grow into perfection. Discipling and teaching should not be confused with each other. Teaching is a follow-up of discipling.

Focus on the common people, even the depressed classes

Much of the energies of the evangelizing agencies are dissipated by not focusing on the responsive. "Win the winnable while they are winnable", says Dr. McGavran. The Harijans and the other depressed castes of India, by the most sober estimate, are the responsive communities in India. No time must be lost in multiplying churches among these people.

Make conversions within the social structure

People need not be asked to change their social customs and other traditional behaviors. To become a Christian does not mean to wear pants and coats. Men and women may be asked to follow Christ still being proud of their culture or caste to which they belong. So let us strive to make conversions with minimum social dislocation.

Christ must increase, Christianity must decrease

I am not saying that Christianity must be done away with. I am only saying that a Christianity which is closely identified with the West must be eventually shipped back to where it came from. When Christ is "lifted up" as the liberator of India, as already He has been, He is going to attract millions of people to Himself. This I can give in writing in my own blood. Christ must be proclaimed as the God of our salvation and as liberator from social, political, and economic depression. Cells of Christians must be formed. The Indian Church must be formed in its own biblical molds.

Plant churches that plant churches

A church is not an end in itself; it is only a means to an end. The Church is a missionary community. Wherever this principle has been applied, the newly organized churches produced daughter churches rapidly. Our ultimate aim must be to plant churches which in turn would plant churches and on and on without end. This could be brought about only through a lay movement. Therefore, it is imperative to keep hammering along at the priesthood of all believers.

Strategize people movements

People in India are not just individuals. There is the extended family and the clan and the caste. The street corner preachings and bazaar preachings and the handing out of tracts, to the passersby may bring in a few stray individuals to the Christian fold. But the most effective and successful way to evangelize is through the families and caste groups who are responsive to the Gospel. Mobilize the Christians to bring their relatives to Christ. Our slogan must be "Families for Christ" and "Relatives for Christ."

Minimize "service missions"

We are not saying that the social gospel must be completely done away with. We only say let these things be done in proportion. Let not priority be given to "service mission."

Restructure seminaries

Seminaries should not be centers of academic pursuit, but idea factories which produce men of action with missionary zeal and vision. If a student has not gained practical knowledge in discipling non-Christians and striven to become an active church planter while in the seminary, he is not going to learn it out in the field. To our knowledge, church planting ministry has been carried out by two of the seminaries in Latin America.[4]

Seminaries in India also should open out-stations to carry out theological education by extension programs.

Indigeneity in theology, worship, and mission

Much has been said about the need of indigenous theology and worship these days, but no one seems to be concerned for an indigenous mission. This is very important in these days when national feelings are so high. We must constantly expose ourselves to new national methods to reach the nationals.

The one I think would be effective along this line is a *"Padayatra"* (foot pilgrimage), which I myself feel burdened to carry out in a few years when the situation ripens. I may begin from Cape Comerin and walk five or ten miles a day, visiting village after village, proclaiming the "good news" and establishing churches on the way, finally reaching Madras.

I am sure there must be still better Indian methods through which the people of India may be discipled. We have to constantly keep ourselves open to the leading of the Holy Spirit to show us new strategies by which an effective church planting ministry may be set in motion. The future of mission in India depends upon our ability to use indigenous methods to disciple the population of our beloved land.

End Notes

1. John Webster Grant, *God's People in India* (Toronto: The Ryerson Press, 1959), p. 9-10.

2. James Canjanan Gamaliel, "The Church in Kerala" (master's thesis, School of World Mission, Fuller Theological Seminary, Pasadena, CA, 1967).

3. Stephen Neil, *A History of Christian Missions* (Great Britain: Penguin Books, 1971), p. 571.

4. Roger S. Greenway, *An Urban Strategy for Latin America* (Grand Rapids: Baker Book House, 1973), p. 152.

Study Questions

1. From the understanding about caste you gained from this article, in what ways can you see that caste could be a help or a hindrance to mission effort?

2. In light of the ten proposals Sargunam makes in this article, what kind of workers are needed in India? What kind of training do they need?

16

Muslim Evangelism

Michael Youssef

In any attempt to evangelize Muslims today, we can hardly afford the mistakes of the past. One of our greatest mistakes has been that of not sufficiently taking into account cultural, linguistic, ethnic, and sociological factors in the background of the people. Nor can we afford the luxury of ancient but erroneous prejudices against the Muslim world.

Perhaps the most damaging mistake of all has been our neglect of Muslims. Hiding behind excuses such as "monolithic Islam," and "Muslims are resistant to the Gospel," we have invested less than 2 percent of North American Protestant missionaries in reaching Muslims. There has been little sowing; there has been little reaping.

The Muslim world, however, has been subjected to the secularizing influences of the West. Past Western domination of present-day independent Muslim nations has not helped the Christian mission, but it did transmit Western ideas and values to a whole generation of Muslim elite.

Some observers felt that these secularizing influences, which have eroded the faith of many in the West in Christ, might well erode Islamic beliefs, too. Little did they suspect the opposite reaction, a revival within Islam in reaction to the secularizing influence of the West.

And yet, in the midst of our miscalculations, prejudices, and neglect, I believe God has made this the hour for Muslim evangelism. Surprising stories from Muslim countries tell us of unprecedented events in the evangelization of Muslims. They reveal that the Muslim world is not everywhere resistant. They give hope to the church to redeem her neglect, to erase her prejudices, and to turn back from former mistakes.

Born in Egypt and ordained to the Anglican ministry in Australia, Michael Youssef was formerly special assistant to the President of the Haggai Institute for Advanced Leadership Training in Atlanta. He is a researcher and lecturer on Muslim evangelism. Adapted from *Unreached Peoples '80*, edited by Dr. C. Peter Wagner and Edward Dayton, Copyright 1980. David C. Cook Publishing Co., Elgin, Illinois. Used by permission.

The Ideological Struggle In The Muslim World—God's Opportunity

We have observed an increase in Islamic militancy in the past ten years. In Pakistan, Iran, Iraq, Egypt, Libya, and Indonesia, militant movements are spreading, some more extensively than others. Ironically, even though most Muslim nations are the signatories of the U.N.'s Declaration on Human Rights, they interpret that declaration in a distinctive way. They reason that, since Islam is a total way of life, the people of a given nation are free under Islam, and since God's law is above human laws and declarations, whatever Islam says is right.

I believe the problem is complicated by more than Islamic militancy. In many cases, Muslim countries that are suspicious of Western influence and Western missions are also susceptible to association with the Russian communist regime. This is illustrated by countries such as Libya, Afghanistan, Algeria, Syria, and Iraq. And although some other countries, such as Indonesia, Egypt, Sudan, and the United Arab Emirates, have not yet opened their doors to missionaries, they are at least allowing them in.

Secularization, both capitalistic and communistic, contributes to the ideological struggle going on in some Muslim countries. The current situation in Iran is a good illustration of this struggle.

In the midst of this kind of struggle and anxiety, the Christian Gospel can be very attractive. We should be watching for stress points in the ideological struggles of the Muslim world. Rather than pulling our people out of such situations, we need to persevere as witnesses. In Iran, for example, a young believer recently led twenty people to Christ in a period of six months! In America, where many Iranians have been stranded by the present government, there are Iranian converts to Christ in almost every major city. Stress produces openness. Restless hearts in search of meaning and peace are finding their rest in Christ.

Another place to watch in the coming days is Afghanistan. Conservative Muslim tribals are up in arms against the Marxist-oriented government of Taraki. After the uprising in Heerat, Russian planes strafed the city for two days, leaving a thousand dead. The general populace, terribly offended by both their own Muslim leaders and their allies, the Russians, have recently shown an uncommon friendliness to Christians passing through the area. There is some sense in which such tragedies can become God's opportunities.

The Use of the Koran as a Bridge

It is of particular relevance to Muslim evangelism to examine the Scriptures and what they show about culturally sensitive approaches to other people. Jesus' approach is especially suggestive. He did not come to preach Judaism, nor did he come to preach salvation through the Law. Yet he never attacks the Law. Rather he shows the Jews that the Law was in fact pointing to him.

Is there a similar way in which we can use the Koran with Muslims? Before I answer, I must make it clear that in no way do I equate the Koran with the Old Testament. I am merely making an analogy. The vast majority of Muslims take the Koran to be the direct word of God. We should meet them where they are.

The Koran contains some magnificent verses about Jesus. So exhilarating and glorifying are these stories that from its pages we see Jesus as the greatest prophet and in a special way close to God. This could not be called the "Gospel in the Koran," but it nevertheless gives the Christian an excellent opportunity to talk to Muslims about Christ.

I am personally convinced that the prophet Muhammad was confused in his understanding of who Jesus was. On the one hand he denied his deity and crucifixion. On the other hand Jesus is called *Kalamet Allah* , "the Word of God" (4:171), and *Rouh Allah* , "the Spirit of God" (2:87). Jesus is significantly quoted as saying, "His (God's) blessing is upon me wherever I go" (19:30). A better translation would be "He (God) has made me blessed wherever I may be." Also, in the Koran Jesus is the only prophet who raises the dead. There is also mention of his miracles and healings and his miraculous virgin birth.

I believe the Koran can be used to bring Muslims to the feet of Jesus. Virtually all converts from Islam say that the God they knew distantly in the Koran they now know more fully in Jesus Christ. As Jesus and his apostles were able to point to the Gospel from the Old Testament, so we can point our Muslim friends to Jesus from the Koran.

I know someone will say, "But Muslim teachers and leaders do not believe that in the Koran Jesus is elevated to deity." This is true. But back in the first century, neither did the Pharisees and other Jewish religious leaders accept Jesus as the fulfillment of the Old Testament prophecies. Yet the Gospel nevertheless spread among those who responded to Christian preaching. Using the Koran as a bridge, we can reach Muslims who have been prepared by God to see Jesus as the one he has sent for their redemption.

The Islamic Monolith: Fact or Fancy?

Underlying our concern for culturally sensitive models is the awareness of the rich diversity within Islam. Muslims are divided into hundreds of "homogeneous units" that differ from each other geographically, ethically, ideologically, culturally, and often theologically. Iran, for example, cannot be called a monolithic society. Ethnic Persians make up only 48 percent of the population. Eight percent of Iran's population is Kurdish, 19 percent Turkish-speaking, 18 percent tribal Gulani, Baluchi, and Luri, and the remaining are divided among many smaller groups. Religiously, Iran's Muslims are divided into Shias, Sunnis, Bahais, Ismailis, Ahl-i-Haqq, Yezidis, communists, secularists, and both progressive and conservative Muslims. This kind of diversity can be observed in dozens of Muslim countries.

Other examples of surprising diversity are the 20,000 Chinese Muslims who have migrated and presently live in Saudi Arabia, 145,000 Kurds living in Kuwait, and 20,000 Circassian Muslims living in Jordan. The 720 million Muslims of the world [*Ed. note: now almost one billion*] speak at least five hundred different languages and are subdivided into probably 3,500 different homogeneous units.

Differing Kinds of Soils—A Clue

Just as there were different kinds of soil in Jesus' parable, so we are likely to find many different kinds of Muslim peoples. Unfortunately, some people treat the whole Muslim world as if it were a single type of soil and erroneously attempt to use only one method on it. It is not, as many who are currently involved in a ministry to Muslims can testify.

Indonesia, for example, is the largest Muslim country in the world, with 121 million Muslims, over 87 percent of the population. Yet Indonesia is not an Islamic state. The number of responsive Muslims to the Christian faith in Indonesia is quite astounding. The Sundanese of Java, for example, long considered resistant to the Gospel, are of varying levels in their commitment to Islam. Some areas are highly orthodox and resistant to Christianity. Others are far less Islamicized. House churches have been successfully planted in nonresistant areas.

The point is that we can find responsive people (good soil) even in the world's most populous Muslim nation. This does not mean we should neglect the unresponsive segment of the population. But it does mean that we should invest our greatest efforts on the fruitful ground and encourage our converts, who appreciate the reasons for resistance to the Gospel, to evangelize the less responsive areas. And we must simultaneously experiment with new strategies.

Opportunities for Cross-Cultural Workers of All Nationalities

Sometimes we can learn from our Muslim friends. For example, there is a growing effort by Saudi Arabia and other Mideastern countries to strengthen the growth of orthodox Islam within Indonesia. Most of the missionaries in that movement are Cairo-trained Arabs sent to Indonesia to teach the Arabic language and Islamic theology.

A suggested strategy, in this case, would be to send Arab Christians as missionaries to these heavily populated Muslim islands of Indonesia. They, too, can teach Arabic, and preach the Gospel. They will be very acceptable because it is prestigious to be an Arabic-speaking person.

Korean Christians are making a far greater impact upon the Muslims in Saudi Arabia than any other group. Saudis expect the adherents of the Greek, Coptic, and Syrian orthodox churches along with the Armenians to be Christians. They expect the Americans, Germans, and British to be at least nominally Christians. But what is baffling to them is how the Koreans, having no Christian background or history, can be dedicated believers in Christ. What could be more significant than a Korean mission in Saudi Arabia, in the form of technical advisors, laborers, doctors, engineers, etc.?

In a recent article, Norman Horner gives some excellent statistical information concerning the Arabian Gulf states. His conviction is that, while these are "arid and sparsely populated regions where the economic and cultural character has undergone more rapid and far-reaching change in the last ten years than has happened almost anywhere else on earth, yet they look to be the promised land for so many foreigners." Of course, the reason for this is obviously the production of oil and all the economic prosperity that accompanies this product. Cultural, economic, and sociological change should be viewed very seriously by missionary-minded people. I believe that cultural distortion and disorientation often provide fertile ground for the Christian to advocate a culturally-relevant evangelism.

However, this is not the only good news about prospects of evangelism in the Gulf area in the eighties. Horner explains that a large influx of foreigners, primarily from India, Pakistan, Iran, Egypt, Lebanon, Europe, and America, now vastly exceeds the population of the natives. Among these people are a sizable number of Christians. In Kuwait, for example, it is estimated that five percent of the population is Christian. In Bahrain, about two percent of the population are Christians; in Qatar, over two percent; in Abu Dhabi, about four percent; in Dubai, a little over three percent. Mind you, the vast majority of these Christians are foreigners. There are very few native Christians, if any. The largest Christian community by far in the Arabian Gulf area is the Indian Christian community. It is estimated that over thirty percent of all Indians living in the Arabian Gulf are Christians.

This is, in my judgment, one of the greatest opportunities for Indian missionaries. That is, Indian missionaries, preferably converts from Islam themselves, should be prepared to work in this area of the world where relative freedom is enjoyed, and there witness for Christ and build his church.

Conclusion

Seven hundred and twenty million Muslims cannot be forgotten by the church. We must not spare any effort to make the Gospel relevant to Islam's various ethnic units.

When Jesus was asked "Which is the greatest commandment of the law?" He replied by quoting Deuteronomy 6:5 "You shall love the Lord your God with all your heart, and with all your soul, and with all your might."

But Jesus added a highly significant clause not found in Deuteronomy, "with all your mind." For full Christian missionary commitment it is necessary not only to dedicate ourselves to evangelism; it is also necessary to think through the most effective ways in which we can carry out Christ's command.

The apostle Paul planned and thought out the best way to allow the Gospel to make its maximum impact. We need to plan Muslim evangelism in the nineties with the same thoroughness. Let us adopt the appropriate means to produce a rich harvest in the Muslim world in our day.

Study Questions

1. What are some of the most convincing facts that have led Michael Youssef to believe this is God's hour for Muslim evangelism?

2. Is there any strategy in this article that is *unique to Muslim evangelism?*

17

South Asia: Vegetables, Fish, and Messianic Mosques

Shah Ali with J. Dudley Woodberry

My Muslim father tried to kill me with a sword when I became a follower of Jesus after comparing the Qu'ran and the Bible. He interpreted my decision as a rejection not only of my faith, but of my family and culture, as well. Historically Christians were largely converts from the Hindu community and had incorporated Hindu words and Western forms into their worship.

In trying to express my faith, I encountered two sets of problems. First, as indicated, Christianity seemed *foreign*. Secondly, attempts by Christians to meet the tremendous human need in the region had frequently led to the attraction of opportunistic, shallow converts and the consequent resentment of the Muslim majority.

Christian Faith in Muslim Dress

I was able to start dealing with the foreignness of Christianity when a missionary hired me to translate the New Testament using Muslim rather than Hindu vocabulary and calling it by its Muslim name, the *Injil Sharif* ("Noble Gospel"). Thousands of *injils* were bought, mostly by Muslims, who now accepted this as the "Gospel" of which the Qu'ran spoke. This approach may be supported not only pragmatically by the amazing results but, more importantly, theologically as well. Unlike the Hindu scriptures, the Qu'ran shares a lot of material with the Bible. In fact, most Muslim theological terms were borrowed from Jews and Christians.[1]

Subsequently, a graduate of Fuller's School of World Mission asked me to train twenty-five couples to live in villages and do agricultural development. Only one couple was from a Muslim background. All the others had problems. Muslims would exchange visits with them but would not eat their food until they began to shower in the morning, hence were ceremonially clean by Muslim law after sleeping with their spouses.

Shah Ali is the pseudonym of a follower of Christ from a Muslim family in South Asia. His identity is being concealed—currently, there is persecution of Christians in his country. He translated the New Testament into his national language using Muslim terms and is training leaders of Messianic mosques. "South Asia: Vegetables, Fish, and Messianic Mosques," *Theology, News and Notes* (March 1992), p. 12-13. Used by permission, Fuller Theological Seminary Pasadena, CA 91182

The Christian couples were called angels because they were so kind, honest, and self-sacrificing, and they prayed to God. However, they were not considered truly religious because they did not perform the Muslim ritual prayer five times a day. Thereafter, we only employed couples who followed Jesus from a Muslim background, and we developed a ritual prayer that retained all the forms and content that Muslims and Christians share but substituted Bible passages for Qu'ranic ones. Little adaptation was necessary, because early Islam borrowed so heavily from Jewish and Christian practice in the formulation of the "pillars" of religious observance (the confession of faith, ritual prayer, almsgiving, fasting, and pilgrimage).[2]

Our Muslim neighbors defined "Christianity" as "a foreign religion of infidels;" so we often referred to ourselves as "Muslims" (literally, "submitters to God"). The necessity of submitting to God is certainly Christian (see James 4:7), and Jesus' disciples call themselves "Muslims" according to the Qu'ran (5:111).[3]

When villages have decided to follow Christ, the people continued to use the mosque for worship of God but now through Christ. Where possible, the former leaders of mosque prayers (*imams*) are trained to continue their role as spiritual leaders.

Persuasion, Power, and People

God used other means as well as contextualization to bring Muslims to faith in Christ. On several occasions I have had public discussions with Muslim teachers (*malvis*) and have been able to show that, contrary to popular belief, the Qu'ran does not name Muhammad as an intercessor. Rather, it states that on the judgment day "intercession will not avail, except [that of] him to whom the Merciful will give permission, and of whose speech He approves" (5:109 Egyptian ed./108 Fluegel ed.). But the *Injil* ("Gospel"), which is from God according to the Qu'ran (5:47/51), not only states that God approves of Jesus (e.g., Mt. 3:17) but that He is the *only* intercessor (1 Tim. 2:5).

God has also shown His power through answered prayer—the recovery of a three-year-old girl who, the doctors said, would die in a few hours; the sending of rain and the stopping of flooding; and the appearance of an unknown man to stop a crowd bent on killing an *imam* who followed Christ.

A conscious effort has been made to foster the movement of groups rather than just individuals to Christ. People have only been baptized if the head of the family was baptized. Effort was made to see that leaders understood the message. A Muslim mystic (Sufi) sheikh, upon learning that the veil of the temple had been rent from top to bottom, threw down his Muslim cap, followed Christ, and brought his followers with him.

Since illiteracy is high, the Bible and training materials are recorded on cassettes, and inexpensive cassette players are made available to the villagers.

There has been persecution. Our training center was closed down. A court case was made against me and three fellow workers. Likewise, there has been friction between the leaders and misunderstanding by other Christian groups. But the movement of people to Christ continues. Most new believers remain in independent Messianic mosques, but some contextualized congregations have joined the major denomination, while still other individuals are absorbed into the traditional, Hindu-background church.

Toward Responsible Self-Help

Besides trying to express our faith in meaningful cultural forms, we have been trying to meet the tremendous human need around us. We want to proclaim the Kingdom and demonstrate its values. Trying to do both presents certain problems. First, there is the problem of using human need for evangelistic purposes—of manipulating people and attracting the insincere. Consequently, we help all the villagers despite their religious affiliation and give no financial help to Jesus mosques or their imams.

Secondly, the former colonizer-colonized dependency easily gets transferred to donor-recipient dependency. Thirdly, even the distribution of donated food from abroad may only help in the city, because of the difficulty of distribution, while giving little incentive to the peasants to produce more because of the artificially reduced price. Fourthly, the introduction of technology may only help those with the skills or the finances to make use of it, while the poorest can just watch the gap between the haves and have-nots widen.

To deal with these problems we have followed such common development practices as loaning planting seed to be replaced at harvest time and providing pumps that are paid for from increased productivity. Now, however, we are adapting a program developed in Southeast Asia which should express holistic Christian concern, deal with the problems outlined, and ensure that the indigenous church remains self-supporting.

The program is training national workers in contextualized church planting and an integrated fish and vegetable cultivation system. The workers are, in turn, sent to needy districts where they are responsible for training local farmers in the easily transferable technology so that they can become self-sufficient. Increased population means less land is available for cultivation, and a poor transportation infrastructure means food must be produced near its consumption.

The intensive food production system was developed elsewhere. In that system, fish ponds are dug and the excavated dirt used for raised vegetable plots. Excess stems and leaves from the vegetables are used to feed the fish, and the waste from the fish is used as fertilizer for the vegetables. These food production centers are within walking distance of regional urban centers for daily sales and provide space for training of regional farmers and leaders of the Jesus mosques.

The concept of Messianic mosques and completed Muslims (following the model of Messianic synagogues and completed Jews) still causes considerable misunderstanding among other Christians. The combining of evangelism and humanitarian ministries by the same people also raises concerns among those who feel Christian agencies should only focus on one or the other. Nevertheless, the models we are developing have been used by God in the raising up of many new disciples and expressing His concern for total persons with physical and spiritual needs. Likewise the Messianic Muslim movement has spilled over into a neighboring country through the normal visiting of relatives; when colleagues and I visited a Southeast Asian country recently, a whole Muslim village began to follow Jesus.

End Notes

1. See Arthur Jeffery, *The Foreign Vocabulary of the Qu'ran* (Oriental Institute, 1938).

2. For the details of this argument see J. D. Woodberry, "Contextualization Among Muslims: Reusing Common Pillars," *The Word Among Us*, ed. Dean S. Gilliland (Word Publishers, 1989), 282-312.

3. In this context, however, they demonstrated their submission by believing in God and his apostle (apparently Muhammad, who had not yet been born).

Study Questions

1. Why do attempts to use meaningful cultural forms and attempts to meet human needs present such problems?

2. Can missionaries call themselves "Muslims" or express their faith in Islamic cultural fashion? Why or why not?

18

On Turning Muslim Stumbling Blocks into Stepping Stones

Warren Chastain

Nate floored me with his question. I found myself unable to give a quick answer to a problem I had mentally wrestled with for two decades! Perhaps it was his Thomas-like, honest doubt which prevented me from delivering a glib, off-the-shelf response. Basically, he was facing the issue: he had a lifetime of service for the Lord before him, but he wondered whether it was wise to sacrifice it for a people as unresponsive as the Muslims. I could easily sympathize with him—and he didn't know half the problem!

Our Stumbling Blocks

The first stumbling block to overcome in Muslim work is in our own mind: the psychological block of our own attitude. Are we willing to lay our lives on the altar? A statement by Bishop Hill captures the heart of the problem:

> Look to the heathen without Christ, and you will find an altar...and may God help you to be a sacrifice.

But who wants that kind of an altar? Most of us prefer the kind where we offer up something else—anything but ourselves! Knives are notoriously hard, sharp, and cold—and made for cutting.

I wondered whether Nate would have asked the question if he were really ready to be a sacrifice. Was his attitude correct? But then I felt a bit guilty about questioning his motives; he was really counting the cost, which the Lord would approve. I was glad I fumbled the answer to Nate's probe. It was better that no answer be given than one that would try to sweeten a knifethrust. It is easier to sing about "laying all on the altar" as long as we ourselves do not end up on the altar. Unfortunately (?), God has engineered the fruit-making process so sacrifice is unavoidable. But man in his ingenuity wants to turn an altar into a stage for seeking applause.

Warren Chastain served as a missionary for 22 years with the Overseas Missionary Fellowship in Thailand, Singapore and Indonesia. He coordinated the translation of the New Testament into the Minangkabau language, planted churches in West Java and Kalimantan, and taught in both government and Christian schools. Chastain currently serves on the staff of the Zwemer Institute in Pasadena, California.

So we must face the question: Are we going into the Lord's service in order to compete for success, to show what we can do, to prove ourselves? If that is our attitude, then Muslim work may be daunting and frustrating. We think of success as what we *achieve* for God, but He values more what we *are*, or what He achieves *in* us. Ultimately we have to be willing to serve on God's terms, whether that means He gives the kind of results we like to see or not.

A bottom-line mentality

Another subjective block which may endanger the church's commitment to Muslim work is our *bottom-line mentality* which suggests that growth is the only significant value. Westerners tend to quantify, to make scientific distinctions based on observation and mathematical calculation. This system has proven its success in dealing with the things of nature which can be observed and counted. This method can glorify God by bringing us true knowledge, but it is harder to apply successfully to the social sciences, and particularly to the spiritual realm. Current Church Growth theory stresses harvests, countable converts and specific churches formed. Thus contemporary missiology provides theoretical and biblical underpinnings to seeking success in terms of evident growth. Church Growth ideas have been a great boon to missions as a corrective to older mission practices which tended to fear large harvests as dangerous to good order and sound doctrine.

But we need to beware of the *bottom-line mentality* which has also developed as a result of the application to missions of (1) modern business managerial practices, and (2) the scientific methods and findings of the social sciences. The result will be that missions will decline to invest money and personnel where specific countable results cannot be counted fairly quickly. This mentality can gain a quasi-biblical justification by arguing that we must be ready to "shake the dust off our feet" when the message is rejected. In terms of evident fruit, it must be admitted that in the past the Christian mission to Islam has largely been a failure in most places. One of the reasons for this failure is the role of violence in Islam. Islam permits the use of social and legal pressures, or even physical violence in both the first stage of *gaining* members, and in the second stage of *retaining* members. Muslims prefer peaceful means, but there are innumerable cases of pressures and violence being used against people who "apostacize" from Islam. But any ideology which must use force to maintain its adherents is admitting its inherent weaknesses. Building the Berlin Wall did not prove the attractiveness of Communism. The "Koranic Curtain" does not prove the strength of Islam. The current Muslim fanaticism suggests the wall is crumbling.

Our *bottom-line mentality* could mean the death-knell of Muslim missions. What missionary would choose a life-long uphill struggle, when he could work somewhere else and be able to write to the home churches glowing success stories about the converts—count 'em! Of course it is not the intention of Church Growth theory to empty the Muslim world of all missionaries, but inevitably people like Nate are going to think twice—and again—and again— before they take a harder road.

The best answer to a false *bottom-line mentality* is to realize that any line man draws is not the bottom line. The real bottom line is the Day of Judgment when we stand before Christ and give account. This does not mean that we cannot draw any lines at all, but, at best, they are merely "tentative lines." So let us be willing to let God draw the bottom line, lest by our own action, we effectively shut out at least one-sixth of the people of the world from an effective preaching of the Gospel.

The second answer to overcoming this *bottom-line mentality* is to fill our minds with a "harvest-mentality." No matter how resistant Islam has been in the past to the Gospel, each new generation is a new opportunity for a God who is unwilling to let any man perish. A harvest mentality is the fruit of two elements: (1) a *knowledge* that Jesus declared that this age, in which he has defeated Satan and risen from the dead, is an age of harvest: "Look unto the fields, for they are white already to harvest" (Jn. 4:35), and (2) *faith* in the Gospel as the power of God unto salvation to every one that believes; and faith in the promise and plan of God. What is this plan of God? It is the winning of at least a representative segment to Christ of peoples from every tribe and tongue on earth (Rev. 5:9, 10). Satan will not ultimately be victorious in shutting out the Gospel from any people group in the world. "Success," in biblical terms, requires the *primary expansion* of the Gospel to the ends of the earth to all tribes. The *secondary expansion* within each tribe, so that each individual is won, is not a requirement for successful completion of the missionary task. This does not mean that the sower does not sow seed in his entire field. We must not criticize the sower for throwing seed on ground that is rocky, full of thorns, or shallow. The sower is not blind, or inept; rather he has a passion to bring life out of all kinds of ground. He will not write anything off, even in the rockiest ground. He has faith that the good seed can cling to life in the hardest places and bear a specially precious harvest.

Muslim Stumbling Blocks

The Incarnation

Turning now from psychological stumbling blocks *in our minds*, let us look at a few key stumbling blocks *in the Muslim mind*. We should be able to sympathize with the Muslim's offense at the great stumbling block of the incarnation. Did God really have to go to all that trouble (as Christianity affirms) to deal with some "foibles" or weaknesses of man (the Muslim estimate of sin)? Can the human state be so bad that God must take on human form and come to earth to correct it? Was Jesus' trip necessary? It is inconceivable to the Muslim that God could be humbled. And to suggest that God must in some way sacrifice Himself is incomprehensible.

Only the Holy Spirit can turn this stumbling block into a stepping stone. But to a thoughtful Muslim the very unthinkableness of the incarnation may hint at its truth. Surely no human mind would dream up such a scheme—and then to glory in it and to make it the foundation of salvation is too grand a concept for some religious hucksters to conceive and peddle. We might also suggest that there is no evidence that God loves man at all if the sacrifice of the incarnation is false. This is the kind of love that is worthy of an infinite God. In fact, if God loves at all, it must be a vast infinite love which only the incarnation and its culmination—the Cross—can demonstrate. As a further help to helping the Muslim believe the incarnation, we might turn his thinking to a problem which Islam has, one which is similar, if not even harder to accept.

Revelation

The Muslim concept of *revelation* seeks to protect God's word from any taint of man's influence. Like the goddess Diana of the Ephesians, the Quran is seen as coming down out of heaven direct to man untouched by human hands. This view seems more honoring to God's revelation, and it makes a more defensible view, avoiding the complexities of the Christian position which has God active within history, and bringing a revelation out of the fire and tribulation of man's experiences.

Many Muslims are unaware of many of the problems inherent within their own theological system. In their zeal to guard the purity and authority of the Word of God, Muslims have conceived of revelation as being a kind of "incarnation" of an attribute of God; that is, God's speech. Since God and his speech must be eternal, the Quran must also be eternal. It is ironic that the holy book which denies the incarnation of Christ is itself supposed to be an incarnation of the speech of God. If it is within the power of God to set apart one of his own attributes and send it down to earth in the form of a book, surely it is not impossible for God to reveal His person in the form of a person who comes to earth. It is not a case of a man being made into a God by the church, but rather God having the power to use the human body which He created in the first place. What we can do to overcome this stumbling block is to shift the focus of discussion to the person of Christ rather than to a battle of books or concepts of revelation.

The Trinity

Another major stumbling block in the mind of the Muslim is his fixation on the concept of the oneness of God. Impatient with the subtleties of the Trinity, the Muslim believes we have some kind of tritheism; and it will not do to answer his $1+1+1=3$ logic with an evasive $1 \times 1 \times 1=1$. A better answer might use the infinity symbol as in $\infty + \infty + \infty = \infty$, but even this is more philosophical than biblical in flavor. The basic problem with the Muslim concept is that it is a mathematical oneness instead of the organic oneness of life; an abstract oneness instead of the composite oneness of personality; a cold, conceptual solitariness, instead of a vital, friendly, loving Father.

In their zeal to fight polytheism, Muslims have opted for this chilling, impersonal Mystery—the "Unknown God." For the Christian to overcome this stumbling block, he must get beyond the mathematics of God to the character of God. We do not worship the number "one" written large; we need to personally know a Father who relates to man. Although the Trinity is unique so that every illustration drawn from nature has shortcomings, we can suggest that in God's creation as one rises from the lower forms of life to the higher we encounter a progression away from simple oneness to a complexity of unity. Each man is one, but he is more complex than a one-celled bacterium. Is it glorifying to God to proclaim him to have a simple mathematical oneness akin to a germ? If the oneness of man involves spiritual aspects as well as physical, surely the oneness of God is not diminished by seeing complexity within that oneness. The mind of man makes a complex one God a possibility; the heart of man makes it a necessity. The Muslim belief in the Quran and the Christian belief in Jesus show they both agree that a bridging of the gap between God and man is necessary. We may suggest that if God is a person, then only a person can reveal a person adequately. If we have only a book then we can know only *about God*, but God himself remains unknown. Even though theological problems like the Trinity and the deity of Christ may be unavoidable, it is better to shift away from those at the beginning to consider a basic issue: how a man is saved.

The Cross

Muslims do not have clearly-defined theology on salvation. A spectrum of answers may be given to the question, "How is a person saved?" The more liberal may say as long as a person believes in one God he can hope for eventual salvation. A traditionalist may demand that a person believe in Muhammad as the preeminent prophet as well as in the one God for salvation. A rigorist may demand godly living in addition to true belief in Allah and His prophet. A fatalist may shrug that no one can ever be sure while another may bring in some kind of purgatory to pay for sins.

The person of Christ is the most attractive means of turning Muslim stumbling blocks into stepping stones. The love of God is revealed in the idea of sacrifice which has been maintained in Islam by a yearly festival where an animal is offered in the Eid sacrifice. We can show from the books of Moses that from the beginning all the prophets acknowledged that sacrifice was the God-ordained way of being reconciled with God. From the days of Adam and Noah, we see God accepting sacrifice. Abraham, by God's direction, sought to offer up his son, so essential was the sacrifice principle. If the Muslim wishes to assert that it was Ishmael, not Isaac, we may bypass a debate and say whichever one was offered, still it is the principle of sacrifice that is undeniable. This brings together the three ideas of salvation, sacrifice, and Jesus as the focus of our discussion, rather than some theological abstractions. This will bring us to the one stumbling stone—the Cross—which will in some way always retain its character as a stumbling stone, even to the Christian, while at the same time becoming a stepping stone to salvation.

We have considered only a few of the theological booby-traps Satan has planted in Islam. The wise Christian witness will study how to defuse each Muslim weapon so that any criticism can be turned positively to the person of Christ and His salvation. By this tactic we cooperate with the God who delights to turn Satan's instruments of death into instruments that bring life. God's weapons are crosses, empty tombs, and willing witnesses.

But missionaries may deny the cross in their own way as well. If we preach a message of ultimate sacrifice but deliver it through a lifestyle which denies sacrifice, we make void our own message. If we preach a message of love in an unloving way, our hearers will doubt that we believe it ourselves. We may thus turn a stepping stone back into a stumbling block.

Study Questions

1. How does Chastain suggest we develop a "harvest" mentality?

2. Why do you think the person of Christ is the most attractive means of turning Muslim stumbling blocks into stepping stones?

19

Keys to Unlocking Muslim Strongholds

Don Newman

Islam stands as the strongest giant against the planting of a church for every people by the year 2000 (Otis). One out of every five people on earth is a Muslim. The heart of Islam and most of its followers live in the part of Africa and Asia known as the 10-40 window. Muslims make up the most resistant and most neglected block of people in the world. There is only one missionary for every one million Muslims.

How can we hope to plant a church in each of the 4,000 unreached Muslim people groups and clearly present the Gospel to the billion Muslims by A.D. 2000? Here is a ring of 10 keys that might just open up the Muslim world to the Gospel.

1. Adopt a Muslim People Group

A number of churches have already adopted a Muslim people group, but many groups remain to be claimed for Christ. With well over 500 Great Commission Christian congregations per unreached people group, it should be possible for a number of congregations to adopt each one. These congregations will then provide the prayer groups along with financial and personnel support to make an effective witness and establish a church in each people group (Stearns).

2. Conduct Strategic Spiritual Warfare

The prince of Persia and the spirit of Babylon are ancient territorial principalities who have resisted the Kingdom of God in Iran and Iraq for centuries. They and similar demonic spirits ruling the Muslim world must be bound before we can snatch the treasures of darkness from Satan's clutches. This can be done through warfare prayer (Wagner) which the gates of hell cannot stand against (Matt. 16:18).

A prayer group for each of the 4,000 Islamic peoples should pray daily and meet monthly to intercede on behalf of these people to clear the air for reception of the Good News.

Don Newman is a pseudonym for a long term worker in Muslim fields. His name has been withheld for security reasons.

The memory of the Crusades is still fresh in Muslim minds after 900 years. It is time to publicly repent of these bitter wars before the entire Muslim world and seek forgiveness and reconciliation.

3. Spread the Word

Islamic leaders are scared to death of the Word of God and will try their best to prevent Muslims from hearing or reading it. The Gospel should be readily available in every Muslim language through radio, cassettes, videos, books, tracts, newspapers, letters, etc. The *Jesus* film is one of the best tools to present the Gospel to both literate and illiterate Muslims.

4. Send in International Church Planting Teams

A team of eight or more international cross-cultural missionaries needs to be operating within a significantly large group of the people being reached. This team should have an incarnational witness, identifying with the people through a simple life style. They should demonstrate the gifts and fruit of the Spirit as they interact with each other and their Muslim friends. They need to be so committed to their people group that they bond with them as they master the culture and language. They must never lose sight of the goal to establish a growing church movement among that people.

5. Use Strategies that Fit the Needs of the People

Since most of the unreached Muslim people groups are in countries that do not grant "missionary visas", creative ways of access need to be found to live in those countries. The team can go as tentmakers, possibly as students, teachers or as providing some service that is appreciated by the government and the people (Wilson). It would help to have a nonresidential missionary based outside the country who can facilitate communications, prayer support, and linking the work of the team with others interested in that people (Garrison).

6. Find a Bridge in their Culture

The team should be searching for cultural and religious beliefs which can serve as a bridge for this group to more readily accept the Gospel (Richardson). The Koran provides stories that can be used to present the Gospel such as Abraham's offering of his son celebrated every year during the Id al-Adha.

7. Start a Socially Acceptable People Movement

Messianic mosques have been appearing in some countries where followers of Jesus do not leave their culture but continue to appear as Muslims while worshipping Jesus (Parshall).

8. Demonstrate God's Love for the Whole Person

Since many Muslim peoples are refugees or are suffering from poverty and starvation, holistic ministries can demonstrate God's love and concern for their physical as well as spiritual needs. Such people find it difficult to understand and accept a Gospel that shows no practical concern for their desperate situation (Elliston).

9. Expect Power Encounters

The majority of Muslims live in fear of jinns, the evil eye, and other expressions of folk Islam. They need to see the power of Christ demonstrated in healing, delivering from demon possession, and conquering the forces of evil. Many Muslims have only come to accept Christ after they have had a vision, dream or dramatic answer to prayer in Jesus' name (Kraft).

10. Demand Obedience to Christ

Those who come to faith need to be discipled in obedience to Christ and gathered into cells where they can be held accountable to follow Jesus whatever the cost. This requires willingness to suffer for Christ and in some cases to die for Him. Until a number of Muslim converts are prepared for this, the church will not grow strong or fast in that society (Patterson).

There are no doubt other keys which can help unlock the door to Muslim cultures so that the Church can be planted in their midst. Let us know what you have found useful so that the lessons learned in one part of the Muslim world can be shared with those working in other areas that Christ may be glorified and the last of the giants can be overcome.

For additional reading see the following:

Elliston, Edgar J. (ed.) *Christian Relief and Development*. Dallas, TX: Word Publishing, 1989.

Garrison, David. *The Nonresidential Missionary*. Monrovia, CA: MARC, 1990.

Kraft, Charles H. *Christianity with Power*. Ann Arbor, MI: Vine Books, 1989.

Otis Jr., George. *The Last of the Giants*. Tarrytown, NY: Ravell Company, 1991.

Parshall, Phil. *Beyond the Mosque*. Grand Rapids, MI: Baker Books, 1985.

Patterson, George. *Church Planting Through Obedience Oriented Teaching*. Pasadena, CA: William Carey Library, 1981.

Stearns, Bill & Amy. *Catch the Vision 2000*. Minneapolis, MN: Bethany House, 1991.

Richardson, Don. *Eternity in Their Hearts*. Ventura, CA: Regal Books, 1984.

Wagner, C. Peter. *Warfare Prayer*. Ventura, CA: Regal Books, 1992.

Wilson, J. Christy. *Today's Tentmakers*. Wheaton, IL: Tyndale House, 1979.

20

Future Prospects For China Ministry — A Dialogue

Jonathan Chao and Tony Lambert

The following is an informal conversation on January 2, 1992, between Jonathan Chao, Director of the Chinese Church Research Center, and Tony Lambert, an OMF (Overseas Missionary Fellowship) China watcher and researcher. Topic for discussion was the "Future Prospects for 1992 with respect to China and China ministry."

Direction of Development

Chao: How do you see China in 1992? What do you think is the likely direction of development?

Lambert: I'd be very cautious in making any predictions. The situation is very volatile. It could change suddenly, or it might be five years down the line. In every area of Chinese life—political, economic, social—you find factors for explosive change in the near future.

There's still a basic contradiction between economic reform and political reform. They are willing to engage in economic reform, but by taking a very hard line political stand, this is in total contradiction to genuine economic reforms. I think there's a key contradiction there. The role of Guangdong and the southern provinces is crucial on how they may react in the near future. Socially and morally in every area of society you have a crisis. You have a growing drug problem and alcoholism. The divorce rate is sky rocketing, particularly amongst intellectuals. From a Christian angle there are serious moral problems involving abortion and infanticide.

I was just told by a Chinese friend visiting North China recently that in the hospitals if people want to have a major operation, it's become quite standard that you have to bribe the surgeon and the medical team with several thousand Reminbi and banquets—both before the operation and after the operation. One wonders how long a society can continue to function in this way. It may be able to be held together by the Party and the army for some years but in the longer term, I think the whole base is crumbling. So therefore I would foresee major change.

Taken from *China PrayerLetter and Ministry Report, no.120*, a periodical of China-Church Research Center. Used with permission.

The major question is: Is there going to be peaceful evolution? Could it be that because the government is standing so obstinately against "peaceful evolution" that the very thing they fear most, i.e., some kind of civil war or bloody catastrophe, they may actually be hastening it along by their intransigence? I am somewhat negative about the political future because I think it may be quite difficult for a liberal alternative to the Communist Party to emerge in the short term, but in the longer term it may well be that the Church and Christianity could provide a new moral base for Chinese society.

Chao: To pick up on the point of this possible emergence of the more liberal section of the Party, I think the development of the world situation will give them encouragement to do so. Last year was a tremendous year—a lot of disasters, a time of tremendous changes in Eastern Europe, and of the Soviet Union.

China now is the last bastion still committed to Marxism. Theoretically they are still committed to it, but practically speaking, they have to find a new way out, to reintegrate themselves to the rest of the nations. The fact that she (China) recognizes Russia shows she's taking a more pragmatic approach.

Also I think there's going to be a greater contact between Taiwan and China and this will aid more toward "peaceful evolution." With the rejection of the Taiwan independence movement by the voters, beginning this year, there's going to be a greater exchange between the two, and that will be a very important factor towards "peaceful evolution," both economically and gradually, perhaps sociologically if not politically.

In China we can expect a gradual erosion of leftist power, that will create room for liberal reformers to emerge again. Five years from now China will definitely be changed, more by internal transformation than by any external force, more by default, because the central government no longer can implement its policies to the grassroots level. In light of this I think the Church inside and outside of China should begin to prepare for a post-communist society involving drastic social and economic changes as well as greater freedom for evangelism, and confusion that comes from opening up.

What do you think the church should do? What would you recommend to foreign missions and churches in Hong Kong for the next five years?

Direction for Mission

Lambert: There's a variety of things we can be doing. One would be to have a much closer cooperation between mission groups and other Christian organizations. There is a lot of informal consultation—particularly in Hong Kong. But I would be quite concerned about groups that are on the fringes of ministry to China or at this time are not committed to China at all—groups that really don't understand China.

In Eastern Europe some quite frightening things are happening with Western groups coming in with more money than sense. A Bulgarian pastor who is doing theological training shared with me that Bulgaria is just being swamped by cults coming in. Also foreign mission agencies who in some cases have a lot of funds are setting the agenda. To give one example, my friend has a vision for an interdenominational Bible college in Bulgaria. There aren't many evangelicals, so it makes sense to have one united Bible college, but other groups are coming—denominational groups mainly from America—demanding denominational colleges because they have money and influence. They can influence some of the local Christian leaders to go their way.

There are signs of this already happening in China with people going in from Hong Kong, Taiwan, and America. One of the sad things is there appears to be much greater division and polarization amongst the Christians in China than there was 10 or 15 years ago. You can't blame it all on the foreigners or overseas Chinese, but I think it is a factor; groups are coming in with their particular doctrines and also their financial aid. Unless it's handled very carefully it just creates further division. It could be a very dangerous situation spiritually, and it's already quite serious now.

But if communism collapses in China and there's a completely "open door," we will probably see groups who know nothing about China wanting to get into the act. Some groups would foolishly want to establish their own denominational "kingdoms" again. So I would hope that there could be much greater liaison and cooperation now between groups, and some form of planning. In terms of practical ministry my own strategy would be very much to say the evangelization of China is being carried on quite successfully at most levels of Chinese society, particularly the grassroots, by Chinese Christians. They certainly need our prayer and our aid for literature and radio and theological training. But they are the ones in charge.

If communism collapses, there will be much greater freedom for things like literature to go in. Possibly literature can be printed on a much wider scale within China. But the problem will be these millions of converts already in the churches and so few pastors, theologically trained leaders, and available literature.

I saw an article from Nanjing Seminary predicting that by the year 2000 the number of Christians in Shanxi Province will have gone up by 2.7 times. Shanxi is by no means one of the areas where you have the fastest growth. So the communists appear to be recognizing that within the next 10 years or so the Church might double or triple. It's a huge number of people flooding into the Church.

I stand open to correction but I think that the Three-Self Movement cannot cope; they have all these elderly pastors. The house church people are doing a lot of good work training, but they still have problems in finding solid people who know the Word of God. There is a major problem with perhaps tens of millions of converts, all kinds of cults springing up in China, groups coming from overseas—the Mormons, etc. It could be pretty chaotic.

The number one priority is to mobilize the Church overseas to prepare to serve the Church in China. To go in at the invitation of Chinese Christian leaders, not to dominate, but to work under and alongside them in key theological training. The West can help, but also people from Japan, Korea, and other Asian countries can have a very strategic role. There may well be other areas of ministry. I don't rule out evangelism, possibly direct pioneer evangelism by foreign Christians, particularly in some of the minority areas. But we have to get over the message that primarily the work of the Gospel will continue to be done by Chinese. Whatever the outside world, I'm thinking particularly of the

Western world, could contribute as a subsidiary may be a very vital supporting role, but it is still subsidiary.

Direction within China

Chao: Yes, I agree with you. Theological education and literature are two primary things, and also the need for an international consultation some time this year or next year on the future evangelization of China, in preparation for a post-communist era that will be emerging in China over the horizon in three to seven years' time.

In terms of policy, we should communicate to the non-Chinese Christian world that we must try our best to assist and confirm the work in China. In terms of ministry,in the next five years we need to first emphasize the training of workers. It is needed both outside for gradual participation in training ministry in China as well as assisting the training program that's being done among house churches, if possible, the Three-Self seminaries.

In a recent Three-Self publication they are now open to the possibility of inviting outside speakers and teachers in their seminaries. They are sending people to study abroad, whereas a year or two ago they were not even open to the idea. In the light of this future transition towards a post-communist era we may have to adopt a revised policy toward the Three-Self, especially in training.

Perhaps some missions can do that and some are doing that. They just need to be aware of the United Front policy. They may be used on the one hand, and on the other hand they could contribute toward equipping the seminaries with good books. As the Three-Self are searching for seminaries to which they will send their students, I would like to encourage evangelical seminaries to open their gates with scholarships, if necessary, to candidates sent by the Three-Self. It's better for them to be trained in evangelical seminaries than for them to go to liberal seminaries.

Lambert: Could I interrupt and pose a question about the TSPM (Three-Self Patriotic Movement)? In Eastern Europe all the "puppet" religious organizations set up by the communists to control the Church collapsed like a pack of cards following the fall of communism. Similarly will the TSPM eventually collapse or disintegrate in China? Will some national church structure emerge that will in a sense come out of the ruins of TSPM that we can work with? Or will things become so fragmented that it will all have to start over again?

Chao: I think that if in China the communist government will evolve slowly toward some more liberal situation, the existing church structures may remain—the ideas may change, the people may change, but the structures may remain. Seminaries and institutions will probably remain, so for lack of any national structure the TSPM may survive but be transformed. It will be less politicized, and be allowed to be more Christian. The local Christians and the churches may demand to Christianize the seminaries as well as the national structures. The national structure I'm not so sure about, but I think the seminaries and institutions may have a better chance to survive.

Lambert: I remember that in late 1987 and 1988 there was a strong movement for reform of the TSPM. So if that was to resurface and continue, I take your point and see that the TSPM perhaps nominally would remain but it could evolve into some kind of National Council of Churches. And possibly it might be more evangelical than any of the bodies we are familiar with in the West!

Chao: Yes. If the United Front Work Department and Religious Affairs Bureau (RAB) officials would withdraw their directives and leave the TSPM and the seminaries to run on their own, they will probably be free to concentrate on church matters. So I think that as China goes through this transition the Church overseas should for the Gospel's sake adopt a more accommodating attitude, one of help, and good will, rather than continual rejection. But that doesn't mean we will be blind-folded to the evils of the past.

Now the churches in Taiwan are beginning to take on more relations with the Church in China. Like the Church in the West, many only go to the Three-Self churches, although a few do go to the house churches. They are not well informed like the Church in Hong Kong in the early 80's. So they need to be informed. On the other hand they need to be guided as to how to work with the Three-Self for the Gospel, rather than be used by the RAB.

Lambert: As I understood it, till fairly recently, in places like Nanjing Theological Seminary, one or two foreigners have been lecturing, but I understood that they were very much liberal in theology. I tend to doubt whether evangelicals would be allowed to lecture.

Chao: I don't think evangelicals will get that much of a welcome in these main city seminaries, but in the regional provincial seminaries where you have the right connection, in a very quiet way some have been able to get a hearing, especially at the county level or some of these informal training sessions. We should adopt a more flexible attitude, and encourage people to take different routes. I will definitely continue to emphasize the encouragement of house church training.

I would like to see more training manuals written that Christians in China can use for training in basic theology. We should also encourage student work, and work among intellectuals and scholars who are genuinely searching, who if they are thoroughly converted, can become future leaders of the Chinese Church.

I think the house church movement has gone to a point of no return; there's no way the government can stop them. In some villages as many as 45% of the population have become Christians; others maybe just 0.5% or 2%. But on the whole it is growing. We should encourage Chinese-speaking foreigners as well as Chinese seminary-trained people to go in a full-time manner as visitors or workers to assist, direct, and teach the intellectuals.

Direction for Leaders

Chao: In the light of the post-communist movement in Europe, China is now so isolated that she has to change. She needs to be realistic. And America also is taking China in a realistic way, putting on pressure but at the same time keeping the relations going. Perhaps China is waiting for some kind of face-saving way for the old timers of China to retire honorably. But so far there's no Gorbachev nor Yeltsin to come forward to provide ideological leaders.

That is a significant difference. In Russia they have intellectuals who were formerly communists who became reformers, who took on political leadership. But in China we don't have many reformers who are ideologically equipped, who at the same time have occupied top positions of leadership, except Zhao Ziyang. But he is not an ideologue. There are very few diehard leftist intellectuals left, and many have already changed their minds.

So I think it's only a matter of time. We do need to pray that God will raise up more liberal-thinking intellectuals who will emerge as political leaders in China. In China they always rely on one top strong leader, without whom things don't move. That is why communism just hasn't worked that well in China or anywhere else for that matter.

Lambert: Yes, I think that the role of the overseas Chinese or the diaspora (People's Republic of China/PRC) overseas is very crucial. We've been involved in outreach to Chinese scholars worldwide for a number of years. We're still learning and seeking what we can do. But there are something like 100,000 PRC scholars and students in America; and probably 80 or 90,000 in Japan. We found out quite recently that in some places like Hungary there could be as many as 20,000 PRC people. There are vast concentrations in Eastern Europe, Australia, UK, Germany, and all over the world.

Many of them are doing serious thinking about the future of China. I don't think that should be ignored in terms of the future impact on the social structures within China, and if they can be won for Christ I think they could have a tremendous impact on China, assuming that many of them do go back eventually, but that is the big question.

I have a fear that if the Christian Church, both within China and outside China, doesn't get its act together in the next five years or ten at the outside, we're going to be left standing on the sidelines. I feel very strongly that this is a God-given opportunity that China certainly has not seen since the May the 4th Movement in 1919. There are large numbers of intellectuals and Chinese students that for the first time are looking at Christianity as an option.

But if the Church does not grapple with that, and in evangelical circles we get stuck in some kind of pietistic rut, then we cannot encourage Chinese scholars who have become Christians to seriously look at society, and all those areas in which they are very deeply interested already. Then I think we're doing China a disservice.

If we look at the long term, surely we need to be doing some serious thinking in these areas ourselves—at least encouraging PRC Christians to get involved. How do you see this?

Chao: I think you are right in that the Chinese people are more than ever open to the Gospel as the only possible solution to the future of China. The Chinese intellectuals always think about saving China! And in the May 4th period the intellectuals rejected the Christian faith, along with other supernatural religious beliefs. Chinese intellectuals adopted materialistic Marxism as a so-called scientific worldview, and followed the revolution for 70 years.

They succeeded in overthrowing the Kuomintang, but they have failed to rebuild a new China. That was the whole purpose, to create a new China, a new society that is free, equal and so on. And the upshot of the experiment is total nationwide frustration and confusion. And there is nothing out of Chinese traditional culture—Confucianism and Taoism—that can rebuild China.

Intellectuals are beginning to understand that Christianity is the only option for reconstructing China. They need to be shown the power of Christian faith for nation building. This is a real opportunity because if China abandons Marxism right away and becomes free, all kinds of materialism may come into China instead.

The intellectuals won't know what to do. At this point they are more open than they will be in the post-communist era. If the Christian faith can convince these intellectuals, then they—when China is in transition, fear and confusion—will eventually come up with some direction.

Lambert: I think that if we look at what is happening in Eastern Europe, it's obviously a wonderful situation in terms of the collapse of totalitarianism, but I think there is a very ugly side as well. One of the problems is that people are seizing freedom. But the danger is "freedom without responsibility." The classic Christian position is "freedom under God."

It's interesting that in Russia, the Orthodox Church does seem to be emerging very rapidly as the moral center for society. But in China, we don't have that. The danger is that there is already a moral and ideological vacuum. If the Gospel is not filling that vacuum, all kinds of other ideologies come in. Perhaps the greatest is the sheer power of materialism.

Direction in Doing

Chao: Yes. So there's a lot of work to be done. If some serious thinking can be done within the next two years, it will give missions' and churches' interest in China a sense of common direction. Otherwise we won't know what to do and confusion may be so big that the work will be beyond any kind of coordination.

Lambert: We have a strong responsibility to not just force a carbon copy of Western capitalist society on China. We must encourage PRC people to do deep theological thinking, biblical thinking, so that they can adapt the Gospel in a thoroughly Chinese manner. There is a danger where quite a lot of young people in China want to go to America to study. There's this cycle where China swings between national xenophobia (everything overseas is dreadful) as happened during the Boxer Rebellion and Cultural Revolution, to the other extreme where everything in the West is wonderful.

So we must encourage people to do some really biblical thinking—to be thoroughly Chinese and biblical. Chinese Solzhenitsins need to emerge! I don't think we've seen that yet, partly because of the pietistic heritage of the Chinese Church. But perhaps now is the time when that kind of person may begin to surface both within China or in the PRC community overseas!

Chao: I agree that the idea of Christianization of Chinese culture and Christian influence of the nations should be spread both among the house churches as well as among the Chinese intellectuals in America or China. We need to provide more of the type of writing dealing with the role of Christianity in the development of Western culture.

Lambert: OMF already has an apologetic literature program—probably about 40 booklets dealing with Christianity and science, philosophy, etc.

Chao: Yes, the important thing is that we need to make a concerted effort and work together to take full advantage of this unprecedented opportunity for the Gospel in China.

Study Questions

1. What problems does the church in China face?

2. What are possible results of a 'open door' policy in China?

3. List some of the developmental and spiritual trends in China according to the dialogue you have just read.

21
Eleven Case Studies of Pioneer Church Planting

This series of case studies focuses exclusively on church planting efforts among peoples which do not have a cluster of evangelizing indigenous churches. Most are quite recent, with the earliest developments occurring during the last thirty years. Each represents "success" to some degree, but this should in no way be construed to suggest that every pioneer church planting effort is successful, easy or quick. It is more often the opposite. Some of these case studies represent experimental efforts that have yet to stand the test of time.

Note the diversity in these studies as well. Some major blocs of unreached peoples—Chinese, Muslim, Hindu, Tribal—are represented. An urban group in Latin America is also included. These peoples live on different continents. Some are urban, others are rural. The diversity properly indicates that missionaries cannot rely on any pat formula for pioneer church planting, but must prayerfully devise unique strategies for unique situations.

The authors also are diverse. Ernie Boehr has been a TEAM (The Evangelical Alliance Mission) missionary in Taiwan. Warren Chastain is a staff member of the Zwemer Institute in Pasadena, California, and served with the Overseas Missionary Fellowship in Indonesia for over twenty years. Clyde Taylor, a former missionary in Latin America, has directed the Evangelical Foreign Missions Association (EFMA) and the National Association of Evangelicals (NAE) and currently serves with the World Relief Corporation, the relief and development arm of the NAE. Phil Elkins directs missionary training for the Mission Training and Resource Center. Greg Livingstone serves as General Director of Frontiers. Ezra Sargunam is the district superintendent for Tamil Nadu with the Church of South India. Jun Balayo serves with O. C. Ministries in the Philippines. William Mial is the Executive Director of Trans World Radio Europe.

Three other authors, as well as the peoples and places they describe, are represented by pseudonyms at their request; "Al Munir" describes the "Gor of Ofir," "Paul Pearlman" describes the "Baranada of Barunda," and "Fatima Mahoumet" describes "Ann Croft" and her work. Likewise, Livingstone's country is referred to as "Sarabia." Taylor also has chosen not to reveal the name of the country where his case study has occurred.

As you read, compare and contrast the case studies. Note the role of the expatriate missionary and of the national worker. Note the methods employed, the obstacles faced and overcome, the time required, the perseverance and creativity demanded. And look for illustrations of principles articulated earlier in this section.

A Pioneer Team in Zambia, Africa

Phillip Elkins

This church planting case study differs from some in that it describes a team of missionaries who banded together *prior* to entering a field. Most efforts are put together by a sending agency and they bring together several people who may meet for the first time in the field. This team came together in 1967 out of a common concern to reach an unreached or "hidden" people whom God had already prepared to be receptive to His redemptive message.

The team took as its model the "Apostolic Band" of the first century. This multi-talented, multi-gifted group had varying degrees of field experience. Stan Shewmaker had already worked in Zambia, Africa for five years; Frank Alexander in Malawi for four years; Phillip and Norma Elkins had been involved in visiting and research of missions in 71 countries and two other couples had been on short-term assignments in Africa. Ages of members ranged from 25 to 33. The five men in the group had degrees in Biblical studies and just prior to leaving for the field completed master's degrees in missiology.

Because of this experience and training, the team felt it could function as its own agency in the same sense that the Paul-Timothy-Luke-Silas "band" of the New Testament did. The group was sent by an "Antioch" congregation in San Fernando, California. This church body recognized that the true "sending" agent was the Holy Spirit (Acts 13: 4, "so being sent by the Holy Spirit") and thus did not consider itself the governing or "decision making" organization. Responsibility for field decisions was left to the team, directed by the Holy Spirit, in partnership with the national Christian leadership on the field.

Early Decisions and Convictions

As the team searched for an unreached people (two years), they concluded the Holy Spirit was leading them to a segment of the Tonga tribe (one of the largest in Zambia, numbering over 300,000) called the Toka-Leya. Ninety-five percent of these people were adherents of an ethnic, or localized, folk-religion (some would use the term *animistic*). Within a twelve-mile radius of where the team settled (the primary target area) were 100 villages with four small congregations that had not grown for several years (a total of 75 Christians).

The team spent most of the first two years (1970-71) learning the language and culture, without engaging in overt evangelistic activities. By the end of 1973 there were four times as many churches (16) and six times the membership (450). Beyond this immediate twelve-mile area, completely new movements were started. For example, in the Moomba chieftaincy, 70 miles to the north, newly trained national Christians planted six churches with 240 members within a few months. This was done in 1973 and involved winning the chief, a third of all the village headmen and both court judges.

I mention this early rapid response to show that we were indeed led to a "ripe pocket" in God's mosaic of peoples. We knew that the national church, motivated and trained, had to be the vehicle to gather the harvest. By 1974 we felt most of the American team could pull out. By 1979, the last two "foreign" families felt they could responsibly move on to another new people to begin the process again. Today a national church continues the process of winning and dis- cipling "to the fringes."

"Methods," "approaches," and "strategy" may be "unspiritual" words in some Christians' vocabulary. I feel in the context of this effort there was validity in the strategy and specific methods followed by the team. In addition to what has been described, I think the first two years in which we were involved as in- depth "learners" of the Tonga world view (language, lifestyle, values, politics, social structure, beliefs, educational systems and other aspects of culture) were essential to our efforts as church planters. My wife and I lived in a village of 175 people and followed a lifestyle closely identified with that of other Toka-Leya families. We learned to "hurt" where they hurt and "feel" what they felt. We identified, not so much to be "accepted," though that is important, but to under- stand and appreciate their culture for its finest and best dimensions. We had to know what parts were already functioning positively within the will and pur- pose of God. We needed to know what had to be confronted and changed to fit the demands of the Kingdom of God.

Perhaps most critical was the need to learn where people had "felt needs" through which God's message of redemption could be accepted as Good News. The message that had been proclaimed as "Gospel" by earlier Christian efforts was in fact perceived as "Bad News." The "Gospel" was perceived as God calling men to have one wife and not to drink beer. Though Christians were saying many other things, this was perceived as the "banner" of the message. Because missionaries showed a major interest in setting up schools for children, the adult population found the message alright for children but almost unthinkable for adults.

Understanding the Tonga World View

During our two years of "incarnational identification," the Tongas' percep- tion of reality (world view) became increasingly clear. Graphically, it might be described to a Westerner as follows:

TONGA WORLD-VIEW

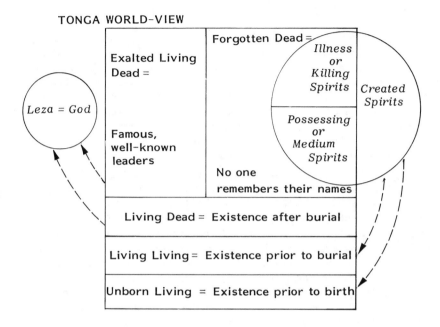

It was to this perception of reality that we had to address our lives and message. Tongas believed that one can affect the *unborn fetus* in another person's body. For example, if a pregnant woman's family had brought death to members of your family, you could enlist the aid of a medicine man to cause the death of the fetus (without having physical contact with the pregnant woman).

The category of *living living* corresponds to our concept of living people with their finite physical limitations. But after physical death this person continues as the *living dead*. The personality, personal enemies, prejudice, taste preferences and so forth, continue intact. Therefore, one can go to the grave of the *living dead* person and request assistance based on a knowledge of that person's personality and the obligations of relationship. Similarly, the *exalted living dead* are to be supplicated on the basis of the status they attained while in the *living living* existence.

The *forgotten dead* are those persons whose names and personalities have passed from living memory. Therefore, no one can now appeal to them, placate them, or appease them. This group represents a dimension of reality which strikes at the heart of the fears, apprehensions and frustrations of the Tonga.

Within this framework of "reality" I will describe how our team of Christians found an opening to speak to felt needs. The Tonga believed that God (*Leza*) created humans and, for a while, lived together with them. But as people became abusive in their relationship with him (in one story a woman strikes God) God left them, and all direct communication became impossible. The only remaining way to speak to God then, is through the living dead or exalted living dead. But the inability to "hear back" from God, to know his personality, to understand whether their needs were adequately communicated, represented an area of *felt need*.

Forgotten ancestors are commonly believed to be the *spirits* which enter people to kill them. A violent illness is associated with such spirits, and unless the person can get this spirit expelled, death will result. Other spirits represent alien forgotten dead (they come from another tribe) which frequently are associated with a long-term, frustrating, but not fatal illness. These spirits also frequently possess the person and use the person as a medium to communicate with the community. The community responds to this possession by special gatherings to dance and sing to the spirit. The purpose of these gatherings is to appease, control and hopefully rid the person of the spirit.

Finally, there are spirits which humans play a role in creating. These particular spirits were the most feared and frustrating for the people with whom I lived. None of the literature I studied on spirits in Africa dealt with this particular spirit, though humanly created spirits do exist in other African tribes.

Our understanding came in this way. A very sick boy was brought to me one day. The child was near death and I felt it was beyond my own limited medical skills to help. I took the parents and child to a hospital, but as I watched the child died. From a Western medical perspective, the child died from complications growing out of malaria and anemia. A year later I attended a village court case where a man was accused of killing this very child. The man finally admitted, after weeks of trial procedures, that he was guilty. The reason was that the man felt he had been wronged by the father of the child and he wanted to create his personal *isaku* spirit. No one during the trial was willing to explain to me what an *isaku* spirit was. People who were normally generous with information would deny knowing anything about these spirits. During this time my wife and I visited a village one evening where none of the women around a fire had their children on their backs. This was very unusual. I asked them why and they explained that it was because there were many *isaku* spirits in their village and they were afraid for the safety of their children. They explained that their children were in huts where they could be watched. When they discovered that I did not know what an *isaku* spirit was they explained only that it was an evil spirit. Since all spirits were considered evil, that was not much help.

As the weeks went by, I finally persuaded a medicine man, who occasionally visited our area, to explain *isaku*. This spirit could be created by people who wanted a being to steal, kill or otherwise serve their own interests. To create an *isaku* one would first have to dig up and decapitate a freshly buried body. The head would be removed in the middle of the night to an isolated area where two paths cross. A fire would be built and certain medicines would be added to it. The ensuing smoke would engulf the head to which portions of certain animals had been attached (snake skin, bird feathers, feet of a rabbit, etc.). This ceremony, if correctly done, would result in a living spirit called *isaku*. The physical part of this spirit was to be kept, fed and hidden. If one properly cared for *isaku*, the person would have his wishes granted. If not properly cared for, *isaku* would kill the person or a member of his family. When a person who owns an *isaku* dies, the relative who inherits the dead person's *name* also inherits their *isaku*. Normally no one would reveal that they had an *isaku*. Thus, if a relative who was asked to receive a name was suspicious that an *isaku* was associated with it, that person might refuse to receive the name.

If anyone inherits a *name*, and unknowingly should have received an *isaku*, they learn of the mistake very painfully. They may arrive home one day to learn that a child has died suddenly.

As our knowledge grew of *isaku* spirits, many gaps in our understanding of the Tonga were eliminated. We grew increasingly conscious of how *powerless* the people felt to adequately deal with *isaku* spirits and those who would create them. This, coupled with the realization that the Tonga felt every death was the result of someone's overt effort to cause it, helped us to understand the extent of much of the animosity and anger between individuals and families.

Responding to Felt Needs

From all of the above insights a picture of *felt needs* emerged to which God could speak meaningfully. The first *Good News* from God for the Tonga was that He had given to us a *Holy Spirit*. The Tongas knew nothing of a good spirit, much less a *Holy Spirit* from God Himself as a gift. We shared that we were not afraid, as they were, of *isaku* spirits because we had residing in us continually a *Spirit* that would not tolerate other spirits. The Spirit in us was more powerful than any other spirit. This explained the lack of fear they had seen in our lives, the joy, the confidence and hope.

The second part of our *Good News* was that the God, which they already knew by name, had *not abandoned them*. The Tonga had left God but He was willing to live among them again. He had already proved His willingness by sending a Son who lived as a human and showed humans how to really live. We explained that one can now talk directly to God about their needs and that this *Son* also serves as a person's special advocate before God. We further explained that God's Son was so concerned to remove the sin and guilt for all of the offensive ways that we live that He Himself accepted the punishment on our behalf.

The Tongas began to realize the verification and proof of what we said was the *Holy Spirit* which lived in us. Lest I be misunderstood by a reader of this, I am not talking about a special gift of speaking in tongues. I am speaking of that which every Christian receives at his *new birth*.

We also spoke of the verification that would come from knowing the Bible. This had little immediate impact, as most of the people could not read. However, the Word is not confined to the printed page. The Word was communicated daily by a God who was willing to reveal Himself in their lives. He revealed Himself one day as we went to a village where we were stopped by a drunken woman who forbade us to come into her village. She said they followed Satan and not God. That night she died and the next day hundreds of people came wanting to know more of God's will for their lives.

The major political leader of our area had been leading the people to the graves of their ancestors annually to solicit rain. When he accepted the *Good News*, he demonstrated his faith by leading his people in a new way. When the first drought occurred he called the people together to spend a day calling to God to give them rain. This was a bold move which exceeded the faith of some of the missionaries. But God honored the boldness and before the sun set the earth was drenched in rain.

In the village where we made our home, almost half of the adult population accepted baptism. At their initiative we all spent a night in prayer before going out as a group to share our faith with another village.

As our team of American missionaries saw more and more churches planted, we began to modify our role as leaders in evangelism and church planting. I believe it was a good strategy for us to identify with the Tongas physically and to provide a physical and spiritual model for evangelism. I know this is a concept that is considered "past" in many circles, but I feel it should still be an emphasis in pioneer mission efforts.

To train an indigenous leadership we set up sixteen extension centers for training every Christian in the basics of the Christian faith, and instituted a special course for those who emerged as church leaders. This was done with the new Christians bearing the cost of the courses. We followed the practice of not subsidizing the construction of buildings, or providing funding for those who entered the preaching ministry.

Prepared for Battle

I cannot close this story without admitting that we, like the team that Paul worked with, experienced some interpersonal conflict and setbacks in our ministry goals, including betrayals by believers and reversions by some of those we had the greatest hopes for. But we accept that as normal in the battle "against the principalities and powers, against the world rulers of this darkness, the spiritual hosts of wickedness in the heavenly places" (Eph. 6: 12).

I think it is important for one to know the Bible well enough to be able to know where the battle is. I think we invite defeat when we do not make the effort to learn the local language well enough to teach effectively in it. I think it is essential that we participate in a real way in the lifestyle and struggles of the people we are sent to. When we do not ground our proclamation on an understanding of a people's hurts and felt needs, and when we allow our own cultural understanding of the Christian message to blind us to what God wants said in a radically different setting and culture, we invite failure.

I heartily commend the team approach for pioneer mission efforts. During the five years I was in Zambia one of our original families left, but others came and were incorporated. In addition, from the very beginning, we tried hard to expand the team leadership to include Tonga Christians. This kind of team approach is not the only way to approach the task, but it was part of what made our five years in Zambia a productive and happy experience.

Establishing a Church in an Unreached Muslim Area

Warren Chastain

Background Information

It would be difficult to find an area on earth subject to direct Western colonial control longer than the Sundanese area of Java—over 350 years under Dutch rule. Of all Muslim peoples, the Sundanese have been under Western ("Christian") domination longer, perhaps, than any other, and have experienced long-term close contact with Europeans with the exploitation (and benefits) of colonialism. For about 267 years (1596 to 1863) missions were not permitted to evangelize the Sundanese—the second largest people of Indonesia, and the eighth largest Muslim ethnic unit in the world. Islam was established in Banten, West Java by 1575 and spread throughout West Java before the Dutch wrested control from the Muslim kingdom and made the area its base for establishing an empire.

Islam became interwoven with indigenous culture so that to the typical Sundanese it appeared as a unified whole which protected him from his long exposure to the chilling blasts of both western supremacy and foreign religion. The robe of Islam is woven from animism, folk Islam, orthodox Islam, and mysticism, which the average villager clings to with a tenacious loyalty even when he is not particularly pious. For 99 percent of the people, to be Sundanese is to be Muslim. This tenacity has tempted Mission Boards many times, since their entrance in 1863, to drop their efforts to reach Sundanese. God, however, has cracked the solid wall of resistance and a few thousand have believed, mostly through the witness of lay-groups operating externally to the mission and church.

Today there is a small Sundanese denomination which is largely ingrown, non-evangelistic, and basically turning away from its Sundanese identity to an Indonesian liturgy, Scriptures, and ministry. Perhaps this was inevitable as other ethnic groups entered the churches to make the Sundanese a minority in their own church. But even if this church exploited its Sundanese culture and were strongly evangelistic, it would still have an enormous task to reach the 28 million Sundanese—a population equal to that of Canada!

The Situation

Before Dutch troops could re-occupy Indonesia after the Japanese surrender in 1945, Indonesian nationalists had proclaimed an independent republic. Four years of violence followed as the Dutch tried to win back the jewel of their empire. A rabid hatred for the Dutch and anything associated with them (including missionaries and Christianity) flamed across the countryside. National Christians suffered, some being killed and others forced from their homes, and evangelism became practically impossible. Between 1950 and 1957 a massive exodus of the remaining Dutch occurred, as the Sukarno government extended its policy of rejection of all Dutch influences—economic, linguistic, cultural, and religious.

Muslim leaders felt that after 350 years of "Christian" domination the golden opportunity to set up an Islamic state had come. Thousands of armed men joined Darul Islam to overthrow the "secular" Sukarno government, and West Java was ravaged in many areas as D.I. guerrillas burned villages, attacked towns and cities, and made the roads unsafe. Atrocities were perpetrated even against other Muslims, so the limited Christian witness that had been done died in most of the Sundanese area.

The Overseas Missionary Fellowship (OMF) was one of the many missions which entered Indonesia as a new field after World War II. Since each missionary needed a national sponsor to get a visa, the OMF contracted my fiancee and me to teach in a new Christian high school run by a Chinese Church in the city of Sukabumi.

Hindrances to the Vision

It would hardly be fair for a mission leader or a church to assign to a first term missionary, still groping in the language and the culture, the job of forming a new church in a distant area where the Gospel was unknown, particularly if Islam was dominant in the area. But it was precisely this challenge that I grasped, moved by such a strong sense of divine calling to establish churches where none existed that I could not be satisfied with merely fulfilling my contractual obligations to the school which took six days a week (and the church, the seventh). Not that I considered the school opportunity insignificant, for a majority of the students were attractive non-Christian Chinese or Muslims and some of them came to faith. But I was determined to try to establish God's Church in an unreached area despite the number of hindrances. I would soon find out how uncooperative Satan would be.

These hindrances included (1) I knew no Sundanese (the language of the villages); (2) School duties took up six days and church the remaining day, so little time was available for new initiatives; (3) Travel was difficult because I had no vehicle until later when I got a scooter; (4) The Islamic guerrilla movement made the roads dangerous, and the "State of Emergency" declared by the government required the missionary to inform the police of all his movements outside his own city. This informing of officials (mostly Muslim) made it difficult to operate in a "low profile" manner; (5) The critical eye of Muslim leaders who actively kept abreast of Christian activities and tried to counter them; (6) Communist agitation against Christianity and Westerners; (7) Difficulty of finding literature on Sundanese culture, knowledge of which was essential in order to present Christ in forms comprehensible to the Sunda people; (8) The residual memories of the brutalities of a war against the Whites made it difficult to accept any message from a "Dutchman"; (9) The strong feeling that to be a Sundanese was to be a Muslim; (10) The lack of Christian literature or Scriptures for evangelistic work; (11) The slanderous idea circulated by some Muslims that the churches bribed people to become Christians—this tended to bring insincere inquirers to our doors or to stigmatize sincere ones; (12) Churches that had forms of worship repellent to potential Muslim converts, or which feared or suspected converts; (13) The negative example of many Christians, as well as the inability to witness of those Christians who were devout; (14) The pervasive lack of vision and expectation of fruit that vitiated any evangelistic outreach (one Dutch missionary told us, "You have to wait ten years before you can begin to witness to a Muslim!"); (15) The short-term nature of the contracts—two years and renewable if the government extended your visa, which was given only for one year at a time; this made long term planning risky, particularly since the government was becoming increasingly pro-Communist; and (16) The lack of a national co-worker who had a burden for the work and time to give.

Beginnings

Sukabumi had a number of ethnic churches already, so I had to look further afield for untouched places. The surrounding villages were crowded with Sundanese whose language I did not know. They were the responsibility of the local Sundanese church. I checked the main roads leading out of Sukabumi and found that the smaller towns all had small fellowships ministering to the Chinese; the Sundanese were neglected, so I decided to have some tracts translated into Sundanese. But there was at least one church in each area—as needy as they were, a greater need would be an area with no witness whatsoever. I had to work in an urban center where I could use Indonesian.

A study of missions in West Java provided further clues which the Lord used to give more precise guidance. Two large areas of West Java had never been opened for missionary work because the colonial government feared outbreaks of Muslim fanaticism. Directly west of Sukabumi was the broad *Banten* region, and to the south the *Jampang* area stretching along the Indian Ocean, both still unoccupied by missionaries. Increased information enabled Betty and I (now married) to focus our prayers. The coastal town of Pelabuhan Ratu (henceforth *PR*) was the largest town along the coast and was located strategically at a road junction joining both Banten and Jampang. A church located there could be a springboard for outreach into two large neglected Sundanese areas. The PR area was important in its own right: there were some 10,000 people in the town itself, and an unknown number in the regions surrounding it.

We continued our prayer and research, concerned lest we launch a project which we might not be able to responsibly fulfill, and fearful that we might jeopardize future progress by making a mistake in our approach. Another problem was getting the agreement and support of the church. They had never tried any outreach project like this before, and they knew that there were only a few Chinese in PR, so there could be no benefit to their own program. They were also concerned for my safety. Terrorists operated just outside the city and often attacked nearby villages. They were merciless even to other Muslims, so would not hesitate to kill a foreign Christian.

We had decided that if God wanted us to reach PR, He would have to bring us into contact with a person who would be willing to request a Bible study in his home. Waiting was discouraging, but eventually we heard about Mr. "Spry," an Indonesian from the outer islands. Would he be merely a nominal Christian, and be wary of evangelism? Would he be fearful for his job and the pressures of the Muslim community? Would he be willing to write out a request to the Police asking to have a Christian meeting in his home (led by a foreigner)? Wary of going directly to Mr. Spry's home (the neighbors might question him), I arranged to meet him when he came to the city. Mr. Spry was an overseer on an estate near PR, a gentle but forceful man who was a true believer! We shared our vision for PR and the struggle it would involve. We thanked God to see him come to share our enthusiasm. Now we could go back to the church leaders with a definite plan; with their approval, we could then start the long process of getting permission from the military, police, Mayor's office, plus the various PR authorities.

The permission-seeking process enabled me to meet most of the leaders of PR, and my trips there using available transportation brought me into contact with a lot of the common people. No advertising campaign was needed, especially later when I traveled by scooter and became known by all. We decided that the timing and structure of the meeting should not look like a church service, which would be perceived by Muslim leaders as a threat. PR was a fishing and farming community, so we sought a time suitable for them and my schedule. Fridays after classes, I would go there and return the next morning to teach. This gave me little time to meet people; Mr. Spry pitched in and made up for my lack. Over the years he had gotten to know the community and had a good reputation. His contacts soon filled the porch where we met around the table eating snacks and studying our way through the Gospel of John.

Growth

I was pleased to be able to report back to the church in Sukabumi that the first convert was a Chinese merchant. After a few visits, I was invited to stay overnight in his home. Curious why I was taking the trouble to come down there (especially when I arrived soaked in rainy season), Mr. Tim soon became exposed to the Bible and to Jesus Christ. After a few months, he believed and became an avid student of the Bible. He grew so quickly that Mr. Tim became one of the leaders of the fellowship.

I extended my contacts with government officials and offered to teach them English. Classes were held in the Police complex, so that I became a person they knew, not just a foreigner to be watched. I knew that when a church did emerge in PR, it might need protection from attacks by fanatics. I realized also that I would be the first target, so it would be good to have a few sympathetic ears in places of authority.

Mr. Spry started to bloom. He had been faithful as a Christian, but a defeatist—living year after year like one odd drop in an ocean of Islam. The Gospel got hold of him and he started to grow. We discussed how the Gospel might become incarnate within Sundanese culture without compromise. He came to see that the Gospel was the power of God to save anybody. Mr. Tim saw remarkable answers to prayer; when the Chinese were being attacked, he saw the fire stop at his house when the market was burning down. Amazing healings occurred in his family in answer to prayer. His business grew by leaps and bounds. He could pray in faith now, and God could use the witness of this transformed life.

We had mixed fellowship of Sundanese, a few Chinese, and other Indonesians. They increasingly realized that it was their own meeting. I could spend so little time with them that to succeed they would have to do the contact work. I was trying to get Mr. Spry to the place where he could take over the leadership. The format of the meetings was so simple—brief prayers, a few songs, and discussing our way through the Gospel of John paragraph by paragraph—that he soon felt willing to attempt the job appropriate to ordained ministers (as he thought). I showed him how to prepare a Bible study, but on his first night he nervously read through his whole sermon, and looked up to find that he still had over three hours to fill (our meetings usually lasted from 7-11 PM). Everyone pitched in and we had a good study, but the ice was broken for Mr. Spry, and he soon was able to lead with confidence.

The First Crisis

The Chief of Police sent an order for me to submit a list of names of everyone who attended the meeting. This was very intimidating even to a person with some education like Mr. Spry, but to some of the poorer people it could easily frighten them all away. I was in a quandary—I felt I would be betraying people who trusted us, particularly since we did not know who would see the list or how it would be used, but if we refused—as I was inclined to do, it could get Mr. Spry into trouble and destroy all our labors. Things had been going so well, it shocked me to see how quickly Satan could ruin it all. We kept it a secret, fearful that if the news got out the whole village would consider it dangerous to visit our meetings. We prayed much. The fingerprints of Satan were all over this demand. It was like the question given to the Lord, "Is it lawful to give a poll-tax to Caesar or not?" (Matthew 22:17). No matter how we answered, it would prevent a church from coming into being. What was the source—local Muslim leaders, the Police Chief himself, or perhaps Intelligence officials in Sukabumi?

Unable to delay any longer, I went down to the Police Station with much inward groaning, still unable to devise a polite way to refuse his order. He was a very short-tempered man who was used to being obeyed, but he was very friendly knowing I had come to submit the list. We chatted a while as I searched for a way to tell him that I had no list. Then I told him that I had come to personally invite him to come to our meetings. I suggested that if he had some reports to fill out for his superiors it would make a much better impression on them if he could say that he had checked it out thoroughly himself. The unstated implication was clear; if the foreigner is being investigated, why depend upon his word? I could sincerely say that I would be quite happy if he attended tomorrow night. He could then make an accurate eyewitness report!

The Police Chief appeared the next night in civilian clothes and enjoyed himself immensely! The members, not knowing the situation, greeted him enthusiastically, and the Chief enjoyed talking about religion and the *Injil*. He went home with a gift of a Bible, and quite convinced that nothing subversive was going on. Everyone in the community knew the Police Chief, and if he could visit the

Christian meeting it gave respectability and acceptance that we were part of the community. Anti-Christian elements had the ground cut out from under them—if they wanted to stir up the community to stop the Christians, the community would think twice.

More people came and the porch got more crowded. Mr. Spry started talking about baptisms and communion. He even wanted a church building. My furlough was approaching, and preparation had to be made for maintaining the meeting. I had hoped that Mr. Spry would feel ready to baptize and break bread, but he had long imbibed the tradition of the clergy laity distinction which limited the sacraments to performance by ordained professionals. He also tended to believe that a real church needed a full time man and a church building. I was sure that these ideas would be detrimental to the rapid extension of the Gospel, but I felt obligated to respect his views. Since I had been teaching them that the church was theirs, I did not feel free to try to impose my will. What was needed was more time for teaching, but my tight school schedule made that impossible.

Mr. Spry was the recognized leader and he started preparing for baptisms. I was inclined to baptize immediately upon belief, but his tradition required a six-month training course. I would be gone by then, after a bit over a year of ministry in PR. I saw a lot of weaknesses in the work, but I was jubilant that God had raised up a fellowship of followers of Jesus in a darkened area. Mr. Spry started plans for a building, but I cautioned him against that. I sensed it would galvanize Muslim opposition, and it would also destroy the family warmth of our gathering. In our present pattern we could carry on the functions of a church without appearing to be a church. To have a minister and a building would flaunt our gains before the Muslims and provoke their reaction. I felt that Mr. Spry already had proven himself to be a minister, and that God would raise up others in time.

Later Developments

Instead of expanding the porch, the fellowship collected their own funds and built a separate building at some sacrifice. Unfortunately, one night it "accidentally" burned down. A few years later other property was bought (adjacent to the Police Station) which still stands, and led by a full-time evangelist supported entirely by the church. A second church has emerged in PR and meets under Mr. Spry's direction. Ten miles to the west another church has emerged near a hotel complex, but this may have developed independently of the PR churches. All succeeding churches are, however, in debt to the first PR church, because by it the Muslim community came to accept the existence of a local Christian body in their midst. That an "alien religion" (as they perceived it) could be established about 1960 in a small town-rural community and grow to the present, suggests many positive qualities in the leadership of the PR Muslim community, who could have incited the forces of intolerance. It also implies the efficiency, skill and goodwill of the Police and governmental apparatus who quietly restrained any fanatic elements. Clearly the Gospel is the power of God—as long as it is preached. The job is not done; there still is not a single missionary in the vast regions that adjoin PR, Banten and Jampang.

A Work of God Among the Hakka in Taiwan

Ernest Boehr

The ministry in the Tungshih area of central Taiwan is an excellent example of how rapidly the Gospel follows along the web of family relationships. It also shows the wisdom of the missionary in guiding the Christians to make functional substitutes and thus satisfy the people's desire to express in a Hakka way their respect of the departed.

The Transformation of Mrs. Chan

The work of God began with the transformation of Mrs. Chan, who had moved with her husband from Cholan in central Taiwan to Kaohsiung, the southern port city. She had been troubled with demons for some years and they really began to bother her when her son wrote from the off-shore island of Chinmen of his fear from the noise of exploding shells from Communist China.

Mrs. Chan went to a monk in Tainan, 50 miles to the north, who was known for his ability to cast out demons. For $15 Mrs. Chan got the advice to make a straw effigy of herself, put her clothes on it and have it buried. She was covered with a fishing net and taken to a dark corner to hide until the effigy was buried. The action was intended to deceive the demons into thinking that she was dead. "Do you think that drove away the demons' she will ask in her testimony. "No!," she will shout. "It didn't help one bit."

About that time an elder's wife from the Hsinsheng Presbyterian Church in Kaohsiung began visiting her and inviting her to church. She had all kinds of excuses but was finally enticed to see some slides on the life of Christ. The demon seized her in the meeting and she ran out, but the pastor came later to see her. He said she would not get rid of the demon without first accepting Christ. He kept on visiting her and teaching her of Christ.

Almost two years later Mrs. Chan woke up early one morning and began breaking the idols on the home altar. Her daughter-in-law thought she was possessed again and called Mr. Chan. He told them to leave Mrs. Chan alone because she was preparing to believe in Jesus. She asked them if they could think

---

Adapted from *Taiwan Church Growth Bulletin*, 1974. Used with permission.

of any help the idols had been in the twenty years they had served them. Since they could think of none, she finished cleaning up the altar and sold to the scrap man what couldn't be burned. She later was baptized and within three years her husband and two sons believed too.

Mrs. Chan's Family and Friends

Mrs. Chan began praying for her brothers and sisters near Tungshih immediately after she was saved. Over a period of ten years she visited them as often as she could, telling them what the Lord had done for her and encouraging them to trust in Christ. One brother was the village elder and he loved to drink. His liver became diseased from too much liquor, so Mrs. Chan prayed that the Lord would both heal his liver and take the taste for liquor from him. When the Lord answered her prayer, she encouraged her brother to trust in Christ. He said they needed to know more and would welcome a preacher to their home.

Mrs. Chan had not lived near Tungshih for many years, so she prayed as she walked to town that the Lord would lead her to the right person. She arrived at the Norwegian Evangelical Lutheran Free Church at seven o'clock in the morning that May day in 1968. Mrs. Johansen was home and she called Miss Cho to interpret what Mrs. Chan was saying. Mrs. Chan told her story and asked Mrs. Johansen to go with her to Henglung.

Mrs. Johansen suggested that she instead should send Miss Ammon, who at that time was in Tungshih and who spoke Hakka. Mrs. Chan objected: "No, the Holy Spirit led me here. You are the one." Then Mrs. Johansen suggested they wait until her husband came back. Again Mrs. Chan objected: "No, someone needs to go in now and each Sunday night as well as one night during the week." Another fellow missionary was available and she went with Miss Cho and Mrs. Chan for the first meeting that day in the Yeh home in Henglung.

Rev. Johansen and Miss Cho began regular meetings in the Yeh home in mid-May in 1968. He spoke in Mandarin and Miss Cho interpreted into Hakka. They wrote out some choruses and a brief prayer asking the Lord's forgiveness and blessing. The oldest women seemed the most responsive. When someone asked about worshipping their ancestors, Rev. Johansen hesitated. Then the oldest brother's wife said: "In all these years that I have offered food to our ancestors not once have they taken what I offered." There were no more questions on ancestor worship.

In May, 1969, Mrs. Chan came again and told Rev. Johansen: "Pastor, tonight you must speak on baptism." Actually he had spoken on salvation and baptism before, but was not planning to give an invitation that night. He did some quick altering of his message and was ready to give the invitation that night when Mrs. Chan came forward to take over. She held a lively invitational meeting until twenty-six had raised their hands professing faith in Christ. At the baptismal service three weeks later, nineteen followed the Lord in baptism—the entire family of the village elder (six people), five members of the third brother's family, three relatives and five friends. The oldest brother had gotten mad and refused to let his family be baptized. They were baptized at a later date.

A Funeral Takes New Meaning

Old mother Yeh passed away in February, 1970, at 94 years of age. She, too, had responded to the Gospel and loved to hear as much as Miss Cho had time to tell her. Her peaceful passing was a wonderful testimony to all, and Mrs. Chan came up from Kaohsiung to make sure the funeral was "Christian." There was no question about keeping idol and ancestor worship out of the ceremony, but a brother-in-law argued hard with Mrs. Chan for reading eulogies to the dead. Rev. Johansen asked if eulogies could be read facing the audience rather than facing the dead. Mrs. Chan agreed to the change.

A group from mother Yeh's side of the family came to express their sorrow by playing Chinese horns, violins and cymbals. Mrs. Chan refused to let them play and the village elder was very chagrined. He explained to Rev. Johansen that the group had come to express their sorrow. Rev. Johansen suggested to Mrs. Chan that the group play at that time and not at the funeral. Mrs. Chan consented and the brother was delighted. He ran up the road to where the group was waiting and told them to come.

The seven-week memorial for old mother Yeh became an excellent opportunity for teaching about life and death and what Christ accomplished in his death and resurrection. Each week for seven weeks, Rev. Johansen went in to Henglung to hold services in the home. This took the place of the heathen rites of having a monk come in each week to report the progress of the soul through hell. It was a very satisfying time for the family. They felt they had done all they could for the departed.

Other Fellowships Begin

During the funeral Mrs. Chan stayed with her youngest sister in Tamap'u, a town nearby. She encouraged her to have meetings in her home. She agreed to the idea, so on Easter Sunday, 1970, Rev. Johansen began services there too. It was not long before the youngest sister and her son believed and were baptized with several older neighbor ladies.

In the meantime, old Mr. Tai, who had been baptized in the Henglung home, asked if they could use the village elder's office in Chungk'o for services. Mr. Yeh was agreeable and Rev. Johansen started services there about the same time as those in Tamap'u. There have been five more baptized in Chungk'o and the group is now renting a small building for services (In November 1980 a new church building was dedicated in Chungk'o).

Since 1969 there have been 50 baptized in the three places. Twenty-three of them are in the immediate Yeh family and three more are close relatives. The remaining twenty-four are friends and neighbors of the family. The meetings in the three places always have a good number of unsaved in attendance because the natural setting of the home is neither foreign nor unnerving. All the meetings are at night when the people have time on their hands.

In the fall of 1972, the Johansens began studying Hakka. Rev. Johansen preaches now in the Hakka dialect. Mrs. Chan continues her ministry of prayer and encouragement. Since 1974, Mrs. Chan has not been in good health. However, the home fellowships in Henglung and Chungk'o continue and the vigorous group in Chungk'o has seen steady growth.

A Flaming Fire in the Maredumilli Jungles

Ezra Sargunam

Prem Sagar, a young man of 22 was called of God for full-time ministry. He came from the West Godavari District of Andhrapradesh to the city of Madras to undergo ministerial training at one of the Bible Schools. During his summer vacation in 1979, he traveled about one hundred miles to spend the holiday at the home of one of his relatives in the East Godavari District. This uncle of Prem Sagar was a forest officer with the government and was living with the family in a forest area called Maredumilli Samithi.

A Flaming Fire

During the time he stayed with his uncle and family, Prem Sagar came to know about the tribal people living in the jungles of Maredumilli Samithi. He met some of these groups and the Lord placed a special burden in his heart to return to work among these tribal people after his seminary training. While he was at the Bible school, Prem Sagar kept talking to me and my colleagues about these hidden people of Maredumilli. However, after seminary training, he was appointed to serve as a member of one of the gospel teams in the city of Madras. Since our committee wasn't too happy to send Prem Sagar to serve in the midst of tribal people all by himself and because no one else came forward to go with him for pioneer ministry in this region, he was stuck with the team in Madras.

Prem Sagar kept praying for these tribal people. As the burden in his heart grew for these unreached and as he began to find out that it might take years before the "bureaucrats" would approve the project of reaching the Maredumilli tribals, Prem Sagar determined before God to do it on his own.

Initially Brother Prem wanted to move to Maredumilli, live with his uncle, and so begin the ministry. It was a real test for him when he came to discover that his uncle had transferred to another area. Nevertheless, the "fire" for ministry among the Maredumilli tribals that was burning in his heart could not be put out. Prem Sagar finally wrote a prayer letter to all of his friends and Christian relatives about his decision, resigned from his services with the gospel team and went entirely on his own in a step of faith to work among the Maredumilli.

It needs more than vision and courage for one to be called to serve among the hidden peoples. One needs to become a "flaming fire". The history of the church has proved that the Lord "maketh His ministers a flaming fire" (Ps.104:4)

Before I elaborate on how this came to be true in the life and ministry of Brother Prem Sagar, let me state briefly here certain characteristics of the people to which he intended to go.

Customs and Cultures of the Maredumilli Tribal People

Maredumilli area covers about 590 square miles and lies on the north east side of Andhrapradesh and south west of Orissa. The entire area is covered by hills and dense forest at an altitude of 1500-4000 feet above sea level. According to India's 1971 census within these jungles are about 30,000 tribal people in 5,800 families living in approximately 330 villages. There are at least two or three legends told about the antiquity of the people. One of the traditions states that these people are descendants of groups who once lived in the plains. They moved with their families into the jungles several hundred years ago when the Muslims carried out a mass killing of people who did not embrace Islam. Once they got settled in these jungles, the tradition said, they never again returned to the plains.

Though the caste system is not commonly found among the tribal people of India, the Maredumilli appear to practice caste to some degree. This is one of the strong arguments in favor of the theory that they once came from the plains. The highest of the caste groups among them are the *Konda Reddies* and the lowest are *Valmikis*.

Since the response to the gospel has been mostly among the *Koyas* and the *Valmikis*, we shall consider briefly the cultural features of these people. They live in huts and lead simple lives. The huts are scattered over hills without regard to caste distinctions. Their clothes are never removed until they are torn or worn to threads. Women wear earrings, nose rings, and bracelets made of various metals. The people go hunting for wild pigs, deer and birds in bands and share the prey among themselves. Both men and women consume "toddy" (an alcoholic beverage made from the *Zeelugu* palm tree). The Koyas and Valmikis do feast on both marriage and funeral occasions. Though they do not have periodic or annual festivals, they observe the harvest of every crop as a time for "merry-making". The crop will not be eaten before the sacrifice of a cock has been made and the blood is sprinkled over the crop, after which they will eat, drink and dance together. They put on tiger and cheetah skins, wear bison horns and peacock feathers and dance in groups.

Marital relations are strictly endogamous. During festivals an unmarried young man (*govu*) can take away the hand of any unmarried maiden (*gubbatty*) and take her as his wife irrespective of the will and pleasure of the maiden and her family. He can also send her away if he is not pleased with her.

The language they speak is a mixture of *Telugu* and *Oriya* and has no script. From the Konda Reddies to Valmikis, they do not have any religion in the strict sense of the term, but they fear the supernatural elements. Sacrifices are made to the supernatural powers like lightning, thunder and rain. Until 1970 these tribes also offered human sacrifices. Though they do not have a clear monotheistic understanding of God, they seem to fear a particular deity by the name of *Khonda Raju*, who is plural. Interestingly enough, they never worship idols, though certain sacred trees are selected under which the sacrifices are made.

They do not follow modern trade systems, since they are scattered in remote areas where there is no proper communication system. They bring such produce as oranges, poultry, and herb medicines, and what they have hunted, on *shanti* days (market days) and barter their goods with the people from the plains for salt, kerosene, and clothes.

The Vision Became a Reality

Prem Sagar left Madras and came to Maredumilli. Living in a small hut under the most trying conditions, Prem began his ministry among the Maredumilli tribes. A few of the Christian relatives and friends back in his home town got behind him by sending him a little money and food. One of his more practical approaches was to meet these tribals on *shanti* days when they would come walking more than 30 miles to barter their goods with the people of the plains.

Since most of the people could neither read nor write, the only method of communication that was open to him was to preach to them at the market on Saturdays. So Prem would stand every Saturday night in one of the entrances to the market and would sing aloud with the help of a tambourine which produced more noise than his singing did. Most of the tribals, on their return journey back into the jungles, would lay down their headloads and listen attentively to the gospel stories. Brother Prem preached to them in the Telugu language which was understood by both the people from the plains as well as the tribals. He followed this with prayers for the sick. Well! Wouldn't anyone like to find healing for their bodies without bothering to give away their wealth to the witch doctor? Many knelt down in prayer for healing, for protection, and for good crops. Several found their prayers answered. The news about the new "Christian Witch Doctor" spread like wildfire throughout the jungles.

Meanwhile, Prem Sagar came across two or three tribals who had apparently attended Christian schools and who had lived and were raised in Christian hostels in Rajamundry, which was about 150 miles away from Maredumilli. These few precious people who were exposed to the message of the gospel still remembered some of the Christian songs. Though they had not become Christians, one of them hung a picture of Christ on the mud walls of his hut. Prem Sagar got all the more excited by the fact that God had already began His work in the Maredumilli area. This particular individual, who also happened to be a tribal leader, had a teen-age daughter who had bad dreams in the night and was filled by the evil spirit. Brother Prem Sagar fasted and prayed for the deliverance of this dear little girl from the demon possession and she was completely delivered. This tribal leader and his family put their trust in Jesus Christ. More and more began to happen.

During these months, Prem Sagar never failed to be in touch with us back in Madras. He had written to us a number of times, challenging us to pray for him. We were left without any option but to get behind this "rebel" who left us before formally informing us of his departure and who had only sent his letter of resignation a month after he had begun his ministry in the Maredumilli area.

Early in the 1980's, I did make an effort to survey Maredumilli area with some of my colleagues. After we had seen and were convinced of God's mighty works, we were definitely prompted by the Holy Spirit to get behind Brother Prem's ministry. Meanwhile, the chief of one of the tribes, who had accepted Christ along with his family, came forward and donated a piece of land, where a semi-permanent church building has since been built. The first converts, seventeen members of five families, were baptized in the summer of 1980. Subsequently 40 other adults have been baptized. Three churches have been planted. Prem Sagar is now married to a very gifted lady, who, though a university graduate, has graciously accepted the call of God to serve with her husband to serve the Lord in the jungles. Three other full-time national missionaries have been appointed by the Indian Missionary Movement, an indigenous mission agency and the missionary arm of the Evangelical Church of India.

The World Evangelical Outreach, who are doing a tremendous ministry among certain hidden peoples around the world, have now taken up the challenge to work alongside the Evangelical Church of India in discipling 30,000 tribals of Maredumilli. The dream of one man, Prem Sagar, is now becoming a reality.

In Conclusion

The strategies employed and the missiological factors behind the Maredumilli movement are obvious.

1. It takes more than a call, vision, courage, conviction, personnel and finances to disciple a hidden people. It takes ministers with a flaming fire. Those whom the Lord makes a flaming fire become so obsessed with the call and purpose in their life that nothing can stop them until they fulfill that assignment. This was very true in the case of Prem Sagar.

2. The powers of darkness in animistic cultures have to be counteracted with power-encounter ministry. Many sick people whom Prem Sagar prayed over were miraculously healed. Demons were cast out, also, as in the case of a tribal chief's daughter. Another person was bitten by a poisonous cobra, and his life was spared because of prayer.

3. The Maredumilli tribals have some kind of monotheistic belief, which was some preparation for them to accept the Christian faith. According to missiological principles, such animistic groups who are remote and do not identify themselves with the mainstream of any one of the major religions, like Hinduism, Buddhism, or Islam, are most responsive to the message of the gospel. This has been very well proven with the Maredumilli tribals.

4. Though the Lord has used Prem Sagar in initiating the movement, he was wise in linking his efforts with a much larger indigenous church planting group, namely, the Evangelical Church of India. He was not fighting the battle on his own. There were others who stood with him in the cause of discipling these precious Maredumilli tribal people.

The Evangelical Church of India, with OMS International at the world level and the Indian Missionary Movement at the national level, are marching towards the goal of 1,000 churches by the turn of the century. Two-hundred of these churches have already been planted. More hidden peoples continue to be identified, and disciples for Christ and multiplied churches are appearing among them. May the Lord of the harvest continue to make his ministers a flaming fire who win the winnable while they are winnable.

Reaching the Baranada People of Barunda

Paul Pearlman

Nestled between Maluwa, Batu, and the blue ocean, Barunda is a tropical nation of fifteen million people. There are some twenty-eight million Baranada; they are the second-largest Muslim ethnic group in Africa. About 60 percent of the ethnic Baranada are Muslims; the remainder are animists. Present-day Barunda is the ancestral homeland of the Baranada people, who are distinct from the surrounding animistic tribes. Barunda, which is unusual for its ethnic homogeneity, is 90 percent Muslim with a 10 percent animist population, mostly of ethnic Baranada background. Eighty-five percent of the ethnic Baranada outside of Barunda are animists, the remainder being Muslims.

The vast majority of the Baranada, both Muslim and animist alike, are subsistence grain farmers. The low-lying terrain of Barunda is ideally suited to such agriculture, but it has been subject to severe weather, including both flooding and droughts. Population is quite dense in areas where arable land is at a premium.

The countryside is socially divided along patrilineal kinship lines. Kinship, which includes the widest possible range of people "related" by blood or marriage, is reckoned in several complex ways and is ingeniously expandable to include close social relationships. The basic community structure is the village, within which there is considerable interrelationship. Households are divided into "eating groups," which are communally run. This household unit symbolizes its mutual interdependence through the preparation and sharing of common food and living quarters. The concept of "community" is a cultural norm traceable well into the animistic past of the Baranada. A person's family membership and place of residence are thus the focal points for all of his activities in the world.

Islam came to the Baranada during the fourteenth century and experienced a rapid growth under the influence of Sufi sheikhs, whose egalitarianism was very appealing during the period of slave trading. The Baranada are Sunni Muslims, for whom the five pillars of Islam are deeply embedded in daily life. The custom of female seclusion is quite strong. Sufi orders also continue to flourish in the rural areas. There are, however, a number of animistic practices the Baranada maintain, one of which is saint worship, as witnessed by the widespread participation in *natu,* "commemorative gatherings," at the tombs of their saints.

The Status of Christianity in Barunda

Christians number some thirty thousand—equally divided between Protestants and Catholics—and comprise less than one percent of the population. The church is derived entirely from Baranada people who have had an animistic background. Despite their common racial background, animists have no dealings with Muslims. The various denominations are almost entirely dependent financially on Western Christian assistance. This applies to church budgetary needs as well as to job opportunities in mission institutions and Western developmental organizations. As pressures continue to increase for the establishment of *shariat*, or Islamic sacred law, in Barunda, the church has been concerned with the growing instances of persecution and social second-class status.

The church, a small, introspective, and often insecure body of believers, has been growing slowly. Twenty-five Protestant mission societies have some 250 missionaries working throughout Barunda, and Catholics 169. There are twelve denominations in the country. Most missionaries work within the established church or are attached to mission-operated institutions. There is a definite trend to place more missionaries in full-time evangelistic outreach.

New Efforts to Reach the Baranada in the Mawasa Area

Despite the Baranada's seeming resistance to the Gospel, some recent breakthroughs have occurred among them under the leadership of the Overseas Christian Missionary Fellowship (OCMF). In 1959, the OCMF entered the town of Mawasa, which has a population of eight thousand in a district of two hundred thousand. Between one and three missionary couples have resided in the town up to the present. Until 1975, their efforts proved fruitless; no church was established and almost no one was led to Christ. Mawasa appeared to be barren and resistant. The OCMF field council determined that it would be expedient to withdraw from that area unless a breakthrough occurred in the ensuing twelve months. Then, the miraculous began to unfold. Through the influence of two Muslim converts, Tabbar and Sadig, the OCMF began to adopt Baranada Muslim forms in their work of communicating the Gospel. Presently there are two worshipping groups of believers in the Mawasa area. Each fellowship is made up of fifteen Muslim converts, almost all of whom are male heads of families. Numerous factors have played a part in the new responsiveness. For example, the response of Christian agencies during natural catastrophe has built up an attitude of goodwill. However, the vast majority of converts cite the Baranada-like quality of the message as being the main reason for their conversion. The Baranada have a highly developed culture and sense of historical tradition. Thus, adapting the forms of the message of the Gospel to fit their patterns and to speak to the needs of their society has been the key factor in establishing the fellowships. The following descriptions of these groups illustrate this point.

Description of Converts

The majority of converts are farmers who, on the average, are barely literate; economically they are self-supporting; and they are close enough sociologically to be able to intermarry. Those who have grown most rapidly spiritually were formerly devout Muslims. Almost all converts are reading the Bible (or having it read to them), praying, and meeting together informally in their village homes for worship—without the presence of a foreign missionary. Witnessing to their neighbors and extended families began on the day of their conversion and has been the major cause of reproduction. Until now, it has not been the missionary who has won these men to the Lord, with a very few exceptions. His role is basically to give spiritual encouragement and biblical teaching. The believers have shown initiative and vision. After a study of 1 Corinthians 12, one group on their own appointed an evangelist, an administrator, a prayer coordinator, and a pastor. A few of the wives and children have accepted Christ, but this area of evangelism still remains an obstacle. There has been an appreciation of the supernatural on a practical level, with visions and dreams of spiritual significance occurring fairly frequently. There is a simple faith that prayer is an instrument of change. Crying out to God and fasting are utilized to effect release from difficulty as well as to bring healing to the afflicted.

Form Adaptations

The apostle Paul in 1 Corinthians 9:19-23 set down some practical theological guidelines for his involvement in the cross-cultural communication of the Gospel. In Barunda, we are seeking to minister within the same liberties and restrictions that Paul experienced. The offense of the nature of God and the atonement of the cross will and must remain. However, there are innumerable peripheral areas that can be subject to alteration without violation of scriptural command or principle. A list of implemented form adaptations follows:

The missionary

1. Our men wear the clothing of the target group, which is the village farmer. Our women wear the local dress and at times have worn the veil covering, which has been very much appreciated by the Muslim and convert community.

2. Several of our men have full beards, which is part of the appearance of a Muslim religious man.

3. Lifestyles are simple.

4. Eating style corresponds to Muslims. No pork is eaten.

5. Time is regarded as more "event oriented" than the traditional time absolutes of the West. Some have adopted the 8 P.M. Barunda suppertime and thus have entered into the social visitation pattern of the society, which takes place each evening between 6 and 8 P.M.

The national

1. A place for washing before prayer is provided for optional use. It is explained that there is no merit attached to such ceremonial washing.

2. Shoes are removed before entering the worship center.

3. All worshippers sit on the floor.

4. Bibles are placed on folding stands such as are used for the Koran.

5. Occasionally, Greek and Hebrew Bibles are placed in a prominent position in front of the worshippers, thus demonstrating our regard for the "original" Bible, such as Muslims feel toward the Arabic Koran.

6. Hands are lifted up Muslim style during prayer times. Prostration is frequently done in Muslim fashion. Some pray with their eyes open, wearing traditional prayer hats.

7. Muslim tunes with Christian words are utilized. Scripture is chanted, as are personal testimonies.

8. The local Muslim dialect, rather than the animist dialect of the Christian church, is spoken and read in the services.

9. Embracing is done in Muslim fashion.

10. Days and times of worship are pragmatically regulated.

11. Fasting is an area of liberty, but is scripturally explained.

12. A Muslim-convert, homogeneous church has developed rather than one of a heterogeneous character.

13. Informal church organization is promoted, basically along the lines of the mosque.

14. The Muslim names of converts are retained.

15. The word Christian is avoided because of negative connotations. Presently Christians are called "followers of Isa" (Jesus).

16. Bible study, prayer, and fasting are emphasized. A higher profile of religious observance is encouraged because Muslims feel Christians are spiritually lazy when they are never seen praying.

17. The converts have chosen their own leadership.

18. The church grows along family and friendship lines.

Financial Considerations

Gifts and employment opportunities from the West have created a horizontal dependence syndrome within the Barunda Christian community. There is little motivation to give sacrificially or to pray about church needs when one is assured budgets will be met with foreign assistance. Christians are given preferential treatment at mission hospitals and schools. A select few are granted theological scholarships abroad. Comparison of lifestyles between nationals and missionaries convinces Barunda Christians that personal sacrifice is not particularly relevant to the "dedicated life." In my view, all of this points to a basic failure on the part of missionaries to live, teach, and administer sound indigenous financial policy in relationship to the national church. The crashing wave of a forced missionary evacuation, which was only barely averted last December, would most likely reduce our practicing Christian community by a minimum of 50 percent. In Mawasa there is a fresh slate. No traditional Christians reside in the area. The emerging Muslim convert church is the only worshipping group present. Our approach has been as follows:

Missionary adjustments

OCMF possesses no compounds or purchased property. This assures mobility as well as a lower financial profile. Missionaries live on as low a lifestyle as emotional and physical health permit. One family presently lives in a small bamboo hut with a mud floor. Others are in simple cement houses rented from Muslim landlords.

Financial relationships with nationals

OCMF aims to preserve the financial autonomy of the convert in relationship to himself, his family, and his peers. Existing economic structures should, at all costs, be preserved. The convert is told from the start that Christianity will only be credible among his Muslim friends if he stands without foreign financial assistance. No option for flight from his village is offered. Jobs, scholarships, and relief are not part and parcel of the Gospel. New believers must learn to stand on their own resources from the commencement of their pilgrimage of faith. OCMF has not been involved in institution or relief work. We have no national evangelists, although we have used Sadiq Jabbar occasionally as volunteer help. The emphasis is on lay witness and ministry.

The Existing Evangelistic Team

At present six foreign missionaries and the forty national believers from among the converted Muslims comprise the major functioning evangelistic team. Other Muslim converts have and will continue to be involved on an itinerant basis. At present, the Baranada church with its animistic background has been very wary of this Islamic-flavored movement. Those Christians are a potential team to assist with evangelism, as are the missionaries of other societies. However, for the time being they have adopted a wait-and-see attitude and are uninvolved in this work.

God Wanted the Matigsalogs Reached

Jun Balayo

Two hours of Toyota land-cruising over newly constructed roads cut through seemingly endless mountains brought us to an altitude of over one thousand feet. The unfamiliar breeze was now cool, soothingly fresh and chilling. From this mountain top one could view the majestic rain forest spread thick and deep as far as one's eyes could see. This vast frontier is the heartland of Mindanao in the Philippines, the ancestral territory of the Matigsalogs, a highland tribe whose favorite habitats are the banks of swift rivers.

The Matigsalogs are a group of people characterized by their shyness and independent-mindedness. Generally, they are peace loving but may suddenly

Reprinted with permission of *Global Church Growth Bulletin*. Copyright January-February 1980, Volume XVII, No. 1.

turn fierce and violent when their cultural rights are violated.

Considered to be the largest cultural group numbering over 80,000 families, the Matigsalogs attracted national attention during a month-long rebellion in July, 1975. The conflict was resolved only after the Matigsalogs, led by Datu Lorenzo Gawilan, obtained from the government a specific area which is now called the "Matigsalog Ancestral Territory."

The way the General Baptists (G.B.) received a mission to reach the Matigsalogs was a bit sensational. Totally devoid of any prior human plans, it could only be explained as part of God's wonderful ways.

The G.B. work started in 1969 when Angel Digdigan, a rather small, unassuming young family man, could not continue with his last year in the Bible school. Utterly frustrated and discouraged, he wandered adrift like a rudderless *banca*. In spite of his name which suggests celestial assets, Angel was no better than a bird with broken wings!

From Empty Bottles to Clear Vessel

Not knowing what to do or where to go, Angel could only roam the barrios in search of empty bottles to buy and then sell. This he did to make a few centavos to keep himself and his family physically and spiritually intact.

Angel could not explain how the Lord led him to the land of the Matigsalogs in Mindanao's hinterland. It was like the experience of the beloved John who was isolated on the Isle of Patmos by the Holy Spirit. All that Angel can recall was that he received God's definite call the moment he was with the people. There the vision became clear and the burden grew heavy.

Beckie, his understanding wife, had entertained thoughts that Angel might have died since she had not heard from him for three months. When at last he suddenly returned home, it was only to fetch his family so that together they would obey a clear vision, a truly exciting mission to reach precious souls in the heartland of the "land of promise."

Blazing the Trail

It does not always require academic trappings before a man can apply his basic principles in pioneering a church planting work. At times it only takes the yieldedness and the willingness of a man to be usable in God's hand. Angel approached the delicate work within the very world of the Matigsalogs. He lived as one with them in their village. His own native hut was made out of split bamboo and cogon grass. He easily learned their dialect. He ate and played with them. His acceptance with the people stems from the fact that Angel's first friend was Datu Madut Tawas, their influential Village Chieftain.

Aware of the basic problems of the Matigsalogs, Angel helped to explain government laws of which the people were ignorant. In the very early part of the evenings Angel and Beckie would teach from 80 to 100 adults and children how to read and write. Since farming was still very primitive, Angel shared with them some simple techniques. He maintained a small vegetable garden for purposes of actual demonstration and as a source of income to support their various projects. This includes a small elementary school which was started in 1971.

As the work expanded gradually through the years, more workers were needed. During a Church Growth Workshop conducted by the O.C. Ministries team for the General Baptists in 1976, Angel presented a dramatic appeal by exhibiting four Datus garbed in their exquisitely hand-woven, colorful, Matigsalog costume. The timeliness of a principle in Church Growth "to direct manpower and logistics to responsive areas" strengthened Angel's call for immediate reinforcement.

The response of the G.B. mission was beyond what Angel expected. Soon an intensified program was decided upon and a General Baptist Tribal Ministry became a major ministry.

Rev. Dean Trivitt, who now resides with his family in Senuda Mission Station among the Matigsalogs, has been designated as missionary in charge. Rev. Robert Carr, a new missionary, directs the Bible School where some Matigsalogs are being trained for the ministry. Mrs. Mary Howard, a missionary nurse, is in charge of a greatly needed Paramedic Program. Angel Digdigan has been given supervisory responsibility over G.B. pioneering and church planting programs with about 14 national workers.

As of April, 1979, encouraging results had already been noted in the G.B. work among the Matigsalogs. Churches increased from four in 1976 to 13. Twenty-two other outstations are being maintained which will eventually be organized into local congregations.

At the height of the rebellion in 1975, Angel was probably the only lowlander who remained with the Matigsalogs when others fled. He may have been the only lowlander who could enter the Matigsalog territory and come out alive when it became a no-man's-land. Angel must have been the only lowlander who dared risk being caught in the crossfire as he passionately interceded and pleaded with the authorities in the cities and the rebels in the mountains to put an end to the senseless shedding of Filipino blood by Filipinos themselves.

It is then no wonder that today the G.B.s enjoy preferential treatment from a grateful people. Such a privilege could only be the fruit of a precious seed of a dedicated life that is totally committed to God's divine call and unreservedly devoted to the people that He seeks to win.

Sarabia: A Case Study of an Indigenous Arab Church

Greg Livingstone

A church lives in Sarabia. A truly indigenous church. The believers are baptized. Nationals are the recognized leaders. Whole families are Christian. Believers meet regularly over the Word of God. The church assumes responsibility for its own financial affairs, spiritual growth, and witness. Long years of faithful labor on the part of missionaries and nationals resulted in such a fellowship. It is one of a precious few gatherings of mature Christians in Sarabia. More are sure to come.

The People of Sarabia

Sarabia's inhabitants include both Arabs and the indigenous people of Berber descent who existed there before the Arabs settled. The Berber population consists of both Arabized Berbers and mountain rural Berbers of different kinds.

The Muslim government of Sarabia assumes that every Sarabian is a Muslim. Though the government could be described as socialist, it is actually an eclectic mixture of Islam, socialism, and the charismatic personalities of the rulers. Sarabia has been independent from France for less than 20 years.

The French colonial influence explains why the educated people speak mostly French, have had their education in French, and in many cases do not even read Arabic well. Since independence, the government has attempted to Arabize the country, but it is evident that until those born after 1970 are in leadership, French will still dominate the culture. The people of the capital city tend therefore to be quite Western in their thinking and cannot be entirely unaffected by French culture with its pessimistic existentialism. Consequently, university students who may have no knowledge of the Sermon on the Mount may be quite familiar with Camus and Sarte.

The people of Sarabia, and particularly those in the capital, are not fanatical Muslims. A small percentage perform the daily prayers, but most are caught up in eking out an existence, especially because of the critical housing shortage. Because most business and commerce is nationalized, people show little motivation to get ahead.

The Beginning Stages of Missionary Work

Although Christian missionaries have worked in Sarabia for one hundred years, they have never been there in great numbers. It may be that the capital city has never had as many as 25 missionaries. Christian work in Sarabia, as in most Muslim lands, ebbs and flows. At one time there were even Arab pastors, salaried by the American Methodist Church, but these no longer exist. Nevertheless, a steady stream of individual Muslims have responded to Christ in the last two decades.

There are no full-time Christian workers among the Sarabians, but for the last 20 years there have been at least four to ten expatriate workers in the city, most of whom have been there a full 20 years. It may be the continuity of the expatriate presence which has enabled a church to take root. Each of these missionaries came to Sarabia with a good working knowledge of Arabic and French and at least half were from secular university backgrounds. One American couple seems to have been the major facilitators in seeing this church started. The husband, now 48 years old, continues as one of the seven elders (the only foreigner).

This American couple, together with a single former Inter-Varsity worker, befriended students in a university reading room (which had once been a Christian bookstore) and there began an investigative Bible study. About ten years ago, the investigative Bible studies led to a believers' Bible study and from there to a worshipping group and finally to an organized church with elders and membership. They still meet in that same room today. It is extremely crowded on a Sunday morning; consequently, they have gone to a multiple-meeting system. Sunday School meets at a different time than worship services, or in private homes during a meeting of adults at the reading room.

The Sarabian Church

Today there may be as many as 75 known believers in the capital city, half of whom are members of the church and are committed to its purposes. Most of these believers are between 18 and 35 years old, with notable exceptions of some who, being older, have provided some credibility and stability to the group. A large percentage of converts have come out of the university or technical colleges; thus, the congregation is very well educated. Perhaps 65 percent of the congregation is Berber in background; this may or may not be a key element. The church was hesitant to appoint the young university students as elders until they were married. I believe, however, that only four of the elders are married, since it is a very long process in prayer and searching and family negotiations to find a Christian mate for one of these brothers .

Mid-week prayer meeting has been a very relevant and dynamic time of dealing with real needs among believers. It has also provided an occasion for salvation of searching Muslims who have been brought there by the Muslim convert church members (note 1 Corinthians 14:14-25). Although the Sarabian elders do organize the services, the style is somewhat similar to the Plymouth Brethren format, namely, a participatory service.

Expatriates provide deeper Bible study and training for six to eight Sarabians at any one time. These Theological Education by Extension (TEE) classes meet in the homes of expatriates.

Burdens and Breakthroughs

Perhaps the biggest problem for Sarabian Christians has been to understand that commitment to Christ (the Head) also entails commitment to Christ's Body. Sarabians do not normally commit themselves to the people outside their own family. Many still fear or find little motivation to identify themselves with the church.

Nonetheless, for several years there has been a good body life, supportive relationships, and a reasonably high trust level (for the Muslim world), all making the Sarabian congregation attractive. As Arabs are able to meet converted Arabs, the credibility of Christ is greatly enhanced. The testimony of an Arab believer is by far the primary means of communicating the Gospel.

Because the police consistently "raid" meetings of believers, those who fear repercussions tend to be frequently absent. However, the believers in the congregation in the capital have taken a bold stand with the police and the result has been a greater courage on the part of the weaker brethren.

It is true, however, that a number of the believers have not even told their families that they are followers of Christ and even their marriages are thought to be Muslim, though both the bride and the groom are in fact believers. Baptism brings such an alienation that it is thought best by most of the congregation to let such realities be discovered slowly. There has not, however, been any organized opposition to break up the congregation or keep it from meeting. Authorities have conducted raids seemingly to discover whether in fact the unauthorized group had any *political* intentions.

Most Sarabians have grown up thinking that Christianity and western lifestyle are synonymous and that therefore Christianity is an inferior and "dirty" religion. Because Islam and politics are totally integrated, it is assumed by the Muslim that western politics and Christianity are as well. For this reason, the rejection of the one brings the rejection of the other. It is a totally new consideration for many that one can be a follower of Christ *and* a good Sarabian.

The church has shown a burden for other parts of its country and is not at all ingrown. A young man, converted in France through Young Life, returned to the university in the capital and through holding evangelistic Bible studies has been able to bring many new students to the congregation. He started a "youth club" that has as many as 40 attending (a Sarabian version of Young Life?). Some of the young people attending this, particularly girls, have found themselves in trouble with the police and therefore their parents. For this reason, these meetings are intermittently halted and restarted.

More Missionaries Needed!

Expatriates enter Sarabia initially as tourists and then enter into Arabic study, for which they can get a resident visa. This is good for perhaps two to three years, which allows enough time to make contact with the people with whom they will eventually secure a job. Job status is required for a long-term visa. These jobs, however, are often limited to six months to a year, and so the expatriate worker is often looking for a new "raison d'etre."

Witnessing opportunities abound because many Sarabians have heard the radio programs from France, have enrolled in Bible correspondence courses, and would like to be visited in order to further "check out" Christianity. A number, if not most, of the believers in the church were initially contacted through radio and Bible correspondence courses. Perhaps web evangelism, in which believers witness to student friends and to relatives, is more common now.

The missionaries in Sarabia, together with the national believers, pray and plan carefully. They have planned to start a new house church in at least four other cities where one to seven believers already exist. One of the leaders from the capital city church is seen as an evangelist-church planter and is helped financially by the church to visit these believers and hold house meetings in these target cities. Nevertheless, both Sarabians and expatriates acknowledge the tremendous need for outside missionaries who can pioneer efforts in the country's fifteen cities with populations of over 100,000 each. Not one has a church.

Looking Back and Ahead

The major reason a church in the capital city emerged in the midst of these hardships is the ability of the pivotal people; that is, three or four Sarabians and three or four missionaries, to always keep the goal of an indigenous church before them. The missionaries established the following criteria for an indigenous church:

1. Baptized Christians;

2. Recognized national elders;

3. Christian families;

4. Regular meetings for ministry of the Word, in a place not provided by foreigners.

5. Group responsibility for its own finances, spiritual activity, discipline, administration of ordinances and witness.

They constantly taught others that this is God's purpose and desire, so that those who accepted Christ's Lordship also made the commitment to the church's existence. Perhaps, because of higher education, the believers have not been as intimidated by social disapproval and government opposition as have believers in other Muslim countries. Perhaps the missionaries that did stay over 20 years have provided a stability and continuity without which the church could not have emerged.

The church in the capital city does provide a model for what could happen in one of the other cities in Sarabia. It has also shown other missionaries what they could do. There are fine prospects for missionaries and willing nationals to team up on compatible intellectual and spiritual levels for church planting in new cities. This will be possible as soon as missionaries who can speak both French and Arabic are available. Such missionaries, however, would need to be persons who understand goal-setting and the means of motivating and coaching national brothers without making them too dependent.

Progress in planting a new church is very slow until there is a "critical mass" of enough believers to make Christianity a viable alternative in the minds of the seekers. The church in the capital began as an investigative Bible study. It may be that Christians from another city could visit the church in the capital to gain a vision of how they may plant an indigenous church in their own city, perhaps also beginning with an investigative Bible study.

An Upper Class People Movement

Clyde W. Taylor

In recent months I have become acquainted with a fascinating movement in Latin America where the Gospel is spreading by a pattern as close to the New Testament pattern as I have ever seen. I'll not name a country, for the leaders do not want any publicity. But what is happening is to the glory of God and represents a quite significant breakthrough.

I learned of it when I was invited to hold a missionary conference in that country a couple of years ago. I was not prepared for what I encountered. I understood the missionary involved had a small work, but I discovered the Gospel was spreading in a way that Dr. McGavran would call a "people movement."

The unusual aspect of this movement is that its faith is spreading almost exclusively among the upper middle and upper classes of the nation. Furthermore, the number of converts involved is relatively high for the size of the segment of society involved. Since the movement is intentionally not highly structured, it is difficult to get accurate statistics; but my extensive conversation with leaders lead me to conclude that a minimum of 2,000 converts were actively involved. The number could easily be as high as 5,000 or more.

Beginnings

The work of the missionary, whom I'll call "John Swanson," began in the 1950's in somewhat typical fashion as he witnessed and evangelized among the responsive lower classes. After several years of ministry in the capital city, he had some 20 to 25 converts whom he was training in his home. He came to realize that he was really not a pastor and preacher—his skills were in music and teaching and so asked another mission to shepherd his little flock.

In 1962, Swanson moved to the second largest city in the nation whereafter studying the methods of Paul in the books of Acts—he changed his approach. He went to the university and started witnessing to students. Within a few months he won 12 of these to Christ whom he then began to train in discipleship. For seven years he led them in their spiritual growth and trained them also in theology, church history, books of the Bible and so on.

While Swanson was writing, translating and mimeographing materials for the daily sessions with his disciples, they were out witnessing to other students. By 1964 they had won and discipled about 300 others. These were all baptized in and some became members of various churches in the city. (At present about a dozen of these early converts are full-time workers in some of these churches.) The movement at this point was focused in small groups meeting in private homes and university lounges.

Churches Grow and Multiply

These early converts, it should be remembered, were all students and therefore single. In time, when some of them graduated and got married, they began thinking in terms of their own church. In 1969, therefore, the first church with five couples was organized in a home and a second church was organized three years later.

In 1977 the first house church, which had grown to 120 members, divided into two separate churches of 60 members each. The second church grew to 160 members and in 1978 divided into two congregations of 80 each. In February of that year another church was formed bringing the total to five house churches with a combined membership of about 500.

This gives a partial picture only of the work, for, in addition to the many who joined existing churches, the leaders of this new movement to Christ estimate that at least 50 percent of their members have scattered to other sections of the country and even the U.S. In many cases they begin the process of witnessing, training new converts and establishing house churches all over again.

Furthermore, cells of believers have been established in many of the universities of the region. I was told, for instance, of a type of church meeting for 35 medical students, another for 15 in the biology department and another for 12 in the technical institute of one university.

In 1964 one of the original 12 leaders graduated and returned to the capital city and began a work along the same lines he had come to know the Lord in and been trained in. Swanson followed him a few years later.

When I visited there in 1979, I was told that there may be as many as 100 Christian cell meetings among the upper classes in the city. These seem to be spreading on their own. The churches (cells) directly identified with Swanson and his workers, however, have grown to 15 with a total membership approaching 1,000. They told me about a number of similar house churches in other cities as well.

An Inside View

One of the unique features of these house churches is that they are made up of members from the upper middle and upper classes of people. The churches in the capital city in particular are made up primarily of those from the highest circles of society. This is not to say that they are unconcerned about the poor and less educated. They have evangelized among them and gained many converts. They discovered, however, that as soon as people from the lower and middle classes began attending their churches, ingathering from among the upper class ceased.

Taking Paul's statement that he became all things to all men, they concluded that if they were going to win upper class people they were going to have to win them with Christians who were likewise from the upper classes. As soon as they gain enough converts from the lower classes, therefore, they organize separate churches for them. For these leaders, it is not a matter of not wanting to associate with those on lower rungs of society, but a matter of how best to win the most people to Jesus Christ on *all* levels.

The growth of this cluster of congregations looks a lot like that of New Testament congregations. The converts meet in homes where they worship, fellowship, study the Word and are sent out to bring others to Christ. Each convert is not so much "followed up" but receives the Gospel in a very personal context to begin with. For example, the group has printed and distributed millions of tracts, but none of them have a name and address printed on them. Instead, the one passing out the tract gives his own name and address. When someone comes to know the Lord, he is immediately given training in discipleship.

I talked with one girl, for example, who meets with four new converts at six a.m. They pray, have fellowship and study the Word until breakfast at seven. She meets for lunch with three other girls who are older Christians. They pray and discuss problems together.

Each church is completely independent, though they all carry the same name. They do not keep any membership lists, but they do seem to know everyone who belongs. They baptize, serve communion and train and ordain their own pastors whom they call "elders." They are not highly structured, but their high level of caring and training binds them together.

It is an interesting paradox that these converts are wealthy but they can expand indefinitely with almost no funds since they meet in their large homes and ordain their own lay and unpaid elders (pastors). But they do give 20 percent of their incomes on the average. With these funds they send out missionaries to other parts of Latin America and even Europe. Money is never mentioned until someone is ready to go to the field and needs support. Then it is not uncommon for someone to say "I'll give $200 a month" and another to say "I'll give $150" and so on. Support is thereby raised very quickly

I heard of one missionary lady who is supported by four of her friends, all executive secretaries. They give her full personal support which is equal to what she would earn as an executive secretary in her home country. They also pay her transportation to and from the field and her ministry needs as well. One of the girls gives 80 percent of her salary, another 60 percent, another 50 percent and another 30 percent. Altogether the fellowship of house churches fully supports 16 missionaries.

The exciting thing about this Christward movement is not just that millionaires, government officials and leading businessmen are becoming believers. The

Lord loves the poorest beggar and his conversion is no less precious in His sight. It's significant that disciple making and church planting is now spreading quickly through a segment of society that has been heretofore unreached. If it can happen in one nation of Latin America, it can happen in others. The Lord of the harvest—of all kinds of crops—will be pleased when it does.

The Impact of Missionary Radio on Church Planting

William Mial

Historically, the role of radio broadcasting of the gospel by missionary radio stations has varied greatly from country to country. In a geographically remote region, such as a river basin area in Venezuela, radio has provided the first contact of the gospel with the listener, ultimately culminating in a nucleus of listeners in a village accepting Jesus Christ as personal Savior and going on to use the Bible study programs on the radio as the focal point of their weekly worship.

In other areas of the world, which are unreachable by any other means than radio due to political restrictions such as in the Soviet Union, we find that gospel missionary radio broadcasting is used by the head of the house to give basic Bible training to his family, and in some cases the radio is used as an evangelist to bring his family to a saving knowledge of Jesus Christ.

The most recent, exciting development in church planting through missionary radio is found in the country of India as a result of the Trans World Radio broadcast from Sri Lanka. The strategy behind this type of ministry is first a presentation of the gospel through various types of radio programs, such as a morning devotional program patterned somewhat after the Hindu morning worship, but of course with gospel music and scripture reading. This attracts a large number of Hindu morning worshippers, providing them with a familiar atmosphere but bringing to them the message of the only true God and the hope of eternal life found in his only Son, Jesus Christ. Various types of traditional and more innovative programming are broadcast throughout the morning and evening in approximately eleven major Indian languages. A variety of Bible correspondence courses are offered and a certain measure of spiritual awareness is developed through this follow-up method.

A less conventional type of follow-up has also been carried on in several language groups in the form of "Seekers Conferences"—three day expanded weekends. Through the mail offering, true seekers of Christianity have the opportunity to register for these special Seekers Conferences. As a result, there has been as much as 100 percent response by these men and women to accept Jesus Christ as personal Savior. In other cases we organize "Radio Rallies," when missionaries are encouraged to attend a series of meetings held over a period of several nights. These are primarily radio listeners, and here again we find a high percentage of response to the gospel, resulting many times in spontaneous desire to follow the Lord in believer's baptism. In the above cases, we make every effort to place these new converts into existing evangelical churches in their particular area.

In sections of India, primarily in Andhra Pradesh, we are finding such a strong wave of popular response to the radio broadcast that we are utilizing a daily 30-minute Bible study transmission. This is providing the core for evangelism and Bible study in many homes.

The President of Trans World Radio, Dr. Paul Freed reported,

> I went into home after home where "house churches" were assembled. People crowd into small houses until there isn't a square foot of standing space left. And this is an everyday occurrence! They work all day, and then begin to arrive for the radio services two hours before the programs even start! In one of the homes I visited, a man had taken a wire and attached it to a speaker outside. When the broadcasts begin in the evening, they can be heard throughout the area surrounding the house.

Although dozens of house groups have been personally visited by Trans World Radio personnel, we are told that the number of house groups in Andhra Pradesh is well over 1,000. The head of the home brings in his neighbor. They listen to the 30-minute transmission. At the conclusion of the program the content of the Bible study is further explained and discussed by the believer. Following this, the believer begins a personal witness to non-Christians who have come to the house Bible study group. This practice is carried out on a seven-day-per-week basis.

Church planting, of course, implies at some point that an adequate number of trained pastors would be available to carry out pastoral responsibilities in these new congregations. This, of course, is a massive undertaking, but missionaries are presently attempting to apply the potentials of radio for a pastoral training program, thus completing the cycle of true church planting and assuring a healthy future development.

Ann Croft and the Fulani

Fatima Mahoumet

Although Ann Croft's father had planted many churches in the U. S. Midwest during her childhood, she wasn't thinking of herself as a missionary when she went to Nigeria. She was simply a teacher of English as a Second Language.

She was able to get to know some of them better, joining them for some meals and eventually reading and discussing stories from the Bible. One student expressed an extraordinary interest in the Bible.

Open Doors

As their friendship grew, her student opened doors for her into the labyrinth of extended family life among the Fulani people in her area. He had many sisters who had married into a number of families in the area. When her student visited them, Ann accompanied him and met each family member.

As a teacher Ann was also respected by the male leaders of the community. At their request, she spent many hours answering their questions about the Bible, helping them to understand more fully the biblical events and characters, including Jesus, which they had encountered in the Quran. In preparation she had done a comparative study of the Quran and Bible, noting their uniqueness, differences and similarities. She used their folk tales as bridges for discussing Scripture.

Soon, Ann had access to every part of the Muslim community. As a woman, she was able to meet the women related to all of her male contacts, even those in the strictest *purdah* (seclusion) who would otherwise be well beyond the sphere of married, let alone single, Christian men. One of the women was especially drawn to Ann. She took her to all the special ceremonies, such as naming ceremonies, weddings and funerals. She helped her with the language and provided many needed bridges of communication and explanations as Ann continued to learn about the Muslim way of life. Ann also learned the traditional stories of her new people and grew to deeply love and appreciate the rich fabric of their lives.

She discovered that being a single woman had its advantages too. In response to questions as to why she was not married, Ann referred to 1 Cor. 7 and a comparable passage in the Quran about single women being able to be totally involved in the work of the Lord. She added that the Bible, unlike the Quran, allowed her to do so well past her 20th birthday. Besides, she remarked, how could she otherwise teach their children and always be available to them any

Adapted from *The Zwemer Institute Newsletter*, Spring 1981. Used with permission of the Zwemer Institute, Pasadena, CA .

time they were having trouble, day or night? She wasn't subject to the demands of marriage or the constraints of *purdah*. She was always free to help.

Caring for Cattle

Ann continued her efforts among the Fulani people of Northern Nigeria.

The Fulani are a largely nomadic people, whose search for good pasture for their cattle has scattered them throughout sub-Saharan West Africa. Strong clan fidelity and six centuries of Muslim evangelism have made them the most effective champions of Islam in West Africa. Of 6.7 million Fulani, only 400 are known Christians.

As Ann studied more about the people to whom God had sent her, she discovered ways of showing the Fulani cattle-herders that they are very special to God. In the Bible she found numerous references to nomadic cattle-herding peoples who played special roles in biblical history.

Knowing the great importance of cattle to them, Ann began to help upgrade the health of the cattle with veterinary medicine and so helped the Fulani begin to cope with some of the economic problems they faced with the growing pressure of urbanization.

Caring for cattle was the way to the Fulani heart. On one occasion she helped a Fulani elder get tuberculosis medicine for his son and worm medicine for himself. But it was not until she gave him medicine for his cows that he said, "Now I know you *really* love us!"

Ann was able to join forces with another mission agency in a distant city that was planning an evangelistic three-day "conference" especially for Fulani. Fulani people were told that it would be a religious conference studying one of the prophets—Abraham, a super-herdsman who had cows and sheep and donkeys and goats and camels. This was a big event for the Fulani, not accustomed to special events just for their people.

At the end of the evangelistic conference, the chief of the area said to Ann that he wanted his people to become part of the Christian community. He had seen that Christians and their Holy Book cared about the needs of his people. Some of the greatest prophets, after all, like Abraham, were cattle-herders too! He also told her that to get a lot of people interested in the Christian faith, one of the best things she could do would be to continue to show a real, genuine interest in every aspect of their culture.

Gathering new believers into viable fellowships is proving to be a tremendous challenge. It is hard enough for some Fulani youth to settle down for Bible school. A permanent location for a tribe would unravel nomadic life. But Ann feels that perhaps now is the time for the Fulani people as they move towards a future that is economically, politically and socially uncertain. She will be there with them, loving and caring for them, believing that God will transform them into a people "gathered...accepted...to the honor of the Lord your God" (Isaiah 60:7).

A Two-Stage Approach to Church Planting in a Muslim Context

Al Munir

The information in the Wycliffe Bible Translators *Ethnologue* on the "Gor" was a shocker. They were one of the most prominent and advanced peoples of Ofir, some 2.5 million strong (in 1930), and there was not a verse of God's Word in their language, no church, no known Christians, and no mission board working among them. As a college student in the 1950's who had a call from God to form churches among unreached peoples, I found the need of the Gor a challenge to prayer and action. Little did I realize that the Gor were not merely a challenge to me. A major spiritual confrontation between the forces of light versus darkness was taking place in one of the largest Muslim countries in the world.

Ofir and the Gor

Most of the Muslim world in the past few decades had recently gained independence from Western domination, which was felt by Muslim leaders to be an unnatural condition for Islam (since they had the truth of God) and a stain on their honor. The new freedom gave opportunity for Islam to regain its proper place of glory and victory: it was the unique historic chance to form an Islamic state. For the Christian, it meant that the Gospel could be dissociated from colonial rule, and it opened a door for new agencies with new visions to reach areas formerly closed to the Gospel.

In Ofir there was more chance of real grappling with the Christian message to take place because being a true national was not equated with being a Muslim. Where the Gospel can get a reasonably fair hearing, it will bear fruit even in Muslim countries. So in Ofir one of the largest turnings to Christ from among Muslims in church history has occurred, but not without a massive struggle.

While some Ofir peoples had been responsive to the Gospel, the Gor had been almost 100% antagonistic. Not only were they unresponsive themselves, but they were the leaders in campaigns attacking the "Christianization" of Ofir. Whispering campaigns and violence occurred, creating tensions, criticisms and suspicion of all Christian activities. They applied their considerable influence and skills to stop growth of churches.

The Gor have been the leaders of Islam for the whole nation. Most of the mosques in the capital are led by Gor. They have supplied most of the intellectual leadership for most of the foremost Muslim social, political and religious organizations. Highly cultured, they have led the way in the development of a national literature. The Gor are an adventurous, activist people who have readily taken up the tools of Western sciences, and have led the way in reconciling Islam with many contrary elements of traditional culture.

There is a strong unity within Gor Islam—all of them being orthodox Sunni of the Shafi School—despite the general national disunity within Islam. The Gor became Muslims in the fifteenth century despite some notable contradictions between the indigenous culture and the Islamic *Sharia*. Quranic law places women under social and economic disadvantage, but Gor inheritance laws grant family lands and property into the hands of the female heirs. The family ties to the land and community are carried on through the women, while the men, when marrying, move into the home of the wife. This matrilineal, matrilocal structure conflicts with the strong patrilineal basis of Islam. Nevertheless, the Gor incline to believe that there is a basic union between Islam and traditional custom. Indeed, the Gor have a reputation of being one of the most fanatically loyal Muslim people in all Ofir. Through the centuries an amazing symbiotic relationship has been worked out so that the old culture actually buttresses Islam despite inherent contradictions.

The union of the Gor way of life and Islam makes it almost impossible for a Gor to seriously conceive of himself ever changing religion, which would be akin to a change of identity and nationality. Since it is the will of God that representatives from every tribe and tongue obey Christ (Rev. 5:9f), the stage is set for a titanic spiritual clash between God and evil among the Gor.

The Battle Begins

God's first move in the 1950's was to call two mission boards to start work to reach the Gor. The "Roger Williams Band," a major denominational board, and the "Hudson Mission," an international mission, both sought to show the love of Christ by medical work. Satanic opposition reared its head right from the beginning as the Hudson Clinic project could not be established even on the border of the Gor heartland. From the year of their receiving a commission to the Gor, a quarter of a century would pass before a Hudson worker would enter Gor territory!

Only after heroic efforts and sacrificial outlay of resources was the Roger Williams Band (RWB) able to enter Gorland. They boldly penetrated to the very heart of the Gor culture, but quickly found that they had stirred up a hornet's nest. Loud screams of protest resounded all the way to the Ofir President and his Cabinet, as well as to the American government! Years of diplomacy would pass before the RWB Hospital could receive patients. Some early evangelistic efforts were made, but came under such attack that the RWB had to promise not to try to convert Muslims in order to get permission to open the hospital. This whole issue became front-page headlines in all Ofir, particularly after bombs were planted in the hospital. Satan countered the RWB penetration by focusing a spotlight on the "Christian threat" so that no witness was possible in the Gor heartland.

While Muslim attention was turned to the "threat" within, God was preparing an inconspicuous maneuver on the distant eastern flank of the Gor heartland. Because Gor men do not inherit the family rice-fields, their society has developed a unique dispersion tradition: the men leave their homeland to seek jobs, education and wealth. This centuries-old tradition, accentuated since World War II, has brought about a dispersion population that may exceed the number of Gor remaining in Gorland. Indeed, in the capital city of Ofir—right on the doorstep of dozens of missions and churches—there are more Gor than there are in the five largest Gor cities at home! Over half of the 6,000,000 Gor were dispersed in areas where the force of tradition was less binding, and they constituted the Gor flank which was exposed but ignored by missions.

Finding a co-worker

The early defeats for the Gospel gave increased evidence that the Gor were unapproachable. God, however, had his key man—a middle-aged Gor businessman who used to be a leader in a progressive Muslim organization. His hatred for the Bible was reversed when he was healed in a hospital by prayer in the name of Jesus. He became a vibrant witness with a gift of evangelism, which he used in Pentecostal circles. "Mr. Raider" knew the Quran and the Bible, was friendly, bold, and zealous, but as a "Dispersion Gor" he found it easy to travel in non-Gor circles and generally ignore the spiritual needs of his own people.

For twenty years I had kept the Gor call in my heart but never found the time or way to reach them. When I heard there was a Gor evangelist I immediately visited him and we struck up a good friendship. I was shocked to find out that he did not believe the Gor were approachable! He had preached in Gorland on a visit and was brought in by the police for interrogation by the Military Intelligence, Muslim leaders, and even the Governor himself! I told him that prayer groups had risen up all over the world who had prayed specially for the Gor people. I told him of my own call, and reminded him that God had a plan for every tribe, including the Gor. In time, I laid out the whole strategy that I had worked out and asked whether he could work with me. He prayed about it and agreed, even though he had a large family to support and I never offered any pay. We were both persuaded that it was God's time to reach the Gor.

The ultimate goal was the formation of a Gor church, but we had no evangelistic literature in the language. I prepared a life of Christ consisting of Bible verses which Raider translated into Gor—the first piece of Christian literature in the language. We had no money for printing it so I took the translation to the Bible Society. They refused it because it did not fit their criteria, nor were the Gor on their budget.

We began another revision process, while continuing to contact people. Raider had a large circle of Gor friends, whom he found more responsive as his expectation and faith grew. I started contacting churches all over the province to find whether there were other hidden Gor believers like Raider. We visited various missions who offered correspondence courses to check for people who were interested enough to study the Bible. In this way we compiled lists of Gor who had been exposed to the Gospel. Pastors gave names of Gor who had married Christians. All of these we tracked down and visited. Raider's gift for personal evangelism sparkled and people started responding. I never heard again any doubts that the Gor could be won to Christ.

Problem one:

Regular meetings were soon established, and the warm fellowship broke down many suspicions. A key decision was made right from the start: we had to decide whether we would try to proceed directly to form a church or not. To reach the Gor people, I was convinced that we needed a specifically Gor fellowship, but the Gor believers were dispersed all over the province and were members of various churches. If we tried to take them out we would be "sheep-stealing." Second, the government discouraged the creation of new churches as did my own mission and my sponsor. Third, if we formed a Gor church it would shock the Gor Muslim leaders into action, whereas I wanted our fellowship to grow as strong as possible before Muslim leaders got wind of us and the retaliation came. Fourth, I wanted to finish our translation work before political pressure could be exerted to stop the project. Fifth, I wanted the church to eventually be formed in such a way that it could not be stigmatized as a foreign plant.

If the church were formed in a two-step process, I (the foreigner) could be off the scene when the second step occurred. The first step was the formation of a para-church organization (a "sodality") which could be done in accord with government regulations and according to Gor tradition. Hundreds of Gor social organizations were found all over Ofir, so a Christian one would not attract attention. The second step could be taken at a time when the Gor group felt they were ready to form the Church. If *they* did it, there would be no danger of the Church expressing American cultural forms, nor would there be an opportunity for me to outlaw elements of Gor culture that might be alien to American ways, but not inherently inimical to the Gospel.

The First Christian Fellowship Among the Gor

Despite the fact that the Gor believers ranged from the very wealthy to the very poor, they enjoyed the fellowship immensely. I had suggested to Raider that the Gor Church would eventually want a Gor hymnal, so the singing and preaching became increasingly Gor (which I could not speak). The Gor lived up to their reputation for intelligence and leadership in our group, so it was easy to take a back seat. I wanted the Fellowship to have a Gor character from top to bottom. Before the group I deferred to Raider so they felt the direction was truly in Gor hands.

Since we had a program and a regular growing fellowship meeting weekly in different homes, we felt ready for formal organization. I was impatient for this because we were open to a charge of being an underground organization, which could bring the government down on our heads. Incorporation would give us legal standing so we could receive funds, own property, sponsor missionaries possibly, and be accepted by other institutions. We could now go before the Bible Society and, as a responsible Gor body, formally request the Society to translate the New Testament into Gor. They could come back to us and ask that we be responsible to provide the translation team.

All agreed that the Gor Christian Fellowship (GCF) had to be incorporated. The dates were set and Gor from all over Ofir were invited to attend to discuss goals, consider a Constitution and the election of officers, and celebrate with a feast and worship. Although we had invited Gor believers from various parts of Ofir, only the provincial contacts could come, but even they crowded the house. For many of them it was an astonishing occasion. Normally each Gor believer thought that he or she was the only Gor Christian in the universe. And each one usually felt that the Gor were impossible to convert. People gave testimonies why they became Christian, and the joy and amazement were inexpressible. For me it was an historic event. My mind went back some 20 years to the 1950's, to all the praying people, to my own call and struggles, and my heart was filled with praise, tears, and joy, for even though the group was not large, there was joy in heaven—some Gor knew Jesus!

Progress Despite Adversity

The goals of GCF were (1) to minister spiritually to those within the group, and (2) to bring the Gospel to unsaved Gor. Since there was no full-time Gor worker, the GCF decided to provide a scholarship to any Gor in a Bible School. Money was collected to help any Gor who was ostracized, or who lost his job because of receiving Christ. A *Bulletin* was to be published to link all the Gor who were dispersed beyond the reach of our local group. Funds for evangelistic expenses were approved. Incorporation required that we organize a book-keeping system and make annual financial reports to the government. This allayed my fear that Satan could undermine the whole work through slipshod handling of funds. Misuse of funds was a disease of Ofir society.

Our regular Bible studies were geared to meet the needs of some members about whose salvation we were not sure. Our membership included all Gor who considered themselves Christian. The GCF had Catholics, Adventists, Pentecostalists and main-line Protestants in it, but the harmony was beautiful because our meeting built on the "Dispersion Gor" tradition of forming a mutual help society, with the exception that ours was Christian.

Raider sometimes mentioned his fears about what Gor Muslim leaders would do when they learned about the Fellowship. But they had *already* done something. Sul was a young man who had been to a number of churches, had taken correspondence courses, had a fair knowledge of the Bible, and professed to be a believer. We all had some doubts, but we tried to help him find a job and to build him up. At this stage, we were still operating quietly in the Gor community; we also had a couple of literature projects we wished to keep private.

But the government keeps a careful watch on all religious organizations. Their own infiltrators found reason to call in a government raid on the headquarters of an extremist Muslim organization in the capital. Letters were there found, written by Sul reporting on GCF activities. He had been planted to try to find or cause some provocation for fanatics to seize upon. Now, however, we were officially registered with the government, and all our actions were legal. We were fearful that our translation work would be interpreted as proselytization of a

Muslim people, but since the GCF was a Christian group we had the right to
have Gor Scriptures.

We prayed and praised God when we received word from the Bible Society
that they had put the Gor New Testament at the top of their priority list. I was
faced with an important decision: I had completed all requirements for a Ph.D in
History and needed only to complete the dissertation—a very time-consuming
task. If I accepted the job of coordinating the project, I would have to drop that as
well as get a release from my responsibilities to my sponsoring church.

The whole GCF got excited about putting God's word into their language for
the first time. We suspected that part of the Gor unresponsiveness of the past
was a result of not presenting Christ in Gor terms. This Gospel in Gor was one
key to the eventual formation of the Gor Church; the other key was the sending
of witnesses. This move of God was not unchallenged: the unseen spiritual conflict sometimes spilled out into the open. The Bible Society held a fund-raising
event for the Gor project in a foreign church in the capital city. The GCF put on a
show of Gor culture to attract donors. A while later newspapers reported that
three men visited the church and stabbed the minister to death. We found out
later that they were Gor fanatics who may have been protesting some other
Christian activity; but my mission leader became more wary of the translation
project, fearing it would be a provocation. At about that time another translation
project into a Muslim language was criticized by a provincial Governor when
some Gospels were indiscriminately placed on railroad trains.

A Possible Obstacle

After the GCF was established in one city, I started visiting the capital, four or
five hours away. I suspected that it would in time become the main center for
reaching the Gor. The formation of a GCF chapter was facilitated because by now
we were known in many churches and we had a nucleus to build on. The first
organizing meeting was held in a mainline church attended by some 30 people.
A new issue arose as I found out that some people in the ecumenical stream were
fascinated with the growth of the new organization and wanted to form a more
"ecumenical" organization. I was shocked at this development because it looked
like a tool to destroy the unity of the Gor and a hindrance to the eventual development of the church. I felt that I should not remain in the background as I
usually did; since I was in the mainline stream myself, I could defend the GCF
and Raider's leadership.

Agreement was reached that as long as the Gor chose their own leaders who
did the work, church politics should not hinder the unity of the witness. No
organizational ties bound the capital GCF to the parent body. I felt that once it
was founded it should eventually take the leading role in reaching the Muslim
Gor. We hope to see other Gor Fellowships throughout Ofir. Our task was to dig
a foundation and set patterns of evangelism, set a tone, and promote a vision of
ministry.

The Gor Fellowship Today

The New Testament has been translated and 50,000 copies of Luke have been printed. Unfortunately, there still is not a single full-time worker (national or foreign) doing evangelism among the Gor. There are at least six Gor pastors in various churches, but no one free for witness to Gor. In Gorland itself there still is no witness to the 3,000,000 Gor. The RWB Hospital still struggles under enormous pressures, a number of transplanted churches exist to minister to non-Muslim ethnic groups, but they are silent to the Gor. When will the Church penetrate the Gor heartland?

A recent (1981) letter from the Gor Fellowship in the capital states they are collecting money for a church building there. When this is done they will move from the first stage of the para-church organization to the second stage of forming of the first church. *[Editor's note: Most mission efforts begin with planting a church and seldom if ever begin a mission structure of any kind.]* The good news is that if the rest of the Christian community continues to ignore the Gor, there exists a body on whom the Spirit can lay the burden to penetrate Gorland itself. But the 200 or so Gor Christians will need a lot of help to reach the six million Gor throughout Ofir.

22

Evangelism: The Leading Partner

Samuel Moffett

The New Testament uses the word *evangelize* in what seems to be a shockingly narrow sense. A whole cluster of verbs, actually, is used to describe evangelism: "preaching the word" (Acts 8:4), "heralding the kingdom" (Luke 9:2), "proclaiming the good news" (Luke 4:18, 8:1). But in essence, what all these words describe is simply the telling of the good news (the Gospel) that Jesus the Messiah is the saving King. Evangelism was the announcement of Christ's kingdom. It was more than an announcement. It was also an invitation to enter that kingdom, by faith and with repentance.

What Evangelism is Not

Evangelism, therefore, is not the whole of the Christian mission. It is only a part of the mission. Jesus and the disciples did many other things besides announce the kingdom and invite response. Evangelism is not worship or sacraments. "Christ did not send me to baptize but to evangelize," said Paul (1 Cor. 1:17).

And it is not church growth or church planting. The planting and growth of the church are surely goals of evangelism and its hoped-for results. But evangelism does not always produce a church or more members for it. Neither is evangelism confined to apologetics. Paul says, "We try to persuade" (2 Cor. 5:11), but insists that he was sent to tell the good news "without using the language of human wisdom" (1 Cor. 1:17, 20).

Finally, evangelism in the New Testament was not confused with Christian service, or Christian action and protest against the world's injustices. A revealing and disturbing incident in the Book of Acts tells how Greek speaking Jews among the early Christians rose as a minority group to complain of discrimination in the distribution of funds. The reply of the apostles seems almost callously narrow: "We cannot neglect the preaching of God's word to handle finances"

Dr. Samuel Moffett was born and raised by missionary parents in Korea. He returned as a missionary to serve first in China and then in Korea, where he served as Dean of the graduate school of the Presbyterian Seminary in Seoul. He now serves as Henry Winters Luce Professor of Ecumenics and Mission Emeritus at Princeton Theological Seminary. He has written numerous articles in missions and theology. Used by permission of the author.

(Acts 6:1, 2 TEV). Of course, they did immediately proceed to do something about the injustice. But they did not call it evangelism.

In Kingdom Context

In the context of the kingdom, however, the evangelistic proclamation was never so narrow that it became isolated from the immediate pressing needs of the poor, the imprisoned, the blind and the oppressed.

Here I am reminded of Korean evangelism. I asked a pastor in the Philadelphia area why his church was growing so fast. "When Koreans come in," he replied, "first I get them jobs; I teach them some English; I help them when they get in trouble with their supervisors. I invite them to church. And then I preach to them the Gospel." That is putting evangelism into context.

But if there is anything worse than taking the text out of context, it is taking the context without the text. Just as Christ's salvation is never to be isolated from the immediate, real needs of the people, neither is it to be identified with those present needs. When Jesus quoted the Old Testament about "good news to the poor" and "freedom for the oppressed," he did so on his own terms. His salvation is not Old Testament *shalom*, and his kingdom is not Israel.

There is nothing quite so crippling to both evangelism and social action as to confuse them in definition or to separate them in practice. Our evangelists sometimes seem to be calling us to accept the King without His kingdom; while our prophets, just as narrow in their own way, seem to be trying to build the kingdom without the saving King.

More Than Balance

There was a time when most Christians believed that evangelism was the only priority. They were wrong. Then the Church swung too far the other way. The only Christian priority for some has been social justice through reconstruction. That, too, is an important priority. But it is not the only one. And when they made it the only clear mission of the Church, the result was a disaster. In trying to speak to the world, they almost lost the Church.

Others tried to restore the balance by pointing out that "Christ mediates God's new covenant through both salvation and service....Christians are called to engage in both evangelism and social action." But even that is not enough. What the Church needs for the future in mission is more than balance. It needs momentum. Not an uneasy truce between faith and works, but a partnership.

Now in most practical, working partnerships, there must be a leading partner, a "first among equals," or nothing gets done. Which should be the leading partner in mission? Evangelism or social action?

I submit that what makes the Christian mission different from other commendable and sincere attempts to improve the human condition is this: in the Christian mission our vertical relationship to God comes first. Our horizontal relationship to our neighbor is "like unto it," and is just as indispensable, but it is still second. The leading partner is evangelism.

This is not to exalt the proclamation at the expense of Christian action. They belong together. But it does insist that, while without the accompanying deeds the good news is scarcely credible, without the word the news is not even comprehensible! Besides, the real good news is not what we in our benevolence do for others, but what God has done for us all in Christ. Evangelism, as has been said, is one beggar telling another where to find bread.

The supreme task of the Church, then, now and for the future, is evangelism. It was the supreme task for the Church of the New Testament. It is also the supreme challenge facing the Church today.

Half the World Unreached

The determining factor in developing evangelistic strategies, I believe, is that evangelism moves always in the direction of the unreached. "It must focus on those without the Gospel." More than one-half of the world's people are still without the simplest knowledge of the good news of God's saving love in Jesus Christ. There is no greater challenge to evangelism in mission than that.

In this connection it may be useful to note that for general strategic evangelistic planning, some missiologists suggest as a rule of thumb that "a group of people are classified as unreached if less than 20 percent claim or are considered to be Christian." Christians are rightly concerned about the grievous unbalances of wealth and food and freedom in the world. What about the most devastating unbalance of all: the unequal distribution of the light of the knowledge of God in Jesus Christ?

I am not overly addicted to statistics. But what does it say about a "six continent approach to evangelism," for example, to find that most of our church mission funds still go to ourselves on the sixth continent, which is between 70 percent and 80 percent at least nominally Christian? Africa, however, is perhaps 40 percent Christian by the same rough and imprecise standards. And Asia, which holds more than one-half of all the people in the world, is only three percent to four percent even nominally Christian.

In the next ten years, the number of non-Christians which will be added to the population of Asia will be greater than the entire present population of the United States multiplied almost three times (650 million, compared to 220 million). Treating all six continents as equals for strategical purposes is a selfish distortion of the evangelistic realities of the world.

One last thought. There is an unexpected bonus to keeping the definition of evangelism simple. It means that anyone can get into the act. One of the happiest lessons I ever learned about evangelism came not from a professional evangelist, but from a watermelon vendor.

It was in a Korean village, and my wife came up to ask him how much a watermelon cost. He was so surprised at finding a long-nosed foreigner who spoke Korean that at first he was struck dumb. He even forgot to tell her the price. There was something more important he wanted to say. He asked, "Are you a Christian?" And when she replied, "Yes," he smiled all over. "Oh, I'm so glad," he said, "because if you weren't I was going to tell you how much you are missing."

If more of us were so happy about what we have found in the Lord Jesus Christ that we couldn't wait to tell those who have not found him how much they are missing, we would need to worry no longer about the future of evangelism.

23

Evangelism as Development

Edward R. Dayton

Development is a many-meaning word. For some it has a sense of Western imperialism: the "developed" country is attempting to impose their own values and desires on "lesser developed" countries. "Developed to what?" they ask. For what? There is a built-in assumption that things are better when they are "developed."

Development has about it the ring of human progress. *Human* progress. It can find its roots in the Age of Enlightenment, when for the first time in history, a large segment of society began to believe that they really could control their destinies. The humanists of the seventeenth and eighteenth centuries were stimulated in their thinking by the great discoveries (for the West!) of the Americas and the African Continent. What we can now see were often coincidences of history worked together to convince them that by dint of hard work and high ideals man could triumph over his situation. The stories of Horatio Alger became the everyday coin of our belief. The Calvin-inspired Protestant ethic became an end in itself. "Progress" was measured by acquisition.

Once the West was won, those who were a part of the grand adventure naturally concluded that what they had been able to accomplish should be a possibility for others. They looked with compassion, mixed with a good degree of superiority, at their neighbors in less "developed" countries and set about to help them develop. Failures outnumbered successes at every turn. The American State Department's Agency for International Development finally concluded that there was little hope for replicating the developed West through massive doses of Western technology. It was a somber, but wise, conclusion.

We are now involved in a fall-back situation of operating on the principle that our mistake was one of scale. To attempt to develop an entire nation was beyond our scope, but there still remains the possibility of *community* development. The

Edward R. Dayton is a management consultant helping mission agencies. He served with World Vision International for 25 years, most recently as Vice-President for Missions and Evangelism with World Vision International. He is the founder of World Vision's Missions and Advance Research and Communications Center (MARC) and has written extensively on management and mission strategy. From *MARC Newsletter*, March 1979.

assumption is that if we can deal with an entire community that is still intact in its community setting, that development is possible. There are many who agree that this is the right approach. We do too.

Now, the goal of community development always was and still remains to bring a group to a place of self-reliance or self-sufficiency: they find within themselves all that is needed to maintain life at a desired level. The fly in the ointment is that the underlying premise of those involved in micro-development, namely, given the right circumstances and resources, mankind is capable of creating for himself a *good* society. The premise is false.

The premise is wrong because man's values are flawed. The natural man is turned in on himself, concerned for himself and his own welfare. Given a choice between his own welfare and the welfare of his society, he will usually erroneously conclude that his own best ends are served by serving himself. This is particularly true if he follows the model of the West. For the model of the West is, "*You* can do it! Look at me. *I* did it!" Or, to put it in the title of a not-so-old popular tune, "I Did It *My* Way."

And so it is quite easy for us to become involved in *valueless* community development. We can look with Christian compassion on a group of people living on the edge of poverty and conclude that if they had a better water system, better farming methods, and basic preventive medicine, they would be all right. Community development is possible. But, along with those changes in material standards there needs to be a change in spiritual standards. There needs to be the announcement of the gospel of the Kingdom, the possibility of a radical change at the core of one's being.

Don't miss the point: It's not a question of material development that is accompanied by the gift of eternal life found in Christ. It's a question of the basic motivation to want to change, to want to find a new relationship with one's neighbor, to want to put spiritual values before material values. Evangelism is at the core of true development. It is the catalyst that makes the rest of the mix take form and endure.

Perhaps an extreme example will make the point. World Vision is currently involved in an area of the world which has recently been resettled by the government. Each family has been given a plot of ground, half of which is to be used for a cash crop controlled by the government and the other half of which can be used for personal use. People have come from many different settings to take advantage of this offer. They each have a means of livelihood. Their material needs are met, but there is a great deal of unrest, strife and social upheaval. Our "development" solution is to support the establishment of a Christian community center that will bring a common value system to the community. The anticipation is that as people become one in Christ they will relate to one another in a new way. Helping to plant a church that will provide the missing values turns out to be the key element of development.

Christians have been uniquely equipped to do development. First, we come to the task with the right motivation. The love of Christ constrains us. The demands of righteousness and justice are upon us. It is not a question of can we, but first a question of *should* we.

Second, Christians come to the task with a balanced sense of the times in which we live and an ability to work out our lives in the midst of the tension that, while we believe we are called upon to work against the forces of evil we find in our world, at the same time we believe that only in Christ's return will that evil be permanently defeated.

But Western Christians live in the midst of what a recent writer has called the Culture of Narcissism, a culture in which the individual is turning in on himself to find a fulfillment or self-understanding or self-awareness or a host of other in-words. We tell ourselves that the society is out of control. Our leaders are found incompetent or corrupt. Our technology threatens to overcome us rather than save us. History loses its meaning for us. What was right seventy years ago is no longer important. Today's problems, we reason, are so different that we will have to make up the rules as we go along. And without recognizing what is happening, we Christians easily follow the same path. We adjust our theology to fit the circumstances we can't change. And therefore it becomes easy for us to conclude that what one values, what one holds most important, probably varies for everyone. And who are we to tell someone else how to live? And that's about the way non-Christian development approaches the task.

The message of the gospel is a radical message. It not only says, "Change your mind about things," it also demands, "Let Christ change your life— think about your sister and your brother. What's important is not how much you acquire but how you live out your life." Salvation is not just eternity. Salvation begins now with a new mind in Christ.

Let's listen again to that message—daily. And if we really believe that Christ changed our life, let's believe that evangelism is a key part of development.

Study Questions

1. What problems would you anticipate if a missionary pursued evangelism without development or development without evangelism?

2. Describe the progression in our understanding of the concept of development.

24

Helping Others Help Themselves: Christian Community Development

Robert C. Pickett and Steven C. Hawthorne

Evangelical Christians are recognizing that social action and evangelism are not opposite poles. They are complementary partners in the task of the church. The task of the church cannot be split into the "social" and "spiritual" dimensions. We are to be the preserving "salt of the earth" as much as are we are to be the evangelizing "light of the world." In many cases, costly service must accompany the gospel proclamation. In almost all cases, tremendous benefit to the well-being of society can and should result from making obedient disciples.

But just what is meant by "social action?" Mentioning the term brings to mind tired warnings against diluting the truth with the "social gospel." Social action is best associated with constructive social change, but the term is used to mean anything from working for women's rights to delivering baskets of food to poor families at Christmas. The term is sufficiently vague to be nearly useless.

Another term is headed to the oblivion of multiple meaning: Development. We hear of International Development, and Christian Development. We read of Developed Countries and Less Developed Countries, and even Least Developed Countries.

What is Development?

There are basically four strategies of alleviating the suffering of a needy world. Each of them has been called "development." These can be considered on

Robert C. Pickett is a professor in community development at William Carey International University in Pasadena, California, and was for 22 years a professor of agronomy at Purdue University. Pickett has worked as a consultant for crop improvement and community development projects in over 100 countries.

Steven C. Hawthorne is part of Hope Chapel in Austin TX and serves with the Antioch Network, helping churches with practical vision to plant new churches among the world's least evangelized peoples. He has led on-site research projects in Asia and the Middle East.

a matrix setting two basic methods against two basic foci of action. Our tactics can bring aid from outside the country or we can seek changes in the structures and life patterns of the people, helping them to effect the changes that they desire. We can either focus on socio-political structures or on meeting basic needs.

Method / Focus	Help from without	Change from within
Structures	Strategy I Economic Growth	Strategy II Political Liberation
Needs	Strategy III Relief	Strategy IV Community Development

The matrix only attempts to begin to distinguish the four approaches. A complete definition of each is beyond the scope of this article.

Each of the approaches has a certain validity. They are, to a great extent, interdependent and complementary. A look at the potential of each approach can help the Christian worker meet basic needs.

Strategy I: Economic Growth

"Economic growth" often is reflected by improvements in the macro-statistics of a country such as higher per capita income level or an improvement in the balance of trade.

The concern for economic growth in the sense of Christian Community Development is for "micro-economic" factors such as adequate food, fuel and health for each family provided locally on a sustainable basis. Any economy must reach decisions about what goods are to be produced, in what quantities and by what methods, and how much of these goods will go to each person or family.

In the Third World or developing countries an accurate assessment must be made of both human and natural resources, along with present problems or limiting factors. The people must be motivated toward development and involved in planning for economic development or growth. Finally, the people must then be adequately trained in the best systems of efficient and sustainable use of the natural resources about them.

One basic problem often overlooked is the effect of grossly inadequate production of many if not most basic items in developing countries. This makes the choice among alternative uses of scarce resources much more difficult. The distribution in most Third World countries becomes inadequate, with many (poor) people being left out and confusion setting in.

The 1960's "Decade of Development" was a period of massive injections of wealth into the economies of the less developed countries. It was thought that benefits derived from booming industry and trade would "trickle down" to the poor. The effort largely failed to bring substantial improvement to the quality of life for the suffering masses. The blessings rarely trickled down to where they were most needed. But economic growth is indeed a viable course of action, when accompanied by careful attention to development on the community level.

Strategy II: Political Liberation

Strategy I aims to bolster the national economy and government. Strategy II tends to see the basic problem to be this very system of national government and commerce. The call is for liberation from oppressive regimes and international trade agreements which intensify the gap between the "haves" and the "have nots." So many have so little. And the gap is widening. The "haves" continue to accumulate. The "have nots" get poorer. But Strategy II is overwhelmingly complex. It includes a wide spectrum of activity from violent revolution to quiet lobbying for human rights.

Christian missions have been a powerful force in matters as varied as land reform, refugee's rights, and the abolition of slavery. Christian missions should continue to be this kind of force. But they must help cultural "insiders" take the leading role in such change; otherwise, such force is a reverse imperialism that still imposes the will of outsiders on the people. Today's missionary force is wise to avoid such interference. Yet, in still another sense, few oppressive political structures stand apart from certain multi-national corporations and international trade agreements. Christians can and should seek to end the injustices in international trade and commerce.

Strategy II is indeed complex, but one thing is clear. It holds little promise of lasting hope without Strategy IV. Time after time, one regime is replaced by one even more oppressive. The liberation all men seek can only be known in the perfect rule of the Messiah Himself at the end of the Age. We are justified in working toward justice and peace; we know that we work with God in doing so. But our efforts will never usher in the Kingdom. Even redeemed humanity cannot govern with the righteousness we ultimately long for.

The converse is also true in many places. (Strategy IV is in some ways contingent on the success of Strategy II.) Development efforts can often come to naught without some attention to the system that may prevent people from partaking of the fruits of community development. It is one thing to give a man rice (Strategy III), it is another thing to help him grow more rice (Strategy IV), and then it is quite another thing to ensure that he may partake of the harvest of rice (Strategy II).

Both Strategies I and II are concerned primarily with structures. A direct focus on either strengthening or overturning structures can often backfire, even with an intention to see needs met. Injustices can be reinforced on the one hand or repeated on the other. Unless people are enabled to help each other live better lives, changes in the system will make little real difference.

Strategy III: Relief

Strategy III aims at survival for victims of war, disaster, and prolonged injustice. Massive relief efforts have been launched by Christian organizations, but they have been called nothing more than a "band-aid" on the desperate wound of humanity. Many such efforts treat the symptoms rather than the disease. Some even feel that relief, if continued, is detrimental in the long run because it takes away the incentive for local production and development. Some say doomed communities should be allowed to pass away to insure the survival of others. However this "lifeboat" mentality has no place in Christian strategy. It amounts to genocide at worst, and the "euthanasia" of an entire community at best. Some have justly criticized relief efforts coupled with evangelism for producing "rice Christians." A "rice Christian" has become a Christian to assure himself and his family of getting a daily dole of food. This is obviously not the best sort of evangelism. At worst it is rank manipulation. If done in this way, evangelism aggravates the situation.

But relief is necessary to break the vicious cycle of survival. An infusion of aid is needed to help people stop "eating their seed-corn," otherwise there is no hope for long-term growth and life. But it is this long-range hope that moves Christians to search for answers to deep-seated problems.

Strategy IV: Community Development

Many factors point to the need for "Community Development. " In the Third World the poorest and those unreached by development are mostly (80% plus or minus) in remote rural areas which suffer from lack of transportation and communication. There is little hope for them to enter into the international trade and buy their basic needs—they must be shown how to produce and meet their own needs themselves in the context of Christian sharing. Development seldom continues well or far if the spiritual needs are not simultaneously being met.

Many people in developing countries become defeatist or fatalistic and think of themselves as poor and incapable. They think their country or area is also poor and lacking in resources. The challenge for the Christian (who ideally is also a developer) is to help the local people see hope—for the abundant life here on earth as well as for the life eternal. After hope comes the need for the local people to become motivated to contribute to their own development. Then comes the adequate assessment of their own personal talents, abilities, and resources as well as the natural resources about them. This can bring release from the syndrome of "we're a poor people in a poor country and cannot improve."

Another factor hindering development is the tendency of many people to look at factors limiting food production, for example, and then blame the lack of adequate programs or performance on the "flood, drought, pests, diseases, etc." The challenge is to adequately assess these problems, make plans to overcome them, and begin adequate production on a renewable basis. The tendency to "find a scape-goat" must be overcome if adequate development is to take place.

There is a place for Christian involvement in all four strategies. But Strategy IV, i.e., Christian Community Development, is the key. Evangelism, in turn, is the key to Strategy IV, when people are freed from their fears or indifference—or even hate—to truly help one another. Community development begins when and where there are hearts of love and hope in a community.

Physical Development Factors

Christian Community Development efforts must address themselves to the whole need complex of a community. Care must be taken to work with the cultural "givens" of the community. Changes must be proven to be desirable. The survival patterns of many communities are so fragile, that unforeseen side effects of improvements can prove disastrous. The risk of doing things differently often appears too great to those at or under a subsistence level of living. Any tools, foods, and new technology must be carefully studied to insure that they are appropriate culturally, and are renewable and sustainable physically. But most community development is a simple matter of a partnership of strengths and common-sense of different cultures. Several basic development factors should be coordinated for holistic development:

1. Water

Pure drinking water is a daily necessity, and water for at least garden irrigation is desirable. Non-potable water is perhaps the greatest purveyor of human physical misery. Diseases and parasites from the water lead to lethargy. Pure water can often be provided by constructing protected wells. Communities can be instructed on how to boil, filter, or chemically treat their water.

2. Sanitation

The prevention of contamination of water and food by diseases and parasites is largely a matter of education. Simple instruction in proper washing of hands and food and the proper disposal and isolation of human and animal wastes can make a great difference.

3. Food

Both the amount of food, i.e., total calories, and the nutritional balance are important. Many people do not have enough to eat, but many more suffer from nutritional deficiencies of protein, vitamins and minerals not present in the usual basic diet of cereals, or in roots and tubers which are high in carbohydrates and starch but deficient in the other necessities. Thus, improvements must be made both in amount of food and in a proper balance of protein, vitamins, and minerals. These nutrients can be provided by such foods as grain legumes (beans, peas, etc.), green leafy vegetables, and other fruits and vegetables that can be grown in intensive home gardens if not generally available. Simple plans for crop rotation and storage can alleviate the "feast and famine" syndrome.

4. Fuel

Wood is by far the number one cooking fuel in the world, particularly in the "hungry half." Native forests are rapidly being cut down in many developing forests, and are long gone in more ancient areas of civilization. The hope for *renewable* firewood production lies in several promising species of fast growing tropical trees including Eucalyptus, Leucaena, Melina, and Pinus species. Several of these are already widely used and are being replanted on hundreds of thousands of acres each year.

5. Health

Westerners are conditioned to think of health as a gift. Health care then is focused on curing diseases with expensive hospital and clinic complexes. In community development efforts, the stress should be in *preventive* medicine. Important components are: teaching sanitation and public health, inoculations, parasite and disease control, and nutrition training. These should be added to whatever curative medicine is present.

6. Shelter and clothing

These should be designed and provided by making maximum use of local crops, e.g., cotton for cloth and bamboo for buildings. Many other plant materials can be used in addition to rock, clay bricks, etc., where available for buildings.

7. Income production

Cash crops are the primary exports and cash earners for most developing countries (except oil-exporting countries). Typical cash crops include coffee, cocoa, sugar cane, rubber, tea, and palm oil, as well as some of the very food crops developing countries need most, such as beans. "Cottage" industries and village cooperatives can be encouraged. Using local labor and materials, these arrangements hold great promise with good marketing technique.

8. Education

In many needy countries there is insufficient education, and literacy rates are very low. Thus literacy often gets first attention in education improvement. Next comes the choice between so-called classical education toward skills useful only at government desks (the biggest employer in many countries) or education toward meeting the needs of the people. The latter desperately needs expansion.

9. Communication and transportation

These two interacting factors are almost unbelievable in their negative effects on the welfare of the people in remote areas. The majority of the people in developing countries live in these areas. Regional or national programs are often necessary to make improvements but the possibilities for local action should be thoroughly studied.

A Team Strategy

There are three kinds of gifts that are needed in Christian Community Development. One is the gift of bringing others to Christ and planting churches. Another is a gift in a needed technical area like food production, health care, literacy, or vocational training. The third is a gift of administration in order to design, implement and evaluate programs to help the people.

A key strategy is to organize teams that have people with special gifts in these three areas of church planting, needed technical expertise, and management. While all these gifts may be found in one person, it would be more advisable to have these tasks assigned to specific members of a team.

Each committed Christian should strive to spread the gospel of Jesus Christ as his first priority. Each member of a team is best trained first as a "generalist" in addition to being trained as a specialist in a specific task. General training can be given to teach basic and practical skills and information that can be shared with the people. This can be on witnessing for Christ, small-scale family food production, health promotion, disease prevention, first aid and simple treatment. Each member can also be trained to be more effective in planning and organizing his or her own work, in leadership, and in controlling (or getting the desired results). The latter means getting information on how the program is doing in order to improve areas that are not doing well.

The Hungry Half and The Unreached Peoples

Thus, while all four strategies for development are necessary, and while all four have weaknesses, community development holds the most promise for the Christian worker desirous of promoting fundamental change in human societies. Community development is consistent with the posture of humility and involvement that Jesus modeled for his disciples. Community development revolves around vigorous yet sensitive evangelism. And the "hungry half" that are most in need of community development are more often than not the "hidden peoples" that are justly receiving increased attention by the Church of Jesus Christ today.

Study Questions

1. Do you agree with the authors' assertion that of the four strategies of development presented, "Community Development holds the most promise?" Why or why not?

2. Explain the inter-relationships between the four approaches.

25

The New Age of Missions: Two-Thirds World Missions

Larry E. Keyes

Editor's note: Although some portions of this article reflect dated statistics, the overview of emerging mission movements and the unique perspective of the decision of involvement and cooperation continues to make this key reading. For updated information on Two-Thirds World missions, see the next article by Keyes' colleague, Larry Pate.

The task of "making disciples" is facing its greatest challenges today. With over three-fourths of the world's billions yet unreached, one great need in missions is a vast new cooperative effort, prioritized in accordance with God's mandate, in order to maximize resources and minimize field duplication.

In 1978, Theodore Williams, General Secretary of the Indian Evangelical Mission said:

> A significant development in the history of the church in our age is the rise of indigenous missionary movements in Asia, Africa and Latin America...The winds of change blowing across Asia, Africa and Latin America and the wind of the Holy Spirit moving upon the church in these continents indicate we are in an exciting period of mission history...Third World missions have just made a beginning.[1]

No longer is Nigeria just a country that receives missionaries; it is a missionary-sending country as well. Nor is Brazil only a nation that receives North American missionaries, but a nation that sends missionaries, even to North America. In 1972, there were at least 203 Third World Missionary Societies which were sending out an estimated 3,404 missionaries. By 1980 there were at least 368

Larry E. Keyes was Field Leader for O.C. Ministries in Sao Paulo, Brazil. During the past nine years he has developed a national ministry of leadership training for church growth and is continuing research into Third World mission agencies. Excerpts taken from "The New Age of Missions: A Study of Third World Missionary Societies", an unpublished dissertation. School of World Mission, Fuller Theological Seminary, 1981. Used with permission.

Third World Missionary Societies sending out an estimated force of 13,000 missionaries. The beginning of a new dimension in missionary involvement has come. The focus of world evangelization is turning towards the Third World. Perhaps the reported explosive growth among Third World mission-sending agencies in the seventies is a sign for the eighties, indicating that the *hour* has arrived for substantial missionary partnership.

In Scripture, God informs us concerning the normalcy of these special and strategic periods of life. One example comes from 2 Corinthians 6:2 where the Apostle Paul describes his evangelistic message and points to a period of decision for all his hearers. "Behold, now is the acceptable time, behold now is the day of salvation." The Greek word he uses for time is *KAIROS* suggesting a definite situation in life which demands a verdict. This is a critical point in one's history where decisions must be made. This "decisive moment" for salvation is now, for there is no other "day."

Elsewhere in his epistles, Paul presents further *KAIROS* situations. He lists additional points in time which involve activities of great importance. Even Jesus, in His evangelistic preaching pointed to a specific period of decision when He said, "The time is fulfilled, and the Kingdom of God is at hand; repent and believe in the gospel" (Mark 1:15). As revealed in Scripture, *KAIROS* is part of life. It is a special period of time which forces us to focus upon priorities and challenges us to make decisions.

The *KAIROS* of World Evangelization

One of the most demanding *KAIROS*-type activities mentioned in the New Testament is the phase of world evangelization. Although the word *KAIROS* is not specifically used, Matthew 24:14 presents an equal situation in all its fullness, for there is a specially designated time period when decisions are made—decisions concerning both those who will be sent and those who will respond to the gospel. And when this period of world witness reaches its climax, "…then the end shall come."

As Christians, in light of this, our faithfulness to Christ's will stirs up an inner tension. For this special phase of human history now demands of us a personal verdict: "How are we going to be involved?" It also demands a sincere decision: "Am I contributing my best towards reaching the yet unreached peoples?"

Historically, many from Western-oriented countries have effectively reached out and witnessed to a myriad of subcultures. Yet for the West to continue reaching as many "new" peoples as before with the same ability is extremely doubtful. Ninety-six percent of Western missionary personnel, it is estimated, are found presently in perfecting ministries. Only four percent are involved primarily in pioneer or frontier missions.[2]

God has raised up at least 13,018 Third World missionaries, and they are reaching additional "unreached peoples." But difficulties for these Third World Agencies likewise exist. Primary needs range from financial to technical, with few solutions in sight.

What would it be like if we could supply these needs? What would happen if half our missionary monies, internationally, were invested specifically in pioneer or frontier missions? How would the Great Commission be altered if several well-trained international teams were strategically placed in the areas ripe for harvest? Serious consideration needs to be given to these questions. An honest analysis of our *own* efforts merits consideration as we enter our *KAIROS* . And a solid inquiry concerning our cooperative spirit, even with other Third World agencies, is necessary.

The New Age of Cooperation

Neither the West nor the Third World is equipped to reach the yet unreached 16,750 peoples[*Ed..Note: now 11,000*] by themselves. Modern missions is beginning to involve feet and faces of all colors. The West is noted for its mission history and surplus funds. The non-West is indispensable for its valuable mentality "from below" and increased vision. Together, with cooperative relationships, we cannot only "give witness to the resurrection of the Lord Jesus" (Acts 4:33), but also increase our effectiveness in world evangelization.

On the basis of my personal correspondence with Third World mission leaders, at least four areas stand out as strategic for international agency cooperation. They are *education, information, finances,* and *techniques.* Each demands equal participation from both Western and non-Western alike, and is based primarily upon purpose or task, rather than specific theologies or experience.

Educational cooperation

One of the first strategic areas of international cooperation must be educational. This includes both advanced courses in missions for career workers and assistance in lay education for those who have pastoral influence, whether foreign missionary or national pastor.

One example of needed educational cooperation is found within the missionary's Bible School training. Stephen J. Akangbe, president of the Evangelical Churches of West Africa begins by saying,

> National churches need more sound Biblical graduate and post-graduate institutions and the general level training to meet the need of everybody of this generation. Seminaries, Bible Colleges, Crash programs, Theological Education by Extension, leadership courses of evangelism, seminars and management courses, workshop and Bible study conferences are all needed. These have their places in our national churches today, for effective witnessing of the Gospel.[3]

However, it is not just any kind of theological training that is referred to here. It is biblical education which graduates students who are successful in church planting. Relevant contextualized courses are needed which are marked by flexibility and commitment to world evangelism. Practical training must be given so that not only does one understand God's mandate and experience the "how," but also comprehends his own gifted area, and his God-designed position in light of the task. Many churches and missions in the Third World have developed their own training programs. But much more *could* be done with cooperation.

This cooperation can be either short or long term, in seminars or mission departments. It can assist in establishing new mission courses or help to glean material from other already existing courses (i.e., the Missionary Training Course at the Institute Injil Indonesia, Batu, Malang, Indonesia). This cooperation can work through residency or extension centers, teaching in person or by tape, through translator or in translated publications. The variations are *many*. The thrust here is that hundreds of missionaries, and perhaps more lay believers throughout the missionary world could benefit from additional missiological education. And it is important to recognize, according to the latest study, that part of this assistance *can* come from non-Western sources.

Informational cooperation

A second strategic area of international cooperation involves providing important researched information to active missionary-sending agencies. Information such as new governmental openings, the location of as yet unreached peoples, newly discovered population trends and societal interests, available support ministries and church growth insight, etc., is a valuable contribution to any frontier endeavor. There are several specialized information-gathering groups which contribute such pertinent trend analysis to cross-cultural societies.

Unintentionally, many research centers find their analysis gaining only limited exposure, usually assisting those agencies who lie in the same region as the researching group. To this extent the extensive research is helpful and valuable. Yet there are hundreds of additional agencies, both in the Third and Western worlds which are located outside this limited region, who are also desirous of receiving new relevant information. Could not their studied insights assist them as well? Could not a loosely-structured, international research network be established whereby, no matter where the agency is located or what denomination it represents those interested could receive pertinent insights, helpful for making future assignments and policies? Research is too painstaking a science and too expensive an art to limit its results to just a region or geographical area. The new age of missions implies international cooperation with research information.

Furthermore, our *KAIROS* demands *new* researched areas. One example concerns tentmaking—those cross-cultural missionaries who earn their salary in the marketplace, while planting churches in evenings and on weekends. Because of the increasing financial difficulties in missionary support, many co-laborers are choosing this alternative method. Like the Apostle Paul (Acts 18: 1-3; 1 Thess. 2:9), they support themselves in the ministry.

Since all indications point to the continued interest in missionary tentmaking worldwide,[4] why could not these study and research centers assist in providing reliable "tentmaking information?" As with other subjects, many centers could divulge key potential jobs to agency headquarters, provide information concerning the most harvestable peoples within the host country, compile lists of existing agencies so that the tentmaker could cooperate with one or more of them while working in the country. A few research centers are doing this. Others need to begin. This related information not only helps agencies organizationally, but spiritually could help stimulate many potential tentmakers towards missionary service. International cooperation in research is crucial.

Financial cooperation

A third strategic area for international cooperation in world evangelization involves financial assistance. An average of 35% of Third World missionaries do *not* receive their promised full salary.

Part of this problem might be resolved if lessons from the past were studied seriously, discovering how "the Karens, the Koreans, those from Oceania were able to solve this problem when wealth was not as easy to obtain as it is today." [5]

Another part of this problem could be resolved if sound financial policies were instituted within certain Third World agencies. Samuel Kim, a Korean missionary who was in Thailand for over seventeen years gives a personal testimony concerning this reality.

> There is a Korean saying, "Cha-Muc-Ku-Ku," which means "counting the fingers." Modern missionary works cannot be carried out by rough finger counting but it must be precise and scientific.

> Since 1956, my wife and I were sent out...to Thailand. We have suffered and become victims of these rough calculating mentalities' abstract missionary maneuvering. Nothing is really specified, including missionary housing, work budget, medical cares, transportations, children's education, etc. But the General Secretary of the board always emphasized the saying that "the Lord provides everything, just pray for the needs." We also needed the Lord's power and needed to pray in our missionary works, but administrational practice and missionary functions are certainly more precise and scientific than prayer.

> I know these kinds of mentalities of rough finger counting sort of figuring is quite common throughout the Third World missions and organizations. We have to correct these out of date methods in order to avoid jeopardy or catastrophe of the Third World mission.[6]

A third way of partially resolving the problem of unpaid salaries and deficit project spending is if additional international financial cooperation was achieved. But to spend money freely without direction or purpose is financial malpractice. Therefore, guidelines must be established for the sake of biblical stewardship.

One guideline could be that of project accounts. Within the Third World, there is a debate over the viability of foreign monies paying national salaries. Good points are expressed by both sides. Perhaps the best general policy, in light of world nationalization and missionary indigenization, is to support special missionary projects, but allow the national churches to pay personal salaries. The basic purpose for suggesting this, of course, is to avoid the depressing problem of foreign dependence. It is demeaning for many missionaries to know that their basic existence is being influenced and determined by foreigners, not by one's own friends and Christian family. It stifles spiritual growth among national believers for there is little "stretch," little faith involved when basic mission salaries are assured from the outside and not dependent from within. The national church must be responsible to support those whom they send as missionaries and to send out no more than what they can adequately support.

At times, however, it is not easy to abide by this second principle of project support. For example, on February 18, 1980, a dear brother from The Christ Church Mission in Nigeria wrote me stating:

> Since 1971, when we erected our theological school, many evangelists, pastors and christian workers have been trained and sent out to plant indigenous churches within nineteen states of Nigeria. Some even went to serve in the Cameroons and Ghana. The Lord Jesus is using these workers to win many souls for himself. Many of them are working to win Muslim believers in Northern Nigeria for Christ...However, some of them have returned home before completing their work and signed contract, before completing their three years. The fact is clear that lack of funds in the ministry to support these workers does not allow them to stay in the field and do a successful service to the end.[7]

What do you do in a situation like this? If you had extra funds available, the immediate tendency would be to invest in this very worthy group and help pay salaries. After all, these national missionaries are planting churches, even evangelizing Muslims in a difficult cross-cultural experience. But what would such assistance eventually do to the indigeneity of the national church? To the spirituality of those believers whose responsibility is to pray for and help support their own missionaries? Would such cooperation enhance their self image and produce greater Christian maturity? These are some of the difficult questions which must be answered before foreign *salary* support becomes credible. However, foreign funds applied towards special time-bounded projects can enhance our *KAIROS* task and compliment national indigeneity, as missionary history reveals.

International cooperation in financial areas can become a significant supportive force in world evangelization. Instead of exercising control over recipients, funds are used with equals towards the accomplishment of one task: the making of disciples in all ethnic peoples. Instead of being a sign of power, money becomes a symbol of cooperative trust. Generosity is expressed because of function and goal, not tradition or denomination. And although such cooperative efforts are difficult, this radical departure from past patterns is needed. While maintaining a conservative theological stance, the need now is to become financially liberal, cooperating regularly with the many rapidly developing missionary agencies "from below."

Technical assistance

The fourth strategic area of international cooperation involves technical assistance. This implies ministry from many "support groups" such as Missionary Aviation Fellowship, Medical Assistance Programs, or Missionary Services, Inc. But it goes beyond this. Many of the larger "nonsupport groups" can render a form of technical aid by assisting in the formation of conferences, missionary consultations or conventions. This is what occurred with the First All Asia Mission Consultation as the Korea International Mission provided time and technical support. David Cho, president of K.I.M., helped plan and promote the consultation.

Also, technical assistance includes loaning office personnel (treasurer, president, founder, etc.) to other agencies in need of ideas or functional models. CLAME (Community of Latin American Evangelical Ministries), the contextualized parent organization for Latin America Mission, has shared their key personnel several times whenever other missionary agencies desire input on agency nationalization. There are *many* ways missionaries can share with one another the diversity of talents and gifts that exist in Christ's body. Each part is a significant contributory function to the whole, without which the body suffers. Thus, in the new age of missions, increased technical assistance must be part of our cooperate stance.

Conclusion

The world is a global village. Missions strategy must adapt to this trend. Edward C. Pentecost, professor of Missions at Dallas Theological Seminary writes,

> The period of internationalization of missions is a period into which we are stepping. The world is shrinking. The world is becoming a world where there is exchange in spite of nationalization. The recognition of internationalization...Missions must move in this direction. Both sides, those from the North American agencies, and those from the Third World must take steps to build relationships—relationships that will be built in a spirit of cooperation and demonstration of confidence and mutual recognition.[8]

By successfully cooperating together in these four suggested areas, new endeavors will be established for world missions. One example of this might be new associational organizations, such as the international network for missionary research.

Another result of our international associative partnership might be the planting of *new missionary agencies* . Whether by encouraging an already known gifted visionary to form a new work (the historical pattern) or by sensing a need and planning an effort to meet that need (the systems pattern), with counsel and cooperation from many sources new pioneer movements can be established.

Cooperation will also produce freshly *restructured agencies* as Western and non-Western societies and churches join hands in missionary partnership. On June 25, 1965, for example, after fourteen years of "wandering in the wilderness" and trying to discern how to identify with Asia's millions, the century-old China Inland Mission became Overseas Missionary Fellowship, with headquarters, activity and personnel resident in Asia.[9] Similarly Latin America Mission spawned CLAME (Community of Latin American Evangelical Ministries) with residency in Costa Rica, and the Sudan Interior Mission's African Missionary Society became part of the Association of Evangelical Churches of West Africa. Because Third World Agencies often prefer non-western structures, meaningful, long-term cooperation can produce valuable restructured societies.

Whatever develops, we must be wise and cautious concerning the duplication of efforts. Just as cooperative endeavors assist world evangelization, too many defeat biblical stewardship.

What do you visualize for the future? What do you foresee as the task of world evangelization grows and becomes more mature? With a sizable missionary force both in the Third World and in the West, with needs and difficulties faced on both sides, with both parts of the one body under the same commander and involved in the same decision-making *KAIROS*, the new age of missions must be one of task-oriented cooperation. Both the Western and non-Western agencies are experienced in mission. Both are maturing and interested in preaching the Gospel of the Kingdom to the whole world. Both desire to be an effective witness to *all the nations* (peoples) before God's appointed end comes (Matt. 24:14). Therefore, let us join friendly hands and purpose in our hearts that everyone may hear before He returns. Let us accept each other as equals, and cooperate together as partners. It is foolishness to think we can do the job alone. As the Apostle Paul exhorts the Romans to "be devoted to one another in brotherly love" and to "give preference to one another in honor" (Romans 12:10), so we must be exhorted to do the same in missions. By accepting God's Word as our authoritative guide, by depending upon the Holy Spirit as our energizing dynamic, and by joining hands internationally as partners we can effectively disciple the nations before He returns.

End Notes

1. Theodore Williams, "Bombay Consultation Papers Released," in Missionary News Service, *MNS Pulse* , 25, no. 12 (June 15, 1978), p.2.

2. Ralph D. Winter, "Penetrating the Last Frontiers," graph (Pasadena, Calif.: U.S. Center for World Mission, 1978).

3. Stephen J. Akangbe, "Three Major Ways That North American Mission Agencies Can Effectively Assist National Churches in the Evangelization of their Countries" (Paper presented at the *EFMA/IFMA Study Conference* , Overland Park, Kansas, November 27-30, 1973), p.2.

4. J. Christy Wilson, Jr., *Today's Tentmakers* (Wheaton: Tyndale House Publishers, 1979), p. 17.

5. Pablo Perez, "How Can North American Mission Agencies Effectively Cooperate with and Encourage Third World Mission Sending Agencies?" (Paper presented at the *EFMA/IFMA Study Conference* , Overland Park, Kansas, November 27-30, 1973), p. 11.

6. Samuel Kim, "Problems of the Third World Missionaries." (Paper presented to C. Peter Wagner at the School of World Mission, Fuller Theological Seminary, May 17, 1973), p. 4.

7. In a personal letter by Rev. O.M. Akpan, dated February 18, 1980.

8. Edward C. Pentecost, "How Can North American Mission Agencies Effectively Cooperate With and Encourage Third World Mission Sending Agencies?" (Paper presented at the *EFMA/IFMA Study Conference* , Overland Park, Kansas, November 27-30, 1973), p. 5.

9. Arthur F. Glasser, "The New Overseas Missionary Fellowship" (Paper presented at the *EFMA Retreat* , Winona Lake, Indiana, October 4-7, 1965), p. 15.

Study Questions

1. What implications does the rising prominence of Third World mission efforts suggest for the preparation of Western missionaries?

2. Which of Keyes' four areas for cooperation do you think will require the most effort? The least effort?

26

The Changing Balance in Global Mission

Larry D. Pate

> Look at the nations and watch—
> and be utterly amazed.
> For I am going to do something in your days
> that you would not believe,
> even if you were told.
> —Habakkuk 1:5 (NIV)

Two years ago, if the rapid decline of the communist nations had been predicted, few would have believed it. We are living in times of dramatic change in the global balance of power, changes that hold great implications for the church.

As the map of world political power is being redrawn, so is the map of missionary activity. Whole nations consisting of scores of ethnolinguistic groups are opening to the outside overnight. At the same time, God is raising up new forces from unexpected quarters to join in the missionary enterprise. Just as the Western world is consolidating its political power, spiritual power is shifting toward the non-Western world. Nowhere is this more evident than in the missionary movement arising among the churches of Asia, Africa, and Latin America. This essay analyzes the growth and development of this movement.

Current Two-Thirds World Missions Studies

The information reported here is the result of two recent studies of the Protestant Two-Thirds World missions movement.[1] The first and largest was commissioned by the Strategy Working Group of the Lausanne Committee for World Evangelization in preparation for Lausanne II in Manila. This information was published as *From Every People: A Handbook of Two-Thirds World Missions with Directory/Histories/Analysis* (Larry D. Pate, MARC, 1989).[2] The second, recently completed by the Two-Thirds World Missions Ministries of OC International (formerly Overseas Crusades) was a study of Protestant Two-Thirds World mis-

---

Larry D. Pate is Director of Two-Thirds World Missions Ministries for OC International, Milpitas, California. He served as a missionary to Bangladesh for six years and was professor of missions at Southern California College for two years before assuming his present position in 1984. He has a Doctor of Missiology degree from the School of World Mission, Fuller Theological Seminary.

sionaries serving with Western agencies.[3]

We have combined the information of these two studies and statistically updated the information to the end of 1990. This yields a fairly comprehensive picture of the growth of the Protestant missions movement from the Two-Thirds World.

The Dramatic Growth of Two-Thirds World Missions

Our research demonstrates that the growth of the non-Western Protestant missions movement continues to be phenomenal. While the growth rate of the the Two-Thirds World evangelical churches is a remarkable 6.7 percent per year,[4] the Two-Thirds World missions movement (which our studies identify as almost entirely evangelical) is growing at 13.3 percent per year. This projects to a phenomenal 248 percent increase every ten years!

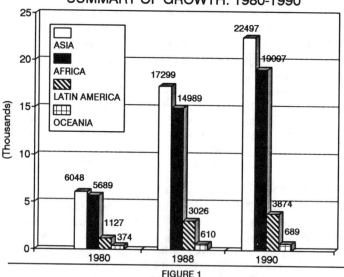

TWO-THIRDS WORLD MISSIONARIES
SUMMARY OF GROWTH: 1980-1990

FIGURE 1

Figure 1 depicts the estimated growth of Two-Thirds World Protestant missionaries by region from 1980 to 1990. Asia has the highest estimated total for 1990, with 22,997 missionaries. Africa follows with an estimated 19,097 missionaries. Latin America, which is experiencing a new-found surge in missionary activity, has an estimated 3,874 missionaries. Oceania has an estimated 689.

The overall growth of Two-Thirds World missionaries may be derived from Figure 1. The missionary total for 1980 is 13,238, with 35,924 for 1988 and a projected total of 46,157 for 1990. This is a net gain of an estimated 32,919 missionaries in just ten years. This very high rate of growth promises to redraw the picture of the global missionary movement.[5]

Two-Thirds World Missionaries in Western Agencies

The study of Protestant Two-Thirds World Missionaries serving with Western Agencies (abbreviated TWMWA) yielded some fascinating insights. The purpose of the study was to discover both the numbers of such missionaries and any relevant information that could shed light on their role in the global missionary movement. By combining this information with existing information on missionaries sent by Two-Thirds World mission agencies, a more comprehensive view of the present and future impact of Two-Thirds World missionaries is possible.

By examining data in resources such as the Mission Handbook USA/Canada Protestant Ministries Overseas (14th edition), we identified more than 400 Western Protestant agencies that were potentially sending agencies of TWMWA missionaries. These agencies were sent a survey to determine if this was the case and to discover pertinent information about these missionaries. Three hundred and seven agencies (70 percent) returned information to us. Of those 307, 86 agencies (or 28 percent) reported Two-Thirds World missionaries among their missionary teams. They reported having sent out 2,402 missionaries fitting our definition. Using statistical analysis, we estimate there are an additional 325 which were not reported, for a total of 2,727.

By comparing the data listed above with some additional data relating to Western Protestant agencies as a whole, the following facts become apparent:

1. The number of Two-Thirds World missionaries serving with Western agencies is not a significant portion of Protestant Western totals. TWMWA missionaries represent only 3 percent of the total Western missionary force of 91,013 (estimated).

2. The vast majority of TWMWA missionaries (92.2 percent) are sent by interdenominational and internationalizing Western agencies rather than by denominational agencies.

3. Western mission agencies have little inclination to send Two-Thirds World missionaries as a part of their missionary teams. Of the 307 reporting agencies, only 86 are actually involved in sending TWMWA missionaries and only 29 are denominational boards. The remaining 221 Western agencies reported no such missionaries at all.

4. A surprising average of 26 percent of the overall funding for TWMWA missionaries comes from the Two-Thirds World. This average is misleading, however, inasmuch as it is mostly due to the success of the larger interdenominational agencies, namely, Youth with a Mission and Operation Mobilization, in garnering strong local support for TWMWA missionaries serving in their home countries. In most other cases, TWMWA missionaries receive only about 1 percent of their support from the Two-Thirds World.

5. Most TWMWA missionaries are involved in long-term ministry. Only 7.8 percent of those reported in the survey are on assignments of two years or less.

6. The number of TWMWA missionaries sent by each agency is not usually very large. Though there was an average of 30 TWMWA missionaries reported per agency, the median was 7. That is, half of the agencies reported 7 or fewer TWMWA missionaries. The average was much higher than the median due to the larger number on the teams of the interdenominational agencies.

TWO-THIRDS WORLD
MISSIONARIES (1990)

2,727 SENT BY WESTERN AGENCIES

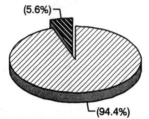

(5.6%)

(94.4%)

46,157 SENT BY TWO-THIRDS WORLD AGENCIES

TOTAL: 48,884

FIGURE 2A

MISSIONARIES SENT BY
WESTERN AGENCIES (1990)

2,727 FROM THE TWO-THIRDS WORLD

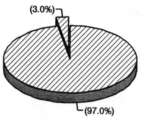

(3.0%)

(97.0%)

88,286 FROM THE WESTERN WORLD

TOTAL: 91,013

FIGURE 2B

A Global View of Protestant Missionaries

By combining the data on the Two-Thirds World missions movement with the data on the Two-Thirds World missionaries serving with Western mission agencies, we can develop a fairly clear picture of the global balance in Protestant missionary personnel.

The two pie charts of Figure 2 represent the above data for the end of 1990. There were approximately 137,170 total Protestant missionaries at the end of 1990.[6] Of this total, an estimated 46,157 were Two-Thirds World missionaries sent out by non-Western agencies. Another 2,727 were Two-Thirds World missionaries sent out as part of Western missionary teams. Finally, 88,286 were Western missionaries sent out by Western agencies.

This establishes the fact that the Two-Thirds World Protestant missions movement has assumed a major portion of the church's responsibility for world evangelism. As of the end of 1990, Two-Thirds World missionaries comprised 35.6 percent of the total Protestant missionary force in the world! These missionaries are not mere statistics. They are living, suffering, struggling, sacrificing, witnessing, and often very effective cross-cultural missionaries, who very well may make a greater impact than their counterparts from the Western world.

A Glance Over the World Missions Horizon

For some time, a number of evangelical missions leaders have been proclaiming the strategic importance of the growth of the Two-Thirds World missions movement. The importance of this movement becomes even clearer when we

TWO-THIRDS WORLD MISSION AGENCIES

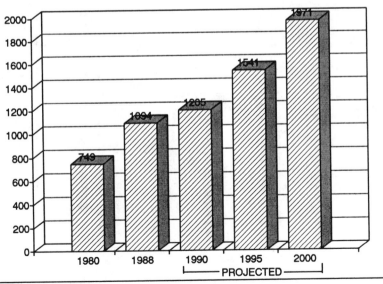

FIGURE 3

project the growth of both Western and non-Western missions to the year 2000.[7]

As stated above, our data indicates the non-Western missions movement increased by an estimated 32,919 missionaries from 1980 to 1990, reflecting an average annual growth of 13.3 percent, or an increase of 248 percent per decade. By comparison, in approximately the same period (1979-1988), the Western missionary movement grew at an annual rate of 4.0 percent, or 48 percent per decade.[8] In other words, in the last decade the Two-Thirds World missions movement has grown more than five times as fast as the Western missions movement.

While not so dramatic, the growth in the number of Two-Thirds World mission agencies is also very substantial. Figure 3 depicts the totals from 1980 to 1988, plus projections to the year 2000. The growth rate from 1980 to 1988 was 62 percent. If the growth of mission agencies in the Two-Thirds World continues as it is, there will be 1,971 non-Western mission agencies in the year 2000.

Figure 4 shows the total number of estimated Protestant missionaries projected to the year 2000, both Western and non-Western. As is pictured, there were an estimated 15,050 Two-Thirds World missionaries in 1980, 38,360 in 1988, and projected totals of 48,884 in 1990, 89,160 in 1995, and 164,230 in the year 2000. These figures include estimates of Two-Thirds World missionaries sent by Western agencies as well as those sent by non-Western agencies.

If both the Western missionary force and the Two-Thirds World missionary force continue to grow at their current rates, the majority of the world's Protestant missionaries will be from the non-Western world by the year 2000. The

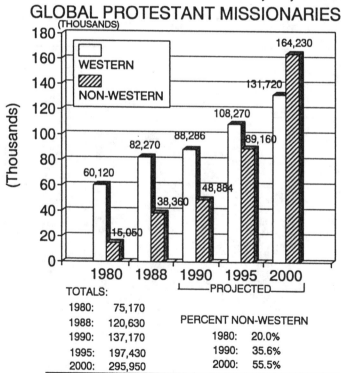

GLOBAL PROTESTANT MISSIONARIES
(THOUSANDS)

TOTALS:

Year	Total
1980:	75,170
1988:	120,630
1990:	137,170
1995:	197,430
2000:	295,950

PERCENT NON-WESTERN

Year	Percent
1980:	20.0%
1990:	35.6%
2000:	55.5%

FIGURE 4

number of Two-Thirds World missionaries would overtake the number of Western missionaries some time in 1998. By 2000, Western missionaries would be approximately 131,700 and Two-Thirds World missionaries would number over 164,200! This would make the non-Western missionary force 55.5 percent of the total Protestant missionaries.

Will the growth continue at this rate? It is important to remember that a projection is not a prediction. Growth rates change from year to year in various regions of the world. External factors such as economics, politics, changes in religious tolerance, financial exchange rates, and changes in government regulations can dramatically affect the rates of growth in a given country. It is impossible to predict what the true growth rate of Two-Thirds World missions will be in the future. The best we can do is project on the basis of what has happened in the past.

The Road to Cooperation in Global Missions

Historical forces are overcoming the inertia of the status quo in many arenas. Political ideologies of the left are collapsing. The balance of economic power is shifting toward Asia, Western Europe, and the Middle East. Around the world, there is a tremendous spiritual vacuum developing in the soul of mankind. If ever the world needed an authentic Gospel witness, it is now.

It may be that the best opportunity for authenticating the Christian Gospel lies in fostering a global missions movement. The Western and the non-Western churches need to find creative ways to partner in the spread of the Gospel. For it is only when churches are committed to each other as much as they are to the message that the Gospel can carry the moral authority and power the world is searching for. With that in mind, here are some possibilities for church and missionary leaders to consider:

1. *The church must learn to understand itself in a global context.* The Two-Thirds World missions movement allows an opportunity to do that. Missions is one arena in which it has been demonstrated that Christians can work together without necessarily stepping on theological and organizational toes. In addition, there are many important missionary tasks which cannot be accomplished otherwise. Some of them are included below.

2. *Global cooperation in missionary training is vital.* The rapid growth of the Two-Thirds World missions movement is creating an emergency need for adequate missionary training. While there are some excellent examples of Two-Thirds World missionary training institutions, many missionaries are sent to the field with little or no training, while others must wait months or even years for a training opportunity. But sending a missionary without training is like commissioning a carpenter without tools! With the number of Two-Thirds World missionaries promising to multiply three and one-half times during this decade, this is a priority issue for Western and non-Western missionary leaders alike.

3. *Global models of support must shift toward the Two-Thirds World.* There is a trend toward internationalization on the part of Western agencies. Organizations like Operation Mobilization, OC International, New Tribes Mission, SIM International (formerly Sudan Interior Mission), and Youth With a Mission have greatly increased the level of non-Western personnel in recent years.

There are very few international Two-Thirds World mission agencies. Projecto Magreb is one such agency that draws personnel and resources from every region of Latin America to focus on the Muslim world. The Christian Missionary Foundation, directed by Reuben Ezemadu, is an international agency in Nigeria that sends some fifty missionaries from nine countries to people groups in seven African countries.

There may come a day when there is no need to distinguish between Western international agencies and non-Western international agencies. For the present, there is a clear distinction. Western agencies may incorporate many Two-Thirds World missionaries into their agencies, allowing them complete international status and equal opportunity for leadership. But their programs tend to be distinctly westernized and they are usually controlled by predominantly Western boards. This does make it difficult for the Two-Thirds World church to identify with them closely, and partner with them directly in missions. It may be possible to increase both their effectiveness and credibility by true internationalization of their leadership structures and ministries.

It may also be time for international mission agencies at their outset to be truly global in their leadership, personnel, and ministries. The emergence of such models would hold great potential for tackling missionary tasks previously not attempted. It would also speak well of the growing level of trust among missions leaders around the globe.

4. *Informational resources must become decentralized.* A major problem confronting the global missions community relates to the growing demand for collection and dissemination of missions information. Principles of the social sciences are increasingly impacting missionary strategy. Concurrently, the technological age has brought new possibilities for collecting and analyzing data on the unreached. These forces are converging to increase the levels of expectation related to missions information.

Such expectations are unrealistic so long as the information is so dependent upon North American personnel and equipment, as is the case now. There must be a rapid decentralization of both data collection and analysis of the data collected if the needed information is to be accurate and applicable to missionary strategy by a global missionary movement. Here is an area in which the Western church could supply needed assistance with equipment and training. Those are among the goals of such international agencies as Global Mapping International, DAWN ministries, and OC International.

This need for decentralization of informational resources is also on the agenda of many non-Western missionary leaders. The Latin American Missions Fellowship (COMIBAM) is an indigenous international association that has done more than any other entity to multiply missionary vision and resources in Latin America. It has recently embarked on a plan to establish national and regional missionary information centers in each country of Latin America. One exists already in Argentina and another is being established in Brazil.

Western churches and missions would do well to invest personnel and equipment in such centers of data collection and distribution. They could easily become an important stimulus for missionary activity and provide tremendously important information for missionary strategies in years to come. Such centers would become important for the entire global missionary enterprise.

5. *Western missionaries must be prepared to shift roles.* The rapid rise of the church in the non-Western world is changing the roles of Western missionaries. Many church-related tasks in which Western missionaries have traditionally been engaged will increasingly fall into the hands of non-Western national leaders. As churches grow, they produce many well-trained and capable leaders who are perhaps even more qualified than the missionaries they will replace. Fewer missionaries will pastor churches and carry out evangelistic campaigns. National churches are producing more and more leaders for these positions. Equally important, those churches are producing enough resources to support those new leaders.

Added to pressure from national churches, the Western missionary will feel pressure from supporting churches. As it becomes increasingly apparent to the churches that many missionary tasks can be accomplished as well or better by less expensive Two-Thirds World missionaries, some of their support will shift toward non-Western missionary activities. As a result, Western missionaries will become more specialized in their roles, leaving more traditional "general missionary" activities to Two-Thirds World Christians and missionaries.

Conclusion

The dramatic growth in Two-Thirds World Missions, coming at a time of unprecedented missionary opportunity, challenges the church to redefine its missionary strategy in global terms.

The comfortable stasis resulting from the tug-of-war between communist and capitalist ideologies is over. Suddenly there's nobody on the other end of the rope! As long as there was tension on the rope, we were comfortable. The West could excuse itself from less immediate threats, such as the environment, world hunger, and the economic marginalization of nations. But while the West sits on its ideological posterior staring at a rope gone slack, the needs and opportunities of a world overdosing on human problems await a message with moral authority and hope.

The greatest hope for the human family and the greatest authority for fulfilling its promise lie in the Gospel of the Kingdom. More than ever, that Gospel is now being proclaimed *from every people to every people!* But the level of hope and impact it carries may very much depend upon how much the church sees itself, and performs its mission, on a global basis.

End Notes

1. For a discussion of the reasons for choosing this term to describe this movement, see Larry D. Pate, *From Every People: A Handbook of Two-Thirds World Missions with Directory/Histories/Analysis* (Monrovia, Calif.: MARC/World Vision International, 1989), pp. 12-14.

2. Pate, *From Every People*, ibid.

3. In order to be included in the figures related to this study, missionaries had to meet the following criteria: 1. they were born of parents of non-Western ethnolinguistic origin and raised in a non-Western country; 2. they are sent out under full missionary

appointment by a Western agency (i.e., they are not local staff members or employees of a mission); and 3. they are working in a language other than their own mother tongue.

4. P. J. Johnstone, *Operation World* (Bromley, Kent, England: STL Publications, 1986), p. 35.

5. These should be considered conservative figures. Every effort throughout this paper has been made to select methods for calculations that do not inflate the figures.

6. These figures include data collected on Western agencies as of the end of 1988 updated to the end of 1990 at the 48 percent decadal growth rate reported earlier in *From Every People*, p. 45. However, figures for TWMWA missionaries have been subtracted from Western totals and added to Two-Thirds World missionary totals. Appropriate adjustments to Two-Thirds World missions totals have also been made where necessary to avoid any duplications.

7. These projections assume the same rate of growth for Western missions as existed from 1979 to 1988, which is 4 percent annual growth. They also assume the same rate of growth for the Two-Thirds World missions that existed from 1980 to 1988, which is 13.3 percent average annual growth.

8. Based on the figures from the 14th edition of the *Mission Handbook: USA/Canada Protestant Ministries Overseas* (Monrovia, Calif.: MARC/World Vision International; and Grand Rapids, Mich.: Zondervan Publishing House). This rate assumes the same growth rate for Western Europe and Australia/New Zealand as for North America.

Study Questions

1. What does the discrepancy between the growth rate of missionaries in the Western church and the Two-Thirds World suggest? What are the relative resources for mission funding? What would the author suggest could be done to benefit both?

2. What is one area of global missions cooperaton in which you and your local church could participate?

27

The Messenger and Mission Structures

Warren W. Webster

Structures for Completing the Missionary Task

In the process of world evangelization, one organizational structure that God has used to spread the gospel and plant churches in nearly every land is that of missionary sending agencies.

Before we can talk meaningfully about the role of such organizations in world evangelization, we need to feel comfortable about their existence.

What are "mission structures" anyway, and what do they do? Have they arisen primarily because of the failure of local churches and local believers to evangelize, or do they have a special strategic role in God's global purposes?

Mission organizations are composed of dedicated Christians who have banded together in a commitment to the Lord and to one another, to make special efforts to cross cultural frontiers, in order to evangelize and disciple those people who have not been reached with the gospel through the normal movements of history and commerce.

Some mission structures are quite simple, consisting of a few individuals sent out by one or more groups of believers. Others are quite large, serving as a vehicle for sending and supporting hundreds—even thousands—of missionaries. Some mission boards or societies are backed by the members of an entire denomination or association of churches; other agencies are church-related but interdenominational; many are parachurch in nature. Some missions focus exclusively on one country or continent; others maintain a broad global outreach. Some specialize in Bible translation, student work, literature or media evangelism; others are involved in a broad spectrum of ministries needed to establish and develop reproducing churches. Some missions function with a church supported centralized budget; many others utilize some type of personalized support.

Warren Webster served fifteen years as a CBFMS missionary among unevangelized Muslim and Hindu people groups in Pakistan where he specialized in linguistic and literature ministries before becoming General Director of the Conservative Baptist Foreign Mission Society. The material in this chapter, first presented as an address at the Urbana 79 Student Missions Convention, was updated and revised by the author for inclusion in this volume.

But the goal of all is the same: to lead men and women to personal faith in Jesus Christ and then to disciple them as responsible members of the ongoing "church, which is his body" (Eph. 1:22-23).

Mission Structures in the New Testament

Sometimes people think that because mission agencies don't seem to be mentioned in the Bible maybe we shouldn't have them. Of course, we also find no mention in Scripture of Sunday schools, hospitals, radio broadcasts, airplanes and many other good things that have proven useful in accomplishing God's purposes. Simply because something cannot be demonstrated in the New Testament does not mean its use cannot be justified in the Lord's service.

We know from Scripture that it is God's will that people and nations everywhere should be reached with the gospel. So committed Christians across the centuries have felt free, under the Spirit's guidance, to use their God-given reason and creativity in utilizing whatever mission structures are needed at the time to carry out God's purposes in fulfillment of the Great Commission.

We do have a "model" or "prototype" for the modern missionary movement in the "apostolic bands" of the New Testament. In Acts 13 we read how the Apostle Paul's first missionary band was formed in Antioch. A group of spiritual leaders in the Antioch church were led by the Holy Spirit to free some of their members for ministry beyond their own community. They obediently released Paul and Barnabas from their local responsibilities and saw them off on a ministry that ultimately included other team members and carried the gospel to many parts of the first-century world. In setting Paul and Barnabas free for this work, the Antioch church had a part in launching something new. Concerning this new movement, Ralph Winter comments:

> It is very important to realize that Paul was not "sent out" by the Antioch congregation, but Paul and Barnabas were "sent off" by the group. Paul reported back but did not ask for orders. His missionary team had all the authority of a local church. They were, in effect, a "traveling church."[1]

Paul may have thought of Antioch as a home base but, notes Winter:

> Once away from Antioch he seemed very much on his own. The little team he formed was economically self-sufficient when occasion demanded. It was also dependent from time to time not alone upon the Antioch church, but upon other churches that had arisen as a result of evangelistic labors.[2]

In time Paul gathered to himself a band of men that included Silas, Luke, Titus, Timothy and others. Peter Wagner says of this early mission structure:

> Paul's missionary band increased in number as the years went by, and from the data we have it seems that Paul himself functioned as the general director and coordinator. He reported back to Antioch from time to time, just as he reported to Jerusalem and the other churches. The church in Philippi most likely was one of the financial supporters of the mission. But the missionary society was not controlled by Antioch or Jerusalem or Philippi, so far as we can determine. The church was the church, and the mission was the mission, right from the beginning.[3]

So early in the New Testament we find embryonic mission structures functioning alongside local church assemblies. The organizational forms of both church and mission were simple, for the New Testament primarily describes first-generation Christianity at a time when the mustard seed of faith had just begun to sprout and had not reached full development. Paul's missionary bands have provided a prototype for subsequent mission structures through which the Lord's obedient disciples in succeeding generations have endeavored to carry out his Commission.

Mission Structures in History

Viewed historically, mission agencies have contributed significantly to the establishing of churches in virtually every nation on the face of the earth. Drawing lessons from the pages of history, Peter Wagner tells us:

> There are some notable exceptions to the rule, but throughout history churches *as churches* have not been particularly effective instruments for carrying the gospel to the regions beyond. The outstanding success stories in world evangelization have usually come from situations in which the church or churches have permitted, encouraged, and supported the formation of specialized *mission structures* to do their missionary work...Those of our own ancestors who inhabited the forests of Northern Europe were largely won to Christ through missionaries working in what is called the monastic movement. [4]

Special structures for missionary outreach are nothing new. Roman Catholic and Nestorian missionaries were active from around A.D. 500. By the eighth century the Nestorian churches of Mesopotamia were involved in an immense missionary outreach through central Asia as far as India and China. Six hundred years before Protestant missions began, Roman Catholic missionary orders had planted themselves around the globe.

When Protestant missionary energies were finally unleashed in the eighteenth century, they made great strides toward catching up with earlier mission efforts. Wagner reports:

> Once missionary societies gained in strength, wonderful things began to happen. More men and women have been led to Christ and more Christian churches have been planted in the world in the 190 years since William Carey than in the eighteen hundred previous years all put together. Missions, then, are not an afterthought to God. They are an integral part of His design for "making disciples of all nations." [5]

Christian missions have made an unprecedented impact on history and society. In addition to establishing vigorous churches and Christian communities, missionaries in the past played an important role in the abolition of slavery, cannibalism, infanticide and widow-burning. From the beginning Christian missionaries introduced biblical perspectives on human values, family life and the role of women. They pioneered medical and health services in many lands as their ministries of compassion to orphans, lepers, the sick, the dying and the disadvantaged demonstrated Christian love in action. In India alone missionaries established over 600 hospitals. Missions have led the way in founding schools, colleges, seminaries and universities as well as in promoting adult literacy education. In Korea they established the largest women's university in the world. Missionaries have made important contributions to scholarship in the areas of linguistics, ethnography, comparative religion and many other fields. They have been leaders in translating and publishing at least one book of the Bible in nearly 2000 languages—spoken by more than 97 percent of the earth's people. This is unquestionably the greatest achievement in communication which the world has ever known!

Missionaries have repeatedly demonstrated the value Christians place on human life through administering emergency relief and rehabilitation when war, famine, flood, earthquake, typhoons and other natural disasters have struck. Through agricultural and vocational training schools, missions have been involved in developmental projects to stimulate self-help and self-sufficiency on the part of growing Christian communities.

All this tremendous vitality and diversity has been motivated by the concern that where there are no Christians there should be Christians, and where churches are few in number they should be strengthened and multiplied.

Strengths of Mission Structures

In determining where and how you might go with the gospel to unreached or "least evangelized" peoples in another culture, mission organizations offer a number of advantages for your consideration:

1. Mission agencies incorporate basic biblical principles of operation and have proven themselves historically as part of God's plan for this age.

2. Mission structures are church related. They arise out of churches and, in turn, produce more churches—often where previously there were none. Jesus said, "I will build my church" (Mt. 16:18). This must be our top priority in missions because it was his. Put in other words: "The mission of the church is missions; the mission of missions is the church." That is one way of emphasizing that every church and every believer has a missionary responsibility, and every mission organization must be committed to planting, strengthening and multiplying churches. In whatever role or capacity Christian workers go abroad they need to be closely related to at least one church at home for prayerful backing and to some assembly of believers abroad for worship, fellowship and witness.

3. One major advantage of mission organizations is that they enable workers to have a full-time ministry and maintain long-term contacts with people they are trying to reach. Missions provide time and opportunity for learning languages and studying culture in order to communicate the gospel effectively. This provision is especially crucial for workers committed to Bible translation or called to witness in rural or primitive areas where self-support is extremely difficult.

4. Missions are able to utilize a broad range of spiritual gifts and abilities dedicated to the Master's use. There are strategic needs, as you would expect, for evangelists and disciplers, for church planters and church development advisers, for Christian education specialists and for teachers in Bible schools and seminaries. But there are also needs for journalists and printers, agriculturists and engi-

neers, doctors and other medical personnel, administrators and accountants, secretaries and bookkeepers, youth workers, teachers of English as a second language—and many others.

5. Another advantage of mission agencies is that they assume responsibility for planning, under God and in the light of his Word, as well as for supervising and evaluating progress toward goals set by prayer and faith. They provide a framework for accountability in order to measure effectiveness. Ongoing training and supervision of missionary personnel for encouragement and fruitfulness contribute to good stewardship of the resources invested in world evangelization.

6. Mission structures supply continuity to the work so it doesn't stop when one person leaves for a time or has to withdraw permanently. They also provide a sense of identity, community and fellowship for witnesses who might otherwise feel isolated and alone. Spiritual gifts exercised within the Body complement one another.

7. Mission agencies have been used of God as a reservoir for renewal, keeping truths about the spiritual lostness of men, the uniqueness of Christ and the urgency of redemption uppermost in the life and ministry of the church.

8. Mission organizations place a strong emphasis upon the power of faith, prayer, the Spirit-filled life, personal evangelism and stewardship of life and resources.

9. Mission structures are responding with great flexibility and creativity to changing times. Missions introduced theological education by extension on a global scale and they are now utilizing gospel telecasts via satellites. They have pioneered in the application of computer science to linguistic analysis, Bible translation and publishing. They are using the most up-to-date language learning methods. They are leading the way in short-term programs which make use of the skills and dedication of students and laypeople. A growing number of missions have programs for liaison with self-supporting Christian workers in secular jobs overseas, in order to provide spiritual fellowship and pastoral care where desired.

10. Missions today are instilling in emerging churches a vision for developing their own mission structures (not necessarily following Western patterns) in response to the unfinished task of evangelizing as yet unreached peoples. One of the bright spots on the world scene is the work of the Holy Spirit in raising up a growing force of non-Western missionaries for new thrusts in cross-cultural evangelism within their own nations and beyond. The number of missionaries rising out of the Third World has reportedly been increasing at an annual rate three times faster than Western missionaries, so it is possible that by the year A.D. 2000 Third World missionaries may comprise half or more of the total world mission force! Western and non-Western missions together are launching many thrusts to contact pockets of people who have been bypassed or neglected in world evangelization.

11. Mission organizations maintain ministries of compassion, including health care, literacy education, community development, and emergency relief

which show the concern for the whole man that has marked Christian missionary work from the beginning.

12. Mission agencies work side by side with overseas churches in a relationship of partnership. Increasingly, responsibility for clinics, schools, publishing programs and outreach ministries started by missionaries is being transferred to national church leadership.

13. Missions encourage and facilitate evangelical cooperation by demonstrating their ability to work together as parts of the One Body.

One obvious disadvantage of traditional mission agencies is that because of their high profile they are frequently prohibited, and generally limited, as to functioning freely within what are sometimes called "Restricted Access Nations." In such situations the creative efforts of national believers augmented by international Christian students, visiting tourists, itinerant and non-residential missionaries, along with self-supporting bi-vocational witnesses ("tentmakers"), are especially strategic.

Mission Structures and You!

In view of all the factors involved, a committed Christian should not be surprised if the Lord leads him or her to give up what might be thought a "normal" means of livelihood in order to follow God's leading in life and ministry. Jesus had to leave the carpenter's shop to begin his mission. His earliest disciples left their nets and tax-collecting to follow him. Even the Apostle Paul, when he went out as a missionary, did not limit himself to tentmaking but gladly received contributions and assistance from friends and churches for his ministry and that of his "apostolic band" (Philippians 4:10-19).

In assessing the strengths and weaknesses of modern mission agencies, Dr. Ralph Winter of the U.S. Center for World Mission concludes that when it comes to cross-cultural communication of the gospel "no one has invented a better mechanism for penetrating new social units than the traditional mission society, whether it be Western, African or Asian, whether it be denominational or interdenominational." [6]

Dr. George Peters states a similar conclusion in his book, *A Biblical Theology of Missions*:

> There is no question in my mind that our times and culture
> demand mission organization and mission societies...God has set
> His seal of approval upon the mission societies thus far. [7]

The advantages of being a member of a respectable mission society are so numerous and so evident that we strongly urge young people to associate themselves with a missionary sending agency. [8]

Just as not every Christian is called to be a missionary in a cross-cultural sense, so mission societies are not for everyone who wants to serve the Lord abroad. The Lord uses many means and methods of sending out messengers with the good news. Since Americans in business overseas outnumber missionaries 100 to 1, we should make every effort to encourage Christians in this vast reservoir of paid-for talent to be effective witnesses.

From your generation we need tens of thousands of Christians from every continent who will seriously commit themselves to world evangelization. We need both donor supported missionaries and self-supporting witnesses. Whether you go as an exchange student or a lecturer, in commerce, industry or government, as an individual or part of a supportive team, as a fully supported missionary or in a self-supporting role—the purpose is the same: "that all nations might believe and obey Jesus Christ" (Romans 16:26)!

End Notes

1. Ralph D. Winter, "Momentum Building in Global Missions," *International Journal of Frontier Missions*, April 1990, p. 58.

2. Ralph D. Winter, "The Two Structures of God's Redemptive Mission,"*Missiology: An International Review*, January 1974, p. 122.

3. C. Peter Wagner, *On the Crest of the Wave, Becoming a World Christian* (Glendale, Calif.: Regal, 1983), pp. 73-74.

4. *Ibid.*, p. 72.

5. *Ibid.*, p. 74.

6. Ralph D. Winter, *Penetrating The Last Frontiers* (Pasadena, Calif.: U.S. Center for World Mission, 1978), p. 14.

7. George W. Peters, *A Biblical Theology of Missions* (Chicago: Moody Press, 1972), pp. 228-29.

8. *Ibid.*, p. 224.

Study Questions

1. What can mission organizations do that ordinary local churches would have difficulty doing by themselves in fulfilling the Great Commission?

2. What are some of the advantages and disadvantages of missionary sending organizations?

28
Tentmakers Needed for World Evangelization

Ruth E. Siemens

Recent events that have radically altered the world's landscape of nations have multiplied the opportunities and the need for tentmakers!

A vast new global job market began to emerge even before the Soviet Union (last of the European colonial empires) began crumbling into independent republics. Its nearby satellite nations and its client states on every continent, bereft of Soviet subsidies, and with no superpowers to play against each other, were already struggling to meet the tough new demands for international aid: market economics, multiparty politics and improved human rights. The worldwide trend toward disassociation, the cross-currents of association (the new European Community, the united Germanys, Yemens, Chinas and Koreas, a western hemisphere bloc, Pacific Rim bloc, etc.), and a new vitality in Arab countries—are reshaping the international job market to provide more openings in more locations than ever before.

What Are Tentmakers And How Do They Serve?

Historically, tentmakers are missions-committed Christians who, like Paul, support themselves in secular work, as they engage in cross-cultural ministry on the job and in their free time.

At the other end of the scale are regular missionaries, who receive church or individual donor support, and are usually perceived as religious workers (even if they do nursing or teaching in a mission institution). In between, is a continuum of combinations of the two options--all valid and biblical. A tentmaker may supplement salary with donor gifts, and a missionary may take a part-time job to augment donor support, or for more contact with non-believers. God leads people to alternate between the modes at different stages of life.

Ruth E. Siemens served for 21 years in Peru, Brazil, Spain and Portugal for the International Fellowship of Evangelical Students (IFES). During six of those years she funded her ministry with tentmaking efforts in education. She is Founder and Director of Global Opportunites, an agency which helps to counsel and link Christian witnesses and international employment opportunities. She also lectures and writes extensively on the subject of tentmaking. Used by permission of the author.

It is important to note that most evangelical expatriates are not tentmakers, because they have little or no commitment to missions or to ministry, unless to their own compatriots. Maybe one percent evangelize citizens of their host country, and qualify as tentmakers.

It is important to note that tentmakers are in full-time spiritual ministry, even when they have full-time employment. The secular job is not an inconvenience, but the God-given context in which tentmakers live out the Gospel in a winsome, wholesome, non-judgmental way, demonstrating personal integrity, doing quality work and developing caring relationships. Because they are under the daily scrutiny of non-believers, they deal with their failures in an open, godly way.

Verbal witness is essential because without words, their exemplary lives merely confuse. Tentmakers do low-key, "fishing" evangelism. Their appropriate comments about God, inserted casually into secular conversations, are "bait" that draw nibbles. They "fish out" the seekers—those "with ears to hear"—without attracting the attention of spiritually hostile listeners around them. The seekers' questions help pace the conversations, as they are ready for more, and show the Christian what to say--the truth they lack, their misconceptions, felt needs, hurts, hangups and obstacles to faith.

This approach reduces evangelism largely to answering questions (Col. 4:5,6 and 1 Pet. 3:14-16), which is easier and more effective than more confrontational approaches. Even veteran Christians can say, "I'm still learning about my faith, but would you like to see what Jesus said?" and take out a pocket Testament for a one-on-one lunch break Bible study. It grows into a weekly home study group, and then into a house church! Natural contact with colleagues, students, patients, clients, neighbors and other social acquaintances, make tentmaking ideal for church planting.

Tentmakers' free-time ministries vary widely. While I worked and evangelized in secular schools, God helped me also to pioneer IVCF-IFES university student movements in Peru and Brazil. A tentmaker couple translated the New Testament for five million Muslims while he did university teaching and she tutored English! A science teacher evangelized his students in rural Kenya, and preached every third Sunday in the local church. A symphony violinist in Singapore had Bible studies with fellow musicians. A faculty person and an engineer set up a Christian bookstore in the Arab Gulf region. A theologically trained graduate student did campus evangelism and taught part-time in an Asian seminary. Some start needed ministries for men, women, children, professional people, prisoners or slum dwellers, literacy or publishing work—or whatever is needed. But evangelism on the job continues to be of major concern.

It is important to note that many tentmakers have theological and missiological training, even though God leads them to work as tentmakers—as lay people rather than as formal missionaries. But in this spiritual struggle for control of the world, not everyone needs officer's training. Foot soldiers must know how to do spiritual battle through prayer and how to use the "sword of the Spirit"—God's Word. They need good personal and small group Bible study skills—for evangelism, discipling, training and worship. All need a brief course on missions, and cultural orientation for their target country.

It is important to note that tentmakers work together in fellowship and accountability groups. At home their churches and friends pray for them, and overseas they work in tentmaker teams, or with a local national church, or as members of a tentmaker sending agency, or as field partners or full members of a regular mission agency, some of which now have tentmaker programs. An English language expatriate church overseas can be helpful, if it does not distract the tentmaker from concentrating on local citizens.

Practical Reasons For Tentmaking

1. Tentmakers can gain entry into restricted-access countries. About half the world's people still live under governments that deny entry to Christian missionaries, but admit people with needed secular expertise. The continuing dissolution of the Marxist world is bringing new freedoms, but ethnic conflict will restrict some. Strong nationalism is the driving force behind anti-communism, (not concern for democratic principles), and nationalism is often hostile to all but its own dominant religion. But economic need will keep doors open for tentmakers. The trend in Islamic countries is toward fanaticism and more aggressive Muslim missionary work around the world. Hinduism and Buddhism have become more aggressive, too. But tentmakers gain entrance--engineers and technicians, educators, health care workers, business people, entrepreneurs, Christians in sports and fine arts.

2. Tentmakers can serve in needy open countries. After a century of missions, Japan is only one percent evangelical. The western European Mediterranean countries have a lower percentage of evangelicals than India, China or sub-Sahara Africa. France has more Muslims than Christians. People who are turned off to organized religion and to clergy (who say religious things because "that's what they get paid for"), are often more willing to listen to lay people.

3. Tentmakers help solve the problem of the cost of missions. They can work for years at little or no expense to the church—not a small matter when mission overheads and country cost-of-living indexes rise steadily. It takes the average candidate couple two and a half years to raise their missionary support. One church reports sixty members training for missions and a church budget that will accomodate only five—not an unusual situation. By sending tentmakers, churches can multiply their missionary efforts, reserving limited funds for those ministries requiring full support.

Prospective missionaries can learn the language and culture as "study abroad" tentmakers, at their own expense or with secular scholarship or internship help. Such a trial period at no cost to the church, might reduce the thirty percent attrition rate—of missionaries who, after costly donor-supported preparation, do not serve a second term.

4. Tentmakers help solve the problem of personnel. Without a great many of them we will never have a large enough missionary force to finish world evangelization, even though missionaries now come from many countries, and even though we do not need to evangelize every person, but to establish in every people group a church that can do so. In spite of exciting progress, the remaining task is daunting!

But the church has vast untapped resources. Many Christians do effective evangelism in the secular world, but cannot see themselves as formal missionaries. God has called them to be his ministers in the financial, commercial, industrial and scientific worlds, in secular education, health care, athletics or fine arts, etc. They move naturally in their own professional circles, understanding the dominant jargon and world view. Their modeling of the Christian life in the workplace may be the most important reason for tentmaking, because it can transform individuals and churches. Missionaries provide excellent models of what religious workers should be, but we need role models abroad for the other ninety-nine percent of the members of a congregation. Tentmakers are a cost-free, parallel force that can complement and assist the work of regular missionaries.

5. Tentmakers are ideal workers for emerging mission agencies. It is exciting that many receiving countries now sending out missionaries! But many cannot easily follow our Western model of donor-supported mission agencies, especially if their currency has little value and their missionaries are going to an expensive country. For Western churches to provide the funds (even where possible) can create problems and stifle the enthusiasm, pride and sense of responsibility of new senders. But tentmaking provides them with an almost cost-free option. Each country has access to the global job market in a different way, most countries have openings abroad for their own citzens—in diplomatic, tourist, airline, foreign trade and mutual aid programs. The "invisible export"—labor, is a major source of income for many countries.

6. The international job market itself is an argument for tentmaking, because it is does not exist by accident, but by God's design. It is his "repopulation program," transferring millions of hard-to-reach people into freer countries (Turks to Germany, Algerians to France, Kurds to Austria, etc.), and opening doors for Christians in hard-to-enter countries—so that many can hear the Gospel! After World War II, the job market grew until four million Americans worked abroad, and millions more from other countries. Mormons and other cults seem to make better use of these opportunities than Christians. Even Muslims make good use of this lay ministry approach. God wants us to take full advantage of international jobs to extend his kingdom.

Every month in the U.S. about forty different kinds of employers advertise several thousand new overseas job openings, for people of all ages (including retirees), in hundreds of careers, for work in every region of the world, in urban, rural and even tribal areas. Americans and Europeans usually need degrees and/or work experience, because governments rightly protect lower level jobs for their own people. But mineral-rich, sparsely populated countries also seek unskilled and semi-skilled workers, mainly from the poorer Asian countries, because most Westerners would not work for the same wages and living conditions, and would be suspect if they did. But these truck drivers and maids earn much more than they could earn in their own countries. In one Muslim city, Pakistani street sweepers share the good news of Jesus Christ!

Most initial contracts are for one to three years, and are usually renewable (serious tentmakers commit themselves to remain abroad as long as God keeps opening doors). Round trip travel is paid for employees and their families. Salaries range from modest but adequate for the cost of living, to high with generous benefits—if one is hired here (to go abroad to seek employment is to risk "local hire," with local pay and no benefits). Some positions are more suitable for ministry than others. Most have no upper age limit, and retired people may opt for part-time work, or expenses-paid voluntary service.

Some tentmakers begin their own businesses. One Christian firm builds high rises, one does high tech manufacturing, another does software applications, some do import-export, several are English language institutes, some restaurants. One person started twenty businesses—including miniature golf! But if experience and capital are required, it can be much more demanding than a salaried position.

Hundreds of study abroad options exist for young people, as well as modestly paid internships, where students and young graduates can work together in teams.

Although tentmaking can help solve a variety of practical problems, the biblical reasons are more important, and a biblical basis is essential for good tentmaking.

Biblical Reasons For Tentmaking

Abraham, Moses, Joseph, Daniel, Amos and others in the Old Testament, maintained themselves while representing God in foreign countries. But it is Paul from whom we derive the concept of tentmaking, whose actions we must examine and whose reasons we must hear. But Paul also reminds us there are two basic approaches to missionary work, one modeled by him and the other by Peter.

Two missionary models: Jesus had called Peter to leave his fishing business forever (Lk. 5:1-11), and when he lapsed, Jesus met him on the beach and asked him to renew his earlier commitment three times (Jn. 21). Years later, in 1 Cor. 9, Paul writes approvingly that Peter and his wife still make their missionary journeys on church support. Paul gives a list of arguments in favor of donor support, and establishes his own right to it as an apostle of Jesus Christ.

But then he says three times (for emphasis) that he himself has never made use of this right. His letter, written near the end of his third journey, must cover his whole ministry. But we need to ask how much he worked, how often he received donor funds, and most important, why he did any manual work at all?

How much did Paul work? What place did it have in his ministry and in his daily schedule?

The first journey. 1 Cor. 9:6 says Paul and Barnabas supported themselves on the first journey and suggests they continued to do so as separate teams.

The second journey. Both of Paul's letters to the Thessalonians say he worked "night and day"—that is, both morning and afternoon shifts.

In Corinth, Paul's job hunting had resulted in employment and lodging with Aquila and Priscilla (Acts 18:1-5), who shared his trade of "tentmaking"—the production of various animal skin products, including tents. Verse five is said to mean Paul worked only until Timothy and Silas arrived from Philippi with money. The Greek suggests rather Paul's great sense of urgency and the surprise of his assistants at how much ministry he had so quickly achieved.

Paul could not have left his tentmaking, because after he had moved on to Ephesus, and Judaizers came to Corinth to discredit Paul's apostleship, they attacked his manual labor. They said it was proof he could not get church support, because he was not an apostle. Unless Paul worked most of the time in Corinth and elsewhere, the attack would be futile, and we would not have Paul's detailed defense of his manual labor in his two Corinthian letters.

The third journey. Near the end of Paul's third year in Ephesus, he begins the defense of his self-support in his first letter to the Corinthians, chapter 9. In 1 Cor. 4:11-12 he had already said, "To this present hour we hunger and thirst, we are ill-clad and buffeted and homeless, and we labor, working with our own hands...." Even in Ephesus.

In Paul's Acts 20 farewell to the Ephesian elders he says, "I coveted no man's silver or gold or apparel. You yourselves know that these hands have ministered to my necessities, and to those who were with me. In all things I have shown you that by so toiling you must also help the weak...." (verses 33-35. The pastors were to continue their self-support, probably not to give to the poor, but to provide a model for easily tempted converts from unsavory backgrounds.)

Paul taught converts "from house to house"—house churches, and preached in the Hall of Tyrannus, probably during the long noon time when the teacher did not need it himself. (F.F. Bruce considers the early Western Text to be accurate in this detail.) Luke remembers that Paul's listeners borrowed his work apron and his handkerchief (the sweat rag around his brow), in hope of healing the sick (Acts 19:11-12)—a poignant glimpse of Paul in work clothes, teaching an audience in work clothes.

Paul's 2 Corinthians, written from Philippi, suggests he worked also in that city (11:12ff). He says that on his forthcoming third visit to Corinth he will work just as has done on previous visits and is doing in Philippi.

That Paul insisted, risking his apostolic authority, suggests that self-support was a non-negotiable aspect of his pioneering. But we must first consider the extent of his church support.

What financial contributions did Paul receive? In 1 Cor. 9 he contrasts two alternatives—support from his converts (which he rejects), and his own earnings. He does not even mention a third possibility—support from churches. But in 2 Cor. 11:8,9 he says he even "robbed churches" to serve the Corinthians. The word "robbed" should alert us to Paul's hyperbole. It was not robbery to receive the gifts brought by "the brethren from Macedonia." He is shaming the Corinthians. The crucial passage is Philippians 4:15-16. Years later, Paul thanks the Philippians for a gift sent to him in prison, where he could not earn. He reminds them that in the pioneering days they were the only ones who ever gave toward his ministry! And they did so a time or two. Paul's enemies said he was probably getting contributions on the sly—a charge he soundly denies (2 Cor. 12:16-18). He even pays his hosts for hospitality—for food and lodging (2 Thess. 3:6-16).

If Paul had received much financial help from any source, his arguments for his manual labor would sound foolish. Why was self-support so important to him? Why did Paul work at all? If his manual work had interfered or slowed down his spiritual ministry, surely God would not have been pleased.

Credibility. Paul says twice (1 Cor. 9:12; 2 Cor. 6:3ff) that he works in order not to put an "obstacle" in the way of the Gospel in the Gentile world. He makes sure his message and motivation will not be suspect. He is not a "peddler of God's Word," not a "people-pleaser" preaching to gain fatter profits. He does not want to be confused with the unscrupulous orators who roamed the empire, exploiting audiences. He is "free from all men"—owes no favors.

Identification. Paul adapts culturally to people, in order to win them—to the Jews as a Jew, to the Greeks as a Greek (an educated Gentile) and to the "weak"—the lower classes, as an artisan (1 Cor. 9:19ff). As a highly educated upper class person, Paul had no trouble making friends with the Asiarchs in Ephesus. But manual labor helps him identify with the lower classes, because most of the people in the empire were at the bottom of the economic scale. His identification with them is not phony—he earns his living (1 Cor. 4:11-12). This costly, incarnational service is not original with Paul. He imitates Jesus, whose identification with us cost him everything (1 Cor. 11:1; Phil. 2:5-11).

Modeling. Paul shows how to live out the Gospel in this idolatrous culture, because no seeker or convert had ever seen it before. He also models a Christian work ethic. In 1 Thess. 3:8 he says, "with toil and labor, we worked night and day that we might not burden any of you, and to give you an example to follow." Work is not optional for Christians. He transforms newly converted thieves, idlers and drunkards into good providers for their families and generous givers to the needy (1 Cor. 6:10,11, Eph. 4:28, 1 Tim. 5:8.). Imagine how these transformed bums affected observers! Paul gives much space in his brief letters to work, because without a strong work ethic, there cannot be godly converts, healthy families, independent churches nor productive societies.

More important, he establishes a pattern for lay ministry. Every convert is to be a full-time, unpaid evangelist--from the moment of conversion. They were to answer the questions of all who asked about their changed lives and new hope. Each convert represented a new beachhead into enemy territory, so they shouldn't usually move or change employment (1 Cor. 7:17-24). Nothing matures new believers like evangelism. Hundreds of homes and workplaces could be reached in a few days.

From the start, Paul's churches were self-reproducing—everyone evangelized. They were self-governing, not dependent on foreign leadership. They were self-supporting, not dependent on foreign funds (he taught Christians to give, but to the poor in their neighborhoods and in Jerusalem). Paul's church planting was only a means to his goal of producing a great world-wide missionary lay movement!

Self-support is a planned part of Paul's pioneering strategy, as a "skilled master builder," who warned others to heed how they built upon his foundation (1 Cor. 3:1ff). Local house church leaders who were appointed almost immediately were to keep their secular jobs. By the time growing congregations needed stronger leadership, it was clear which leaders had the respect of local Christians and non-believers, local funds were available for their support, and the pattern of unpaid evangelists was well established. Paid ministry was the exception. Paul never allowed his churches to become dependent on foreign funds or leadership.

How did Paul's strategy work out? Although Paul's evangelists were from unsavory, uneducated, pagan backgrounds, with neither anthropological nor missiological training, most had received the Lord at enormous risk, and they risked their lives to take it to others.

In ten years (the three journeys took a decade), Paul and his friends (one small team), without support (no donor funds), evangelized six whole provinces, in a hostile environment. They did it by winning and mobilizing the largely uneducated, unpaid converts. In just over twenty years, Paul could say, "From Jerusalem to Illyricum I have fully preached the gospel of Christ....I no longer have any room for work in these regions..." (Rom. 15:19-24). He had evangelized the Greek-speaking half of the Roman empire, and now turned to the more Latin half--including Rome and Spain.

But how can he claim to be through with the Greek half, when neither he nor his team seem to have left the main cities? Paul said he was debtor to all classes, including the barbarians—those who were not native Greek speakers (Rom. 1:14-16). The Empire was never more than a chain of city colonies and military out-posts, each with its own customs, local laws and deities, respected by Roman authorities. Neither the Greeks nor the Romans had ever tried to integrate or to educate the hinterlands. Many languages were used, even in the cities—by the lower class laborers. (Remember Lystra in Acts 14?)

By turning these multi-lingual, lower class converts into unpaid evangelists, Paul virtually guaranteed the evangelization of the hinterlands, as converts ran to share the Gospel in their home towns, and village people located their friends in the city. Converts took the Gospel home, clothed in their own language and culture. After a few months in Philippi, Paul speaks of Macedonian churches. Paul's first follow-up letter to the Thessalonians says the Gospel has already sounded out from them through the whole region! Corinth spreads the Gospel through Achaia. Paul stays in Ephesus three years, but Luke writes that after two, "all Asia had already heard"—the whole province! It was indigenous, exponential growth!

Speed matters in hostile cultures. The Gospel spread so quickly that by the time the opposition had geared up, it was too late to put out the fire.

We need to give much more attention to the different aspects of Paul's pioneering strategy and see how to apply it today—for example, by sending both models together. Donald MacGavran said that church growth requires a large group of unpaid evangelists. But it is not easy to produce them, if the only models are missionaries on full donor support.

Conclusion

A study of Paul's practice and teaching supports the definition of tentmaking at the beginning of this paper, provides a biblical basis and biblical rationale, and it does so in balance with donor-supported ministry. A biblical definition of tentmaking, plus knowledge of the global job market and current tentmaker practice, eliminates most of the long list of "disadvantages" usually found in tentmaker articles; and the others are not weaknesses of tentmaking, but limitations imposed by restrictive governments.

Both models are equally biblical and needed, but too little importance has been given to tentmaking. What matters is how God leads each person. Since God leads us largely through information prayerfully evaluated, a test of a Christian's missions commitment is the effort made to get information on all the kinds of options both missionary approaches provide. Get in touch with mission agencies and tentmaker ministries.

Prospective tentmakers should acquire degrees and work experience, develop personal and small group Bible study skills (inductive!), increase their friendship and "fishing" evangelism, especially with internationals, take at least a short course in missions, maybe a course on church planting. They can work on a foreign language. Students may want to do a Junior year abroad. They can choose from a wide range of overseas vacation service options with mission agencies or tentmaking ministries, with donor support, or take a modestly paid vacation job or short-term job abroad. Ask God to guide and then trust he is doing so through information he helps you find.

With many more tentmakers (in the newly amplified global job market) and many more missionaries, all working together under our Commander-in-Chief, Jesus Christ, we can "fill the earth with the knowledge of the Lord as the waters cover the sea!" (Isaiah 11:9).

Study Questions

1. What types of support, if not financial, does a tentmakers need? Which support needs would be best met locally? Which might be met at a distance?

2. What new structures need to be developed for churches and tentmakers to cooperate effectively?

29

You Can So Get There From Here

MARC

It's not easy to become an effective missionary. The road from the "here" of North America to the "there" of effective service is filled with roadblocks.

Step 1: Personal Spiritual Discipleship

You are a Christian. You have made a commitment to serve Christ. You believe He may be leading you to become a cross-cultural missionary. Dedication is not enough. You need to grow in Christ.

Pray. Pray-ers become doers. The same disciples Jesus commanded to pray for workers for the white harvest (Matthew 9) were the ones sent forth to the harvest (Matthew 10). Every surge of missionary activity has grown out of personal prayer. If you're serious about being sent, your concern for those who need to be reached will drive you to pray for the missionaries trying to reach them, as well as the people themselves.

Prayer should be fed on facts. Match your prayer with well-focused information. Constantly try to discover and define the need of the world. Relate the facts to a missionary you know. Take part in his support.

Study God's Word. Do you have a consistent program of exposing yourself not only to what the Bible says but what it calls you to do? Are you in a study group with others attempting to understand God's will for them?

Fellowship. When we became Christians we became part of the Body of Christ (1 Corinthians 12). Each of us has been gifted to build up the others. How are you finding Christian fellowship? Find or begin a mission fellowship on campus. Get involved!

Witness. The most effective way to communicate the gospel is by telling others what Christ has done for you. To want to speak for Christ "out there" without sharing Him with others "here" would be contradictory. Gifts of sharing are developed in practice. You become what you do. To become a cross-cultural witness means being a witness now.

MARC is the Missions Advanced Research and Communications Center, a division of World Vision International in Duarte, California. Adapted from *You Can So Get There From Here*, a MARC publication. Copyright 1979, World Vision International, Monrovia, California. Used with permission.

Step 2: Church Support

The Bible never sees Christians as whole unless they are in fellowship. Romans 12 and 1 Corinthians 12 tell us that we are part of one another. You need to be worshipping, fellowshipping, and working with a local church wherever you are. This may mean that you will need a church-away-from-home as well as the local church in your hometown. If you became a Christian after you had left home for school, it may mean establishing two church bases.

Get Involved: on campus, in training school, or on the field. Prospective missionaries need a mission agency and a local church which provides not only the people, but also the prayers and the finances.

Share your new commitment with your local church. Ask them to give you the spiritual guidance every Christian needs. Some churches take pastoral candidates or missionary candidates "under care." They recognize the candidates' calling and seek to stay with them through their training and into their career.

If your church does not have a strong missions program, ask them to give you a special person or couple who can counsel and pray with you. Share what you're learning about yourself. Even if your local church is unaware of the process of getting to the mission field, you still need the prayer and counsel of older Christians, and you need to be accountable to a local church.

As you pray and plan, try to discover God's career path for you. As the church helps you, they too will catch a vision. You and the church need to consider how they will relate to you. Will there be some kind of commissioning? What might be their long term commitment to you?

Step 3: Basic Education

Is the academic program that you were pursuing when you made this new commitment adequate for what lies ahead? If it is not, can you find the courses you need in your present college, or will you have to change colleges? Or perhaps you will be able to augment your basic college education with other courses.

You need a good basic and general education. You'll also need Biblical training and an introduction to cross-cultural communication found in the social sciences.

If you're an undergraduate student you can fit in courses in social and cultural anthropology and sociology. Take other courses like international relations or regional world histories. Certain economics courses will help. Try a course on the theory of language.

You'll need some understanding of the world's religions and of Church history, particularly missions history. Most of all you need basic courses in Bible, hermeneutics (how to study the Bible), and theology.

There is a growing number of summer programs and correspondence courses that will give you the basics in Bible study and missions work even if you're enrolled in a secular college.

Some North America mission agencies will take candidates with a Bible or Christian college education and send them overseas after a few weeks of orientation. You probably won't feel adequately prepared or satisfied with the job you can do if you go on that basis. You could become another missionary dropout.

Step 4: Exposure to Other Cultures

Not until we have actually lived in another culture do we really understand the tremendous differences. For the most part, cultures are neither right nor wrong, they're just different. Some people are more adequately equipped to be a bridge between their own culture and the one to which they are attempting to communicate Christ.

Cross-cultural experience cannot be obtained through books, although these will help you to prepare. You need actual experience as soon as possible. A number of colleges offer a year of study in another country, usually living in the home of nationals who speak English. Some Christian colleges offer an inter-term study trip to a mission field.

Short-term missionary experiences are available. They vary from three months to two years. Some agencies are specifically designed to give younger men and women a short-term experience, such as Youth With A Mission and Operation Mobilization. Others are part of a larger program. Some short-termers do specific work. Others go as learners.

Look through available resources. Choose specific programs that fit your overall career plan. If possible, choose an agency and/or work among a people with whom you think you might eventually like to work.

Don't overlook cross-cultural experiences in the United States or Canada. You'll be surprised at how many different cultures surround you. Such experiences are not as effective as moving outside of the country. It's too easy for us to return to "home-base." Nevertheless, they do sharpen our sense of cultural differences.

Step 5: On-the-job Experience at Home

If unreached people are to understand what it means to be part of one Body, you must understand it yourself.

You need to be attending a church. You need to be a part of a smaller fellowship within the church. But you need to go further than that. You need to be *serving* in a local church. There are many ways in which you could do this. You can teach a Sunday school class. You could be part of an evangelism witnessing team. You could be a summer intern in your church or another church.

Talk over your situation with your pastor. Seek ways to find a number of different tasks within the church which will help you to experience your gifts and to sharpen your understanding of what God would have you to do.

Don't overlook the value of training received from jobs to raise money for school. There is something to be learned from any job. Missionaries have to be self-sufficient and imaginative, finding new ways to do routine tasks more effectively. There is no job that cannot be made more interesting and more productive if it is approached with the simple belief that God has placed you in it for a purpose and expects you to do your best.

Step 6: Advanced Training

By this stage you may have completed your basic academic training. You may have had some on-the-job training within a church and hopefully also in some situation in which you were earning a living. You probably will have spent at least one short period of time in another culture, and perhaps as long as two years in a short-term or cross-cultural experience. Now comes the question of the kind of advanced training you are going to need. This step like others before it or after it may be done in parallel, for there are a number of things that you have to consider at the same time.

Focus on what kind of a missionary you want to become—for instance, a church planter trying to reach the unreached. Is God calling you to work with distant tribal groups or within the burgeoning cities around the world?

Perhaps God has revealed to you a particular continent or country within which He wants you to work. It may be that you have had opportunity to study the many unreached people groups that have been identified and have felt led by the Spirit to attempt to reach a particular one. All these factors will enter into the extent and type of advanced training that you will need.

Some fundamentals are a must, such as a working knowledge of the Scriptures and a good understanding of the culture from which the Scriptures have been written. Without this you will be unable to effectively communicate God's Word within another culture.

You must have adequate theological preparation, an understanding of the history of thought within the Church, the way men and women through the ages have worked out their understanding of what God has been saying to us.

You must have training in the social sciences which complements the history and present effectiveness of missions.

Step 7: Agency Contact and Candidacy

Romans 10:15 asks "And how can men preach unless they are sent?" Experience shows that missionaries sent within the framework of an agency are most effective.

There are more than 700 North American agencies with ministry outside the United States. They range from those with thousands of missionaries to those with just a handful. Some minister all over the world. Others work just in one country. Many have broad and all-encompassing ministries. Others have very specific ministries such as literature distribution or mission aviation. Some are directly affiliated with a denomination. Many are nondenominational. Some agencies are very much involved in church planting while others may consider their major role to give service to the existing church.

Begin with a familiar mission agency. If you are a member of a denomination, get information about its mission first.

A key source for information on North American Protestant agencies is the *Mission Handbook: North American Protestant Ministries Overseas.*

Write to the Candidate Secretary. Someone in each agency will go over procedures from application to accreditation and appointment. Contact several immediately. The initiative is yours. The place God wants you is worth seeking in faith. Don't let anyone tell you that seeking is unspiritual. Scriptures encourage the right kind of seeking, and that includes both jobs and the gifts to do them.

Step 8: Assignment Search

Seek the task

It is important that you ask God specifically as to what role you are to play in seeing a strong and effective church planted within each people group around the world. This list of steps has been designed with the *church planter* in mind. This is where the need is greatest. There are over two billion people and thousands of people groups within which there are no Christians. Without those called specifically to go to these unreached people with an understanding of their language, their culture, and their needs, there can be no church.

Seek the target

But there are a number of the many different missionary tasks also needed. And regardless of what you now believe is the task to which God is calling you, you will find it extremely useful to think about a particular people group with whom God wants you to be involved. Study some people group, perhaps several. Look for God's leading to be shown by a match between your abilities and character, and the characteristics of the situation of the people. Avoid snap judgments and being attracted too easily to "youth" or some exotic adventure. Patiently wait for God's leading to mature you, and be reinforced by interaction with the agency. Saul was "called" at his conversion in Acts 9, but he was "sent" by the church in Acts 13.

Seek with a team

Most sending agencies are happy to search with you for your place in the harvest. They are interested in matching your gifts to the task to be done. Probably you will be asked to take tests of linguistic ability, vocational preference, and psychological tests. These are tools and not final answers. For instance, research has shown that motivation is as important as natural aptitude for success in language learning.

There are subsequent steps of Language and Culture Learning, Apprenticeship/Internship, Senior Missionary, and Ongoing Education. But these are some steps that you can take to plan your missionary career.

They are steps that you will have to continually review. You will need those who will be supporting you in prayer and counsel as you work through. Pray much. Believe a great God. Anticipate that He is at work in you. What a fantastic thought!

And don't let anyone tell you it can't or shouldn't be done. Last year 35,000 men and women had the determination to work for seven to ten years beyond college to receive a Ph.D. degree in the United States, most without trusting the Lord for help. Many thousands more pursued secular careers overseas. How much greater the rewards of preparation and perseverance in Christ's mission!

Study Questions

1. Judging from your own experience or from the experience of others, what has been the route to missionary service? How does it compare with the route outlined in this article?

2. Would you put these steps in any different order or suggest doing any of them simultaneously?

30

Serving as Senders

Steven C. Hawthorne

College student Ken went to the annual missions banquet without coercion. But he went without his friends as well—they all seemed to be busy that night. The church social hall was festooned with potted plants and stuffed monkeys to simulate actual jungle conditions. That way everybody could feel like they were involved. The missionary had piled baskets and arrowheads and blankets and other curios on a table in the back. Ken was disappointed. Just like last year. He had hoped for something a bit more exciting. He had been getting interested in evangelism. Some friends at school had been witnessing and talking about world evangelization. Ken was interested in getting involved in some way. But he wasn't sure about being a missionary. That seemed a bit too dull.

Missionary Mike, the guest speaker that evening, was hurriedly trying to prepare some notes for his message in the back room. He couldn't remember the pastor's name. This was the fifth church he had visited in four days. But he had some great new ideas for his message. Someone a few churches back had told him it was a bit dull. Missionary Mike had been thinking about how to get more laymen involved in missions. The key, he felt, was to keep them interested, give them something they could do easily and not get pushy. Mike had some great new ideas.

The slides seemed all the same to Ken. He couldn't remember if this was the same missionary as last year. But the message was a bit different.

"Everyone is a missionary," Missionary Mike declared, "and wherever you are is a mission field." This seemed plausible to Ken. Most people nodded some kind of agreement. Mike was encouraged and droned on about different mission fields.

"Some can go, others can give, and some can pray." Ken was just a student. He knew which of the three categories was his—he would pray. But the mission-

---

Steven C. Hawthorne is part of Hope Chapel in Austin TX and serves with the Antioch Network, helping churches with practical vision to plant new churches among the world's least evangelized peoples. He has led on-site research projects in Asia and the Middle East.

ary didn't say much about the needs of the people in the country. He went on about what the missionaries had done successfully and what they needed.

Ken knew what to expect at the closing. Sure enough, an appeal to the young people to be willing to go anywhere God would lead them. Ken stood with the rest. He really had no choice; it was expected. But he knew as well that he was not expected actually to go. It was a mere display of openness to God's will.

He was open. But there just didn't seem like there was a way for him to get involved. But that was confusing. He witnessed on campus. Wasn't he a missionary already? Well, he would try to pray more. He had a flyer with the missionary's name and picture on it.

Scenarios like this constantly repeat themselves: lonely missionaries on "deputation" trying to give the best impression of their work to stimulate giving, but seldom sharing their heart, seldom sensing support. Good-hearted laymen and students wanting to be more involved, but lacking knowledge of any clear way that they can help. Very few "helper" categories are specified. Prayer for missionaries quickly fades from the agenda of prayer meetings until the next missionary visit. But everybody is glad to have the missionary around. It makes them feel better. At least *someone* is out there evangelizing the world.

There is an underlying confusion. On the one hand, "everyone is a missionary," and on the other hand, missions is for that special spiritual elite (or in some cases, the well-meaning misfit). Let's face it, we have allowed missions to become a "to be or not to be" thing. If you are a missionary, then the world is your parish, but if you aren't a missionary, then you can leave the task of world evangelization with those who are. It only intensifies the confusion to chatter about all of us being missionaries. This is nonsense. If we are all missionaries, then *no one* is a missionary. The label is stretched beyond usefulness. Of course, we are all called to be witnesses wherever we are, but "all are not apostles, are they?" We are not all sent to bring the gospel to a people among whom "Christ is not named."

We have heard the analogy between the church and a football game: The two dozen desperately need rest and the twenty thousand desperately need exercise. We need more active players and fewer passive spectators in the cause of missions. (Are we even good spectators?) Why so few participants? How can we move beyond this "to be or not to be" impasse?

GETTING OUR GOALS BEFORE OUR ROLES

Attitude Check

A close look at certain aspects of our notion of freedom and our quest for fulfillment may shed light on why so few participate in a task so great as world evangelization. Most Americans are raised with a basic precept that we all have inalienable rights to "life, liberty, and the pursuit of happiness." This usually comes out to mean that life *is* liberty and the pursuit of happiness.

The Western values that cluster around liberty and happiness are worth a careful scrutiny. At best, they are limiting to Christian obedience; at worst, they are disastrous.

Freedom

We tend to think of freedom in terms of personal autonomy. Think for yourself. Do your own thing. Privacy. Don't invade another's "space." Make your own decisions. This all fits in well with our brand of individualism. Our exalted model of the "rugged individualist" excuses much of our reluctance to make commitments or to join organizations that would limit our options.

Fulfillment

Our focus on "going it alone" is akin to our sense of "looking out for number one." Our culture has been described as essentially narcissistic. This is not to say that we incessantly navel-gaze or that we have a prima donna lifestyle of the mythical Narcissus who loved to look at his reflection. But we are a people of inordinate self-interest. We tend to view life as "me and (or versus) the world." We tend to value things or persons as they serve our particular interests. In other words, it is quite easy in our pattern of life in the West to increasingly orient our lives around ourselves. Self-love is easily tangled with the more acceptable experiences of happiness, fun, and fulfillment.

So what does "missions" sound like to some of us caught up in acting autonomously and serving themselves? It sounds exceedingly dull, terribly unsafe, and particularly wasteful of the potential experiences of life. At best, missions sounds like a fulfilling career, if only it can be shown to be exciting, reasonably safe, and the most rewarding way to spend a life. The missions career may be a viable option for some of us if we can be assured that our education and skills will not be wasted (tentmakers!?). Or if we can be assured that we are not entering a binding contract which would severely limit our choices for our futures (short-term missions!?). There is nothing wrong with tentmaking and short terms, but what is profoundly wrong is the choice of *roles* without careful thought on the question of *goals*. In a society where the autonomy and self-interest of the individual is assured, it is only natural that we wouldn't think of meddling with someone's life goals. That is each one's personal business. We feel this profoundly.

"Followship"

Let's consider how Jesus dealt with a similar cultural patterning in his day. When Jesus called some fishermen to join him, he summed up his commanding invitation with two words, "Follow me." This did not mean to woodenly imitate him or play follow the leader like so many ducklings. It meant "drop what you are doing and go where I'm going." Serve the Father *with* me. Take on *my* goals. It may mean a rather radical redefinition of your role in life (a fisher of *men* ?), but come with me.

Although it was not an invitation to merely tag along, Jesus did get such a following. At one point he turned to such a group of believers, "If anyone wants to come after me...let him follow me." Following is apparently more than merely "coming after" him. How does one follow? "Let him deny himself, take up his cross and follow me" (Mark 8:34).

Take note that Jesus did not say, "deny yourself a new car" or "deny yourself a TV show." Jesus was not speaking of self-denial. He spoke of denial of self. Denial of self is to release one's claim to autonomy. It is to break up the all-too-natural pattern of things, people, and God himself, quietly orbiting around myself.

"Let him take up his cross." Jesus hadn't been crucified yet, nor had he specifically spoken of the manner of his death, so this word about the cross must have really come out of the blue. They could only have understood it in one way. A condemned person in the Roman Empire carried a cross from the place of sentencing to the place of execution. There was no extended period of waiting for execution, like our "death row." Once a person took up that cross, he was considered a goner. He really had very little choice about his future. His life was out of his hands. Consider the value system of a person with a noose around their neck! If we express it positively, Jesus said that a person was to follow him with all the abandon and release of one who no longer has a real stake in this world. This is true freedom—not merely "another word for nothin' left to lose," but the abandon of doing that for which he was created and called—and doing it with Jesus. Jesus called his disciples to deliberately and daily live with such a value system.

Jesus went on to explain why. "Whoever wishes to save his life shall lose it, and whoever loses his life for my sake and the gospel's shall save it" (Mark 8:35). Jesus isn't speaking of "life" as physical existence. "Life" here means one's own aspirations, dreams, and ambitions. Seeking to preserve a self-image, or to pursue a self-determined ambition will inevitably fail. But to give up small and self-oriented ambitions in order to know him and make him known is to live indeed. Note that Jesus said both for *my sake*, and the *gospel's*. Beware of orienting your entire life around the mere mechanics of seeing the gospel proclaimed throughout the world. Many have labored for the Kingdom without enjoying the King. A life that revolves around the *person* of Jesus will never fail to find deep sustained fulfillment in his global gospel *purpose*.

So we can say that to follow Jesus is to have fellowship with Jesus (and with others so called)! How about the term "followship" with Jesus to express the antidote to our craving for fulfillment? "Followship" connotes life in intimate fellowship with the King and his servants, pursuing his goals. "Followship" is knowing him *personally* and serving him *purposefully*. It means losing all but gaining more in Christ.

Friendship

What about our desire for an autonomous style of freedom? Jesus said, "You are my friends if you do what I command you" (John 15:14). What an amazing statement! We usually define friendship as unconditional mutual appreciation and enjoyment. You can do whatever you please in a friendship.

Jesus effectually combines the roles of slave and friend. "No longer do I call you slaves, for a slave does not know what his master is doing. I have called you friends, for all things that I have heard from my Father I have made known to you" (John 15:15). The friend has an intimate and responsible knowledge of the wishes and intentions of his companion that the slave can never have with his master. Jesus does not call us to the blind obedience of a slave. He has revealed the Father's purpose to gather to himself some from every people. We usually think of friendship as a relationship by mutual choice. But Jesus reminds his disciples that his choice was prior. "You did not choose me, but I chose you and appointed you" (John 15:16). This prior choice means that Jesus is the leading partner, determining what the friendship is all about. Jesus makes it clear that the friendship is an appointment to bear fruit. "I chose you and appointed you that you should go and bear fruit." The "fruit" means something more than the character of the disciple. "Your fruit should remain" can only mean a lasting impact on other lives. But it is left to us to bring it about through prayer: "and whatever you ask in my name he may give to you" (John 15:16). What fruit will we bear? He has left the overall plan with us, his friends, but with a chance to find a lasting part to play through "going" and "asking in his name." This is freedom indeed—a responsibility with power.

Cause Before Career

We can sum all this up simply. Jesus wants us to follow his *goals* before we choose our *roles*. He calls us to his *cause* before our *career*. Instead of pursuing the elusive value of *freedom*, He offers us the reality of a fruit-bearing *friendship*. Instead of seeking a fading *self-fulfillment*, Jesus offers us the genuine experience of "*followship*," following him in his global purpose.

Making this kind of commitment to Christ has world-sized implications. It is the "World-Christian" decision to take on personal responsibility for reaching the unreached, orienting one's entire life around his global purpose. Does this mean that everyone is a missionary? No, but it means that in order to go you must be willing to stay, and in order to stay you must be willing to go.

Several hundred young people (and more every day) throughout the world are committing themselves to God in this way:

> By the grace of God and for His glory, I commit my entire life to obeying His commission of Matthew 28:18-20 wherever and however He leads me, giving priority to the peoples currently beyond the reach of the gospel (Romans 15:20-21). I will also endeavor to impart this vision to others.

This declaration was forged at the International Student Consultation on Frontier Missions, held in Edinburgh, Scotland, in November, 1980.

The "wherever" and the "however" clause still leaves open the basic role distinction of going or sending. It is no longer a self-determined *decision* to go or send. It is a matter of guidance. But it is not a matter of passively waiting for God to lead. He has ordained *us* that *we* should go and bear fruit!

Instead of assuming that we are called to stay unless we hear otherwise, what would happen if we assumed that we were called to go unless we received guidance to send? We must actively seek what David Bryant calls a "world-sized part in the task of world evangelization." We should attempt to go as far as God would lead us in being directly involved in making disciples among the world's most unreached peoples.

FINDING A WORLD-SIZED PART

Once we have taken his "friendship" and his "followship," putting his cause before our careers, it is abundantly possible to find our "world-sized" part. Missions is no longer a "to be or not to be" choice; it is a matter of participation in his plan. To find our part, either as one who goes or one who sends, we need to do three things: "Teaming"—developing *partnership* ; "dreaming"—exploring in *prayer* ; and "scheming"—making *plans.*

Teaming

"Teaming" begins simply by joining with other like-minded World Christians to pray for the world and for each other. Teaming is the development of committed relationships oriented toward world evangelization. Partnerships emerge without respect to the particular roles of each individual in the task. It is what Paul calls "fellowship in the gospel." Meet regularly with "World Christians" who may be in your church or campus fellowship. Consider traveling a distance to meet with your team. Cells of fellowship in the gospel are invaluable in providing the context where you can honestly work through frustrations and conflicts in finding your part in the task.

Without such a band of World Christians surrounding us, we quickly slip into a sense of being a one man-band—the only missions enthusiast in the crowd. Be sure to get with someone else who cares about missions.

Dreaming

"Dreaming" is an exercise of attempting to lay aside tired, limited images of who we are and who God is. Dreamers dare to consider by *hope* God's ultimate global purposes and to imagine by *faith* the part God may give them in fulfilling that purpose. Dreams are world-sized scenarios, informed by Scripture, rooted in reality, and bathed in prayer. They are always corporate visions. What will God do with *us*? What task can *we* fulfill in his plan? Bold dreams shared in fellowship mean clearer pictures of God's plans and roles for individuals in the group.

An excellent guidebook for dreaming is *Set World Christian Dreams Free!* by David Bryant, available from Inter-Varsity Missions.

Scheming

"Scheming" is a matter of shaping dreams into hard, bold plans. Set short term goals together that will stretch you somewhat. Establish a first step that you can't help but accomplish. Plan so that you will know when and if you have failed or succeeded.

Such plans cannot really succeed apart from the efforts that have gone on before. Don't close yourself in. Be sure to check with the leadership of your church, if they are not involved in your team already. Educate yourself by acquainting yourself with a few agencies that are doing something similar to your dream. Perhaps they have tried and failed. Perhaps they are doing it differently but better. You may find that your plans are ahead of the times, or well behind the times. Your plans will bear most fruit if they are part of larger efforts. Approach other mission efforts with a willingness to incorporate your dreams into their work.

In all of this, your highest priority should be your commitment to follow Christ wherever He would lead. What is God himself calling you to do? Two good indicators are: What *counsel* do you receive from family and Christians you trust? What spiritual *gifts* have emerged clearly through what God has done through you before? Seek counsel as a team. What spiritual giftings are in your midst?

If you spend a few weeks and months teaming, dreaming, and scheming, you should be able to get a much better idea of your role—a missionary or a sender.

SERVING AS SENDERS

But what is a sender? What do they do that no one else can? For lack of a clear idea of what senders do, we can easily slip back into the "to be or not to be" dichotomy and leave missions to an elite class of "missionaries."

Active Participants

Senders do not merely provide a ride to the airport for departing missionaries. The support they give does more than channel survival substance in minimal quantity, like the air in the "lifeline" of a deep-sea diving suit.

Perhaps it is improper to speak of a sender in the singular. It is not an individual role. A sender is an integral part of a team. He is not the "waterboy" on the sidelines. Sending is a team effort focused on a jointly held task.

This task orientation can be confusing. We tend to identify ourselves by position, status, and role, more than what we do day by day. An individual sender participates in a mission effort but holds other positions and roles as well. There are a few "full-time" sending roles, but most senders will not have a comprehensive one-word description of themselves. Sending in most cases is not a clearly defined role.

This lack of definition partly explains the passive nature of most missions support. Passive support can be encouraged by statements like, "Some can go, some can give, and others can pray." One indigenous Indian mission agency has called the bluff of those too willing to "just pray." They use the motto "you can go or you can give, but you cannot just pray." They are challenging *passive* sending. In most missions support, much money is given, many prayers are offered, but usually in response to requests for prayer and disclosures of need. A true team of senders does not wait to be reminded to pray or give. They are *active* participants with specific missionaries or mission efforts keeping the entire cause in view.

Such senders are vital. Perhaps as many as three ardent mission activists are needed for every effective missionary on the field. The ratio is probably much higher. If we need 200,000 new missionaries from all over the world to finish the task of pioneer church planting, how many more senders will we need? The prospect of additional tentmaking missionaries who support themselves will not diminish but accentuate the need for more caring, involved senders.

The Philippians: Active Senders

The Philippian church exemplified the heart of *active* sending. They gave and prayed for Paul, but they went well beyond the minimum. Paul called them partners in the *grace* (Phil. 1:7) God had given him. This grace they shared was not simply what we call "saving grace"; it was "the grace given to me to preach to the nations the riches of Christ" (Eph. 3:8). Paul said, "We have received *grace* and apostleship to bring about the obedience of faith among all the nations, for his name's sake" (Romans 1:5). God had not given the task to Paul alone, but God had *graced* Paul, and the Philippians with Paul, to reach the nations. This is the heart of sending, a partnership in the gospel—owning the task together. This is in fact the very term Paul uses to describe his relationship with the Philippians. He rejoiced in their "fellowship" or "partnership" (Greek: koinonia) in the gospel (Phil. 1:5). Paul makes it quite clear that the "gospel" means "the progress of the gospel" (Phil. 1:12).

The Philippians really *knew* Paul. He even said, "I have you in my heart" (Phil. 1:7). It is this heart-level knowledge that will enable senders to respond to needs unasked, and to pray for problems and difficulties unique to the particular personality and situation of the missionary. Missionaries need to know above all that they are loved and understood.

The Philippians gave sacrificially. They gave as consistently as they could. (Phil. 4:10-19). Apparently they hadn't been able to get funds through to Paul while he was traveling, in custody, from Jerusalem to Rome. And they were a praying church. Paul found the core group of the converts at a place of prayer (Acts 16:16). And surely they continued to pray for Paul.

The Philippians went so far as to send one of their best men to visit and serve Paul (Phil. 2:25). Shuttling servants like Epaphroditus can be a prime method of supporting missionaries and is increasingly possible today. A visit by serving, caring friends can refresh the vision and work of all. Senders are informed from an insider's perspective. Missionaries are understood and encouraged. The visit of Epaphroditus demonstrated the involvement of the entire church. They were indeed active participants in the missions task.

How To Serve As Senders

How can we serve as senders? Many of our churches and fellowships don't have the advantage of participating "from the first day" in the gospel as did the Philippians (Phil. 1:5). We must learn how. There are at least four key activities that every band of senders must do. They are not "steps" to be followed in succession. All of them need to work together: Define the task, Search and Send, Train, and Keep a church base.

Define the task

Senders must *define the task* clearly. Unless each sender knows his part of the task, it can easily become a project for spare time or merely the subject of a monthly meeting. Vigorous sending usually demands a daily involvement.

Pray. Plan creatively together how you will pray daily for your missionaries. Some senders have developed a "prayer chain," praying throughout all or part of the day. Others have devised their own weekly prayer guides about their missionaries. The methods vary endlessly, but remember to pray 'beyond' your missionaries. Pray for those things and people for which your missionaries themselves agonize in prayer. And pray for those you are not directly supporting.

Give. Much support is given in the spirit of giving alms: spare change to the nameless needy. Support must be both missions- and missionary-oriented. Missions-oriented giving is sacrificially given for the cause. The Order for World Evangelization (1605 Elizabeth St., Pasadena, CA 91104) is a group of senders who have covenanted to live at the same economic level of certain missionaries and give all surplus to missions.

Missionary-oriented giving is done in response to particular needs of particular missionaries. The Friends Missionary Prayer Band in India supports their missionaries by bands of senders committed to a missionary couple. These bands treat the needs of the missionaries as if they were their own: "If the missionaries don't eat, we won't eat."

Giving can only be sustained if church members are truly sending by caring for missionaries. Once again, knowing the missionaries personally is essential. Communication by letter and gifts should be continual. If your sender team plans to give regularly, agree on how to earn, collect and handle the funds. Be sure that each person knows the needs of the missionary. Be clear about everyone's part in giving. Some senders will commit themselves to a fixed regular sum. Other teams pool whatever they have monthly. Take care not to present your missionary with "faith-stretchers" of missed support. Others use centralized budgets in their church and denomination. Take care that this does not take the edge off the urgency of your giving.

Serve. You can serve your missionary by sending a delegation to visit, help, and encourage on the field. Be sure such visits are approved ahead of time by the missionary and his mission board. Be sure to serve your missionary on furlough. Furloughs can be agonizing rat-races of travel and slightly "edited," surface-level glory stories given to disinterested and unknown churches. Many missionaries dread furlough. But some missionaries are supported by senders from one or two churches. For these, furloughs become times of rest, study, and encouragement in relationships. Plan for housing and special times.

Know. Be prepared for this by knowing your missionaries. Plan to keep up a friendly investigation into other areas of life than just the ministry. Know your missionaries as whole people in whole families, with whole histories, and with a whole list of strengths and weaknesses. Understand your missionaries as real people. Keep letting them know you care. Send them communication that indicates you think of them more as fellow disciples than as elite "super missionaries." Most sending teams will divide the responsibility of keeping communication varied and regular.

Search and Send

The second activity is to *Search and Send*. God may lead your team to set apart someone from your own World-Christian fellowship. But God may lead you to search for others to support. Contact agencies. Eagerly and prayerfully seek to participate in the support of missionaries already on the field.

But *sending* also means that senders will actively recruit and send new missionaries. Senders obey the Lord in praying that he would thrust out laborers. One sender prayed through the Wheaton College yearbook regularly years ago. During the years he prayed, there were extraordinary numbers of missionary recruits. Evangelist Luis Palau tells how he became burdened for the world. One sender with a missionary heart asked Luis to pray with him regularly. They began to pray for the surrounding neighborhood, and then for the city, until they were praying with ever larger maps before them. Fired by this vision caught by prayer, Luis Palau has been instrumental in major evangelistic efforts throughout the world. Senders will encourage new recruits in their church, young and old, to be missionaries or to be senders with them. Contact also "Senders," (c/o Caleb, 10 West Dry Creek Circle, Littleton, CO 80120).

Train

Senders need training in three areas. A survey course on missions will enable them to grasp what the missionary is doing and why he is doing it. Senders will also need training in how to serve and know their missionaries, and how to spread the vision of missions to other potential senders and missionaries. A basic missions overview can be gained from a variety of sources. One of the best is the Perspectives Study Program (1605 Elizabeth St., Pasadena, CA 91104). Senders should continually expand the base of their knowledge of missions. Reading material abounds. Missionaries must take pains to inform their senders about the realities and the complexities of the task they face. Genuine support can only take place with this knowledge. Updates are continually needed.

Keep a church base

Senders must keep their efforts linked with a local church. The local church is the only adequate base for long-term missions support. Student groups can have lasting impact, however, if they integrate their sending activities with a local church. A band of senders will rarely constitute an entire church. But the entire church needs to take part. The Association of Church Missions Committees in Wheaton, IL, has identified five areas in which the local church needs to have a vital and growing ministry: Support, Sending, Stimulation, Strategy, and Leadership. Senders can work to see their church growing in each of these five areas.

Support is usually spoken of in terms of financial giving. *Support* is handled by some churches by a centralized budget. Other churches encourage their members to give individually. Both means of collecting and distributing funds have strengths and weaknesses. But more basic than giving is the care of existing missionaries by truly knowing them. A *Sending* church will care for its own missionaries and cultivate new missionaries. This is largely a matter of prayerful and careful *Stimulation* of missions interest in the church. Senders will seek ways to share their burden for world evangelization in Sunday School, in youth meetings, in discipleship gatherings, and prayer meetings. Missions conferences are marvelous events, but even more frequent occasions can expose the plight of the unreached of the world and the possibility of reaching them today. But most missions vision education will not take place from the platform. Missions must be *taught*, but the heart of the vision is *caught* by joining in prayer. The Frontier Fellowship is a program designed to stimulate daily personal involvement in frontier missions. Participants commit themselves to collect their loose change and pray for Unreached Peoples daily. Daily prayer guides and materials for monthly meetings have been developed (Global Prayer Digest, 1605 Elizabeth St., Pasadena, California 91104).

A church faces numerous possibilities for missions involvement, far more than is possible for any congregation. There should be a general plan or *Strategy* in which achievable and measurable goals are set in all areas of the missions ministry.

Leadership in strategy and policy are best handled by a group of trusted men and women who are knowledgeable and trained in missions. The Association of Church Missions Committees (ACMC, P.O. Box ACMC, Wheaton, IL 60189) is an interchurch organization of such local church mission leaders who have developed extensive materials and conferences designed to help the local church in all phases of its sending ministry.

The Cost of Sending

Cross-cultural or counter-cultural

Missions need not be a "to be or not to be" decision. Whether you go or stay, you will be an ardent activist in the cause of world evangelization. But do consider that if you want to continue to orient your entire life around finishing the task, it will probably be easier for you to "go" in some ways than to "stay." If you go as a missionary, you will have a clearly defined niche in the American social mosaic: a missionary. Granted, it is something close to the general category of "wierdo" or fanatic; but at least you can introduce yourself with a one-word title—missionary. But if you dare stay and order your life around sending others as missionaries, you will not be readily understood. Missionary work is *cross*-cultural, but active sending can be *counter*-cultural.

Unknown yet well-known

Senders will probably lead what appear to many to be fairly normal lives. Most will hold jobs and have families. They will be noted for their zeal to make disciples wherever they are. But they will be caught up in a war that many of their friends and relatives do not or will not acknowledge. Their hearts bleed for people they have never seen. They discipline themselves to doggedly love friends that they see once every four or five years. They give away up to half or more of what they earn. Their lives are simple. A glad soberness attends their lives. They speak often of distant peoples. They relish extended times of prayer. Theirs is a joyous detachment and yet an earnest involvement in the affairs of the world.

Senders cannot easily *explain* who they are or what they do to those who do not understand the cause. Jesus, the greatest *sender* of all, never quite satisfied those who asked, "Who are you?" But the sender's identity is secure in him who promised: "If anyone follows me, let him serve me,...and the Father himself will honor him "(John 12:26).

Study Questions

1. Why do we tend to view missions as one career option among many?

2. How does Jesus call to "follow me" challenge aspects of the American value system? What does this have to do with missions?

3. What is the difference between active and passive senders?

4. Restate the five ways that the Philippian church served as senders. How can your fellowship engage in these activities?

31
Preparation: Pay the Price!

Phil Elkins

I am frequently asked by Americans, "What kind of training do I need to be an effective missionary?" My response is, "What kind of missionary do you want to be?" If you want to follow the Apostle Paul and be a church planter in differing cultural environments, the requirements are pretty stiff. If you want an evangelistic ministry among American servicemen stationed in Japan, the requirements are much less. This latter task for the committed American Christian is no less holy, but one's life experience in America puts one in a much better position to do that job than it does to plant a church among an isolated tribe in Southeast Asia.

Servants and Master Builders

First, read with me some passages from 1 Cor. 3:5-13: "Who is Apollos? And who is Paul? We are simply *servants*, by whom you were led to believe. Each one of us does the work the Lord gave him to do: I planted the seed, Apollos watered the plant....There is no difference between the person who *plants* and the person who *waters*;....Using the gift that God gave me, I did the work of an *expert builder* and laid the foundation, and another person is building on it. But everyone must be careful how they build...the quality of each person's work will be seen when the Day of Christ exposes it. For the Day's fire will reveal everyone's work; the fire will test it and show its real quality."

There are several observations I want to draw from this passage. The first is that regardless of one's role or task, that person is a *servant*. Second, there are distinct roles and jobs that different people are called to do. Third, Paul's gift and role in church planting was that of an *expert builder* (some translations say *master builder*). Fourth, God is concerned with the quality of the work we do and commits Himself to judge the quality of our efforts.

Now the President of Mission Training and Resource Center, Phil Elkins was for five years a member of a missionary team among the Tonga tribe in Zambia. He has also directed the Cross-Cultural Studies program of Fuller Theological Seminary's School of World Mission. Used by permission of the author.

Let me try to illustrate this and some additional comments with the following grid.

WHAT KIND OF SERVANT?

Servant	Piece Work Job Assigned Single responsibility Limited Training and Experience	Apprentice	Teacher	Orderly Aide
Servant and Steward	More Responsible More Authority Greater Experience and Training Greater Investment	Foreman	Principal	Physician's Assistant
Servant and Master Builder	Added Experience and Training Faces More Alternatives Decisions Affect Many Major Responsibility	Architect	Super- intendent	Medical Doctor

Regardless of one's life work and position, we are all servants. In the above listing of nine professions, none can be considered better or more noble or holy. But, as one moves from the three positions on the top squares to those at the bottom, the experience and training required to fulfill the task and position increases. The authority and responsibilities of a principal are greater than a teacher, but no more sacred or honorable. The school superintendent has to deal with options, alternatives, and decisions which in turn affect the lives of principals and teachers, the facilities they use, and students they teach. The architect carries the responsibility to provide guidance and directions for the foreman, who in turn is responsible for delegating tasks to apprentices.

A doctor is expected to know how to do what an orderly or physician's assistant does. But, for a physician's assistant to be a doctor, he or she must have more training and experience to be able to handle competently the additional responsibility. We would object strenuously to a physician's assistant, who without paying the price to qualify as a physician began to call himself "Doctor" and tell us, "I think I can do the job, let me practice on you!"

DEFINING THE MISSIONARY ROLE

Missionary roles can be defined in terms of cultural distance. Ralph Winter has suggested the terms E-0, E-1, E-2, and E-3 to describe the distance of the missionary from the target people. The categories on the left describe servant roles and how they are influenced by experience, training, and the ability to handle responsibility. As one contemplates a shift from E-0 Servant to E-l, E-2, or E-3 Servant, the task becomes increasingly difficult and would require an increased amount of training to do an effective job. Similarly, as one moves from E-0 Servant to E-0 Steward or Master Builder, more experience and training are necessary. The difference between aptitude, training and experience is greatest as one contrasts E-0 Servant and the square representing E-3 Master Builder. To function within the latter category, one must be prepared to pay the price of years of preparation (including internship).

Let me briefly describe each of the above three church planting categories. The E-1 *Master Builder* is a friend of mine. He served one church as pastor for over a decade. Later, he entered a radio-preaching ministry. As time went on, he decided to plant new churches in areas where he had a large radio response. He would then be in a position to help people like the "Yankee Pastor" with 20 years of preaching and nurturing experience to plant a new church in Guilford, Connecticut. An inexperienced but committed resident of Guilford could assist both of the above people through his knowledge of the town and through his personal witness. This inexperienced person could, in time, get the necessary training and experience to serve as a *steward* or eventually in a *master builder* role. But, he would need to seek a balance between his personal knowledge of the community and the kind of theological training necessary for those performing this kind of ministry.

The same could be said for the 23 year-old "WASP." Before she entered a drastically different culture in an E-3 situation, she should have some experience witnessing in her own culture. She should have enough training to be able to learn the language and adjust her lifestyle radically. She might not have a good perception of how to plant churches, but should seek guidance from those already doing effective work. Her role, at first, would be that of an apprentice and learner. She might never want to move beyond the role of apprentice and learner, but rather to return to her own country to serve world evangelism in a different way. However, if her aspiration is to be an effective church planter among Indian tribes in Colombia, she must anticipate years of academic training and internship.

The Price of Preparation

It is my strong personal conviction that pioneer church planting is at least as complicated as learning to be a surgeon. Everyone desiring to become a surgeon knows he must receive much classroom training, read widely, pass standardized examinations, and then do extensive internship. Aspiring physicians who want to perform heart transplants, or enter some other specialty, know they must pay the price of added study and internship. Physicians wanting to practice as psychiatrists must complete years of additional preparation to meet that goal.

A friend of mine, an outstanding pastor, decided to become a lawyer. His goal was to represent people before the Supreme Court of the United States. His goal was high and he calculated the price. He knew he had at least three years of

DEFINING THE MISSIONARY ROLE

	E-0 SPIRITUAL NURTURE NOT CONVERSION GROWTH	E-1 CHURCH PLANTING WITHIN YOUR CULTURE	E-2 CHURCH PLANTING IN SIMILAR CULTURE	E-3 CHURCH PLANTING IN A CULTURE RADICALLY DIFFERENT
SERVANT	Sunday School teacher in a Community Church	Inexperienced but committed Christian excited about planting a new church in his town --Guilford, Conn.	25 year-old WASP witnessing to University students in Columbia	23 year-old WASP witnessing to Amazon Indian tribe in Columbia
SERVANT/ STEWARD	Sunday School Director--same church	Yankee pastor-- 20 years experience, assisting in planting a new church	WASP Bible translator starting one church in Ladino town	WASP Bible translator starting a church in a single Amazon village
SERVANT/ MASTER BUILDER	Senior pastor	A successful church planter in many parts of the United States	WASP 10 year veteran church planter among Ladinos in Colombia	WASP 10 year veteran church planter among Indian tribes in Colombia

E = Evangelism

1, 2, 3 = The higher the number, the greater the cultural distance from the sending community

WASP = White Anglo-Saxon Protestant

law school, stiff bar examinations, and additional years of specialized practice before he could represent a client before the Supreme Court. He found many attorneys who could counsel him on the minimum educational and experiential requirements to be effective in his anticipated job.

When it comes to preparing to be an effective missionary, the task of getting good counsel is much more difficult than it was for my attorney friend. It is difficult because of the practice of labeling all who function in overseas ministries with the one term, *missionary*. Frequently the career missionaries themselves do not communicate the broader and more complex picture because they are under severe pressure to raise funds and recruit for their particular ministry, project and field. The result is that one finds little clarity and definition is provided for the extremely complex number of tasks and roles which missionaries are called upon to perform.

A great deal of energy has been expended recently in focusing attention on the unreached and hidden peoples of the world. For Western Christians, these peoples are a radically different culture (E-3). The complexities of reaching them would, at least from a human perspective, probably exceed those faced by the Apostle Paul and his team companions. Yet, notice the extraordinary efforts God took to prepare Paul, a Jew, to go to the Gentiles. He was a mature man when he accepted Christ. At that time he had already received extraordinary training under Gamaliel, a well respected doctor of the Jewish Law.

Paul had already developed a reputation for his religious zeal and leadership. In spite of this, God worked in preparing Paul for at least 13 more years, including a time of tutorship under Barnabas (an outstanding Christian leader and missionary). The necessity of this extensive time of preparation becomes clear as we read of his missionary church planting efforts in the book of Acts. His spiritual fiber had to be strong. His theological perspective had to be mature and more flexible than the apostles and church leaders back home (in Jerusalem). He had to have the personal confidence to withstand attacks from outside and within the Christian faith. He even had to withstand and confront Peter publicly. Today, the task that Paul faced is complicated by nearly 2,000 years of history, innumerable divisions within Christendom, and a population at least ten times as large.

Specialization

Another dimension is illustrated by the following chart, used by C. Peter Wagner in one of his courses at Fuller Theological Seminary.

MISSIONARIES? YES—BUT WHAT KIND?

This expands the previous model I used. There I spoke only of the nine categories relating to missions as evangelism and church planting (E-1, E-2, E-3). Here N-1, N-2, N-3 could be expanded into those same nine categories. It is *not* the intention of the above model to isolate church planting from Christian nurture and social service. I believe in a holistic approach to the task. But aspects of the training needed for effective social service and church planting differ significantly. One should not lump the training as all being the same, though both need the same basics.

MISSIONARIES? YES--BUT WHAT KIND?

CULTURAL DISTANCE FROM SENDING COMMUNITY

		0	1	2	3
Evangelism & Church Planting	E	E-0	E-1	E-2	E-3
Christian Nurture	N	N-0	N-1	N-2	N-3
Social Service	S	S-0	S-1	S-2	S-3
		Christian Community	Non-X'n Community	Similar Culture	Distinct Culture
		MONOCULTURAL MINISTRY		CROSS-CULTURAL MINISTRY	

PRIMARY VOCATIONAL RESPONSIBILITY

Stained-Glass Barrier

Cultural Barrier

Sometimes physicians are teamed with people who are involved in church planting and evangelism; most frequently they are not. Sometimes their perspective is, "I am a Christian and a specialist in medicine [or nutrition, engineering, education, etc.]. I don't know anything about church planting, cross-cultural evangelism or how missions operate, but I want to help. Is there a place for me?" Someone says "yes" too quickly and they go straight to the field. Their response should be, "Yes, you are needed, but you need some additional specialty training to prepare you to use your vocational skills in a cross-cultural context. Before you go, learn the basics involved in being an effective witness, church planter and disciple in a radical new environment. It is an extremely complex task to apply your skills toward the development of a strong national church."

Getting the Basics

What are these basics that everyone needs prior to entering the field? A person needs a solid introductory course in missions taught by one or more experienced missionaries who are professionally trained in the discipline of missiology. Many undergraduate colleges and seminaries offer such a course. If the course includes experiential dimensions of learning, so much the better. Preceding, or during this training, should be solid college level biblical training. This should be followed by three to twelve months of field experience under the tutorship of a competent, effective missionary or national church leader.

This experience should be followed by further biblical studies which speak to the issues of contextualizing the Gospel. They should separate biblical and church customs from the universal messages. Additional time should be spent in learning the skills of language acquisition (how to learn a language *outside* the classroom). Other basics at this stage include missionary anthropology (cultural

A Model for Missionary Training

TRAINING AND EXPERIENCE LEVELS	TYPE OF PREPARATION		
	CLASSROOM	FIELD TRAINING	EXPERIENCE
LEVEL I – Pre-Mission: Four to five years of undergraduate work.	College Undergraduate: Bible, sociology, anthropology & theory of language, French or Spanish.	One year formal education in another culture and language.	Four summers or interterms with two different agencies and fields.
LEVEL II – Mission Training: Three to four years of graduate work.	University graduate study: theology, biblical studies, Greek, missionary anthropology and sociology, communication theory and practice.	One to two years of field work in area near expected service.	Field work done in cooperation with and under supervision of selected mission agency.
LEVEL III – Intern: Two years of language acquisition and people study.	None	Coaching by senior missionary and former professors via correspondence. Language study.	Assignment to specific people group. Language study among group.
LEVEL IV – Associate Missionary: Two to six years of work on field.	Nine months of field work at School of World Mission at end of field work. Review, evaluate.	Supervision by senior missionary.	Work with mission team attempting to evangelize assigned group.
LEVEL V – Missionary: Two to six years of work on field.	None	Supervision of associate missionaries.	Decision on assignment to new field or continuance in present field.
LEVEL VI – Senior Missionary: Four to eight years of field work and teaching.	Two years of graduate study leading to PhD or equivalent.	Teaching of trainees and interns. Field evaluation assignments.	Decision to return to a people or to a field teaching situation.

anthropology is helpful but needs applications), cross-cultural communication, and extensive studies of what causes churches to grow and what retards growth on the mission field.

By the time you have done the above, you will not need further guidance from this article. You will have your data base for selecting an agency or experienced missionary or national church to apprentice yourself with. You will know what additional training you need for the area of specialization God is calling you to.

If you desire to serve as a missionary in another culture, I hope you have *not* been discouraged by the above comments. They are *not* intended to frustrate, but to challenge you to give the best you have to offer. Those of us who have been used by God as church planters in other cultures are conscious we are made of clay, prone to sin, frequently break God's heart, and are "average" humans. But God's love challenges us to think His great thoughts, respond to His great acts, attempt great things for His glory.

I would encourage you to read closely the comments of two of my most respected colleagues, Edward R. Dayton and David Fraser, in their book, *Planning Strategies for World Evangelism* , 1980, pp. 243-251. They suggest different levels of training and experience. Where the one term, missionary, has been used, they recommend six terms according to the level of service. Let me encourage you to be challenged by this model.

Finally, they quote in their book from an outstanding missionary educator, J. Herbert Kane. This shall serve as my concluding thought:

> There's still a prevailing notion that one can major in any subject in college or seminary and be a good missionary. No special courses are necessary! Most leading missions have a minimum requirement—one year of Bible—nothing is said of missions! I think this is a great mistake. To go overseas without missionary anthropology, cross-cultural communication, area studies, missionary life at work—to say nothing of the history of missions and non-Christian religions, is an act of consummate folly!

Study Questions

1. How does a missionary's role, field of service, and specialization affect the level and extent of training required?

2. What specific training do you feel that an E-3 pioneer church planter would need?

3. What are the basics of preparation that Elkins thinks that *anyone* needs prior to entering the mission field?

32

Lifestyle for Servants of Christ (at Home and Overseas)

David H. Adeney

Before leaving England fifty-six years ago for my first seven-year term of service in China, I was greatly influenced by a man of God who had served as a missionary bishop in Africa. Before going overseas, Bishop Taylor Smith had kept a four-word motto on his desk: "AS NOW, SO THEN." He often reminded us that going overseas will not suddenly turn you into a saint. What you are now will determine what kind of missionary you will be in the future. There are not two kinds of lifestyles: one for home and the other for overseas. If you are considering missionary service, adopt *now* the lifestyle you expect to follow in the coming years.

This does not mean that there will not be changes in our lifestyle. Throughout our lives we should be learning more and more of what is involved in living as a true disciple of the Lord Jesus and be able to adapt to different situations.

Paul's Lifestyle

The clearest description of a missionary's lifestyle is found in Paul's message to the Ephesian elders in Acts 20.

Paul's lifestyle was a direct result of the vision he received at the beginning of his Christian life. Years later he could say, "I was not disobedient to the heavenly vision." His compelling desire was to see the Gentiles presented as an offering to God. His life-long purpose, to preach where Christ had not been named, deter-

David Adeney's first term of service with the China Inland Mission (now Overseas Missionary Fellowship) from 1934 to 1941 was spent in a church planting ministry in the rural areas of Henan. After World War II he returned to work with CIM and the China Inter-Varsity Fellowship, visiting Chinese students in universities all over China. After the Revolution he served first as missions director of IVCF USA and then moved with his family to Hong Kong to work for 12 years as regional director for East Asia of the International Fellowship of Evangelical Students. He is currently a vice-president of the IFES. The Adeney family lived in Singapore where David served for 8 years as dean of the Discipleship Training Centre. After China began to open he made a number of return visits. He started the Pray for China Fellowship and served as North American Coordinator for the China Program of the Overseas Missionary Fellowship. He was also Professor of Christian Mission at New College, Berkeley. He is currently Minister at Large for the OMF.

mined the kind of life he lived. His whole attitude in life was summed up in Acts 20:24, "I do not count my life of any value or as precious to myself, if only I may accomplish my course and the ministry which I received from the Lord Jesus, to testify to the gospel of the grace of God."

Instead of seeking to preserve a comfortable way of living he chose to offer up his life completely in the service of the Lord Jesus and His kingdom. The great need today is for people who share Paul's vision and are prepared, like him, to dedicate their whole lives to the task of finishing the work that Christ has committed to his disciples.

God gives fresh vision at different stages of our life. During our first seven years in China the vision was to see churches established in the unevangelised market towns and villages of Henan. When we returned to China in 1946 our aim was to see a Christian witness established on every Chinese University campus. Ten years later we were looking at universities throughout East Asia seeking to establish and build up national student movements in each country. When a Chinese fellow-worker took my place in the leadership of the International Fellowship of Evangelical Students in Asia the call came to start the Discipleship Training Centre in Singapore to prepare Asian graduates for leadership in the church in Asia. When we reached the official age for retirement God gave a fresh vision and we started the Pray for China Fellowship seeking to keep the church in the West informed of what God is doing through the rapidly growing Christian communities in China.

The vision that God gives in every stage of life determines our lifestyle. If I am convinced that God has a certain task for me to fulfill, my whole manner of life must contribute to that overall objective. Those who enter a highly specialized profession such as medicine often find that they are required to make changes in their lifestyle in order to qualify as a doctor. How much more willing we should be to accept changes that will fit us for service as true ambassadors for Jesus Christ.

A self-centred vision wrapped in material things will result in a lifestyle characterised by love of the world. But a vision of the Kingdom of God—and a deep desire to serve our generation according to the purpose of God—will produce a lifestyle worthy of God's calling. If you have already begun to sense a deep concern for some area of need or some unreached peoples in the world today, this may be an indication that God is calling you to some specific ministry. It may also lead to significant changes in your lifestyle in the coming days.

Identification

When we look in detail at the things which were basic in Paul's lifestyle we find in Acts 20:18 that he refers to his having lived among the people to whom he is speaking. Paul had spent almost 3 years in Ephesus and the people had come to know him very well. His own background was very different from that of the Ephesian Christians but they had become very dear to him. He reminded them that "I did not cease night or day to admonish everyone with tears." In his letter to the Ephesians he also asked them to pray very especially for him, "that utterance may be given me in opening my mouth boldly to proclaim the mystery of the gospel" (Eph. 5:18, 19). This indicates a very close relationship, both giving and receiving.

This long-term close relationship is sometimes lacking in present day missionary work. Short term missions have become very popular. They certainly provide valuable learning experiences and often lead the participants into a longer period of service. But effective missionary work requires far more than a few weeks' visit. Too many young missionaries only go overseas for one term of three or four years, not realising that their most fruitful ministry is yet to come. Workers are needed who have had a prolonged exposure to a new culture and have mastered the language so that they truly become part of the Christian family in the land of their adoption. This applies not only to regular missionaries relating to the national church but also to Christian professionals in a restricted access nation. The longer that they can stay the more valuable will be their service.

Overconfident?

Paul goes on to speak of "serving the Lord with all humility." In his letter to the Corinthians he writes about "the meekness and gentleness of Christ."

The greatest barrier to effective missionary service is pride, which often takes very subtle and unrecognized forms.

When I arrived in China, the general director of the China Inland Mission was D.E. Hoste, an old man, a member of the Cambridge Seven. Enthusiastically I talked to him about the student work at Cambridge and our plans for an evangelistic mission.

He was interested, but I remember only one sentence of his response. "Beware," he said, "of national pride which shows itself just like a man who has been eating garlic."

I was to experience this danger. During my first term in China, much of my self-confidence had to be stripped away.

I had been active in student and young people's work, and had served as missionary secretary of the British Inter-Varsity. But now I found myself handicapped by my lack of language, working among country people, many of whom were illiterate. I would have liked to go into a university center to work with students, but God saw that I needed to go to the "university of the countryside" and learn from these simple village Christians, living in their homes and sharing in their way of life. Years later, the desire to do student work would be fulfilled, but only after the humbling experience of those early years.

I shall never forget the way in which a Chinese pastor ministered to me during a time of spiritual depression. I went to live with him in what was known as "The Spiritual Work Team." I was refreshed as he opened up the Scriptures. And I was amazed when, responding to an invitation to go and pray with him, I found him flat on his face, pouring out his soul in confession to God.

It is easy for a young worker to be judgmental and fail to appreciate the strengths of those with whom we are sent to work. I had to learn through mistakes.

I remember once telling a Chinese fellow-worker that I felt there was something lacking in his message. He was deeply offended. I had failed to speak in a spirit of love and humility.

Years later, the leader of one of the IFES national movements emphasized this need for humility. "There are two kinds of missionaries who come to our country," he said. "The first comes full of ideas and plans. He asks us to help him with some new evangelistic project. In contrast, there is the missionary who comes with a much more sensitive approach to the new culture into which he is entering. He asks how he can be of help to *us*. He has something to contribute, but he does not push himself. He is ready to listen and learn."

This kind of missionary has no wish to see national Christians follow a Western pattern. He wants them to be completely identified with their own cultural and political background, as long as it does not prevent them from manifesting the life of the kingdom of God in "righteousness, peace and joy in the Holy Spirit."

We may so easily in our methods and approach appear to be Americans or British first and Christians second. Without true humility, it is all too easy to set up Western organizations which depend upon Western leadership, even though national leaders may nominally be in control. Only Westerners with a truly humble spirit will be able to enter into the kind of partnership which is so desperately needed in the church today. There must be true equality, with each one contributing the varied gifts received from the Lord.

Shared Sorrows

In the same verse Paul also speaks of great conflicts and sufferings. Nothing binds people together so much as sharing in trials.

In the early days of World War II, we shared in the sorrows and dangers of our fellow believers in China. And they shared in ours. I shall always remember our Chinese fellow workers standing with us by the side of the little grave where our second child was buried, praying that as God had taken our treasure to be with him, our hearts might be drawn closer to heaven.

When we went out with the evangelistic bands to country villages, sometimes in brigand-infested areas, we lived together in often very primitive conditions. We shared simple air-raid shelters in our garden when the Japanese bombers rained their bombs on our town.

Later, we shared the heartache of seeing some students give up their faith during the communist revolution. Since then, our brothers and sisters in China have entered far more deeply into the fellowship of Christ's suffering.

One of the most moving experiences of my recent visit to China took place when a door opened and a white-haired man greeted me with the words, "I am Stephen." Actually he spoke in Chinese and used his Chinese name. I had not recognized him. In the thirty years since we last met, he had greatly changed. Twenty years of hard labor in prison and labor camp had left their marks on him.

I had known him as a keen young graduate dedicated to serving the Lord, especially in the field of literature. In the early years, before his books were taken away, he would translate helpful passages and send them to his friends. Later, pulling a cart and doing other rough forms of manual labor, he felt that his experience was that of Job.

As I talked and prayed with Stephen and saw the reality of his faith, I was reminded of James's words, "Behold, we call those happy who were steadfast. You have heard of the steadfastness of Job, and you have seen the purpose of the Lord, how the Lord is compassionate and merciful" (Jas. 5:11). I realised afresh that the Christian lifestyle is one which is not offended by trials and temptations. No effective work can be done without a willingness to endure hardship as a good soldier of Jesus Christ.

Hudson Taylor, speaking to his fellow workers after a year full of difficulties and dangers said, "We have put to the proof his faithfulness, his power to support in trouble and to give patience under afflictions as well as to deliver from danger. I trust we are all fully satisfied that we are God's servants sent by him to the various places we occupy. We did not come to China because missionary work here was either safe or easy but because he had called us."

True motivation is essential. Only those who realise when they face trials that it is "for Jesus' sake" are likely to remain steadfast till the end. In Calcutta, India, Mother Theresa reminded a group of new workers that if they came just because they were sent or even out of compassion for the poor they would likely fail. The only satisfactory motivation, she said, is devotion to Jesus Christ.

Spreading the Word

In Acts 20:20-21 we see that Paul's lifestyle was characterized by untiring zeal in proclaiming the Word of God. "I did not shrink from declaring to you anything that was profitable, and teaching you in public and from house to house, testifying both to Jews and to Greeks of repentance to God and of faith in our Lord Jesus Christ." Like Christ (Jn. 17:8) Paul could say "I have given them the words which thou gavest me." He told the Thessalonian Christians that he had boldness to speak to them the gospel of God under much opposition.

God is still looking for men and women with this kind of boldness and zeal to proclaim his Word. But the Word of God must come to me personally with deep conviction if I am to communicate it with power and authority to others.

I discovered the power of the Word of God in my own life during a time of depression when I was strongly tempted to give up. Almost in desperation, I turned to John's Gospel and read it all through at one sitting. God spoke to me through it and I realized again that faith comes through the hearing of the Word of Christ.

To be really effective, the messenger must be disciplined, carefully guarding his times of fellowship with God. If I am to plant churches or strengthen student groups, I must be prepared to teach the Word of God in all kinds of situations. Whether it be in leading a small Bible study group, instructing others in the ministry of teaching, or opening up the Scriptures from the pulpit, I must be known for my love of the Word of God.

I must also learn how to help my national fellow-workers think through ways in which biblical principles can help in solving the perplexing problems of modern society.

Material Goods

Another characteristic of Paul's lifestyle is found in Acts 20:33 where we read, "I coveted no one's silver or gold or apparel." He is an example in his attitude toward material things. He knew times of hardship and financial strain when he worked with his own hands to support himself and his fellow workers. At other times he was well provided for with gifts from the churches. A missionary's lifestyle may well vary according to his area of work. We must always aim to avoid a disparity between our own lifestyle and that of the people around us.

During our first term in China we lived in a simple, two-room Chinese house, at the end of the church building, with an outhouse. To us it seemed a very simple home, but to those from the countryside who lived in very primitive dwellings, it must have seemed luxurious. Later, when working with students in a large city, we shared a house with our Chinese Inter-Varsity staff co-workers. In Hong Kong our apartment was comparable to one in this country. Many of the students with whom we worked came from more luxurious homes, while others lived in tiny flats and crowded government high-rise housing estates.

In Singapore when we started the Discipleship Training Centre it was important for us to live in the same house with students and other members of the staff. Learning to cope with cross-cultural community life was an essential part of the training.

The important thing was not the size of the house. What really mattered was to have a house in which our Chinese friends would always feel at home. We wanted to be an example of not coveting silver or gold, for in an economy in which inflation is rampant, it is terribly easy to become preoccupied with prices and opportunities for bargains.

Far more important than the type of home in which we live is our attitude toward the people. They want to know if we really belong to them.

You Are the Message

Like Ezekiel, the missionary's whole life is the message. The life of Christ has to shine forth from his or her life. True identification with the people will entail deep concern for every area of society and a sympathetic entering into the social, political and economic problems together with a sharing of whatever trials and tests may come.

If the way should ever open again for me to live in China, I would want to share with the people in the house churches. I would not want to go back to the Western church buildings, or to the ecclesiastical organizations of the past. I would have to learn from those who have experienced so much of what it means to suffer for the sake of Christ. I would want to contribute, under the guidance of the Holy Spirit, insights given to me from the Word of God. But I trust I would not seek to impose customs and patterns of Western Christianity which are not essential to the witness of the church which is living and serving in a communist society. I would want the believers to live as truly Chinese Christians, steadfast in faith and able to adjust to the economic and political changes in society. For the transforming power of the gospel to which they bear witness is not only for the individual but also for the society in which they live. And I would seek to identify as closely as possible with them.

To rejoice with those who rejoice, to weep with those who weep, to learn from the experiences of God's people, and to give, not only the gospel but one's own self, is surely the only way that the lifestyle of the messenger can fulfill God's purpose.

Study Questions

1. What do you anticipate would happen to the man or woman who went to the field as a missionary full of ideas and plans, and desirous of enlisting the help of nationals to fulfill them?

2. How does a man of God attain humility, willingness to endure hardship, conviction in the Word of God, a simple lifestyle, and biblical leadership? Do our educational programs today provide the context for the cultivation of these qualities?

33

Reconsecration to a Wartime, Not a Peacetime, Lifestyle

Ralph D. Winter

The Queen Mary, lying in repose in the harbor at Long Beach, California, is a fascinating museum of the past. Used both as a luxury liner in peacetime and a troop transport during the Second World War, its present status as a museum the length of three football fields affords a stunning contrast between the lifestyles appropriate in peace and war. On one side of a partition you see the dining room reconstructed to depict the peacetime table setting that was appropriate to the wealthy patrons of high culture for whom a dazzling array of knives and forks and spoons held no mysteries. On the other side of the partition the evidences of wartime austerities are in sharp contrast. One metal tray with indentations replaces fifteen plates and saucers. Bunks, not just double but eight tiers high, explain why the peace-time complement of 3000 gave way to 15,000 people on board in wartime. How repugnant to the peacetime masters this transformation must have been! To do it took a national emergency, of course. The survival of a nation depended upon it. The essence of the Great Commission today is that the survival of many millions of people depends on its fulfillment.

But obedience to the Great Commission has more consistently been poisoned by affluence than by anything else. The antidote for affluence is reconsecration. Consecration is by definition the "setting apart of things for a holy use." Affluence did not keep Borden of Yale from giving his life in Egypt. Affluence didn't stop Francis of Assisi from moving against the tide of his time.

Curiously enough, while the Protestant tradition has no significant counterpart to the Catholic orders within its U.S. base (unless we think of the more recent campus evangelistic organizations such as Inter-Varsity, Campus Crusade, and Navigators) nevertheless the entire Protestant missionary tradition has

After serving ten years as a missionary among Mayan Indians in western Guatemala, Ralph D. Winter spent the next ten years as a professor of missions at the School of World Mission at Fuller Theological Seminary. He is the founder of the U.S. Center for World Mission in Pasadena, California, a cooperative center focused on people groups still lacking a culturally relevant church. Winter has also been instrumental in the formation of the movement called Theological Education by Extension, the William Carey Library publishing house, the American Society of Missiology, the Perspectives Study Program and the International Society for Frontier Missiology. Since March of 1990 he has been the President of the William Carey International University.

always stressed a practical measure of austerity and simplicity as well as a parity of level of consumption within its missionary ranks. Widespread reconsecration leading to a reformed lifestyle with wartime priorities is not likely to be successful (even in an age of increasing awareness of the lifestyle issue itself) unless Protestantism can develop patterns of consecration among the people back home that are comparable to what has characterized the Protestant missionary movement for nearly two hundred years.

There will only be a way if there is a will. But we will find there is no will

- so long as the Great Commission is thought impossible to fulfill;
- so long as anyone thinks that the problems of the world are hopeless or that, conversely, they can be solved merely by politics or technology;
- so long as our home problems loom larger to us than anyone else's;
- so long as people enamored of Eastern culture do not understand that Chinese and Muslims can and must as easily become evangelical Christians without abandoning their cultural systems as did the Greeks in Paul's day;
- so long as modern believers, like the ancient Hebrews, get to thinking that God's sole concern is the blessing of our nation;
- so long as well paid evangelicals, both pastors and people, consider their money a gift from God to spend however they wish on themselves rather than a responsibility from God to help others in spiritual and economic need;
- so long as we do not understand that he who would seek to save his life shall lose it.

America today is a save-yourself society if there ever was one. But does it really work? The underdeveloped societies suffer from one set of diseases: tuberculosis, malnutrition, pneumonia, parasites, typhoid, cholera, typhus, etc. Affluent America has virtually invented a whole new set of diseases: obesity, arteriosclerosis, heart disease, strokes, lung cancer, venereal disease, cirrhosis of the liver, drug addiction, alcoholism, divorce, battered children, suicide, murder. Take your choice. Labor saving machines have turned out to be body killing devices. Our affluence has allowed both mobility and isolation of the nuclear family and as a result our divorce courts, our prisons and our mental institutions are flooded. In saving ourselves we have nearly lost ourselves.

How hard have we tried to save others? Consider the fact that the U.S. evangelical slogan "Pray, give or go" allows people merely to pray, if that is their choice! By contrast the Friends Missionary Prayer Band of South India numbers 8000 people in their prayer bands and supports 80 full-time missionaries in North India. If my denomination (with its unbelievably greater wealth per person) were to do that well, we would not be sending 500 missionaries, but 26,000. In spite of their true poverty, those poor people in South India are sending 50 times as many cross-cultural missionaries as we are! This fact reminds me of the title of a book, *The Poor Pay More* . They may very well pay more for the things they buy, but they are apparently willing to pay more for the things they believe. No wonder the lukewarm non-sacrificing believer is a stench in the nostrils of God. Luis Palau (1977) in a new book speaks of "unyielding mediocrity" in America today. When will we recognize the fact that the wrath of God spoken of the Bible is far less directed at those who sit in darkness than it is against those who refuse to share what they have?

How hard have we tried to save others? The nearly two billion dollars American evangelicals give per year to mission agencies is one fourth of what they spend on weight-loss programs. A person must overeat by at least two dollars worth of food per month to maintain one excess pound of flesh. Yet two dollars per month is more than what 90% of all Christians in America give to missions. If the average mission supporter is only five pounds overweight, it means he spends (to his own hurt) at least five times as much as he gives for missions. If he were to choose simple food (as well as not overeat) he could give ten times as much as he does to mission and not modify his standard of living in any other way!

Where does this line of reasoning lead? It means that the overall lifestyle to which Americans have acquiesced has led us to a place where we are hardening our hearts and our arteries simultaneously. Is our nation not described by Isaiah?

> My people are like the dead branches of a tree...a foolish nation, a witless, stupid people....The only language they can understand is punishment. So God will send against them foreigners who speak strange gibberish! Only then will they listen to Him! They could have rest in their own land if they would obey Him, if they were kind and good (Isa. 27:11; 28:11, 12).

Or, hear Ezekiel:

> They come as though they are sincere and sit before you listening. But they have no intention of doing what I tell them to; they talk very sweetly about loving the Lord, but with their hearts they are loving their money....

> My sheep wandered through the mountains and hills and over the face of the earth, and there was no one to search for them or care about them....As I live, says the Lord God...you were no real shepherds at all, for you didn't search for them (my flock). You fed yourselves and let them starve....Therefore, the Lord God says: I will surely judge between these fat shepherds and their scrawny sheep...and I will notice which is plump and which is thin, and why! (Eze. 33:31; 34:6; 34:8,20, 22b).

We must learn that Jesus meant it when He said, "Unto whomsoever much is given, of him shall much be required." I believe that *God cannot expect less from us as our Christian duty to save other nations than our own nation in wartime conventionally requires of us in order to save our own nation.* This means that we must be willing to adopt a wartime lifestyle if we are to play fair with the clear intent of scripture that the poor of this earth, the people who sit in darkness, shall see a great light. Otherwise, again Isaiah, "I faint when I hear what God is planning" (Isa. 21:3).

The essential tactic to adopt a wartime lifestyle is to build on pioneer mission perspective and to do so by a very simple and dramatic method. Those who are awakened from the grogginess and stupor of our times can, of course, go as missionaries. But they can also *stay home and deliberately and decisively adopt a missionary support level as their standard of living and their basis of lifestyle, regardless of their income.* This will free up an unbelievable amount of money—so much in fact that if a million average Presbyterian households were to live within the average Presbyterian minister's salary, it would create at least two billion dollars a year. Yet that happens to be only one-seventh of the amount Americans spend on tobacco. But what a mighty gift to the nations if carefully spent on developmental missions!

In order to help families shift to a wartime lifestyle, two organizations are proposing a six-step plan that will lead gradually (with both education and coaching) to the adoption of the salary provisions of an existing mission agency, the remainder of their income, at their own discretion at every point, being dedicated to what they believe to be the highest mission priority. The United Presbyterian Order for World Evangelization is a denominational sister of the general Order for World Evangelization. The twofold purpose of each of these organizations is 1) to imbue individuals and families with a concern for reaching the Unreached Peoples and 2) to assist them in practical ways to live successfully within the maximum limits of expenditure as defined by an agreed upon existing mission structure.

Even missionary families need help in staying within their income limitations, but ironically, no more so than people with twice their income. These organizations believe that families can be healthier and happier by identifying themselves with the same discipline with which missionary families are coping. For two hundred years it has been the undeviating pattern of all Protestant missionary agencies to establish a single standard for all their overseas personnel, adjusted of course to known costs of living and for various kinds of special circumstances. Some boards extend this system to their home office staff. No agency (until now) has gone the one logical step further—namely, to offer to the donors themselves this unique and long tested system. In view of the widespread concern of our time for a simple lifestyle, it would seem that this is an idea whose time has come.

We have Weight Watcher Clinics all over the country. We have Total Woman Clinics. Why not mission-focused Family Lifestyle Clinics? How much more significant these clinics will be with ends as noble as the Great Commission!

To reconsecrate ourselves to a wartime lifestyle will involve a mammoth upheaval for a significant minority. It will not go uncontested—any more than did the stern warnings of Isaiah and Ezekiel. But we do not need to defend our campaign. It is not ours.

Study Questions

1. Do you think that obedience to the Great Commission can be poisoned by affluence? Explain and give examples.

2. What are additional ways Americans might reconsecrate themselves to a wartime lifestyle?

34
The Non-Essentials of Life

Roberta Winter

Scene 1: Summer 1951

(It was our second date. Ralph and I were sitting on the grass close to the Rose Bowl, getting acquainted. We had first met just two weeks before.)

"I want you to know I'm a rather...uh...radical person," Ralph told me. "My mother has often despaired of me. At one point I even refused to wear dress clothes to church."

I waited for his explanation. He seemed to be dressed like everyone else—sport shirt and slacks. Nothing elaborate, but nothing weird.

"Some of my friends and I had been reading about various saints down through history, and we just couldn't see why God would not expect as much of us as of them. Take neckties, for example. It didn't seem right to buy neckties when people elsewhere were starving. I figure Americans must own $500,000,000 worth of neckties."

"But you wear them now, don't you?" I asked

"Yes, but not for the usual reasons. I wear them only to keep from scaring away the natives." And he laughed as he motioned with his hand to some people sitting a little ways away.

I didn't fully understand what he was saying. Gradually I realized that, as Paul said, we don't live to ourselves alone (1 Cor. 10). Our conviction of how the Lord wants us to live must be balanced by its effect on others. Does our style of living lead others to Christ or become a barrier to keep them from Him? As I came to understand, I was more able to enunciate what for us both has become a basic principle of life:

Roberta Winter has written *I Will Do a New Thing* (William Carey Library). She and her husband Ralph D. Winter founded the U.S. Center for World Mission in Pasadena California. Reprinted by permission from the February 1980 issue of *Moody Monthly*.

Principle One: *Our lifestyle must please the Lord, yet it should not in small matters be so shockingly different from those among whom we walk as to make unintelligible the message we wish to convey.*

That day in the park was certainly not *my* first exposure to a simple lifestyle. Born during the depression, I could remember birthdays celebrated with one lead pencil. Yet we now could have meat every day. If I needed a dress, I could get one. Furthermore, long before I met Ralph, God has touched my lifestyle when I asked myself, "Would I follow what the Lord wanted me to do if no one understood?"

As we talked that day I knew it would be exciting and challenging to marry this man. He told me of little economies here and there, but mostly he talked of his dreams, his ideals, his goals that had derived from his walk with the Lord.

I was fascinated with those dreams. Some were just dreams. Others were becoming realities. Because of his efforts as a student in seminary, a group of Christians were in "closed" Afghanistan teaching English and starting an engineering school.

He was excited about his doctoral studies in linguistics because he wanted to make the biblical languages more useful to the average pastor and missionary. Already he had a card file of the Greek lexicon which he hoped to arrange in order of the biblical text to avoid the endless flipping of pages to look up a word. In his head were the ideas behind the *Word Study Concordance* and the *Word Study New Testament* (jointly published in 1978 by Tyndale and William Carey Library).

I caught a glimpse that day of the excitement Ralph felt in doing something creative for the Lord, something that would make a difference in the spread of the gospel. Any excitement I might have ever felt for new clothes and a beautiful home paled in comparison to his.

Much later I learned that John Wesley had also been caught up in this same kind of excitement and had called it "the expulsive power of a new affection." Wesley could have become wealthy, but he was so excited accomplishing things for the Lord that he could not be bothered. When he died, he owned only two silver spoons, but was known and loved in the smallest towns of England because of the light he had brought.

During the first few years after marriage, our problem was not whether we should live simply. Once we chose the dreams, we had no alternative. Ralph was in graduate school. And though I could have earned a good salary as a registered nurse, I preferred to become a part of those dreams by working with him in his graduate studies.

I would nurse for a while to build up a reserve, then do research for him until the reserve was gone. We repeated the cycle as often as necessary. After he finished his dissertation, our first two children were born. Then I could neither nurse nor do library research.

By now Ralph had returned to seminary, and we had to make ends meets on what he earned as a student pastor and as a part time engineer. Our income was so meager that when we became missionaries, it tripled.

Scene 2: June 1957

(We had just arrived at our post in the mountains of Guatemala. Our assignment was to work with a dozen congregations among the Mam Indians, one of the poorest groups of people in this hemisphere.)

I was embarrassed. The truck with all our belongings arrived dust-covered from the trip over the narrow dirt road which led through the mountain pass into our valley. We collected all our barrels and mattresses and our gas-powered wringer washer—something we considered a "must" with our three small children. A crowd of curious onlookers surrounded us—and all that stuff!

"Why do they stare?" I thought with a twinge of irritation. And then, sure enough, a young man asked the question I had been dreading:

"How much did that cost?"

Barefoot, wearing clothes on which even the patches were patched, he pointed to a mattress. He also kept eyeing the washing machine, obviously wondering what on earth that could be. Never in all his life had he seen a machine like that! Mattresses he had seen, to be sure—bags stuffed with straw that rustled and pricked with every move and all too soon became infested with vermin.

What could I tell him? We had bought what seemed to us to be so little. Yet I knew that a month's salary for that young man would not begin to buy a mattress. And I felt defensive.

I could have sold all that was luxurious in the eyes of these people. I could more quickly identify with them if I did.

And yet I also knew that without those machines and little "luxuries" I would be tied to housework. These things could allow me to do in an hour what might otherwise take all day. Even hiring outside help would be luxurious in their eyes.

And I didn't want all my missionary experience to be housework. Surely God had called me to more than that! Thus I had to choose between simplicity in how my *money* was spent and simplicity in how my *time* was spent.

Nevertheless, I could not close my eyes to the dire poverty of these dear people. I could not forget that John said: "If someone who is supposed to be a Christian has money enough to live well, and sees a brother in need, and won't help him—how can God's love be within him?"(1 John 3:17, LB).

It took us some months to adjust to the uncomfortable idea that we would always have more "things" than these people. I doubt if we could have survived on their economic level, but in the long run we did everything we could to live in a way to which they could at least aspire.

We bought only the kinds of equipment which they as a group could afford. We even avoided small luxuries like soda pop, a useless temptation they could ill afford.

I learned in those years a new principle:

Principle Two: *A simple lifestyle in the U.S. can still seem extravagant to most of the people in the world. Yet our geographic isolation does not reduce our obligation in God's eye to people at a distance.*

Scene Three: Fall 1961

(We had just returned on furlough after our first five years in Guatemala. Ralph and I stepped into an American drug store to fill a prescription. I waited twenty minutes for the druggist and came back to find Ralph standing near the cash register rather bemused, looking back at a long counter filled with pink, fluffy giraffes, purple elephants, and green monkeys.)

"Roberta, I've walked around this entire store, and there's not one thing here I would take home even if they gave it to me." He motioned toward the counters filled with bric-a-brac, poorly made furniture, discount jewelry, and endless toys. "Do they really think they can unload this stuff on thinking people?"

We're still not sure.

After Guatemala, the U.S. society seemed gorged and glutted with trivialities—things that soon would be more junk at garage sales. But our four young daughters were dazzled by all that.

"Daddy, do we have enough money to buy...?" they would ask.

And he would inevitably reply, "Of course we can! But do we want it?" A long discussion would follow, setting "things" in their proper perspective without making the girls feel deprived and poor.

Furloughs were always a problem. From being the wealthiest people in our Guatemala community, we became poor missionaries in the eyes of others. Yet our missionary salary had always seemed adequate. It was adjusted year by year to our cost of living. We were provided with money to cover most of our medical and dental expenses. We even had the unheard-of benefit of a fund set aside to help with the college education of our children. Because we worked overseas, we paid no income tax. And our home was provided.

Even in the States it was not hard for us to live on our missionary salary because we knew we were here temporarily. Thus we were not tempted to keep up our with friends at home. Moreover, we knew that back on the field we would neither need nor want a stereo, a television, or the latest fad in kitchen appliances.

Yet while here, we never hesitated to buy something which would simplify our lives, giving us more time to spend on more important things. But *we* determined what we wanted. *We*, not television ads nor social pressure, decided what would help us. And we tried to teach our daughters what to us had become a principle of life:

Principle Three: *We don't really need most of the things our culture would push off on us. Once we learn to resist social pressure, it is far easier to determine what we really want or need.*

Scene 4: Winter 1968

(After our second furlough, due to several pressing circumstances, we remained in the States. Ralph became a professor in the recently established School of World Mission at Fuller Theological Seminary, and we suddenly found ourselves in a different world. From time to time Ralph had to attend important functions and entertain visiting dignitaries. Because they no longer needed a three bedroom home, my parents-in-law moved

into a small apartment, giving us their home and all its furniture. One day my sister came to see me.)

"Roberta, you're probably going to be in the States for a while. Why don't you buy some new furniture? This heavy Spanish-look is really out of date."

I was caught off guard. The furniture was much better than any we had ever owned. True, the sofa needed to be recovered and the table refinished. But I liked the style. Why spend money on something my sister would choose?

Ralph and I discussed her suggestion that night.

"Does the furniture look that bad?" I asked. "Or do you think that we have become unconscious of what looks good?"

"Don't worry, Roberta," he said. "We decided a long time ago not to let others dictate our lifestyle. We have enough money to buy new furniture if we want, but that does not *force* us to buy it. Why can't we continue to live as if we were still missionaries on furlough, buying only what we need? If we let others know that we *choose* to live that way, maybe they'll quit worrying about us."

Let me state this idea a different way:

Principle Four: *There ought not be any connection between what is earned and what needs to be spent. You don't buy things just because you have the money.*

With this principle, money in-evitably accumulates. We followed this principle while missionaries; so when it seemed necessary to start a new publishing house specializing in books on missions, we were able to do it. That in turn encouraged us in a much greater venture, the U.S. Center for World Mission.

Not quite the same, a group of 120 people in Minneapolis have lived for years on only a portion of their group income and used the rest to support dozens of their members as missionaries. What would happen to this world if more evangelical Christians were to realize that God blessed them with money in order to make them a blessing, not to pamper them.

What an immense amount of money would be released for highly strategic causes! How much easier it would be to understand that Christ did not ask us to be "successes" but servants (Mark 10:44).

Scene 5: Summer 1978

(We were seated around a long table at the newly established U.S. Center for World Mission. There were twenty of us with notebooks of accounting sheets and a copy of our support-raising manual at each elbow.)

"One of the first things you'll have to learn in raising your support is how to live within your income," Ralph told them. "Our support level is basically the same as Campus Crusade's. To those of you who have worked at well-paying jobs, this will seem very meager.

"To some of you who are just out of college, it may seem like too much. We want all of you to have enough for your needs, and a little besides for you to use as the Lord directs. I believe it is an important exercise to give money to someone else.

"Parkinson enunciated a law which says the 'expenses rise to meet income.' I believe there should be another which says 'when income falls, expenses also fall.

"Most people have no idea where their money goes. Consequently, the thought of living on less scares them. In order to know exactly how we were coming out, our family has used a basic family accounting system.

"Month by month we can tell how our net worth is changing. This helps us decide if we are spending more than we should. We end up each month with both a profit and loss statement and a balance sheet just like a commercial enterprise."

I could tell my husband was beyond most of them. But little by little he explained a simplified process of double entry bookkeeping.

The lessons were important, even for those who never really mastered them. For months many of our staff were living on far less than their full support, and they were amazed at how well they got by. God supplied in unusual ways, and they learned how to buy more efficiently.

Very basic, however, was the fact that we were all in this together. Beyond the suggestions and clues we could give each other, we developed a certain sense of comradeship best stated in another principle:

Principle Five: *It is much easier to adopt a simple lifestyle if you join a support group which covenants together to live on less.*

Among other equally valuable lessons, we learned that God really *does* take care of us if we make His concerns our highest priority (Luke 12:31, LB).

We learned that simplicity of life means far more than how we spend our money. It also means being willing to live to the Lord, unworried about making a good impression (Col. 3:12b, LB).

It means being willing to be God's servants in the jobs where He has placed us, recognizing that even Christ was under authority to serve rather than to be served. We learned that our money, like our lives, was ours only because He gave it to us to use; consequently it was at His beck and call whenever He saw fit.

As a group learning how to live in this new way, we came to value what Jesus meant when He said, "Only those who throw away their lives for my sake and for the sake of the Good News will ever know what it means to really live" (Mark 8:35, LB).

Scene 6: March 16, 1979

(Three generations gathered around a book, reading one paragraph at a time: Dr. and Mrs. McGavran in their eighties and highly revered as missionary statesmen, Ralph and myself now in the middle years, and eight young people. The book was John R. Mott's account of the early days of the Student Volunteer Movement for Foreign Missions, written in 1892.)

"Can we do it again?" This was the unspoken question on every heart.

"In 1807 four other students, praying for the world, said, 'We can do it if we will!' When they said that, there were no mission societies in America and only one or two in England. Almost all of Protestant mission work was still ahead of them.

"Today we have more than 600 mission agencies in America alone," Ralph said. "We also have thousands, perhaps millions, of evangelical young people. Not all will catch the vision of the unreached frontiers, but Singapore alone has 600 Chinese young people now ready to go."

"But look," Brad insisted, "both in 1807 and in 1892 the students had a watchword. We've also got to have something that will challenge the hearts of our generation."

"How about 'A Church for Every People by the Year 2000'? "someone asked.

The air was electric. Never have I felt such a holy awe as I sensed that night.

Could we do it? Could *they* do it? Dr. McGavran's life was mainly spent, ours perhaps well over. During the next twenty years the job of missions would have to be the responsibility of these young people and thousands more like them.

Others their age were absorbed with getting better paying jobs or with furnishing homes. Not these! They had caught a higher vision. Their hearts were caught up in the awe of knowing God's hand on their shoulders.

Others their age in earlier times had also experienced this awe, this "expulsive power of a new affection" which dwarfed all lesser pursuits.

For Peter, fishing for mere fish lost its attraction.

The very proper young Wesley abandoned his high church connections for the field and mining camps because God's hand was on him.

Carey, just a poor village cobbler, became history's foremost missionary statesman, meddling in everything from education to commerce to law to Bible translation, all for the sake of the gospel.

Wilberforce poured his riches into legislation for the slaves. And the list goes on and on.

I've often wondered, given the chance, what Christ would have done with the rich young ruler—the only one about whom it is written, "Jesus looked at him and loved him" (Mark 10:21, NIV). But he ended up a rich unknown. Could he have become a Paul, a Luther, a Wesley?

But he was rich, and "the attractions of this world and the delights of wealth, and the search for success and lure of nice things came in and crowded out God's message from his heart, so that no crop was produced" (Mark 4:19).

Principle Six: *The foundation of the simple lifestyle is "the expulsive power of a new affection."*

It is this which dims worldly goals and makes money itself seem unimportant.

It is this love of Christ and His cause which makes life become real living.

It is this Henry Varley spoke of when he said, "The world has yet to see what God can do with a man who is wholly committed to Him."

It is this new affection that makes the simplest lifestyle really glorious!

35

Obey the Vision Through Prayer

David Bryant

> Of highest priority, then, I urge that supplications, prayers, inter-
> cessions, and thanksgivings be made for all men, for kings and for
> all who are in high positions...this will provide an openness for
> the Gospel because the society at large will be quiet and peaceable.
> Furthermore, this will bring you favor and respect among those
> you are trying to reach. Of course, this is all to the good—this is
> precisely what God wants to see happen—because our Father
> desires that all men be saved and come to the knowledge of the
> truth about His Son. (I Timothy 2:1-4 paraphrased.)

Prayer is the one world-sized mission available to *all* Christians. Through it
we can love any of the world's unreached peoples, even at the "ends of the
earth." Prayer provides us a way to get involved in world evangelization without
a moment of delay. Our lives can begin counting right now for Christ's global
cause.

Don't ever underestimate the mission of prayer. There's nothing placid about
it! *Prayer is action!* By prayer we step out in advance of all the other results we
expect to see through any other ways we get involved in world outreach. In the
final analysis, World Christians who pray aren't opting for one of many "mission
activities." Rather, they have entered into the one mission upon which all the
others *depend* for fulfillment. The greatest impact any of us can ever have on the
world missionary movement is to saturate it with prayer and lead other Christians to pray with us.

An excellent example of prayer's impact on world missions was the Great
Awakening of 1790-1830. This sweeping movement of Christians in Britain, and

Under the leadership of David Bryant, Concerts of Prayer International is uniting and equipping Christians worldwide to pray. As a
member of the National Prayer Committee in the U.S., the Commission on Church Renewal of the World Evangelical Fellowship, and
the Intercessory Working Group for the Lausanne Committee for
World Evangelization, David Bryant helps foster urban prayer movements in many countries. Formerly a pastor and later missions specialist with Inter-Varsity Christian Fellowship, he authored the
modern missions classic, *In The Gap*. Taken from, "Obey the Vision
Through Prayer," David Bryant. Copyright 1980, Inter-Varsity Chris-
tain Fellowship, and used by permission of Inter-Varsity Press.

eventually throughout the world, sprang from hundreds of spontaneous small groups that prayed specifically for "the revival of religion and the spread of Christ's Kingdom world-wide." The results were staggering!

One world-sized result was the call of William Carey—a London cobbler turned mission strategist, turned missionary to India, turned "the father of the modern missionary movement." It all began for him as he met monthly with a local prayer cell to bring the nations before God in whole nights of intercession, and as he prayed over a world map at his cobbler's bench.

In 1806, six students from Williams College in Massachusetts prayed together for world missions under a New England haystack during an afternoon thunderstorm. God sent them forth from there to fulfill their prayers by forming one of the first Protestant missionary societies in North America.

To these fruits of prayer during the Awakening we could add: the formation of the Religious Tract Society, of the British and Foreign Bible Societies, of the London Missionary Society, and the Church Missionary Society and New York Missionary Society. Fortunately, such significant historical advances in missions are available to any generation that learns to pray in the *world* dimension.

Why is this? For one thing, World Christian praying *releases* God's work into every corner of the world, for every kind of need, among all kinds of people. True, this is a great mystery. How do we explain the interaction between God's sovereignty and man's activities of faith? Nonetheless, Paul urged the Ephesian Christians to give prayer for the whole world the highest priority ("first of all" in the RSV) in their corporate life. It remains just as crucial today.

Not only is it crucial, but it is equally exciting! What if you could travel anywhere in the world, to anyone in deep need, and stretch forth a loving hand to help them? Did you ever stop to think that prayer allows you to have such a limitless mission? As far as God can go—geographically, culturally, spiritually—prayer can go. Distance, social status or language create no barriers for our God and for what He ultimately does with our faithfulness in praying. Our requests actually touch people where they are because God is there to touch them according to what we ask. Is that not exciting?

Harold Lindsell in *When You Pray* (Baker Book House, 1975) confirms this view of prayer's limitless power in missions:

> Distance is no bar, space no barrier, to reaching the remotest place on earth. Nor is the power of prayer diminished by the distance between the person who prays and the person prayed for. Men and nations can and do have their destinies. Decided by God's praying people who, through intercessory prayer, wield power greater than the armed might of the nations of earth. (pp. 52-53)

When all is said and done—when all the best laid mission strategies of the Church are set in motion—prayer remains the major way for us to penetrate every human barrier in the world that keeps out the Gospel. After all, prayer penetrates the two ultimate barriers every time: The darkened hearts of sinners and the resistive powers of Satan.

We must credit our praying for the world as a *specific act of love* for the world. Have you caught a vision of Christ's global cause? Do you want to effectively obey that vision? Are you ready to reach out in love to an unreached world day-by-day? Then, give prayer highest priority. What a way to love the world! Your prayers will establish a "beachhead" in places the Gospel has never come so that other missionary activity can gather up the victories created by your cry of faith. It will bring God's love to bear deeply on those who previously knew nothing of it.

Have you ever been helpless and totally dependent on someone else to guide you, or feed you or run your errands? Of course, all of us were infants at one time! In the same way, our prayers do for people what they often cannot do for themselves. For unbelievers, our prayers stand in the gap between them and the God who loves them, as we intercede that they might see and understand clearly who Jesus is. In love we challenge the Forces of Darkness pitted against the Gospel and, therefore, against unreached peoples as well. Certainly lost sinners cannot fight this battle for themselves!

To say it another way: *prayer is love at war.* The world missionary movement can be defined as a battle of *wills:* Satan's will against God's; Satan's obedient hosts, committed to destroying those made in God's image, against Christ's redeemed disciples, committed to bringing God's healing love to the nations. Humanly speaking, only believers—those whom Christ has first freed from the rule of sin and evil—can fight this battle. Those trapped in Darkness have nothing at their disposal to do this, even if they wanted to. But the promise of Scripture is that as we are persistent in faith, with desires and requests consistent with Christ's global cause, the Kingdom can break through where it has never come before.

An Indian Christian, a member of an indigenous Indian missionary movement, gave me this contrast between most people in India (where there are millions who have never once heard of Christ) and those in the States: "In America you have darkness, but in India we have *deep* darkness." Above all we may ever pray for, our prayers for those in deepest darkness—for no opportunity to receive it through present church and missionary efforts—are the most strategic. As we pray for them, we are challenging the purposes of our Enemy to prevail over the nations; we are invading territory for which he has not been previously challenged. And it is war.

John caught the splendor of this war of love:

> And another angel came and stood at the altar with a golden
> censer; and he was given much incense to mingle with the prayers
> of all the saints upon the golden altar before the throne; and the
> smoke of the incense rose with the prayers of the saints from the
> hand of the angel before God. Then the angel took the censer and
> filled it with fire from the altar and threw it on the earth; and there
> were peals of thunder, loud noises, flashes of lightening, and an
> earthquake. (Revelation 8:3-5)

To be honest, however, there is a "risk" for the World Christian himself in such a prayer strategy. Not only will it change the world but it can also change *us* in the process. Through prayer for earth's unreached we draw "dangerously" close to the compassionate heart of Christ Himself. We are stretched in prayer to want to love, actively love, the whole world. Our longing to become a blessing to the families of earth and to bring them Christ's salvation will intensify. World-sized praying will make us more willing and ready than every other world mission His love leads us into.

Someone has said that the *scope* of our praying will determine the scope of our concern and of all our actions. No one can pray for the ends of the earth enthusiastically for very long, unless they are prepared, at the same time, to become an important part of the answer themselves!

WHAT SHOULD WORLD CHRISTIANS PRAY FOR?

Dick Eastman, director of World Literature Crusade's *Change the World School of Prayer* seminars, writes:

> Prayer is serving on an executive committee for World Evangelization...To pray for World Evangelization is to serve on a "Great Commission Fulfillment Committee" that meets daily in the courts of heaven. It is not only a time of fellowship, it is a time of action!

What should this "executive committee's" agenda be? There are at least *two overriding concerns* for all prayer with a world dimension: (1) prayer for the *fulfillment* of Christ's global cause, so that all things may eventually be summed up in Him to the Father's glory (Eph. 1:10). (2) prayer for the *fulness* of Christ's global body so that we can carry out our world-sized mission together. Fulfillment and fulness—the two important concerns for strategic intercession.

These two areas are found in the important prayer model that Jesus gave us in Matthew 6:9-13. To illustrate, we could paraphrase Him this way:

Fulfillment:

> Our gracious Father to whom all the resources and the eternal praises of Heaven belong: Reveal Your glory, so that all peoples may praise you! Expand your Kingdom to the ends of the earth—let it break through in the Gospel wherever it has never come before! Fulfill Your grand purpose of redemption for all the nations!...and as you do this, we also ask...

Fulness:

> Provide us and Your people around the world with the essentials we need to live and work with Christ in fulfilling His cause in our generation. Preserve the circle of love that binds Your people to Yourself and to one another, here and around the world, so that we can more effectively move out in the critical challenge of loving those yet to be reached for Christ in every nation.

> Empower us and Your Church around the world to win over all opposition and all trials, so that Your salvation may break through every barrier especially those erected by the Evil One himself.

More specifically, in private and group prayer meetings, a World Christian might concentrate on some of these crucial issues:

Fulfillment

1. That God would be glorified throughout the earth, among all peoples everywhere, especially those currently beyond the reach of the Gospel.

2. That the Church worldwide might be unified in a singleness of purpose to fulfill the Great Commission in our generation, especially among the 2.5 billion people who can only be reached by major, new cross-cultural missionary efforts.

3. For Satan to be bound. That Christ's victory on the cross would break Satan's hold on nations and cultures.

4. For world leaders and world events, that these might positively affect the free course of the Gospel world-wide.

5. For specific unreached people groups currently beyond the reach of the Gospel (there are at least 11,000 such groups).

6. For a church to be planted within every people group (providing God's Kingdom with a base of operation in each group) in this generation.

7. For current missionary work, involving the over 60,000 Protestant missionaries, including 15,000 sent from Third World churches.[Ed. note: See Pate, p. D—229 for updated statistics]

8. For new cross-cultural messengers of the churches to be sent out from the churches that already exist—we need hundreds of thousands of more missionaries world-wide.

9. That God would deploy a new force of self-supporting ("tent-making") witnesses to relocate among those peoples of the earth closed to professional missionaries.

10. For those places and peoples where the doors are open for hundreds of more laborers to enter the harvest—that the doors would remain open and the laborers soon be found to send.

11. That God's Spirit raise up a new movement of senders—people who know for sure God has called them to send out a new force of cross-cultural missionaries, and who embrace that calling with the same vision and sacrifice that they ask of those who go.

12. That Christians become increasingly sensitive to those peoples right around them who are currently beyond the reach of the Gospel.

Fulness

1. New awareness of God's holiness and the Church's need to be holy.

2. Fresh sense of God's love and a rekindling of the Church's love for Him.

3. That all Christians would become transparent before God and each other in repentance and reconciliation.

4. That God would educate His people about His heart for the world and about the challenge today.

5. That He would fill us with hearts of compassion for earth's unreached, so that we're ready to die for them.

6. That God would renew our world vision and our faith to move forward to face the challenge among the nations, beginning with the challenge where we are.

7. That God would bring commitment to Christ's global cause among the hundreds of thousands of Christian students world-wide, and would prepare them to assume leadership and sacrifice to carry out that commitment.

8. That the Church would be filled with victorious optimism in keeping with God's love and purposes for the whole earth.

Extraordinary Prayer

Extraordinary prayer is *not* determined so much by how long one prays or how often, but rather that we *do* pray for those things most on God's heart, and that we do so together—"in concert"—in Jesus' name.

After years of working with groups to encourage vital, extraordinary prayer, Concerts of Prayer have developed. These join major denominational, nondenominational groups and various ministries to foster united, large scale Prayer Rallies for spiritual awakening and world evangelization. Recently over 10,000 have gathered in Minneapolis for such an event.

In Concerts of Prayer, people are directed through prayers specifically for fulness and fulfillment . A sample gathering might look like the following, with the time in minutes by each section:

Celebration and Praise (10)

Preparation: Welcome and Preview (20)

Dedication and Invitation (5)

Seeking Fulness/Awakening in the Church (30)

Seeking Fulfillment/Mission among the Nations (30)

Testimonies: What Has God Said to Us Here? (10)

Finale: Offering of Selves in Praise and Prayer (15)

Dr. A. T. Pierson once said, "There has never been a spiritual awakening in any country or locality that did not begin in united prayer." Dr. J. Edwin Orr concurs, "History is full of exciting results as God has worked through concerted, united, sustained prayer."

Study Questions

1. Why is it that prayer is rarely seen as "highest priority"?

2. What relationships does Bryant suggest between prayer and action?

3. Explain what is meant by "Prayer is love at war."

36

What it Means to Be a World Christian

David Bryant

What, then, shall we call this discovery that can change us so radically and yet make us so healthy? And, what shall we call those who have experienced it?

By now it should be obvious that *all* Christians are born again *into* the Gap between God's world-wide purpose and the fulfillment of it. But there's more than one kind of *response* to that Gap.

Some are asleep, some are on retreat, and some are determined to stand in the Gap, particularly at its widest end where billions await the opportunity to hear of Christ for the first time. Some are heading into the "sunrise of missions" while others huddle in the shadows. Many move along at a sluggish pace, changing little in the Gap because of their own internal gap-of-unbelief. Others run the race before them setting no limits on how, where, or among whom God will use them.

Some are trapped in boxes of pea-sized Christianity, full of myths about missions that rob them of incentive to care about the unreached. Others have broken though into cause-Christianity, ready to reach out with God's love to the ends of the earth. They are determined to make Christ's global cause the unifying focus—the context—for all they are and do in the Gap. Yielded to the mediator, they are willing to be broken and remolded to fit in the Gap wherever they can make the most strategic impact. In turn, they're growing to know Christ, obey Him, and glorify Him as the mediator.

So, what shall we call the discovery that redirects Christians toward the needs of the Gap? And how shall we distinguish those who have made it?

Some Christians in the Gap are stunted by selfishness and petty preoccupations or by a cautious obedience and love reserved for the closest and easiest to

Under the leadership of David Bryant, Concerts of Prayer International is uniting and equipping Christians worldwide to pray. As a member of the National Prayer Committee in the U.S., the Commission on Church Renewal of the World Evangelical Fellowship, and the Intercessory Working Group for the Lausanne Committee for World Evangelization, David Bryant helps foster urban prayer movements in many countries. Formerly a pastor and later missions specialist with Inter-Varsity Christian Fellowship, he authored the modern missions classic, *In The Gap*. Reprinted by permission of Inter-Varsity Missions, 1979. *In The Gap*, pp.71-76. Inter-Varsity Missions, Madison, Wisconsin

care about. How shall we distinguish the others in the Gap whose growth in discipleship is unmistakable, with a vitality that comes only to those who help bring lost sinners from many nations home?

What shall we call this distinct group of Christians who have taken a stand that says:

> We want to accept personal responsibility for reaching some of earth's unreached, especially from among the billions at the widest end of the Gap who can only be reached through major new efforts by God's people. Among every people group where there is no vital, evangelizing Christian community there should be one, there must be one, there shall be one. Together we want to help make this happen.

For a moment, let's call them WORLD CHRISTIANS. Of course, any new term might be misunderstood. For example, some might think I said "worldly" Christians, not World Christians. By now we know, however, if you are one, you can't be the other. If you are one you don't *want* to be the other!

No, the term is not in your Bible concordance. Don't worry. It isn't another cliche like the words of the bumper sticker that read "Honk-if-the-Rapture-starts." Nor is it an attempt to label some new spiritual elite who have a corner on a super-secret blessing. Rather, the term describes what all of us are meant to be and what some of us have started to become.

The term "World Christian" may have been coined first by Daniel Fleming in a 1920 YMCA book entitled *Marks of a World Christian*. More recently the term has appeared in publications of such groups as the World Team missions, Conservation Baptist Foreign Missionary Society, United Presbyterian Center for Mission Studies, the Mission Renewal Teams, Inc., and the Fellowship of World Christians, as well as Campus Crusade for Christ and Inter-Varsity Christian Fellowship.

A World Christian isn't better than other Christians. But by God's grace, he has made a discovery so important that life can never be the same again. He has discovered the truth about the Gap, the fact that he is already in it, and the call of Christ to believe, think, plan, and act accordingly. By faith, he has chosen to *stand* in the Gap as a result.

Some World Christians are missionaries who stand in the Gap by physically crossing major human barriers (cultural, political, etc.) to bring the Gospel to those who can hear no other way. But every Christian is meant to be a World Christian, whether you physically "go", or "stay at home" to provide the sacrificial love, prayers, training, money, and quality of corporate life that backs the witness of those who "go".

World Christians are day-to-day disciples for whom Christ's global cause has become the integrating, overriding priority for all that He is for them. Like disciples should, they actively investigate all that their Master's Great Commission means. Then they act on what they learn.

World Christians are Christians whose life-directions have been solidly transformed by a world vision. This is not a term for frustrated Christians who feel trapped into the world missionary movement and sporadically push a few buttons to say they've done their part. Having caught a vision, World Christians want to keep that vision and obey it unhesitatingly.

World Christians are (in Corrie Ten Boom's phrase) tramps for the Lord who have left their hiding places to roam the Gap with the Savior. They are heaven's expatriates, camping where the Kingdom is best served. They are earth's dispossessed, who've journeyed forth to give a dying world not only the Gospel but their own souls as well. They are members of God's global dispersion down through history and out through the nations, reaching the unreached and blessing the families of earth.

By taking three steps we become World Christians. First, World Christians *catch* a world vision. They see the cause the way God sees it. They see the full scope of the Gap. Next, World Christians *keep* that world vision. They put the cause at the heart of their life in Christ. They put their life at the heart of the Gap. Then World Christians *obey* their world vision. Together they develop a strategy that makes a lasting impact on the cause, particularly at the widest end of the Gap.

Many years ago a World Christian named John R. Mott, leader of the Student Volunteer Movement that sent out 20,000 new missionaries, outlined similar steps:

> An enterprise which aims at the evangelization of the whole world in a generation, and contemplates the ultimate establishment of the Kingdom of Christ, requires that its leaders be Christian statesmen with far-seeing views, with comprehensive plans, with power of initiative, and with victorious faith.

Catch! Keep! Obey!—these are the three steps to becoming a World Christian. Let's examine them a little more closely in outline form:

Step One: Catch a World Vision

See God's world-wide *purpose* in Christ

See a world full of *possibilities* through Christ

See a world full of *people* without Christ

See my world-sized *part* with Christ

Step Two: Keep a World Vision

Be a World Christian

Join with other World Christians

Plan to obey the vision

Step Three: Obey a World Vision

Obey as you regularly *build* your vision

Obey as you *reach-out* directly in love

Obey as you *give* your vision to other Christians

How can someone know if they've taken these three basic steps toward becoming a world Christian? Here are some important clues:

STEP ONE: Have I caught a world vision?

> PURPOSE: Do I see the big picture of Christ's global cause from God's point of view?

> POSSIBILITIES: Do I see the Church's potential in our generation for closing the Gap between God's world-wide purpose and its fulfillment?

> PEOPLE: Do I see the great scope of earth's unreached peoples, especially the billions at the widest end of the Gap who have yet to clearly hear the Gospel?

> PART: Do I believe that I, along with other Christians, can have a strategic impact on Christ's global cause right now?

STEP TWO: Have I kept a world vision?

> BE: Am I willing to stand in the Gap with Christ, to unite my whole relationship with Him around His global cause?

> JOIN: Am I willing to team-up with other World Christians to stand in the Gap together?

> PLAN: Am I willing to design specific ways to obey my world vision and help close the Gap?

STEP THREE: Do I obey a world vision?

> BUILD: Do I take time to study the cause? Am I letting my world vision grow?

> REACH-OUT: Do I personally get involved in the cause? Am I helping to reach unreached peoples, especially at the widest end of the Gap?

> GIVE: Do I transfer my vision to other Christians? Am I seeking more World Christians to stand in the Gap and serve the cause?

Ultimately, however, becoming a World Christian goes beyond "steps" that we take. It is the gracious work of Christ Himself! Our faith must always be in Him, not in any simple three-step process. It is Christ who opens us up to catch His world vision. He alone anchors us to that vision and then empowers us to effectively obey it. With the hymn writer all World Christians appeal to Christ: "Be Thou my Vision, Oh Lord of my Heart."

Study Questions

1. Can you explain biblical support for the idea of being a World Christian?

2. How does a World Christian compare with a missionary in function and responsibility?

37

The Missionary Problem
is a Personal One

Andrew Murray

Andrew Murray was a well-known and influential pastor of the Dutch Reformed Church in nineteenth-century South Africa. The author of a wide range of devotional literature, including With Christ in the School of Prayer, *Murray was invited to address an interdenominational missionary conference in New York in April of 1900. Unable to attend due to the Boer War in South Africa, Murray nonetheless expressed his concern that the conference agenda was lacking. He commented, "I had received the impression that while very naturally the chief attention was directed to the work on the field, the work at the home base, in preparing the Church for doing its part faithfully, hardly had the place which its importance demands." After observing that post-conference reports also hardly dealt with this topic, Murray penned* Key to the Missionary Problem, *the "missionary problem" referring to the paucity of missionary zeal, funds, and workers. This excerpt is the heart of his book.*

In a report of the Student Missionary Conference of 1900, the Appendix contained a statement: IF there were only one Christian in the world, and he worked and prayed a year to win one friend to Christ, and IF these two then continued each year to win one more, and "IF every person thus led into the kingdom led another to Christ every year, in thirty-one years every person in the world would be won for Christ." The mathematical progression showed that at the end of the thirty-one years there would be over two billion Christians.

Some may doubt the validity of calculations which lie altogether beyond the range of possibility or the promises of God's Word. Others may question the correctness of a calculation which appears to count upon all who become Christians living for thirty-one years, while we know that something like one-thirtieth of the earth's population dies each year. Leaving such questions aside, I wish simply to take the principle which forms the basis of the calculation. I wish to point out what the effect would be if the substantial truth it contains were really believed and preached, and practiced. That truth is: *Christ meant every believer to be a soul-winner.* Or rather, for this is the deeper truth in which the former has its root and strength, that every believer had been saved with the express purpose that he should make the saving of other souls the main, the supreme end of his existence in the world.

From *Key to the Missionary Problem*, pp. 125-136. Taken from copyrighted material. Used by permission of the Christian Literature Crusade, Fort Washington, PA 19034.

If ever I feel the need of the teaching of the Holy Spirit for myself and my readers it is when I come to this point. We so easily accept general statements without realizing fully what they imply. It is only when we are brought face to face with them, and challenged to apply and act upon them, that the secret unbelief comes out that robs them of their power. Only by the Holy Spirit can we look beyond the present state of the Church and the great majority of Christians, and realize what actually is the will of our God concerning His people, and what He has actually made possible to them in the grace of His Holy Spirit. When we teach the Church our motto must be: *Every believer a soul-winner!* This alone will give a sure foundation for our missionary appeal and our hope for an immediate and sufficient response to the call to make Christ known to every person.

But is this statement, *every believer a soul-winner*, literally true and binding? Is it not something impractical? Something beyond the reach of the majority of true but weak believers? The very fact that this truth seems strange to so many and so difficult for any but the spiritual mind to grasp as possible and obligatory, is the most urgent reason to teach it. Let us see the ground on which it rests.

Nature teaches us that it must be so: It is an essential part of the new nature. We see it in every child who loves to tell of his happiness and to bring others to share his joys. We expect to find in every human heart a feeling of compassion for the poor and the suffering. So why should it be thought strange that every child of God is called to take part in making known the happiness he has found, to concern himself about those who are perishing, to have compassion on them, and work for their salvation? *Every believer a soul-winner!* What can be more natural?

Christ called His disciples the light of the world. The believer is an intelligent being—his light does not shine as a blind force of nature, but is the voluntary reaching out of his heart towards those who are in darkness. He longs to bring the light to them, to do all he can do to make them acquainted with Christ Jesus. The light is often used to illustrate the silent influence which good works and a consistent life may have. Yes, this is an essential element, but it means a great deal more. It does not mean, as is often thought, that I am to be content with finding my own salvation, and trusting that my example will do others good. No! Even as Christ's example derived its power from the fact that it was a life lived for us and given up on our behalf, so the true power of the Christian's influence lies in the love that gives itself away in seeking the happiness of others. As God is light and love, it is love that makes the Christian the light of the world. *Every believer a soul-winner* —this is indeed the law of the Spirit of life in Christ Jesus.

How could it be otherwise? As God is love, so is he that loveth born of God. Love is God's highest glory, His everlasting blessedness. God's children bear His image, share His blessedness, and are the heirs of His glory. But this cannot be in any other way than by their living a life of love. The new life in them is a life of love; how can it manifest itself but in loving as God loves, in loving those whom God loves? It is God's own love that is shed abroad in our hearts. Christ prayed "that the love wherewith Thou lovest Me may be in them." It is the love of Christ, the love with which He loved us, that constrains us. Love cannot change its nature when it flows down from God into us: it still loves the evil ones and the unworthy. Christ's love has no way, now that He is in heaven, of reaching the souls for whom He died, for whom He longs, but through us. Surely nothing can be more natural and true than the blessed message: *Every believer redeemed to be a soul-winner.*

But why, if it is so simple and so sure, are so many words needed to prove and enforce it? Alas! Because the Church is in a weak and sickly state, and tens of thousands of its members have never learned that this is one of the choicest treasures of their heritage. They are content with the selfish thought of personal salvation, and even in the struggle for holiness never learn the Divine purpose for their salvation. And there are tens of thousands more who have some thought of its being part of their calling, yet who have looked upon it as a command beyond their strength. They have never known that, as a law and a power of their inmost nature, its fulfillment is meant to be a normal function of a healthy body in joy and strength.

Even the commandments of our Lord Jesus may be to us as great a burden as the law of Moses, bringing bondage and condemnation, unless we know the two-fold secret that brings the power of performance. That secret is first what we have already named—the faith that *love is the inward law of our new nature* and that the Spirit of God's law is within us to enable us gladly to love, and bless, and save those around us. Second, that it is the *surrender to a life of close following* and continual fellowship with the Lord Jesus rejoicing in Him, forsaking all for Him, yielding all to the service of His love—that our spiritual nature can be strengthened. Then the work of winning souls becomes the highest joy and fulfillment of the Christian life. To those who in some measure understand this, there is nothing strange in the thought: *Every believer a soul-winner!* This ought to be the theme of every pastor's preaching and every believer's life.

But even this is not all. Many will agree that every believer is called upon to live and work for others, but still looks upon this as only a secondary thing, additional and subordinate to the primary interest of working out his own salvation. *Every believer a soul-winner* —that does not mean, *among other things,* but *first of all* as the chief reason of his existence. We all agree in saying that the one and supreme end of the Church is to bring the world to Christ. We know that God gave Him the Church as his body. The one purpose was that it should be to its Head what everybody is on earth—the living organ or instrument through which the purposes and the work of the head can be carried out. What is true of the Head, is true of the Body; what is true of the Body, is true of each individual member—even the very weakest. As in the Head, Christ Jesus, as in the Body, the Church, so in every believer, the supreme, the sole end of our being is the saving of souls. It is in this, above everything, that God is glorified. "I have chosen you, and ordained you, that ye should go and should bring forth fruit."

Many may be brought to agree to this truth and yet have to confess that they do not feel its full force. Many a minister may feel how little he is able to preach it, compared with the full conviction with which he preaches grace for salvation. It is well that we should give such confessions careful consideration. Where does the difficulty come in? This union with the Lord Jesus, to participate in His saving work to such an extent that without us He cannot do it, that through us

He will and can accomplish it in Divine power, is a deep spiritual mystery. It is an honor altogether too great for us to understand. It is a fellowship and union and partnership so intimate and Divine that the Holy Spirit alone must reveal it to us.

To simple, childlike souls the reality of it comes without their knowing how. Some have lived long in the Christian life and lost the first love, and to them everything has to come by the slow way of the understanding. Such people need humility to give up preconceived opinions, and the confidence of being able to grasp spiritual truths. They also need patient waiting for the Spirit to work such truth in their inmost parts. Above all, we need to turn away from the world, with its spirit and wisdom, and return to closer fellowship with Jesus Christ, from whom alone come light and love. *Every believer ordained to be first and foremost a soul-winner.* Simple though it sounds, it will cost much to many before it has mastered them.

We are often at a loss to understand the need of much continued communion with God. And yet it is the same as with the things of earth. Take the gold put into the furnace. Exposed to insufficient heat, it gets heated but not melted. Exposed to an intense heat for only a short time, and then taken out again, it is not melted. It needs an intense and continuous heat, before the precious but hard metal is prepared for the goldsmith's work. So it is with the fire of God's love. They who would know it in its power, and in power to proclaim and convey it to others, must keep in contact with the love of Christ. They must know it in its intensity, and know what it is to continue in it till their whole being realized that love can reach all, and melt all. It can make even the coldest and weakest child of God a lover and seeker of souls. In that intense and continuous fire a pastor, a leader, can learn to witness in power to the truth—*Every believer a soul-winner.*

What has this to do with our missionary discussion? We seek to make it the keynote of this book—*The missionary problem is a personal one.* If the Church is really to take up its work, it is not enough that we speak of the obligation resting upon the present generation to make Christ known to everyone. True education must always deal with the individual mind. To the general command must always be added the personal one. Nelson's signal "England expects every man to do his duty," was a personal appeal addressed to every seaman, not just his fleet. As we seek to find out why, with such millions of Christians, the real army of God that is fighting the hosts of darkness is so small, the only answer is—lack of heart. The enthusiasm of the kingdom is missing. And that is because there is so little enthusiasm for *the King* . Though much may be done by careful organization and strict discipline and good generalship to make the best of the few troops we have, there is nothing that can so restore confidence and courage as the actual presence of a beloved King, to whom every heart beats warm in loyalty and devotion.

The missionary appeal must go deeper and seek to deal with the very root of the evil. If there is no desire for soul-winning at home, how can the interest in the distant unevangelized be truly deep or spiritual? There may be many motives to which we appeal effectively in asking for supplies of men and money—the compassion of a common humanity, the alleviation of the evils of pagan people, the elevation of fellow-human beings in the scale of human life, the claims of our church or society. But the true and highest motive is the only one that will really call forth the spiritual power of the Church, for the work to be done.

If the missionary appeal to this generation to bring the gospel to every person is to be successful, the Church will have to gird itself for the work in a very different way from what it has been doing. The most serious question the Church has to face just now—in fact, the only real difficulty of the missionary problem is how she is to be awakened as a whole to the greatness and glory of the task entrusted to her and led to engage in it with all her heart and strength. The only answer to that question—the key to the whole situation appears to be the simple truth: *The missionary problem is a personal one.* The Lord Jesus Christ is the Author and Leader of Mission. Whoever stands right with Him, and abides in Him, will be ready to know and do His will. It is simply a matter of *being near enough to Him to hear His voice and so devoted to Him and His love as to be ready to do all His will.* Christ's whole relation to each of us is an intensely personal one. He loved me and gave Himself for *me.* My relation to Him is an entirely personal one. He gave Himself a ransom for me, and I am His, to live for *Him* and *His* glory. He has breathed His love into my heart, and I love Him. He tells me that, as a member of His Body, He needs me for His service, and in love I gladly yield myself to Him. He wants nothing more than that I should tell this to others, prove to them how He loves, how He enables us to love, and how blessed is a life in His love.

The personal element of the missionary problem must be put in the foreground. Every missionary sermon or meeting must give the love of Christ the first place. If Christians are in a low, cold, worldly state, the first object must be to wait on God in prayer and faith for His Holy Spirit to lead them to a true devotion to Jesus Christ. Will that be an apparent loss of time in not beginning at once with the ordinary missionary information and pleas? Ah, no—it will soon be made up. Weak believers who are glad to hear and give, must be lifted to the consciousness of the wonderful spiritual privilege of offering *themselves* to Christ to live for His kingdom. They must be encouraged to believe that the Lord who loves them, greatly prizes their love, and will enable them to bring it to Him. They must learn that Christ's love asks for whole-hearted devotion, and that the more they sacrifice, the more will that love possess them. As definitely as we labor to secure the interest and the gifts of each individual, even more so must be labor to bring each one into contact with Christ Himself.

At first it may appear as if we are aiming too high. In many congregations the response may be very weak. Let the pastor give himself to study the missionary problem in this light. Let him put it to his people, clearly and perseveringly: You have been redeemed to be the witnesses and messengers of Christ's love. To fit you for it, His love has been given you, and shed abroad in your heart. As He loves you, He loves the whole world. He wants those who know it to tell those who don't know it. His love to you and to them, your love to Him and to them call you to do it. It is your highest privilege, it will be your highest happiness and perfection. As Christ gave Himself, give *yourself* wholly to this work of love.

Study Questions

1. What does Murray mean when he claims that the missionary problem is a *personal* one?

2. If the missionary problem is a personal one, how should this affect strategies for recruiting new missionaries and new "senders"?

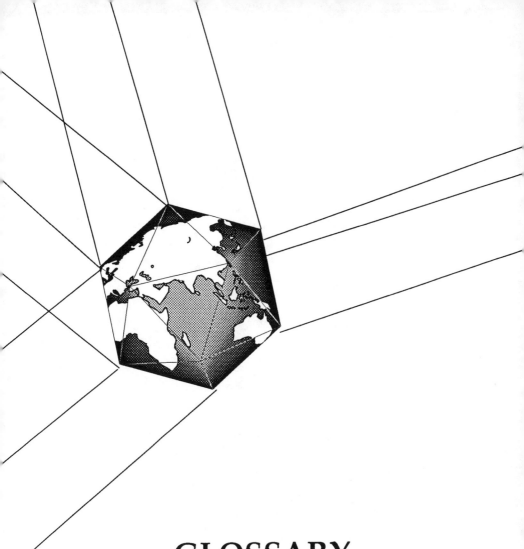

GLOSSARY ,
SCRIPTURE INDEX,
& INDEX

E

Glossary

INTRODUCTION

The following is a glossary of some of the main concepts and terms used in the Perspectives Reader. Further suggestions for inclusion would be most welcome.

ANIMISM —The attribution of soul to inanimate objects and natural phenomena (Shorter Oxford Dictionary). Animism accepts the reality of spiritual forces and beings (see p. D—107).

BEING-IN-THE-WAY STRATEGY—"…at first appears to be no strategy at all. People who adopt this strategy believe that it is not necessary to plan. They have no specific intentions about the future. They assume that God will lead" (p. D—37).

BELIEFS—What is considered to be "true" within a culture. A distinction should be drawn between (a) operating beliefs—beliefs that affect values and behavior; and (b) theoretical beliefs—beliefs that have little practical impact on values and behavior (p. C—5).

BIBLICAL CONCEPT OF MYSTERY—See: MYSTERY

BIBLICAL CONCEPT OF NATION—See: NATION

BIBLICAL REALIST—A person who realizes the power of evil in the world yet is prepared to venture forth in the mission of world-wide evangelization. Not a "rosy optimist" (expecting the Gospel to conquer the world), nor a "despairing pessimist" (feeling the task is hopeless)—(see p. A—80).

BICULTURALISM—An ability to move between two cultures (home and adopted) and to live in either without experiencing culture shock (pp. C—14-15).

BICULTURAL BRIDGE—The relationship between missionaries and their national counterparts (see p. C—24).

"BOBO" THEORY OF CHRISTIANITY—This is the mistaken assumption that the Christian faith "Blinked Out" after the Apostles and then "Blinked On" again with the Protestant Reformation. It needs to be stressed that this is an incorrect assumption (see p. B—6).

BONDING—In nature—the sense of attachment and belonging established between parent and child following birth. In the missionary context—the sense of attachment and belonging established between missionary and host community following contact (see pp. C—107-119).

BRIDGES OF GOD—Naturally occurring networks of kinship or group membership that can be used for the transmission of the Gospel. Note McGavran's comment: "In order to be called a bridge, the connection must be large enough to provide not merely for the baptism of individuals, but for the baptism of enough groups in a short enough time and a small enough area to create a People Movement in the other community" (p. B—155-156).

The CHURCH—The church is the Body of Christ, the community of the Holy Spirit, the people of God. It is the community of the King and the agent in the world for God's plan for the reconciliation of all things (see p. B—142).

A CHURCH—"A church is a congregation of disciples who obey the commands of the Lord Jesus Christ. These are repentant, baptized believers who celebrate the Lord's Supper, love one another, show compassion to their neighbors, pray, give and evangelize" (p. D—85).

CLOSURE—A commitment to setting definite goals and developing specific means to accomplish the task of the Great Commission within a specified time frame. "Closure strategy says it is not enough for us today to go across the world and do a good job. We must work toward finishing the task" (p. D—62).

COMITY—The practice of designating a mission agency to be responsible for the evangelism of particular pieces of territory. The custom produced "denominationalism by geography" but it was intended to prevent double occupancy of a region, the overlapping of mission programs and hence unnecessary waste of personnel and resources (see p. B—70).

CONCEPT FULFILLMENT—The process by which redemptive analogies within a culture are identified and used to contextualize the Gospel message and thus bring the analogies to fulfillment (see pp. C—59-63).

CONGLOMERATE CHURCH—A church that is made up of people from several different segments of a society. It is made up of individuals who one by one have come out of several different societies, castes or tribes.

CONTEXTUALIZATION OF THE GOSPEL—Examining the Gospel in the light of the respondent world view and then adapting the message, encoding it in such a way that it can become meaningful to respondents (see p. C—45-46). Presenting the gospel in forms that are appropriate to the local culture and society (see p. C—192).

CULTURE: A range of definitions are offered:

Kwast: The "patterned way of doing things" within a particular society. The "superglue"that binds people together and gives them a sense of identity and continuity (see p. C—4). Culture can also be seen as "learned and shared ways of perceiving" or "shared cognitive orientation" (see p. C—5).

Hiebert: "…the integrated system of learned patterns of behavior, ideas and products characteristic of a society" (p. C—9). It is thus a "mental map" of the world that provides guidelines for action (p. C—9). It can also be seen as "the symbol systems… that people create in order to think and communicate" (p. C—10).

Kluckhohn: "…a way of thinking, feeling, believing. It is the group's knowledge stored up for future use" (quoted on p. C—35).

Luzbetak: "…a design for living. It is a plan according to which society adapts itself to its physical, social and ideational environment". "Cultures are but different answers to essentially the same human problems" (quoted on p. C—35).

Hesselgrave: "Any given culture is made up of folkways, modes and mores, language, human productions, and social structures…One might compare culture to a large and intricate tapestry. The tapestry is made up of numberless threads, various colors, larger shadings and lines—all of which go to make up the overall mosaic or pattern which in turn serves in interpreting any part. Culture is also this wholeness, this larger reality" (p. C—43).

Lausanne Committee: "Culture is an integrated system of beliefs…, of values…, of customs…, and of institutions which express these…, which binds a society together and gives it a sense of identity, dignity, security and continuity" (p. C—164).

CULTURE SHOCK—"…the sense of confusion and disorientation we face when we move into another culture" (p. C—13). This can also lead to disillusionment and depression (p. C—13).

CULTURAL MEGASPHERE—A major cultural bloc e.g., Muslim, Han Chinese, etc. (p. B—178).

CULTURAL MACROSPHERE—A group of societies within a cultural megasphere that have certain cultural similarities within and between them e.g., Cantonese-speaking people (p. B—178).

CULTURAL MINISPHERE—A distinct group (usually defined by language dialect) within a cultural macrosphere. It should be noted that these may number over a million people (see p. B—178).

CULTURE CHRISTIANITY—"A Christian message that is distorted by the materialistic, consumer culture of the West" (p. A—7).

CULTURE PROBE—Studying a culture with the purpose of discovering redemptive analogies within it (see p. C—63).

DOUBLE CULTURAL IMPERIALISM—Imposing our culture on others and despising theirs (p. A—7).

DYNAMIC EQUIVALENCE—This can be applied either to Bible translation or to church formation. A dynamic equivalence translation "seeks to convey to contemporary readers meanings equivalent to those conveyed to the original readers, by using appropriate cultural forms" (p. C—82). Likewise, a dynamic equivalence church would "preserve the essential meanings and functions which the New Testament predicated of the church, but would seek to express these in forms equivalent to the originals but appropriate to the local culture" (p. C—82).

DYNAMIC EQUIVALENCE TRANSLATIONS OF THE GOSPEL—Translations in which the "meaning" of the Gospel item is preserved cross-culturally even if it is presented in a different "form" (see pp. C—21, C—182).

ECCLESIOCENTRISM—Ecclesiastical ethnocentrism. The view that the way we do things in our church or denomination is the only right way. All other churches are wrong in their ritual and beliefs where they differ from us (p. A—54).

EPOCHS OF REDEMPTIVE HISTORY

1. 2000 to 1600 BC: The Patriarchs

2.1600 to 1200 BC: The Captivity

3. 1200 to 800 BC: The Judges

4. 800 to 400 BC: The Kings

5. 400 to 0 BC : Second Captivity and Diaspora

  CHRIST'S BIRTH

6. 0 to 400 AD : Winning the Romans

7. 400 to 800 AD: Winning the Barbarians

8. 800 to 1200 AD: Winning the Vikings

9. 1200 to 1600 AD: Winning the Saracens

10. 1600 to 2000 AD: To the Ends of the Earth

ETHNOCENTRISM—Cultural narrow-mindedness. The view that the way we do things in our culture is the only right way of doing things. All other ways are wrong (see p. A—54). The tendency to " judge the behavior of people in other cultures by the values and assumptions of our own" (see p. C—21).

ETHNOCENTRIC RESTRICTION OF THE GOSPEL—Focusing on the "top line" of the Abrahamic covenant (I will bless you) and ignoring the "bottom line" (and in you shall all the nations be blessed).

EVANGELISM—"To evangelize is to spread the good news that Jesus Christ died for our sins and was raised from the dead according to the Scriptures, and that as the reigning Lord he now offers the forgiveness of sins and the liberating gift of the Spirit to all who repent and believe" (quoted on page 5 of the Lausanne Covenant,). The activity of reaching out from an existing church within a cultural minisphere where the missiological breakthrough of establishing a viable church has taken place (p. B—180-181).

E-0 EVANGELISM—Same-culture renewal evangelism of church members (p. B—180-181).

E-0.5 EVANGELISM—Same-culture evangelism of those on the fringe of the church e.g., nominal Christians (p. B—184).

E-1 EVANGELISM—The situation where the evangelist is working within his/her own cultural sphere ("culturally near"—e .g.,Judea) . It is also referred to as "near neighbor evangelism " (see pp. B—179, 181, 184, 186).

E-2 EVANGELISM—The situation where there are some cultural and language differences between the evangelist and hearer but these are not a major hindrance to communication ("culturally close"—e.g., Samaria) (see pp. B—179, B—181-186).

E-2.5 EVANGELISM—Cross-cultural evangelism of non-Christians in a similar but quite different culture (p. B—184-185).

E-3 EVANGELISM—The situation where there is maximum cultural distance between evangelist and hearer ("culturally far"—e.g., the ends of the earth) (see pp. B—179, 181-186).

EXOCENTRIC PROGRESSION OF THE GOSPEL—"...in Jerusalem, and in all of Judea, etc." (Acts 1:8).

EYE-OPENER—"...establishing a beachhead for the truth in the understanding" of people (p. C—64). Using what is familiar in a person's life, or something which they cherish, to establish an openness to the Gospel (a redemptive analogy) and thus help to turn them "from darkness to light" (see p. C—64).

FORMAL CORRESPONDENCE—This concept can be applied either to Bible translation or to church formation. In either case it implies "...a slavish imitation, whether in translating a word into another language or exporting a church model to another culture" (p. C—182).

FORM ADAPTATION—The process by which missionaries adapt aspects of their lifestyle (dress, eating, etc.) and Christian worship to conform to the lifestyle and culture of the target group (see pp. C—184-185).

The GREAT CENTURY—According to Latourette this was the period between 1800 and 1914. It is equivalent to Winter's First Era of Christian mission.

HETEROGENEOUS SOCIETY—"Heterogeneous societies are primarily of two types: (1) urban societies that contain urban-structured minority groups, similar, for example, to the African-American subculture within American life; and (2) urban societies that include face-to-face subsocieties (see diagrams on pages C—91-92).

HIDDEN PEOPLE GROUPS-See Unreached People Groups

HOMOGENEOUS SOCIETY—"...one in which most or all of the people participate in the common life in more or less the same way. Such groups may have class differences and distinctions of leadership and positions of authority, but the society is nevertheless an integrated whole, sharing much the same system of values; it is not merely an aggregate of subcultures which operate along quite different lines" (p. B—42).

INCARNATIONAL IDENTIFICATION—The identification of missionaries with the culture and way of life of the people being targeted (see pp. D—164-165).

INDIGENIZATION OF THE GOSPEL—Presenting the Gospel in such a way that it is consistent with the principles and assumptions of the indigenous culture while at the same time being authentic to Biblical foundations (p. C—21).

INDIGENOUS CHURCH—"...a group of believers who live out their life, including their socialized Christian activity, in the patterns of the local society, and for whom any transformation of that society comes out of their felt needs under the guidance of the Holy Spirit and the Scriptures" (C—153).

INVOLUNTARY MISSION OUTREACH—The situation where, when the people of God are unwilling to share His blessing, they are invaded by or sent into exile in other nations with whom the blessing should have been shared (see p. B—4-5). This is also referred to as the "involuntary-go" mechanism.

KINGDOM OF GOD—This always refers to God's reign, rule and sovereignty and never to the realm or people over whom it is exercised (see p. A—66).

MISSION FIELD—An area where there are no churches (see p. A—124).

MISSION SOCIETIES—"...dedicated Christians who have banded together in a commitment to the Lord and to one another to make special efforts to cross cultural frontiers in order to evangelize and disciple those who would not otherwise be reached with the gospel in the normal movements of history and commerce" (p. D—239).

MISSION STATION APPROACH—An approach whereby missionaries and their converts lived separately from the indigenous people. This is also referred to as the "gathered colony" approach (see p. B—142-143).

MISSIONARY BAND—An independent unit, organized around committed, experienced Christian workers who join as a result of a separate decision from church membership (see p. B—46-47).

MISSIONARY MECHANISMS—(a) voluntary-go; (b) involuntary-go; (c) voluntary-come; and (d) involuntary-come (see lesson 6 for a fuller discussion).

MISSIONS—FRONTIER—Cross-cultural evangelism by a different-culture worker within a cultural minisphere where no missiological breakthrough has occurred, i.e., within an Unreached People Group (see p. B—181).

MISSIONS—REGULAR—Cross-cultural evangelism by a different- culture worker within a cultural minisphere where a missiological breakthrough has taken place, i.e., within a Reached People Group (see p. B—181).

MISSIOLOGICAL BREAKTHROUGH—The establishment of a viable church within an otherwise Unreached People Group. This is achieved by Frontier Missions (see p. B—181).

MODALITY—"A structured fellowship in which there is no distinction of sex or age", e.g., the New Testament church, a denomination or a local congregation (see pp. B—49-50).

MYSTERY (Biblical concept of)—Something which God has kept secret or hidden from man but which is now disclosed as part of God's redemptive purpose (see p. A—67).

NATION (Biblical concept of)—An ethnic unit or people group (Greek=ethnos; Hebrew=gam or mishpahgeh) rather than a country or politically defined group (see pp. B—176-177).

NEW TESTAMENT CHURCH—Organized along the lines of the Jewish synagogue, it included "the community of the faithful" in any given place, both old and young, male and female, Jew and Greek (see p. B—46).

NEW UNIVERSALISM—The teaching that because Christ died for all, then all people will ultimately be saved (see p. A—150).

NEW WIDER HOPE THEORY—Those who live by the light they have will be saved on the merits of Christ's death. This is a more conservative version of the New Universalism (see p. A—150).

ONLY ONE NAME THEORY—Only those who "call on the name of the Lord" (Rom 10:13) will be saved (see p. A—150).

P-O CONVERSION—Conversion of people who are nominal Christians. The cultural distance between church and convert is nil (p. B—182).

P-1 CONVERSION—Conversion of people who do not consciously consider themselves to be Christians but who are part of the same cultural minisphere as an indigenous church. The cultural distance between church and convert is minimal (p.B—182).

P-2 CONVERSION—Conversion of people who are not the same but only similar culturally to a cultural minisphere possessing an indigenous church. The cultural distance between church and convert is significant (p. B—182-183).

P-3 CONVERSION—Conversion of people from a cultural megasphere where there is no indigenous church. The cultural distance between church and convert is substantial (p. B—183).

PEOPLE GROUP— "A significantly large sociological grouping of individuals who perceive themselves to have a common affinity for one another because of their shared language, religion, ethnicity, residence, occupation, class or caste, situation etc., or combinations of these." For evangelistic purposes it is, "The largest group within which the Gospel can spread as a church planting movement without encountering barriers of understanding or acceptance." Note that the elements of "largest" or MAXimum sized and sufficiently UNIfied to be without insuperable barriers underlies *the alternate name for this kind of a group*, namely a UNIMAX group. Note also, that the first part of this definition gives rise to the concept of sociopeople, described further on in the same article in the *Perspectives Study Guide*. ("Basic Concepts of Frontier Missiology," *Study Guide*, p. E-2, 4)

PEOPLE MOVEMENTS—The process by which whole people groups come to Christ (see p. B—140).

PLAN-SO-FAR STRATEGY—This assumes that we will plan to begin the work and God will do the rest. This strategy does not focus on outcomes, but on beginnings.

REACHED PEOPLE GROUP—A cultural minisphere (a Unimax group) within which there exists a body of Christians with the potential to evangelize its own people and thus does not require cross-cultural evangelism (p. B—180).

REDEMPTIVE ANALOGIES—Catalyzing elements within a culture that anticipate aspects of the Gospel. Their God-ordained purpose is to pre-condition the mind to recognize Jesus as Saviour (p. C—60).

RICE CHRISTIANS—People who become Christians simply for the material benefits that this will bring to themselves and to their families (see p. D—211).

ROLE—"Behavioral expectations" associated with a particular status (see page 381). Note that all interpersonal relationships can be broken down into "complementary role pairs", e.g., teacher-student, parent-child, etc (see p. C—25).

SOCIAL STRUCTURE—The way in which statuses and roles are organized together to form a society (see p. C—24).

SODALITY—"A structured fellowship in which membership involves an adult second decision beyond modality membership and may be limited by either age or sex or marital status" (see p. B—50).

SOTERIOLOGICAL THEME OF THE BIBLE —God's work of rescuing and saving the nations (see p. A—51).

SPONTANEOUS EXPANSION—The situation whereby new converts are: "formed into churches which from the beginning are fully equipped with all spiritual authority to multiply themselves without any necessary reference to the foreign missionaries" (p. B—154).

STANDARD SOLUTION STRATEGY—"...works out a particular way of doing things, then uses this same approach in every situation" (p. D—37).

STATUS—A position in a social system occupied by an individual, e.g., teacher, father, mother, student (see p. C—25).

STRATEGY—"A strategy is an overall approach, plan or way of describing how we will go about reaching our goal or solving our problem. It is not concerned with details" (p. D—36).

SYNCRETISM—"The mixture of old meanings (from the receiving culture) with the new (from the Gospel) so that the essential nature of each is lost" (page 378). "...Harmful carry-overs from the old way of life..." (page 533). This inevitably involves the contamination of Christian faith, ritual or belief through the incorporation into these of inappropriate cultural items. The attempt to reconcile differing philosophical or religious systems into one, e.g., "all religions are one and we are going to the same place" (p. D—132).

TENTMAKER MISSIONARY—"...a trained, experienced Christian worker, with missionary motivation, who is led by God into a cross-cultural ministry, to make Him known, at his own expense, in the context of secular employment or study" (p. D—246).

THREE-SELF FORMULA—The goal of missions is to plant and foster the development of churches which will be self-governing, self-supporting and self-propagating (see B—67).

TWENTY FIVE UNBELIEVABLE YEARS—This refers to the period from 1945 to 1969. In 1945 Europeans controlled nearly 99.5% of the non-Western world. By 1969 this had been reduced to only 5%. These years also saw the "unbelievable" upsurge of Christianity in the non-Western world (see p. B—19).

UNIMAX GROUP—See definition of People Group.

UNIQUE SOLUTION STRATEGY—"...assumes that every situation we face is different, that each one requires its own special strategy. It assumes that we can find a way, that there is an answer. It assumes that we should make statements of faith (set goals) about the future. It assumes that standard solutions probably will not work. We believe that there are some approaches that can be used to discover God's strategy for each unique situation" (pp. D—37-38).

UNREACHED PEOPLE GROUP—A cultural minisphere (a Unimax group) that does not have a cluster of indigenous, growing, evangelizing congregations and thus requires cross-cultural evangelism (p. B—180).

UNIVERSALISM —The teaching that because God is good, all people will ultimately be saved (see p. A—149).

VALUES—What is considered to be "good", "beneficial" or "best" within a society. Values provide "pre-set" decisions that a culture makes between choices commonly faced by its people. They define what "should" or "ought" to be done in order to fit in or conform to a society's way of life (see p. C—4).

VIABLE CHURCH—"...a sufficiently developed indigenous Christian tradition, capable of evangelizing its own people without cross-cultural help" (p. B—180). A church that has within itself the evangelistic capacity to spread the Good News through the rest of its sociological grouping .

WEB EVANGELISM —The process by which believers witness to friends and relatives (see p. D—192).

WIDER HOPE THEORY —Not all will be saved but many who have not heard the gospel will be saved because God is just and would not condemn the sincere seeker after truth (see p. A—150).

WORLD CHRISTIAN—A Christian who has caught the vision of God's global purpose, who has responded to that vision in practical ways and whose lifestyle has been transformed in obedience to the demands of that vision (see pp D—306-D—307).

WORLD EVANGELIZATION—The nature of world evangelization is the communication of the Good News. The purpose is to give individuals and groups a valid opportunity to accept Jesus Christ. The goal is that of persuading men and women to accept Jesus Christ as Lord and Saviour, and to serve Him in the fellowship of His church .

WORLD VIEW (or WORLDVIEW): A range of definitions are offered:

Kwast: What is considered to be "real" within a culture. This is concerned with the "great and ultimate questions of reality" (see page 363) and as such forms the core of culture. "Every culture assumes specific answers to these questions, and those answers control and integrate every function, every aspect, and component of the culture" (p. C—5).

Hiebert: "At the center... of a culture are the basic assumptions the people have about the nature of reality and of right and wrong. Taken together, they are referred to as the people's world view" (p. C—12).

Hesselgrave: "...the way people see or perceive the world, the way they 'know' it to be. What men see is in part what is there. It is partly who we are. But these combine to form one reality, one world view" (p. C—44).

Lausanne Committee: "...a general understanding of the nature of the universe and of one's place in it" (p. C—163).

Scripture Index

Index

L

Language acquisition B—100; C—102,
C—112-113

Latin America, evangelization of
B—196-197

Lausanne Committee for World Evangelization D—119-128

Lausanne Congress on World Evangelization (1974) B—161

Lausanne Covenant A—5, 7

Laymen's Missionary Movement
B—90-93

Learner role C—102; D—164

Liberation motif in Old Testament
A—2

Liberation, political and development
D—22, 215

Lifestyle,
missionary D—281-287
simple C—114; D—285-286, 292-298
wartime D—288-291

Light received brings more light
A—152-153

Little Flock assembly D—95

Livingstone, David B—80, 124

London Missionary Society B—36,
B—65-66

Lordship of Christ C—177, 179

Love of God A—17, 19-20, 23

Lull, Raymond B—16, 59, 120

Luther, Martin B—53

M

Make disciples A—63

Mandate for world evangelization
A—3

Maredumilli, evangelization of
D—178-181

Marshman, Joshua B—66

Marxism B—33

Material culture C—11, 34

Matigsalog people, evangelization of
D—187-188

McDonald, Hamish C—141-148

McGavran, Donald B—41-42

Medicine, role in nineteenth-century
missions of B—69-70

Messiah A—98

Millennium A—70

Mills, Samuel J., Jr. B—81

Mission Aviation Fellowship B—42;
C—141, 143-144

Mission activity, four stages of
B—36-37

Mission compounds C—133

Mission mechanisms B—3-21

Mission societies,
advantages of D—242-244
as "means" for world evangelization
B—101-102
candidacy in D—258-259
contributions of D—241
role of D—239

Mission station approach to evangelization B—142, 145-147, 148

Mission stations B—66-67

Mission,
message in A—71-75
motive for A—78-82
nature of A—75-78

Missionaries, deployment of B—188

Missionary band B—46-47

Missionary finances C—131-132

Missionary housing C—133

Missionary lifestyle D—184

Missionary motif in Old Testament
A—52-53

Missionary preparation,
levels of D—276-277
necessity for D—275

"Missionary problem" D—310-314

Missionary service,
steps to D—255-260

X,Y

Z